PROGRAMMING WITH MICROSOFT® VISUAL BASIC® 2012

SIXTH EDITION

PROGRAMMING WITH MICROSOFT® VISUAL BASIC® 2012

DIANE ZAK

COURSE TECHNOLOGY
CENGAGE Learning®

Australia • Brazil • Japan • Korea • Mexico • Singapore • Spain • United Kingdom • United States

COURSE TECHNOLOGY
CENGAGE Learning®

Programming with Microsoft® Visual Basic® 2012, Sixth Edition
Diane Zak

Executive Editor: Kathleen McMahon
Senior Product Manager: Alyssa Pratt
Editorial Assistant: Sarah Ryan
Brand Marketing Manager: Kay Stefanski
Senior Content Project Manager: Matthew Hutchinson
Quality Assurance: Nicole Spoto
Art Director: Cheryl Pearl, GEX
Cover Designer: Cheryl Pearl, GEX
Print Buyer: Julio Esperas
Proofreader: Kathy Orrino
Indexer: Alexandra Nickerson
Compositor: Integra Software Services Pvt. Ltd.

Library of Congress Control Number: 2012956117

ISBN-13: 978-1-285-07792-5

ISBN-10: 1-285-07792-X

Course Technology
20 Channel Center Street
Boston, MA 02210
USA

Cengage Learning is a leading provider of customized learning solutions with office locations around the globe, including Singapore, the United Kingdom, Australia, Mexico, Brazil and Japan. Locate your local office at **international.cengage.com/region**

Cengage Learning products are represented in Canada by Nelson Education, Ltd.

For your course and learning solutions, visit **www.cengage.com.**

Purchase any of our products at your local college store or at our preferred online store **www.cengagebrain.com.**

Instructors: Please visit **login.cengage.com** and log in to access instructor-specific resources.

Printed in the United States of America
1 2 3 4 5 6 18 17 16 15 14 13

Brief Contents

Contents

Preface

Programming with Microsoft Visual Basic 2012, Sixth Edition uses Visual Basic 2012, an object-oriented language, to teach programming concepts. This book is designed for a beginning programming course. However, it assumes students are familiar with basic Windows skills and file management.

Organization and Coverage

Programming with Microsoft Visual Basic 2012, Sixth Edition contains an Overview and 14 chapters that present hands-on instruction; it also contains five appendices (A through E). An additional appendix (Appendix F) covering multiple-form applications and the FontDialog, ColorDialog, and TabControl tools is available online at *www.cengagebrain.com*.

In the chapters, students with no previous programming experience learn how to plan and create their own interactive Windows applications. GUI design skills, OOP concepts, and planning tools (such as TOE charts, pseudocode, and flowcharts) are emphasized throughout the book. The chapters show students how to work with objects and write Visual Basic statements such as If...Then...Else, Select Case, Do...Loop, For...Next, and For Each...Next. Students also learn how to create and manipulate variables, constants, strings, sequential access files, structures, classes, and arrays. Chapter 12 shows students how to create both static and dynamic Web applications. In Chapter 13, students learn how to connect an application to a Microsoft Access database, and then use Language Integrated Query (LINQ) to query the database. Chapter 14 continues the coverage of databases, introducing the student to more advanced concepts and Structured Query Language (SQL). Appendix A, which can be covered after Chapter 3, teaches students how to locate and correct errors in their code. The appendix shows students how to step through their code and also how to create breakpoints. Appendix B recaps the GUI design guidelines mentioned in the chapters, and Appendix C lists the Visual Basic conversion functions. The Visual Basic 2012 Cheat Sheet contained in Appendix D summarizes important concepts covered in the chapters, such as the syntax of statements, methods, and so on. The Cheat Sheet provides a convenient place for students to locate the information they need as they are creating and coding their applications. Appendix E contains Case Projects that can be assigned after completing specific chapters in the book.

Approach

Programming with Microsoft Visual Basic 2012, Sixth Edition teaches programming concepts using a task-driven rather than a command-driven approach. By working through the chapters, which are each motivated by a realistic case, students learn how to develop applications they are likely to encounter in the workplace. This is much more effective than memorizing a list of commands out of context. The book motivates students by demonstrating why they need to learn the concepts and skills covered in each chapter.

Features

Programming with Microsoft Visual Basic 2012, Sixth Edition is an exceptional textbook because it also includes the following features:

READ THIS BEFORE YOU BEGIN This section is consistent with Course Technology's unequaled commitment to helping instructors introduce technology into the classroom. Technical considerations and assumptions about hardware, software, and default settings are listed in one place to help instructors save time and eliminate unnecessary aggravation.

YOU DO IT! BOXES These boxes provide simple applications that allow students to demonstrate their understanding of a concept before moving on to the next concept. The YOU DO IT! boxes are located almost exclusively in Lesson A of each chapter.

VISUAL STUDIO 2012 METHODS The book focuses on Visual Studio 2012 methods rather than on Visual Basic functions. This is because the Visual Studio methods can be used in any .NET language, whereas the Visual Basic functions can be used only in Visual Basic. Exceptions to this are the Val and Format functions, which are introduced in Chapter 2. These functions are covered in the book simply because it is likely that students will encounter them in existing Visual Basic programs. However, in Chapter 3, the student is taught to use the TryParse method and the Convert class methods rather than the Val function. Also in Chapter 3, the Format function is replaced with the ToString method.

OPTION STATEMENTS All programs include the Option Explicit, Option Strict, and Option Infer statements.

START HERE ARROWS These arrows indicate the beginning of a tutorial steps section in the book.

DATABASES, LINQ, AND SQL The book includes two chapters (Chapters 13 and 14) on databases. LINQ is covered in Chapter 13. SQL is covered in Chapter 14.

FIGURES Figures that introduce new statements, functions, or methods contain both the syntax and examples of using the syntax. Including the syntax in the figures makes the examples more meaningful, and vice versa.

CHAPTER CASES Each chapter begins with a programming-related problem that students could reasonably expect to encounter in business, followed by a demonstration of an application that could be used to solve the problem. Showing the students the completed application before they learn how to create it is motivational and instructionally sound. By allowing the students to see the type of application they will be able to create after completing the chapter, the students will be more motivated to learn because they can see how the programming concepts they are about to learn can be used and, therefore, why the concepts are important.

LESSONS Each chapter is divided into three lessons—A, B, and C. Lesson A introduces the programming concepts that will be used in the completed application. The concepts are illustrated with code examples and sample applications. The user interface for each sample application is provided to the student. Also provided are tutorial-style steps that guide the student on coding, running, and testing the application. Each sample application allows the student to observe how the current concept can be used before the next concept is introduced. In Lessons B and/or C, the student creates the application required to solve the problem specified in the Chapter Case.

APPENDICES Appendix A, which can be covered after Chapter 3, teaches students how to locate and correct errors (syntax, logic, and run time) in their code. The appendix shows students how to step through their code and also how to create breakpoints. Appendix B summarizes the GUI design guidelines taught in the chapters, making it easier for the student to follow the guidelines when designing an application's interface. Appendix C lists the Visual Basic conversion functions. Appendix D contains a Cheat Sheet that summarizes important concepts covered in the chapters, such as the syntax of statements, methods, and so on. The Cheat Sheet provides a convenient place for students to locate the information they need as they are creating and coding their applications. Appendix E contains Case Projects that can be assigned after completing specific chapters in the book. Appendix F, which is available online at *www.cengagebrain.com*, covers multiple-form applications and the FontDialog, ColorDialog, and TabControl tools.

GUI DESIGN TIP BOXES The GUI DESIGN TIP boxes contain guidelines and recommendations for designing applications that follow Windows standards. Appendix B provides a summary of the GUI design guidelines covered in the chapters.

TIP These notes provide additional information about the current concept. Examples include alternative ways of writing statements or performing tasks, as well as warnings about common mistakes made when using a particular command and reminders of related concepts learned in previous chapters.

SUMMARY Each lesson contains a Summary section that recaps the concepts covered in the lesson.

KEY TERMS Following the Summary section in each lesson is a listing of the key terms introduced throughout the lesson, along with their definitions.

REVIEW QUESTIONS Each lesson contains Review Questions designed to test a student's understanding of the lesson's concepts.

EXERCISES The Review Questions in each lesson are followed by Exercises, which provide students with additional practice of the skills and concepts they learned in the lesson. The Exercises are designated as INTRODUCTORY, INTERMEDIATE, ADVANCED, DISCOVERY, and SWAT THE BUGS. The DISCOVERY Exercises encourage students to challenge and independently develop their own programming skills while exploring the capabilities of Visual Basic 2012. The SWAT THE BUGS Exercises provide an opportunity for students to detect and correct errors in an application's code.

New to This Edition!

VIDEOS These notes direct students to videos that accompany each chapter in the book. The videos explain and/or demonstrate one or more of the chapter's concepts. The videos have been revised from the previous edition and are available via the optional CourseMate for this text.

NEW CHAPTER CASES, EXAMPLES, APPLICATIONS, REVIEW QUESTIONS, AND EXERCISES The chapters contain new Chapter Cases, code examples, sample applications, Review Questions, and Exercises.

APPENDIX D (VISUAL BASIC 2012 CHEAT SHEET) This appendix summarizes important concepts covered in the chapters (such as the syntax of statements, methods, and so on) and provides a quick reference for students.

APPENDIX E (CASE PROJECTS) This appendix contains Case Projects that can be assigned after completing specific chapters in the book.

Chapters 4, 5, and 7

The following two topics were moved from Chapter 4 to Chapter 5: the TryParse method's return value and the comparison of Boolean values. The Financial.Pmt method was removed from Chapter 4. In the previous edition of the book, independent Sub procedures were introduced in Chapter 5 and then covered more fully in Chapter 7. In this edition, independent Sub procedures are now covered in one place: Chapter 7.

Steps and Figures

The tutorial-style steps in the book assume you are using Microsoft Visual Studio Professional 2012 and a system running either Microsoft Windows 8 or Microsoft Windows 7. The figures in the book reflect how your screen will look if you are using a Microsoft Windows 8 system. Your screen may appear slightly different in some instances if you are using a Microsoft Windows 7 system. Any major differences between the screens for both versions of Microsoft Windows are indicated in the figures.

Instructor Resources

The following teaching tools are available for download at our Instructor Companion Site. Simply search for this text at *login.cengage.com*. An instructor login is required.

ELECTRONIC INSTRUCTOR'S MANUAL The Instructor's Manual that accompanies this textbook includes additional instructional material to assist in class preparation, including items such as Sample Syllabi, Chapter Outlines, Technical Notes, Lecture Notes, Quick Quizzes, Teaching Tips, Discussion Topics, and Additional Case Projects.

EXAMVIEW® This textbook is accompanied by ExamView, a powerful testing software package that allows instructors to create and administer printed, computer (LAN-based), and Internet exams. ExamView includes hundreds of questions that correspond to the topics covered in this text, enabling students to generate detailed study guides that include page references for further review. The computer-based and Internet testing components allow students to take exams at their computers, and also save the instructor time by grading each exam automatically.

POWERPOINT PRESENTATIONS This book offers Microsoft PowerPoint slides for each chapter. These are included as a teaching aid for classroom presentation, to make available to students on the network for chapter review, or to be printed for classroom distribution. Instructors can add their own slides for additional topics they introduce to the class.

SOLUTION FILES Solutions to the Lesson applications and the end-of-lesson Review Questions and Exercises are provided.

DATA FILES Data Files are necessary for completing the computer activities in this book. Data Files can also be downloaded by students at *www.cengagebrain.com.*

CourseMate

The more you study, the better the results. Make the most of your study time by accessing everything you need to succeed in one place. Read your textbook, take notes, review flashcards, watch videos, and take practice quizzes online. CourseMate goes beyond the book to deliver what you need! Learn more at *www.cengage.com/coursemate.*

The *Visual Basic* CourseMate includes:

- **Video Lessons:** Each chapter is accompanied by several video lessons that help to explain important chapter concepts. These videos were created and narrated by the author.
- An interactive eBook, quizzes, flashcards, and more!

Instructors may add CourseMate to the textbook package, or students may purchase CourseMate directly at *www.cengagebrain.com.*

Acknowledgments

Writing a book is a team effort rather than an individual one. I would like to take this opportunity to thank my team, especially Alyssa Pratt (Senior Project Manager), Sreejith Govindan (Full Service Project Manager), Nicole Spoto (Quality Assurance), Matt Hutchinson (Content Project Manager), Kathy Orrino (Proofreader), and the compositors at Integra. Thank you for your support, enthusiasm, patience, and hard work. Last, but certainly not least, I want to thank the following reviewers for their invaluable ideas and comments: Mary Brock: Mississippi University for Women; John Buerck: Saint Louis University; Jane Hammer: Valley City University; Donna Petty: Wallace Community College; and Helen Schneider: The University of Findlay. And a special thank you to Sally Douglas (College of Central Florida) for suggesting the YOU DO IT! boxes.

Diane Zak

Read This Before You Begin

Technical Information

Data Files

You will need data files to complete the computer activities in this book. Your instructor may provide the data files to you. You may obtain the files electronically at *www.cengagebrain.com*, and then navigating to the page for this book.

Each chapter in this book has its own set of data files, which are stored in a separate folder within the VB2012 folder. The files for Chapter 1 are stored in the VB2012\Chap01 folder. Similarly, the files for Chapter 2 are stored in the VB2012\Chap02 folder. Throughout this book, you will be instructed to open files from or save files to these folders.

You can use a computer in your school lab or your own computer to complete the steps and Exercises in this book.

Using Your Own Computer

To use your own computer to complete the computer activities in this book, you will need the following:

- A Pentium® 4 processor, 1.6 GHz or higher, personal computer running Microsoft Windows. This book was written using Microsoft Windows 8, and Quality Assurance tested using Microsoft Windows 7.
- Either Microsoft Visual Studio 2012 or the Express Editions of Microsoft Visual Studio 2012 (namely, Microsoft Visual Studio Express 2012 for Windows Desktop and Microsoft Visual Studio Express 2012 for Web) installed on your computer. This book was written and Quality Assurance tested using Microsoft Visual Studio Professional 2012 and Microsoft Visual Studio Express 2012 for Web. At the time of this writing, you can download a free copy of the Express Editions at *www.microsoft.com/visualstudio/eng/products/visual-studio-express-products*.

Figures

The figures in this book reflect how your screen will look if you are using Microsoft Visual Studio Professional 2012 and a Microsoft Windows 8 system. Your screen may appear slightly different in some instances if you are using another version of either Microsoft Visual Studio or Microsoft Windows.

Visit Our Web Site

Additional materials designed for this textbook might be available at *www.cengagebrain.com*. Search this site for more details.

To the Instructor

To complete the computer activities in this book, your students must use a set of data files. These files can be obtained electronically at *www.cengagebrain.com*.

The material in this book was written using Microsoft Visual Studio Professional 2012 on a Microsoft Windows 8 system. It was Quality Assurance tested using Microsoft Visual Studio Professional 2012 on a Microsoft Windows 7 system, and using Microsoft Visual Studio Express 2012 for Web on a Microsoft Windows 8 system.

OVERVIEW

An Introduction to Programming

After studying the Overview, you should be able to:

- Define the terminology used in programming
- Explain the tasks performed by a programmer
- Understand the employment opportunities for programmers and software engineers
- Run a Visual Basic 2012 application
- Understand how to use the chapters effectively

Programming a Computer

In essence, the word **programming** means *giving a mechanism the directions to accomplish a task*. If you are like most people, you've already programmed several mechanisms, such as your digital video recorder (DVR), cell phone, or coffee maker. Like these devices, a computer also is a mechanism that can be programmed.

The directions given to a computer are called **computer programs** or, more simply, **programs**. The people who write programs are called **programmers**. Programmers use a variety of special languages, called **programming languages**, to communicate with the computer. Some popular programming languages are Visual Basic, C#, C++, and Java. In this book, you will use the Visual Basic programming language.

The Programmer's Job

When a company has a problem that requires a computer solution, typically it is a programmer who comes to the rescue. The programmer might be an employee of the company; or he or she might be a freelance programmer, which is a programmer who works on temporary contracts rather than for a long-term employer.

First the programmer meets with the user, which is the person (or persons) responsible for describing the problem. In many cases, this person or persons also will eventually use the solution. Depending on the complexity of the problem, multiple programmers may be involved, and they may need to meet with the user several times. Programming teams often contain subject matter experts, who may or may not be programmers. For example, an accountant might be part of a team working on a program that requires accounting expertise. The purpose of the initial meetings with the user is to determine the exact problem and to agree on a solution.

Overview-Programmers video

After the programmer and user agree on the solution, the programmer begins converting the solution into a computer program. During the conversion phase, the programmer meets periodically with the user to determine whether the program fulfills the user's needs and to refine any details of the solution. When the user is satisfied that the program does what he or she wants it to do, the programmer rigorously tests the program with sample data before releasing it to the user. In many cases, the programmer also provides the user with a manual that explains how to use the program. As this process indicates, the creation of a good computer solution to a problem—in other words, the creation of a good program—requires a great deal of interaction between the programmer and the user.

Employment Opportunities

When searching for a job in computer programming, you will encounter ads for "computer programmers" as well as for "computer software engineers." Although job titles and descriptions vary, computer software engineers typically are responsible for designing an appropriate solution to a user's problem, while computer programmers are responsible for translating the solution into a language that the computer can understand. The process of translating the solution is called **coding**.

Overview-Programmer Qualities video

Keep in mind that, depending on the employer and the size and complexity of the user's problem, the design and coding tasks may be performed by the same employee, no matter what his or her job title is. In other words, it's not unusual for a software engineer to code her solution, just as it's not unusual for a programmer to have designed the solution he is coding.

Programmers and software engineers need to have strong problem-solving and analytical skills, as well as the ability to communicate effectively with team members, end users, and other nontechnical personnel. Typically, computer software engineers are expected to have at least a bachelor's degree in software engineering, computer science, or mathematics, along with practical work experience, especially in the industry in which they are employed. Computer programmers usually need at least an associate's degree in computer science, mathematics, or information systems, as well as proficiency in one or more programming languages.

Computer programmers and software engineers are employed by companies in almost every industry, such as telecommunications companies, software publishers, financial institutions, insurance carriers, educational institutions, and government agencies. The Bureau of Labor Statistics predicts that employment of computer software engineers will increase by 28% from 2010 to 2020. The employment of computer programmers, on the other hand, will increase by 12% over the same period. In addition, consulting opportunities for freelance programmers and software engineers are expected to increase as companies look for ways to reduce their payroll expenses.

There is a great deal of competition for programming and software engineering jobs, so jobseekers will need to keep up to date with the latest programming languages and technologies. A competitive edge may be gained by obtaining vendor-specific or language-specific certifications. More information about computer programmers and computer software engineers can be found on the Bureau of Labor Statistics Web site at *www.bls.gov*.

Visual Basic 2012

In this book, you will learn how to create programs using the Visual Basic 2012 programming language. Visual Basic 2012 is an **object-oriented programming language**, which is a language that allows the programmer to use objects to accomplish a program's goal. An **object** is anything that can be seen, touched, or used. In other words, an object is nearly any *thing*. The objects in an object-oriented program can take on many different forms. Programs written for the Windows environment typically use objects such as check boxes, list boxes, and buttons. A payroll program, on the other hand, might utilize objects found in the real world, such as a time card object, an employee object, and a check object.

Every object in an object-oriented program is created from a **class**, which is a pattern that the computer uses to create the object. The class contains the instructions that tell the computer how the object should look and behave. An object created from a class is called an **instance** of the class and is said to be **instantiated** from the class. An analogy involving a cookie cutter and cookies is often used to describe a class and its objects: the class is the cookie cutter, and the objects instantiated from the class are the cookies. You will learn more about classes and objects throughout this book.

Visual Basic 2012 is one of the languages included in Visual Studio 2012, which is available in many different editions. The most robust edition is Visual Studio Ultimate 2012, followed by Visual Studio Premium 2012, Visual Studio Professional 2012, and then the Express editions of Visual Studio 2012. Microsoft plans to release four different Express editions: Visual Studio Express 2012 for Windows 8, Visual Studio Express 2012 for Web, Visual Studio Express 2012 for Windows Desktop, and Visual Studio Express 2012 for Windows Phone. Each of these products include an **integrated development environment (IDE)**, which is an environment that contains all of the tools and features you need to create, run, and test your programs.

You can use Visual Basic to create programs, called **applications**, for the Windows environment or for the Web. A Windows application has a Windows user interface and runs on a personal computer. A **user interface** is what the user sees and interacts with while an application is running. Examples of Windows applications include graphics programs, data-entry systems, and games. A Web application, on the other hand, has a Web user interface and runs on a server. You access a Web application using your computer's browser. Examples of Web applications include e-commerce applications available on the Internet, and employee handbook applications accessible on a company's intranet. You also can use Visual Basic to create applications for tablet PCs and mobile devices, such as cell phones and PDAs (personal digital assistants).

A Visual Basic 2012 Demonstration

In the following set of steps, you will run a Visual Basic 2012 application that shows you some of the objects you will learn about in the chapters. For now, it is not important for you to understand how these objects were created or why the objects perform the way they do. Those questions will be answered in the chapters.

START HERE

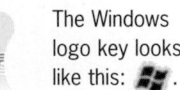

The Windows logo key looks like this: .

To run the Visual Basic 2012 application:

1. Press and hold down the **Windows logo** key on your keyboard as you tap the letter **r**. The Run dialog box opens. Release the logo key.
2. Click the **Browse** button to open the Browse dialog box. Locate and then open the VB2012\Overview folder on your computer's hard disk or on the device designated by your instructor.
3. Click **Monthly Payment Calculator (Monthly Payment Calculator.exe)** in the list of filenames. (Depending on how Windows is set up on your computer, you may see the .exe extension on the filename.) Click the **Open** button. The Browse dialog box closes and the Run dialog box appears again.
4. Click the **OK** button in the Run dialog box. After a few moments, the Monthly Payment Calculator application shown in Figure 1 appears on the screen. The interface contains a text box, list box, buttons, radio buttons, and labels. You can use the application to calculate the monthly payment for a car loan.

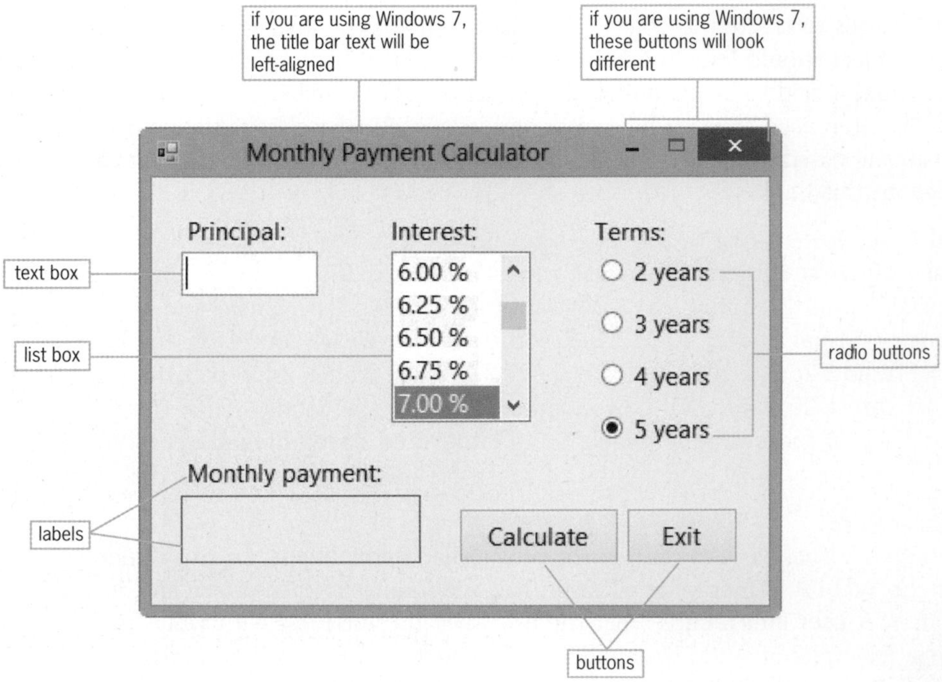

Figure 1 Monthly Payment Calculator application

Don't be concerned if some of the letters on your screen are underlined. You can show/hide the underlined letters by pressing the Alt key.

5. Use the application to calculate the monthly payment for a $20,000 loan at 6.75% interest for five years. Type **20000** in the Principal text box and then click **6.75 %** in the Interest list box. The radio button corresponding to the five-year term is already selected, so you just need to click the **Calculate** button to compute the monthly payment. The application indicates that your monthly payment would be $393.67. See Figure 2.

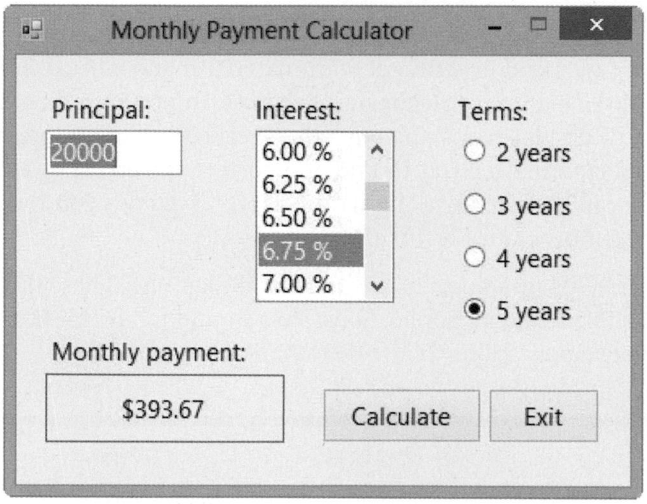

Figure 2 Computed monthly payment

6. Now determine what your monthly payment would be if you borrowed $10,000 at 8% interest for four years. Type **10000** in the Principal text box. Scroll down the Interest list box and then click **8.00 %**. Click the **4 years** radio button and then click the **Calculate** button. The Monthly payment box shows $244.13.
7. Click the **Exit** button to close the application.

Using the Chapters Effectively

This book is designed for a beginning programming course. However, it assumes students are familiar with basic Windows skills and file management. The chapters in this book will help you learn how to write programs using Microsoft Visual Basic 2012. The chapters are designed to be used at your computer. Begin by reading the text that explains the concepts. When you come to the numbered steps, follow the steps on your computer. Read each step carefully and completely before you try it. As you work, compare your screen with the figures to verify your results. The figures in this book reflect how your screen will look if you are using Visual Studio Professional 2012 and a Microsoft Windows 8 system. Your screen may appear slightly different in some instances if you are using a different edition of Visual Studio or if you are using another version of Microsoft Windows. Don't worry if your screen display differs slightly from the figures. The important parts of the screen display are labeled in each figure. Just be sure you have these parts on your screen.

Do not worry about making mistakes; that's part of the learning process. Tip notes identify common problems and explain how to get back on track. They also provide additional information about a procedure—for example, an alternative method of performing the procedure.

Tip notes are designated by the icon.

Each chapter is divided into three lessons. You might want to take a break between lessons. Following each lesson is a Summary section that lists the important elements of the lesson. After the Summary section is a listing of the key terms (including definitions) covered in the lesson. Following the Key Terms section are questions and exercises designed to review and reinforce the lesson's concepts. You should complete all of the end-of-lesson questions and several exercises before continuing to the next lesson. It takes a great deal of practice to acquire the skills needed to create good programs, and future chapters assume that you have mastered the information found in the previous chapters.

Some of the end-of-lesson exercises are Discovery exercises, which allow you to both "discover" the solutions to problems on your own and experiment with material that is not covered in the chapter. Some lessons also contain one or more Debugging exercises. In programming, the term **debugging** refers to the process of finding and fixing any errors, called bugs, in a program. Debugging exercises provide opportunities for you to find and correct the errors in existing applications. Appendix A, which can be covered along with Chapter 3, guides you through the process of locating and correcting a program's errors (bugs).

Throughout the book you will find GUI (graphical user interface) design tips. These tips contain guidelines and recommendations for designing applications. You should follow these guidelines and recommendations so that your applications follow the Windows standards.

Summary

- Programs are the step-by-step instructions that tell a computer how to perform a task.
- Programmers use various programming languages to communicate with the computer.
- The creation of a good program requires a great deal of interaction between the programmer and the user.
- Programmers rigorously test a program with sample data before releasing the program to the user.
- It's not unusual for the same person to perform the duties of both a software engineer and a programmer.
- An object-oriented programming language, such as Visual Basic 2012, allows programmers to use objects to accomplish a program's goal. An object is anything that can be seen, touched, or used.
- Every object in an object-oriented program is instantiated (created) from a class, which is a pattern that tells the computer how the object should look and behave. An object is referred to as an instance of the class.
- The process of locating and correcting the errors (bugs) in a program is called debugging.

Key Terms

Applications—programs created for the Windows environment, the Web, or mobile devices

Class—a pattern that the computer uses to create (instantiate) an object

Coding—the process of translating a solution into a language that the computer can understand

Computer programs—the directions given to computers; also called programs

Debugging—the process of locating and correcting the errors (bugs) in a program

IDE—integrated development environment

Instance—an object created (instantiated) from a class

Instantiated—the process of creating an object from a class

Integrated development environment—an environment that contains all of the tools and features you need to create, run, and test your programs; also called an IDE

Object—anything that can be seen, touched, or used

Object-oriented programming language—a programming language that allows the programmer to use objects to accomplish a program's goal

Programmers—the people who write computer programs

Programming—the process of giving a mechanism the directions to accomplish a task

Programming languages—languages used to communicate with a computer

Programs—the directions given to computers; also called computer programs

User interface—what the user sees and interacts with while an application is running

CHAPTER 1

An Introduction to Visual Basic 2012

Creating a Splash Screen

In this chapter, you will use Visual Basic 2012, Microsoft's newest version of the Visual Basic language, to create a splash screen for the Red Tree Inn. A splash screen is the first image that appears when an application is started. It is used to introduce the application and to hold the user's attention while the application is being read into the computer's internal memory.

Previewing the Splash Screen

Before you start the first lesson in this chapter, you will preview a completed splash screen. The splash screen is contained in the VB2012\Chap01 folder.

START HERE

To preview a completed splash screen:

1. Press and hold down the **Windows logo** key on your keyboard as you tap the letter **r**. The Run dialog box opens. Release the logo key.
2. Click the **Browse** button to open the Browse dialog box. Locate and then open the VB2012\Chap01 folder on your computer's hard disk or on the device designated by your instructor.
3. Click **RTI Splash** (**RTI Splash.exe**) in the list of filenames. (Depending on how Windows is set up on your computer, you may see the .exe extension on the filename.) Click the **Open** button. The Browse dialog box closes and the Run dialog box appears again.
4. Click the **OK** button in the Run dialog box. After a few moments, the splash screen shown in Figure 1-1 appears on the screen. The splash screen closes when six seconds have elapsed.

The Windows logo key looks like this: .

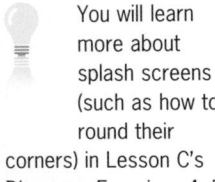

You will learn more about splash screens (such as how to round their corners) in Lesson C's Discovery Exercises 4, 5, and 6.

Figure 1-1 Splash screen for the Red Tree Inn
Photo courtesy of Diane Zak

Chapter 1 is designed to help you get comfortable with the Visual Studio 2012 integrated development environment. As you learned in the Overview, an integrated development environment (IDE) is an environment that contains all of the tools and features you need to create, run, and test your programs. As do all the chapters in this book, Chapter 1 contains three lessons. You should complete a lesson in full and do all of the end-of-lesson questions and several exercises before continuing to the next lesson.

LESSON A

After studying Lesson A, you should be able to:

- Start and customize Visual Studio 2012
- Create a Visual Basic 2012 Windows application
- Manage the windows in the IDE
- Set the properties of an object
- Restore a property to its default setting
- Save a solution
- Close and open an existing solution

The Splash Screen Application

In this chapter, you will create a splash screen using Visual Basic 2012. The following set of steps will guide you in starting Visual Studio Professional 2012 from either Windows 8 or Windows 7. Your steps may differ slightly if you are using a different edition of Visual Studio 2012.

To start Visual Studio Professional 2012:

START HERE

1. *Windows 8*: If necessary, tap the **Windows logo** key to switch to the Windows 8 tile-based mode, and then click the **Visual Studio 2012** tile.

   Windows 7: Click the **Start** button on the Windows 7 taskbar and then point to **All Programs**. Click **Microsoft Visual Studio 2012** on the All Programs menu and then click **Visual Studio 2012**.

2. If the Choose Default Environment Settings dialog box appears, click **Visual Basic Development Settings** and then click **Start Visual Studio**.

3. Click **WINDOW** on the menu bar, click **Reset Window Layout**, and then click the **Yes** button. When you start Visual Studio Professional 2012, your screen will appear similar to Figure 1-2. However, your menu bar may contain underlined letters, called access keys. You will learn about access keys in Chapter 2. (You can show/hide the access keys by pressing the Alt key on your keyboard.)

The Ch01A video demonstrates all of the steps contained in Lesson A. You can view the video either before or after completing the lesson.

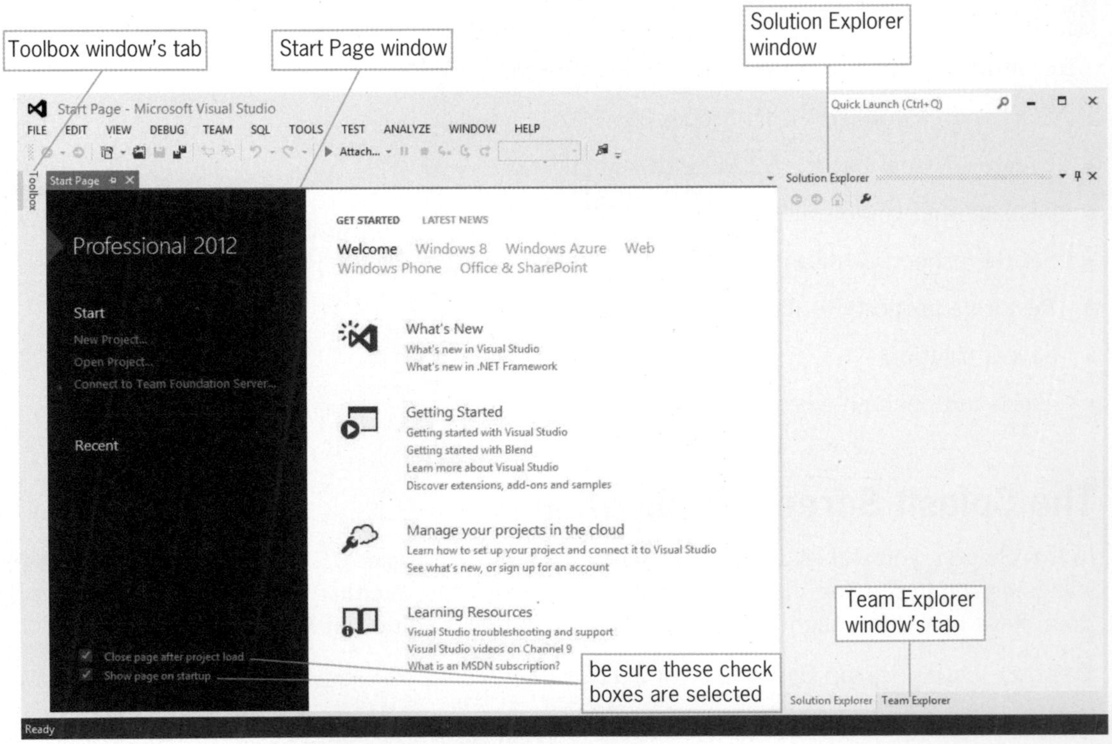

Figure 1-2 Microsoft Visual Studio Professional 2012 startup screen

Note: To select a different window layout, click TOOLS on the menu bar, click Import and Export Settings, select the Reset all settings radio button, click the Next button, select the appropriate radio button, click the Next button, click the settings collection you want to use, and then click the Finish button.

Next, you will configure Visual Studio so that your screen agrees with the figures and tutorial steps in this book. As mentioned in the Overview, the figures reflect how your screen will look if you are using Visual Studio Professional 2012 and a Microsoft Windows 8 system. Your screen may appear slightly different in some instances if you are using a different edition of Visual Studio or if you are using another version of Microsoft Windows. Don't worry if your screen display differs slightly from the figures.

START HERE

To configure Visual Studio:

1. Click **TOOLS** on the menu bar and then click **Options** to open the Options dialog box. Click the **Projects and Solutions** node. Use the information shown in Figure 1-3 to select and deselect the appropriate check boxes. (Your dialog box will look slightly different if you are using Windows 7. For example, the title bar text will be left-aligned rather than centered, and the buttons on the title bar will look different.) When you are finished, click the **OK** button to close the Options dialog box.

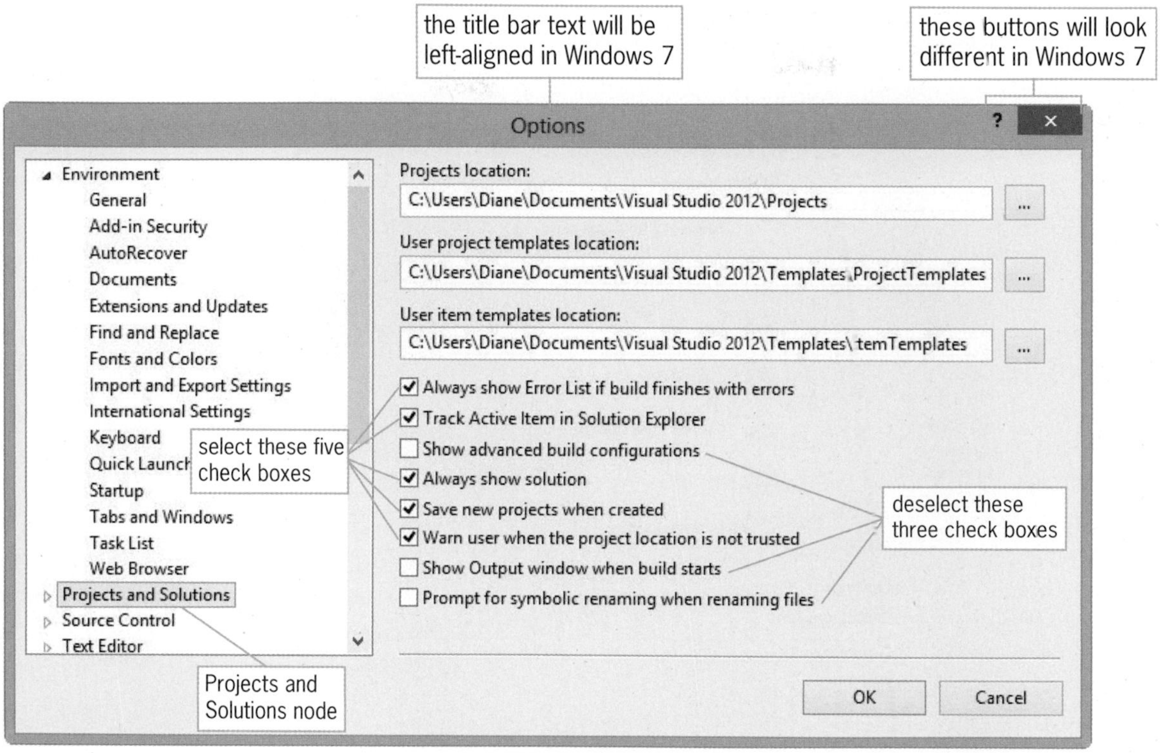

Figure 1-3 Options dialog box

The splash screen will be a Windows application, which means it will have a Windows user interface and run on a desktop computer. Recall that a user interface is what the user sees and interacts with while an application is running. Windows applications in Visual Basic are composed of solutions, projects, and files. A solution is a container that stores the projects and files for an entire application. Although the solutions in this book contain only one project, a solution can contain several projects. A project also is a container, but it stores only the files associated with that particular project.

START HERE

To create a Visual Basic 2012 Windows application:

1. Click **FILE** on the menu bar and then click **New Project** to open the New Project dialog box.
2. If necessary, expand the **Visual Basic** node in the Installed Templates list, and then (if necessary) click **Windows**.
3. If necessary, click **Windows Forms Application** in the middle column of the dialog box.
4. Change the name entered in the Name box to **Splash Project**.
5. Click the **Browse** button to open the Project Location dialog box. Locate and then click the **VB2012\Chap01** folder. Click the **Select Folder** button to close the Project Location dialog box.
6. If necessary, select the **Create directory for solution** check box in the New Project dialog box. Change the name entered in the Solution name box to **Splash Solution**. Figure 1-4 shows the completed New Project dialog box in Visual Studio Professional 2012. (Your dialog box will look slightly different if you are using Windows 7 or a different edition of Visual Studio.) The drive letter may be different from the one shown

in the figure if you are saving to a device other than your computer's hard drive—for example, if you are saving to a flash drive.

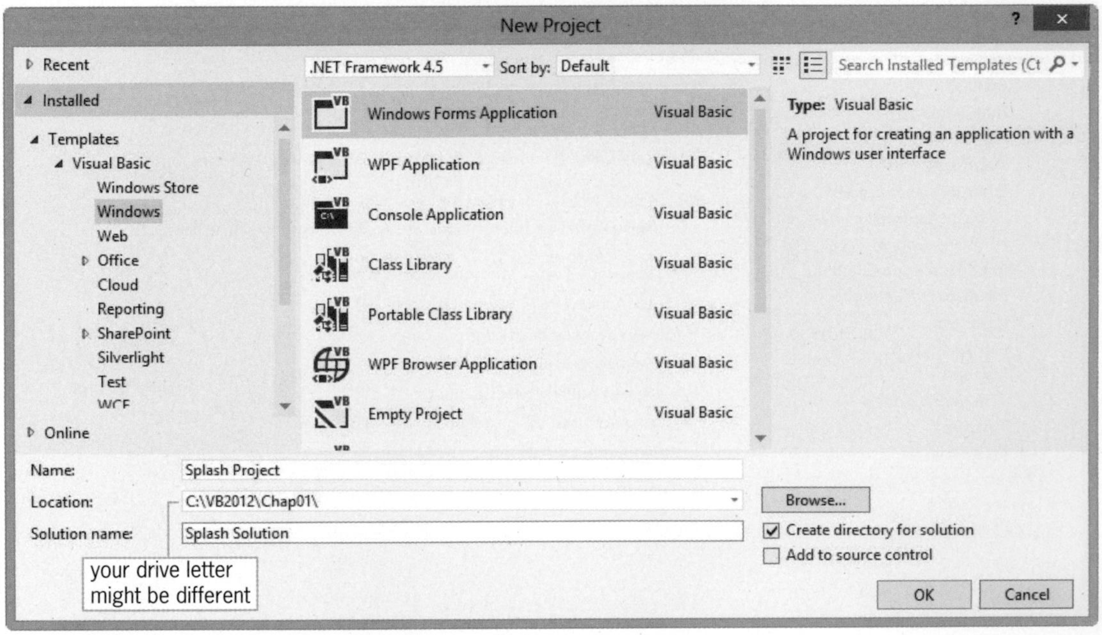

Figure 1-4 Completed New Project dialog box in Visual Studio Professional 2012

7. Click the **OK** button to close the New Project dialog box. The computer creates a solution and adds a Visual Basic project to the solution. The names of the solution and project, along with other information pertaining to the project, appear in the Solution Explorer window. See Figure 1-5. In addition to the windows shown earlier in Figure 1-2, three other windows appear in the IDE: Windows Form Designer, Properties, and Data Sources. (Don't be concerned if different properties appear in your Properties window.)

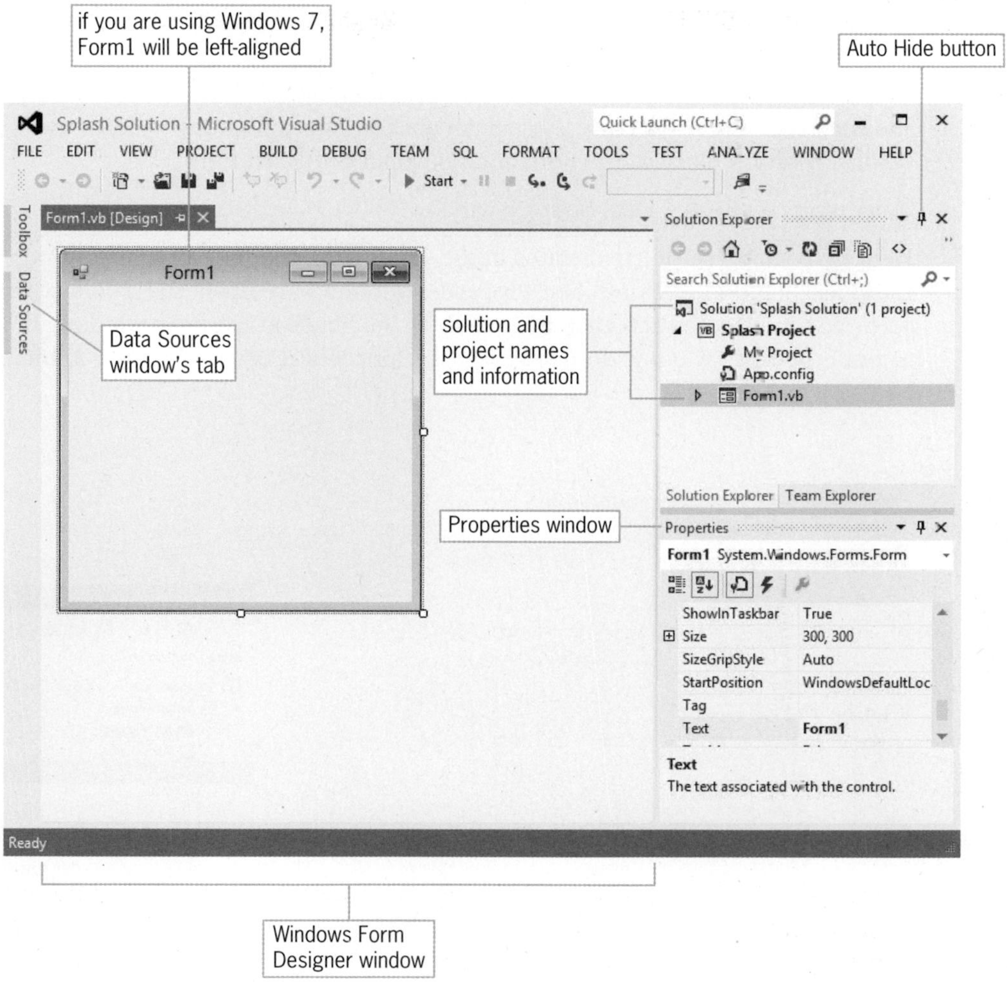

Figure 1-5 Solution and Visual Basic project

If you want to size the Solution Explorer window to match Figure 1-5, position your mouse pointer on the window's left border until the mouse pointer becomes a sizing pointer (a horizontal line with an arrowhead at each end), and then drag the border to either the left or the right.

Managing the Windows in the IDE

In most cases, you will find it easier to work in the IDE if you either close or auto-hide the windows you are not currently using. The easiest way to close an open window is to click the Close button on the window's title bar. In most cases, the VIEW menu provides an appropriate option for opening a closed window. Rather than closing a window, you also can auto-hide it. You auto-hide a window using the Auto Hide button (refer to Figure 1-5) on the window's title bar. The Auto Hide button is a toggle button: clicking it once activates it, and clicking it again deactivates it. The Toolbox and Data Sources windows in Figure 1-5 are auto-hidden windows.

START HERE

To close, open, auto-hide, and display windows in the IDE:

1. Click the **Close** button on the Properties window's title bar to close the window. Now, click **VIEW** on the menu bar and then click **Properties Window** to open the window.
2. If your IDE contains the Team Explorer window, click the **Team Explorer** tab and then click the **Close** button on the window's title bar.
3. Click the **Auto Hide** (vertical pushpin) button on the Solution Explorer window. The Solution Explorer window is minimized and appears as a tab on the edge of the IDE.
4. To temporarily display the Solution Explorer window, click the **Solution Explorer** tab. Notice that the Auto Hide button is now a horizontal pushpin rather than a vertical

pushpin. To return the Solution Explorer window to its auto-hidden state, click the **Solution Explorer** tab again.

5. To permanently display the Solution Explorer window, click the **Solution Explorer** tab and then click the **Auto Hide** (horizontal pushpin) button on the window's title bar. The vertical pushpin replaces the horizontal pushpin on the button.
6. If necessary, close the Data Sources window.
7. Figure 1-6 shows the current status of the windows in the IDE. Only the Windows Form Designer, Solution Explorer, and Properties windows are open; the Toolbox window is auto-hidden. If necessary, click **Form1.vb** in the Solution Explorer window. If the items in the Properties window do not appear in alphabetical order, click the **Alphabetical** button.

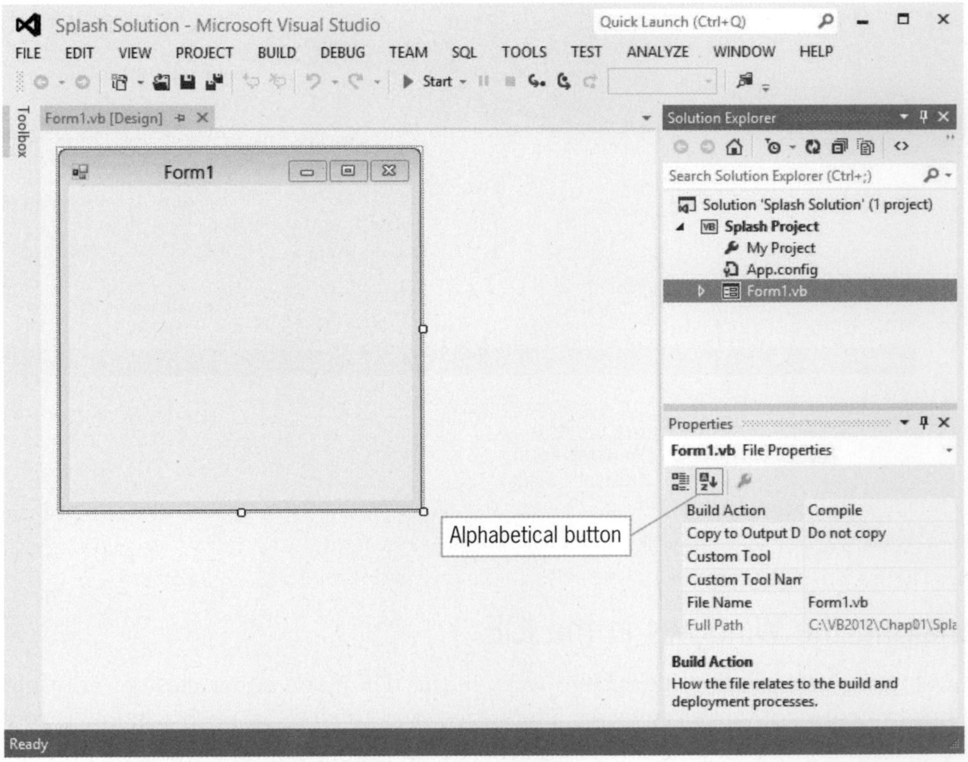

Figure 1-6 Current status of the windows in the IDE

To reset the window layout in the IDE, click WINDOW on the menu bar, click Reset Window Layout, and then click the Yes button.

In the next several sections, you will take a closer look at the Windows Form Designer, Solution Explorer, and Properties windows. (The Toolbox window is covered in Lesson B.)

The Windows Form Designer Window

Figure 1-7 shows the **Windows Form Designer window**, where you create (or design) your application's graphical user interface, more simply referred to as a **GUI**. Only a Windows Form object appears in the designer window shown in the figure. A **Windows Form object**, or **form**, is the foundation for the user interface in a Windows application. You create the user interface by adding other objects, such as buttons and text boxes, to the form. Notice that a title bar appears at the top of the form. The title bar contains a default caption (Form1) along with Minimize, Maximize, and Close buttons. (The title bar text will be left-aligned in Windows 7.) At the top of the designer window is a tab labeled Form1.vb [Design]. Form1.vb is the name of the file (on your computer's hard disk or on another device) that contains the Visual Basic instructions associated with the form, and [Design] identifies the window as the designer window.

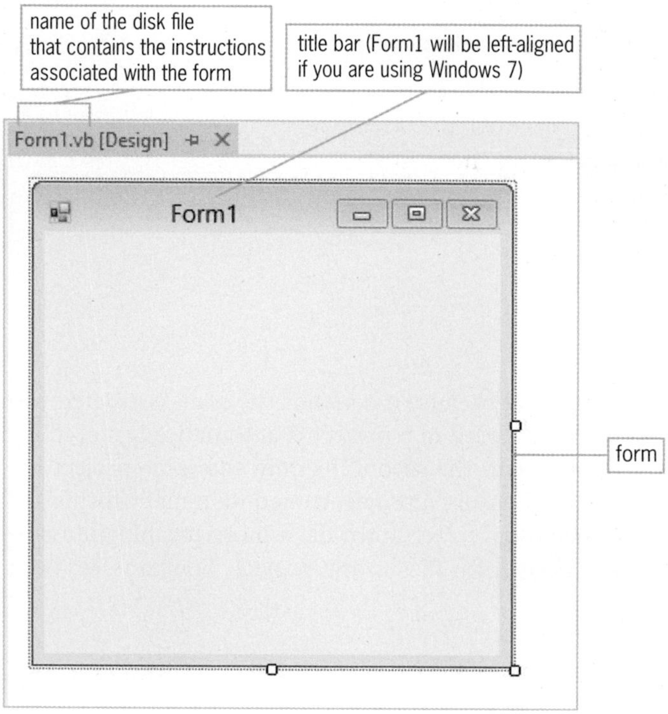

Figure 1-7 Windows Form Designer window

As you learned in the Overview, all objects in an object-oriented program are instantiated (created) from a class. A form, for example, is an instance of the Windows Form class. The form is automatically instantiated for you when you create a Windows application.

Recall that a class is a pattern that the computer uses to create an object.

The Solution Explorer Window

The **Solution Explorer window** displays a list of the projects contained in the current solution and the items contained in each project. Figure 1-8 shows the Solution Explorer window for the Splash Solution, which contains one project named Splash Project. Within the Splash Project are the My Project folder and two files named App.config and Form1.vb. The project also contains other items, which are typically kept hidden. However, you can display the additional items by clicking the Show All Files button. You would click the button again to hide the items. The .vb on the Form1.vb filename indicates that the file is a Visual Basic source file. A **source file** is a file that contains program instructions, called **code**. The Form1.vb file contains the code associated with the form displayed in the designer window. You can view the code using the Code Editor window, which you will learn about in Lesson B.

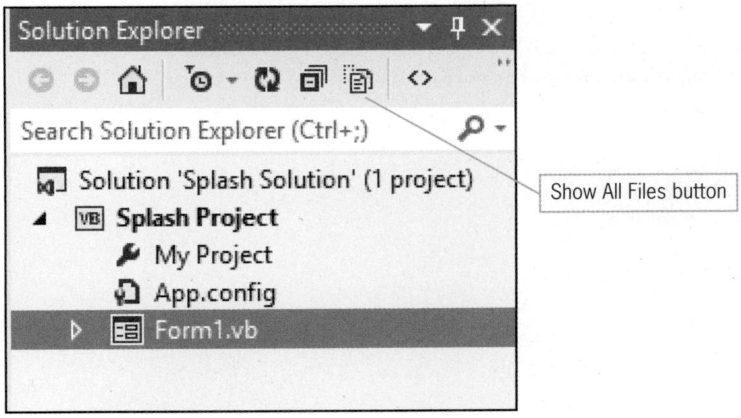

Figure 1-8 Solution Explorer window

The Form1.vb source file is referred to as a **form file** because it contains the code associated with a form. The code associated with the first form included in a project is automatically stored in a form file named Form1.vb. The code associated with the second form in the same project is stored in a form file named Form2.vb, and so on. Because a project can contain many forms and, therefore, many form files, it is a good practice to give each form file a more meaningful name. Doing this will help you keep track of the various form files in the project. You can use the Properties window to change the filename.

The Properties Window

As is everything in an object-oriented language, a file is an object. Each object has a set of attributes that determine its appearance and behavior. The attributes are called **properties** and are listed in the **Properties window**. When an object is created, a default value is assigned to each of its properties. The Properties window shown in Figure 1-9 lists the default values assigned to the properties of the Form1.vb file. (You do not need to widen your Properties window to match Figure 1-9.) As indicated in the figure, the Properties window includes an Object box and a Properties list. The **Object box** contains the name of the selected object. In this case, it contains Form1.vb, which is the name of the form file. The **Properties list** has two columns. The left column displays the names of the selected object's properties. You can use the Alphabetical and Categorized buttons to display the names either alphabetically or by category, respectively. However, it's usually easier to work with the Properties window when the properties are listed in alphabetical order, as they are in Figure 1-9. The right column in the Properties list is called the **Settings box** and displays the current value (or setting) of each of the object's properties. A brief description of the selected property appears in the Description pane.

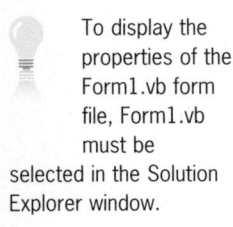

To display the properties of the Form1.vb form file, Form1.vb must be selected in the Solution Explorer window.

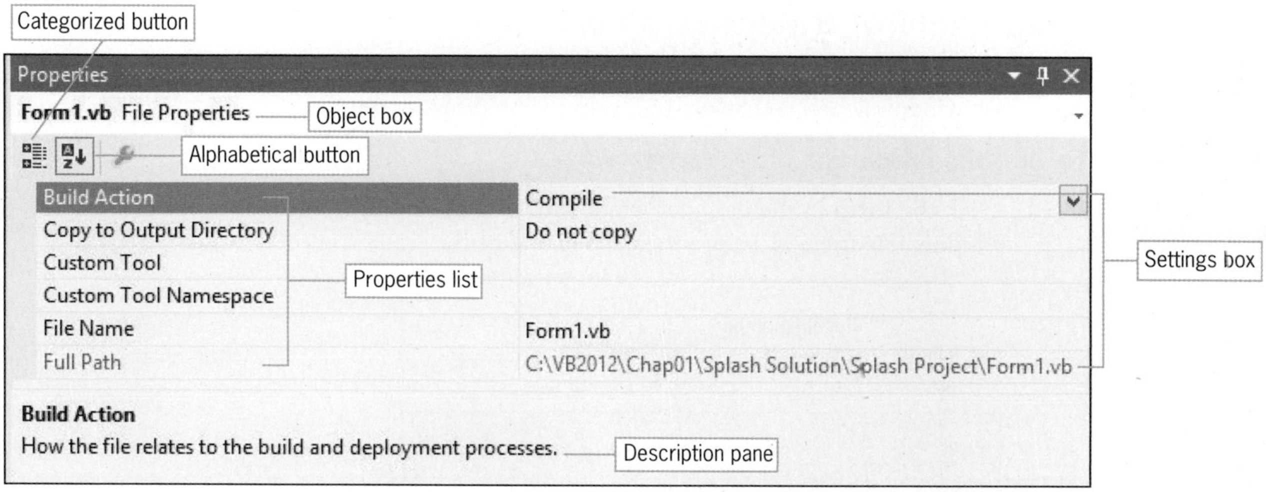

Figure 1-9 Properties window

To use the Properties window to change the form file's name:

START HERE

1. Form1.vb should be selected in the Solution Explorer window. Click **File Name** in the Properties list and then type **Splash Form.vb**. Be sure to include the .vb extension on the filename; otherwise, the computer will not recognize the file as a source file.
2. Press **Enter**. Splash Form.vb appears in the Solution Explorer and Properties windows and on the designer window's tab, as shown in Figure 1-10.

You also can change the File Name property by right-clicking Form1.vb in the Solution Explorer window and then clicking Rename on the context menu.

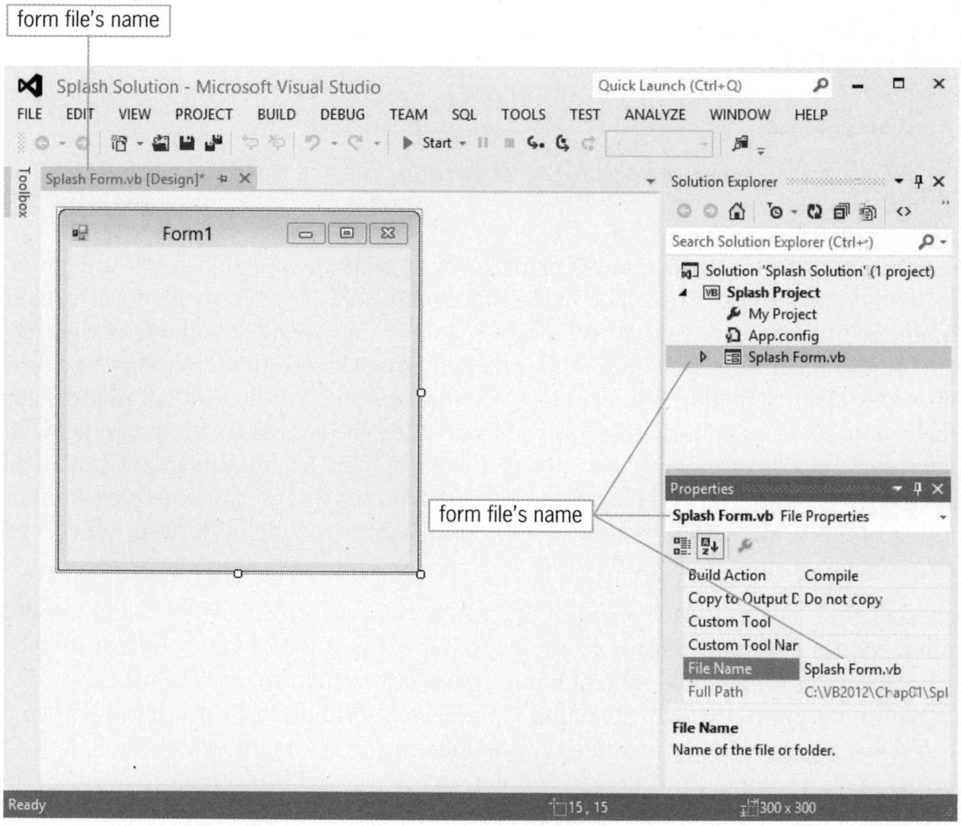

Figure 1-10 Form file's name shown in various locations

Properties of a Windows Form

Like a file, a Windows form also has a set of properties. The form's properties will appear in the Properties window when you select the form in the designer window.

START HERE

To view the properties of the form:

1. Click the **form** in the designer window to display the form's properties in the Properties window. Figure 1-11 shows a partial listing of the properties of a Windows form.

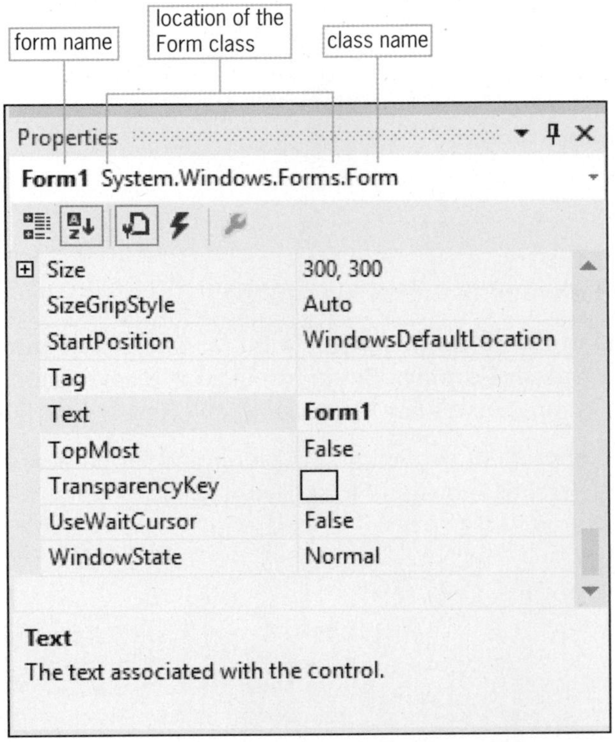

Figure 1-11 Properties window showing a partial listing of the form's properties

Notice that Form1 System.Windows.Forms.Form appears in the Object box in Figure 1-11. Form1 is the name of the form. The name is automatically assigned to the form when the form is instantiated (created). In System.Windows.Forms.Form, Form is the name of the class used to instantiate the form. System.Windows.Forms is the namespace that contains the Form class definition. A **class definition** is a block of code that specifies (or defines) an object's appearance and behavior. All class definitions in Visual Basic 2012 are contained in namespaces, which you can picture as blocks of memory cells inside the computer. Each **namespace** contains the code that defines a group of related classes. The System.Windows.Forms namespace contains the definition of the Windows Form class. It also contains the class definitions for objects you add to a form, such as buttons and text boxes.

The period that separates each word in System.Windows.Forms.Form is called the **dot member access operator**. Similar to the backslash (\) in a folder path, the dot member access operator indicates a hierarchy, but of namespaces rather than folders. In other words, the backslash in the path D:\VB2012\Chap01\Splash Solution\Splash Project\Splash Form.vb indicates that the Splash Form.vb file is contained in (or is a member of) the Splash Project folder, which is a member of the Splash Solution folder, which is a member of the Chap01 folder, which is a member of the VB2012 folder, which is a member of the D: drive. Likewise, the name System.Windows.Forms.Form indicates that the Form class is a member of the Forms namespace, which is a member of the Windows namespace, which is a member of the System namespace. The dot member access operator allows the computer to locate the Form class in the computer's internal memory, similar to the way the backslash (\) allows the computer to locate the Splash Form.vb file on your computer's disk.

The Name Property

As you do to a form file, you should assign a more meaningful name to a Windows form because doing so will help you keep track of the various forms in a project. Unlike a file, a Windows form has a Name property rather than a File Name property. You use the name entered in an object's Name property to refer to the object in code, so each object must have a unique name. The name you assign to an object must begin with a letter and contain only letters, numbers, and the underscore character. The name cannot include punctuation characters or spaces.

There are several conventions for naming objects in Visual Basic. In this book, you will use a naming convention called Hungarian notation. Names in Hungarian notation begin with a three (or more) character ID that represents the object's type, with the remaining characters in the name representing the object's purpose. For example, using Hungarian notation, you might assign the name frmSplash to the current form. The "frm" identifies the object as a form, and "Splash" reminds you of the form's purpose. Hungarian notation names are entered using **camel case**, which means you enter the ID characters in lowercase and then capitalize the first letter of each subsequent word in the name. Camel case refers to the fact that the uppercase letters appear as "humps" in the name because they are taller than the lowercase letters.

START HERE

To change the name of the form:

1. Drag the scroll box in the Properties window to the top of the vertical scroll bar. As you scroll, notice the various properties associated with a form. Also notice that the items within parentheses appear at the top of the Properties list.
2. Click **(Name)** in the Properties list. Type **frmSplash** and press **Enter**. An asterisk (*) appears on the designer window's tab. The asterisk indicates that the form has been changed since the last time it was saved.

The Text Property

In addition to changing the form's Name property, you also should change its Text property, which controls the text displayed in the form's title bar. Form1 is the default value assigned to the Text property of the first form in a project. In this case, "Red Tree Inn" would be a more descriptive value.

START HERE

To set the Text property of the form:

1. Scroll down the Properties window until you see the Text property in the Properties list and then click **Text**.
2. Type **Red Tree Inn** and press **Enter**. The new text appears in the property's Settings box and also in the form's title bar.

The Name and Text properties of a Windows form should always be changed to more meaningful values. The Name property is used by the programmer when coding the application. The Text property, on the other hand, is read by the user while the application is running.

The StartPosition Property

When an application is started, the computer uses the form's StartPosition property to determine the form's initial position on the screen. The frmSplash form represents a splash screen, which typically appears in the middle of the screen.

START HERE

To center a form on the screen when the application is started:

1. Click **StartPosition** in the Properties list and then click the **list arrow** in the Settings box.
2. Click **CenterScreen** in the list.

The Font Property

A form's Font property determines the type, style, and size of the font used to display the text on the form. A font is the general shape of the characters in the text. Segoe UI, Tahoma, and Microsoft Sans Serif are examples of font types. Font styles include regular, bold, and italic. The numbers 9, 12, and 18 are examples of font sizes, which typically are measured in points, with one **point** equaling 1/72 of an inch. The recommended font for applications created for systems running Windows 8, Windows 7, or Windows Vista is Segoe UI because it offers improved readability. Segoe is pronounced SEE-go, and UI stands for user interface. For most of the elements in the interface, you will use a font size of 9-point. However, to make the figures in the book more readable, some of the interfaces created in this book will use a larger font size.

START HERE

To set the form's Font property:

1. Click **Font** in the Properties list and then click the **...** (ellipsis) button in the Settings box to open the Font dialog box.
2. Locate and then click the **Segoe UI** font in the Font box. Click **9** in the Size box and then click the **OK** button. (Don't be concerned if the size of the form changes.)

The Size Property

As you can with any Windows object, you can size a form by selecting it and then dragging the sizing handles that appear around it. You also can size an object by selecting it and then pressing and holding down the Shift key as you press the up, down, right, or left arrow key on your keyboard. In addition, you can set the object's Size property.

START HERE

To set the form's Size property:

1. Click **Size** in the Properties list. Notice that the Size property contains two numbers separated by a comma and a space. The first number represents the width of the form, measured in pixels. The second number represents the height, also measured in pixels. A pixel, which is short for "picture element," is one spot in a grid of thousands of such spots that form an image either produced on the screen by a computer or printed on a page by a printer.
2. Type **605, 334** in the Size property's Settings box and press **Enter**. Expand the Size property by clicking the **plus box** that appears next to the property. Notice that the first number listed in the property represents the width, and the second number represents the height. Click the **minus box** to collapse the property.

Setting and Restoring a Property's Value

In the next set of steps, you will practice setting and then restoring a property's value. More specifically, you will set and then restore the value of the form's BackColor property, which determines the background color of the form.

To set and then restore the form's BackColor property value:

START HERE

1. Click **BackColor** in the Properties list and then click the **list arrow** in the Settings box. Click the **Custom** tab and then click a **red square** to change the background color of the form to red.
2. Now, right-click **BackColor** in the Properties list and then click **Reset** on the context menu. The background color of the form returns to its default setting. Figure 1-12 shows the status of the form in the IDE.

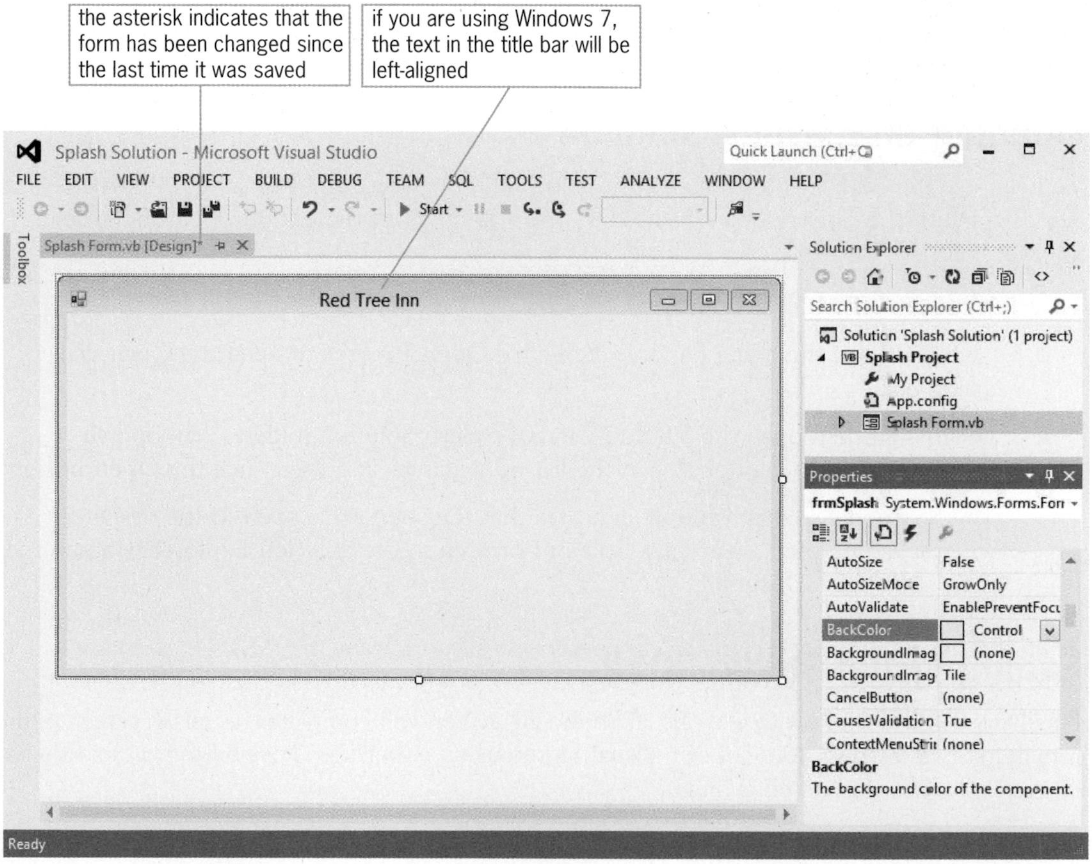

Figure 1-12 Status of the form in the IDE

Saving a Solution

The asterisk (*) that appears on the designer tab in Figure 1-12 indicates that a change was made to the form since the last time it was saved. It is a good idea to save the current solution every 10 or 15 minutes so that you will not lose a lot of your work if the computer loses power. You can save the solution by clicking FILE on the menu bar and then clicking Save All. You also can click the Save All button on the Standard toolbar. When you save the solution, the computer saves any changes made to the files included in the solution. It also removes the asterisk that appears on the designer window's tab.

The Save All button on the Standard toolbar looks like this: .

To save the current solution:

START HERE

1. Click **FILE** on the menu bar and then click **Save All**. The asterisk is removed from the designer window's tab, indicating that all changes made to the form have been saved.

Closing the Current Solution

When you are finished working on a solution, you should close it. Closing a solution closes all projects and files contained in the solution.

START HERE

To close the Splash Solution:

1. Click **FILE** on the menu bar. Notice that the menu contains a Close option and a Close Solution option. The Close option closes the designer window in the IDE; however, it does not close the solution itself. Only the Close Solution option closes the solution.
2. Click **Close Solution**. The Solution Explorer window indicates that no solution is currently open in the IDE.

Opening an Existing Solution

You can use the FILE menu to open an existing solution. The names of solution files end with .sln. If a solution is already open in the IDE, you will be given the option of closing it before another solution is opened.

START HERE

To open the Splash Solution:

1. Click **FILE** on the menu bar and then click **Open Project** to open the Open Project dialog box.
2. Locate and then open the VB2012\Chap01\Splash Solution folder. Click **Splash Solution** (Splash Solution.sln) in the list of filenames and then click the **Open** button.
3. The Solution Explorer window indicates that the solution is open. If the designer window is not open, right-click **Splash Form.vb** in the Solution Explorer window and then click **View Designer**.

Exiting Visual Studio 2012

Finally, you will learn how to exit Visual Studio 2012. You will complete the splash screen in the remaining two lessons. You can exit Visual Studio using either the Close button on its title bar or the Exit option on its FILE menu.

START HERE

To exit Visual Studio 2012:

1. Click **FILE** on the menu bar and then click **Exit**.

Lesson A Summary

- To start Visual Studio 2012:

  If you are using Windows 8, tap the Windows logo key (if necessary) to switch to the Windows 8 tile-based mode and then click the Visual Studio 2012 tile. If you are using Windows 7, click the Start button on the Windows 7 taskbar, point to All Programs, click Microsoft Visual Studio 2012, and then click Visual Studio 2012.

- To select a different window layout:

  Click TOOLS on the menu bar, click Import and Export Settings, select the Reset all settings radio button, click the Next button, select the appropriate radio button, click the Next button, click the settings collection you want to use, and then click the Finish button.

- To configure Visual Studio:

  Click TOOLS, click Options, click the Projects and Solutions node, and then use the information shown earlier in Figure 1-3 to select and deselect the appropriate check boxes. Click the OK button.

- To create a Visual Basic 2012 Windows application:

  Start Visual Studio 2012. Click FILE, click New Project, expand the Visual Basic node, click Windows, and then click Windows Forms Application. Enter an appropriate name and location in the Name and Location boxes, respectively. Select the Create directory for solution check box. Enter an appropriate name in the Solution name box and then click the OK button.

- To reset the window layout in the IDE:

  Click WINDOW, click Reset Window Layout, and then click the Yes button.

- To close and open a window in the IDE:

  Close the window by clicking the Close button on its title bar. Use the appropriate option on the VIEW menu to open the window.

- To auto-hide a window in the IDE:

  Click the Auto Hide (vertical pushpin) button on the window's title bar.

- To temporarily display an auto-hidden window in the IDE:

  Click the window's tab.

- To permanently display an auto-hidden window in the IDE:

  Click the window's tab to display the window, and then click the Auto Hide (horizontal pushpin) button on the window's title bar.

- To set the value of a property:

  Select the object whose property you want to set and then select the appropriate property in the Properties list. Type the new property value in the selected property's Settings box, or choose the value from the list, color palette, or dialog box.

- To give a more meaningful name to an object:

  Set the object's Name property.

- To control the text appearing in the form's title bar:

  Set the form's Text property.

- To specify the starting location of the form:

  Set the form's StartPosition property.

- To specify the type, style, and size of the font used to display text on the form:

  Set the form's Font property.

- To size a form:

  Drag the form's sizing handles. You also can set the form's Size, Height, and Width values in the Properties window. In addition, you can select the form and then press and hold down the Shift key as you press the up, down, left, or right arrow key on your keyboard.

- To change the background color of a form:

  Set the form's BackColor property.

- To restore a property to its default setting:

  Right-click the property in the Properties list and then click Reset.

- To save a solution:

  Click FILE on the menu bar and then click Save All. You also can click the Save All button on the Standard toolbar.

- To close a solution:

  Click FILE on the menu bar and then click Close Solution.

- To open an existing solution:

  Click FILE on the menu bar and then click Open Project. Locate and then open the application's solution folder. Click the solution filename, which ends with .sln. Click the Open button. If the designer window is not open, right-click the form file's name in the Solution Explorer window and then click View Designer.

- To exit Visual Studio 2012:

  Click the Close button on the Visual Studio 2012 title bar. You also can click FILE on the menu bar and then click Exit.

Lesson A Key Terms

Camel case—used when entering object names in Hungarian notation; the practice of entering the object's ID characters in lowercase and then capitalizing the first letter of each subsequent word in the name

Class definition—a block of code that specifies (or defines) an object's appearance and behavior

Code—program instructions

Dot member access operator—a period; used to indicate a hierarchy

Form—the foundation for the user interface in a Windows application; also called a Windows Form object

Form file—a file that contains the code associated with a Windows form

GUI—acronym for graphical user interface

Namespace—a block of memory cells inside the computer; contains the code that defines a group of related classes

Object box—the section of the Properties window that contains the name of the selected object

Point—used to measure font size; 1/72 of an inch

Properties—the attributes that control an object's appearance and behavior

Properties list—the section of the Properties window that lists both the names and the values of the selected object's properties

Properties window—the window that lists an object's attributes (properties)

Settings box—the right column of the Properties list; displays each property's current value (setting)

Solution Explorer window—the window that displays a list of the projects contained in the current solution and the items contained in each project

Source file—a file that contains code

Windows Form Designer window—the window in which you create an application's GUI

Windows Form object—the foundation for the user interface in a Windows application; referred to more simply as a form

Lesson A Review Questions

1. When a form has been modified since the last time it was saved, what appears on its tab in the designer window?
   a. an ampersand (&)
   b. an asterisk (*)
   c. a percent sign (%)
   d. a plus sign (+)

2. You use the ________ window to set the characteristics that control an object's appearance and behavior.
   a. Characteristics
   b. Object
   c. Properties
   d. Toolbox

3. The ________ window lists the projects and files included in a solution.
   a. Object
   b. Project
   c. Properties
   d. Solution Explorer

4. The names of solution files in Visual Basic 2012 end with ________ .
   a. .prg
   b. .sln
   c. .src
   d. .vb

5. Which of the following statements is true?
   a. You can auto-hide a window by clicking the Auto-Hide (vertical pushpin) button on its title bar.
   b. An auto-hidden window appears as a tab on the edge of the IDE.
   c. You temporarily display an auto-hidden window by clicking its tab.
   d. all of the above

6. The ________ property controls the text displayed in a form's title bar.
   a. Caption
   b. Text
   c. Title
   d. TitleBar

7. You give an object a more meaningful name by setting the object's ________ property.
   a. Application
   b. Caption
   c. Name
   d. Text

8. The ________ property determines the initial position of a form when the application is started.
   a. InitialLocation
   b. Location
   c. StartLocation
   d. StartPosition
9. Explain the difference between a form's Text property and its Name property.
10. Explain the difference between a form file and a form.
11. What does the dot member access operator indicate in the text System.Windows.Forms.Label?

Lesson A Exercises

INTRODUCTORY

1. If necessary, start Visual Studio 2012 and permanently display the Solution Explorer window. Use the FILE menu to open the Carter Solution (Carter Solution.sln) file, which is contained in the VB2012\Chap01\Carter Solution folder. If necessary, right-click the form file's name in the Solution Explorer window and then click View Designer. Change the form's Name property to frmMain. Change the form's BackColor property to light purple. Change the form's Font property to Segoe UI, 9pt. Change the form's StartPosition property to CenterScreen. Change the form's Text property to Carter Sales. Click FILE on the menu bar and then click Save All to save the solution. Click FILE on the menu bar and then click Close Solution to close the solution.

INTRODUCTORY

2. If necessary, start Visual Studio 2012 and permanently display the Solution Explorer window. Create a Visual Basic Windows application. Use the following names for the solution and project, respectively: Turner Solution and Turner Project. Save the application in the VB2012\Chap01 folder. Change the form file's name to Main Form.vb. Change the form's name to frmMain. The form's title bar should say Turner Inc.; set the appropriate property. The form should be centered on the screen when it first appears; set the appropriate property. Change the background color of the form to light pink. Any text on the form should appear in the Segoe UI, 12pt font; set the appropriate property. Save and then close the solution.

INTRODUCTORY

3. If necessary, start Visual Studio 2012 and permanently display the Solution Explorer window. Create a Visual Basic Windows application. Use the following names for the solution and project, respectively: Hillside Solution and Hillside Project. Save the solution in the VB2012\Chap01 folder. Change the form file's name to Main Form.vb. Change the form's name to frmMain. The form's title bar should say Hillside Shopping Center; set the appropriate property. The form should be centered on the screen when it first appears; set the appropriate property. Any text on the form should appear in the Segoe UI, 9pt font; set the appropriate property. Save and then close the solution.

LESSON B

After studying Lesson B, you should be able to:

- Add a control to a form
- Set the properties of a label, picture box, and button control
- Select multiple controls
- Center controls on the form
- Open the Project Designer window
- Start and end an application
- Enter code in the Code Editor window
- Terminate an application using the `Me.Close()` instruction
- Run the project's executable file

The Toolbox Window

The Ch01B video demonstrates all of the steps contained in Lesson B. You can view the video either before or after completing the lesson.

In Lesson A, you learned about the Windows Form Designer, Solution Explorer, and Properties windows. In this lesson, you will learn about the **Toolbox window**, referred to more simply as the toolbox. The **toolbox** contains the tools you use when creating your application's user interface. Each tool represents a class from which an object, such as a button or text box, can be instantiated. The instantiated objects, called **controls**, will appear on the form.

START HERE

To open the Splash Solution from Lesson A and then display the Toolbox window:

1. If necessary, start Visual Studio 2012 and open the Solution Explorer window.
2. Open the Splash Solution (Splash Solution.sln) file contained in the VB2012\Chap01\Splash Solution folder. If necessary, open the designer window.
3. Permanently display the Properties and Toolbox windows and then auto-hide the Solution Explorer window.
4. If necessary, expand the Common Controls node in the toolbox. Rest your mouse pointer on the word **Label** in the toolbox. The tool's purpose appears in a box. See Figure 1-13.

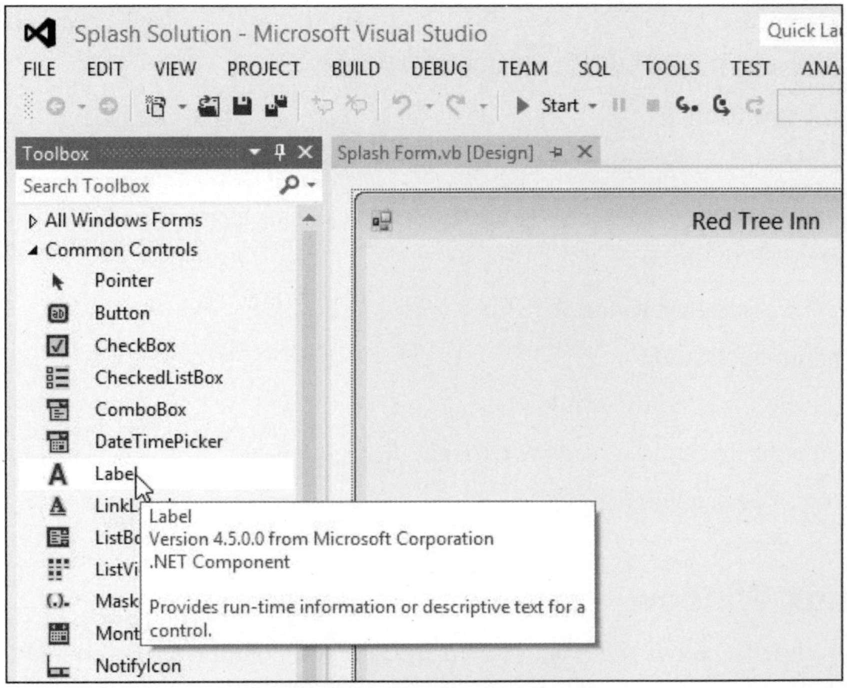

Figure 1-13 Toolbox window showing the purpose of the Label tool

The Label Tool

You use the Label tool to add a label control to a form. The purpose of a **label control** is to display text that the user is not allowed to edit while the application is running. In this case, for example, you do not want the user to change the name of the inn or the "A relaxing place to stay!" message. Therefore, you will display the information using two label controls.

START HERE

To use the Label tool to instantiate a label control:

1. Click the **Label** tool in the toolbox, but do not release the mouse button. Hold down the mouse button as you drag the mouse pointer to the lower-left corner of the form. As you drag the mouse pointer, you will see a solid box, an outline of a rectangle, and a plus box following the mouse pointer. The blue lines that appear between the form's left and bottom borders and the label's left and bottom borders are called margin lines because their size is determined by the contents of the label's Margin property. The purpose of the margin lines is to assist you in spacing the controls properly on the form. See Figure 1-14.

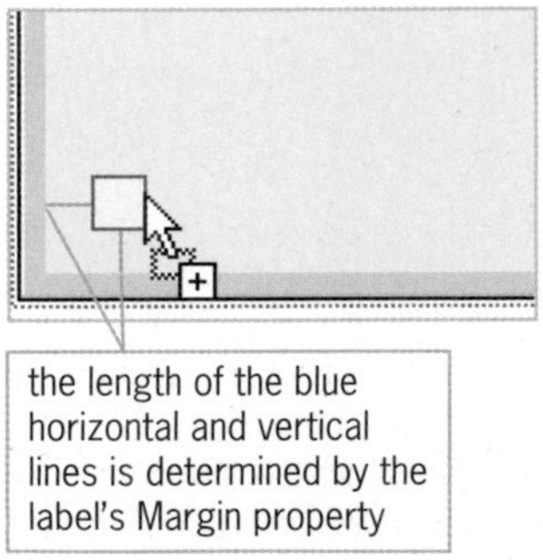

Figure 1-14 Label tool being dragged to the form

2. Release the mouse button. A label control appears on the form. See Figure 1-15. (If the wrong control appears on the form, right-click the control, click Delete, and then repeat Steps 1 and 2.) Notice that Label1 System.Windows.Forms.Label appears in the Object box in the Properties window. (You may need to widen the Properties window to view the entire contents of the Object box.) Label1 is the default name assigned to the label control. System.Windows.Forms.Label indicates that the control is an instance of the Label class, which is defined in the System.Windows.Forms namespace.

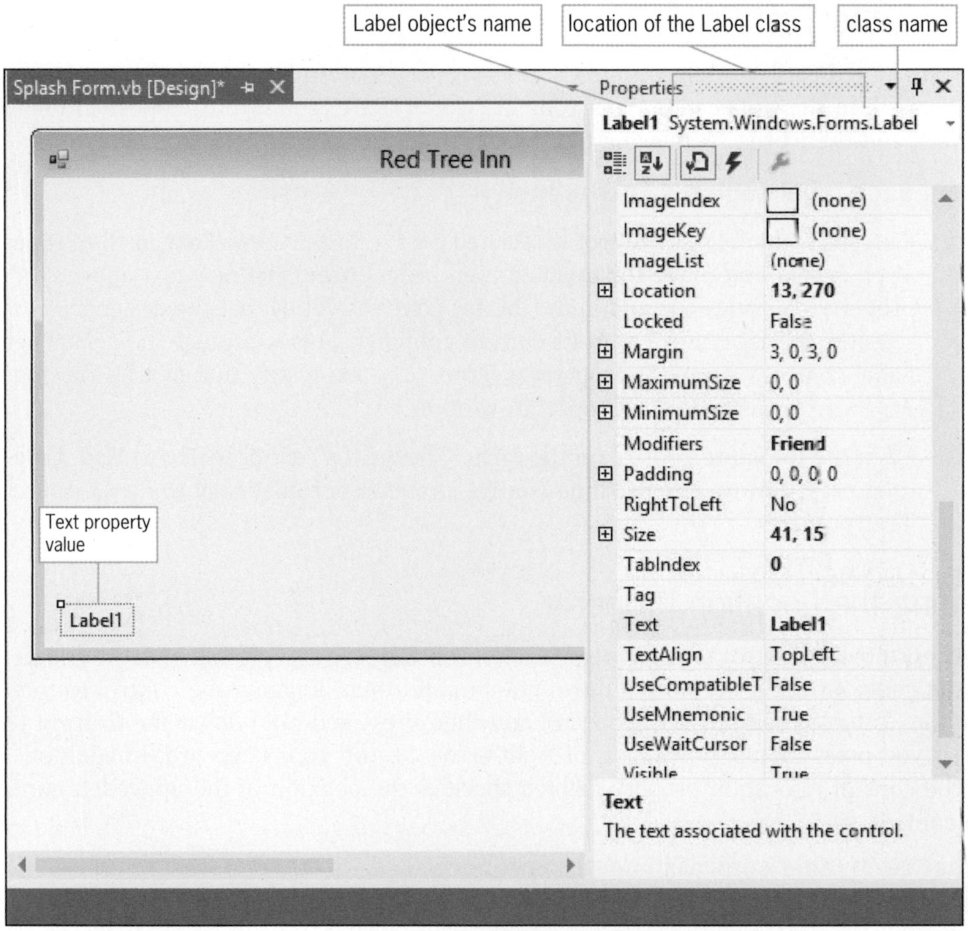

Figure 1-15 Label control added to the form

You also can add a control to the form by clicking a tool in the toolbox and then clicking the form. In addition, you can click a tool in the toolbox, place the mouse pointer on the form, and then press the left mouse button and drag the mouse pointer until the control is the desired size. You also can double-click a tool in the toolbox.

Recall from Lesson A that a default value is assigned to each of an object's properties when the object is created. Label1 is the default value assigned to the Text and Name properties of the first label control added to a form. The value of the Text property appears inside the label control, as indicated in Figure 1-15.

START HERE

To add another label control to the form:

1. Click the **Label** tool in the toolbox and then drag the mouse pointer to the form, positioning it above the existing label control. (Do not worry about the exact location.)
2. Release the mouse button. Label2 is assigned to the control's Text and Name properties.

Some programmers assign meaningful names to all of the controls in an interface, while others do so only for controls that are either coded or referred to in code. In subsequent chapters in this book, you will follow the latter convention. In this chapter, however, you will assign a meaningful name to each control in the interface. The three-character ID used for naming labels is lbl.

START HERE

To assign meaningful names to the label controls:

1. Click the **Label1** control on the form. This selects the control and displays its properties in the Properties window. Click **(Name)** in the Properties list. Type **lblName** in the Settings box and then press **Enter**.
2. Click the **Label2** control on the form. Change the control's name to **lblMsg** and then press **Enter**.

Setting the Text Property

As you learned earlier, a label control's Text property determines the value that appears inside the control. In this application, you want the words "Red Tree Inn" to appear in the lblName control, and the words "A relaxing place to stay!" to appear in the lblMsg control.

START HERE

To set each label control's Text property:

1. Currently, the lblMsg control is selected on the form. Click **Text** in the Properties list. Type **A relaxing place to stay!** and then press **Enter**. The new text appears in the Text property's Settings box and in the lblMsg control. Notice that the designer automatically sizes the lblMsg control to fit its current contents. This is because the default setting of a Label control's AutoSize property is True. (You can verify that fact by viewing the AutoSize property in the Properties window.)
2. Click the **lblName** control on the form. Change its Text property to **Red Tree Inn** and then press **Enter**. The lblName control stretches automatically to fit the contents of its Text property.

Setting the Location Property

You can move a control to a different location on the form by placing your mouse pointer on the control until it becomes a move pointer, and then dragging the control to the desired location. You also can select the control and then press and hold down the Control (Ctrl) key as you press the up, down, left, or right arrow key on your keyboard. In addition, you can set the control's Location property, which specifies the position of the upper-left corner of the control.

The move pointer looks like this: ✥.

START HERE

To set each label control's Location property:

1. Click the **lblMsg** control to select it. Click **Location** in the Properties list. Expand the Location property by clicking its **plus box**. The X value specifies the number of pixels from the left border of the form to the left border of the control. The Y value specifies the number of pixels between the top border of the form and the top border of the control. In other words, the X value refers to the control's horizontal location on the form, whereas the Y value refers to its vertical location.
2. Type **315, 175** in the Location property and then press **Enter**. The lblMsg control moves to its new location. Click the **minus box** to collapse the property.
3. In addition to selecting a control by clicking it on the form, you also can select a control by clicking its entry (name and class) in the Object box in the Properties window. Click the **list arrow** in the Properties window's Object box, and then click **lblName System.Windows.Forms.Label** in the list. Set the control's Location property to **315, 130**.

Changing a Property For Multiple Controls

In Lesson A, you changed the form's Font property to Segoe UI, 9pt. When you add a control to the form, the control's Font property is set to the same value as the form's Font property. Using object-oriented programming terminology, the control "inherits" the Font attribute of the form. In this case, for example, the lblName and lblMsg controls inherit the form's Font property setting: Segoe UI, 9pt.

At times, you may want to use a different font type, style, or size for a control's text. One reason for doing this is to bring attention to a specific part of the screen. In the splash screen, for example, you can make the text in the two label controls more noticeable by increasing the size of the font used to display the text. You can change the font size for both controls at the same time by clicking one control and then pressing and holding down the Ctrl (Control) key as you click the other control on the form. You can use the Ctrl+click method to select as many controls as you want. To cancel the selection of one of the selected controls, press and hold down the Ctrl key as you click the control. To cancel the selection of all of the selected controls, release the Ctrl key and then click the form or an unselected control on the form.

To easily select a group of controls on a form, place the mouse pointer slightly above and to the left of the first control you want to select, and then press and hold down the left mouse button as you drag the mouse pointer. A dotted rectangle will appear as you drag. When all of the controls you want to select are within (or at least touched by) the dotted rectangle, release the mouse button. All of the controls surrounded or touched by the dotted rectangle will be selected.

START HERE

To select both label controls and then set their Font property:

1. Verify that the lblName control is selected. Press and hold down the **Ctrl** (Control) key as you click the **lblMsg** control, and then release the Ctrl key. Both controls are selected, as shown in Figure 1-16.

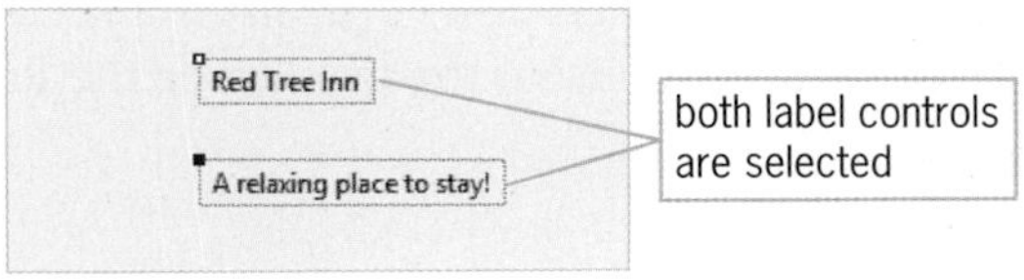

Figure 1-16 Label controls selected on the form

2. Open the Font dialog box by clicking **Font** in the Properties list and then clicking the **...** (ellipsis) button in the Settings box. Click **18** in the Size box, and then click the **OK** button to close the Font dialog box. The text in the two label controls appears in the new font size.
3. Click the **form** to deselect the label controls.
4. Click the **lblName** control and then use its Font property to change its font style to **Bold**.
5. Click the **lblMsg** control and then use its Font property to change its font style to **Italic**.

Using the Format Menu

The Format menu provides options for manipulating the controls on the form. The Align option, for example, allows you to align two or more controls by their left, right, top, or bottom borders. You can use the Make Same Size option to make two or more controls the same width and/or height. Before you can use the Format menu to change the alignment or size of two or more controls, you first must select the controls. The first control you select should always be

To experiment with the Align and Make Same Size options, complete Discovery Exercise 4 at the end of this lesson.

the one whose size and/or location you want to match. For example, to align the left border of the Label2 control with the left border of the Label1 control, you first select the Label1 control and then select the Label2 control. However, to make the Label1 control the same size as the Label2 control, you must select the Label2 control before selecting the Label1 control. The first control you select is referred to as the **reference control**. The reference control will have white sizing handles, whereas the other selected controls will have black sizing handles.

The Format menu also has a Center in Form option that centers one or more controls either horizontally or vertically on the form. In the next set of steps, you will use the Center in Form option to center the two label controls vertically on the form.

START HERE

To center the label controls vertically on the form:

1. Verify that the lblMsg control is selected. Ctrl+click the **lblName** control. Both label controls are now selected.
2. Click **FORMAT** on the menu bar, point to **Center in Form**, and then click **Vertically**.
3. Click **FILE** on the menu bar and then click **Save All** to save the solution.

The PictureBox Tool

The splash screen you previewed at the beginning of the chapter showed two images. You can include an image on a form using a **picture box control**, which you instantiate using the PictureBox tool.

START HERE

To add two picture box controls to the form:

1. Click the **PictureBox** tool in the toolbox and then drag the mouse pointer to the upper-left corner of the form. Release the mouse button. The picture box control's properties appear in the Properties list, and a box containing a triangle appears in the upper-right corner of the control. The box is referred to as the task box because, when you click it, it displays a list of tasks associated with the control. Each task in the list is associated with one or more properties. You can set the properties using the task list or the Properties window.
2. Click the **task box** on the PictureBox1 control. See Figure 1-17.

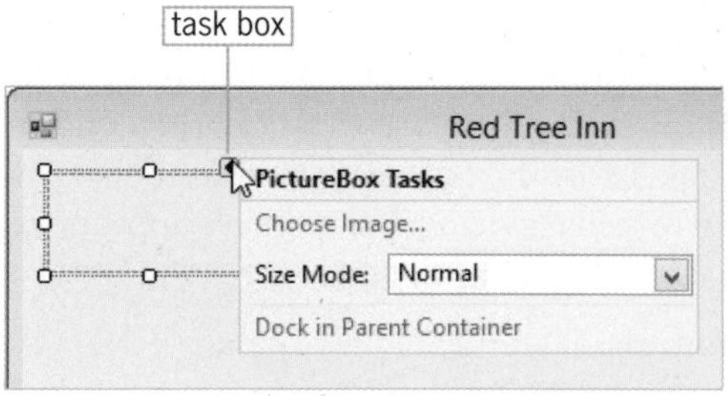

Figure 1-17 Open task list for a picture box

3. Click **Choose Image** to open the Select Resource dialog box. The Choose Image task is associated with the Image property in the Properties window.
4. To include the image file within the project itself, the Project resource file radio button must be selected in the Select Resource dialog box. Verify that the radio button is selected, and then click the **Import** button to open the Open dialog box.

5. Open the VB2012\Chap01 folder. Click **RedTreeInn** (**RedTreeInn.jpg**) in the list of filenames and then click the **Open** button. See Figure 1-18.

Figure 1-18 Completed Select Resource dialog box
Photo courtesy of Diane Zak

6. Click the **OK** button to close the Select Resource dialog box. A small portion of the image appears in the picture box control on the form, and Splash_Project.My.Resources. Resources.RedTreeInn appears in the control's Image property in the Properties window.
7. Click the **list arrow** in the Size Mode box in the task list and then click **StretchImage** in the list. Click the **picture box** control to close the task list.
8. The three-character ID used when naming picture box controls is pic. Use the Properties window to change the picture box's name to **picRedTree**.
9. If necessary, place your mouse pointer on the picture box control and then drag it to the location shown in Figure 1-19 (on the next page). Then place your mouse pointer on the sizing handle located in the lower-right corner of the picture box. Drag the sizing handle until the picture box is the size shown Figure 1-19 and then release the mouse button. (You also can set the Location and Size properties to 12, 12 and 245, 270, respectively.)
10. On your own, add another picture box control to the form. Position the picture box in the upper-right corner of the form. The control should display the image stored in the **RTI.png** file, which is contained in the VB2012\Chap01 folder. Change its size mode to **StretchImage**. Change the control's name to **picRti**. Position and size the control as shown in Figure 1-19.

Figure 1-19 Picture boxes added to the form
Photo courtesy of Diane Zak

The Button Tool

Every application should give the user a way to exit the program. Most Windows applications accomplish this task using either an Exit option on a FILE menu or an Exit button. In this lesson, the splash screen will provide a button for ending the application. In Windows applications, a **button control** is commonly used to perform an immediate action when clicked. The OK and Cancel buttons are examples of button controls found in many Windows applications.

START HERE

To add a button control to the form:

1. Use the Button tool in the toolbox to add a button control to the form. Position the control in the lower-right corner of the form.
2. The three-character ID used when naming button controls is btn. Change the button control's name to **btnExit**.
3. The button control's Text property determines the text that appears on the button's face. Set the button control's Text property to **Exit**.
4. Save the solution.

Starting and Ending an Application

Now that the user interface is complete, you can start the splash screen application to see how it will appear to the user. Before you start an application for the first time, you should open the Project Designer window and verify the name of the **startup form**, which is the form that the computer automatically displays each time the application is started. You can open the Project Designer window by right-clicking My Project in the Solution Explorer window and then clicking Open on the context menu. Or, you can click PROJECT on the menu bar and then click <*project name*> Properties on the menu.

START HERE

To verify the name of the startup form:

1. Auto-hide the Toolbox and Properties windows. Temporarily display the Solution Explorer window. Right-click **My Project** in the Solution Explorer window and then click **Open** to open the Project Designer window.
2. If necessary, click the **Application** tab to display the Application pane, which is shown in Figure 1-20. If frmSplash does not appear in the Startup form list box, click the **Startup form** list arrow and then click **frmSplash** in the list.

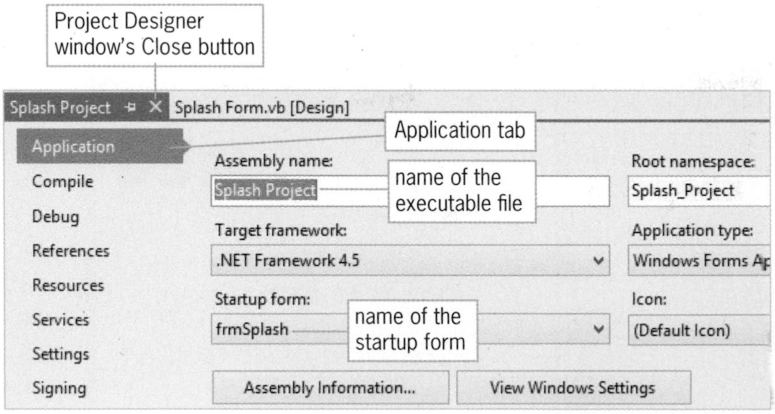

Figure 1-20 Application pane in the Project Designer window

You can start an application by clicking DEBUG on the menu bar and then clicking Start Debugging. You also can press the F5 key on your keyboard or click the Start button on the Standard toolbar. When you start a Visual Basic application, the computer automatically creates a file that can be run outside of the IDE (such as from the Run dialog box in Windows). The file is referred to as an **executable file**. The executable file's name is the same as the project's name, except it ends with .exe. The name of the executable file for the Splash Project, for example, is Splash Project.exe. However, you can use the Project Designer window to change the executable file's name. The computer stores the executable file in the project's bin\Debug folder. In this case, the Splash Project.exe file is stored in the VB2012\Chap01\Splash Solution\Splash Project \bin\Debug folder. When you are finished with an application, you typically give the user only the executable file because it does not allow the user to modify the application's code. To allow someone to modify the code, you need to provide the entire solution.

To change the name of the executable file, and then start and end the application:

START HERE

1. The Project Designer window should still be open. Change the filename in the Assembly name box to **Red Tree Splash**. Save the solution and then close the Project Designer window by clicking its **Close** button. (Refer to Figure 1-20 for the location of the Close button.)
2. Click **DEBUG** on the menu bar and then click **Start Debugging** to start the application. See Figure 1-21. (Do not be concerned about any windows that appear at the bottom of the screen.)

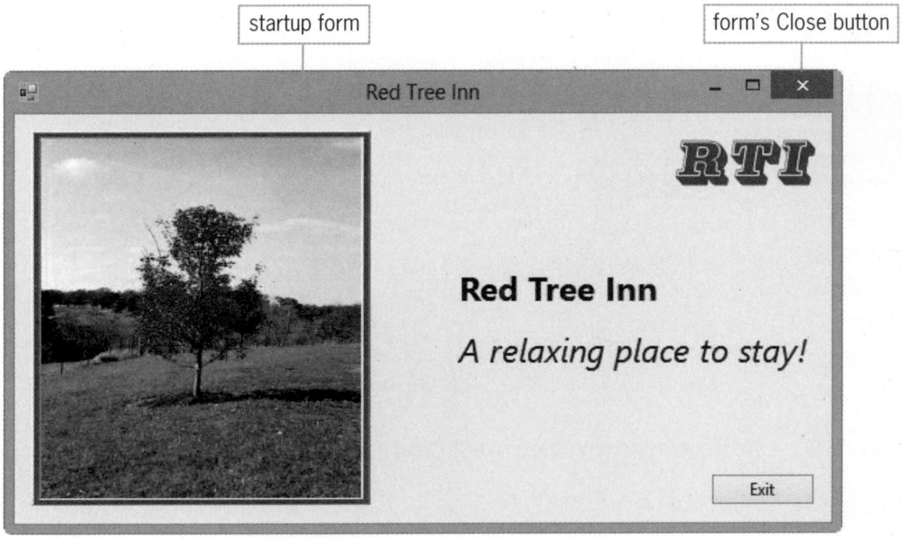

Figure 1-21 Result of starting the splash screen application
Photo courtesy of Diane Zak

3. Recall that the purpose of the Exit button is to allow the user to end the application. Click the **Exit** button on the splash screen. The button does not end the application; this is because you have not yet entered the instructions that tell the button how to respond when clicked.
4. Click the **Close** button on the form's title bar to stop the application. (You also can click the designer window to make it the active window, then click DEBUG on the menu bar, and then click Stop Debugging.)

The Code Editor Window

After creating your application's interface, you can begin entering the Visual Basic instructions (code) that tell the controls how to respond to the user's actions. Those actions—such as clicking, double-clicking, or scrolling—are called **events**. You tell an object how to respond to an event by writing an **event procedure**, which is a set of Visual Basic instructions that are processed only when the event occurs. You enter the procedure's code in the Code Editor window. In this lesson, you will write a Click event procedure for the Exit button, which should end the application when it is clicked.

START HERE

To open the Code Editor window:

1. Right-click the **form** and then click **View Code** on the context menu. The Code Editor window opens in the IDE, as shown in Figure 1-22. The Code Editor window contains the Class statement, which is used to define a class in Visual Basic. In this case, the Class statement begins with the `Public Class frmSplash` clause and ends with the `End Class` clause. Within the Class statement you enter the code to tell the form and its objects how to react to the user's actions.

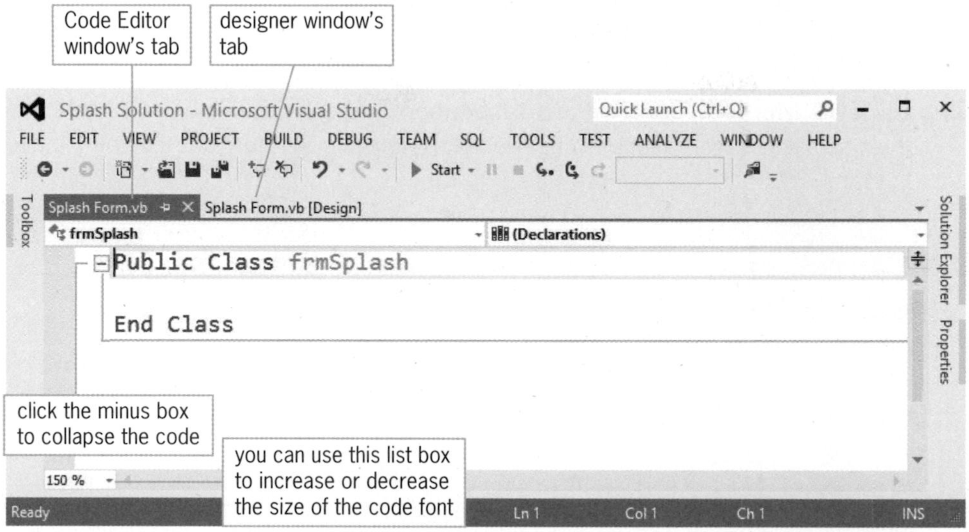

Figure 1-22 Code Editor window opened in the IDE

The `Public` keyword in the Class statement indicates that the class can be used by code defined outside of the class.

If the Code Editor window contains many lines of code, you might want to hide the sections of code that you are not presently working with or that you do not want to print. You hide a section (or region) of code by clicking the minus box that appears next to it. To unhide a region of code, you click the plus box that appears next to the code. Hiding and unhiding the code is also referred to as collapsing and expanding the code, respectively.

START HERE

To collapse and expand a region of code in the Code Editor window:

1. Click the **minus box** that appears next to the `Public Class frmSplash` clause in the Code Editor window. Doing this collapses the Class statement, as shown in Figure 1-23.

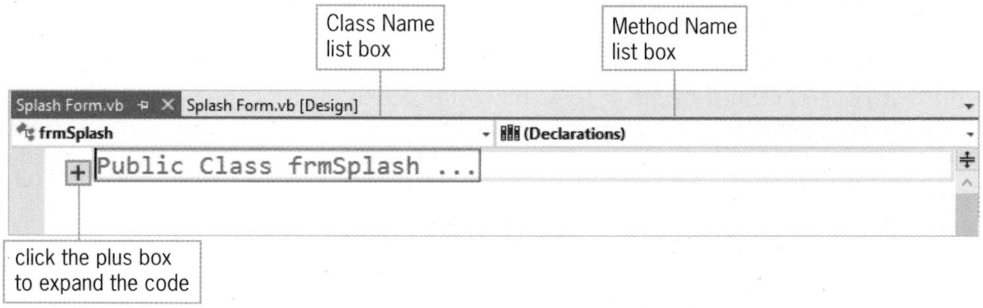

Figure 1-23 Code collapsed in the Code Editor window

2. Now click the **plus box** to expand the code.

As Figure 1-23 indicates, the Code Editor window contains a Class Name list box and a Method Name list box. The **Class Name list box** lists the names of the objects included in the user interface. The **Method Name list box** lists the events to which the selected object is capable of responding. In object-oriented programming (**OOP**), an event is considered a behavior of an object because it represents an action to which the object can respond. In the context of OOP, the Code Editor window "exposes" an object's behaviors to the programmer. You use the Class Name and Method Name list boxes to select the object and event, respectively, that you want to code. In this case, you will select btnExit in the Class Name list box and Click in the Method Name list box. This is because you want the application to end when the Exit button is clicked.

START HERE

To select the btnExit control's Click event:

1. Click the **Class Name** list arrow and then click **btnExit** in the list.
2. Click the **Method Name** list arrow and then click **Click** in the list. A code template for the btnExit control's Click event procedure appears in the Code Editor window. See Figure 1-24.

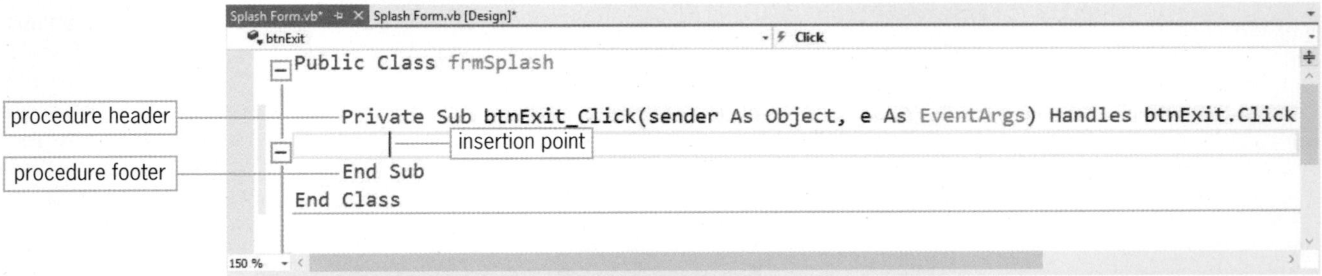

Figure 1-24 btnExit control's Click event procedure

The Code Editor provides the code template to help you follow the rules of the Visual Basic language. The rules of a programming language are called its **syntax**. The first line in the code template is called the **procedure header**, and the last line is called the **procedure footer**. The procedure header begins with the two keywords `Private Sub`. A **keyword** is a word that has a special meaning in a programming language. Keywords appear in a different color from the rest of the code. The `Private` keyword in Figure 1-24 indicates that the button's Click event procedure can be used only within the current Code Editor window. The `Sub` keyword is an abbreviation of the term **sub procedure**, which is a block of code that performs a specific task. Following the `Sub` keyword is the name of the object, an underscore, the name of the event, and parentheses containing some text. For now, you do not have to be concerned with the text that appears between the parentheses. After the closing parenthesis is `Handles btnExit.Click`. This part of the procedure header indicates that the procedure handles (or is associated with) the btnExit control's Click event. It tells the computer to process the procedure only when the btnExit control is clicked.

The code template ends with the procedure footer, which contains the keywords `End Sub`. You enter your Visual Basic instructions at the location of the insertion point, which appears between the Private Sub and End Sub clauses in Figure 1-24. The Code Editor automatically indents the line between the procedure header and footer. Indenting the lines within a procedure makes the instructions easier to read and is a common programming practice. In this case, the instruction you enter will tell the btnExit control to end the application when it is clicked.

The Me.Close() Instruction

The `Me.Close()` instruction tells the computer to close the current form. If the current form is the only form in the application, closing it terminates the entire application. In the instruction, `Me` is a keyword that refers to the current form, and `Close` is one of the methods available in Visual Basic. A **method** is a predefined procedure that you can call (or invoke) when needed. For example, if you want the computer to close the current form when the user clicks the Exit button, you enter the `Me.Close()` instruction in the button's Click event procedure. Notice the empty set of parentheses after the method's name in the instruction. The parentheses are required when calling some Visual Basic methods. However, depending on the method, the parentheses may or may not be empty. If you forget to enter the empty set of parentheses, the Code Editor will enter them for you when you move the insertion point to another line in the Code Editor window.

START HERE

To code the btnExit control's Click event procedure:

1. You can type the `Me.Close()` instruction on your own or use the Code Editor window's IntelliSense feature. In this set of steps, you will use the IntelliSense feature. Type **me.** (be sure to type the period, but don't press Enter). When you type the period, the IntelliSense feature displays a list of properties, methods, and so on from which you can select.

   Note: If the list of choices does not appear, the IntelliSense feature may have been turned off on your computer system. To turn it on, click TOOLS on the menu bar and then click Options. Expand the Text Editor node and then click Basic. Select the Auto list members check box and then click the OK button.

2. If necessary, click the **Common** tab. The Common tab displays the most commonly used items, whereas the All tab displays all of the items. Type **cl** (but don't press Enter). The IntelliSense feature highlights the Close method in the list. See Figure 1-25.

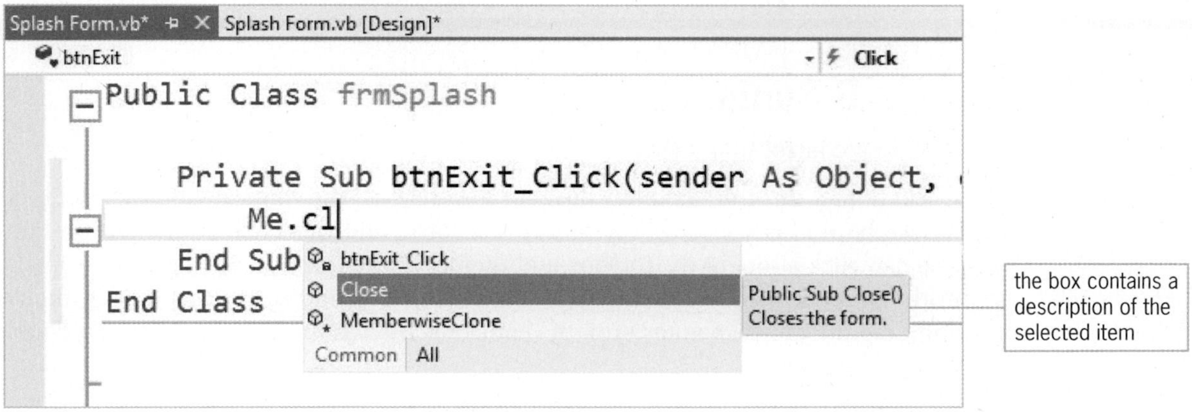

Figure 1-25 List displayed by the IntelliSense feature

3. Press **Tab** to include the Close method in the instruction and then press **Enter**. See Figure 1-26.

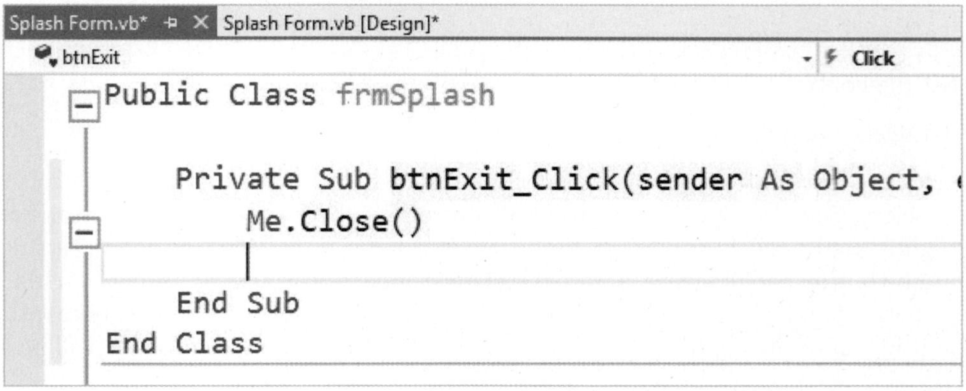

Figure 1-26 Completed Click event procedure for the btnExit control

It's a good idea to test a procedure after you have coded it. By doing this, you'll know where to look if an error occurs. You can test the Exit button's Click event procedure by starting the application and then clicking the button. When the button is clicked, the computer will process the `Me.Close()` instruction contained in the procedure.

START HERE

To test the Exit button's Click event procedure and the executable file:

1. Save the solution and then press the **F5** key to start the application. The splash screen appears.
2. Click the **Exit** button to end the application. Close the Code Editor window and then close the solution.
3. Press and hold down the **Windows logo** key on your keyboard as you tap the letter **r**. When the Run dialog box opens, release the logo key.
4. Click the **Browse** button. Locate and then open the VB2012\Chap01\Splash Solution\Splash Project\bin\Debug folder. Click **Red Tree Splash** (**Red Tree Splash.exe**) and then click the **Open** button.
5. Click the **OK** button in the Run dialog box. When the splash screen appears, click the **Exit** button.

Lesson B Summary

- To add a control to a form:

  Click a tool in the toolbox, but do not release the mouse button. Hold down the mouse button as you drag the tool to the form, and then release the mouse button. You also can click a tool in the toolbox and then click the form. In addition, you can click a tool in the toolbox, place the mouse pointer on the form, and then press the left mouse button and drag the mouse pointer until the control is the desired size. You also can double-click a tool in the toolbox.

- To display text that the user cannot edit while the application is running:

  Use the Label tool to instantiate a label control. Set the label control's Text property.

- To move a control to a different location on the form:

  Drag the control to the desired location. You also can set the control's Location property. In addition, you can select the control and then press and hold down the Ctrl (Control) key as you press the up, down, right, or left arrow key on your keyboard.

- To specify the type, style, and size of the font used to display text in a control:

  Set the control's Font property.

- To select multiple controls on a form:

  Click the first control you want to select, then Ctrl+click each of the other controls you want to select. You also can select a group of controls on the form by placing the mouse pointer slightly above and to the left of the first control you want to select, then pressing the left mouse button and dragging. A dotted rectangle appears as you drag. When all of the controls you want to select are within (or at least touched by) the dotted rectangle, release the mouse button. All of the controls surrounded or touched by the dotted rectangle will be selected.

- To cancel the selection of one or more controls:

  You cancel the selection of one control by pressing and holding down the Ctrl key as you click the control. You cancel the selection of all of the selected controls by releasing the Ctrl key and then clicking the form or an unselected control on the form.

- To center one or more controls on the form:

  Select the controls you want to center. Click FORMAT on the menu bar, point to Center in Form, and then click either Horizontally or Vertically.

- To align the borders of two or more controls on the form:

  Select the reference control and then select the other controls you want to align. Click FORMAT on the menu bar, point to Align, and then click the appropriate option.

- To make two or more controls on the form the same size:

  Select the reference control and then select the other controls you want to size. Click FORMAT on the menu bar, point to Make Same Size, and then click the appropriate option.

- To display a graphic in a control in the user interface:

  Use the PictureBox tool to instantiate a picture box control. Use the task box or Properties window to set the control's Image and SizeMode properties.

- To display a standard button that performs an action when clicked:

  Use the Button tool to instantiate a button control.

- To verify or change the names of the startup form and/or executable file:

  Use the Application pane in the Project Designer window. You can open the Project Designer window by right-clicking My Project in the Solution Explorer window, and then clicking Open on the context menu. Or, you can click PROJECT on the menu bar and then click *<project name>* Properties on the menu.

- To start and stop an application:

  You can start an application by clicking DEBUG on the menu bar and then clicking Start Debugging. You also can press the F5 key on your keyboard or click the Start button on the Standard toolbar. You can stop an application by clicking the form's Close button. You also can first make the designer window the active window, and then click DEBUG on the menu bar and then click Stop Debugging.

- To open the Code Editor window:

  Right-click the form and then click View Code on the context menu.

- To display an object's event procedure in the Code Editor window:

  Open the Code Editor window. Use the Class Name list box to select the object's name, and then use the Method Name list box to select the event.

- To allow the user to close the current form while an application is running:

  Enter the `Me.Close()` instruction in an event procedure.

- To run a project's executable file:

  Open the Run dialog box in Windows. Click the Browse button. Locate and then open the project's bin\Debug folder. Click the executable file's name. Click the Open button to close the Browse dialog box, and then click the OK button.

Lesson B Key Terms

Button control—the control commonly used to perform an immediate action when clicked

Class Name list box—appears in the Code Editor window; lists the names of the objects included in the user interface

Controls—objects (such as a label, a picture box, or a button) added to a form

Event procedure—a set of Visual Basic instructions that tell an object how to respond to an event

Events—actions to which an object can respond; examples include clicking and double-clicking

Executable file—a file that can be run outside of the Visual Studio IDE, such as from the Run dialog box in windows; the file has an .exe extension on its filename

Keyword—a word that has a special meaning in a programming language

Label control—the control used to display text that the user is not allowed to edit while an application is running

Method—a predefined Visual Basic procedure that you can call (invoke) when needed

Method Name list box—appears in the Code Editor window; lists the events to which the selected object is capable of responding

OOP—acronym for object-oriented programming

Picture box control—the control used to display an image on a form

Procedure footer—the last line in a procedure

Procedure header—the first line in a procedure

Reference control—the first control selected in a group of controls; this is the control whose size and/or location you want the other selected controls to match

Startup form—the form that appears automatically when an application is started

Sub procedure—a block of code that performs a specific task

Syntax—the rules of a programming language

Toolbox—refers to the Toolbox window

Toolbox window—the window that contains the tools used when creating an interface; each tool represents a class; referred to more simply as the toolbox

Lesson B Review Questions

1. The purpose of the ________ control is to display text that the user is not allowed to edit while the application is running.
   a. Button
   b. DisplayBox
   c. Label
   d. PictureBox

2. The text displayed on a button's face is stored in the button's ________ property.
   a. Caption
   b. Label
   c. Name
   d. Text

3. The Format menu contains options that allow you to ________.
   a. align two or more controls
   b. center one or more controls horizontally on the form
   c. make two or more controls the same size
   d. all of the above

4. You can use the ________ instruction to terminate a running application.
   a. `Me.Close()`
   b. `Me.Done()`
   c. `Me.Finish()`
   d. `Me.Stop()`

5. Define the term "syntax."

Lesson B Exercises

INTRODUCTORY

1. Open the Carpenters Solution (Carpenters Solution.sln) file contained in the VB2012\Chap01\Carpenters Solution folder. If necessary, open the designer window.
   a. Change the form file's name to Main Form.vb.
   b. Change the form's name to frmMain. Change its Font property to Segoe UI, 9pt. The form's title bar should say ICA; set the appropriate property. The form should be centered on the screen when it first appears; set the appropriate property.
   c. Add a label control to the form. The label should contain the text "International Carpenters Association" (without the quotation marks); set the appropriate property. Display the label's text in italics using the Segoe UI, 16pt font. The label should be located 20 pixels from the top of the form, and it should be centered horizontally on the form.
   d. Add a picture box control to the form. The control should display the image stored in the ICA.png file, which is contained in the VB2012\Chap01 folder. Set the picture box's size mode to StretchImage. Change the size of the picture box to 290, 110. Center the picture box on the form, both vertically and horizontally.
   e. Add a button control to the form. Position the button in the lower-right corner of the form. Change the button's name to btnExit. The button should display the text "Exit" (without the quotation marks); set the appropriate property.
   f. Open the Code Editor window. Enter the `Me.Close()` instruction in the btnExit control's Click event procedure.
   g. Display the Project Designer window. Verify that the name of the startup form is frmMain. Also, use the Assembly name box to change the executable file's name to ICA. Close the Project Designer window.
   h. Save the solution and then start the application. Use the Exit button to stop the application. Close the Code Editor window and then close the solution.
   i. Use the Run dialog box to run the project's executable file, which is contained in the project's bin\Debug folder.

INTERMEDIATE

2. Create a Visual Basic Windows application. Use the following names for the solution and project, respectively: Costello Solution and Costello Project. Save the application in the VB2012\Chap01 folder. Change the form file's name to Main Form.vb. Create the user interface shown in Figure 1-27. The picture box should display the image stored in the DollarSign.png file, which is contained in the VB2012\Chap01 folder. Change the form's Font property to Segoe UI, 9pt. You can use any font style and size for the label controls. The form should be centered on the screen when the application is started. Code the Exit button so that it closes the application when it is clicked. Use the Project Designer window to verify that the name of the startup form is correct, and to change the executable file's name to Costello Motors. Save the solution and then start the application. Use the Exit button to stop the application. Close the Code Editor window and then close the solution. Use the Run dialog box to run the project's executable file, which is contained in the project's bin\Debug folder.

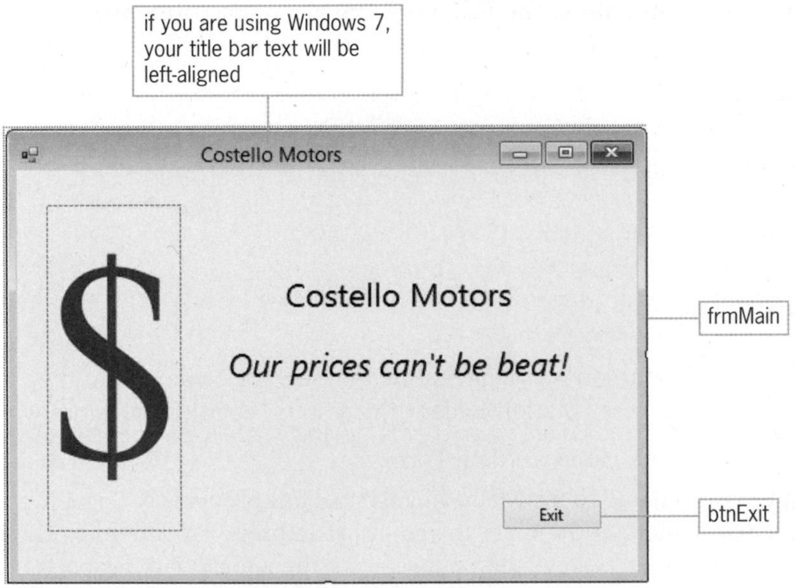

Figure 1-27 User interface for the Costello Motors application

INTERMEDIATE

3. Create a Visual Basic Windows application. Use the following names for the solution and project, respectively: Tabatha Solution and Tabatha Project. Save the application in the VB2012\Chap01 folder. Change the form file's name to Main Form.vb. Create the user interface shown in Figure 1-28. Change the form's Font property to Segoe UI, 9pt. You can use any font style and size for the label control. The form should be centered on the screen when the application is started. Assign appropriate names to the form and button. The picture box should display the image stored in the BandB.png file, which is contained in the VB2012\Chap01 folder. Code the Exit button so that it closes the application when it is clicked. Save the solution and then start the application. Use the Exit button to stop the application. Close the Code Editor window and then close the solution. Use the Run dialog box to run the project's executable file, which is contained in the project's bin\Debug folder.

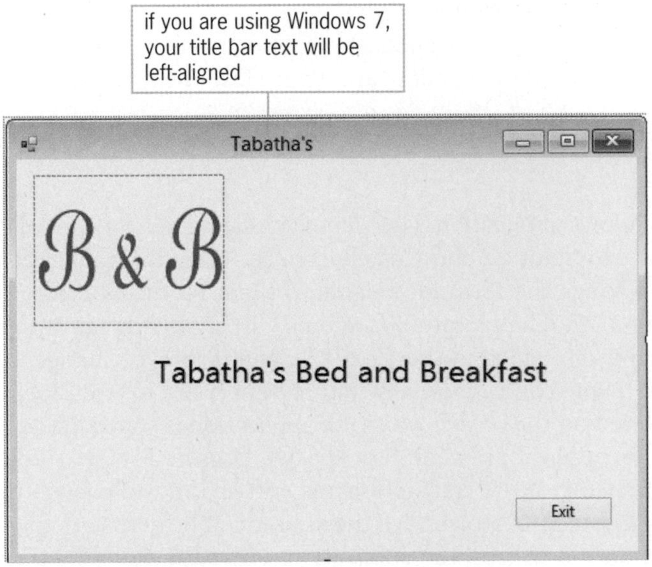

Figure 1-28 User interface for the Tabatha's Bed and Breakfast application

DISCOVERY

4. In this exercise, you learn about the FORMAT menu's Align and Make Same Size options.

   a. Open the Format Solution (Format Solution.sln) file contained in the VB2012\Chap01\Format Solution folder. If necessary, open the designer window.
   b. Click the Button2 control, and then press and hold down the Ctrl (Control) key as you click the other two button controls. Release the Ctrl key. Notice that the sizing handles on the first button you selected (Button2) are white, while the sizing handles on the other two buttons are black. The Align and Make Same Size options on the FORMAT menu use the control with the white sizing handles as the reference control when aligning and sizing the selected controls. First, you will practice with the Align option by aligning the three buttons by their left borders. Click FORMAT, point to Align, and then click Lefts. The left borders of the Button1 and Button3 controls are aligned with the left border of the Button2 control, which is the reference control.
   c. The Make Same Size option makes the selected objects the same height, width, or both. Here again, the first object you select determines the size. Click the form to deselect the three buttons. Click Button1, Ctrl+click Button2, and then Ctrl+click Button3. Click FORMAT, point to Make Same Size, and then click Both. The height and width of the Button2 and Button3 controls now match the height and width of the reference control (Button1).
   d. Click the form to deselect the buttons. Save and then close the solution.

LESSON C

After studying Lesson C, you should be able to:

- Set the properties of a timer control
- Delete a control from the form
- Delete code from the Code Editor window
- Code a timer control's Tick event procedure
- Prevent the user from sizing a form
- Remove and/or disable a form's Minimize, Maximize, and Close buttons
- Print an application's code and interface

The Ch01C video demonstrates all of the steps contained in Lesson C. You can view the video either before or after completing the lesson.

Using the Timer Tool

In Lesson B, you added an Exit button to the splash screen created for the Red Tree Inn. Splash screens usually do not contain an Exit button. Instead, they use a timer control to automatically remove themselves from the screen after a set period of time. In this lesson, you will remove the Exit button from the splash screen and replace it with a timer control.

START HERE

To open the Splash Solution from Lesson B:

1. If necessary, start Visual Studio 2012 and open the Solution Explorer window.
2. Open the Splash Solution (Splash Solution.sln) file contained in the VB2012\Chap01\Splash Solution folder. If necessary, open the designer window.
3. Permanently display the Properties and Toolbox windows and then auto-hide the Solution Explorer window.

You instantiate a timer control using the Timer tool, which is located in the Components section of the toolbox. When you drag the Timer tool to the form and then release the mouse button, the timer control will be placed in the component tray rather than on the form. The **component tray** is a special area of the IDE. Its purpose is to store controls that do not appear in the user interface during **run time**, which occurs while an application is running. In other words, the timer will not be visible to the user when the interface appears on the screen.

The Boolean values (True and False) are named after the English mathematician George Boole.

The purpose of a **timer control** is to process code at one or more regular intervals. The length of each interval is specified in milliseconds and entered in the timer's Interval property. A millisecond is 1/1000 of a second; in other words, there are 1000 milliseconds in a second. The timer's state—either running or stopped—is determined by its Enabled property, which can be set to either the Boolean value True or the Boolean value False. When its Enabled property is set to True, the timer is running; when it is set to False, the timer is stopped. If the timer is running, its Tick event occurs each time an interval has elapsed. Each time the Tick event occurs, the computer processes any code contained in the Tick event procedure. If the timer is stopped, the Tick event does not occur and, therefore, any code entered in the Tick event procedure is not processed.

START HERE

To add a timer control to the splash screen:

1. If necessary, expand the Components node in the toolbox. Click the **Timer** tool and then drag the mouse pointer to the form. (Do not worry about the exact location.) When you release the mouse button, a timer control appears in the component tray at the bottom of the IDE.

2. The three-character ID used when naming timer controls is tmr. Change the timer's name to **tmrExit**, and then set its Enabled property to **True**.
3. You will have the timer end the application after six seconds, which are 6000 milliseconds. Set the timer's Interval property to **6000** and press **Enter**. See Figure 1-29.

Figure 1-29 Timer control placed in the component tray
Photo courtesy of Diane Zak

You no longer need the Exit button, so you can delete it and its associated code. You then will enter the `Me.Close()` instruction in the timer's Tick event procedure.

To delete the Exit button and its code, and then code and test the timer:

START HERE

1. Auto-hide the Toolbox and Properties windows. Click the **Exit** button to select it and then press **Delete** to delete the control from the form.
2. Deleting a control from the form does not delete the control's code, which remains in the Code Editor window. Open the Code Editor window by right-clicking the **form** and then clicking **View Code**. Select (highlight) the entire Click event procedure for the btnExit control, including the blank line above the procedure, as shown in Figure 1-30.

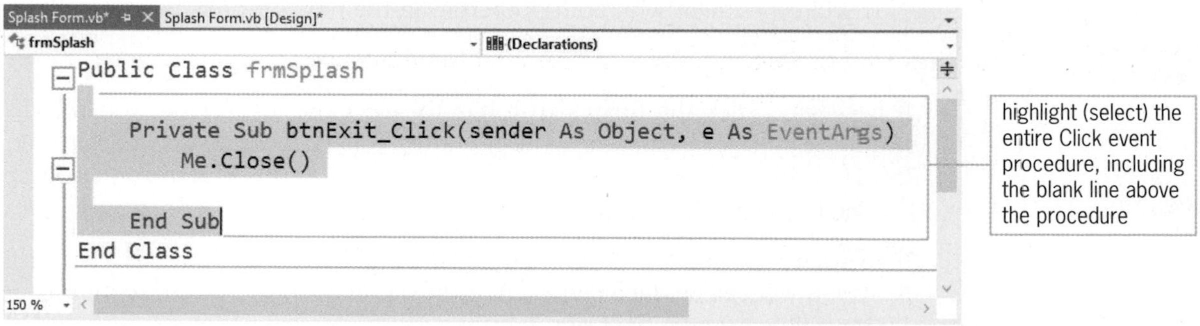

Figure 1-30 Exit button's Click event procedure selected in the Code Editor window

3. Press **Delete** to delete the selected code from the Code Editor window.
4. Use the Class Name and Method Name list boxes to open the code template for the tmrExit control's Tick event procedure. Type **Me.Close()** and press **Enter**.
5. Save the solution and then start the application. The splash form appears on the screen.

6. Place your mouse pointer on the form's right border until it becomes a horizontal sizing pointer, and then drag the form's border to the left. Notice that you can change the form's size during run time. Typically, a user is not allowed to change the size of a splash screen. You can prevent the user from sizing the form by changing the form's FormBorderStyle property, which you will do in the next section.

The horizontal sizing pointer looks like this: ⇔.

7. When six seconds have elapsed, the application ends and the splash form disappears. Click the **Splash Form.vb [Design]** tab to make the designer window the active window.

Setting the FormBorderStyle Property

A form's FormBorderStyle property determines the border style of the form. For most applications, you will leave the property at its default setting, Sizable. Doing this allows the user to change the form's size by dragging its borders while the application is running. When a form represents a splash screen, however, you typically set the FormBorderStyle property to either None or FixedSingle. The None setting removes the form's border, whereas the FixedSingle setting draws a fixed, thin line around the form.

START HERE

To change the FormBorderStyle property:

1. Click the **form's title bar** to select the form. Temporarily display the Properties window, and then set the FormBorderStyle property to **FixedSingle**.
2. Save the solution and then start the application. Try to size the form by dragging one of its borders. You will notice that you cannot size the form using its border.
3. When six seconds have elapsed, the application ends. Start the application again. Notice that the splash screen's title bar contains a Minimize button, a Maximize button, and a Close button. As a general rule, most splash screens do not contain these elements. You will learn how to remove the elements, as well as the title bar itself, in the next section. Here again, the application ends after six seconds have elapsed.

The MinimizeBox, MaximizeBox, and ControlBox Properties

You can use a form's MinimizeBox property to disable the Minimize button that appears on the form's title bar. Similarly, you can use the MaximizeBox property to disable the Maximize button. You will experiment with both properties in the next set of steps.

START HERE

To experiment with the MinimizeBox and MaximizeBox properties:

1. If necessary, click the **form's title bar** to select the form. First, you will disable the Minimize button. Temporarily display the Properties window, and then set the form's MinimizeBox property to **False**. Notice that the Minimize button appears dimmed (grayed-out) on the title bar. This indicates that the button is not available for use.
2. Now you will enable the Minimize button and disable the Maximize button. Set the MinimizeBox property to **True**, and then set the MaximizeBox property to **False**. Now only the Maximize button appears dimmed (grayed-out) on the title bar.

3. Now observe what happens if both the MinimizeBox and MaximizeBox properties are set to False. Set the MinimizeBox property to **False**. (The MaximizeBox property is already set to False.) Notice that when both properties are set to False, the buttons are not disabled; instead, they are removed from the title bar.
4. Now return the buttons to their original state by setting the form's MinimizeBox and MaximizeBox properties to **True**.

Unlike most applications, splash screens typically do not contain a title bar. You can remove the title bar by setting the form's ControlBox property to False, and then removing the text from its Text property. You will try this next.

START HERE

You will learn more about splash screens (such as how to round their corners) in this lesson's Discovery Exercises 4, 5, and 6.

To remove the title bar from the splash screen:

1. Set the form's ControlBox property to **False**. Doing this removes the title bar elements (icon and buttons) from the form; however, it does not remove the title bar itself. To remove the title bar, you must delete the contents of the form's Text property. Select the text in the Text property. Press **Delete** and then press **Enter**.
2. Save the solution and then start the application. The splash screen appears without a title bar. See Figure 1-31. The application ends after six seconds have elapsed.

Figure 1-31 Completed splash screen
Photo courtesy of Diane Zak

Printing the Application's Code and Interface

You should always print a copy of your application's code because the printout will help you understand and maintain the application in the future. To print the code, the Code Editor window must be the active (current) window. You also should print a copy of the application's user interface.

START HERE

To print the splash screen's interface and code:

1. The designer window should be the active window. Tap the **Print Screen** (Prnt Scrn or PrtSc) key on your keyboard; doing this places a picture of the interface on the Clipboard. Start Microsoft Word (or any application that can display a picture) and open a new document (if necessary). Press **Ctrl+v** to paste the contents of the Clipboard in the document. If your computer is connected to a printer, use the application to print the document. Close Microsoft Word (or the application you used to display the picture) without saving the document.

Ch01C-Snipping Tool

Note: If the Print Screen key does not work on your computer, you may be able to use the Windows Snipping Tool to take a picture of your interface and then save the picture to a file for printing. See the Ch01C-Snipping Tool video.

2. Click the **Splash Form.vb** tab to make the Code Editor window the active window. Click **FILE** on the menu bar, and then click **Print** to open the Print dialog box. See Figure 1-32. Notice that you can include line numbers in the printout. You also can choose to hide the collapsed regions of code. Currently, the Hide collapsed regions check box is grayed-out because no code is collapsed in the Code Editor window.

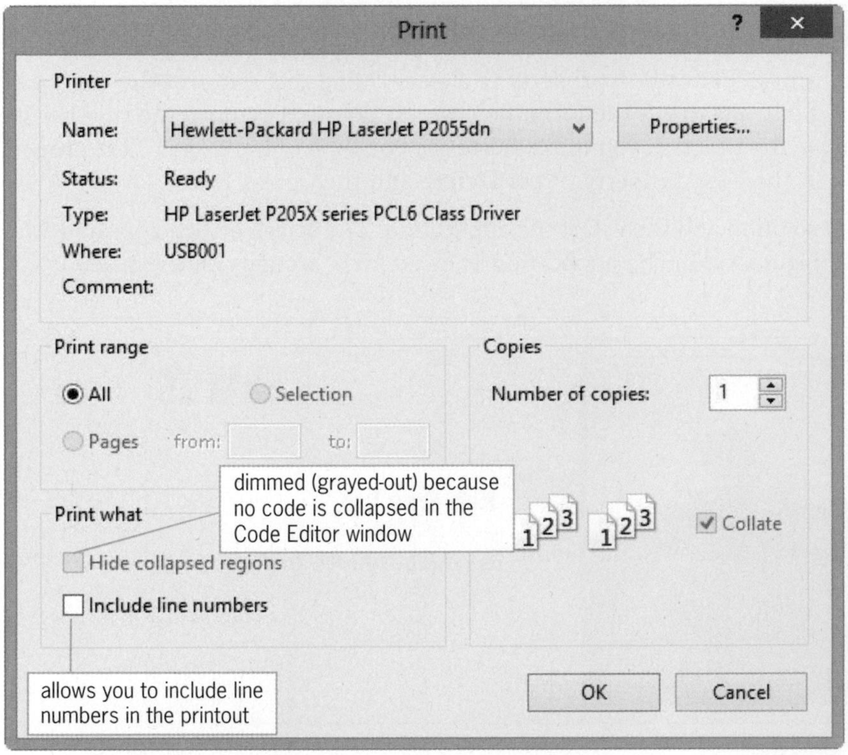

Figure 1-32 Print dialog box

3. If your computer is connected to a printer, click the **OK** button to begin printing; otherwise, click the **Cancel** button. If you clicked the OK button, your printer prints the code.
4. Close the Code Editor window and then close the solution.

Lesson C Summary

- To process code at specified intervals of time:

  Use the Timer tool to instantiate a timer control. Set the timer's Interval property to the number of milliseconds for each interval. Turn on the timer by setting its Enabled property to True. Enter the timer's code in its Tick event procedure.

- To delete a control:

  Select the control you want to delete and then press Delete. If the control contains code, open the Code Editor window and delete the code contained in the control's event procedures.

- To control the border style of the form:

  Set the form's FormBorderStyle property.
- To enable/disable the Minimize button on the form's title bar:

  Set the form's MinimizeBox property.
- To enable/disable the Maximize button on the form's title bar:

  Set the form's MaximizeBox property.
- To control whether the icon and buttons appear in the form's title bar:

  Set the form's ControlBox property.
- To print the user interface:

  Make the designer window the active window. Tap the Print Screen (Prnt Scrn or PrtSc) key. Start an application that can display a picture (such as Microsoft Word) and open a new document (if necessary). Press Ctrl+v to paste the contents of the Clipboard in the document. Use the application to print the document. Close the application you used to display the picture.
- To print the Visual Basic code:

  Make the Code Editor window the active window. Collapse any code you do not want to print. Click FILE on the menu bar and then click Print. If you don't want to print the collapsed code, select the Hide collapsed regions check box. If you want to print line numbers, select the Include line numbers check box. Click the OK button in the Print dialog box.

Lesson C Key Terms

Component tray—a special area in the IDE; stores controls that do not appear in the interface during run time

Run time—the state of an application while it is running

Timer control—the control used to process code at one or more regular intervals

Lesson C Review Questions

1. If a timer is running, the code in its ________ event procedure is processed each time an interval has elapsed.
   a. Interval
   b. Tick
   c. Timed
   d. Timer

2. Which of the following is false?
   a. When you add a timer control to a form, the control appears in the component tray.
   b. The user can see a timer control during run time.
   c. You stop a timer by setting its Enabled property to False.
   d. The number entered in a timer's Interval property represents the number of milliseconds for each interval.

3. To disable the Minimize button on a form's title bar, set the form's ________ property to False.
   a. ButtonMinimize
   b. Minimize
   c. MinimizeBox
   d. MinimizeButton

4. You can remove the Minimize, Maximize, and Close buttons from a form's title bar by setting the form's ________ property to False.
   a. ControlBox
   b. ControlButton
   c. TitleBar
   d. TitleBarElements

5. Explain how you delete a control that contains code.

Lesson C Exercises

INTRODUCTORY

1. In this exercise, you modify an existing form by replacing its Exit button with a timer.
   a. Open the Williams Solution (Williams Solution.sln) file contained in the VB2012\Chap01\Williams Solution folder. If necessary, open the designer window.
   b. Delete the Exit button from the form and then delete the button's code from the Code Editor window.
   c. Return to the designer window. Add a timer control to the form. Change the timer's name to tmrExit. Set the timer's Enabled property to True. The timer should end the application after eight seconds have elapsed; set the appropriate property. Enter the `Me.Close()` instruction in the appropriate event procedure in the Code Editor window.
   d. Save the solution and then start the application. When eight seconds have elapsed, the application ends.
   e. Set the form's FormBorderStyle property to FixedSingle. Also, remove the elements (icon and buttons) and text from the form's title bar.
   f. Save the solution and then start the application. Close the Code Editor window and then close the solution.

INTERMEDIATE

2. Create a Visual Basic Windows application. Use the following names for the solution and project, respectively: Faces Solution and Faces Project. Save the application in the VB2012\Chap01 folder. Change the form file's name to Main Form.vb. Create the interface shown in Figure 1-33. The picture boxes should display the images stored in the Face1.png and Face2.png files, which are contained in the VB2012\Chap01 folder. Include a timer that ends the application after five seconds have elapsed. Save the solution and then start the application. Now, remove the icon and buttons from the form's title bar. Also, use the Project Designer window to change the executable file's name to Faces. Save the solution and then start the application. Close the Code Editor window and then close the solution. Use the Run dialog box in Windows to run the Faces.exe file, which is contained in the project's bin\Debug folder.

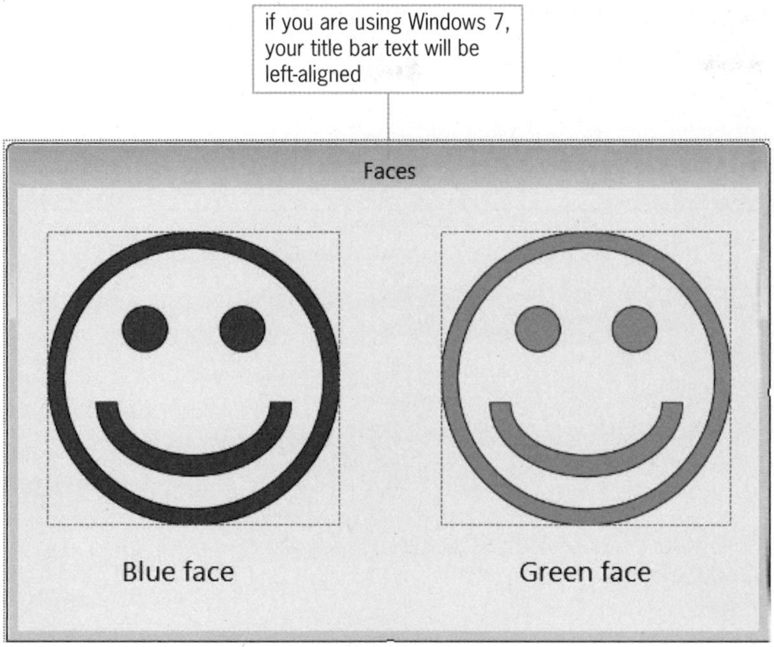
if you are using Windows 7, your title bar text will be left-aligned
Faces
Blue face
Green face

Figure 1-33 Interface for the Faces application

3. Create a Visual Basic Windows application. Name the solution, project, and form file My Splash Solution, My Splash Project, and Splash Form.vb. Save the application in the VB2012\Chap01 folder. Create your own splash screen. Save the solution and then start the application. Close the Code Editor window and then close the solution. INTERMEDIATE

4. The Internet contains a vast amount of code snippets that you can use in your Visual Basic applications. And in many cases, you can use the snippet without fully understanding each line of its code. In this exercise, you will use a code snippet that rounds the corners on a splash screen. DISCOVERY

   a. Open the Rounded Corners Solution (Rounded Corners Solution.sln) file contained in the VB2012\Chap01\Rounded Corners Solution folder. If necessary, open the designer window.

   b. For the code snippet to work properly, the splash screen cannot have a border. Therefore, change the form's FormBorderStyle property to None.

   c. Change the form's BackColor property to black.

   d. Save the application and then start the solution. Notice that the splash screen contains the standard corners, which are not rounded. Click the Exit button to end the application.

   e. Open the Code Editor window. Select (highlight) the lines of code contained in the form's Load event procedure, which is processed when the application is run and the form is loaded into the computer's internal memory. See Figure 1-34.

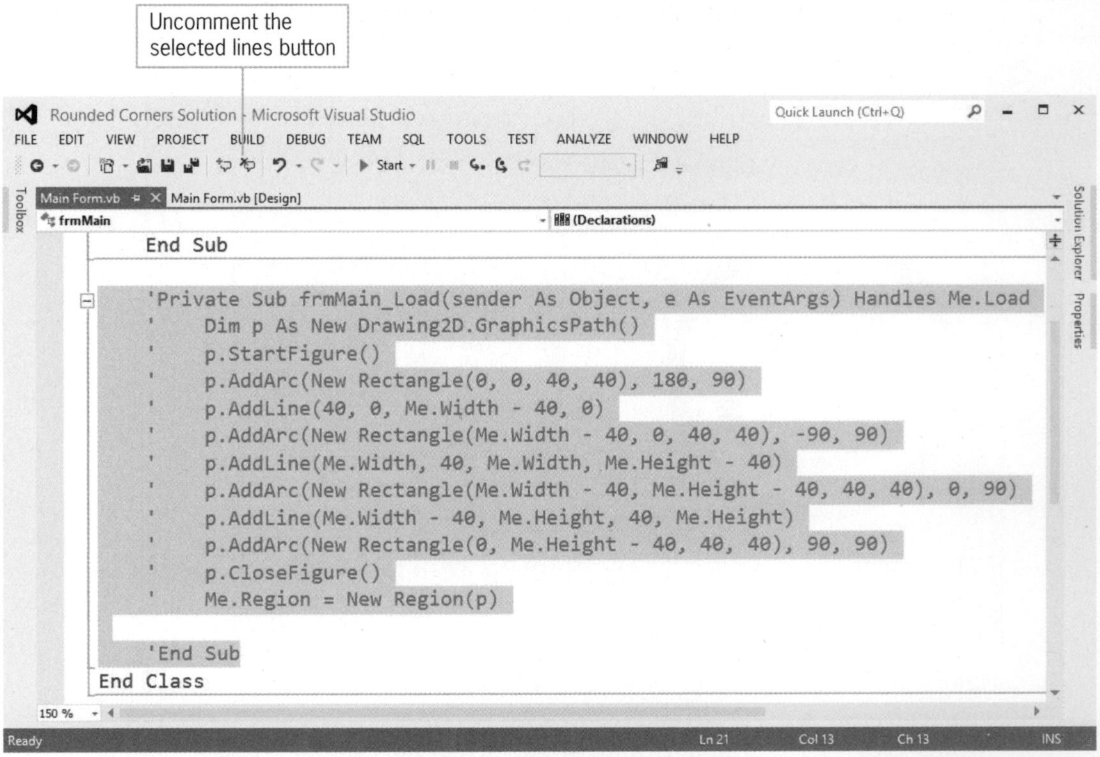

Figure 1-34 Form's Load event procedure selected in the Code Editor window

f. Click the Uncomment the selected lines button on the Standard toolbar. (Refer to Figure 1-34 for the button's location.) Save the solution and then start the application. The splash screen now has rounded corners. See Figure 1-35.

Figure 1-35 Splash screen with rounded corners

g. Click the Exit button to end the application. Close the Code Editor window and then close the solution.

DISCOVERY

5. In this exercise, you will create a splash screen that has a transparent background.

a. Open the Petal Solution (Petal Solution.sln) file contained in the VB2012\Chap01\Petal Solution folder. If necessary, open the designer window.

b. Add a picture box control to the form. The picture box should display the image stored in the PetalShop.png file, which is contained in the VB2012\Chap01 folder. Set the picture box's size mode to StretchImage. Set its name property to picPetal. Position and size the picture box as shown in Figure 1-36.

Figure 1-36 Correct location and size of picture box

c. Click the form's title bar to select the form. Set the form's FormBorderStyle property to None.

d. Click TransparencyKey in the Properties window. The TransparencyKey property determines the color that will appear transparent when the application is run. For example, you can make the form transparent by setting its TransparencyKey property to the same color as its BackColor property. Click the TransparencyKey property's list arrow, then click the System tab, and then click Control.

e. Open the Code Editor window. Open the code template for the picPetal control's Click event procedure. Type Me.Close() and press Enter.

f. Save the solution and then start the application. Because the color specified in the form's BackColor property is the same as the color specified in the TransparencyKey property, the form appears transparent. As a result, the splash screen shows only the image contained in the picture box. See Figure 1-37.

cPetal_Click(sender As Object, e As EventArgs) Handles picP
The Petal Shop

Figure 1-37 Splash screen with a transparent background

g. Click the picture box to end the application. Close the Code Editor window and then close the solution.

DISCOVERY

6. In this exercise, you will learn how to display a splash screen followed by another form.

a. Open the Two Form Solution (Two Form Solution.sln) file contained in the VB2012\Chap01\Two Form Solution folder. If necessary, open the Solution Explorer and designer windows. Notice that the project contains one form named Splash Form.vb.

b. Now you will add a new form to the project. Click PROJECT on the menu bar, then click Add Windows Form, and then click the Add button. Change the new form file's name to Main Form.vb. Change the form's name to frmMain, and then set its StartPosition property to CenterScreen. Also set its Text property to Main Form.

c. Right-click My Project in the Solution Explorer window and then click Open. Change the entry in the Startup form box to frmMain. Change the entry in the Splash screen box to frmSplash. Close the Project Designer window.

d. Save the solution and then start the application. The splash screen (frmSplash) appears first. After a few seconds, the splash screen disappears automatically and the startup form (frmMain) appears. Click the Close button on the startup form's title bar, and then close the solution.

DISCOVERY

7. In this exercise, you learn how to display a tooltip. Open the ToolTip Solution (ToolTip Solution.sln) file contained in the VB2012\Chap01\ToolTip Solution folder. If necessary, open the designer window. Click the ToolTip tool in the toolbox and then drag the tool to the form. Notice that a tooltip control appears in the component tray rather than on the form. Set the btnExit control's ToolTip on ToolTip1 property to "Ends the application" (without the quotation marks). Save the solution and then start the application. Hover your mouse pointer over the Exit button. The tooltip "Ends the application" appears in a tooltip box. Click the Exit button and then close the solution.

SWAT THE BUGS

8. Open the Debug Solution (Debug Solution.sln) file contained in the VB2012\Chap01\Debug Solution folder. If necessary, open the designer window. Start the application. The application is not working correctly because the splash screen does not disappear after four seconds have elapsed. Click DEBUG on the menu bar and then click Stop Debugging. Locate and then correct the error(s). Save the solution and then start the application again to verify that it is working correctly. Close the Code Editor window and then close the solution.

CHAPTER 2

Designing Applications

Creating the Play It Again Movies Application

In this chapter, you create an application that prints a sales receipt for Play It Again Movies, a small store that sells used movies in both DVD and Blu-ray format. The DVD and Blu-ray discs sell for $7 each. The application will allow the salesclerk to enter the current date and the number of DVDs and Blu-rays sold to a customer. It then will calculate and display the total number of discs sold and the total sales amount.

Previewing the Play It Again Movies Application

Before you start the first lesson in this chapter, you will preview the completed application. The application is contained in the VB2012\Chap02 folder.

START HERE

To preview the completed application:

1. Use the Run dialog box to run the Play It Again (Play It Again.exe) file contained in the VB2012\Chap02 folder. The interface shown in Figure 2-1 appears on the screen. (The image in the picture box was downloaded from the Open Clip Art Library at *http://openclipart.org.*) In addition to the picture box, label, and button controls that you learned about in Chapter 1, the interface contains three text boxes. A text box gives a user an area in which to enter data.

To open the Run dialog box, press and hold down the Windows logo key as you tap the letter r, and then release the logo key.

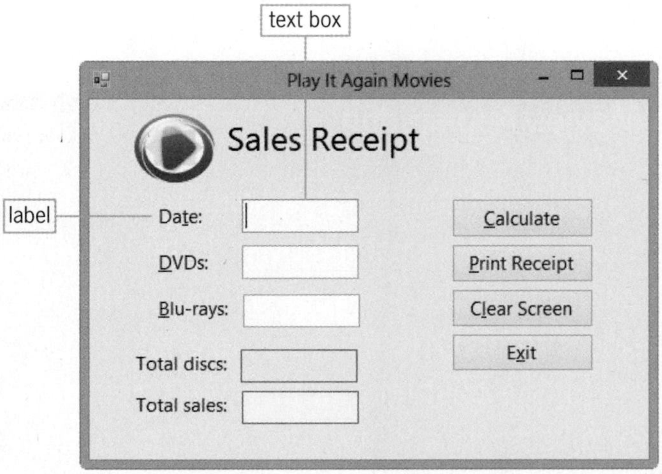

Figure 2-1 Play It Again Movies interface
OpenClipArt.org/John Diamond / diamonjohn

Note: If the underlined letters, called access keys, do not appear on your screen, press the Alt key on your keyboard. You will learn about access keys in Lesson B.

2. The insertion point is located in the first text box. The label control to the left of the text box identifies the information the user should enter. Type **11/15/2014** as the date, and then press **Tab** twice to move the insertion point to the Blu-rays text box.
3. Type **5** in the Blu-rays box and then press **Shift+Tab** (press and hold down the Shift key as you tap the Tab key) to move the insertion point to the DVDs text box.
4. Type **3** in the DVDs box and then click the **Calculate** button. The button's Click event procedure calculates and displays the total number of discs sold (8) and the total sales ($56.00).
5. Click the **Blue-rays** text box. Change the number 5 in the box to **2**, and then click the **Calculate** button. The button's Click event procedure recalculates the total number of discs sold (5) and the total sales ($35.00). See Figure 2-2.

Figure 2-2 Completed sales receipt
OpenClipArt.org/John Diamond / diamonjohn

6. Click the **Print Receipt** button. The sales receipt appears in the Print preview window. (It may take a few seconds for the window to open.) Click the **Zoom** button's list arrow and then click **75%**. If necessary, size the Print preview window to view the entire sales receipt. See Figure 2-3.

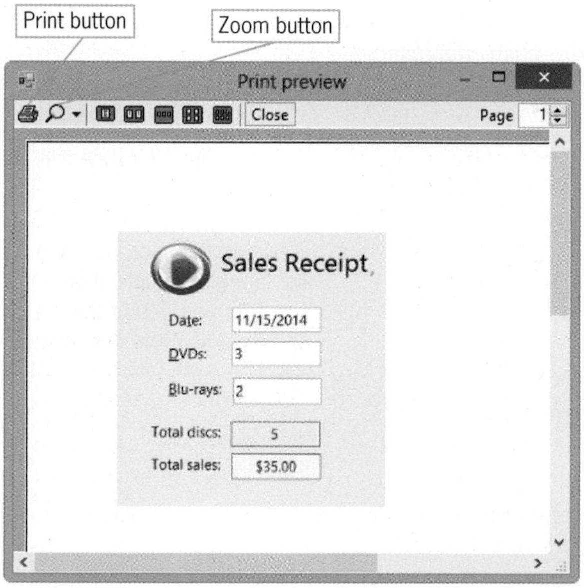

Figure 2-3 Print preview window
OpenClipArt.org/John Diamond / diamonjohn

7. If your computer is connected to a printer, click the **Print** button (the printer) on the Print preview window's toolbar to send the output to the printer.
8. Click the **Close** button on the Print preview window's toolbar.
9. Click the **Clear Screen** button to remove the sales information (except the date) from the form, and then click the **Exit** button to end the application.

The Play It Again Movies application is an object-oriented program because it uses objects (such as buttons and text boxes) to accomplish its goal. In Lesson A, you will learn how a programmer plans an object-oriented program. You will create the Play It Again Movies application in Lessons B and C. Be sure to complete each lesson in full and do all of the end-of-lesson questions and several exercises before continuing to the next lesson.

LESSON A

After studying Lesson A, you should be able to:

- Plan an object-oriented Windows application in Visual Basic 2012
- Complete a TOE (Task, Object, Event) chart
- Follow the Windows standards regarding the layout and labeling of controls

Creating an Object-Oriented Application

As Figure 2-4 indicates, the process a programmer follows when creating an object-oriented (OO) application is similar to the process a builder follows when building a home. Like a builder, a programmer first meets with the client to discuss the client's wants and needs; both then create a plan for the project. After the client approves the plan, the builder builds the home's frame, whereas the programmer builds the user interface, which is the application's frame. Once the frame is built, the builder completes the home by adding the electrical wiring, walls, and so on. The programmer, on the other hand, completes the application by adding the necessary code to the user interface. When the home is complete, the builder makes a final inspection and corrects any problems before the customer moves in. Similarly, the programmer tests the completed application and fixes any problems, called bugs, before releasing the application to the user. The final step in both processes is to assemble the project's documentation (paperwork), which then is given to the customer/user.

A builder's process	A programmer's process
1. Meet with the client	1. Meet with the client
2. Plan the home (blueprint)	2. Plan the application (TOE chart)
3. Build the frame	3. Build the user interface
4. Complete the home	4. Code the application
5. Inspect the home and fix any problems	5. Test and debug the application
6. Assemble the documentation	6. Assemble the documentation

Figure 2-4 Processes used by a builder and a programmer

You will learn how to plan an OO application in this lesson. Steps three through six of the process are covered in Lessons B and C.

Planning an Object-Oriented Application

As any builder will tell you, the most important aspect of a home is not its beauty. Rather, it is how closely the home matches the buyer's wants and needs. The same is true of an OO application. For an application to fulfill the wants and needs of the user, it is essential for the programmer to plan the application jointly with the user. It cannot be stressed enough that the only way to guarantee the success of an application is to actively involve the user in the planning phase. The steps for planning an OO application are listed in Figure 2-5.

Planning an OO application

1. Identify the tasks the application needs to perform
2. Identify the objects to which you will assign the tasks
3. Identify the events required to trigger an object into performing its assigned tasks
4. Draw a sketch of the user interface

Figure 2-5 Steps for planning an OO application

You can use a TOE (Task, Object, Event) chart to record the application's tasks, objects, and events, which are identified in the first three steps of the planning phase. In the next section, you begin completing a TOE chart for the Play It Again Movies application. The first step is to identify the application's tasks.

Identifying the Application's Tasks

Realizing that it is essential to involve the user when planning the application, you meet with the store manager of Play It Again Movies, Ms. Kranz, to determine her requirements. You ask Ms. Kranz to bring a sample of the store's current sales receipt; the sample is shown in Figure 2-6. Viewing a store's (or company's) current forms and procedures will help you gain a better understanding of the application you need to create. You also can use the current form as a guide when designing the user interface.

Play It Again Movies
Sales Receipt

Date:	5/2/2014
DVDs:	2
Blu-rays:	3
Total discs:	5
Total sales:	$35.00

Figure 2-6 Sample of the store's current sales receipt

When identifying the major tasks an application needs to perform, it is helpful to ask the questions italicized in the following bulleted items. The answers pertaining to the Play It Again Movies application follow each question.

- *What information will the application need to display on the screen and/or print on the printer?* The application should display and also print the following information: the date, the number of DVDs sold, the number of Blu-rays sold, the total number of discs sold, and the total sales amount.
- *What information will the user need to enter into the user interface to display and/or print the desired information?* The salesclerk (the user) must enter the date, the number of DVDs sold, and the number of Blu-rays sold.
- *What information will the application need to calculate to display and/or print the desired information?* The application needs to calculate the total number of discs sold and the total sales amount.

- *How will the user end the application?* All applications should provide a way for the user to end the application. The Play It Again Movies application will use an Exit button for this task.
- *Will previous information need to be cleared from the screen before new information is entered?* The sales information will need to be cleared from the screen before the next customer's sales information is entered.

Figure 2-7 shows the application's tasks listed in a TOE chart. The tasks do not need to be listed in any particular order. In this case, the data entry tasks are listed first, followed by the calculation tasks, the display and printing tasks, the application ending task, and the screen clearing task.

Task	Object	Event
Get the following sales information from the user: Current date Number of DVDs sold Number of Blu-rays sold		
Calculate total discs sold and total sales amount		
Display the following information: Current date Number of DVDs sold Number of Blu-rays sold Total discs sold Total sales amount		
Print the sales receipt		
End the application		
Clear screen for the next sale		

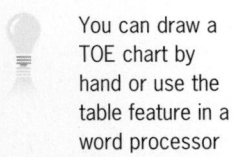

You can draw a TOE chart by hand or use the table feature in a word processor (such as Microsoft Word).

Figure 2-7 Tasks entered in a TOE chart

Identifying the Objects

After completing the Task column of the TOE chart, you then assign each task to an object in the user interface. For this application, the only objects you will use besides the Windows form itself are the button, label, and text box controls. As you already know, you use a label to display information that you do not want the user to change while the application is running, and you use a button to perform an action immediately after the user clicks it. You use a **text box** to give the user an area in which to enter data.

The first task listed in Figure 2-7 is to get the sales information from the user. For each order, the salesclerk will need to enter the current date, the number of DVDs sold, and the number of Blu-rays sold. Because you need to provide the salesclerk with areas in which to enter the information, you will assign the first task to three text boxes—one for each item of information. The three-character ID used when naming text boxes is txt, so you will name the text boxes txtDate, txtDvd, and txtBluRay.

The second task listed in the TOE chart is to calculate both the total number of discs sold and the total sales amount. So that the salesclerk can calculate these amounts at any time, you will assign the task to a button named btnCalc.

The third task listed in the TOE chart is to display the sales information along with the total number of discs sold and the total sales amount. The sales information is displayed automatically when the user enters that information in the three text boxes. The total discs sold and total sales amount, however, are not entered by the user. Instead, those amounts are calculated by the btnCalc control. Because the user should not be allowed to change the calculated results, you will have the btnCalc control display the total discs sold and total sales amount in two label controls named lblTotalDiscs and lblTotalSales. If you look ahead to Figure 2-8, you will notice that "(from btnCalc)" was added to the Task column for both display tasks.

The fourth task listed in the TOE chart is to print the sales receipt. Here again, you will assign the task to a button so that the salesclerk has control over when the sales receipt is printed. You will name the button btnPrint.

The last two tasks listed in the TOE chart are "End the application" and "Clear screen for the next sale." You will assign the tasks to buttons named btnExit and btnClear; doing this gives the user control over when the tasks are performed. Figure 2-8 shows the TOE chart with the Task and Object columns completed.

Task	Object	Event
Get the following sales information from the user:		
Current date	txtDate	
Number of DVDs sold	txtDvds	
Number of Blu-rays sold	txtBluRays	
Calculate total discs sold and total sales amount	btnCalc	
Display the following information:		
Current date	txtDate	
Number of DVDs sold	txtDvds	
Number of Blu-rays sold	txtBluRays	
Total discs sold (from btnCalc)	lblTotalDiscs	
Total sales amount (from btnCalc)	lblTotalSales	
Print the sales receipt	btnPrint	
End the application	btnExit	
Clear screen for the next sale	btnClear	

Figure 2-8 Tasks and objects entered in a TOE chart

Identifying the Events

After defining the application's tasks and assigning the tasks to objects in the interface, you then determine which event (if any) must occur for an object to carry out its assigned task. The three text boxes listed in the TOE chart in Figure 2-8 are assigned the task of getting and displaying the sales information. Text boxes accept and display information automatically, so no special event is necessary for them to do their assigned task. The two label controls listed in the TOE chart are assigned the task of displaying the total number of discs sold and the total sales amount. Label controls automatically display their contents; so, here again, no special event needs to occur. (Recall that the two label controls will get their values from the btnCalc control.) The remaining objects listed in the TOE chart are the four buttons. You will have the buttons perform their assigned tasks when the user clicks them. Figure 2-9 shows the completed TOE chart.

Task	Object	Event
Get the following sales information from the user:		
Current date	txtDate	None
Number of DVDs sold	txtDvds	None
Number of Blu-rays sold	txtBluRays	None
Calculate total discs sold and total sales amount	btnCalc	Click
Display the following information:		
Current date	txtDate	None
Number of DVDs sold	txtDvds	None
Number of Blu-rays sold	txtBluRays	None
Total discs sold (from btnCalc)	lblTotalDiscs	None
Total sales amount (from btnCalc)	lblTotalSales	None
Print the sales receipt	btnPrint	Click
End the application	btnExit	Click
Clear screen for the next sale	btnClear	Click

Figure 2-9 Completed TOE chart ordered by task

If the application you are creating is small, as is the Play It Again Movies application, you can use the TOE chart in its current form to help you write the Visual Basic code. When the application is large, however, it is often helpful to rearrange the TOE chart so that it is ordered by object rather than by task. To do so, you list all of the objects in the Object column of a new TOE chart, being sure to list each object only once. Then list each object's tasks and events in the Task and Event columns, respectively. Figure 2-10 shows the rearranged TOE chart ordered by object rather than by task.

Task	Object	Event
1. Calculate total discs sold and total sales amount 2. Display total discs sold and total sales amount in lblTotalDiscs and lblTotalSales	btnCalc	Click
Print the sales receipt	btnPrint	Click
End the application	btnExit	Click
Clear screen for the next sale	btnClear	Click
Display total discs sold (from btnCalc)	lblTotalDiscs	None
Display total sales amount (from btnCalc)	lblTotalSales	None
Get and display the sales information	txtDate, txtDvds, txtBluRays	None

Figure 2-10 Completed TOE chart ordered by object

After completing the TOE chart, the next step is to draw a rough sketch of the user interface.

Drawing a Sketch of the User Interface

Although the TOE chart lists the objects to include in the interface, it does not indicate where the objects should be placed on the form. While the design of an interface is open to creativity, there are some guidelines to which you should adhere so that your interface is consistent with the Windows standards. This consistency will give your interface a familiar look, which will make your application easier to both learn and use. The guidelines are referred to as GUI (graphical user interface) guidelines.

The first GUI guideline covered in this book pertains to the organization of the controls in the interface. In Western countries, the user interface should be organized so that the information flows either vertically or horizontally, with the most important information always located in the upper-left corner of the interface. In a vertical arrangement, the information flows from top to bottom: the essential information is located in the first column of the interface, while secondary information is placed in subsequent columns. In a horizontal arrangement, on the other hand, the information flows from left to right: the essential information is placed in the first row of the interface, with secondary information placed in subsequent rows.

Some companies have their own standards for interfaces used within the company. A company's standards supersede the Windows standards.

Related controls should be grouped together using either white (empty) space or one of the tools located in the Containers section of the toolbox. Examples of tools found in the Containers section include the GroupBox, Panel, and TableLayoutPanel tools. The difference between a panel and a group box is that, unlike a group box, a panel can have scroll bars. However, unlike a panel, a group box has a Text property that you can use to indicate the contents of the control. Unlike the panel and group box controls, the table layout panel control provides a table structure in which you place other controls.

The Ch02A-Containers video demonstrates how to use the group box, panel, and table layout panel controls.

Figures 2-11 and 2-12 show two different sketches of the Play It Again Movies interface. In Figure 2-11 the information is arranged vertically, and white space is used to group related controls together. In Figure 2-12 the information is arranged horizontally, with related controls grouped together using a group box. Each box and button in both figures is labeled so the user knows its purpose. For example, the "Date:" label tells the user the type of information to enter in the box that appears to its right. Similarly, the "Calculate" caption on the first button indicates the action the button will perform when it is clicked.

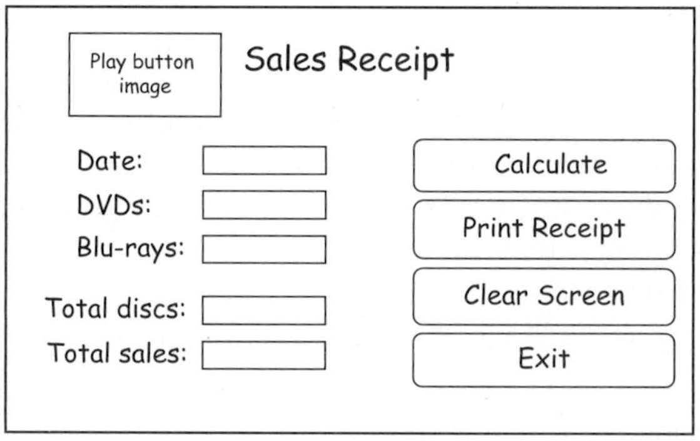

Figure 2-11 Vertical arrangement of the Play It Again Movies application

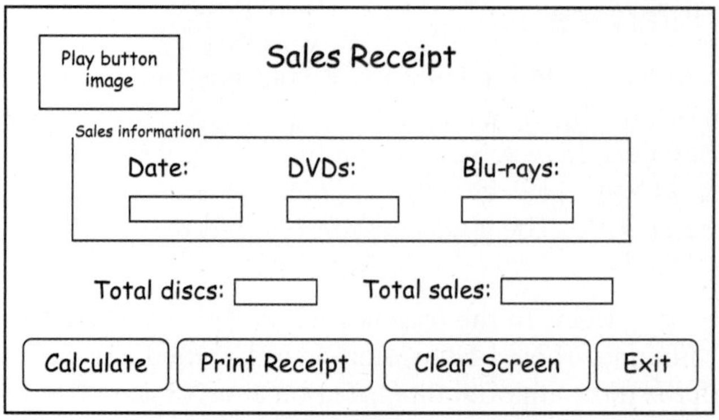

Figure 2-12 Horizontal arrangement of the Play It Again Movies application

Most times, program output (such as the result of calculations) is displayed in a label control in the interface. Label controls that display program output should be labeled to make their contents obvious to the user. In the interfaces shown in Figures 2-11 and 2-12, the "Total discs:" and "Total sales:" labels identify the contents of the lblTotalDiscs and lblTotalSales controls, respectively.

The text contained in an identifying label should be meaningful and left-aligned within the label. In most cases, an identifying label should be from one to three words only and appear on one line. In addition, the identifying label should be positioned either above or to the left of the control it identifies. An identifying label should end with a colon (:), which distinguishes it from other text in the user interface (such as the heading text "Sales Receipt"). Some assistive technologies, which are technologies that provide assistance to individuals with disabilities, rely on the colons to make this distinction. The Windows standard is to use sentence capitalization for identifying labels. **Sentence capitalization** means you capitalize only the first letter in the first word and in any words that are customarily capitalized.

As you learned in Chapter 1, buttons are identified by the text that appears on the button's face. The text is often referred to as the button's caption. The caption should be meaningful, be from one to three words only, and appear on one line. A button's caption should be entered using **book title capitalization**, which means you capitalize the first letter in each word, except for articles, conjunctions, and prepositions that do not occur at either the beginning or end of the caption. If the buttons are stacked vertically, as they are in Figure 2-11, all the buttons should be the same height and width. If the buttons are positioned horizontally, as they are in Figure 2-12, all the buttons should be the same height, but their widths may vary if necessary. In a group of buttons, the most commonly used button typically appears first—either on the top (in a vertical arrangement) or on the left (in a horizontal arrangement).

When positioning the controls in the interface, place related controls close to each other and be sure to maintain a consistent margin from the edges of the form. Also, it's helpful to align the borders of the controls wherever possible to minimize the number of different margins appearing in the interface. Doing this allows the user to more easily scan the information. You can align the borders using the snap lines that appear as you are building the interface. Or, you can use the FORMAT menu to align (and also size) the controls.

In this lesson you learned some basic guidelines to follow when sketching a graphical user interface (GUI). You will learn more GUI guidelines in the remaining lessons and in subsequent chapters. You can find a complete list of the GUI guidelines in Appendix B of this book.

GUI DESIGN TIP Layout and Organization of the User Interface

- Organize the user interface so that the information flows either vertically or horizontally, with the most important information always located in the upper-left corner of the interface.
- Group related controls together using either white (empty) space or one of the tools from the Containers section of the toolbox.
- Use a label to identify each text box in the user interface. Also use a label to identify other label controls that display program output. The label text should be meaningful, be from one to three words only, and appear on one line. Left-align the text within the label, and position the label either above or to the left of the control it identifies. Enter the label text using sentence capitalization, and follow the label text with a colon (:).
- Display a meaningful caption on the face of each button. The caption should indicate the action the button will perform when clicked. Enter the caption using book title capitalization. Place the caption on one line and use from one to three words only.
- When a group of buttons are stacked vertically, each button in the group should be the same height and width. When a group of buttons are positioned horizontally, each button in the group should be the same height. In a group of buttons, the most commonly used button is typically placed first in the group.
- Align the borders of the controls wherever possible to minimize the number of different margins appearing in the interface.

Lesson A Summary

- To create an OO application:
  1. Meet with the client
  2. Plan the application
  3. Build the user interface
  4. Code the application
  5. Test and debug the application
  6. Assemble the documentation
- To plan an OO application in Visual Basic 2012:
  1. Identify the tasks the application needs to perform
  2. Identify the objects to which you will assign the tasks
  3. Identify the events required to trigger an object into performing its assigned tasks
  4. Draw a sketch of the user interface
- To assist you in identifying the major tasks an application needs to perform, ask the following questions:
  1. What information will the application need to display on the screen and/or print on the printer?
  2. What information will the user need to enter into the user interface to display and/or print the desired information?

3. What information will the application need to calculate to display and/or print the desired information?
4. How will the user end the application?
5. Will prior information need to be cleared from the screen before new information is entered?

Lesson A Key Terms

Book title capitalization—the capitalization used for a button's caption; refers to capitalizing the first letter in each word, except for articles, conjunctions, and prepositions that do not occur at either the beginning or end of the caption

Sentence capitalization—the capitalization used for identifying labels; refers to capitalizing only the first letter in the first word and in any words that are customarily capitalized

Text box—a control that provides an area in the form for the user to enter data

Lesson A Review Questions

1. When designing a user interface, the most important information should be placed in the ____________ corner of the interface.
   a. lower-left
   b. lower-right
   c. upper-left
   d. upper-right

2. A button's caption should be entered using ____________.
   a. book title capitalization
   b. sentence capitalization
   c. either book title capitalization or sentence capitalization

3. Which of the following statements is false?
   a. The text contained in identifying labels should be left-aligned within the label.
   b. An identifying label should be positioned either above or to the right of the control it identifies.
   c. Identifying labels should be entered using sentence capitalization.
   d. Identifying labels should end with a colon (:).

4. Listed below are the four steps you should follow when planning an OO application. Put the steps in the proper order by placing a number (1 through 4) on the line to the left of the step.

   ____________ Identify the objects to which you will assign the tasks

   ____________ Draw a sketch of the user interface

   ____________ Identify the tasks the application needs to perform

   ____________ Identify the events required to trigger an object into performing its assigned tasks

5. Listed below are the six steps you should follow when creating an OO application. Put the steps in the proper order by placing a number (1 through 6) on the line to the left of the step.

    ______________ Test and debug the application

    ______________ Build the user interface

    ______________ Code the application

    ______________ Assemble the documentation

    ______________ Plan the application

    ______________ Meet with the client

Lesson A Exercises

INTRODUCTORY

1. At the end of the year, each salesperson at Shiloh Products is paid a bonus of 1% of his or her annual sales. The company's payroll clerk wants an application that will compute the bonus after he or she enters the salesperson's ID and annual sales. Prepare a TOE chart ordered by task, and then rearrange the TOE chart so that it is ordered by object. Be sure to include buttons that allow the user to both clear and print the screen. Draw a sketch of the user interface. (You will create the interface in Lesson B's Exercise 1 and then code the application in Lesson C's Exercise 1.)

INTERMEDIATE

2. Carson Carpets wants an application that allows the salesclerk to enter a floor's length and width measurements in feet. The application should calculate the floor's area in both square feet and square yards. Prepare a TOE chart ordered by task, and then rearrange the TOE chart so that it is ordered by object. Be sure to include buttons that allow the user to both clear and print the screen. Draw a sketch of the user interface. (You will create the interface in Lesson B's Exercise 2 and then code the application in Lesson C's Exercise 4.)

INTERMEDIATE

3. KJ Inc. divides its sales territory into four regions: North, South, East, and West. The sales manager wants an application that allows him to enter the current year's sales for each region and the projected increase (expressed as a decimal number) for each region. He wants the application to compute the following year's projected sales for each region. As an example, if the sales manager enters 10000 as the current sales for the South region, and then enters .05 (the decimal equivalent of 5%) as the projected increase, the application should display 10500 as the next year's projected sales. Prepare a TOE chart ordered by task, and then rearrange the TOE chart so that it is ordered by object. Be sure to include buttons that allow the user to both clear and print the screen. (You will create the interface in Lesson B's Exercise 3 and then code the application in Lesson C's Exercise 5.)

LESSON B

After studying Lesson B, you should be able to:

- Build the user interface using your TOE chart and sketch
- Follow the Windows standards regarding the use of graphics, fonts, and color
- Set a control's BorderStyle, AutoSize, and TextAlign properties
- Add a text box to a form
- Lock the controls on the form
- Assign access keys to controls
- Set the TabIndex property

Building the User Interface

In Lesson A, you planned the Play It Again Movies application. Planning the application is the second of the six steps involved in creating an OO application. Now you are ready to tackle the third step, which is to build the user interface. You use the TOE chart and sketch you created in the planning step as guides when building the interface, which involves placing the appropriate controls on the form and setting the applicable properties of the controls. To save you time, the VB2012\Chap02\Play It Again Solution folder contains a partially completed application for Play It Again Movies. When you open the solution, you will find that most of the user interface has been created and most of the properties have been set. You will complete the interface in this lesson.

START HERE

To open the partially completed application:

1. If necessary, start Visual Studio 2012 and open the Solution Explorer window. Open the Play It Again Solution (Play It Again Solution.sln) file contained in the VB2012\Chap02\Play It Again Solution folder. If necessary, open the designer window.
2. Permanently display the Properties and Toolbox windows and then auto-hide the Solution Explorer window. Figure 2-13 shows the partially completed interface, which resembles the sketch shown in Figure 2-11 in Lesson A.

Figure 2-13 Partially completed interface for the Play It Again Movies application
OpenClipArt.org/John Diamond / diamonjohn

The application's user interface follows the GUI guidelines covered in Lesson A. The information is arranged vertically, and the controls are aligned wherever possible. Each text box and button, as well as each label control that displays program output, is labeled so the user knows the control's purpose. The text contained in the identifying labels is entered using sentence capitalization. In addition, the text ends with a colon and is left-aligned within the label. The identifying labels are positioned to the left of the controls they identify. Each button's caption is entered using book title capitalization. The button captions and identifying labels appear on one line and do not exceed the three-word limit. Because the buttons are stacked in the interface, each button has the same height and width, and the most commonly used button (Calculate) is placed at the top of the button group.

When building the user interface, keep in mind that you want to create a screen that no one notices. Interfaces that contain a lot of different colors, fonts, and graphics may get "oohs" and "aahs" during their initial use, but they become tiresome after a while. The most important point to remember is that the interface should not distract the user from doing his or her work. The next three sections provide some guidelines to follow regarding the use of these elements in an interface.

The graphics, font, and color guidelines do not pertain to game applications.

Including Graphics in the User Interface

The human eye is attracted to pictures before text, so use graphics sparingly. Designers typically include graphics to either emphasize or clarify a portion of the screen. However, a graphic also can be used merely for aesthetic purposes, as long as it is small and placed in a location that does not distract the user. The small graphic in the Play It Again Movies interface is included for aesthetics only. The graphic is purposely located in the upper-left corner of the interface, which is where you want the user's eye to be drawn first anyway. The graphic adds a personal touch to the sales receipt form without being distracting to the user.

GUI DESIGN TIP Adding Graphics

- Use graphics sparingly. If the graphic is used solely for aesthetics, use a small graphic and place it in a location that will not distract the user.

Selecting Fonts for the Interface

As you learned in Chapter 1, an object's Font property determines the type, style, and size of the font used to display the object's text. You should use only one font type (typically Segoe UI) for all of the text in the interface, and use no more than two different font sizes. In addition, avoid using italics and underlining in an interface because both font styles make text difficult to read. The use of bold text should be limited to titles, headings, and key items that you want to emphasize.

GUI DESIGN TIP Selecting Font Types, Styles, and Sizes

- Use only one font type (typically Segoe UI) for all of the text in the interface.
- Use no more than two different font sizes in the interface.
- Avoid using italics and underlining because both font styles make text difficult to read.
- Limit the use of bold text to titles, headings, and key items that you want to emphasize.

Adding Color to the Interface

The human eye is attracted to color before black and white; therefore, use color sparingly in an interface. It is a good practice to build the interface using black, white, and gray first, and then add color only if you have a good reason to do so. Keep the following three points in mind when deciding whether to include color in an interface:

1. People who have some form of either color blindness or color confusion will have trouble distinguishing colors.
2. Color is very subjective: A color that looks pretty to you may be hideous to someone else.
3. A color may have a different meaning in a different culture.

Usually, it is best to use black text on a white, off-white, or light gray background because dark text on a light background is the easiest to read. You should never use a dark color for the background or a light color for the text. This is because a dark background is hard on the eyes, and light-colored text can appear blurry.

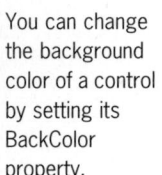

You can change the background color of a control by setting its BackColor property.

If you are going to include color in an interface, limit the number of colors to three, not including white, black, and gray. Be sure that the colors you choose complement each other. Although color can be used to identify an important element in the interface, you should never use it as the only means of identification. In the Play It Again Movies interface, for example, the colored box helps the salesclerk quickly locate the total sales amount. However, color is not the only means of identifying the contents of that box; the box also has an identifying label (Total sales:).

GUI DESIGN TIP Selecting Colors

- Build the interface using black, white, and gray. Only add color if you have a good reason to do so.
- Use white, off-white, or light gray for the background. Use black for the text.
- Never use a dark color for the background or a light color for the text. A dark background is hard on the eyes, and light-colored text can appear blurry.
- Limit the number of colors in an interface to three, not including white, black, and gray. The colors you choose should complement each other.
- Never use color as the only means of identification for an element in the interface.

The BorderStyle, AutoSize, and TextAlign Properties

A control's border is determined by its **BorderStyle property**, which can be set to None, FixedSingle, or Fixed3D. Controls with a BorderStyle property set to None have no border. Setting the BorderStyle property to FixedSingle surrounds the control with a thin line, and setting it to Fixed3D gives the control a three-dimensional appearance. In most cases, a text box's BorderStyle property should be left at the default setting: Fixed3D. The BorderStyle property for each text box in the Play It Again Movies interface follows this convention.

The appropriate setting for a label control's BorderStyle property depends on the control's purpose. Label controls that identify other controls (such as those that identify text boxes) should have a BorderStyle property setting of None, which is the default setting. This is the setting for each identifying label in the Play It Again Movies interface. Label controls that display program output, such as those that display the result of a calculation, typically have a BorderStyle property setting of FixedSingle. The BorderStyle property of the lblTotalSales control in the Play It Again Movies interface is set to FixedSingle. You should avoid setting a label control's BorderStyle property to Fixed3D because, in Windows applications, a control with a three-dimensional appearance implies that it can accept user input.

A label control's **AutoSize property** determines whether the control automatically sizes to fit its current contents. The appropriate setting depends on the label's purpose. Label controls that identify other controls use the default setting: True. However, you typically set to False the AutoSize property of label controls that display program output.

A label control's **TextAlign property** determines the alignment of the text within the label. The TextAlign property can be set to nine different values, such as TopLeft, MiddleCenter, and BottomRight. In the next set of steps, you will change the AutoSize, BorderStyle, and TextAlign properties of the lblTotalDiscs control. (The AutoSize, BorderStyle, and TextAlign properties of the lblTotalSales control have already been set.) You also will delete the contents of the control's Text property and then size the control to match the lblTotalSales control.

To change the properties of the lblTotalDiscs control and then size the control:

START HERE

1. Click the **lblTotalDiscs** control, which contains the text Label7. Set the following properties:

AutoSize	**False**
BorderStyle	**FixedSingle**

2. Click **TextAlign** in the Properties list and then click the **list arrow** in the Settings box. Click the center button to change the property's setting to MiddleCenter.
3. Click **Text** in the Properties list and then select (highlight) Label7. Press **Delete** (or **Backspace**) and then press **Enter**.
4. Click the **lblTotalSales** control and then press and hold down the Ctrl key as you click the **lblTotalDiscs** control. Click **FORMAT** on the menu bar, point to **Make Same Size**, and then click **Both**.
5. Click the **form** to deselect the two labels.

GUI DESIGN TIP Setting the BorderStyle Property of a Text Box or Label

- Keep the BorderStyle property of text boxes at the default setting: Fixed3D.
- Keep the BorderStyle property of identifying labels at the default setting: None.
- Set to FixedSingle the BorderStyle property of labels that display program output, such as those that display the result of a calculation.
- In Windows applications, a control that contains data that the user is not allowed to edit does not usually appear three-dimensional. Therefore, avoid setting a label control's BorderStyle property to Fixed3D.

GUI DESIGN TIP Setting the AutoSize Property of a Label

- Keep the AutoSize property of identifying labels at the default setting: True.
- In most cases, set to False the AutoSize property of label controls that display program output.

Adding a Text Box Control to the Form

A text box is an instance of the TextBox class.

As mentioned earlier, a text box provides an area in the form for the user to enter data. Missing from the Play It Again Movies interface is the text box for entering the number of Blu-rays sold. You will add the missing text box in the next set of steps.

START HERE

To add the missing text box to the form:

1. Use the TextBox tool in the toolbox to add a text box to the form. Position the text box immediately below the text box labeled DVDs.
2. Change the text box's name to **txtBluRays** and press **Enter**.
3. Next, you will make the Blu-rays text box the same size as the DVDs text box. Click the **txtDvds** control and then Ctrl+click the **txtBluRays** control. Click **FORMAT** on the menu bar, point to **Make Same Size**, and then click **Both**.
4. You can align the Blu-rays text box using either the FORMAT menu or the snap lines. You will use the snap lines. Click the **form** to deselect the DVDs and Blu-rays text boxes. Place your mouse pointer on the txtBluRays control, and then press and hold down the left mouse button as you drag the control to the location shown in Figure 2-14. The blue snap lines help you align the Blu-rays text box with the DVDs text box. The pink snap line allows you to align the text in the Blu-rays text box with the text in its identifying label.

Figure 2-14 Snap lines shown in the interface
OpenClipArt.org/John Diamond / diamonjohn

5. When the Blu-rays text box is in the correct location, release the mouse button.

Locking the Controls on a Form

After placing all of the controls in their appropriate locations, it is a good idea to lock the controls on the form. Locking the controls prevents them from being moved inadvertently as you work in the IDE. You can lock the controls by clicking the form (or any control on the form) and then clicking the Lock Controls option on the FORMAT menu; you can follow the same procedure to unlock the controls. You also can lock and unlock the controls by right-clicking the form (or any control on the form) and then clicking Lock Controls on the context menu. When a control is locked, a small lock appears in the upper-left corner of the control.

A locked control can be deleted. It also can be moved by setting its Location property.

START HERE

To lock the controls on the form and then save the solution:

1. Right-click the **form** and then click **Lock Controls**. A small lock appears in the upper-left corner of the form.
2. Save the solution. Try dragging one of the controls to a different location on the form. You will not be able to do so.

Assigning Access Keys

The text in many of the controls shown in Figure 2-14 contains an underlined letter. The underlined letter is called an **access key**, and it allows the user to select an object using the Alt key in combination with a letter or number. For example, you can select the Exit button in the Play It Again Movies interface by pressing Alt+x because the letter x is the Exit button's access key. Access keys are not case sensitive. Therefore, you can select the Exit button by pressing either Alt+x or Alt+X. If you do not see the underlined access keys while an application is running, you can show them temporarily by pressing the Alt key. (To always display access keys in Windows 7, see the Summary section at the end of this lesson.)

You should assign access keys to each of the controls (in the interface) that can accept user input. Examples of such controls include text boxes and buttons. This is because the user can enter information in a text box and click a button. The only exceptions to this rule are the OK and Cancel buttons, which typically do not have access keys in Windows applications. It is important to assign access keys for the following reasons:

1. They allow a user to work with the application even when their mouse becomes inoperative.
2. They allow users who are fast typists to keep their hands on the keyboard.
3. They allow people who cannot work with a mouse, such as people with disabilities, to use the application.

You assign an access key by including an ampersand (&) in the control's caption or identifying label. If the control is a button, you include the ampersand in the button's Text property, which is where a button's caption is stored. If the control is a text box, you include the ampersand in the Text property of its identifying label. (As you will learn later in this lesson, you also must set the TabIndex properties of the text box and its identifying label appropriately.) You enter the ampersand to the immediate left of the character you want to designate as the access key. For example, to assign the letter x as the access key for the Exit button, you enter E&xit in the button's Text property. To assign the letter D as the access key for the txtDvds control, you enter &DVDs: in the Text property of its identifying label.

Each access key in an interface should be unique. The first choice for an access key is the first letter of the caption or identifying label, unless another letter provides a more meaningful association. For example, the letter x is the access key for an Exit button because it provides a more meaningful association than does the letter E. If you can't use the first letter (perhaps because it is already used as the access key for another control) and no other letter provides a more meaningful association, then use a distinctive consonant in the caption or label. The last choices for an access key are a vowel or a number.

Missing from the interface shown in Figure 2-14 are the access keys for the Calculate button and Date text box. You will assign those access keys in the next set of steps. However, notice that the Total discs: and Total sales: labels also do not have access keys. This is because those labels do not identify controls that accept user input; rather, they identify other label controls. Recall that users cannot access label controls while an application is running, so it is inappropriate to assign an access key to their identifying labels.

START HERE

To assign access keys to the Calculate button and Date text box:

1. Click the **Calculate** button. Change the button's Text property to **&Calculate** and then press **Enter**. The letter C in the button's caption is now underlined.
2. Click the **Date:** label, which identifies the txtDate control. Change the label's Text property to **Da&te:** and then press **Enter**. The letter t is now underlined.

GUI DESIGN TIP Assigning Access Keys

- Assign a unique access key to each control that can accept user input.
- When assigning an access key to a control, use the first letter of the control's caption or identifying label, unless another letter provides a more meaningful association. If you can't use the first letter and no other letter provides a more meaningful association, then use a distinctive consonant. Lastly, use a vowel or a number.

Controlling the Tab Order

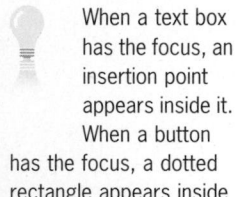

When a text box has the focus, an insertion point appears inside it. When a button has the focus, a dotted rectangle appears inside its darkened border.

While you are creating the interface, each control's **TabIndex property** contains a number that represents the order in which the control was added to the form. The first control added to a form has a TabIndex value of 0; the second control has a TabIndex value of 1, and so on. The TabIndex values determine the **tab order**, which is the order in which each control receives the **focus** when the user either presses the Tab key or employs an access key while an application is running. A control whose TabIndex is 2 will receive the focus immediately after the control whose TabIndex is 1, and so on. When a control has the focus, it can accept user input. Not all controls have a TabIndex property; a PictureBox control, for example, does not have a TabIndex property.

Most times, you will need to reset the TabIndex values for an interface. This is because controls rarely are added to a form in the desired tab order. To determine the appropriate TabIndex values, you first make a list of the controls that can accept user input. The list should reflect the order in which the user will want to access the controls. In the Play It Again Movies interface, the user typically will want to access the txtDate control first, followed by the txtDvds control, the txtBluRays control, the btnCalc control, and so on.

If a control that accepts user input is identified by a label control, you also include the label control in the list. (A text box is an example of a control that accepts user input and is identified by a label control.) You place the name of the label control immediately above the name of the control it identifies in the list. In the Play It Again Movies interface, the Label2 control (which contains Date:) identifies the txtDate control. Therefore, Label2 should appear immediately above txtDate in the list.

The names of controls that do not accept user input and are not used to identify controls that do should be listed at the bottom of the list; these names do not need to appear in any specific order. After listing the control names, you then assign each control in the list a TabIndex value, beginning with the number 0. If a control does not have a TabIndex property, you do not assign it a TabIndex value in the list. You can tell whether a control has a TabIndex property by viewing its Properties list.

Figure 2-15 shows the list of controls and TabIndex values for the Play It Again Movies interface. Notice that the TabIndex value assigned to each text box's identifying label is one number less than the value assigned to the text box itself. For example, the Label2 control has a TabIndex value of 0 and its corresponding text box (txtDate) has a TabIndex value of 1. For a text box's access key (which is defined in the identifying label) to work appropriately, you must be sure to set the identifying label's TabIndex property to a value that is one number less than the value stored in the text box's TabIndex property.

Controls that accept user input, along with their identifying labels	**TabIndex value**
Label2 (Date:)	0
txtDate	1
Label3 (DVDs:)	2
txtDvds	3
Label4 (Blu-rays:)	4
txtBluRays	5
btnCalc	6
btnPrint	7
btnClear	8
btnExit	9
Other controls	
Label1 (Sales Receipt)	10
Label5 (Total discs:)	11
Label6 (Total sales:)	12
lblTotalDiscs	13
lblTotalSales	14
PictureBox1	N/A

Figure 2-15 List of controls and TabIndex values

You can set each control's TabIndex property using either the Properties window or the Tab Order option on the VIEW menu. The Tab Order option is available only when the designer window is the active window.

To set the TabIndex values and then verify the tab order:

START HERE

1. Click the **form** to make the designer window the active window. Click **VIEW** on the menu bar and then click **Tab Order**. The current TabIndex values appear in blue boxes on the form. (The picture box does not have a TabIndex property.)
2. You begin specifying the desired tab order by clicking the first control you want in the tab order. According to Figure 2-15, the first control in the tab order should be the Label2 control, which displays the Date: text. Click the **blue box that contains the number 1**. (You also can click the Label2 control directly.) The number 0 replaces the number 1 in the box, and the color of the box changes from blue to white to indicate that you have set the control's TabIndex value.

3. The second control in the tab order should be the txtDate control, which currently has a TabIndex value of 10. Click the **blue box that contains the number 10**. The number 1 replaces the number 10 in the box, and the color of the box changes from blue to white.

4. Use the information shown in Figure 2-16 to set the TabIndex properties for the remaining controls, which have TabIndex values of 2 through 14. Be sure to set the values in numerical order. If you make a mistake, press the Esc key to remove the TabIndex boxes from the form, and then repeat Steps 1 through 4. When you have finished setting all of the TabIndex values, the color of the boxes will automatically change from white to blue, as shown in Figure 2-16.

Figure 2-16 TabIndex boxes showing the correct TabIndex values
OpenClipArt.org/John Diamond / diamonjohn

You also can remove the TabIndex boxes using the Tab Order option on the VIEW menu.

5. Press **Esc** to remove the TabIndex boxes from the form.

6. Save the solution and then start the application. If the access keys do not appear in the interface, press the **Alt** key. When you start an application, the computer sends the focus to the control whose TabIndex is 0. In the Play It Again Movies interface, that control is the Label2 (Date:) control. However, because label controls cannot receive the focus, the computer sends the focus to the next control in the tab order sequence (txtDate). The blinking insertion point indicates that the text box has the focus and is ready to receive input from you. See Figure 2-17.

Figure 2-17 Play It Again Movies interface
OpenClipArt.org/John Diamond / diamonjohn

7. Type **5/6/2014** in the Date text box. The information you entered is recorded in the text box's Text property.
8. In Windows applications, the Tab key moves the focus forward, and the Shift+Tab key combination moves the focus backward. Press **Tab** to move the focus to the DVDs text box, and then press **Shift+Tab** to move the focus back to the Date text box.
9. Now use the Tab key to verify the tab order of the controls in the interface. Press **Tab**, slowly, three times. The focus moves to the DVDs text box, then to the Blu-rays text box, and then to the Calculate button. Notice that when a button has the focus, a dotted rectangle appears inside its darkened border. Press **Tab**, slowly, three more times. The focus moves to the Print Receipt button, then to the Clear Screen button, and finally to the Exit button.
10. Pressing the Enter key when a button has the focus invokes the button's Click event, causing the computer to process any code contained in the Click event procedure. Press **Enter** to have the computer process the Exit button's Click event procedure, which contains the `Me.Close()` instruction. The application ends.
11. You also can move the focus using a text box's access key. Start the application. If the access keys do not appear in the interface, press the **Alt** key to display them. Now, press **Alt+b** to move the focus to the Blu-rays text box. Then press **Alt+t** to move the focus to the Date text box. Lastly, press **Alt+d** to move the focus to the DVDs text box.
12. Unlike pressing a text box's access key, which moves the focus, pressing a button's access key invokes the button's Click event. Press **Alt+x** to invoke the Exit button's Click event, which ends the application.
13. Close the solution.

GUI DESIGN TIP Using the TabIndex Property to Control the Focus

- Assign a TabIndex value (starting with 0) to each control in the interface, except for controls that do not have a TabIndex property. The TabIndex values should reflect the order in which the user will want to access the controls.
- To allow users to access a text box using the keyboard, assign an access key to the text box's identifying label. Set the identifying label's TabIndex property to a value that is one number less than the value stored in the text box's TabIndex property.

Lesson B Summary

- To use appropriate graphics, fonts, and colors in an interface:

  Refer to the GUI guidelines listed in Appendix B for this chapter's lesson.
- To specify a control's border:

  Set the control's BorderStyle property.
- To specify whether a label control should automatically size to fit its current contents:

  Set the label control's AutoSize property.
- To specify the alignment of the text within a label control:

  Set the label control's TextAlign property.

- To lock/unlock the controls on the form:

  Right-click the form or any control on the form and then select Lock Controls on the context menu. You also can click the Lock Controls option on the FORMAT menu.

- To assign an access key to a control:

  Type an ampersand (&) in the Text property of the control or identifying label. The ampersand should appear to the immediate left of the character that you want to designate as the access key.

- To provide keyboard access to a text box:

  Assign an access key to the text box's identifying label. Set the identifying label's TabIndex property to a value that is one number less than the text box's TabIndex value.

- To employ an access key:

  If necessary, press the Alt key to display the access keys, and then release the key. Press and hold down the Alt key as you tap the access key.

- To set the tab order:

  Set each control's TabIndex property to a number (starting with 0) that represents the order in which the control should receive the focus. You can set the TabIndex property using either the Properties window or the Tab Order option on the VIEW menu.

- To always display access keys in Windows 7:

  Click the Start button on the Windows 7 taskbar. Click Control Panel and then click Appearance and Personalization. In the Ease of Access Center section, click Turn on easy access keys. Select the Underline keyboard shortcuts and access keys check box, and then click the OK button. Close the Control Panel window.

Lesson B Key Terms

Access key—the underlined character in an object's identifying label or caption; allows the user to select the object using the Alt key in combination with the underlined character

AutoSize property—determines whether a control automatically sizes to fit its current contents

BorderStyle property—determines the appearance of a control's border

Focus—indicates that a control is ready to accept user input

Tab order—the order in which each control receives the focus when the user either presses the Tab key or employs an access key while an application is running

TabIndex property—specifies a control's position in the tab order

TextAlign property—determines the alignment of the text within a control

Lesson B Review Questions

1. Which property determines the tab order for the controls in an interface?

   a. SetOrder

   b. SetTab

   c. TabIndex

   d. TabOrder

2. An Exit button's access key is always the letter ________________.
   a. E
   b. x
   c. i
   d. t

3. You assign an access key using a control's ________________ property.
   a. Access
   b. Caption
   c. Key
   d. Text

4. Which of the following specifies the letter D as the access key?
   a. &Display
   b. #Display
   c. ^Display
   d. D&isplay

5. Explain the method for providing keyboard access to a text box.

Lesson B Exercises

INTRODUCTORY

1. Open the Shiloh Solution (Shiloh Solution.sln) file contained in the VB2012\Chap02\Shiloh Solution folder. If necessary, open the designer window. Figure 2-18 shows the completed interface. Add the missing txtSales and lblBonus controls to the form. Set the lblBonus control's TextAlign property to MiddleCenter. Lock the controls on the form. Assign the access keys (shown in the figure) to the text boxes and buttons. Set the TabIndex values appropriately. Save the solution and then start the application. Verify that the tab order is correct. Also verify that the access keys work appropriately. Use the Exit button to end the application. Close the solution. (You will code the Calculate, Print, and Clear Screen buttons in Lesson C's Exercise 1.)

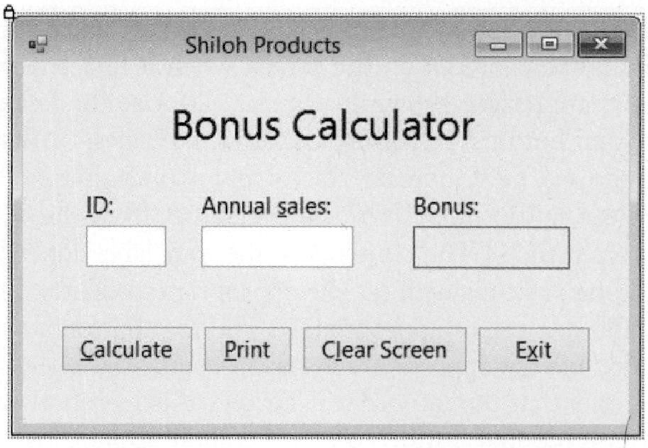

Figure 2-18 Shiloh Products user interface

INTERMEDIATE

2. Create a Visual Basic Windows application. Use the following names for the solution and project respectively: Carson Solution and Carson Project. Save the application in the VB2012\Chap02 folder. Change the form file's name to Main Form.vb. Change the form's name to frmMain. The form should be centered on the screen when it first appears; set the appropriate property. Create the interface shown in Figure 2-19. Use the following names for the text boxes, labels, and buttons: txtLength, txtWidth, lblAreaSqFt, lblAreaSqYd, btnCalc, btnPrint, btnClear, and btnExit. (Or, use the names from the TOE chart you created in Lesson A's Exercise 2.) The contents of the lblAreaSqFt and lblAreaSqYd controls should be centered; set the appropriate property. Lock the controls on the form. Set the TabIndex values appropriately. The Exit button should end the application when it is clicked; code the appropriate event procedure. Save the solution and then start the application. Verify that the tab order is correct. Also verify that the access keys work appropriately. Use the Exit button to end the application. Close the solution. (You will code the Calculate, Print, and Clear buttons in Lesson C's Exercise 4.)

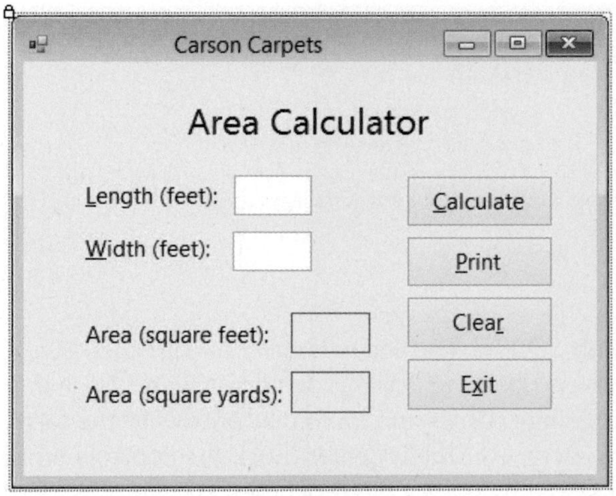

Figure 2-19 Carson Carpets user interface

INTERMEDIATE

3. Create a Visual Basic Windows application. Use the following names for the solution and project respectively: KJ Solution and KJ Project. Save the application in the VB2012\Chap02 folder. Change the form file's name to Main Form.vb. Change the form's name to frmMain. The form should be centered on the screen when it first appears; set the appropriate property. Create the interface shown in Figure 2-20. Use the following names for the text boxes, labels, and buttons: txtNsales, txtSsales, txtEsales, txtWsales, txtNincrease, txtSincrease, txtEincrease, txtWincrease, lblNorth, lblSouth, lblEast, lblWest, btnCalc, btnPrint, btnClear, and btnExit. (Or, use the names from the TOE chart you created in Lesson A's Exercise 3.) The contents of the four label controls that display the projected sales should be right-aligned; set the appropriate property. Lock the controls on the form. Set the TabIndex values appropriately. The Exit button should end the application when it is clicked; code the appropriate event procedure. Save the solution and then start the application. Verify that the tab order is correct. Also verify that the access keys work appropriately. Use the Exit button to end the application. Close the solution. (You will code the Calculate, Print, and Clear buttons in Lesson C's Exercise 5.)

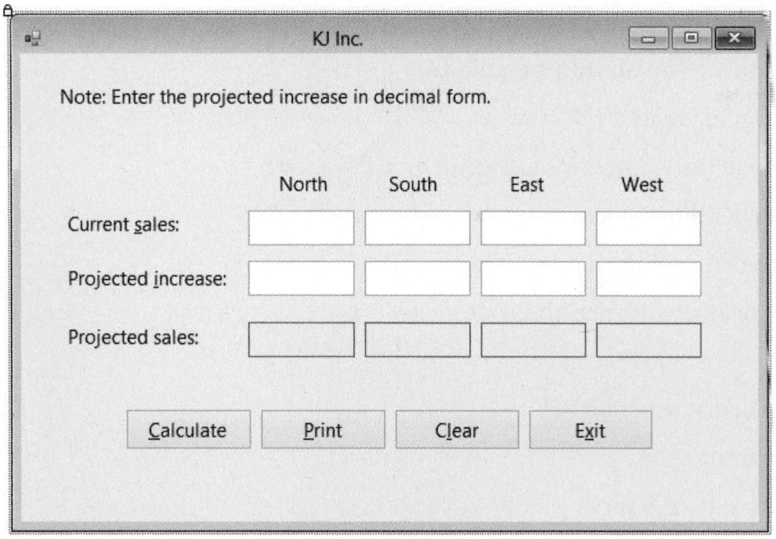

Figure 2-20 KJ Inc. user interface

INTERMEDIATE

4. Open the Age Solution (Age Solution.sln) file contained in the VB2012\Chap02\Age Solution folder. If necessary, open the designer window. The application allows the user to enter the year you were born and the current year. When it is coded, the Calculate button will calculate your age by subtracting your birth year from the current year. Lay out and organize the interface so that it follows all of the GUI design guidelines you have learned so far. (Refer to Appendix B for a listing of the guidelines covered in Chapter 1 and in Lessons A and B of Chapter 2.) Lock the controls on the form. Code the Exit button's Click event procedure so it ends the application. Save the solution and then start the application. Verify that the tab order is correct. Also verify that the access keys work appropriately. Use the Exit button to end the application. Close the solution. (You will code the Calculate and Print buttons in Lesson C's Exercise 2.)

LESSON C

After studying Lesson C, you should be able to:

- Code an application using its TOE chart
- Plan an object's code using either pseudocode or a flowchart
- Write an assignment statement
- Send the focus to a control during run time
- Include internal documentation in the code
- Write arithmetic expressions
- Use the Val and Format functions
- Print an interface from code
- Locate and correct syntax errors

Coding the Application

In Lessons A and B, you created a TOE chart and user interface for the Play It Again Movies application. The user interface and TOE chart are shown in Figures 2-21 and 2-22, respectively.

Figure 2-21 Play It Again Movies user interface from Lesson B
OpenClipArt.org/John Diamond / diamonjohn

Task	Object	Event
1. Calculate total discs sold and total sales amount 2. Display total discs sold and total sales amount in lblTotalDiscs and lblTotalSales	btnCalc	Click
Print the sales receipt	btnPrint	Click
End the application	btnExit	Click
Clear screen for the next sale	btnClear	Click
Display total discs sold (from btnCalc)	lblTotalDiscs	None
Display total sales amount (from btnCalc)	lblTotalSales	None
Get and display the sales information	txtDate, txtDvds, txtBluRays	None

Figure 2-22 TOE chart (ordered by object) for Play It Again Movies

After planning an application and building its user interface, you then can begin coding the application. You code an application so that the objects in the interface perform their assigned tasks when the appropriate event occurs. The objects and events that need to be coded, as well as the tasks assigned to each object and event, are listed in the application's TOE chart. The TOE chart in Figure 2-22 indicates that only the four buttons require coding, as they are the only objects with an event listed in the third column of the chart.

Before you begin coding an object's event procedure, you should plan it. Many programmers use planning tools such as pseudocode or flowcharts. You do not need to create both a flowchart and pseudocode for a procedure; you need to use only one of these planning tools. The tool you use is really a matter of personal preference. For simple procedures, pseudocode works just fine. When a procedure becomes more complex, however, the procedure's steps may be easier to understand in a flowchart. The programmer uses either the procedure's pseudocode or its flowchart as a guide when coding the procedure.

Using Pseudocode to Plan a Procedure

Pseudocode uses short phrases to describe the steps a procedure must take to accomplish its goal. Even though the word "pseudocode" might be unfamiliar to you, you have already written pseudocode without even realizing it. Consider the last time you gave directions to someone. You wrote each direction down on paper, in your own words; your directions were a form of pseudocode.

Figure 2-23 shows the pseudocode for the procedures that need to be coded in the Play It Again Movies application. Notice that the btnExit control's Click event procedure will simply end the application. The btnCalc control's Click event procedure will calculate the total discs sold and the total sales amount, and then display the calculated results in the appropriate label controls in the interface. The btnPrint control's Click event procedure will print the sales receipt. The btnClear control's Click event procedure will prepare the screen for the next sale. It will do this by removing the previous sale's information—in this case, the number of DVDs sold, the number of Blu-rays sold, the total number of discs sold, and the total sales—from the appropriate controls in the interface. It then will send the focus to the txtDvds control so the user can begin entering the next sale. You may be wondering why the event procedure doesn't clear the date entered in the txtDate control, and why it sends the focus to the txtDvds control rather than to the txtDate control. After the salesclerk enters the date the first time, there is no reason to have him or her enter it again for subsequent sales because the date will be the same.

```
btnExit Click event procedure
end the application

btnCalc Click event procedure
1. calculate total discs sold = DVDs sold + Blu-rays sold
2. calculate total sales = total discs sold * disc price
3. display total discs sold and total sales in lblTotalDiscs and lblTotalSales

btnPrint Click event procedure
print the sales receipt

btnClear Click event procedure
1. clear the contents of the txtDvds and txtBluRays text boxes
2. clear the contents of the lblTotalDiscs and lblTotalSales controls
3. send the focus to the txtDvds control so the user can begin entering the next sale
```

Figure 2-23 Pseudocode for the Play It Again Movies application

Using a Flowchart to Plan a Procedure

Unlike pseudocode, which consists of short phrases, a **flowchart** uses standardized symbols to show the steps a procedure must follow to reach its goal. Figure 2-24 shows the flowcharts for the procedures that need to be coded in the Play It Again Movies application. The logic illustrated in the flowcharts is the same as the logic shown in the pseudocode in Figure 2-23. The flowcharts contain three different symbols: an oval, a rectangle, and a parallelogram. The oval symbol is called the **start/stop symbol**. The start and stop ovals indicate the beginning and end, respectively, of the flowchart. The rectangles are called **process symbols**. You use the process symbol to represent tasks such as making assignments and calculations. The parallelogram in a flowchart is called the **input/output symbol** and is used to represent input tasks (such as getting information from the user) and output tasks (such as displaying information). The parallelograms in Figure 2-24 represent output tasks. The lines connecting the symbols in a flowchart are called **flowlines**.

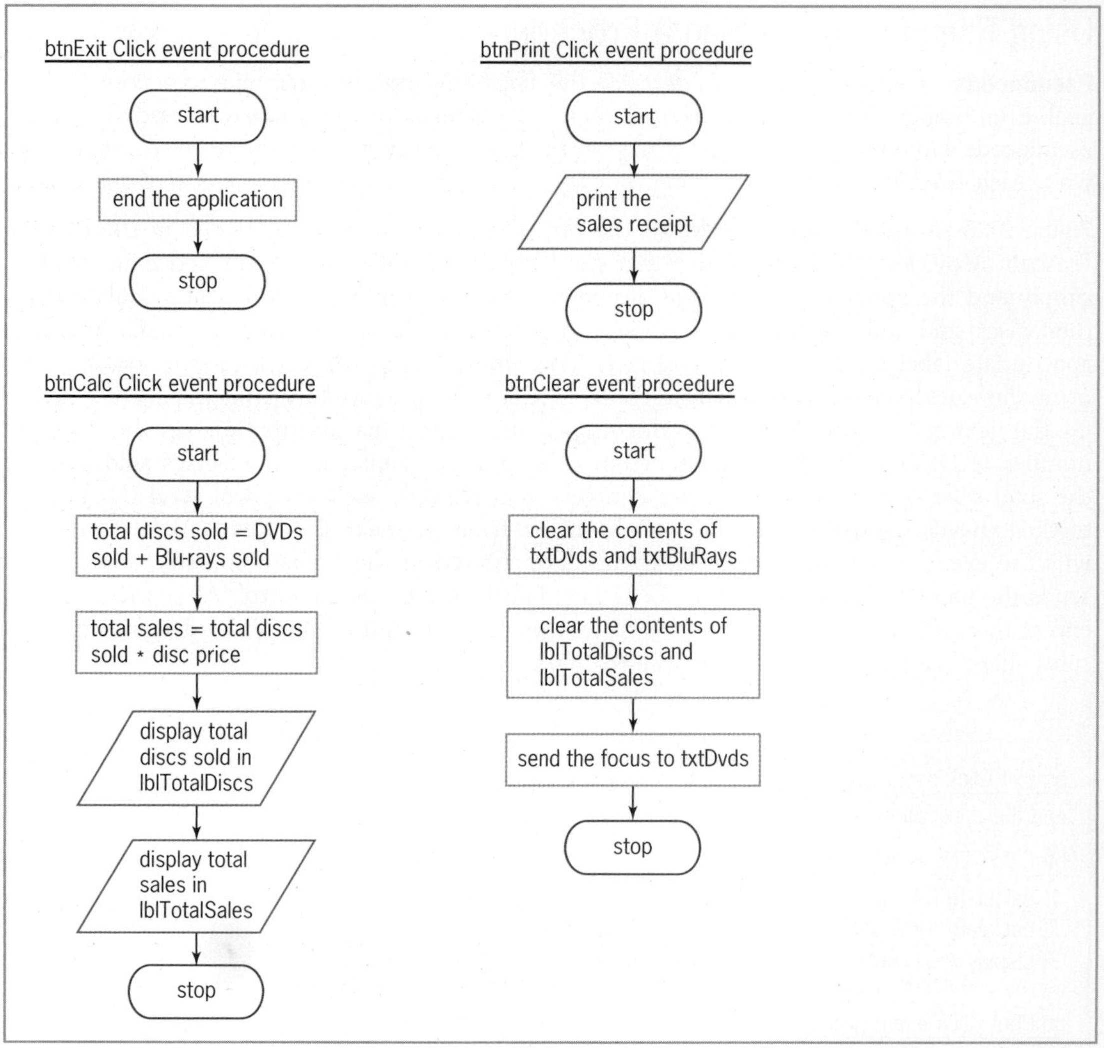

Figure 2-24 Flowcharts for Play It Again Movies

Coding the btnClear Control's Click Event Procedure

According to its pseudocode and flowchart, the btnClear control's Click event procedure should clear the Text property of two of the three text boxes and two of the labels in the interface. It then should send the focus to the txtDvds control. You can clear the Text property of an object by assigning a zero-length string to it. A **string** is defined as zero or more characters enclosed in quotation marks. The word "Jones" is a string. Likewise, "45" is a string, but 45 (without the quotes) is a number. "Jones" is a string with a length of five because there are five characters between the quotation marks. "45" is a string with a length of two because there are two characters between the quotation marks. Following this logic, a **zero-length string**, also called an **empty string**, is a set of quotation marks with nothing between them, like this: "". Assigning a zero-length string to the Text property of an object during run time removes the contents of the object. You also can clear an object's Text property by assigning the value **String.Empty** to it while an application is running. When you do this, the computer assigns an empty string to the Text property, thereby removing its contents.

You also can use the Clear method to clear the contents of a text box. The Clear method is covered in Discovery Exercise 14 at the end of this lesson.

Assigning a Value to a Property during Run Time

In Chapter 1, you learned how to use the Properties window to set an object's properties during design time, which is when you are building the interface. You also can set an object's properties during run time; you do this using an assignment statement. An **assignment statement** is one of many different types of Visual Basic instructions. Its purpose is to assign a value to something (such as to the property of an object) while an application is running.

The syntax of an assignment statement is shown in Figure 2-25 along with examples of using the syntax. In the syntax, *object* and *property* are the names of the object and property, respectively, to which you want the value of the *expression* assigned. The expression can be a string, a keyword, a number, or a calculation. You use a period to separate the object name from the property name. Recall that the period is the dot member access operator. In this case, the operator indicates that the *property* is a member of the *object*. You use an equal sign between the *object.property* information and the *expression*. The equal sign in an assignment statement is called the **assignment operator**.

Assigning a Value to a Property during Run Time

Syntax
object.property = *expression*

Examples
```
txtState.Text = "Montana"
txtName.Text = String.Empty
btnCalc.Visible = False
lblDue.Width = 120
lblProduct.Text = 6 + 3
```

Figure 2-25 Syntax and examples of assigning a value to a property during run time

When the computer processes an assignment statement, it assigns the value of the expression that appears on the right side of the assignment operator to the object and property that appear on the left side of the assignment operator. The assignment statement `txtState.Text = "Montana"`, for example, assigns the string "Montana" to the txtState control's Text property. Similarly, the assignment statement `txtName.Text = String.Empty` assigns the empty string to the Text property of the txtName control. You will use assignment statements to code the btnClear control's Click event procedure.

START HERE

To open the btnClear control's Click event procedure:

1. If necessary, start Visual Studio 2012 and open the Solution Explorer window. Open the Play It Again Solution (Play It Again Solution.sln) file from Lesson B. The file is contained in the VB2012\Chap02\Play It Again Solution folder. If necessary, open the designer window.
2. Auto-hide the Solution Explorer window. If necessary, auto-hide the Properties and Toolbox windows.
3. Open the Code Editor window. Notice that the btnExit control's Click event procedure has already been coded.
4. Use the Class Name and Method Name list boxes to open the code template for the btnClear control's Click event procedure.
5. Press **Enter** to insert a blank line below the procedure header.

According to its pseudocode and flowchart (shown earlier in Figures 2-23 and 2-24), the procedure should clear the contents of the txtDvds and txtBluRays text boxes. You can do this using either the *textbox*`.Text = String.Empty` instruction or the *textbox*`.Text = ""` instruction, where *textbox* is the name of the appropriate text box. You will assign the String.Empty value to the Text property of both text boxes. As you learned in Chapter 1, you can either type the Visual Basic instructions on your own or use the IntelliSense feature that is built into the Code Editor. In the next set of steps, you will use the IntelliSense feature.

START HERE

To begin coding the btnClear control's Click event procedure:

1. First, you will enter the `txtDvds.Text = String.Empty` assignment statement in the procedure. Type the two letters **tx** and then (if necessary) click the **Common** tab. The IntelliSense feature lists the names of the three text boxes. See Figure 2-26.

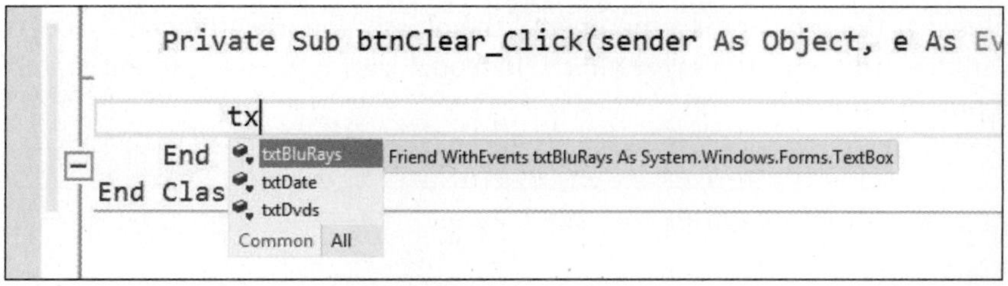

Figure 2-26 Listing of text box names

2. Type **tdv** to highlight txtDvds in the list and then press **Tab** to enter txtDvds in the assignment statement.
3. Now type **.** (a period) to display a listing of the properties and methods of the txtDvds control. If Text is not highlighted in the list, type **te**. At this point, you can either press the Tab key to enter the Text property in the assignment statement, or you can type the character that follows Text in the statement. In this case, the next character is the assignment operator. Type = to enter the Text property and an equal sign in the statement.
4. Next, type **st** to highlight String in the list, and then type **.e** to highlight Empty. Press **Enter**. The `txtDvds.Text = String.Empty` statement appears in the Code Editor window. See Figure 2-27.

```
    Private Sub btnClear_Click(sender As Object, e

        txtDvds.Text = String.Empty
        |
    End Sub
End Class
```

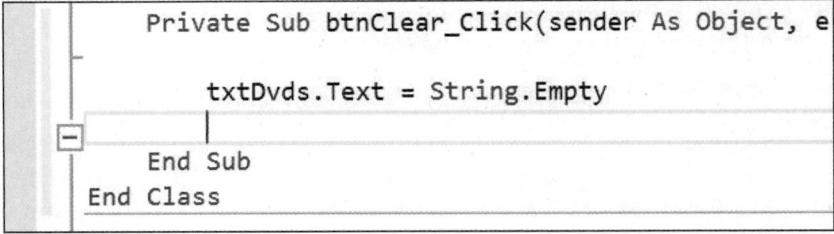

Figure 2-27 First assignment statement entered in the procedure

When entering code, you can type the names of commands, objects, and properties in lowercase letters. When you move to the next line in the Code Editor window, the Code Editor automatically changes your code to reflect the proper capitalization of those elements. This provides a quick way of verifying that you entered an object's name and property correctly, and that you entered the code using the correct syntax. If the capitalization does not change, it means that the Code Editor does not recognize the object, command, or property. In this book you will always be given the complete instruction to enter, including the appropriate capitalization. Keep in mind that you can either type the instruction on your own or use the IntelliSense feature to enter the instruction.

START HERE

To continue coding the btnClear control's Click event procedure:

1. Type **txtBluRays.Text = String.Empty** and press **Enter**.
2. Next, the procedure should clear the contents of the lblTotalDiscs and lblTotalSales controls. Enter the following two assignment statements. Press **Enter** twice after typing the last statement.

   lblTotalDiscs.Text = String.Empty
   lblTotalSales.Text = String.Empty

The last step in the procedure's pseudocode and flowchart is to send the focus to the txtDvds control. You can accomplish this task using the Focus method. Recall that a method is a predefined Visual Basic procedure that you can call (or invoke) when needed.

Using the Focus Method

You can use the **Focus method** to move the focus to a specified control while an application is running. As you learned in Lesson B, a control that has the focus can accept user input. The Focus method's syntax is *object*.**Focus()**, in which *object* is the name of the object to which you want the focus sent.

START HERE

To enter the Focus method in the btnClear control's Click event procedure:

1. Type **txtDvds.Focus()** and press **Enter**.
2. Save the solution.

Internally Documenting the Program Code

It is a good practice to include comments, called internal documentation, as reminders in the Code Editor window. Programmers use comments to indicate a procedure's purpose and also to explain various sections of a procedure's code. Including comments in your code will make the code more readable and easier to understand by anyone viewing it. You create a comment in Visual Basic by placing an apostrophe (') before the text that represents the comment. The computer ignores everything that appears after the apostrophe on that line.

Although it is not required, some programmers use a space to separate the apostrophe from the comment text; you will follow that convention in this book.

START HERE

To add comments to the btnClear control's Click event procedure:

1. Click the **blank line** above the `txtDvds.Text = String.Empty` statement. Type **' prepare screen for the next sale** (be sure to type the apostrophe followed by a space) and press **Enter**. Notice that comments appear in a different color from the rest of the code.
2. Click the **blank line** above the `txtDvds.Focus()` statement. Type **' send the focus to the DVDs box** and then click the **blank line** above the procedure's End Sub clause. See Figure 2-28.

```
Private Sub btnClear_Click(sender As Object, e As
    ' prepare screen for the next sale

    txtDvds.Text = String.Empty
    txtBluRays.Text = String.Empty
    lblTotalDiscs.Text = String.Empty
    lblTotalSales.Text = String.Empty
    ' send the focus to the DVDs box
    txtDvds.Focus()

End Sub
```

Figure 2-28 btnClear control's Click event procedure

It is a good idea to test a procedure after you have coded it because, by doing so, you will know where to look if an error occurs.

START HERE

To test the btnClear control's Click event procedure:

1. Save the solution and then start the application. Type **5** in the Date, DVDs, and Blu-rays boxes. You haven't coded the Calculate button yet, so the Total discs and Total sales boxes are empty at this point. Therefore, you will only be able to observe whether the Clear Screen button clears the two text boxes and moves the focus appropriately. You will need to test the Clear Screen button again after the Calculate button is coded.
2. Click the **Clear Screen** button. The computer processes the instructions contained in the button's Click event procedure. The instructions remove the contents of the two text boxes (and also the contents of the two labels, which are currently empty), and then send the focus to the DVDs box. Click the **Exit** button to end the application.

Many programmers also use comments to document the project's name and purpose, the programmer's name, and the date the code was either created or modified. Such comments are placed above the Public Class clause in the Code Editor window. The area above the Public Class clause is called the **General Declarations section**.

START HERE

To include comments in the General Declarations section:

1. Click **before the letter P** in the `Public Class frmMain` line and then press **Enter** to insert a blank line. Now, click the **blank line**.
2. Type the comments shown in Figure 2-29 and then save the solution. In the comments, replace <your name> and <current date> with your name and the current date, respectively.

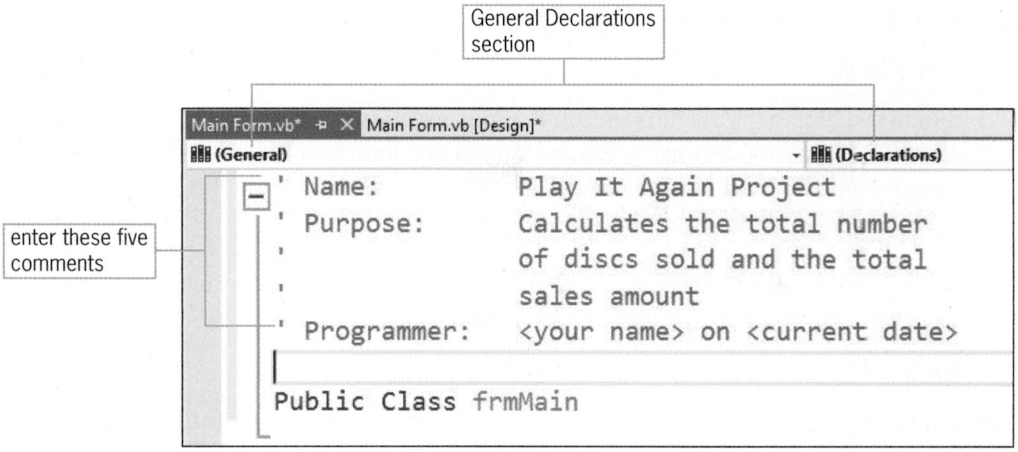

Figure 2-29 Comments entered in the General Declarations section

Coding the btnPrint Control's Click Event Procedure

Visual Basic provides the **PrintForm tool** for printing an interface from code. The tool is contained in the Visual Basic PowerPacks section of the toolbox. When you drag the PrintForm tool to a form, the instantiated print form control appears in the component tray. You can use the control to send the printout either to the Print preview window or directly to the printer. The syntax for printing the interface from code is shown in Figure 2-30 along with examples of using the syntax. As the figure indicates, the printing task requires two statements. The first statement specifies the output destination, and the second statement tells the computer to start the print operation.

Printing the Interface from Code

Syntax
object.**PrintAction = Printing.PrintAction.***destination*
object.**Print()**

destination	Purpose
`PrintToPreview`	sends the printout to the Print preview window
`PrintToPrinter`	sends the printout to the printer

Example 1
```
PrintForm1.PrintAction =
    Printing.PrintAction.PrintToPreview
PrintForm1.Print()
```
sends the output to the Print preview window

Example 2
```
PrintForm1.PrintAction =
    Printing.PrintAction.PrintToPrinter
PrintForm1.Print()
```
sends the output directly to the printer

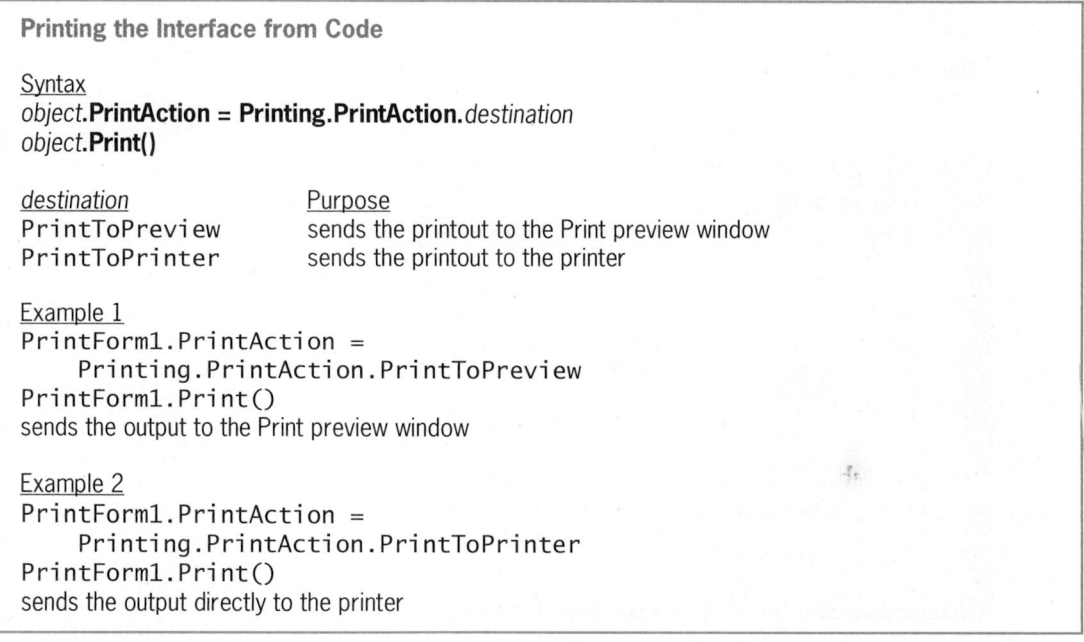

Figure 2-30 Syntax and examples of printing the interface from code

START HERE

To add a print form control to the application:

1. Click the designer window's tab to make the designer window the active window.
2. Temporarily display the toolbox. Scroll down the toolbox until you see the Visual Basic PowerPacks section. If necessary, expand the section's node. Click **PrintForm**, and then drag your mouse pointer to the form. When you release the mouse button, a print form control appears in the component tray.

You will have the Print Receipt button send the sales receipt to the Print preview window rather than directly to the printer. By doing so, the user will have more control over when the receipt is printed.

START HERE

To begin coding the btnPrint control's Click event procedure:

1. Return to the Code Editor window. Open the code template for the btnPrint control's Click event procedure, and then enter the comment and statements shown in Figure 2-31.

enter this comment and two lines of code

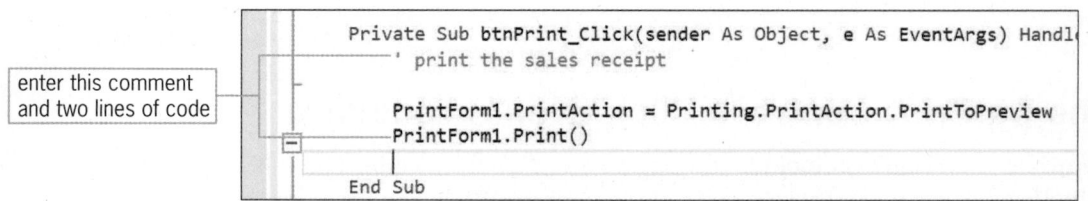

```
Private Sub btnPrint_Click(sender As Object, e As EventArgs) Handl
    ' print the sales receipt

    PrintForm1.PrintAction = Printing.PrintAction.PrintToPreview
    PrintForm1.Print()

End Sub
```

Figure 2-31 Comment and printing instructions entered in the procedure

2. Save the solution and then start the application. If necessary, press **Alt** to display the access keys. Click the **Print Receipt** button. A printout of the interface appears in the Print preview window. (It may take a few seconds for the window to open.) Click the **Zoom** button's list arrow and then click **75%**. See Figure 2-32. Notice that the four buttons appear on the sales receipt. You will fix that problem in the next set of steps.

Zoom button's list arrow

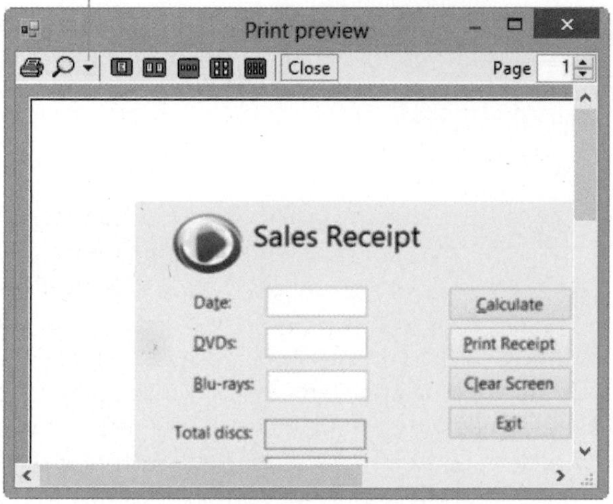

Figure 2-32 Print preview window
OpenClipArt.org/John Diamond / diamonjohn

3. You won't need to print the sales receipt, so click the **Close** button on the Print preview window's toolbar, and then click the **Exit** button in the interface.

You can prevent the buttons from appearing on the printed receipt by hiding them on the form *before* the receipt is printed, and then showing them again *after* the receipt is printed. In this case, you will hide the buttons by reducing the width of the form by 165 pixels. You can do this using the statement `Me.Width = Me.Width - 165`. As you learned in Chapter 1, `Me` is a keyword that refers to the current form. After the sales receipt is printed, you will increase the form's width by the same amount so that the buttons appear once again on the form.

START HERE

To finish coding the btnPrint control's Click event procedure:

1. Enter the additional two assignment statements shown in Figure 2-33.

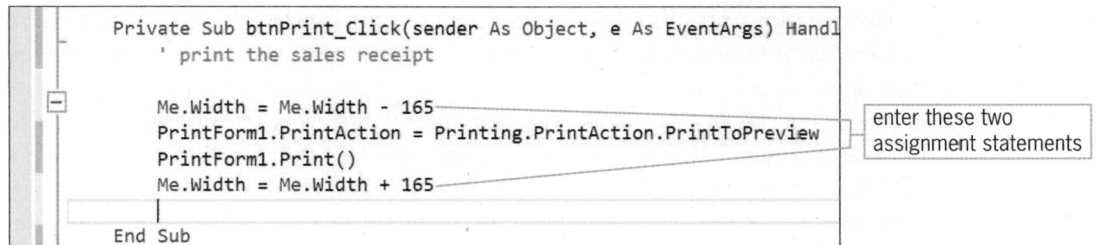

```
Private Sub btnPrint_Click(sender As Object, e As EventArgs) Handl
    ' print the sales receipt

    Me.Width = Me.Width - 165
    PrintForm1.PrintAction = Printing.PrintAction.PrintToPreview
    PrintForm1.Print()
    Me.Width = Me.Width + 165

End Sub
```

enter these two assignment statements

Figure 2-33 Completed Click event procedure for the btnPrint control

2. Save the solution and then start the application. Enter **5** in the Date, DVDs, and Blu-rays boxes.
3. Click the **Print Receipt** button to display the sales receipt in the Print preview window. Notice that the four buttons do not appear on the sales receipt.
4. If your computer is connected to a printer, click the **Print** button (the printer) on the Print preview window's toolbar.
5. Click the **Close** button on the Print preview window's toolbar, and then click the **Exit** button in the interface.

Before you can code the btnCalc control's Click event procedure, you need to learn how to write arithmetic expressions in Visual Basic. **Note**: You have learned a lot so far in this lesson. You may want to take a break at this point before continuing.

Writing Arithmetic Expressions

Most applications require the computer to perform at least one calculation. You instruct the computer to perform a calculation by writing an arithmetic expression, which is an expression that contains one or more arithmetic operators. Figure 2-34 lists the most commonly used arithmetic operators available in Visual Basic, along with their precedence numbers. The precedence numbers indicate the order in which the computer performs the operation in an expression. Operations with a precedence number of 1 are performed before operations with a precedence number of 2, and so on. However, you can use parentheses to override the order of precedence because operations within parentheses are always performed before operations outside parentheses.

Operator	Operation	Precedence number
^	exponentiation (raises a number to a power)	1
–	negation (reverses the sign of a number)	2
*, /	multiplication and division	3
\	integer division	4
Mod	modulus (remainder) arithmetic	5
+, –	addition and subtraction	6

Figure 2-34 Most commonly used arithmetic operators

Although the negation and subtraction operators listed in Figure 2-34 use the same symbol (a hyphen), there is a difference between both operators: the negation operator is unary, whereas the subtraction operator is binary. Unary and binary refer to the number of operands required by the operator. Unary operators require one operand; binary operators require two operands. For example, the expression –10 uses the negation operator to turn its one operand (the positive number 10) into a negative number. The expression 8 – 2, on the other hand, uses the subtraction operator to subtract its second operand (the number 2) from its first operand (the number 8).

Two of the arithmetic operators listed in Figure 2-34 might be less familiar to you: the integer division operator (\) and the modulus (remainder) operator (Mod). You use the **integer division operator** to divide two integers (whole numbers) and then return the result as an integer. For instance, the expression 211 \ 4 results in 52, which is the integer result of dividing 211 by 4. (If you use the standard division operator [/] to divide 211 by 4, the result is 52.75 rather than 52.) You might use the integer division operator in a program that determines the number of quarters, dimes, and nickels to return as change to a customer. For example, if a customer should receive 53 cents in change, you could use the expression 53 \ 25 to determine the number of quarters to return; the expression evaluates to 2.

The **modulus operator** (sometimes referred to as the remainder operator) is also used to divide two numbers, but the numbers do not have to be integers. After dividing the numbers, the modulus operator returns the remainder of the division. For instance, 211 Mod 4 equals 3, which is the remainder of 211 divided by 4. A common use for the modulus operator is to determine whether a number is even or odd. If you divide the number by 2 and the remainder is 0, the number is even; if the remainder is 1, however, the number is odd. Figure 2-35 shows several examples of using the integer division and Mod operators.

Examples	Results
211 \ 4	52
211 Mod 4	3
53 \ 25	2
53 Mod 25	3
75 \ 2	37
75 Mod 2	1
100 \ 2	50
100 Mod 2	0

Figure 2-35 Examples of the integer division and Mod (remainder) operators

You may have noticed that some of the operators listed in Figure 2-34, like the addition and subtraction operators, have the same precedence number. When an expression contains more than one operator having the same priority, those operators are evaluated from left to right.

In the expression 7 – 8 / 2 + 5, for instance, the division (/) is performed first, then the subtraction (–), and then the addition (+). The result of the expression is the number 8, as shown in Example 1 in Figure 2-36. You can use parentheses to change the order in which the operators in an expression are evaluated. For instance, as Example 2 in Figure 2-36 shows, the expression 7 – (8 / 2 + 5) evaluates to –2 rather than to 8. This is because the parentheses tell the computer to perform the division first, then the addition, and then the subtraction.

<u>Example 1</u>	
Original expression	7 – 8 / 2 + 5
The division is performed first	7 – 4 + 5
The subtraction is performed next	3 + 5
The addition is performed last	8
<u>Example 2</u>	
Original expression	7 – (8 / 2 + 5)
The division is performed first	7 – (4 + 5)
The addition is performed next	7 – 9
The subtraction is performed last	–2

Figure 2-36 Expressions containing more than one operator having the same precedence

The Ch02C-Arithmetic Operators video provides more examples of using arithmetic operators.

When entering an arithmetic expression in code, you do not enter a comma or special characters, such as the dollar sign or percent sign. If you want to include a percentage in an arithmetic expression, you do so using its decimal equivalent; for example, you enter .05 rather than 5%.

Coding the btnCalc Control's Click Event Procedure

According to its pseudocode and flowchart (shown earlier in Figures 2-23 and 2-24), the btnCalc control's Click event should calculate the total number of discs sold by adding together the number of DVDs sold and the number of Blu-rays sold. The number of DVDs sold is recorded in the txtDvds control's Text property as the user enters that information in the interface. Likewise, the number of Blu-rays sold is recorded in the txtBluRays control's Text property. You can use an assignment statement to first add together the Text property of the two text boxes, and then assign the sum to the Text property of the lblTotalDiscs control. The total discs sold calculation is illustrated in Figure 2-37.

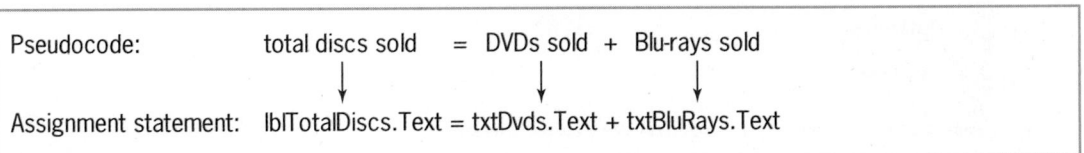

Pseudocode:	total discs sold	=	DVDs sold	+	Blu-rays sold
	↓		↓		↓
Assignment statement:	lblTotalDiscs.Text	=	txtDvds.Text	+	txtBluRays.Text

Figure 2-37 Illustration of the total discs sold calculation

Next, the procedure should calculate the total sales by multiplying the total number of discs sold (which is recorded in the lblTotalDiscs control) by the disc price ($7). The total sales should be displayed in the lblTotalSales control. The total sales calculation is illustrated in Figure 2-38.

Pseudocode: total sales = total discs sold * disc price

Assignment statement: lblTotalSales.Text = lblTotalDiscs.Text * 7

Figure 2-38 Illustration of the total sales calculation

Finally, the procedure should display the total discs sold and total sales amount in the appropriate label controls. The assignment statements shown in Figures 2-37 and 2-38 accomplish this task.

START HERE

To code the btnCalc control's Click event procedure and then test it:

1. Open the code template for the btnCalc control's Click event procedure. Type **' calculate number of discs sold and total sales** and press **Enter** twice.
2. Next, enter the following two assignment statements:

   lblTotalDiscs.Text = txtDvds.Text + txtBluRays.Text

   lblTotalSales.Text = lblTotalDiscs.Text * 7
3. Save the solution and then start the application. Click the **DVDs** text box. Type **2** and then press **Tab**. Type **5** as the number of Blu-rays sold and then click the **Calculate** button. The button's Click event procedure calculates the total number of discs sold and total sales, displaying the results in the two label controls. As Figure 2-39 indicates, the displayed results are incorrect. Instead of mathematically adding the two sales quantities together, giving 7, the second sales quantity was appended to the first sales quantity, giving 25. When the total discs sold amount is incorrect, the total sales will also be incorrect because the total discs sold amount is used in the total sales calculation.

Remember that you can use the Alt key to show/hide the access keys.

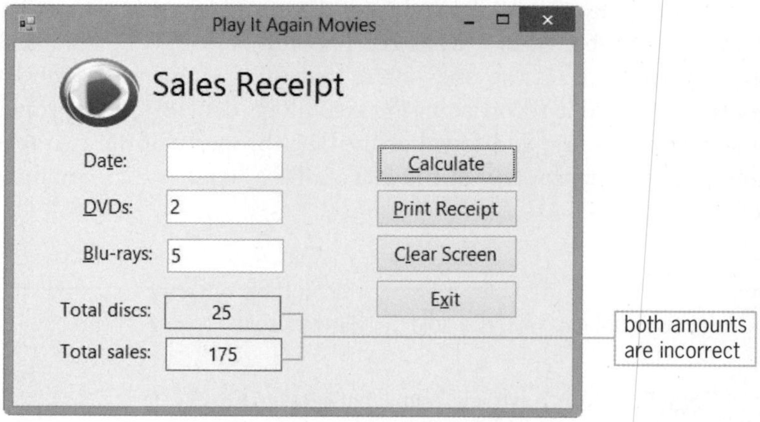

Figure 2-39 Interface showing the incorrect results of the calculations

OpenClipArt.org/John Diamond / diamonjohn

4. Click the **Exit** button to end the application.

Even though you do not see the quotation marks around the value, a value stored in the Text property of an object is treated as a string rather than as a number. Adding strings together does not give you the same result as adding numbers together. For example, adding the string "2" to the string "5" results in the string "25", whereas adding the number 2 to the number 5 results in the number 7. To add together the contents of two text boxes, you need to tell the computer to treat the contents as numbers rather than as strings. The easiest way, although not one of the preferred ways, is to use the Val function. However, because this lesson's topics are difficult for many beginning programmers, we'll use the Val function in this lesson (and only in this lesson) so as not to complicate those topics.

The Val Function

A **function** is a predefined procedure that performs a specific task and then returns a value after completing the task. The **Val function**, for instance, temporarily converts a string to a number and then returns the number. The number is stored in the computer's internal memory only while the function is processing.

The syntax of the Val function is shown in Figure 2-40. The item within the parentheses is called an argument and represents information that the function needs to perform its task. In this case, the *string* argument represents the string you want treated as a number. Because the Val function must be able to interpret the string as a numeric value, the string cannot include a letter, a comma, or a special character (such as the dollar sign or percent sign); it can, however, include a period or a space. When the Val function encounters an invalid character in its *string* argument, it stops converting the string to a number at that point. Figure 2-40 shows some examples of how the Val function converts various strings.

Val Function

Syntax
Val(*string***)**

Example	Numeric result
`Val("456")`	456
`Val("24,500")`	24
`Val("123X")`	123
`Val("25%")`	25
`Val("  12  34  ")`	1234
`Val("$56.88")`	0
`Val("Abc")`	0
`Val("")`	0

Figure 2-40 Syntax and examples of the Val function

To include the Val function in the btnCalc control's code:

START HERE

1. Change the two assignment statements as follows:

   lblTotalDiscs.Text = Val(txtDvds.Text) + Val(txtBluRays.Text)
   lblTotalSales.Text = Val(lblTotalDiscs.Text) * 7

2. Save the solution. The changes made to the procedure are highlighted in Figure 2-41.

```
Private Sub btnCalc_Click(sender As Object, e As EventArgs) Handles
    ' calculate number of discs sold and total sales

    lblTotalDiscs.Text = Val(txtDvds.Text) + Val(txtBluRays.Text)
    lblTotalSales.Text = Val(lblTotalDiscs.Text) * 7

End Sub
```

Figure 2-41 Val function entered in the assignment statements

3. Start the application. Enter **2** in the DVDs box and enter **5** in the Blu-rays box. Click the **Calculate** button. The application correctly calculates and displays the total number of discs sold (7) and total sales amount (49). See Figure 2-42.

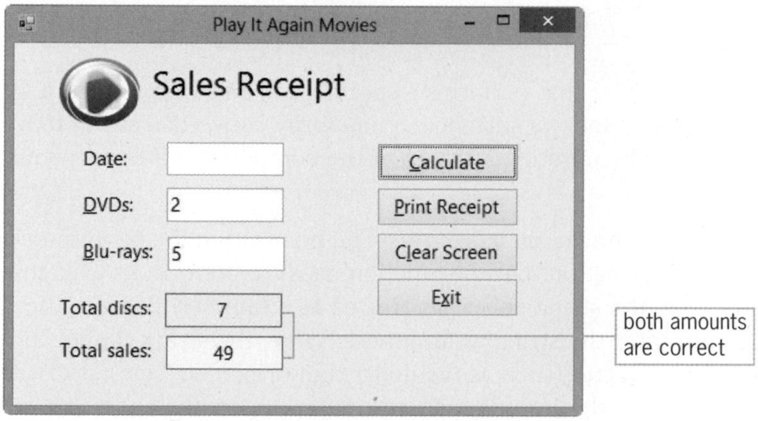

Figure 2-42 Interface showing the correct results of the calculations
OpenClipArt.org/John Diamond / diamonjohn

4. In the next section, you will improve the appearance of the total sales amount by including a dollar sign, a thousands separator, and two decimal places. Click the **Exit** button.

The Format Function

You can use the **Format function** to improve the appearance of numbers in an interface. The function's syntax is shown in Figure 2-43. The *expression* argument specifies the number, date, time, or string whose appearance you want to format. The *style* argument can be a predefined Visual Basic format style, some of which are explained in the figure. It also can be a string containing special symbols that indicate how you want the expression displayed. (You can display the Help screen for the Format function to learn more about these special symbols.) In this case, you will use one of the predefined format styles.

Format Function

Syntax

Format(*expression*, *style***)**

Format style	Description
Currency	Formats the number with a dollar sign, two decimal places, and (if appropriate) a thousands separator; negative numbers are enclosed in parentheses
Fixed	Formats the number with at least one digit to the left of the decimal point and two digits to the right of the decimal point
Standard	Formats the number with at least one digit to the left of the decimal point, two digits to the right of the decimal point, and (if appropriate) a thousands separator
Percent	Multiplies the number by 100 and then formats the result with a percent sign and two digits to the right of the decimal point

Figure 2-43 Format function's syntax and some of the predefined format styles

To format the total sales amount:

START HERE

1. Enter the following statement in the blank line below the total sales assignment statement:

   lblTotalSales.Text = Format(lblTotalSales.Text, "Currency")

2. Save the solution. The change made to the procedure is highlighted in Figure 2-44.


```
Private Sub btnCalc_Click(sender As Object, e As EventArgs) Handles
    ' calculate number of discs sold and total sales

    lblTotalDiscs.Text = Val(txtDvds.Text) + Val(txtBluRays.Text)
    lblTotalSales.Text = Val(lblTotalDiscs.Text) * 7
    lblTotalSales.Text = Format(lblTotalSales.Text, "Currency")

End Sub
```

Figure 2-44 Format function entered in the procedure

You also can include the Format function in the statement that calculates the total sales, like this: `lblTotalSales.Text = Format(Val(lblTotalDiscs.Text) * 7, "Currency")`.

3. Start the application. Enter **4/16/2014** in the Date box, **100** in the DVDs box, and **100** in the Blu-rays box. Click the **Calculate** button. See Figure 2-45.

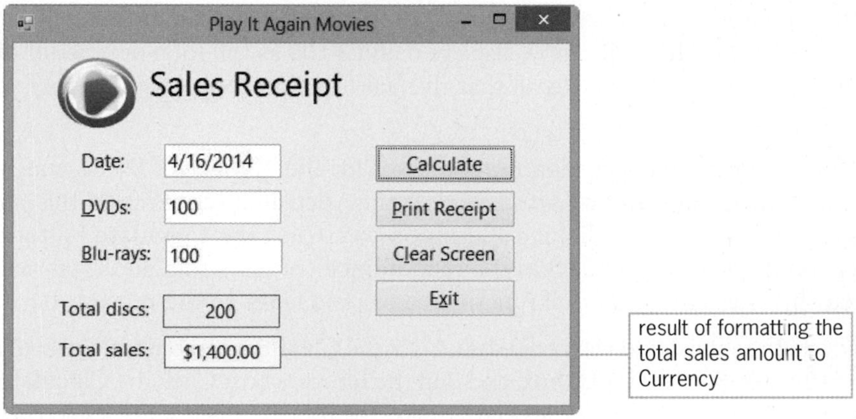

Figure 2-45 Formatted total sales amount shown in the interface
OpenClipArt.org/John Diamond / diamonjohn

4. Click the **Exit** button.

You have completed the first four of the six steps involved in creating an OO application: meeting with the client, planning the application, building the user interface, and coding the application. The fifth step is to test and debug the application.

Testing and Debugging the Application

You test an application by starting it and entering some sample data. The sample data should include both valid and invalid data. **Valid data** is data that the application is expecting the user to enter, whereas **invalid data** is data that the application is not expecting the user to enter. The Play It Again Movies application, for instance, expects the user to enter a numeric value in the DVDs box; it does not expect the user to enter a letter. In most cases, invalid data is a result of a typing error made by the user. You should test an application as thoroughly as possible to ensure that it displays the correct output when valid data is entered, and does not end abruptly when invalid data is entered.

Debugging refers to the process of locating and correcting the errors, called **bugs**, in a program. Program bugs are typically categorized as syntax errors, logic errors, or run time errors. As you learned in Chapter 1, the term "syntax" refers to the set of rules you must follow when using a programming language. A **syntax error** occurs when you break one of the language's rules. Most syntax errors are a result of typing errors that occur when entering instructions, such as typing `Me.Clse()` instead of `Me.Close()`. The Code Editor detects most syntax errors as you enter the instructions.

Logic errors, on the other hand, are much more difficult to find because the Code Editor cannot detect them for you. A **logic error** can occur for a variety of reasons, such as forgetting to enter an instruction or entering the instructions in the wrong order. Some logic errors occur as a result of calculation statements that are correct syntactically but incorrect mathematically. For example, consider the statement `lblSquared.Text = Val(txtNum.Text) + Val(txtNum.Text)`, which is supposed to square the number entered in the txtNum control. The statement's syntax is correct; however, the statement is incorrect mathematically because you square a value by multiplying it by itself, not by adding it to itself.

A **run time error** is an error that occurs while an application is running. An expression that attempts to divide a value by the number 0 will result in a run time error. You will learn more about run time errors as you progress through this book.

START HERE

To test and debug the Play It Again Movies application:

1. Start the application. First, test the application by clicking the **Calculate** button without entering any data. The application displays 0 and $0.00 as the total number of discs sold and total sales, respectively. (Recall that the Val function converts the empty string to the number 0.)
2. Now you will test the application using a letter for the number of DVDs and Blu-rays sold. Click the **Clear Screen** button to clear the calculated results from the label controls. Enter **p** in the DVDs and Blu-rays boxes. Click the **Calculate** button. The application displays 0 and $0.00 as the total number of discs sold and total sales, respectively. (Recall that the Val function converts a letter to the number 0.)
3. Finally, test the application with valid data. Click the **Clear Screen** button. Enter **6/10/2014** in the Date box, **6** in the DVDs box, and **3** in the Blu-rays box. Click the **Calculate** button. The application correctly calculates and displays the total number of discs sold (9) and total sales amount ($63.00).
4. Click the **Print Receipt** button. If your computer is connected to a printer, print the sales receipt. Close the Print preview window.
5. Click the **Clear Screen** button and then practice with other entries to see how the application responds. When you are finished testing the application, click the **Exit** button to end the application.

In the following set of steps, you will introduce syntax errors in the application's code. You also will learn how to locate and correct the errors.

START HERE

To introduce syntax errors in the code and also debug the code:

1. Change the statement in the btnExit control's Click event procedure to **Me.Clse()** and then click the **blank line** above the procedure header. The jagged blue line indicates that the statement contains a syntax error. To debug the code, change the statement to **Me.Close()** and then click the **blank line** above the procedure header. The jagged blue line disappears.
2. In the btnCalc control's Click event procedure, delete the ending parenthesis in the last assignment statement and then click the **blank line** below the statement. The jagged

blue line indicates that the statement contains a syntax error. The red rectangle indicates that the Code Editor has some suggestions for fixing the error.

3. Hover your mouse pointer over the red rectangle until you see the Error Correction Options box, and then click the **list arrow** in the box. A suggestion for fixing the error appears in the Error Correction window. See Figure 2-46. [Don't be concerned if your Error Correction window appears above (rather than below) the red rectangle.]

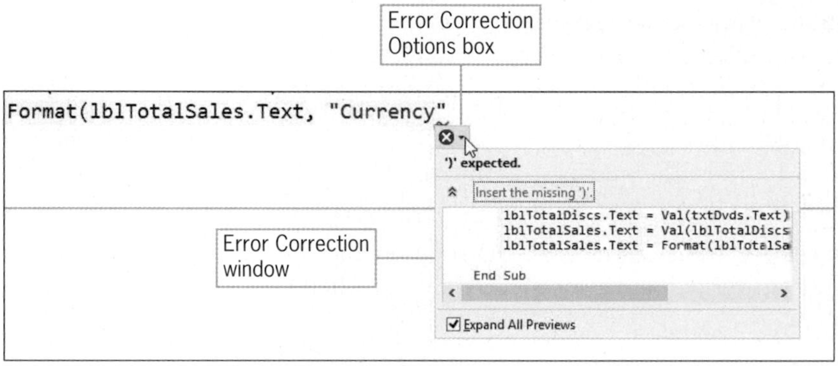

Figure 2-46 Suggestion for fixing the error

4. Move the scroll bar in the Error Correction window all the way to the right. The window indicates that the missing parenthesis will be inserted at the end of the assignment statement that contains the syntax error. You can type the missing parenthesis yourself. Or, you can simply click the suggestion in the Error Correction window. Click the **Insert the missing ')'.** suggestion to insert the missing parenthesis.

5. In this step, you will observe what happens when you start an application whose code contains a syntax error. First, delete the ending parenthesis in the last assignment statement in the btnCalc control's Click event procedure, and then click the **blank line** below the statement. Save the solution and then start the application. The message dialog box shown in Figure 2-47 appears.

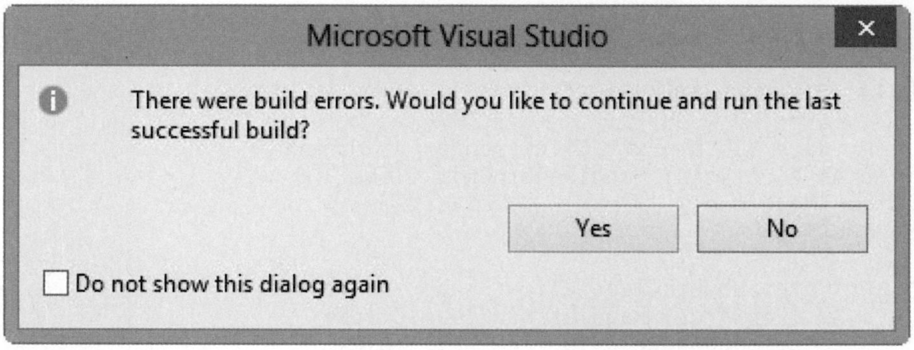

Figure 2-47 Message dialog box

6. Click the **No** button. The Error List window shown in Figure 2-48 opens at the bottom of the IDE. The window indicates that the code contains one error, and it provides both a description and the location of the error in the Code Editor window.

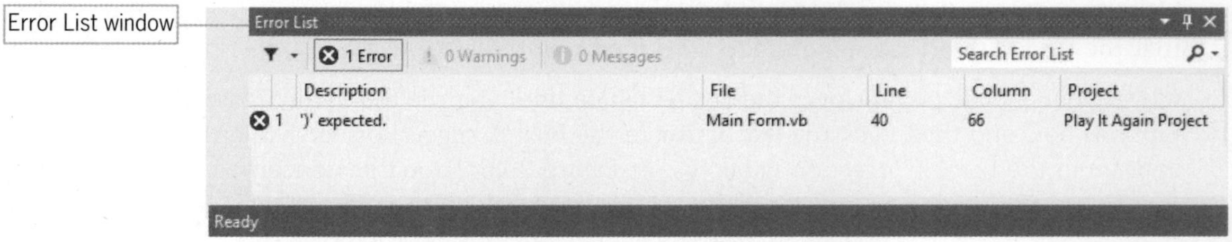

Figure 2-48 Error List window in the IDE

7. Double-click the **error message** in the Error List window. The Code Editor opens the Error Correction window shown earlier in Figure 2-46. Click the **Insert the missing ')'.** suggestion to insert the missing parenthesis. The Code Editor inserts the missing parenthesis and then removes the error message from the Error List window.
8. Close the Error List window. Save the solution and then start the application. Test the application to verify that it works correctly, and then click the **Exit** button to end the application.
9. Close the Code Editor window and then close the solution.

Assembling the Documentation

After you have tested an application thoroughly, you can move to the last step involved in creating an OO application: assemble the documentation. Assembling the documentation refers to putting your planning tools and a printout of the application's interface and code in a safe place, so you can refer to them if you need to change the application in the future. Your planning tools include the TOE chart, a sketch of the user interface, and either the flowcharts or pseudocode. The code for the Play It Again Movies application is shown in Figure 2-49.

```
' Name:         Play It Again Project
' Purpose:      Calculates the total number
'               of discs sold and the total
'               sales amount
' Programmer:   <your name> on <current date>

Public Class frmMain

    Private Sub btnExit_Click(sender As Object,
    e As EventArgs) Handles btnExit.Click
        Me.Close()
    End Sub

    Private Sub btnClear_Click(sender As Object,
    e As EventArgs) Handles btnClear.Click
        ' prepare screen for the next sale

        txtDvds.Text = String.Empty
        txtBluRays.Text = String.Empty
        lblTotalDiscs.Text = String.Empty
        lblTotalSales.Text = String.Empty
        ' send the focus to the DVDs box
        txtDvds.Focus()

    End Sub

```

Figure 2-49 Play It Again Movies code *(continues)*

(continued)

```
    Private Sub btnPrint_Click(sender As Object,
    e As EventArgs) Handles btnPrint.Click
       ' print the sales receipt

       Me.Width = Me.Width - 165
       PrintForm1.PrintAction =
       Printing.PrintAction.PrintToPreview
         PrintForm1.Print()
       Me.Width = Me.Width + 165

    End Sub

    Private Sub btnCalc_Click(sender As Object,
    e As EventArgs) Handles btnCalc.Click
       ' calculate number of discs sold and total sales

       lblTotalDiscs.Text = Val(txtDvds.Text) +
         Val(txtBluRays.Text)
       lblTotalSales.Text = Val(lblTotalDiscs.Text) * 7
       lblTotalSales.Text =
         Format(lblTotalSales.Text, "Currency")

    End Sub
End Class
```

Figure 2-49 Play It Again Movies code

Lesson C Summary

- To plan an object's code:

  Use pseudocode or a flowchart.

- To clear the text property of an object while an application is running:

  Assign either the String.Empty value or the empty string ("") to the object's Text property.

- To assign a value to an object's property while an application is running:

  Use an assignment statement that follows the syntax *object.property* = *expression*.

- To move the focus to an object while an application is running:

  Use the Focus method. The method's syntax is *object*.**Focus()**.

- To create a comment in Visual Basic:

  Begin the comment text with an apostrophe (').

- To divide two integers and then return the result as an integer:

  Use the integer division operator (\).

- To divide two numbers and then return the remainder:

  Use the modulus (remainder) operator (Mod).

- To print the interface during run time:

  Use the PrintForm tool to instantiate a print form control. The tool is located in the Visual Basic PowerPacks section of the toolbox.

- To temporarily convert a string to a number:

  Use the Val function. The function's syntax is **Val(*string*)**.
- To improve the appearance of numbers in the user interface:

  Use the Format function. The function's syntax is **Format(*expression*, *style*)**.

Lesson C Key Terms

Assignment operator—the equal sign in an assignment statement

Assignment statement—an instruction that assigns a value to something, such as to the property of an object

Bugs—the errors in a program

Debugging—the process of locating and correcting the bugs (errors) in a program

Empty string—a set of quotation marks with nothing between them (""); also called a zero-length string

Flowchart—a planning tool that uses standardized symbols to show the steps a procedure must take to accomplish its goal

Flowlines—the lines connecting the symbols in a flowchart

Focus method—moves the focus to a specified control during run time

Format function—used to improve the appearance of numbers in an interface

Function—a procedure that processes a specific task and returns a value

General Declarations section—the area above the Public Class clause in the Code Editor window

Input/output symbol—the parallelogram in a flowchart; used to represent input and output tasks

Integer division operator—represented by a backslash (\); divides two integers and then returns the quotient as an integer

Invalid data—data that an application is not expecting the user to enter

Logic error—occurs when you neglect to enter an instruction or enter the instructions in the wrong order; also occurs as a result of calculation statements that are correct syntactically but incorrect mathematically

Modulus operator—represented by the keyword `Mod`; divides two numbers and returns the remainder of the division

PrintForm tool—used to instantiate a print form control; located in the Visual Basic PowerPacks section of the toolbox

Process symbols—the rectangle symbols in a flowchart; used to represent assignment and calculation tasks

Pseudocode—a planning tool that uses phrases to describe the steps a procedure must take to accomplish its goal

Run time error—an error that occurs while an application is running; an example is an expression that attempts to divide by zero

Start/stop symbol—the oval symbol in a flowchart; used to indicate the beginning and end of the flowchart

String—zero or more characters enclosed in quotation marks

String.Empty—the value that represents the empty string in Visual Basic

Syntax error—occurs when an instruction in an application's code breaks one of a programming language's rules

Val function—temporarily converts a string to a number and then returns the number

Valid data—data that an application is expecting the user to enter

Zero-length string—a set of quotation marks with nothing between them (""); also called an empty string

Lesson C Review Questions

1. Which of the following assignment statements will not calculate correctly?
   a. `lblTotal.Text = Val(txtSales1.Text) + Val(txtSales2.Text)`
   b. `lblTotal.Text = 4 - Val(txtSales1.Text)`
   c. `lblTotal.Text = Val(txtQuantity.Text + 3)`
   d. All of the above assignment statements will calculate correctly.
2. The ______________ function temporarily converts a string to a number, and then returns the number.
   a. Format
   b. FormatNumber
   c. StringToNumber
   d. Val
3. Which symbol is used in a flowchart to represent an output task?
   a. circle
   b. oval
   c. parallelogram
   d. rectangle
4. What value is assigned to the lblNum control when the `lblNum.Text = 99 \ 25` instruction is processed by the computer?
5. What value is assigned to the lblNum control when the `lblNum.Text = 99 Mod 25` instruction is processed by the computer?

Lesson C Exercises

Note: In several of the exercises in this lesson, you perform the second through sixth steps involved in creating an OO application. Recall that the six steps are:

1. Meet with the client.
2. Plan the application. (Prepare a TOE chart that is ordered by object, and then draw a sketch of the user interface.)
3. Build the user interface. (Refer to Appendix B for a listing of the GUI guidelines you have learned so far. To help you remember the names of the controls as you are coding, print the application's interface and then write the names next to each object.)
4. Code the application. (Write pseudocode for each of the objects that will be coded. Include appropriate comments in the code.)
5. Test and debug the application.
6. Assemble the documentation (your planning tools and a printout of the interface and code).

INTRODUCTORY

1. In this exercise, you complete the application saved in Lesson B's Exercise 1. Open the Shiloh Solution (Shiloh Solution.sln) file contained in the VB2012\Chap02\Shiloh Solution folder. If necessary, open the designer window.

   a. At the end of the year, each salesperson at Shiloh Products is paid a bonus of 1% of his or her annual sales. Code the Calculate button using the Val function. Use the Format function to display the bonus with a dollar sign, a thousands separator, and two decimal places.

   b. Code the Clear Screen button. Send the focus to the ID text box.

   c. Add a print form control to the application, and then code the Print button. Send the printout to the Print preview window. To hide the buttons in the printout, reduce the form's height by 75 pixels before printing, and then increase the height by the same amount after printing.

   d. Add appropriate comments in the General Declarations section and in the coded procedures.

   e. Save the solution and then start the application. Enter the following valid ID and sales amount: AB65 and 5000. The bonus should be $50.00. If your computer is connected to a printer, print the interface.

   f. Clear the screen. Now test the application using invalid data. More specifically, test it without entering any data. Then test it using a letter as the sales amount.

   g. Close the Code Editor window and then close the solution.

INTRODUCTORY

2. In this exercise, you complete the application saved in Lesson B's Exercise 4. Open the Age Solution (Age Solution.sln) file contained in the VB2012\Chap02\Age Solution folder. If necessary, open the designer window. The Calculate button should calculate your age by subtracting your birth year from the current year. Code the Calculate button using the Val function. Add a print form control to the application, and then code the Print button. Send the printout (which should not include the buttons) to the Print preview window. Add appropriate comments in the General Declarations section and in the coded procedures. Save the solution and then start the application. Test the application using your birth year and the current year. Also test it without entering any data. Finally, test it using a $ sign for the birth year and a % sign for the current year. Close the Code Editor window and then close the solution.

INTRODUCTORY

3. ABC Company wants an application that displays the company's net annual profit or loss. The company's accountant will enter the following two pieces of information: the company's total annual revenue and its total annual expenses.

   a. Create a Visual Basic Windows application. Use the following names for the solution and project, respectively: ABC Solution and ABC Project. Save the application in the VB2012\Chap02 folder. Change the form file's name to Main Form.vb. Change the form's name to frmMain.

   b. Perform the steps involved in creating an OO application. (See the Note at the beginning of the Exercises section.) Include buttons that allow the user to both clear and print the screen. Send the printout (which should not include the buttons) to the Print preview window. Code the application using the Val and Format functions. Add appropriate comments in the General Declarations section and in the coded procedures.

c. Test the application using the following revenue and expenses, respectively: 115000 and 64500. Then test it without entering any data. Also test it using a letter as the revenue and expenses. Finally, test it using 50 and 75 as the revenue and expenses, respectively.

d. Close the Code Editor window and then close the solution.

INTERMEDIATE

4. In this exercise, you complete the application saved in Lesson B's Exercise 2. Open the Carson Solution (Carson Solution.sln) file contained in the VB2012\Chap02\Carson Solution folder. If necessary, open the designer window.

   a. The Carson Carpets application should calculate the area of a floor in both square feet and square yards. Code the Calculate button using the Val function. Use the Format function to display the calculated results using the Standard format style.

   b. Code the Clear button. Send the focus to the Length text box.

   c. Add a print form control to the application, and then code the Print button. Send the printout (which should include the buttons) to the Print preview window.

   d. Add appropriate comments in the General Declarations section and in the coded procedures.

   e. Save the solution and then start the application. Test the application using 10 as the length and 12 as the width. If your computer is connected to a printer, print the interface.

   f. Clear the screen. Now test the application using invalid data. More specifically, test it without entering any data. Then test it using a letter as the length and width measurements.

   g. Close the Code Editor window and then close the solution.

INTERMEDIATE

5. In this exercise, you complete the application saved in Lesson B's Exercise 3. Open the KJ Solution (KJ Solution.sln) file contained in the VB2012\Chap02\KJ Solution folder. If necessary, open the designer window.

   a. The KJ Inc. application should calculate the projected sales for each sales region. Code the Calculate button using the Val function. Use the Format function to display the calculated results using the Standard format style.

   b. Code the Clear button. Send the focus to the Current sales text box in the North column.

   c. Add a print form control to the application, and then code the Print button. Send the printout (which should not include the buttons) to the Print preview window.

   d. Add appropriate comments in the General Declarations section and in the coded procedures.

   e. Save the solution and then start the application. Test the application using the following valid data:

North sales and percentage:	25000, .1
South sales and percentage:	10000, .05
East sales and percentage:	10000, .04
West sales and percentage:	15000, .11

   f. Test the application without entering any data. Also test it using letters as the sales and percentage amounts.

   g. Close the Code Editor window and then close the solution.

INTERMEDIATE

6. In this exercise, you modify the Play It Again Movies application from the chapter. Use Windows to make a copy of the Play It Again Solution folder contained in the VB2012\Chap02 folder. Rename the copy Modified Play It Again Solution. Open the Play It Again Solution (Play It Again Solution.sln) file contained in the Modified Play It Again Solution folder. Open the designer window. Modify the interface so that it allows the user to enter the disc price. Also modify the application's code. Save the solution and then start and test the application. Close the Code Editor window and then close the solution.

INTERMEDIATE

7. Create a Visual Basic Windows application. Use the following names for the solution and project, respectively: Average Solution and Average Project. Save the application in the VB2012\Chap02 folder. Change the form file's name to Main Form.vb. Change the form's name to frmMain. The application should display the average of any three numbers entered by the user. Perform the steps involved in creating an OO application. (See the Note at the beginning of the Exercises section.) Include buttons that allow the user to both clear and print the screen. Send the printout (which should include the buttons) to the Print preview window. Display the average with two decimal places. Code the application using the Val and Format functions. Add appropriate comments in the General Declarations section and in the coded procedures. Use the following three numbers to test the application: 27, 9, and 18. Also test it without entering any data. Finally, test it using letters for the input. Close the Code Editor window and then close the solution.

INTERMEDIATE

8. Timbers is having a 20% off sale. The store manager wants an application that allows the clerk to enter the original price of an item. The application should display the discount and new price. Create a Visual Basic Windows application. Use the following names for the solution and project, respectively: Timbers Solution and Timbers Project. Save the application in the VB2012\Chap02 folder. Change the form file's name to Main Form.vb. Change the form's name to frmMain. Perform the steps involved in creating an OO application. (See the Note at the beginning of the Exercises section.) Include buttons that allow the user to both clear and print the screen. Send the printout (which should not include the buttons) to the Print preview window. Code the application using the Val function. Format the discount and new price using the Standard format style. Add appropriate comments in the General Declarations section and in the coded procedures. Test the application using valid and invalid data. Close the Code Editor window and then close the solution.

INTERMEDIATE

9. The store manager of Reader Haven needs an inventory application. The application should allow him to enter the title of a book, the number of paperback versions of the book currently in inventory, the number of hardcover versions of the book currently in inventory, the cost of the paperback version, and the cost of the hardcover version. The application should display the value of the paperback versions of the book, the value of the hardcover versions of the book, the total number of paperback and hardcover versions, and the total value of the paperback and hardcover versions combined. Create a Visual Basic Windows application. Use the following names for the solution and project, respectively: Reader Haven Solution and Reader Haven Project. Save the application in the VB2012\Chap02 folder. Change the form file's name to Main Form.vb. Change the form's name to frmMain. Perform the steps involved in creating an OO application. (See the Note at the beginning of the Exercises section.) Include buttons that allow the user to both clear and print the screen. Send the printout (which should not include the buttons) to the Print preview window. Code the application using the Val and Format functions. Format the calculated dollar amounts to show a dollar sign,

thousands separator, and two decimal places. Add appropriate comments in the General Declarations section and in the coded procedures. Use the valid and invalid data shown here when testing the application. Close the Code Editor window and then close the solution.

Book Title:	Summer Nights
Paperback versions: 100	Paperback cost: 40
Hardcover versions: 50	Hardcover cost: 75

Book Title:	Kitchen Helpers
Paperback versions: A	Paperback cost: B
Hardcover versions: C	Hardcover cost: D

10. Carol's favorite crackers have 50 calories per serving. In this case, a serving is 10 crackers. Carol wants an application that displays the number of calories she consumes during her midnight snack of crackers. Create a Visual Basic Windows application. Use the following names for the solution and project, respectively: Calories Solution and Calories Project. Save the application in the VB2012\Chap02 folder. Change the form file's name to Main Form.vb. Change the form's name to frmMain. Perform the steps involved in creating an OO application. (See the Note at the beginning of the Exercises section.) Include buttons that allow the user to both clear and print the screen. Send the printout (which should not include the buttons) to the Print preview window. Code the application using the Val function. Add appropriate comments in the General Declarations section and in the coded procedures. Test the application using both valid and invalid data. Close the Code Editor window and then close the solution. INTERMEDIATE

11. Zander Typing Services charges $0.12 per typed envelope and $0.40 per typed page. The company accountant wants an application to help her prepare bills. She will enter the customer's name, the number of typed envelopes, and the number of typed pages. The application should calculate and display the customer's total bill. Create a Visual Basic Windows application. Use the following names for the solution and project, respectively: Zander Solution and Zander Project. Save the application in the VB2012\Chap02 folder. Change the form file's name to Main Form.vb. Change the form's name to frmMain. Perform the steps involved in creating an OO application. (See the Note at the beginning of the Exercises section.) Test the application using both valid and invalid data. Close the Code Editor window and then close the solution. INTERMEDIATE

12. Yardley Company needs an application that allows the shipping clerk to enter the quantity of an item in inventory and the number of the items that can be packed in a box for shipping. When the shipping clerk clicks a button, the application should compute and display both the number of full boxes that can be packed and the number of items left over. Create a Visual Basic Windows application. Use the following names for the solution and project, respectively: Yardley Solution and Yardley Project. Save the application in the VB2012\Chap02 folder. Change the form file's name to Main Form.vb. Change the form's name to frmMain. Perform the steps involved in creating an OO application. (See the Note at the beginning of the Exercises section.) Save the solution and then start the application. Yardley Company has 73 items in inventory. If five of the items can fit into a box for shipping, how many full boxes can the company ship and how many items will remain in inventory? Close the Code Editor window and then close the solution. ADVANCED

13. The payroll clerk at Lawry Inc. wants an application that displays an employee's net pay. The application should allow the payroll clerk to enter the employee's name, hours worked, and rate of pay. For this application, you do not have to worry about overtime because this company does not allow anyone to work more than 40 hours. The ADVANCED

application should calculate and display the gross pay, the federal withholding tax (FWT), the Social Security tax (FICA), the state income tax, and the net pay. The FWT is 20% of the gross pay. The FICA tax is 8% of the gross pay. The state income tax is 3% of the gross pay. Create a Visual Basic Windows application. Use the following names for the solution and project, respectively: Lawry Solution and Lawry Project. Save the application in the VB2012\Chap02 folder. Change the form file's name to Main Form.vb. Change the form's name to frmMain. Perform the steps involved in creating an OO application. (See the Note at the beginning of the Exercises section.) Format the calculated amounts using the Standard format style. Test the application using both valid and invalid data. Close the Code Editor window and then close the solution.

DISCOVERY

14. In this exercise, you learn about a text box's Clear method, which can be used to remove the contents of the text box while an application is running. Use Windows to make a copy of the Play It Again Solution folder from the chapter. Rename the copy Discovery Play It Again Solution. Open the Play It Again Solution (Play It Again Solution.sln) file contained in the Discovery Play It Again Solution folder. Open the designer window. The Clear method's syntax is *textbox*.**Clear()**. Use the Clear method in the btnClear control's Click event procedure to remove the contents of the txtDvds and txtBluRays controls. (You cannot use the Clear method to remove the contents of label controls.) Save the solution and then start the application. Enter any date and sales amounts, and then click the Calculate button. Click the Clear Screen button to verify that the Clear method worked correctly. Close the Code Editor window and then close the solution.

SWAT THE BUGS

15. Open the Debug Solution (Debug Solution.sln) file contained in the VB2012\Chap02\Debug Solution folder. If necessary, open the designer window. Open the Code Editor window. Locate and then correct the syntax errors in the code. Save the solution and then start and test the application. If necessary, correct any other errors in the code. Close the Code Editor window and then close the solution.

CHAPTER 3

Using Variables and Constants

Revising the Play It Again Movies Application

In this chapter, you modify the Play It Again Movies application from Chapter 2. The modified application will calculate a 3% sales tax and then display the result in the interface. It also will display the name of the salesclerk who entered the sales information.

Previewing the Modified Play It Again Movies Application

Before you start the first lesson in this chapter, you will preview the completed application contained in the VB2012\Chap03 folder.

START HERE

To preview the completed application:

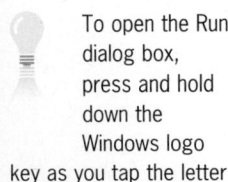

To open the Run dialog box, press and hold down the Windows logo key as you tap the letter r, and then release the logo key.

1. Use the Run dialog box to run the Play It Again (Play It Again.exe) file contained in the VB2012\Chap03 folder. A sales receipt similar to the one created in Chapter 2 appears on the screen.
2. Type **8/8/2014** in the Date box, **5** in the DVDs box, and **8** in the Blu-rays box.
3. Although the Calculate button does not have the focus, you can select it by pressing the Enter key because it is the default button in the interface. You will learn how to designate a default button in Lesson B. Press **Enter** to calculate both the total number of discs sold and the total sales amount. A Name Entry dialog box appears and requests the salesclerk's name, as shown in Figure 3-1.

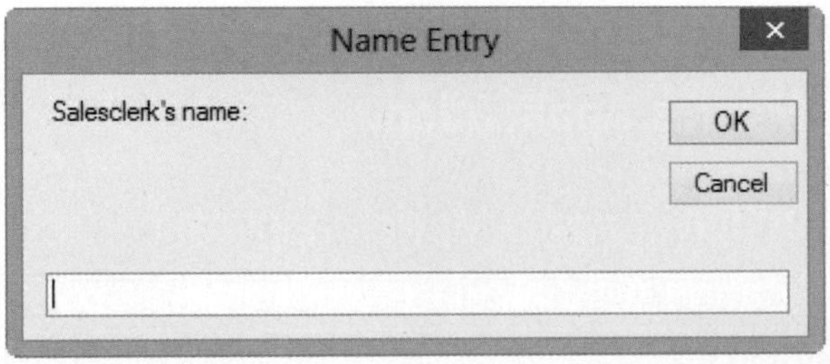

Figure 3-1 Name Entry dialog box

4. Type **Kevin Cooper** and then press **Enter** to select the dialog box's OK button. The completed sales receipt is shown in Figure 3-2. The application uses string concatenation, which is covered in Lesson B, to display the sales tax amount and salesclerk's name on the receipt.

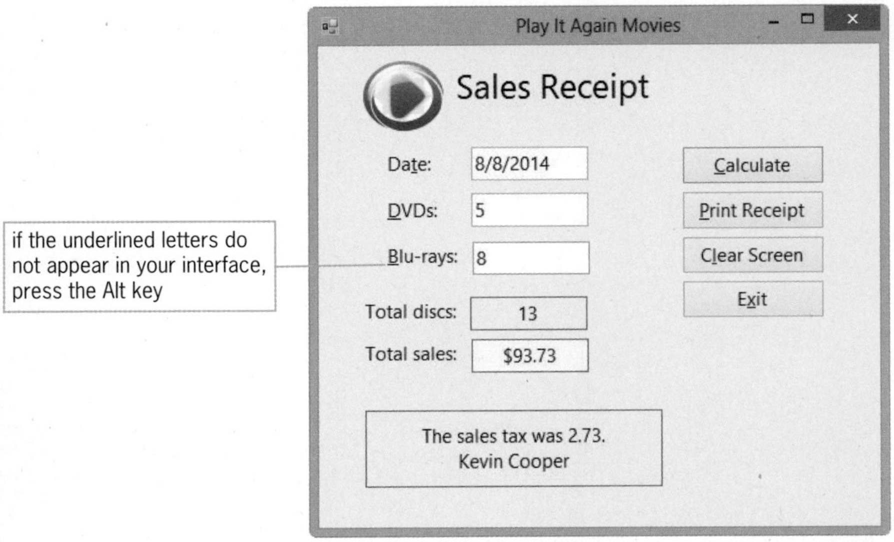

Figure 3-2 Completed sales receipt
OpenClipArt.org/John Diamond / diamonjohn

5. Change the number of DVDs sold to **4**. The application clears the contents of the label controls that display the total number of discs sold, the total sales amount, and the message. In Lesson C, you will learn how to clear the contents of a control when a change is made to the value stored in a different control.
6. Click the **Calculate** button. The Name Entry dialog box appears and displays the salesclerk's name. Press **Enter** to select the dialog box's OK button. The application recalculates the total number of discs sold, the total sales amount, and the sales tax amount, and then displays the information on the sales receipt.
7. Click the **Clear Screen** button to clear the sales information (except the date) from the form, and then click the **Exit** button to end the application.

In Lesson A, you will learn how to store information, temporarily, in memory locations inside the computer. You will modify the Play It Again Movies application in Lessons B and C. Be sure to complete each lesson in full and do all of the end-of-lesson questions and several exercises before continuing to the next lesson.

LESSON A

After studying Lesson A, you should be able to:

- Declare variables and named constants
- Assign data to an existing variable
- Convert string data to a numeric data type using the TryParse method
- Convert numeric data to a different data type using the Convert class methods
- Explain the scope and lifetime of variables and named constants
- Explain the purpose of Option Explicit, Option Infer, and Option Strict

Using Variables to Store Information

Ch03A-Variables video

In the Play It Again Movies application from Chapter 2, all of the sales information is temporarily stored in the properties of the controls on the sales receipt form. For example, the numbers of DVDs and Blu-rays sold are stored in the Text properties of the txtDvds and txtBluRays controls, respectively. Recall that the btnCalc control's Click event procedure uses the Text properties of those controls to calculate the total number of discs sold, like this: `lblTotalDiscs.Text = Val(txtDvds.Text) + Val(txtBluRays.Text)`. The application then uses the lblTotalDiscs control's Text property to calculate the total sales amount, like this: `lblTotalSales.Text = Val(lblTotalDiscs.Text) * 7`.

Besides storing data in the properties of controls, a programmer also can temporarily store data in memory locations inside the computer. The memory locations are called **variables** because the contents of the locations can change (vary) as the application is running. It may be helpful to picture a variable as a small box inside the computer. You can enter and store data in the box, but you cannot actually see the box. One use for a variable is to hold information that is not stored in a control on the form. For example, if you didn't need to display the total number of discs sold on the Play It Again Movies sales receipt, you could eliminate the lblTotalDiscs control from the form and store the total number of discs sold in a variable instead. You then would use the value stored in the variable, rather than the value stored in the Text property of the lblTotalDiscs control, in the total sales calculation.

You also can use a variable to store the data contained in a control's property, such as the data contained in a control's Text property. Programmers typically do this when the data is a numeric amount that will be used in a calculation. As you will learn in the next section, assigning numeric data to a variable allows you to control the preciseness of the data. It also makes your code run more efficiently because the computer can process data stored in a variable much faster than it can process data stored in the property of a control.

Every variable has a data type, name, scope, and lifetime. First, you will learn how to select an appropriate data type for a variable.

Don't be overwhelmed by the number of data types listed in Figure 3-3. This book will use only the Boolean, Decimal, Double, Integer, and String data types.

Selecting a Data Type for a Variable

Each variable used in an application should be assigned a data type by the programmer. The **data type** determines the type of data the variable can store. Figure 3-3 describes most of the basic data types available in Visual Basic 2012. Each data type is a class, which means that each data type is a pattern from which one or more objects—in this case, variables—are instantiated (created).

Data type	Stores	Memory Required
Boolean	a logical value (True, False)	2 bytes
Char	one Unicode character	2 bytes
Date	date and time information Date range: January 1, 0001 to December 31, 9999 Time range: 0:00:00 (midnight) to 23:59:59	8 bytes
Decimal	a number with a decimal place Range with no decimal place: +/–79,228,162,514,264,337,593,543,950,335 Range with a decimal place: +/–7.9228162514264337593543950335	16 bytes
Double	a number with a decimal place Range: +/–4.94065645841247 X 10^{-324} to +/–1.79769313486231 X 10^{308}	8 bytes
Integer	integer Range: –2,147,483,648 to 2,147,483,647	4 bytes
Long	integer Range: –9,223,372,036,854,775,808 to 9,223,372,036,854,775,807	8 bytes
Object	data of any type	4 bytes
Short	integer Range: –32,768 to 32,767	2 bytes
Single	a number with a decimal place Range: +/–1.401298 X 10^{-45} to +/–3.402823 X 10^{38}	4 bytes
String	text; 0 to approximately 2 billion characters	

Figure 3-3 Basic data types in Visual Basic

As Figure 3-3 indicates, variables assigned the Integer, Long, or Short data type can store integers, which are whole numbers. A whole number is a positive or negative number that does not have any decimal places. The differences among these three data types are in the range of integers each type can store and the amount of memory each type needs to store the integer.

The Decimal, Double, and Single variables can store numbers containing a decimal place. Here again, the differences among these three data types are in the range of numbers each type can store and the amount of memory each type needs to store the numbers. However, calculations involving Decimal variables are not subject to the small rounding errors that may occur when using Double or Single variables. In most cases, the small rounding errors do not create any problems in an application. One exception to this is when the application contains complex equations dealing with money, where you need accuracy to the penny. In those cases, the Decimal data type is the best type to use.

The Char data type can store one Unicode character, while the String data type can store from zero to approximately two billion Unicode characters. **Unicode** is the universal coding scheme for characters. It assigns a unique numeric value to each character used in the written languages of the world. (For more information, see The Unicode Standard at *www.unicode.org*.)

Also listed in Figure 3-3 are the Boolean, Date, and Object data types. You use a Boolean variable to store a Boolean value (either True or False), and a Date variable to store date and time information. The Object data type can store any type of data. However, your application will pay a price for this flexibility: It will run more slowly because the computer has to determine the type of data currently stored in an Object variable. It is best to avoid using the Object data type.

The applications in this book will use the Integer data type for variables that will store integers used in calculations, even when the integers are small enough to fit into a Short variable. This is because a calculation containing Integer variables takes less time to process than the equivalent calculation containing Short variables. Either the Decimal data type or the Double data type will be used for numbers that contain decimal places and are used in calculations. The applications will use the String data type for variables that contain either text or numbers not used in calculations, and the Boolean data type to store Boolean values.

Selecting a Name for a Variable

In addition to assigning a data type to an application's variables, the programmer also must assign a name to each variable. The name, also called the identifier, should describe the contents of the variable. A good variable name is one that is meaningful right after you finish a program and also years later when you (or perhaps a co-worker) need to modify the program. There are several conventions for naming variables in Visual Basic. In this book, you will use Hungarian notation, which is the same naming convention used for controls. Variable names in Hungarian notation begin with a three-character ID that represents the variable's data type. The three-character IDs for the most commonly used data types are listed in Figure 3-4 along with examples of variable names. Like control names, variable names are entered using camel case, which means you lowercase the ID and then uppercase the first letter of each word in the name.

Data type	ID	Example
Boolean	bln	`blnInsured`
Decimal	dec	`decGrossPay`
Double	dbl	`dblSales`
Integer	int	`intNumSold`
String	str	`strFirstName`

Figure 3-4 Three-character IDs and examples

Figure 3-5 lists the rules for naming variables and includes examples of valid and invalid variable names.

Rules for Naming Variables

1. The name must begin with a letter or an underscore.
2. The name can contain only letters, numbers, and the underscore character. No punctuation characters, special characters, or spaces are allowed in the name.
3. Although the name can contain thousands of characters, 32 characters is the recommended maximum number of characters to use.
4. The name cannot be a reserved word, such as `Sub` or `Double`.

Valid names

`intFeb_Income, decSales2014, dblEastRegion, strName, blnIsValid`

Invalid names	Problem
`4thQuarter`	the name must begin with a letter or an underscore
`dblWest Region`	the name cannot contain a space
`strFirst.Name`	the name cannot contain punctuation
`decSales$East`	the name cannot contain a special character

Figure 3-5 Variable naming rules and examples

Declaring a Variable

Now that you know how to select an appropriate data type and name for a variable, you can learn how to declare a variable in code. Declaring a variable tells the computer to set aside a small section of its internal memory, and it allows you to refer to the section by the variable's name. The size of the section is determined by the variable's data type. You declare a variable using a declaration statement. Figure 3-6 shows the syntax of a declaration statement and includes examples of declaring variables. The {`Dim` | `Private` | `Static`} portion of the syntax indicates that you can select only one of the keywords appearing within the braces. In most instances, you declare a variable using the `Dim` keyword. (You will learn about the `Private` and `Static` keywords later in this lesson.)

`Dim` comes from the word "dimension," which is how programmers in the 1960s referred to the process of allocating the computer's memory. "Dimension" refers to the "size" of something.

Variable Declaration Statement

Syntax
{**Dim** | **Private** | **Static**} *variableName* **As** *dataType* [= *initialValue*]

Example 1
```
Dim intNumSold As Integer
Dim dblTaxRate As Double
```
declares an Integer variable named `intNumSold` and a Double variable named `dblTaxRate`; the variables are automatically initialized to 0

Example 2
```
Dim decPay As Decimal
```
declares a Decimal variable named `decPay`; the variable is automatically initialized to 0

Example 3
```
Dim blnInsured As Boolean = True
```
declares a Boolean variable named `blnInsured` and initializes it using the keyword `True`

Example 4
```
Dim strMsg As String = "Good Night"
```
declares a String variable named `strMsg` and initializes it using the string "Good Night"

Figure 3-6 Syntax and examples of a variable declaration statement

In the syntax, *variableName* and *dataType* are the variable's name and data type, respectively. As mentioned earlier, a variable is considered an object in Visual Basic and is an instance of the class specified in the *dataType* information. The `Dim intNumSold As Integer` statement, for example, creates a variable (object) named `intNumSold`. The `intNumSold` variable (object) is an instance of the Integer class.

InitialValue in the syntax is the value you want stored in the variable when it is created in the computer's internal memory. The square brackets in the syntax indicate that the "= *initialValue*" part of a variable declaration statement is optional. If you do not assign an initial value to a variable when it is declared, the computer stores a default value in the variable. The default value depends on the variable's data type. A variable declared using one of the numeric data types is automatically initialized to—in other words, given a beginning value of—the number 0. The computer automatically initializes a Boolean variable using the keyword `False`, and a Date variable to 1/1/0001 12:00:00 AM. Object and String variables are automatically initialized using the keyword `Nothing`. Variables initialized to `Nothing` do not actually contain the word "Nothing"; rather, they contain no data at all.

Assigning Data to an Existing Variable

In Chapter 2, you learned how to use an assignment statement to assign a value to a control's property during run time. An assignment statement is also used to assign a value to a variable during run time; the syntax for doing this is shown in Figure 3-7. In the syntax, *expression* can contain items such as literal constants, object properties, variables, keywords, or arithmetic operators. A **literal constant** is an item of data whose value does not change while the application is running; examples include the string literal constant "Mary" and the numeric literal constant 500. When the computer processes an assignment statement, it assigns the value of the expression that appears on the right side of the assignment operator (=) to the variable (memory location) whose name appears on the left side of the assignment operator. In other words, the computer evaluates the expression and then stores the result in the variable.

Assigning a Value to a Variable during Run Time

Syntax
variableName = *expression*

Note: In each of the following examples, the data type of the expression assigned to the variable is the same as the data type of the variable itself.

Example 1
`intNumber = 25`
assigns the integer 25 to the `intNumber` variable

Example 2
`strName = "Karen"`
assigns the string "Karen" to the `strName` variable

Example 3
`strCity = txtCity.Text`
assigns the string contained in the txtCity control's Text property to the `strCity` variable

Example 4
`dblInterestRate = .09`
assigns the Double number .09 to the `dblInterestRate` variable

Example 5
`decTaxRate = .06D`
converts the Double number .06 to Decimal and then assigns the result to the `decTaxRate` variable

Example 6
`dblBonus = dblSales * .05`
multiplies the contents of the `dblSales` variable by the Double number .05 and then assigns the result to the `dblBonus` variable

Figure 3-7 Syntax and examples of assigning a value to a variable during run time

The data type of the expression assigned to a variable should be the same data type as the variable itself; this is the case in all of the examples included in Figure 3-7. The assignment statement in Example 1 stores the numeric literal constant 25 (an integer) in an Integer variable named `intNumber`. Similarly, the assignment statement in Example 2 stores the string literal constant "Karen" in a String variable named `strName`. Notice that string literal constants are enclosed in quotation marks, but numeric literal constants and variable names are not. The quotation marks differentiate a string from both a number and a variable name. In other words, "500" is a string, but 500 is a number. Similarly, "Karen" is a string, but Karen (without the quotation marks) would be interpreted by the computer as the name of a variable. When the computer processes an assignment statement that assigns a string to a String variable, it assigns only the characters that appear between the quotation marks; it does not assign the quotation marks themselves.

The assignment statement in Example 3 assigns the string contained in the txtCity control's Text property to a String variable named `strCity`. (Recall that the value stored in the Text property of an object is always treated as a string.) The assignment statement in Example 4 assigns the Double number .09 to a Double variable named `dblInterestRate`. This is because a numeric literal constant that has a decimal place is automatically treated as a Double number in Visual Basic. When entering a numeric literal constant, you do not enter a comma or special characters, such as the dollar sign or percent sign. If you want to include a percentage in an assignment statement, you do so using its decimal equivalent; for example, you enter .09 rather than 9%.

The `decTaxRate = .06D` statement in Example 5 shows how you convert a numeric literal constant of the Double data type to the Decimal data type, and then assign the result to a Decimal variable. The D that follows the number .06 in the statement is one of the literal type characters in Visual Basic. A **literal type character** forces a literal constant to assume a data type other than the one its form indicates. In this case, the D forces the Double number .06 to assume the Decimal data type.

You will learn about another literal type character, the letter C, in Chapter 8.

Finally, the `dblBonus = dblSales * .05` statement in Example 6 in Figure 3-7 multiplies the contents of the `dblSales` variable by the Double number .05 and then assigns the result to the `dblBonus` variable. When an assignment statement's expression contains the name of a variable, the computer uses the value stored inside the variable to evaluate the expression.

A variable can store only one value at any one time. When you use an assignment statement to assign another value to the variable, the new value replaces the existing value. The code shown in Figure 3-8 illustrates this point. The declaration statement in the code creates the `intQuantity` variable and initializes it to the number 0. The first assignment statement then replaces the number 0 with the number 25. The second assignment statement multiplies the contents of the `intQuantity` variable (25) by the number 2, giving 50. It then replaces the number 25 stored in the variable with the number 50. Notice that the calculation appearing on the right side of the assignment operator is performed first, and then the result is assigned to the variable whose name appears on the left side of the assignment operator.

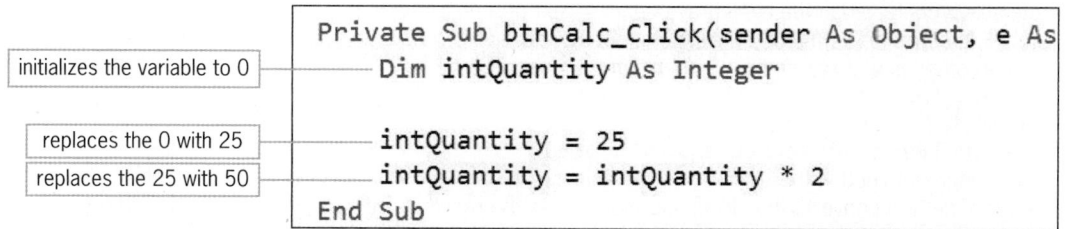

```
Private Sub btnCalc_Click(sender As Object, e As
    Dim intQuantity As Integer

    intQuantity = 25
    intQuantity = intQuantity * 2
End Sub
```

initializes the variable to 0 (Dim intQuantity As Integer)

replaces the 0 with 25 (intQuantity = 25)

replaces the 25 with 50 (intQuantity = intQuantity * 2)

Figure 3-8 Assignment statements entered in the btnCalc_Click procedure

In all of the assignment statements shown in Figures 3-7 and 3-8, the expression's data type is the same as the variable's data type. At times, however, you may need to store a value of a different data type in a variable. You can change the value's data type to match the variable's data type using either the TryParse method or one of the methods in the Convert class.

The TryParse Method

You will learn more about the TryParse method in Chapter 5.

Like the Val function, which you learned about in Chapter 2, the **TryParse method** converts a string to a number. However, unlike the Val function, which returns a Double number, the TryParse method allows the programmer to specify the number's data type; for this reason, most programmers prefer to use the TryParse method. Every numeric data type in Visual Basic has a TryParse method that converts a string to that particular data type.

Figure 3-9 shows the basic syntax of the TryParse method and includes examples of using the method. In the syntax, *dataType* is one of the numeric data types available in Visual Basic. The dot member access operator in the TryParse method's syntax indicates that the method is a member of the *dataType* class. The method's arguments (*string* and *numericVariableName*) represent information that the method needs to perform its task. The *string* argument is the string you want converted to a number of the *dataType* type. The *string* argument is typically either the Text property of a control or the name of a String variable. The *numericVariableName* argument is the name of a numeric variable in which the TryParse method can store the number. The numeric variable must have the same data type as specified in the *dataType* portion of the syntax. For example, when using the TryParse method to convert a string to a Double number, you need to provide the method with the name of a Double variable in which to store the number.

The TryParse method parses its *string* argument to determine whether the string can be converted to a number. In this case, the term "parse" means to look at each character in the string. If the string can be converted, the TryParse method converts the string to a number and then stores the number in the variable specified in the *numericVariableName* argument. If the TryParse method determines that the string cannot be converted to the appropriate data type, it assigns the number 0 to the variable.

TryParse Method

Basic syntax
dataType.**TryParse(***string*, *numericVariableName***)**

Example 1
```
Double.TryParse(txtDue.Text, dblDue)
```
If the string contained in the txtDue control's Text property can be converted to a Double number, the TryParse method converts the string and then stores the result in the `dblDue` variable; otherwise, it stores the number 0 in the variable.

Example 2
```
Decimal.TryParse(txtNetPay.Text, decNetPay)
```
If the string contained in the txtNetPay control's Text property can be converted to a Decimal number, the TryParse method converts the string and then stores the result in the `decNetPay` variable; otherwise, it stores the number 0 in the variable.

Example 3
```
Integer.TryParse(strScore, intScore)
```
If the string contained in the `strScore` variable can be converted to an Integer number, the TryParse method converts the string and then stores the result in the `intScore` variable; otherwise, it stores the number 0 in the variable.

Figure 3-9 Basic syntax and examples of the TryParse method

Figure 3-10 shows how the TryParse method of the Double, Decimal, and Integer data types would convert various strings. As the figure indicates, the three methods can convert a string that contains only numbers. They also can convert a string that contains a leading sign, as well as one that contains leading or trailing spaces. In addition, the Double.TryParse and Decimal.TryParse methods can convert a string that contains a decimal point or a comma. However, none of the three methods can convert a string that contains a dollar sign, a percent sign, a letter, or a space within the string.

string	Double.TryParse	Decimal.TryParse	Integer.TryParse
"62"	62	62	62
"–9"	–9	–9	–9
"12.55"	12.55	12.55	0
"–4.23"	–4.23	–4.23	0
"1,457"	1457	1457	0
" 33 "	33	33	33
"$5"	0	0	0
"7%"	0	0	0
"122a"	0	0	0
"1 345"	0	0	0
empty string	0	0	0

Figure 3-10 Results of the TryParse method for the Double, Decimal, and Integer data types

The Convert Class

At times, you may need to convert a number (rather than a string) from one data type to another. Visual Basic provides several ways of accomplishing this task. One way is to use the Visual Basic conversion functions, which are listed in Appendix C in this book. You also can use one of the methods defined in the **Convert class**. In this book you will use the Convert class methods because they can be used in any of the languages built into Visual Studio. The conversion functions, on the other hand, can be used only in the Visual Basic language. The more commonly used methods in the Convert class are the ToDecimal, ToDouble, ToInt32, and ToString methods. The methods convert a value to the Decimal, Double, Integer, and String data types, respectively.

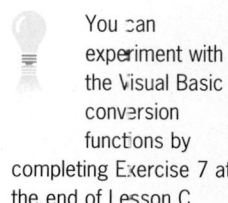

You can experiment with the Visual Basic conversion functions by completing Exercise 7 at the end of Lesson C.

The syntax for using the Convert class methods is shown in Figure 3-11 along with examples of using the methods. The dot member access operator in the syntax indicates that the *method* is a member of the Convert class. In most cases, the *value* argument is a numeric value that you want converted either to the String data type or to a different numeric data type (for example, from Double to Decimal). Although you can use the Convert methods to convert a string to a numeric data type, the TryParse method is the recommended method to use for that task. This is because, unlike the Convert methods, the TryParse method does not produce an error when it tries to convert the empty string. Instead, the TryParse method assigns the number 0 to its *numericVariableName* argument.

Convert Class Methods

Syntax
Convert.*method***(***value***)**

Example 1
`decRate = Convert.ToDecimal(.15)`
converts the Double number .15 to Decimal and then assigns the result to the `decRate` variable

Example 2
`lblQuantity.Text = Convert.ToString(intQuantity)`
converts the integer stored in the `intQuantity` variable to String and then assigns the result to the lblQuantity control's Text property

Example 3
`decBonus = decSales * Convert.ToDecimal(.05)`
converts the Double number .05 to Decimal, then multiplies the result by the contents of the `decSales` variable, and then assigns that result to the `decBonus` variable

Figure 3-11 Syntax and examples of the Convert class methods

In the statement shown in Example 1, the Convert.ToDecimal method converts the Double number .15 to Decimal. (Recall that a number with a decimal place is automatically treated as a Double number in Visual Basic.) The statement then assigns the result to the `decRate` variable. You also could write the statement as `decRate = .15D`. However, many programmers would argue that using the Convert.ToDecimal method, rather than the literal type character D, makes the code clearer.

In Example 2's statement, the Convert.ToString method converts the integer stored in the `intQuantity` variable to String before the statement assigns the result to the lblQuantity control's Text property. The statement in Example 3 uses the Convert.ToDecimal method to convert the Double number .05 to Decimal. The statement multiplies the result by the contents of the `decSales` variable and then assigns the product to the `decBonus` variable. You also could write this statement as `decBonus = decSales * .05D`.

YOU DO IT 1!

Create a Visual Basic Windows application named YouDoIt 1. Save the application in the VB2012\Chap03 folder. Add a text box, a label, and a button to the form. The button's Click event procedure should store the contents of the text box in a Double variable named `dblCost`. It then should display the variable's contents in the label. Code the procedure. Save the solution and then start and test the application. Close the solution.

Note: You have learned a lot so far in this lesson. You may want to take a break at this point before continuing.

The Scope and Lifetime of a Variable

Ch03A-Scope and Lifetime

Besides a name, data type, and initial value, every variable also has a scope and a lifetime. A variable's **scope** indicates where the variable can be used in an application's code, and its **lifetime** indicates how long the variable remains in the computer's internal memory. Variables can have class scope, procedure scope, or block scope. However, most of the variables used in an application will have procedure scope. This is because fewer unintentional errors occur in applications when the variables are declared using the minimum scope needed, which usually is procedure scope.

A variable's scope and lifetime are determined by where you declare the variable—in other words, where you enter the variable's declaration statement. Typically, you enter the declaration statement either in a procedure (such as an event procedure) or in the Declarations section of a form. A form's Declarations section is not the same as the General Declarations section, which you learned about in Chapter 2. The General Declarations section is located above the Public Class clause in the Code Editor window, whereas the **form's Declarations section** is located between the Public Class and End Class clauses. Variables declared in a form's Declarations section have class scope. Variables declared in a procedure, on the other hand, have either procedure scope or block scope, depending on where in the procedure they are declared. In the next two sections, you will learn about procedure scope variables and class scope variables. Variables having block scope are covered in Chapter 4.

Variables can also have namespace scope and are referred to as namespace variables, global variables, or public variables. Such variables can lead to unintentional errors in a program and should be avoided, if possible. For this reason, they are not covered in this book.

Variables with Procedure Scope

When you declare a variable in a procedure, the variable is called a **procedure-level variable**. Procedure-level variables have **procedure scope** because they can be used only by the procedure in which they are declared. Procedure-level variables are typically declared at the beginning of a procedure, and they remain in the computer's internal memory only while the procedure is running. Procedure-level variables are removed from memory when the procedure in which they are declared ends. In other words, a procedure-level variable has the same lifetime as the procedure that declares it. As mentioned earlier, most of the variables in your applications will be procedure-level variables.

Procedure-level variables are also called local variables and their scope is often referred to as local scope.

The Discount Calculator application that you view next illustrates the use of procedure-level variables. As the interface shown in Figure 3-12 indicates, the application allows the user to enter a sales amount. It then calculates and displays either a 15% discount or a 20% discount, depending on the button selected by the user.

In the *Static Variables* section of this chapter, you will learn how to declare a procedure-level variable that remains in the computer's memory even when the procedure in which it is declared ends.

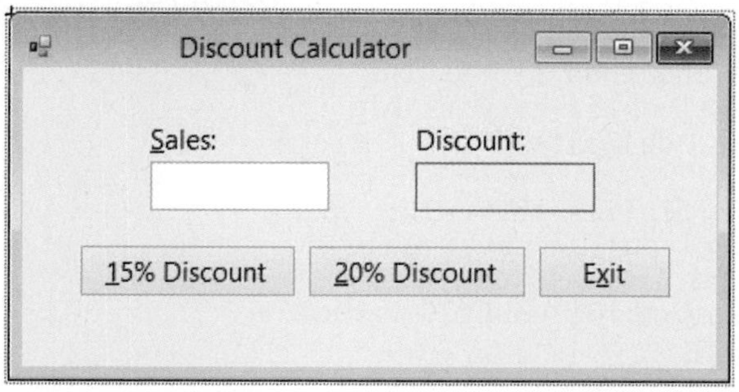

Figure 3-12 User interface for the Discount Calculator application

Figure 3-13 shows the Click event procedures for the 15% Discount and 20% Discount buttons. The comments in the figure indicate the purpose of each line of code. When each procedure ends, its procedure-level variables are removed from the computer's memory. The variables will be created again the next time the user clicks the button.

```
Private Sub btnDisc15_Click(sender As Object, e As EventArgs)
Handles btnDisc15.Click
    ' calculates and displays a 15% discount

    ' the Dim statements declare two procedure-level
    ' variables that can be used only within the
    ' btnDisc15_Click procedure
    Dim dblSales As Double
    Dim dblDiscount15 As Double

    ' the TryParse method converts the contents of the
    ' txtSales control to Double and then stores the
    ' result in the procedure-level dblSales variable
    Double.TryParse(txtSales.Text, dblSales)

    ' the assignment statement multiplies the value
    ' stored in the procedure-level dblSales variable
    ' by the Double number 0.15 and then assigns the
    ' result to the procedure-level dblDiscount15 variable
    dblDiscount15 = dblSales * 0.15

    ' the Convert method converts the value stored in the
    ' procedure-level dblDiscount15 variable to String, and
    ' the assignment statement assigns the result to the
    ' lblDiscount control's Text property
    lblDiscount.Text = Convert.ToString(dblDiscount15)
End Sub
```

these variables will be removed from memory when the btnDisc15_Click procedure ends

```
Private Sub btnDisc20_Click(sender As Object, e As EventArgs)
Handles btnDisc20.Click
    ' calculates and displays a 20% discount

    ' the Dim statements declare two procedure-level
    ' variables that can be used only within the
    ' btnDisc20_Click procedure
    Dim dblSales As Double
    Dim dblDiscount20 As Double

    ' the TryParse method converts the contents of the
    ' txtSales control to Double and then stores the
    ' result in the procedure-level dblSales variable
    Double.TryParse(txtSales.Text, dblSales)

    ' the assignment statement multiplies the value
    ' stored in the procedure-level dblSales variable
    ' by the Double number 0.2 and then assigns the
    ' result to the procedure-level dblDiscount20 variable
    dblDiscount20 = dblSales * 0.2

    ' the Convert method converts the value stored in the
    ' procedure-level dblDiscount20 variable to String, and
    ' the assignment statement assigns the result to the
    ' lblDiscount control's Text property
    lblDiscount.Text = Convert.ToString(dblDiscount20)
End Sub
```

these variables will be removed from memory when the btnDisc20_Click procedure ends

Figure 3-13 Click event procedures using procedure-level variables

Notice that both procedures in Figure 3-13 declare a variable named `dblSales`. When you use the same name to declare a variable in more than one procedure, each procedure creates its own variable when the procedure is invoked. Each procedure also destroys its own variable when the procedure ends. In other words, although both procedures in Figure 3-13 declare a variable named `dblSales`, each `dblSales` variable will refer to a different section in the computer's internal memory, and each will be both created and destroyed independently from the other.

START HERE

To code and then test the Discount Calculator application:

1. If necessary, start Visual Studio 2012. Open the Discount Calculator Solution (Discount Calculator Solution.sln) file contained in the VB2012\Chap03\Discount Calculator Solution-Procedure-level folder. If necessary, open the designer window and auto-hide the Solution Explorer, Properties, and Toolbox windows. The user interface shown earlier in Figure 3-12 appears on the screen.
2. Open the Code Editor window. See Figure 3-14. For now, do not be concerned about the three Option statements that appear in the window. You will learn about the Option statements later in this lesson. Replace <your name> and <current date> in the comments with your name and the current date, respectively.

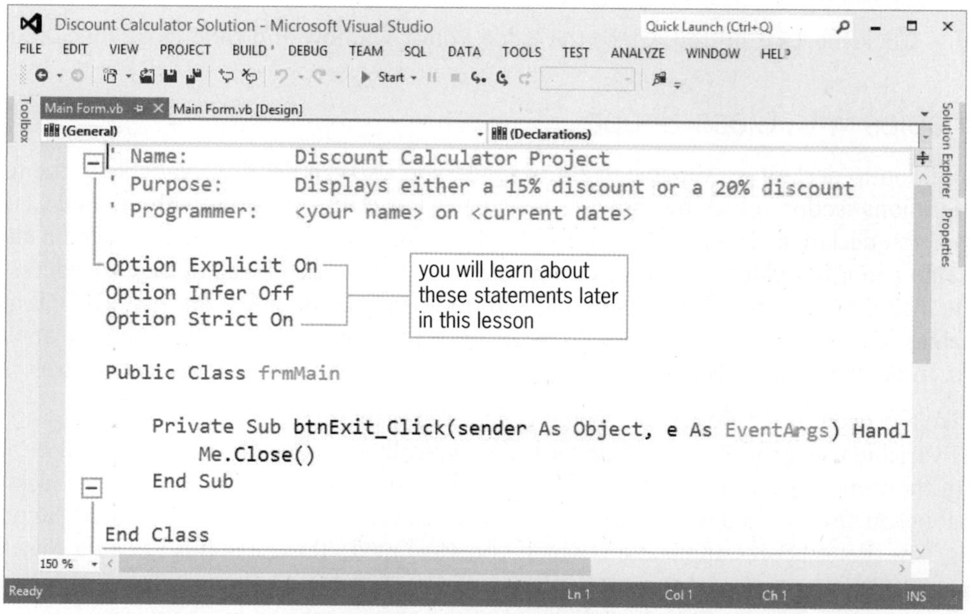

Figure 3-14 Code Editor window for the Discount Calculator application

3. Open the code template for the btnDisc15 control's Click event procedure. Also open the code template for the btnDisc20 control's Click event procedure. In the procedures, enter the comments and code shown earlier in Figure 3-13.
4. Save the solution and then start the application. If necessary, press **Alt** to display the access keys in the interface.
5. First, calculate and display a 15% discount on $600. If you do not see the blinking insertion point in the Sales box, click the **Sales** box. Type **600** in the Sales box and then click the **15% Discount** button. The number 90 appears in the Discount box, as shown in Figure 3-15.

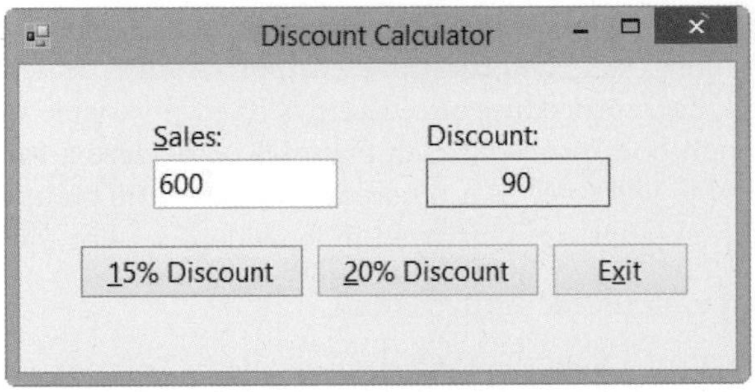

Figure 3-15 Discount shown in the interface

6. Change the sales amount to the letter **a** and then click the **15% Discount** button. The number 0 appears in the Discount box.
7. Change the sales amount to **1000** and then click the **20% Discount** button. The number 200 appears in the Discount box.
8. Change the sales amount to the letter **s** and then click the **20% Discount** button. The number 0 appears in the Discount box.
9. Click the **Exit** button. Close the Code Editor window and then close the solution.

Variables with Class Scope

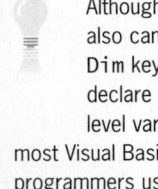

> Although you also can use the `Dim` keyword to declare a class-level variable, most Visual Basic programmers use the `Private` keyword so that the scope is more obvious to anyone reading the code.

In addition to declaring a variable in a procedure, you also can declare a variable in the form's Declarations section, which begins with the Public Class clause and ends with the End Class clause. When you declare a variable in the form's Declarations section, the variable is called a **class-level variable** and it has **class scope**. Class-level variables can be used by all of the procedures in the form, including the procedures associated with the controls contained on the form. Class-level variables retain their values and remain in the computer's internal memory until the application ends. In other words, a class-level variable has the same lifetime as the application itself.

Unlike a procedure-level variable, which is declared using the `Dim` keyword, you declare a class-level variable using the `Private` keyword. You typically use a class-level variable when you need more than one procedure in the same form to use the same variable. However, a class-level variable can also be used when a procedure needs to retain a variable's value after the procedure ends. The Total Scores application, which you view next, illustrates this use of a class-level variable. The application's interface is shown in Figure 3-16. As the interface indicates, the application calculates and displays the total of the scores entered by the user.

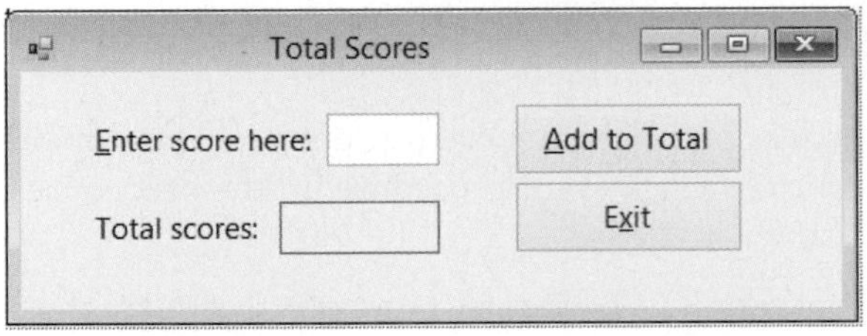

Figure 3-16 User interface for the Total Scores application

Figure 3-17 shows the Total Scores application's code. The code uses a class-level variable named `decTotal` to accumulate (add together) the scores entered by the user. Class-level variables are declared after the Public Class clause, but before the first Private Sub clause, in the form's Declarations section.

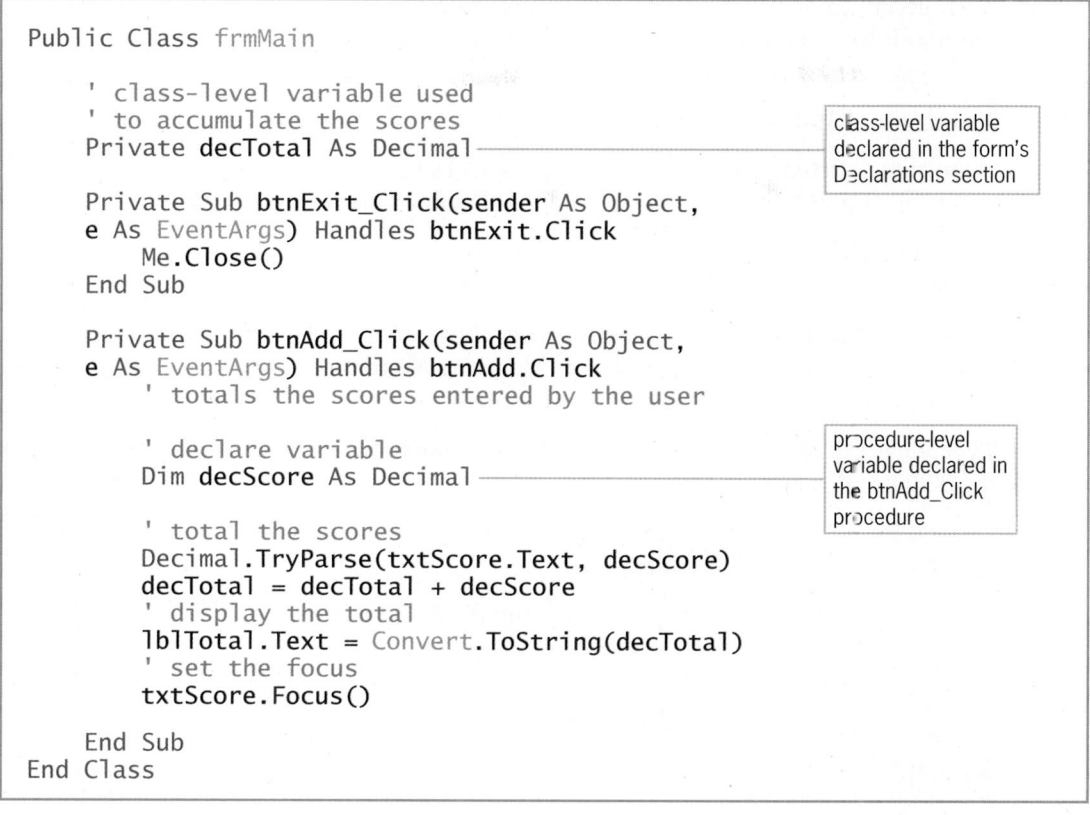

```
Public Class frmMain

    ' class-level variable used
    ' to accumulate the scores
    Private decTotal As Decimal

    Private Sub btnExit_Click(sender As Object,
    e As EventArgs) Handles btnExit.Click
        Me.Close()
    End Sub

    Private Sub btnAdd_Click(sender As Object,
    e As EventArgs) Handles btnAdd.Click
        ' totals the scores entered by the user

        ' declare variable
        Dim decScore As Decimal

        ' total the scores
        Decimal.TryParse(txtScore.Text, decScore)
        decTotal = decTotal + decScore
        ' display the total
        lblTotal.Text = Convert.ToString(decTotal)
        ' set the focus
        txtScore.Focus()

    End Sub
End Class
```

class-level variable declared in the form's Declarations section

procedure-level variable declared in the btnAdd_Click procedure

Figure 3-17 Total Scores application's code using a class-level variable

When the user starts the Total Scores application, the computer will process the `Private decTotal As Decimal` statement first. The statement creates and initializes the class-level `decTotal` variable. The variable is created and initialized only once, when the application starts. It remains in the computer's internal memory until the application ends.

Each time the user clicks the Add to Total button, the button's Click event procedure creates and initializes a procedure-level variable named `decScore`. The TryParse method then converts the contents of the txtScore control to Decimal, storing the result in the `decScore` variable. The first assignment statement in the procedure adds the contents of the procedure-level `decScore` variable to the contents of the class-level `decTotal` variable. At this point, the `decTotal` variable contains the sum of all of the scores entered so far. The last assignment statement in the procedure converts the contents of the `decTotal` variable to String and then assigns the result to the lblTotal control. The procedure then sends the focus to the txtScore control. When the procedure ends, the computer removes the procedure-level `decScore` variable from its memory. However, it does not remove the class-level `decTotal` variable. The `decTotal` variable is removed from the computer's memory only when the application ends.

To code and then test the Total Scores application:

START HERE

1. Open the Total Scores Solution (Total Scores Solution.sln) file contained in the VB2012 \Chap03\Total Scores Solution-Class-level folder. If necessary, open the designer window. The user interface shown earlier in Figure 3-16 appears on the screen.
2. Open the Code Editor window. Here again, do not be concerned about the three Option statements that appear in the window. You will learn about the Option statements later in this lesson. Replace <your name> and <current date> in the comments with your name and the current date, respectively.

3. First, declare the class-level `decTotal` variable in the form's Declarations section. Click the **blank line** below the `' to accumulate the scores` comment and then enter the following declaration statement:

   Private decTotal As Decimal

4. Open the code template for the btnAdd control's Click event procedure. In the procedure, enter the comments and code shown earlier in Figure 3-17.

5. Save the solution and then start the application. If necessary, press **Alt** to display the access keys.

   Note: The figures in this book will usually show the interface's access keys. However, from now on, you will not be instructed to press Alt to display the access keys. Instead, you can choose whether or not to display them.

6. Type **95** as the score and then click the **Add to Total** button. The number 95 appears in the Total scores box.

7. Change the score to **87** and then click the **Add to Total** button. The number 182 appears in the Total scores box.

8. Change the score to **100** and then click the **Add to Total** button. The number 282 appears in the Total scores box, as shown in Figure 3-18.

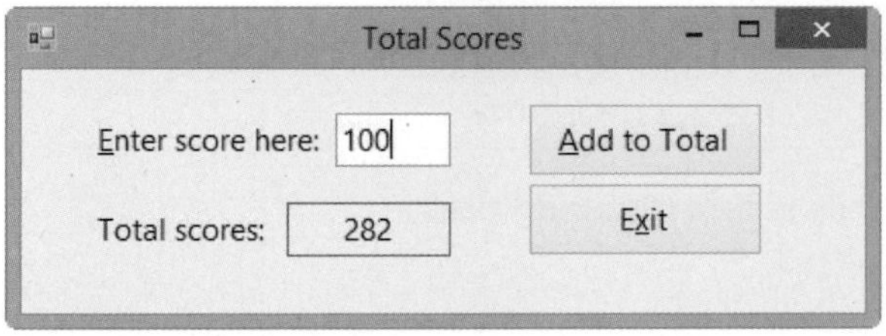

Figure 3-18 Interface showing the total of the scores you entered

9. Click the **Exit** button. Close the Code Editor window and then close the solution.

Static Variables

Recall that you can declare a variable using the `Dim`, `Private`, or `Static` keywords. You already know how to use the `Dim` and `Private` keywords to declare procedure-level and class-level variables, respectively. In this section, you will learn how to use the `Static` keyword to declare a special type of procedure-level variable, called a static variable.

A **static variable** is a procedure-level variable that remains in memory, and also retains its value, even when the procedure in which it is declared ends. Like a class-level variable, a static variable is not removed from the computer's internal memory until the application ends. However, unlike a class-level variable, which can be used by all of the procedures in a form, a static variable can be used only by the procedure in which it is declared. In other words, a static variable has a narrower (or more restrictive) scope than does a class-level variable. As mentioned earlier, you can prevent many unintentional errors from occurring in an application by declaring the variables using the minimum scope needed.

The `Static` keyword can be used only in a procedure.

In the previous section, you viewed the interface and code for the Total Scores application, which uses a class-level variable to accumulate the scores entered by the user. Rather than using a class-level variable for that purpose, you also can use a static variable, as shown in the code in Figure 3-19.

```
Public Class frmMain

    Private Sub btnExit_Click(sender As Object,
    e As EventArgs) Handles btnExit.Click
        Me.Close()
    End Sub

    Private Sub btnAdd_Click(sender As Object,
    e As EventArgs) Handles btnAdd.Click
        ' totals the scores entered by the user

        ' declare variables
        Dim decScore As Decimal
        Static decTotal As Decimal

        ' total the scores
        Decimal.TryParse(txtScore.Text, decScore)
        decTotal = decTotal + decScore
        ' display the total
        lblTotal.Text = Convert.ToString(decTotal)
        ' set the focus
        txtScore.Focus()

    End Sub
End Class
```

modified comment

static variable declared in the btnAdd_Click procedure

Figure 3-19 Total Scores application's code using a static variable

The first time the user clicks the Add to Total button, the button's Click event procedure creates and initializes (to 0) a procedure-level variable named `decScore` and a static variable named `decTotal`. The TryParse method then converts the contents of the txtScore control to Decimal, storing the result in the `decScore` variable. The first assignment statement in the procedure adds the contents of the `decScore` variable to the contents of the `decTotal` variable. The last assignment statement in the procedure converts the contents of the `decTotal` variable to String and assigns the result to the lblTotal control. The procedure then sends the focus to the txtScore control. When the procedure ends, the computer removes the variable declared using the `Dim` keyword (`decScore`) from its internal memory. But it does not remove the variable declared using the `Static` keyword (`decTotal`).

Each subsequent time the user clicks the Add to Total button, the computer re-creates and re-initializes the `decScore` variable declared in the button's Click event procedure. However, it does not re-create or re-initialize the `decTotal` variable because that variable, as well as its current value, is still in the computer's memory. After re-creating and re-initializing the `decScore` variable, the computer processes the remaining instructions contained in the button's Click event procedure. Here again, each time the procedure ends, the `decScore` variable is removed from the computer's internal memory. The `decTotal` variable is removed only when the application ends.

To use a static variable in the Total Scores application:

START HERE

1. Open the Total Scores Solution (Total Scores Solution.sln) file contained in the Total Scores Solution-Static folder. If necessary, open the designer window. The user interface shown earlier in Figure 3-16 appears on the screen.
2. Open the Code Editor window. (Recall that you will learn about the Option statements later in this lesson.) Replace <your name> and <current date> in the comments with your name and the current date, respectively.

3. Delete the comments and Private declaration statement entered in the form's Declarations section.
4. Modify the btnCalc control's Click event procedure so that it uses a static variable rather than a class-level variable. Use the code shown in Figure 3-19 as a guide.
5. Save the solution and then start the application.
6. Use the application to total the following three scores: 95, 87, and 100. Be sure to click the Add to Total button after typing each score. Also be sure to delete the previous score before entering the next score. When you are finished entering the scores, the number 282 appears in the Total scores box, as shown earlier in Figure 3-18.
7. Click the **Exit** button. Close the Code Editor window and then close the solution.

YOU DO IT 2!

Create a Visual Basic Windows application named YouDoIt 2. Save the application in the VB2012\Chap03 folder. Add a label and a button to the form. The button's Click event procedure should add the number 1 to the contents of a class-level Integer variable named `intNumber`. It then should display the variable's contents in the label. Code the application. Save the solution and then start and test the application. Now change the class-level variable to a static variable. Save the solution and then start and test the application. Close the solution.

Named Constants

In addition to using literal constants and variables in your code, you also can use named constants. Like a variable, a **named constant** is a memory location inside the computer. However, unlike the value stored in a variable, the value stored in a named constant cannot be changed while the application is running. You create a named constant using the **Const statement**. The statement's syntax is shown in Figure 3-20. In the syntax, *expression* is the value you want stored in the named constant when it is created in the computer's internal memory. The expression's value must have the same data type as the named constant. The expression can contain a literal constant, another named constant, or an arithmetic operator; however, it cannot contain a variable or a method.

Declaring a Named Constant

Syntax
[Private] Const *constantName* **As** *dataType* = *expression*

Example 1
```
Const dblPI As Double = 3.141593
```
declares `dblPI` as a Double named constant and initializes it to the Double number 3.141593

Example 2
```
Const intLIMIT As Integer = 70
```
declares `intLIMIT` as an Integer named constant and initializes it to the integer 70

Example 3
```
Const strCOMPANY As String = "Merring Co."
```
declares `strCOMPANY` as a String named constant and initializes it to the string "Merring Co."

Example 4
```
Private Const decTAX_RATE As Decimal = .025D
```
declares `decTAX_RATE` as a Decimal named constant and initializes it to the Decimal number .025

the D literal type character changes the number from Double to Decimal

Figure 3-20 Syntax and examples of the Const statement

To differentiate the name of a constant from the name of a variable, many programmers lowercase the three-character ID that represents the constant's data type and then uppercase the remaining characters in the name, as shown in the examples in Figure 3-20. When entered in a procedure, the Const statements shown in the first three examples create procedure-level named constants. To create a class-level named constant, you precede the `Const` keyword with the `Private` keyword, as shown in Example 4. In addition, you enter the Const statement in the form's Declarations section. Notice that Example 4 uses the literal type character D to convert the Double number .025 to Decimal. The Convert.ToDecimal method was not used for this purpose because, as mentioned earlier, the expression assigned to a named constant cannot contain a method.

Named constants make code more self-documenting and easier to modify because they allow you to use meaningful words in place of values that are less clear. The named constant `dblPI`, for example, is much more meaningful than the number 3.141593, which is the value of pi rounded to six decimal places. Once you create a named constant, you then can use the constant's name, rather than its value, in the application's code. Unlike the value stored in a variable, the value stored in a named constant cannot be inadvertently changed while the application is running. Using a named constant to represent a value has another advantage: If the value changes in the future, you will need to modify only the Const statement in the program, rather than all of the program statements that use the value.

The Area Calculator application that you view next illustrates the use of a named constant. As the interface shown in Figure 3-21 indicates, the application allows the user to enter the radius of a circle. It then calculates and displays the circle's area. The formula for calculating the area of a circle is πr^2, where π stands for pi (3.141593).

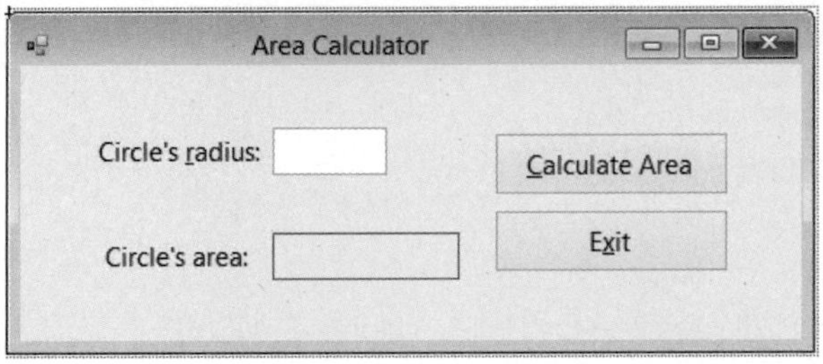

Figure 3-21 User interface for the Area Calculator application

You also can calculate the area using the expression `dblPI * dblRadius ^ 2`.

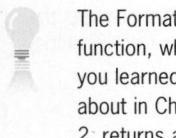

The Format function, which you learned about in Chapter 2, returns a string.

Figure 3-22 shows the code for the Calculate Area button's Click event procedure. The declaration statements in the procedure declare and initialize a named constant and two variables. The TryParse method converts the contents of the txtRadius control to Double, storing the result in the `dblRadius` variable. The first assignment statement in the procedure calculates the circle's area using the values stored in the `dblPI` named constant and `dblRadius` variable; it then assigns the result to the `dblArea` variable. The Format function in the second assignment statement formats the contents of the `dblArea` variable and then displays the resulting string in the lblArea control. When the procedure ends, the computer removes the named constant and two variables from its internal memory.

```
Private Sub btnCalc_Click(sender As Object, e As EventArgs)
Handles btnCalc.Click
    ' calculates the area of a circle

    ' declare named constant and variables
    Const dblPI As Double = 3.141593
    Dim dblRadius As Double
    Dim dblArea As Double

    ' calculate and display the area
    Double.TryParse(txtRadius.Text, dblRadius)
    dblArea = dblPI * dblRadius * dblRadius
    lblArea.Text = Format(dblArea, "Standard")

End Sub
```

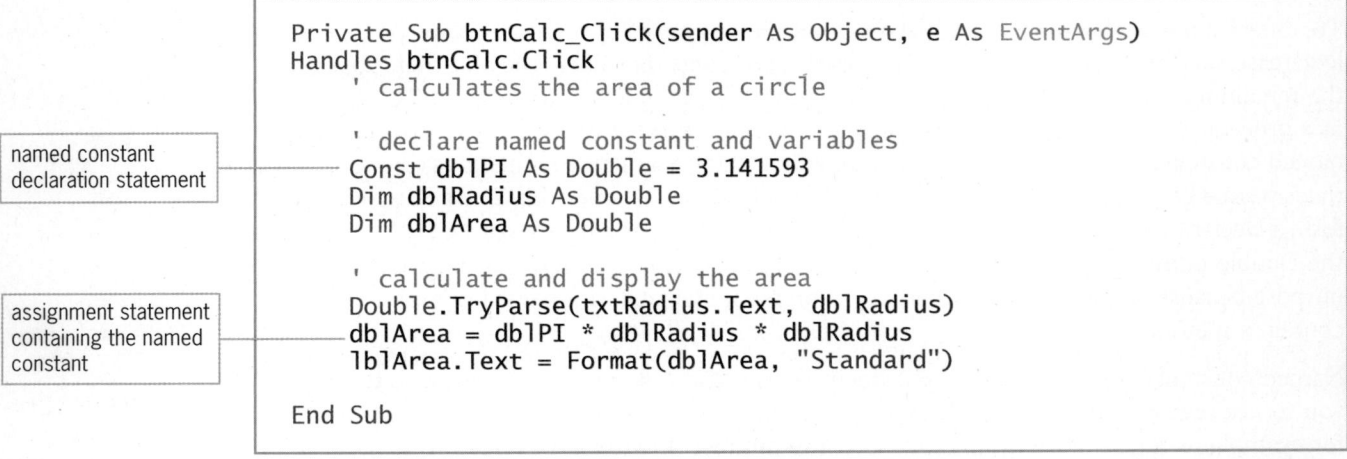

named constant declaration statement (callout: `Const dblPI As Double = 3.141593`)

assignment statement containing the named constant (callout: `dblArea = dblPI * dblRadius * dblRadius`)

Figure 3-22 Calculate Area button's Click event procedure

START HERE

To code and then test the Area Calculator application:

1. Open the Area Calculator Solution (Area Calculator Solution.sln) file contained in the VB2012\Chap03\Area Calculator Solution folder. If necessary, open the designer window. The user interface shown earlier in Figure 3-21 appears on the screen.
2. Open the Code Editor window. (You will learn about the Option statements in the next section.) Replace <your name> and <current date> in the comments with your name and the current date, respectively.
3. Open the code template for the btnCalc control's Click event procedure, and then enter the comments and code shown earlier in Figure 3-22.
4. Save the solution and then start the application.
5. Type **10** in the Circle's radius box and then click the **Calculate Area** button. The number 314.16 appears in the Circle's area box, as shown in Figure 3-23.

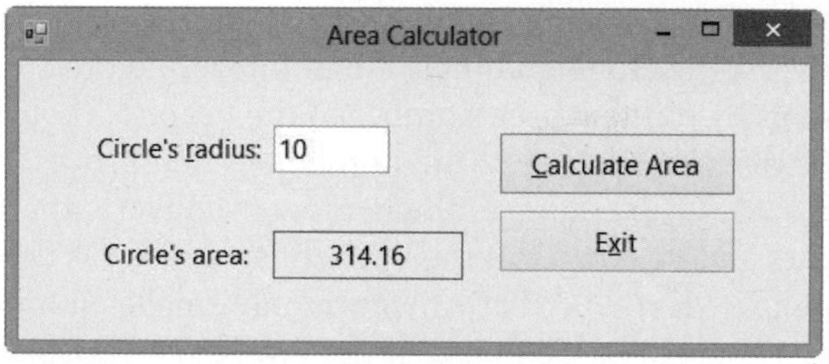

Figure 3-23 Interface showing the circle's area

6. Click the **Exit** button. Close the Code Editor window and then close the solution.

Option Statements

Finally, you will learn about the three Option statements shown earlier in Figure 3-14. The Option statements appeared in the Code Editor window for all of the applications you viewed in this lesson—namely, the Discount Calculator, Total Scores, and Area Calculator applications. You will learn about the Option Explicit and Option Infer statements first.

Option Explicit and Option Infer

It is important to declare every variable used in your code. This means every variable should appear in a declaration statement, such as a Dim or Private statement. The declaration statement is important because it allows you to control the variable's data type. Declaration statements also make your code more self-documenting. However, a word of caution is in order at this point: In Visual Basic you can create variables "on the fly." This means that if a statement in your code refers to an undeclared variable, Visual Basic will create the variable for you and assign the Object data type to it. Recall that the Object type is not a very efficient data type, and its use should be limited.

Because it is so easy to forget to declare a variable—and so easy to misspell a variable's name while coding, thereby inadvertently creating an undeclared variable—Visual Basic provides a statement that tells the Code Editor to flag any undeclared variables in your code. The statement, `Option Explicit On`, must be entered in the General Declarations section of the Code Editor window. When you also enter the `Option Infer Off` statement in the General Declarations section, the Code Editor ensures that every variable and named constant is declared with a data type. In other words, the statement tells the computer not to infer (or assume) a memory location's data type based on the data assigned to the memory location.

Recall that the General Declarations section is located above the Public Class clause in the Code Editor window.

Option Strict

As you learned earlier, the data type of the value assigned to a memory location should be the same as the data type of the memory location itself. If the value's data type does not match the memory location's data type, the computer uses a process called **implicit type conversion** to convert the value to fit the memory location. For example, when processing the statement `Dim dblLength As Double = 9`, the computer converts the integer 9 to the Double number 9.0 before storing the value in the `dblLength` variable. When a value is converted from one data type to another data type that can store either larger numbers or numbers with greater precision, the value is said to be **promoted**. In this case, if the `dblLength` variable is used subsequently in a calculation, the results of the calculation will not be adversely affected by the implicit promotion of the number 9 to the number 9.0.

On the other hand, if you inadvertently assign a Double number to a memory location that can store only integers, the computer converts the Double number to an integer before storing the value in the memory location. It does this by rounding the number to the nearest whole number and then truncating (dropping off) the decimal portion of the number. When processing the statement `Dim intScore As Integer = 78.4`, for example, the computer converts the Double number 78.4 to the integer 78 before storing the integer in the `intScore` variable. When a value is converted from one data type to another data type that can store only smaller numbers or numbers with less precision, the value is said to be **demoted**. If the `intScore` variable is used subsequently in a calculation, the implicit demotion of the number 78.4 to the number 78 will probably cause the calculated results to be incorrect.

With implicit type conversions, data loss can occur when a value is converted from one data type to a narrower data type, which is a data type with less precision or smaller capacity. You can eliminate the problems that occur as a result of implicit type conversions by entering the `Option Strict On` statement in the General Declarations section of the Code Editor window. When the `Option Strict On` statement appears in an application's code, the computer uses the type conversion rules listed in Figure 3-24. The figure also includes examples of these rules.

Type Conversion Rules

1. Strings will not be implicitly converted to numbers. The Code Editor will display a warning message when a statement attempts to use a string where a number is expected.

   Incorrect: `dblSales = txtSales.Text`
   Correct: `Double.TryParse(txtSales.Text, dblSales)`

2. Numbers will not be implicitly converted to strings. The Code Editor will display a warning message when a statement attempts to use a number where a string is expected.

   Incorrect: `lblBonus.Text = decBonus`
   Correct: `lblBonus.Text = Convert.ToString(decBonus)`

3. Wider data types will not be implicitly demoted to narrower data types. The Code Editor will display a warning message when a statement attempts to use a wider data type where a narrower data type is expected.

   Incorrect: `Dim decRate As Decimal = .05`
   Correct: `Dim decRate As Decimal =.05D`
   Correct: `Dim decRate As Decimal = Convert.ToDecimal(.05)`

4. Narrower data types will be implicitly promoted to wider data types.

   Correct: `dblAverage = dblTotal / intNum`

Figure 3-24 Rules and examples of type conversions

According to the first rule, the computer will not implicitly convert a string to a number. As a result, the Code Editor will issue the warning message "Option Strict On disallows implicit conversions from 'String' to 'Double'" when your code contains the statement `dblSales = txtSales.Text`. This is because the statement tells the computer to store a string in a Double variable. As you learned earlier, you should use the TryParse method to explicitly convert a string to the Double data type before assigning it to a Double variable. In this case, the appropriate statement to use is `Double.TryParse(txtSales.Text, dblSales)`.

According to the second rule, the computer will not implicitly convert a number to a string. Therefore, the Code Editor will issue an appropriate warning message when your code contains the statement `lblBonus.Text = decBonus`; this is because the statement assigns a number to a string. Recall that you can use the Convert class methods to explicitly convert a number to the String data type. An appropriate statement to use here is `lblBonus.Text = Convert.ToString (decBonus)`.

The third rule states that wider data types will not be implicitly demoted to narrower data types. A data type is wider than another data type if it can store either larger numbers or numbers with greater precision. Because of this rule, a Double number will not be implicitly demoted to the Decimal or Integer data types. If your code contains the statement `Dim decRate As Decimal = .05`, the Code Editor will issue an appropriate warning message because the statement assigns a Double number to a Decimal variable. The correct statement to use in this case is either `Dim decRate As Decimal = .05D` or `Dim decRate As Decimal = Convert.ToDecimal(.05)`.

According to the last rule listed in Figure 3-24, the computer will implicitly convert narrower data types to wider data types. For example, when processing the statement `dblAverage = dblTotal / intNum`, the computer will implicitly promote the integer stored in the `intNum` variable to Double before dividing it into the contents of the `dblTotal` variable. The result, a Double number, will be assigned to the `dblAverage` variable.

Figure 3-25 shows the three Option statements entered in the General Declarations section of the Code Editor window. If a project contains more than one form, the statements must be entered in each form's Code Editor window.

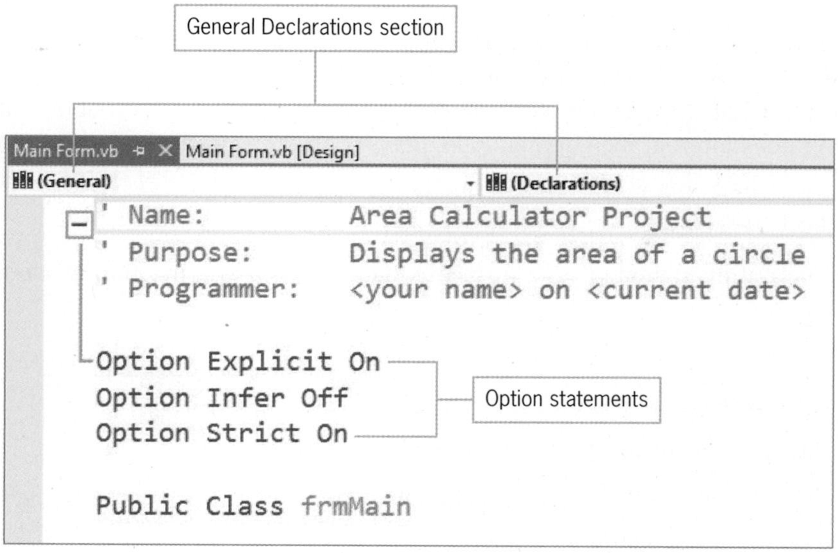

Figure 3-25 Option statements entered in the General Declarations section

In Visual Basic 2012, the default setting for Option Explicit and Option Infer is On, whereas the default setting for Option Strict is Off.

Rather than entering the Option statements in the Code Editor window, you also can set the options using either the Project Designer window or the Options dialog box. However, it is strongly recommended that you enter the Option statements in the Code Editor window because doing so makes your code more self-documenting and ensures that the options are set appropriately. The steps for setting the options in the Project Designer window and Options dialog box are listed in the Lesson A Summary section.

YOU DO IT 3!

Create a Visual Basic Windows application named YouDoIt 3. Save the application in the VB2012\Chap03 folder. Add a text box, a label, and a button to the form. In the General Declarations section of the Code Editor window, enter the following three Option statements: `Option Explicit On`, `Option Strict Off`, and `Option Infer Off`. In the button's Click event procedure, declare a Double variable named `dblNum`. Use an assignment statement to assign the contents of the text box to the Double variable. Then, use an assignment statement to assign the contents of the Double variable to the label. Save the solution and then start and test the application. Stop the application. Now change the `Option Strict Off` statement to `Option Strict On`, and then make the necessary modifications to the code. Save the solution and then start and test the application. Close the solution.

Lesson A Summary

- To declare a variable:

  The syntax of a variable declaration statement is {**Dim** | **Private** | **Static**} *variableName* **As** *dataType* [= *initialValue*]. Use camel case for a variable's name.

- To declare a procedure-level variable:

  Enter the variable declaration statement in a procedure; use the `Dim` keyword to declare a procedure-level variable that will be removed from the computer's internal memory when the procedure ends; use the `Static` keyword to declare a procedure-level variable that remains in the computer's internal memory, and also retains its value, until the application ends.

- To declare a class-level variable:

  Enter the variable declaration statement in a form's Declarations section; use the `Private` keyword.

- To use an assignment statement to assign data to an existing variable:

  Use the syntax *variableName* = *expression*.

- To force a Double literal constant to assume the Decimal data type:

  Append the letter D to the end of the Double literal constant.

- To convert a string to a numeric data type:

  Use the TryParse method. The method's syntax is *dataType*.**TryParse(***string*, *numeric-VariableName***)**.

- To convert a numeric value to a different data type:

  Use one of the Convert methods. Each method's syntax is **Convert.***method***(***value***)**.

- To create a named constant:

  Use the Const statement. The statement's syntax is [**Private**] **Const** *constantName* **As** *dataType* = *expression*. Enter the three-character ID in lowercase, and the remainder of the name in uppercase.

- To create a procedure-level named constant:

  Enter the Const statement (without the `Private` keyword) in a procedure.

- To create a class-level named constant:

  Enter the Const statement, preceded by the keyword `Private`, in a form's Declarations section.

- To prevent the computer from creating an undeclared variable:

  Enter the `Option Explicit On` statement in the General Declarations section of the Code Editor window.

- To prevent the computer from inferring a variable's data type:

  Enter the `Option Infer Off` statement in the General Declarations section of the Code Editor window.

- To prevent the computer from making implicit type conversions that may result in a loss of data:

  Enter the `Option Strict On` statement in the General Declarations section of the Code Editor window.

- To use the Project Designer window to set Option Explicit, Option Strict, and Option Infer for an entire project:

  Open the solution that contains the project. Right-click My Project in the Solution Explorer window and then click Open to open the Project Designer window. Click the Compile tab. Use the Option explicit, Option strict, and Option infer boxes to set the options. Save the solution and then close the Project Designer window.

- To use the Options dialog box to set Option Explicit, Option Strict, and Option Infer for all of the projects you create:

  Click TOOLS on the Visual Studio menu bar and then click Options. When the Options dialog box opens, expand the Projects and Solutions node and then click VB Defaults. Use the Option Explicit, Option Strict, and Option Infer boxes to set the options. Click the OK button to close the Options dialog box.

Lesson A Key Terms

Class scope—the scope of a class-level variable; refers to the fact that the variable can be used by any procedure in the form

Class-level variable—a variable declared in a form's Declarations section; the variable has class scope

Const statement—the statement used to create a named constant

Convert class—contains methods that return the result of converting a value to a specified data type

Data type—indicates the type of data a memory location (variable or named constant) can store

Demoted—the process of converting a value from one data type to another data type that can store only smaller numbers or numbers with less precision

Form's Declarations section—located between the Public Class and End Class clauses in the Code Editor window; the section of the Code Editor window where class-level variables are declared

Implicit type conversion—the process by which a value is automatically converted to fit the memory location to which it is assigned

Lifetime—indicates how long a variable or named constant remains in the computer's internal memory

Literal constant—an item of data whose value does not change during run time

Literal type character—a character (such as the letter D) appended to a literal constant for the purpose of forcing the literal constant to assume a different data type (such as Decimal)

Named constant—a computer memory location whose contents cannot be changed during run time; created using the Const statement

Procedure scope—the scope of a procedure-level variable; refers to the fact that the variable can be used only by the procedure in which it is declared

Procedure-level variable—a variable declared in a procedure; the variable has procedure scope

Promoted—the process of converting a value from one data type to another data type that can store either larger numbers or numbers with greater precision

Scope—indicates where a memory location (variable or named constant) can be used in an application's code

Static variable—a procedure-level variable that remains in memory, and also retains its value, until the application (rather than the procedure) ends

TryParse method—used to convert a string to a number of a specified data type

Unicode—the universal coding scheme that assigns a unique numeric value to each character used in the written languages of the world

Variables—computer memory locations where programmers can temporarily store data, as well as change the data, while an application is running

Lesson A Review Questions

1. Which of the following keywords is used to declare a class-level variable?
   a. `Class`
   b. `Dimension`
   c. `Global`
   d. `Private`

2. Which of the following is a data item whose value does not change during run time?
   a. literal constant
   b. literal variable
   c. named constant
   d. variable

3. Which of the following statements declares a procedure-level variable that remains in the computer's memory until the application ends?
   a. `Dim Static intScore As Integer`
   b. `Private Static intScore As Integer`
   c. `Static intScore As Integer`
   d. both b and c

4. Which of the following keywords can be used to declare a procedure-level variable?
   a. `Dim`
   b. `Procedure`
   c. `Static`
   d. both a and c

5. Which of the following statements declares a class-level variable?
   a. `Class intNum As Integer`
   b. `Private intNum As Integer`
   c. `Private Class intNum As Integer`
   d. `Private Dim intNum As Integer`

6. Which of the following declares a procedure-level String variable?
   a. `Dim String strCity`
   b. `Dim strCity As String`
   c. `Private strCity As String`
   d. `String strCity`

7. Which of the following are computer memory locations that can temporarily store information?
   a. Literal constants
   b. Named constants
   c. Variables
   d. both b and c

8. If Option Strict is set to On, which of the following statements will assign the contents of the txtSales control to a Double variable named `dblSales`?
   a. `dblSales = txtSales.Text`
   b. `dblSales = txtSales.Text.Convert.ToDouble`
   c. `Double.TryParse(txtSales.Text, dblSales)`
   d. `TryParse.Double(txtSales.Text, dblSales)`

9. Which of the following declares a named constant having the Double data type?
   a. `Const dblRATE As Double = .09`
   b. `Const dblRATE As Double`
   c. `Constant dblRATE = .09`
   d. both a and b

10. If Option Strict is set to On, which of the following statements assigns the sum of two Integer variables to the Text property of the lblTotal control.
    a. `lblTotal.Text = Convert.ToInteger(intN1 + intN2)`
    b. `lblTotal.Text = Convert.ToInt32(intN1 + intN2)`
    c. `lblTotal.Text = Convert.ToString(intN1) + Convert.ToString(intN2)`
    d. none of the above

11. Which of the following statements prevents data loss due to implicit type conversions?
    a. `Option Explicit On`
    b. `Option Strict On`
    c. `Option Implicit Off`
    d. `Option Convert Off`

Lesson A Exercises

INTRODUCTORY

1. A procedure needs to store an employee's name and net pay amount (which may have decimal places). Write the appropriate Dim statements to declare the necessary procedure-level variables.

INTRODUCTORY

2. A procedure needs to store a person's height and weight. The height may have a decimal place; the weight will always be a whole number. Write the appropriate Dim statements to declare the necessary procedure-level variables.

INTRODUCTORY

3. A procedure needs to store the name of an inventory item, the number of units in stock at the beginning of the current month, the number of units purchased during the current month, the number of units sold during the current month, and the number of units in stock at the end of the current month. The number of units is always a whole number. Write the appropriate Dim statements to declare the necessary procedure-level variables.

INTRODUCTORY

4. Write an assignment statement that assigns Alabama to a String variable named `strState`.

INTRODUCTORY

5. Write an assignment statement that assigns the word July to a String variable named `strMonth`. Also write assignment statements that assign the numbers 4 and 20 to Integer variables named `intMomBirthday` and `intDadBirthday`, respectively.

INTRODUCTORY

6. Write the statement to declare the procedure-level `decINTEREST_RATE` named constant whose value is .075.

INTRODUCTORY

7. Write the statement to store the contents of the txtQuantity control in an Integer variable named `intQuantity`.

INTRODUCTORY

8. Write the statement to assign the contents of an Integer variable named `intPopulation` to the lblPopulation control.

INTRODUCTORY

9. An application needs to store the name of an item and its price (which may contain a decimal place). Write the appropriate Private statements to declare the necessary class-level variables.

INTRODUCTORY

10. Write an assignment statement that subtracts the contents of the `dblExpenses` variable from the contents of the `dblIncome` variable and then assigns the result to the `dblNet` variable.

INTRODUCTORY

11. Open the Shiloh Solution (Shiloh Solution.sln) file contained in the VB2012\Chap03\Shiloh Solution folder. If necessary, open the designer window. At the end of the year, each salesperson at Shiloh Products is paid a bonus of 1% of his or her annual sales.
    a. Open the Code Editor window. In the General Declarations section, enter your name, the current date, and the three Option statements. Use variables and the TryParse method to code the Calculate button. Use the Format function to display the bonus with a dollar sign, a thousands separator, and two decimal places.
    b. Save the solution and then start the application. Enter the following valid ID and sales amount: DB12 and 9500. The bonus should be $95.00. If your computer is connected to a printer, print the interface.
    c. Clear the screen. Now test the application using invalid data. More specifically, test it without entering any data. Then test it using a letter as the sales amount.
    d. Close the Code Editor window and then close the solution.

INTRODUCTORY

12. Open the Age Solution (Age Solution.sln) file contained in the VB2012\Chap03\Age Solution folder. If necessary, open the designer window. The Calculate button should

calculate your age this year by subtracting your birth year from the current year. Open the Code Editor window. In the General Declarations section, enter your name, the current date, and the three Option statements. Use variables, the TryParse method, and the Convert.ToString method to code the Calculate button. Save the solution and then start the application. Test the application without entering any data. Then test it using your birth year and the current year. Finally, test it using a $ sign for the birth year and a % sign for the current year. Close the Code Editor window and then close the solution.

13. Write an assignment statement that increases the contents of the `decSalary` variable by 2%. INTERMEDIATE

14. Write an assignment statement that adds together the values stored in the `decRegion1` and `decRegion2` variables, and then assigns the result to a String variable named `strTotalSales`. INTERMEDIATE

15. Write the statement to declare a String variable that can be used by two procedures in the same form. Name the variable `strEmployeeName`. Also specify where you will need to enter the statement in the Code Editor window and whether the variable is a procedure-level or class-level variable. INTERMEDIATE

16. Open the Happy Flooring Solution (Happy Flooring Solution.sln) file contained in the VB2012\Chap03\Happy Flooring Solution folder. If necessary, open the designer window. The application should calculate the area of a floor in square yards. Open the Code Editor window. In the General Declarations section, enter your name, the current date, and the three Option statements. Use variables and the TryParse method to code the Calculate button. Use the Format function to display the calculated results using the Standard format style. Save the solution and then start the application. Test the application using 10 as the length and 12 as the width. Now test the application using invalid data. More specifically, test it without entering any data. Then test it using a letter as the length and width measurements. Close the Code Editor window and then close the solution. INTERMEDIATE

17. Open the Mason Solution (Mason Solution.sln) file contained in the VB2012\Chap03\Mason Solution folder. If necessary, open the designer window. The application should calculate the projected sales for each sales region. INTERMEDIATE

    a. Open the Code Editor window. In the General Declarations section, enter your name, the current date, and the three Option statements. Use variables and the TryParse method to code the Calculate button. Use the Format function to display the calculated results using the Standard format style.

    b. Save the solution and then start the application. Test the application using the following valid sales and increase percentage amounts. The percentage amounts are shown in decimal form.

Region 1 sales and percentage:	150000, .15
Region 2 sales and percentage:	175500, .12
Region 3 sales and percentage:	100300, .11

    c. Test the application without entering any data. Also test it using letters as the sales and percentage amounts.

    d. Close the Code Editor window and then close the solution.

DISCOVERY

18. In this exercise, you experiment with procedure-level and class-level variables. Open the Scope Solution (Scope Solution.sln) file contained in the VB2012\Chap03\Scope Solution folder. The Scope application allows the user to calculate either a 5% or 10% commission on a sales amount. It displays the sales and commission amounts in the lblSales and lblCommission controls, respectively.

    a. Open the Code Editor window and then open the code template for the btnSales control's Click event procedure. Code the procedure so that it declares a variable named `dblSales`. The procedure also should use an assignment statement to assign the number 500 to the variable. In addition, the procedure should display the contents of the variable in the lblSales control on the form.

    b. Save the solution and then start the application. Click the Display Sales button. What does the button's Click event procedure display in the lblSales control? When the Click event procedure ends, what happens to the `dblSales` variable? Click the Exit button.

    c. Open the code template for the btnComm5 control's Click event procedure. In the procedure, enter an assignment statement that multiplies a variable named `dblSales` by .05, assigning the result to the lblCommission control. When you press the Enter key after typing the assignment statement, a jagged line appears below `dblSales` in the instruction. The jagged line indicates that the code contains a syntax error. To determine the problem, rest your mouse pointer on the variable name, `dblSales`. The message in the box indicates that the variable is not declared. In other words, the btnComm5 control's Click event procedure cannot locate the variable's declaration statement, which you previously entered in the btnSales control's Click event procedure. As you learned in Lesson A, only the procedure in which a variable is declared can use the variable. No other procedure is even aware that the variable exists.

    d. Now observe what happens when you use the same name to declare a variable in more than one procedure. Insert a blank line above the assignment statement in the btnComm5 control's Click event procedure. In the blank line, type a statement that declares the `dblSales` variable, and then click the assignment statement to move the insertion point away from the current line. Notice that the jagged line disappears from the assignment statement. Save the solution and then start the application. Click the Display Sales button. The contents of the `dblSales` variable declared in the btnSales control's Click event procedure (500) appears in the lblSales control. Click the 5% Commission button. Why does the number 0 appear in the lblCommission control? What happens to the `dblSales` variable declared in the btnComm5 control's Click event procedure when the procedure ends? Click the Exit button. As this example shows, when you use the same name to declare a variable in more than one procedure, each procedure creates its own procedure-level variable. Although the variables have the same name, each refers to a different location in memory.

    e. Next, you use a class-level variable in the application. Click the blank line above the btnExit control's Click event procedure. The Class Name and Method Name boxes show frmMain and (Declarations), respectively. Press Enter to insert a blank line. In the blank line, enter a statement that declares a class-level variable named `dblSales`.

    f. Delete the Dim statement from the btnSales control's Click event procedure. Also delete the Dim statement from the btnComm5 control's Click event procedure.

    g. Open the code template for the btnComm10 control's Click event procedure. In the procedure, enter an assignment statement that multiplies the `dblSales` variable by .1, assigning the result to the lblCommission control.

h. Save the solution and then start the application. The variable declaration statement in the form's Declarations section creates the `dblSales` variable and initializes it to 0. Click the Display Sales button. The button's Click event procedure stores the number 500 in the `dblSales` variable and then displays the contents of the variable (500) in the lblSales control. Click the 5% Commission button. The button's Click event procedure multiplies the contents of the `dblSales` variable (500) by .05 and then displays the result (25) in the lblCommission control. Click the 10% Commission button. The button's Click event procedure multiplies the contents of the `dblSales` variable (500) by .1 and then displays the result (50) in the lblCommission control. As this example shows, any procedure in the form can use a class-level variable. Click the Exit button. What happens to the class-level `dblSales` variable when the application ends? Close the Code Editor window and then close the solution.

19. Open the Debug Solution (Debug Solution.sln) file contained in the VB2012\Chap03\Debug Solution-Lesson A folder. The application is supposed to display the number of times the Count button is pressed, but it is not working correctly. SWAT THE BUGS

a. Start the application. Click the Count button. The message indicates that you have pressed the Count button once, which is correct. Click the Count button several more times. The message still displays the number 1. Click the Exit button.

b. Open the Code Editor window and study the code. What are two ways that you can use to correct the code? Which way is the preferred way? Modify the code using the preferred way. Save the solution and then start the application. Click the Count button several times. Each time you click the Count button, the message should change to indicate the number of times the button was pressed.

c. Click the Exit button. Close the Code Editor window and then close the solution.

LESSON B

After studying Lesson B, you should be able to:

- Include procedure-level and class-level variables in an application
- Concatenate strings
- Get user input using the InputBox function
- Include the ControlChars.NewLine constant in code
- Designate the default button for a form
- Format numbers using the ToString method

Modifying the Play It Again Movies Application

Your task in this chapter is to modify the Play It Again Movies application created in Chapter 2. The modified application will calculate and display a 3% sales tax. It also will display the name of the salesclerk who entered the sales information. Before making modifications to an application's existing code, you should review the application's documentation and revise the necessary documents. In this case, you need to revise the application's TOE chart and also the pseudocode for the Calculate button. The revised TOE chart is shown in Figure 3-26. The changes made to the original TOE chart from Chapter 2 are shaded in the figure. (You will view the revised pseudocode for the Calculate button later in this lesson.)

Task	Object	Event
1. Calculate total discs sold and total sales amount 2. Display total discs sold and total sales amount in lblTotalDiscs and lblTotalSales 3. Calculate the sales tax 4. Display sales tax and salesclerk's name in lblMessage	btnCalc	Click
Print the sales receipt	btnPrint	Click
End the application	btnExit	Click
Clear screen for the next sale	btnClear	Click
Display total discs sold (from btnCalc)	lblTotalDiscs	None
Display total sales amount (from btnCalc)	lblTotalSales	None
Get and display the sales information	txtDate, txtDvds, txtBluRays	None
Get the salesclerk's name	frmMain	Load
Display sales tax and salesclerk's name (from btnCalc)	lblMessage	None

Figure 3-26 Revised TOE chart for the Play It Again Movies application

Notice that the revised TOE chart includes two additional objects (the form and a label control), as well as an additional event (Load). A form's **Load event** occurs when the application is started and the form is displayed the first time. According to the TOE chart, the Load event is responsible for getting the salesclerk's name. Also notice that the btnCalc control's Click event procedure now has two additional tasks: It must calculate the sales tax and also display the sales tax and salesclerk's name in the lblMessage control.

To open the Play It Again Movies application:

START HERE

1. If necessary, start Visual Studio 2012. Open the Play It Again Solution (Play It Again Solution.sln) file contained in the VB2012\Chap03\Play It Again Solution folder. If necessary, open the designer window. Figure 3-27 shows the application's user interface.

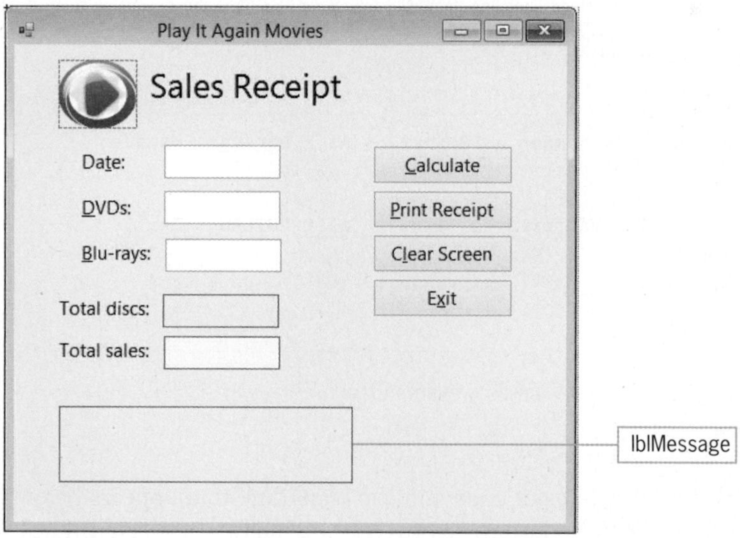

Figure 3-27 Modified user interface for the Play It Again Movies application
OpenClipArt.org/John Diamond / diamonjohn

Two modifications were made to the application created in Chapter 2: The lblMessage control was added to the interface and the statement `lblMessage.Text = String.Empty` was added to the btnClear control's Click event procedure. The statement will remove the contents of the lblMessage control when the user clicks the Clear Screen button.

Modifying the Calculate Button's Code

Currently, the Calculate button uses the Val function and the Text properties of controls to calculate the total number of discs sold and total sales amount. In this lesson, you will modify the button's code to use the TryParse method and variables.

To begin modifying the application's code:

START HERE

1. Open the Code Editor window. Replace <your name> and <current date> with your name and the current date, respectively.
2. The code will contain variables, so you will enter the three Option statements in the Code Editor window. Click the **blank line** above the `Public Class frmMain` clause and then press **Enter** to insert another blank line. Enter the following three statements:

   Option Explicit On
   Option Strict On
   Option Infer Off

3. Scroll down the Code Editor window until the entire btnCalc_Click procedure is visible. Notice that jagged blue lines appear below the expressions in the two calculations. The jagged lines indicate that the expressions contain one or more syntax errors.
4. Position your mouse pointer on the first jagged blue line, as shown in Figure 3-28. An error message appears in a box. (If the box does not appear after a few seconds have

elapsed, try moving your mouse pointer to a different location on the jagged blue line.) The error message says "Option Strict On disallows implicit conversions from 'Double' to 'String'." You received this error message because the expression on the right side of the assignment operator results in a Double number, and the assignment statement is attempting to assign that Double number to the Text property of a control. (Recall that the Val function returns a Double number, and the Text property of a control is a string.)

mouse pointer

```
Private Sub btnCalc_Click(sender As Object, e As EventArgs) Handles |
    ' calculate number of discs sold and total sales

    lblTotalDiscs.Text = Val(txtDvds.Text) + Val(txtBluRays.Text)
    lblTotalSales.Text =  Option Strict On disallows implicit conversions from 'Double' to 'String'.
    lblTotalSales.Text = Format(lblTotalSales.Text, "Currency")

End Sub
```

Figure 3-28 A jagged blue line indicates a syntax error

5. Highlight (select) the three lines of code and the blank line that appears below them, as shown in Figure 3-29. Press **Delete** to remove the highlighted (selected) lines from the procedure.

```
Private Sub btnCalc_Click(sender As Object, e As EventArgs) Handles |
    ' calculate number of discs sold and total sales

    lblTotalDiscs.Text = Val(txtDvds.Text) + Val(txtBluRays.Text)
    lblTotalSales.Text = Val(lblTotalDiscs.Text) * 7
    lblTotalSales.Text = Format(lblTotalSales.Text, "Currency")

End Sub
```

highlight (select) these lines and then press Delete

Figure 3-29 Lines to delete from the procedure

Figure 3-30 shows the revised pseudocode and flowchart for the btnCalc control's Click event procedure. Changes made to the original pseudocode and flowchart from Chapter 2 are shaded in the figure. The Click event procedure includes two additional calculations: one for the subtotal and one for the sales tax. The subtotal is computed by multiplying the total number of discs sold by the disc price. The sales tax is computed by multiplying the subtotal by the sales tax rate. Notice that the total sales expression has changed; it now adds the subtotal to the sales tax. Lastly, the Click event procedure displays the sales tax and the salesclerk's name in the lblMessage control.

btnCalc Click event procedure
1. calculate total discs sold = DVDs sold + Blu-rays sold
2. calculate subtotal = total discs sold * disc price
3. calculate sales tax = subtotal * sales tax rate
4. calculate total sales = subtotal + sales tax
5. display total discs sold and total sales in lblTotalDiscs and lblTotalSales
6. display sales tax and salesclerk's name in lblMessage

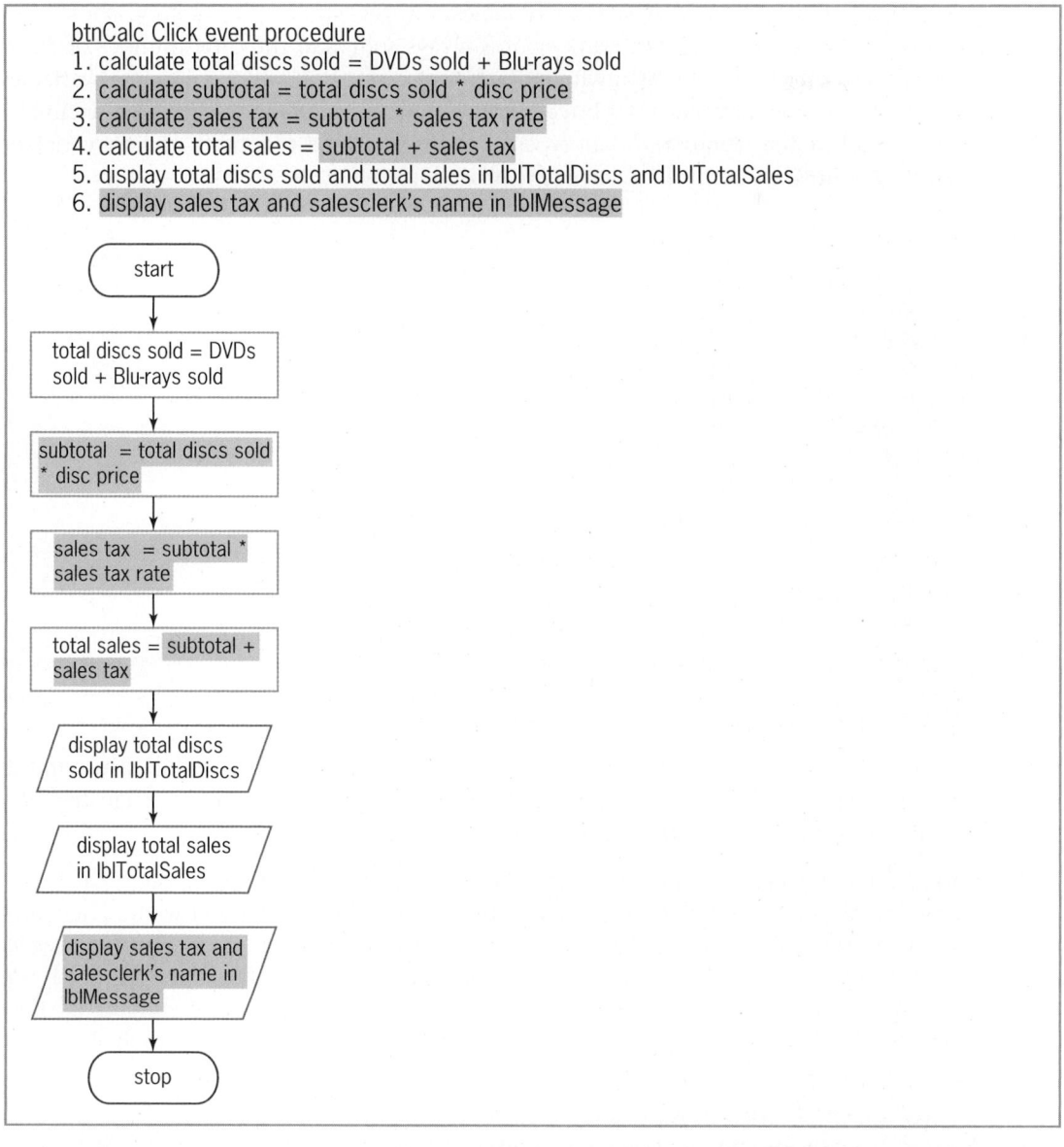

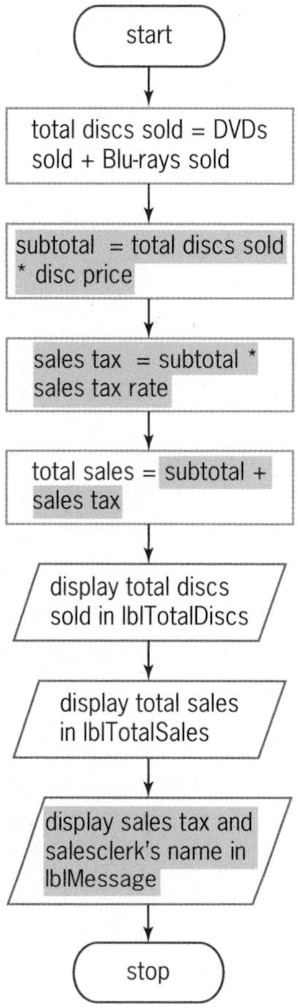
start
total discs sold = DVDs sold + Blu-rays sold
subtotal = total discs sold * disc price
sales tax = subtotal * sales tax rate
total sales = subtotal + sales tax
display total discs sold in lblTotalDiscs
display total sales in lblTotalSales
display sales tax and salesclerk's name in lblMessage
stop

Figure 3-30 Revised pseudocode and flowchart for the btnCalc control's Click event procedure

Before you begin coding a procedure, you first study the procedure's pseudocode to determine the variables and named constants (if any) the procedure will use. When determining the named constants, look for items whose value should be the same each time the procedure is invoked. In the btnCalc control's Click event procedure, the disc price and sales tax rate will always be $7 and .03 (the decimal equivalent of 3%), respectively; therefore, you will assign both values to Decimal named constants. At this point, you may be wondering why the disc price is assigned to a Decimal constant rather than to an Integer constant. Although the disc price does not currently contain any decimal places, it is possible that the price may include a decimal place in the future. By using the Decimal data type now, you can change the constant's value to include a decimal place without having to remember to also change its data type.

When determining a procedure's variables, look in the pseudocode for items whose value is allowed to change each time the procedure is processed. In the btnCalc control's Click event procedure, the numbers of DVDs and Blu-rays sold will likely be different each time the procedure is processed. As a result, the total number of discs sold, subtotal, sales tax, and total sales amounts will also vary because they are based on the numbers of DVDs and Blu-rays sold.

Therefore, you will assign those six values to variables. Integer variables are a good choice for storing the number of DVDs sold, the number of Blu-rays sold, and the total number of discs sold because a customer can buy only a whole number of discs. You will use Decimal variables to store the subtotal, sales tax, and total price because these amounts may contain a decimal place. Figure 3-31 lists the names and data types of the two named constants and six variables you will use in the btnCalc control's Click event procedure.

Named constant/Variable	Data type
decDISC_PRICE	Decimal
decTAX_RATE	Decimal
intDvds	Integer
intBluRays	Integer
intTotalDiscs	Integer
decSubtotal	Decimal
decSalesTax	Decimal
decTotalSales	Decimal

Figure 3-31 List of named constants and variables

START HERE

To declare the named constants and variables:

1. The insertion point should be located in the blank line above the End Sub clause in the btnCalc control's Click event procedure. If necessary, press **Tab** twice to align the blinking insertion point with the apostrophe in the comment.

2. First, you will declare the named constants. When declaring named constants and variables, be sure to enter the name using the exact capitalization you want. Then, any time you want to refer to the named constant or variable in the code, you can enter its name using any case. The Code Editor will automatically adjust the name to match the case used in the declaration statement. Enter the following declaration statements. (For now, don't be concerned about the jagged green line that appears below each statement after you press Enter.)

   Const decDISC_PRICE As Decimal = 7D
   Const decTAX_RATE As Decimal = .03D

3. Next, enter the following six variable declaration statements. Press **Enter** twice after typing the last statement.

   Dim intDvds As Integer
   Dim intBluRays As Integer
   Dim intTotalDiscs As Integer
   Dim decSubtotal As Decimal
   Dim decSalesTax As Decimal
   Dim decTotalSales As Decimal

4. Place your mouse pointer on the jagged green line that appears below the last Dim statement. A warning message appears in a box, as shown in Figure 3-32. The message alerts you that the `decTotalSales` variable has been declared but has not been used yet. In other words, the variable name does not appear in any other statement in the code. The jagged green line will disappear when you include the variable name in another statement in the procedure.

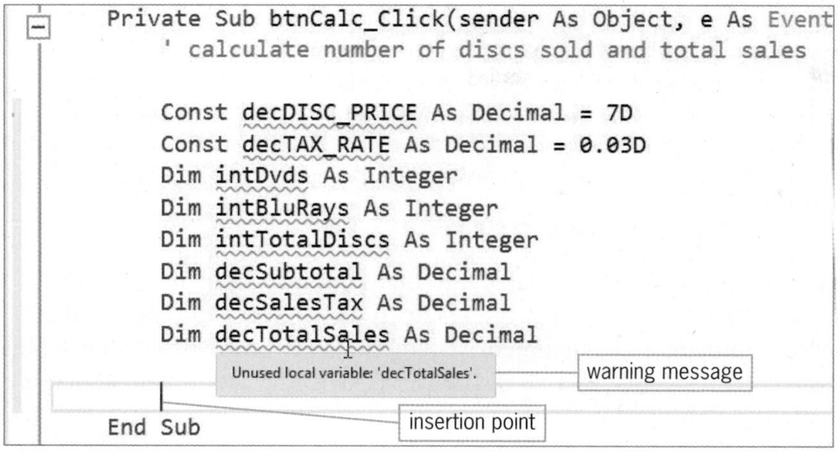

Figure 3-32 Const and Dim statements entered in the procedure

After declaring the named constants and variables, you can begin coding either each step in the procedure's pseudocode or each symbol (other than the start and stop ovals) in its flowchart. Keep in mind that some steps and symbols may require more than one line of code. You will use the pseudocode shown earlier in Figure 3-30 to code the procedure. The first step in the pseudocode calculates the total number of discs sold by adding the number of DVDs sold to the number of Blu-rays sold. The numbers of DVDs and Blu-rays sold are stored in the Text properties of the txtDvds and txtBluRays controls, respectively. You will use the TryParse method to convert the Text properties to integers and then store the results in the `intDvds` and `intBluRays` variables. You then will use an assignment statement to add together the contents of both variables, assigning the sum to the `intTotalDiscs` variable.

To continue coding the btnCalc control's Click event procedure:

START HERE

1. The insertion point should be positioned as shown earlier in Figure 3-32. Enter the following comment and TryParse methods. When you press Enter after typing each TryParse method, the Code Editor removes the jagged green line that appears below the respective variable's Dim statement.

```
' calculate total number of discs sold
Integer.TryParse(txtDvds.Text, intDvds)
Integer.TryParse(txtBluRays.Text, intBluRays)
```

2. Next, you will enter an assignment statement that calculates the total number of discs sold. Type the following assignment statement and then press **Enter** twice. (Notice that all of the variables in the assignment statement have the same data type: Integer.)

```
intTotalDiscs = intDvds + intBluRays
```

3. The second step in the pseudocode calculates the subtotal by multiplying the total number of discs sold by the disc price. You will assign the subtotal to the `decSubtotal` variable. Enter the following comment and assignment statement. Press **Enter** twice after typing the assignment statement. When processing the assignment statement, the computer will implicitly convert the integer stored in the `intTotalDiscs` variable to Decimal before multiplying it by the decimal number stored in the `decDISC_PRICE` constant. It then will assign the result to the `decSubtotal` variable.

```
' calculate the subtotal
decSubtotal = intTotalDiscs * decDISC_PRICE
```

4. The third step in the pseudocode calculates the sales tax by multiplying the subtotal by the sales tax rate. You will assign the sales tax to the `decSalesTax` variable. Enter the following comment and assignment statement. Press **Enter** twice after typing the assignment statement. (Notice that the variables and named constant in the assignment statement have the same data type: Decimal.)

   ' calculate the sales tax
   decSalesTax = decSubtotal * decTAX_RATE

5. The fourth step in the pseudocode calculates the total sales by adding together the subtotal and the sales tax. You will assign the result to the `decTotalSales` variable. Enter the following comment and assignment statement. Press **Enter** twice after typing the assignment statement. (Notice that all of the variables in the assignment statement have the same data type: Decimal.)

   ' calculate the total sales
   decTotalSales = decSubtotal + decSalesTax

6. Step 5 in the pseudocode displays the total number of discs sold and total sales in their respective label controls. The total number of discs sold and total sales are stored in the `intTotalDiscs` and `decTotalSales` variables, respectively. Because both variables have a numeric data type, you will need to convert their contents to the String data type before assigning the contents to the label controls. You can use the ToString method of the Convert class to make the conversions. Enter the following comment and assignment statements. Press **Enter** twice after typing the last assignment statement.

   ' display total amounts
   lblTotalDiscs.Text = Convert.ToString(intTotalDiscs)
   lblTotalSales.Text = Convert.ToString(decTotalSales)

7. The last step in the pseudocode displays both the sales tax and the salesclerk's name in the lblMessage control. For now, you will display only the sales tax. Enter the following comment and assignment statement:

   ' display tax and salesclerk's name
   lblMessage.Text = Convert.ToString (decSalesTax)

8. Save the solution. Figure 3-33 shows the code entered in the btnCalc control's Click event procedure.

```
Private Sub btnCalc_Click(sender As Object, e As EventArgs)
Handles btnCalc.Click
    ' calculate number of discs sold and total sales

    Const decDISC_PRICE As Decimal = 7D
    Const decTAX_RATE As Decimal = 0.03D
    Dim intDvds As Integer
    Dim intBluRays As Integer
    Dim intTotalDiscs As Integer
    Dim decSubtotal As Decimal
    Dim decSalesTax As Decimal
    Dim decTotalSales As Decimal

    ' calculate total number of discs sold
    Integer.TryParse(txtDvds.Text, intDvds)
    Integer.TryParse(txtBluRays.Text, intBluRays)
    intTotalDiscs = intDvds + intBluRays
```

Figure 3-33 Code entered in the btnCalc control's Click event procedure *(continues)*

(continued)

```
    ' calculate the subtotal
    decSubtotal = intTotalDiscs * decDISC_PRICE

    ' calculate the sales tax
    decSalesTax = decSubtotal * decTAX_RATE

    ' calculate the total sales
    decTotalSales = decSubtotal + decSalesTax

    ' display total amounts
    lblTotalDiscs.Text = Convert.ToString(intTotalDiscs)
    lblTotalSales.Text = Convert.ToString(decTotalSales)

    ' display tax and salesclerk's name
    lblMessage.Text = Convert.ToString(decSalesTax)

End Sub
```

Figure 3-33 Code entered in the btnCalc control's Click event procedure

To start and then test the application:

START HERE

1. Start the application. Type **4/9/2014** in the Date box, **5** in the DVDs box, and **3** in the Blu-rays box. Click the **Calculate** button. The total number of discs sold, total sales, and sales tax appear in the interface, as shown in Figure 3-34. However, it's not obvious to the user that the 1.68 is the sales tax. You can fix this problem by displaying the message "The sales tax was" before the sales tax amount. Before you can accomplish this task, you need to learn how to concatenate (link together) strings. String concatenation is covered in the next section.

Figure 3-34 Calculated amounts shown in the interface
OpenClipArt.org/John Diamond / diamonjohn

2. Click the **Clear Screen** button to clear the sales receipt (except for the date), and then click the **Exit** button.

Concatenating Strings

You use the **concatenation operator**, which is the ampersand (**&**), to concatenate (connect or link together) strings. For the Code Editor to recognize the ampersand as the concatenation operator, the ampersand must be both preceded and followed by a space. Figure 3-35 shows some examples of string concatenation.

You also can use the plus sign (+) to concatenate strings. To avoid confusion, however, you should use the plus sign for addition and the ampersand for concatenation.

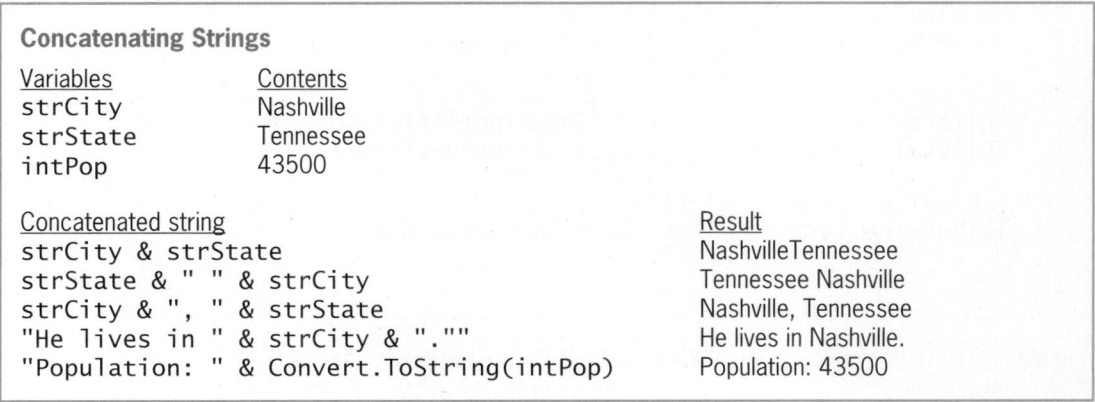

Concatenating Strings

Variables	Contents
strCity	Nashville
strState	Tennessee
intPop	43500

Concatenated string	Result
`strCity & strState`	NashvilleTennessee
`strState & " " & strCity`	Tennessee Nashville
`strCity & ", " & strState`	Nashville, Tennessee
`"He lives in " & strCity & "."`	He lives in Nashville.
`"Population: " & Convert.ToString(intPop)`	Population: 43500

Figure 3-35 Examples of string concatenation

You will use the concatenation operator to concatenate the following three strings: "The sales tax was ", the contents of the `decSalesTax` variable after it has been converted to a string, and ".". Using the examples shown in Figure 3-35 as a guide, the correct assignment statement is `lblMessage.Text = "The sales tax was " & Convert.ToString(decSalesTax) & "."`. The assignment statement is rather long and, depending on the size of the font used in your Code Editor window, you may not be able to view the entire statement without scrolling the window. The Code Editor allows you to break a line of code into two or more physical lines, as long as the break comes either before a closing parenthesis or after one of the following: a comma, an opening parenthesis, or an operator (arithmetic, assignment, comparison, logical, or concatenation). If you want to break a line of code anywhere else, you will need to use the **line continuation character**, which is an underscore (_) that is immediately preceded by a space. However, if you use the line continuation character, it must appear at the end of a physical line of code. In this case, you will break the assignment statement after the first concatenation operator.

START HERE

To concatenate the strings and then test the code:

1. Change the last assignment statement in the procedure as shown in Figure 3-36. The modifications are shaded in the figure.

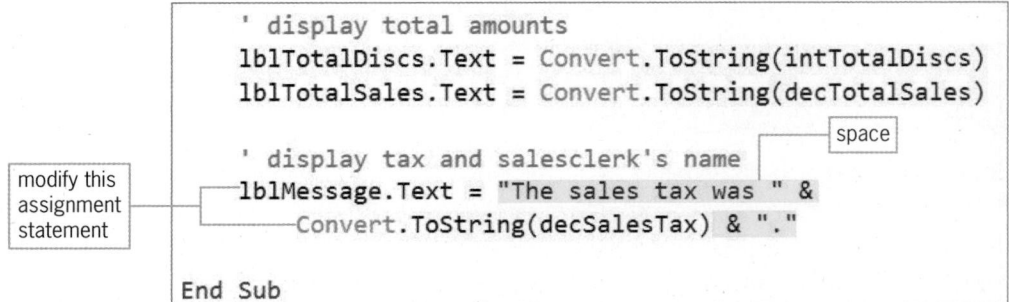

```
    ' display total amounts
    lblTotalDiscs.Text = Convert.ToString(intTotalDiscs)
    lblTotalSales.Text = Convert.ToString(decTotalSales)

    ' display tax and salesclerk's name
    lblMessage.Text = "The sales tax was " &
        Convert.ToString(decSalesTax) & "."

End Sub
```

modify this assignment statement

space

Figure 3-36 String concatenation included in the assignment statement

2. Save the solution and then start the application. Type **4/9/2014** in the Date box, **5** in the DVDs box, and **3** in the Blu-rays box. Click the **Calculate** button. The lblMessage control contains the sentence "The sales tax was 1.68.". See Figure 3-37.

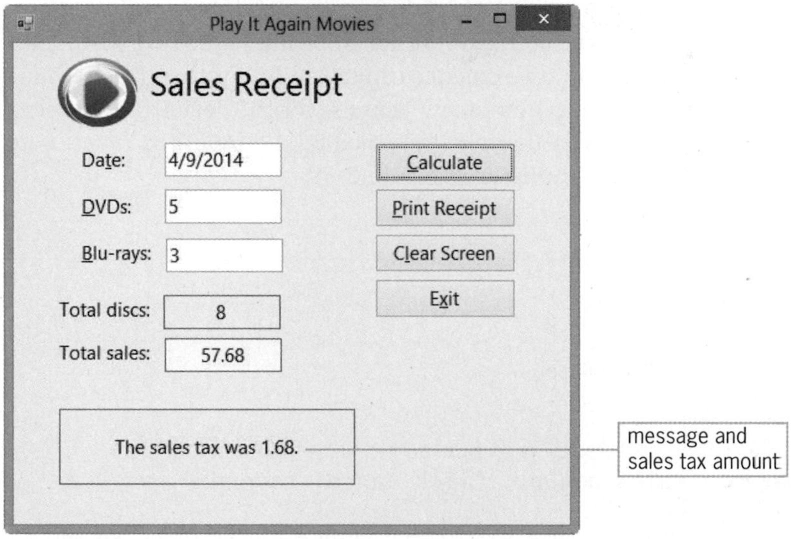

Figure 3-37 Concatenated strings displayed in the lblMessage control
OpenClipArt.org/John Diamond / diamonjohn

3. Click the **Exit** button.

You also need to display the salesclerk's name in the lblMessage control. You can use the InputBox function to obtain the name from the user.

The InputBox Function

The **InputBox function** displays an input dialog box, which is one of the standard dialog boxes available in Visual Basic. An example of an input dialog box is shown in Figure 3-38. The message in the dialog box should prompt the user to enter the appropriate information in the input area. The user closes the dialog box by clicking the OK button, Cancel button, or Close button. The value returned by the InputBox function depends on the button the user chooses. If the user clicks the OK button, the function returns the value contained in the input area of the dialog box; the return value is always treated as a string. If the user clicks either the Cancel button in the dialog box or the Close button on the dialog box's title bar, the function returns an empty (or zero-length) string.

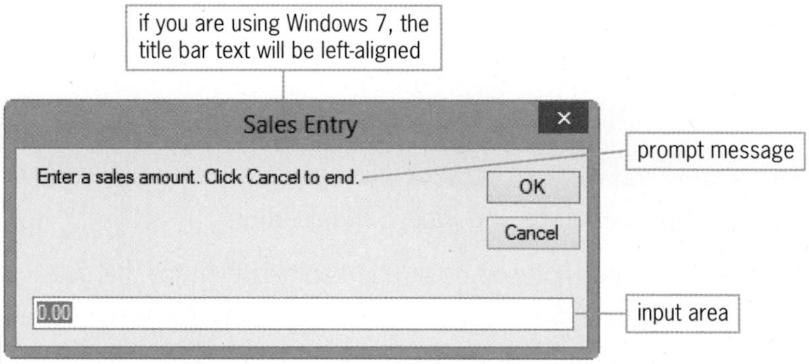

Figure 3-38 Example of an input dialog box

Figure 3-39 shows the basic syntax of the InputBox function. The *prompt* argument contains the message to display inside the dialog box. The optional *title* and *defaultResponse* arguments control the text that appears in the dialog box's title bar and input area, respectively. If you omit the *title* argument, the project name appears in the title bar. If you omit the *defaultResponse* argument, a blank input area appears when the dialog box opens. The *prompt, title,* and *defaultResponse* arguments can be string literal constants, String named constants, or String variables. The Windows standard is to use sentence capitalization for the prompt, but book title capitalization for the title. The capitalization (if any) you use for the defaultResponse depends on the text itself. In most cases, you assign the value returned by the InputBox function to a String variable, as shown in the first three examples in Figure 3-39.

Using the InputBox Function

Syntax
InputBox(*prompt*[, *title*][, *defaultResponse*]**)**

Example 1
```
strSales =
  InputBox("Enter a sales amount. Click Cancel to end.",
  "Sales Entry", "0.00")
```
Displays the input dialog box shown in Figure 3-38. When the user closes the dialog box, the assignment statement assigns the function's return value to the `strSales` variable.

Example 2
```
strCity = InputBox("City name:", "City")
```
Displays an input dialog box that shows City name: as the prompt, City in the title bar, and an empty input area. When the user closes the dialog box, the assignment statement assigns the function's return value to the `strCity` variable.

Example 3
```
Const strPROMPT As String = "Enter the discount rate:"
Const strTITLE As String = "Discount Rate"
strRate = InputBox(strPROMPT, strTITLE, ".00")
```
Displays an input dialog box that shows the contents of the `strPROMPT` constant as the prompt, the contents of the `strTITLE` constant in the title bar, and .00 in the input area. When the user closes the dialog box, the assignment statement assigns the function's return value to the `strRate` variable.

Example 4
```
Integer.TryParse(InputBox("How old are you?",
     "Discount Verification"), intAge)
```
Displays an input dialog box that shows How old are you? as the prompt, Discount Verification in the title bar, and an empty input area. When the user closes the dialog box, the TryParse method converts the function's return value from String to Integer and then stores the result in the `intAge` variable.

Figure 3-39 Basic syntax and examples of the InputBox function

The InputBox function's syntax also includes optional *XPos* and *YPos* arguments for specifying the dialog box's horizontal and vertical positions, respectively. If both arguments are omitted, the dialog box appears centered on the screen.

GUI DESIGN TIP InputBox Function's Prompt and Title Capitalization

- Use sentence capitalization for the prompt, but book title capitalization for the title.

You will use the InputBox function to prompt the salesclerk to enter his or her name. The function should be entered in the form's Load event procedure because that is the procedure responsible for getting the salesclerk's name. Recall that a form's Load event occurs before the form appears on the screen. After the Load event procedure obtains the salesclerk's name, you will have the Calculate button's Click event procedure concatenate the name to the message displayed in the lblMessage control.

Before entering the InputBox function in the Load event procedure, you must decide where to declare the String variable that will store the function's return value. In other words, should the variable have procedure scope or class scope? When deciding, consider the fact that the form's Load event procedure needs to store a value in the variable, and the Calculate button's Click event procedure needs to display the variable's value in the lblMessage control. Recall from Lesson A that when two procedures in the same form need access to the same variable, you declare the variable as a class-level variable by entering its declaration statement in the form's Declarations section.

START HERE

To continue coding the Play It Again Movies application:

1. Scroll to the top of the Code Editor window. Click the **blank line** immediately below the `Public Class frmMain` clause. When you do so, frmMain and (Declarations) appear in the Class Name and Method Name boxes, respectively. Press **Enter** to insert a blank line.
2. First, you will declare a class-level String variable named `strClerk`. Enter the comment and declaration statement shown in Figure 3-40.

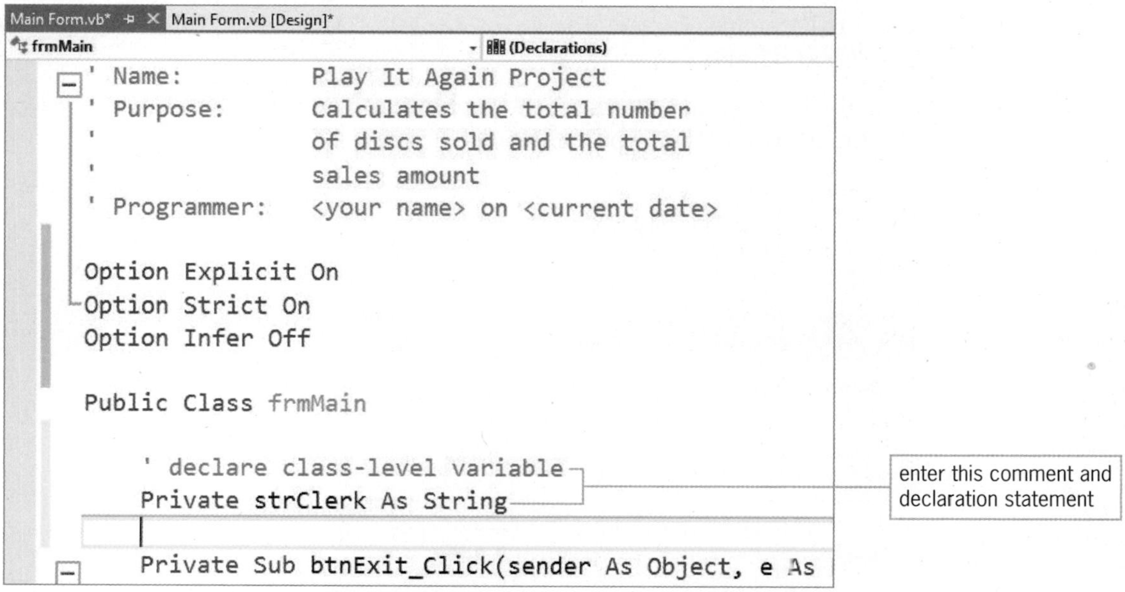

Figure 3-40 Class-level variable declared in the form's Declarations section

3. Now you will enter the InputBox function in the form's Load event procedure. You access the form's procedures by selecting (frmMain Events) in the Class Name list box. Click the **Class Name** list arrow and then click **(frmMain Events)** in the list. Click the **Method Name** list arrow to view a list of the form's procedures. Scroll down the list until you see Load, and then click **Load** in the list. The frmMain Load event procedure appears in the Code Editor window.
4. To make the assignment statement that contains the InputBox function shorter and easier to understand, you will create named constants for the function's *prompt* and *title* arguments, and then use the named constants (rather than the longer strings) in the

function. You are using named constants rather than variables because the prompt and title will not change as the application is running. Enter the comments and code shown in Figure 3-41.

enter these two comments and three lines of code

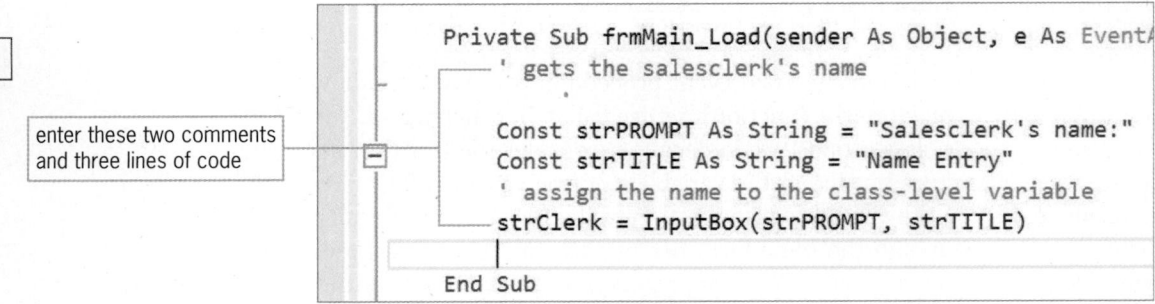

```
Private Sub frmMain_Load(sender As Object, e As EventA
    ' gets the salesclerk's name

    Const strPROMPT As String = "Salesclerk's name:"
    Const strTITLE As String = "Name Entry"
    ' assign the name to the class-level variable
    strClerk = InputBox(strPROMPT, strTITLE)

End Sub
```

Figure 3-41 frmMain Load event procedure

5. Next, you will concatenate the `strClerk` variable to the message assigned to the lblMessage control. Locate the btnCalc control's Click event procedure. Click **immediately after the closing quotation mark** in the `Convert.ToString (decSalesTax) & "."` line. Press the **spacebar** to enter a space character after the closing quotation mark. Type **&** and then press **Enter**. Now type **strClerk** and then click the **blank line** above the End Sub clause. The modified assignment statement is shown here: `lblMessage.Text = "The sales tax was " & Convert.ToString(decSalesTax) & "." & strClerk`.
6. Save the solution and then start the application. The Name Entry dialog box created by the InputBox function appears first. See Figure 3-42.

if you are using Windows 7, the title bar text will be left-aligned

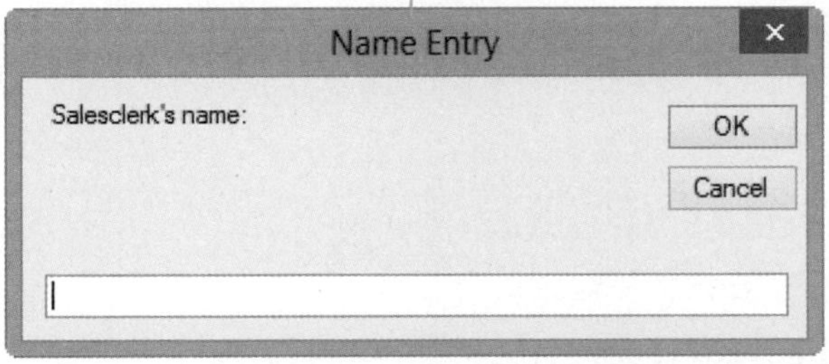

Figure 3-42 Dialog box created by the InputBox function

7. Type your name in the input area of the dialog box and then click the **OK** button. The sales receipt appears. Type **4** in the DVDs box and then click the **Calculate** button. Notice that your name appears much too close to the period in the lblMessage control. You can correct the spacing problem by replacing the period (`"."`) in the assignment statement with a period and two spaces (`".  "`). Or, you can use the ControlChars.NewLine constant to display the salesclerk's name on the next line in the lblMessage control. Click the **Exit** button.

The ControlChars.Newline Constant

The **ControlChars.NewLine constant** instructs the computer to advance the insertion point to the next line in a control. (You also can use it to advance the insertion point in a file or on the printer.) Whenever you want to start a new line, you simply enter the ControlChars.NewLine constant at the appropriate location in your code. In this case, you want to advance to a new line after displaying the period—in other words, before displaying the salesclerk's name—in the lblMessage control.

START HERE

To display the salesclerk's name on a separate line in the lblMessage control:

1. In the btnCalc control's Click event procedure, modify the last assignment statement as indicated in Figure 3-43. The modifications are shaded in the figure.

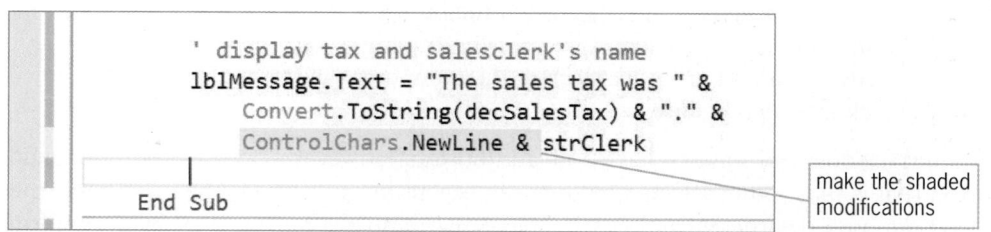

```
' display tax and salesclerk's name
lblMessage.Text = "The sales tax was " &
    Convert.ToString(decSalesTax) & "." &
    ControlChars.NewLine & strClerk

End Sub
```

make the shaded modifications

Figure 3-43 Modified assignment statement

The ControlChars.NewLine constant is an intrinsic constant, which is a named constant built into Visual Basic.

2. Save the solution and then start the application. The Name Entry dialog box shown in Figure 3-44 appears first. The blinking insertion point indicates that the dialog box's input area has the focus. However, notice that the OK button in the dialog box has a darkened border, even though it does not have the focus. In Windows terminology, a button that has a darkened border when it does not have the focus is called the default button. You can select a default button by pressing Enter at any time.

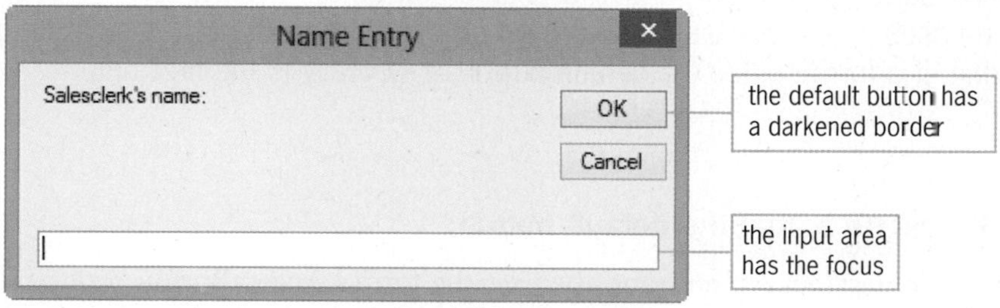
Name Entry
Salesclerk's name:
OK
Cancel
the default button has a darkened border
the input area has the focus

Figure 3-44 Name Entry input dialog box

3. Type **Martin Lapinski** and then press **Enter**. The sales receipt appears.
4. Type **10/10/2014** in the Date box and **5** in the DVDs box. Click the **Calculate** button. The salesclerk's name now appears on a separate line in the lblMessage control, as shown in Figure 3-45. Click the **Exit** button.

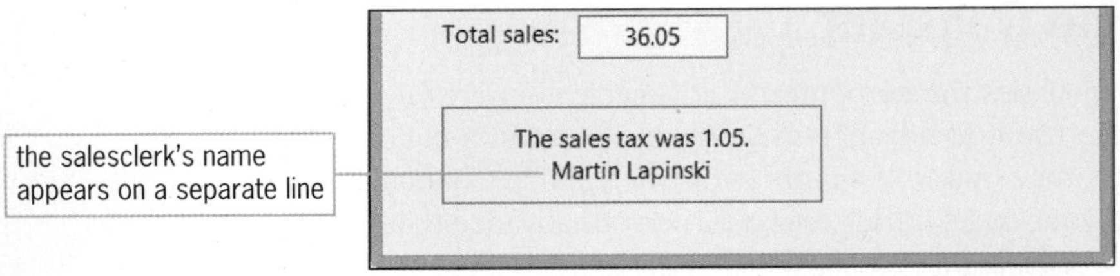
Total sales:
36.05
The sales tax was 1.05.
Martin Lapinski
the salesclerk's name appears on a separate line

Figure 3-45 Salesclerk's name shown on the sales receipt

Designating a Default Button

As you already know from using Windows applications, you can select a button either by clicking it or by pressing the Enter key when the button has the focus. If you make a button the **default button**, you also can select it by pressing the Enter key even when the button does not have the focus. When a button is selected, the computer processes the code contained in the button's Click event procedure.

Forms also have a CancelButton property that specifies the button whose Click event procedure is processed when the user presses the Esc key. This property is covered in Exercise 12 at the end of this lesson.

An interface does not have to have a default button. However, if one is used, it should be the button that is most often selected by the user, except in cases where the tasks performed by the button are both destructive and irreversible. For example, a button that deletes information should not be designated as the default button unless the application provides a way for the information to be restored. If you assign a default button in an interface, it typically is the first button on the left when the buttons are positioned horizontally, but the first button on the top when they are stacked vertically. A form can have only one default button. You specify the default button (if any) by setting the form's AcceptButton property to the name of the button.

GUI DESIGN TIP Assigning a Default Button

- The default button should be the button that is most often selected by the user, except in cases where the tasks performed by the button are both destructive and irreversible. If a form contains a default button, it typically is the first button.

START HERE

To make the Calculate button the default button:

1. Return to the designer window and then set the form's AcceptButton property to **btnCalc**. A darkened border appears around the Calculate button.
2. Save the solution and then start the application. Type your name in the Name Entry dialog box and then press **Enter**. The sales receipt appears.
3. Click the **DVDs box**. Type **5** and then press **Enter** to select the Calculate button. The numbers 5 and 36.05 appear in the Total discs and Total sales boxes, respectively. In addition, the message "The sales tax was 1.05." and your name appear in the lblMessage control. Click the **Exit** button.

Finally, you will modify the btnCalc control's Click event procedure so that it displays a dollar sign and comma (if appropriate) in the total sales amount.

Using the ToString Method to Format Numbers

Numbers representing monetary amounts are usually displayed with either zero or two decimal places and may include a dollar sign and a thousands separator. Similarly, numbers representing percentage amounts are usually displayed with zero or more decimal places and a percent sign. Specifying the number of decimal places and the special characters to display in a number is called **formatting**. In Chapter 2, you learned how to use the Format function to format a number for output as a string. Although you can still use the Format function in Visual Basic 2012, many programmers now use the ToString method because the method can be used in any of the languages built into Visual Studio.

The ToString method's syntax is shown in Figure 3-46. In the syntax, *numericVariableName* is the name of a numeric variable. The **ToString method** formats the number stored in the numeric variable and then returns the result as a string. The *formatString* argument in the syntax specifies the format you want to use. The *formatString* argument must take the form "*Axx*", where *A* is an alphabetic character called the format specifier, and *xx* is a sequence of digits called the precision specifier. The format specifier must be one of the built-in format characters. The most commonly used format characters are listed in Figure 3-46. Notice that you can use either an uppercase letter or a lowercase letter as the format specifier. When used with one of the format characters listed in the figure, the precision specifier controls the number of digits that will appear after the decimal point in the formatted number. Also included in Figure 3-46 are examples of using the ToString method.

Using the ToString Method to Format a Number

Syntax
numericVariableName.**ToString(***formatString***)**

Format specifier (Name)	Description
C or c (Currency)	formats the string with a dollar sign; includes a thousands separator (if appropriate); negative values are enclosed in parentheses
N or n (Number)	similar to the Currency format, but does not include a dollar sign and negative values are preceded by a minus sign
F or f (Fixed-point)	same as the Number format, but does not include a thousands separator
P or p (Percent)	multiplies the numeric variable's value by 100 and formats the result with a percent sign; negative values are preceded by a minus sign

Example 1
```
Dim intPropertyTax As Integer = 1250
lblTax.Text = intPropertyTax.ToString("C2")
```
assigns the string "$1,250.00" to the lblTax control's Text property

Example 2
```
Dim decDue As Decimal = 63.775D
lblDue.Text = decDue.ToString("N2")
```
assigns the string "63.78" to the lblDue control's Text property

Example 3
```
Dim dblRate As Double = .04
lblRate.Text = dblRate.ToString("P0")
```
assigns the string "4 %" to the lblRate control's Text property

Figure 3-46 Syntax and examples of the ToString method

In the Play It Again Movies application, you will display the total sales amount with a dollar sign, thousands separator, and two decimal places.

START HERE

To format the total sales:

1. Return to the Code Editor window. In the btnCalc_Click procedure, change the `lblTotalSales.Text = Convert.ToString(decTotalSales)` statement as follows:

   lblTotalSales.Text = decTotalSales.ToString("C2")

2. Save the solution and then start the application. Type **Kate Hansen** and then press **Enter**. The sales receipt appears.

3. Type **7/20/2014** in the Date box, **4** in the DVDs box, and **10** in the Blu-rays box. Press **Enter** to select the Calculate button. The total sales amount appears with a dollar sign, a thousands separator, and two decimal places. See Figure 3-47.

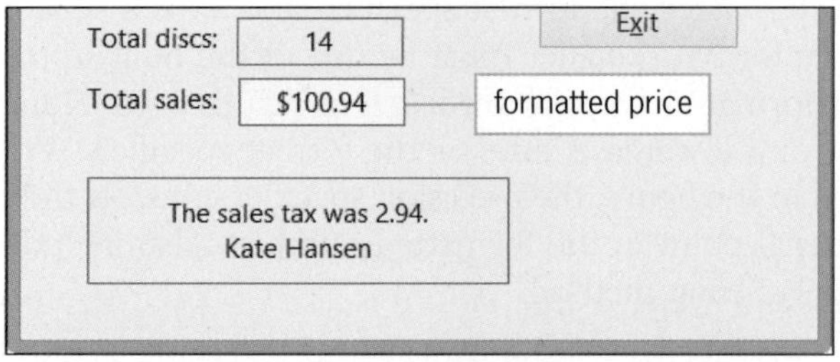

Figure 3-47 Formatted total sales amount shown on the sales receipt

4. Click the **Exit** button. Close the Code Editor window and then close the solution.

Figure 3-48 shows the application's code at the end of Lesson B.

```
' Name:          Play It Again Project
' Purpose:       Calculates the total number
'                of discs sold and the total
'                sales amount
' Programmer:    <your name> on <current date>

Option Explicit On
Option Strict On
Option Infer Off

Public Class frmMain

    ' declare class-level variable
    Private strClerk As String

    Private Sub btnExit_Click(sender As Object,
    e As EventArgs) Handles btnExit.Click
        Me.Close()
    End Sub

    Private Sub btnClear_Click(sender As Object,
    e As EventArgs) Handles btnClear.Click
        ' prepare screen for the next sale

```

Figure 3-48 Play It Again Movies application's code at the end of Lesson B *(continues)*

(*continued*)

```
        txtDvds.Text = String.Empty
        txtBluRays.Text = String.Empty
        lblTotalDiscs.Text = String.Empty
        lblTotalSales.Text = String.Empty
        lblMessage.Text = String.Empty
        ' send the focus to the DVDs box
        txtDvds.Focus()

    End Sub

    Private Sub btnPrint_Click(sender As Object,
    e As EventArgs) Handles btnPrint.Click
        ' print the sales receipt

        Me.Width = Me.Width - 165
        PrintForm1.PrintAction =
            Printing.PrintAction.PrintToPreview
        PrintForm1.Print()
        Me.Width = Me.Width + 165

    End Sub

    Private Sub btnCalc_Click(sender As Object,
    e As EventArgs) Handles btnCalc.Click
        ' calculate number of discs sold and total sales

        Const decDISC_PRICE As Decimal = 7D
        Const decTAX_RATE As Decimal = 0.03D
        Dim intDvds As Integer
        Dim intBluRays As Integer
        Dim intTotalDiscs As Integer
        Dim decSubtotal As Decimal
        Dim decSalesTax As Decimal
        Dim decTotalSales As Decimal

        ' calculate total number of discs sold
        Integer.TryParse(txtDvds.Text, intDvds)
        Integer.TryParse(txtBluRays.Text, intBluRays)
        intTotalDiscs = intDvds + intBluRays

        ' calculate the subtotal
        decSubtotal = intTotalDiscs * decDISC_PRICE

        ' calculate the sales tax
        decSalesTax = decSubtotal * decTAX_RATE

        ' calculate the total sales
        decTotalSales = decSubtotal + decSalesTax

        ' display total amounts
        lblTotalDiscs.Text = Convert.ToString(intTotalDiscs)
        lblTotalSales.Text = decTotalSales.ToString("C2")

        ' display tax and salesclerk's name
        lblMessage.Text = "The sales tax was " &
            Convert.ToString(decSalesTax) & "." &
            ControlChars.NewLine & strClerk

    End Sub

```

Figure 3-48 Play It Again Movies application's code at the end of Lesson B *(continues)*

(*continued*)

```
    Private Sub frmMain_Load(sender As Object,
    e As EventArgs) Handles Me.Load
        ' gets the salesclerk's name

        Const strPROMPT As String = "Salesclerk's name:"
        Const strTITLE As String = "Name Entry"
        ' assign the name to the class-level variable
        strClerk = InputBox(strPROMPT, strTITLE)

    End Sub
End Class
```

Figure 3-48 Play It Again Movies application's code at the end of Lesson B

Lesson B Summary

- To concatenate strings:

  Use the concatenation operator (&). Be sure to include a space before and after the ampersand.

- To display an input dialog box:

  Use the InputBox function. The function's syntax is **InputBox(***prompt*[, *title*] [, *defaultResponse*]**)**. The *prompt, title,* and *defaultResponse* arguments can be string literal constants, String named constants, or String variables. Use sentence capitalization for the prompt, but book title capitalization for the title.

  If the user clicks the OK button, the InputBox function returns the value contained in the input area of the dialog box. The return value is always treated as a string. If the user clicks either the dialog box's Cancel button or its Close button, the InputBox function returns an empty string.

- To advance the insertion point to the next line:

  Use the ControlChars.NewLine constant in code.

- To break up a long instruction into two or more physical lines in the Code Editor window:

  Break the line after a comma, after an opening parenthesis, before a closing parenthesis, or after an operator (arithmetic, assignment, comparison, logical, or concatenation). You also can use the line continuation character, which is an underscore (_). The line continuation character must be immediately preceded by a space and appear at the end of a physical line of code.

- To make a button the default button:

  Set the form's AcceptButton property to the name of the button.

- To format a number for output as a string:

  Use the ToString method. The method's syntax is *numericVariableName***.ToString(***formatString***)**.

Lesson B Key Terms

&—the concatenation operator

Concatenation operator—the ampersand (&); used to concatenate strings; must be both preceded and followed by a space character

ControlChars.NewLine constant—used to advance the insertion point to the next line

Default button—a button that can be selected by pressing the Enter key even when the button does not have the focus

Formatting—specifying the number of decimal places and the special characters to display in a number

InputBox function—a Visual Basic function that displays an input dialog box containing a message, OK and Cancel buttons, and an input area

Line continuation character—an underscore that is immediately preceded by a space and located at the end of a physical line of code; used to split a long instruction into two or more physical lines in the Code Editor window

Load event—an event associated with a form; occurs when the application is started and the form is displayed the first time

ToString method—formats a number stored in a numeric variable and then returns the result as a string

Lesson B Review Questions

1. The name of a form's default button is specified in the ____________ property.
   a. button's AcceptButton
   b. button's DefaultButton
   c. form's AcceptButton
   d. form's DefaultButton

2. The InputBox function displays a dialog box containing which of the following?
   a. input area
   b. OK and Cancel buttons
   c. prompt
   d. all of the above

3. Which of the following is the concatenation operator?
   a. @
   b. &
   c. $
   d. #

4. Which of the following Visual Basic constants advances the insertion point to the next line?
   a. Advance
   b. ControlChars.Advance
   c. ControlChars.NewLine
   d. none of the above

5. The `strWord1` and `strWord2` variables contain the strings "Input" and "Box", respectively. Which of the following will display the string "InputBox" (one word) in the lblWord control?

   a. `lblWord.Text = strWord1 & strWord2`

   b. `lblWord.Text = "strWord1 " & "strWord2 "`

   c. `lblWord.Text = strWord1 @ strWord2`

   d. `lblWord.Text = strWord1 # strWord2`

6. The `strCity` and `strState` variables contain the strings "Tampa" and "Florida", respectively. Which of the following will display the string "Tampa, Florida" (the city, a comma, a space, and the state) in the lblCityState control?

   a. `lblCityState.Text = strCity , & strState`

   b. `lblCityState.Text = strCity & "," & strState`

   c. `lblCityState.Text = "strCity" & ", " & "strState"`

   d. none of the above

7. Which of the following statements correctly assigns the InputBox function's return value to a Double variable named `dblNum`?

   a.
   ```
   Double.TryParse(InputBox(strMSG,
          "Number"), dblNum)
   ```

   b.
   ```
   dblNum = Double.TryParse(
          InputBox(strMSG, "Number"))
   ```

   c. `dblNum = InputBox(strMSG, "Number")`

   d.
   ```
   TryParse.Double(InputBox(strMSG,
          "Number"), dblNum)
   ```

8. Which of the following statements correctly assigns the InputBox function's return value to a String variable named `strCity`?

   a.
   ```
   String.TryParse(InputBox(strMSG,
          "City"), strCity)
   ```

   b.
   ```
   strCity = String.TryParse(
          InputBox(strMSG, "City"))
   ```

   c. `strCity = InputBox(strMSG, "City")`

   d. none of the above

9. The InputBox function's prompt argument should be entered using ______________.

   a. book title capitalization

   b. sentence capitalization

10. If the `decPay` variable contains the number 1200.76, which of the following statements displays the number as $1,200.76?

    a. `lblPay.Text = decPay.ToString("N2")`

    b. `lblPay.Text = decPay.ToString("F2")`

    c. `lblPay.Text = decPay.ToString("D2")`

    d. `lblPay.Text = decPay.ToString("C2")`

Lesson B Exercises

1. The `strFirst` and `strLast` variables contain the strings "Dolly" and "Pershing", respectively. Write an assignment statement to display the string "Pershing, Dolly" in the lblName control. INTRODUCTORY

2. The `strCity` variable contains the string "Bowling Green". Write an assignment statement to display the string "Our office is in Bowling Green, KY." in the lblMsg control. INTRODUCTORY

3. In this exercise, you modify the Play It Again Movies application from this lesson. Use Windows to make a copy of the Play It Again Solution folder. Rename the copy Modified Play It Again Solution. Open the Play It Again Solution (Play It Again Solution.sln) file contained in the Modified Play It Again Solution folder. Open the designer window. Modify the btnCalc control's Click event procedure so that it displays the sales tax amount with a dollar sign, two decimal places, and a thousands separator (if necessary). Save the solution and then start and test the application. Close the Code Editor window and then close the solution. INTRODUCTORY

4. Open the Gross Pay Solution (Gross Pay Solution.sln) file contained in the VB2012\Chap03\Gross Pay Solution folder. If necessary, open the designer window. The application calculates and displays an employee's gross pay. Make the Calculate button the default button. Open the Code Editor window and enter the three Option statements in the General Declarations section. Review the code in the Calculate button's Click event procedure. Modify the procedure's code to use variables. (Do not use the Val function.) Use the ToString method to display the gross pay amount with a dollar sign, two decimal places, and a thousands separator (if necessary). Save the solution and then start the application. Test the application by calculating the gross pay for an employee working 35 hours at $9.75 per hour. Close the Code Editor window and then close the solution. INTRODUCTORY

5. The `strFirst`, `strMiddle`, `strLast`, and `strNickname` variables contain the strings "Karl", "G.", "Perillo", and "KG", respectively. Write an assignment statement that will display the string "My name is Karl G. Perillo, but you can call me KG." in the lblMsg control. INTERMEDIATE

6. Open the Fairmont Solution (Fairmont Solution.sln) file contained in the VB2012\Chap03\Fairmont Solution folder. If necessary, open the designer window. The application allows the sales manager to enter the sales made in three states. It then calculates and displays both the total sales made and the total commission earned in the three states. INTERMEDIATE

   a. Make the Calculate button the default button.

   b. Enter the appropriate Option statements in the Code Editor window.

   c. Code the Exit button so that it ends the application when it is clicked.

   d. Use the pseudocode shown in Figure 3-49 to code the Calculate button's Click event procedure. Be sure to use variables. (Do not use the Val function.) The commission rate is 3%. Use the ToString method to display a thousands separator (if necessary) and two decimal places in the total sales and commission amounts.

   e. Save the solution and then start the application. Test the application by calculating the total sales and commission for the following amounts: Illinois sales of 36000, Indiana sales of 34500, and Alaska sales of 23675.

   f. Close the Code Editor window and then close the solution.

```
btnCalc Click event procedure
1. calculate total sales = Illinois sales + Indiana sales + Alaska sales
2. calculate commission = total sales * commission rate
3. display total sales and commission in lblTotalSales and lblTotalComm
4. send the focus to the txtIll control
```

Figure 3-49 Pseudocode for Exercise 6

INTERMEDIATE

7. In this exercise, you modify the Fairmont application from Exercise 6. Use Windows to make a copy of the Fairmont Solution folder. Rename the copy Modified Fairmont Solution. Open the Fairmont Solution (Fairmont Solution.sln) file contained in the Modified Fairmont Solution folder. Open the designer window. Code the form's Load event procedure so that it uses the InputBox function to ask the user for the commission rate before the form appears. Modify the code in the btnCalc control's Click event procedure so that it uses the commission rate entered by the user. Save the solution and then start the application. When you are prompted to enter the commission rate, type .1 (the decimal equivalent of 10%) and then click the OK button. Test the application using 56000 as the Illinois sales, 64000 as the Indiana sales, and 39000 as the Alaska sales. Close the Code Editor window and then close the solution.

INTERMEDIATE

8. Open the Turner Solution (Turner Solution.sln) file contained in the VB2012\Chap03\Turner Solution folder. If necessary, open the designer window. The application calculates the new hourly pay for each of three job codes, given the current hourly pay for each job code and the raise percentage (entered as a decimal number). The application should display the message "Raise percentage: *XX*" in a label control on the form. The *XX* in the message should be replaced by the actual raise percentage.

   a. Code the Exit button so that it ends the application when it is clicked.

   b. Before the form appears, use the InputBox function to prompt the personnel clerk to enter the raise percentage in decimal form. You will use the raise percentage to calculate the new hourly pay for each job code.

   c. Use the pseudocode shown in Figure 3-50 to code the Calculate button's Click event procedure. Be sure to use variables. (Do not use the Val function.) Create a named constant for the "Raise percentage:" message. Format the new hourly pay amounts using the "N2" *formatString*. Format the raise rate (in the message) using the "P0" *formatString*.

   d. Save the solution and then start the application. When you are prompted to enter the raise percentage, type .05 (the decimal equivalent of 5%) and then click the OK button. Use the following information to calculate the new hourly pay for each job code:

Current hourly pay for job code 1:	5
Current hourly pay for job code 2:	6.5
Current hourly pay for job code 3:	8.75

   e. Close the Code Editor window and then close the solution.

```
btnCalc Click event procedure
1. calculate each new hourly pay = current hourly pay * raise rate + current hourly pay
2. display the new hourly pays in the appropriate label controls
3. display the message and raise rate in the lblMessage control
4. send the focus to the txtCurrent1 control
```


Figure 3-50 Pseudocode for Exercise 8

INTERMEDIATE

9. Create a Visual Basic Windows application. Use the following names for the solution and project, respectively: Red Lion Solution and Red Lion Project. Save the application in the VB2012\Chap03 folder. Change the form file's name to Main Form.vb. Change the form's name to frmMain. The application's interface should allow the owner of the Red Lion photo studio to enter the studio's quarterly sales amount. The application should display the amount of state, county, and city sales tax the studio must pay. It also should display the total sales tax. The sales tax rates for the state, county, and city are 3%, 1%, and 0.5%, respectively. Be sure to use variables. (Do not use the Val function.) Use the ToString method to display a thousands separator (if necessary) and two decimal places in each of the sales tax amounts. Also include a dollar sign in the total sales tax amount. Save the solution and then start and test the application. Close the Code Editor window and then close the solution.

INTERMEDIATE

10. Create a Visual Basic Windows application. Use the following names for the solution and project, respectively: Martin Motors Solution and Martin Motors Project. Save the application in the VB2012\Chap03 folder. Change the form file's name to Main Form.vb. Change the form's name to frmMain. Jerry Martin of Martin Motors wants an application that allows him to enter the annual sales made at each of three dealerships. The application should calculate the total annual sales and also the percentage that each dealership contributed to the total annual sales. Save the solution and then start and test the application. Close the Code Editor window and then close the solution.

ADVANCED

11. In this exercise, you modify the Turner application from Exercise 8. The modified application will allow the user to enter a separate raise percentage for each job code. Use Windows to make a copy of the Turner Solution folder. Rename the copy Modified Turner Solution. Open the Turner Solution (Turner Solution.sln) file contained in the Modified Turner Solution folder. Open the designer window.

    a. Modify the application's code so that it asks the personnel clerk to enter the raise for each job code separately. Display the following information on separate lines in the lblMessage control. Be sure to replace the *XX* in each line with the appropriate raise percentage. (You may need to change the size of the form and/or lblMessage control.)

       Job Code 1: XX %
       Job Code 2: XX %
       Job Code 3: XX %

b. Save the solution and then start the application. When you are prompted to enter the raise percentages for the job codes, use .03 for job code 1, .05 for job code 2, and .04 for job code 3. Use the following information to calculate the new hourly pay for each job code:

Current hourly pay for job code 1:	5
Current hourly pay for job code 2:	6.5
Current hourly pay for job code 3:	8.75

c. Close the Code Editor window and then close the solution.

DISCOVERY

12. In this exercise, you learn about the CancelButton property of a Windows form. Open the Cancel Solution (Cancel Solution.sln) file contained in the VB2012\Chap03\Cancel Solution folder.

a. Open the Code Editor window and review the existing code. Start the application. Type your first name in the text box and then press Enter to select the Clear button, which is the form's default button. The Clear button removes your name from the text box. Click the Undo button. Your name reappears in the text box. Click the Exit button.

b. Return to the designer window. Set the form's CancelButton property to btnUndo. Doing this tells the computer to process the code in the Undo button's Click event procedure when the user presses the Esc key. Save the solution and then start the application. Type your first name in the text box and then press Enter to select the Clear button. Press Esc to select the Undo button. Your name reappears in the text box. Close the Code Editor window and then close the solution.

LESSON C

After studying Lesson C, you should be able to:

- Include a static variable in code
- Code the TextChanged event procedure
- Create a procedure that handles more than one event

Modifying the Load and Click Event Procedures

Currently, the Play It Again Movies application allows the user to enter the salesclerk's name only when the application first starts. In this lesson you will modify the code so that it asks for the name each time the Calculate button is clicked. This will allow another salesclerk to enter his or her name on the sales receipt without having to start the application again.

As you learned in Lesson B, you should review an application's documentation and revise the necessary documents before making modifications to the code. Figure 3-51 shows the revised TOE chart. Changes made to the TOE chart from Lesson B are shaded in the figure. Notice that the Calculate button's Click event procedure, rather than the form's Load event procedure, is now responsible for getting the salesclerk's name.

Task	Object	Event
1. Get the salesclerk's name 2. Calculate total discs sold and total sales amount 3. Display total discs sold and total sales amount in lblTotalDiscs and lblTotalSales 4. Calculate the sales tax 5. Display sales tax and salesclerk's name in lblMessage	btnCalc	Click
Print the sales receipt	btnPrint	Click
End the application	btnExit	Click
Clear screen for the next sale	btnClear	Click
Display total discs sold (from btnCalc)	lblTotalDiscs	None
Display total sales amount (from btnCalc)	lblTotalSales	None
Get and display the sales information	txtDate, txtDvds, txtBluRays	None
~~Get the salesclerk's name~~	~~frmMain~~	~~Load~~
Display sales tax and salesclerk's name (from btnCalc)	lblMessage	None

Figure 3-51 Revised TOE chart for the Play It Again Movies application in Lesson C

Figure 3-52 shows the revised pseudocode for the Calculate button's Click event procedure. Changes made to the pseudocode from Lesson B are shaded in the figure.

```
btnCalc Click event procedure
1. get the salesclerk's name
2. calculate total discs sold = DVDs sold + Blu-rays sold
3. calculate subtotal = total discs sold * disc price
4. calculate sales tax = subtotal * sales tax rate
5. calculate total sales = subtotal + sales tax
6. display total discs sold and total sales in lblTotalDiscs and lblTotalSales
7. display sales tax and salesclerk's name in lblMessage
```

Figure 3-52 Revised pseudocode for the Calculate button in Lesson C

First, you will open the Play It Again Movies application from Lesson B. You then will move the code contained in the form's Load event procedure to the btnCalc control's Click event procedure.

START HERE

To open the Play It Again Movies application and then move some of the code:

1. If necessary, start Visual Studio 2012. Open the Play It Again Solution (Play It Again Solution.sln) file from Lesson B. The file is contained in the VB2012\Chap03\Play It Again Solution folder. If necessary, open the designer window.
2. Open the Code Editor window. Locate the form's Load event procedure, and then highlight the two Const statements in the procedure. Press **Ctrl+x** to cut the two Const statements from the procedure.
3. Locate the btnCalc_Click procedure. Click the **blank line** above the first Const statement in the procedure, and then press **Enter** to insert a new blank line. With the insertion point in the new blank line, press **Ctrl+v**. The two Const statements that you cut from the Load event procedure now appear in the Click event procedure. (Don't be concerned about the jagged green lines that appear below the two Const statements. The lines will disappear when you use the constants in another statement within the procedure.)
4. Return to the form's Load event procedure. Highlight the second comment and the assignment statement. Press **Ctrl+x** to remove the comment and the assignment statement from the procedure.
5. Return to the btnCalc_Click procedure. Click the **blank line** below the last Dim statement, and then press **Enter** to insert a new blank line. With the insertion point in the new blank line, press **Ctrl+v**. The comment and assignment statement that you cut from the Load event procedure now appear in the Click event procedure. Press **Enter** to insert a new blank line below the assignment statement, and then delete the `class-level` text from the comment.
6. Return to the form's Load event procedure and then delete the entire procedure from the Code Editor window.

Now that you have moved the InputBox function from the form's Load event procedure to the btnCalc_Click procedure, only one procedure—the btnCalc_Click procedure—needs to use the `strClerk` variable. Therefore, you should change the variable from a class-level variable to a procedure-level variable. You can do this by moving the variable's declaration statement from the form's Declarations section to the btnCalc_Click procedure. In addition, you will need to change the keyword in the declaration statement from `Private` to `Dim`. Recall that you use the `Private` keyword to declare class-level variables, but you use the `Dim` keyword to declare procedure-level variables.

To move the declaration statement and then modify it:

START HERE

1. Delete the `' declare class-level variable` comment from the form's Declarations section. Highlight the `Private strClerk As String` statement, and then press **Ctrl+x** to cut the statement from the Declarations section.
2. Click the **blank line** below the last Dim statement in the btnCalc_Click procedure. Press **Ctrl+v** to paste the Private statement in the procedure, and then press **Enter** to insert a blank line below the statement.
3. The jagged blue line below the `Private` keyword indicates that the statement contains a syntax error. Rest your mouse pointer on the `Private` keyword. The error message indicates that the `Private` keyword is not valid on a local variable declaration. Change `Private` in the variable declaration statement to **Dim**.
4. Save the solution and then start the application. Click the **Calculate** button. Type your name in the Name Entry dialog box and then press **Enter**. The message "The sales tax was 0.00." and your name appear in the lblMessage control.
5. Click the **Calculate** button again. Notice that the Name Entry dialog box requires the user to enter the salesclerk's name again. It would be more efficient for the user if the salesclerk's name appeared as the default response the second and subsequent times the Calculate button is clicked.
6. Click the **Cancel** button in the dialog box. The InputBox function returns an empty string, so no name appears in the lblMessage control. Click the **Exit** button.

To display the salesclerk's name in the dialog box when the Calculate button is clicked the second and subsequent times, you can declare the `strClerk` variable as either a class-level variable or a static variable, and then use the variable as the *defaultResponse* argument in the InputBox function. In this case, a static variable is a better choice because static variables have a lesser (more restrictive) scope than class-level variables. Recall that a static variable is really just a special type of procedure-level variable. As you learned in Lesson A, fewer unintentional errors occur in applications when variables are declared using the minimum scope needed. In this case, the minimum scope required for the `strClerk` variable is procedure scope because only one procedure needs to use the variable.

To declare the strClerk variable as a static variable and then modify the InputBox function:

START HERE

1. In the btnCalc_Click procedure, change the `Dim` in the `Dim strClerk As String` statement to **Static**.
2. Now change the statement that contains the InputBox function as follows, and then click the **blank line** below the statement:

   strClerk = InputBox(strPROMPT, strTITLE, strClerk)
3. Save the solution and then start the application. Type **1/25/2014** in the Date box, **5** in the DVDs box, and **3** in the Blu-rays box. Press **Enter**. Type your name in the Name Entry dialog box and then press **Enter**. The application calculates and displays the total discs sold (8) and total sales ($57.68). In addition, the message "The sales tax was 1.68." and your name appear in the lblMessage control.
4. Change the number of DVDs sold to **2**. At this point, the calculated amounts on the sales receipt are incorrect because they do not reflect the change in the number of DVDs sold. To display the correct amounts, you will need to recalculate the amounts by selecting the Calculate button. Press **Enter** to select the Calculate button. Your name appears highlighted in the input area of the Name Entry dialog box.

5. Press **Enter** to select the dialog box's OK button. The application calculates and displays the total discs sold (5) and total sales ($36.05). The message "The sales tax was 1.05." and your name appear in the lblMessage control. Click the **Exit** button.

Having the previously calculated amounts remain on the screen when a change is made to the interface could be misleading. A better approach is to clear the amounts when a change is made to either the number of DVDs sold or the number of Blu-rays sold.

Coding the TextChanged Event Procedure

A control's **TextChanged event** occurs when a change is made to the contents of the control's Text property. This can happen as a result of either the user entering data into the control or the application's code assigning data to the control's Text property. In the next set of steps, you will code the txtDvds_TextChanged event procedure so that it clears the contents of the lblTotalDiscs, lblTotalSales, and lblMessage controls when the user changes the number of DVDs sold.

START HERE

To code the txtDvds_TextChanged event procedure:

1. Open the code template for the txtDvds control's TextChanged event procedure. Type the following comment and then press **Enter** twice.

   ' clears the total discs, total sales, and message

2. Enter the following three assignment statements:

   lblTotalDiscs.Text = String.Empty
   lblTotalSales.Text = String.Empty
   lblMessage.Text = String.Empty

3. Save the solution and then start the application. Type **1/25/2014** in the Date box, **5** in the DVDs box, and **3** in the Blu-rays box. Press **Enter**. Type your name in the Name Entry dialog box and then press **Enter**. The application calculates and displays the total discs sold (8), total sales ($57.68), and sales tax (1.68).
4. Change the number of DVDs sold to **2**. When you make this change, the txtDvds_TextChanged procedure clears the total discs sold, total sales, and message information from the form. Click the **Exit** button.

Recall that you also want to clear the calculated amounts when a change is made to the number of Blu-rays sold. You could code the TextChanged event procedure for the txtBluRays control separately, as you did with the txtDvds control. However, you also can create one procedure for the computer to process when the TextChanged event of either of the two controls occurs.

Associating a Procedure with Different Objects and Events

The `Handles` clause in an event procedure's header indicates the object and event associated with the procedure. The Handles clause in Figure 3-53, for example, indicates that the procedure is associated with the TextChanged event of the txtDvds control. As a result, the procedure will be processed when the txtDvds control's TextChanged event occurs.

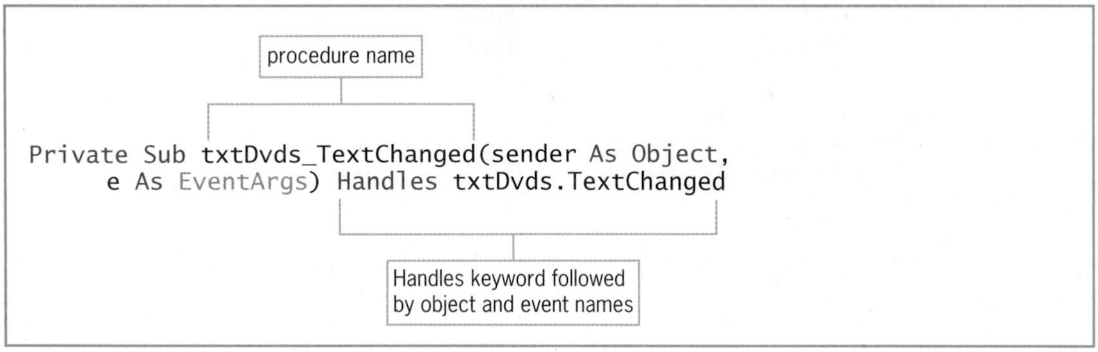

Figure 3-53 TextChanged event procedure associated with the txtDvds control

Although an event procedure's name contains the names of its associated object and event, separated by an underscore, that is not a requirement. You can change the name of an event procedure to almost anything you like, as long as the name follows the same rules for naming variables. Unlike variable names, however, procedure names are usually entered using **Pascal case**, which means you capitalize the first letter in the name and the first letter of each subsequent word in the name. For example, you can change the name of the procedure in Figure 3-53 from txtDvds_TextChanged to ClearLabels and the procedure will still work correctly. This is because the Handles clause, rather than the event procedure's name, determines when the procedure is invoked.

You can associate a procedure with more than one object and event, as long as each event contains the same parameters in its procedure header. To do so, you list each object and event in the procedure's Handles clause. You separate the object and event with a period, like this: *object.event.* You use a comma to separate each *object.event* from the next *object.event.* In the next set of steps, you will change the name of the txtDvds_TextChanged procedure to ClearLabels. You then will associate the ClearLabels procedure with the txtDvds.TextChanged and txtBluRays.TextChanged events.

START HERE

To change the procedure's name and then associate the procedure with different objects and events:

1. Change `txtDvds_TextChanged`, which appears after Private Sub in the procedure header, to **ClearLabels**.
2. In the ClearLabels procedure header, click **immediately before the letter H** in the keyword `Handles`. Type _ (an underscore, which is the line continuation character). Be sure there is a space between the ending parenthesis and the underscore.
3. Press **Enter** to move the Handles clause to the next line in the procedure.
4. Click **immediately after TextChanged** in the Handles clause. The ClearLabels procedure is already associated with the txtDvds.TextChanged event. You just need to associate it with the txtBluRays.TextChanged event. Type **,** (a comma). Scroll the list of object names until you see txtBluRays. Click **txtBluRays** in the list, and then press **Tab** to enter the object name in the Handles clause.
5. Type **.** (a period). Scroll the list of event names (if necessary) until you see TextChanged. Click **TextChanged** and then press **Tab**. Figure 3-54 shows the completed ClearLabels procedure.

line continuation character

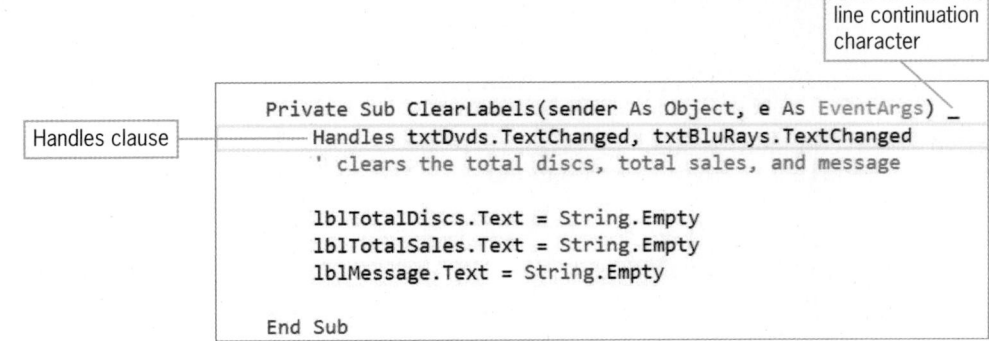

Handles clause

```
Private Sub ClearLabels(sender As Object, e As EventArgs) _
    Handles txtDvds.TextChanged, txtBluRays.TextChanged
    ' clears the total discs, total sales, and message

    lblTotalDiscs.Text = String.Empty
    lblTotalSales.Text = String.Empty
    lblMessage.Text = String.Empty

End Sub
```

Figure 3-54 Completed ClearLabels procedure

6. Save the solution and then start the application. Type **8/8/2014** in the Date box, **5** in the DVDs box, and **3** in the Blu-rays box. Press **Enter**. Type your name in the Name Entry dialog box and then press **Enter**. The application calculates and displays the total discs sold (8), total sales ($57.68), and sales tax (1.68).
7. Change the number of DVDs sold to **2**. The ClearLabels procedure clears the total discs sold, total sales, and message information from the form.
8. Press **Enter** to select the Calculate button, and then press **Enter** to select the OK button in the Name Entry dialog box. The application calculates and displays the total discs sold (5), total sales ($36.05), and sales tax (1.05).
9. Change the number of Blu-rays sold to **4**. The ClearLabels procedure clears the total discs sold, total sales, and message information from the form.
10. Press **Enter** to select the Calculate button. Type **Sarah Wilson** in the Name Entry dialog box, and then press **Enter** to select the OK button. The application calculates and displays the total discs sold (6), total sales ($43.26), and sales tax (1.26). See Figure 3-55.

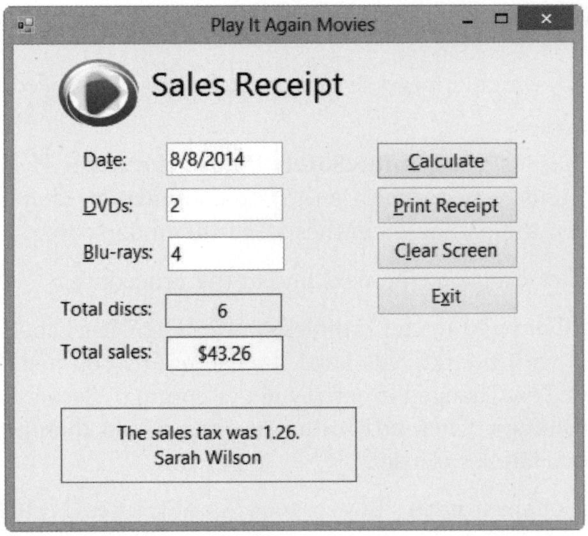

Figure 3-55 Completed Sales Receipt

OpenClipArt.org/John Diamond / diamonjohn

11. Click the **Exit** button. Close the Code Editor window and then close the solution.

Figure 3-56 shows the application's code at the end of Lesson C.

```
' Name:         Play It Again Project
' Purpose:      Calculates the total number
'               of discs sold and the total
'               sales amount
' Programmer:   <your name> on <current date>

Option Explicit On
Option Strict On
Option Infer Off

Public Class frmMain

   Private Sub btnExit_Click(sender As Object,
   e As EventArgs) Handles btnExit.Click
       Me.Close()
   End Sub

   Private Sub btnClear_Click(sender As Object,
   e As EventArgs) Handles btnClear.Click
       ' prepare screen for the next sale

       txtDvds.Text = String.Empty
       txtBluRays.Text = String.Empty
       lblTotalDiscs.Text = String.Empty
       lblTotalSales.Text = String.Empty
       lblMessage.Text = String.Empty
       ' send the focus to the DVDs box
       txtDvds.Focus()

   End Sub

   Private Sub btnPrint_Click(sender As Object,
   e As EventArgs) Handles btnPrint.Click
       ' print the sales receipt

       Me.Width = Me.Width - 165
       PrintForm1.PrintAction =
         Printing.PrintAction.PrintToPreview
       PrintForm1.Print()
       Me.Width = Me.Width + 165

   End Sub

   Private Sub btnCalc_Click(sender As Object,
   e As EventArgs) Handles btnCalc.Click
       ' calculate number of discs sold and total sales

       Const strPROMPT As String = "Salesclerk's name:"
       Const strTITLE As String = "Name Entry"
       Const decDISC_PRICE As Decimal = 7D
```

Figure 3-56 Play It Again Movies application's code at the end of Lesson C *(continues)*

(continued)

```
        Const decTAX_RATE As Decimal = 0.03D
        Dim intDvds As Integer
        Dim intBluRays As Integer
        Dim intTotalDiscs As Integer
        Dim decSubtotal As Decimal
        Dim decSalesTax As Decimal
        Dim decTotalSales As Decimal
        Static strClerk As String

        ' assign the name to the variable
        strClerk = InputBox(strPROMPT, strTITLE, strClerk)

        ' calculate total number of discs sold
        Integer.TryParse(txtDvds.Text, intDvds)
        Integer.TryParse(txtBluRays.Text, intBluRays)
        intTotalDiscs = intDvds + intBluRays

        ' calculate the subtotal
        decSubtotal = intTotalDiscs * decDISC_PRICE

        ' calculate the sales tax
        decSalesTax = decSubtotal * decTAX_RATE

        ' calculate the total sales
        decTotalSales = decSubtotal + decSalesTax

        ' display total amounts
        lblTotalDiscs.Text = Convert.ToString(intTotalDiscs)
        lblTotalSales.Text = decTotalSales.ToString("C2")

        ' display tax and salesclerk's name
        lblMessage.Text = "The sales tax was " &
            Convert.ToString(decSalesTax) & "." &
            ControlChars.NewLine & strClerk

    End Sub

    Private Sub ClearLabels(sender As Object, e As EventArgs) _
        Handles txtDvds.TextChanged, txtBluRays.TextChanged
        ' clears the total discs, total sales, and message

        lblTotalDiscs.Text = String.Empty
        lblTotalSales.Text = String.Empty
        lblMessage.Text = String.Empty

    End Sub
End Class
```

Figure 3-56 Play It Again Movies application's code at the end of Lesson C

Lesson C Summary

- To create a procedure-level variable that retains its value until the application ends:

  Declare the variable in a procedure, using the `Static` keyword. The variable will remain in memory until the application ends.

- To process code when a change is made to the contents of a control's Text property:

  Enter the code in the control's TextChanged event procedure.

- To associate a procedure with more than one object or event:

  List each object and event (using the syntax *object.event*) after the `Handles` keyword in the procedure header. Use a comma to separate each object and event from the previous object and event.

Lesson C Key Terms

Pascal case—used when entering procedure names; the process of capitalizing the first letter in the name and the first letter of each subsequent word in the name

TextChanged event—occurs when a change is made to the contents of a control's Text property

Lesson C Review Questions

1. Which of the following events occurs when a change is made to the contents of a text box?
   a. Change
   b. Changed
   c. TextChanged
   d. TextChange

2. A ______________ variable is a procedure-level variable that retains its value after the procedure in which it is declared ends.
   a. constant
   b. static
   c. stationary
   d. term

3. Which of the following clauses associates a procedure with the TextChanged event of the txtMid and txtFinal controls?
   a. `Associates txtMid_TextChanged, txtFinal_TextChanged`
   b. `Handled txtMid_TextChanged, txtFinal_TextChanged`
   c. `Controls txtMid.TextChanged And txtFinal.TextChanged`
   d. `Handles txtMid.TextChanged, txtFinal.TextChanged`

4. Which of the following statements declares a procedure-level variable that is removed from the computer's memory when the procedure ends?
   a. `Const intCounter As Integer`
   b. `Dim intCounter As Integer`
   c. `Local intCounter As Integer`
   d. `Static intCounter As Integer`

5. Which of the following statements declares a procedure-level variable that retains its value after the procedure in which it is declared ends?
   a. `Const intCounter As Integer`
   b. `Dim intCounter As Constant`
   c. `Dim intCounter As Integer`
   d. `Static intCounter As Integer`

Lesson C Exercises

INTRODUCTORY

1. Open the CityState Solution (CityState Solution.sln) file contained in the VB2012\Chap03\CityState Solution folder. Code the form's Load event procedure so that it uses two InputBox functions to prompt the user to enter the name of a city and the name of a state. Assign the results of both functions to variables. Code the Display button's Click event procedure so that it displays the city name followed by a comma, a space, and the state name in the lblCityState control. Save the solution and then start and test the application. Close the Code Editor window and then close the solution.

INTRODUCTORY

2. In this exercise, you create an application that converts American dollars to the Euro, the Swiss franc, and the South African rand. Create a Visual Basic Windows application. Use the following names for the solution and project, respectively: Converter Solution and Converter Project. Save the application in the VB2012\Chap03 folder. Change the form file's name to Main Form.vb. Change the form's name to frmMain. Create the interface shown in Figure 3-57. Make the Convert button the default button. Code the application appropriately. Use the Internet to determine the appropriate conversion rates. Be sure to use variables in your code. (Do not use the Val function.) The calculated amounts should be displayed with two decimal places. Clear the calculated amounts when a change is made to the number of dollars. Save the solution and then start and test the application. Close the Code Editor window and then close the solution.

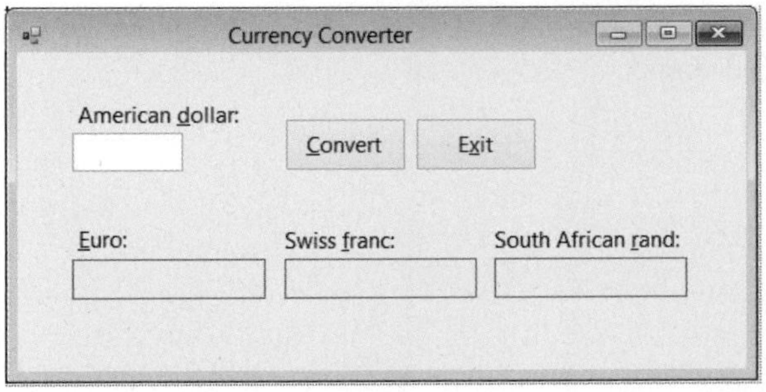

Figure 3-57 Interface for Exercise 2

INTERMEDIATE

3. In this exercise, you create an application that allows your friend Miranda to enter the number of pennies she has in a jar. The application should calculate the number of dollars, quarters, dimes, nickels, and pennies she will receive when she cashes in the pennies at a bank. Create a Visual Basic Windows application. Use the following names for the solution and project, respectively: Pennies Solution and Pennies Project. Save the application in the VB2012\Chap03 folder. Change the form file's name to Main Form.vb. Change the form's name to frmMain. Create the interface shown in Figure 3-58. Make the Calculate button the default button. Code the application appropriately. (It might be helpful to review the information in Figures 2-34 and 2-35 in Chapter 2.) Clear the calculated amounts when a change is made to the number of pennies entered by the user. Save the solution and then start the application. Test the application twice, using the following data: 706 pennies and 533 pennies. Close the Code Editor window and then close the solution.

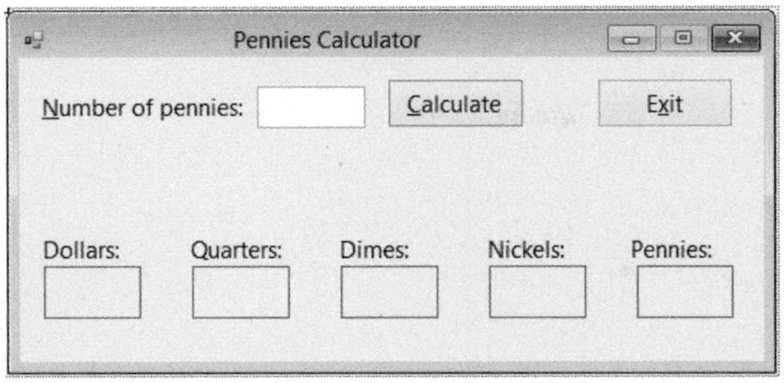

Figure 3-58 Interface for Exercise 3

4. Create a Visual Basic Windows application. Use the following names for the solution and project, respectively: Car Solution and Car Project. Save the application in the VB2012\Chap03 folder. Change the form file's name to Main Form.vb. Change the form's name to frmMain. The application's interface should allow the user to enter his or her monthly car expenses. The expenses should include the loan payment, insurance payment, oil change, maintenance, car washes, and gas. You will need a text box for each individual expense for each month. The application should calculate and display each month's total expenses, as well as the total expenses for the year. Save the solution and then start and test the application.

INTERMEDIATE

5. Create a Visual Basic Windows application. Use the following names for the solution and project, respectively: Credit Card Solution and Credit Card Project. Save the application in the VB2012\Chap03 folder. Change the form file's name to Main Form.vb. Change the form's name to frmMain. Create an interface that allows the user to enter the total monthly amount charged to his or her credit card for the following five categories of expenses: Merchandise, Restaurants, Gasoline, Travel/Entertainment, Services, and Supermarkets. The application should calculate and display each month's total charges, as well as the total annual amount he or she charged. The application also should calculate and display the percentage that each category contributed to the total annual amount charged. Save the solution and then start and test the application.

INTERMEDIATE

6. In this exercise, you create an application that can help students in grades 1 through 6 learn how to make change. The application should allow the student to enter the amount of money a customer owes and the amount of money the customer paid. It then should calculate the amount of change, as well as the number of dollars, quarters, dimes, nickels, and pennies to return to the customer. For now, you do not have to worry about the situation where the amount owed is greater than the amount paid. You can assume that the customer pays either the exact amount or more than the exact amount. Create a Visual Basic Windows application. Use the following names for the solution, project, and form file, respectively: Change Solution, Change Project, and Main Form.vb. Save the application in the VB2012\Chap03 folder. Create the interface shown in Figure 3-59. Make the Calculate Change button the default button. Code the application appropriately. (It might be helpful to review the information in Figures 2-34 and 2-35 in Chapter 2.) Clear the calculated amounts when a change is made to either the amount owed or amount paid. Save the solution and then start the application. Test the application three times, using the following data: 75.33 as the amount owed and 80.00 as the amount paid, 39.67 as the amount owed and 50.00 as the amount paid, and 45.55 as the amount owed and 45.55 as the amount paid. Close the Code Editor window and then close the solution.

ADVANCED

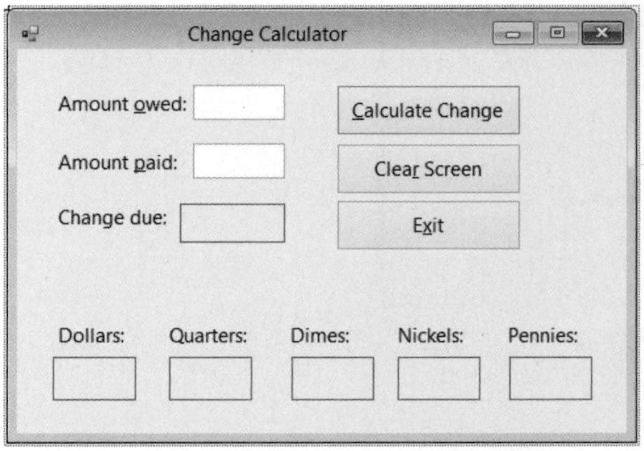

Figure 3-59 Interface for Exercise 6

DISCOVERY

7. In this exercise, you experiment with the Visual Basic conversion functions listed in Appendix C. Open the Conversion Functions Solution (Conversion Functions Solution.sln) file contained in the VB2012\Chap03\Conversion Functions Solution folder. Start the application. Test the application using 4 and 10 as the item price and number purchased, respectively. What appears in the Total price box when you click the Calculate button? Now delete the number 10 from the Number purchased box. What appears in the Total price box when you click the Calculate button? Stop the application. Modify the code so that it uses the Visual Basic conversion functions listed in Appendix C. For example, to convert the item price to Decimal, use `decPrice = CDec(txtPrice.Text)`. Save the solution and then start the application. Test the application using 4 and 10 as the item price and number purchased, respectively. What appears in the Total price box when you click the Calculate button? Now delete the number 10 from the Number purchased box. What happens when you click the Calculate button? Stop the application by clicking DEBUG on the menu bar and then clicking Stop Debugging. What does this exercise tell you about the difference between the TryParse methods and the Visual Basic conversion functions? Close the Code Editor window and then close the solution.

SWAT THE BUGS

8. Open the Debug Solution (Debug Solution.sln) file contained in the VB2012\Chap03\Debug Solution-Lesson C folder. If necessary, open the designer window. Start and then test the application. Locate and correct any errors. When the application is working correctly, close the Code Editor window and then close the solution.

CHAPTER 4

The Selection Structure

Creating the Covington Resort Application

In this chapter, you will create a reservation application for Covington Resort. The application should allow the user to enter the following information: the number of rooms to reserve, the length of stay (in nights), the number of adult guests, and the number of child guests. Each room can accommodate a maximum of six guests. The resort charges $284 per room per night. It also charges a 15.25% sales and lodging tax, which is based on the room charge. In addition, there is a $15 resort fee per room per night. The application should display the total room charge, the sales and lodging tax, the resort fee, and the total due.

Previewing the Covington Resort Application

Before you start the first lesson in this chapter, you will preview the completed application. The application is contained in the VB2012\Chap04 folder.

START HERE

To preview the completed application:

1. Use the Run dialog box to run the Covington (Covington.exe) file contained in the VB2012\Chap04 folder. The application's user interface appears on the screen.
2. Type **1** in the Rooms box, **2** in the Nights box, **2** in the Adults box, and **3** in the Children box. Click the **Calculate** button. The application calculates and displays the charges shown in Figure 4-1.

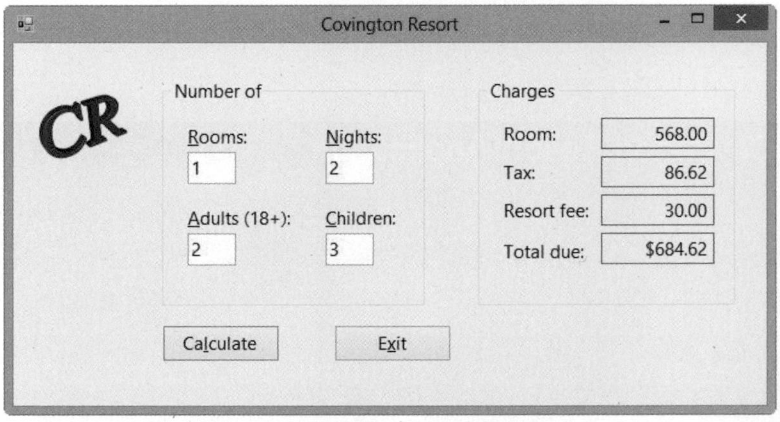

Figure 4-1 Interface showing the calculated amounts

3. Recall that only 6 guests are allowed in a room. Change the number of adults to **4** and then click the **Calculate** button. The message box shown in Figure 4-2 appears on the screen. You will learn how to create a message box in Lesson B.

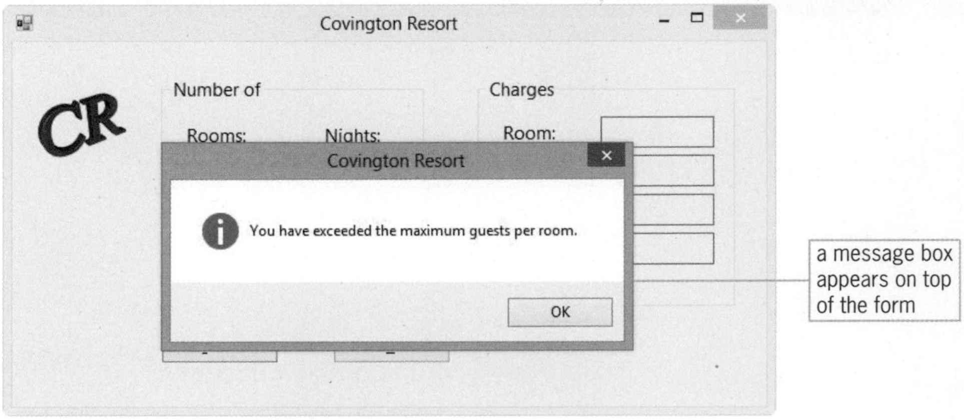

Figure 4-2 Message box

4. Click the **OK** button to close the message box. Try typing a **$** in the Nights box. Notice that the text box does not accept the $ key. You will learn how to prevent a text box from accepting unwanted characters in Lesson C.

5. Change the number of nights and number of adults to **1** and **2**, respectively. Also change the number of children to **2**. Click the **Calculate** button. The application calculates and displays the charges shown in Figure 4-3.

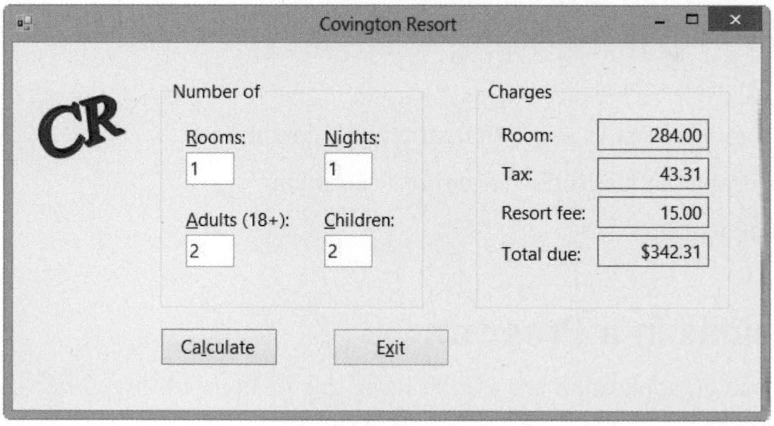

Figure 4-3 New charges shown in the interface

6. Click the **Exit** button to end the application.

The Covington Resort application uses the selection structure, which you will learn about in Lesson A. In Lesson B, you will complete the application's interface and also begin coding the application. You will finish coding the application in Lesson C. Be sure to complete each lesson in full and do all of the end-of-lesson questions and several exercises before continuing to the next lesson.

LESSON A

After studying Lesson A, you should be able to:

- Write pseudocode for the selection structure
- Create a flowchart to help you plan an application's code
- Write an If ... Then ... Else statement
- Include comparison operators in a selection structure's condition
- Include logical operators in a selection structure's condition
- Change the case of a string

Making Decisions in a Program

All of the procedures in an application are written using one or more of three basic control structures: sequence, selection, and repetition. The procedures in the previous three chapters used the sequence structure only. When one of the procedures was invoked during run time, the computer processed its instructions sequentially—in other words, in the order the instructions appeared in the procedure. Every procedure you write will contain the sequence structure. Many times, however, a procedure will need the computer to make a decision before selecting the next instruction to process. A procedure that calculates an employee's gross pay, for example, typically has the computer determine whether the number of hours an employee worked is greater than 40. The computer then would select either an instruction that computes regular pay only or an instruction that computes regular pay plus overtime pay. Procedures that need the computer to make a decision require the use of the selection structure (also called the decision structure).

The **selection structure** indicates that a decision (based on some condition) needs to be made, followed by an appropriate action derived from that decision. But how does a programmer determine whether a problem's solution requires a selection structure? The answer to this question is by studying the problem specification. The first problem specification you will examine in this lesson involves an evil scientist named Dr. N. The problem specification and an illustration of the problem are shown in Figure 4-4 along with a solution to the problem. The solution, which is written in pseudocode, requires only the sequence structure.

Ch04A video

Problem Specification

Dr. N is sitting in a chair in his lair, facing a control deck and an electronic screen. At times, visitors come to the door located at the rear of the lair. Before pressing the blue button on the control deck to open the door, Dr. N likes to view the visitor on the screen. He can do so by pressing the orange button on the control deck. Write the instructions that direct Dr. N to view the visitor first, and then open the door and say "Welcome".

Solution
1. press the orange button on the control deck to view the visitor on the screen
2. press the blue button on the control deck to open the door
3. say "Welcome"

Figure 4-4 A problem that requires the sequence structure only
Image by Diane Zak; Created with Reallusion CrazyTalk Animator

Now we'll make a slight change to the problem specification from Figure 4-4. In this case, Dr. N should open the door only if the visitor knows the secret password. The modified problem specification and solution are shown in Figure 4-5. The solution contains both the sequence and selection structures. The selection structure's condition directs Dr. N to make a decision about the visitor's password. More specifically, he needs to determine whether the visitor's password matches the secret password. The **condition** in a selection structure must be phrased so that it evaluates to an answer of either true or false. In this case, either the visitor's password matches the secret password (true) or it doesn't match the secret password (false). Only if both passwords are the same does Dr. N need to follow the two indented instructions. The selection structure in Figure 4-5 is referred to as a **single-alternative selection structure** because it requires one or more actions to be taken *only* when its condition evaluates to true. Other examples of single-alternative selection structures include "if it's raining, take an umbrella" and "if you are driving your car at night, turn your car's headlights on".

Problem Specification

Dr. N is sitting in a chair in his lair, facing a control deck and an electronic screen. At times, visitors come to the door located at the rear of the lair. Before pressing the blue button on the control deck to open the door, Dr. N likes to view the visitor on the screen. He can do so by pressing the orange button on the control deck. Write the instructions that direct Dr. N to view the visitor first, and then ask the visitor for the password. He should open the door and say "Welcome" only if the visitor knows the secret password.

Solution

1. press the orange button on the control deck to view the visitor on the screen
2. ask the visitor for the password
3. if the visitor's password matches the secret password
    press the blue button on the control deck to open the door
    say "Welcome"
   end if

condition

followed only when the condition is true

Figure 4-5 A problem that requires the sequence structure and a single-alternative selection structure

In pseudocode, most programmers use the words "if" and "end if" to denote the beginning and end, respectively, of a selection structure. They also indent the instructions within the selection structure.

Figure 4-6 shows a modified version of the previous problem specification. In this version, Dr. N will say "Sorry, you are wrong" and then destroy the visitor if the passwords do not match. Also shown in Figure 4-6 are two possible solutions to the problem; both solutions produce the same result. The condition in Solution 1's selection structure determines whether the visitor's password is *correct*. If it is correct, Dr. N will open the door and welcome the visitor to his lair. Otherwise, he will tell the visitor that the password is wrong and then destroy the visitor. The condition in Solution 2's selection structure, on the other hand, determines whether the visitor's password is *incorrect*. If it is incorrect, Dr. N will tell the visitor that the password is wrong and then destroy the visitor; otherwise, he will open the door and welcome the visitor to his lair.

Problem Specification

Dr. N is sitting in a chair in his lair, facing a control deck and an electronic screen. At times, visitors come to the door located at the rear of the lair. Before pressing the blue button on the control deck to open the door, Dr. N likes to view the visitor on the screen. He can do so by pressing the orange button on the control deck. Write the instructions that direct Dr. N to view the visitor first, and then ask the visitor for the password. He should open the door and say "Welcome" only if the visitor knows the secret password. If the visitor does not know the secret password, Dr. N should say "Sorry, you are wrong" and then destroy the visitor by pressing the big red button on the control deck.

Solution 1

```
1. press the orange button on the control deck to view the visitor on the screen
2. ask the visitor for the password
                                   condition
3. if the visitor's password matches the secret password
         press the blue button on the control deck to open the door  ┐
         say "Welcome"                                               ┘ true path
   else
         say "Sorry, you are wrong"                                  ┐
         press the big red button on the control deck to destroy the visitor ┘ false path
   end if
```

Solution 2

```
1. press the orange button on the control deck to view the visitor on the screen
2. ask the visitor for the password
                                   condition
3. if the visitor's password does not match the secret password
         say "Sorry, you are wrong"                                  ┐
         press the big red button on the control deck to destroy the visitor ┘ true path
   else
         press the blue button on the control deck to open the door  ┐
         say "Welcome"                                               ┘ false path
   end if
```

Figure 4-6 A problem that requires the sequence structure and a dual-alternative selection structure

Unlike the selection structure in Figure 4-5, which provides instructions for Dr. N to follow *only* when the selection structure's condition is true, the selection structures in Figure 4-6 require Dr. N to perform one set of instructions when the condition is true but a different set of instructions when the condition is false. The instructions to follow when the condition evaluates to true are called the **true path**. The true path begins with the "if" and ends with either the "else" (if there is one) or the "end if". The instructions to follow when the condition evaluates to false are called the **false path**. The false path begins with the "else" and ends with the "end if". For clarity, the instructions in each path should be indented as shown in Figure 4-6. Selection structures that contain instructions in both paths, like the ones in Figure 4-6, are referred to as **dual-alternative selection structures**.

Flowcharting a Selection Structure

As you learned in Chapter 2, many programmers use flowcharts (rather than pseudocode) when planning solutions to problems. Figures 4-7 and 4-8 show two problem specifications along with the correct solutions in flowchart form. (So that you can compare both planning tools, the corresponding pseudocode is also included in the figures.) The diamond in a flowchart is called the **decision symbol** because it is used to represent the condition (decision) in both the selection and repetition structures. The diamonds in Figures 4-7 and 4-8 represent the condition in a selection structure. The flowchart in Figure 4-7 contains a single-alternative selection structure. You can tell that it's a single-alternative selection structure because it requires a set of actions to be taken only when its condition evaluates to true. Figure 4-8's flowchart contains a dual-alternative selection structure. You can tell that it's a dual-alternative selection structure because it requires two different sets of actions: one to be taken only when its condition evaluates to true, and the other to be taken only when its condition evaluates to false.

Problem Specification

Jerrili's Trading Store wants an application that allows a salesclerk to enter an item's price and the quantity purchased by a customer. When the quantity purchased is over 10, the customer is given a 20% discount. The application should calculate and display the total amount the customer owes.

Pseudocode for the Calculate button's Click event procedure

```
1. store price and quantity purchased in variables
2. total owed = price * quantity purchased
3. if the quantity purchased is over 10
       discount = total owed * .2
       total owed = total owed – discount
   end if
4. display total owed in lblTotal
```

Flowchart for the Calculate button's Click event procedure

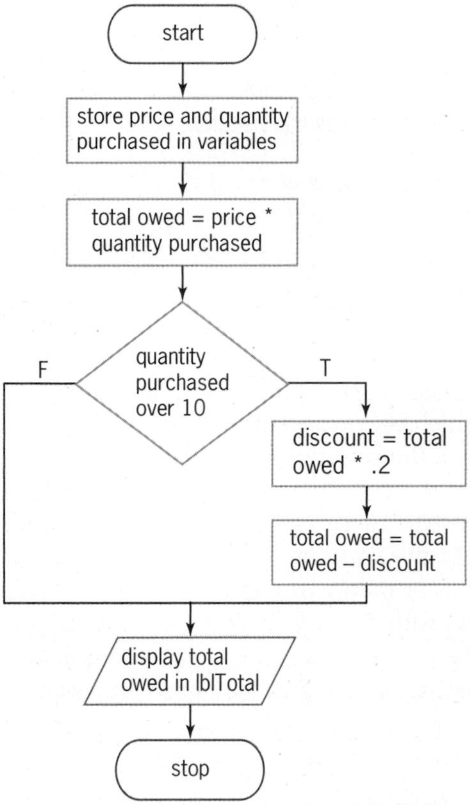

Figure 4-7 Pseudocode and flowchart showing a single-alternative selection structure

Problem Specification

Mary Kettleson wants an application that calculates and displays her annual bonus, given her annual sales amount. Mary receives a 2% bonus when her annual sales are over $15,000; otherwise, she receives a 1.5% bonus.

Pseudocode for the Calculate button's Click event procedure

```
1. store sales in a variable
2. if the sales are over 15000
         bonus = sales * .02
   else
         bonus = sales * .015
   end if
3. display bonus in lblBonus
```

Flowchart for the Calculate button's Click event procedure

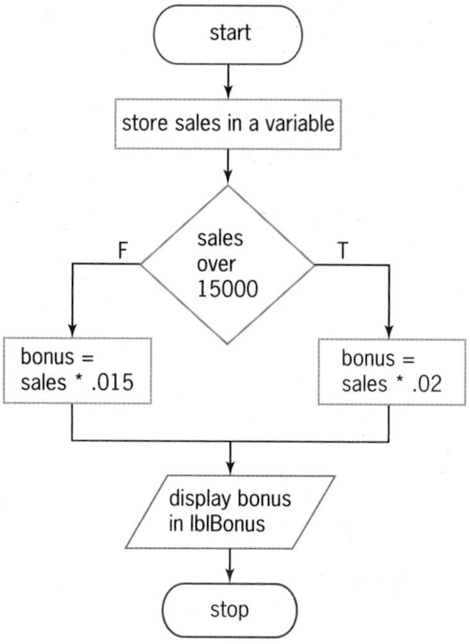

Figure 4-8 Pseudocode and flowchart showing a dual-alternative selection structure

The condition in Figure 4-7's diamond checks whether the customer purchased more than 10 items. It's necessary to do this because the customer receives a 20% discount when more than 10 items are purchased. The condition in Figure 4-8's diamond, on the other hand, determines whether Mary's sales are over $15,000. In this case, the result (either true or false) determines whether Mary receives a 2% or 1.5% bonus. Notice that the conditions in both diamonds evaluate to either true or false only. Also notice that both diamonds have one flowline entering the symbol and two flowlines leaving the symbol. One of the flowlines leading out of a diamond in a flowchart should be marked with a "T" (for true) and the other should be marked with an "F" (for false). The "T" flowline points to the next instruction to be processed when the condition evaluates to true. In Figure 4-7, the next instruction calculates the 20% discount; in Figure 4-8, it calculates the 2% bonus. The "F" flowline points to the next instruction to be processed when the condition evaluates to false. In Figure 4-7, that instruction displays the total owed; in Figure 4-8, it calculates the 1.5% bonus. You also can mark the flowlines leading out of a diamond with a "Y" and an "N" (for yes and no).

Coding Selection Structures in Visual Basic

Visual Basic provides the **If ... Then ... Else statement** for coding single-alternative and dual-alternative selection structures. The statement's syntax is shown in Figure 4-9. The square brackets in the syntax indicate that the Else portion, referred to as the Else clause, is optional. Recall, however, that boldfaced items in a statement's syntax are required. In this case, the keywords `If`, `Then`, and `End If` are required. The `Else` keyword is necessary only in a dual-alternative selection structure.

Italicized items in the syntax indicate where the programmer must supply information. In the If ... Then ... Else statement, the programmer must supply the *condition* that the computer needs to evaluate before further processing can occur. The condition must be a Boolean expression, which is an expression that results in a Boolean value (True or False). Besides providing the condition, the programmer must provide the statements to be processed in the true path and (optionally) in the false path. The set of statements contained in each path is referred to as a **statement block**. (In Visual Basic, a statement block is a set of statements terminated by an Else, End If, Loop, or Next clause. You will learn about the Loop and Next clauses in Chapters 6 and 7.)

Also included in Figure 4-9 are two examples of using the If...Then...Else statement to code selection structures. Example 1 shows how you use the statement to code the single-alternative selection structure shown earlier in Figure 4-7. Example 2 shows how you use the statement to code the dual-alternative selection structure shown earlier in Figure 4-8. Both examples contain the greater-than comparison operator (>), which you will learn about in the next section.

If...Then...Else Statement

Syntax
If *condition* **Then**
    statement block to be processed when the condition is true
[**Else**
    statement block to be processed when the condition is false]
End If

Figure 4-9 Syntax and examples of the If ... Then ... Else statement *(continues)*

(continued)

Example 1
```
Private Sub btnCalc_Click(sender As Object,
e As EventArgs) Handles btnCalc.Click
    ' calculate total owed

    Dim dblPrice As Double
    Dim intQuantity As Integer
    Dim dblTotal As Double
    Dim dblDiscount As Double

    ' store user input in variables
    Double.TryParse(txtPrice.Text, dblPrice)
    Integer.TryParse(txtQuantity.Text, intQuantity)

    ' calculate total owed
    dblTotal = dblPrice * intQuantity
    ' subtract discount, if necessary
    If intQuantity > 10 Then
       dblDiscount = dblTotal * 0.2
       dblTotal = dblTotal - dblDiscount
    End If
    ' display total owed
    lblTotal.Text = dblTotal.ToString("C2")
End Sub
```
single-alternative selection structure

Example 2
```
Private Sub btnCalc_Click(sender As Object,
e As EventArgs) Handles btnCalc.Click
    ' calculate the annual bonus

    Dim dblSales As Double
    Dim dblBonus As Double

    ' store sales in a variable
    Double.TryParse(txtSales.Text, dblSales)

    ' calculate and display bonus
    If dblSales > 15000 Then
       dblBonus = dblSales * 0.02
    Else
       dblBonus = dblSales * 0.015
    End If
    lblBonus.Text = dblBonus.ToString("C2")
End Sub
```
dual-alternative selection structure

Figure 4-9 Syntax and examples of the If ... Then ... Else statement

START HERE

To code and then test the Jerrili and Kettleson applications:

1. If necessary, start Visual Studio 2012. Open the Jerrili Solution (Jerrili Solution.sln) file contained in the VB2012\Chap04\Jerrili Solution folder. If necessary, open the designer window.
2. Open the Code Editor window. Replace <your name> and <current date> in the comments with your name and the current date, respectively.
3. Open the code template for the btnCalc control's Click event procedure. Enter the comments and code shown in Example 1 in Figure 4-9.
4. Save the solution and then start the application. First, calculate the total owed when the customer purchases 9 items at $5 per item; the total owed should be $45.00. Type **5** in the Item's price box and then type **9** in the Quantity purchased box. Click the **Calculate** button. The button's Click event procedure displays $45.00 in the Total owed box, as shown in Figure 4-10.

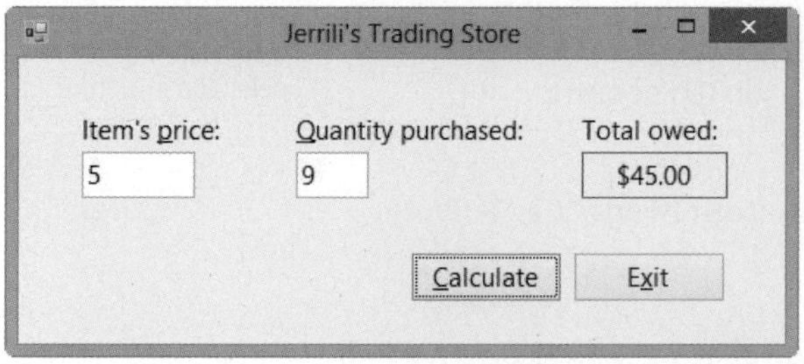

Figure 4-10 Jerrili's interface showing the total owed

5. Now, calculate the total owed when the customer purchases 20 items at $5 per item; the total owed should be $80.00. Change the quantity purchased to **20** and then click the **Calculate** button. $80.00 appears in the Total owed box.
6. Click the **Exit** button. Close the Code Editor window and then close the solution.
7. Open the Kettleson Solution (Kettleson Solution.sln) file contained in the VB2012\Chap04\Kettleson Solution folder. If necessary, open the designer window.
8. Open the Code Editor window. Replace <your name> and <current date> in the comments with your name and the current date, respectively.
9. Open the code template for the btnCalc control's Click event procedure. Enter the comments and code shown in Example 2 in Figure 4-9.
10. Save the solution and then start the application. First, calculate the bonus when the sales are $25,000; the bonus should be $500.00. Type **25000** in the Annual sales box and then click the **Calculate** button. The button's Click event procedure displays $500.00 in the Annual bonus box, as shown in Figure 4-11.

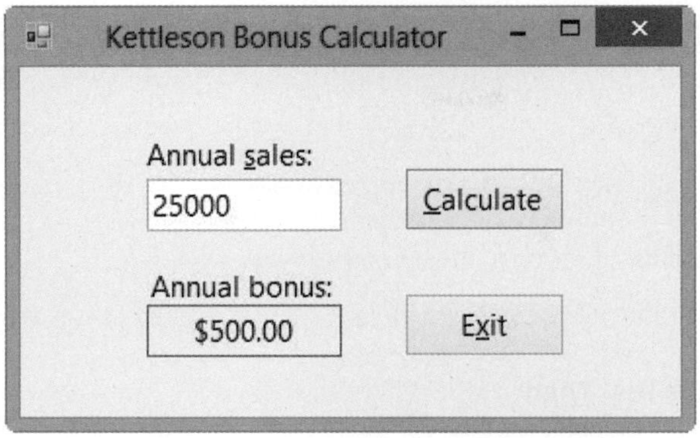

Figure 4-11 Kettleson interface showing the bonus

11. Now, calculate the bonus when the sales are $10,000; the bonus should be $150.00. Change the annual sales to **10000** and then click the **Calculate** button. $150.00 appears in the Annual bonus box.
12. Click the **Exit** button. Close the Code Editor window and then close the solution.

YOU DO IT 1!

Create a Visual Basic Windows application named YouDoIt 1. Save the application in the VB2012\Chap04 folder. Add a text box, a label, and a button to the form. The button's Click event procedure should display the string "Over 1" in the label when the value in the text box is greater than the number 1; otherwise, it should display the string "Not Over 1". Code the procedure. Save the solution and then start and test the application. Close the solution.

As mentioned earlier, an If...Then...Else statement's condition must be a Boolean expression, which is an expression that evaluates to either True or False. The expression can contain variables, constants, properties, methods, keywords, arithmetic operators, comparison operators, and logical operators. You already know about variables, constants, properties, methods, keywords, and arithmetic operators. You will learn about comparison operators and logical operators in this lesson. We'll begin with comparison operators.

Comparison Operators

Figure 4-12 lists the most commonly used **comparison operators** in Visual Basic. Comparison operators (also referred to as relational operators) are used in expressions to compare two values. When making comparisons, keep in mind that equal to (=) is the opposite of not equal to (<>), greater than (>) is the opposite of less than or equal to (<=), and less than (<) is the opposite of greater than or equal to (>=). Expressions containing a comparison operator always evaluate to a Boolean value: either True or False. Also included in Figure 4-12 are examples of using comparison operators in an If...Then...Else statement's condition.

Comparison Operators

Operator	Operation
=	equal to
>	greater than
>=	greater than or equal to
<	less than
<=	less than or equal to
<>	not equal to

Example 1
```
If decNorthSales = decSouthSales Then
```
The condition evaluates to True when both variables contain the same value; otherwise, it evaluates to False.

Example 2
```
If intAge >= 65 Then
```
The condition evaluates to True when the value stored in the `intAge` variable is greater than or equal to 65; otherwise, it evaluates to False.

Example 3
```
If decTotal < 500.75D Then
```
The condition evaluates to True when the value stored in the `decTotal` variable is less than 500.75; otherwise, it evaluates to False. You also can write the condition as `decTotal < Convert.ToDecimal(500.75)`.

Example 4
```
If dblCommission <= 1500 Then
```
The condition evaluates to True when the value stored in the `dblCommission` variable is less than or equal to 1500; otherwise, it evaluates to False.

Example 5
```
If strState <> "KY" Then
```
The condition evaluates to True when the `strState` variable does not contain the string "KY"; otherwise, it evaluates to False.

Figure 4-12 Listing and examples of commonly used comparison operators

Unlike arithmetic operators, comparison operators in Visual Basic do not have an order of precedence. When an expression contains more than one comparison operator, the computer evaluates the comparison operators from left to right in the expression. Comparison operators are evaluated after any arithmetic operators in an expression. For example, when processing the expression 3 + 6 < 16 / 2, the computer will evaluate the two arithmetic operators before it evaluates the comparison operator. The result of the expression is the Boolean value False, as shown in Figure 4-13. Also included in the figure are the evaluation steps for two other expressions that contain arithmetic and comparison operators.

Evaluation Steps	Result
Original expression	3 + 6 < 16 / 2
The division is performed first	3 + 6 < 8
The addition is performed next	9 < 8
The < comparison is performed last	False

Figure 4-13 Evaluation steps for expressions containing arithmetic and comparison operators *(continues)*

(continued)

Evaluation Steps	Result
Original expression	6 * 2 * 3 >= 6 * 6
The first multiplication is performed first	12 * 3 >= 6 * 6
The second multiplication is performed next	36 >= 6 * 6
The remaining multiplication is performed next	36 >= 36
The >= comparison is performed last	True
Original expression	7 + 6 * 4 * 2 – 1 > 50
The first multiplication is performed first	7 + 24 * 2 – 1 > 50
The remaining multiplication is performed next	7 + 48 – 1 > 50
The addition is performed next	55 – 1 > 50
The subtraction is performed next	54 > 50
The > comparison is performed last	True

Figure 4-13 Evaluation steps for expressions containing arithmetic and comparison operators

YOU DO IT 2!

On a piece of paper, write down the answers to the following four expressions:

4 + 3 * 2 > 2 * 10 – 11

8 + 3 – 6 + 85 < 5 * 26

10 / 5 + 3 – 6 * 2 > 0

75 / 25 + 2 * 5 * 6 <= 8 * 8

Next, create a Visual Basic Windows application named YouDoIt 2. Save the application in the VB2012\Chap04 folder. Add four labels and a button to the form. The button's Click event procedure should display the results of the four expressions shown here. Code the procedure. Save the solution and then start and test the application. Compare the application's results with your answers. Close the solution.

In the next two sections, you will view two procedures that contain a comparison operator in an If…Then…Else statement's condition. The first procedure uses a single-alternative selection structure, and the second procedure uses a dual-alternative selection structure.

Using Comparison Operators: Swapping Numeric Values

Figure 4-14 shows a sample run of an application that displays the lowest and highest of two scores entered by the user. Figure 4-15 shows the pseudocode and flowchart for the Display button's Click event procedure. The procedure contains a single-alternative selection structure whose condition determines whether the first score entered by the user is greater than the second score. If it is, the selection structure's true path takes the appropriate action.

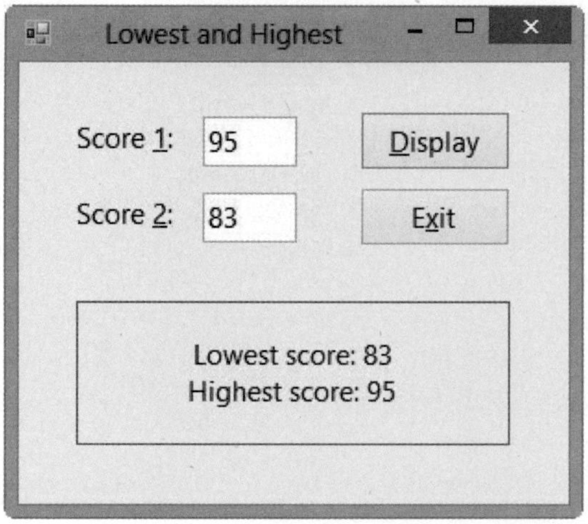

Figure 4-14 Sample run of the Lowest and Highest application

Pseudocode for the Display button's Click event procedure

1. store the two scores in two variables
2. if the score in the first variable is greater than the score in the second variable
        swap both scores so that the first variable contains the lowest of the two scores
   end if
3. display the lowest and highest scores (and appropriate messages) in lblMessage

Flowchart for the Display button's Click event procedure

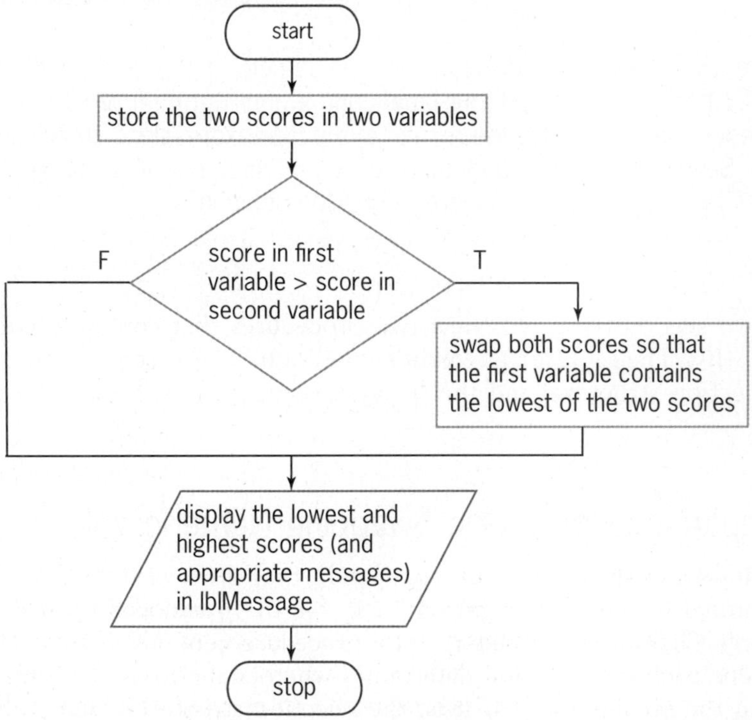

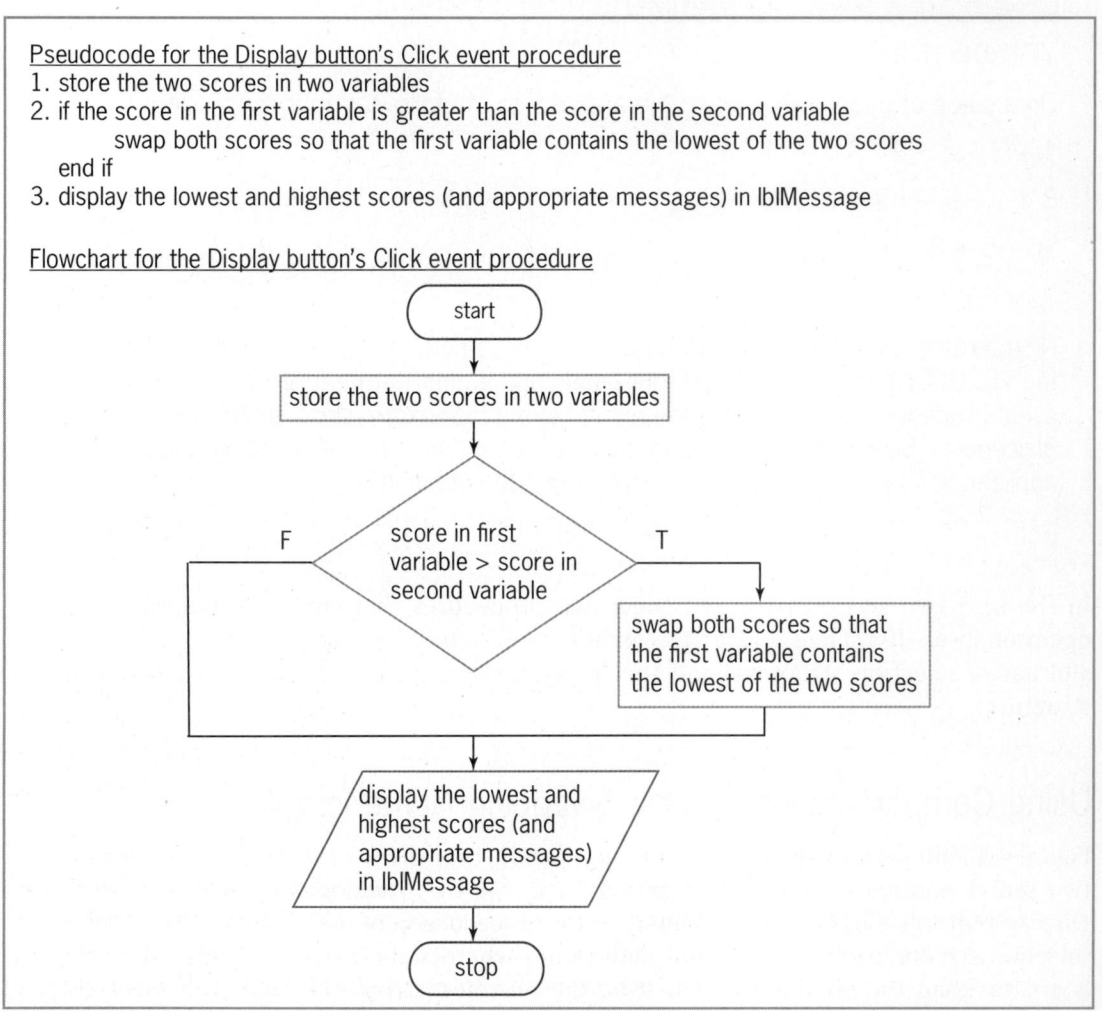

Figure 4-15 Pseudocode and flowchart containing a single-alternative selection structure

Figure 4-16 shows the code entered in the Display button's Click event procedure. The condition in the If clause compares the contents of the `intScore1` variable with the contents of the `intScore2` variable. If the value in the `intScore1` variable is greater than the value in the `intScore2` variable, the condition evaluates to True and the four instructions in the If ... Then ... Else statement's true path swap both values. Swapping the values places the smaller number in the `intScore1` variable and places the larger number in the `intScore2` variable. If the condition evaluates to False, on the other hand, the true path instructions are skipped over because the `intScore1` variable already contains a number that is smaller than (or possibly equal to) the number stored in the `intScore2` variable.

```
Private Sub btnDisplay_Click(sender As Object,
e As EventArgs) Handles btnDisplay.Click
    ' display the lowest and highest scores

    Dim intScore1 As Integer
    Dim intScore2 As Integer

    ' store input in variables
    Integer.TryParse(txtScore1.Text, intScore1)
    Integer.TryParse(txtScore2.Text, intScore2)

    ' swap scores, if necessary
    If intScore1 > intScore2 Then
        Dim intTemp As Integer
        intTemp = intScore1
        intScore1 = intScore2
        intScore2 = intTemp
    End If

    ' display lowest and highest scores
    lblMessage.Text = "Lowest score: " &
        Convert.ToString(intScore1) &
        ControlChars.NewLine &
        "Highest score: " &
        Convert.ToString(intScore2)
End Sub
```

comparison operator

single-alternative selection structure

Figure 4-16 Display button's Click event procedure

The first instruction in the If ... Then ... Else statement's true path declares and initializes a variable named `intTemp`. Like a variable declared at the beginning of a procedure, a variable declared within a statement block—referred to as a **block-level variable**—remains in memory until the procedure ends. However, unlike a variable declared at the beginning of a procedure, block-level variables have block scope rather than procedure scope. A variable that has **block scope** can be used only within the statement block in which it is declared. More specifically, it can be used only below its declaration statement within the statement block. In this case, the procedure-level `intScore1` and `intScore2` variables can be used anywhere below their Dim statements within the Display button's Click event procedure, but the block-level `intTemp` variable can be used only after its Dim statement within the If ... Then ... Else statement's true path.

You may be wondering why the `intTemp` variable was not declared at the beginning of the procedure, along with the other variables. Although there is nothing wrong with declaring the `intTemp` variable in that location, there is no reason to create the variable until it is needed, which (in this case) is only when a swap is necessary.

The second instruction in the If... Then... Else statement's true path assigns the value in the `intScore1` variable to the `intTemp` variable. If you do not store the `intScore1` variable's value in the `intTemp` variable, the value will be lost when the computer processes the next statement, `intScore1 = intScore2`, which replaces the contents of the `intScore1` variable with the contents of the `intScore2` variable. Finally, the `intScore2 = intTemp` instruction assigns the `intTemp` variable's value to the `intScore2` variable; this completes the swap. Figure 4-17 illustrates the concept of swapping, assuming the user enters the numbers 95 and 83 in the txtScore1 and txtScore2 controls, respectively.

	`intScore1`	`intScore2`	`intTemp`
values stored in the variables immediately before the `intTemp = intScore1` statement is processed	95	83	0
result of the `intTemp = intScore1` statement	95	83	95
result of the `intScore1 = intScore2` statement	83	83	95
result of the `intScore2 = intTemp` statement	83	95	95

the values were swapped

Figure 4-17 Illustration of the swapping concept

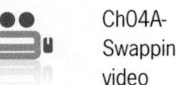

Ch04A-Swapping video

START HERE

To code and then test the Lowest and Highest application:

1. Open the Lowest and Highest Solution (Lowest and Highest Solution.sln) file contained in the VB2012\Chap04\Lowest and Highest Solution folder. If necessary, open the designer window.
2. Open the Code Editor window. Replace <your name> and <current date> in the comments with your name and the current date, respectively.
3. Open the code template for the btnDisplay control's Click event procedure. Enter the comments and code shown earlier in Figure 4-16.
4. Save the solution and then start the application. Type **95** in the Score 1 box and then type **83** in the Score 2 box. Click the **Display** button. The button's Click event procedure displays the lowest and highest scores, as shown earlier in Figure 4-14.
5. Click the **Exit** button. Close the Code Editor window and then close the solution.

Using Comparison Operators: Displaying the Sum or Difference

Figure 4-18 shows a sample run of an application that displays either the sum of two numbers entered by the user or the difference between both numbers. Figure 4-19 shows the pseudocode and flowchart for the Calculate button's Click event procedure. The procedure uses a dual-alternative selection structure to determine the appropriate operation to perform.

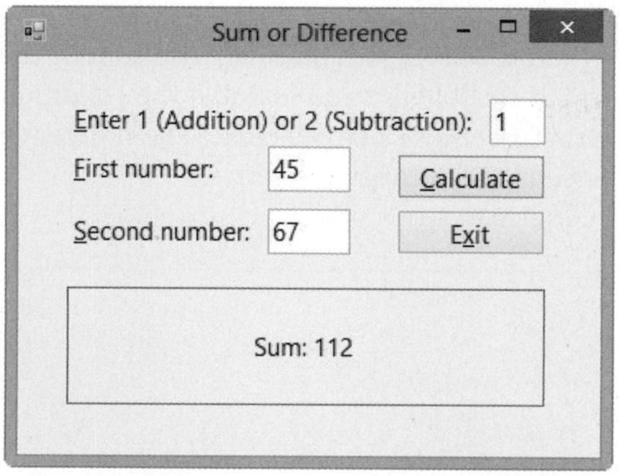

Figure 4-18 Sample run of the Sum or Difference application

<u>Pseudocode for the Calculate button's Click event procedure</u>

1. store operation, first number, and second number in variables
2. if the operation is "1", which indicates Addition
        calculate the sum by adding together the first number and the second number
        display the message "Sum:" along with the sum in lblAnswer
   else
        calculate the difference by subtracting the second number from the first number
        display the message "Difference:" along with the difference in lblAnswer
   end if

<u>Flowchart for the Calculate button's Click event procedure</u>

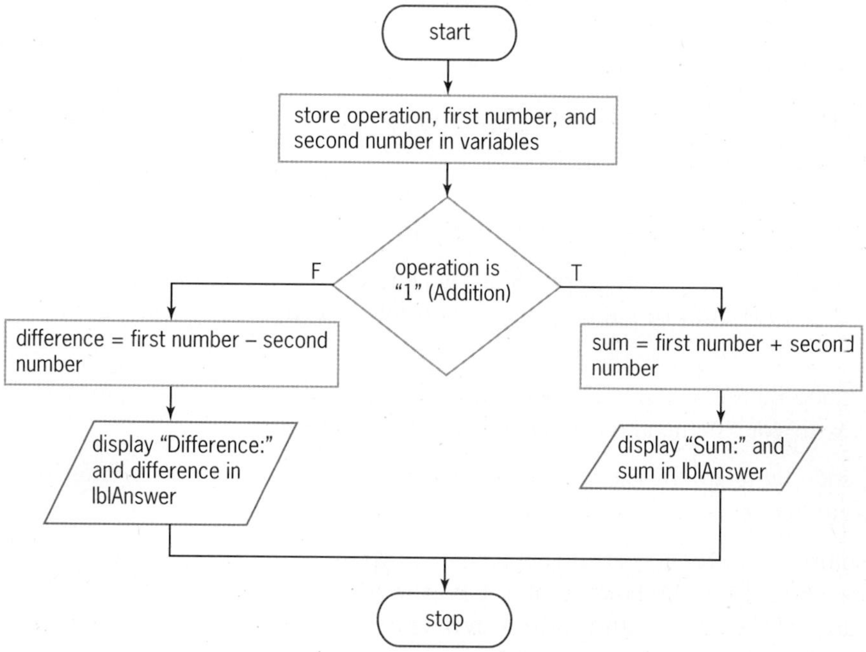

Figure 4-19 Flowchart and pseudocode containing a dual-alternative selection structure

Figure 4-20 shows the code entered in the Calculate button's Click event procedure. The Dim statements in the procedure declare four procedure-level variables. The next three statements store the contents of the text boxes in the appropriate variables. The condition in the If clause compares the contents of the `strOperation` variable with the string "1". If the condition evaluates to True, the statements in the selection structure's true path calculate the sum of the numbers entered by the user and then display the sum in the lblAnswer control. If the condition evaluates to False, the statements in the selection structure's false path calculate the difference between both numbers and then display the difference in the lblAnswer control.


```
Private Sub btnCalc_Click(sender As Object,
e As EventArgs) Handles btnCalc.Click
    ' calculate either a sum or a difference

    Dim strOperation As String
    Dim dblNum1 As Double
    Dim dblNum2 As Double
    Dim dblAnswer As Double

    ' store input in variables
    strOperation = txtOperation.Text
    Double.TryParse(txtFirst.Text, dblNum1)
    Double.TryParse(txtSecond.Text, dblNum2)

    ' calculate and display the sum or difference
    If strOperation = "1" Then
       dblAnswer = dblNum1 + dblNum2
       lblAnswer.Text =
           "Sum: " & Convert.ToString(dblAnswer)
    Else
       dblAnswer = dblNum1 - dblNum2
       lblAnswer.Text =
           "Difference: " & Convert.ToString(dblAnswer)
    End If
End Sub
```

comparison operator

dual-alternative selection structure

Figure 4-20 Calculate button's Click event procedure

START HERE

To code and then test the Sum or Difference application:

1. Open the Sum or Difference Solution (Sum or Difference Solution.sln) file contained in the VB2012\Chap04\Sum or Difference Solution folder. If necessary, open the designer window.
2. Open the Code Editor window. Replace <your name> and <current date> in the comments with your name and the current date, respectively.
3. Open the code template for the btnCalc control's Click event procedure. Enter the comments and code shown in Figure 4-20.
4. Save the solution and then start the application. Type **1** in the Enter 1 (Addition) or 2 (Subtraction) box, **45** in the First number box, and **67** in the Second number box. Click the **Calculate** button. The button's Click event procedure displays the sum of both numbers, as shown earlier in Figure 4-18.
5. Change the 1 in the Enter 1 (Addition) or 2 (Subtraction) box to **2** and then click the **Calculate** button. The button's Click event procedure displays the difference between both numbers (–22).
6. Click the **Exit** button. Close the Code Editor window and then close the solution.

YOU DO IT 3!

Create a Visual Basic Windows application named YouDoIt 3. Save the application in the VB2012\Chap04 folder. Add a text box, a label, and a button to the form. If the user enters the number 1 in the text box, the button's Click event procedure should display the result of multiplying the number 20 by the number 5; otherwise, it should display the result of dividing the number 20 by the number 5. Code the procedure. Save the solution and then start and test the application. Close the solution.

YOU DO IT 4!

Create a Visual Basic Windows application named YouDoIt 4. Save the application in the VB2012\Chap04 folder. Add two text boxes, a label, and a button to the form. The button's Click event procedure should assign the contents of the text boxes to Double variables named `dblNum1` and `dblNum2`. It then should divide the contents of the `dblNum1` variable by the contents of the `dblNum2` variable, assigning the result to a Double variable named `dblAnswer`. Display the answer in the label. Code the procedure. Save the solution and then start the application. Test the application using the numbers 6 and 2; the number 3 appears in the label control. Now test it using the numbers 6 and 0. The word "Infinity" appears in the label control because, as in math, division by 0 is not possible. Add a selection structure to the procedure. The selection structure should perform the division only if the contents of the dblNum2 variable is not 0. Save the solution and then start and test the application. Close the solution.

Logical Operators

An If…Then…Else statement's condition can also contain logical operators. Visual Basic provides six logical operators, which are listed along with their order of precedence in Figure 4-21. Keep in mind, however, that logical operators are evaluated after any arithmetic or comparison operators in an expression. All of the **logical operators**, with the exception of the Not operator, allow you to combine two or more conditions, called sub-conditions, into one compound condition. The compound condition will always evaluate to either True or False, which is why logical operators are often referred to as Boolean operators. Also included in Figure 4-21 are examples of using logical operators in the If…Then…Else statement's condition.

Logical Operators

Operator	Operation	Precedence number
Not	reverses the truth-value of the condition; True becomes False, and False becomes True	1
And	all sub-conditions must be true for the compound condition to evaluate to True	2
AndAlso	same as the And operator, except performs short-circuit evaluation	2
Or	only one of the sub-conditions needs to be true for the compound condition to evaluate to True	3
OrElse	same as the Or operator, except performs short-circuit evaluation	3
Xor	one and only one of the sub-conditions can be true for the compound condition to evaluate to True	4

Example 1
```
If Not blnIsInsured Then
```
The condition evaluates to True when the `blnIsInsured` variable contains the Boolean value False; otherwise, it evaluates to False. The clause also could be written more clearly as `If blnIsInsured = False Then`.

Example 2
```
If dblRate > 0 AndAlso dblRate < 0.15 Then
```
The compound condition evaluates to True when the value in the `dblRate` variable is greater than 0 and, at the same time, less than 0.15; otherwise, it evaluates to False.

Example 3
```
If strState = "AK" AndAlso decSales > 1999.99D Then
```
The compound condition evaluates to True when the `strState` variable contains the string "AK" and, at the same time, the value in the `decSales` variable is greater than 1999.99; otherwise, it evaluates to False.

Example 4
```
If strState = "AK" OrElse decSales > 1999.99D Then
```
The compound condition evaluates to True when the `strState` variable contains the string "AK" or when the value in the `decSales` variable is greater than 1999.99; otherwise, it evaluates to False.

Example 5
```
If strCoupon1 = "USE" Xor strCoupon2 = "USE" Then
```
The compound condition evaluates to True when only one of the variables contains the string "USE"; otherwise, it evaluates to False.

Figure 4-21 Listing and examples of logical operators

You already are familiar with logical operators because you use them on a daily basis. Examples of this include the following:

if you finished your homework *and* you studied for tomorrow's exam, watch a movie

if your cell phone rings *and* (it's your spouse calling *or* it's your child calling), answer the phone

if you are driving your car *and* (it's raining *or* it's foggy *or* there is bug splatter on your windshield), turn your car's wipers on

As mentioned earlier, all expressions containing a logical operator evaluate to either True or False only. The tables shown in Figure 4-22, called **truth tables**, summarize how the computer evaluates the logical operators in an expression.

Truth Tables

Not operator

value of *condition*	value of Not *condition*
True	False
False	True

And operator

sub-condition1	sub-condition2	sub-condition1 And sub-condition2
True	True	True
True	False	False
False	True	False
False	False	False

AndAlso operator

sub-condition1	sub-condition2	sub-condition1 AndAlso sub-condition2
True	True	True
True	False	False
False	(not evaluated)	False

Or operator

sub-condition1	sub-condition2	sub-condition1 Or sub-condition2
True	True	True
True	False	True
False	True	True
False	False	False

OrElse operator

sub-condition1	sub-condition2	sub-condition1 OrElse sub-condition2
True	(not evaluated)	True
False	True	True
False	False	False

Xor operator

sub-condition1	sub-condition2	sub-condition1 Xor sub-condition2
True	True	False
True	False	True
False	True	True
False	False	False

Figure 4-22 Truth tables for the logical operators

As the figure indicates, the **Not operator** reverses the truth-value of the *condition*. If the value of the *condition* is True, then the value of Not *condition* is False. Likewise, if the value of the *condition* is False, then the value of Not *condition* is True.

When you use either the **And operator** or the **AndAlso operator** to combine two sub-conditions, the resulting compound condition evaluates to True only when both sub-conditions are True. If either sub-condition is False or if both sub-conditions are False, then the compound condition evaluates to False. The difference between the And and AndAlso operators is that the And operator always evaluates both sub-conditions, while the AndAlso operator performs a **short-circuit evaluation**, which means it does not always evaluate sub-condition2. Because both sub-conditions combined with the AndAlso operator need to be True for the compound condition to evaluate to True, the AndAlso operator does not evaluate sub-condition2 when sub-condition1 is False; this makes the AndAlso operator more efficient than the And operator.

Notice that when you combine two sub-conditions using either the **Or operator** or the **OrElse operator**, the compound condition evaluates to True when either one or both of the sub-conditions is True. The compound condition will evaluate to False only when both sub-conditions are False. The difference between the Or and OrElse operators is that the Or operator always evaluates both sub-conditions, while the OrElse operator performs a short-circuit evaluation. In this case, because only one of the sub-conditions combined with the OrElse operator needs to be True for the compound condition to evaluate to True, the OrElse operator does not evaluate sub-condition2 when sub-condition1 is True. As a result, the OrElse operator is more efficient than the Or operator.

Finally, when you combine conditions using the Xor operator, the compound condition evaluates to True only when one and only one sub-condition is True. If both sub-conditions are True or both sub-conditions are False, then the compound condition evaluates to False. In the next section, you will use the truth tables to determine which logical operator to use in an If…Then…Else statement's condition.

Using the Truth Tables

When ordering from Warren's Web site, customers using their Warren credit card to pay for their order receive free shipping on order amounts over $100. In the procedure that determines the free-shipping eligibility, the order amount and credit card name are stored in variables named `dblOrderAmount` and `strCreditCard`, respectively. Therefore, you can phrase sub-condition1 in the If…Then…Else statement as `dblOrderAmount > 100`, and phrase sub-condition2 as `strCreditCard = "Warren"`. Which logical operator should you use to combine both sub-conditions into one compound condition? We'll use the truth tables from Figure 4-22 to answer this question.

For a customer to receive free shipping at Warren's, both sub-condition1 (`dblOrderAmount > 100`) and sub-condition2 (`strCreditCard = "Warren"`) must be True at the same time. If either one or both of the sub-conditions are False, then the compound condition should be False and the customer should not receive free shipping. According to the truth tables, all of the logical operators except Xor evaluate a compound condition as True when both sub-conditions are True. However, only the And and AndAlso operators evaluate the compound condition as False when either one or both of the sub-conditions are False. In this case, we'll use the AndAlso operator because it is more efficient than the And operator. Therefore, the correct compound condition to use here is `dblOrderAmount > 100 AndAlso strCreditCard = "Warren"`.

Unlike Warren's Web site, Houston's Web site has the following shipping policy: Customers who belong to Houston's free shipping club are always entitled to free shipping; all other customers receive free shipping only when their order amount is over $100. In the procedure that determines the free-shipping eligibility, the order amount and club information are stored in variables named `dblOrderAmount` and `strClub`, respectively. Therefore, you can phrase sub-condition1 in the If…Then…Else statement as `dblOrderAmount > 100`, and phrase sub-condition2 as `strClub = "Member"`. Now which logical operator should you use to combine both sub-conditions into one compound condition? Here again, we'll use the truth tables from Figure 4-22 to answer this question.

For a customer to receive free shipping at Houston's, at least one of the sub-conditions needs to be True. In other words, either the customer's order needs to be over $100 or the customer needs to be a member of the free shipping club. As the truth tables indicate, the Or and OrElse operators are the only operators that evaluate the compound condition as True when at least one of the sub-conditions is True. In this case, we'll use the OrElse operator because it is more efficient than the Or operator. Therefore, the correct compound condition to use here is `dblOrderAmount > 100 OrElse strClub = "Member"`.

Finally, assume that when placing an order at Houston's, a customer is allowed to use only one of two coupons. If a procedure uses the variables `strCoupon1` and `strCoupon2` to keep track of the coupons, you can phrase sub-condition1 as `strCoupon1 = "USE"` and phrase sub-condition2 as `strCoupon2 = "USE"`. Now which operator should you use to combine both sub-conditions? According to the truth tables, the Xor operator is the only operator that evaluates the compound condition as True when one and only one condition is True. Therefore, the correct compound condition to use here is `strCoupon1 = "USE" Xor strCoupon2 = "USE"`.

Using Logical Operators: Calculating Gross Pay

A procedure needs to calculate and display an employee's gross pay. To keep this example simple, no one at the company works more than 40 hours per week and everyone earns the same hourly rate, $10.75. Before making the gross pay calculation, the procedure should verify that the number of hours entered by the user is greater than or equal to 0 but less than or equal to 40. Programmers refer to the process of verifying that the input data is within the expected range as **data validation**. In this case, if the number of hours is valid, the procedure should calculate and display the gross pay. Otherwise, it should display an error message alerting the user that the number of hours is incorrect.

Figure 4-23 shows two examples of code that calculates and displays the gross pay. Both examples contain a dual-alternative selection structure whose compound condition includes a logical operator. The compound condition in Example 1 uses the AndAlso operator to determine whether the value stored in the `dblHours` variable is greater than or equal to 0 and, at the same time, less than or equal to 40. If the compound condition evaluates to True, the selection structure's true path calculates and displays the gross pay; otherwise, its false path displays the "Incorrect number of hours" message. The compound condition in Example 2, on the other hand, uses the OrElse operator to determine whether the value stored in the `dblHours` variable is either less than 0 or greater than 40. If the compound condition evaluates to True, the selection structure's true path displays the "Incorrect number of hours" message; otherwise, its false path calculates and displays the gross pay. Both examples in Figure 4-23 produce the same result and simply represent two different ways of performing the same task.

Procedures Containing Logical Operators

Example 1– using the AndAlso operator

```
PrivateSub btnCalc_Click(sender As Object,
e As EventArgs) Handles btnCalc.Click
    ' calculate the gross pay

    Const dblRATE As Double = 10.75
    Dim dblHours As Double
    Dim dblGross As Double

    ' store hours in a variable
    Double.TryParse(txtHours.Text, dblHours)

    If dblHours >= 0 AndAlso dblHours <= 40 Then
        ' calculate and display gross pay
        dblGross = dblHours * dblRATE
        lblGross.Text = dblGross.ToString("C2")
    Else
        lblGross.Text = "Incorrect number of hours"
    End If
End Sub
```

Figure 4-23 Examples of using the AndAlso and OrElse logical operators *(continues)*

(continued)

Example 2– using the OrElse operator

```
Private Sub btnCalc_Click(sender As Object,
e As EventArgs) Handles btnCalc.Click
    ' calculate the gross pay

    Const dblRATE AsDouble = 10.75
    Dim dblHours AsDouble
    Dim dblGross AsDouble

    ' store hours in a variable
    Double.TryParse(txtHours.Text, dblHours)

    If dblHours < 0 OrElse dblHours > 40 Then
       lblGross.Text = "Incorrect number of hours"
    Else
       ' calculate and display gross pay
       dblGross = dblHours * dblRATE
       lblGross.Text = dblGross.ToString("C2")
    End If
End Sub
```

Figure 4-23 Examples of using the AndAlso and OrElse logical operators

START HERE

To code and then test the Gross Pay Calculator application:

1. Open the Gross Pay Solution (Gross Pay Solution.sln) file contained in the VB2012\Chap04\Gross Pay Solution folder. If necessary, open the designer window.
2. Open the Code Editor window. Replace <your name> and <current date> in the comments with your name and the current date, respectively.
3. Locate the code template for the btnCalc control's Click event procedure. Enter the comments and code from either of the two examples shown in Figure 4-23.
4. Save the solution and then start the application. Type **30** in the Hours worked box and then press **Enter** to select the Calculate button. The button's Click event procedure displays the gross pay amount in the Gross pay box. See Figure 4-24.

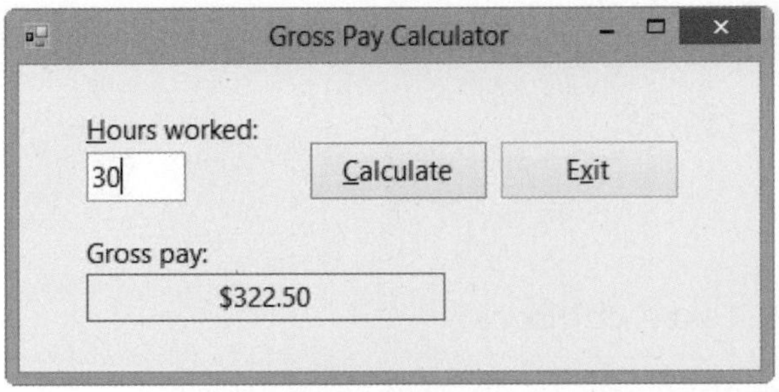

Figure 4-24 Sample run of the application using valid data

5. Change the number of hours worked to **43** and then press **Enter**. The Calculate button's Click event procedure displays the "Incorrect number of hours" message in the Gross pay box. See Figure 4-25.

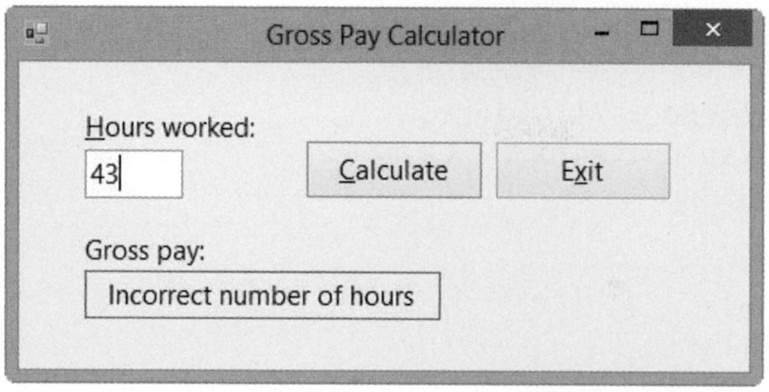

Figure 4-25 Sample run of the application using invalid data

6. Click the **Exit** button. Close the Code Editor window and then close the solution.

YOU DO IT 5!

Create a Visual Basic Windows application named YouDoIt 5. Save the application in the VB2012\Chap04 folder. Add a text box, a label, and a button to the form. If the user enters a number that is either less than 0 or greater than 100, the button's Click event procedure should display the string "Invalid number" in the label; otherwise, it should display the string "Valid number". Code the procedure. Save the solution and then start and test the application. Close the solution.

In addition to comparing numeric values, as well as comparing numbers treated as strings, an If...Then...Else statement's condition also can compare strings containing letters.

Comparing Strings Containing Letters

A procedure needs to display the words "Senior discount" when the user enters the letter Y in the txt65AndOver control, and the words "No discount" when the user enters anything else. Figure 4-26 shows four ways of writing the procedure's code.

Procedures Containing String Comparisons

Example 1 – using the OrElse operator

```
Private Sub btnDisplay_Click(sender As Object,
e As EventArgs) Handles btnDisplay.Click
    ' display appropriate message

    Dim strSenior As String
    ' store input in a variable
    strSenior = txt65AndOver.Text
    ' display message
    If strSenior = "Y" OrElse strSenior = "y" Then
       lblMsg.Text = "Senior discount"
    Else
       lblMsg.Text = "No discount"
    End If
End Sub
```

Figure 4-26 Examples of using string comparisons in a procedure *(continues)*

(continued)

Example 2 – using the AndAlso operator
```
Private Sub btnDisplay_Click(sender As Object,
e As EventArgs) Handles btnDisplay.Click
    ' display appropriate message

    Dim strSenior As String
    ' store input in a variable
    strSenior = txt65AndOver.Text
    ' display message
    If strSenior <> "Y" AndAlso strSenior <> "y" Then
       lblMsg.Text = "No discount"
    Else
       lblMsg.Text = "Senior discount"
    End If
End Sub
```

Example 3 – inefficient solution
```
Private Sub btnDisplay_Click(sender As Object,
e As EventArgs) Handles btnDisplay.Click
    ' display appropriate message

    Dim strSenior As String
    ' store input in a variable
    strSenior = txt65AndOver.Text
    ' display message
    If strSenior = "Y" OrElse strSenior = "y" Then
       lblMsg.Text = "Senior discount"
    End If
    If strSenior <> "Y" AndAlso strSenior <> "y" Then
       lblMsg.Text = "No discount"
    End If
End Sub
```

unnecessary evaluation

Example 4 – using the ToUpper method
```
PrivateSub btnDisplay_Click(sender As Object,
e As EventArgs) Handles btnDisplay.Click
    ' display appropriate message

    Dim strSenior As String
    ' store input in a variable
    strSenior = txt65AndOver.Text
    ' display message
    If strSenior.ToUpper = "Y" Then
       lblMsg.Text = "Senior discount"
    Else
       lblMsg.Text = "No discount"
    End If
End Sub
```

Figure 4-26 Examples of using string comparisons in a procedure

The compound condition in Example 1 determines whether the value stored in the `strSenior` variable is either the uppercase letter Y or the lowercase letter y. When the variable contains one of those two letters, the compound condition evaluates to True and the selection structure's true path displays the words "Senior discount" on the screen; otherwise, its false path displays the words "No discount". You may be wondering why you need to compare the contents of the `strSenior` variable with both the uppercase and lowercase forms of the letter Y. As is true in many programming languages, string comparisons in Visual Basic are case sensitive, which means that the uppercase version of a letter is not the same as its lowercase counterpart. So, although a human being recognizes Y and y as being the same letter, a computer does not; to a computer, a Y is different from a y. The reason for this differentiation is that each character on the computer keyboard is stored using a different Unicode character in the computer's internal memory.

In Example 2 in Figure 4-26, the compound condition determines whether the value stored in the `strSenior` variable is not equal to the uppercase letter Y and also not equal to the lowercase letter y. When the variable does not contain either of those two letters, the compound condition evaluates to True and the selection structure's true path displays the words "No discount" on the screen; otherwise, its false path displays the words "Senior discount".

Rather than using a dual-alternative selection structure, as in Examples 1 and 2, Example 3 uses two single-alternative selection structures. Although the selection structures in Example 3 produce the same results as the ones in Examples 1 and 2, they do so less efficiently. To illustrate this point, assume that the user enters the letter Y in the txt65AndOver control. The compound condition in the first selection structure in Example 3 determines whether the value stored in the `strSenior` variable is equal to either Y or y. The compound condition evaluates to True, so the first selection structure's true path displays the words "Senior discount". Although the appropriate words ("Senior discount") already appear in the interface, the procedure still evaluates the second selection structure's compound condition to determine whether to display the "No discount" message. The second evaluation is unnecessary and makes Example 3's code less efficient than the code shown in Examples 1 and 2.

The selection structure in Example 4 in Figure 4-26 also contains a string comparison in its condition. However, notice that the condition does not use a logical operator; rather, it uses the ToUpper method. You will learn about the ToUpper method in the next section.

Converting a String to Uppercase or Lowercase

As already mentioned, string comparisons in Visual Basic are case-sensitive, which means that the string "Yes" is not the same as either the string "YES" or the string "yes". Because of this, a problem may occur when you need to compare strings that are either entered by the user or read from a file. This is due to the fact that you cannot always control the case of the string. Although you can change a text box's CharacterCasing property from its default value of Normal to either Upper (which converts the user's entry to uppercase) or Lower (which converts the user's entry to lowercase), you may not want to change the case of the user's entry as he or she is typing it. And it's entirely possible that you may not be aware of the case of strings that are read from a file. To fix the comparison problem, you can use either the **ToUpper method** or the **ToLower method** to temporarily convert the string to either uppercase or lowercase, respectively, and then use the converted string in the comparison.

You will use the CharacterCasing property in Exercise 16 at the end of this lesson.

Figure 4-27 shows the syntax of the ToUpper and ToLower methods and includes examples of using the methods. In each syntax, *string* is usually either the name of a String variable or the Text property of an object. Both methods copy the contents of the *string* to a temporary location in the computer's internal memory. The methods convert the temporary string to the appropriate case (if necessary) and then return the temporary string. Keep in mind that the ToUpper and ToLower methods do not change the contents of the *string*; they change the contents of the temporary location only. In addition, the ToUpper and ToLower methods affect only letters of the alphabet, which are the only characters that have uppercase and lowercase forms.

ToUpper and ToLower Methods

<u>Syntax</u>
string.**ToUpper**
string.**ToLower**

<u>Example 1</u>
`If strSenior.ToUpper = "Y" Then`
compares the uppercase version of the string stored in the `strSenior` variable with the uppercase letter Y

<u>Example 2</u>
`If strName1.ToUpper = strName2.ToUpper Then`
compares the uppercase version of the string stored in the `strName1` variable with the uppercase version of the string stored in the `strName2` variable

<u>Example 3</u>
`If strSenior.ToLower <> "y" Then`
compares the lowercase version of the string stored in the `strSenior` variable with the lowercase letter y

<u>Example 4</u>
`If "london" = txtCity.Text.ToLower Then`
compares the lowercase string "london" with the lowercase version of the string stored in the txtCity control's Text property

<u>Example 5</u>
`lblName.Text = strCustomer.ToUpper`
assigns the uppercase version of the string stored in the `strCustomer` variable to the lblName control's Text property

<u>Example 6</u>
```
strName = strName.ToUpper
txtState.Text = txtState.Text.ToLower
```
changes the contents of the `strName` variable to uppercase, and changes the contents of the txtState control's Text property to lowercase

Figure 4-27 Syntax and examples of the ToUpper and ToLower methods

When using the ToUpper method in a comparison, be sure that everything you are comparing is uppercase, as shown in Examples 1 and 2; otherwise, the comparison will not evaluate correctly. For instance, the clause `If strSenior.ToUpper = "y" Then` is not correct: The condition will always evaluate to False because the uppercase version of a letter will never be equal to its lowercase counterpart. Likewise, when using the ToLower method in a comparison, be sure that everything you are comparing is lowercase, as shown in Examples 3 and 4. The statement in Example 5 temporarily converts the contents of the `strCustomer` variable to uppercase and then assigns the result to the lblName control. As Example 6 indicates, you also can use the ToUpper and ToLower methods to permanently convert the contents of either a String variable or a control's Text property to uppercase or lowercase, respectively.

Using the ToUpper and ToLower Methods: Displaying a Message

A procedure needs to display the message "On Mount Rushmore" when the user enters the name of any of the four Mount Rushmore presidents; otherwise, the procedure should display the message "Not on Mount Rushmore". Figure 4-28 shows three ways of writing the procedure's code.

Procedures Containing the ToUpper and ToLower Methods

Example 1 – using the ToUpper method in a condition

```
Private Sub btnDisplay_Click(sender As Object,
e As EventArgs) Handles btnDisplay.Click
    ' display an appropriate message

    Dim strName As String

    strName = txtName.Text
    If strName.ToUpper = "GEORGE WASHINGTON" OrElse
       strName.ToUpper = "THOMAS JEFFERSON" OrElse
       strName.ToUpper = "ABRAHAM LINCOLN" OrElse
       strName.ToUpper = "THEODORE ROOSEVELT" Then
       lblMsg.Text = "On Mount Rushmore"
    Else
       lblMsg.Text = "Not on Mount Rushmore"
    End If
EndSub
```

Example 2 – using the ToUpper method in an assignment statement

```
Private Sub btnDisplay_Click(sender As Object,
e As EventArgs) Handles btnDisplay.Click
    ' display an appropriate message

    Dim strName As String

    strName = txtName.Text.ToUpper
    If strName = "GEORGE WASHINGTON" OrElse
       strName = "THOMAS JEFFERSON" OrElse
       strName = "ABRAHAM LINCOLN" OrElse
       strName = "THEODORE ROOSEVELT" Then
       lblMsg.Text = "On Mount Rushmore"
    Else
       lblMsg.Text = "Not on Mount Rushmore"
    End If
End Sub
```

Example 3 – using the ToLower method in an assignment statement

```
Private Sub btnDisplay_Click(sender As Object,
e As EventArgs) Handles btnDisplay.Click
    ' display an appropriate message

    Dim strName AsString

    strName = txtName.Text.ToLower
    If strName <> "george washington" AndAlso
       strName <> "thomas jefferson" AndAlso
       strName <> "abraham lincoln" AndAlso
       strName <> "theodore roosevelt" Then
       lblMsg.Text = "Not on Mount Rushmore"
    Else
       lblMsg.Text = "On Mount Rushmore"
  End If
End Sub
```

Figure 4-28 Examples of using the ToUpper and ToLower methods in a procedure

When the computer processes the compound condition in Example 1, it temporarily converts the contents of the `strName` variable to uppercase and then compares the result to the string "GEORGE WASHINGTON". If the comparison evaluates to False, the computer again temporarily converts the contents of the variable to uppercase, this time comparing the result to the string "THOMAS JEFFERSON". If the comparison evaluates to False, the computer again temporarily converts the contents of the variable to uppercase; this time, it compares the result to the string "ABRAHAM LINCOLN". If the comparison evaluates to False, the computer once again temporarily converts the contents of the variable to uppercase, comparing the result to the string "THEODORE ROOSEVELT". Notice that, depending on the result of each condition, the computer might need to temporarily convert the contents of the `strName` variable to uppercase four times.

Example 2 in Figure 4-28 provides a more efficient way of writing Example 1's code. The `strName = txtName.Text.ToUpper` statement in Example 2 temporarily converts the contents of the txtName control's Text property to uppercase and then assigns the result to the `strName` variable. The compound condition then compares the contents of the `strName` variable (which now contains uppercase letters) to the string "GEORGE WASHINGTON". If the comparison evaluates to False, the computer compares the variable's contents to the string "THOMAS JEFFERSON". If this comparison evaluates to False, the computer compares the variable's contents to the string "ABRAHAM LINCOLN". If this comparison evaluates to False, the computer compares the variable's contents to the string "THEODORE ROOSEVELT". Notice that the value in the txtName control's Text property is converted to uppercase only once, rather than four times. However, although Example 2's code is more efficient than Example 1's code, there may be times when you will not want to change the case of the string stored in a variable. For example, you may need to display (on the screen or in a printed report) the variable's contents using the exact case entered by the user.

The `strName = txtName.Text.ToLower` statement in Example 3 in Figure 4-28 temporarily converts the contents of the txtName control's Text property to lowercase and then assigns the result to the `strName` variable. The compound condition in Example 3 is processed similarly to the compound condition in Example 2. However, the comparisons are made using lowercase letters rather than uppercase letters, and the comparisons test for inequality rather than equality. The three examples in Figure 4-28 produce the same result and simply represent different ways of performing the same task.

START HERE

To code and then test the Mount Rushmore application:

1. Open the Mount Rushmore Solution (Mount Rushmore Solution.sln) file contained in the VB2012\Chap04\ Mount Rushmore Solution folder. If necessary, open the designer window.
2. Open the Code Editor window. Replace <your name> and <current date> in the comments with your name and the current date, respectively.
3. Open the code template for the btnDisplay control's Click event procedure. Enter the code shown in any of the three examples shown earlier in Figure 4-28.
4. Save the solution and then start the application. Type **george washington** in the Name box and then press **Enter** to select the Display button. The button's Click event procedure displays the "On Mount Rushmore" message in the lblMsg control. See Figure 4-29.

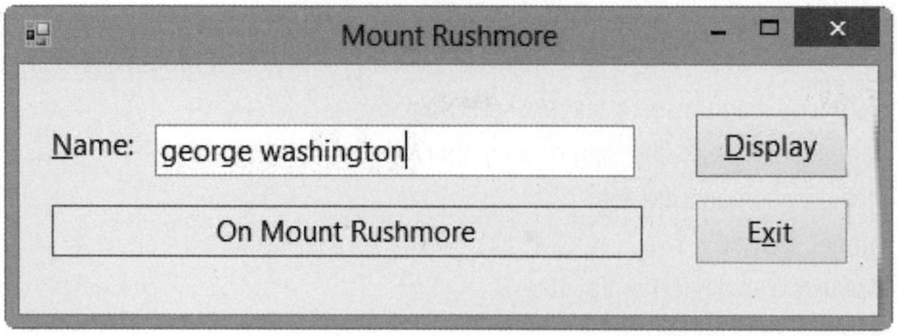

Figure 4-29 Message shown in the interface

5. Change the name to **john adams** and then press **Enter**. The button's Click event procedure displays the "Not on Mount Rushmore" message.
6. On your own, test the code using the names of the other three presidents on Mount Rushmore.
7. When you are finished testing the code, click the **Exit** button. Close the Code Editor window and then close the solution.

YOU DO IT 6!

Create a Visual Basic Windows application named YouDoIt 6. Save the application in the VB2012\Chap04 folder. Add a text box, a label, and a button to the form. If the user enters the letter A (in either uppercase or lowercase), the button's Click event procedure should display the string "Addition" in the label; otherwise, it should display the string "Subtraction". Code the procedure. Save the solution and then start and test the application. Close the solution.

Summary of Operators

Figure 4-30 shows the order of precedence for the arithmetic, concatenation, comparison, and logical operators you have learned so far. Recall that operators with the same precedence number are evaluated from left to right in an expression. Notice that logical operators are evaluated after any arithmetic operators or comparison operators in an expression. As a result, when the computer processes the expression 30 > 75 / 3 AndAlso 5 < 10 * 2, it evaluates the arithmetic operators first, followed by the comparison operators and then the logical operator. The expression evaluates to True, as shown in the example included in Figure 4-30. (Keep in mind that you can use parentheses to override the order of precedence.)

Ch04A-Operators video

Operator	Operation	Precedence number
^	exponentiation (raises a number to a power)	1
–	negation (reverses the sign of a number)	2
*, /	multiplication and division	3
\	integer division	4
Mod	modulus (remainder) arithmetic	5
+, –	addition and subtraction	6
&	concatenation	7
=, >, >=, <, <=, <>	equal to, greater than, greater than or equal to, less than, less than or equal to, not equal to	8
Not	reverses the truth-value of the condition; True becomes False, and False becomes True	9
AndAlso, And	all sub-conditions must be True for the compound condition to evaluate to True	10
OrElse, Or	only one of the sub-conditions needs to be True for the compound condition to evaluate to True	11
Xor	one and only one of the sub-conditions can be True for the compound condition to evaluate to True	12

Example

Evaluation steps	Result
Original expression	30 > 75 / 3 AndAlso 5 < 10 * 2
75 / 3 is evaluated first	30 > 25 AndAlso 5 < 10 * 2
10 * 2 is evaluated second	30 > 25 AndAlso 5 < 20
30 > 25 is evaluated third	True AndAlso 5 < 20
5 < 20 is evaluated fourth	True AndAlso True
True AndAlso True is evaluated last	True

Figure 4-30 Listing of arithmetic, concatenation, comparison, and logical operators

Lesson A Summary

- To code single-alternative and dual-alternative selection structures:

  Use the If…Then…Else statement. The statement's syntax is shown in Figure 4-9.

- To compare two values:

  Use the comparison operators listed in Figure 4-12.

- To swap the values contained in two variables:

  Assign the first variable's value to a temporary variable. Assign the second variable's value to the first variable, and then assign the temporary variable's value to the second variable. An illustration of the swapping concept is shown in Figure 4-17.

- To create a compound condition:

  Use the logical operators and truth tables listed in Figures 4-21 and 4-22, respectively.

- To convert the user's text box entry to either uppercase or lowercase as the user is typing the text:

  Change the text box's CharacterCasing property from Normal to either Upper or Lower.

- To temporarily convert a string to uppercase:

  Use the ToUpper method. The method's syntax is *string*.**ToUpper**.
- To temporarily convert a string to lowercase:

  Use the ToLower method. The method's syntax is *string*.**ToLower**.
- To evaluate an expression containing arithmetic, comparison, and logical operators:

  Evaluate the arithmetic operators first, followed by the comparison operators and then the logical operators. Figure 4-30 shows the order of precedence for the arithmetic, concatenation, comparison, and logical operators you have learned so far.

Lesson A Key Terms

And operator—one of the logical operators; when used to combine two sub-conditions, the resulting compound condition evaluates to True only when both sub-conditions are True; it evaluates to False when one or both of the sub-conditions are False

AndAlso operator—one of the logical operators; same as the And operator, but more efficient because it performs a short-circuit evaluation

Block scope—the scope of a variable declared within a statement block; a variable with block scope can be used only within the statement block in which it is declared, and only after its declaration statement

Block-level variable—a variable declared within a statement block; the variable has block scope

Comparison operators—operators used to compare values in an expression; also called relational operators

Condition—specifies the decision you are making and must be phrased so that it evaluates to an answer of either true or false

Data validation—the process of verifying that a program's input data is within the expected range

Decision symbol—the diamond in a flowchart; used to represent the condition in selection and repetition structures

Dual-alternative selection structure—a selection structure that requires one set of actions to be performed when the structure's condition evaluates to True, but a different set of actions to be performed when the structure's condition evaluates to False

False path—contains the instructions to be processed when a selection structure's condition evaluates to False

If . . . Then . . . Else statement—used to code single-alternative and dual-alternative selection structures in Visual Basic

Logical operators—operators used to combine two or more sub-conditions into one compound condition; also called Boolean operators

Not operator—one of the logical operators; reverses the truth-value of a condition

Or operator—one of the logical operators; when used to combine two sub-conditions, the resulting compound condition evaluates to True when at least one of the sub-conditions is True; it evaluates to False only when both sub-conditions are False

OrElse operator—one of the logical operators; same as the Or operator, but more efficient because it performs a short-circuit evaluation

Selection structure—one of the three basic control structures; tells the computer to make a decision based on some condition and then select the appropriate action; also called the decision structure

Short-circuit evaluation—refers to the way the computer evaluates two sub-conditions connected by either the AndAlso or OrElse operators; when the AndAlso operator is used, the computer does not evaluate sub-condition2 when sub-condition1 is False; when the OrElse operator is used, the computer does not evaluate sub-condition2 when sub-condition1 is True

Single-alternative selection structure—a selection structure that requires a special set of actions to be performed only when the structure's condition evaluates to True

Statement block—in a selection structure, the set of statements terminated by an Else or End If clause

ToLower method—temporarily converts a string to lowercase

ToUpper method—temporarily converts a string to uppercase

True path—contains the instructions to be processed when a selection structure's condition evaluates to True

Truth tables—tables that summarize how the computer evaluates the logical operators in an expression

Lesson A Review Questions

1. What is the scope of variables declared in an If... Then... Else statement's true path?
   a. only the true path in the If... Then... Else statement
   b. the entire application
   c. the procedure in which the If... Then... Else statement appears
   d. the entire If... Then... Else statement

2. Which of the following is a valid condition for an If... Then... Else statement?
   a. `intQuantity > 0 AndAlso < 500`
   b. `intQuantity < 0 AndAlso intQuantity > 5000`
   c. `intQuantity < 0 OrElse intQuantity > 5000`
   d. `intQuantity > 0 OrElse > 500`

3. Which of the following If clauses compares the string contained in the txtId control with the state abbreviation Tx? (Be sure the clause will handle Tx, TX, tx, and tX.)
   a. `If txtId.Text = ToUpper("TX") Then`
   b. `If txtId.Text = ToLower("tx") Then`
   c. `If ToUpper(txtId.Text) = "TX" Then`
   d. `If txtId.Text.ToUpper = "TX" Then`

4. The six logical operators are listed below. Indicate their order of precedence by placing a number (1, 2, and so on) on the line to the left of the operator. (If two or more operators have the same precedence, assign the same number to each.)

   _______________ Xor

   _______________ And

   _______________ Not

   _______________ Or

   _______________ AndAlso

   _______________ OrElse

5. An expression can contain arithmetic, comparison, and logical operators. Indicate the order of precedence for the three types of operators by placing a number (1, 2, or 3) on the line to the left of the operator type.

   ______________ Arithmetic

   ______________ Logical

   ______________ Comparison

6. The expression 6 > 12 `OrElse` 4 < 5 evaluates to ______________.
   a. True
   b. False

7. The expression 6 + 3 > 7 `AndAlso` 11 > 2 * 5 evaluates to ______________.
   a. True
   b. False

8. The expression 8 >= 4 + 6 `OrElse` 5 > 6 `AndAlso` 4 < 7 evaluates to ______________.
   a. True
   b. False

9. The expression 7 + 3 * 2 > 5 * 3 `AndAlso True` evaluates to ______________.
   a. True
   b. False

10. The expression 5 * 4 > 6 ^ 2 evaluates to ______________.
    a. True
    b. False

11. The expression 5 * 4 > 6 ^ 2 `AndAlso True OrElse False` evaluates to ______________.
    a. True
    b. False

Use the selection structure shown in Figure 4-31 to answer Questions 12 through 14.

```
If intNum >= 500 Then
      intNum = intNum * 5
Else
      intNum = intNum * 3
End If
```

Figure 4-31 Code for Review Questions 12 through 14

12. If the `intNum` variable contains the number 90, what value will be in the variable after the selection structure in Figure 4-31 is processed?

    a. 0
    b. 90
    c. 270
    d. 450

13. If the `intNum` variable contains the number 1000, what value will be in the variable after the selection structure in Figure 4-31 is processed?

    a. 0
    b. 1000
    c. 3000
    d. 5000

14. If the `intNum` variable contains the number 500, what value will be in the variable after the selection structure in Figure 4-31 is processed?

    a. 0
    b. 500
    c. 1500
    d. 2500

Lesson A Exercises

INTRODUCTORY

1. Draw the flowchart corresponding to the pseudocode shown in Figure 4-32.

```
if the sales are less than or equal to 10,000
        display "3% bonus"
else
        display "5% bonus"
end if
```

Figure 4-32 Pseudocode for Exercise 1

INTRODUCTORY

2. Write an If…Then…Else statement that displays the string "Vegetable" in the lblType control when the txtFood control contains the string "Corn" (in any case).

INTRODUCTORY

3. Write an If…Then…Else statement that displays the string "Please enter the invoice number" in the lblMsg control when the txtInvoiceNum control does not contain any data.

INTRODUCTORY

4. Write an If…Then…Else statement that displays the string "Incorrect quantity" in the lblMsg control when the `intQuantity` variable contains a number that is less than 0; otherwise, display the string "Valid quantity".

INTRODUCTORY

5. Write an If…Then…Else statement that displays the string "Time to reorder" in the lblMsg control when the `intNumUnits` variable contains a number that is less than 5; otherwise, display the string "We have enough in stock".

INTRODUCTORY

6. Write an If…Then…Else statement that assigns the number 35 to the `intCommission` variable when the `decSales` variable contains a number that is less than or equal to $250; otherwise, assign the number 50.

7. Write an If ... Then ... Else statement that displays the value 25 in the lblShipping control when the `strState` variable contains the string "Alaska" (in any case); otherwise, display the value 15. INTRODUCTORY

8. Write an If ... Then ... Else statement that displays the string "Cat" in the lblAnimal control when the `strAnimal` variable contains the letter "C" (in any case); otherwise, display the string "Dog". Also draw the flowchart. INTRODUCTORY

9. A procedure should calculate a 2.5% commission when the `strCommType` variable contains the string "Prime" (in any case); otherwise, it should calculate a 2% commission. The commission is calculated by multiplying the commission rate by the contents of the `dblSales` variable. Display the commission in the lblComm control. Draw the flowchart and then write the Visual Basic code. INTRODUCTORY

10. In this exercise, you modify the Kettleson application from this lesson. Use Windows to make a copy of the Kettleson Solution folder. Rename the copy Modified Kettleson Solution. Open the Kettleson Solution (Kettleson Solution.sln) file contained in the Modified Kettleson Solution folder. Open the designer and Code Editor windows. Locate the btnCalc_Click procedure. Change the selection structure's condition so that it tests for the opposite of what it does now, then make the appropriate modifications to the selection structure's true and false paths. Save the solution and then start the application. Test the application twice, using 25000 and 15000 as the annual sales. Close the Code Editor window and then close the solution. INTRODUCTORY

11. Assume that a customer purchases either a Harris Brothers item or a Jacob Co. item. If the item is a sweater manufactured by Harris Brothers, the customer is entitled to a 5% discount. Write the Visual Basic code for a procedure that calculates and displays the discount (if any) and the new price. Use the variables `strManufacturer`, `strItem`, `dblPrice`, and `dblDiscount`. Format the discount and new price using the "C2" format. Display the calculated amounts in the lblDiscount and lblNewPrice controls. INTERMEDIATE

12. Write the Visual Basic code that swaps the values stored in the `decLow` and `decHigh` variables, but only if the value stored in the `decHigh` variable is less than the value stored in the `decLow` variable. INTERMEDIATE

13. In this exercise, you modify the Sum or Difference application from this lesson. Use Windows to make a copy of the Sum or Difference Solution folder. Rename the copy Modified Sum or Difference Solution. Open the Sum or Difference Solution (Sum or Difference Solution.sln) file contained in the Modified Sum or Difference Solution folder. Open the designer window. Change the Label1's text from "Enter 1 (Addition) or 2 (Subtraction):" to "Enter A (Addition) or S (Subtraction):". Open the Code Editor window. Make the appropriate modifications to the btnCalc_Click procedure. The user should be able to enter the operation letter in either uppercase or lowercase. Save the solution and then start and test the application. Close the Code Editor window and then close the solution. INTERMEDIATE

14. In this exercise, you modify the Jerrili application from this lesson. Use Windows to make a copy of the Jerrili Solution folder. Rename the copy Modified Jerrili Solution. Open the Jerrili Solution (Jerrili Solution.sln) file contained in the Modified Jerrili Solution folder. Open the designer and Code Editor windows. Jerrili's now gives a discount to all of its customers. The discount rate is 20% when the quantity purchased is at least 10, and 15% when the quantity purchased is less than 10. Make the appropriate modifications to the btnCalc_Click procedure. Save the solution and then start and test the application. Close the Code Editor window and then close the solution. INTERMEDIATE

15. Open the Shipping Solution (Shipping Solution.sln) file contained in the VB2012\Chap04\Shipping Solution folder. If necessary, open the designer window. INTERMEDIATE

The Display button's Click event procedure should display the message "We ship to this state." if the user enters one of the following state IDs: TN, KY, or IN. If the user enters an ID other than these, the procedure should display the "We don't ship to this state." message. The user should be able to enter the ID in uppercase, lowercase, or a combination of uppercase and lowercase. Code the procedure. Save the solution and then start and test the application. Close the Code Editor window and then close the solution.

DISCOVERY

16. In this exercise, you learn how to use a text box's CharacterCasing property. Open the CharCase Solution (CharCase Solution.sln) file contained in the VB2012\Chap04\CharCase Solution folder. If necessary, open the designer window.

    a. Open the Code Editor window and study the code contained in the btnDisplay_Click procedure. The code compares the contents of the txtId control with the strings "AB12", "XY59", and "TV45". However, it does not convert the contents of the text box to uppercase. Start the application. Enter ab12 as the ID and then click the Display button. The button's Click event procedure displays the "Invalid ID" message, which is incorrect. Click the Exit button.

    b. Use the Properties window to change the txtId control's CharacterCasing property to Upper. Save the solution and then start the application. Enter ab12 as the ID. Notice that the letters appear in uppercase in the text box. Click the Display button. The button's Click event procedure displays the "Valid ID" message, which is correct. Click the Exit button. Close the Code Editor window and then close the solution.

LESSON B

After studying Lesson B, you should be able to:

- Group objects using a GroupBox control
- Create a message box using the MessageBox.Show method
- Determine the value returned by a message box

Creating the Covington Resort Application

Recall that your task in this chapter is to create a reservation application for Covington Resort. The application will allow the user to enter the following information: the number of rooms to reserve, the length of stay (in nights), the number of adults, and the number of children. As you may remember, each room can accommodate a maximum of six people. The resort charges $284 per room per night. It also charges a 15.25% sales and lodging tax, which is based on the room charge. In addition, there is a $15 resort fee per room per night. The application should display the total room charge, the sales and lodging tax, the total resort fee, and the total due.

Ch04B video

To open the partially completed Covington Resort application:

START HERE

1. If necessary, start Visual Studio 2012. Open the Covington Resort Solution (Covington Resort Solution.sln) file contained in the VB2012\Chap04\Covington Resort Solution folder. If necessary, open the designer window. The interface contains one group box. In the next section, you will add another group box to the interface. See Figure 4-33.

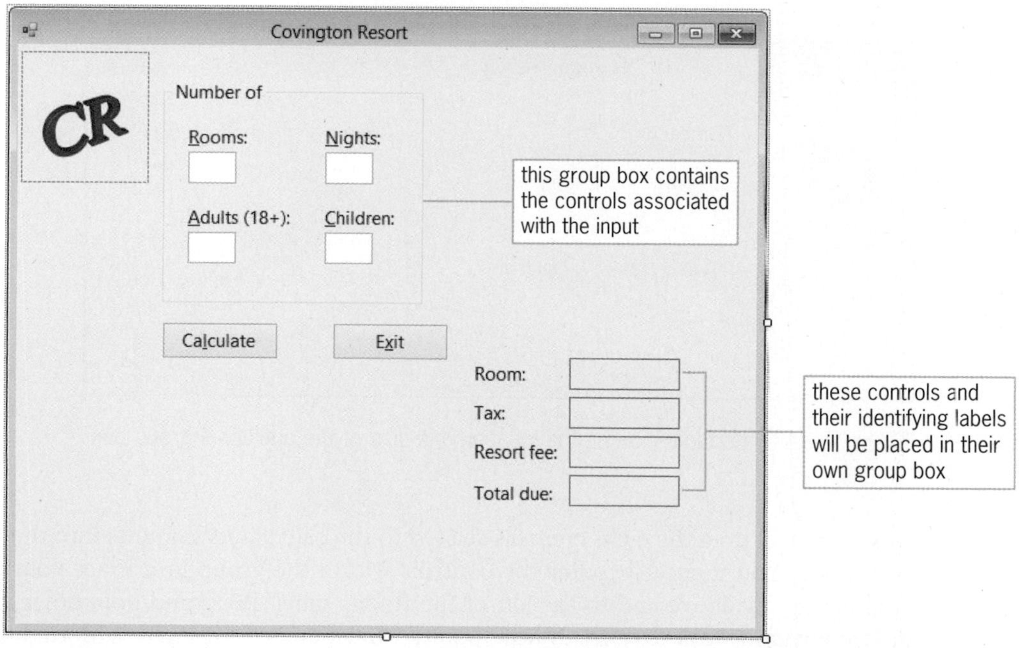

Figure 4-33 Partially completed interface for Covington Resort

Adding a Group Box to the Form

You use the GroupBox tool, which is located in the Containers section of the toolbox, to add a group box to the interface. A **group box** serves as a container for other controls and is typically used to visually separate related controls from other controls on the form. For example, the group box shown in Figure 4-33 visually separates the input controls from the rest of the controls. You can include an identifying label on a group box by setting the group box's Text property. Labeling a group box is optional; but if you do label it, the label should be entered using sentence capitalization. Keep in mind that a group box and its controls are treated as one unit. When you move a group box, the controls inside the group box also move. Likewise, when you delete a group box, the controls inside the group box are also deleted.

GUI DESIGN TIP Labeling a Group Box

- Use sentence capitalization for the optional identifying label, which is entered in the group box's Text property.

START HERE

To add a group box to the interface:

1. If necessary, expand the Containers node in the toolbox. Click the **GroupBox** tool and then drag the mouse pointer to the form. You do not need to worry about the exact location. Release the mouse button. The GroupBox1 control appears on the form.
2. Change the group box's Text property to **Charges**, then position and size the group box as shown in Figure 4-34.

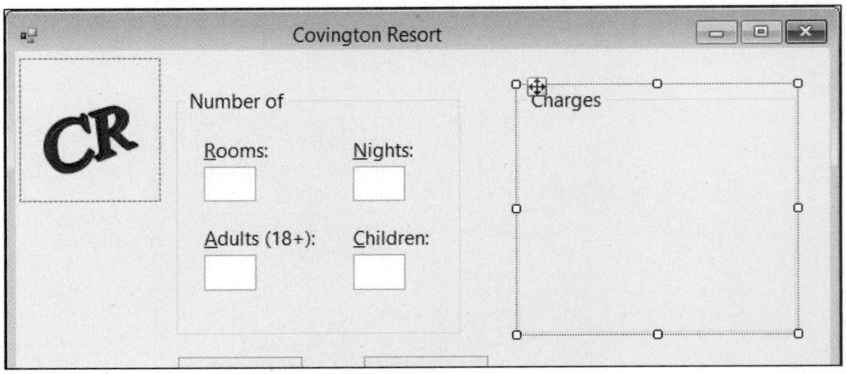

Figure 4-34 Interface showing the location and size of the additional group box

3. Next, you will drag the eight controls related to the calculated amounts into the Charges group box. You then will center the controls within the group box. Place your mouse pointer slightly above and to the left of the Room: label. Press and hold down the left mouse button as you drag the mouse pointer down and to the right. A dotted rectangle appears as you drag. Continue to drag until the dotted rectangle surrounds the eight controls, as shown in Figure 4-35.

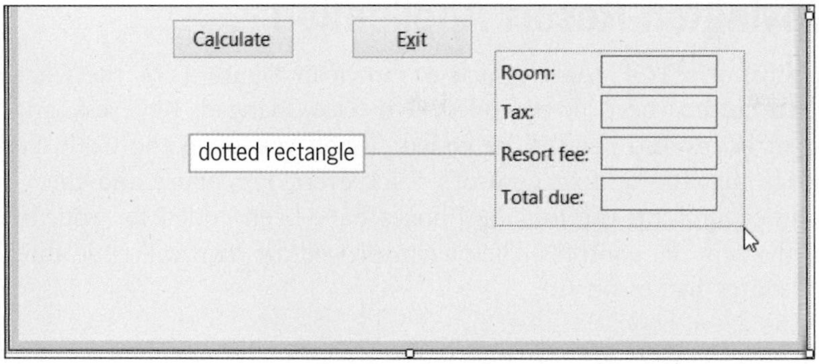

Figure 4-35 Dotted rectangle surrounding the eight controls

4. When the dotted rectangle surrounds the eight controls, release the mouse button to select the eight controls. Place your mouse pointer on one of the selected controls. The mouse pointer turns into the move pointer. Press and hold down the left mouse button as you drag the selected controls into the Charges group box, then release the mouse button.
5. Use the Format menu to center the selected controls both horizontally and vertically in the group box.
6. Click the **form** to deselect the controls. Use the sizing handle to move the form's bottom border closer to the buttons (you can look ahead to Figure 4-36), and then lock the controls on the form.
7. Click **View** on the menu bar and then click **Tab Order**. Notice that the TabIndex values of the controls contained within each group box begin with the TabIndex value of the group box itself. This indicates that the controls belong to the group box rather than to the form. As mentioned earlier, if you move or delete the group box, the controls that belong to the group box will also be moved or deleted. The numbers that appear after the period in the TabIndex values indicate the order in which each control was added to the group box.
8. Use the information shown in Figure 4-36 to set each control's TabIndex value.

You also can select more than one control by clicking the first control and then pressing and holding down the Ctrl (Control) key as you click the other controls you want to select. The move pointer mentioned in Step 4 looks like this: .

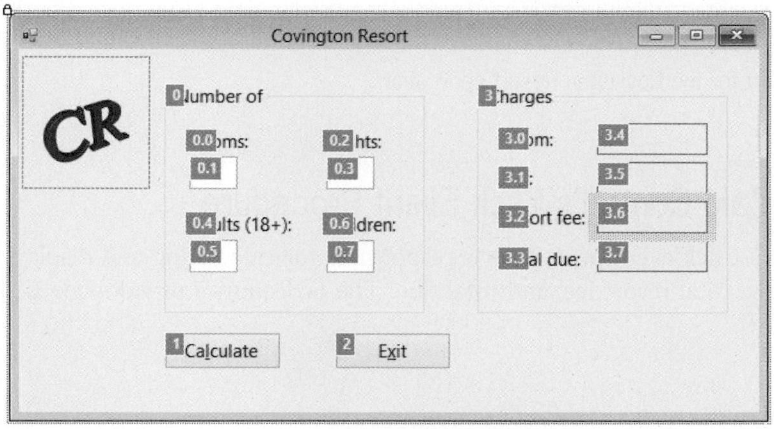

Figure 4-36 Correct TabIndex values for the interface

9. When you are finished setting the TabIndex values, press **Esc** to remove the TabIndex boxes, and then save the solution.

Coding the Covington Resort Application

According to the application's TOE chart, which is shown in Figure 4-37, the Click event procedures for the two buttons need to be coded. The TextChanged, KeyPress, and Enter events for the four text boxes also need to be coded. When you open the Code Editor window, you will notice that the btnExit control's Click event procedure and the TextChanged event procedures for the four text boxes have been coded for you. In this lesson, you will code the btnCalc control's Click event procedure. You will code the KeyPress and Enter event procedures in Lesson C.

Task	Object	Event
1. Calculate the total room charge, tax, total resort fee, and total due 2. Display the calculated amounts in lblRoomChg, lblTax, lblResortFee, and lblTotalDue	btnCalc	Click
End the application	btnExit	Click
Display the total room charge (from btnCalc)	lblRoomChg	None
Display the tax (from btnCalc)	lblTax	None
Display the total resort fee (from btnCalc)	lblResortFee	None
Display the total due (from btnCalc)	lblTotalDue	None
Get and display the number of rooms reserved, number of nights, number of adults, and number of children	txtRooms, txtNights, txtAdults, txtChildren	None
Clear the contents of lblRoomChg, lblTax, lblResortFee, and lblTotalDue	txtRooms, txtNights, txtAdults, txtChildren	TextChanged
Allow the text box to accept only numbers and the Backspace key	txtRooms, txtNights, txtAdults, txtChildren	KeyPress
Select the contents of the text box	txtRooms, txtNights, txtAdults, txtChildren	Enter

Figure 4-37 TOE chart for the Covington Resort application

Coding the btnCalc Control's Click Event Procedure

The btnCalc control's Click event procedure is responsible for calculating and displaying the total room charge, tax, total resort fee, and total due. The procedure's pseudocode is shown in Figure 4-38.

btnCalc Click event procedure

1. store user input (numbers of rooms reserved, nights, adults, and children) in variables
2. calculate the total number of guests = number of adults + number of children
3. calculate the number of rooms required = total number of guests / maximum number of guests per room, which is 6
4. if the number of rooms reserved < number of rooms required

        display the message "You have exceeded the maximum guests per room."

    else

        calculate total room charge = number of rooms reserved * number of nights * daily room charge of $284

        calculate tax = total room charge * tax rate of 15.25%

        calculate total resort fee = number of rooms reserved * number of nights * daily resort fee of $15

        calculate total due = total room charge + tax + total resort fee

        display total room charge, tax, total resort fee, and total due

    end if

Figure 4-38 Pseudocode for the btnCalc control's Click event procedure

START HERE

To begin coding the btnCalc control's Click event procedure:

1. Open the Code Editor window. Replace <your name> and <current date> in the comments with your name and the current date, respectively.
2. Open the code template for the btnCalc control's Click event procedure. Type the comments shown in Figure 4-39, and then position the insertion point as shown in the figure.

```
Private Sub btnCalc_Click(sender As Object, e As EventArg
    ' calculate and display total room charge,
    ' tax, total resort fee, and total due

    ' declare named constants and variables
    |
End Sub
```

enter these three comments

position the insertion point here

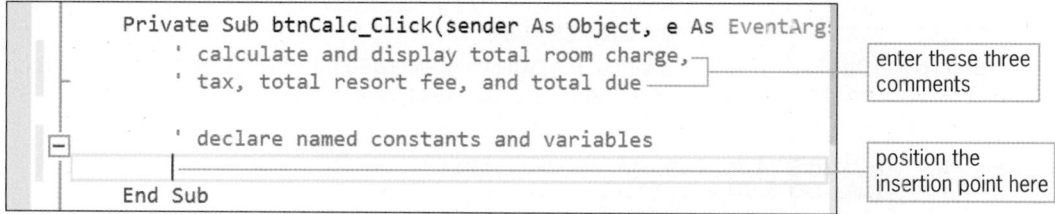

Figure 4-39 Comments and Dim statements entered in the procedure

Now, study the procedure's pseudocode to determine any named constants or variables the procedure will use. When determining the named constants, look for items whose value should remain the same each time the procedure is invoked. In the btnCalc_Click procedure, those items are the maximum number of guests per room, the daily room charge, the tax rate, the daily resort fee, and the message. Figure 4-40 shows the named constants that the procedure will use for these items. The named constants will make the code easier to understand. In addition, they will allow you (or another programmer) to quickly locate those values should they need to be changed in the future.

Named constants	Values
intMAX_PER_ROOM	6
intDAILY_ROOM_CHG	284
dblTAX_RATE	0.1525 (the decimal equivalent of 15.25%)
intDAILY_RESORT_FEE	15
strMSG	"You have exceeded the maximum guests per room."

Figure 4-40 Listing of named constants and their values

When determining the procedure's variables, look in the pseudocode for items whose value is allowed to change each time the procedure is processed. In the btnCalc_Click procedure, those values are the four input items, the number of guests, the number of rooms required, the room charge, the tax, the resort fee, and the total due. Figure 4-41 shows the variables that the procedure will use for these items.

Variable names	Stores
intRoomsReserved	the number of rooms to reserve
intNights	the number of nights
intAdults	the number of adult guests
intChildren	the number of child guests
intNumGuests	the total number of guests, which is calculated by adding together the number of adult guests and the number of child guests
dblRoomsRequired	the number of rooms required, which is calculated by dividing the total number of guests by the maximum guests per room (may contain a decimal place)
intTotalRoomChg	the total room charge, which is calculated by multiplying the number of rooms to reserve by the number of nights and then multiplying the result by the daily room charge
dblTax	the tax, which is calculated by multiplying the total room charge by the tax rate
intTotalResortFee	the total resort fee, which is calculated by multiplying the number of rooms to reserve by the number of nights and then multiplying the result by the daily resort fee
dblTotalDue	the total due, which is calculated by adding together the total room charge, tax, and total resort fee

Figure 4-41 Listing of variables and what each stores

START HERE

To continue coding the btnCalc control's Click event procedure:

1. Enter the Const and Dim statements shown in Figure 4-42, and then position the insertion point as shown in the figure.

```
' declare named constants and variables
Const intMAX_PER_ROOM As Integer = 6
Const intDAILY_ROOM_CHG As Integer = 284
Const dblTAX_RATE As Double = 0.1525
Const intDAILY_RESORT_FEE As Integer = 15
Const strMSG As String = "You have exceeded the maximum guests per room."
Dim intRoomsReserved As Integer
Dim intNights As Integer
Dim intAdults As Integer
Dim intChildren As Integer
Dim intNumGuests As Integer
Dim dblRoomsRequired As Double
Dim intTotalRoomChg As Integer
Dim dblTax As Double
Dim intTotalResortFee As Integer
Dim dblTotalDue As Double

|
End Sub
```

enter these Const and Dim statements

position the insertion point here

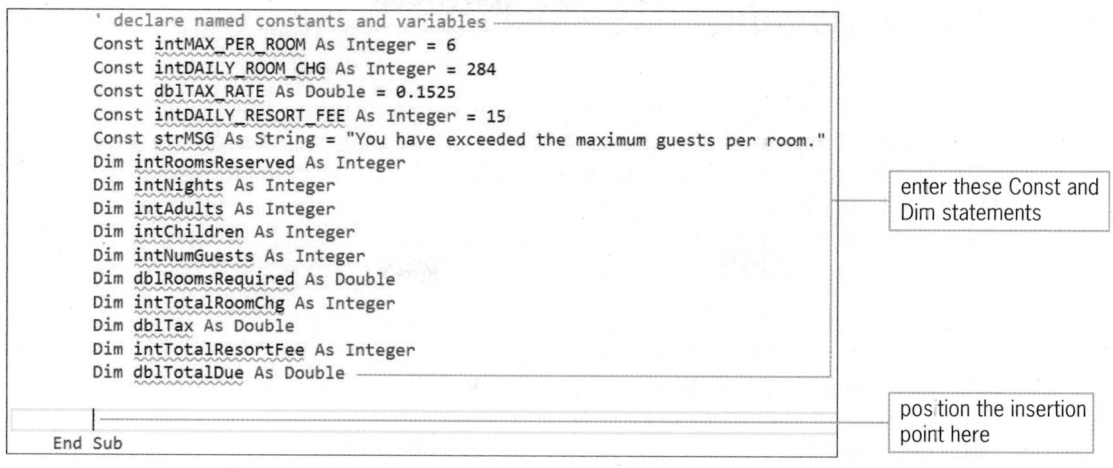

Figure 4-42 Const and Dim statements entered in the procedure

2. Step 1 in the pseudocode is to store the input items in variables. Enter the following comment and TryParse methods. Press **Enter** twice after typing the last TryParse method.

   ' store input in variables
   Integer.TryParse(txtRooms.Text, intRoomsReserved)
   Integer.TryParse(txtNights.Text, intNights)
   Integer.TryParse(txtAdults.Text, intAdults)
   Integer.TryParse(txtChildren.Text, intChildren)

Using a blank line to separate related blocks of code in the Code Editor window makes the code easier to read and understand.

3. Step 2 in the pseudocode calculates the total number of guests by adding together the number of adult guests and the number of child guests. Enter the following comment and assignment statement:

   ' calculate total number of guests
   intNumGuests = intAdults + intChildren

4. Step 3 in the pseudocode calculates the number of rooms required by dividing the total number of guests by the maximum number of guests per room. Enter the following comment and assignment statement. Press **Enter** twice after typing the assignment statement.

   ' calculate number of rooms required
   dblRoomsRequired = intNumGuests / intMAX_PER_ROOM

5. Step 4 in the pseudocode is a selection structure that determines whether the number of rooms reserved is adequate for the number of guests. If the number of reserved rooms is less than the number of required rooms, the selection structure's true path displays an appropriate message. In the next section, you will learn how to display the message in a message box. For now, enter the following comments and If clause. When you press Enter after typing the If clause, the Code Editor will automatically enter the End If clause for you.

   ' determine whether number of reserved
   ' rooms is adequate and then either display a
   ' message or calculate and display the charges
   If intRoomsReserved < dblRoomsRequired Then

6. Save the solution.

The MessageBox.Show Method

At times, an application may need to communicate with the user during run time; one means of doing this is through a message box. You display a message box using the **MessageBox.Show method**. The message box contains text, one or more buttons, and an icon. Figure 4-43 shows the method's syntax and also lists the meaning of each argument. The figure also includes examples of using the method. Figures 4-44 and 4-45 show the message boxes created by the two examples. (Your message boxes will look slightly different if you are using Windows 7.)

MessageBox.Show Method

Syntax

MessageBox.Show(text, *caption*, *buttons*, *icon*[, *defaultButton*]**)**

Argument	Meaning
text	text to display in the message box; use sentence capitalization
caption	text to display in the message box's title bar; use book title capitalization

buttons	buttons to display in the message box; can be one of the following constants:
	`MessageBoxButtons.AbortRetryIgnore`
	`MessageBoxButtons.OK` (default setting)
	`MessageBoxButtons.OKCancel`
	`MessageBoxButtons.RetryCancel`
	`MessageBoxButtons.YesNo`
	`MessageBoxButtons.YesNoCancel`

icon	icon to display in the message box; typically, one of the following constants:
	`MessageBoxIcon.Exclamation`
	`MessageBoxIcon.Information`
	`MessageBoxIcon.Stop`

defaultButton	button automatically selected when the user presses Enter; can be one of the following constants:
	`MessageBoxDefaultButton.Button1` (default setting)
	`MessageBoxDefaultButton.Button2`
	`MessageBoxDefaultButton.Button3`

Example 1

```
MessageBox.Show("Record deleted.", "Payroll",
     MessageBoxButtons.OK, MessageBoxIcon.Information)
```

displays an information message box that contains the message "Record deleted."

Example 2

```
MessageBox.Show("Delete this record?", "Payroll",
     MessageBoxButtons.YesNo, MessageBoxIcon.Exclamation,
     MessageBoxDefaultButton.Button2)
```

displays a warning message box that contains the message "Delete this record?"

Figure 4-43 Syntax and examples of the MessageBox.Show method

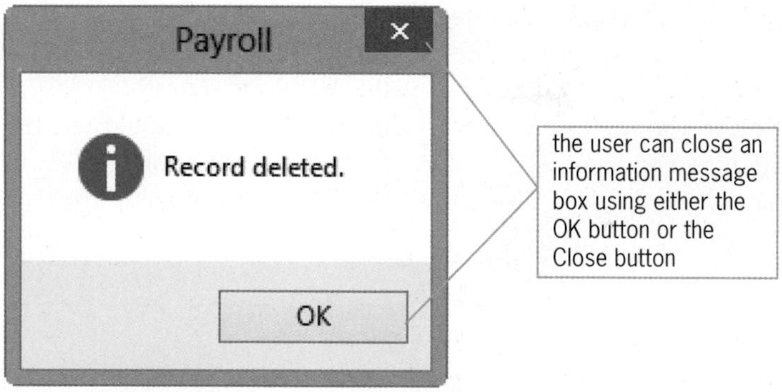
Payroll
Record deleted.
OK
the user can close an information message box using either the OK button or the Close button

Figure 4-44 Message displayed by the code in Example 1 in Figure 4-43

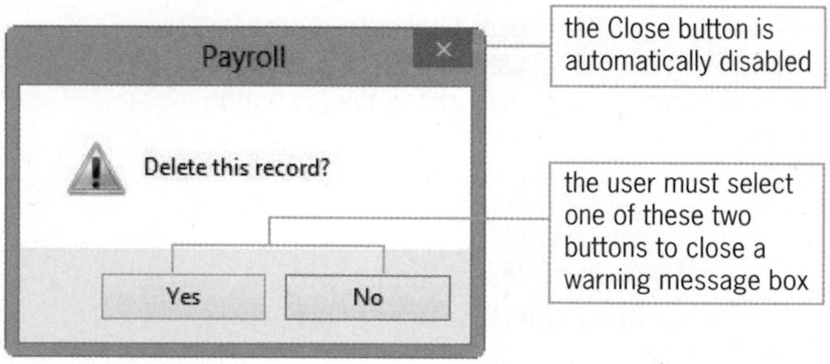
Payroll
Delete this record?
Yes
No
the Close button is automatically disabled
the user must select one of these two buttons to close a warning message box

Figure 4-45 Message displayed by the code in Example 2 in Figure 4-43

GUI DESIGN TIP MessageBox.Show Method

- Use sentence capitalization for the *text* argument, but book title capitalization for the *caption* argument.
- Display the Exclamation icon to alert the user that he or she must make a decision before the application can continue. You can phrase the message as a question. These message boxes typically contain more than one button.
- Display the Information icon along with an OK button in a message box that displays an informational message.
- Display the Stop icon to alert the user of a serious problem that must be corrected before the application can continue.
- The default button in the message box should be the one that represents the user's most likely action, as long as that action is not destructive.

After displaying the message box, the MessageBox.Show method waits for the user to choose one of the buttons. It then closes the message box and returns an integer indicating the button chosen by the user. Sometimes you are not interested in the value returned by the MessageBox.Show method. This is the case when the message box is for informational purposes only, like the message box shown in Figure 4-44. Many times, however, the button selected by the user determines the next task performed by the computer. Selecting the Yes button in the message box shown in Figure 4-45 tells the application to delete the record; selecting the No button tells it *not* to delete the record.

Figure 4-46 lists the integer values returned by the MessageBox.Show method. Each value is associated with a button that can appear in a message box. The figure also lists the DialogResult values assigned to each integer, and the meaning of the integers and DialogResult values. As the figure indicates, the MessageBox.Show method returns the integer 6 when the user selects the Yes button. The integer 6 is represented by the DialogResult value, `Windows.Forms.DialogResult.Yes`. When referring to the method's return value in code, you should use the DialogResult values rather than the integers because the values make the code more self-documenting and easier to understand. Figure 4-46 also shows two examples of using the MessageBox.Show method's return value.

MessageBox.Show Method's Return Values

Integer	DialogResult value	Meaning
1	`Windows.Forms.DialogResult.OK`	user chose the OK button
2	`Windows.Forms.DialogResult.Cancel`	user chose the Cancel button
3	`Windows.Forms.DialogResult.Abort`	user chose the Abort button
4	`Windows.Forms.DialogResult.Retry`	user chose the Retry button
5	`Windows.Forms.DialogResult.Ignore`	user chose the Ignore button
6	`Windows.Forms.DialogResult.Yes`	user chose the Yes button
7	`Windows.Forms.DialogResult.No`	user chose the No button

Example 1

```
Dim dlgButton As DialogResult
dlgButton =
      MessageBox.Show("Delete this record?", "Payroll",
      MessageBoxButtons.YesNo, MessageBoxIcon.Exclamation,
      MessageBoxDefaultButton.Button2)
If dlgButton = Windows.Forms.DialogResult.Yes Then
      instructions to delete the record
End If
```

Example 2

```
If MessageBox.Show("Play another game?", "Math Monster",
      MessageBoxButtons.YesNo,
      MessageBoxIcon.Exclamation) = Windows.Forms.DialogResult.Yes Then
      instructions to start another game
Else   ' No button
      instructions to close the game application
End If
```

Figure 4-46 Values returned by the MessageBox.Show method

In the first example in Figure 4-46, the MessageBox.Show method's return value is assigned to a DialogResult variable named `dlgButton`. The selection structure in the example compares the contents of the `dlgButton` variable with the `Windows.Forms.DialogResult.Yes` value. In the second example, the method's return value is not stored in a variable. Instead, the method appears in the selection structure's condition, where its return value is compared with the `Windows.Forms.DialogResult.Yes` value. The selection structure in Example 2 performs one set of tasks when the user selects the Yes button in the message box, but a different set of tasks when the user selects the No button. Many programmers document the Else portion of the selection structure as shown in Figure 4-46 because it makes it clear that the Else portion is processed only when the user selects the No button.

In the Covington Resort application, the btnCalc_Click procedure should display an appropriate message when the number of rooms reserved is less than the number of rooms required. You will use the MessageBox.Show method to display the message in a message box. The message box is for informational purposes only. Therefore, it should contain the Information icon and the OK button, and you do not need to be concerned with its return value.

To add the MessageBox.Show method to the btnCalc_Click procedure:

START HERE

1. The insertion point should be positioned in the blank line above the End If clause. Enter the following lines of code:

```
MessageBox.Show(strMSG, "Covington Resort",
        MessageBoxButtons.OK,
        MessageBoxIcon.Information)
```


Completing the btnCalc_Click Procedure

Recall that Step 4 in the btnCalc_Click procedure's pseudocode is a selection structure that determines whether the number of rooms reserved is adequate for the number of guests. In the previous section, you completed the selection structure's true path. You will complete the false path in this section. According to the pseudocode, the false path should calculate and display the total room charge, tax, total resort fee, and total due.

To complete the btnCalc_Click procedure and then test it:

START HERE

1. In the blank line above the End If clause, type **else** and press **Enter**.
2. The total room charge is calculated by first multiplying the number of rooms reserved by the number of nights and then multiplying the result by the daily room charge of $284. Enter the following comment and assignment statement:

```
' calculate charges
intTotalRoomChg = intRoomsReserved *
    intNights * intDAILY_ROOM_CHG
```

3. The tax is calculated by multiplying the total room charge by the tax rate of 15.25%. Enter the following assignment statement:

```
dblTax = intTotalRoomChg * dblTAX_RATE
```

4. The total resort fee is calculated by first multiplying the number of rooms reserved by the number of nights and then multiplying the result by the daily resort fee of $15. Enter the following assignment statement:

```
intTotalResortFee = intRoomsReserved *
    intNights * intDAILY_RESORT_FEE
```

5. The total due is calculated by adding together the total room charge, tax and total resort fee. Enter the following assignment statement:

```
dblTotalDue = intTotalRoomChg +
    dblTax + intTotalResortFee
```

6. Finally, you will display the calculated amounts in the interface. Press **Enter** to insert another blank line below the last assignment statement. Enter the following comment and assignment statements:

```
' display charges
lblRoomChg.Text = intTotalRoomChg.ToString("N2")
lblTax.Text = dblTax.ToString("N2")
lblResortFee.Text = intTotalResortFee.ToString("N2")
lblTotalDue.Text = dblTotalDue.ToString("C2")
```

7. If necessary, delete the blank line above the End If clause.

8. Save the solution and then start the application. Type **1** in the Rooms box, **2** in the Nights box, **4** in the Adults box, and **4** in the Children box. Click the **Calculate** button. The message box shown in Figure 4-47 opens.

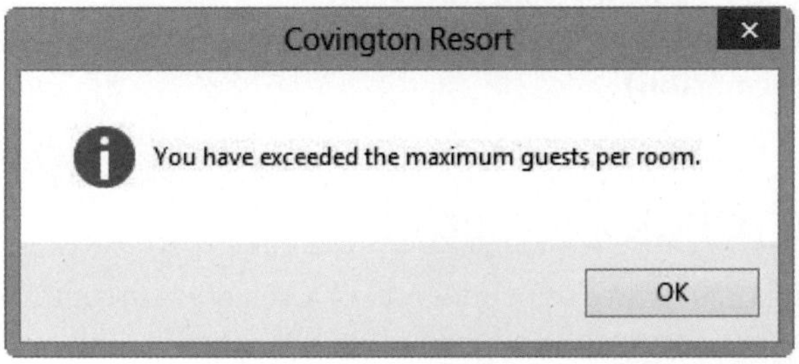

Figure 4-47 Message box created by the MessageBox.Show method

9. Click the **OK** button to close the message box. Change the number of adults to **2**. Also change the number of children to **2**. Click the **Calculate** button. The total room charge, tax, total resort fee, and total due appear in the interface. See Figure 4-48.

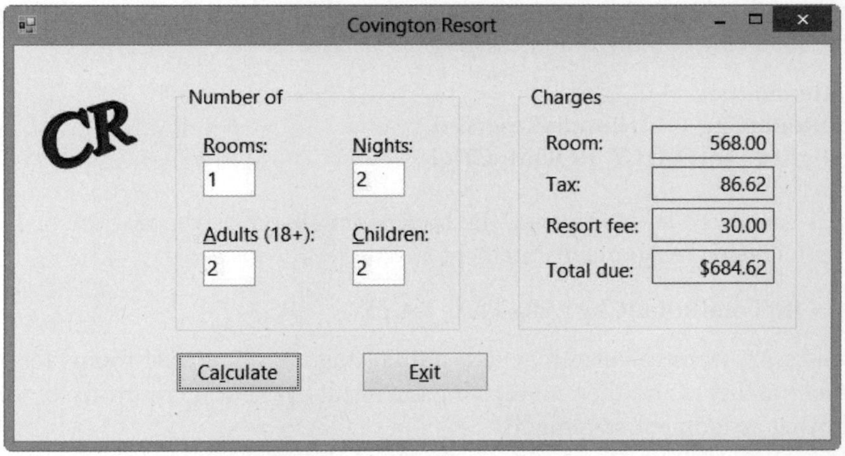

Figure 4-48 Calculated amounts shown in the interface

10. Click the **Exit** button.

Figure 4-49 shows the application's code at the end of Lesson B.

```
' Name:         Covington Resort Project
' Purpose:      Display the total room charge, tax,
'               total resort fee, and total due
' Programmer:   <your name> on <current date>

Option Explicit On
Option Strict On
Option Infer Off

Public Class frmMain

   Private Sub btnExit_Click(sender As Object,
   e As EventArgs) Handles btnExit.Click
       Me.Close()
   End Sub

   Private Sub ClearLabels(sender As Object, e As EventArgs) _
       Handles txtRooms.TextChanged, txtNights.TextChanged,
       txtAdults.TextChanged, txtChildren.TextChanged
       ' clear calculated amounts

       lblRoomChg.Text = String.Empty
       lblTax.Text = String.Empty
       lblResortFee.Text = String.Empty
       lblTotalDue.Text = String.Empty
   End Sub

   Private Sub btnCalc_Click(sender As Object,
   e As EventArgs) Handles btnCalc.Click
       ' calculate and display total room charge,
       ' tax, total resort fee, and total due

       ' declare named constants and variables
       Const intMAX_PER_ROOM As Integer = 6
       Const intDAILY_ROOM_CHG As Integer = 284
       Const dblTAX_RATE As Double = 0.1525
       Const intDAILY_RESORT_FEE As Integer = 15
       Const strMSG As String =
         "You have exceeded the maximum guests per room."
       Dim intRoomsReserved As Integer
       Dim intNights As Integer
       Dim intAdults As Integer
       Dim intChildren As Integer
       Dim intNumGuests As Integer
       Dim dblRoomsRequired As Double
       Dim intTotalRoomChg As Integer
       Dim dblTax As Double
       Dim intTotalResortFee As Integer
       Dim dblTotalDue As Double

       ' store input in variables
```

Figure 4-49 Covington Resort application's code at the end of Lesson B *(continues)*

(continued)

```
        Integer.TryParse(txtRooms.Text, intRoomsReserved)
        Integer.TryParse(txtNights.Text, intNights)
        Integer.TryParse(txtAdults.Text, intAdults)
        Integer.TryParse(txtChildren.Text, intChildren)

        ' calculate total number of guests
        intNumGuests = intAdults + intChildren
        ' calculate number of rooms required
        dblRoomsRequired = intNumGuests / intMAX_PER_ROOM

        ' determine whether number of reserved
        ' rooms is adequate and then either display a
        ' message or calculate and display the charges
        If intRoomsReserved < dblRoomsRequired Then
            MessageBox.Show(strMSG, "Covington Resort",
                 MessageBoxButtons.OK,
                 MessageBoxIcon.Information)
        Else
            ' calculate charges
            intTotalRoomChg = intRoomsReserved *
                 intNights * intDAILY_ROOM_CHG
            dblTax = intTotalRoomChg * dblTAX_RATE
            intTotalResortFee = intRoomsReserved *
                 intNights * intDAILY_RESORT_FEE
            dblTotalDue = intTotalRoomChg +
                 dblTax + intTotalResortFee

            ' display charges
            lblRoomChg.Text = intTotalRoomChg.ToString("N2")
            lblTax.Text = dblTax.ToString("N2")
            lblResortFee.Text = intTotalResortFee.ToString("N2")
            lblTotalDue.Text = dblTotalDue.ToString("C2")
        End If
    End Sub
End Class
```

Figure 4-49 Covington Resort application's code at the end of Lesson B

Lesson B Summary

- To group controls together using a group box:

  Use the GroupBox tool to add a group box to the form. Drag controls from either the form or the toolbox into the group box. To include an optional identifying label on a group box, set the group box's Text property. The TabIndex value of a control contained within a group box is composed of two numbers separated by a period. The number to the left of the period is the TabIndex value of the group box itself. The number to the right of the period indicates the order in which the control was added to the group box.

- To display a message box that contains text, one or more buttons, and an icon:

  Use the MessageBox.Show method. The method's syntax is **MessageBox.Show(***text, caption, buttons, icon*[*, defaultButton*]**)**. Refer to Figure 4-43 for a description of each argument. The figure also contains examples of using the method to display a message box. Refer to Figure 4-46 for a listing and description of the method's return values.

Lesson B Key Terms

Group box—a control that is used to contain other controls; instantiated using the GroupBox tool, which is located in the Containers section of the toolbox

MessageBox.Show method—displays a message box that contains text, one or more buttons, and an icon; allows an application to communicate with the user while the application is running

Lesson B Review Questions

1. Which of the following statements is false?
   a. When you delete a group box, the controls contained within the group box are also deleted.
   b. Moving a group box also moves all of the controls contained within the group box.
   c. A group box's Label property specifies its identifying label.
   d. You can drag a control from the form into a group box.

2. What is the TabIndex value of the first control added to a group box whose TabIndex value is 3?
   a. 3
   b. 3.0
   c. 3.1
   d. none of the above

3. You use the ______________ constant to include the Exclamation icon in a message box.
   a. `MessageBox.Exclamation`
   b. `MessageBox.IconExclamation`
   c. `MessageBoxIcon.Exclamation`
   d. `MessageBox.WarningIcon`

4. If a message is for informational purposes only and does not require the user to make a decision, the message box should display which of the following?
   a. an OK button and the Information icon
   b. an OK button and the Exclamation icon
   c. a Yes button and the Information icon
   d. any button and the Information icon

5. If the user clicks the Yes button in a message box, the message box returns the number 6, which is equivalent to which value?
   a. `Windows.Forms.DialogResultButton.Yes`
   b. `Windows.Forms.DialogResult.Yes`
   c. `Windows.Forms.DialogResult.YesButton`
   d. none of the above

Lesson B Exercises

INTRODUCTORY

1. In this exercise, you create an application for Jonas Manufacturing. Create a Visual Basic Windows application. Use the following names for the solution and project, respectively: Jonas Solution and Jonas Project. Save the application in the VB2012\Chap04 folder. Change

the form file's name to Main Form.vb. Change the form's name to frmMain. The application's interface, which is shown in Figure 4-50, allows the user to enter an employee's current salary and pay grade. The application should display the employee's raise and new salary in a message box. Employees having a pay grade of 1 receive a 3% raise; all other employees receive a 2% raise. Use the ToString method to display a thousands separator (if necessary) and two decimal places in the raise and new salary. Code the application. (Be sure to use variables. Do not use the Val function.) Save the solution and then start and test the application. Close the Code Editor window and then close the solution.

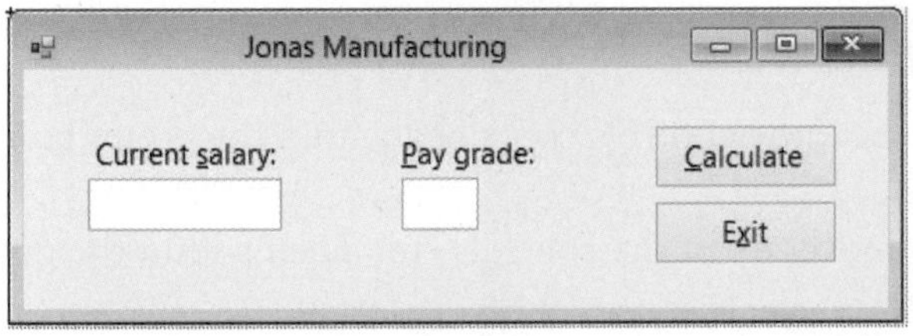

Figure 4-50 Interface for Exercise 1

INTRODUCTORY

2. In this exercise, you modify the application from Exercise 1. Use Windows to make a copy of the Jonas Solution folder. Rename the copy Modified Jonas Solution. Open the Jonas Solution (Jonas Solution.sln) file contained in the Modified Jonas Solution folder. Open the designer window. Modify the code so that employees having a pay grade of 1, 2, or 3 receive a 3% raise. All other employees should receive a 2% raise. Save the solution and then start and test the application. Close the Code Editor window and then close the solution.

INTERMEDIATE

3. Tea Time Company wants an application that allows a clerk to enter the number of pounds of tea ordered, the price per pound, and whether the customer should be charged a $15 shipping fee. The application should calculate and display the total amount the customer owes. Create a Visual Basic Windows application. Use the following names for the solution and project, respectively: Tea Time Solution and Tea Time Project. Save the application in the VB2012\Chap04 folder. Change the form file's name to Main Form.vb. Change the form's name to frmMain. The total amount owed should be removed from the interface when a change is made to the contents of a text box in the interface. Use the MessageBox.Show method to determine whether the user should be charged for shipping. (Use the examples in Figure 4-46 as a guide.) Code the application. (Be sure to use variables. Do not use the Val function.) Save the solution and then start and test the application. Close the Code Editor window and then close the solution.

INTERMEDIATE

4. Marcy's Department store is having a BoGoHo (Buy One, Get One Half Off) sale. The store manager wants an application that allows the salesclerk to enter the prices of two items. The application should calculate and display the total amount the customer owes. The half-off should always be taken on the item having the lowest price. Use the MessageBox.Show method to display the amount the customer saved. For example, if the two items cost $24.99 and $10, the half-off would be taken on the $10 item, and the message box would indicate that the customer saved $5.00. Create a Visual Basic Windows application. Use the following names for the solution and project, respectively: Marcy Solution and Marcy Project. Save the application in the VB2012\Chap04 folder. Change the form file's name to Main Form.vb. Change the form's name to frmMain. The total amount owed should be removed from the interface when a change is made to the contents of a text box in the interface. Code the application. (Be sure to use variables. Do not use the Val function.) Save the solution and then start and test the application. Close the Code Editor window and then close the solution.

INTERMEDIATE

5. In this exercise, you create an application for Corondo Industries. Create a Visual Basic Windows application. Use the following names for the solution and project, respectively: Corondo Solution and Corondo Project. Save the application in the VB2012\Chap04 folder. Change the form file's name to Main Form.vb. Change the form's name to frmMain. The application's interface, which is shown in Figure 4-51, allows the user to enter the quantity ordered and product price. The application should calculate the discount (if any) and total due. Before calculating the discount, the btnCalc control's Click event procedure should display the message "Are you a wholesaler?" in a message box. Only wholesalers receive a discount, which is 10%. The discount and total due should be removed from the interface when a change is made to the contents of a text box in the interface. Code the application. Save the solution and then start the application. Test the application by calculating the total due for a wholesaler ordering 4 units of product at $10 per unit. Then, test the application by calculating the total due for a non-wholesaler ordering 2 units of product at $5 per unit. Close the Code Editor window and then close the solution.

Figure 4-51 Interface for Exercise 2

ADVANCED

6. Open the Division Solution (Division Solution.sln) file contained in the VB2012\Chap04\Division Solution folder. If necessary, open the designer window. The interface allows the user to enter two numbers. The Calculate button's Click event procedure should calculate and display the result of dividing the larger number by the smaller number. However, keep in mind that an application will end abruptly if a statement attempts to divide a number by zero. This is because, as in math, division by zero is not allowed. Therefore, if the smaller number is 0, the application should display the "Cannot divide by 0" message. Code the application. (Be sure to use variables. Do not use the Val function.) Save the solution and then start the application. Test the application using 150.72 and 3 as the two numbers, then test it using 4 and 100. Also test it using 0 and 5, and then using 0 and –3. Close the Code Editor window and then close the solution.

LESSON C

After studying Lesson C, you should be able to:

- Prevent the entry of unwanted characters in a text box
- Select the existing text in a text box

Coding the KeyPress Event Procedures

Ch04C video

To complete the Covington Resort application, you need to code the KeyPress and Enter event procedures for the four text boxes. You will code the KeyPress event procedures first.

START HERE

To open the Covington Resort application:

1. If necessary, start Visual Studio 2012. Open the Covington Resort Solution (Covington Resort Solution.sln) file from Lesson B. The file is contained in the VB2012\Chap04\Covington Resort Solution folder. If necessary, open the designer window.

The application provides text boxes for the user to enter the numbers of rooms, nights, adults, and children. The user should enter those items using only numbers. The items should not contain any letters, spaces, punctuation marks, or special characters. Unfortunately, you can't stop the user from trying to enter an inappropriate character into a text box. However, you can prevent the text box from accepting the character; you do this by coding the text box's KeyPress event procedure.

START HERE

To view the code template for the txtRooms control's KeyPress event procedure:

1. Open the Code Editor window and then open the code template for the txtRooms control's KeyPress event procedure. See Figure 4-52.

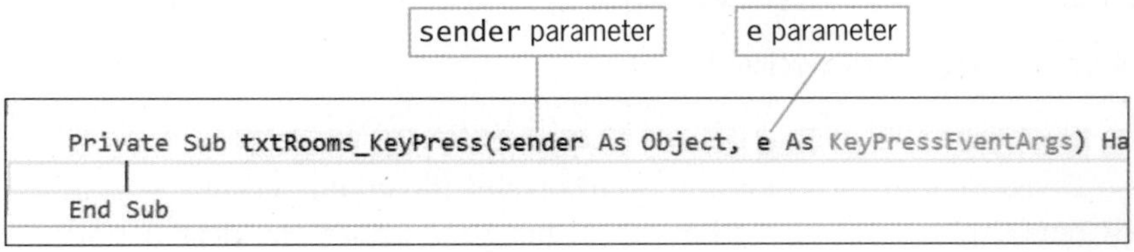
sender parameter
e parameter
Private Sub txtRooms_KeyPress(sender As Object, e As KeyPressEventArgs) Ha
End Sub

Figure 4-52 Code template for the txtRooms control's KeyPress event procedure

A control's **KeyPress event** occurs each time the user presses a key while the control has the focus. The procedure associated with the KeyPress event has two parameters, which appear within the parentheses in the procedure header: `sender` and `e`. A **parameter** represents information that is passed to the procedure when the event occurs. When the KeyPress event occurs, a character corresponding to the pressed key is sent to the KeyPress event's `e` parameter. For example, when the user presses the period (.) while entering data into a text box, the text box's KeyPress event occurs and a period is sent to the event's `e` parameter. Similarly, when the Shift key along with a letter is pressed, the uppercase version of the letter is sent to the `e` parameter.

To prevent a text box from accepting an inappropriate character, you first use the `e` parameter's **KeyChar property** to determine the pressed key. (KeyChar stands for "key character.") You then use the `e` parameter's **Handled property** to cancel the key if it is an inappropriate one. You cancel the key by setting the Handled property to True, like this: `e.Handled = True`.

Figure 4-53 shows examples of using the KeyChar and Handled properties in the KeyPress event procedure. The condition in Example 1's selection structure compares the contents of the KeyChar property with a dollar sign. If the condition evaluates to True, the `e.Handled = True` instruction in the selection structure's true path cancels the $ key before it is entered in the txtSales control. You can use the selection structure in Example 2 to allow the text box to accept only numbers and the Backspace key (which is used for editing). You refer to the Backspace key on your keyboard using Visual Basic's **ControlChars.Back constant**.

The KeyPress event automatically allows the use of the Delete key for editing.

Controlling the Characters Accepted by a Text Box

Example 1

```
Private Sub txtSales_KeyPress(sender As Object,
e As KeyPressEventArgs) Handles txtSales.KeyPress
    ' prevents the text box from accepting the dollar sign

    If e.KeyChar = "$" Then
        e.Handled = True
    End If
End Sub
```

Example 2

```
Private Sub txtAge_KeyPress(sender As Object,
e As KeyPressEventArgs) Handles txtAge.KeyPress
    ' allows the text box to accept only numbers
    ' and the Backspace key

    If (e.KeyChar < "0" OrElse e.KeyChar > "9") AndAlso
        e.KeyChar <> ControlChars.Back Then
        e.Handled = True
    End If
End Sub
```

Figure 4-53 Examples of using the KeyChar and Handled properties in the KeyPress event procedure

According to the application's TOE chart, each text box's KeyPress event procedure should allow the text box to accept only numbers and the Backspace key. All other keys should be canceled. (The TOE chart is shown in Figure 4-37 in Lesson B.)

To allow the four text boxes to accept only numbers and the Backspace key:

START HERE

1. Change txtRooms_KeyPress in the procedure header to **CancelKeys**.
2. Click **immediately before the)** (closing parenthesis) in the procedure header and then press **Enter** to move the parenthesis and Handles clause to the next line in the procedure. (You can look ahead to Figure 4-54.)
3. Click **at the end of the Handles clause**. Type the following text and press **Enter**. (Be sure to type the comma before and after txtNights.KeyPress.)

   , txtNights.KeyPress,

4. Now type the following text and press **Enter**:

   txtAdults.KeyPress, txtChildren.KeyPress

5. Enter the following comments. Press **Enter** twice after typing the second comment.

   ' allows the text box to accept only numbers and
   ' the Backspace key

6. Enter the following If clause. When you press Enter after typing Then, the Code Editor will automatically enter the End If clause for you.

   If (e.KeyChar < "0" OrElse e.KeyChar > "9") AndAlso
   e.KeyChar <> ControlChars.Back Then

7. Enter the following comment and assignment statement:

   ' cancel the key
   e.Handled = True

8. If necessary, delete the blank lines above the End If and End Sub clauses. Figure 4-54 shows the completed CancelKeys procedure, which is associated with each text box's KeyPress event.


```
Private Sub CancelKeys(sender As Object, e As KeyPressEventArgs
                       ) Handles txtRooms.KeyPress, txtNights.KeyPress,
                   txtAdults.KeyPress, txtChildren.KeyPress
    ' allows the text box to accept only numbers and
    ' the Backspace key

    If (e.KeyChar < "0" OrElse e.KeyChar > "9") AndAlso
        e.KeyChar <> ControlChars.Back Then
        ' cancel the key
        e.Handled = True
    End If
End Sub
```

the procedure is associated with each text box's KeyPress event

Figure 4-54 CancelKeys procedure

In the next set of steps, you will test the CancelKeys procedure to verify that it allows the text boxes to accept only numbers and the Backspace key.

START HERE

To test the CancelKeys procedure:

1. Save the solution and then start the application.
2. Try entering a letter in the Rooms box, and then try entering a dollar sign. Now, type **10** in the Rooms box and then press **Backspace** to delete the 0. The Rooms box now contains only the number 1.
3. Try entering a letter in the Nights box, and then try entering a percent sign. Now, type **21** in the Nights box and then press **Backspace** to delete the 1. The Nights box now contains only the number 2.
4. Try entering a letter in the Adults box, and then try entering an ampersand. Now, type **20** in the Adults box and then press **Backspace** to delete the 0. The Adults box now contains only the number 2.
5. Try entering a letter in the Children box, and then try entering a period. Now, type **13** in the Children box and then press **Backspace** to delete the 3. The Children box now contains only the number 1.

6. Click the **Calculate** button to display the calculated amounts in the interface.
7. Press **Tab** twice to move the focus to the Rooms box. Notice that the insertion point appears at the end of the number 1. It is customary in Windows applications to have a text box's existing text selected (highlighted) when the text box receives the focus. You will learn how to select the existing text in the next section. Click the **Exit** button to end the application.

Coding the Enter Event Procedures

To complete the Covington Resort application, you just need to code the Enter event procedures for the four text boxes. A text box's **Enter event** occurs when the text box receives the focus, which can happen as a result of the user tabbing to the control or using the control's access key. It also occurs when the Focus method is used to send the focus to the control. In the current application, the Enter event procedure for each text box is responsible for selecting (highlighting) the contents of the text box. When the text is selected in a text box, the user can remove the text simply by pressing a key on the keyboard, such as the letter n; the pressed key—in this case, the letter n—replaces the selected text.

Visual Basic provides the **SelectAll method** for selecting a text box's existing text. The method's syntax is shown in Figure 4-55 along with an example of using the method. In the syntax, *textbox* is the name of the text box whose contents you want to select.

SelectAll Method
Syntax
textbox.**SelectAll( )**

Example
```
txtId.SelectAll()
```
selects the contents of the txtId control

Figure 4-55 Syntax and an example of the SelectAll method

You will use the SelectAll method to select the contents of the four text boxes in the Covington Resort application. You will enter the method in each text box's Enter event procedure so that the method is processed when the text box receives the focus.

To code each text box's Enter event procedure and then test the procedures:

START HERE

1. Open the code template for the txtRooms control's Enter event procedure. Type the following comments and then press **Enter** twice:

   ' selects the contents when the
   ' text box receives the focus

2. Type **txtRooms.SelectAll()** and then click the **blank line** below the last comment.
3. Open the code template for the txtNights control's Enter event procedure. Copy the comments and SelectAll method from the txtRooms_Enter procedure to the txtNights_Enter procedure. Change txtRooms in the SelectAll method to **txtNights** and then click the **blank line** below the last comment.
4. Open the code template for the txtAdults control's Enter event procedure. Copy the comments and SelectAll method from the txtRooms_Enter procedure to the

txtAdults_Enter procedure. Change txtRooms in the SelectAll method to **txtAdults** and then click the **blank line** below the last comment.

5. Open the code template for the txtChildren control's Enter event procedure. Copy the comments and SelectAll method from the txtRooms_Enter procedure to the txtChildren_Enter procedure. Change txtRooms in the SelectAll method to **txtChildren** and then click the **blank line** below the last comment.
6. Save the solution and then start the application. Type **1** in the Rooms box, **1** in the Nights box, **2** in the Adults box, and **2** in the Children box. Click the **Calculate** button to display the calculated amounts in the interface.
7. Press **Tab** twice to move the focus to the Rooms box. The txtRooms_Enter procedure selects the contents of the text box, as shown in Figure 4-56.

the existing text is selected when the text box receives the focus

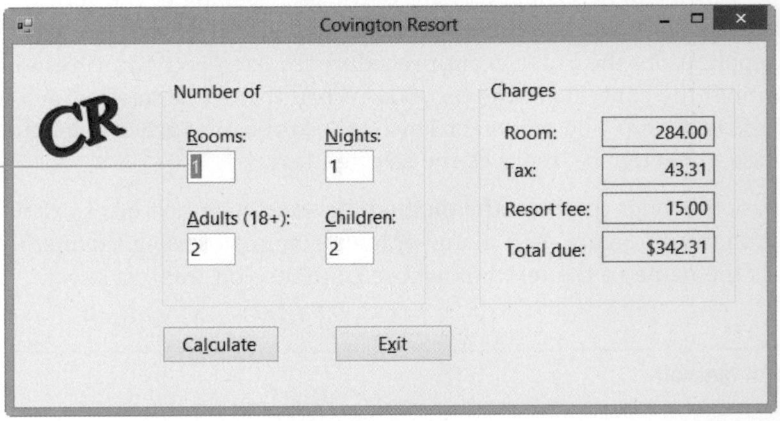

Figure 4-56 Existing text selected in the txtRooms control

8. Press **Tab** three times, slowly, to move the focus to each of the other three text boxes. Each text box's Enter event procedure selects the contents of the text box.
9. Click the **Exit** button. Close the Code Editor window and then close the solution.

Figure 4-57 shows the application's code at the end of Lesson C.

```
' Name:         Covington Resort Project
' Purpose:      Display the total room charge, tax,
'               total resort fee, and total due
' Programmer:   <your name> on <current date>

Option Explicit On
Option Strict On
Option Infer Off

Public Class frmMain

    Private Sub btnExit_Click(sender As Object,
    e As EventArgs) Handles btnExit.Click
        Me.Close()
    End Sub

```

Figure 4-57 Covington Resort application's code at the end of Lesson C *(continues)*

(continued)

```
Private Sub txtRooms_Enter(sender As Object,
e As EventArgs) Handles txtRooms.Enter
    ' selects the contents when the
    ' text box receives the focus

    txtRooms.SelectAll()
End Sub

Private Sub txtNights_Enter(sender As Object,
e As EventArgs) Handles txtNights.Enter
    ' selects the contents when the
    ' text box receives the focus

    txtNights.SelectAll()
End Sub

Private Sub txtAdults_Enter(sender As Object,
e As EventArgs) Handles txtAdults.Enter
   ' selects the contents when the
   ' text box receives the focus

   txtAdults.SelectAll()
End Sub

Private Sub txtChildren_Enter(sender As Object,
e As EventArgs) Handles txtChildren.Enter
    ' selects the contents when the
    ' text box receives the focus

    txtChildren.SelectAll()
End Sub

Private Sub CancelKeys(sender As Object,
e As KeyPressEventArgs
          ) Handles txtRooms.KeyPress, txtNights.KeyPress,
            txtAdults.KeyPress, txtChildren.KeyPress
    ' allows the text box to accept only numbers and
    ' the Backspace key

    If (e.KeyChar < "0" OrElse e.KeyChar > "9") AndAlso
        e.KeyChar <> ControlChars.Back Then
        ' cancel the key
        e.Handled = True
    End If
End Sub

Private Sub ClearLabels(sender As Object, e As EventArgs) _
    Handles txtRooms.TextChanged, txtNights.TextChanged,
  txtAdults.TextChanged, txtChildren.TextChanged
    ' clear calculated amounts

    lblRoomChg.Text = String.Empty
    lblTax.Text = String.Empty
    lblResortFee.Text = String.Empty
    lblTotalDue.Text = String.Empty
End Sub
```

Figure 4-57 Covington Resort application's code at the end of Lesson C *(continues)*

(continued)

```
    Private Sub btnCalc_Click(sender As Object,
    e As EventArgs) Handles btnCalc.Click
        ' calculate and display total room charge,
        ' tax, total resort fee, and total due

        ' declare named constants and variables
        Const intMAX_PER_ROOM As Integer = 6
        Const intDAILY_ROOM_CHG As Integer = 284
        Const dblTAX_RATE As Double = 0.1525
        Const intDAILY_RESORT_FEE As Integer = 15
        Const strMSG As String =
              "You have exceeded the maximum guests per room."
        Dim intRoomsReserved As Integer
        Dim intNights As Integer
        Dim intAdults As Integer
        Dim intChildren As Integer
        Dim intNumGuests As Integer
        Dim dblRoomsRequired As Double
        Dim intTotalRoomChg As Integer
        Dim dblTax As Double
        Dim intTotalResortFee As Integer
        Dim dblTotalDue As Double

        ' store input in variables
        Integer.TryParse(txtRooms.Text, intRoomsReserved)
        Integer.TryParse(txtNights.Text, intNights)
        Integer.TryParse(txtAdults.Text, intAdults)
        Integer.TryParse(txtChildren.Text, intChildren)

        ' calculate total number of guests
        intNumGuests = intAdults + intChildren
        ' calculate number of rooms required
        dblRoomsRequired = intNumGuests / intMAX_PER_ROOM

        ' determine whether number of reserved
        ' rooms is adequate and then either display a
        ' message or calculate and display the charges
        If intRoomsReserved < dblRoomsRequired Then
            MessageBox.Show(strMSG, "Covington Resort",
                            MessageBoxButtons.OK,
                            MessageBoxIcon.Information)
        Else
            ' calculate charges
            intTotalRoomChg = intRoomsReserved *
                intNights * intDAILY_ROOM_CHG
            dblTax = intTotalRoomChg * dblTAX_RATE
            intTotalResortFee = intRoomsReserved *
                intNights * intDAILY_RESORT_FEE
            dblTotalDue = intTotalRoomChg +
                dblTax + intTotalResortFee

            ' display charges
            lblRoomChg.Text = intTotalRoomChg.ToString("N2")
            lblTax.Text = dblTax.ToString("N2")
            lblResortFee.Text = intTotalResortFee.ToString("N2")
            lblTotalDue.Text = dblTotalDue.ToString("C2")
        End If
    End Sub
End Class
```

Figure 4-57 Covington Resort application's code at the end of Lesson C

Lesson C Summary

- To allow a text box to accept only certain keys:

  Code the text box's KeyPress event procedure. The key the user pressed is stored in the e.KeyChar property. You use the `e.Handled = True` statement to cancel the key pressed by the user.

- To select the existing text in a text box:

  Use the SelectAll method. The method's syntax is *textbox*.**SelectAll()**.

- To process code when a control receives the focus:

  Enter the code in the control's Enter event procedure.

Lesson C Key Term

ControlChars.Back constant—the Visual Basic constant that represents the Backspace key on your keyboard

Enter event—occurs when a control receives the focus, which can happen as a result of the user either tabbing to the control or using the control's access key; also occurs when the Focus method is used to send the focus to the control

Handled property—a property of the KeyPress event procedure's `e` parameter; when assigned the value True, it cancels the key pressed by the user

KeyChar property—a property of the KeyPress event procedure's `e` parameter; stores the character associated with the key pressed by the user

KeyPress event—occurs each time the user presses a key while a control has the focus

Parameter—an item contained within parentheses in a procedure header; represents information passed to the procedure when the procedure is invoked

SelectAll method—used to select all of the text contained in a text box

Lesson C Review Questions

1. A control's ________________ event occurs each time a user presses a key while the control has the focus.

   a. Focus
   b. Key
   c. KeyFocus
   d. KeyPress

2. When entered in the appropriate event procedure, which of the following statements cancels the key pressed by the user?

   a. `e.Cancel = True`
   b. `e.Cancel = False`
   c. `e.Handled = True`
   d. `e.Handled = False`

3. Which of the following If clauses determines whether the user pressed the Backspace key?

   a. `If e.KeyChar = ControlChars.Back Then`
   b. `If e.KeyChar = Backspace Then`
   c. `If e.KeyChar = ControlChars.Backspace Then`
   d. `If ControlChars.BackSpace = True Then`

4. Which of the following If clauses determines whether the user pressed the % key?
   a. `If ControlChars.PercentSign = True Then`
   b. `If e.KeyChar = "%" Then`
   c. `If e.KeyChar = Chars.PercentSign Then`
   d. `If KeyChar.ControlChars = "%" Then`

5. When a user tabs to a text box, the text box's ____________ event occurs.
   a. Access
   b. Enter
   c. TabOrder
   d. TabbedTo

6. Which of the following tells the computer to highlight all of the text contained in the txtName control?
   a. `txtName.SelectAll()`
   b. `txtName.HighlightAll()`
   c. `Highlight(txtName)`
   d. `SelectAll(txtName.Text)`

Lesson C Exercises

INTRODUCTORY

1. Open the State ID Solution (State ID Solution.sln) file contained in the VB2012\Chap04\State ID Solution folder. If necessary, open the designer window. The txtState control should accept only letters and the Backspace key; code the appropriate procedure. When the txtState control receives the focus, its existing text should be selected; code the appropriate procedure. Save the solution and then start the application. Test the application with both valid data (uppercase and lowercase letters and the Backspace key) and invalid data (numbers and special characters). Close the Code Editor window and then close the solution.

INTRODUCTORY

2. Use Windows to make a copy of the Play It Again Solution folder contained in the VB2012\Chap04 folder. Rename the copy Play It Again Solution-Introductory. Open the Play It Again Solution (Play It Again Solution.sln) file contained in the Play It Again Solution-Introductory folder. Open the designer window. When a text box receives the focus, its existing text should be selected; code the appropriate procedures. The Date text box should accept only numbers, the slash (/), the hyphen (-), and the Backspace key; code the appropriate procedure. The DVDs and Blu-rays boxes should accept only numbers and the Backspace key; code the appropriate procedures. Save the solution and then start and test the application. Close the Code Editor window and then close the solution.

INTRODUCTORY

3. Open the MessageBox Value Solution (MessageBox Value Solution.sln) file contained in the VB2012\Chap04\MessageBox Value Solution folder. If necessary, open the designer window. Open the Code Editor window. The btnCalc control's Click event procedure should use the MessageBox.Show method to ask whether the user wants to include a dollar sign in the gross pay amount. Include Yes and No buttons in the message box. If the user clicks the Yes button, the procedure should display the gross pay amount using the "C2" format. If the user clicks the No button, the procedure should display the gross pay amount using the "N2" format. Modify the btnCalc control's code. In addition, when the text box receives the focus, its existing text should be selected; code the appropriate procedure. Save the solution and then start and test the application. Close the Code Editor window and then close the solution.

INTRODUCTORY

4. Create a Visual Basic Windows application. Use the following names for the solution and project, respectively: Concert Solution and Concert Project. Save the application in the VB2012\Chap04 folder. Change the form file's name to Main Form.vb. Change the form's name to frmMain. The interface, which is shown in Figure 4-58, allows the user to enter the number of concert tickets purchased. Each concert ticket costs $75.50. A customer is allowed to purchase a maximum of 25 tickets at a time. The application displays the total amount a customer owes for the concert tickets. Code the application. Allow the text box to accept only numbers and the Backspace key. Clear the total due when a change is made to the number of tickets purchased. When the text box receives the focus, select its existing text. The Calculate button's Click event procedure should display the "You can purchase up to 25 tickets only." message when the number of tickets is greater than 25. It should display the total due with a dollar sign and two decimal places. Save the solution and then start and test the application. Close the Code Editor window and then close the solution.

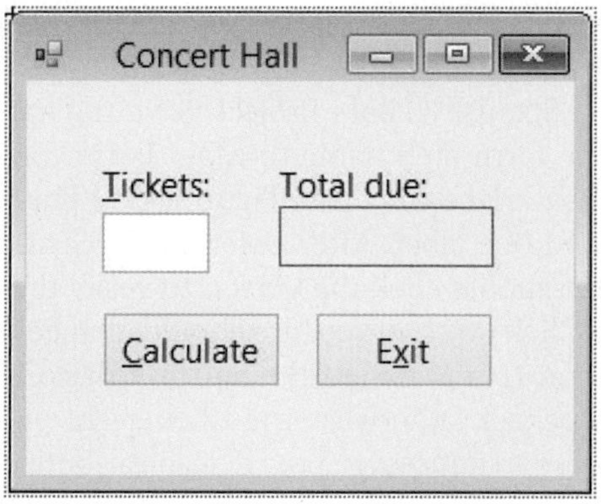

Figure 4-58 Interface for Exercise 4

INTRODUCTORY

5. Create a Visual Basic Windows application. Use the following names for the solution and project, respectively: Mortgage Solution and Mortgage Project. Save the application in the VB2012\Chap04 folder. Change the form file's name to Main Form.vb. Change the form's name to frmMain. Generally speaking, most prospective homeowners can afford a mortgage that is between 2 and 2.5 times their annual gross income. Create an interface that allows the user to enter his or her annual gross income. The application should display the lower and upper ends of the mortgage range. The text box in which the user enters the gross income should accept only numbers, the period, and the Backspace key, and it should have its existing text highlighted when it receives the focus. Save the solution and then start and test the application. Close the Code Editor window and then close the solution.

INTRODUCTORY

6. Create a Visual Basic Windows application. Use the following names for the solution and project, respectively: Hinsbrook Solution and Hinsbrook Project. Save the application in the VB2012\Chap04 folder. Change the form file's name to Main Form.vb. Change the form's name to frmMain. A third-grade teacher at Hinsbrook Elementary School wants an application that allows a student to enter the amount of money a customer owes and the amount of money the customer paid. The application should calculate and display the amount of change. Display an appropriate message when the amount paid is less than the amount owed. The text boxes in which the user enters the amounts owed and paid should accept only numbers, the period, and the Backspace key, and they should have their existing text highlighted when they receive the focus. Save the solution and then start and test the application. Close the Code Editor window and then close the solution.

INTERMEDIATE

7. In this exercise, you modify the application from Exercise 6. Use Windows to make a copy of the Hinsbrook Solution folder. Rename the copy Modified Hinsbrook Solution. Open the Hinsbrook Solution (Hinsbrook Solution.sln) file contained in the Modified Hinsbrook Solution folder. Open the designer window. Modify the interface and code so that they also display the number of dollars, quarters, dimes, nickels, and pennies to return to the customer. Save the solution and then start and test the application. Close the Code Editor window and then close the solution.

INTERMEDIATE

8. Open the Zip Shipping Solution (Zip Shipping Solution.sln) file contained in the VB2012\Chap04\Zip Shipping Solution folder. If necessary, open the designer window. Code the Display Shipping Charge button's Click event procedure. The procedure should display $15.00 as the shipping charge for the following ZIP codes: 42164, 45134, 60345, and 42544. All other ZIP codes are charged $17.75 for shipping. Save the solution and then start and test the application. Close the Code Editor window and then close the solution.

INTERMEDIATE

9. In this exercise, you create an application designed to teach the Spanish words for red, blue, and green. The Spanish words are rojo, azul, and verde, respectively. Create a Visual Basic Windows application. Use the following names for the solution and project, respectively: Spanish Colors Solution and Spanish Colors Project. Save the application in the VB2012\Chap04 folder. Change the form file's name to Main Form.vb. Change the form's name to frmMain. Create the interface shown in Figure 4-59. The interface contains three text boxes, five buttons, and one label. After entering the Spanish word corresponding to a button's color, the user should click the button to verify the entry. If the Spanish word is correct, the button's Click event procedure should change the color of the text box to match the button's color. (Hint: Assign the button's BackColor property to the text box's BackColor property.) Otherwise, the Click event procedure should display the appropriate Spanish word in a message box. The Clear button should change each text box's background color to white, using the Visual Basic constant `Color.White`; it also should clear the contents of each text box. Save the solution and then start and test the application. Close the Code Editor window and then close the solution.

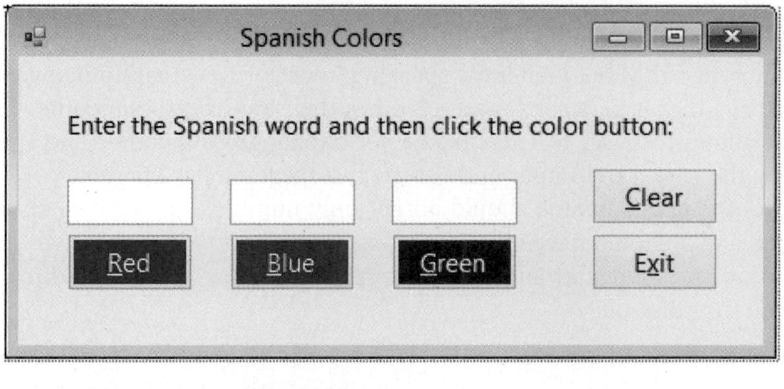

Figure 4-59 Interface for Exercise 9

INTERMEDIATE

10. Create a Visual Basic Windows application. Use the following names for the solution and project, respectively: Allenton Solution and Allenton Project. Save the application in the VB2012\Chap04 folder. Change the form file's name to Main Form.vb. Change the form's name to frmMain. Allenton Water Department wants an application that calculates a customer's monthly water bill. The application's interface, which is shown in Figure 4-60, allows the user to enter the current and previous meter readings. The

application should calculate and display the number of gallons of water used and the total charge for the water. The charge for water is $1.75 per 1000 gallons. However, there is a minimum charge of $16.67. (In other words, every customer must pay at least $16.67.) Display the total charge with a dollar sign and two decimal places. The text boxes should accept only numbers and the Backspace key. Clear the number of gallons used and the total charge when a change is made to the contents of a text box on the form. When a text box receives the focus, select its existing text. Save the solution and then start and test the application. Close the Code Editor window and then close the solution.

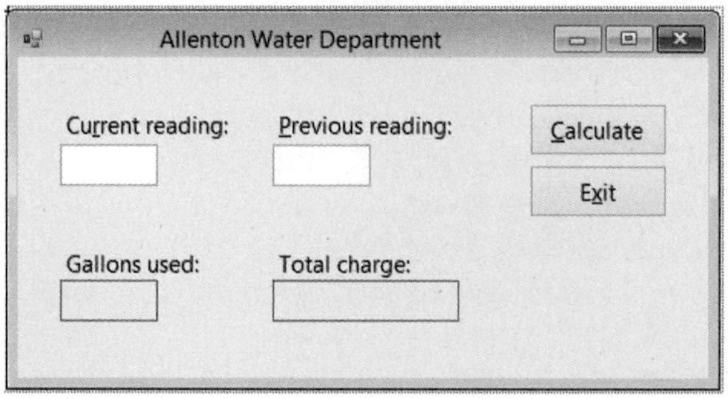

Figure 4-60 Interface for Exercise 10

11. In this exercise, you modify the application from Exercise 2. Use Windows to make a copy of the Play It Again Solution-Introductory folder. Rename the copy Play It Again Solution-Intermediate. Open the Play It Again Solution (Play It Again Solution.sln) file contained in the Play It Again Solution-Intermediate folder. Open the designer and Code Editor windows. If the txtDvds control does not contain any data, the btnCalc control's Click event procedure should assign the number 0 to the text box's Text property. Likewise, if the txtBluRays control does not contain any data, the btnCalc control's Click event procedure should assign the number 0 to the text box's Text property. Modify the procedure's code. Save the solution and then start and test the application. Close the Code Editor window and then close the solution.

INTERMEDIATE

12. Create a Visual Basic Windows application. Use the following names for the solution and project, respectively: Treasures Solution and Treasures Project. Save the application in the VB2012\Chap04 folder. Change the form file's name to Main Form.vb. Change the form's name to frmMain. Create the interface shown in Figure 4-61. When the user clicks the Calculate button, the button's Click event procedure should add the item price to the total of the prices already entered; this amount represents the subtotal owed by the customer. The procedure should display the subtotal on the form. It also should display a 2% sales tax, the shipping charge, and the grand total owed by the customer. The grand total is calculated by adding together the subtotal, the 2% sales tax, and a $10 shipping charge. For example, if the user enters 30.55 as the price and then clicks the Calculate button, the button's Click event procedure should display 30.55 as the subtotal, 0.61 as the sales tax, 10.00 as the shipping charge, and 41.16 as the total due. If the user subsequently enters 20 as the price and then clicks the Calculate button, the button's Click event procedure should display 50.55 as the subtotal, 1.01 as the sales tax, 10.00 as the shipping charge, and 61.56 as the total due. However, when the subtotal is at least $100, the shipping charge is 0.00. Code the application. Save the solution and then start and test the application. Close the Code Editor window and then close the solution.

ADVANCED

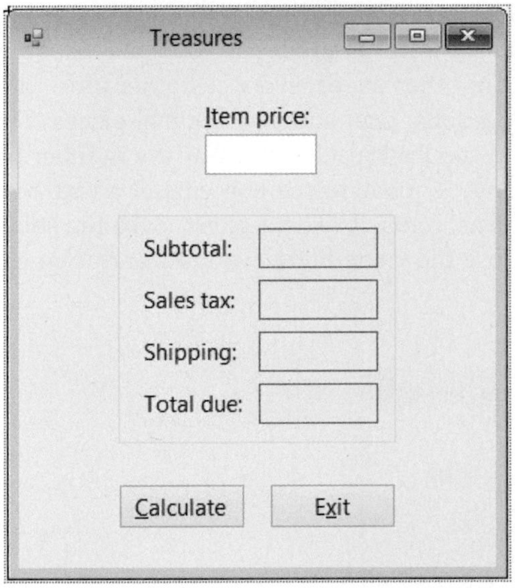

Figure 4-61 Interface for Exercise 12

DISCOVERY

13. In this exercise, you learn how to specify the maximum number of characters that can be entered in a text box. Open the Zip Solution (Zip Solution.sln) file contained in the VB2012\Chap04\Zip Solution folder. If necessary, open the designer window. Click the txtZip control. Look in the Properties list for a property that allows you to specify the maximum number of characters that can be entered in the text box. When you locate the property, set its value to 10. Save the solution and then start the application. Test the application by trying to enter more than 10 characters in the text box. Close the solution.

SWAT THE BUGS

14. Open the Debug Solution (Debug Solution.sln) file contained in the VB2012\Chap04\Debug Solution folder. Open the Code Editor window and review the existing code. The btnCalc control's Click event procedure should calculate a 5% commission when the code entered by the user is 1, 2, or 3 and, at the same time, the sales amount is greater than $5,000; otherwise, the commission rate is 3%. Also, the CancelKeys procedure should allow the two text boxes to accept only numbers, the period, and the Backspace key.

    a. Start the application. Type the number 1 in the Code box and then press the Backspace key. Notice that the Backspace key is not working correctly. Stop the application and then make the appropriate change to the CancelKeys procedure.

    b. Save the solution and then start the application. Type the number 12 in the Code box and then press the Backspace key to delete the 2. The Code box now contains the number 1.

    c. Type 2000 in the Sales amount box and then click the Calculate button. A message box appears and indicates that the commission amount is $100.00 (5% of $2,000), which is incorrect; it should be $60.00 (3% of $2,000). Close the message box. Stop the application and then make the appropriate change to the btnCalc control's Click event procedure.

    d. Save the solution and then start the application. Type the number 1 in the Code box. Type 2000 in the Sales amount box and then click the Calculate button. The message box should indicate that the commission amount is $60.00. Close the message box.

e. Test the application using the following codes and sales amounts:

Code	Sales amount
1	7000
2	5000
2	5000.75
3	175.55
3	9000.65
4	2000
4	6700

f. When you are finished testing the application, close the Code Editor window and then close the solution.

CHAPTER 5

More on the Selection Structure

Revising the Covington Resort Application

In this chapter, you will modify the Covington Resort application from Chapter 4. In addition to the previous input data, the application's interface will now allow the user to select the number of beds (either two queen beds or one king bed), the view (either standard or atrium), and whether the guest should be charged a vehicle parking fee. The resort charges $284 for two queen beds with a standard view, $325 for two queen beds with an atrium view, $290 for one king bed with a standard view, and $350 for one king bed with an atrium view. The vehicle parking fee is $12.75 per night. In addition to displaying the total room charge, the sales and lodging tax, the resort fee, and the total due, the application should now also display the total parking fee.

Previewing the Modified Covington Resort Application

Before you start the first lesson in this chapter, you will preview the completed application. The application is contained in the VB2012\Chap05 folder.

START HERE

To preview the completed application:

1. Use the Run dialog box to run the Covington (Covington.exe) file contained in the VB2012\Chap05 folder. The application's user interface appears on the screen. Type **1**, **1**, **2**, and **2** in the Rooms, Nights, Adults, and Children boxes, respectively. Click the **Calculate** button. See Figure 5-1.

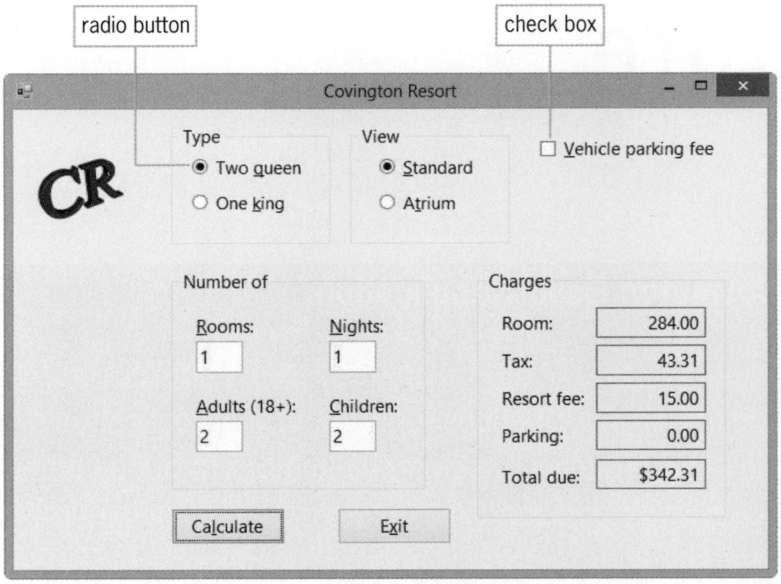

Figure 5-1 Interface showing the calculated amounts

2. The interface contains radio buttons and a check box. These controls are covered in Lesson B. Click the **One king** and **Atrium** radio buttons to select both. Also click the **Vehicle parking fee** check box to select it. A check mark appears inside the check box. Click the **Calculate** button. See Figure 5-2.

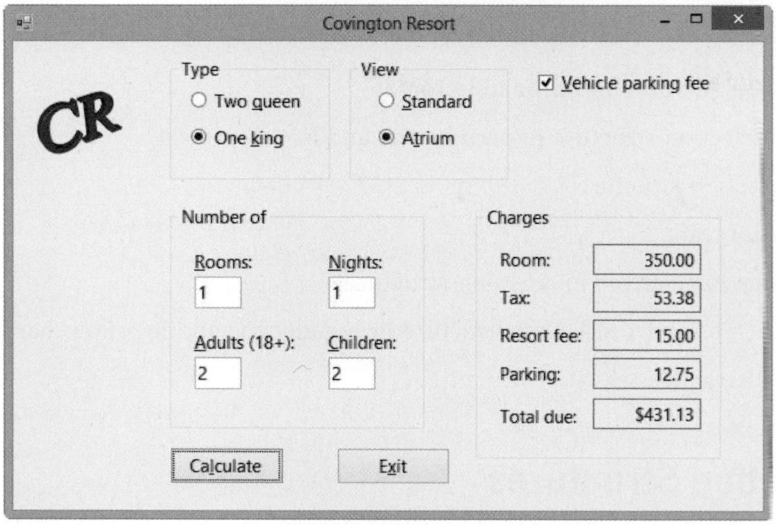

Figure 5-2 Recalculated amounts shown in the interface

3. Click the **Exit** button to end the application.

The modified Covington Resort application uses nested selection structures, which you will learn about in Lesson A. You also will learn about multiple-alternative selection structures. In Lesson B, you will add a radio button and a check box to the Covington Resort application's interface; you also will modify the application's code. In Lesson C, you will learn how to use the TryParse method for data validation. You also will learn how to generate random integers and how to hide and show controls during runtime. Be sure to complete each lesson in full and do all of the end-of-lesson questions and several exercises before continuing to the next lesson.

LESSON A

After studying Lesson A, you should be able to:

- Include a nested selection structure in pseudocode and in a flowchart
- Code a nested selection structure
- Desk-check an algorithm
- Recognize common logic errors in selection structures
- Include a multiple-alternative selection structure in pseudocode and in a flowchart
- Code a multiple-alternative selection structure

Nested Selection Structures

In Chapter 4, you learned that you use the selection structure when you want the computer to make a decision and then select the appropriate path—either the true path or the false path—based on the result. Both paths in a selection structure can include instructions that declare variables, perform calculations, and so on. In this chapter, you will learn that both paths can also include other selection structures. When either a selection structure's true path or its false path contains another selection structure, the inner selection structure is referred to as a **nested selection structure** because it is contained (nested) within the outer selection structure.

A programmer determines whether a problem's solution requires a nested selection structure by studying the problem specification. The first problem specification you will examine in this chapter involves a basketball player named Maleek. The problem specification and an illustration of the problem are shown in Figure 5-3, along with an appropriate solution. The solution requires a selection structure, but not a nested one. This is because only one decision—whether the basketball went through the hoop—is necessary.

Ch05A video

Problem Specification

Maleek is practicing for an upcoming basketball game. Write the instructions that direct Maleek to shoot the basketball and then say one of two phrases, depending on whether or not the basketball went through the hoop.

Result of shot	Phrase
Basketball went through the hoop	I did it!
Basketball did not go through the hoop	Missed it!

Solution

1. shoot the basketball [condition]
2. if the basketball went through the hoop
   say "I did it!" — true path
   else
   say "Missed it!" — false path
   end if

Figure 5-3 A problem that requires the selection structure
Image by Diane Zak; Created with Reallusion CrazyTalk Animator; OpenClipArt.org/Tom Kolter/tawm1972

Now we'll make a slight change to the problem specification shown in Figure 5-3. This time, Maleek should say either one or two phrases, depending not only on whether or not the ball went through the hoop, but also on where he was standing when he made the basket. Figure 5-4 shows the modified problem specification and solution. The modified solution contains an outer dual-alternative selection structure and a nested dual-alternative selection structure. The outer selection structure begins with "if the basketball went through the hoop", and it ends with the last "end if". The last "else" belongs to the outer selection structure and separates the structure's true path from its false path. Notice that the instructions in both paths are indented within the outer selection structure. Indenting in this manner clearly indicates the instructions to be followed when the basketball went through the hoop, as well as the ones to be followed when the basketball did not go through the hoop.

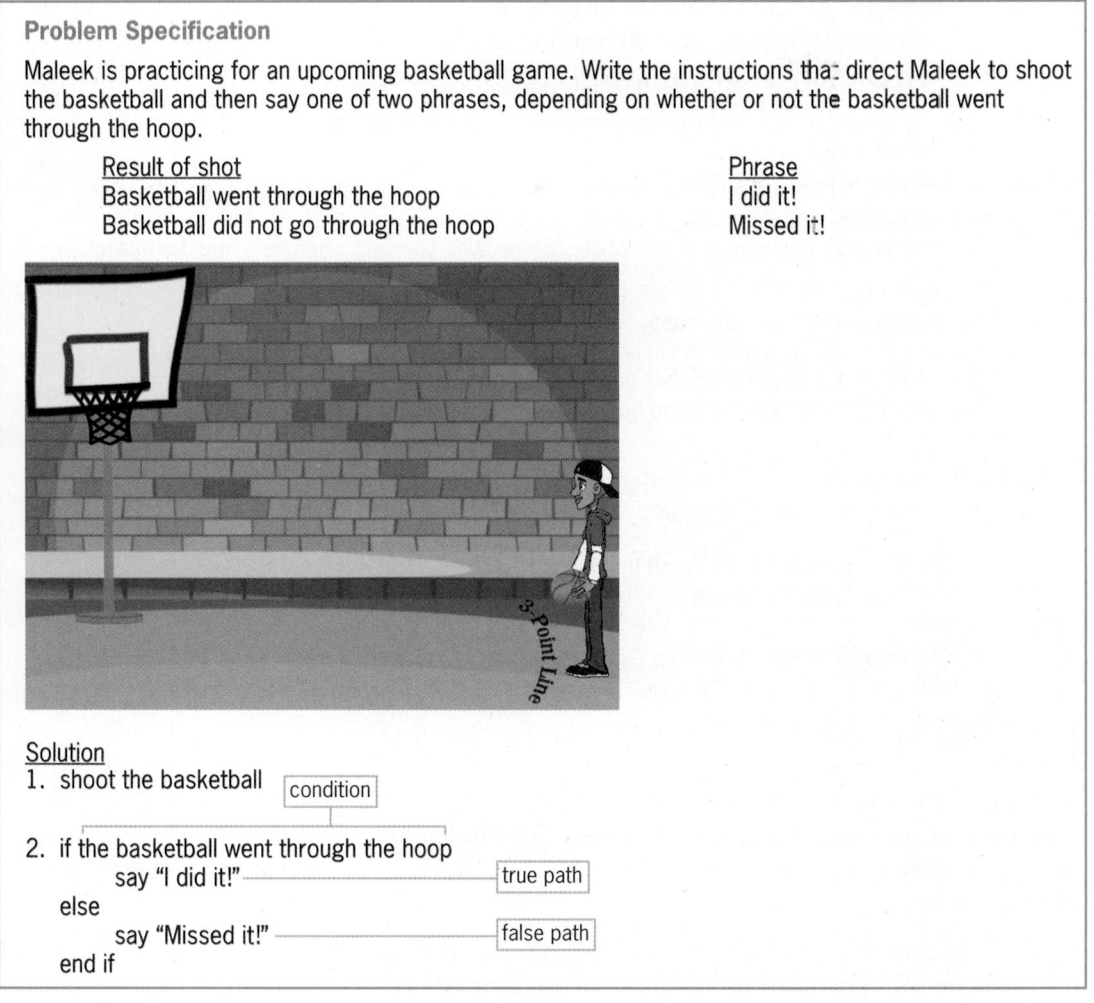

The nested selection structure in Figure 5-4 appears in the outer selection structure's true path. The nested selection structure begins with "if Maleek was either inside or on the 3-point line", and it ends with the first "end if". The indented "else" belongs to the nested selection structure and separates the nested structure's true path from its false path. For clarity, the instructions in the nested selection structure's true and false paths are indented within the structure. For a nested selection structure to work correctly, it must be contained entirely within either the outer selection structure's true path or its false path. The nested selection structure in Figure 5-4, for example, appears entirely within the outer selection structure's true path.

Problem Specification

Maleek is practicing for an upcoming basketball game. Write the instructions that direct Maleek to shoot the basketball and then say either one or two of four phrases, depending on whether or not the basketball went through the hoop and also where Maleek was standing when he made the basket.

Result of shot	Phrase
Basketball went through the hoop	I did it!
Maleek made the basket from either inside or on the 3-point line	2 points for me
Maleek made the basket from behind the 3-point line	3 points for me
Basketball did not go through the hoop	Missed it!

Solution

```
1. shoot the basketball
2. if the basketball went through the hoop
        say "I did it!"
        if Maleek was either inside or on the 3-point line
              say "2 points for me"
        else
              say "3 points for me"
        end if
   else
        say "Missed it!"
   end if
```

nested dual-alternative selection structure

outer dual-alternative selection structure

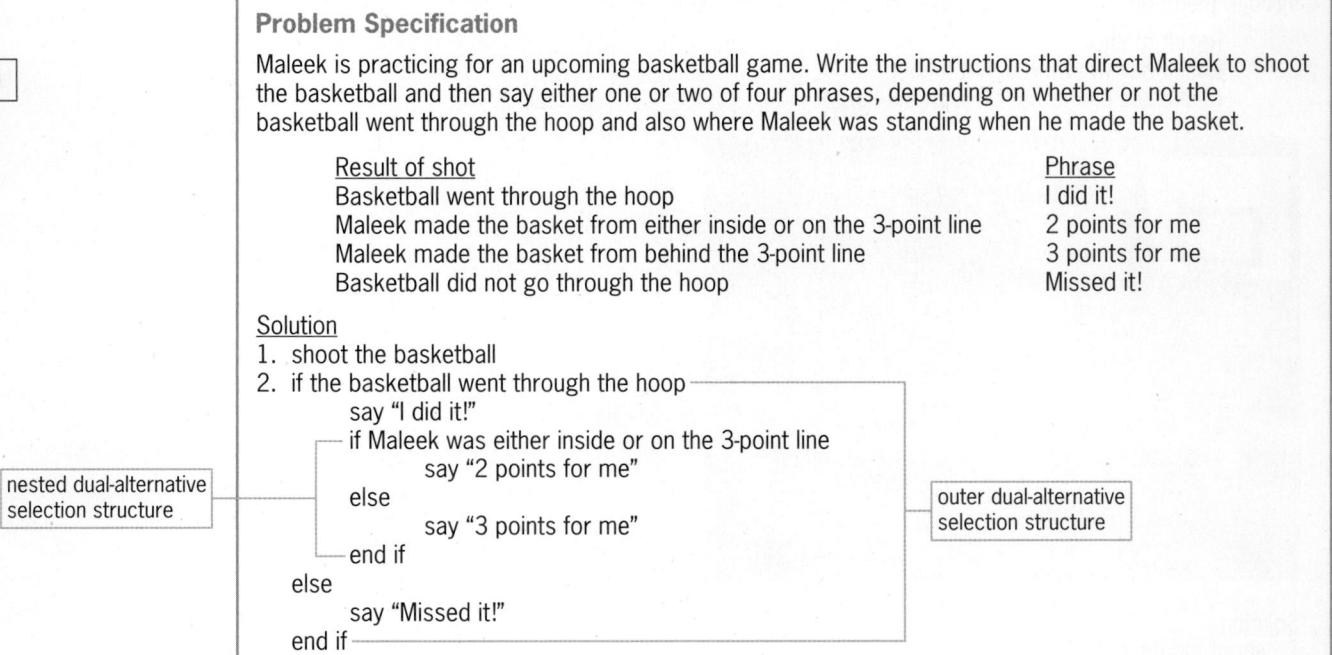

Figure 5-4 A problem that requires a nested selection structure

Figure 5-5 shows a modified version of the previous problem specification, along with the modified solution. In this version of the problem, Maleek should still say "Missed it!" when the basketball misses its target. However, if the basketball hits the rim, he also should say "So close". In addition to the nested dual-alternative selection structure from the previous solution, the modified solution also contains a nested single-alternative selection structure, which appears in the outer selection structure's false path. The nested single-alternative selection structure begins with "if the basketball hit the rim", and it ends with the second "end if". Notice that the nested single-alternative selection structure is contained entirely within the outer selection structure's false path.

Problem Specification

Maleek is practicing for an upcoming basketball game. Write the instructions that direct Maleek to shoot the basketball and then say either one or two of five phrases, depending on whether or not the basketball went through the hoop and also where Maleek was standing when he made the basket.

Result of shot	Phrase
Basketball went through the hoop	I did it!
Maleek made the basket from either inside or on the 3-point line	2 points for me
Maleek made the basket from behind the 3-point line	3 points for me
Basketball did not go through the hoop	Missed it!
Maleek's missed shot hit the rim	So close

Solution

```
1. shoot the basketball
2. if the basketball went through the hoop
        say "I did it!"
        if Maleek was either inside or on the 3-point line
              say "2 points for me"
        else
              say "3 points for me"
        end if
   else
        say "Missed it!"
        if the basketball hit the rim
              say "So close"
        end if
   end if
```

nested dual-alternative selection structure

nested single-alternative selection structure

outer dual-alternative selection structure

Figure 5-5 A problem that requires two nested selection structures

Flowcharting a Nested Selection Structure

Figure 5-6 shows a problem specification for a voter eligibility application. The application determines whether a person can vote and then displays one of three messages. The appropriate message depends on the person's age and voter registration status. For example, if the person is younger than 18 years old, the program should display the message "You are too young to vote." However, if the person is at least 18 years old, the program should display one of two messages. The correct message to display is determined by the person's voter registration status. If the person is registered, then the appropriate message is "You can vote."; otherwise, it is "You must register before you can vote." Notice that determining the person's voter registration status is important only *after* his or her age is determined. Because of this, the decision regarding the age is considered the primary decision, while the decision regarding the registration status is considered the secondary decision because whether it needs to be made depends on the result of the primary decision. A primary decision is always made by an outer selection structure, while a secondary decision is always made by a nested selection structure.

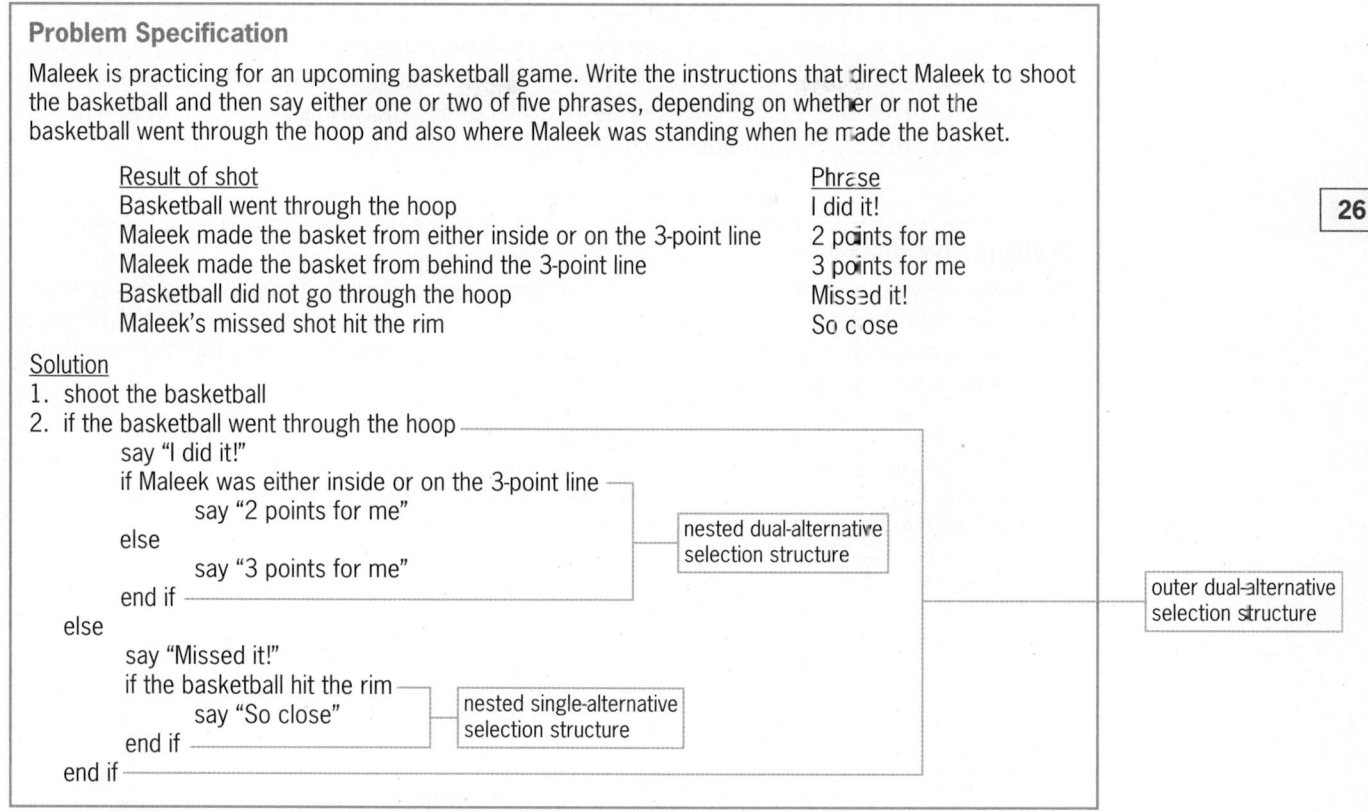

Also included in Figure 5-6 is a correct solution to the voter eligibility problem in flowchart form. The first diamond in the flowchart represents the outer selection structure's condition, which checks whether the age entered by the user is greater than or equal to 18. If the condition evaluates to false, it means that the person is not old enough to vote. In that case, the outer selection structure's false path will display the "You are too young to vote." message before the outer selection structure ends. However, if the outer selection structure's condition evaluates to true, it means that the person *is* old enough to vote. Before displaying the appropriate message, the outer selection structure's true path gets the registration status from the user. It then uses a nested selection structure to determine whether the person is registered and then take the appropriate action. The nested selection structure's condition is represented by the second diamond in Figure 5-6. If the person is registered, the nested selection structure's true path displays the "You can vote." message; otherwise, its false path displays the "You must register before you can vote." message. After the appropriate message is displayed, the nested and outer selection structures end. Notice that the nested selection structure is processed only when the outer selection structure's condition evaluates to true.

Problem Specification

The Danville city manager wants an application that determines voter eligibility and displays one of three messages. The messages and the criteria for displaying each message are shown here. The application's interface will provide a text box for entering the prospective voter's age. It will use a message box to ask the user whether the person is registered to vote.

<u>Message</u>	<u>Criteria</u>
You are too young to vote.	person is younger than 18 years old
You can vote.	person is at least 18 years old and is registered to vote
You must register before you can vote.	person is at least 18 years old but is not registered to vote

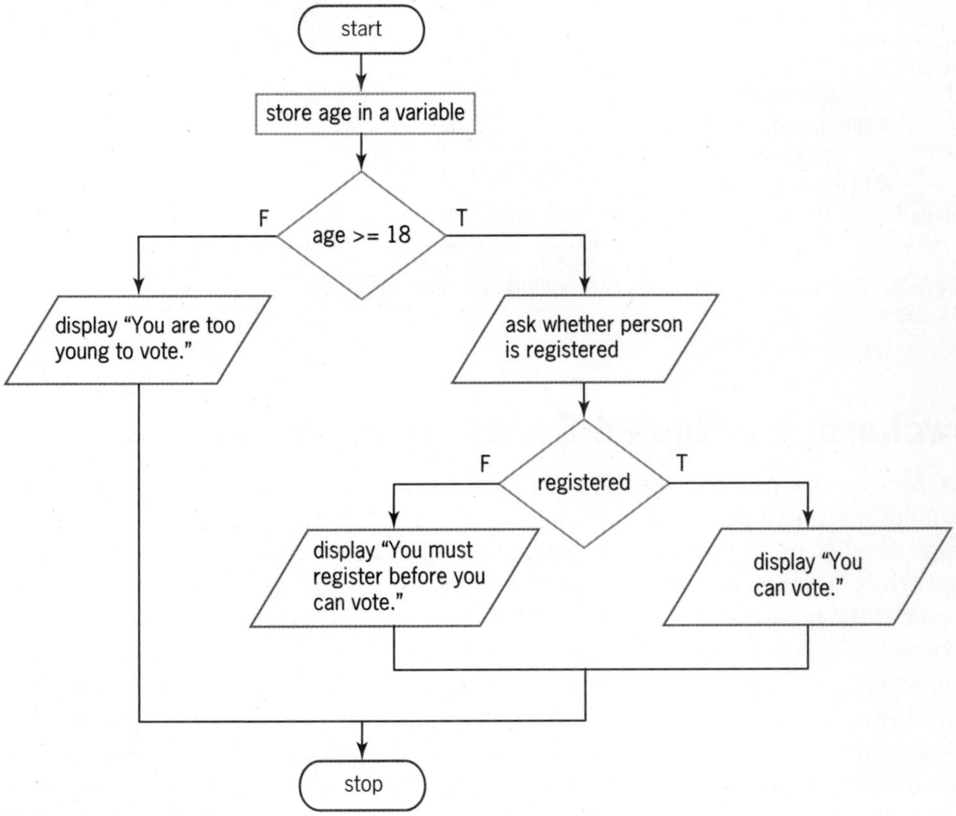

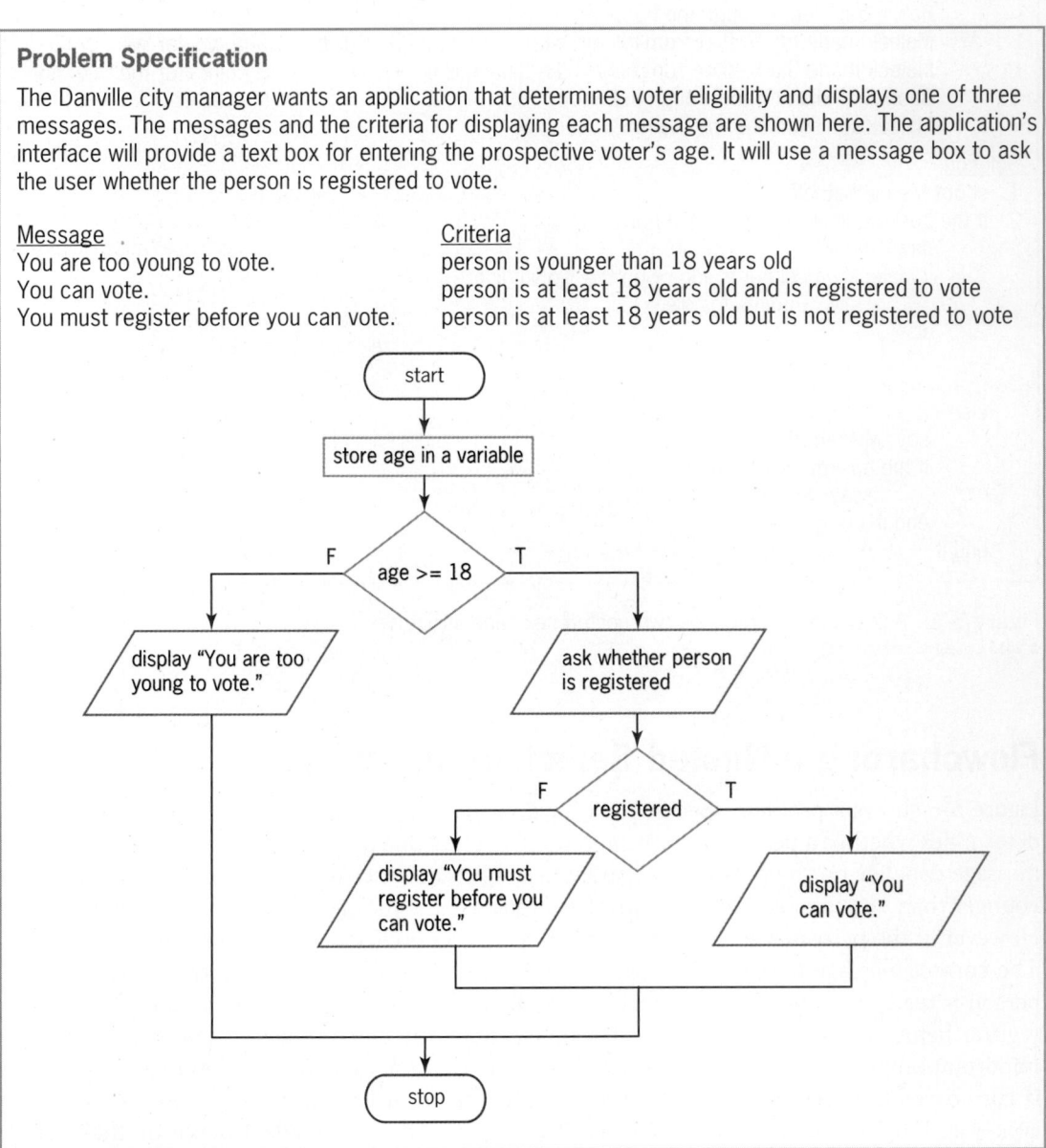

Figure 5-6 Problem specification and a correct solution for the voter eligibility problem

Even small problems can have more than one solution. Figure 5-7 shows another correct solution, also in flowchart form, for the voter eligibility problem. As in the previous solution, the outer selection structure in this solution determines the age (the primary decision), and the nested selection structure determines the voter registration status (the secondary decision). In this solution, however, the outer selection structure's condition is the opposite of the one in Figure 5-6: It checks whether the age is less than 18, rather than checking if it is greater than or equal to 18. (Recall that *less than* is the opposite of *greater than or equal to*.) In addition, the nested selection structure appears in the outer selection structure's false path in this solution, which means it will be processed only when the outer selection structure's condition evaluates to false. The solutions in Figures 5-6 and 5-7 produce the same results. Neither solution is better than the other. Each simply represents a different way of solving the same problem.

Problem Specification

The Danville city manager wants an application that determines voter eligibility and displays one of three messages. The messages and the criteria for displaying each message are shown here. The application's interface will provide a text box for entering the prospective voter's age. It will use a message box to ask the user whether the person is registered to vote.

Message	Criteria
You are too young to vote.	person is younger than 18 years old
You can vote.	person is at least 18 years old and is registered to vote
You must register before you can vote.	person is at least 18 years old but is not registered to vote

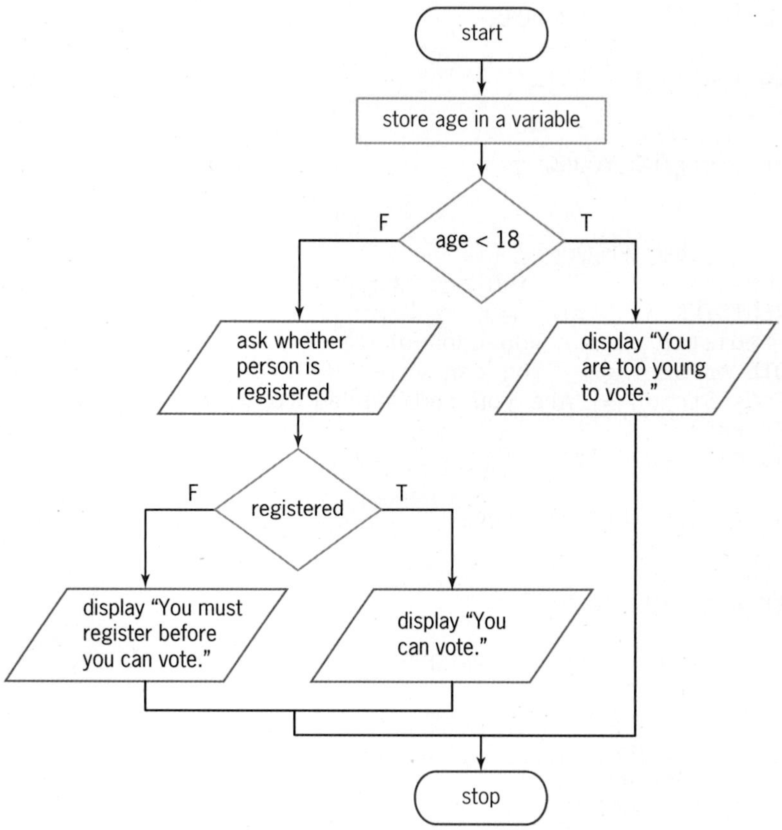

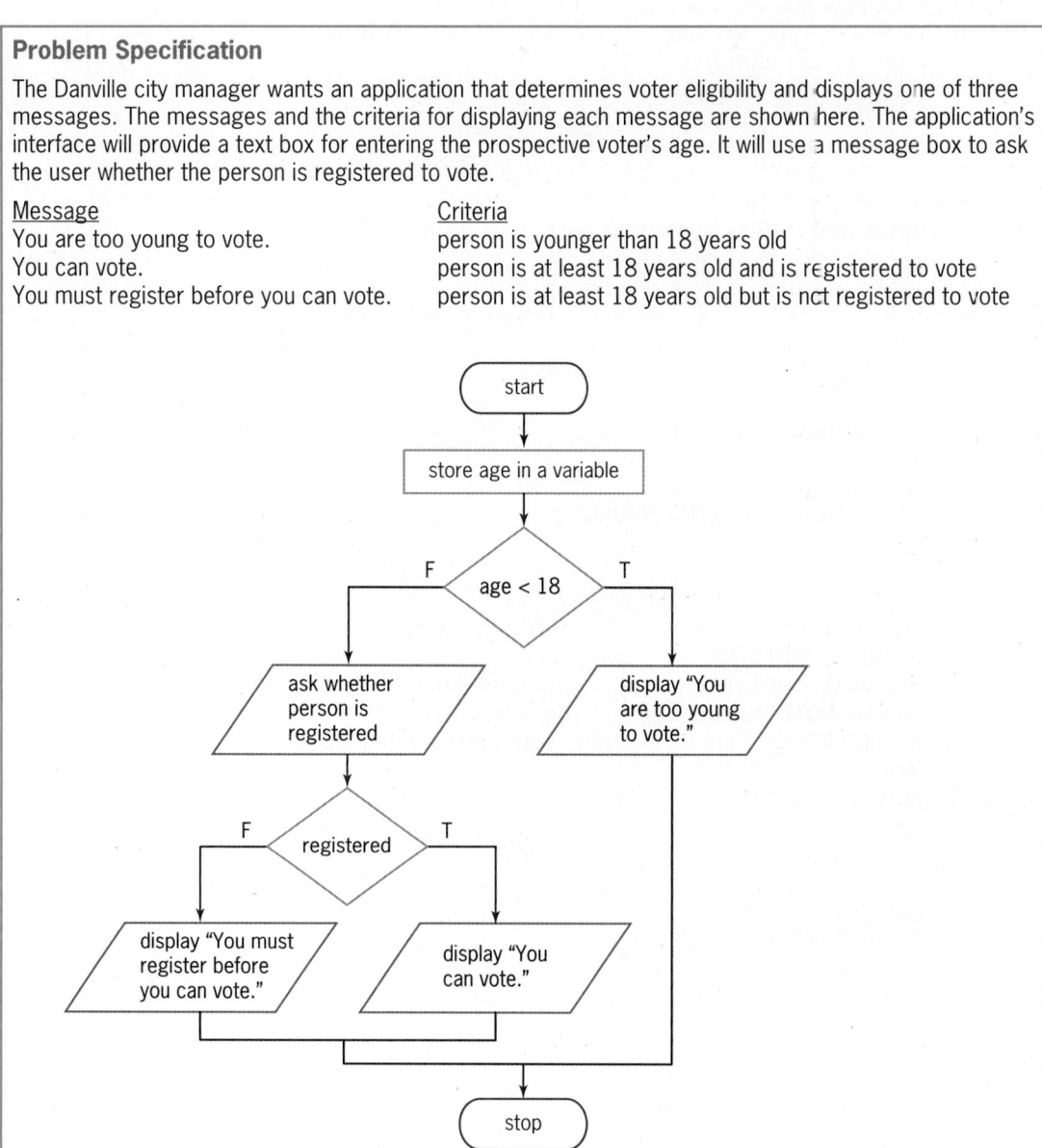

Figure 5-7 Another correct solution for the voter eligibility problem

Coding a Nested Selection Structure

Figure 5-8 shows examples of code that could be used for the voter eligibility application. The first example corresponds to the flowchart in Figure 5-6, and the second example corresponds to the flowchart in Figure 5-7.

Example 1: Code for the flowchart in Figure 5-6

```
Const strTOO_YOUNG As String = "You are too young to vote."
Const strMUST_REGISTER As String =
     "You must register before you can vote."
Const strCAN_VOTE As String = "You can vote."
Const strPROMPT As String = "Are you registered to vote?"
Dim intAge As Integer
Dim dlgButton As DialogResult

Integer.TryParse(txtAge.Text, intAge)

If intAge >= 18 Then
     dlgButton = MessageBox.Show(strPROMPT,
                 "Voter Eligibility",
                 MessageBoxButtons.YesNo,
                 MessageBoxIcon.Exclamation)
     If dlgButton = Windows.Forms.DialogResult.Yes Then
          lblMsg.Text = strCAN_VOTE
     Else
          lblMsg.Text = strMUST_REGISTER
     End If
Else
     lblMsg.Text = strTOO_YOUNG
End If
```

Example 2: Code for the flowchart in Figure 5-7

```
Const strTOO_YOUNG As String = "You are too young to vote."
Const strMUST_REGISTER As String =
     "You must register before you can vote."
Const strCAN_VOTE As String = "You can vote."
Const strPROMPT As String = "Are you registered to vote?"
Dim intAge As Integer
Dim dlgButton As DialogResult

Integer.TryParse(txtAge.Text, intAge)

If intAge < 18 Then
     lblMsg.Text = strTOO_YOUNG
Else
     dlgButton = MessageBox.Show(strPROMPT,
                 "Voter Eligibility",
                 MessageBoxButtons.YesNo,
                 MessageBoxIcon.Exclamation)
     If dlgButton = Windows.Forms.DialogResult.Yes Then
          lblMsg.Text = strCAN_VOTE
     Else
          lblMsg.Text = strMUST_REGISTER
     End If
End If
```

Figure 5-8 Code for the flowcharts in Figures 5-6 and 5-7

START HERE

To code and then test the Voter Eligibility application:

1. If necessary, start Visual Studio 2012. Open the Voter Solution (Voter Solution.sln) file contained in the VB2012\Chap05\Voter Solution folder. If necessary, open the designer window.
2. Open the Code Editor window. Replace <your name> and <current date> in the comments with your name and the current date, respectively.

3. Locate the btnDisplay_Click procedure. Enter the code shown in either of the examples in Figure 5-8.
4. Save the solution and then start the application. Type **17** in the Age box and then click the **Display Message** button. The "You are too young to vote." message appears in the lblMsg control. See Figure 5-9.

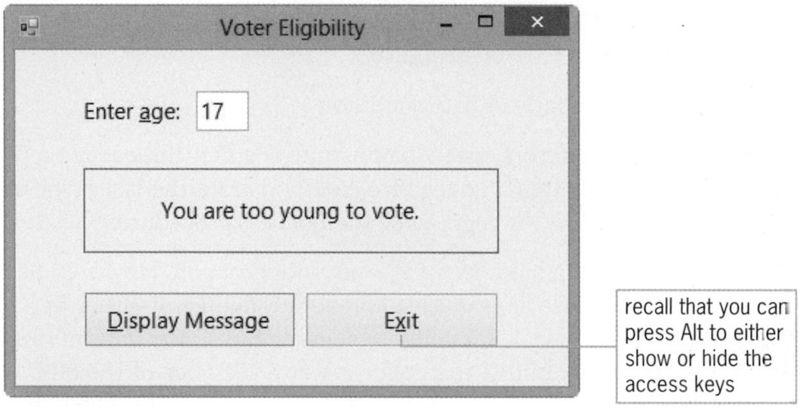

Figure 5-9 Sample run of the Voter Eligibility application

5. Change the age to **21** and then press **Enter**. A message box opens and displays the "Are you registered to vote?" message. Press **Enter** to select the Yes button. The "You can vote." message appears in the lblMsg control.
6. Click the **Display Message** button and then click the **No** button in the message box. The "You must register before you can vote." message appears in the lblMsg control.
7. Click the **Exit** button. Close the Code Editor window and then close the solution.

YOU DO IT 1!

Create a Visual Basic Windows application named YouDoIt 1. Save the application in the VB2012\Chap05 folder. Add a label and two buttons to the form. The application should display the price of a CD (compact disc) in the label. The prices are shown here. Code the first button's Click event procedure using a nested selection structure in the outer selection structure's true path. Code the second button's Click event procedure using a nested selection structure in the outer selection structure's false path. Use message boxes with Yes and No buttons to get the coupon information from the user. Save the solution and then start and test the application. Close the solution.

Price	Criteria
\$12	customer does not have a coupon
\$10	customer has a \$2 coupon
\$ 8	customer has a \$4 coupon

Logic Errors in Selection Structures

In the next few sections, you will observe some of the common logic errors made when writing selection structures. Being aware of these errors will help prevent you from making them. In most cases, logic errors in selection structures are a result of one of the following four mistakes:

1. using a compound condition rather than a nested selection structure
2. reversing the decisions in the outer and nested selection structures
3. using an unnecessary nested selection structure
4. including an unnecessary comparison in a condition

To better understand these four logic errors, we'll demonstrate the first three using a procedure that displays the appropriate fee to charge a golfer. We'll demonstrate the last error using a procedure that displays a bonus rate. We'll begin with the golf fee procedure.

Harper Golf Club charges every golfer a basic fee of $25 per round of golf. However, if the golfer is not a member of the golf club, he or she is charged an additional fee of either $15 on a weekday or $20 on a weekend. Notice that the golfer's membership status determines whether the golfer is charged an additional amount. If the golfer is not a member of the club, then whether it's either a weekday or a weekend determines the appropriate additional amount. In this case, the decision regarding the membership status is the primary decision, while the decision regarding where the day falls in the week is the secondary decision. The pseudocode shown in Figure 5-10 represents a correct algorithm for the golf fee procedure. An **algorithm** is the set of step-by-step instructions for accomplishing a task.

Problem Specification

Harper Golf Club wants an application that displays the appropriate fee to charge a golfer. The club's fees are as follows:

Basic fee for members and non-members	$25
Additional fee for non-members on a weekday	15
Additional fee for non-members on a weekend	20

Correct algorithm

```
1. golf fee = 25
2. if non-member
        if weekday
          add 15 to the golf fee
        else
          add 20 to the golf fee
        end if
   end if
3. display the golf fee
```

Figure 5-10 A correct algorithm for the golf fee procedure

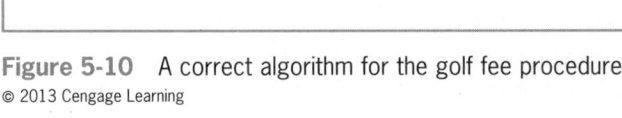

You also can write the nested selection structure's if clause in Figure 5-10 as follows: if weekend. However, you then would need to reverse the instructions in the true and false paths.

Ch05A-Harper Correct Desk-Check video

You can verify that the algorithm in Figure 5-10 works correctly by desk-checking it. **Desk-checking** refers to the process of reviewing the algorithm while seated at your desk rather than in front of the computer. Desk-checking is also called **hand-tracing** because you use a pencil and paper to follow each of the algorithm's instructions by hand. You desk-check an algorithm to verify that it is not missing any instructions and that the existing instructions are correct and in the proper order.

Before you begin the desk-check, you first choose a set of sample data for the input values, which you then use to manually compute the expected output values. Figure 5-11 shows the input values you will use to desk-check Figure 5-10's algorithm four times; it also includes the expected output values.

Desk-check	Membership Status	Day Information	Expected Golf Fee
1	member	weekday	$25
2	member	weekend	$25
3	non-member	weekday	$40
4	non-member	weekend	$45

Figure 5-11 Sample data and expected results for the algorithm shown in Figure 5-10

Step 1 in Figure 5-10's algorithm assigns $25 as the golf fee. Next, the condition in the outer selection structure in Step 2 determines whether the golfer is not a club member. For the first desk-check, the condition evaluates to False because the golfer *is* a club member. As a result, the outer selection structure ends. Notice that the nested selection structure is not processed when the outer selection structure's condition is false. This is because the day of the week information is not important when the golfer is a club member. The last step in the algorithm displays the expected golf fee of $25.

Now we'll desk-check the algorithm using the second set of test data: member and weekend. Step 1 in Figure 5-10's algorithm assigns $25 as the golf fee. Next, the condition in the outer selection structure in Step 2 determines whether the golfer is not a club member. Here again, the condition evaluates to False because the golfer *is* a club member. As a result, the outer selection structure ends. The last step in the algorithm displays the expected golf fee, $25.

Next, we'll desk-check the algorithm using the third set of test data: non-member and weekday. Step 1 in Figure 5-10's algorithm assigns $25 as the golf fee. Next, the condition in the outer selection structure in Step 2 determines whether the golfer is not a club member. In this case, the condition evaluates to True, so the nested selection structure's condition checks whether the person is golfing on a weekday. This condition also evaluates to True, so the nested selection structure's true path adds $15 to the basic golf fee, giving $40; after doing this, both selection structures end. The last step in the algorithm displays the expected golf fee, $40.

Finally, we'll desk-check the algorithm using the fourth set of test data: non-member and weekend. Step 1 in Figure 5-10's algorithm assigns $25 as the golf fee. Next, the condition in the outer selection structure in Step 2 determines whether the golfer is not a club member. The condition evaluates to True, so the nested selection structure's condition checks whether the person is golfing on a weekday. This condition evaluates to False, so the nested selection structure's false path adds $20 to the basic golf fee, giving $45; after doing this, both selection structures end. The last step in the algorithm displays the expected golf fee of $45. The results of desk-checking the algorithm using the data from Figure 5-11 agree with the expected values also shown in the figure.

First Logic Error: Using a Compound Condition Rather Than a Nested Selection Structure

A common error made when writing selection structures is to use a compound condition in the outer selection structure when a nested selection structure is needed. Figure 5-12 shows an example of this error in the golf fee algorithm. The correct algorithm is included in the figure for comparison. Notice that the incorrect algorithm uses one selection structure rather than two selection structures and that the selection structure contains a compound condition. Consider why the selection structure in the incorrect algorithm cannot be used in place of the selection structures in the correct one. In the correct algorithm, the outer and nested selection structures indicate that a hierarchy exists between the membership status and day of the week decisions: The status decision is always made first, followed by the day of the week decision (if necessary). In the incorrect algorithm, the compound condition indicates that no hierarchy exists between the status and day decisions. Consider how this difference changes the algorithm.

<u>Correct algorithm</u>

```
1. golf fee = 25
2. if non-member
      if weekday
         add 15 to the golf fee
      else
         add 20 to the golf fee
      end if
   end if
3. display the golf fee
```

<u>Incorrect algorithm</u>

```
1. golf fee = 25
2. if non-member and weekday
      add 15 to the golf fee
   else
      add 20 to the golf fee
   end if
3. display the golf fee
```

uses a compound condition instead of a nested selection structure

Figure 5-12 Correct algorithm and an incorrect algorithm containing the first logic error

To understand why the incorrect algorithm in Figure 5-12 will not work correctly, you will desk-check it using the same test data used to desk-check the correct algorithm. Step 1 in the incorrect algorithm assigns $25 as the golf fee. Next, the compound condition in Step 2 determines whether the golfer is not a club member and, at the same time, the person is golfing on a weekday. Using the first set of test data (member and weekday), the compound condition evaluates to False because the golfer *is* a club member. As a result, the selection structure's false path adds $20 to the golf fee, giving $45, and then the selection structure ends. The last step in the incorrect algorithm displays $45 as the golf fee, which is not correct; the correct fee is $25, as shown earlier in Figure 5-11.

Ch05A-First Logic Error Desk-Check video

Now we'll desk-check the incorrect algorithm using the second set of test data: member and weekend. Step 1 in the incorrect algorithm assigns $25 as the golf fee. Next, the compound condition in Step 2 determines whether the golfer is not a club member and, at the same time, the person is golfing on a weekday. Here again, the compound condition evaluates to False: this time because the golfer *is* a club member and is *not* golfing on a weekday. As a result, the selection structure's false path adds $20 to the golf fee, giving $45, and then the selection structure ends. The last step in the incorrect algorithm displays $45 as the golf fee, which is not correct; the correct fee is $25, as shown earlier in Figure 5-11.

Next, we'll desk-check the incorrect algorithm using the third set of test data: non-member and weekday. Step 1 in the incorrect algorithm assigns $25 as the golf fee. Next, the compound condition in Step 2 determines whether the golfer is not a club member and, at the same time, the person is golfing on a weekday. In this case, the compound condition evaluates to True, so the selection structure's true path adds $15 to the golf fee, giving $40, and then the selection structure ends. The last step in the incorrect algorithm displays the expected golf fee, $40. Even though its selection structure is phrased incorrectly, the incorrect algorithm produces the same result as the correct algorithm using the third set of test data.

Finally, we'll desk-check the incorrect algorithm in Figure 5-12 using the fourth set of test data: non-member and weekend. Step 1 in the incorrect algorithm assigns $25 as the golf fee. Next, the compound condition in Step 2 determines whether the golfer is not a club member and, at the same time, the person is golfing on a weekday. The compound condition evaluates to False because the person is *not* golfing on a weekday. As a result, the selection structure's false path adds $20 to the golf fee, giving $45, and then the selection structure ends. The last step in the incorrect algorithm displays the expected golf fee, $45. Here again, even though its selection structure is phrased incorrectly, the incorrect algorithm produces the same result as the correct algorithm using the fourth set of test data.

Figure 5-13 shows the desk-check table for the incorrect algorithm from Figure 5-12. As indicated in the figure, the results of the third and fourth desk-checks are correct, but the results of the first and second desk-checks are not correct.

Desk-check	Membership Status	Day Information	Expected Golf Fee	Actual Result
1	member	weekday	$25	$45 (incorrect)
2	member	weekend	$25	$45 (incorrect)
3	non-member	weekday	$40	$40 (correct)
4	non-member	weekend	$45	$45 (correct)

Figure 5-13 Results of desk-checking the incorrect algorithm from Figure 5-12

The importance of desk-checking an algorithm several times using different data cannot be emphasized enough. In this case, if you had used only the last two sets of data to desk-check the incorrect algorithm, you would not have discovered that the algorithm did not work as intended.

Second Logic Error: Reversing the Outer and Nested Decisions

Another common error made when writing selection structures is to reverse the decisions made by the outer and nested structures. Figure 5-14 shows an example of this error in the golf fee algorithm. The correct algorithm is included in the figure for comparison. Unlike the selection structures in the correct algorithm, which determine the membership status before determining the day of the week, the selection structures in the incorrect algorithm determine the day of the week before determining the membership status. Consider how this difference changes the algorithm. In the correct algorithm, the selection structures indicate that only non-members pay an additional amount. The selection structures in the incorrect algorithm, on the other hand, indicate that the additional amount is paid by anyone golfing on a weekday. Figure 5-15 shows the results of desk-checking the incorrect algorithm. As indicated in the figure, only two of the four results are correct.

Ch05A-Second Logic Error Desk-Check Video

Correct algorithm	Incorrect algorithm
1. golf fee = 25	1. golf fee = 25
2. if non-member	2. if weekday
if weekday	if non-member
add 15 to the golf fee	add 15 to the golf fee
else	else
add 20 to the golf fee	add 20 to the golf fee
end if	end if
end if	end if
3. display the golf fee	3. display the golf fee

the outer and nested decisions are reversed

Figure 5-14 Correct algorithm and an incorrect algorithm containing the second logic error

Desk-check	Membership Status	Day Information	Expected Golf Fee	Actual Result
1	member	weekday	\$25	\$45 (incorrect)
2	member	weekend	\$25	\$25 (correct)
3	non-member	weekday	\$40	\$40 (correct)
4	non-member	weekend	\$45	\$25 (incorrect)

Figure 5-15 Results of desk-checking the incorrect algorithm from Figure 5-14

Third Logic Error: Using an Unnecessary Nested Selection Structure

Another common error made when writing selection structures is to include an unnecessary nested selection structure. In most cases, a selection structure containing this error will still produce the correct results. However, it will do so less efficiently than selection structures that are properly structured. Figure 5-16 shows an example of this error in the golf fee algorithm. The correct algorithm is included in the figure for comparison. Unlike the correct algorithm, which contains two selection structures, the inefficient algorithm contains three selection structures. The condition in the third selection structure determines whether the day is a weekend and is processed only when the second selection structure's condition evaluates to False. In other words, it is processed only when the day is not a weekday. However, if the day is not a weekday, then it would have to be a weekend, so the third selection structure is unnecessary. Figure 5-17 shows the results of desk-checking the inefficient algorithm. Although the results of the four desk-checks are correct, the result of the second desk-check is obtained in a less efficient manner.

Ch05A-Third Logic Error Desk-Check video

Correct algorithm	Inefficient algorithm
1. golf fee = 25	1. golf fee = 25
2. if non-member	2. if non-member
if weekday	if weekday
add 15 to the golf fee	add 15 to the golf fee
else	else
add 20 to the golf fee	if weekend
end if	add 20 to the golf fee
end if	end if
3. display the golf fee	end if
	end if
	3. display the golf fee

unnecessary nested selection structure

Figure 5-16 Correct algorithm and an inefficient algorithm containing the third logic error

Desk-check	Membership Status	Day Information	Expected Golf Fee	Actual Result
1	member	weekday	$25	$25 (correct)
2	member	weekend	$25	$25 (correct)
3	non-member	weekday	$40	$40 (correct)
4	non-member	weekend	$45	$45 (correct)

result obtained in a less efficient manner

Figure 5-17 Results of desk-checking the inefficient algorithm from Figure 5-16

Credit to Come

Fourth Logic Error: Including an Unnecessary Comparison in a Condition

Another common error made when writing selection structures is to include an unnecessary comparison in a condition. Like selection structures containing the third logic error, selection structures containing this error also produce the correct results in an inefficient way. We'll demonstrate this error using the bonus rate procedure created for the Carrington Company. Figure 5-18 shows the problem specification, a correct algorithm, and an inefficient algorithm that contains the fourth logic error.

Ch05A-Fourth Logic Error Desk-Check video

Problem Specification

Carrington Company wants an application that displays the rate to use when calculating a salesperson's bonus. The rates are as follows:

Sales ($)	Bonus Rate
Less than 0	0
0 – 5,000	1%
Over 5,000	1.5%

Correct algorithm

```
1. if sales < 0
        rate = 0
   else
        if sales <= 5000
             rate = .01
        else
             rate = .015
        end if
   end if
2. display the rate
```

Inefficient algorithm

```
1. if sales < 0
        rate = 0
   else
        if sales >= 0 and sales <= 5000
             rate = .01
        else
             rate = .015
        end if
   end if
2. display the rate
```

unnecessary comparison

Figure 5-18 Problem specification, a correct algorithm, and an inefficient algorithm

In Figure 5-18, you also can write the nested selection structure's if clause in the correct algorithm as follows: if sales > 5000. However, you then would need to reverse the instructions in the true and false paths.

Unlike the nested selection structure in the correct algorithm, the nested selection structure in the inefficient algorithm contains a compound condition that compares the sales to both 0 and 5000. Consider why the comparison to 0 in the compound condition is unnecessary. If the sales *are* less than 0, the outer selection structure's condition will evaluate to True. As a result, the outer selection structure's true path will assign the number 0 as the rate before the outer selection structure ends. In other words, sales that are less than 0 will be handled by the outer selection structure's true path. The nested selection structure's condition will be evaluated only when the sales are greater than or equal to 0. Therefore, the comparison to 0 is unnecessary in the compound condition. Figure 5-19 shows the results of desk-checking the correct and inefficient algorithms. Although the results of the three desk-checks for the inefficient algorithm are correct, the results of the second and third desk-checks are obtained in a less efficient manner.

Correct Algorithm Desk-check	Sales	Expected Rate	Actual Result
1	–300	0	0 (correct)
2	1000	.01	.01 (correct)
3	5001	.015	.015 (correct)

Inefficient Algorithm Desk-check	Sales	Expected Rate	Actual Result
1	–300	0	0 (correct)
2	1000	.01	.01 (correct)
3	5001	.015	.015 (correct)

results obtained in a less efficient manner

Figure 5-19 Results of desk-checking the algorithms from Figure 5-18

Note: You have learned a lot so far in this lesson. You may want to take a break at this point before continuing.

Multiple-Alternative Selection Structures

Figure 5-20 shows the problem specification for the Allen High School application. The application's solution requires a selection structure that can choose from several different letter grades. As the figure indicates, when the letter grade is A, the selection structure should display the message "Excellent". When the letter grade is B, the selection structure should display the message "Above Average", and so on. Selection structures containing several alternatives are referred to as **multiple-alternative selection structures** or **extended selection structures**.

Problem Specification

Mrs. Jackson teaches math at Allen High School. She wants an application that displays a message based on a letter grade she enters. The valid letter grades and their corresponding messages are shown here. If the letter grade is not valid, the application should display the "Incorrect Grade" message.

Letter grade	Message
A	Excellent
B	Above Average
C	Average
D	Below Average
F	Below Average

Figure 5-20 Problem specification for the Allen High School problem

Figure 5-21 shows the pseudocode and flowchart for a procedure in the Allen High School application. The diamond in the flowchart represents a multiple-alternative selection structure's condition. Recall that the diamond is also used to represent the condition in both the single-alternative and dual-alternative selection structures. However, unlike the diamond in both of those selection structures, the diamond in a multiple-alternative selection structure has several flowlines (rather than only two flowlines) leading out of the symbol. Each flowline represents a possible path and must be marked appropriately, indicating the value or values necessary for the path to be chosen.


```
1. change the grade entered by the user to uppercase
2. if the grade is one of the following:
         A        display "Excellent"
         B        display "Above Average"
         C        display "Average"
         D, F     display "Below Average"
   else
         display "Incorrect Grade"
   end if
```

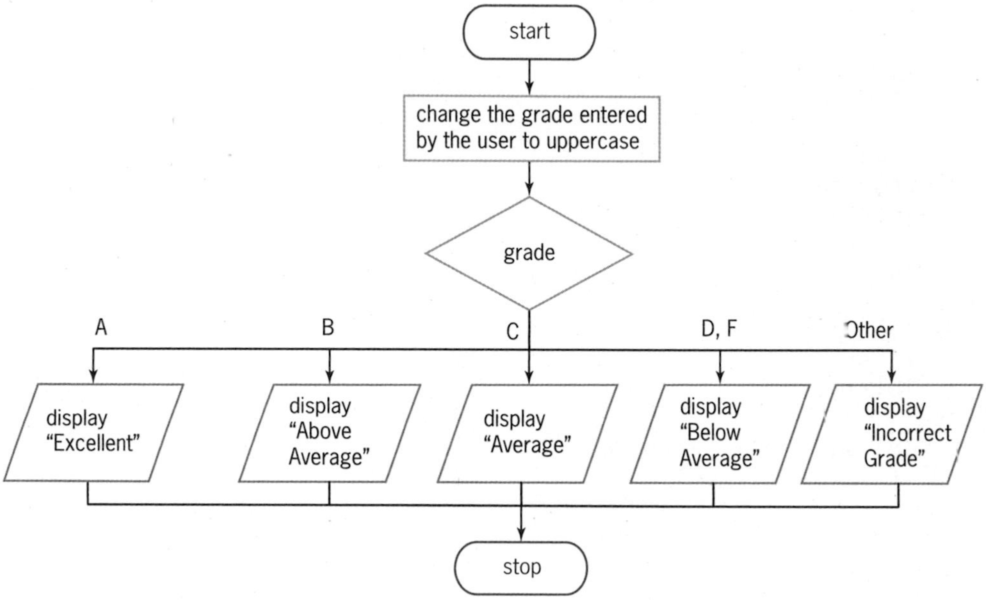

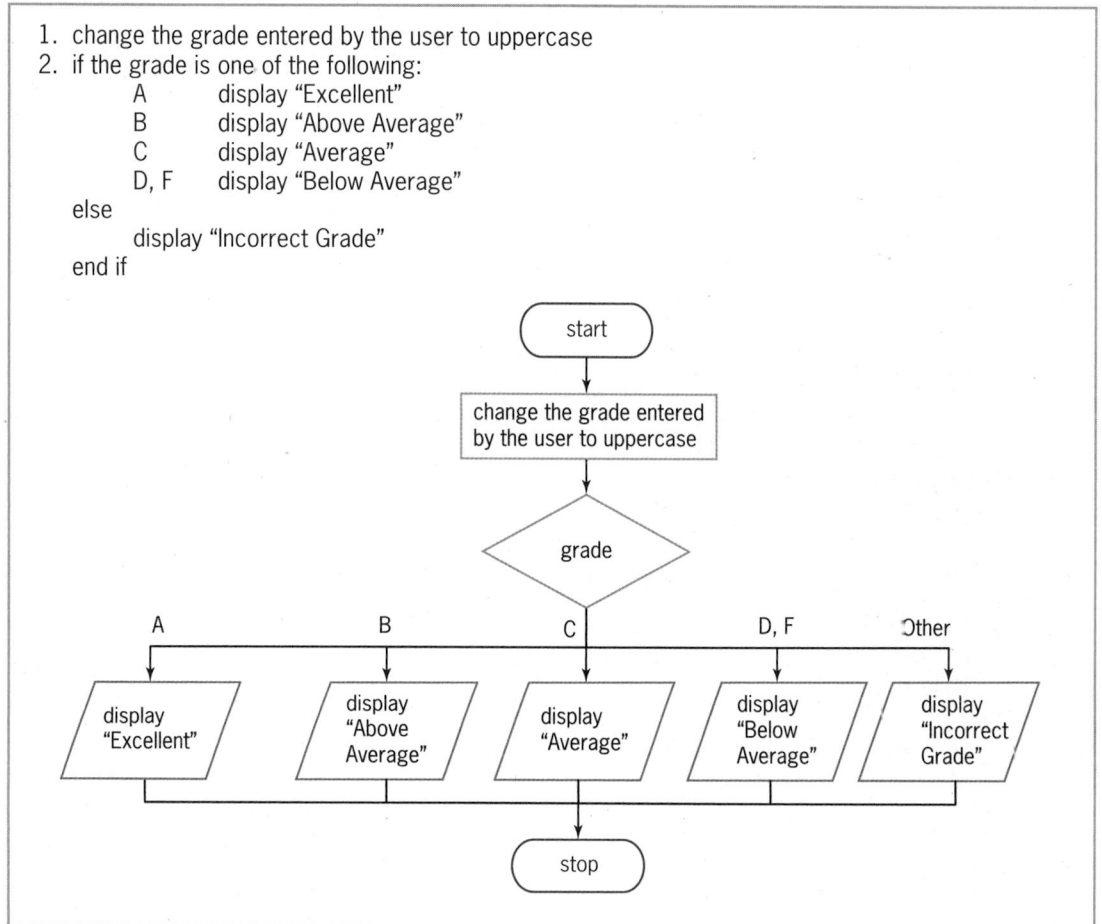

Figure 5-21 Pseudocode and flowchart containing a multiple-alternative selection structure

Figure 5-22 shows two versions of the code corresponding to the multiple-alternative selection structure from Figure 5-21; both versions use If...Then...Else statements. Although both versions produce the same result, Version 2 provides a more convenient way of coding a multiple-alternative selection structure.

Version 1
```
Dim strGrade As String

strGrade = txtGrade.Text.ToUpper
If strGrade = "A" Then
    lblMsg.Text = "Excellent"
Else
    If strGrade = "B" Then
        lblMsg.Text = "Above Average"
    Else
        If strGrade = "C" Then
            lblMsg.Text = "Average"
        Else
            If strGrade = "D" OrElse strGrade = "F" Then
                lblMsg.Text = "Below Average"
            Else
                lblMsg.Text = "Incorrect Grade"
            End If
        End If
    End If
End If
```
(Callouts: "you get here when the grade is not A" — at If strGrade = "B"; "you get here when the grade is not A and not B" — at If strGrade = "C"; "you get here when the grade is not A, B, or C" — at If strGrade = "D" OrElse...; "you get here when the grade is not A, B, C, D, or F" — at lblMsg.Text = "Incorrect Grade"; "four End If clauses are required")

Version 2
```
Dim strGrade As String

strGrade = txtGrade.Text.ToUpper
If strGrade = "A" Then
    lblMsg.Text = "Excellent"
ElseIf strGrade = "B" Then
    lblMsg.Text = "Above Average"
ElseIf strGrade = "C" Then
    lblMsg.Text = "Average"
ElseIf strGrade = "D" OrElse strGrade = "F" Then
    lblMsg.Text = "Below Average"
Else
    lblMsg.Text = "Incorrect Grade"
End If
```
(Callout: "only one End If clause is required")

Figure 5-22 Two versions of the code containing a multiple-alternative selection structure

START HERE

To code and then test the Allen High School application:

1. Open the Grade Solution (Grade Solution.sln) file contained in the VB2012\Chap05\Grade Solution-If folder. If necessary, open the designer window.
2. Open the Code Editor window. Replace <your name> and <current date> in the comments with your name and the current date, respectively.
3. Locate the btnDisplay_Click procedure. Enter the code from Version 2 in Figure 5-22.
4. Save the solution and then start the application. Type the letter **a** and then press **Enter**. The "Excellent" message appears in the interface. See Figure 5-23.

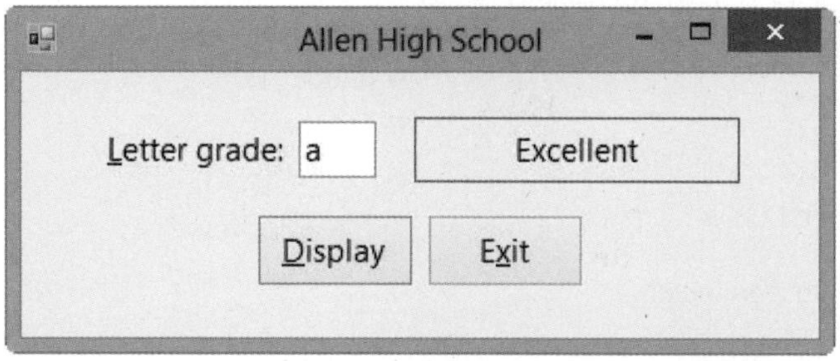

Figure 5-23 Excellent message shown in the interface

5. On your own, test the application using the following grades: **b**, **c**, **d**, **x**, and **f**. When you are finished testing, click the **Exit** button. Close the Code Editor window and then close the solution.

YOU DO IT 2!

Create a Visual Basic Windows application named YouDoIt 2. Save the application in the VB2012\Chap05 folder. Add a text box, a label, and a button to the form. The button's Click event procedure should display (in the label) either the price of a concert ticket or an error message. The ticket price is based on the code entered in the text box, as shown here. Code the procedure. Save the solution and then start and test the application. Close the solution.

Code	Ticket price
1	$15
2	$15
3	$25
4	$35
5	$37
Other	Invalid code

The Select Case Statement

When a multiple-alternative selection structure has many paths from which to choose, it is often simpler and clearer to code the selection structure using the **Select Case statement** rather than several If...Then...Else statements. The Select Case statement's syntax is shown in Figure 5-24. The figure also shows how you can use the statement to code the multiple-alternative selection structure from Figure 5-22.

Select Case Statement

Syntax

Select Case *selectorExpression*
    Case *expressionList1*
        instructions for the first Case
    [**Case** *expressionList2*
        instructions for the second Case]
    [**Case** *expressionListN*
        instructions for the Nth Case]
    [**Case Else**
        instructions for when the selectorExpression does not match any of the expressionLists]
End Select

Example

```
Dim strGrade As String

strGrade = txtGrade.Text.ToUpper
Select Case strGrade
    Case "A"
        lblMsg.Text = "Excellent"
    Case "B"
        lblMsg.Text = "Above Average"
    Case "C"
        lblMsg.Text = "Average"
    Case "D", "F"
        lblMsg.Text = "Below Average"
    Case Else
        lblMsg.Text = "Incorrect Grade"
End Select
```

the *selectorExpression* needs to match only one of these values

Figure 5-24 Syntax and an example of the Select Case statement

The Select Case statement begins with the keywords `Select Case`, followed by a *selectorExpression*. The selectorExpression can contain any combination of variables, constants, keywords, functions, methods, operators, and properties. In the example in Figure 5-24, the selectorExpression is a String variable named `strGrade`. The Select Case statement ends with the End Select clause. Between the Select Case and End Select clauses are the individual Case clauses. Each Case clause represents a different path that the computer can follow. It is customary to indent each Case clause and the instructions within each Case clause, as shown in the figure. You can have as many Case clauses as necessary in a Select Case statement. However, if the Select Case statement includes a Case Else clause, the Case Else clause must be the last clause in the statement.

Each of the individual Case clauses, except the Case Else clause, must contain an *expressionList*, which can include one or more expressions. To include more than one expression in an expressionList, you separate each expression with a comma, as in the expressionList `Case "D", "F"`. The selectorExpression needs to match only one of the expressions listed in an expressionList. The data type of the expressions must be compatible with the data type of the selectorExpression. If the selectorExpression is numeric, the expressions in the Case clauses should be numeric. Likewise, if the selectorExpression is a string, the expressions should be strings. In the example in Figure 5-24, the selectorExpression (`strGrade`) is a string, and so are the expressions `"A"`, `"B"`, `"C"`, `"D"`, and `"F"`.

The Select Case statement looks more complicated than it really is. When processing the statement, the computer simply compares the value of the selectorExpression with the value or values listed in each of the Case clauses, one Case clause at a time beginning with the first. If the selectorExpression matches at least one of the values listed in a Case clause, the computer processes only the instructions contained in that Case clause. After the Case clause instructions are processed, the Select Case statement ends and the computer skips to the instruction following the End Select clause. For instance, if the `strGrade` variable in the example shown in Figure 5-24 contains the letter A, the computer will display the "Excellent" message and then skip to the instruction following the End Select clause. Similarly, if the `strGrade` variable contains the letter F, the computer will display the "Below Average" message and then skip to the instruction following the End Select clause. Keep in mind that if the selectorExpression matches a value in more than one Case clause, only the instructions in the first match's Case clause are processed.

Ch05A-Select Case video

If the selectorExpression does *not* match any of the values listed in any of the Case clauses, the next instruction processed depends on whether the Select Case statement contains a Case Else clause. If there *is* a Case Else clause, the computer processes the instructions in that clause and then skips to the instruction following the End Select clause. (Recall that the Case Else clause and its instructions immediately precede the End Select clause.) If there *isn't* a Case Else clause, the computer just skips to the instruction following the End Select clause.

START HERE

To use the Select Case statement to code the Allen High School application:

1. Open the Grade Solution (Grade Solution.sln) file contained in the VB2012\Chap05\Grade Solution-Select Case folder. If necessary, open the designer window.
2. Open the Code Editor window. Replace <your name> and <current date> in the comments with your name and the current date, respectively.
3. Locate the btnDisplay_Click procedure. Enter the code shown in Figure 5-24.
4. Save the solution and then start the application. Type the letter **a** and then press **Enter**. The "Excellent" message appears in the interface, as shown earlier in Figure 5-23.
5. On your own, test the application using the following grades: **b**, **c**, **d**, **x** and **f**. When you are finished testing, click the **Exit** button. Close the Code Editor window and then close the solution.

Specifying a Range of Values in a Case Clause

In addition to specifying one or more discrete values in a Case clause, you also can specify a range of values, such as the values 1 through 4 or values greater than 10. You do this using either the keyword `To` or the keyword `Is`. You use the `To` keyword when you know both the upper and lower values in the range. The `Is` keyword is appropriate when you know only one end of the range (either the upper or lower end). Figure 5-25 shows the syntax for using both keywords. It also contains an example of a Select Case statement that assigns a price based on the number of items ordered. According to the price chart shown in the figure, the price for 1 to 5 items is $25 each. Using discrete values, the first Case clause would look like this: `Case 1, 2, 3, 4, 5`. However, a more convenient way of writing that range of numbers is to use the `To` keyword, like this: `Case 1 To 5`. The expression `1 To 5` specifies the range of numbers from 1 to 5, inclusive. The expression `6 To 10` in the second Case clause in the example specifies the range of numbers from 6 through 10. Notice that both Case clauses state both the lower (1 and 6) and upper (5 and 10) values in each range.

If you neglect to type the `Is` keyword in an expressionList—for example, if you enter `Case > 10`—the Code Editor will change the clause to `Case Is > 10`.

The third Case clause, `Case Is > 10`, contains the `Is` keyword rather than the `To` keyword. Recall that you use the `Is` keyword when you know only one end of the range of values. In this case, you know only the lower end of the range, 10. The `Is` keyword is always used in combination with one of the following comparison operators: =, <, <=, >, >=, <>. The `Case Is > 10` clause specifies all numbers greater than the number 10. Because `intQuantity` is an Integer variable, you also can write this Case clause as `Case Is >= 11`. The Case Else clause in the example in

Figure 5-25 is processed only when the `intQuantity` variable contains a value that is not included in any of the previous Case clauses.

Specifying a Range of Values in a Case Clause

Syntax
Case *smallest value in the range* **To** *largest value in the range*
Case Is *comparisonOperator value*

Example
The ABC Corporation's price chart is shown here:

Quantity ordered	Price per item
1 – 5	$25
6 – 10	$23
More than 10	$20
Less than 1	$0

```
Select Case intQuantity
    Case 1 To 5
        intPrice = 25
    Case 6 To 10
        intPrice = 23
    Case Is > 10
        intPrice = 20
    Case Else
        intPrice = 0
End Select
```

Figure 5-25 Syntax and an example of specifying a range of values

Be sure to test your code thoroughly because the computer will not display an error message when the value preceding To in a Case clause is greater than the value following To. Instead, the Select Case statement will not give the correct results.

START HERE

To code and then test the ABC Corporation application:

1. Open the ABC Solution (ABC Solution.sln) file contained in the VB2012\Chap05\ABC Solution folder. If necessary, open the designer window.
2. Open the Code Editor window. Replace <your name> and <current date> in the comments with your name and the current date, respectively.
3. Locate the btnDisplay_Click procedure. Click the **blank line** below the `' determine the price per item` comment and then enter the Select Case statement shown in Figure 5-25.
4. Save the solution and then start the application. Type **7** in the Quantity ordered box and then press **Enter**. $23.00 appears in the Price per item box. See Figure 5-26.

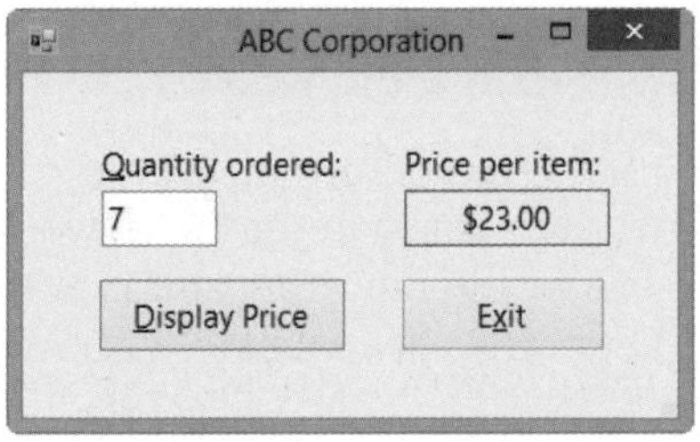

Figure 5-26 Price per item shown in the interface

5. On your own, test the application using **6**, **11**, and **0** as the quantity ordered. When you are finished testing, click the **Exit** button. Close the Code Editor window and then close the solution.

YOU DO IT 3!

Create a Visual Basic Windows application named YouDoIt 3. Save the application in the VB2012\Chap05 folder. Add a text box, a label, and a button to the form. The button's Click event procedure should display (in the label) either the price of a concert ticket or an error message. The ticket price is based on the code entered in the text box, as shown here. Code the procedure using the Select Case statement. Save the solution and then start and test the application. Close the solution.

Code	Ticket price
1	$15
2	$15
3	$25
4	$35
5	$37
Other	Invalid code

Lesson A Summary

- To create a selection structure that evaluates both a primary and a secondary decision:

  Place (nest) the secondary decision's selection structure within either the true or false path of the primary decision's selection structure.

- To verify that an algorithm works correctly:

  Desk-check (hand-trace) the algorithm.

- To code a multiple-alternative selection structure:

  Use either If...Then...Else statements or the Select Case statement.

- To specify a range of values in a Select Case statement's Case clause:
  Use the `To` keyword when you know both the upper and lower values in the range. Use the `Is` keyword when you know only one end of the range. The `Is` keyword is used in combination with one of the following comparison operators: =, <, <=, >, >=, <>.

Lesson A Key Terms

Algorithm—a set of step-by-step instructions for accomplishing a task

Desk-checking—the process of using sample data to manually walk through the steps in an algorithm; also called hand-tracing

Extended selection structures—another name for multiple-alternative selection structures

Hand-tracing—another term for desk-checking

Multiple-alternative selection structures—selection structures that contain several alternatives; also called extended selection structures; can be coded using either If...Then...Else statements or the Select Case statement

Nested selection structure—a selection structure that is wholly contained (nested) within either the true or false path of another selection structure

Select Case statement—used to code a multiple-alternative selection structure in Visual Basic

Lesson A Review Questions

Use the code shown in Figure 5-27 to answer Review Questions 1 through 4.

```
If intNum > 1000 Then
    intNum = intNum * 3
ElseIf intNum > 500 Then
    intNum = intNum * 2
End If
```

Figure 5-27 Code for Review Questions 1 through 4

1. If the `intNum` variable contains the number 600, what value will be in the variable after the code in Figure 5-27 is processed?
   a. 0
   b. 600
   c. 1200
   d. 1800

2. If the `intNum` variable contains the number 1000, what value will be in the variable after the code in Figure 5-27 is processed?
   a. 0
   b. 1000
   c. 2000
   d. 3000

3. If the `intNum` variable contains the number 500, what value will be in the variable after the code in Figure 5-27 is processed?
   a. 0
   b. 500
   c. 1000
   d. 1500

4. If the `intNum` variable contains the number 2000, what value will be in the variable after the code in Figure 5-27 is processed?
   a. 0
   b. 2000
   c. 4000
   d. 6000

Use the code shown in Figure 5-28 to answer Review Questions 5 through 8.

```
If intId = 1 Then
    lblName.Text = "Janet"
ElseIf intId = 2 Then
    lblName.Text = "Mark"
ElseIf intId = 3 OrElse intId = 4 Then
    lblName.Text = "Jerry"
Else
    lblName.Text = "Sue"
End If
```

Figure 5-28 Code for Review Questions 5 through 8

5. What will the code in Figure 5-28 display when the `intId` variable contains the number 2?
   a. Janet
   b. Jerry
   c. Mark
   d. Sue

6. What will the code in Figure 5-28 display when the `intId` variable contains the number 4?
   a. Janet
   b. Jerry
   c. Mark
   d. Sue

7. What will the code in Figure 5-28 display when the `intId` variable contains the number 3?
   a. Janet
   b. Jerry
   c. Mark
   d. Sue

8. What will the code in Figure 5-28 display when the `intId` variable contains the number 8?
   a. Janet
   b. Jerry
   c. Mark
   d. Sue

9. A nested selection structure can appear ______________.
   a. only in an outer selection structure's false path
   b. only in an outer selection structure's true path
   c. in either an outer selection structure's true path or its false path

10. Which of the following Case clauses is valid in a Select Case statement whose selectorExpression is an Integer variable named `intCode`?

    a. `Case Is > 7`

    b. `Case 3, 5`

    c. `Case 1 To 4`

    d. all of the above

Use the code shown in Figure 5-29 to answer Review Questions 11 through 13.

```
Select Case intId
    Case 1
        lblName.Text = "Janet"
    Case 2 To 4
        lblName.Text = "Mark"
    Case 5, 7
        lblName.Text = "Jerry"
    Case Else
        lblName.Text = "Sue"
End Select
```

Figure 5-29 Code for Review Questions 11 through 13

11. What will the code in Figure 5-29 display when the `intId` variable contains the number 2?

    a. Janet

    b. Mark

    c. Jerry

    d. Sue

12. What will the code in Figure 5-29 display when the `intId` variable contains the number 3?

    a. Janet

    b. Mark

    c. Jerry

    d. Sue

13. What will the code in Figure 5-29 display when the `intId` variable contains the number 6?

    a. Janet

    b. Mark

    c. Jerry

    d. Sue

14. List the four errors commonly made when writing selection structures. Which errors produce the correct results, but in a less efficient way?

15. Explain the meaning of the term "desk-checking."

Lesson A Exercises

INTRODUCTORY

1. Travis is standing in front of two containers: one marked Trash and the other marked Recycle. In his right hand, he is holding a bag that contains either trash or recyclables. Travis needs to lift the lid from the appropriate container (if necessary), then drop the bag in the container, and then put the lid back on the container. Write an appropriate algorithm, using only the instructions listed in Figure 5-30.

```
else
end if
drop the bag of recyclables in the Recycle container
drop the bag of trash in the Trash container
if the bag contains trash
if the lid is on the Recycle container
if the lid is on the Trash container
lift the Recycle container's lid using your left hand
lift the Trash container's lid using your left hand
put the lid back on the Recycle container using your left hand
put the lid back on the Trash container using your left hand
```

Figure 5-30 Instructions for Exercise 1

INTRODUCTORY

2. Caroline is at a store's checkout counter. She'd like to pay for her purchase using one of her credit cards—either her Discovery card or her Vita card, but preferably her Discovery card. However, she is not sure whether the store accepts either card. If the store doesn't accept either card, she will need to pay cash for the items. Write an appropriate algorithm, using only the instructions listed in Figure 5-31.

```
else
end if
pay for your items using your Vita card
pay for your items using your Discovery card
pay for your items using cash
if the store accepts the Vita card
if the store accepts the Discovery card
ask the store clerk whether the store accepts the Vita card
ask the store clerk whether the store accepts the Discovery card
```

Figure 5-31 Instructions for Exercise 2

INTRODUCTORY

3. What is wrong with the algorithm shown in Figure 5-32?


```
1. shoot the basketball
2. if the basketball went through the hoop
        say "I did it!"
   else
        if the basketball did not go through the hoop
              say "Missed it!"
        end if
   end if
```

Figure 5-32 Algorithm for Exercise 3

INTRODUCTORY

4. Write the Visual Basic code for the algorithm shown in Figure 5-10 in this lesson. The membership status (either N for non-member or M for member) is stored, in uppercase, in a variable named `strStatus`. The day of the week information (either D for weekday or E for weekend) is stored, in uppercase, in a variable named `strDay`. Assign the fee to a variable named `intFee`. Display the fee in the lblFee control.

INTRODUCTORY

5. Write the Visual Basic code that displays the message "Highest honors" when a student's test score is 90 or above. When the test score is 70 through 89, display the message "Good job". For all other test scores, display the message "Retake the test". The test score is stored in the `intScore` variable. Display the appropriate message in the lblMsg control. Code the multiple-alternative selection structure using the If...Then...Else statement.

INTRODUCTORY

6. Rewrite the code from Exercise 5 using the Select Case statement.

INTRODUCTORY

7. Open the Movie Ticket Solution (Movie Ticket Solution.sln) file contained in the VB2012\Chap05\Movie Ticket Solution folder. If necessary, open the designer window. Use the If...Then...Else statement to code the If...Then...Else button's Click event procedure. Use the Select Case statement to code the Select Case button's Click event procedure. Both procedures should display the appropriate ticket price, which is based on the customer's age as shown here. Save the solution and then start the application. Test each button's Click event procedure five times, using the numbers 1, 3, 64, 65, and 70.

Age	Price ($)
Under 3	0
3 to 64	9
65 and over	6

INTERMEDIATE

8. Does the algorithm in Figure 5-33 give you the same results as the solution shown in Figure 5-4 in this lesson? If not, why not?

```
1. shoot the basketball
2. if the basketball went through the hoop and Maleek was either inside or on the 3-point line
       say "I did it!"
       say "2 points for me"
   else
       if Maleek was behind the 3-point line
             say "I did it!"
             say "3 points for me"
       else
             say "Missed it!"
       end if
   end if
```

Figure 5-33 Algorithm for Exercise 8

INTERMEDIATE

9. Does the algorithm in Figure 5-34 give you the same results as the solution shown in Figure 5-4 in this lesson? If not, why not?

```
1. shoot the basketball
2. if the basketball did not go through the hoop
       say "Missed it!"
   else
       say "I did it!"
       if Maleek was either inside or on the 3-point line
             say "2 points for me"
       else
             say "3 points for me"
       end if
   end if
```

Figure 5-34 Algorithm for Exercise 9

INTERMEDIATE

10. Open the Rate Solution (Rate Solution.sln) file contained in the VB2012\Chap05\Rate Solution folder. If necessary, open the designer window. Use the Select Case statement to finish coding the Display button's Click event procedure. Use the partial flowchart shown in Figure 5-35 as a guide. Display the rate formatted with a percent sign and no decimal places. Save the solution and then start and test the application. Close the Code Editor window and then close the solution.

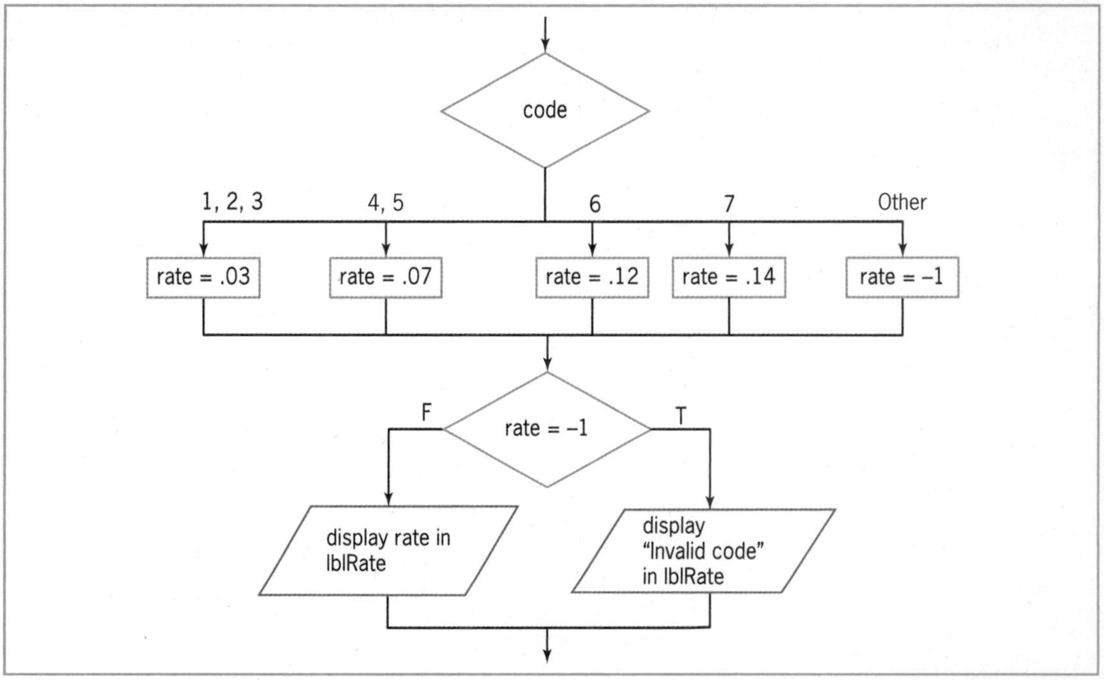

Figure 5-35 Flowchart for Exercise 10

INTERMEDIATE

11. Open the Kettleson Solution (Kettleson Solution.sln) file contained in the VB2012\Chap05\Kettleson Solution folder. Open the Code Editor window. The txtSales control should accept only numbers, the period, and the Backspace key; code the appropriate procedure. Now, locate the btnCalc_Click procedure. The procedure calculates a 2% bonus when the annual sales are over $15,000; otherwise, it calculates a 1.5% bonus. Modify the procedure to use the bonus rates shown here. Use the If...Then...Else statement to code the multiple-alternative selection structure. Save the solution and then start the application. Test the application seven times, using 2500, 16000, 15000, 15000.99, 20000, 50000, and 65000 as the annual sales. Close the Code Editor window and then close the solution.

Annual sales ($)	Bonus rate
0 – 15,000	1.5%
15,000.01 – 25,000	2%
25,000.01 – 50,000	3%
Over 50,000	4%

INTERMEDIATE

12. In this exercise, you modify the Kettleson application from Exercise 11. Use Windows to make a copy of the Kettleson Solution folder. Rename the copy Modified Kettleson Solution. Open the Kettleson Solution (Kettleson Solution.sln) file contained in the Modified Kettleson Solution folder. Open the designer and Code Editor windows. Locate the btnCalc_Click procedure. Code the multiple-alternative selection structure using the Select Case statement rather than the If...Then...Else statement. Save the solution and then start the application. Test the application seven times, using 2500, 16000, 15000, 15000.99, 20000, 50000, and 65000 as the annual sales. Close the Code Editor window and then close the solution.

INTERMEDIATE

13. Open the Jerrili Solution (Jerrili Solution.sln) file contained in the VB2012\Chap05\Jerrili Solution folder. Open the Code Editor window. The txtPrice control should accept only numbers, the period, and the Backspace key; code the appropriate

procedure. The txtQuantity control should accept only numbers and the Backspace key; code the appropriate procedure. Jerrili's now uses the discount rates shown here. Make the appropriate modifications to the btnCalc_Click procedure. Save the solution and then start and test the application. Close the Code Editor window and then close the solution.

Quantity purchased	Discount rate
0 – 5	0
6 – 15	2%
16 – 30	3%
Over 30	4%

14. Open the Bonus Solution (Bonus Solution.sln) file contained in the VB2012\Chap05\Bonus Solution folder. If necessary, open the designer window. Open the Code Editor window. The Calculate button's Click event procedure should assign the number 25 to the `intBonus` variable when the user enters a sales amount that is greater than or equal to $100, but less than or equal to $250. When the user enters a sales amount that is greater than $250, the procedure should assign the number 50 to the variable. When the user enters a sales amount that is less than $100, the procedure should assign the number 0 as the bonus. Use the If...Then...Else statement to code the multiple-alternative selection structure. Save the solution and then start the application. Test the Calculate button's code three times, using sales amounts of 100, 300, and 40. Close the Code Editor window and then close the solution.

INTERMEDIATE

15. In this exercise, you modify the Bonus application from Exercise 14. Use Windows to make a copy of the Bonus Solution folder. Rename the copy Modified Bonus Solution. Open the Bonus Solution (Bonus Solution.sln) file contained in the Modified Bonus Solution folder. Open the designer and Code Editor windows. Locate the btnCalc_Click procedure. Code the multiple-alternative selection structure using the Select Case statement rather than the If...Then...Else statement. Save the solution and then start the application. Test the Calculate button's code three times, using sales amounts of 100, 300, and 40. Close the Code Editor window and then close the solution.

INTERMEDIATE

16. Open the Blane Solution (Blane Solution.sln) file contained in the VB2012\Chap05\Blane Solution folder. If necessary, open the designer window. Blane Ltd. sells economic development software to cities around the country. The company is having its annual user's forum next month. The price per person depends on the number of people a user registers. The first 3 people a user registers are charged $150 per person. Registrants 4 through 10 are charged $100 per person. Registrants over 10 are charged $60 per person. For example, if a user registers 8 people, then the total amount owed is $950. The $950 is calculated by first multiplying 3 by 150, giving 450. You then multiply 5 by 100, giving 500. You then add the 500 to the 450, giving 950. Display the total amount owed in the lblTotalOwed control. Use the Select Case statement to complete the Calculate button's Click event procedure. Save the solution and then start and test the application. Close the Code Editor window and then close the solution.

ADVANCED

LESSON B

After studying Lesson B, you should be able to:

- Include a group of radio buttons in an interface
- Designate a default radio button
- Include a check box in an interface
- Compare Boolean values

Modifying the Covington Resort Application

Your task in this chapter is to modify the Covington Resort application created in Chapter 4. In addition to the previous input data, the application's interface will now allow the user to select the number of beds (either two queen beds or one king bed), the view (either standard or atrium), and whether the guest should be charged a vehicle parking fee of $12.75 per night. In addition to displaying the total room charge, the sales and lodging tax, the resort fee, and the total due, the application should now also display the total parking fee. Figure 5-36 shows the application's revised TOE chart. The changes made to the original TOE chart from Chapter 4 are shaded in the figure.

Task	Object	Event
1. Calculate the total room charge, tax, total resort fee, total parking fee, and total due 2. Display the calculated amounts in lblRoomChg, lblTax, lblResortFee, lblParkingFee, and lblTotalDue	btnCalc	Click
End the application	btnExit	Click
Display the total room charge (from btnCalc)	lblRoomChg	None
Display the tax (from btnCalc)	lblTax	None
Display the total resort fee (from btnCalc)	lblResortFee	None
Display the total parking fee (from btnCalc)	lblParkingFee	None
Display the total due (from btnCalc)	lblTotalDue	None
Specifies whether the guest should be charged the vehicle parking fee	chkParkingFee	None
Get and display the number of rooms reserved, number of nights, number of adults, and number of children	txtRooms, txtNights, txtAdults, txtChildren,	None
Get number of beds	radQueen, radKing	None
Get room view	radStandard, radAtrium	None

Figure 5-36 Revised TOE chart for the Covington Resort application *(continues)*

(continued)

Task	Object	Event
Clear the contents of lblRoomChg, lblTax, lblResortFee, lblParkingFee, and lblTotalDue	txtRooms, txtNights, txtAdults, txtChildren	TextChanged
	radQueen, radKing, radStandard, radAtrium, chkParkingFee	CheckedChanged
Allow the text box to accept only numbers and the Backspace key	txtRooms, txtNights, txtAdults, txtChildren	KeyPress
Select the contents of the text box	txtRooms, txtNights, txtAdults, txtChildren	Enter

Figure 5-36 Revised TOE chart for the Covington Resort application

The revised TOE chart indicates that the interface will now include six additional controls: a label, a check box, and four radio buttons. The additional label will be used to display the total parking fee. The check box will allow the user to specify whether the vehicle parking fee is applicable to the guest. Two of the four radio buttons will allow the user to specify the number of beds, while the other two will allow him or her to specify the room view.

To open the Covington Resort application:

START HERE

1. If necessary, start Visual Studio 2012. Open the Covington Resort Solution (Covington Resort Solution.sln) file contained in the VB2012\Chap05\Covington Resort Solution folder. If necessary, open the designer window. See Figure 5-37. Four of the additional six controls listed in the TOE chart have already been added to the interface.
   The interface also includes two group boxes that will serve as containers for the radio buttons. (Controls whose purpose is to contain other controls are usually not listed in the TOE chart.) Missing from the interface are the Atrium radio button and the Vehicle parking fee check box.

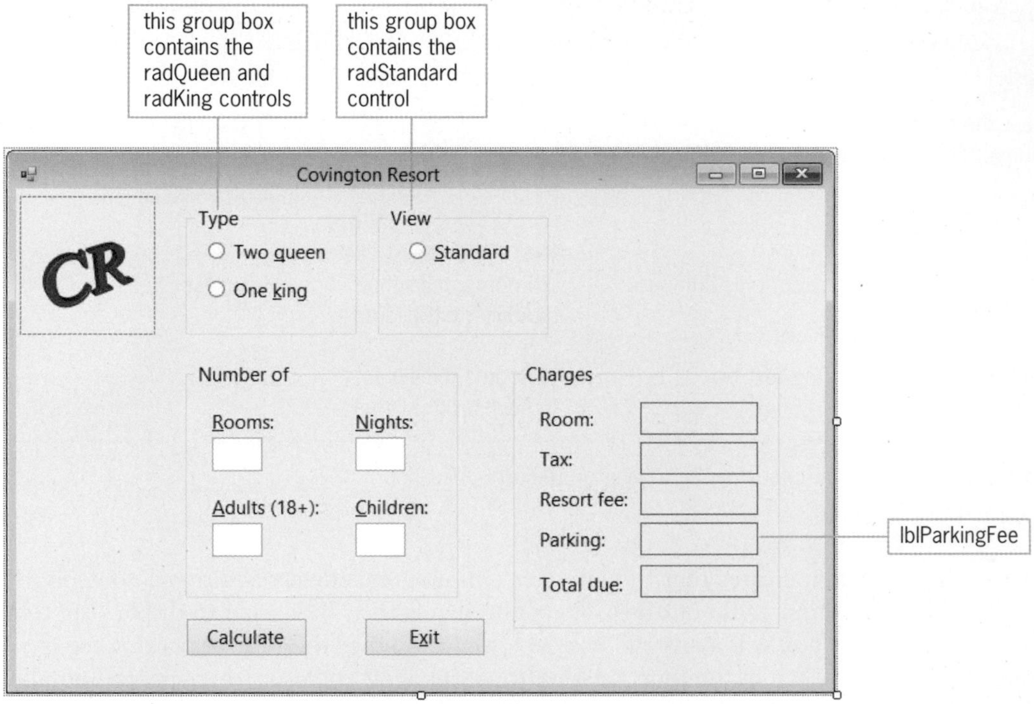

Figure 5-37 Partially completed interface for the Covington Resort application

Adding a Radio Button to the Interface

Ch05B video

You create a radio button using the RadioButton tool in the toolbox. **Radio buttons** allow you to limit the user to only one choice from a group of two or more related but mutually exclusive choices. Each radio button in an interface should be labeled so the user knows the choice it represents. You enter the label using sentence capitalization in the radio button's Text property. Each radio button should also have a unique access key that allows the user to select the button using the keyboard. The three-character ID for a radio button's name is rad.

The Covington Resort interface will use two groups of radio buttons: one for selecting the number of beds and one for selecting the room view. To include two groups of radio buttons in an interface, at least one of the groups must be placed within a container, such as a group box. Otherwise, the radio buttons are considered to be in the same group and only one can be selected at any one time. In this case, the radio buttons pertaining to the number of beds are contained in the Type group box, and the radio buttons pertaining to the room view are contained in the View group box. Placing each group of radio buttons in a separate group box allows the user to select one button from each group. During run time, you can determine whether a radio button is selected or unselected by looking at the value in its Checked property. If the property contains the Boolean value True, the radio button is selected. If it contains the Boolean value False, the radio button is not selected.

Keep in mind that the minimum number of radio buttons in a group is two; this is because the only way to deselect a radio button is to select another radio button. The recommended maximum number of radio buttons in a group is seven. In the next set of steps, you will add the missing Atrium radio button to the View group box.

START HERE

To add the Atrium radio button to the View group box:

1. Click the **RadioButton** tool in the toolbox and then drag the mouse pointer into the View group box, placing it below the Standard radio button. Release the mouse button. The RadioButton1 control appears in the group box.

2. Change the RadioButton1 control's name to **radAtrium**, and then change its Text property to **A&trium**. If necessary, position the radio button as shown in Figure 5-38.

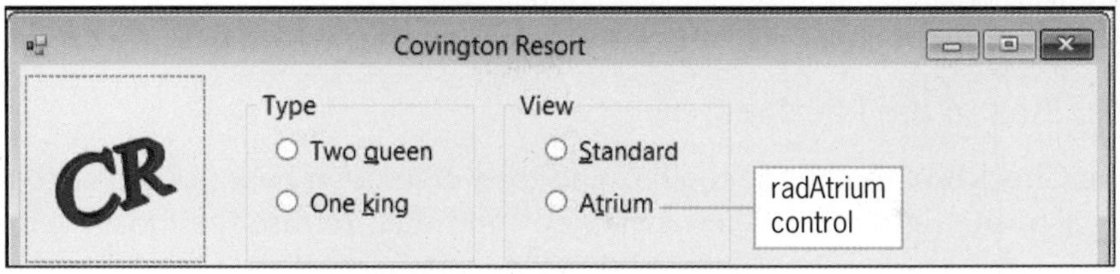

Figure 5-38 Atrium radio button added to the View group box

It is customary in Windows applications to have one of the radio buttons in each group already selected when the user interface first appears. The automatically selected radio button is called the **default radio button** and is either the radio button that represents the user's most likely choice or the first radio button in the group. You designate the default radio button by setting the button's **Checked property** to the Boolean value True.

START HERE

To designate a default radio button in each group:

1. Click the **Two queen** radio button and then use the Properties window to set the radio button's Checked property to **True**. When you do this, a colored dot appears inside the button's circle to indicate that the button is selected.
2. Now set the Standard radio button's Checked property to **True**.

GUI DESIGN TIP Radio Button Standards

- Use radio buttons to limit the user to one choice in a group of related but mutually exclusive choices.
- The minimum number of radio buttons in a group is two and the recommended maximum number is seven.
- The label in the radio button's Text property should be entered using sentence capitalization.
- Assign a unique access key to each radio button in an interface.
- Use a container (such as a group box) to create separate groups of radio buttons. Only one button in each group can be selected at any one time.
- Designate a default radio button in each group of radio buttons.

Adding a Check Box to the Interface

You create a check box using the CheckBox tool in the toolbox. Like radio buttons, check boxes can be either selected or deselected. Also like radio buttons, you can determine whether a check box is selected by looking at the value in its Checked property during run time: A True value indicates that the check box is selected, whereas a False value indicates that it is not selected. However, unlike radio buttons, **check boxes** provide one or more independent and nonexclusive items from which the user can choose. Whereas only one button in a group of radio buttons can be selected at any one time, any number of check boxes on a form can be selected at the same time. Each check box in an interface should be labeled to make its purpose obvious. You enter the label using sentence capitalization in the check box's Text property. Each check box should also have a unique access key that allows the user to select it using the keyboard. The three-character ID for a check box's name is chk.

START HERE

To add a check box to the interface:

1. Click the **CheckBox** tool in the toolbox and then drag the mouse pointer onto the form. Position it to the right of the View group box and then release the mouse button.
2. Change the CheckBox1 control's name to **chkParkingFee**, and then change its Text property to **&Vehicle parking fee**. Position the check box as shown in Figure 5-39.

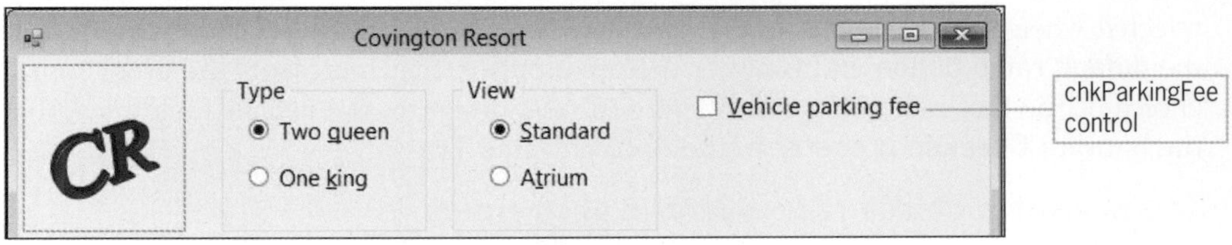

Figure 5-39 Vehicle parking fee check box added to the interface

GUI DESIGN TIP Check Box Standards

- Use check boxes to allow the user to select any number of choices from a group of one or more independent and nonexclusive choices.
- The label in the check box's Text property should be entered using sentence capitalization.
- Assign a unique access key to each check box in an interface.

Now that you have completed the user interface, you can lock the controls in place and then set each control's TabIndex property.

START HERE

To lock the controls and then set each control's TabIndex property:

1. Right-click the **form** and then click **Lock Controls** on the context menu.
2. Click **VIEW** on the menu bar and then click **Tab Order**. Use the information shown in Figure 5-40 to set the TabIndex values for the controls. (As you learned in Chapter 2, picture boxes do not have a TabIndex property.) When you are finished, press **Esc** to remove the TabIndex boxes from the form.

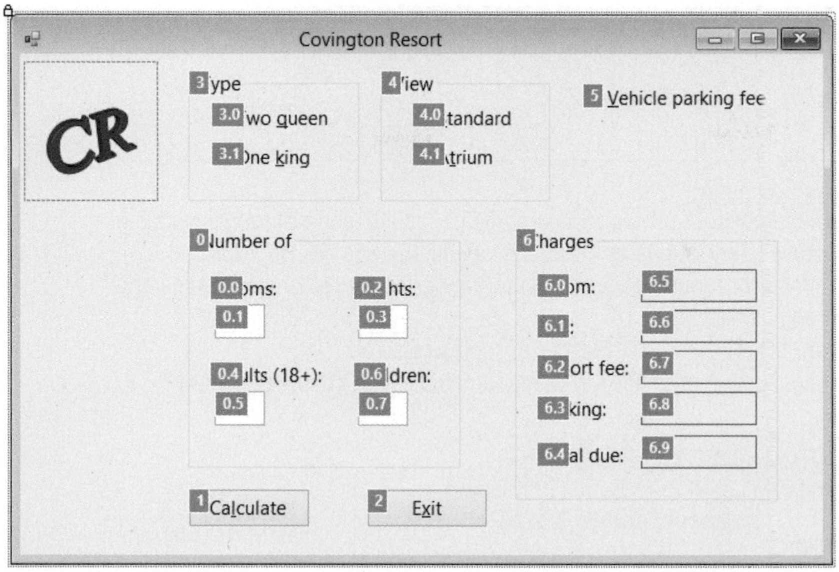

Figure 5-40 Correct TabIndex values

Next, you will start the application to observe how you select and deselect radio buttons and check boxes.

START HERE

To select and deselect radio buttons and check boxes:

1. Save the solution and then start the application. Notice that the Two queen and Standard radio buttons are already selected.
2. You can select a different radio button by clicking it. You can click either the circle or the text that appears inside the radio button. Click the **One king** radio button. The computer selects the One king radio button as it deselects the Two queen radio button. This is because both radio buttons belong to the same group and only one radio button in a group can be selected at any one time.
3. Click the **Atrium** radio button. The computer selects the Atrium radio button as it deselects the Standard radio button. Here again, the radio buttons associated with the room view belong to the same group, so selecting one deselects the other.
4. You can select a check box by clicking either the square or the text that appears inside the control. Click the **Vehicle parking fee** check box to select it. A check mark appears inside the check box to indicate that the check box is selected. Now, click the **Vehicle parking fee** check box again. This time the check box is deselected, as the absence of the check mark indicates.
5. Click the **Exit** button.

Modifying the Calculate Button's Code

According to the application's TOE chart (shown earlier in Figure 5-36), the Calculate button's Click event procedure will now need to calculate and display the total parking fee. However, that is not the only modification you will need to make to the procedure. You will also need to change the way it calculates the total room charge because the daily room charge now depends on both the number of beds and the room view. Figure 5-41 shows the modified pseudocode for the btnCalc_Click procedure. The changes made to the original pseudocode from Chapter 4 are shaded in the figure. Notice that the outer selection structure's false path now includes a nested dual-alternative selection structure and a nested single-alternative selection structure. Each path in the nested dual-alternative selection structure also contains a nested dual-alternative selection structure.

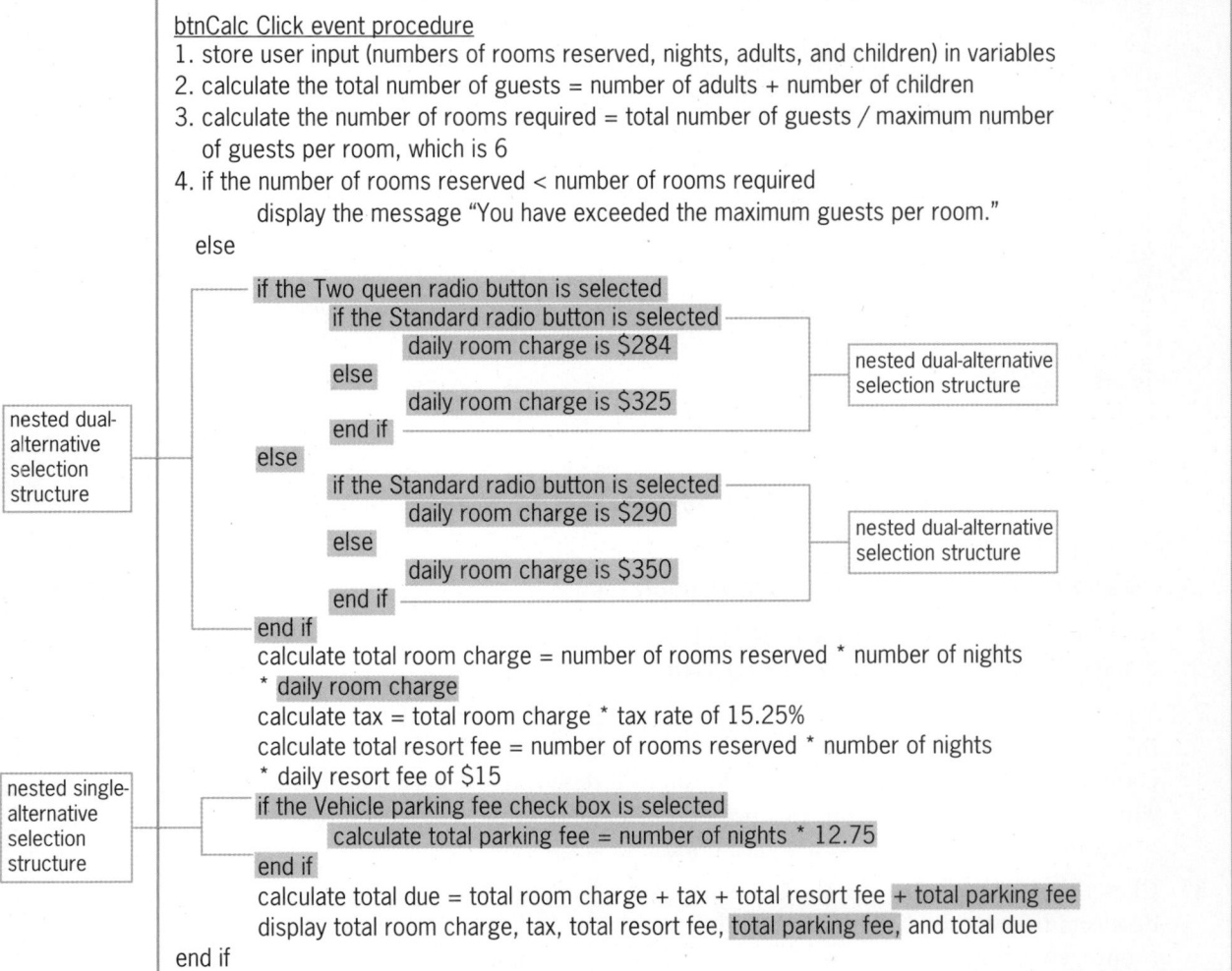

```
btnCalc Click event procedure
1. store user input (numbers of rooms reserved, nights, adults, and children) in variables
2. calculate the total number of guests = number of adults + number of children
3. calculate the number of rooms required = total number of guests / maximum number
   of guests per room, which is 6
4. if the number of rooms reserved < number of rooms required
        display the message "You have exceeded the maximum guests per room."
   else
        if the Two queen radio button is selected
              if the Standard radio button is selected
                    daily room charge is $284
              else
                    daily room charge is $325
              end if
        else
              if the Standard radio button is selected
                    daily room charge is $290
              else
                    daily room charge is $350
              end if
        end if
        calculate total room charge = number of rooms reserved * number of nights
        * daily room charge
        calculate tax = total room charge * tax rate of 15.25%
        calculate total resort fee = number of rooms reserved * number of nights
        * daily resort fee of $15
        if the Vehicle parking fee check box is selected
              calculate total parking fee = number of nights * 12.75
        end if
        calculate total due = total room charge + tax + total resort fee + total parking fee
        display total room charge, tax, total resort fee, total parking fee, and total due
   end if
```

nested dual-alternative selection structure (outer if/else on the Two queen radio button)

nested dual-alternative selection structure (each inner if/else on the Standard radio button)

nested single-alternative selection structure (if the Vehicle parking fee check box is selected)

Figure 5-41 Modified pseudocode for the btnCalc_Click procedure

Figure 5-42 contains a list of the named constants and variables the btnCalc_Click procedure will now use. The changes made to the list of named constants and variables from Chapter 4 are shaded in the figure. Notice that the procedure will no longer use the `intDAILY_ROOM_CHG` named constant, whose value is $284. In the modified Covington Resort application, the daily room charge varies depending on the radio buttons selected in the interface. Therefore, the btnCalc_Click procedure will need four named constants to represent the four different daily room charges ($284, $325, $290, and $350). The fifth named constant you will add to the procedure, `dblDAILY_PARKING_FEE`, will store the daily vehicle parking fee, which is $12.75. The two additional variables added to the procedure will store the total parking fee and the appropriate daily room charge.

Named constants	Values
intMAX_PER_ROOM	6
~~intDAILY_ROOM_CHG~~	~~284~~
intDAILY_ROOM_CHG_QUEEN_STAND	284
intDAILY_ROOM_CHG_QUEEN_ATRIUM	325
intDAILY_ROOM_CHG_KING_STAND	290
intDAILY_ROOM_CHG_KING_ATRIUM	350
dblDAILY_PARKING_FEE	12.75
dblTAX_RATE	0.1525 (the decimal equivalent of 15.25%)
intDAILY_RESORT_FEE	15
strMSG	"You have exceeded the maximum guests per room."

Variable names	Stores
intRoomsReserved	the number of rooms to reserve
intNights	the number of nights
intAdults	the number of adult guests
intChildren	the number of child guests
intNumGuests	the total number of guests, which is calculated by adding together the number of adult guests and the number of child guests
dblRoomsRequired	the number of rooms required, which is calculated by dividing the total number of guests by the maximum guests per room (may contain a decimal place)
dblParkingFee	the total parking fee, which is calculated by multiplying the number of nights by the daily parking fee
intDailyRoomChg	the daily room charge, which depends on the number of beds and room view
intTotalRoomChg	the total room charge, which is calculated by multiplying the number of rooms to reserve by the number of nights and then multiplying the result by the daily room charge
dblTax	the tax, which is calculated by multiplying the total room charge by the tax rate
intTotalResortFee	the total resort fee, which is calculated by multiplying the number of rooms to reserve by the number of nights and then multiplying the result by the daily resort fee
dblTotalDue	the total due, which is calculated by adding together the total room charge, tax, total resort fee, and total parking fee

Figure 5-42 Modified list of named constants and variables

To begin modifying the btnCalc_Click procedure:

START HERE

1. Open the Code Editor window. Replace <your name> and <current date> in the comments with your name and the current date, respectively.
2. Locate the btnCalc_Click procedure. First, you'll modify the Const section of the procedure. Delete the second Const statement, which says `Const intDAILY_ROOM_CHG As Integer = 284`, and then enter the five Const statements indicated in Figure 5-43.

enter these Const statements

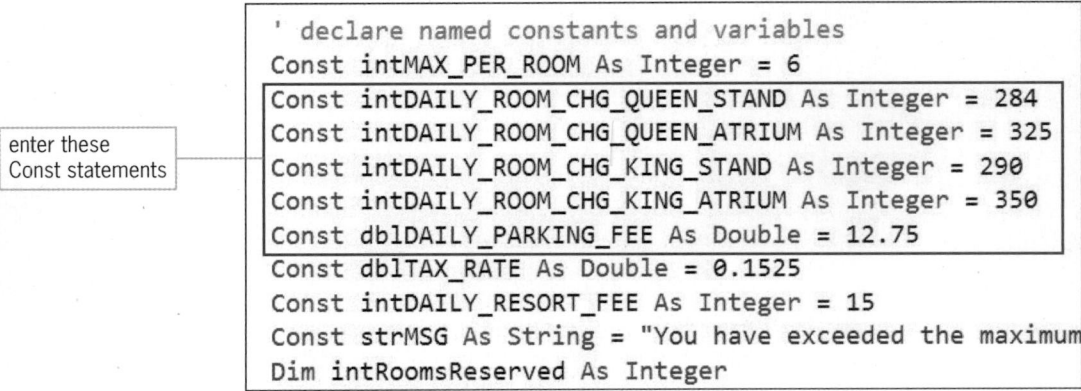

```
' declare named constants and variables
Const intMAX_PER_ROOM As Integer = 6
Const intDAILY_ROOM_CHG_QUEEN_STAND As Integer = 284
Const intDAILY_ROOM_CHG_QUEEN_ATRIUM As Integer = 325
Const intDAILY_ROOM_CHG_KING_STAND As Integer = 290
Const intDAILY_ROOM_CHG_KING_ATRIUM As Integer = 350
Const dblDAILY_PARKING_FEE As Double = 12.75
Const dblTAX_RATE As Double = 0.1525
Const intDAILY_RESORT_FEE As Integer = 15
Const strMSG As String = "You have exceeded the maximum
Dim intRoomsReserved As Integer
```

Figure 5-43 Named constants added to the procedure

3. Next, you'll modify the Dim section of the procedure. Insert a blank line below the `Dim dblRoomsRequired As Double` statement, and then enter the two Dim statements indicated in Figure 5-44.

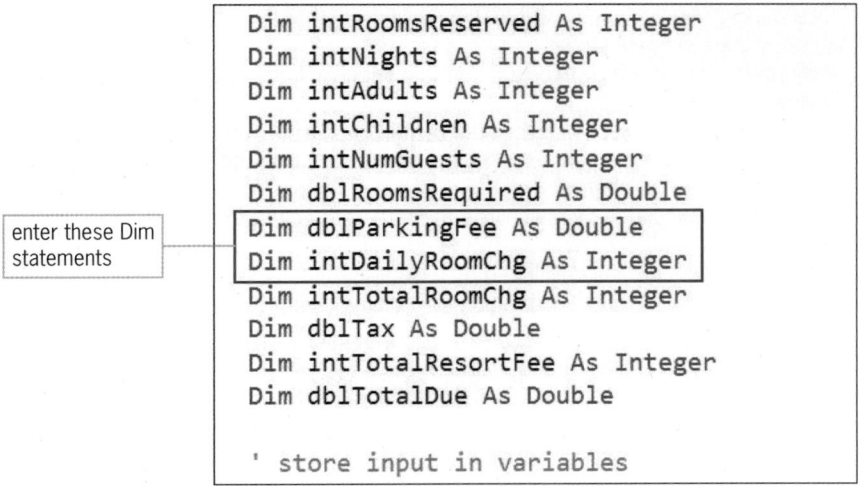

enter these Dim statements

```
Dim intRoomsReserved As Integer
Dim intNights As Integer
Dim intAdults As Integer
Dim intChildren As Integer
Dim intNumGuests As Integer
Dim dblRoomsRequired As Double
Dim dblParkingFee As Double
Dim intDailyRoomChg As Integer
Dim intTotalRoomChg As Integer
Dim dblTax As Double
Dim intTotalResortFee As Integer
Dim dblTotalDue As Double

' store input in variables
```

Figure 5-44 Variables added to the procedure

According to the pseudocode shown earlier in Figure 5-41, you need to add three nested dual-alternative selection structures to the outer selection structure's false path. The conditions in the nested selection structures will determine whether the Two queen and Standard radio buttons are selected. As you learned earlier, you can determine whether a radio button is selected or unselected by looking at the value in its Checked property. If the property contains the Boolean value True, the radio button is selected. If it contains the Boolean value False, the radio button is not selected.

Comparing Boolean Values

In addition to comparing numbers and strings, you also can compare Boolean values in If...Then...Else and Select Case statements. Examples of such comparisons are shown in Figure 5-45.

Comparing Boolean Values

Example 1

```
If blnIsInsured Then
```

The condition evaluates to True when the `blnIsInsured` variable contains the Boolean value True; otherwise, it evaluates to False. You also can write the If clause like this: `If blnIsInsured = True Then`.

Example 2

```
If Not blnIsInsured Then
```

The condition evaluates to True when the `blnIsInsured` variable contains the Boolean value False; otherwise, it evaluates to True. You also can write the If clause like this: `If blnIsInsured = False Then`.

Example 3

```
If chkParkingFee.Checked Then
```

The condition evaluates to True when the chkParkingFee check box is selected; otherwise, it evaluates to False. You also can write the If clause like this: `If chkParkingFee.Checked = True Then`.

Example 4

```
Select Case chkParkingFee.Checked
    Case True
        instructions to process when the check box is selected
    Case False
        instructions to process when the check box is not selected
End Select
```

The instructions in the first Case clause will be processed when the chkParkingFee check box is selected; the instructions in the second Case clause will be processed when the check box is not selected.

Example 5

```
Select Case True
    Case radStandard.Checked
        instructions to process when the radStandard radio button is selected
    Case radAtrium.Checked
        instructions to process when the radAtrium radio button is selected
End Select
```

The instructions in the first Case clause will be processed when the radStandard radio button is selected; the instructions in the second Case clause will be processed when the radAtrium radio button is selected.

Figure 5-45 Examples of comparing Boolean values

The first two examples in Figure 5-45 use a Boolean variable named `blnIsInsured`. You learned about the Boolean data type in Chapter 3. Recall that a Boolean variable can store either the Boolean value True or the Boolean value False. The condition in Example 1 will evaluate to True when the `blnIsInsured` variable contains the Boolean value True. As the figure indicates, you also can write the condition as `blnIsInsured = True`. The condition in Example 2, on the other hand, will evaluate to True when the `blnIsInsured` variable contains the Boolean value False.

This is because the Not operator, which you learned about in Chapter 4, reverses the truth-value of a *condition*. In other words, if `blnIsInsured` is True, then `Not blnIsInsured` would have to be False because False is the opposite of True. Although most programmers would use the Not operator in this condition, you also can write the condition as `blnIsInsured = False`.

The condition in Example 3 in Figure 5-45 will evaluate to True when the chkParkingFee check box is selected. Notice that you also can phrase the condition as `chkParkingFee.Checked = True`. Examples 4 and 5 show how you can use a Boolean value in a Select Case statement. In Example 4, the check box's Checked property is used as the selectorExpression. Recall that the value in the Checked property indicates whether the check box is selected (True) or unselected (False). The instructions in the `Case True` clause will be processed when the check box is selected; otherwise, the instructions in the `Case False` clause will be processed. Because a check box's Checked property can only be either True or False, you can replace the `Case False` clause with `Case Else`.

In Example 5 in Figure 5-45, the Boolean value True is used as the selectorExpression. The first Case clause compares the selectorExpression with the radStandard control's Checked property. If the Standard radio button is selected, the computer processes only the instructions in the first Case clause. If the Standard radio button is not selected, the second Case clause compares the selectorExpression with the radAtrium control's Checked property. If the Atrium radio button is selected, the computer processes only the instructions in the second Case clause. Because the Standard and Atrium radio buttons are the only buttons in their group, you can replace the second Case clause with `Case Else`.

START HERE

To finish modifying the btnCalc_Click procedure:

1. First, you'll enter the three nested dual-alternative selection structures. Insert a blank line below the `' calculate charges` comment, and then enter the nested selection structures indicated in Figure 5-46. The nested selection structures determine the selected radio buttons and then assign the appropriate daily room charge to the `intDailyRoomChg` variable.

enter these selection structures

```
Else
    ' calculate charges
    If radQueen.Checked Then
        If radStandard.Checked Then
            intDailyRoomChg = intDAILY_ROOM_CHG_QUEEN_STAND
        Else
            intDailyRoomChg = intDAILY_ROOM_CHG_QUEEN_ATRIUM
        End If
    Else
        If radStandard.Checked Then
            intDailyRoomChg = intDAILY_ROOM_CHG_KING_STAND
        Else
            intDailyRoomChg = intDAILY_ROOM_CHG_KING_ATRIUM
        End If
    End If
    intTotalRoomChg = intRoomsReserved *
        intNights * intDAILY_ROOM_CHG
    dblTax = intTotalRoomChg * dblTAX_RATE
```

Figure 5-46 Nested dual-alternative selection structures entered in the procedure

You can also write the If clauses in Figure 5-46 as `If radQueen.Checked = True Then` and `If radStandard.Checked = True`.

2. In the line below the nested selection structures, change intDAILY_ROOM_CHG to **intDailyRoomChg**.

3. You also need to include a single-alternative selection structure that determines whether the Vehicle parking fee check box is selected. If it is, the procedure should calculate the total parking fee by multiplying the number of nights by the daily parking fee. Insert a blank line above the statement that calculates the total due, and then enter the selection structure indicated in Figure 5-47.

```
intTotalResortFee = intRoomsReserved *
    intNights * intDAILY_RESORT_FEE
If chkParkingFee.Checked Then
    dblParkingFee = intNights * dblDAILY_PARKING_FEE
End If
dblTotalDue = intTotalRoomChg +
    dblTax + intTotalResortFee
```

enter this selection structure

Figure 5-47 Nested single-alternative selection structure entered in the procedure

You can also write the If clause in Figure 5-47 as follows: If chkParkingFee.Checked = True Then.

4. Finally, you need to add the total parking fee to the total due and also display the total parking fee in the lblParkingFee control. Make the modifications indicated in Figure 5-48.

```
    dblTotalDue = intTotalRoomChg +
        dblTax + intTotalResortFee + dblParkingFee

    ' display charges
    lblRoomChg.Text = intTotalRoomChg.ToString("N2")
    lblTax.Text = dblTax.ToString("N2")
    lblResortFee.Text = intTotalResortFee.ToString("N2")
    lblParkingFee.Text = dblParkingFee.ToString("N2")
    lblTotalDue.Text = dblTotalDue.ToString("C2")
End If
```

enter this code

enter this statement

Figure 5-48 Final modifications made to the procedure

5. Save the solution and then start the application. Type **1**, **1**, and **2** in the Rooms, Nights, and Adults boxes, respectively, and then click the **Calculate** button. See Figure 5-49.

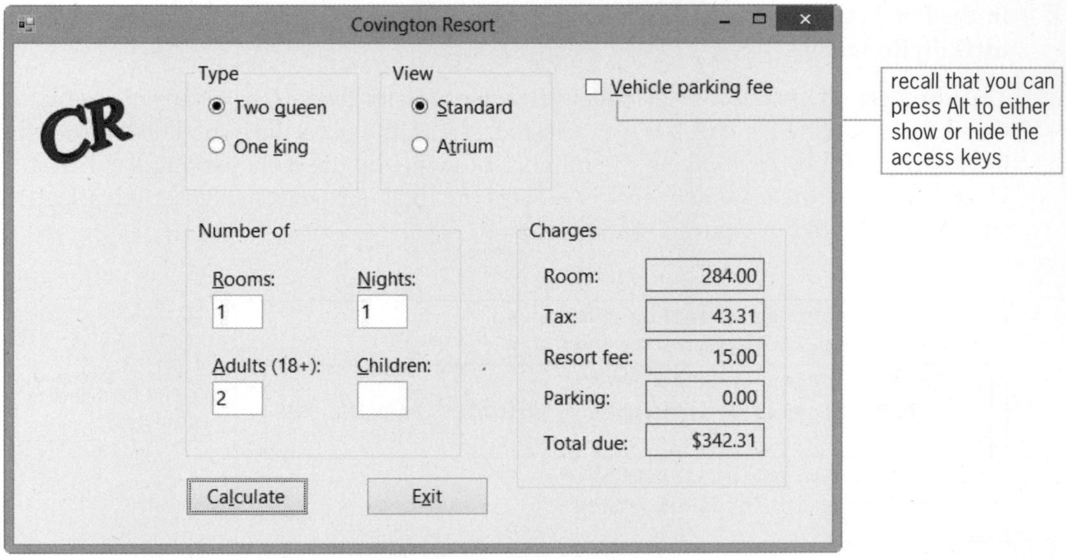

Figure 5-49 Calculated amounts shown in the interface

6. Now click the **Atrium** radio button. Notice that the calculated amounts still appear in the interface. You will fix that problem in the next section. Change the number of nights to **2** and then click the **Calculate** button. The total due is now $779.13.
7. Click the **Vehicle parking fee** check box. Here too, the calculated amounts still appear in the interface. You will fix this problem in the next section. Click the **Calculate** button. The total due is now $804.63.
8. Click the **Exit** button.

Modifying the ClearLabels Procedure

According to the application's TOE chart (shown earlier in Figure 5-36), the CheckedChanged events of the radio buttons and check box need to be coded. The **CheckedChanged event** occurs when the value in a control's Checked property changes. For example, when you select a check box, its Checked property changes from False to True; this change invokes the check box's CheckedChanged event. Likewise, when you deselect a check box, its Checked property changes from True to False, thereby invoking its CheckedChanged event. When you select a radio button, its Checked property changes from False to True and its CheckedChanged event occurs. In addition, the Checked property of the previously selected radio button in the same group changes from True to False, thereby invoking that radio button's CheckedChanged event.

The TOE chart indicates that the CheckedChanged events should clear the contents of five label controls in the interface; the ClearLabels procedure that you created in Chapter 4 will perform that task. All you need to do is add the `lblParkingFee.Text = String.Empty` statement to the procedure, and then include the CheckedChanged events for the radio buttons and check box in the procedure's Handles cause.

To modify and then test the ClearLabels procedure:

START HERE

1. Locate the ClearLabels procedure and then make the modifications indicated in Figure 5-50. (Be sure to type the comma after `txtChildren.TextChanged` in the Handles clause.)

```
Private Sub ClearLabels(sender As Object, e As EventArgs) _
    Handles txtRooms.TextChanged, txtNights.TextChanged,
    txtAdults.TextChanged, txtChildren.TextChanged,
    radQueen.CheckedChanged, radKing.CheckedChanged,
    radStandard.CheckedChanged, radAtrium.CheckedChanged,
    chkParkingFee.CheckedChanged
    ' clear calculated amounts

    lblRoomChg.Text = String.Empty
    lblTax.Text = String.Empty
    lblResortFee.Text = String.Empty
    lblParkingFee.Text = String.Empty
    lblTotalDue.Text = String.Empty
End Sub
```

be sure to type the comma

enter this code

enter this statement

Figure 5-50 ClearLabels procedure

2. Save the solution and then start the application. Type **1**, **1**, and **2** in the Rooms, Nights, and Adults boxes, respectively, and then click the **Calculate** button. The total due is $342.31, as shown earlier in Figure 5-49.
3. Click the **Atrium** radio button. The ClearLabels procedure removes the calculated amounts from the interface. Click the **Calculate** button. The total due is now $389.56.
4. Click the **Vehicle parking fee** check box. The ClearLabels procedure removes the calculated amounts from the interface. Click the **Calculate** button. The total due is now $402.31.
5. On your own, verify that the ClearLabels procedure removes the calculated amounts when the One king radio button is clicked, and also when the Standard radio button is clicked.
6. Click the **Exit** button. Close the Code Editor window and then close the solution.

Figure 5-51 shows the application's code at the end of Lesson B.

```
' Name:          Covington Resort Project
' Purpose:       Display the total room charge, tax,
'                total resort fee, total parking fee,
'                and total due
' Programmer:    <your name> on <current date>

Option Explicit On
Option Strict On
Option Infer Off

Public Class frmMain

     Private Sub btnExit_Click(sender As Object,
     e As EventArgs) Handles btnExit.Click
        Me.Close()
     End Sub

     Private Sub txtRooms_Enter(sender As Object,
     e As EventArgs) Handles txtRooms.Enter
        ' selects the contents when the
        ' text box receives the focus

        txtRooms.SelectAll()
     End Sub

     Private Sub txtNights_Enter(sender As Object,
     e As EventArgs) Handles txtNights.Enter
        ' selects the contents when the
        ' text box receives the focus

        txtNights.SelectAll()
     End Sub

     Private Sub txtAdults_Enter(sender As Object,
     e As EventArgs) Handles txtAdults.Enter
        ' selects the contents when the
        ' text box receives the focus

        txtAdults.SelectAll()
     End Sub

     Private Sub txtChildren_Enter(sender As Object,
     e As EventArgs) Handles txtChildren.Enter
        ' selects the contents when the
        ' text box receives the focus

        txtChildren.SelectAll()
     End Sub

     Private Sub CancelKeys(sender As Object,
     e As KeyPressEventArgs
        ) Handles txtRooms.KeyPress, txtNights.KeyPress,
```

Figure 5-51 Covington Resort application's code at the end of Lesson B *(continues)*

(continued)

```
        txtAdults.KeyPress, txtChildren.KeyPress
        ' allows the text box to accept only numbers and
        ' the Backspace key

        If (e.KeyChar < "0" OrElse e.KeyChar > "9") AndAlso
            e.KeyChar <> ControlChars.Back Then
            ' cancel the key
            e.Handled = True
        End If
    End Sub

    Private Sub ClearLabels(sender As Object,
    e As EventArgs) _
        Handles txtRooms.TextChanged, txtNights.TextChanged,
        txtAdults.TextChanged, txtChildren.TextChanged,
        radQueen.CheckedChanged, radKing.CheckedChanged,
        radStandard.CheckedChanged, radAtrium.CheckedChanged,
        chkParkingFee.CheckedChanged
        ' clear calculated amounts

        lblRoomChg.Text = String.Empty
        lblTax.Text = String.Empty
        lblResortFee.Text = String.Empty
        lblParkingFee.Text = String.Empty
        lblTotalDue.Text = String.Empty
    End Sub

    Private Sub btnCalc_Click(sender As Object,
    e As EventArgs) Handles btnCalc.Click
        ' calculate and display total room charge,
        ' tax, total resort fee, total parking fee,
        ' and total due

        ' declare named constants and variables
        Const intMAX_PER_ROOM As Integer = 6
        Const intDAILY_ROOM_CHG_QUEEN_STAND As Integer = 284
        Const intDAILY_ROOM_CHG_QUEEN_ATRIUM As Integer = 325
        Const intDAILY_ROOM_CHG_KING_STAND As Integer = 290
        Const intDAILY_ROOM_CHG_KING_ATRIUM As Integer = 350
        Const dblDAILY_PARKING_FEE As Double = 12.75
        Const dblTAX_RATE As Double = 0.1525
        Const intDAILY_RESORT_FEE As Integer = 15
        Const strMSG As String =
            "You have exceeded the maximum guests per room."
        Dim intRoomsReserved As Integer
        Dim intNights As Integer
        Dim intAdults As Integer
        Dim intChildren As Integer
        Dim intNumGuests As Integer
        Dim dblRoomsRequired As Double
        Dim dblParkingFee As Double
        Dim intDailyRoomChg As Integer
```

Figure 5-51 Covington Resort application's code at the end of Lesson B *(continues)*

(continued)

```
        Dim intTotalRoomChg As Integer
        Dim dblTax As Double
        Dim intTotalResortFee As Integer
        Dim dblTotalDue As Double

        ' store input in variables
        Integer.TryParse(txtRooms.Text, intRoomsReserved)
        Integer.TryParse(txtNights.Text, intNights)
        Integer.TryParse(txtAdults.Text, intAdults)
        Integer.TryParse(txtChildren.Text, intChildren)

        ' calculate total number of guests
        intNumGuests = intAdults + intChildren
        ' calculate number of rooms required
        dblRoomsRequired = intNumGuests / intMAX_PER_ROOM

        ' determine whether number of reserved
        ' rooms is adequate and then either display a
        ' message or calculate and display the charges
        If intRoomsReserved < dblRoomsRequired Then
           MessageBox.Show(strMSG, "Covington Resort",
           MessageBoxButtons.OK,
           MessageBoxIcon.Information)
        Else
           ' calculate charges
           If radQueen.Checked Then
              If radStandard.Checked Then
                 intDailyRoomChg = intDAILY_ROOM_CHG_QUEEN_STAND
              Else
                 intDailyRoomChg = intDAILY_ROOM_CHG_QUEEN_ATRIUM
              End If
           Else
              If radStandard.Checked Then
                 intDailyRoomChg = intDAILY_ROOM_CHG_KING_STAND
              Else
                 intDailyRoomChg = intDAILY_ROOM_CHG_KING_ATRIUM
              End If
           End If
            intTotalRoomChg = intRoomsReserved *
               intNights * intDailyRoomChg
            dblTax = intTotalRoomChg * dblTAX_RATE
            intTotalResortFee = intRoomsReserved *
               intNights * intDAILY_RESORT_FEE
            If chkParkingFee.Checked Then
              dblParkingFee = intNights * dblDAILY_PARKING_FEE
            End If
            dblTotalDue = intTotalRoomChg +
              dblTax + intTotalResortFee + dblParkingFee

            ' display charges
            lblRoomChg.Text = intTotalRoomChg.ToString("N2")
            lblTax.Text = dblTax.ToString("N2")
            lblResortFee.Text = intTotalResortFee.ToString("N2")
            lblParkingFee.Text = dblParkingFee.ToString("N2")
            lblTotalDue.Text = dblTotalDue.ToString("C2")
        End If
    End Sub
End Class
```

Figure 5-51 Covington Resort application's code at the end of Lesson B

Lesson B Summary

- To limit the user to only one choice in a group of two or more related but mutually exclusive choices:

  Use the RadioButton tool to add two or more radio buttons to the form. To include two groups of radio buttons on a form, at least one of the groups must be placed within a container, such as a group box.

- To allow the user to select any number of choices from a group of one or more independent and nonexclusive choices:

  Use the CheckBox tool to add one or more check box controls to the form.

- To determine whether a radio button or check box is selected or unselected:

  Use the Checked property of the radio button or check box. The property will contain the Boolean value True if the control is selected; otherwise, it will contain the Boolean value False.

- To process code when the value in the Checked property of a radio button or check box changes:

  Enter the code in the radio button's or check box's CheckedChanged event procedure.

Lesson B Key Terms

Check boxes—controls used to offer the user one or more independent and nonexclusive choices

Checked property—the property of radio button and check box controls that indicates whether or not the control is selected; contains either the Boolean value True or the Boolean value False

CheckedChanged event—an event associated with radio buttons and check boxes; occurs when the value in a control's Checked property changes

Default radio button—the radio button that is automatically selected when an interface first appears

Radio buttons—controls used to limit the user to only one choice from a group of two or more related but mutually exclusive choices

Lesson B Review Questions

1. What is the minimum number of radio buttons in a group?

   a. one

   b. two

   c. three

   d. There is no minimum number of radio buttons.

2. If a check box is not selected, what value is contained in its Checked property?

   a. True

   b. Unchecked

   c. False

   d. Unselected

3. The text appearing in check boxes and radio buttons should be entered using ________________.
   a. sentence capitalization
   b. book title capitalization
   c. either book title capitalization or sentence capitalization

4. It is customary in Windows applications to designate a default check box.
   a. True
   b. False

5. A form contains six radio buttons. Three of the radio buttons are contained in a group box. How many of the radio buttons on the form can be selected at the same time?
   a. one
   b. two
   c. three
   d. six

6. A form contains six check boxes. Three of the check boxes are contained in a group box. How many of the check boxes on the form can be selected at the same time?
   a. one
   b. two
   c. three
   d. six

7. If a radio button is selected, its ________________ property contains the Boolean value True.
   a. Checked
   b. On
   c. Selected
   d. Selection

8. Which of the following If clauses will evaluate to True when the Bonus check box is selected?
   a. `If chkBonus.Check = True Then`
   b. `If chkBonus.Checked Then`
   c. `If chkBonus.Selected = True Then`
   d. `If chkBonus.Selected Then`

9. Which of the following events occurs when a check box is clicked?
   a. Check
   b. Checked
   c. CheckedChange
   d. CheckedChanged

10. If the `blnSenior` variable contains the Boolean value False, then the `Not blnSenior` condition will evaluate to ________________.
    a. True
    b. False

Lesson B Exercises

INTRODUCTORY

1. In this exercise, you modify the Covington Resort application from this lesson. Use Windows to make a copy of the Covington Resort Solution folder. Rename the copy Covington Resort Solution-Select Case. Open the Covington Resort Solution (Covington Resort Solution.sln) file contained in the Covington Resort Solution-Select Case folder. Open the designer and Code Editor windows. In the btnCalc_Click procedure, replace the If...Then...Else statement that determines the number of beds with the Select Case statement. Save the solution and then start and test the application. Close the Code Editor window and then close the solution.

INTRODUCTORY

2. In this exercise, you create an application for Moonbucks Coffee. Create a Visual Basic Windows application. Use the following names for the solution and project, respectively: Moonbucks Solution and Moonbucks Project. Save the application in the VB2012\Chap05 folder. Change the form file's name to Main Form.vb. Change the form's name to frmMain. The application's interface, which is shown in Figure 5-52, allows the user to specify the size of the coffee a customer is ordering and whether the coffee should be decaffeinated. The price for each coffee size is shown in the interface; however, the store must also charge a 5% sales tax. The Calculate button should calculate the total price of a cup of coffee. It then should display (in the label control) a message that indicates the coffee size, total price, and whether the coffee is decaf or regular. Use the If...Then...Else statement to code the multiple-alternative selection structure. The Print button should print the interface. The CheckedChanged event procedures for the radio buttons and check box should clear the message from the label control. Code the application. Save the solution and then start and test the application. Close the Code Editor window and then close the solution.

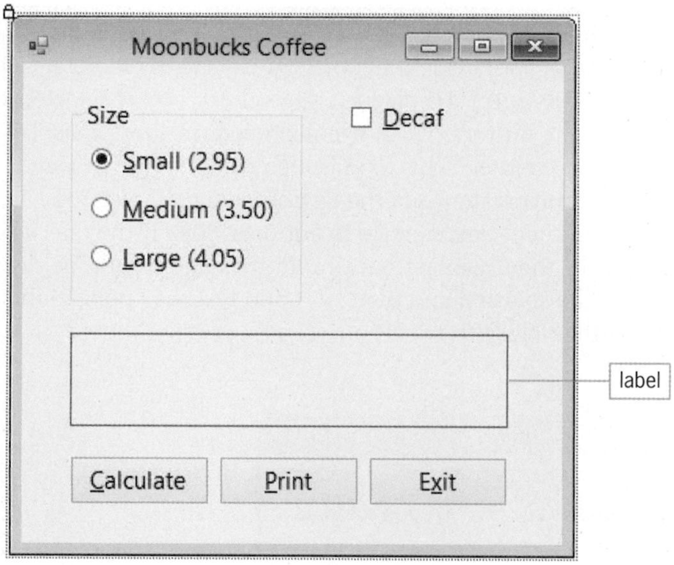

Figure 5-52 Interface for Exercise 2

INTRODUCTORY

3. In this exercise, you modify the Moonbucks Coffee application from Exercise 2. Use Windows to make a copy of the Moonbucks Solution folder. Rename the copy Modified Moonbucks Solution. Open the Moonbucks Solution (Moonbucks Solution.sln) file contained in the Modified Moonbucks Solution folder. Open the designer and Code Editor windows. Use the Select Case statement to code the multiple-alternative selection structure in the Calculate button's Click event procedure. Save the solution and then start and test the application. Close the Code Editor window and then close the solution.

INTERMEDIATE

4. In this exercise, you code an application that allows the user to select one radio button from each of two groups: a State group and a City group. Open the Geography Solution (Geography Solution.sln) file contained in the VB2012\Chap05\Geography Solution folder. If necessary, open the designer window. When a radio button is selected, its CheckedChanged event procedure should clear the contents of the lblMsg control. The Verify Answer button's Click event procedure should verify that the selected city is the capital of the selected state. If it is, the procedure should display the message "Correct"; otherwise, it should display the message "Incorrect". Code the procedure using one dual-alternative selection structure. Save the solution and then start and test the application. Close the Code Editor window and then close the solution.

INTERMEDIATE

5. In this exercise, you create an application that allows the user to enter both the number of calories and the number of grams of fat contained in a specific food. Create a Visual Basic Windows application. Use the following names for the solution and project, respectively: Fat Solution and Fat Project. Save the application in the VB2012\Chap05 folder. Change the form file's name to Main Form.vb. Change the form's name to frmMain. Create the interface shown in Figure 5-53. The application should calculate and display two values: the food's fat calories (the number of calories attributed to fat) and its fat percentage (the ratio of the food's fat calories to its total calories). You calculate the number of fat calories in a food by multiplying the number of fat grams contained in the food by the number 9 because each gram of fat contains 9 calories. To calculate the fat percentage, you divide the food's fat calories by its total calories and then multiply the result by 100. If the Display message check box is selected when the Calculate button is clicked, the button's Click event procedure should display one of two messages in a message box: either "This food is high in fat" or "This food is not high in fat". The first message is appropriate when the fat percentage is over 30%. The second message is appropriate when the fat percentage is not over 30%. If the check box is not selected when the user clicks the Calculate button, no message should be displayed. Code the application. Save the solution and then start and test the application. Close the Code Editor window and then close the solution.

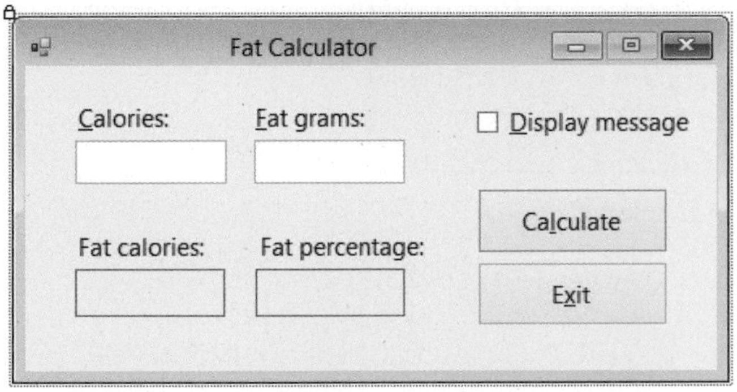

Figure 5-53 Interface for Exercise 5

INTERMEDIATE

6. In this exercise, you modify the Covington Resort application from this lesson. Use Windows to make a copy of the Covington Resort Solution folder. Rename the copy Modified Covington Resort Solution. Open the Covington Resort Solution (Covington Resort Solution.sln) file contained in the Modified Covington Resort Solution folder. Open the designer window.

   a. Currently, the application calculates the total parking fee by multiplying the daily parking fee by the number of nights. However, this calculation is based on the assumption that the guest will have only one vehicle to park, when it is entirely possible that he or she may have two or more vehicles. Add a label control and a text box to the form, positioning both below the check box. Change the label's Text property to N&umber of vehicles:. The user will enter the number of vehicles in the additional text box. When the user selects the check box, display the number 1 in the text box. When the user deselects the check box, clear the contents of the text box. (Hint: A check box also has a Click event.)

   b. Open the Code Editor window. The code should now calculate the total parking fee by multiplying the daily parking fee by the number of nights, and then multiplying that result by the number of vehicles. As is currently done, the parking fee should be charged only when the check box is selected. If the check box is selected and the text box is empty, display the number 1 in the text box. Make the appropriate modifications to the code. Save the solution and then start and test the application. Close the Code Editor window and then close the solution.

INTERMEDIATE

7. In this exercise, you create an application for Hinsbrook Health Club. Create a Visual Basic Windows application. Use the following names for the solution and project, respectively: Hinsbrook Solution and Hinsbrook Project. Save the application in the VB2012\Chap05 folder. Change the form file's name to Main Form.vb. Change the form's name to frmMain. The application should display the number of daily calories needed to maintain a person's current weight. The formulas for calculating the number of daily calories are shown in Figure 5-54. Create a suitable interface, and then code the application. Save the solution and then start and test the application. Close the Code Editor window and then close the solution.

Gender	Activity Level	Total Daily Calories Formula
Female	Moderately active	weight * 12 calories per pound
Female	Relatively inactive	weight * 10 calories per pound
Male	Moderately active	weight * 15 calories per pound
Male	Relatively inactive	weight * 13 calories per pound

Figure 5-54 Formulas for Exercise 7

ADVANCED

8. In this exercise, you create an application that converts U.S. dollars (entered as a whole number) to a different currency. Create a Visual Basic Windows application. Use the following names for the solution and project, respectively: Currency Solution and Currency Project. Save the application in the VB2012\Chap05 folder. Change the form file's name to Main Form.vb. Change the form's name to frmMain. The number of U.S. dollars should always be an integer that is greater than or equal to 0. Create an interface that allows the user to select from the listing of currencies shown in Figure 5-55. Use the Internet to research the current exchange rates. Code the application. Save the solution and then start and test the application. Close the Code Editor window and then close the solution.

Currency
Canadian dollar
Euro
Indian rupee
Japanese yen
Mexican peso
South African rand
British pound

Figure 5-55 Currencies for Exercise 8

ADVANCED

9. Shopper Stoppers wants an application that displays the number of reward points a customer earns each month. The reward points are based on the customer's membership type and total monthly purchase amount, as shown in Figure 5-56. Create a Visual Basic Windows application. Use the following names for the solution and project, respectively: Shopper Solution and Shopper Project. Save the application in the VB2012\Chap05 folder. Change the form file's name to Main Form.vb. Change the form's name to frmMain. Create a suitable interface. Code the application. Display the reward points as whole numbers. Save the solution and then start and test the application. Close the Code Editor window and then close the solution.

Membership Type	Total Monthly Purchase ($)	Reward Points
Basic	Less than 100	5% of the total monthly purchase
	100 and over	7% of the total monthly purchase
Standard	Less than 150	6% of the total monthly purchase
	150 – 299.99	8% of the total monthly purchase
	300 and over	10% of the total monthly purchase
Premium	Less than 200	7% of the total monthly purchase
	200 and over	15% of the total monthly purchase

Figure 5-56 Reward points for Exercise 9

DISCOVERY

10. Create a Visual Basic Windows application. Use the following names for the solution and project, respectively: Songs Solution and Songs Project. Save the application in the VB2012\Chap05 folder. Change the form file's name to Main Form.vb. Change the form's name to frmMain.

    a. Create the interface shown in Figure 5-57. The four radio buttons contain song titles. The Artist Name button's Click event procedure should display the name of the artist associated with the selected radio button. The names of the artists are Andrea Bocelli, Michael Jackson, Beyonce, and Josh Groban. Code the application. Save the solution and then start and test the application.

b. Now, remove the Artist Name button from the interface. Also remove the button's code from the Code Editor window. Code the application so that the artist name automatically appears when a radio button is selected. Save the solution and then start the application. The name Andrea Bocelli should appear in the Artist box because the Because We Believe radio button is selected. Click the Billie Jean radio button. The name Michael Jackson should appear in the Artist box. Close the Code Editor window and then close the solution.

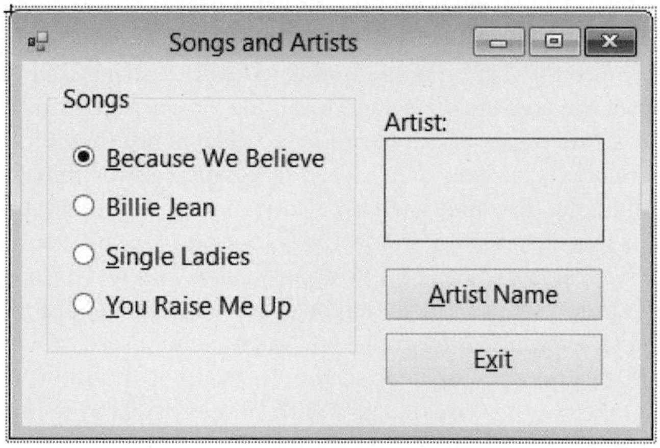

Figure 5-57 Interface for Exercise 10

LESSON C

After studying Lesson C, you should be able to:

- Determine the success of the TryParse method
- Generate random numbers
- Show and hide a control while an application is running

Using the TryParse Method for Data Validation

In Chapter 3, you learned how to use the TryParse method to convert a string to a number of a specific data type. Recall that if the conversion is successful, the TryParse method stores the number in the variable specified in the method's *numericVariableName* argument; otherwise, it stores the number 0 in the variable. What you didn't learn in Chapter 3 was that in addition to storing a number in the variable, the TryParse method also returns a Boolean value that indicates whether the conversion was successful (True) or unsuccessful (False). You can assign the value returned by the TryParse method to a Boolean variable, as shown in the syntax and example in Figure 5-58. You then can use a selection structure to take the appropriate action based on the result of the conversion. For example, you might want a selection structure's true path to calculate an employee's gross pay only when the user's input (hours worked and pay rate) can be converted to numbers; otherwise, its false path should display an "Input Error" message.

Using the Boolean Value Returned by the TryParse Method

Syntax

booleanVariable = *dataType*.**TryParse(***string*, *numericVariableName***)**

Example

```
blnIsValid = Double.TryParse(txtSales.Text, dblSales)
```

	Result of assignment statement	
Test data	`dblSales`	`blnIsValid`
"12"	12.0	True
"25.7"	25.7	True
"Ab"	0	False
"25%"	0	False
"" (empty string)	0	False

Figure 5-58 Syntax and an example of using the Boolean value returned by the TryParse method

Study the assignment statement shown in the example in Figure 5-58. The TryParse method in the statement will attempt to convert the string stored in the txtSales control's Text property to a Double number. If the conversion is successful, the method stores the Double number in the `dblSales` variable and also returns the Boolean value True. If the conversion is not successful, the method stores the number 0 in the `dblSales` variable and returns the Boolean value False. The assignment statement assigns the return value (either True or False) to the `blnIsValid` variable.

Now look at the test data and results shown in Figure 5-58. Notice that the TryParse method can convert, to the Double data type, a string composed of numbers and an optional period. Also notice that when the conversion is successful, the `dblSales` variable contains the numeric equivalent of the string, and the `blnIsValid` variable contains the Boolean value True. On the other hand, the TryParse method will fail if the string contains a letter or a special character, or if the string is the empty string. Notice that when the conversion is unsuccessful, the `dblSales` variable contains the number 0, and the `blnIsValid` variable contains the Boolean value False.

To use the Boolean value returned by the TryParse method:

START HERE

1. If necessary, start Visual Studio 2012. Open the New Pay Solution (New Pay Solution.sln) file contained in the VB2012\Chap05\New Pay Solution folder. If necessary, open the designer window.
2. Open the Code Editor window. Replace <your name> and <current date> in the comments with your name and the current date, respectively.
3. Locate the btnCalc_Click procedure. Before modifying the code to use the Boolean value returned by the TryParse method, you will observe how the procedure currently works. Start the application. Type **10** in the Old pay box and then click the **Calculate** button. Even though no raise rate was entered, the button's Click event procedure displays an amount in the New pay box; in this case, it displays the old pay amount of $10.00.
4. Type **a** in the Raise rate box and then click the **Calculate** button. Here again, the procedure displays $10.00 in the New pay box, even though the raise rate is invalid. See Figure 5-59. (Recall that you can press Alt to either show or hide the access keys.)

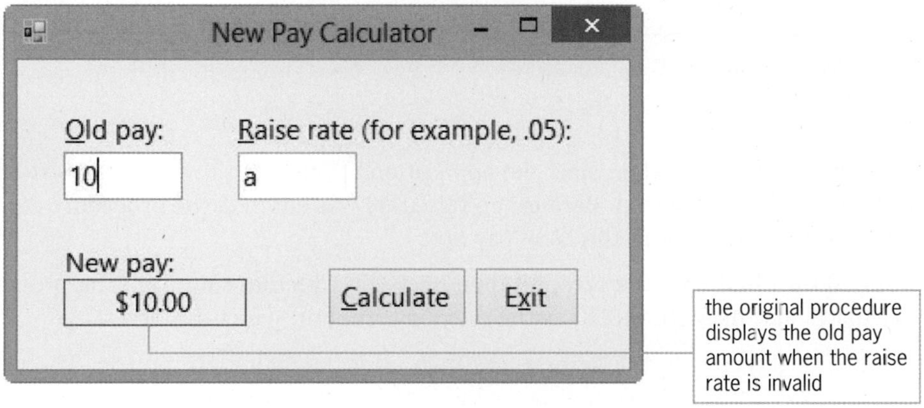

Figure 5-59 Sample run of the original Click event procedure

5. Change the raise rate to **.05** and then click the **Calculate** button. The procedure displays $10.50 in the New pay box, which is correct. Click the **Exit** button.
6. Use the code shown in Figure 5-60 to modify the btnCalc_Click procedure. The modifications are shaded in the figure.

```
Private Sub btnCalc_Click(sender As Object,
e As EventArgs) Handles btnCalc.Click
    ' calculates and displays the new pay

    Dim dblOld As Double
    Dim dblRate As Double
    Dim dblNew As Double
    Dim blnIsOldOk As Boolean
    Dim blnIsRateOk As Boolean

    ' convert the input to numbers
    blnIsOldOk = Double.TryParse(txtOld.Text, dblOld)
    blnIsRateOk = Double.TryParse(txtRate.Text, dblRate)

    ' determine whether the conversions were successful
    If blnIsOldOk AndAlso blnIsRateOk Then
        ' calculate and display the new pay
       dblNew = dblOld + dblOld * dblRate
       lblNew.Text = dblNew.ToString("C2")
    Else
       lblNew.Text = "Invalid data"
    End If

    ' set the focus
    txtOld.Focus()
End Sub
```

Figure 5-60 Modified btnCalc_Click procedure

7. Save the solution and then start the application. Type **10** in the Old pay box and then click the **Calculate** button. Because no raise rate was entered, the procedure displays the "Invalid data" message in the New pay box.
8. Type **.05** in the Raise rate box and then click the **Calculate** button. The procedure calculates and displays $10.50 as the new pay amount, which is correct.
9. Change the old pay to the letter **a** and then click the **Calculate** button. The procedure displays the "Invalid data" message, which is correct.
10. Click the **Exit** button. Close the Code Editor window and then close the solution.

YOU DO IT 4!

Create a Visual Basic Windows application named YouDoIt 4. Save the application in the VB2012\Chap05 folder. Add a text box, a label, and a button to the form. If the user enters a value that can be converted to the Integer data type, the button's Click event procedure should display the integer in the label; otherwise, it should display the string "Can't be converted". Code the procedure. Save the solution and then start the application. Test the application using the following values: 12, 12.75, 2, $45, 3, 5%, 6, and the empty string. Close the solution.

Generating Random Integers

Most computer game programs contain at least one multiple-alternative selection structure; most also use random numbers. You already know how to write multiple-alternative selection structures. In this section, you will learn how to generate random integers. If you want to learn how to generate random numbers containing a decimal place, refer to Exercise 13 at the end of this lesson.

Most programming languages provide a **pseudo-random number generator**, which is a device that produces a sequence of numbers that meet certain statistical requirements for randomness. Pseudo-random numbers are chosen with equal probability from a finite set of numbers. The chosen numbers are not completely random because a definite mathematical algorithm is used to select them. However, they are sufficiently random for practical purposes. The pseudo-random number generator in Visual Basic is an object whose data type is Random.

Figure 5-61 shows the syntax for generating random integers in Visual Basic, and it includes examples of using the syntax. As the figure indicates, you first create a **Random object** to represent the pseudo-random number generator in your application's code. You create the Random object by declaring it in a Dim statement. You enter the Dim statement in the procedure that will use the number generator. After the Random object is created, you can use the object's Random.Next method to generate random integers. In the method's syntax, *randomObjectName* is the name of the Random object. The *minValue* and *maxValue* arguments in the syntax must be integers, and minValue must be less than maxValue. The **Random.Next method** returns an integer that is greater than or equal to minValue, but less than maxValue. You will use random integers to code the Roll 'Em Game application, which simulates the rolling of two dice.

Generating Random Integers

Syntax
Dim *randomObjectName* **As New Random**
randomObjectName.**Next(***minValue*, *maxValue***)**

Example 1
```
Dim randGen As New Random
intNum = randGen.Next(1, 51)
```
The Dim statement creates a Random object named `randGen`. The `randGen.Next(1, 51)` expression generates a random integer that is greater than or equal to 1, but less than 51. The assignment statement assigns the random integer to the `intNum` variable.

Example 2
```
Dim randGen As New Random
intNum = randGen.Next(-10, 0)
```
The Dim statement creates a Random object named `randGen`. The `randGen.Next(-10, 0)` expression generates a random integer that is greater than or equal to –10, but less than 0. The assignment statement assigns the random integer to the `intNum` variable.

Figure 5-61 Syntax and examples of generating random integers

START HERE

To open the Roll 'Em Game application:

1. Open the Roll Em Solution (Roll Em Solution.sln) file contained in the VB2012\Chap05\Roll Em Solution folder. If necessary, open the designer window. The interface is shown in Figure 5-62. (The die images were downloaded from the Open Clip Art Library at *http://openclipart.org*.)

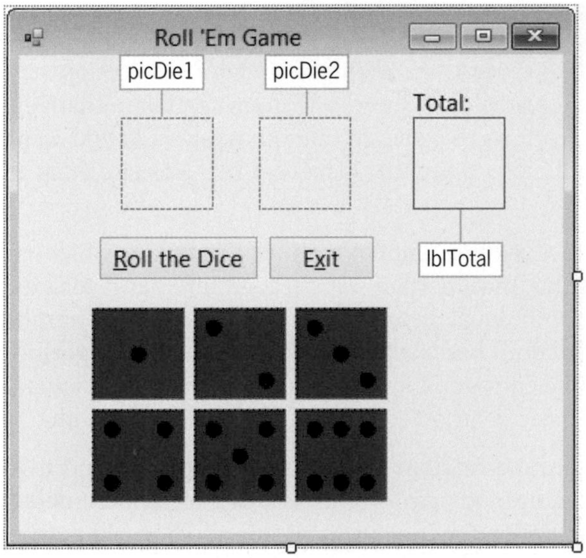

Figure 5-62 Roll 'Em Game application's interface
OpenClipArt.org/orsonj

2. Open the Code Editor window. Replace <your name> and <current date> in the comments with your name and the current date, respectively.

When the user clicks the Roll the Dice button, the button's Click event procedure will generate two random integers from 1 through 6. It will use the random integers to select one of the images located below the buttons in the interface. The images are named picOneDot, picTwoDots, picThreeDots, picFourDots, picFiveDots, and picSixDots. The procedure will display the selected images in the picDie1 and picDie2 controls. It also will total the number of dots appearing on both dice and then display the total in the lblTotal control. Figure 5-63 shows the pseudocode for the Roll the Dice button's Click event procedure.

```
btnRoll Click event procedure
1. generate a random integer from 1 through 6 and assign to a variable named intNum1
2. generate a random integer from 1 through 6 and assign to a variable named intNum2
3. use the intNum1 variable's value to display the appropriate image in the picDie1 control
       if intNum1 contains:
       1   display the picOneDot image
       2   display the picTwoDots image
       3   display the picThreeDots image
       4   display the picFourDots image
       5   display the picFiveDots image
       6   display the picSixDots image
```

Figure 5-63 Pseudocode for the Roll the Dice button's Click event procedure *(continues)*

(continued)

4. use the intNum2 variable's value to display the appropriate image in the picDie2 control
    if intNum2 contains:
    1 display the picOneDot image
    2 display the picTwoDots image
    3 display the picThreeDots image
    4 display the picFourDots image
    5 display the picFiveDots image
    6 display the picSixDots image
5. calculate the total number of dots on both dice by adding together the integers stored in the intNum1 and intNum2 variables
6. display the total in the lblTotal control

Figure 5-63 Pseudocode for the Roll the Dice button's Click event procedure

To code the Roll the Dice button's Click event procedure:

START HERE

1. Open the code template for the btnRoll control's Click event procedure. Type the following comment and then press **Enter** twice:

   ' simulates a game of rolling dice

2. First, you will declare the random number generator. Type the following Dim statement and then press **Enter**:

   Dim randGen As New Random

3. Next, you will declare the `intNum1` and `intNum2` variables, which will store the random integers. You also will declare an Integer variable to store the total of the dots on both dice. Enter the following three Dim statements. Press **Enter** twice after typing the last Dim statement.

   Dim intNum1 As Integer
   Dim intNum2 As Integer
   Dim intTotal As Integer

4. The first two steps in the pseudocode are to generate two random integers from 1 through 6 and assign them to the `intNum1` and `intNum2` variables. To generate integers in that range, you will need to use 1 for the Random.Next method's *minValue* argument, and 7 for its *maxValue* argument. Enter the following comment and two assignment statements. Press **Enter** twice after typing the second assignment statement.

   ' assign random integer from 1 through 6
   intNum1 = randGen.Next(1, 7)
   intNum2 = randGen.Next(1, 7)

5. Step 3 in the pseudocode uses the `intNum1` variable's value to display the appropriate image in the picDie1 control. Enter the following comment and Select Case statement:

```
' display appropriate image in picDie1
Select Case intNum1
   Case 1
         picDie1.Image = picOneDot.Image
   Case 2
         picDie1.Image = picTwoDots.Image
   Case 3
         picDie1.Image = picThreeDots.Image
   Case 4
         picDie1.Image = picFourDots.Image
   Case 5
         picDie1.Image = picFiveDots.Image
   Case 6
         picDie1.Image = picSixDots.Image
End Select
```

6. Similarly, Step 4 uses the `intNum2` variable's value to display the appropriate image in the picDie2 control. Insert another blank line above the End Sub clause and then enter the following comment and Select Case statement:

```
' display appropriate image in picDie2
Select Case intNum2
   Case 1
         picDie2.Image = picOneDot.Image
   Case 2
         picDie2.Image = picTwoDots.Image
   Case 3
         picDie2.Image = picThreeDots.Image
   Case 4
         picDie2.Image = picFourDots.Image
   Case 5
         picDie2.Image = picFiveDots.Image
   Case 6
         picDie2.Image = picSixDots.Image
End Select
```

7. The last two steps in the pseudocode calculate the total number of dots on both dice and then display the result in the lblTotal control. Insert another blank line above the End Sub clause and then enter the following comment and assignment statements:

```
' calculate and display total number of dots
intTotal = intNum1 + intNum2
lblTotal.Text = intTotal.ToString()
```

8. Save the solution and then start the application. Click the **Roll the Dice** button. See Figure 5-64. Because random numbers are used to select the appropriate images for the picDie1 and picDie2 controls, your dice and total might be different from the dice and total shown in the figure.

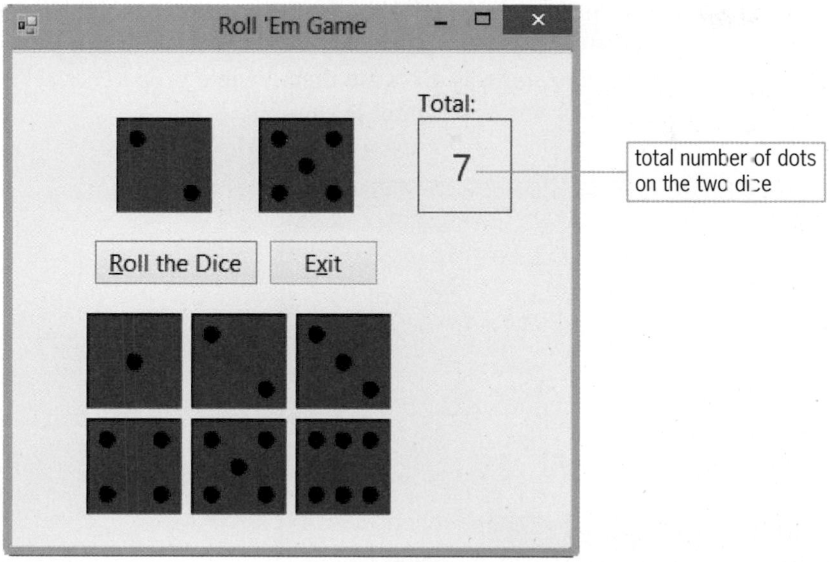

Figure 5-64 Result of clicking the Roll the Dice button
OpenClipArt.org/orsonj

9. Click the **Roll the Dice** button several more times to verify that different images appear in the picDie1 and picDie2 controls. Also verify that the number in the Total box is correct. When you are finished testing the application, click the **Exit** button.

YOU DO IT 5!

Create a Visual Basic Windows application named YouDoIt 5. Save the application in the VB2012\Chap05 folder. Add a label and a button to the form. The button's Click event procedure should display an integer from 1 through 10 in the label. Code the procedure. Save the solution and then start and test the application. Close the solution.

Showing and Hiding a Control

The six picture boxes located at the bottom of the form should not appear while the application is running. You can hide them by changing their **Visible property** from True to False. Setting a control's Visible property to False makes the control invisible during runtime. However, you will still be able to see the control in the designer window.

To hide the six picture boxes and then resize the form:

START HERE

1. Close the Code Editor window. Select the six picture boxes located at the bottom of the form, and then use the Properties window to change the Visible property to **False**. Click the **form** to deselect the picture boxes.

2. Drag the form's bottom sizing handle up until the form is approximately the size shown in Figure 5-65. Don't be concerned that you can still see a portion of the picOneDot, picTwoDots, and picThreeDots controls. Because their Visible property is set to False, the controls won't appear while the application is running.

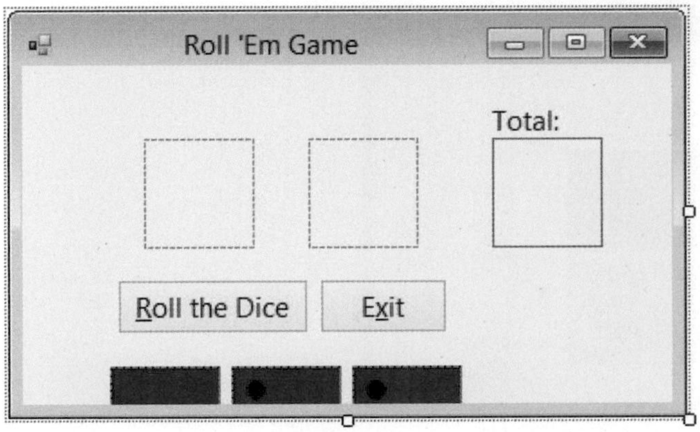

Figure 5-65 Resized form
OpenClipArt.org/orsonj

3. Lock the controls on the form. Save the solution and then start the application. Click the **Roll the Dice** button. See Figure 5-66. Notice that the picture boxes located at the bottom of the form are hidden from view.

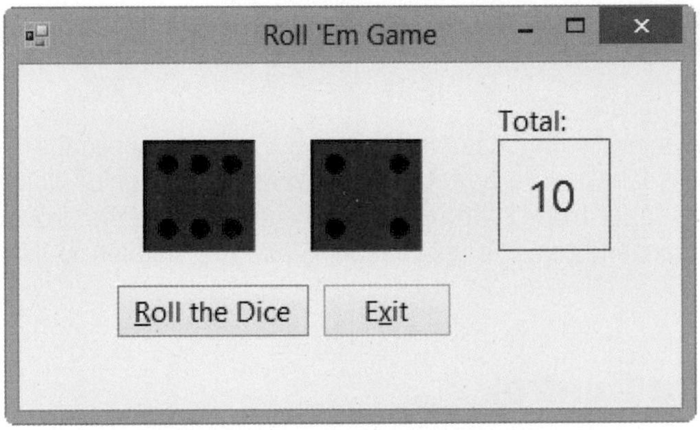

Figure 5-66 Interface with six of the picture boxes hidden
OpenClipArt.org/orsonj

4. Click the **Exit** button and then close the solution.

Figure 5-67 shows the code entered in the Roll the Dice button's Click event procedure.

```
Private Sub btnRoll_Click(sender As Object,
e As EventArgs) Handles btnRoll.Click
    ' simulates a game of rolling dice

    Dim randGen As New Random
    Dim intNum1 As Integer
    Dim intNum2 As Integer
    Dim intTotal As Integer

    ' assign random integer from 1 through 6
    intNum1 = randGen.Next(1, 7)
    intNum2 = randGen.Next(1, 7)

    ' display appropriate image in picDie1
    Select Case intNum1
        Case 1
            picDie1.Image = picOneDot.Image
        Case 2
            picDie1.Image = picTwoDots.Image
        Case 3
            picDie1.Image = picThreeDots.Image
        Case 4
            picDie1.Image = picFourDots.Image
        Case 5
            picDie1.Image = picFiveDots.Image
        Case 6
            picDie1.Image = picSixDots.Image
    End Select

    ' display appropriate image in picDie2
    Select Case intNum2
        Case 1
            picDie2.Image = picOneDot.Image
        Case 2
            picDie2.Image = picTwoDots.Image
        Case 3
            picDie2.Image = picThreeDots.Image
        Case 4
            picDie2.Image = picFourDots.Image
        Case 5
            picDie2.Image = picFiveDots.Image
        Case 6
            picDie2.Image = picSixDots.Image
    End Select

    ' calculate and display total number of dots
    intTotal = intNum1 + intNum2
    lblTotal.Text = intTotal.ToString()

End Sub
```

Figure 5-67 Roll the Dice button's Click event procedure

Lesson C Summary

- To determine whether the TryParse method converted a string to a number of the specified data type:

  Use the syntax *booleanVariable* = *dataType*.**TryParse(***string***,** *numericVariableName***)**. The TryParse method returns the Boolean value True when the string can be converted to the numeric *dataType*; otherwise, it returns the Boolean value False.

- To generate random integers:

  Create a Random object to represent the pseudo-random number generator. Typically, the syntax for creating a Random object is **Dim** *randomObjectName* **As New Random**. You then use the Random.Next method to generate a random integer. The method's syntax is *randomObjectName*.**Next(***minValue***,** *maxValue***)**. The Random.Next method returns an integer that is greater than or equal to minValue, but less than maxValue. In most cases, the Random.Next method's return value is assigned to a variable.

- To show or hide a control while an application is running:

  Set the control's Visible property to the Boolean value True to show the control during runtime. Set the control's Visible property to the Boolean value False to hide the control during runtime.

Lesson C Key Terms

Pseudo-random number generator—a device that produces a sequence of numbers that meet certain statistical requirements for randomness; the pseudo-random generator in Visual Basic is an object whose data type is Random

Random object—represents the pseudo-random number generator in Visual Basic

Random.Next method—used to generate a random integer that is greater than or equal to a minimum value, but less than a maximum value

Visible property—determines whether a control is visible in the interface while an application is running

Lesson C Review Questions

1. If the txtPrice control contains the value 75, what value will the `Decimal.TryParse(txtPrice.Text, decPrice)` method return?
   a. False
   b. True
   c. 75
   d. 75.00

2. Which of the following statements will hide the picCar control?
   a. `picCar.Hide`
   b. `picCar.Hide = True`
   c. `picCar.Invisible = True`
   d. `picCar.Visible = False`

3. Which of the following statements declares an object to represent the pseudo-random number generator in a procedure?
   a. `Dim randGen As New RandomNumber`
   b. `Dim randGen As New Generator`
   c. `Dim randGen As New Random`
   d. `Dim randGen As New RandomObject`

4. Which of the following statements generates a random integer from 1 to 25, inclusive?
   a. `intNum = randGen.Next(1, 25)`
   b. `intNum = randGen.Next(1, 26)`
   c. `intNum = randGen(1, 25)`
   d. `intNum = randGen.NextNumber(1, 26)`

5. If the txtAge control is empty, the `blnIsOk = Integer.TryParse(txtAge.Text, intAge)` statement will store ______________ in the `intAge` variable and also assign ______________ to the `blnIsOk` variable.
   a. 0, True
   b. 0, False
   c. False, the empty string
   d. the empty string, False

Lesson C Exercises

1. Open the Kelley Solution (Kelley Solution.sln) file contained in the VB2012\Chap05\Kelley Solution folder. If necessary, open the designer and Code Editor windows. Locate the btnCalc_Click procedure. The procedure should display the message "Please enter a number" in the lblBonus control when the contents of the txtSales control cannot be converted to a Double number. Otherwise, it should multiply the contents of the `dblSales` variable by 10% and display the result in the lblBonus control. Make the appropriate modifications to the procedure's code. Save the solution and then start and test the application. Close the Code Editor window and then close the solution. INTRODUCTORY

2. Create a Visual Basic Windows application. Use the following names for the solution and project, respectively: Lottery Solution and Lottery Project. Save the application in the VB2012\Chap05 folder. Change the form file's name to Main Form.vb. Change the form's name to frmMain. Create the interface shown in Figure 5-68. The image for the picture box is stored in the VB2012\Chap05\BagOfMoney.png file. (The image was downloaded from the Open Clip Art Library at *http://openclipart.org*.) The Select Numbers button should display six lottery numbers. Each lottery number can range from 1 through 54 only. (An example of six lottery numbers would be: 4 8 35 15 20 3.) Code the application. For now, do not worry if the lottery numbers are not unique. You will learn how to display unique numbers in Chapter 9. Save the solution and then start and test the application. Close the Code Editor window and then close the solution. INTRODUCTORY

Figure 5-68 Interface for Exercise 2
OpenClipArt.org/johnny_automatic

INTRODUCTORY

3. Open the Sum Solution (Sum Solution.sln) file contained in the VB2012\Chap05\Sum Solution folder. If necessary, open the designer window. The Calculate button's Click event procedure should calculate the sum of the two values entered by the user, and then display the result in the lblSum control. Calculate and display the sum only when both values can be converted to the Integer data type; otherwise, display the message "Please enter two integers" in a message box. Code the procedure. Save the solution and then start and test the application. Close the Code Editor window and then close the solution.

INTERMEDIATE

4. Create a Visual Basic Windows application. Use the following names for the solution and project, respectively: Concert Solution and Concert Project. Save the application in the VB2012\Chap05 folder. Change the form file's name to Main Form.vb. Change the form's name to frmMain. Create the interface shown in Figure 5-69. The three text boxes should be invisible when the application starts. When the user selects a check box, its corresponding text box should appear in the interface and remain visible until the user deselects the check box. The user will enter the number of tickets he or she wants to purchase in the appropriate text box. Keep in mind that the user can purchase any combination of tickets, such as 3 box tickets and 5 lawn tickets, or 2 pavilion tickets, 1 box ticket, and 2 lawn tickets. The application should calculate and display the total number of tickets purchased and the total price. The tickets for box, pavilion, and lawn seats are $75, $30, and $21, respectively. Save the solution and then start and test the application. Close the Code Editor window and then close the solution.

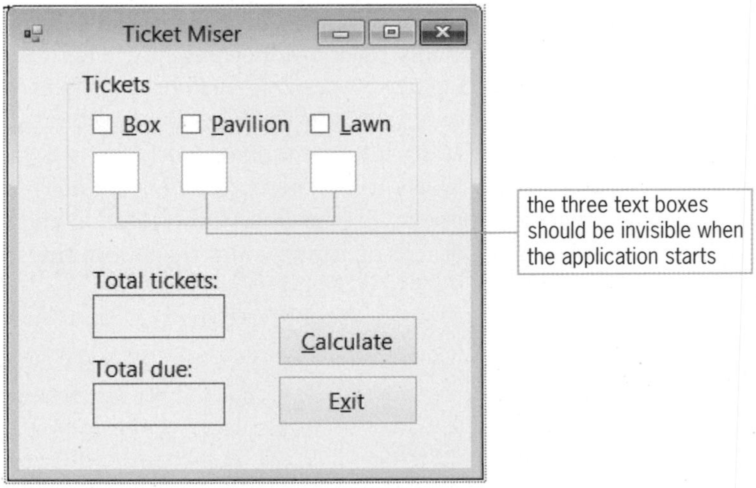

Figure 5-69 Interface for Exercise 4

INTERMEDIATE

5. Create a Visual Basic Windows application. Use the following names for the solution and project, respectively: Guessing Game Solution and Guessing Game Project. Save the application in the VB2012\Chap05 folder. Change the form file's name to Main Form.vb. Change the form's name to frmMain. The application should generate a random integer from 1 through 25, inclusive. It then should give the user as many chances as necessary to guess the integer. If the user guesses the integer, the application should display the "You are correct. The random integer is *x*." message, where *x* is the random integer. If the user's guess is less than the random integer, the application should display the "Guess higher" message. If the user's guess is greater than the random integer, the application should display the "Guess lower" message. Create a suitable interface, and then code the application. Save the solution and then start and test the application. Close the Code Editor window and then close the solution.

INTERMEDIATE

6. In this exercise, you modify the application from Exercise 5. Use Windows to make a copy of the Guessing Game Solution folder. Rename the copy Modified Guessing Game Solution. Open the Guessing Game Solution (Guessing Game Solution.sln) file contained in the Modified Guessing Game Solution folder. Open the designer and Code Editor windows. Allow the user to make only five incorrect guesses. When the user has made the fifth incorrect guess, display the random integer. Save the solution and then start and test the application. Close the Code Editor window and then close the solution.

INTERMEDIATE

7. Create a Visual Basic Windows application. Use the following names for the solution and project, respectively: Willowbrook Solution and Willowbrook Project. Save the application in the VB2012\Chap05 folder. Change the form file's name to Main Form.vb. Change the form's name to frmMain. Create the interface shown in Figure 5-70. The application should calculate and display a club member's monthly dues, which includes the basic monthly fee and any additional monthly charges for tennis ($30), golf ($25), and racquetball ($20). Code the application. Save the solution and then start and test the application. Close the Code Editor window and then close the solution.

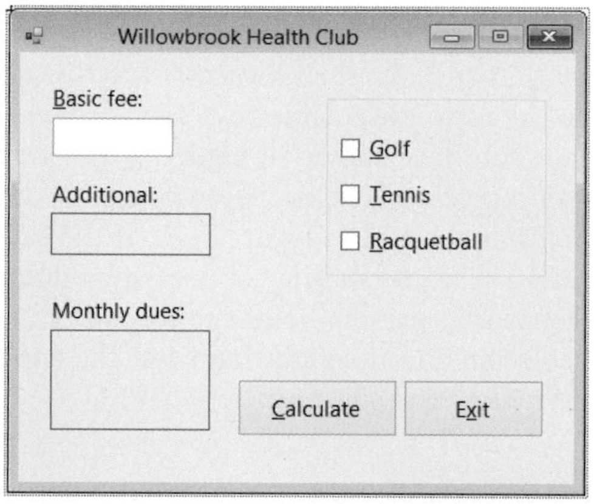

Figure 5-70 Interface for Exercise 7

INTERMEDIATE

8. Open the Juarez Solution (Juarez Solution.sln) file contained in the VB2012\Chap05\Juarez Solution folder. If necessary, open the designer window.

   a. The Display Grade button's Click event procedure should display a letter grade that is based on the average of three test scores. See Figure 5-71. Each test is worth 100 points. The procedure should display an appropriate message if any of the test scores cannot be converted to the Double data type. Code the Click event procedure.

b. When the user makes a change to the contents of a text box, the application should remove the contents of the lblGrade control. Code the appropriate event procedures.

c. The application should select a text box's existing text when the text box receives the focus. Code the appropriate event procedures.

d. Save the solution and then start and test the application. Use the following scores for the first test: 90, 95, and 100. The grade should be an A. Use the following scores for the second test: 83, 72, and 65. Use the following scores for the third test: 40, 30, and 20. Next, test the application using letters, and then test it using an empty text box. Close the Code Editor window and then close the solution.

Average	Grade
90 – 100	A
80 – 89	B
70 – 79	C
60 – 69	D
Below 60	F

Figure 5-71 Grade information for Exercise 8

INTERMEDIATE

9. Open the Gross Pay Solution (Gross Pay Solution.sln) file contained in the VB2012\Chap05\Gross Pay Solution folder. If necessary, open the designer window. The Calculate button's Click event procedure should calculate an employee's gross pay. Employees working more than 40 hours receive time and one-half for the hours over 40. The procedure should display an appropriate message if the user's input cannot be converted to a Decimal number. Code the procedure. Save the solution and then start and test the application. Close the Code Editor window and then close the solution.

INTERMEDIATE

10. Create a Visual Basic Windows application. Use the following names for the solution and project, respectively: Marshall Solution and Marshall Project. Save the application in the VB2012\Chap05 folder. Change the form file's name to Main Form.vb. Change the form's name to frmMain. Create the interface shown in Figure 5-72. Each salesperson at Marshall Sales Corporation receives a commission based on the amount of his or her sales. The commission rates are shown in Figure 5-73. If the salesperson has been with the company more than 10 years, he or she receives an additional $500. If the salesperson is classified as a traveling salesperson, he or she receives an additional $700. Code the application. Save the solution and then start and test the application. Close the Code Editor window and then close the solution.

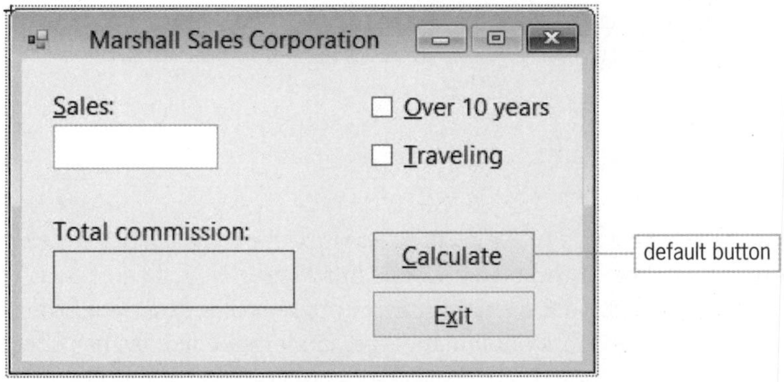

Figure 5-72 Interface for Exercise 10

Sales ($)	Commission
1 – 100,000.99	2% of sales
100,001 – 400,000.99	$2,000 plus 5% of the sales over $100,000
400,001 and over	$17,000 plus 10% of the sales over $400,000

Figure 5-73 Commission rates for Exercise 10

ADVANCED

11. In this exercise, you create an application for Sunnyside Products. The application calculates and displays the price of an order, based on the number of units ordered and the customer's status (either wholesaler or retailer). The price per unit is shown in Figure 5-74. Create a Visual Basic Windows application. Use the following names for the solution and project, respectively: Sunnyside Solution and Sunnyside Project. Save the application in the VB2012\Chap05 folder. Change the form file's name to Main Form.vb. Change the form's name to frmMain. Design an appropriate interface. Use radio buttons to determine the customer's status. Code the application. Save the solution and then start and test the application. Close the Code Editor window and then close the solution.

Wholesaler		**Retailer**	
Number of Units	Price per Unit ($)	Number of Units	Price per Unit ($)
1–10	20	1–5	30
11 and over	15	6–15	28
		16 and over	25

Figure 5-74 Pricing chart for Exercise 11

ADVANCED

12. In this exercise, you modify the Covington Resort application from Lesson B's Exercise 6. Use Windows to make a copy of the Modified Covington Resort Solution folder. Rename the copy Modified Covington Resort Solution-Advanced. Open the Covington Resort Solution (Covington Resort Solution.sln) file contained in the Modified Covington Resort Solution-Advanced folder. Open the designer window. Change the Visible property of the Number of vehicles: label and its associated text box to False in the Properties window. The label and text box should appear in the interface only when the check box is selected. If the check box is subsequently deselected, the application should hide the label and text box once again. Save the solution and then start and test the application. Close the Code Editor window and then close the solution.

DISCOVERY

13. This exercise will show you how to generate and display random numbers containing decimal places. Open the Random Double Solution (Random Double Solution.sln) file contained in the VB2012\Chap05\Random Double Solution folder. If necessary, open the designer window.

    a. Open the Code Editor window. You can use the Random.NextDouble method to return a random number that is greater than or equal to 0.0, but less than 1.0. The syntax of the Random.NextDouble method is *randomObjectName*.**NextDouble**. Code the btnDisplay_Click procedure so that it displays a random number in the lblNumber control. Save the solution and then start the application. Click the Display Random Number button several times. Each time you click the button, a random number that is greater than or equal to 0.0, but less than 1.0, appears in the lblNumber control.

b. You can use the following formula to generate random numbers within a specified range: (*maxValue* – *minValue* + **1**) * *randomObjectName*.**NextDouble** + *minValue*. For example, if the Random object's name is `randGen`, the formula `(10 - 1 + 1) * randGen.NextDouble + 1` generates random numbers that are greater than or equal to 1.0, but less than 11.0. Modify the btnDisplay_Click procedure to display a random number that is greater than or equal to 25.0, but less than 51.0. Display two decimal places in the number.

c. Save the solution and then start the application. Click the Display Random Number button several times. Each time you click the button, a random number that is greater than or equal to 25.0, but less than 51.0, appears in the lblNumber control. Close the Code Editor window and then close the solution.

SWAT THE BUGS

14. The purpose of this exercise is to demonstrate the importance of testing an application thoroughly. Open the Debug Solution (Debug Solution.sln) file contained in the VB2012\Chap05\Debug Solution folder. If necessary, open the designer and Code Editor windows. The application displays a shipping charge, which is based on the total price entered by the user. If the total price is greater than or equal to $100 but less than $501, the shipping charge is $10. If the total price is greater than or equal to $501 but less than $1,001, the shipping charge is $7. If the total price is greater than or equal to $1,001, the shipping charge is $5. No shipping charge is due if the total price is less than $100. Start the application. Test the application using the following total prices: 100, 501, 1500, 500.75, 30, 1000.33, and 2000. Notice that the application does not always display the correct shipping charge. Correct the application's code. Save the solution and then start and test the application again. Close the Code Editor window and then close the solution.

CHAPTER 6

The Repetition Structure

Creating the Gross Pay Application

In this chapter, you create an application that allows the user to enter the number of hours an employee worked and his or her rate of pay. The number of hours worked and pay rate will be entered using list boxes. The hours worked list box will display numbers from 0.5 through 40.0 in increments of 0.5 (for example, 0.5, 1.0, 1.5, 2.0, and so on). The pay rate list box will display numbers from 8.00 through 15.00, also in increments of 0.5. The application will calculate and display the employee's gross pay.

Previewing the Gross Pay Application

Before you start the first lesson in this chapter, you will preview the completed application. The application is contained in the VB2012\Chap06 folder.

START HERE

To preview the completed application:

1. Use the Run dialog box to run the Gross Pay (Gross Pay.exe) file contained in the VB2012\Chap06 folder. The application's user interface appears on the screen. The interface contains two list boxes. List box controls are covered in Lesson C.
2. Click **38.5** in the Hours list box, and then click the **Calculate** button. The gross pay amount ($385.00) appears in the interface. See Figure 6-1.

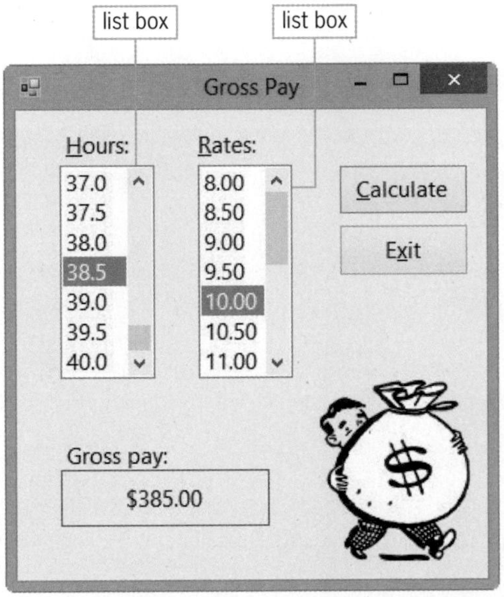

Figure 6-1 Gross pay shown in the interface
OpenClipArt.org/johnny_automatic

3. Click the **Exit** button to end the application.

The Gross Pay application uses the repetition structure, which is covered in Lessons A and B. You will code the Gross Pay application in Lesson C. Be sure to complete each lesson in full and do all of the end-of-lesson questions and several exercises before continuing to the next lesson.

LESSON A

After studying Lesson A, you should be able to:

- Differentiate between a looping condition and a loop exit condition
- Explain the difference between a pretest loop and a posttest loop
- Include pretest and posttest loops in pseudocode and in a flowchart
- Write a Do...Loop statement
- Stop an infinite loop
- Utilize counters and accumulators
- Explain the purpose of the priming and update reads
- Abbreviate assignment statements using the arithmetic assignment operators
- Code a counter-controlled loop using the For...Next statement

Repeating Program Instructions

Recall that all of the procedures in an application are written using one or more of three control structures: sequence, selection, and repetition. You learned about the sequence and selection structures in previous chapters. This chapter covers the repetition structure. Programmers use the **repetition structure**, referred to more simply as a **loop**, when they need the computer to repeatedly process one or more program instructions. The loop contains a condition that controls whether the instructions are repeated. In many programming languages, the condition can be phrased in one of two ways. It can either specify the requirement for repeating the instructions or specify the requirement for *not* repeating them. The requirement for repeating the instructions is referred to as the **looping condition** because it indicates when the computer should continue "looping" through the instructions. The requirement for *not* repeating the instructions is referred to as the **loop exit condition** because it tells the computer when to exit (or stop) the loop. Every looping condition has an opposing loop exit condition; one is the opposite of the other.

Some examples may help illustrate the difference between the looping condition and the loop exit condition. You've probably heard the old adage "Make hay while the sun shines." The "while the sun shines" is the looping condition because it tells you when to *continue* making hay. The adage could also be phrased as "Make hay until the sun is no longer shining." In this case, the "until the sun is no longer shining" is the loop exit condition because it indicates when you should *stop* making hay. In the phrase, "Keep your car's windshield wipers on while it is raining," the "while it is raining" is the looping condition. To use the loop exit condition, you would change the phrase to "Keep your car's windshield wipers on until it stops raining." Similarly, the idiom "While the cat's away, the mice will play" uses the looping condition "While the cat's away" to indicate when the mice will continue playing. You could also phrase the idiom using a loop exit condition, like this: "Until the cat returns, the mice will play." In this case, the loop exit condition indicates when the mice will stop playing. As mentioned earlier, the looping and loop exit conditions are the opposite of each other.

The programmer determines whether a problem's solution requires a loop by studying the problem specification. The first problem specification you will examine in this chapter involves a superheroine named Isis. The problem specification and an illustration of the problem are shown in Figure 6-2, along with a correct solution written in pseudocode. The solution uses only the sequence and selection structures because no instructions need to be repeated.

Ch06A video

Problem Specification

A superheroine named Isis must prevent a poisonous yellow spider from attacking King Khafra and Queen Rashida. Isis has one weapon at her disposal: a laser beam that shoots out from her right hand. Unfortunately, Isis gets only one shot at the spider, which is flying around the palace looking for the king and queen. Before taking the shot, she needs to position both her right arm and her right hand toward the spider. After taking the shot, she should return her right arm and right hand to their original positions. In addition, she should say "You are safe now. The spider is dead." if the laser beam hit the spider; otherwise, she should say "Run for your lives, my king and queen!"

Solution

1. position both your right arm and your right hand toward the spider
2. shoot a laser beam at the spider
3. return your right arm and right hand to their original positions
4. if the laser beam hit the spider
        say "You are safe now. The spider is dead."
    else
        say "Run for your lives, my king and queen!"
    end if

Figure 6-2 A problem that requires the sequence and selection structures
Image by Diane Zak; Created with Reallusion CrazyTalk Animator

Now let's change the problem specification slightly. This time, rather than taking only one shot, Isis can take as many shots as needed to destroy the poisonous yellow spider. Because of this, she will never need to tell the king and queen to run for their lives again. Figure 6-3 shows the modified problem specification along with two solutions. (As mentioned in Chapter 5, even small problems can have more than one solution.) Both solutions contain the sequence and repetition structures. The repetition structure in Solution 1 begins with the "repeat while the laser beam did not hit the spider" clause and ends with the "end repeat while" clause. The repetition structure in Solution 2, on the other hand, begins with the "repeat until the laser beam hits the spider" clause and ends with the "end repeat until" clause. The instructions between both clauses are called the **loop body** and are indented to indicate that they are part of the repetition structure.

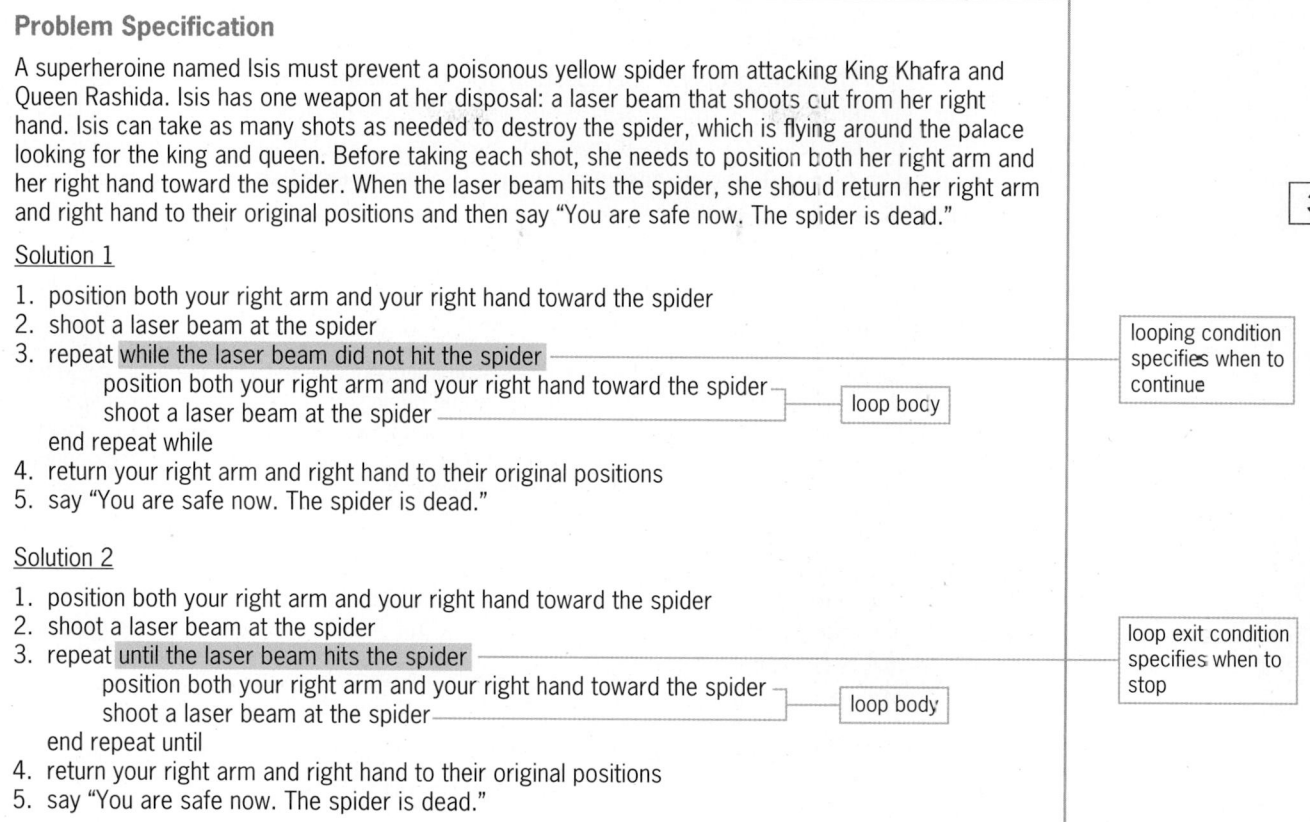

Problem Specification

A superheroine named Isis must prevent a poisonous yellow spider from attacking King Khafra and Queen Rashida. Isis has one weapon at her disposal: a laser beam that shoots out from her right hand. Isis can take as many shots as needed to destroy the spider, which is flying around the palace looking for the king and queen. Before taking each shot, she needs to position both her right arm and her right hand toward the spider. When the laser beam hits the spider, she should return her right arm and right hand to their original positions and then say "You are safe now. The spider is dead."

Solution 1

```
1. position both your right arm and your right hand toward the spider
2. shoot a laser beam at the spider
3. repeat while the laser beam did not hit the spider
        position both your right arm and your right hand toward the spider
        shoot a laser beam at the spider
   end repeat while
4. return your right arm and right hand to their original positions
5. say "You are safe now. The spider is dead."
```

looping condition specifies when to continue

loop body

Solution 2

```
1. position both your right arm and your right hand toward the spider
2. shoot a laser beam at the spider
3. repeat until the laser beam hits the spider
        position both your right arm and your right hand toward the spider
        shoot a laser beam at the spider
   end repeat until
4. return your right arm and right hand to their original positions
5. say "You are safe now. The spider is dead."
```

loop exit condition specifies when to stop

loop body

Figure 6-3 A problem that requires the sequence and repetition structures

The shaded portion in each solution in Figure 6-3 specifies the repetition structure's condition. The condition in Solution 1 is phrased as a looping condition because it tells Isis when to *continue* repeating the instructions. In this case, she should repeat the instructions as long as (or while) the laser beam did not hit the spider. The condition in Solution 2 is phrased as a loop exit condition because it tells Isis when to *stop* repeating the instructions. In this case, she should stop when the laser beam hits the spider. Notice that the loop exit condition is the opposite of the looping condition. Whether you use a looping condition or a loop exit condition, the condition must evaluate to a Boolean value.

YOU DO IT 1!

Using only the seven instructions shown here, write two solutions for printing the pages in a document that contains at least one page. Use a looping condition in the first solution. Use a loop exit condition in the second solution.

```
end repeat until
end repeat while
print the next page
print the first page
repeat until there are no more pages to print
repeat while there is another page to print
say "Done printing"
```

The Savings Account Application

Figure 6-4 shows the next problem specification you will examine in this chapter, along with the pseudocode and code for the Calculate button's Click event procedure. The procedure requires only the sequence structure. It does not need a selection structure or a loop because no decisions need to be made and no instructions need to be repeated to calculate and display the account balance at the end of the year.

Problem Specification

Create an application that displays the balance in a savings account at the end of the year, given the amount of money deposited into the savings account at the beginning of the year and the annual interest rate. The interest is compounded annually and no withdrawals or additional deposits are made during the year. The interest rate will be entered in decimal form. The application's interface should provide a Calculate button for displaying the account balance.

Pseudocode for the Calculate button's Click event procedure

1. store deposit in balance variable
2. store interest rate in rate variable
3. interest = balance * rate
4. add interest to balance
5. display balance

Code for the Calculate button's Click event procedure

```
Dim dblBalance As Double
Dim dblRate As Double
Dim dblInterest As Double
Double.TryParse(txtDeposit.Text, dblBalance)
Double.TryParse(txtRate.Text, dblRate)
dblInterest = dblBalance * dblRate
dblBalance = dblBalance + dblInterest
lblBalance.Text = "You will have " &
    dblBalance.ToString("C2") &
    " at the end of 1 year."
```

Figure 6-4 Problem specification, pseudocode, and code for the Savings Account application

START HERE

To run the Savings Account application:

1. If necessary, start Visual Studio 2012. Open the Savings Solution (Savings Solution.sln) file contained in the VB2012\Chap06\Savings Solution folder. If necessary, open the designer window.
2. Open the Code Editor window. Replace <your name> and <current date> in the comments with your name and the current date, respectively.
3. Locate the btnCalc_Click procedure. The procedure contains the code shown in Figure 6-4.
4. Save the solution and then start the application. Enter **5000** as the deposit and **.03** as the annual interest rate. Click the **Calculate** button. The button's Click event procedure displays the message shown in Figure 6-5.

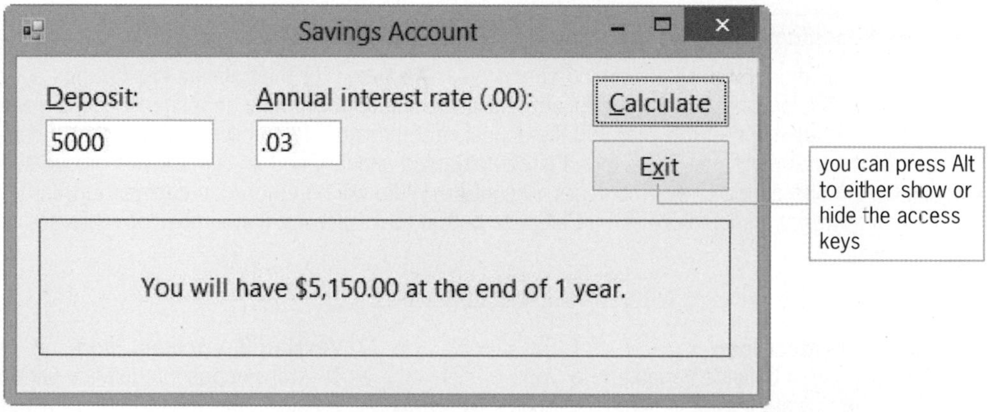

Figure 6-5 Sample run of the Savings Account application

5. Click the **Exit** button.

Now we'll make a slight change to the problem specification from Figure 6-4. The Savings Account application will now need to display the number of years required for the savings account to reach one-quarter of a million dollars, and the balance in the account at that time. Consider the changes you will need to make to the Calculate button's original pseudocode.

The first two steps in the original pseudocode are to store the input items (deposit and interest rate) in variables; the modified pseudocode will still need both of these steps. Steps 3 and 4 calculate the interest and then add the interest to the savings account balance. The modified pseudocode will need to repeat both of those steps either while the balance is less than one-quarter of a million dollars (looping condition) or until the balance is greater than or equal to one-quarter of a million dollars (loop exit condition). Here too, notice that the loop exit condition is the opposite of the looping condition. The loop in the modified pseudocode will also need to keep track of the number of times the instructions in Steps 3 and 4 are processed because each time represents a year. The last step in the original pseudocode displays the account balance. The modified pseudocode will need to display the account balance as well as the number of years.

The modified problem specification is shown in Figure 6-6 along with four versions of the modified pseudocode for the Calculate button's Click event procedure. (Here again, notice that even small procedures can have many solutions.) Only the loop is different in each version.

Problem Specification

Create an application that displays the number of years required for the balance in a savings account to reach at least one-quarter of a million dollars, given the amount of money deposited into the savings account at the beginning of the year and the annual interest rate. The application should also display the account balance at that time. The interest is compounded annually and no withdrawals or additional deposits are made during any of the years. The interest rate will be entered in decimal form. The application's interface should provide a Calculate button for displaying the number of years and the account balance.

Pseudocode for the Calculate button's Click event procedure

Version 1 – pretest loop

```
1. store deposit in balance variable
2. store interest rate in rate variable
3. repeat while balance < 250,000
       interest = balance * rate
       add interest to balance
       add 1 to number of years
   end repeat while
4. display balance and number of years
```

looping condition specifies when to continue (points to step 3)

Version 2 – pretest loop

```
1. store deposit in balance variable
2. store interest rate in rate variable
3. repeat until balance >= 250,000
       interest = balance * rate
       add interest to balance
       add 1 to number of years
   end repeat until
4. display balance and number of years
```

loop exit condition specifies when to stop (points to step 3)

Version 3 – posttest loop

```
1. store deposit in balance variable
2. store interest rate in rate variable
3. repeat
       interest = balance * rate
       add interest to balance
       add 1 to number of years
   end repeat while balance < 250,000
4. display balance and number of years
```

looping condition specifies when to continue (points to end repeat while)

Version 4 – posttest loop

```
1. store deposit in balance variable
2. store interest rate in rate variable
3. repeat
       interest = balance * rate
       add interest to balance
       add 1 to number of years
   end repeat until balance >= 250,000
4. display balance and number of years
```

loop exit condition specifies when to stop (points to end repeat until)

Figure 6-6 Modified problem specification and pseudocode for the Calculate button's Click event procedure

The loops in Versions 1 and 2 in Figure 6-6 are pretest loops. In a **pretest loop**, the condition appears at the beginning of the loop, indicating that it is evaluated *before* the instructions within the loop are processed. The condition in Version 1 is a looping condition because it tells the computer when to continue repeating the loop instructions. Version 2's condition, on the other hand, is a loop exit condition because it tells the computer when to stop repeating the instructions. Depending on the result of the evaluation, the instructions in a pretest loop may never be processed. For example, if the original deposit entered by the user is greater than or equal to 250,000 (one-quarter of a million), the "while balance < 250,000" looping condition in Version 1 will evaluate to False and the loop instructions will be skipped over. Similarly, the "until balance >= 250,000" loop exit condition in Version 2 will evaluate to True, causing the loop instructions to be bypassed.

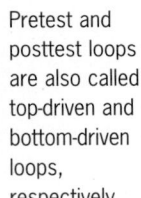

Pretest and posttest loops are also called top-driven and bottom-driven loops, respectively.

The loops in Versions 3 and 4 in Figure 6-6, on the other hand, are posttest loops. In a **posttest loop**, the condition appears at the end of the loop, indicating that it is evaluated *after* the instructions within the loop are processed. The condition in Version 3 is a looping condition, whereas the condition in Version 4 is a loop exit condition. Unlike the instructions in a pretest loop, the instructions in a posttest loop will always be processed at least once. In this case, if the original deposit entered by the user is greater than or equal to 250,000, the instructions in the two posttest loops will be processed once before the loop ends. Posttest loops should be used only when you are certain that the loop instructions should be processed at least once.

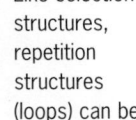

Like selection structures, repetition structures (loops) can be nested.

The Visual Basic language provides three different statements for coding loops: Do...Loop, For...Next, and For Each...Next. The Do...Loop statement can be used to code both pretest and posttest loops, whereas the For...Next and For Each...Next statements are used only for pretest loops. You will learn about the Do...Loop and For...Next statements in this lesson. The For Each...Next statement is covered in Chapter 9.

The Do...Loop Statement

Figure 6-7 shows two versions of the syntax for the **Do...Loop statement**: one for coding a pretest loop and the other for coding a posttest loop. In both versions of the syntax, the statement begins with the Do clause and ends with the Loop clause. Between both clauses, you enter the instructions you want the computer to repeat. The {While | Until} portion in each syntax indicates that you can select only one of the keywords appearing within the braces. You follow the keyword with a *condition*, which can be phrased as either a looping condition or a loop exit condition. You use the `While` keyword in a looping condition to specify that the loop body should be processed *while* (in other words, as long as) the condition is true. You use the `Until` keyword in a loop exit condition to specify that the loop body should be processed *until* the condition becomes true, at which time the loop should stop. Like the condition in an If...Then...Else statement, the condition in a Do...Loop statement can contain variables, constants, properties, methods, keywords, and operators; it also must evaluate to a Boolean value. The condition is evaluated with each repetition of the loop and determines whether the computer processes the loop body. Notice that the keyword (either `While` or `Until`) and the condition appear in the Do clause in a pretest loop, but they appear in the Loop clause in a posttest loop.

> You can use the `Exit Do` statement to exit the Do...Loop statement before the loop has finished processing. You may need to do this if the computer encounters an error when processing the loop instructions.

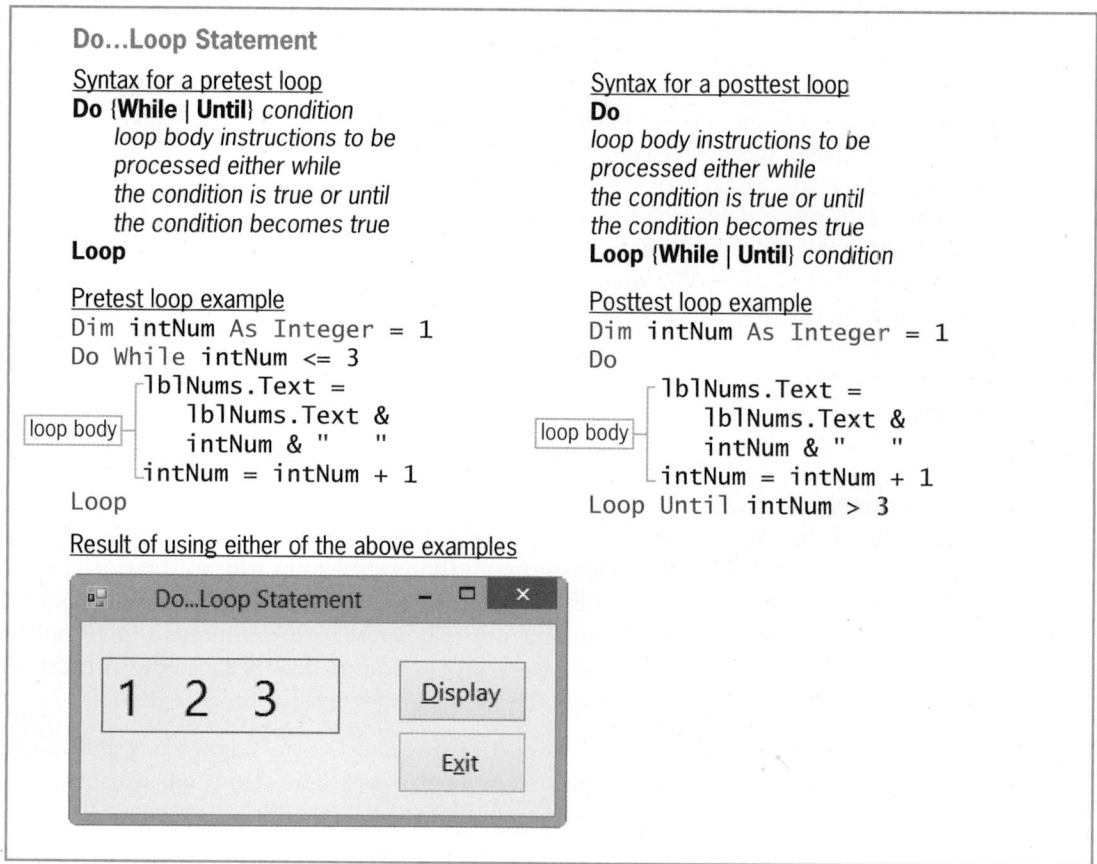

Do...Loop Statement

Syntax for a pretest loop
Do {**While** | **Until**} *condition*
loop body instructions to be processed either while the condition is true or until the condition becomes true
Loop

Syntax for a posttest loop
Do
loop body instructions to be processed either while the condition is true or until the condition becomes true
Loop {**While** | **Until**} *condition*

Pretest loop example

```
Dim intNum As Integer = 1
Do While intNum <= 3
    lblNums.Text =
        lblNums.Text &
        intNum & "   "
    intNum = intNum + 1
Loop
```

(loop body: the lblNums.Text and intNum = intNum + 1 statements)

Posttest loop example

```
Dim intNum As Integer = 1
Do
    lblNums.Text =
        lblNums.Text &
        intNum & "   "
    intNum = intNum + 1
Loop Until intNum > 3
```

(loop body: the lblNums.Text and intNum = intNum + 1 statements)

Result of using either of the above examples

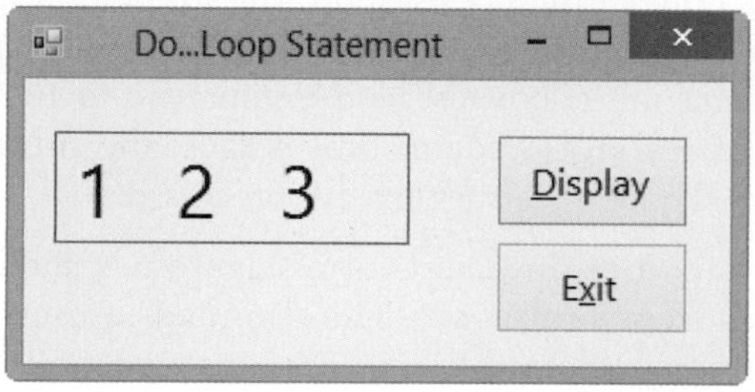

Figure 6-7 Syntax versions and examples of the Do...Loop statement

Figure 6-7 also shows examples of using both syntax versions to display the numbers 1, 2, and 3 in a label control, and it includes a sample run of an application that contains either example. Figure 6-8 describes the way the computer processes the code shown in the examples.

Processing steps for the pretest loop example

1. The `intNum` variable is created and initialized to 1.
2. The Do clause checks whether the value in the `intNum` variable (1) is less than or equal to 3. It is, so the loop body instructions display the number 1 in the lblNums control and then add 1 to the contents of the `intNum` variable, giving 2.
3. The Loop clause returns processing to the Do clause (the beginning of the loop).
4. The Do clause checks whether the value in the `intNum` variable (2) is less than or equal to 3. It is, so the loop body instructions display the numbers 1 and 2 (separated by spaces) in the lblNums control and then add 1 to the contents of the `intNum` variable, giving 3.
5. The Loop clause returns processing to the Do clause (the beginning of the loop).
6. The Do clause checks whether the value in the `intNum` variable (3) is less than or equal to 3. It is, so the loop body instructions display the numbers 1, 2, and 3 (separated by spaces) in the lblNums control and then add 1 to the contents of the `intNum` variable, giving 4.
7. The Loop clause returns processing to the Do clause (the beginning of the loop).
8. The Do clause checks whether the value in the `intNum` variable (4) is less than or equal to 3. It isn't, so the loop ends. Processing will continue with the statement following the Loop clause.

Processing steps for the posttest loop example

1. The `intNum` variable is created and initialized to 1.
2. The Do clause marks the beginning of the posttest loop.
3. The loop body instructions display the number 1 in the lblNums control and then add 1 to the contents of the `intNum` variable, giving 2.
4. The Loop clause checks whether the value in the `intNum` variable (2) is greater than 3. It isn't, so processing returns to the Do clause (the beginning of the loop).
5. The loop body instructions display the numbers 1 and 2 (separated by spaces) in the lblNums control and then add 1 to the contents of the `intNum` variable, giving 3.
6. The Loop clause checks whether the value in the `intNum` variable (3) is greater than 3. It isn't, so processing returns to the Do clause (the beginning of the loop).
7. The loop body instructions display the numbers 1, 2, and 3 (separated by spaces) in the lblNums control and then add 1 to the contents of the `intNum` variable, giving 4.
8. The Loop clause checks whether the value in the `intNum` variable (4) is greater than 3. It is, so the loop ends. Processing will continue with the statement following the Loop clause.

Ch06A-Do Loop video

Figure 6-8 Processing steps for the loop examples from Figure 6-7

Although both examples in Figure 6-7 produce the same results, pretest and posttest loops are not always interchangeable. For instance, if the `intNum` variable in the pretest loop in Figure 6-7 is initialized to 10 rather than to 1, the instructions in the pretest loop will not be processed because the `intNum` <= 3 condition (which is evaluated before the instructions are processed) evaluates to False. However, if the `intNum` variable in the posttest loop is initialized to 10 rather than to 1, the instructions in the posttest loop will be processed one time because the `intNum` > 3 condition is evaluated after (rather than before) the loop instructions are processed.

It's often easier to understand loops when viewed in flowchart form. Figure 6-9 shows the flowcharts associated with the loop examples from Figure 6-7. The diamond in each flowchart indicates the beginning of a repetition structure (loop). Like the diamond in a selection structure, the diamond in a repetition structure contains a condition that evaluates to either True or False only. The condition determines whether the instructions within the loop are processed. Also like the diamond in a selection structure, the diamond in a repetition structure has one flowline entering the symbol and two flowlines leaving the symbol. The two flowlines leading out of the diamond should be marked so that anyone reading the flowchart can distinguish the true path from the false path. Typically, the flowlines are marked with a "T" (for true) and an "F" (for false); however, they also can be marked with a "Y" (for yes) and an "N" (for no). In the pretest loop's flowchart, a circle or loop is formed by the flowline entering the diamond combined with the diamond and the symbols and flowlines within the true path. In the posttest loop's flowchart, the loop (circle) is formed by all of the symbols in the false path. It is this loop (circle) that distinguishes the repetition structure from the selection structure in a flowchart.

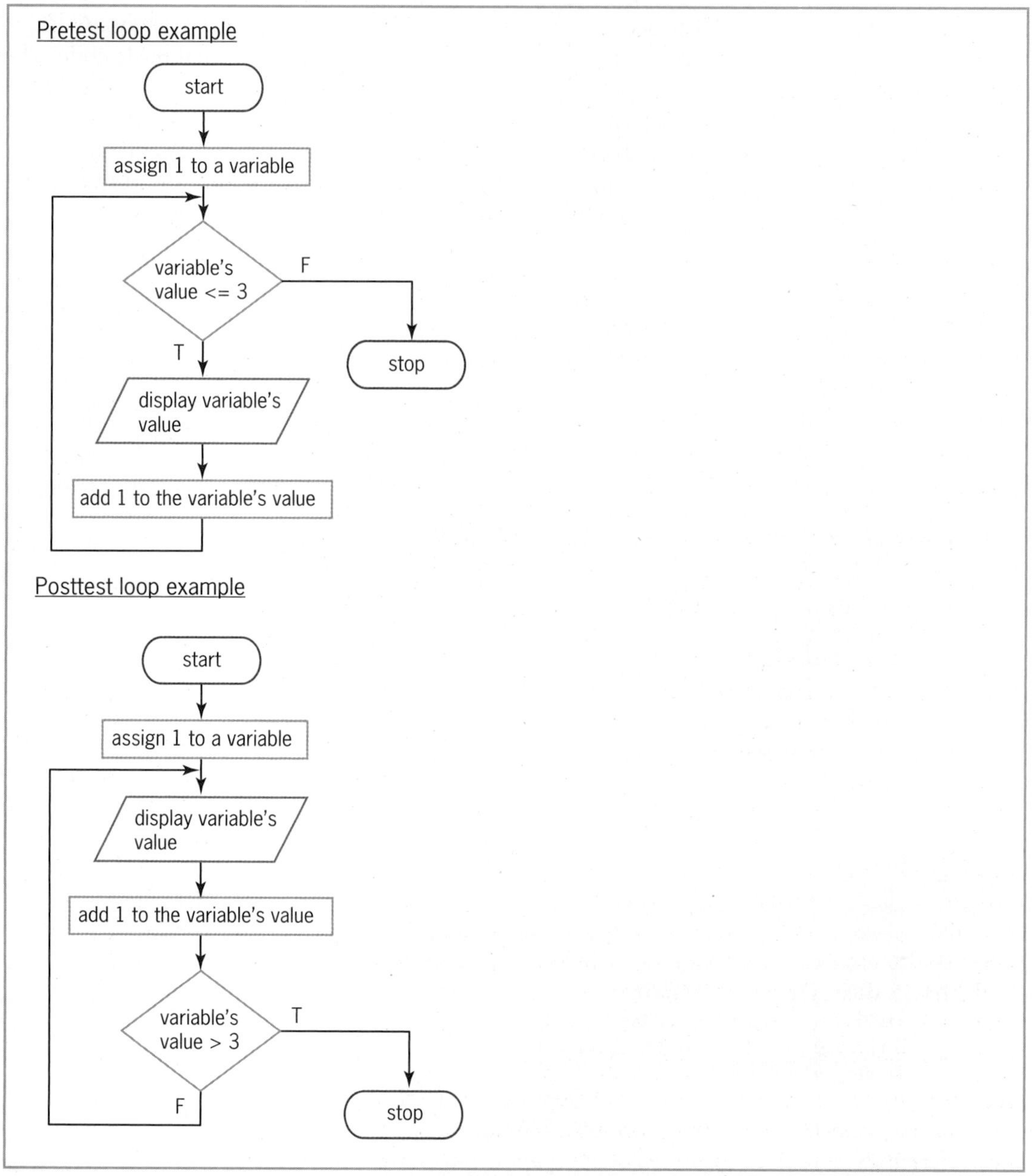

Figure 6-9 Flowcharts for the loop examples from Figure 6-7

YOU DO IT 2!

Close the Savings Account application's solution, if necessary. Create a Visual Basic Windows application named YouDoIt 2. Save the application in the VB2012\Chap06 folder. Add two buttons to the form. Both buttons should display the following numbers in message boxes: 1, 3, 5, and 7. Code the first button's Click event procedure using a pretest loop. Code the second button's Click event procedure using a posttest loop. Save the solution and then start and test the application. Close the solution.

Coding the Modified Savings Account Application

Earlier, in Figure 6-6, you viewed four versions of the modified pseudocode for the Calculate button's Click event procedure in the Savings Account application. Figure 6-10 shows the pseudocode from Version 1. It also shows the corresponding Visual Basic code. The changes made to the original pseudocode and code, shown earlier in Figure 6-4, are shaded in Figure 6-10. The looping condition in the Do...Loop statement tells the computer to repeat the loop body as long as (or while) the number in the `dblBalance` variable is less than 250,000 (one-quarter of a million). You also can use a loop exit condition in the Do clause, like this: `Do Until dblBalance >= 250000`. (Recall that >= is the opposite of <.)

Problem Specification

Create an application that displays the number of years required for the balance in a savings account to reach at least one-quarter of a million dollars, given the amount of money deposited into the savings account at the beginning of the year and the annual interest rate. The application should also display the account balance at that time. The interest is compounded annually and no withdrawals or additional deposits are made during any of the years. The interest rate will be entered in decimal form. The application's interface should provide a Calculate button for displaying the number of years and the account balance.

version 1 from Figure 6-6

Pseudocode for the Calculate button's Click event procedure

```
1. store deposit in balance variable
2. store interest rate in rate variable
3. repeat while balance < 250,000
       interest = balance * rate
       add interest to balance
       add 1 to number of years
   end repeat while
4. display balance and number of years
```

Code for the Calculate button's Click event procedure

```
Dim dblBalance As Double
Dim dblRate As Double
Dim dblInterest As Double
Dim intYears As Integer
Double.TryParse(txtDeposit.Text, dblBalance)
Double.TryParse(txtRate.Text, dblRate)
Do While dblBalance < 250000
    dblInterest = dblBalance * dblRate
    dblBalance = dblBalance + dblInterest
    intYears = intYears + 1
Loop
lblBalance.Text = "You will have " &
    dblBalance.ToString("C2") &
    " in " & intYears.ToString & " years."
```

Figure 6-10 Problem specification, pseudocode, and code for the modified Savings Account application

START HERE

To modify the Savings Account application:

1. If necessary, open the Savings Solution (Savings Solution.sln) file contained in the VB2012\Chap06\Savings Solution folder. Then, if necessary, open the designer and Code Editor windows and then locate the btnCalc_Click procedure.
2. Make the modifications shaded in Figure 6-10 to the btnCalc_Click procedure.
3. Save the solution and then start the application. Enter **50000** as the deposit and **.04** as the annual interest rate. Click the **Calculate** button. The button's Click event procedure displays the message shown in Figure 6-11.

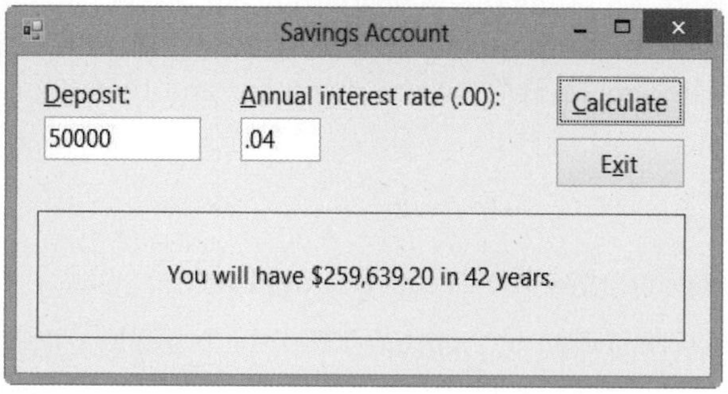

Figure 6-11 Sample run of the modified Savings Account application

4. Now, delete the **50000** in the Deposit box and then click the **Calculate** button. After a short period of time, a run time error occurs and the error message box shown in Figure 6-12 appears on the screen. (It may take as long as 30 seconds for the error message box to appear.) Place your mouse pointer on `intYears`, as shown in the figure.

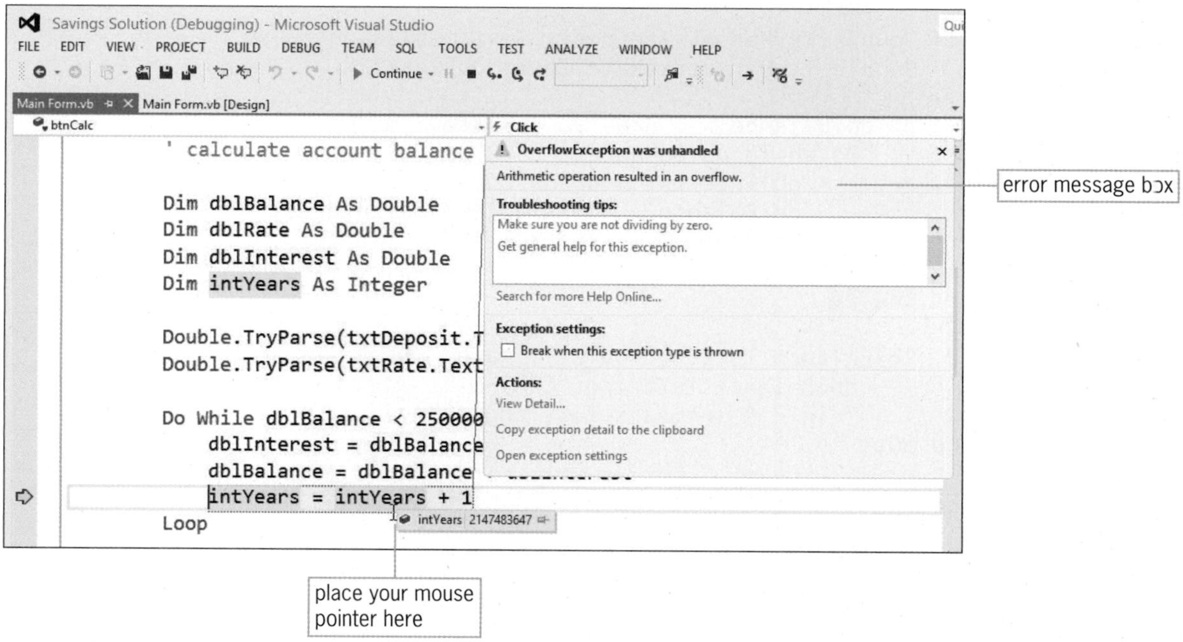

Figure 6-12 Screen showing the error message box

The error message informs you that an arithmetic operation—in this case, adding 1 to the `intYears` variable—resulted in an overflow. An overflow error occurs when the value assigned to a memory location is too large for the location's data type. (An overflow error is similar to trying to fill an 8 ounce glass with 10 ounces of water.) In this case, the `intYears` variable already contains the highest value that can be stored in an Integer variable (2,147,483,647 according to Figure 3-3 in Chapter 3). Therefore, when the `intYears = intYears + 1` statement attempts to increase the variable's value by 1, an overflow error occurs. But why does the `intYears` variable contain 2,147,483,647? In this case, because you didn't provide the initial deposit amount, the loop's condition (`dblBalance < 250000`) always evaluated to True; it never evaluated to False, which is required for stopping the loop. A loop that has no way to end is called an **infinite loop** or an **endless loop**. An infinite loop will also occur if you enter an initial deposit that is less than 250,000, but you neglect to enter an interest rate. You can stop a program that has an infinite loop by clicking DEBUG on the menu bar and then clicking Stop Debugging.

START HERE

To continue testing the application:

1. Click **DEBUG** on the menu bar and then click **Stop Debugging**.
2. Add the shaded selection structure shown in Figure 6-13 to the btnCalc_Click procedure.

```
Private Sub btnCalc_Click(sender As Object,
e As EventArgs) Handles btnCalc.Click
    ' calculate account balance

    Dim dblBalance As Double
    Dim dblRate As Double
    Dim dblInterest As Double
    Dim intYears As Integer

    Double.TryParse(txtDeposit.Text, dblBalance)
    Double.TryParse(txtRate.Text, dblRate)

    If dblBalance > 0 AndAlso dblRate > 0 Then
        Do While dblBalance < 250000
            dblInterest = dblBalance * dblRate
            dblBalance = dblBalance + dblInterest
            intYears = intYears + 1
        Loop
    End If

    lblBalance.Text = "You will have " &
        dblBalance.ToString("C2") &
        " in " & intYears.ToString & " years."
End Sub
```

Figure 6-13 Selection structure added to the procedure

3. Save the solution and then start the application. Click the **Calculate** button. Notice that no overflow error occurs. Instead, the Calculate button's Click event procedure displays the message "You will have $0.00 in 0 years."

4. Enter **50000** as the deposit and **.04** as the annual interest rate. Click the **Calculate** button. The button's Click event procedure displays the message shown earlier in Figure 6-11.

5. On your own, test the application using different deposits and annual interest rates. When you are finished, click the **Exit** button. Close the Code Editor window and then close the solution.

The Click event procedure shown in Figure 6-13 used a counter to keep track of the number of years. It also used an accumulator to keep track of the account balance. Counters and accumulators are covered in the next section.

Counters and Accumulators

Some procedures require you to calculate a subtotal, a total, or an average. You make these calculations using a loop that includes a counter, an accumulator, or both. A **counter** is a numeric variable used for counting something, such as the number of employees paid in a week. An **accumulator** is a numeric variable used for accumulating (adding together) something, such as the total dollar amount of a week's payroll. The `intYears` variable in the code shown earlier in Figure 6-13 is a counter because it keeps track of the number of years required for the account balance to reach 250,000. The `dblBalance` variable in the code is an accumulator because it adds together the annual interest amounts.

Two tasks are associated with counters and accumulators: initializing and updating. **Initializing** means to assign a beginning value to the counter or accumulator. Typically, counters and accumulators are initialized to the number 0. However, they can be initialized to any number, depending on the value required by the procedure's code. The initialization task is performed before the loop is processed because it needs to be performed only once. **Updating** refers to the process of either adding a number to (called **incrementing**) or subtracting a number from (called **decrementing**) the value stored in the counter or accumulator. The number can be either positive or negative, integer or non-integer. A counter is always updated by a constant amount—typically the number 1. An accumulator, on the other hand, is usually updated by an amount that varies. Accumulators are usually updated by incrementing rather than by decrementing. The assignment statement that updates a counter or an accumulator is placed in the body of a loop. This is because the update task must be performed each time the loop instructions are processed.

Figure 6-14 shows the syntax used for updating counters and accumulators, and it includes examples of using the syntax. (You also can use arithmetic assignment operators to update counters and accumulators. You will learn about those operators later in this lesson.) In the syntax for counters, notice that *counterVariable* appears on both sides of the assignment operator (=). The syntax tells the computer to add (or subtract) the *constantValue* to (from) the *counterVariable* first, and then place the result back in the *counterVariable*. If the `intYears` variable contains the number 1, then the update statement `intYears = intYears + 1` will change the variable's contents to 2. In the syntax for accumulators, *accumulatorVariable* appears on both sides of the assignment operator (=). This syntax tells the computer to add the *value* to (or subtract the *value* from) the *accumulatorVariable* first, and then place the result back in the *accumulatorVariable*. If the `dblBalance` and `dblInterest` variables contain the numbers 2015.41 and 10.15, respectively, then the update statement `dblBalance = dblBalance + dblInterest` will change the `dblBalance` variable's contents to 2025.56.

Updating Counters and Accumulators

<u>Syntax for counters</u>
counterVariable = *counterVariable* {+ | –} *constantValue*

<u>Examples for counters</u>
```
intYears = intYears + 1
intStudents = intStudents - 1
intEvenNum = intEvenNum + 2
```

<u>Syntax for accumulators</u>
accumulatorVariable = *accumulatorVariable* {+ | –} *value*

<u>Examples for accumulators</u>
```
dblBalance = dblBalance + dblInterest
intSum = intSum + intNum
dblTotalSales = dblTotalSales + dblSales
```

Figure 6-14 Syntax and examples of update statements for counters and accumulators

Ch06-Eddie Game video

Game programs make extensive use of counters and accumulators. The partial game program shown in Figure 6-15, for example, uses a counter to keep track of the number of smiley faces that Eddie (the character in the figure) destroys. After he destroys three smiley faces and then jumps through the manhole, he advances to the next level in the game, as shown in the figure.

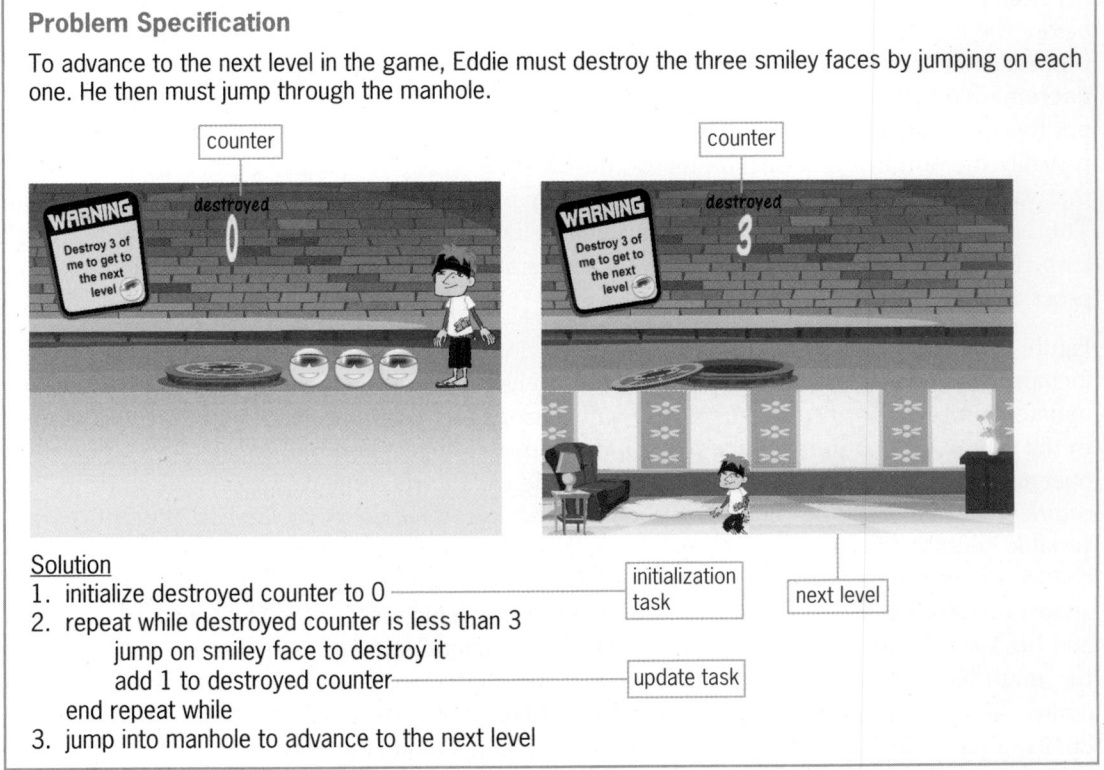

Problem Specification

To advance to the next level in the game, Eddie must destroy the three smiley faces by jumping on each one. He then must jump through the manhole.

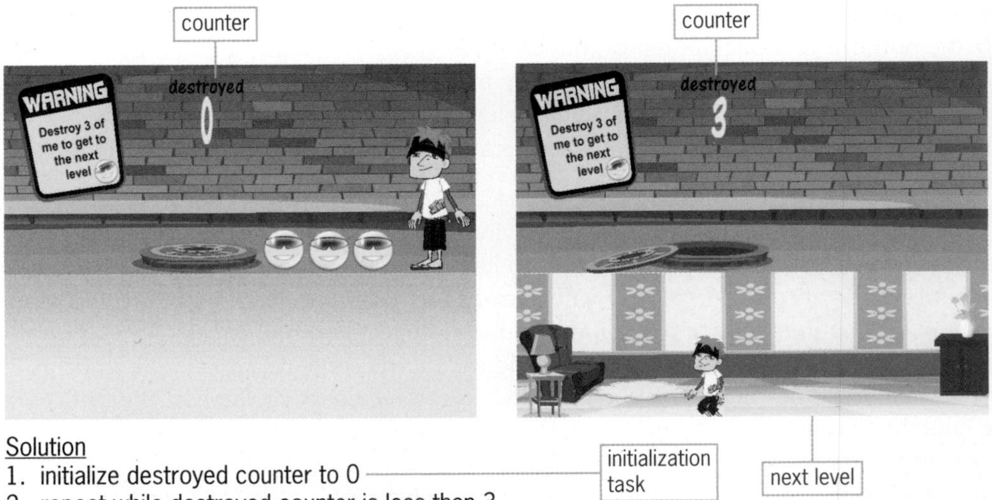

<u>Solution</u>
1. initialize destroyed counter to 0 — initialization task
2. repeat while destroyed counter is less than 3
   jump on smiley face to destroy it
   add 1 to destroyed counter — update task
   end repeat while
3. jump into manhole to advance to the next level

Figure 6-15 Example of a partial game program that uses a counter

The Addition Application

Figure 6-16 shows the problem specification for the Addition application. The application uses an accumulator to add together (accumulate) the numbers entered by the user. In this application, the accumulator is a class-level variable named `intSum`. The figure also shows the pseudocode for the Add and Start Over buttons' Click event procedures. In addition, it shows a sample run of the application.

Problem Specification

Create an application that calculates the sum of the integers entered by the user, and also displays a list of the integers and their sum. The application's interface should provide a text box for entering the integers, and another text box for displaying the list of integers entered. It also should provide a label for displaying the sum. In addition to an Exit button, the interface should provide an Add button and a Start Over button. The Add button's Click event procedure should perform the calculation and display tasks, using an accumulator to total the integers. The accumulator should be a class-level Integer variable.The Start Over button should reset the accumulator to 0 and also clear the existing data from the screen. Use the following names for the controls in the interface: txtNumber, txtList, lblSum, btnAdd, btnStartOver, and btnExit. Use the following names for the variables: intNum and intSum (accumulator).

Add button's Click event procedure
1. display (in the txtList control) the integer entered by the user
2. add the integer entered by the user to the intSum accumulator
3. display the intSum accumulator's value in the lblSum control
4. send the focus to the txtNumber control and select its existing text

Start Over button's Click event procedure
1. reset intSum accumulator to 0
2. clear the contents of the txtNumber, txtList, and lblSum controls
3. send the focus to the txtNumber control

Sample run

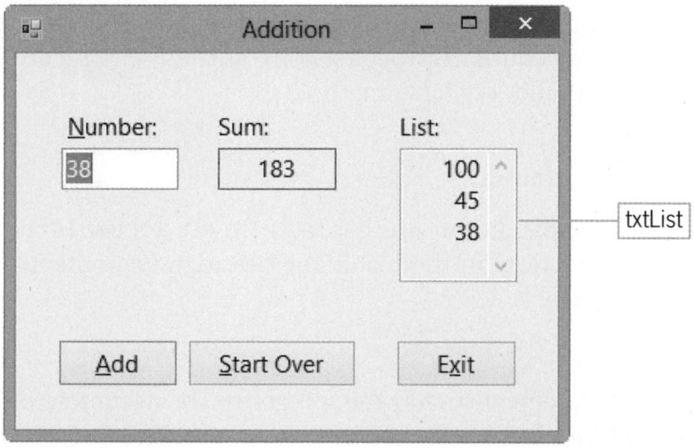

Figure 6-16 Problem specification, pseudocode, and a sample run for the Addition application

The txtList control in the interface has its Multiline and ReadOnly properties set to True, and its ScrollBars property set to Vertical. When a text box's **Multiline property** is set to True, the text box can both accept and display multiple lines of text; otherwise, only one line of text can be entered in the text box. Changing a text box's **ReadOnly property** from its default value (False) to True prevents the user from changing the contents of the text box during run time. A text box's **ScrollBars property** specifies whether the text box has no scroll bars (the default), a horizontal scroll bar, a vertical scroll bar, or both horizontal and vertical scroll bars. The txtList control also has its TextAlign property set to Right.

First, you will code the Add button's Click event procedure.

START HERE

To code the Add button's Click event procedure:

1. Open the Addition Solution (Addition Solution.sln) file contained in the VB2012\Chap06\Addition Solution folder. If necessary, open the designer window.
2. Open the Code Editor window. Replace <your name> and <current date> in the comments with your name and the current date, respectively.
3. Open the code template for the btnAdd control's Click event procedure. Enter the following comments. Press **Enter** twice after typing the second comment.

   ' accumulates the numbers
   ' entered by the user

4. Now type the following Dim statement and then press **Enter** twice:

   Dim intNum As Integer

5. Step 1 in the pseudocode for the Add button is to display (in the txtList control) the integer entered by the user. Enter the following comment and assignment statement. Press **Enter** twice after typing the assignment statement.

   ```
   ' display number in the list
   txtList.Text = txtList.Text &
       txtNumber.Text & ControlChars.NewLine
   ```

6. Step 2 is to add the integer entered by the user to the `intSum` accumulator. Before you can enter the appropriate assignment statement, you need to convert the user's input to a number. You also need to declare the `intSum` variable, which should be a class-level Integer variable. A class-level variable is appropriate in this case because the variable will need to be used by two different procedures: the Add button's Click event procedure and the Start Over button's Click event procedure. First, you'll convert the user's input to a number. Enter the following comment and TryParse method:

   ```
   ' convert input to a number
   Integer.TryParse(txtNumber.Text, intNum)
   ```

7. Next, you'll declare the class-level variable. Locate the `' class-level accumulator` comment in the form's Declarations section. In the blank line below the comment, enter the following declaration statement:

   Private intSum As Integer

8. Now you can enter the assignment statement to add the integer to the accumulator. Return to the btnAdd_Click procedure. Click the **blank line above the End Sub clause**. Enter the following comment and assignment statement:

   ```
   ' add the number to the sum
   intSum = intSum + intNum
   ```

9. The last two steps in the Add button's pseudocode are to display the accumulator's value in the appropriate label control and then send the focus to the txtNumber control and select its existing text. Enter the comments and lines of code indicated in Figure 6-17.

```
Private Sub btnAdd_Click(sender As Object,
e As EventArgs) Handles btnAdd.Click
    ' accumulates the numbers
    ' entered by the user

     Dim intNum As Integer

     ' display number in the list
     txtList.Text = txtList.Text &
         txtNumber.Text & ControlChars.NewLine

     ' convert input to a number
     Integer.TryParse(txtNumber.Text, intNum)
     ' add the number to the sum
     intSum = intSum + intNum
     ' display the sum
     lblSum.Text = intSum.ToString()
     ' send the focus and select the text
     txtNumber.Focus()
     txtNumber.SelectAll()
End Sub
```

enter these comments and lines of code

Figure 6-17 Completed btnAdd_Click procedure

In the next set of steps, you will test the btnAdd_Click procedure to verify that it is working correctly.

To test the Add button's Click event procedure:

START HERE

1. Save the solution and then start the application. Type the following three numbers, pressing Enter after typing each one: **100**, **45**, and **38**. The three numbers appear in the txtList control, and 183 appears in the Sum box, as shown earlier in Figure 6-16.
2. Now type the following three numbers, pressing Enter after typing each one: **87**, **450**, and **7**. The number 727 appears in the Sum box, and a scroll box appears on the txtList control. The scroll box allows you to view the numbers that are not currently displayed in the control. See Figure 6-18.

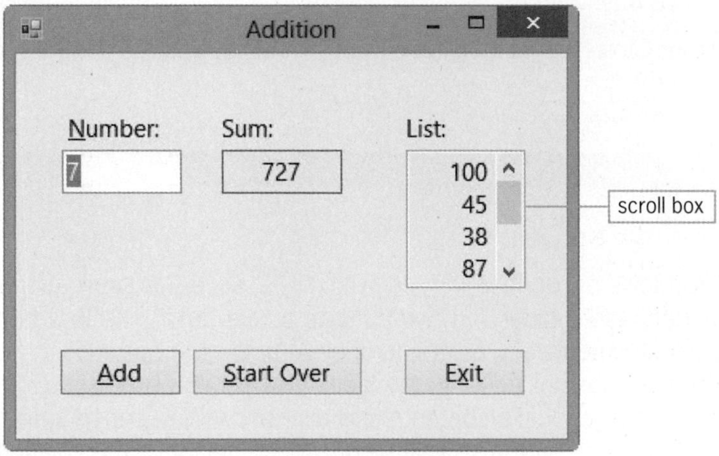

Figure 6-18 Scroll box on the txtList control

3. Use the scroll box on the txtList control to scroll through the list of numbers contained in the txtList control, and then click the **Exit** button.

Next, you will complete the Addition application by coding its Start Over button's Click event procedure.

START HERE

To code and then test the Start Over button's Click event procedure:

1. Open the code template for the btnStartOver control's Click event procedure. Type the following comment and then press **Enter** twice:

   ' resets accumulator, clears screen, sets focus

2. According to its pseudocode (shown earlier in Figure 6-16), the procedure should reset the accumulator variable to 0. It also should clear the contents of the two text boxes and the lblSum control, and then send the focus to the txtNumber control. Enter the five lines of code indicated in Figure 6-19.

```
Private Sub btnStartOver_Click(sender As Object,
e As EventArgs) Handles btnStartOver.Click
    ' resets accumulator, clears screen, sets focus

    intSum = 0
    txtNumber.Text = String.Empty
    txtList.Text = String.Empty
    lblSum.Text = String.Empty
    txtNumber.Focus()

End Sub
```

enter these five lines of code

Figure 6-19 Completed btnStartOver_Click procedure

3. Save the solution and then start the application. Type any three numbers, pressing Enter after typing each one. Then click the **Start Over** button. The button's Click event procedure clears the contents of the txtNumber, txtList, and lblSum controls.
4. Recall that the Start Over button's Click event procedure also resets the `intSum` accumulator variable to 0. To verify that fact, type the following two numbers, pressing Enter after typing each one: **2** and **5**. The correct sum, 7, appears in the Sum box.
5. Click the **Exit** button. Close the Code Editor window and then close the solution.

YOU DO IT 3!

Create a Visual Basic Windows application named YouDoIt 3. Save the application in the VB2012\Chap06 folder. Add a label and two buttons to the form. The first button's Click event procedure should keep track of the number of times the button is clicked, always displaying the current count in the label. The second button's Click event procedure should clear the label's contents and also allow the user to start counting from 0 again. Code each button's Click event procedure. Save the solution and then start and test the application. Close the solution.

The Sales Express Application

Figure 6-20 shows the problem specification for the Sales Express application, which uses a loop, a counter, and an accumulator to calculate the average sales amount entered by the sales manager. The figure also shows the pseudocode for the Calculate and Start Over buttons' Click event procedures. In addition, it shows a sample run of the application.

Problem Specification

Sales Express wants an application that allows the sales manager to enter each salesperson's annual sales amount, and then calculate and display the average sales amount. The application's interface should provide a Calculate button for these tasks. The button's Click event procedure should use the InputBox function for entering the sales amounts; it should display the amounts in a text box in the interface. The procedure should use a counter to keep track of the number of sales amounts entered and an accumulator to total the amounts. When the sales manager has finished entering the sales amounts, the procedure should calculate the average amount by dividing the value stored in the accumulator by the value stored in the counter. It then should display the average amount in a label control. If the sales manager does not enter any sales amounts, the procedure should display the message "N/A" (for "not available") in the label control. The interface should also provide a Start Over button that clears the previous sales amounts entered by the user and also the average sales amount. Use the following names for the controls in the interface: txtList, lblAvg, btnCalc, btnStartOver, and btnExit. Use the following names for the variables: strInputSales, decSales, intNumSales (counter), decTotalSales (accumulator), and decAvg.

<u>Calculate button's Click event procedure</u>

```
1. initialize the intNumSales counter to 0
2. initialize the decTotalSales accumulator to 0
3. get a sales amount from the user                         [priming read]
4. repeat while the user entered a sales amount
       display the sales amount in the txtlist control
       add 1 to the intNumSales counter
       add the sales amount to the decTotalSales accumulator
       get a sales amount from the user                     [update read]
   end repeat while
5. if the value in the intNumSales counter is greater than 0
       average sales = decTotalSales accumulator / intNumSales counter
       display average sales in lblAvg control
   else
       display "N/A" in lblAvg control
   end if
```

<u>Start Over button's Click event procedure</u>

clear the contents of the txtList and lblAvg controls

Figure 6-20 Problem specification, pseudocode, and a sample run for the Sales Express application *(continues)*

(continued)

Sample run

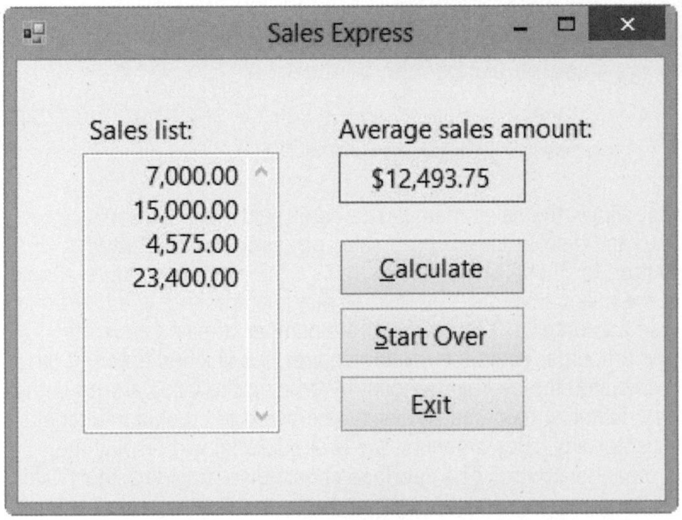

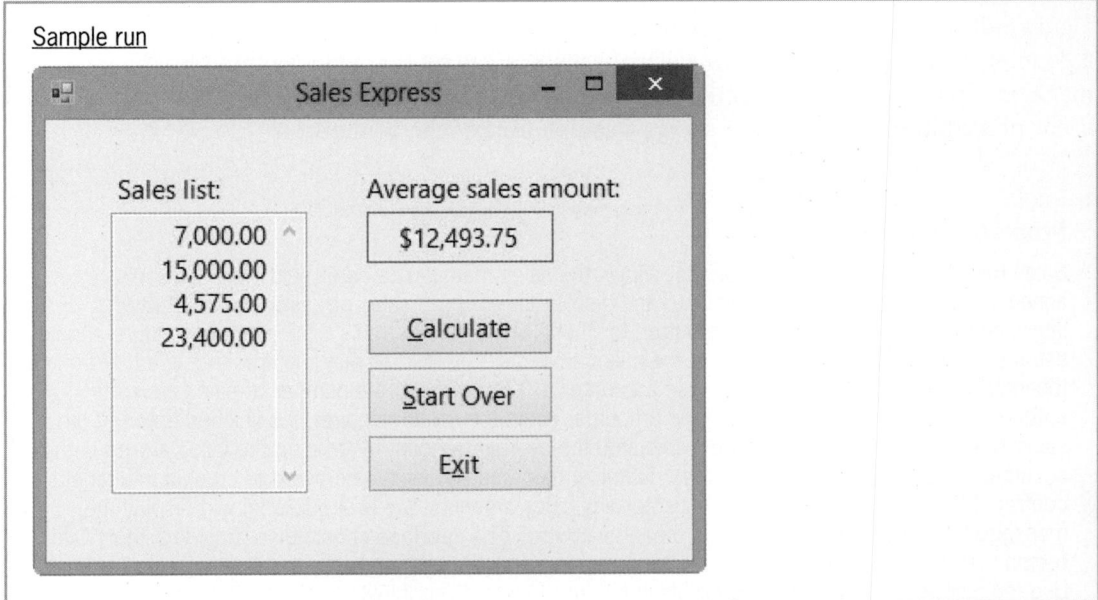

Figure 6-20 Problem specification, pseudocode, and a sample run for the Sales Express application

Notice that the Calculate button's pseudocode contains two "get a sales amount from the user" instructions. One of the instructions appears above the loop, and the other appears as the last instruction in the loop body. The "get a sales amount from the user" instruction above the loop is referred to as the **priming read** because it is used to prime (prepare or set up) the loop. The priming read initializes the loop condition by providing its first value. In this case, the priming read gets only the first sales amount from the user. Because the loop is a pretest loop, the first sales amount determines whether the instructions in the loop body are processed at all. If the loop body instructions *are* processed, the "get a sales amount from the user" instruction in the loop body gets the remaining sales amounts (if any) from the user. This instruction is referred to as the **update read** because it allows the user to update the value of the input item (in this case, the sales amount) associated with the loop's condition. The update read is often an exact copy of the priming read.

The importance of the update read cannot be stressed enough. If you don't include the update read in the loop body, there will be no way to enter a value that will stop the loop after it has been processed the first time. This is because the priming read is processed only once and gets only the first sales amount from the user. Without the update read, the loop will have no way of stopping on its own. As you learned earlier, a loop that has no way to end is called an infinite (or endless) loop. Recall that you can stop an infinite loop by clicking DEBUG on the menu bar and then clicking Stop Debugging.

Figure 6-21 shows the Calculate button's Click event procedure in flowchart form, with the priming and update reads shaded. Notice that the priming read's parallelogram is located above the diamond that represents the loop's condition, while the update read's parallelogram is located at the end of the loop body.

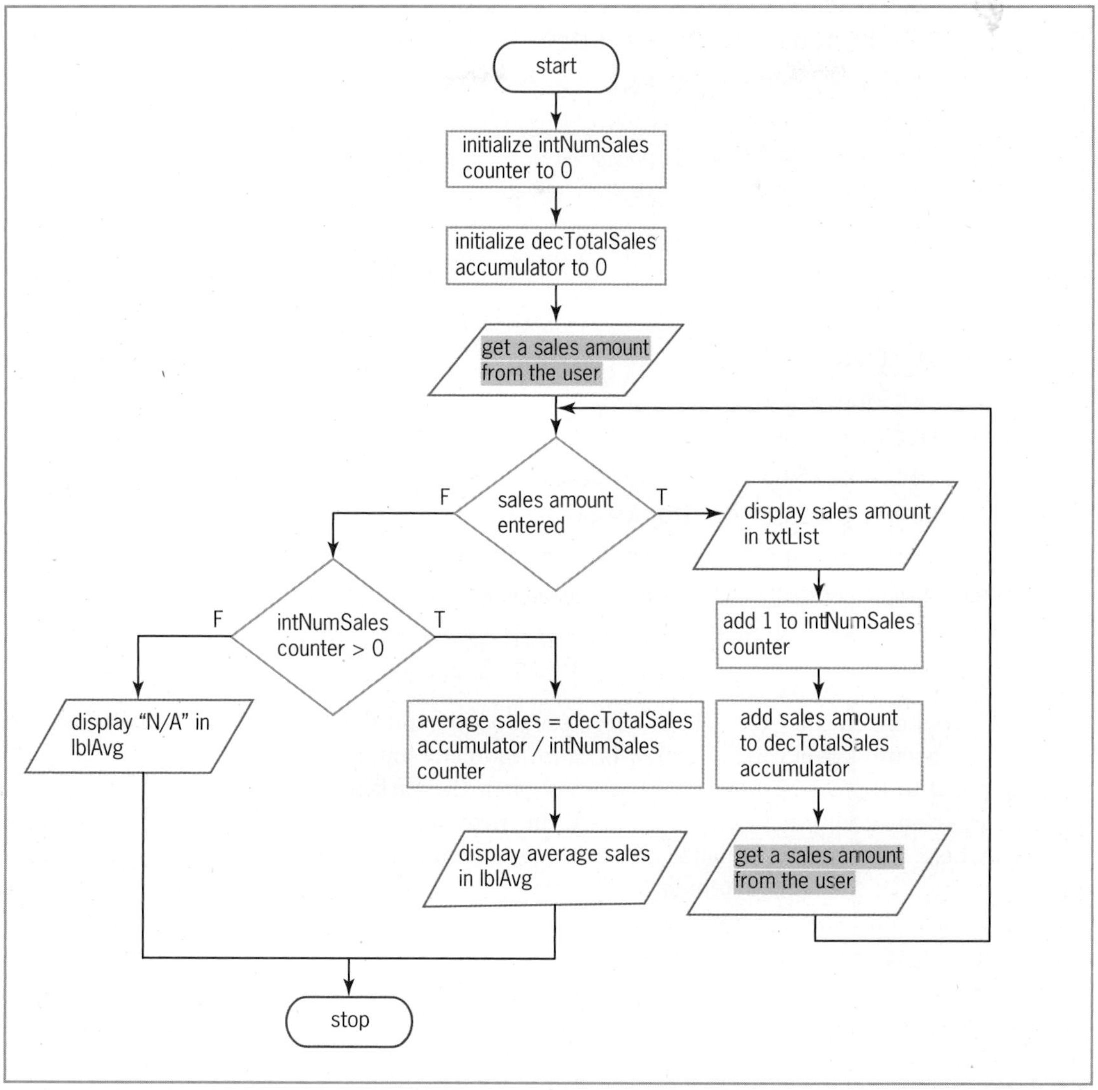

Figure 6-21 Flowchart for the Calculate button's Click event procedure

To open the Sales Express application:

START HERE

1. Open the Sales Express Solution (Sales Express Solution.sln) file contained in the VB2012\Chap06\Sales Express Solution folder. If necessary, open the designer window.
2. Open the Code Editor window. Replace <your name> and <current date> in the comments with your name and the current date, respectively.
3. Locate the btnCalc_Click procedure. The procedure declares the two named constants and five variables shown in Figure 6-22. The named constants and `strInputSales` variable will be used, along with the InputBox function, to get a sales amount from the user. The `decSales` variable will store the sales amount after it has been converted to Decimal. The `intNumSales` variable will be the counter that keeps track of the number of sales amounts entered, and the `decTotalSales` variable will accumulate the sales amounts. The `decAvgSales` variable will store the average sales amount after it has been calculated.

```
Private Sub btnCalc_Click(sender As Object, e As
    ' calculates the average sales amount

    Const strPROMPT As String =
        "Enter a sales amount. " &
        ControlChars.NewLine &
        "Click Cancel or leave blank to end."
    Const strTITLE As String = "Sales Entry"
    Dim strInputSales As String
    Dim decSales As Decimal
    Dim intNumSales As Integer
    Dim decTotalSales As Decimal
    Dim decAvgSales As Decimal
```

Figure 6-22 Named constants and variables declared in the btnCalc_Click procedure

The first two steps in the Calculate button's pseudocode and flowchart are to initialize the counter and accumulator variables to 0. Because the Dim statement automatically assigns the number 0 to Integer and Decimal variables when the variables are created, you do not need to enter any additional code to initialize the `intNumSales` and `decTotalSales` variables. In cases where you need to initialize a counter or accumulator to a value other than 0, you can do so either in the Dim statement that declares the variable or in an assignment statement. For example, to initialize the `intNumSales` variable to the number 1, you could use either the declaration statement `Dim intNumSales As Integer = 1` or the assignment statement `intNumSales = 1` in your code. However, to use the assignment statement, the `intNumSales` variable must be declared before the assignment statement is processed.

START HERE

To code and then test the Calculate button's Click event procedure:

1. The next step in the pseudocode and flowchart gets the first sales amount from the user. Click the **blank line** below the `' get first sales amount` comment and then enter the following assignment statement:

   strInputSales = InputBox(strPROMPT, strTITLE, "0")

2. Next, you need to enter a pretest loop whose condition determines whether the user entered a sales amount. If no sales amount was entered, the InputBox function will return the empty string. In this case, you want the loop body instructions processed only when the function returns a value other than the empty string. Click the **blank line** below the `' repeat as long as the user enters a sales amount` comment and then enter the following Do While clause. When you press Enter after typing the clause, the Code Editor will automatically enter a Loop clause for you.

   Do While strInputSales <> String.Empty

3. If the user entered a sales amount, the instructions in the loop body should display the sales amount in the txtList control, then update the counter and accumulator, and then get another sales amount from the user. Enter the loop body indicated in Figure 6-23.

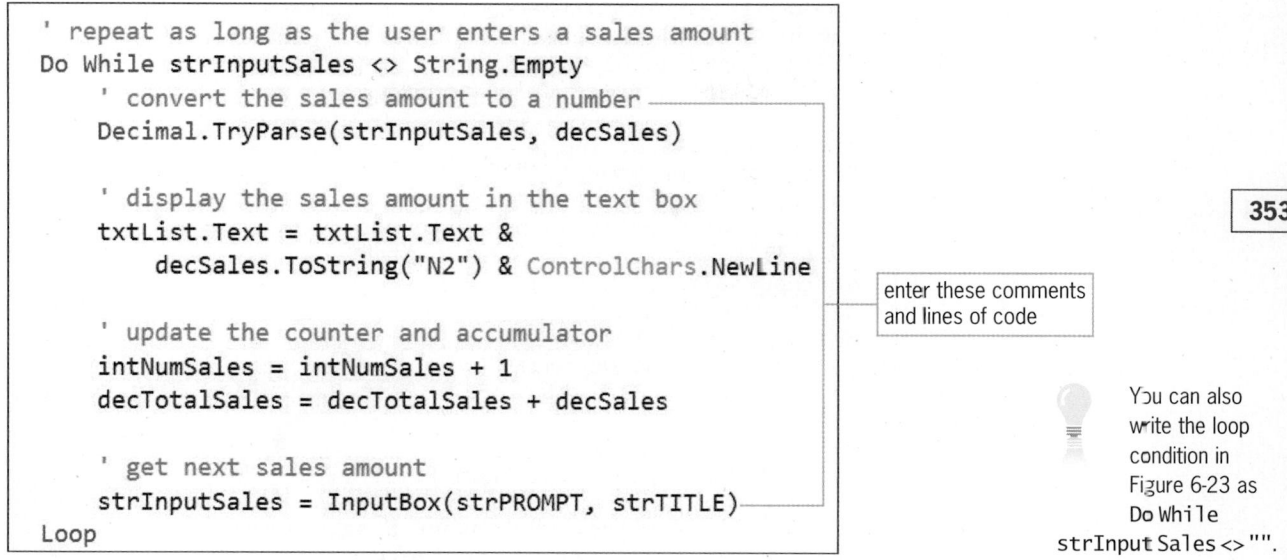

```
' repeat as long as the user enters a sales amount
Do While strInputSales <> String.Empty
    ' convert the sales amount to a number
    Decimal.TryParse(strInputSales, decSales)

    ' display the sales amount in the text box
    txtList.Text = txtList.Text &
        decSales.ToString("N2") & ControlChars.NewLine

    ' update the counter and accumulator
    intNumSales = intNumSales + 1
    decTotalSales = decTotalSales + decSales

    ' get next sales amount
    strInputSales = InputBox(strPROMPT, strTITLE)
Loop
```

enter these comments and lines of code

Figure 6-23 Loop entered in the btnCalc_Click procedure

You can also write the loop condition in Figure 6-23 as `Do While strInputSales <> ""`.

4. When the user has finished entering sales amounts, the loop ends and processing continues with Step 5 in the pseudocode (or the second diamond in the flowchart). Step 5 is a selection structure whose condition verifies that the value stored in the `intNumSales` variable is greater than the number 0. This verification is necessary because the first instruction in the selection structure's true path uses the variable as the divisor when calculating the average sales amount. Before using a variable as the divisor in an expression, you should always verify that the variable does not contain the number 0 because, as in mathematics, division by zero is not possible. Dividing by zero in a procedure will cause the application to end abruptly with an error. Click the **blank line** below the `' verify that the counter is greater than 0` comment. Enter the following If clause. When you press Enter after typing the clause, the Code Editor will automatically enter an End If clause for you.

   If intNumSales > 0 Then

5. If the counter's value is greater than 0, the selection structure's true path should calculate and display the average sales amount; otherwise, it should display the string "N/A". Complete the selection structure's true and false paths as indicated in Figure 6-24.

```
Private Sub btnCalc_Click(sender As Object,
e As EventArgs) Handles btnCalc.Click
    ' calculates the average sales amount

    Const strPROMPT As String =
        "Enter a sales amount. " &
        ControlChars.NewLine &
        "Click Cancel or leave blank to end."
    Const strTITLE As String = "Sales Entry"
    Dim strInputSales As String
    Dim decSales As Decimal
    Dim intNumSales As Integer
    Dim decTotalSales As Decimal
    Dim decAvgSales As Decimal

    ' get first sales amount
    strInputSales = InputBox(strPROMPT, strTITLE, "0")

    ' repeat as long as the user enters a sales amount
    Do While strInputSales <> String.Empty
        ' convert the sales amount to a number
        Decimal.TryParse(strInputSales, decSales)

        ' display the sales amount in the text box
        txtList.Text = txtList.Text &
            decSales.ToString("N2") & ControlChars.NewLine

        ' update the counter and accumulator
        intNumSales = intNumSales + 1
        decTotalSales = decTotalSales + decSales

        ' get next sales amount
        strInputSales = InputBox(strPROMPT, strTITLE)
    Loop

    ' verify that the counter is greater than 0
    If intNumSales > 0 Then
        decAvgSales = decTotalSales / intNumSales
        lblAvg.Text = decAvgSales.ToString("C2")
    Else
        lblAvg.Text = "N/A"
    End If
End Sub
```

enter these four lines of code

Figure 6-24 Completed btnCalc_Click procedure

6. Save the solution and then start the application. Click the **Calculate** button. Use the Sales Entry dialog box to enter the following four sales amounts, one at a time: **7000**, **15000**, **4575**, and **23400**.

7. Click the **Cancel** button in the dialog box. The sales amounts appear in the txtList control, and the number $12,493.75 appears in the Average sales amount box, as shown earlier in Figure 6-20.

8. Click the **Exit** button.

To complete the application, you just need to code the Start Over button's Click event procedure. According to its pseudocode, shown earlier in Figure 6-20, the procedure is responsible for clearing the contents of the txtList and lblAvg controls.

To code and then test the Start Over button's Click event procedure:

START HERE

1. Open the code template for the btnStartOver control's Click event procedure. Enter the comment and code shown in Figure 6-25.

```
Private Sub btnStartOver_Click(sender As Object,
    ' clear screen

    txtList.Text = String.Empty
    lblAvg.Text = String.Empty
End Sub
```

enter this comment and these two lines of code

Figure 6-25 Completed btnStartOver_Click procedure

2. Save the solution and then start the application. Click the **Calculate** button. Use the Sales Entry dialog box to enter any two sales amounts, one at a time, and then click the **Cancel** button. The sales amounts and average sales amount appear in the interface.
3. Click the **Start Over** button to clear the sales amounts and average sales amount from interface. Click the **Exit** button. Close the Code Editor window and then close the solution.

YOU DO IT 4!

Create a Visual Basic Windows application named YouDoIt 4. Save the application in the VB2012\Chap06 folder. Add three labels and a button to the form. The button's Click event procedure should allow the user to enter one or more prices. It then should display (in the labels) the number of prices entered, the total of the prices entered, and the average price entered. If the user does not enter any numbers, the procedure should display the string "None" in the three labels. Code the button's Click event procedure using a pretest loop and the InputBox function. Save the solution and then start and test the application. Close the solution.

Arithmetic Assignment Operators

In addition to the standard arithmetic operators listed in Figure 2-34 in Chapter 2, Visual Basic also provides several arithmetic assignment operators. You can use the **arithmetic assignment operators** to abbreviate an assignment statement that contains an arithmetic operator. However, the assignment statement must have the following format, in which *variableName* is the name of the same variable: *variableName* = *variableName arithmeticOperator value*. For example, you can use the multiplication assignment operator (*=) to abbreviate the statement `dblPrice = dblPrice * 1.05` as follows: `dblPrice *= 1.05`. Both statements tell the computer to multiply the contents of the `dblPrice` variable by 1.05 and then store the result in the `dblPrice` variable.

Figure 6-26 shows the syntax for using an arithmetic assignment operator. Notice that each arithmetic assignment operator consists of an arithmetic operator followed immediately by the assignment operator (=). The arithmetic assignment operators do not contain a space; in other words, the multiplication assignment operator is *=, not * =. Including a space in an arithmetic assignment operator is a common syntax error. Figure 6-26 also includes examples of using arithmetic assignment operators to abbreviate assignment statements. To abbreviate an assignment statement, you simply remove the variable name that appears on the left side of the assignment operator (=), and then put the assignment operator immediately after the arithmetic operator.

Arithmetic Assignment Operators

Syntax
variableName arithmeticAssignmentOperator value

Operator	Purpose
+=	addition assignment
-=	subtraction assignment
*=	multiplication assignment
/=	division assignment

Example 1
Original statement: `intAge = intAge + 1`
Abbreviated statement: `intAge += 1`
Both statements add 1 to the number stored in the `intAge` variable and then assign the result to the variable.

Example 2
Original statement: `decPrice = decPrice - decDiscount`
Abbreviated statement: `decPrice -= decDiscount`
Both statements subtract the number stored in the `decDiscount` variable from the number stored in the `decPrice` variable and then assign the result to the `decPrice` variable.

Example 3
Original statement: `dblPrice = dblPrice * 1.05`
Abbreviated statement: `dblPrice *= 1.05`
Both statements multiply the number stored in the `dblPrice` variable by 1.05 and then assign the result to the variable.

Example 4
Original statement: `dblNum = dblNum / 2`
Abbreviated statement: `dblNum /= 2`
Both statements divide the number stored in the `dblNum` variable by 2 and then assign the result to the variable.

Figure 6-26 Syntax and examples of the arithmetic assignment operators

START HERE

To use the arithmetic assignment operators in the Sales Express application:

1. Use Windows to make a copy of the Sales Express Solution folder. Rename the copy Sales Express Solution-Arithmetic Assignment.
2. Open the Sales Express Solution (Sales Express Solution.sln) file contained in the Sales Express Solution-Arithmetic Assignment folder. Open the designer window.
3. Open the Code Editor window. Locate the btnCalc_Click procedure. Modify the statements that update the counter and accumulator variables as shown in Figure 6-27.

```
' update the counter and accumulator
intNumSales += 1
decTotalSales += decSales
```

modify these two statements as shown

Figure 6-27 Modified update statements using arithmetic assignment operators

4. Save the solution and then start the application. Click the **Calculate** button. Use the Sales Entry dialog box to enter the following three sales amounts: **100**, **140**, and **220**. Click the **Cancel** button in the dialog box. The sales amounts appear in the txtList control, and the number $153.33 appears in the Average sales amount box.
5. Click the **Exit** button. Close the Code Editor window and then close the solution.

Note: You have learned a lot so far in this lesson. You may want to take a break at this point before continuing.

The For...Next Statement

Unlike the Do...Loop statement, which can be used to code both pretest and posttest loops, the **For...Next statement** can be used to code only a specific type of pretest loop, called a counter-controlled loop. A **counter-controlled loop** is a loop whose processing is controlled by a counter. You use a counter-controlled loop when you want the computer to process the loop instructions a precise number of times. Although you can also use the Do...Loop statement to code a counter-controlled loop, the For...Next statement provides a more compact and convenient way of writing that type of loop.

Figure 6-28 shows the For...Next statement's syntax and includes examples of using the statement. It also shows the tasks performed by the computer when processing the statement. You enter the loop body, which contains the instructions you want the computer to repeat, between the statement's For and Next clauses. The *counterVariableName* that appears in both clauses is the name of a numeric variable. The computer will use the variable to keep track of (in other words, count) the number of times the loop body instructions are processed. Although, technically, you do not need to specify the name of the counter variable in the Next clause, doing so is highly recommended because it makes your code more self-documenting.

For...Next Statement

Syntax

For *counterVariableName* [**As** *dataType*] = *startValue* **To** *endValue* [**Step** *stepValue*]
    loop body instructions
Next *counterVariableName*

stepValue	Loop body processed when	Loop ends when
positive number	counter's value <= *endValue*	counter's value > *endValue*
negative number	counter's value >= *endValue*	counter's value < *endValue*

Example 1

```
For intNum As Integer = 10 To 12
    MessageBox.Show(intNum.ToString)
Next intNum
```

loop body

displays 10, 11, and 12 in message boxes

Example 2

```
Dim strCity As String
For intX As Integer = 5 To 1 Step -1
    strCity = InputBox("City:", "City Entry")
    txtCities.Text = txtCities.Text &
        strCity & ControlChars.NewLine
Next intX
```

loop body

displays five city names in the txtCities control

Example 3

```
Dim dblRate As Double
For dblRate = 0.05 To 0.1 Step 0.01
    lblRates.Text = lblRates.Text &
        dblRate.ToString("P0") &
        ControlChars.NewLine
Next dblRate
```

loop body

displays 5 %, 6 %, 7 %, 8 %, 9 %, and 10 % in the lblRates control

Processing tasks

1. If the counter variable is declared in the For clause, the variable is created and then initialized to the *startValue*; otherwise, it is just initialized to the *startValue*. The initialization task is done only once, at the beginning of the loop.
2. The counter's value is compared with the *endValue* to determine whether the loop should end. If the *stepValue* is a positive number, the comparison determines whether the counter's value is greater than the *endValue*. If the *stepValue* is a negative number, the comparison determines whether the counter's value is less than the *endValue*. Notice that the computer evaluates the loop condition before processing the instructions within the loop.
3. If the comparison from task 2 evaluates to True, the loop ends and processing continues with the statement following the Next clause. Otherwise, the loop body instructions are processed and then task 4 is performed.
4. Task 4 is performed only when the comparison from task 2 evaluates to False. In this task, the *stepValue* is added to the counter's value, and then tasks 2, 3, and 4 are repeated until the loop condition evaluates to True.

Figure 6-28 For...Next statement's syntax, examples, and processing tasks

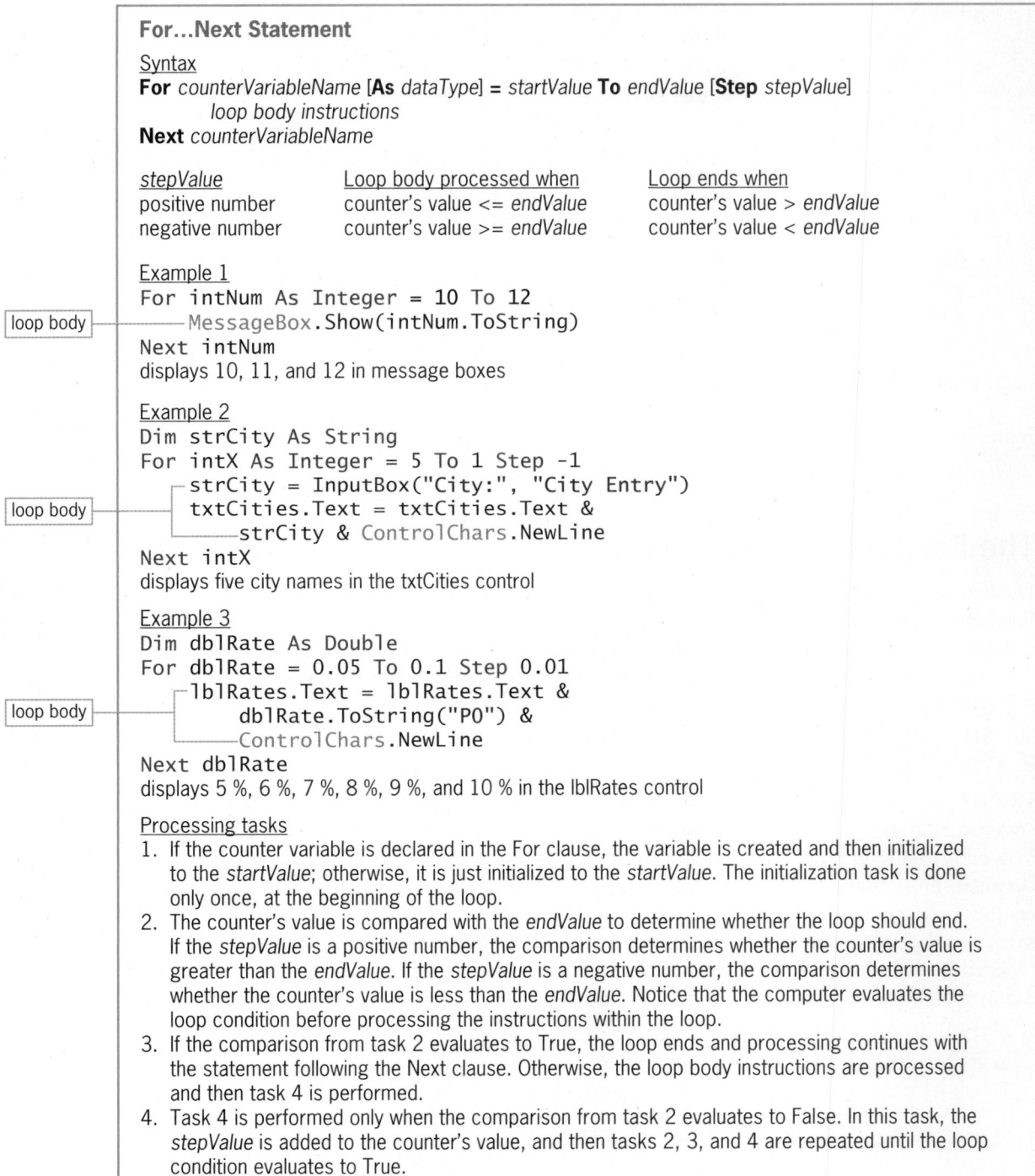

You can use the As *dataType* portion of the For clause to declare the counter variable, as shown in the first two examples in Figure 6-28. When you declare a variable in the For clause, the variable has block scope and can be used only within the For...Next loop. Alternatively, you can declare the counter variable in a Dim statement, as shown in Example 3. As you know, a variable declared in a Dim statement at the beginning of a procedure has procedure scope and can be used within the entire procedure. When deciding where to declare the counter variable, keep in mind that if the variable is needed only by the For...Next loop, then it is a better programming practice to declare the variable in the For clause. As mentioned in Chapter 3, fewer unintentional errors occur in applications when the variables are declared using the minimum scope needed. Block-level variables have the smallest scope, followed by procedure-level variables and then class-level variables. You should declare the counter variable in a Dim statement only when its value is required by statements outside the For...Next loop in the procedure.

The *startValue*, *endValue*, and *stepValue* items in the For clause control the number of times the loop body is processed. The startValue and endValue tell the computer where to begin and end counting, respectively. The stepValue tells the computer how much to count by—in other words, how much to add to the counter variable each time the loop body is processed. If you omit the stepValue, a stepValue of positive 1 is used. In Example 1 in Figure 6-28, the startValue is 10, the endValue is 12, and the stepValue (which is omitted) is 1. Those values tell the computer to start counting at 10 and, counting by 1s, stop at 12—in other words, count 10, 11, and 12. The computer will process the instructions in Example 1's loop body three times.

The startValue, endValue, and stepValue items must be numeric and can be either positive or negative, integer or non-integer. As indicated in Figure 6-28, if the stepValue is a positive number, the startValue must be less than or equal to the endValue for the loop instructions to be processed. For instance, the `For intNum As Integer = 10 To 12` clause is correct, but the `For intNum As Integer = 12 To 10` clause is not correct because you cannot count from 12 (the startValue) to 10 (the endValue) by adding increments of 1 (the stepValue). If, on the other hand, the stepValue is a negative number, then the startValue must be greater than or equal to the endValue for the loop instructions to be processed. As a result, the `For intNum As Integer = 5 To 1 Step -1` clause is correct, but the `For intNum As Integer = 1 To 5 Step -1` clause is not correct because you cannot count from 1 to 5 by adding increments of negative 1. Adding increments of a negative 1 is the same as decrementing by 1.

You can use the `Exit For` statement to exit the For...Next statement before the loop has finished processing. You may need to do this if the computer encounters an error when processing the loop instructions.

Figure 6-29 describes the steps the computer follows when processing the loop shown in Example 1 in Figure 6-28. As Step 2 indicates, the loop's condition is evaluated before the loop body is processed. This is because the loop created by the For...Next statement is a pretest loop. Notice that the `intNum` variable contains the number 13 when the For...Next statement ends. The number 13 is the first integer that is greater than the loop's endValue of 12.

Processing steps for Example 1

1. The For clause creates the `intNum` variable and initializes it to 10.
2. The For clause compares the `intNum` value (10) with the endValue (12) to determine whether the loop should end. 10 is not greater than 12, so the MessageBox.Show method displays the number 10 in a message box, and then the For clause increments `intNum` by 1, giving 11.
3. The For clause compares the `intNum` value (11) with the endValue (12) to determine whether the loop should end. 11 is not greater than 12, so the MessageBox.Show method displays the number 11 in a message box, and then the For clause increments `intNum` by 1, giving 12.
4. The For clause compares the `intNum` value (12) with the endValue (12) to determine whether the loop should end. 12 is not greater than 12, so the MessageBox.Show method displays the number 12 in a message box, and then the For clause increments `intNum` by 1, giving 13.
5. The For clause compares the `intNum` value (13) with the endValue (12) to determine whether the loop should end. 13 is greater than 12, so the loop ends. Processing will continue with the statement following the Next clause.

Figure 6-29 Processing steps for Example 1 in Figure 6-28

Ch06A-For Next video

You will use the For...Next statement to code a different version of the Saving Account application coded earlier in this lesson.

A Different Version of the Savings Account Application

The problem specification for the original Savings Account application is shown earlier in Figure 6-4, along with the pseudocode and code for the Calculate button's Click event procedure. As you may remember, the procedure calculates and displays the balance in a savings account at the end of the year, given the amount of money deposited into the savings account at the beginning of the year and the annual interest rate. A sample run of the original application is shown earlier in Figure 6-5.

Figure 6-30 shows the problem specification for a slightly different version of the Savings Account application. In this version, the Calculate button's Click event procedure will need to display the balance in the savings account at the end of each of five years. Figure 6-30 also shows the modified pseudocode and corresponding code for the Calculate button's Click event procedure. The modifications made to the original problem specification, pseudocode, and code are shaded in the figure. In addition, the figure shows a sample run of the modified application.

Problem Specification

Create an application that displays the balance in a savings account at the end of each of five years, given the amount of money deposited into the savings account at the beginning of the year and the annual interest rate. The interest is compounded annually and no withdrawals or additional deposits are made during any of the years. The interest rate will be entered in decimal form. The application's interface should provide a Calculate button for displaying the account balances.

Pseudocode for the Calculate button's Click event procedure

1. store deposit in balance variable
2. store interest rate in rate variable
3. display Year and Balance column headings
4. repeat for years from 1 to 5 in increments of 1
        interest = balance * rate
        add interest to balance
        display year number and balance
    end repeat for

Code for the Calculate button's Click event procedure

```
Dim dblBalance As Double
Dim dblRate As Double
Dim dblInterest As Double
Double.TryParse(txtDeposit.Text, dblBalance)
Double.TryParse(txtRate.Text, dblRate)
lblBalance.Text = "Year          Balance" &
    ControlChars.NewLine
For intYear As Integer = 1 To 5
    dblInterest = dblBalance * dblRate
    dblBalance = dblBalance + dblInterest
    lblBalance.Text = lblBalance.Text &
        intYear.ToString & "               " &
        dblBalance.ToString("C2") &
        ControlChars.NewLine
Next intYear
```

Figure 6-30 Problem specification, pseudocode, code, and sample run for another version of the Savings Account application *(continues)*

(continued)

Sample run

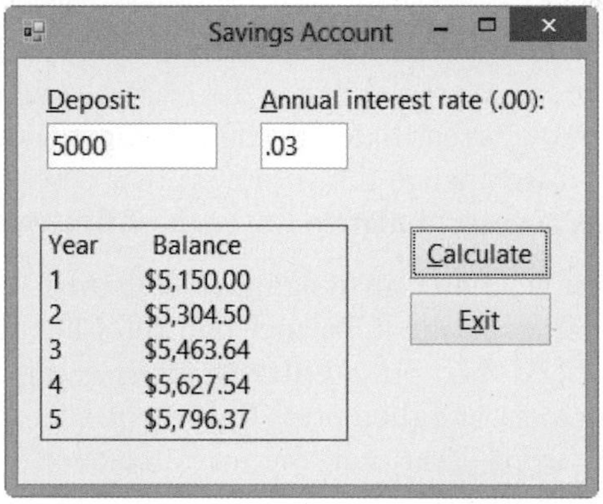

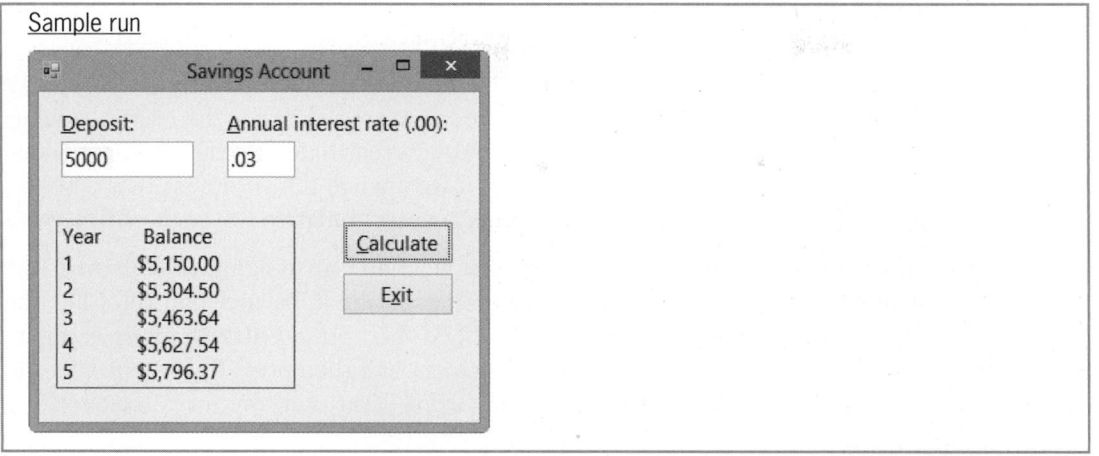

Figure 6-30 Problem specification, pseudocode, code, and sample run for another version of the Savings Account application

Figure 6-31 shows the flowchart for the Calculate button's Click event procedure. Many programmers use a hexagon, which is a six-sided figure, to represent the For clause in a flowchart. Within the hexagon, you record the four items contained in a For clause: *counterVariableName, startValue, endValue,* and *stepValue.* The counterVariableName and stepValue are placed at the top and bottom, respectively, of the hexagon. The startValue and endValue are placed on the left and right side, respectively. The hexagon in Figure 6-31 indicates that the counterVariableName is `intYear`, the startValue is 1, the endValue is 5, and the stepValue is 1. Notice that a greater than sign (>) precedes the endValue in the hexagon. The > sign indicates that the loop will end when the counter variable's value is greater than 5.

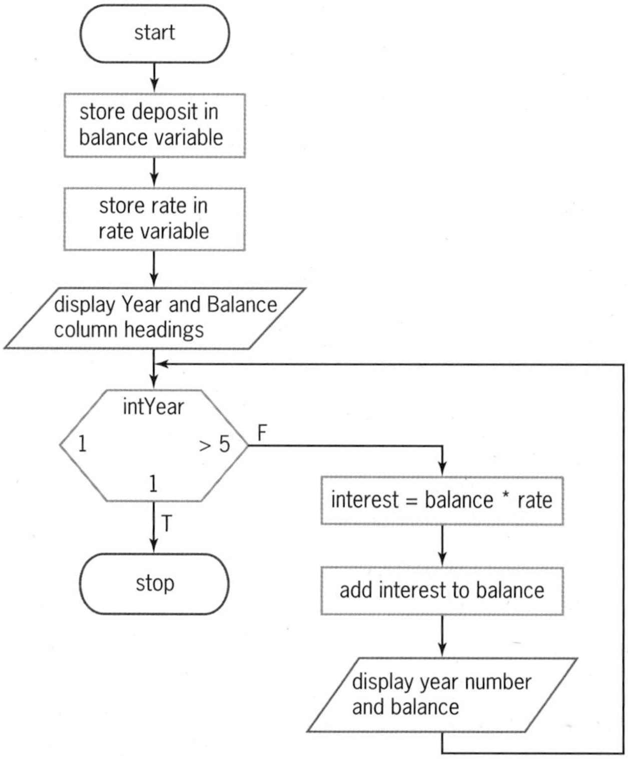

Figure 6-31 Flowchart for the Calculate button's Click event procedure

START HERE

To code and then test this version of the Savings Account application:

1. Open the Savings Solution (Savings Solution.sln) file contained in the VB2012\Chap06\Savings Solution-For Next folder. If necessary, open the designer window.
2. Open the Code Editor window. The window contains the code for the original Savings Account application. Replace <your name> and <current date> in the comments with your name and the current date, respectively. Also change the comment that describes the application's purpose to **Display a savings account balance for each of five years**.
3. Locate the btnCalc_Click procedure. First, you will enter an assignment statement that will display the Year and Balance column headings in the lblBalance control. Click the **blank line below the last TryParse method** and then press **Enter** to insert another blank line. Type the following assignment statement and then press **Enter** twice. Be sure to include eight space characters between the word "Year" and the word "Balance".

   lblBalance.Text = "Year   Balance" &
   ControlChars.NewLine

4. Now, enter the following For clause. When you press Enter after typing the clause, the Code Editor will automatically enter a Next clause for you.

   For intYear As Integer = 1 To 5

5. Change the `Next` clause to **Next intYear**.
6. Move the three assignment statements that appear below the `Next intYear` clause into the For...Next loop, as shown in Figure 6-32. Then modify the last assignment statement as indicated in the figure. Include eight space characters between the quotation marks in the last assignment statement.

```
Private Sub btnCalc_Click(sender As Object,
e As EventArgs) Handles btnCalc.Click
    ' calculate account balance

    Dim dblBalance As Double
    Dim dblRate As Double
    Dim dblInterest As Double

    Double.TryParse(txtDeposit.Text, dblBalance)
    Double.TryParse(txtRate.Text, dblRate)

    lblBalance.Text = "Year        Balance" &
        ControlChars.NewLine

    For intYear As Integer = 1 To 5
        dblInterest = dblBalance * dblRate
        dblBalance = dblBalance + dblInterest

        lblBalance.Text = lblBalance.Text &
            intYear.ToString & "        " &
            dblBalance.ToString("C2") &
            ControlChars.NewLine
    Next intYear
End Sub
```

move these three statements into the loop, then modify the last statement

Figure 6-32 Completed btnCalc_Click procedure

7. Save the solution and then start the application. Type **5000** and **.03** in the Deposit and Annual interest rate boxes and then click the **Calculate** button. The savings account balance at the end of each of the five years appears in the interface, as shown earlier in Figure 6-30.

8. Click the **Exit** button. Close the Code Editor window and then close the solution.

Comparing the For...Next and Do...Loop Statements

As mentioned earlier, you can code a counter-controlled loop using either the For...Next statement or the Do...Loop statement; however, the For...Next statement is more convenient to use. Figure 6-33 shows an example of using both loops to display the string "Hi" three times. Notice that, when using the Do...Loop statement to code a counter-controlled loop, you must include a statement to declare and initialize the counter variable, as well as a statement to update the counter variable. In addition, you must include the appropriate comparison in the Do clause. In a For...Next statement, the declaration, initialization, update, and comparison tasks are handled by the For clause.

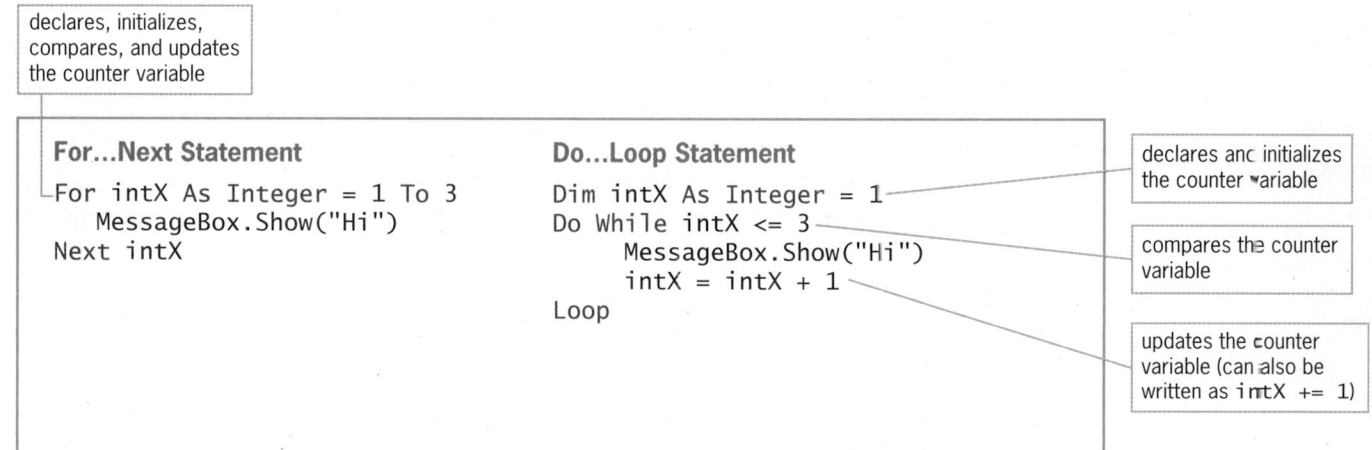

declares, initializes, compares, and updates the counter variable

For...Next Statement

```
For intX As Integer = 1 To 3
   MessageBox.Show("Hi")
Next intX
```

Do...Loop Statement

```
Dim intX As Integer = 1
Do While intX <= 3
     MessageBox.Show("Hi")
     intX = intX + 1
Loop
```

declares and initializes the counter variable

compares the counter variable

updates the counter variable (can also be written as `intX += 1`)

Figure 6-33 Comparison of the For...Next and Do...Loop statements

YOU DO IT 5!

Create a Visual Basic Windows application named YouDoIt 5. Save the application in the VB2012\Chap06 folder. Add two labels and a button to the form. The button's Click event procedure should display the number of integers from 14 through 23 in one of the labels, and the sum of those integers in the other label. Code the procedure using the For...Next statement. Save the solution and then start and test the application. Close the solution.

Lesson A Summary

- To have the computer repeatedly process one or more program instructions while the looping condition is true (or until the loop exit condition has been met):

  Use a repetition structure (loop). You can code a repetition structure in Visual Basic using one of the following statements: For...Next, Do...Loop, and For Each...Next. (The For Each...Next statement is covered in Chapter 9.)

- To use the Do...Loop statement to code a loop:

  Refer to Figure 6-7 for the two versions of the Do...Loop statement's syntax. The Do...Loop statement can be used to code both pretest and posttest loops. In a pretest loop, the loop condition appears in the Do clause; it appears in the Loop clause in a posttest loop. The loop condition must evaluate to a Boolean value.

- To represent the loop condition in a flowchart:

  Use the decision symbol, which is a diamond.

- To stop an endless (infinite) loop:

  Click DEBUG on the menu bar and then click Stop Debugging.

- To use a counter:

  Initialize and update the counter. The initialization is done outside of the loop that uses the counter; the update is done within the loop. You update a counter by either incrementing or decrementing its value by a constant amount, which can be either positive or negative, integer or non-integer.

- To use an accumulator:

  Initialize and update the accumulator. The initialization is done outside of the loop that uses the accumulator; the update is done within the loop. In most cases, you update an accumulator by incrementing (rather than by decrementing) its value by an amount that varies. The amount can be either positive or negative, integer or non-integer.

- To abbreviate an assignment statement:

  Use the arithmetic assignment operators listed in Figure 6-26. The assignment statement you want to abbreviate must follow this format, in which *variableName* is the name of the same variable: *variableName* = *variableName arithmeticOperator value*.

- To use the For...Next statement to code a counter-controlled loop:

  Refer to Figure 6-28 for the For...Next statement's syntax. The statement can be used to code pretest loops only. In the syntax, counterVariableName is the name of a numeric variable that the computer will use to keep track of the number of times the loop body instructions are processed. The number of iterations is controlled by the For clause's startValue, endValue, and stepValue. The startValue, endValue, and stepValue must be numeric and can be positive or negative, integer or non-integer. If you omit the stepValue, a stepValue of positive 1 is used.

- To flowchart a For...Next loop:

  Many programmers use a hexagon to represent the For clause. Inside the hexagon, you record the counter variable's name and its startValue, stepValue, and endValue.

Lesson A Key Terms

Accumulator—a numeric variable used for accumulating (adding together) something

Arithmetic assignment operators—composed of an arithmetic operator followed by the assignment operator; used to abbreviate an assignment statement that has the following format, in which *variableName* is the name of the same variable: *variableName* = *variableName arithmeticOperator value*

Counter—a numeric variable used for counting something

Counter-controlled loop—a loop whose processing is controlled by a counter; the loop body will be processed a precise number of times

Decrementing—decreasing a value

Do...Loop statement—a Visual Basic statement that can be used to code both pretest loops and posttest loops

Endless loop—a loop whose instructions are processed indefinitely; also called an infinite loop

For...Next statement—a Visual Basic statement that is used to code a specific type of pretest loop, called a counter-controlled loop

Incrementing—increasing a value

Infinite loop—another name for an endless loop

Initializing—the process of assigning a beginning value to a memory location, such as a counter or accumulator variable

Loop—another name for the repetition structure

Loop body—the instructions within a loop

Loop exit condition—the requirement that must be met for the computer to stop processing the loop body instructions

Looping condition—the requirement that must be met for the computer to continue processing the loop body instructions

Multiline property—determines whether a text box can accept and display only one line of text or multiple lines of text

Posttest loop—a loop whose condition is evaluated *after* the instructions in its loop body are processed

Pretest loop—a loop whose condition is evaluated *before* the instructions in its loop body are processed

Priming read—the input instruction that appears above the loop that it controls; used to get the first input item from the user

ReadOnly property—controls whether the user is allowed to change the contents of a text box during run time

Repetition structure—the control structure used to repeatedly process one or more program instructions; also called a loop

ScrollBars property—a property of a text box; specifies whether the text box has scroll bars

Update read—the input instruction that appears within a loop and is associated with the priming read

Updating—the process of either adding a number to or subtracting a number from the value stored in a counter or accumulator variable

Lesson A Review Questions

1. Which of the following clauses stops the loop when the value in the `intPopulation` variable is less than the number 5000?

   a. `Do While intPopulation >= 5000`

   b. `Do Until intPopulation < 5000`

   c. `Loop While intPopulation >= 5000`

   d. all of the above

2. Which of the following statements can be used to code a loop whose instructions you want processed 10 times?

   a. Do...Loop

   b. For...Next

   c. either a or b

3. The instructions in a ______________ loop might not be processed at all, whereas the instructions in a ______________ loop are always processed at least once.

   a. posttest, pretest

   b. pretest, posttest

4. How many times will the MessageBox.Show method in the following code be processed?

```
Dim intCount As Integer
Do While intCount > 4
   MessageBox.Show("Hello")
   intCount = intCount + 1
Loop
```

   a. 0

   b. 1

   c. 4

   d. 5

5. How many times will the MessageBox.Show method in the following code be processed?

```
Dim intCount As Integer
Do
   MessageBox.Show("Hello")
   intCount += 1
Loop While intCount > 4
```

   a. 0

   b. 1

   c. 4

   d. 5

6. How many times will the MessageBox.Show method in the following code be processed?

```
For intCount As Integer = 6 To 13 Step 2
   MessageBox.Show("Hello")
Next intCount
```

   a. 3
   b. 4
   c. 5
   d. 8

7. The computer will stop processing the loop in Review Question 6 when the `intCount` variable contains the number ________________.

   a. 11
   b. 12
   c. 13
   d. 14

8. A procedure allows the user to enter one or more values. The first input instruction will get the first value only and is referred to as the ________________ read.

   a. entering
   b. initializer
   c. priming
   d. starter

Refer to Figure 6-34 to answer Review Questions 9 through 12.

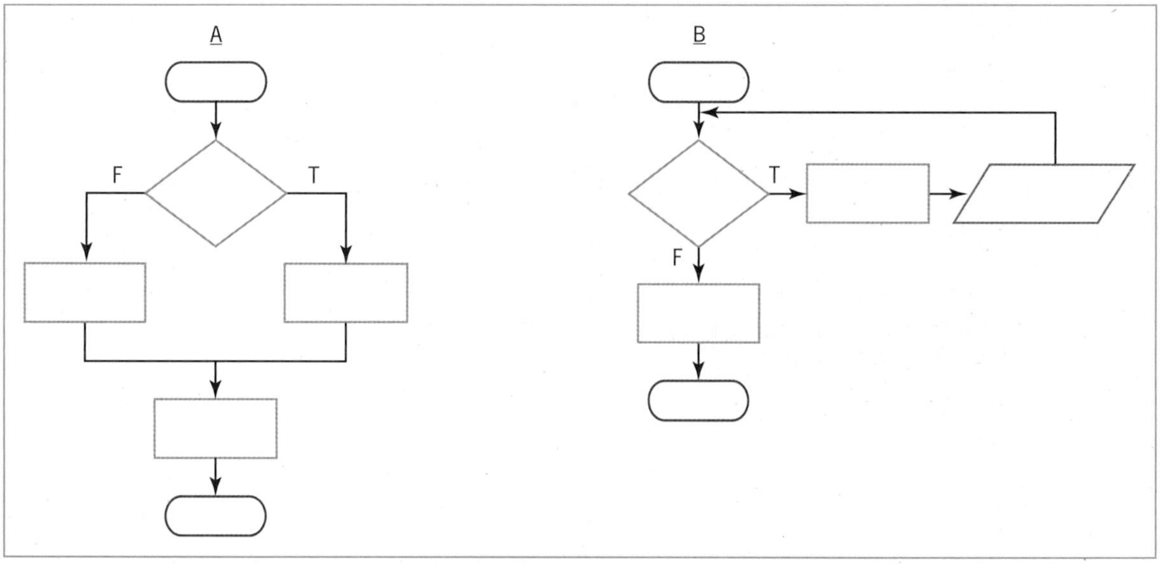

Figure 6-34 Flowcharts for Review Questions 9 through 12 *(continues)*

(continued)

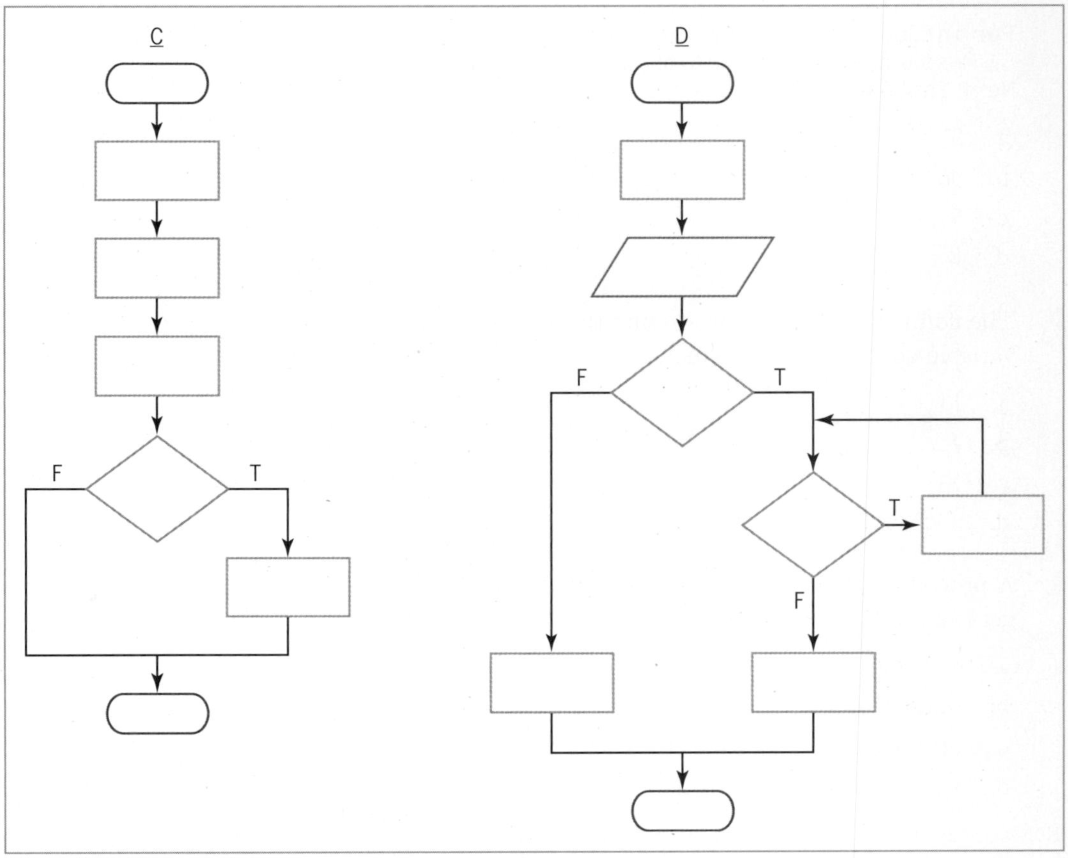

Figure 6-34 Flowcharts for Review Questions 9 through 12

9. Which of the following control structures are used in flowchart A in Figure 6-34? (Select all that apply.)
    a. sequence
    b. selection
    c. repetition

10. Which of the following control structures are used in flowchart B in Figure 6-34? (Select all that apply.)
    a. sequence
    b. selection
    c. repetition

11. Which of the following control structures are used in flowchart C in Figure 6-34? (Select all that apply.)
    a. sequence
    b. selection
    c. repetition

12. Which of the following control structures are used in flowchart D in Figure 6-34? (Select all that apply.)
    a. sequence
    b. selection
    c. repetition

13. Which of the following statements is equivalent to the statement `dblTotal = dblTotal + dblScore`?
    a. `dblTotal += dblScore`
    b. `dblScore += dblTotal`
    c. `dblTotal =+ dblScore`
    d. `dblScore =+ dblTotal`

14. Which of the following For clauses indicates that the loop instructions should be processed as long as the `intX` variable's value is less than 100?
    a. `For intX As Integer = 10 To 100`
    b. `For intX As Integer = 10 To 99`
    c. `For intX As Integer = 10 To 101`
    d. all of the above

15. The loop controlled by the correct For clause from Review Question 14 will end when the `intX` variable contains the number ______________.
    a. 100
    b. 111
    c. 101
    d. 110

Lesson A Exercises

1. Write a Visual Basic Do clause that processes the loop instructions as long as the value in the `intTotal` variable is greater than the number 0. Use the `While` keyword. Now rewrite the Do clause using the `Until` keyword. INTRODUCTORY
2. Write a Visual Basic Do clause that stops the loop when the value in the `intQuantity` variable is less than or equal to the value in the `intOrdered` variable. Use the `Until` keyword. Now rewrite the Do clause using the `While` keyword. INTRODUCTORY
3. Write a Visual Basic Loop clause that processes the loop instructions as long as the value in the `strAnswer` variable is either Y or y. Use the `While` keyword. Now rewrite the Loop clause using the `Until` keyword. INTRODUCTORY
4. Write a Visual Basic Do clause that processes the loop instructions as long as the value in the `strState` variable is not "Finished" (in any case). Use the `While` keyword. Now rewrite the Do clause using the `Until` keyword. INTRODUCTORY
5. What will the following code display in message boxes? INTRODUCTORY

```
Dim intX As Integer
Do While intX < 4
   MessageBox.Show(intX.ToString)
   intX += 1
Loop
```

INTRODUCTORY

6. What will the following code display in message boxes?

```
Dim intX As Integer
Do
  MessageBox.Show(intX.ToString)
  intX = intX + 1
Loop Until intX > 4
```

INTRODUCTORY

7. Write a Visual Basic assignment statement that updates the `intTotal` counter variable by 2.

INTRODUCTORY

8. Write a Visual Basic assignment statement that updates the `decTotal` accumulator variable by the value stored in the `decSales` variable.

INTERMEDIATE

9. Figure 6-35 shows a problem specification, two illustrations, and two solutions containing loops.

   a. Will both loops work when Sherri is one or more steps away from the fountain, as shown in Illustration A? If not, why not?

   b. Will both loops work when Sherri is directly in front of the fountain, as shown in Illustration B? If not, why not?

Problem Specification

Sherri is standing an unknown number of steps away from the Burlington Fountain. Write the instructions that direct Sherri to walk from her current location to the fountain.

Illustration A

Illustration B

Solution 1– pretest loop

```
repeat while you are not directly in front of the fountain
      walk forward
end repeat while
```

Solution 2 – posttest loop

```
repeat
      walk forward
end repeat while you are not directly in front of the fountain
```

Figure 6-35 Information for Exercise 9

Image by Diane Zak; Created with Reallusion CrazyTalk Animator

INTERMEDIATE

10. Write a Visual Basic assignment statement that updates the `intTotal` counter variable by –3.

INTERMEDIATE

11. Write a Visual Basic assignment statement that subtracts the contents of the `decReturns` variable from the contents of the `decSales` accumulator variable.

12. Modify Solution 2 shown earlier in Figure 6-3. The solution should now keep track of the number of times Isis's laser beam missed the spider. After saying "You are safe now. The spider is dead", Isis should say one of the following: "I got him immediately.", "I missed him one time.", or "I missed him *x* times." (where *x* is the value in the counter). INTERMEDIATE

13. Write the Visual Basic code for a pretest loop that uses an Integer variable named `intOdd` to display the odd integers from 7 through 19 in the lblOddNums control. Use the For...Next statement. Display each number on a separate line in the control. Now create a Visual Basic Windows application to test your code. Use the following names for the solution and project, respectively: Odd Numbers Solution and Odd Numbers Project. Save the application in the VB2012\Chap06 folder. Add a button and a label to the interface. Enter your code in the button's Click event procedure. Save the solution and then start and test the application. Close the Code Editor window and then close the solution. INTERMEDIATE

14. Rewrite the pretest loop from Exercise 13 using the Do...Loop statement. Add another button to the interface created in Exercise 13. Enter your code from this exercise in the button's Click event procedure. Save the solution and then start and test the application. Close the Code Editor window and then close the solution. INTERMEDIATE

15. Change the pretest loop from Exercise 13 to a posttest loop. Add another button to the interface used in Exercise 14. Enter your code from this exercise in the button's Click event procedure. Save the solution and then start and test the application. Close the Code Editor window and then close the solution. INTERMEDIATE

16. Write the Visual Basic code that corresponds to the flowchart shown in Figure 6-36. Display the calculated results on separate lines in the lblCount control. INTERMEDIATE

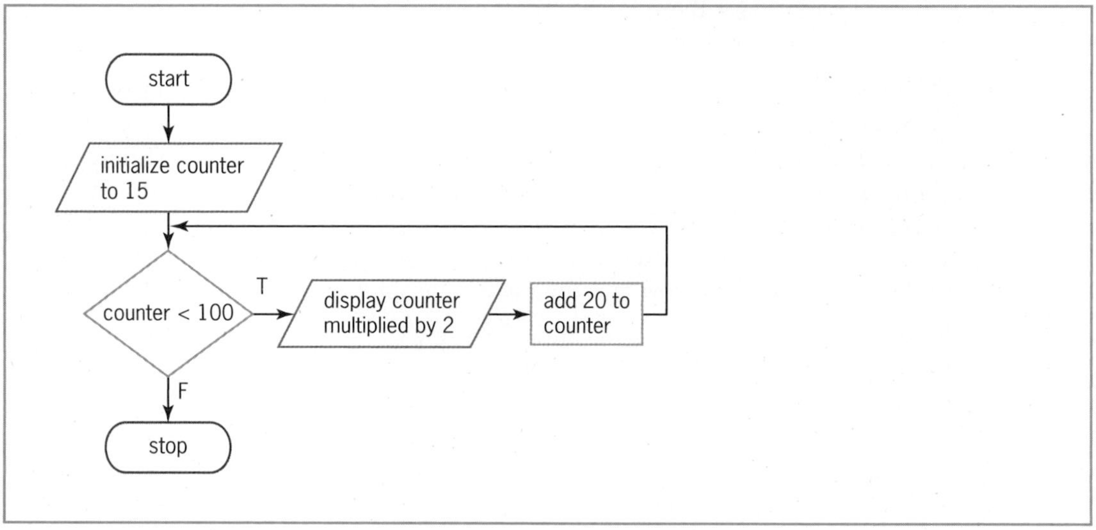

Figure 6-36 Flowchart for Exercise 16

17. Write a For...Next statement that displays the numbers from 9 through 81, in increments of 9, in the lblNums control. Display each number on a separate line in the control. INTERMEDIATE

18. Write a For...Next statement that calculates and displays the squares of the even numbers from 2 through 26. Display the results in the lblNums control. Display each number on a separate line in the control. INTERMEDIATE

INTERMEDIATE

19. What will the following code display?

```
Dim intTotal As Integer
Do While intTotal <= 5
  MessageBox.Show(intTotal.ToString)
  intTotal += 2
Loop
```

INTERMEDIATE

20. What will the following code display?

```
Dim intTotal As Integer = 1
Do
  MessageBox.Show(intTotal.ToString)
  intTotal = intTotal + 2
Loop Until intTotal >= 3
```

INTERMEDIATE

21. In this exercise, you modify one of the Savings Account applications from this lesson. Use Windows to make a copy of the Savings Solution folder. Rename the copy Savings Solution-Intermediate. Open the Savings Solution (Savings Solution.sln) file contained in the Savings Solution-Intermediate folder. Open the designer window. Rather than using $250,000 as the savings goal, the user should be able to enter any savings goal. Modify the interface and code appropriately. Save the solution and then start and test the application. Close the Code Editor window and then close the solution.

INTERMEDIATE

22. In this exercise, you modify the Addition application from this lesson. Use Windows to make a copy of the Addition Solution folder. Rename the copy Addition Solution-Intermediate. Open the Addition Solution (Addition Solution.sln) file contained in the Addition Solution-Intermediate folder. Open the designer window. The application should also keep track of the number of integers entered and the average integer entered; both numbers should be displayed in the interface. Modify the interface and code appropriately. Save the solution and then start and test the application. Close the Code Editor window and then close the solution.

INTERMEDIATE

23. In this exercise, you modify one of the Savings Account applications from this lesson. Use Windows to make a copy of the Savings Solution-For Next folder. Rename the copy Savings Solution-Do While. Open the Savings Solution (Savings Solution.sln) file contained in the Savings Solution-Do While folder. Open the designer and Code Editor windows. Change the For...Next statement in the btnCalc_Click procedure to a Do...Loop statement. Save the solution and then start and test the application. Close the Code Editor window and then close the solution.

INTERMEDIATE

24. In this exercise, you create an application for Koby Coffee House. Create a Visual Basic Windows application. Use the following names for the solution and project, respectively: Koby Solution and Koby Project. Save the application in the VB2012\Chap06 folder. Change the form file's name to Main Form.vb. Change the form's name to frmMain. The application's interface is shown in Figure 6-37. The Add to Total button's Click event procedure should accumulate the prices entered in the text box, always displaying the accumulated value plus a 3% sales tax in the Total due box. In other words, if the user enters the number 5 in the text box, the Total due box should say $5.15. If the user subsequently enters the number 10, the Total due box should say $15.45. The Next Order button should allow the user to start accumulating the values for the next order. Create the interface and then code the application. Save the solution and then start and test the application. Close the Code Editor window and then close the solution.

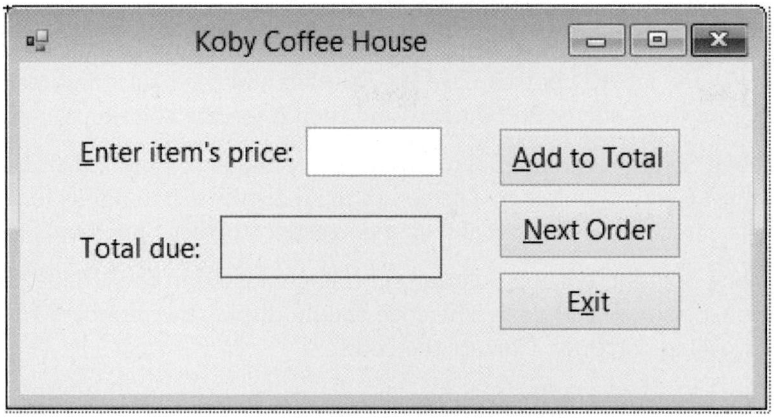

Figure 6-37 Interface for Exercise 24

25. In this exercise, you create an application for Sharon's Chocolates. Create a Visual Basic Windows application. Use the following names for the solution and project, respectively: Sharon Solution and Sharon Project. Save the application in the VB2012\Chap06 folder. Change the form file's name to Main Form.vb. Change the form's name to frmMain. The application's interface is shown in Figure 6-38. The Calculate button's Click event procedure should use a loop and the InputBox function to get the prices of the chocolates purchased by the user. It then should accumulate the prices. When the user has finished entering the prices for the current order, the procedure should display the accumulated value, plus a 5% sales tax, in the Total due box. Create the interface and then code the application. Save the solution and then start and test the application. Close the Code Editor window and then close the solution. INTERMEDIATE

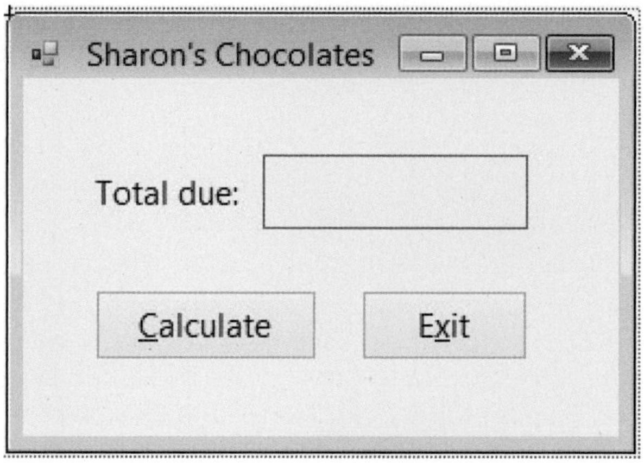

Figure 6-38 Interface for Exercise 25

26. In this exercise, you modify the Sales Express application from this lesson. Use Windows to make a copy of the Sales Express Solution folder. Rename the copy Sales Express Solution-Advanced. Open the Sales Express Solution (Sales Express Solution.sln) file contained in the Sales Express Solution-Advanced folder. Open the designer and Code Editor windows. Each time the Calculate button is clicked, the user will enter five sales amounts. Change the Do...Loop statement in the btnCalc_Click procedure to a For... Next statement. If a sales amount cannot be converted to a number, use the `Exit For` statement to exit the loop. (Hint: Refer to Chapter 5's Lesson C for how to use the ADVANCED

TryParse method for data validation.) Calculate the average only when the user enters five valid sales amounts; otherwise, display an appropriate message in a message box and the number 0 in the lblAvg control. Save the solution and then start and test the application. Close the Code Editor window and then close the solution.

SWAT THE BUGS

27. Open the Debug Solution (Debug Solution.sln) file contained in the VB2012\Chap06\Debug Solution-Lesson A-27 folder. The code should display a 10% bonus for each sales amount that is entered, but it is not working correctly. Correct the code.

SWAT THE BUGS

28. Open the Debug Solution (Debug Solution.sln) file contained in the VB2012\Chap06\Debug Solution-Lesson A-28 folder. The code should display the numbers 1 through 4, but it is not working correctly. Correct the code.

SWAT THE BUGS

29. Open the Debug Solution (Debug Solution.sln) file contained in the VB2012\Chap06\Debug Solution-Lesson A-29 folder. The code should display the numbers 10 through 1, but it is not working correctly. Correct the code.

SWAT THE BUGS

30. Open the Debug Solution (Debug Solution.sln) file contained in the VB2012\Chap06\Debug Solution-Lesson A-30 folder. The code should display a 5% commission for each sales amount that is entered, but it is not working correctly. Correct the code.

LESSON B

After studying Lesson B, you should be able to:

- Nest repetition structures
- Refresh the screen
- Delay program execution

Nested Repetition Structures

Like selection structures, repetition structures can be nested, which means you can place one loop (called the nested or inner loop) within another loop (called the outer loop). Both loops can be pretest loops, or both can be posttest loops. Or, one can be a pretest loop and the other a posttest loop.

A clock uses nested loops to keep track of the time. For simplicity, consider a clock's minute and second hands only. The second hand on a clock moves one position, clockwise, for every second that has elapsed. After the second hand moves 60 positions, the minute hand moves one position, also clockwise. The second hand then begins its journey around the clock again. Figure 6-39 shows the logic used by a clock's minute and second hands. As the figure indicates, an outer loop controls the minute hand, while the inner (nested) loop controls the second hand. Notice that the entire nested loop is contained within the outer loop; this must be true for the loop to be nested and for it to work correctly. The next iteration of the outer loop (which controls the minute hand) occurs only after the nested loop (which controls the second hand) has finished processing.

```
repeat for minutes from 0 through 59
     repeat for seconds from 0 through 59 ----------
          move second hand 1 position, clockwise   |---- nested loop
     end repeat for seconds ------------------------
     move minute hand 1 position, clockwise
end repeat for minutes
```

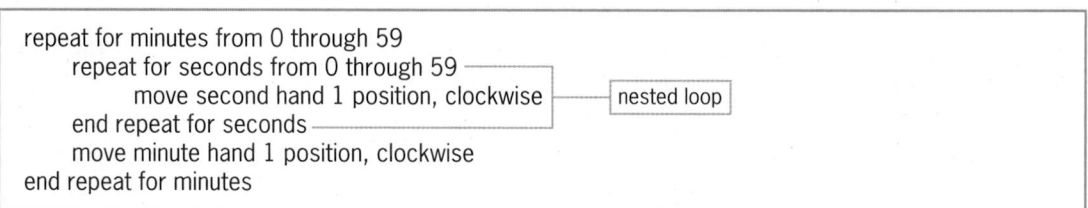

Figure 6-39 Logic used by a clock's minute and second hands

To code and then test the Clock application:

START HERE

1. If necessary, start Visual Studio 2012. Open the Clock Solution (Clock Solution.sln) file contained in the VB2012\Chap06\Clock Solution folder. If necessary, open the designer window. See Figure 6-40.

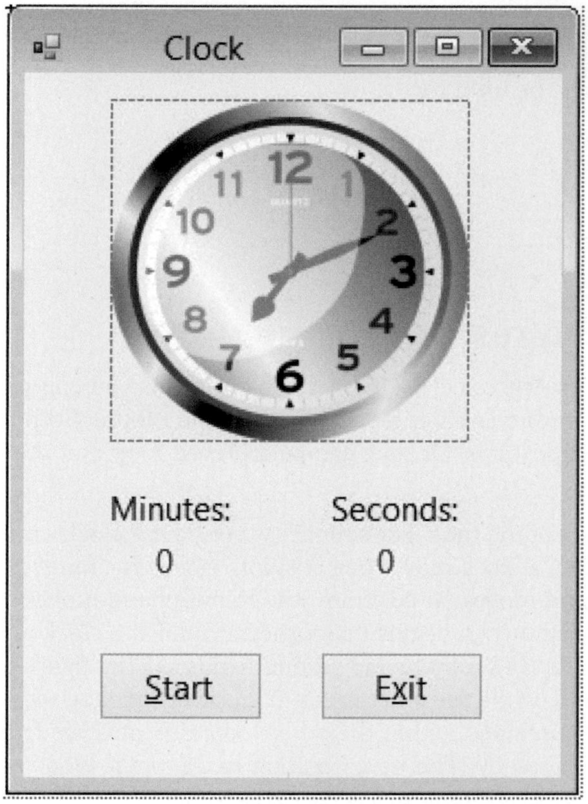

Figure 6-40 Clock application's interface
OpenClipArt.org/filtre

2. Open the Code Editor window. Replace <your name> and <current date> in the comments with your name and the current date, respectively.

3. Open the code template for the btnStart control's Click event procedure. The procedure will use an outer loop to display the number of minutes, and a nested loop to display the number of seconds. For simplicity in watching the minutes and seconds tick away, you will display minute values from 0 through 2, and display second values from 0 through 5. Enter the following comments. Press **Enter** twice after typing the last comment.

```
' displays minutes (from 0 through 2 only)
' and seconds (from 0 through 5 only)
```

4. Now enter the following outer and nested loops:

```
For intMinutes As Integer = 0 To 2
    lblMinutes.Text = intMinutes.ToString
    For intSeconds As Integer = 0 To 5
        lblSeconds.Text = intSeconds.ToString
    Next intSeconds
Next intMinutes
```

5. Save the solution and then start the application. Click the **Start** button. The computer processes the code entered in the button's Click event procedure so quickly that you don't get a chance to see each of the values assigned to the labels. Instead, only the final values (2 and 5) appear in the interface. You can fix this problem by refreshing the interface and then delaying program execution each time the value in the lblSeconds control changes.

The Refresh and Sleep Methods

You can refresh (or redraw) the interface using the form's Refresh method. The **Refresh method** ensures that the computer processes any previous lines of code that affect the interface's appearance. The Refresh method's syntax is `Me.Refresh()`, in which `Me` refers to the current form. You can delay program execution using the **Sleep method** in the following syntax: `System.Threading.Thread.Sleep(`*milliseconds*`)`. The *milliseconds* argument is the number of milliseconds to suspend the program. A millisecond is 1/1000 of a second; in other words, there are 1000 milliseconds in a second. In the Clock application, you will delay program execution for a half of a second, which is 500 milliseconds.

START HERE

To include the Refresh and Sleep methods in the procedure and then test the code:

1. Enter the additional comment and two lines of code indicated in Figure 6-41.

```
Private Sub btnStart_Click(sender As Object, e As EventArg
    ' displays minutes (from 0 through 2 only)
    ' and seconds (from 0 through 5 only)

    For intMinutes As Integer = 0 To 2
        lblMinutes.Text = intMinutes.ToString
        For intSeconds As Integer = 0 To 5
            lblSeconds.Text = intSeconds.ToString
            ' refresh interface and then pause execution
            Me.Refresh()
            System.Threading.Thread.Sleep(500)
        Next intSeconds
    Next intMinutes
End Sub
```

enter this comment and these two lines of code

Figure 6-41 Refresh and Sleep methods added to the procedure

2. Save the solution and then start the application. Click the **Start** button. The number 0 appears in the lblMinutes control, and the numbers 0 through 5 appear (one at a time) in the lblSeconds control. Notice that the number of minutes is increased by 1 when the number of seconds changes from 5 to 0. When the procedure ends, the lblMinutes and lblSeconds controls contain the numbers 2 and 5, respectively. (If you want to end the procedure before it has finished processing, click the form in the designer window, click DEBUG on the menu bar, and then click Stop Debugging.)
3. Click the **Exit** button. Close the Code Editor window and then close the solution.

Trixie at the Diner

A programmer determines whether a problem's solution requires a nested loop by studying the problem specification. The first problem specification you will examine in this chapter involves a waitress named Trixie. The problem specification and an illustration of the problem are shown in Figure 6-42, along with an appropriate solution. The solution requires a loop because the instructions for telling each table about the daily specials must be repeated for every table that needs to be waited on. However, the solution does not require a nested loop. This is because the instructions within the loop should be followed only once per table.

Problem Specification

A waitress named Trixie works at a local diner. The diner just opened for the day and there are customers already sitting at several of the tables. Write the instructions that direct Trixie to go over to each table that needs to be waited on and tell the customers about the daily specials.

Solution
repeat for each table that needs to be waited on
        go to a table that needs to be waited on
        tell the customers at the table about the daily specials
end repeat for

follow these instructions for each table

Figure 6-42 Problem specification and solution that requires a loop
Image by Diane Zak; Created with Reallusion CrazyTalk Animator

Now we'll add some additional tasks for Trixie to perform. This time, after telling the customers at a table about the daily specials, Trixie should take each customer's order and then submit the order for the entire table to the cook. Figure 6-43 shows the modified problem specification along with the modified solution, which requires a nested loop. The outer loop begins with "repeat for each table that needs to be waited on", and it ends with the last "end repeat for". The nested loop begins with "repeat for each customer at the table", and it ends with the first "end repeat for". Here again, notice that the entire nested loop is contained within the outer loop. Recall that this is a requirement for the loop to be nested and work correctly.

Problem Specification

A waitress named Trixie works at a local diner. The diner just opened for the day and there are customers already sitting at several of the tables. Write the instructions that direct Trixie to go over to each table that needs to be waited on and tell the customers about the daily specials. While at each table, Trixie should take each customer's order. She then should submit the order for the entire table to the cook.

Solution

```
repeat for each table that needs to be waited on
        go to a table that needs to be waited on
        tell the customers at the table about the daily specials
        repeat for each customer at the table
                ask the customer for his or her order
                record the order on the order slip for that table
        end repeat for
        go over to the cook at the counter
        tear the appropriate order slip from the order pad
        give the order slip to the cook
end repeat for
```

follow these instructions for each customer at the current table

follow these instructions for each table

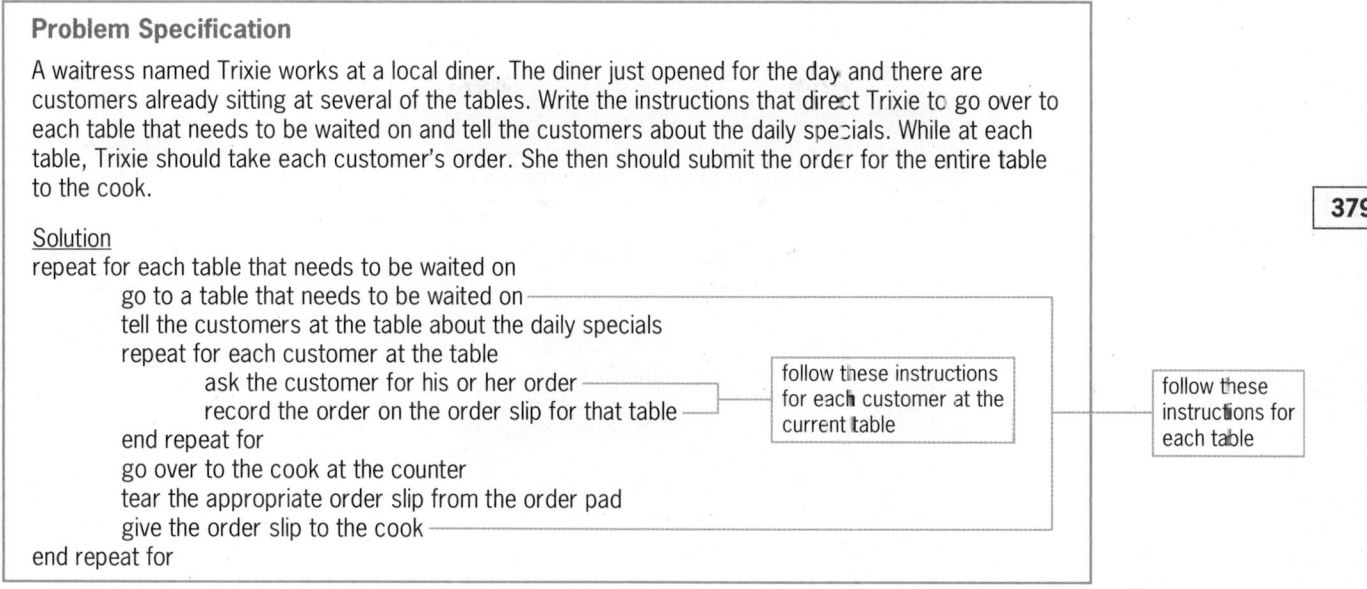

Figure 6-43 Modified problem specification and solution that requires a nested loop

Revisiting the Savings Account Application

In this section, you will code another version of the Savings Account application from Lesson A. In this version, the application will display the balance in the savings account at the end of each of five years, using rates from 3% to 7%. The solution to this problem will require two loops, one nested within the other. The outer loop will control the years, which range from 1 to 5 in increments of 1. The inner loop will control the rates, which range from 3% to 7% in increments of 1%. Figure 6-44 shows the problem specification for this version of the application. It also shows the modified pseudocode and corresponding code for the Calculate button's Click event procedure. The modifications made to the problem specification, pseudocode, and code from Figure 6-30 in Lesson A are shaded in Figure 6-44. In addition, the figure shows a sample run of this version of the application. Notice that this version displays the output in a text box rather than in a label. A text box is used in this case because the output will contain many lines of text. Rather than using a large label to display the output, you can use a smaller text box that provides a vertical scroll bar. The scroll bar will allow the user to view the output that is not currently showing in the text box.

Problem Specification

Create an application that displays the balance in a savings account at the end of each of five years, given the amount of money deposited into the savings account at the beginning of the year and using annual interest rates of 3% to 7% in increments of 1%. The interest is compounded annually and no withdrawals or additional deposits are made during any of the years. ~~The interest rate will be entered in decimal form.~~ The application's interface should provide a Calculate button for displaying the account balances.

<u>Pseudocode for the Calculate button's Click event procedure</u>

```
1. store deposit in balance variable
2. store interest rate in rate variable
3. display Year, Rate, and Balance column headings
4. repeat for years from 1 to 5 in increments of 1
       display year number
       repeat for rates from 3% to 7% in increments of 1%
             interest = balance * rate
             add interest to balance
             display rate and balance
       end repeat for
   end repeat for
```

<u>Code for the Calculate button's Click event procedure</u>

```
Dim dblBalance As Double
Dim dblInterest As Double
Double.TryParse(txtDeposit.Text, dblBalance)
txtBalance.Text = "Year" & ControlChars.Tab &
    "Rate" & ControlChars.Tab & "Balance" &
    ControlChars.NewLine
For intYear As Integer = 1 To 5
    txtBalance.Text = txtBalance.Text &
        intYear.ToString & ControlChars.NewLine
    For dblRate As Double = 0.03 To 0.07 Step 0.01
        dblInterest = dblBalance * dblRate
        dblBalance = dblBalance + dblInterest
        txtBalance.Text = txtBalance.Text &
            ControlChars.Tab & dblRate.ToString("P0") &
            ControlChars.Tab & dblBalance.ToString("C2") &
            ControlChars.NewLine
    Next dblRate
Next intYear
```

<u>Sample run</u>

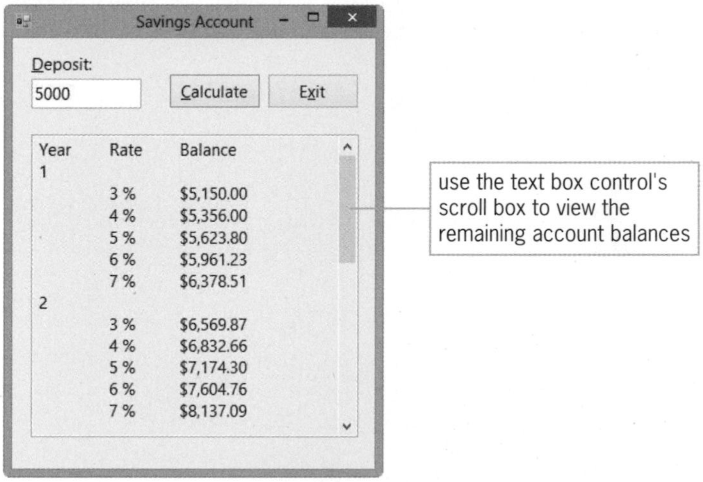

Figure 6-44 Problem specification, pseudocode, code, and sample run for another version of the Savings Account application

START HERE

To code this version of the Savings Account application:

1. Open the Savings Solution (Savings Solution.sln) file contained in the VB2012\Chap06\Savings Solution-Nested folder. If necessary, open the designer window.
2. Open the Code Editor window. Replace <your name> and <current date> in the comments with your name and the current date, respectively.
3. Locate the btnCalc_Click procedure. The procedure contains the Dim statements that declare the `dblBalance` and `dblInterest` variables. It also contains the TryParse method that converts the user's input (the deposit) to the Double data type. In addition, it contains an assignment statement that displays the "Year", "Rate", and "Balance" headings in the txtBalance control. Notice that the assignment statement uses the ControlChars.Tab and ControlsChars.NewLine constants, which represent the Tab and Enter keys, respectively.
4. Click the **blank line** below the `' calculate and display account balances` comment. First, you will enter the loop that controls the years. Enter the following For clause:

   For intYear As Integer = 1 To 5
5. Change the Next clause to **Next intYear**.
6. According to its pseudocode, the procedure should display the year number next. Click the **blank line below the For clause**, and then enter the following lines of code:

   txtBalance.Text = txtBalance.Text &
   intYear.ToString & ControlChars.NewLine
7. Next, you will enter the loop that controls the interest rates. Enter the following For clause:

   For dblRate As Double = .03 To .07 Step .01
8. Change the Next clause to **Next dblRate**.
9. According to its pseudocode, the procedure should calculate the interest and balance next. Click the **blank line below the nested For clause**, and then enter the following assignment statements. Press **Enter** twice after typing the second assignment statement.

   dblInterest = dblBalance * dblRate
   dblBalance = dblBalance + dblInterest
10. The last step in the procedure's pseudocode displays the rate and balance. Type the lines of code indicated in Figure 6-45.

Although both loops in Figure 6-45 are pretest loops, you also can use two posttest loops or a combination of a pretest and a posttest loop.

```
Private Sub btnCalc_Click(sender As Object,
e As EventArgs) Handles btnCalc.Click
    ' calculate account balances for each of
    ' five years, using rates from 3% to 7%
    ' in increments of 1%

    Dim dblBalance As Double
    Dim dblInterest As Double

    Double.TryParse(txtDeposit.Text, dblBalance)

    txtBalance.Text = "Year" & ControlChars.Tab &
        "Rate" & ControlChars.Tab & "Balance" &
        ControlChars.NewLine

    ' calculate and display account balances
    For intYear As Integer = 1 To 5
        txtBalance.Text = txtBalance.Text &
            intYear.ToString & ControlChars.NewLine
        For dblRate As Double = 0.03 To 0.07 Step 0.01
            dblInterest = dblBalance * dblRate
            dblBalance = dblBalance + dblInterest

            txtBalance.Text = txtBalance.Text &
                ControlChars.Tab & dblRate.ToString("P0") &
                ControlChars.Tab & dblBalance.ToString("C2") &
                ControlChars.NewLine
        Next dblRate
    Next intYear
End Sub
```

enter these four lines of code

Figure 6-45 Completed btnCalc_Click procedure

In the next set of steps, you will test the btnCalc_Click procedure to verify that it is working correctly.

START HERE

To test this version of the Savings Account application:

1. Save the solution and then start the application. Type **5000** in the Deposit box and then click the **Calculate** button. The account balances appear in the txtBalance control, as shown earlier in Figure 6-44.
2. Use the control's scroll box to verify that the control contains the account balances for five years, using rates from 3% to 7%.
3. Click the **Exit** button. Close the Code Editor window and then close the solution.

A Caution about Real Numbers

Numbers with a decimal place are called **real numbers**. Unfortunately, not all real numbers can be stored precisely in the computer's internal memory. Many can be stored only as an approximation, which may lead to unexpected results when two real numbers are compared with each other. For example, sometimes a `Double` number that is the result of a calculation doesn't compare precisely with the same number stored as a literal constant. This is the reason it is so important to test your application's code thoroughly. In the next set of steps, you will observe how the comparison problem would affect the Savings Account application that you completed in the previous section.

To modify the Savings Account application from the previous section:

START HERE

1. Use Windows to make a copy of the Savings Solution-Nested folder. Rename the copy Modified Savings Solution-Nested.
2. Open the Savings Solution (Savings Solution.sln) file contained in the Modified Savings Solution-Nested folder. Open the designer window.
3. Open the Code Editor window. Locate the btnCalc_Click procedure. Now let's assume that the user still wants to display the account balances for each of the five years, but for rates from 3% to 6% (rather than from 3% to 7%). In the nested For clause, change 0.07 to **0.06**.
4. Save the solution and then start the application. Click the **Calculate** button. See Figure 6-46. Notice that the information associated with the 6% rate is missing from the txtBalance control.

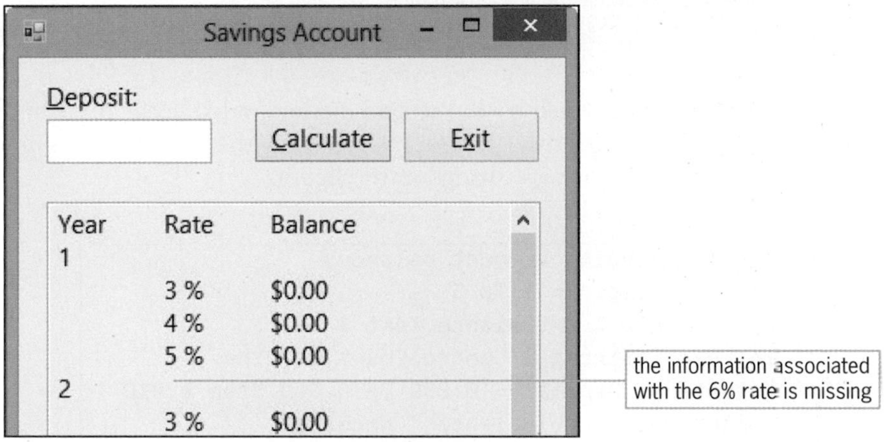

Figure 6-46 Interface showing that the 6% information is missing

5. Click the **Exit** button.

Consider why the loop that controls the interest rates failed to display the 6% rate information. Recall that the For clause in that loop looks like this: `For dblRate As Double = 0.03 To 0.06 Step 0.01`. The clause tells the computer to stop processing the loop instructions when the value in the `dblRate` variable is greater than 0.06 (the endValue). This indicates that when the For clause updates the `dblRate` variable to 0.06 and then compares that value with the 0.06 literal constant (the clause's endValue), the value in the `dblRate` variable is viewed as *greater* than the literal constant, so the loop ends prematurely. To fix this problem, you can either increase the literal constant's value slightly (for example, you can use 0.0600001) or use the Decimal data type for the loop that controls the rates. You will try both methods in the next set of steps.

To fix the comparison problem in the Savings Account application:

START HERE

1. First, you'll increase the literal constant's value. Change 0.06 in the nested For clause to **0.0600001**. Save the solution and then start the application. Click the **Calculate** button. See Figure 6-47. The txtBalance control now includes the information pertaining to the 6% rate.

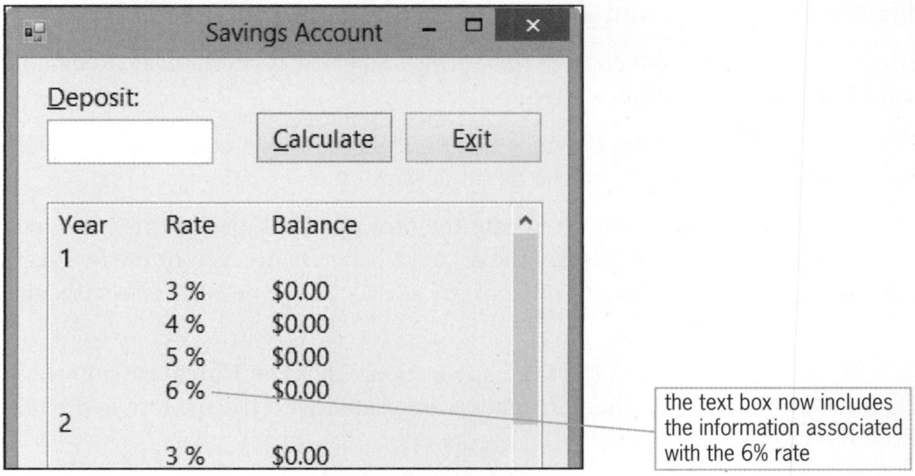

Figure 6-47 Interface showing the 6% information

2. Click the **Exit** button. Now you'll try the second method of fixing the problem, which is to use the Decimal data type for the interest rates. Modify the nested loop as indicated in Figure 6-48. The modifications are shaded in the figure.

```
' calculate and display account balances
For intYear As Integer = 1 To 5
    txtBalance.Text = txtBalance.Text &
        intYear.ToString & ControlChars.NewLine
    For decRate As Decimal = 0.03D To 0.06D Step 0.01D
        dblInterest = dblBalance * decRate
        dblBalance = dblBalance + dblInterest

        txtBalance.Text = txtBalance.Text &
            ControlChars.Tab & decRate.ToString("P0") &
            ControlChars.Tab & dblBalance.ToString("C2")
            ControlChars.NewLine
    Next decRate
```

make the shaded modifications

Figure 6-48 Modifications made to the nested loop that controls the interest rates

3. Save the solution and then start the application. Click the **Calculate** button. The 6% rate information appears in the txtBalance control, as shown earlier in Figure 6-47.
4. Click the **Exit** button. Close the Code Editor window and then close the solution.

Lesson B Summary

- To nest a repetition structure (loop):

  Place the entire inner loop within the outer loop.

- To refresh the interface:

  Use the Refresh method. The method's syntax is **Me.Refresh()**.

- To pause program execution:

  Use the Sleep method. The method's syntax is **System.Threading.Thread.Sleep(*milliseconds*)**.

Lesson B Key Terms

Real numbers—numbers with a decimal place

Refresh method—can be used to refresh (redraw) a form

Sleep method—can be used to delay program execution

Lesson B Review Questions

1. What will the following code display in the lblAsterisks control?

```
For intX As Integer = 1 To 2
   For intY As Integer = 1 To 3
      lblAsterisks.Text = lblAsterisks.Text & "*"
   Next intY
   lblAsterisks.Text = lblAsterisks.Text &
      ControlChars.NewLine
Next intX
```

   a. ***
   ***

   b. ***
   ***
   ***

   c. **
   **
   **

   d. ***
   ***
   ***
   ***

2. What will the following code display in the lblSum control?

```
Dim intSum As Integer
Dim intY As Integer
Do While intY < 3
   For intX As Integer = 1 To 4
      intSum = intSum + intX
   Next intX
   intY = intY + 1
Loop
lblSum.Text = Convert.ToString(intSum)
```

   a. 5
   b. 8
   c. 15
   d. 30

3. Which of the following statements pauses program execution for 1 second?
   a. `System.Threading.Thread.Pause(1000)`
   b. `System.Threading.Thread.Pause(1)`
   c. `System.Threading.Thread.Sleep(1000)`
   d. `System.Threading.Thread.Sleep(100)`

Lesson B Exercises

INTRODUCTORY

1. In this exercise, you modify the Clock application from this lesson. Use Windows to make a copy of the Clock Solution folder. Rename the copy Clock Solution-Introductory. Open the Clock Solution (Clock Solution.sln) file contained in the Clock Solution-Introductory folder. Open the designer and Code Editor windows. Change the outer For...Next statement to a Do...Loop statement. Save the solution and then start and test the application. Close the Code Editor window and then close the solution.

INTRODUCTORY

2. In this exercise, you modify one of the Savings Account applications from this lesson. Use Windows to make a copy of the Modified Savings Solution-Nested folder. Rename the copy Savings Solution-Nested-Introductory. Open the Savings Solution (Savings Solution.sln) file contained in the Savings Solution-Nested-Introductory folder. Open the designer and Code Editor windows. Change the For...Next statement that controls the rates to a Do...Loop statement. Save the solution and then start and test the application. Close the Code Editor window and then close the solution.

INTERMEDIATE

3. In this exercise, you modify the Clock application from this lesson. Use Windows to make a copy of the Clock Solution folder. Rename the copy Clock Solution-Intermediate. Open the Clock Solution (Clock Solution.sln) file contained in the Clock Solution-Intermediate folder. Open the designer and Code Editor windows. Change both For...Next statements to Do... Loop statements. Save the solution and then start and test the application. Stop the application. Close the Code Editor window, then close the solution.

INTERMEDIATE

4. In this exercise, you modify one of the Savings Account applications from this lesson. Use Windows to make a copy of the Modified Savings Solution-Nested folder. Rename the Savings Solution-Nested-Intermediate. Open the Savings Solution (Savings Solution.sln) file contained in the Savings Solution-Nested-Intermediate folder. Open the designer and Code Editor windows. Change both For...Next statements to Do...Loop statements. Save the solution and then start and test the application. Close the Code Editor window and then close the solution.

INTERMEDIATE

5. Professor Arkins wants an application that allows him to assign a grade to any number of students. Each student's grade is based on three test scores, with each test worth 100 points. The application should total the test scores and then assign the appropriate grade using the information shown in Figure 6-49. Open the Grade Calculator Solution (Grade Calculator Solution.sln) file contained in the VB2012\Chap06\Grade Calculator Solution folder. If necessary, open the designer window. Code the application. Save the solution and then start and test the application. Close the Code Editor window and then close the solution.

Total points earned	Grade
270–300	A
240–269	B
210–239	C
180–209	D
below 180	F

Figure 6-49 Grade information for Exercise 5

INTERMEDIATE

6. Create a Visual Basic Windows application. Use the following names for the solution and project, respectively: Table Solution and Table Project. Save the application in the VB2012\Chap06 folder. Change the form file's name to Main Form.vb. Change the form's name to frmMain. The application should display a table consisting of four rows and five columns. The first column should contain the numbers 1 through 4. The second and subsequent columns should contain the result of multiplying the number in the first column by the numbers 2 through 5. Create a suitable interface and then code the application. Save the solution and then start and test the application. Close the Code Editor window and then close the solution.

INTERMEDIATE

7. Create a Visual Basic Windows application. Use the following names for the solution and project, respectively: Raises Solution and Raises Project. Save the application in the VB2012\Chap06 folder. Change the form file's name to Main Form.vb. Change the form's name to frmMain. At the beginning of every year, Khalid receives a raise on his previous year's salary. He wants a program that calculates and displays the amount of his annual raises for the next three years, using rates of 3%, 4%, 5%, and 6%. Create a suitable interface and then code the application. Save the solution and then start and test the application. Close the Code Editor window and then close the solution.

ADVANCED

8. Create a Visual Basic Windows application. Use the following names for the solution and project, respectively: Bar Chart Solution and Bar Chart Project. Save the application in the VB2012\Chap06 folder. Change the form file's name to Main Form.vb. Change the form's name to frmMain. The application should allow the user to enter the ratings for five different movies. Each rating should be a number from 1 through 10 only. The application should graph the ratings using a horizontal bar chart consisting of five rows, one row for each movie. Each row should contain from one to 10 plus signs (+). The number of plus signs depends on the movie's rating. Create a suitable interface and then code the application. Save the solution and then start and test the application. Close the Code Editor window and then close the solution.

ADVANCED

9. Open the Car Solution (Car Solution.sln) file contained in the VB2012\Chap06\Car Solution folder. (The image in the picture box was downloaded from the Open Clip Art Library at *http://openclipart.org*.) The Click Me button's Click event procedure should make the "I WANT THIS CAR!" message blink 10 times. In other words, the message should disappear and then reappear, disappear and then reappear, and so on. Use the For...Next statement. Save the solution and then start and test the application. Close the Code Editor window and then close the solution.

LESSON C

After studying Lesson C, you should be able to:

- Include a list box on a form
- Select a list box item from code
- Determine the selected item in a list box

Creating the Gross Pay Application

Your task in this chapter is to create an application that allows the user to enter the number of hours an employee worked and his or her rate of pay. The number of hours worked and pay rate will be entered using list boxes. The hours worked list box will display numbers from 0.5 through 40.0 in increments of 0.5. The pay rate list box will display numbers from 8.00 through 15.00, also in increments of 0.5. The application will calculate and display the employee's gross pay. Figure 6-50 shows the application's TOE chart.

Task	Object	Event
End the application	btnExit	Click
1. Calculate the gross pay 2. Display the grossPay in lblGross	btnCalc	Click
1. Fill lstHours and lstRates with values 2. Select a default value in lstHours and lstRates	frmMain	Load
Display the gross pay (from btnCalc)	lblGross	None
Get and display the hours worked and pay rate Clear lblGross	lstHours, lstRates	None SelectedValueChanged

Figure 6-50 TOE chart for the Gross Pay application

START HERE

To open the partially-completed Gross Pay application:

1. If necessary, start Visual Studio 2012. Open the Gross Pay Solution (Gross Pay Solution.sln) file contained in the VB2012\Chap06\Gross Pay Solution folder. If necessary, open the designer window. The interface contains four labels, two buttons, a picture box, and a list box. Missing from the interface is the list box for entering the pay rates.

Including a List Box in an Interface

You add a list box to an interface using the ListBox tool in the toolbox. A **list box** displays a list of items from which the user can select zero items, one item, or multiple items. The number of items the user can select is controlled by the list box's **SelectionMode property**. The default value for the property, One, allows the user to select only one item at a time. In the Gross Pay application, you will use the default value for each list box's SelectionMode property. (You can learn more about the property in Exercise 13 at the end of this lesson.)

If you have only two items to offer the user, you should use two radio buttons rather than a list box.

Although you can make a list box any size you want, you should follow the Windows standard, which is to display a minimum of three items and a maximum of eight items at a time. If you have more items than can fit into the list box, the control automatically displays a scroll bar for viewing the complete list of items. You should use a label control to provide keyboard access to the list box. For the access key to work correctly, you must set the label's TabIndex property to a value that is one number less than the list box's TabIndex value.

START HERE

To complete the user interface:

1. Click the **ListBox** tool in the toolbox and then drag the mouse pointer to the form. Position the mouse pointer below the Rates: label and then release the mouse button.
2. The three-character ID for list box names is lst. Change the list box's name to **lstRates**. Do not be concerned that the list box's name appears inside the control. The name will not appear when the application is started.
3. Use the FORMAT menu to make the lstRates control the same size as the lstHours control. Then use the FORMAT menu to align the tops of both list boxes.
4. Lock the controls on the form and then use the information in Figure 6-51 to set the TabIndex values. When you are finished, press **Esc** to remove the TabIndex boxes from the form, and then save the solution.

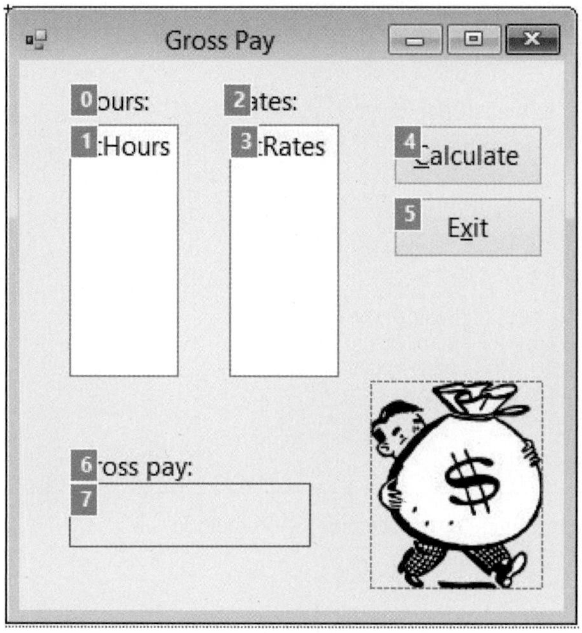

Figure 6-51 Correct TabIndex values
OpenClipArt.org/johnny_automatic

Adding Items to a List Box

The items in a list box belong to a collection called the **Items collection**. A **collection** is a group of individual objects treated as one unit. The first item in the Items collection appears as the first item in the list box. The second item in the collection appears as the second item in the list box, and so on. A unique number identifies each item in the Items collection; the unique number is called an index. The first item in the collection (which also is the first item in the list box) has an index of 0, the second item has an index of 1, and so on. You specify each item to display in a list box using the Items collection's **Add method**.

Figure 6-52 shows the Add method's syntax and includes examples and the results of using the method. In the syntax, *object* is the name of the list box control, and the *item* argument is the text you want to add to the control's list. The three Add methods in Example 1 will add the strings "Dog", "Cat", and "Horse" to the lstAnimal control. In Example 2, the Add method appears in the body of a pretest loop that repeats its instructions for `intCode` values of 100 through 105. As a result, the Add method will add the values 100, 101, 102, 103, 104, and 105 (each converted to the String data type) to the lstCode control. You also can write the Add method in Example 2 as follows: `lstCode.Items.Add(Convert.ToString(intCode))`. In most cases, you enter the Add methods in a form's Load event procedure because you typically want the list box to display its values when the form first appears on the screen.

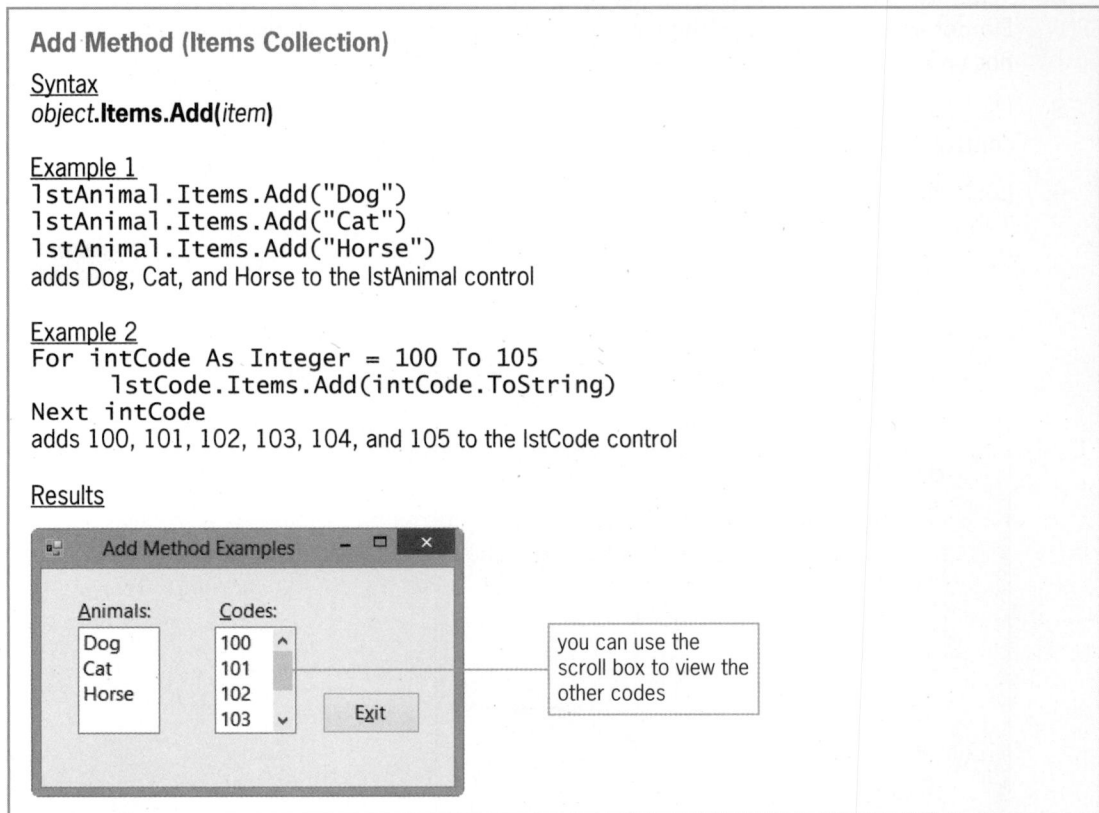

Add Method (Items Collection)

Syntax
object.**Items.Add(***item***)**

Example 1
```
lstAnimal.Items.Add("Dog")
lstAnimal.Items.Add("Cat")
lstAnimal.Items.Add("Horse")
```
adds Dog, Cat, and Horse to the lstAnimal control

Example 2
```
For intCode As Integer = 100 To 105
     lstCode.Items.Add(intCode.ToString)
Next intCode
```
adds 100, 101, 102, 103, 104, and 105 to the lstCode control

Results

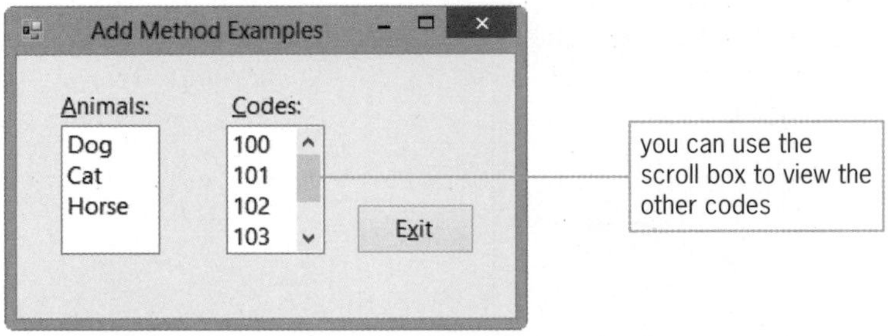

To learn more about list boxes, complete Exercises 13, 14, and 15 at the end of this lesson.

Figure 6-52 Syntax, examples, and results of the Items collection's Add method

The Sorted Property

The position of an item in a list box depends on the value stored in the list box's **Sorted property**. When the Sorted property is set to False (the default value), the item is added at the end of the list. The Sorted property of both list boxes in Figure 6-52 is set to False. When the Sorted property is set to True, the item is sorted along with the existing items and then placed in its proper position in the list. Visual Basic sorts the list box items in dictionary order, which means that numbers are sorted before letters, and a lowercase letter is sorted before its uppercase equivalent. The items in a list box are sorted based on the leftmost characters in each item. As a result, the items "Personnel", "Inventory", and "Payroll" will appear in the following order when the lstDepartment control's Sorted property is set to True: Inventory, Payroll, Personnel. Likewise, the items 1, 2, 3, and 10 will appear in the following order when the lstNumber control's Sorted property is set to True: 1, 10, 2, 3. Both list boxes are shown in Figure 6-53.

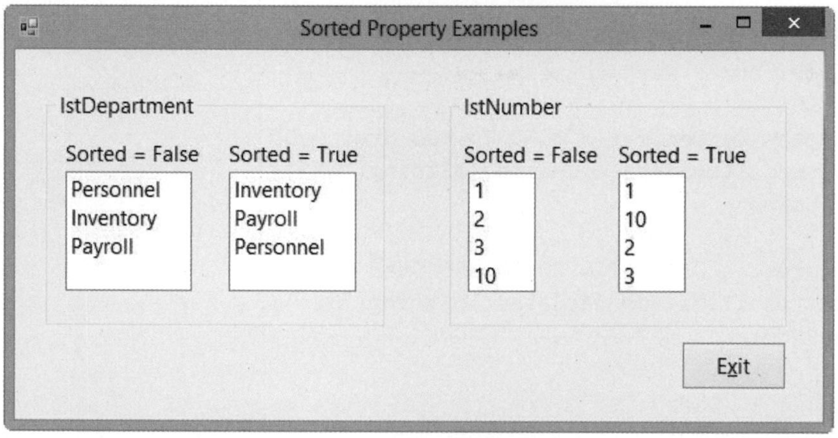

Figure 6-53 Examples of the list box's Sorted property

The requirements of the application you are creating determine whether you display the list box items in either sorted order or the order in which they are added to the list box. If several list items are selected much more frequently than other items, you typically leave the list box's Sorted property set to False and then add the frequently used items first to ensure that they appear at the beginning of the list. However, if the list box items are selected fairly equally, you typically set the list box's Sorted property to True because it is easier to locate items when they appear in a sorted order.

GUI DESIGN TIP List Box Standards

- A list box should contain a minimum of three items.
- A list box should display a minimum of three items and a maximum of eight items at a time.
- Use a label control to provide keyboard access to the list box. Set the label's TabIndex property to a value that is one number less than the list box's TabIndex value.
- List box items are either arranged by use, with the most used entries appearing first in the list, or sorted in ascending order.

Coding the Gross Pay Application

When the Gross Pay interface appears on the screen, the appropriate hours and rates should be listed in the lstHours and lstRates controls, respectively. You can accomplish this by entering the appropriate Add methods in the form's Load event procedure.

To specify the hours and rates to display in the list boxes:

START HERE

1. Open the Code Editor window. Replace <your name> and <current date> in the comments with your name and the current date, respectively.
2. Click the **Class Name** list arrow and then click **(frmMain Events)**. Click the **Method Name** list arrow and then click **Load**. Enter the comment and For...Next loops shown in Figure 6-54. (Be sure to change the Next clauses as shown in the figure.)

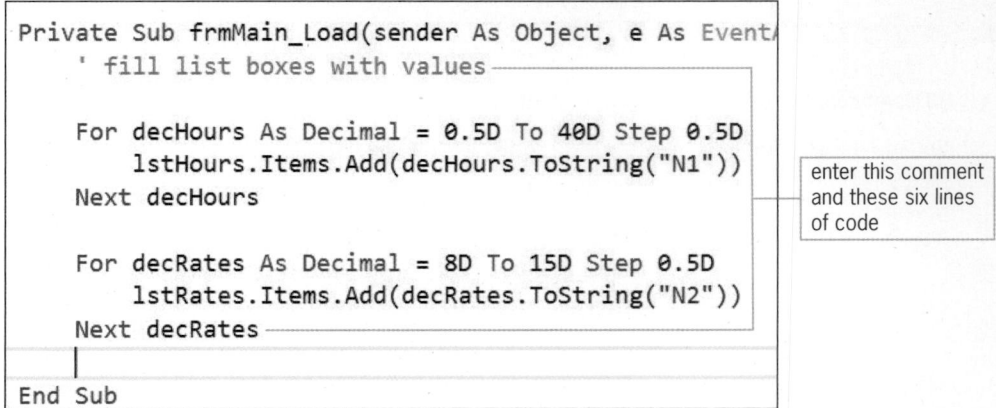

```
Private Sub frmMain_Load(sender As Object, e As Event
    ' fill list boxes with values

    For decHours As Decimal = 0.5D To 40D Step 0.5D
        lstHours.Items.Add(decHours.ToString("N1"))
    Next decHours

    For decRates As Decimal = 8D To 15D Step 0.5D
        lstRates.Items.Add(decRates.ToString("N2"))
    Next decRates

End Sub
```

enter this comment and these six lines of code

Figure 6-54 For...Next loops entered in the Load event procedure

3. Save the solution and then start the application. Scroll down the Hours list box to verify that it contains numbers from 0.5 through 40.0, in increments of 0.5. Also scroll down the Rates list box to verify that it contains numbers from 8.00 through 15.00, also in increments of 0.5.

4. Scroll to the top of the Rates list box and then click **8.00** in the list. Now scroll to the top of the Hours list box and then click **2.0** in the list. When you select an item in a list box, the item appears highlighted in the list, as shown in Figure 6-55. In addition, the item's value and index are stored in the list box's SelectedItem property and SelectedIndex property, respectively. Click the **Exit** button.

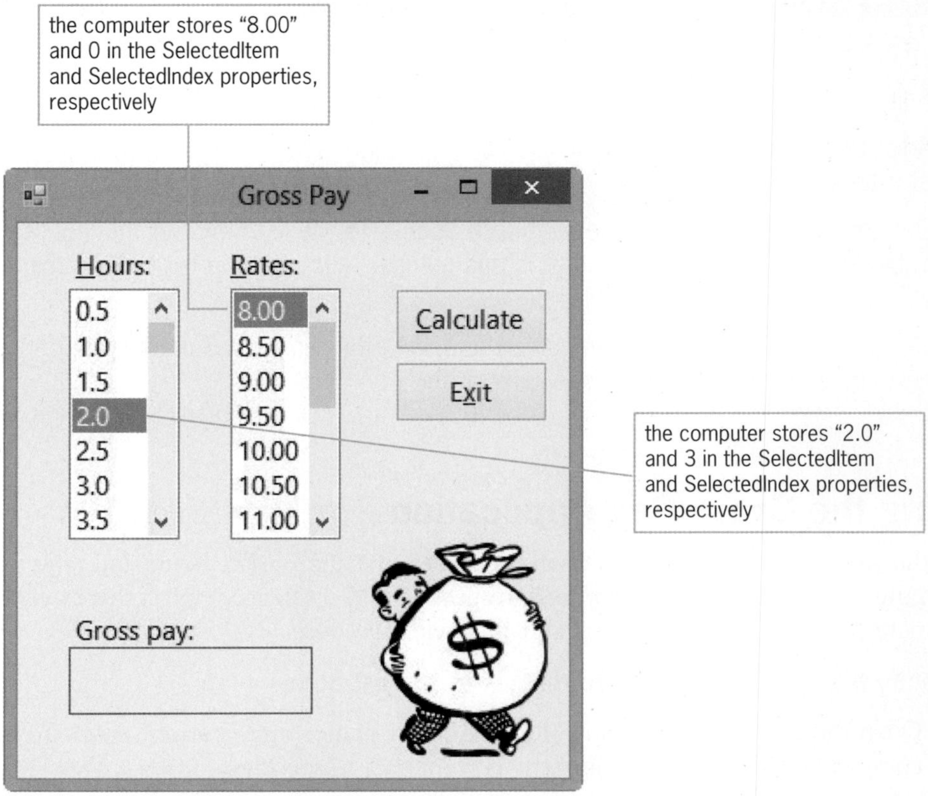

Figure 6-55 Items selected in the list boxes
OpenClipArt.org/johnny_automatic

The SelectedItem and SelectedIndex Properties

You can use either the **SelectedItem property** or the **SelectedIndex property** to determine whether an item is selected in a list box. When no item is selected, the SelectedItem property contains the empty string, and the SelectedIndex property contains the number –1 (negative 1). Otherwise, the SelectedItem and SelectedIndex properties contain the value of the selected item and the item's index, respectively. Figure 6-56 shows examples of using the SelectedItem and SelectedIndex properties. (The examples refer to the list boxes shown earlier in Figure 6-52.)

SelectedItem and SelectedIndex Properties

Example 1 (SelectedItem property)
```
lblAnimal.Text = Convert.ToString(lstAnimal.SelectedItem)
```
The item selected in the lstAnimal control is converted to String before being assigned to the lblAnimal control's Text property.

Example 2 (SelectedItem property)
```
If Convert.ToInt32(lstCode.SelectedItem) = 103 Then
```
The item selected in the lstCode control is converted to Integer before being compared to the integer 103. You also can convert the selected item to String and then compare the result with the string "103" as follows: `If Convert.ToString(lstCode.SelectedItem) = "103"`.

Example 3 (SelectedItem property)
```
If Convert.ToString(lstCode.SelectedItem) <> String.Empty Then
```
The item selected in the lstCode control is converted to String before being compared with the empty string.

Example 4 (SelectedIndex property)
```
MessageBox.Show(lstAnimal.SelectedIndex.ToString)
```
The index of the item selected in the lstAnimal control is converted to String and then displayed in a message box. You also can use the following statement:
`MessageBox.Show(Convert.ToString(lstAnimal.SelectedIndex))`.

Example 5 (SelectedIndex property)
```
If lstCode.SelectedIndex = 0 Then
```
The index of the item selected in the lstCode control is compared with the number 0.

Figure 6-56 Examples of the list box's SelectedItem and SelectedIndex properties

If a list box allows the user to make only one selection, it is customary in Windows applications to have one of the list box items already selected when the interface appears. The selected item, called the **default list box item**, should be either the item selected most frequently or the first item in the list. You can use either the SelectedItem property or the SelectedIndex property to select the default list box item from code, as shown in the examples in Figure 6-57. (The examples refer to the list boxes shown earlier in Figure 6-52.) In most cases, you enter the appropriate code in the form's Load event procedure.

Selecting the Default List Box Item

Example 1 (SelectedItem property)
```
lstAnimal.SelectedItem = "Cat"
```
selects the Cat item in the lstAnimal control

Example 2 (SelectedItem property)
```
lstCode.SelectedItem = "101"
```
selects the 101 item in the lstCode control

Example 3 (SelectedIndex property)
```
lstCode.SelectedIndex = 2
```
selects the third item in the lstCode control

Figure 6-57 Examples of selecting the default list box item

START HERE

To select a default item in the lstHours and lstRates controls:

1. Click the **blank line** below the `Next decHours` clause in the form's Load event procedure. Most employees work 40 hours per week, so you'll have the Load event procedure automatically select that value in the Hours list box. Enter the following assignment statement:

   lstHours.SelectedItem = "40.0"

2. In the Rates list box, you will have the procedure automatically select the 10.00 value. That value is the fifth item in the list box, which means its index is 4. You can select the item using either the `lstRates.SelectedItem = "10.00"` statement or the `lstRates.SelectedIndex = 4` statement. Click the **blank line** below the `Next decRates` clause, and then enter the following assignment statement:

   lstRates.SelectedIndex = 4

3. Save the solution and then start the application. The form's Load event procedure fills the list boxes with values and then selects the default item in each list. See Figure 6-58.

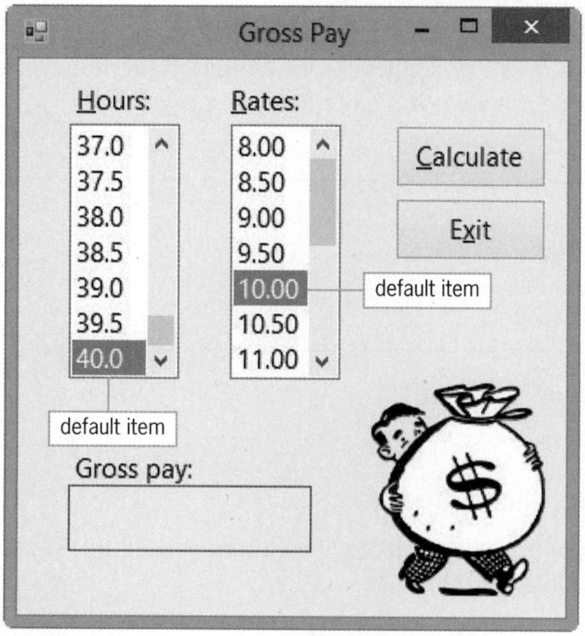

Figure 6-58 Default item selected in each list box

OpenClipArt.org/johnny_automatic

4. Click the **Exit** button.

GUI DESIGN TIP Default List Box Item

- If a list box allows the user to make only one selection, a default item should be selected when the interface first appears. The default item should be either the item selected most frequently or the first item in the list. However, if a list box allows more than one selection at a time, you do not select a default item.

The SelectedValueChanged and SelectedIndexChanged Events

Each time either the user or a statement selects an item in a list box, the list box's **SelectedValueChanged event** and its **SelectedIndexChanged event** occur. You can use the procedures associated with these events to perform one or more tasks when the selected item has changed. In the Gross Pay application, for example, you will use each list box's SelectedValueChanged procedure to clear the gross pay amount from the interface.

To code each list box's SelectedValueChanged event procedure:

START HERE

1. Open the code template for the lstHours control's SelectedValueChanged event procedure. Type **' clear the gross pay** and then press **Enter** twice. Now type **lblGross.Text = String.Empty** and press **Enter**.
2. Change `lstHours_SelectedValueChanged` in the Public Sub clause to **ClearLabel**, and then type the following at the end of the Handles clause (be sure to type the comma): **, lstRates.SelectedValueChanged**.
3. Save the solution.

Coding the Calculate Button's Click Event Procedure

In this section, you will complete the Gross Pay application by coding the btnCalc_Click procedure. The procedure's pseudocode is shown in Figure 6-59.

```
btnCalc Click event procedure
1. store the user input (hours and pay rate) in variables
2. calculate the gross pay = hours * pay rate
3. display the gross pay in the lblGross control
```

Figure 6-59 Pseudocode for the btnCalc_Click procedure

START HERE

To code and then test the btnCalc_Click procedure:

1. Open the code template for the btnCalc control's Click event procedure. Type the following comment and then press **Enter** twice:

   ' calculate gross pay

2. Recall that before you begin coding a procedure, you first study the procedure's pseudocode to determine the variables and named constants (if any) the procedure will use. In this case, the procedure will not use any named constants; however, it will use three variables. The `decHours` and `decRate` variables will store the items selected in the Hours and Rates list boxes, respectively. The `decGross` variable will store the gross pay amount. Enter the following three Dim statements. Press **Enter** twice after typing the last Dim statement.

   Dim decHours As Decimal
   Dim decRate As Decimal
   Dim decGross As Decimal

3. The first step in the pseudocode is to store the user input in variables. Enter the TryParse methods shown in Figure 6-60, and then position the insertion point as shown in the figure.

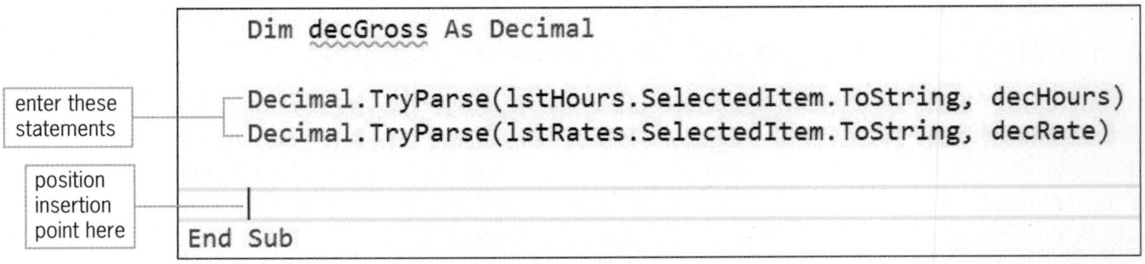

Figure 6-60 TryParse methods entered in the btnCalc_Click procedure

4. The second step in the pseudocode calculates the gross pay. Enter the following assignment statement:

   decGross = decHours * decRate

5. The last step in the pseudocode displays the gross pay in the lblGross control. Enter the following assignment statement:

   lblGross.Text = decGross.ToString("C2")

6. Save the solution and then start the application. Click the **Calculate** button. $400.00 appears in the Gross pay box. See Figure 6-61.

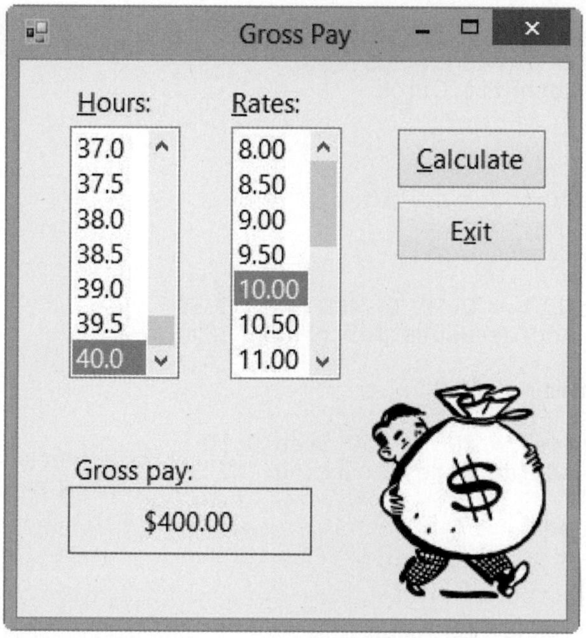

Figure 6-61 Gross pay shown in the interface
OpenClipArt.org/johnny_automatic

7. Click **38.5** in the Hours list box. The list box's SelectedValueChanged procedure removes the gross pay from the lblGross control. Click the **Calculate** button. $385.00 appears in the Gross pay box.

8. Click **13.50** in the Rates list box. The list box's SelectedValueChanged procedure removes the gross pay from the lblGross control. Click the **Calculate** button. $519.75 appears in the Gross pay box.

9. Click the **Exit** button. Close the Code Editor window and then close the solution.

Figure 6-62 shows the application's code.

```
' Name:         Gross Pay Project
' Purpose:      Displays an employee's gross pay
' Programmer:   <your name> on <current date>

Option Explicit On
Option Strict On
Option Infer Off

Public Class frmMain

    Private Sub btnExit_Click(sender As Object,
    e As EventArgs) Handles btnExit.Click
        Me.Close()
    End Sub

    Private Sub frmMain_Load(sender As Object,
    e As EventArgs) Handles Me.Load
        ' fill list boxes with values

        For decHours As Decimal = 0.5D To 40D Step 0.5D
            lstHours.Items.Add(decHours.ToString("N1"))
        Next decHours
        lstHours.SelectedItem = "40.0"

        For decRates As Decimal = 8D To 15D Step 0.5D
            lstRates.Items.Add(decRates.ToString("N2"))
        Next decRates
        lstRates.SelectedIndex = 4

    End Sub

    Private Sub ClearLabel(sender As Object,
    e As EventArgs) Handles lstHours.SelectedValueChanged,
    lstRates.SelectedValueChanged
        ' clear the gross pay

        lblGross.Text = String.Empty

    End Sub

    Private Sub btnCalc_Click(sender As Object,
    e As EventArgs) Handles btnCalc.Click
        ' calculate gross pay

        Dim decHours As Decimal
        Dim decRate As Decimal
        Dim decGross As Decimal

        Decimal.TryParse(lstHours.SelectedItem.ToString,
        decHours)
        Decimal.TryParse(lstRates.SelectedItem.ToString,
        decRate)

        decGross = decHours * decRate
        lblGross.Text = decGross.ToString("C2")

    End Sub
End Class
```

Figure 6-62 Gross Pay application's code

Lesson C Summary

- To add a list box to a form:

  Use the ListBox tool in the toolbox.

- To specify whether the user can select zero items, one item, or multiple items in a list box:

  Set the list box's SelectionMode property.

- To add items to a list box:

  Use the Items collection's Add method. The method's syntax is *object*.**Items.Add(***item***)**. In the syntax, *object* is the name of the list box control, and the *item* argument is the text you want to add to the control's list.

- To automatically sort the items in a list box:

  Set the list box's Sorted property to True.

- To determine the item selected in a list box, or to select a list box item from code:

  Use either the list box's SelectedItem property or its SelectedIndex property.

- To perform tasks when a different item is selected in a list box:

  Enter the code in either the list box's SelectedValueChanged procedure or its SelectedIndexChanged procedure.

Lesson C Key Terms

Add method—the Items collection's method used to add items to a list box

Collection—a group of individual objects treated as one unit

Default list box item—the item automatically selected in a list box when the interface appears on the screen

Items collection—the collection composed of the items in a list box

List box—a control used to display a list of items from which the user can select zero items, one item, or multiple items

SelectedIndex property—stores the index of the item selected in a list box

SelectedIndexChanged event—occurs when an item is selected in a list box

SelectedItem property—stores the value of the item selected in a list box

SelectedValueChanged event—occurs when an item is selected in a list box

SelectionMode property—determines the number of items that can be selected in a list box

Sorted property—specifies whether the list box items should appear in the order they are entered or in sorted order

Lesson C Review Questions

1. Which of the following methods is used to add items to a list box?

   a. Add

   b. AddList

   c. Item

   d. ItemAdd

2. The items in a list box belong to the ______________ collection.
   a. Items
   b. List
   c. ListItems
   d. Values

3. Which of the following properties stores the index of the item selected in a list box?
   a. Index
   b. SelectedIndex
   c. Selection
   d. SelectionIndex

4. Which of the following statements selects the "Horse" item, which appears third in the lstAnimal control?
   a. `lstAnimal.SelectedIndex = 2`
   b. `lstAnimal.SelectedIndex = 3`
   c. `lstAnimal.SelectedItem = 2`
   d. `lstAnimal.SelectedItem = 3`

5. The ______________ event occurs when the user selects a different item in a list box.
   a. SelectionChanged
   b. SelectedItemChanged
   c. SelectedValueChanged
   d. none of the above

Lesson C Exercises

INTRODUCTORY

1. In this exercise, you modify the Gross Pay application from this lesson. Use Windows to make a copy of the Gross Pay Solution folder. Rename the copy Modified Gross Pay Solution. Open the Gross Pay Solution (Gross Pay Solution.sln) file contained in the Modified Gross Pay Solution folder. Open the designer and Code Editor windows. Locate the form's Load event procedure. Change both For...Next statements to Do...Loop statements. Save the solution and then start and test the application. Close the Code Editor window and then close the solution.

INTRODUCTORY

2. In this exercise, you create an application that displays the ZIP code (or codes) corresponding to the city name selected in a list box. The city names and ZIP codes are shown in Figure 6-63. Create a Visual Basic Windows application. Use the following names for the solution and project, respectively: Zip Solution and Zip Project. Save the application in the VB2012\Chap06 folder. Change the form file's name to Main Form.vb. Change the form's name to frmMain.
   a. Create the interface shown in Figure 6-64. The items in the list box should be sorted; set the appropriate property.
   b. Code the application. The form's Load event procedure should add the city names shown in Figure 6-63 to the list box and then select the first name in the list. The list box's SelectedValueChanged event procedure should assign the item selected in the list box to a variable. It then should use the Select Case statement to display the city's ZIP code(s).

c. Save the solution and then start and test the application. Close the Code Editor window and then close the solution.

City	ZIP Code(s)
Park Ridge	60068
Barrington	60010, 60011
Glen Ellyn	60137, 60138
Algonquin	60102
Crystal Lake	60012

Figure 6-63 Information for Exercise 2

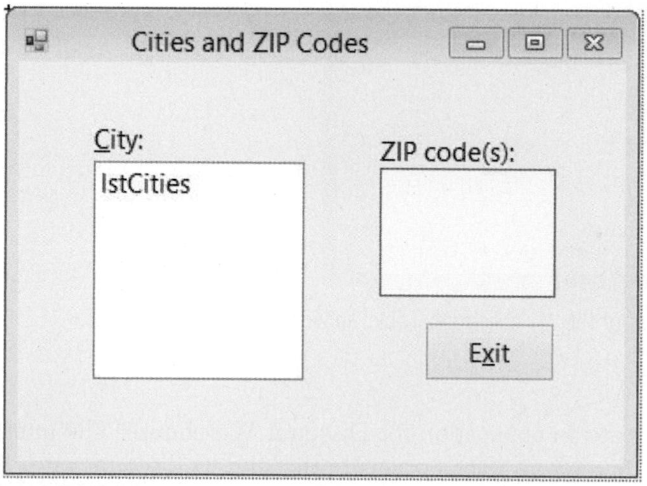

Figure 6-64 Interface for Exercise 2

INTRODUCTORY

3. In this exercise, you modify the application from Exercise 2. Use Windows to make a copy of the Zip Solution folder. Rename the copy Modified Zip Solution. Open the Zip Solution (Zip Solution.sln) file contained in the Modified Zip Solution folder. Open the designer and Code Editor windows. Modify the list box's SelectedValueChanged event procedure so that it assigns the index of the item selected in the list box to a variable. Modify the Select Case statement so that it displays the ZIP code(s) corresponding to the index stored in the variable. Save the solution and then start and test the application. Close the Code Editor window and then close the solution.

INTRODUCTORY

4. In this exercise, you create an application that displays the name of the state corresponding to the area code selected in a list box. Create a Visual Basic Windows application. Use the following names for the solution and project, respectively: Area Code Solution and Area Code Project. Save the application in the VB2012\Chap06 folder. Change the form file's name to Main Form.vb. Change the form's name to frmMain. Add five area codes of your choosing to the list box. When the user clicks an area code, the name of its corresponding state should appear in a label control. Create a suitable interface and then code the application. Save the solution and then start and test the application. Close the Code Editor window and then close the solution.

INTRODUCTORY

5. In this exercise, you create an application that displays a multiplication table similar to the one shown in Figure 6-65. Open the Multiplication Solution (Multiplication Solution.sln) file contained in the VB2012\Chap06\Multiplication Solution folder.

Code the application. Save the solution and then start and test the application. Close the Code Editor window and then close the solution.

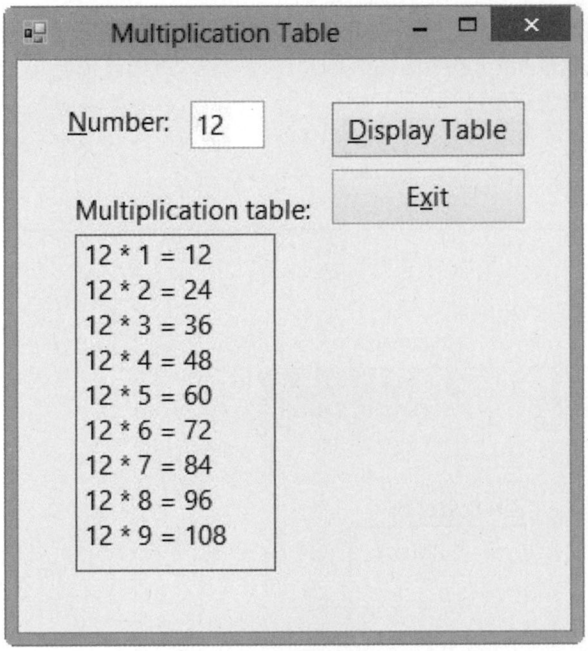

Figure 6-65 Sample run of the Multiplication Table application from Exercise 5

INTERMEDIATE

6. In this exercise, you create an application for Discount Warehouse. The interface should allow the user to enter an item's original price and its discount rate. The discount rates should range from 10% through 40% in increments of 5%. Use a text box for entering the original price, and use a list box for entering the discount rates. The application should display the amount of the discount and also the discounted price. Create a Visual Basic Windows application. Use the following names for the solution and project, respectively: Discount Solution and Discount Project. Save the application in the VB2012\Chap06 folder. Change the form file's name to Main Form.vb. Change the form's name to frmMain. Create a suitable interface and then code the application. Save the solution and then start and test the application. Close the Code Editor window and then close the solution.

INTERMEDIATE

7. In this exercise, you modify the Gross Pay application from this lesson. Use Windows to make a copy of the Gross Pay Solution folder. Rename the copy Gross Pay Solution-Intermediate. Open the Gross Pay Solution (Gross Pay Solution.sln) file contained in the Gross Pay Solution-Intermediate folder. Open the designer and Code Editor windows. Modify the form's Load event procedure to display hours from 0.5 through 50.0 in the lstHours control. If an employee worked more than 40 hours, he or she should receive time and one-half for the hours worked over 40. Make the appropriate modifications to the btnCalc control's Click event procedure. Save the solution and then start and test the application. Close the Code Editor window and then close the solution.

INTERMEDIATE

8. Mills Skating Rink holds a weekly ice-skating competition. Competing skaters must perform a two-minute program in front of a panel of judges. The number of judges varies from week to week. At the end of a skater's program, each judge assigns a score of 0 through 10 to the skater. The manager of the ice rink wants an application that allows him to enter each judge's score for a specific skater. The application should calculate and display the skater's average score. It also should display the skater's total score and

the number of scores entered. Figure 6-66 shows a sample run of the application, assuming the manager entered two scores: 8 and 6. (You enter a score by selecting it from the list box and then clicking the Record Score button.) Create a Visual Basic Windows application. Use the following names for the solution and project, respectively: Mills Solution and Mills Project. Save the application in the VB2012\ Chap06 folder. Change the form file's name to Main Form.vb. Change the form's name to frmMain. Create the interface shown in Figure 6-66 and then code the application. Save the solution and then start and test the application. Close the Code Editor window and then close the solution.

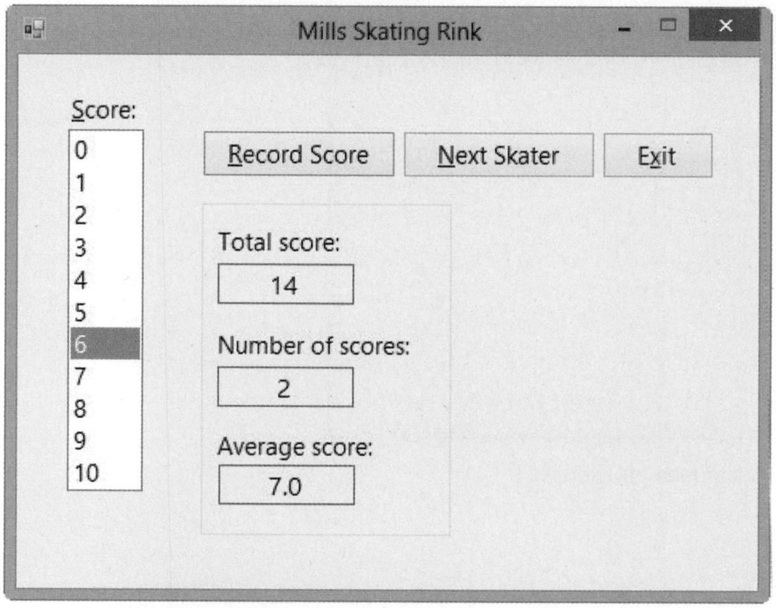

Figure 6-66 Sample run of the Mills Skating Rink application from Exercise 8

9. In this exercise, you create an application that allows the user to enter the gender (either F or M) and GPA for any number of students. The application should calculate the average GPA for all students, the average GPA for male students, and the average GPA for female students. The list box should list GPAs from 1.0 through 4.0 in increments of 0.1. (For example, 1.0, 1.1, 1.2, 1.3, and so on.) Create a Visual Basic Windows application. Use the following names for the solution and project, respectively: GPA Solution and GPA Project. Save the application in the VB2012\ Chap06 folder. Change the form file's name to Main Form.vb. Change the form's name to frmMain. Create the interface shown in Figure 6-67 and then code the application. Save the solution and then start and test the application. Close the Code Editor window and then close the solution.

INTERMEDIATE

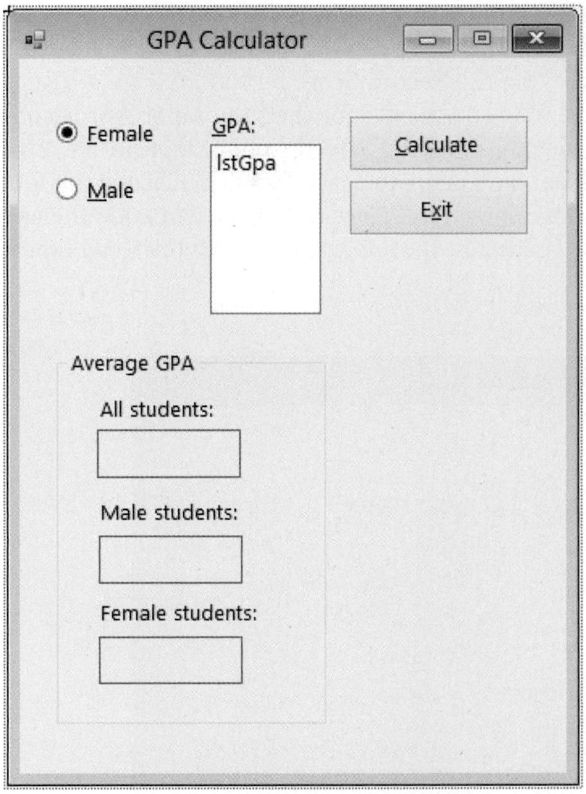

Figure 6-67 Interface for Exercise 9

ADVANCED

10. In this exercise, you code an application that allows the user 10 chances to guess a random number generated by the computer. The random number should be an integer from 1 through 50, inclusive. Each time the user makes an incorrect guess, the application should display a message that tells the user either to guess a higher number or to guess a lower number. When the user guesses the random number, the application should display a "Congratulations!" message. If the user is not able to guess the random number after 10 tries, the application should display the random number in a message. Open the Random Solution (Random Solution.sln) file contained in the VB2012\Chap06\Random Solution folder. If necessary, open the designer window. Code the application. Save the solution and then start and test the application. Close the Code Editor window and then close the solution.

ADVANCED

11. In this exercise, you code an application that displays the first 10 Fibonacci numbers: 1, 1, 2, 3, 5, 8, 13, 21, 34, and 55. Notice that, beginning with the third number in the series, each Fibonacci number is the sum of the prior two numbers. In other words, 2 is the sum of 1 plus 1, 3 is the sum of 1 plus 2, 5 is the sum of 2 plus 3, and so on. Open the Fibonacci Solution (Fibonacci Solution.sln) file contained in the VB2012\Chap06\Fibonacci Solution folder. If necessary, open the designer window. Code the application. Display the numbers in the lblNumbers control. Save the solution and then start and test the application. Close the Code Editor window and then close the solution.

ADVANCED

12. The accountant at Sonheim Manufacturing Company wants an application that calculates an asset's annual depreciation. The accountant will enter the asset's cost, useful life (in years), and salvage value (which is the value of the asset at the end of its useful life). Use a list box to display the useful life, which should range from 3 through 20 years. The application should use the double-declining balance method to calculate the annual depreciation amounts; it then should display the amounts in the interface.

You can use the Financial.DDB method to calculate the depreciation. The method's syntax is **Financial.DDB(*cost, salvage, life, period*)**. In the syntax, the *cost*, *salvage*, and *life* arguments are the asset's cost, salvage value, and useful life, respectively. The *period* argument is the period for which you want the depreciation amount calculated. The method returns the depreciation amount as a Double number. Figure 6-68 shows a sample depreciation schedule for an asset with a cost of $1000, a useful life of 4 years, and a salvage value of $100. Create a Visual Basic Windows application. Use the following names for the solution and project, respectively: Sonheim Solution and Sonheim Project. Save the application in the VB2012\Chap06 folder. Change the form file's name to Main Form.vb. Change the form's name to frmMain. Create the interface shown in Figure 6-68. Set the txtSchedule control's Multiline and ReadOnly properties to True, and set its ScrollBars property to Vertical. Code the application. Save the solution and then start and test the application. Close the Code Editor window and then close the solution.

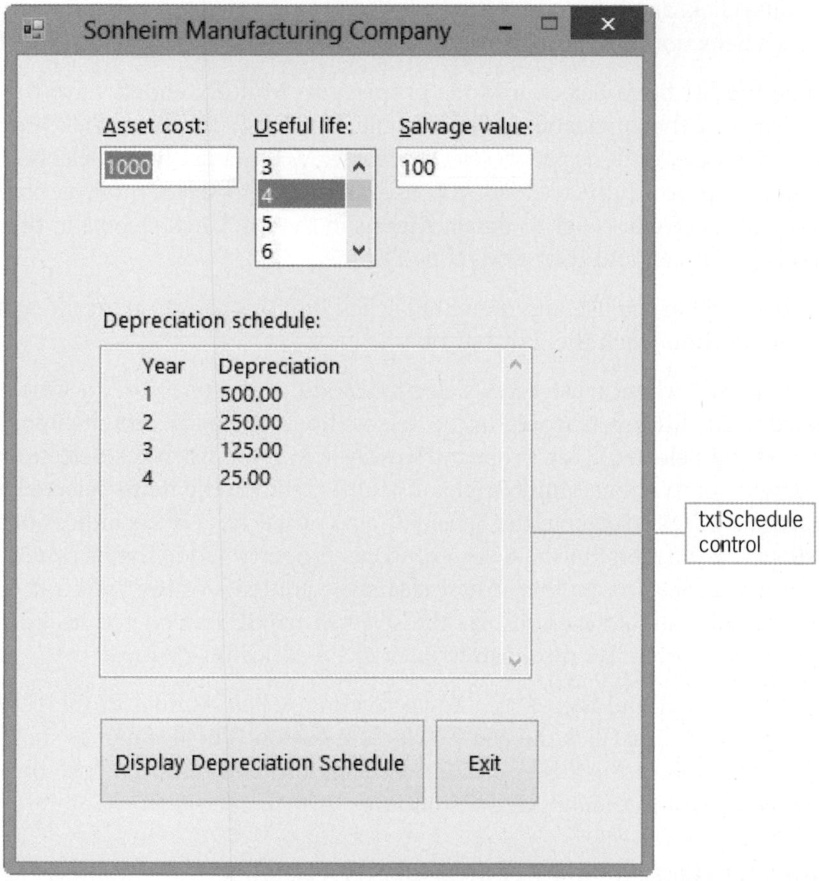

Figure 6-68 Sample run of the Sonheim Manufacturing Company application for Exercise 12

13. In this exercise, you learn how to create a list box that allows the user to select more than one item at a time. Open the Multi Solution (Multi Solution.sln) file contained in the VB2012\Chap06\Multi Solution folder. If necessary, open the designer window. The interface contains a list box named lstNames. The list box's Sorted and SelectionMode properties are set to True and One, respectively. DISCOVERY

a. Open the Code Editor window. The form's Load event procedure adds five names to the lstNames control. Code the btnSingle control's Click event procedure so that it displays, in the lblResult control, the item selected in the list box. For example, if the user clicks Debbie in the list box and then clicks the Single Selection button, the name Debbie should appear in the lblResult control. (Hint: Use the Convert.ToString method.)

b. Save the solution and then start the application. Click Debbie in the list box, then click Ahmad, and then click Bill. Notice that when the list box's SelectionMode property is set to One, you can select only one item at a time in the list.

c. Click the Single Selection button. The name Bill appears in the lblResult control. Click the Exit button.

d. Change the list box's SelectionMode property to MultiSimple. Save the solution and then start the application. Click Debbie in the list box, then click Ahmad, then click Bill, and then click Ahmad. Notice that when the list box's SelectionMode property is set to MultiSimple, you can select more than one item at a time in the list. Also notice that you click to both select and deselect an item. (You also can use Ctrl+click and Shift+click, as well as press the Spacebar, to select and deselect items when the list box's SelectionMode property is set to MultiSimple.) Click the Exit button.

e. Change the list box's SelectionMode property to MultiExtended. Save the solution and then start the application. Click Debbie in the list, and then click Jim. Notice that in this case, clicking Jim deselects Debbie. When a list box's SelectionMode property is set to MultiExtended, you use Ctrl+click to select multiple items in the list. You also use Ctrl+click to deselect items in the list. Click Debbie in the list, then Ctrl+click Ahmad, and then Ctrl+click Debbie.

f. Next, click Bill in the list, and then Shift+click Jim; this selects all of the names from Bill through Jim. Click the Exit button.

g. As you know, when a list box's SelectionMode property is set to One, the item selected in the list box is stored in the SelectedItem property, and the item's index is stored in the SelectedIndex property. However, when a list box's SelectionMode property is set to either MultiSimple or MultiExtended, the items selected in the list box are stored (as strings) in the SelectedItems property, and the indices of the items are stored (as integers) in the SelectedIndices property. Code the btnMulti control's Click event procedure so that it first clears the contents of the lblResult control. The procedure should then display the selected names (which are stored in the SelectedItems property) on separate lines in the lblResult control.

h. Save the solution and then start the application. Click Ahmad in the list box, and then Shift+click Jim. Click the Multi-Selection button. The five names should appear on separate lines in the lblResult control. Click the Exit button. Close the Code Editor window and then close the solution.

DISCOVERY

14. In this exercise, you learn how to use the Items collection's Insert, Remove, RemoveAt, and Clear methods. You also learn how to use the Items collection's Count property. Open the Items Solution (Items Solution.sln) file contained in the VB2012\Chap06\Items Solution folder. If necessary, open the designer window.

a. The Items collection's Insert method allows you to add an item at a desired position in a list box during run time. The Insert method's syntax is *object*.**Items.Insert(***position*, *item***)**, where *position* is the index of the item. Code the Insert button's Click event procedure so it adds your name as the fourth item in the list box.

b. The Items collection's Remove method allows you to remove an item from a list box during run time. The Remove method's syntax is *object*.**Items.Remove(***item***)**, where *item* is the item's value. Code the Remove button's Click event procedure so it removes your name from the list box.

c. Like the Remove method, the Items collection's RemoveAt method also allows you to remove an item from a list box while an application is running. However, in the RemoveAt method, you specify the item's index rather than its value. The RemoveAt method's syntax is *object*.**Items.RemoveAt(***index***)**, where *index* is the item's index. Code the Remove At button's Click event procedure so it removes the second name from the list box.

d. You can use the Items collection's Clear method to remove all items from a list box during run time. The Clear method's syntax is *object*.**Items.Clear()**. Code the Clear button's Click event procedure so it clears the items from the list box.

e. The Items collection's Count property stores the number of items contained in a list box. Code the Count button's Click event procedure so it displays (in a message box) the number of items listed in the lstNames control.

f. Save the solution and then start and test the application. Close the Code Editor window and then close the solution.

DISCOVERY

15. In this exercise, you learn how to use the String Collection Editor window to fill a list box with values. Open the ListBox Solution (ListBox Solution.sln) file contained in the VB2012\Chap06\ListBox Solution folder. If necessary, open the designer window. Open the Code Editor window. Remove the Add methods and the For...Next statement from the form's Load event procedure. Close the Code Editor window. Click the lstAnimal control on the form. Click the Items property in the Properties list and then click the ellipsis (...) button in the Settings box. The String Collection Editor window opens. Type Dog and then press Enter. Type Cat and then press Enter. Finally, type Horse and then press Enter. Click the OK button to close the dialog box. Use the String Collection Editor window to enter the following codes in the lstCode control: 100, 101, 102, 103, 104, and 105. Save the solution and then start the application. Close the solution.

SWAT THE BUGS

16. Open the Debug Solution (Debug Solution.sln) file contained in the VB2012\Chap06\Debug Solution-Lesson C folder. If necessary, open the designer window. Open the Code Editor window and review the existing code. Start and then test the application. Be sure to include non-integers in your test data. (If you need to stop an endless loop, click DEBUG on the menu bar and then click Stop Debugging.) Correct any errors in the code. Save the solution and then start and test the application again. Close the Code Editor window and then close the solution.

CHAPTER 7

Sub and Function Procedures

Creating the Cerruti Company Application

In this chapter, you create an application for Lucy Malkin, the payroll manager at Cerruti Company. Currently, Ms. Malkin manually calculates each employee's weekly gross pay, federal withholding tax (FWT), Social Security and Medicare (FICA) tax, and net pay. Making these calculations manually is both time-consuming and prone to mathematical errors. Ms. Malkin has asked you to create an application that she can use to perform the payroll calculations both efficiently and accurately.

Previewing the Cerruti Company Application

Before you start the first lesson in this chapter, you will preview the completed application. The application is contained in the VB2012\Chap07 folder.

START HERE

To preview the completed application:

1. Use the Run dialog box to run the Cerruti (Cerruti.exe) file contained in the VB2012\Chap07 folder. The application's user interface appears on the screen.
2. Type **Georgia Manero** in the Name box and then click the **Married** radio button.
3. Scroll down the Hours list box and then click **41.0** in the list. Scroll down the Rate list box and then click **13.00** in the list.
4. The interface contains a combo box that allows you to either type the number of withholding allowances or select the number from a list. Click the **list arrow** in the Allowances combo box and then click **3** in the list.
5. Click the **Calculate** button. The gross pay, taxes, and net pay appear in the interface. See Figure 7-1.

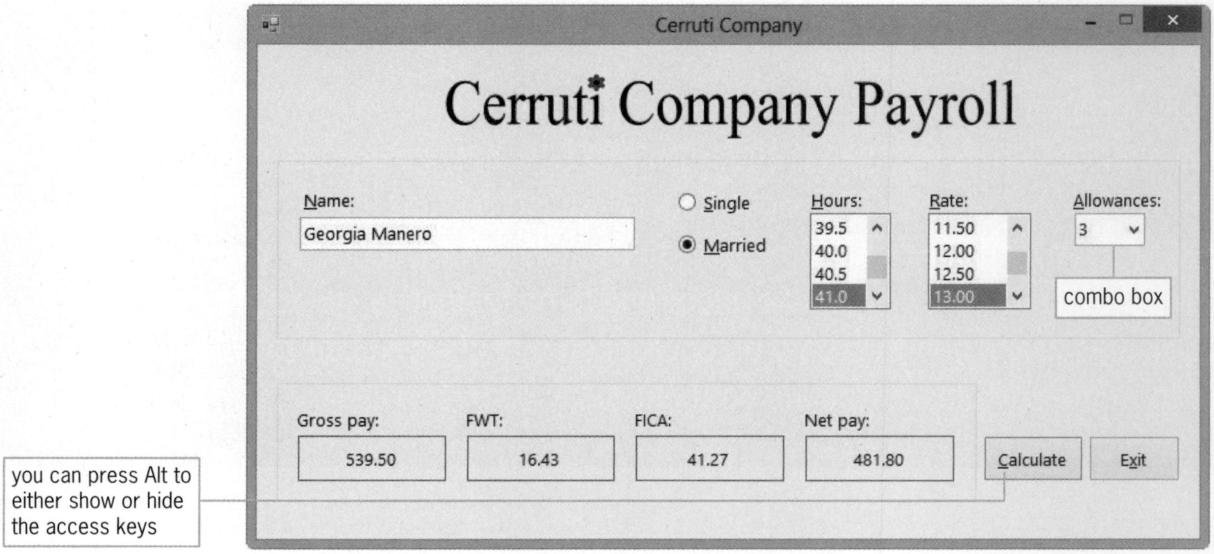

Figure 7-1 Interface showing the payroll calculations

6. Click the **Exit** button. The "Do you want to exit?" message appears in a message box. See Figure 7-2.

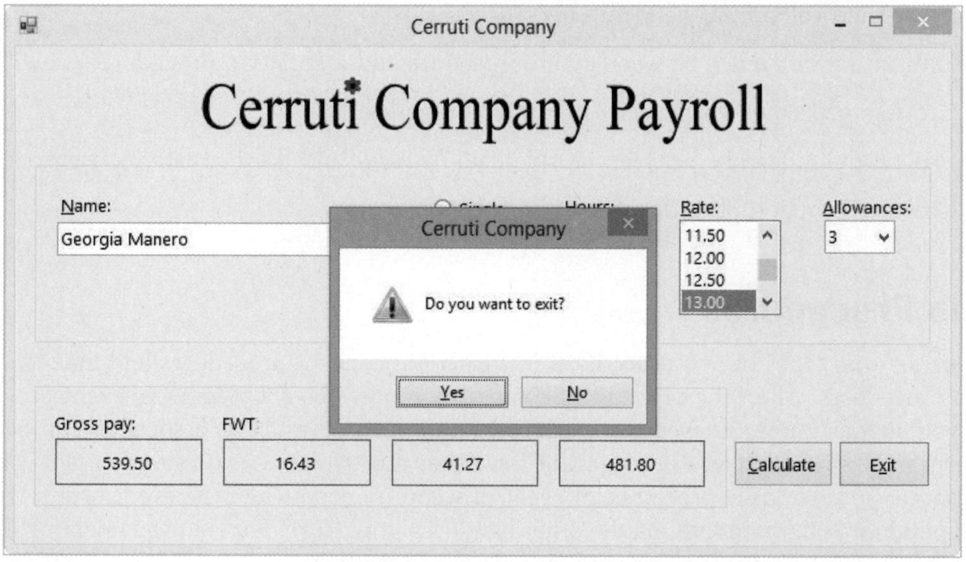

Figure 7-2 Message box containing a confirmation message

7. Click the **No** button. Notice that the form remains on the screen. In Lesson C, you will learn how to prevent the computer from closing a form.
8. Click the **Exit** button and then click the **Yes** button in the message box. The application ends.

The Cerruti Company application uses a combo box and a Function procedure. You will learn about Function procedures, more simply referred to as functions, in Lesson A. Combo boxes are covered in Lesson B. You will code the Cerruti Company application in Lesson C. Be sure to complete each lesson in full and do all of the end-of-lesson questions and several exercises before continuing to the next lesson.

LESSON A

After studying Lesson A, you should be able to:

- Create and call an independent Sub procedure
- Explain the difference between a Sub procedure and a Function procedure
- Create a procedure that receives information passed to it
- Explain the difference between passing data *by value* and passing data *by reference*
- Create a Function procedure

Sub Procedures

There are two types of Sub procedures in Visual Basic: event procedures and independent Sub procedures. All of the procedures coded in the previous chapters were event procedures. As you already know, an event procedure is a Sub procedure that is associated with a specific object and event, such as a button's Click event or a text box's TextChanged event. The computer automatically processes an event procedure's code when the event occurs. An **independent Sub procedure**, on the other hand, is a procedure that is independent of any object and event. An independent Sub procedure is processed only when called (invoked) from code. In Visual Basic, you invoke an independent Sub procedure using the **Call statement**.

Programmers use independent Sub procedures for several reasons. First, they allow the programmer to avoid duplicating code when different sections of a program need to perform the same task. Rather than enter the code in each of those sections, the programmer can enter the code in a procedure and then have each section call the procedure to perform its task when needed. Second, consider an event procedure that must perform many tasks. To keep the event procedure's code from getting unwieldy and difficult to understand, the programmer can assign some of the tasks to one or more independent Sub procedures. Doing this makes the event procedure easier to code because it allows the programmer to concentrate on one small piece of the code at a time. And finally, independent Sub procedures are used extensively in large and complex programs, which typically are written by a team of programmers. The programming team will break up the program into small and manageable tasks, and then assign some of the tasks to different team members to be coded as independent Sub procedures. Doing this allows more than one programmer to work on the program at the same time, decreasing the time it takes to write the program.

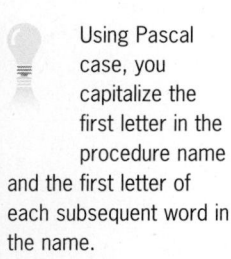

Using Pascal case, you capitalize the first letter in the procedure name and the first letter of each subsequent word in the name.

Figure 7-3 shows the syntax of both an independent Sub procedure and the Call statement in Visual Basic. Like event procedures, independent Sub procedures have a procedure header and a procedure footer. In most cases, the procedure header begins with the `Private` keyword, which indicates that the procedure can be used only within the current Code Editor window. Following the `Private` keyword is the `Sub` keyword, which identifies the procedure as a Sub procedure. After the `Sub` keyword is the procedure name. The rules for naming an independent Sub procedure are the same as those for naming variables; however, procedure names are usually entered using Pascal case. The Sub procedure's name should indicate the task the procedure performs. It is a common practice to begin the name with a verb. For example, a good name for a Sub procedure that displays two random integers is DisplayRandomIntegers.

Independent Sub Procedure and Call Statement

Syntax of an independent Sub procedure
Private Sub *procedureName*(*[parameterList]*)
statements
End Sub

Syntax of the Call statement
Call *procedureName*(*[argumentList]*)

Example 1
```
Private Sub DisplayRandomIntegers()
    Dim randGen As New Random
    lblNum1.Text = randGen.Next(1, 11).ToString
    lblNum2.Text = randGen.Next(1, 11).ToString
End Sub

Call DisplayRandomIntegers()
```
calls (invokes) the DisplayRandomIntegers procedure

Example 2
```
Private Sub DisplaySum(dblScore1 As Double,
                       dblScore2 As Double)
    Dim dblSum As Double
    dblSum = dblScore1 + dblScore2
    lblSum.Text = dblSum.ToString
End Sub

Call DisplaySum(45.9, 73.6)
or
Call DisplaySum(dblMidterm, dblFinal)
```
either of these Call statements can be used to invoke the DisplaySum procedure

Figure 7-3 Syntax and examples of an independent Sub procedure and the Call statement

Following the procedure name in the procedure header is a set of parentheses that contains an optional *parameterList*. The parameterList lists the data type and name of one or more parameters. As you learned in Chapter 4, a parameter represents information that is passed to a procedure when the procedure is invoked. Each parameter in the parameterList has procedure scope and each stores an item of data. The data is passed to the procedure through the Call statement's *argumentList*. The number of arguments should agree with the number of parameters. If the parameterList does not contain any parameters, as shown in Example 1 in Figure 7-3, then an empty set of parentheses follows the procedure name in the Call statement. However, if the parameterList contains one parameter, then the argumentList should have one argument. Similarly, a procedure that contains three parameters requires three arguments in the Call statement that invokes it. (Refer to the Tip on this page for an exception to this general rule.)

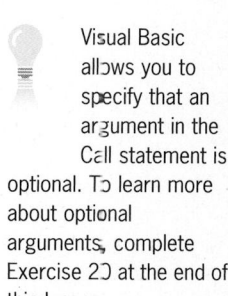

Visual Basic allows you to specify that an argument in the Call statement is optional. To learn more about optional arguments, complete Exercise 20 at the end of this lesson.

In addition to having the same number of arguments as parameters, the data type and order (or position) of each argument should agree with the data type and order (position) of its corresponding parameter. If the first parameter has a data type of String and the second a data type of Double, then the first argument in the Call statement should have the String data type and the second should have the Double data type. This is because when the procedure is called, the computer stores the value of the first argument in the procedure's first parameter, the value of the second argument in its second parameter, and so on. For instance, when processing the first Call statement shown in Example 2 in Figure 7-3, the computer will store the Double number 45.9 in the `dblScore1` parameter and then store the Double number 73.6 in the `dblScore2` parameter.

An argument can be a literal constant (as shown in the first Call statement in Example 2 in Figure 7-3), a named constant, a keyword, or a variable (as shown in the second Call statement in Example 2 in Figure 7-3). However, in most cases, the argument will be a variable.

Passing Variables

The internal memory of a computer is similar to a large post office. Like each post office box, each memory cell has a unique address.

Ch07A video

Each variable declared in a program has both a value and a unique address that represents the location of the variable in the computer's internal memory. Visual Basic allows you to pass either a copy of the variable's value or its address to the receiving procedure. Passing a copy of a variable's value is referred to as **passing by value**, whereas passing its address is referred to as **passing by reference**. The method you choose—*by value* or *by reference*—depends on whether you want the receiving procedure to have access to the variable in memory. In other words, it depends on whether you want to allow the receiving procedure to change the variable's contents.

Although the idea of passing information *by value* and *by reference* may sound confusing at first, it is a concept with which you are already familiar. We'll use the illustrations shown in Figure 7-4 to demonstrate this fact. Assume you have a savings account at a local bank. (Think of the savings account as a variable.) During a conversation with your friend Joan, you mention the amount of money you have in the account, as shown in Illustration A. Sharing this information with Joan is similar to passing a variable *by value*. Knowing the balance in your savings account does not give Joan access to the account. It merely provides information that she can use to compare with the amount of money she has saved.

Now we'll use the savings account example to demonstrate passing information *by reference*. (Here again, think of your savings account as a variable.) To either deposit money in your account or withdraw money from your account, you must provide the bank teller with your account number, as shown in Illustration B in Figure 7-4. The account number represents the location of your account at the bank and allows the teller to change the account balance. Giving the teller your bank account number is similar to passing a variable *by reference*. The account number allows the teller to change the contents of your bank account, similar to the way a variable's address allows the receiving procedure to change the contents of the variable.

Figure 7-4 Illustrations of passing *by value* and passing *by reference*
Image by Diane Zak; Created with Reallusion CrazyTalk Animator

Passing Variables by Value

To pass a variable *by value*, you include the keyword `ByVal` before the name of its corresponding parameter in the receiving procedure's parameterList. When you pass a variable *by value*, the computer passes a copy of the variable's contents to the receiving procedure. When only a copy of the contents is passed, the receiving procedure is not given access to the variable in memory. Therefore, it cannot change the value stored inside the variable. It is appropriate to pass a variable *by value* when the receiving procedure needs to *know* the variable's contents, but it does not need to *change* the contents. In this section, you will finish coding the Favorite Title application, which passes two variables *by value* to an independent Sub procedure.

To begin coding the Favorite Title application:

START HERE

1. If necessary, start Visual Studio 2012. Open the Favorite Title Solution (Favorite Title Solution.sln) file contained in the VB2012\Chap07\Favorite Title Solution folder. If necessary, open the designer window. See Figure 7-5.

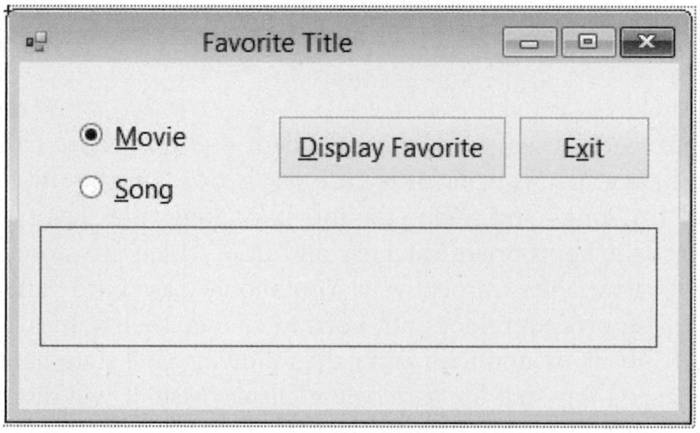

Figure 7-5 Favorite Title application's interface

2. Open the Code Editor window. Replace <your name> and <current date> in the comments with your name and the current date, respectively.
3. Locate the btnDisplay_Click event procedure. See Figure 7-6. Depending on which radio button is selected, the event procedure gets the title of the user's favorite movie or song.

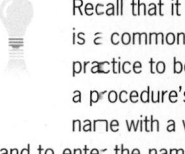

Recall that it is a common practice to begin a procedure's name with a verb and to enter the name using Pascal case.

```
Private Sub btnDisplay_Click(sender As Object, e As EventArgs) Ha
    ' gets the title and then calls
    ' a procedure to display the title

    Dim strCategory As String
    Dim strTitle As String

    If radMovie.Checked Then
        strCategory = "movie"
        strTitle =
            InputBox("Your favorite movie?", "Movie")
    Else
        strCategory = "song"
        strTitle = InputBox("Your favorite song?", "Song")
    End If


End Sub
```

Figure 7-6 Partially-coded btnDisplay_Click event procedure

4. Before the event procedure ends, it will call an independent Sub procedure named DisplayMsg to display the message "Your favorite *category* is *title*." In the message, *category* is either "movie" or "song", and *title* is the movie or song title. The Call statement will need to pass the appropriate category and title, which are stored in the `strCategory` and `strTitle` variables, respectively. You should pass both variables *by value* because the DisplayMsg procedure does not need to change their values. Click the **blank line** above the End Sub clause and then enter the following Call statement. (Don't be concerned about the jagged line that appears below DisplayMsg; it will disappear when you create the procedure in the next set of steps.)

   Call DisplayMsg(strCategory, strTitle)

Next, you will create the DisplayMsg procedure. The procedure will store the two String values it receives from the Call statement in two parameters named `strType` and `strName`. Some programmers enter independent Sub procedures above the first event procedure, while others enter them below the last event procedure. Still others enter them either immediately above or immediately below the procedure from which they are invoked. Whichever way is chosen, however, all independent Sub procedures must appear between the Public Class and End Class clauses and outside of any other procedure. In this book, the independent Sub procedures will be entered above the first event procedure in the Code Editor window.

START HERE

To finish coding the Favorite Title application:

1. If necessary, scroll to the top of the Code Editor window. Click the **blank line** below the `' independent Sub procedure` clause and then enter the DisplayMsg procedure shown in Figure 7-7. Notice that when you press Enter after typing the procedure header, the Code Editor automatically enters the procedure footer (`End Sub`) for you.

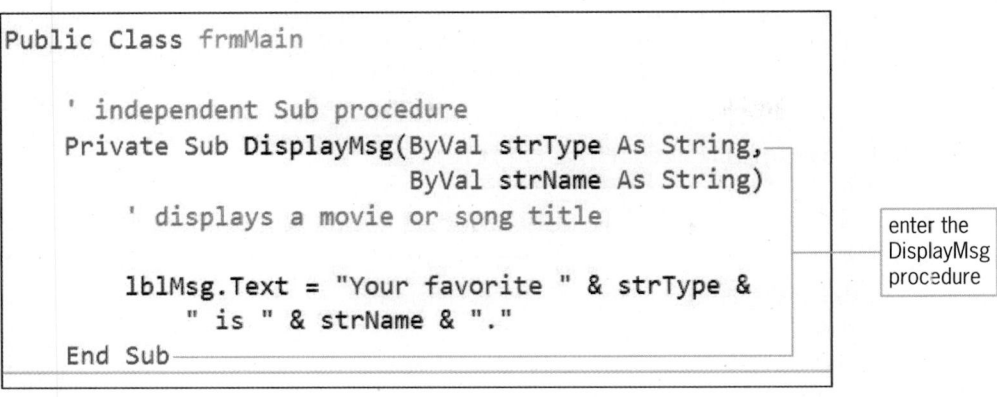

```
Public Class frmMain

    ' independent Sub procedure
    Private Sub DisplayMsg(ByVal strType As String,
                           ByVal strName As String)
        ' displays a movie or song title

        lblMsg.Text = "Your favorite " & strType &
            " is " & strName & "."
    End Sub
```

enter the DisplayMsg procedure

Figure 7-7 DisplayMsg procedure

2. Save the solution and then start the application. Click the **Display Favorite** button. The InputBox function in the button's Click event procedure prompts you to enter the name of your favorite movie. Type **Gone with the Wind** in the Movie dialog box and then press **Enter**. The Call statement in the event procedure invokes the DisplayMsg procedure, passing it a copy of the value stored in the `strCategory` variable (movie) and a copy of the value stored in the `strTitle` variable (Gone with the Wind). The DisplayMsg procedure header stores the values passed to it in its `strType` and `strName` parameters. The assignment statement in the procedure then displays the message shown in Figure 7-8 in the lblMsg control.

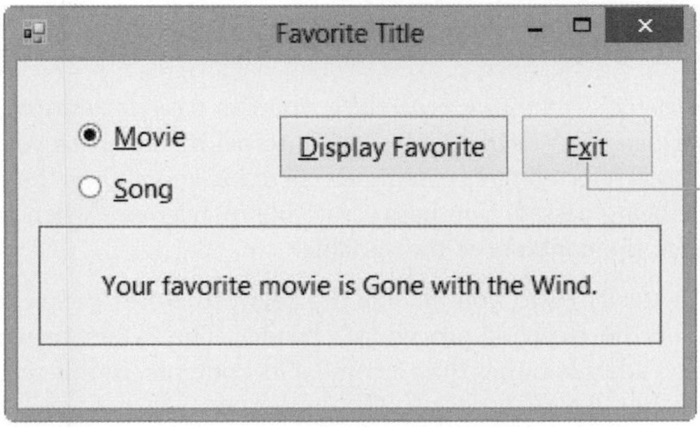

you can press Alt to either show or hide the access keys

Figure 7-8 Message shown in the interface

3. Click the **Song** radio button and then click the **Display Favorite** button. Type the name of your favorite song in the Song dialog box and then press **Enter**. A message containing the name of your favorite song appears in the lblMsg control.
4. Click the **Exit** button. Close the Code Editor window and then close the solution.

Figure 7-9 shows the DisplayMsg procedure header and the Call statement that invokes the procedure. Notice that the number, data type, and order (position) of the arguments in the Call statement match the number, data type, and order (position) of the corresponding parameters in the DisplayMsg procedure header. Also notice that the names of the arguments do not need to be identical to the names of the corresponding parameters. In fact, to avoid confusion, you should use different names for the arguments and parameters.

```
Private Sub DisplayMsg(ByVal strType As String,     parameterList
                       ByVal strName As String)

Call DisplayMsg(strCategory, strTitle)
                      argumentList
```

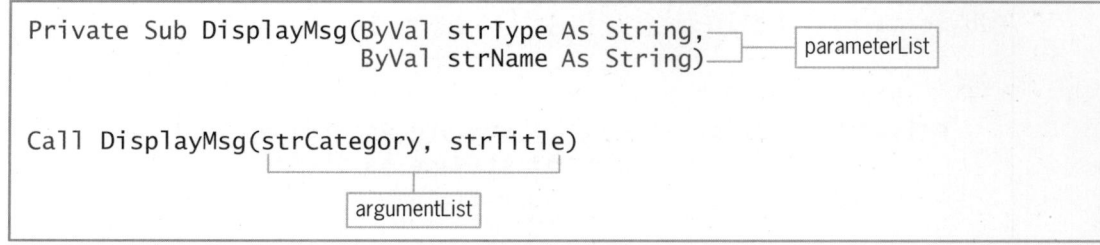

Figure 7-9 DisplayMsg procedure header and Call statement

The Call statement does not indicate whether a variable is being passed *by value* or *by reference*. To make that determination, you need to look at the receiving procedure's header.

YOU DO IT 1!

Create a Visual Basic Windows application named YouDoIt 1. Save the application in the VB2012\Chap07 folder. Add a text box, a label, and a button to the form. The button's Click event procedure should assign the text box value to a Double variable and then pass a copy of the variable's value to an independent Sub procedure named ShowDouble. The ShowDouble procedure should multiply the variable's value by 2 and then display the result in the label control. Code the button's Click event procedure and the ShowDouble procedure. Save the solution and then start and test the application. Close the solution.

Passing Variables by Reference

Instead of passing a copy of a variable's value to a procedure, you can pass its address. In other words, you can pass the variable's location in the computer's internal memory. As you learned earlier, passing a variable's address is referred to as passing *by reference*, and it gives the receiving procedure access to the variable being passed. You pass a variable *by reference* when you want the receiving procedure to change the contents of the variable.

To pass a variable *by reference* in Visual Basic, you include the keyword `ByRef` before the name of the corresponding parameter in the receiving procedure's header. The `ByRef` keyword tells the computer to pass the variable's address rather than a copy of its contents. In this section, you will modify the Gross Pay application from Chapter 6. The application will now use an independent Sub procedure named CalcGross to calculate the gross pay. The Call statement that invokes the CalcGross procedure will have three variables in its argumentList. The first two variables will be passed *by value*; the third will be passed *by reference*.

START HERE

To open the Gross Pay application from Chapter 6:

1. Open the Gross Pay Solution (Gross Pay Solution.sln) file contained in the VB2012\Chap07\Gross Pay Solution-Sub folder. If necessary, open the designer window. See Figure 7-10. Recall that the application calculates and displays an employee's gross pay, which is based on the hours worked and pay rate entered by the user.

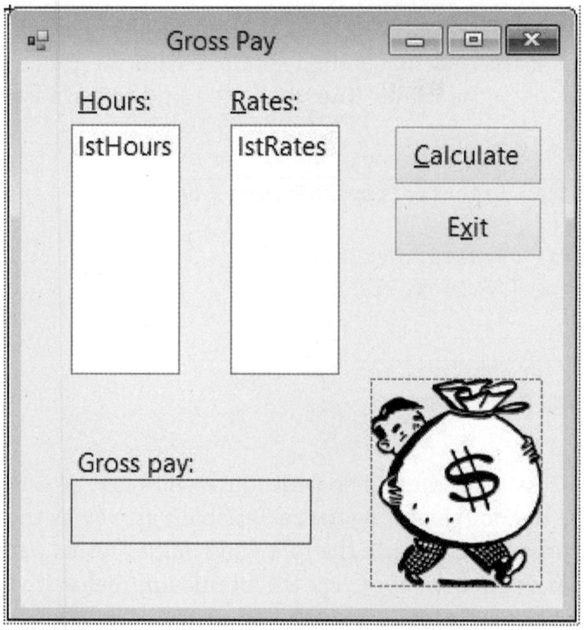

Figure 7-10 Gross Pay application's interface
OpenClipArt.org/johnny_automatic

2. Open the Code Editor window. Replace <your name> and <current date> in the comments with your name and the current date, respectively.

3. Locate the btnCalc_Click procedure. The procedure's code from Chapter 6 is shown in Figure 7-11.

```
Private Sub btnCalc_Click(sender As Object, e As EventArgs) Han
    ' calculate gross pay

    Dim decHours As Decimal
    Dim decRate As Decimal
    Dim decGross As Decimal

    Decimal.TryParse(lstHours.SelectedItem.ToString, decHours)
    Decimal.TryParse(lstRates.SelectedItem.ToString, decRate)

    decGross = decHours * decRate
    lblGross.Text = decGross.ToString("C2")

End Sub
```

this assignment statement calculates the gross pay

Figure 7-11 btnCalc_Click procedure from Chapter 6

Before displaying the gross pay, the btnCalc_Click procedure will call an independent Sub procedure named CalcGross to calculate the gross pay. For the CalcGross procedure to perform its task, it needs to know the number of hours worked and the pay rate; those values are stored in the `decHours` and `decRate` variables, respectively. The CalcGross procedure will not need to change the values stored in the variables, so you will pass the variables *by value*. However, the CalcGross procedure also needs to know where to store the gross pay after it has been calculated. To have the procedure store the gross pay in the `decGross` variable, you will need to pass the variable's address to the procedure. In other words, you will need to pass the variable *by reference*.

START HERE

To modify the application's code and then test the code:

1. Replace the assignment statement that calculates the gross pay with the Call statement shown in Figure 7-12, and then click the **blank line** above the End Sub clause.

replace the assignment statement with this Call statement

```
    Decimal.TryParse(lstRates.SelectedItem.ToString, decRate)

    Call CalcGross(decHours, decRate, decGross)
    lblGross.Text = decGross.ToString("C2")

End Sub
```

Figure 7-12 Call statement entered in the procedure

2. Now you will create the CalcGross procedure. The procedure will need to receive a copy of the values stored in the `decHours` and `decRate` variables, as well as the address of the `decGross` variable. The procedure will use the following names for its parameters: `decHoursWkd`, `decPayRate`, and `decGrossPay`. Click the **blank line** below the `Public Class frmMain` clause and then press **Enter** to insert another blank line. Enter the CalcGross procedure shown in Figure 7-13.

enter the CalcGross procedure

```
Public Class frmMain

    Private Sub CalcGross(ByVal decHoursWkd As Decimal,
                          ByVal decPayRate As Decimal,
                          ByRef decGrossPay As Decimal)
        ' calculate gross pay for btnCalc_Click

        decGrossPay = decHoursWkd * decPayRate
    End Sub
```

Figure 7-13 CalcGross procedure

3. Save the solution and then start the application. Click **38.5** in the Hours list box, and then click **9.00** in the Rates list box. Click the **Calculate** button. $346.50 appears in the Gross pay box, as shown in Figure 7-14.

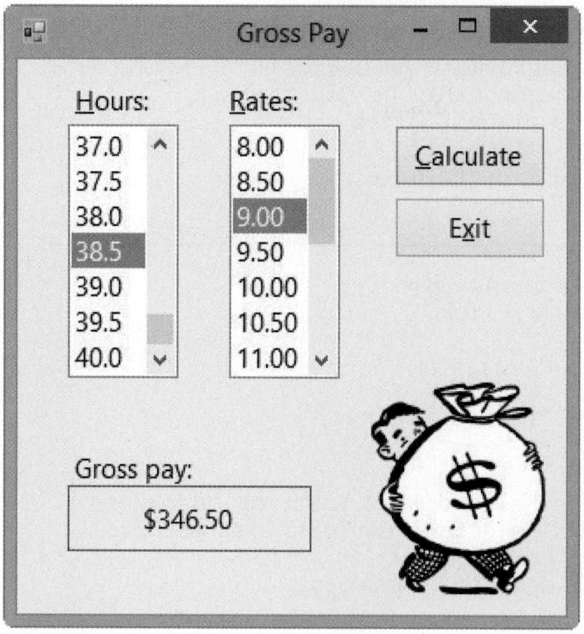

Figure 7-14 Gross pay shown in the interface
OpenClipArt.org/johnny_automatic

4. Click the **Exit** button. Close the Code Editor window and then close the solution.

Figure 7-15 shows the CalcGross and btnCalc_Click procedures. Here again, notice that the number, data type, and order (position) of the arguments in the Call statement match the number, data type, and order (position) of the corresponding parameters in the CalcGross procedure header. Also notice that the names of the arguments are not identical to the names of their corresponding parameters. The `ByVal` in the parameterList indicates that the first two variables in the argumentList are passed *by value.* The `ByRef` in the parameterList indicates that the third variable is passed *by reference.*

```
Private Sub CalcGross(ByVal decHoursWkd As Decimal,
                      ByVal decPayRate As Decimal,
                      ByRef decGrossPay As Decimal)
    ' calculate gross pay for btnCalc_Click

    decGrossPay = decHoursWkd * decPayRate
End Sub
```

parameterList

```
Private Sub btnCalc_Click(sender As Object,
e As EventArgs) Handles btnCalc.Click
    ' calculate gross pay

    Dim decHours As Decimal
    Dim decRate As Decimal
    Dim decGross As Decimal

    Decimal.TryParse(lstHours.SelectedItem.ToString, decHours)
    Decimal.TryParse(lstRates.SelectedItem.ToString, decRate)

    Call CalcGross(decHours, decRate, decGross)

    lblGross.Text = decGross.ToString("C2")

End Sub
```

arguments passed *by value*

argument passed *by reference*

The Call statement does not indicate whether a variable is being passed *by value* or *by reference*. To make that determination, you need to look at the receiving procedure's header.

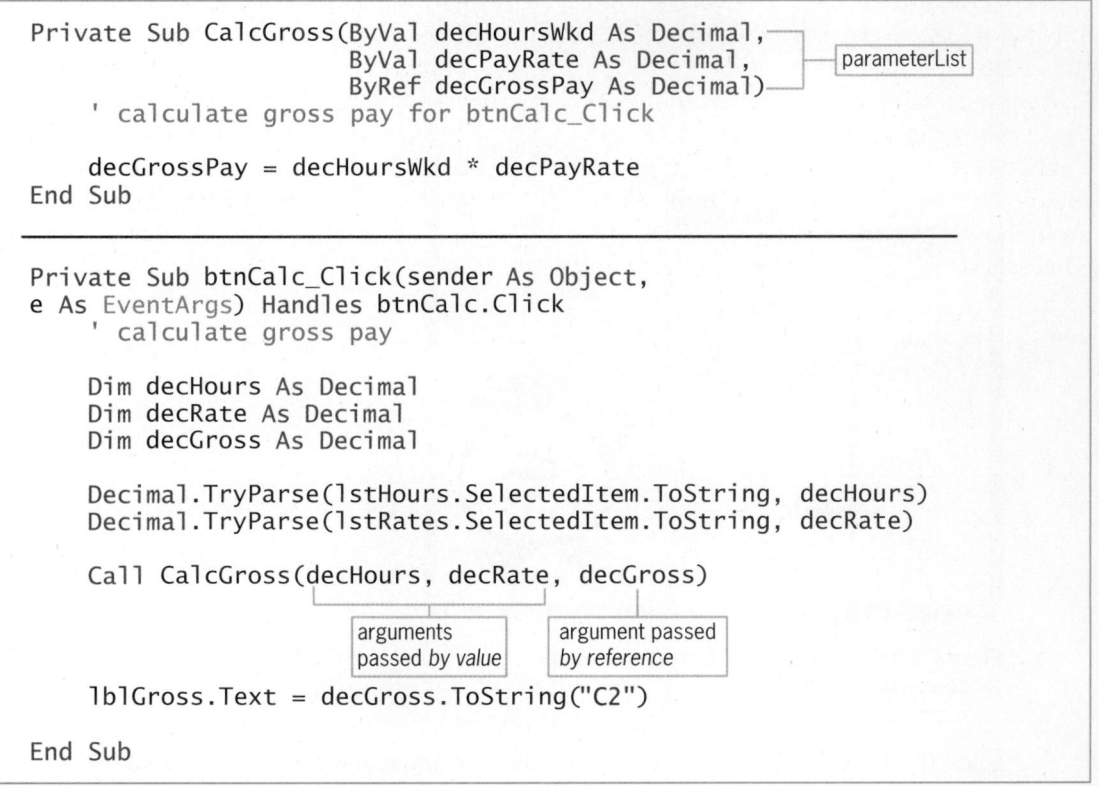

Figure 7-15 CalcGross and btnCalc_Click procedures

Desk-checking the procedures shown in Figure 7-15 will help clarify the difference between passing *by value* and passing *by reference*. When the user clicks the Calculate button after selecting 38.5 and 9.00 as the hours and pay rate, respectively, the Dim statements in the btnCalc_Click procedure create and initialize three Decimal variables. Next, the two TryParse methods store the hours and pay rate in the `decHours` and `decRate` variables. Figure 7-16 shows the contents of the variables before the Call statement is processed.

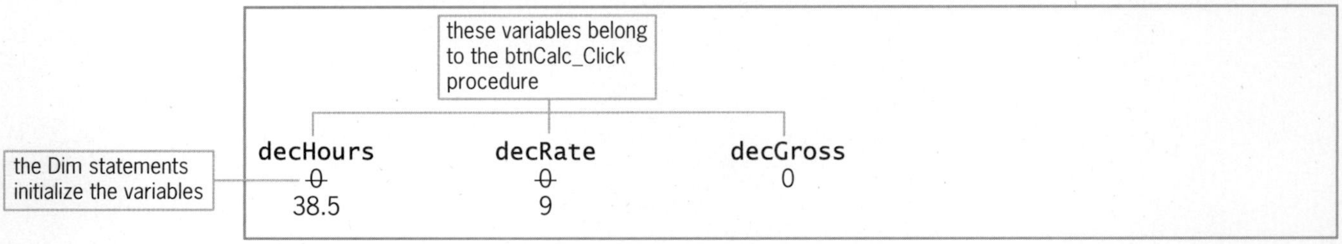

Figure 7-16 Desk-check table before the Call statement is processed

The computer processes the Call statement next. The statement invokes the CalcGross procedure, passing it three arguments. At this point, the computer temporarily leaves the Click event procedure to process the code contained in the CalcGross procedure; the procedure header is processed first. The `ByVal` keyword indicates that the first two parameters are receiving values from the Call statement—in this case, copies of the numbers stored in the `decHours` and `decRate` variables. As a result, the computer creates the `decHoursWkd` and `decPayRate` variables listed in the parameterList, and stores the numbers 38.5 and 9, respectively, in the variables.

The ByRef keyword indicates that the third parameter is receiving the address of a variable. When you pass a variable's address to a procedure, the computer uses the address to locate the variable in its internal memory. It then assigns the parameter name to the memory location. In this case, the computer locates the decGross variable in memory and assigns the name decGrossPay to it. As indicated in the desk-check table shown in Figure 7-17, the memory location now has two names: one assigned by the btnCalc_Click procedure and the other assigned by the CalcGross procedure. Although both procedures can access the memory location, each procedure uses a different name to do so. The btnCalc_Click procedure uses the name decGross, whereas the CalcGross procedure uses the name decGrossPay.

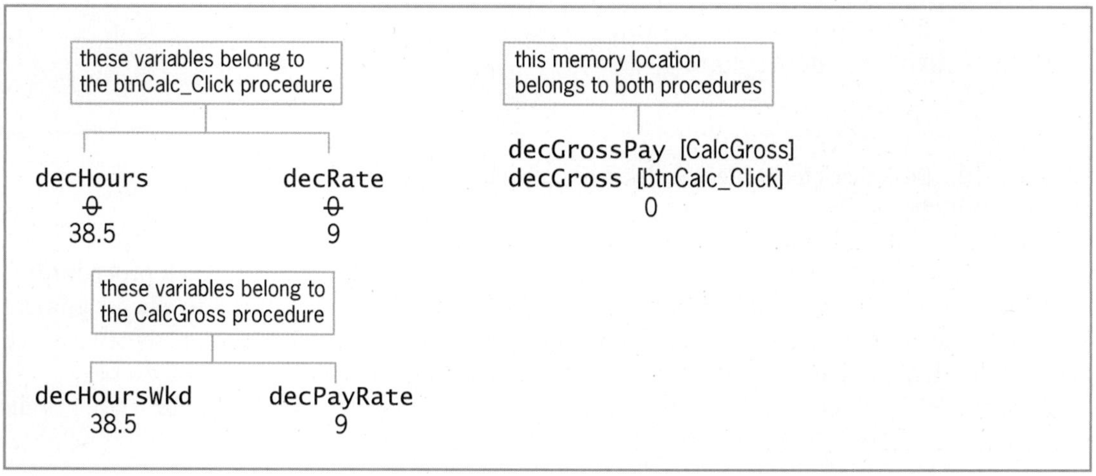

Figure 7-17 Desk-check table after the Call statement and CalcGross procedure header are processed

The decGross variable is recognized only within the btnCalc_Click procedure, and the decGrossPay variable is recognized only within the CalcGross procedure.

After processing the CalcGross procedure header, the computer processes the statement contained in the procedure. The statement calculates the gross pay by multiplying the contents of the decHoursWkd variable (38.5) by the contents of the decPayRate variable (9), and then assigns the result (346.5) to the decGrossPay variable. Figure 7-18 shows the desk-check table after the calculation statement is processed. Notice that changing the value in the decGrossPay variable also changes the value in the decGross variable. This is because both variable names refer to the same location in memory.

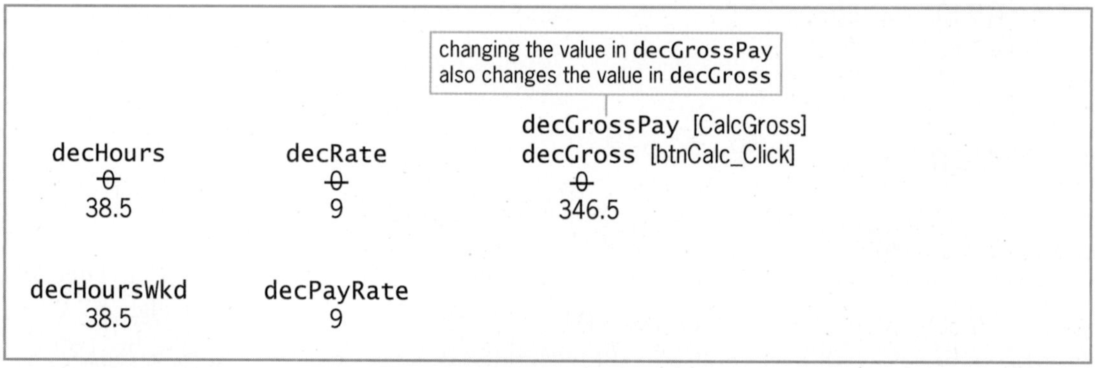

Figure 7-18 Desk-check table after the statement in the CalcGross procedure is processed

The CalcGross procedure's End Sub clause is processed next and ends the procedure. At this point, the computer removes the `decHoursWkd` and `decPayRate` variables from memory. It also removes the `decGrossPay` name from the appropriate location in memory, as indicated in Figure 7-19. Notice that the `decGross` memory location now has only one name: the name assigned to it by the btnCalc_Click procedure.

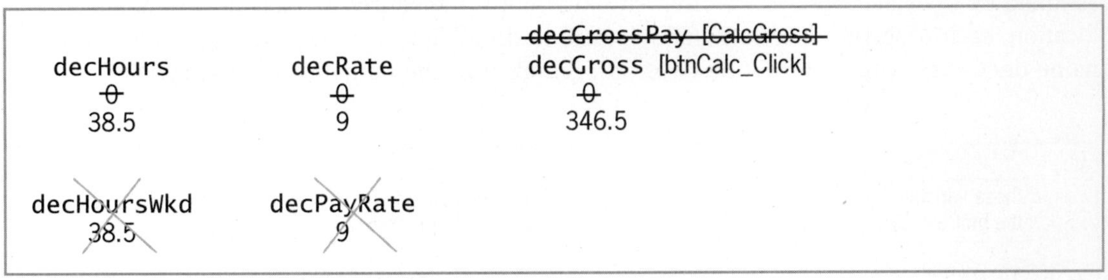

Figure 7-19 Desk-check table after the CalcGross procedure ends

After the CalcGross procedure ends, the computer returns to the btnCalc_Click procedure to finish processing the event procedure's code. More specifically, it returns to the assignment statement located below the Call statement. After processing the assignment statement, which displays the gross pay in the lblGross control, the computer processes the Click event procedure's End Sub clause. When the Click event procedure ends, the computer removes the procedure's variables (`decHours`, `decRate`, and `decGross`) from memory.

YOU DO IT 2!

Create a Visual Basic Windows application named YouDoIt 2. Save the application in the VB2012\Chap07 folder. Add a text box, a label, and a button to the form. The button's Click event procedure should assign the text box value to an Integer variable and then pass a copy of the variable's value, along with the address of a different Integer variable, to an independent Sub procedure named CalcDouble. The CalcDouble procedure should multiply the first Integer variable's value by 2 and then store the result in the second Integer variable. The button's Click event procedure should display the contents of the second Integer variable in the label control. Code the button's Click event procedure and the CalcDouble procedure. Save the solution and then start and test the application. Close the solution.

Function Procedures

In addition to creating Sub procedures in Visual Basic, you also can create Function procedures. The difference between both types of procedures is that a **Function procedure** returns a value after performing its assigned task, whereas a Sub procedure does not return a value. Function procedures are referred to more simply as **functions**. The illustration shown in Figure 7-20 may help clarify the difference between Sub procedures and functions. Sarah and her two siblings are planning a surprise birthday party for their mother. Being the oldest of the three children, Sarah will handle most of the party plans herself. However, she does need to delegate some tasks to her brother (Jacob) and sister (Sonja). She delegates the task of putting up the decorations (streamers, balloons, and so on) to Jacob, and delegates the task of getting the birthday present (a bottle of perfume) to Sonja. Like a Sub procedure, Jacob will perform his task but won't need to return anything to Sarah after doing so. However, like a function, Sonja will perform her task and then return a value (the bottle of perfume) to Sarah for wrapping.

Figure 7-20 Illustration of a Sub procedure and a function
Image by Diane Zak; Created with Reallusion CrazyTalk Animator

Figure 7-21 provides another example of the difference between a Sub procedure and a function. In Illustration A, Helen is at the ticket counter in her local movie theater, requesting a ticket for the current movie. Helen gives the ticket agent a $5 bill and expects a ticket in return. The ticket agent is similar to a function in that he performs his task (fulfilling Helen's request for a ticket) and then returns a value (a ticket) to Helen. Compare that with Illustration B, where Helen and her granddaughter, Penelope, are at the Blast Off Games arcade. Helen wants Penelope to have fun, so she gives Penelope a $5 bill to play some games. But, unlike with the ticket agent, Helen expects nothing from Penelope in return. This is similar to the way a Sub procedure works. Penelope performs her task (having fun by playing games), but doesn't need to return any value to her grandmother.

Illustration A

Helen:
1. ask ticket agent for a senior ticket
2. give ticket agent $5
3. receive senior ticket from ticket agent

Ticket agent (function):
1. take $5 from Helen
2. give Helen a senior ticket

Illustration B

Helen:
1. tell Penelope to have fun playing games
2. give Penelope $5

Penelope (Sub procedure):
1. take $5 from Helen
2. buy game tickets with the $5
3. play games and have fun

Figure 7-21 Another example of the difference between a Sub procedure and a function
Image by Diane Zak; Created with Reallusion CrazyTalk Animator; OpenClipArt.org/rg1024

Figure 7-22 shows the syntax and examples of functions in Visual Basic. Notice that unlike a Sub procedure, a function's header and footer contain the `Function` keyword rather than the `Sub` keyword. A function's header also includes the `As` *dataType* section, which specifies the data type of the value the function will return. The value is returned by the **Return statement**, which typically is the last statement within a function. The statement's syntax is `Return` *expression*, where *expression* represents the one and only value that will be returned to the statement that invoked the function. The data type of the *expression* must agree with the data type specified in the `As` *dataType* section of the header. Like a Sub procedure, a function can receive information either *by value* or *by reference*. The information it receives is listed in its parameterList.

Function Procedure

Syntax
Private Function *procedureName*(**[***parameterList***]**) **As** *dataType*
statements
Return *expression*
End Function

(callout: specifies the data type of the return value)

Example 1
```
Private Function GetNewPrice(ByVal dblOld As Double) As Double
    ' increases current price by 5% and returns new price

    Dim dblNew As Double
    dblNew = dblOld * 1.05
    Return dblNew
End Function
```

(callout: returns the dblNew variable's value to the statement that invoked the function)

Example 2
```
Private Function GetNewPrice(ByVal dblOld As Double) As Double
    ' increases current price by 5% and returns new price
    Return dblOld * 1.05
End Function
```

(callout: calculates and returns the new price to the statement that invoked the function)

Figure 7-22 Syntax and examples of functions

As with Sub procedures, you can enter your functions anywhere in the Code Editor window, as long as you enter them between the Public Class and End Class clauses and outside of any other procedure. In this book, the functions will be entered above the first event procedure in the Code Editor window. Like Sub procedure names, function names are entered using Pascal case and typically begin with a verb. The name should indicate the task the function performs. The GetNewPrice name used in the examples in Figure 7-22 indicates that each function returns a new price.

You can invoke a function from one or more places in an application's code. You invoke a function that you create in exactly the same way as you invoke one of Visual Basic's built-in functions, such as the InputBox function. You do this by including the function's name and arguments (if any) in a statement. The number, data type, and position of the arguments should agree with the number, data type, and position of the function's parameters. In most cases, the statement that invokes a function assigns the function's return value to a variable. However, it also may use the return value in a calculation or simply display the return value. Figure 7-23 shows examples of invoking the GetNewPrice function from Figure 7-22. The `GetNewPrice(dblPrice)` entry in each example invokes the function, passing it the value stored in the `dblPrice` variable.

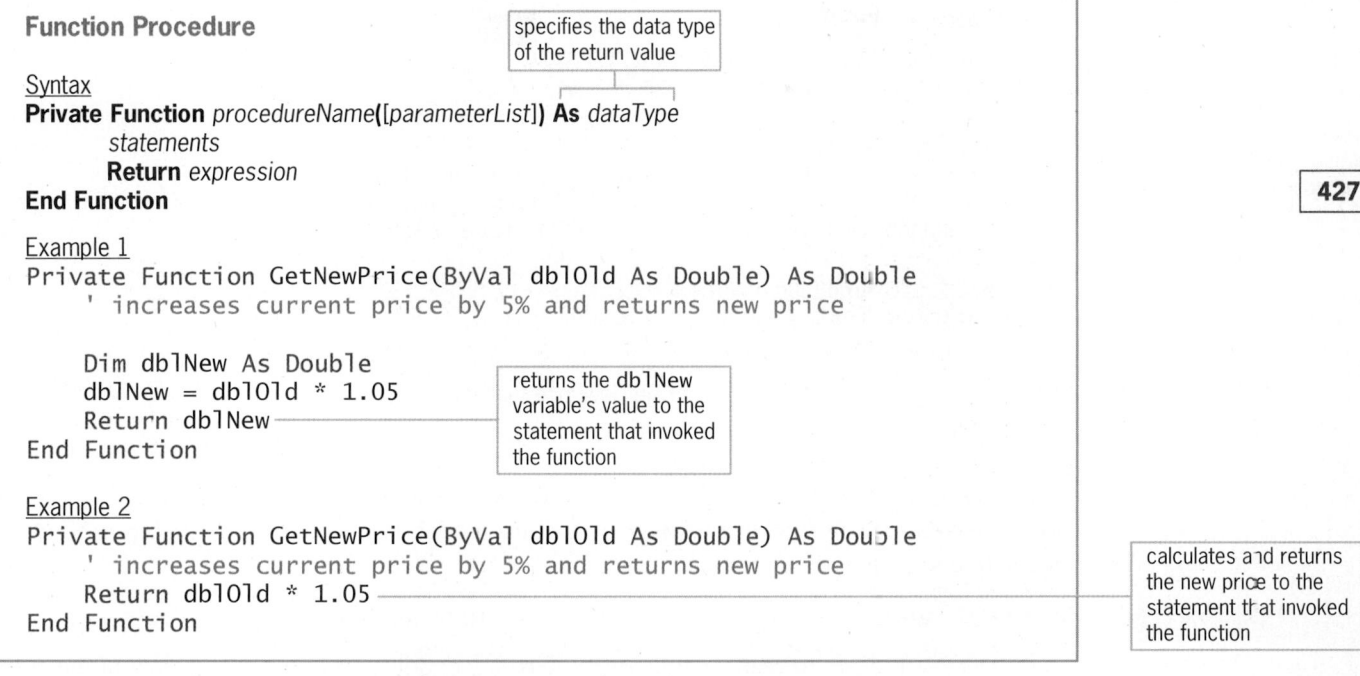

Invoking a Function

Example 1 – assigning the return value to a variable
```
dblNewPrice = GetNewPrice(dblPrice)
```

Example 2 – using the return value in a calculation
```
dblTotalDue = intQuantity * GetNewPrice(dblPrice)
```
the assignment statement multiplies the function's return value by the value in the `intQuantity` variable and then assigns the result to the `dblTotalDue` variable

Example 3 – displaying the return value
```
lblNewPrice.Text = GetNewPrice(dblPrice).ToString("C2")
```

Figure 7-23 Examples of invoking the GetNewPrice function

In the next set of steps, you will modify the Gross Pay application that you completed in the previous section. The modified application will use a function (rather than a Sub procedure) to calculate and return the gross pay.

START HERE

To modify the Gross Pay application to use a function:

1. Use Windows to make a copy of the Gross Pay Solution-Sub folder. Rename the copy Gross Pay Solution-Function. Open the Gross Pay Solution (Gross Pay Solution.sln) file contained in the Gross Pay Solution-Function folder. Open the designer window.
2. Open the Code Editor window. First, you will change the CalcGross Sub procedure to a function. Change the `Sub` keyword in the CalcGross procedure header to **Function** and then click the **blank line** above the procedure. The Code Editor automatically changes the procedure's footer to `End Function`.
3. The CalcGross function will return the gross pay to the statement that invoked the function. Therefore, unlike the CalcGross Sub procedure, it won't need the address of a variable in which to store the gross pay. Delete the entire third line from the function header. The third line contains `ByRef decGrossPay As Decimal)`. Then replace the comma in the second line of the function header with **)** (a closing parenthesis).
4. Recall that the data type of the function's return value is specified at the end of the procedure header. The CalcGross function will return the gross pay as a Decimal number. The insertion point should be located after the closing parenthesis in the function header. Press the **Spacebar**, type **As Decimal**, and then click the **blank line** below the comment in the procedure.
5. When you removed `ByRef decGrossPay As Decimal` from the function header, the `decGrossPay` variable was no longer declared. As a result, a jagged line appears below the variable's name in the assignment statement. In order to use the variable, the function will need to declare it in a Dim statement. The insertion point should be located below the comment in the function. Press **Enter** to insert another blank line and then enter the following Dim statement:

   Dim decGrossPay As Decimal
6. Finally, you need to tell the function to return the gross pay to the statement that invoked the function. Insert a blank line above the End Function clause. In the blank line, enter the following Return statement:

   Return decGrossPay

7. The CalcGross function is now complete, but you still need to modify the btnCalc_Click procedure. Locate the btnCalc_Click procedure. You will need to replace the Call statement with a statement that invokes the CalcGross function (rather than the CalcGross Sub procedure). The statement will assign the function's return value to the `decGross` variable. Like the Sub procedure, the function will need the statement to pass the values stored in the `decHours` and `decRate` variables because those values are needed to calculate the gross pay. However, the function will not need the statement to pass the address of the `decGross` variable because the statement itself will store the gross pay in the variable. Change the Call statement to the following assignment statement and then click the **blank line** above the End Sub clause:

   decGross = CalcGross(decHours, decRate)

8. Save the solution and then start the application. Click **38.5** in the Hours list box and **9.00** in the Rates list box. Click the **Calculate** button. The gross pay is $346.50, as shown earlier in Figure 7-14.
9. Click the **Exit** button. Close the Code Editor window and then close the solution.

Figure 7-24 shows the code entered in the CalcGross function and btnCalc_Click procedure. The modified lines of code are shaded in the figure.

```
Private Function CalcGross(ByVal decHoursWkd As Decimal,
                           ByVal decPayRate As Decimal) As Decimal
    ' calculate gross pay for btnCalc_Click

    Dim decGrossPay As Decimal

    decGrossPay = decHoursWkd * decPayRate
    Return decGrossPay

End Function
```

```
Private Sub btnCalc_Click(sender As Object,
e As EventArgs) Handles btnCalc.Click
    ' calculate gross pay

    Dim decHours As Decimal
    Dim decRate As Decimal
    Dim decGross As Decimal

    Decimal.TryParse(lstHours.SelectedItem.ToString, decHours)
    Decimal.TryParse(lstRates.SelectedItem.ToString, decRate)

    decGross = CalcGross(decHours, decRate)
    lblGross.Text = decGross.ToString("C2")

End Sub
```

invokes the function and assigns the return value to the `decGross` variable

Figure 7-24 CalcGross function and btnCalc_Click procedure

YOU DO IT 3!

Create a Visual Basic Windows application named YouDoIt 3. Save the application in the VB2012\Chap07 folder. Add a text box, a label, and a button to the form. The button's Click event procedure should assign the text box value to an Integer variable and then pass a copy of the variable's value to a function named GetBonus. The GetBonus function should multiply the integer it receives by 10% and then return the result. The button's Click event procedure should display the function's return value in the label control. Code the GetBonus function and the button's Click event procedure. Save the solution and then start and test the application. Close the solution.

Lesson A Summary

- To create an independent Sub procedure:

  Refer to the syntax shown in Figure 7-3.

- To call an independent Sub procedure:

  Use the Call statement. The statement's syntax is **Call** *procedureName*(**[***argumentList***]**).

- To pass information to a Sub or Function procedure:

  Include the information in the Call statement's argumentList. In the parameterList in the procedure header, include the names of memory locations that will store the information. The number, data type, and order (position) of the arguments in the argumentList should agree with the number, data type, and order (position) of the parameters in the parameterList.

- To pass a variable *by value* to a procedure:

  Include the `ByVal` keyword before the parameter name in the procedure header's parameterList. Because only a copy of the variable's value is passed, the receiving procedure cannot access the variable.

- To pass a variable *by reference*:

  Include the `ByRef` keyword before the parameter name in the procedure header's parameterList. Because the variable's address is passed, the receiving procedure can change the contents of the variable.

- To create a Function procedure:

  Refer to the syntax shown in Figure 7-22.

Lesson A Key Terms

Call statement—the Visual Basic statement used to invoke (call) an independent Sub procedure

Function procedure—a procedure that returns a value after performing its assigned task

Functions—another name for Function procedures

Independent Sub procedure—a procedure that is independent of any object and event; the procedure is processed only when called (invoked) from code

Passing by reference—refers to the process of passing a variable's address to a procedure so that the value in the variable can be changed

Passing by value—refers to the process of passing a copy of a variable's value to a procedure

Return statement—the Visual Basic statement that returns a function's value to the statement that invoked the function

Lesson A Review Questions

1. Which of the following is false?
   a. A function can return only one value to the statement that invoked it.
   b. A Sub procedure can accept only one item of data passed to it.
   c. The parameterList in a procedure header is optional.
   d. At times, a memory location inside the computer's internal memory may have more than one name.

2. The items listed in the Call statement are referred to as ________________.
   a. arguments
   b. parameters
   c. passers
   d. none of the above

3. Each memory location listed in the parameterList in the procedure header is referred to as ________________.
   a. an address
   b. a constraint
   c. a parameter
   d. a value

4. To determine whether a variable is being passed to a procedure *by value* or *by reference,* you will need to examine ________________.
   a. the Call statement
   b. the procedure header
   c. the statements entered in the procedure
   d. either a or b

5. Which of the following statements invokes the GetArea Sub procedure, passing it two variables *by value*?
   a. `Call GetArea(dblLength, dblWidth)`
   b. `Call GetArea(ByVal dblLength, ByVal dblWidth)`
   c. `Invoke GetArea(dblLength, dblWidth)`
   d. `GetArea(dblLength, dblWidth) As Double`

6. Which of the following is a valid header for a procedure that receives a copy of the value stored in a String variable?
   a. `Private Sub DisplayName(ByContents strName As String)`
   b. `Private Sub DisplayName(ByValue strName As String)`
   c. `Private Sub DisplayName ByVal(strName As String)`
   d. none of the above

7. Which of the following is a valid header for a procedure that receives an integer followed by a number with a decimal place?
   a. `Private Sub GetFee(intBase As Integer, decRate As Decimal)`
   b. `Private Sub GetFee(ByRef intBase As Integer, ByRef decRate As Decimal)`
   c. `Private Sub GetFee(ByVal intBase As Integer, ByVal decRate As Decimal)`
   d. none of the above

8. Which of the following is false?
   a. The order of the arguments listed in the Call statement should agree with the order of the parameters listed in the receiving procedure's header.
   b. The data type of each argument in the Call statement should match the data type of its corresponding parameter in the procedure header.
   c. The name of each argument in the Call statement should be identical to the name of its corresponding parameter in the procedure header.
   d. When you pass information to a procedure *by value*, the procedure stores the value of each item it receives in a separate memory location.

9. Which of the following instructs a function to return the contents of the `dblBonus` variable?
   a. `Return dblBonus`
   b. `Return ByVal dblBonus`
   c. `Send dblBonus`
   d. `SendBack dblBonus`

10. Which of the following is a valid header for a procedure that receives the address of a Decimal variable followed by an integer?
    a. `Private Sub GetFee(ByVal decX As Decimal, ByAdd intY As Integer)`
    b. `Private Sub GetFee(decX As Decimal, intY As Integer)`
    c. `Private Sub GetFee(ByRef decX As Decimal, ByRef intY As Integer)`
    d. none of the above

11. Which of the following is a valid header for a procedure that is passed the number 15?
    a. `Private Function GetTax(ByVal intRate As Integer) As Decimal`
    b. `Private Function GetTax(ByAdd intRate As Integer) As Decimal`
    c. `Private Sub CalcTax(ByVal intRate As Integer)`
    d. both a and c

12. If the statement `Call CalcNet(decNetPay)` passes the variable's address, the variable is said to be passed ______________.
    a. *by address*
    b. *by content*
    c. *by reference*
    d. *by value*

13. Which of the following is false?

    a. When you pass a variable *by reference*, the receiving procedure can change its contents.

    b. To pass a variable *by reference* in Visual Basic, you include the `ByRef` keyword before the variable's name in the Call statement.

    c. When you pass a variable *by value*, the receiving procedure creates a procedure-level variable that it uses to store the value passed to it.

    d. Unless you specify otherwise, a variable in Visual Basic will be passed *by value*.

14. A Sub procedure named GetEndingInventory is passed four Integer variables named `intBegin`, `intSales`, `intPurchases`, and `intEnding`. The procedure should calculate the ending inventory using the beginning inventory, sales, and purchase amounts passed to the procedure. The result should be stored in the `intEnding` variable. Which of the following procedure headers is correct?

    a. `Private Sub GetEndingInventory(ByVal intB As Integer, ByVal intS As Integer, ByVal intP As Integer, ByRef intFinal As Integer)`

    b. `Private Sub GetEndingInventory(ByVal intB As Integer, ByVal intS As Integer, ByVal intP As Integer, ByVal intFinal As Integer)`

    c. `Private Sub GetEndingInventory(ByRef intB As Integer, ByRef intS As Integer, ByRef intP As Integer, ByVal intFinal As Integer)`

    d. `Private Sub GetEndingInventory(ByRef intB As Integer, ByRef intS As Integer, ByRef intP As Integer, ByRef intFinal As Integer)`

15. Which of the following statements should you use to call the GetEndingInventory procedure described in Review Question 14?

    a. `Call GetEndingInventory(intBegin, intSales, intPurchases, intEnding)`

    b. `Call GetEndingInventory(ByVal intBegin, ByVal intSales, ByVal intPurchases, ByRef intEnding)`

    c. `Call GetEndingInventory(ByRef intBegin, ByRef intSales, ByRef intPurchases, ByRef intEnding)`

    d. `Call GetEndingInventory(ByVal intBegin, ByVal intSales, ByVal intPurchases, ByVal intEnding)`

16. The memory locations listed in the parameterList in a procedure header have procedure scope and are removed from the computer's internal memory when the procedure ends.

    a. True

    b. False

17. Which of the following statements invokes the GetDiscount function, passing it the contents of two Decimal variables named `decSales` and `decRate`? The statement should assign the function's return value to the `decDiscount` variable.

    a. `decDiscount = Call GetDiscount(decSales, decRate)`

    b. `Call GetDiscount(decSales, decRate, decDiscount)`

    c. `decDiscount = GetDiscount(decSales, decRate)`

    d. none of the above

18. Explain the difference between a Sub procedure and a Function procedure.
19. Explain the difference between passing a variable *by value* and passing it *by reference*.
20. Explain the difference between invoking a Sub procedure and invoking a function.

Lesson A Exercises

INTRODUCTORY

1. Write the code for a Sub procedure that receives a Double number passed to it. The procedure should divide the number by 2 and then display the result in the lblNum control. Name the procedure DivideByTwo. Then write a statement to invoke the procedure, passing it the number 87.8.

INTRODUCTORY

2. Write the code for a Sub procedure named GetCountry. The procedure should prompt the user to enter the name of a country, storing the user's response in its `strName` parameter. Then write a statement to invoke the procedure, passing it the `strCountry` variable.

INTRODUCTORY

3. Write the code for a function named GetCountry. The function should prompt the user to enter the name of a country and then return the user's response. Then write a statement to invoke the GetCountry function. Display the function's return value in a message box.

INTRODUCTORY

4. Write the code for a Sub procedure that receives three Double variables: the first two *by value* and the last one *by reference*. The procedure should divide the first variable by the second variable and then store the result in the third variable. Name the procedure CalcQuotient.

INTRODUCTORY

5. Write the code for a function that receives a copy of the value stored in an Integer variable. The function should divide the value by 2 and then return the result, which may contain a decimal place. Name the function GetQuotient. Then write an appropriate statement to invoke the function, passing it the `intNumber` variable. Assign the function's return value to the `dblAnswer` variable.

INTRODUCTORY

6. In this exercise, you experiment with passing variables *by value* and *by reference*. Open the Passing Solution (Passing Solution.sln) file contained in the VB2012\Chap07\Passing Solution folder. If necessary, open the designer window.
   a. Open the Code Editor window and review the existing code. Notice that the `strMyName` variable is passed *by value* to the GetName procedure. Start the application. Click the Display Name button. When prompted to enter a name, type your name and press Enter. Explain why the btnDisplay control's Click event procedure does not display your name in the lblName control. Stop the application.
   b. Modify the btnDisplay control's Click event procedure so that it passes the `strMyName` variable *by reference* to the GetName procedure. Save the solution and then start the application. Click the Display Name button. When prompted to enter a name, type your name and press Enter. This time, your name appears in the lblName control. Explain why the btnDisplay control's Click event procedure now works correctly. Stop the application. Close the Code Editor window and then close the solution.

INTRODUCTORY

7. In this exercise, you modify the Favorite Title application from this lesson. Use Windows to make a copy of the Favorite Title Solution folder. Rename the copy Modified Favorite Title Solution. Open the Favorite Title Solution (Favorite Title Solution.sln) file contained in the Modified Favorite Title Solution folder. Open the designer window. Modify the interface and code to allow the user to also enter the title of his or her favorite book. Save the solution and then start and test the application. Close the Code Editor window and then close the solution.

8. In this exercise, you modify one of the Gross Pay applications from this lesson. Use Windows to make a copy of the Gross Pay Solution-Sub folder. Rename the copy Modified Gross Pay Solution-Sub. Open the Gross pay Solution (Gross Pay Solution.sln) file contained in the Modified Gross Pay Solution-Sub folder. Open the designer window. Modify the code to display hours from 0.5 to 60.0 (rather than to 40.0), and pay rates from 8.00 to 30.00 (rather than to 15.00). Also modify the code to give employees double-time for the hours worked over 40. Save the solution and then start and test the application. Close the Code Editor window and then close the solution. INTERMEDIATE

9. In this exercise, you modify one of the Gross Pay applications from this lesson. Use Windows to make a copy of the Gross Pay Solution-Function folder. Rename the copy Modified Gross Pay Solution-Function. Open the Gross pay Solution (Gross Pay Solution.sln) file contained in the Modified Gross Pay Solution-Function folder. Open the designer window. Modify the code to display hours from 0.5 to 60.0 (rather than to 40.0). Also modify the code to give employees time and one-half for the hours worked over 37.5. However, if the employee worked more than 50 hours, he or she should receive time and one-half for the hours from 38 through 50, and then double-time for the hours over 50. Save the solution and then start and test the application. Close the Code Editor window and then close the solution. INTERMEDIATE

10. Open the Average Solution (Average Solution.sln) file contained in the VB2012\Chap07\Average Solution folder. If necessary, open the designer window. Open the Code Editor window and review the existing code. The btnAvg_Click procedure should use a function to calculate and return the average score. Complete the application's code. Save the solution and then start and test the application. Close the Code Editor window and then close the solution. INTERMEDIATE

11. Open the Math Solution (Math Solution.sln) file contained in the VB2012\Chap07\Math Solution folder. If necessary, open the designer window. Open the Code Editor window and review the existing code. The btnCalc_Click procedure should use an independent Sub procedure to calculate both the sum of and the difference between the two numbers entered by the user. When calculating the difference, always subtract the smaller number from the larger number. Complete the application's code. Save the solution and then start and test the application. Close the Code Editor window and then close the solution. INTERMEDIATE

12. Open the Temperature Solution (Temperature Solution.sln) file contained in the VB2012\Chap07\Temperature Solution-Sub folder. If necessary, open the designer window. Code the application so that it uses two independent Sub procedures: one to convert a temperature from Fahrenheit to Celsius, and the other to convert a temperature from Celsius to Fahrenheit. Save the solution and then start and test the application. Close the Code Editor window and then close the solution. INTERMEDIATE

13. Open the Temperature Solution (Temperature Solution.sln) file contained in the VB2012\Chap07\Temperature Solution-Function folder. If necessary, open the designer window. Code the application so that it uses two functions: one to convert a temperature from Fahrenheit to Celsius, and the other to convert a temperature from Celsius to Fahrenheit. Save the solution and then start and test the application. Close the Code Editor window and then close the solution. INTERMEDIATE

14. Create a Visual Basic Windows application. Use the following names for the solution and project, respectively: Pine Lodge Solution and Pine Lodge Project. Save the application in the VB2012\Chap07 folder. Change the form file's name to Main Form.vb. Change the form's name to frmMain. Create the interface shown in Figure 7-25. The lstRates control should display three nightly room rates: 125.00, 175.00, and 220.00. The lstPercents control should display numbers from 10 through 20 in increments of 5. The label that displays the discounted rate should be cleared when a change is made to INTERMEDIATE

either list box. The Calculate button's Click event procedure should use a function to calculate and return the discounted nightly room rate. The Click event procedure should display the discounted rate with a dollar sign and two decimal places. Code the application. Save the solution and then start the application. First, calculate the discounted rate based on a nightly rate of 125.00 and a discount percentage of 10. The discounted rate should be $112.50. Now test the application using the other nightly rates and discount percentages. Close the Code Editor window and then close the solution.

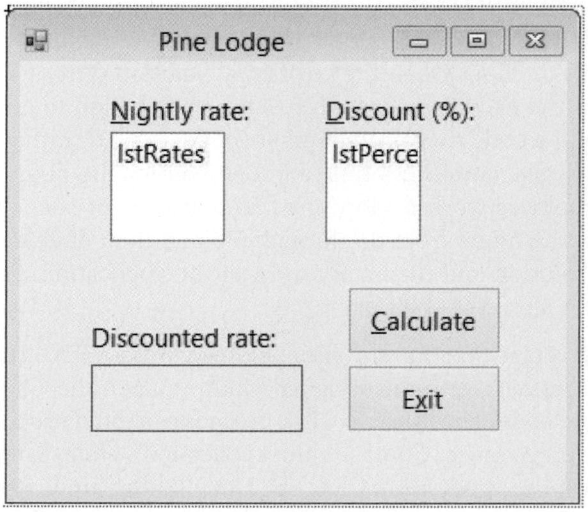

Figure 7-25 Interface for Exercise 14

INTERMEDIATE

15. In this exercise, you modify the application from Exercise 14. Use Windows to make a copy of the Pine Lodge Solution folder. Rename the copy Modified Pine Lodge Solution. Open the Pine Lodge Solution (Pine Lodge Solution.sln) file contained in the Modified Pine Lodge Solution folder. Open the designer and Code Editor windows. Change the function to a Sub procedure and then make the necessary modifications to the Calculate button's Click event procedure. Save the solution and then start and test the application. Close the Code Editor window and then close the solution.

INTERMEDIATE

16. In this exercise, you modify one of the Savings Account applications that you coded in Chapter 6's Lesson A. Use Windows to copy the Savings Solution folder from the VB2012\Chap06 folder to the VB2012\Chap07 folder. Open the Savings Solution (Savings Solution.sln) file contained in the VB2012\Chap07\Savings Solution folder. Open the designer and Code Editor windows. Modify the code so it uses a function to calculate and return the account balance. Save the solution and then start and test the application. Close the Code Editor window and then close the solution.

INTERMEDIATE

17. In this exercise, you modify the application from Exercise 16. Use Windows to make a copy of the Savings Solution folder. Rename the copy Modified Savings Solution. Open the Savings Solution (Savings Solution.sln) file contained in the Modified Savings Solution folder. Open the designer and Code Editor windows. Change the function to a Sub procedure and then make the necessary modifications to the code. Save the solution and then start and test the application. Close the Code Editor window and then close the solution.

ADVANCED

18. Create a Visual Basic Windows application. Use the following names for the solution and project, respectively: Rainfall Solution and Rainfall Project. Save the application in the VB2012\Chap07 folder. Change the form file's name to Main Form.vb. Change the form's name to frmMain. Create the interface shown in Figure 7-26. The user will enter one or more monthly rainfall amounts, one at a time, in the text box. The button's Click event procedure should use a Sub procedure to calculate both the total and the average of the rainfall amounts entered so far. The Click event procedure should display the calculated results in the label controls. Code the application. Save the solution and then start and test the application. Close the Code Editor window and then close the solution.

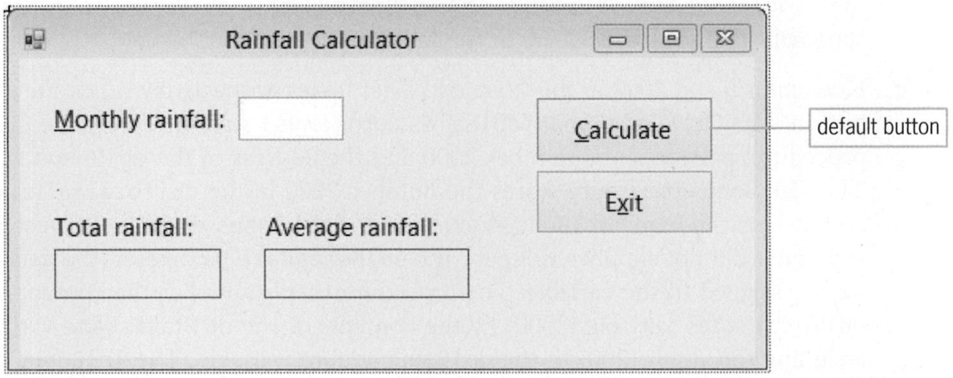

Figure 7-26 Interface for Exercise 18

ADVANCED

19. In this exercise, you modify the application from Exercise 18. Use Windows to make a copy of the Rainfall Solution folder. Rename the copy Modified Rainfall Solution. Open the Rainfall Solution (Rainfall Solution.sln) file contained in the Modified Rainfall Solution folder. Open the designer and Code Editor windows. Modify the code to use two Function procedures (rather than one Sub procedure) to calculate the total and average rainfall amounts. Save the solution and then start and test the application. Close the Code Editor window and then close the solution.

DISCOVERY

20. In this exercise, you learn how to specify that one or more arguments are optional in a Call statement. Open the Optional Solution (Optional Solution.sln) file contained in the VB2012\Chap07\Optional Solution folder. If necessary, open the designer window.

    a. Open the Code Editor window and review the existing code. The btnCalc_Click procedure contains two Call statements. The first Call statement passes three variables to the CalcBonus procedure. The second call statement, however, passes only two variables to the procedure. (Do not be concerned about the jagged line that appears below the second Call statement.) Notice that the `dblRate` variable is omitted from the second Call statement. You indicate that the `dblRate` variable is optional in the Call statement by including the keyword `Optional` before the variable's corresponding parameter in the procedure header. You enter the `Optional` keyword before the `ByVal` keyword. You also assign a default value that the procedure will use for the missing parameter when the procedure is called. You assign the default value by entering the assignment operator and the default value after the parameter. In this case, you will assign the number .1 as the default value for the `dblRate` variable. (Optional parameters must be listed at the end of the procedure header.)

b. Change the `ByVal dblBonusRate As Double` in the procedure header appropriately. Save the solution and then start the application. Enter a and 1000 in the Code and Sales boxes, respectively. Click the Calculate button. Type .05 and press Enter. The `Call CalcBonus(dblSales, dblBonus, dblRate)` statement calls the CalcBonus procedure, passing it the number 1000, the address of the `dblBonus` variable, and the number .05. The CalcBonus procedure stores the number 1000 in the `dblTotalSales` variable. It also assigns the name `dblBonusAmount` to the `dblBonus` variable and stores the number .05 in the `dblBonusRate` variable. The procedure then multiplies the contents of the `dblTotalSales` variable (1000) by the contents of the `dblBonusRate` variable (.05), assigning the result (50) to the `dblBonusAmount` variable. The `lblBonus.Text = dblBonus.ToString("C2")` statement then displays $50.00 in the lblBonus control.

c. Now enter b and 2000 in the Code and Sales boxes, respectively. Click the Calculate button. The `Call CalcBonus(dblSales, dblBonus)` statement calls the CalcBonus procedure, passing it the number 2000 and the address of the `dblBonus` variable. The CalcBonus procedure stores the number 2000 in the `dblTotalSales` variable and assigns the name `dblBonusAmount` to the `dblBonus` variable. Because the Call statement did not supply a value for the `dblBonusRate` parameter, the default value (.1) is assigned to the variable. The procedure then multiplies the contents of the `dblTotalSales` variable (2000) by the contents of the `dblBonusRate` variable (.1), assigning the result (200) to the `dblBonusAmount` variable. The `lblBonus.Text = dblBonus.ToString("C2")` statement then displays $200.00 in the lblBonus control. Stop the application. Close the Code Editor window and then close the solution.

SWAT THE BUGS

21. Open the Debug Solution (Debug Solution.sln) file contained in the VB2012\Chap07\Debug Solution-Lesson A folder. If necessary, open the designer window. Open the Code Editor window and review the existing code. Start the application. Enter 100, 200.55, and .04 in the Store 1 sales, Store 2 sales, and Commission rate boxes, respectively. Click the Calculate Commission button. Notice that the application is not working properly. Correct the application's code. Save the solution and then start and test the application again. Close the Code Editor window and then close the solution.

LESSON B

After studying Lesson B, you should be able to:

- Include a combo box in an interface
- Add items to a combo box
- Select a combo box item from code
- Determine the number of items in the list portion of a combo box
- Sort the items in the list portion of a combo box
- Determine the item either selected or entered in a combo box
- Code a combo box's TextChanged event procedure

Including a Combo Box in an Interface

In many interfaces, combo boxes are used in place of list boxes. You use the ComboBox tool in the toolbox to add a combo box to an interface. A **combo box** is similar to a list box in that it allows the user to select from a list of choices. However, unlike a list box, the full list of choices in a combo box can be hidden, allowing you to save space on the form. Also unlike a list box, a combo box contains a text field. Depending on the style of the combo box, the text field may or may not be editable by the user.

Three styles of combo boxes are available in Visual Basic. The style is controlled by the combo box's **DropDownStyle property**, which can be set to Simple, DropDown (the default), or DropDownList. Each style of combo box contains a text portion and a list portion. When the DropDownStyle property is set to either Simple or DropDown, the text portion of the combo box is editable. However, in a Simple combo box the list portion is always displayed, while in a DropDown combo box the list portion appears only when the user clicks the combo box's list arrow. When the DropDownStyle property is set to the third style, DropDownList, the text portion of the combo box is not editable and the user must click the combo box's list arrow to display the list of choices.

Figure 7-27 shows an example of each combo box style. You should use a label control to provide keyboard access to the combo box, as shown in the figure. For the access key to work correctly, you must set the label's TabIndex property to a value that is one number less than the combo box's TabIndex value. Like the items in a list box, the items in the list portion of a combo box are either arranged by use, with the most used entries listed first, or sorted in ascending order. To sort the items in the list portion of a combo box, you set the combo box's Sorted property to True.

If you want to experiment with the combo boxes shown in Figure 7-27, open the application contained in the Combo Box Styles solution folder.

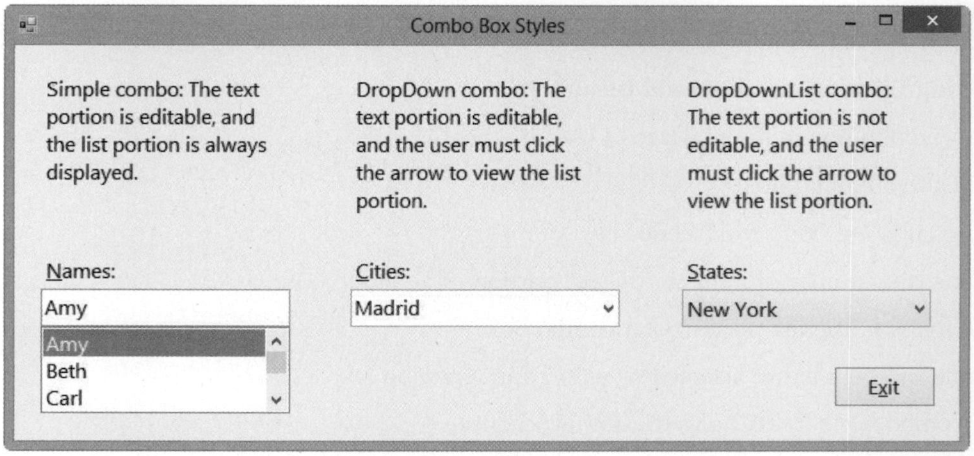

Figure 7-27 Examples of the combo box styles

Figure 7-28 shows the code used to fill the combo boxes in Figure 7-27 with values. As you do with a list box, you use the Items collection's Add method to add an item to a combo box. Like the first item in a list box, the first item in a combo box has an index of 0. You can use any of the following properties to select a default item, which will appear in the text portion of the combo box: SelectedIndex, SelectedItem, or Text. If no item is selected, the SelectedItem and Text properties contain the empty string, and the SelectedIndex property contains –1 (negative one). If you need to determine the number of items in the list portion of a combo box, you can use the Items collection's Count property. The property's syntax is *object*.`Items.Count`, in which *object* is the name of the combo box.

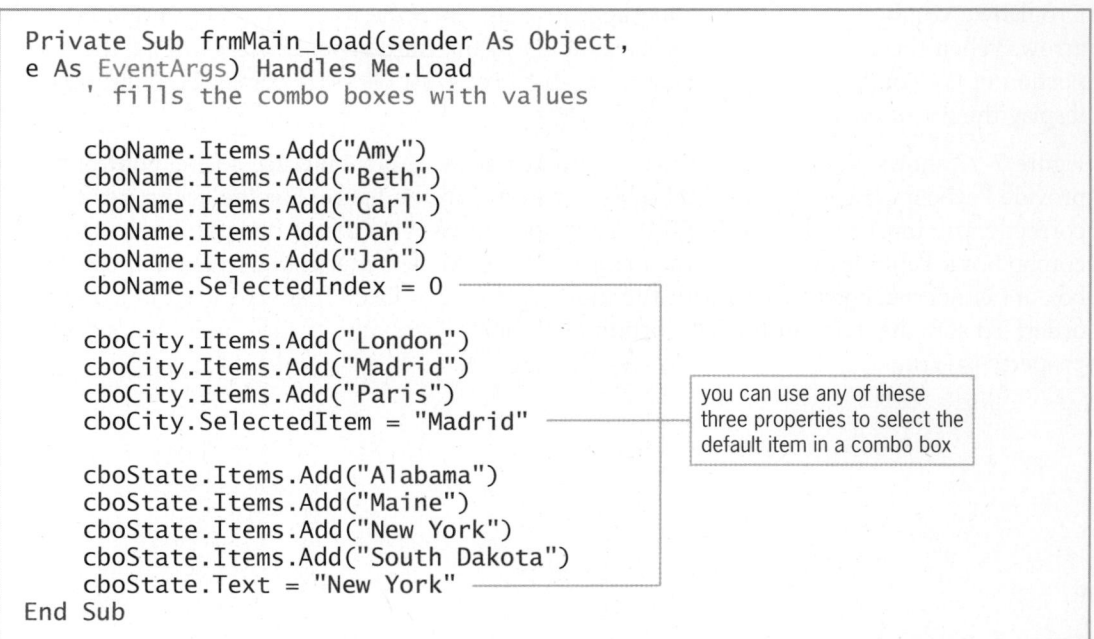

```
Private Sub frmMain_Load(sender As Object,
e As EventArgs) Handles Me.Load
    ' fills the combo boxes with values

    cboName.Items.Add("Amy")
    cboName.Items.Add("Beth")
    cboName.Items.Add("Carl")
    cboName.Items.Add("Dan")
    cboName.Items.Add("Jan")
    cboName.SelectedIndex = 0

    cboCity.Items.Add("London")
    cboCity.Items.Add("Madrid")
    cboCity.Items.Add("Paris")
    cboCity.SelectedItem = "Madrid"

    cboState.Items.Add("Alabama")
    cboState.Items.Add("Maine")
    cboState.Items.Add("New York")
    cboState.Items.Add("South Dakota")
    cboState.Text = "New York"
End Sub
```

you can use any of these three properties to select the default item in a combo box

Figure 7-28 Code associated with the combo boxes in Figure 7-27

GUI DESIGN TIP Combo Box Standards

- Use a label control to provide keyboard access to a combo box. Set the label's TabIndex property to a value that is one number less than the combo box's TabIndex value.
- Combo box items are either arranged by use, with the most used entries appearing first in the list, or sorted in ascending order.

It is easy to confuse a combo box's SelectedItem property with its Text property. The SelectedItem property contains the value of the item selected in the list portion of the combo box, whereas the Text property contains the value that appears in the text portion. A value can appear in the text portion as a result of the user either selecting an item in the list portion of the control or typing an entry in the text portion itself. It also can appear in the text portion as a result of a statement that assigns a value to the control's SelectedIndex, SelectedItem, or Text property.

If the combo box is a DropDownList style, where the text portion is not editable, you can use the SelectedItem and Text properties interchangeably. However, if the combo box is either a Simple or DropDown style, where the user can type an entry in the text portion, you should use the Text property because it contains the value either selected or entered by the user. When the value in the text portion of a combo box changes, the combo box's TextChanged event occurs. In the next set of steps, you will modify one of the Gross Pay applications from Lesson A. The modified application will use a combo box rather than a list box.

START HERE

To modify one of the Gross Pay applications from Lesson A:

1. Use Windows to make a copy of the Gross Pay Solution-Function folder from Lesson A. Rename the copy Gross Pay Solution-Function-ComboBox.
2. If necessary, start Visual Studio 2012. Open the Gross Pay Solution (Gross Pay Solution.sln) file contained in the Gross Pay Solution-Function-ComboBox folder. Open the designer window.
3. First, you will replace the Rates list box with a DropDownList combo box. Unlock the controls on the form. Click the **lstRates** control and then press **Delete**. Click the **ComboBox** tool in the toolbox and then drag the mouse pointer to the form. Position the mouse pointer below the Rates: label and then release the mouse button. Change the combo box's DropDownStyle property to **DropDownList**.
4. The three-character ID for combo box names is cbo. Change the combo box's name to **cboRates**.
5. Now use the FORMAT menu to make the combo box the same width as the lstHours control.
6. Lock the controls on the form and then use the information shown in Figure 7-29 to set the TabIndex values.

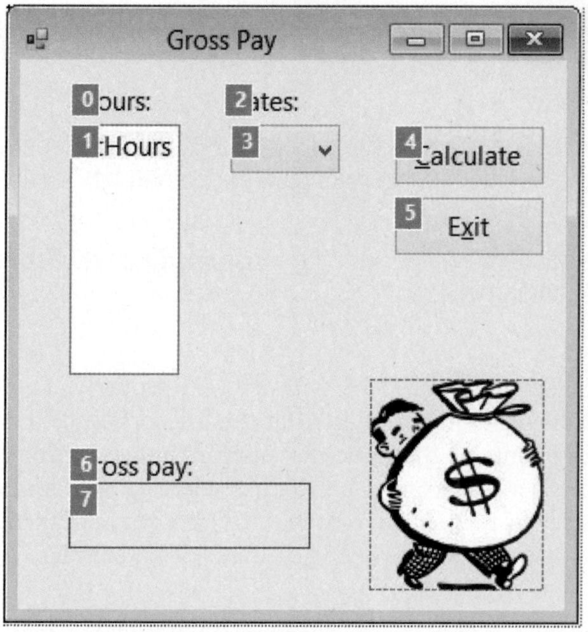

Figure 7-29 Correct TabIndex values
OpenClipArt.org/johnny_automatic

7. Press **Esc** to remove the TabIndex boxes from the form.
8. Open the Code Editor window and locate the form's Load event procedure. Change both occurrences of `lstRates` to **cboRates**. In addition, change `list boxes` in the first comment to **a list box and a combo box**.
9. Locate the btnCalc_Click procedure. Replace `lstRates.SelectedItem.ToString` in the second TryParse method with **cboRates.Text**.
10. Locate the ClearLabel procedure. Enter **, cboRates.TextChanged** at the end of the Handles clause. (Be sure to type the comma.)
11. Save the solution and then start the application. Click the **list arrow** in the Rates combo box and then click **9.00** in the list. Click the **Calculate** button. $360.00 appears in the Gross pay box, as shown in Figure 7-30.

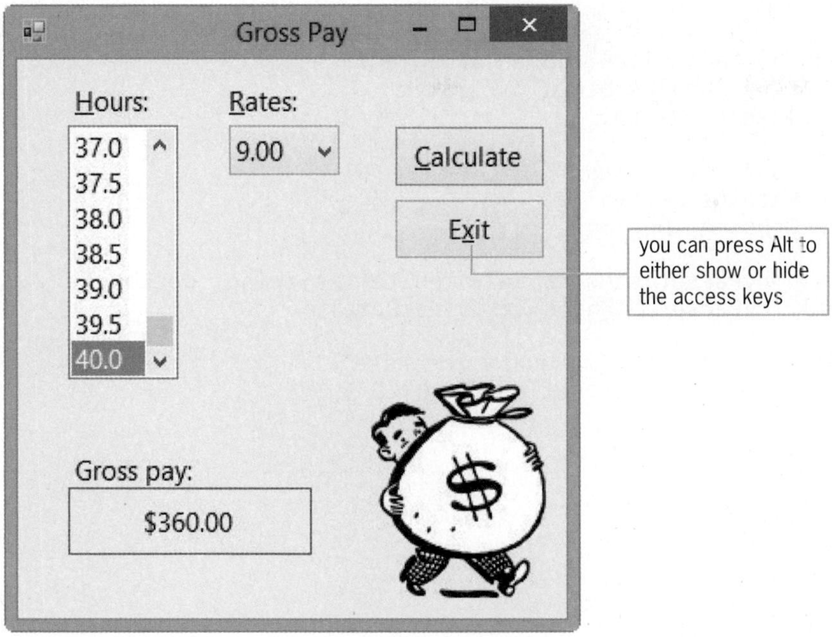

Figure 7-30 Gross pay amount shown in the interface
OpenClipArt.org/johnny_automatic

12. Click the **Exit** button. Close the Code Editor window and then close the solution.

Figure 7-31 shows the code entered in the form's Load event procedure, the ClearLabel procedure, and the btnCalc_Click procedure. The modifications made to the original code from Lesson A are shaded in the figure.

```
Private Sub frmMain_Load(sender As Object,
e As EventArgs) Handles Me.Load
    ' fill a list box and a combo box with values

    For decHours As Decimal = 0.5D To 40D Step 0.5D
        lstHours.Items.Add(decHours.ToString("N1"))
    Next decHours
    lstHours.SelectedItem = "40.0"

    For decRates As Decimal = 8D To 15D Step 0.5D
        cboRates.Items.Add(decRates.ToString("N2"))
    Next decRates
    cboRates.SelectedIndex = 4

End Sub

Private Sub ClearLabel(sender As Object,
e As EventArgs) Handles lstHours.SelectedValueChanged,
cboRates.TextChanged
    ' clear the gross pay

    lblGross.Text = String.Empty

End Sub
```

Figure 7-31 Modified code for the Gross Pay application *(continues)*

(continued)

```
Private Sub btnCalc_Click(sender As Object,
e As EventArgs) Handles btnCalc.Click
    ' calculate gross pay

    Dim decHours As Decimal
    Dim decRate As Decimal
    Dim decGross As Decimal

    Decimal.TryParse(lstHours.SelectedItem.ToString, decHours)
    Decimal.TryParse(cboRates.Text, decRate)

    decGross = CalcGross(decHours, decRate)
    lblGross.Text = decGross.ToString("C2")

End Sub
```

Figure 7-31 Modified code for the Gross Pay application

Lesson B Summary

- To add a combo box to a form:

  Use the ComboBox tool in the toolbox.

- To specify the style of a combo box:

  Set the combo box's DropDownStyle property.

- To add items to a combo box:

  Use the Items collection's Add method. The method's syntax is *object*.**Items.Add(***item***)**. In the syntax, *object* is the name of the combo box, and *item* is the text you want added to the list portion of the control.

- To automatically sort the items in the list portion of a combo box:

  Set the combo box's Sorted property to True.

- To determine the number of items in the list portion of a combo box:

  Use the Items collection's Count property. Its syntax is *object*.**Items.Count**, in which *object* is the name of the combo box.

- To select a combo box item from code:

  Use any of the following properties: SelectedIndex, SelectedItem, or Text.

- To determine the item either selected in the list portion of a combo box or entered in the text portion:

  Use the combo box's Text property. However, if the combo box is a DropDownList style, you also can use the SelectedIndex or SelectedItem property.

- To process code when the value in a combo box's Text property changes:

  Enter the code in the combo box's TextChanged event procedure.

Lesson B Key Terms

Combo box—a control that allows the user to select from a list of choices and also has a text field that may or may not be editable

DropDownStyle property—determines the style of a combo box

Lesson B Review Questions

1. Which property is used to specify a combo box's style?
   a. ComboBoxStyle
   b. DropDownStyle
   c. DropStyle
   d. Style

2. The items in a combo box belong to which collection?
   a. Items
   b. List
   c. ListBox
   d. Values

3. Which of the following selects the Cat item, which appears third in the cboAnimal control?
   a. `cboAnimal.SelectedIndex = 2`
   b. `cboAnimal.SelectedItem = "Cat"`
   c. `cboAnimal.Text = "Cat"`
   d. all of the above

4. The item that appears in the text portion of a combo box is stored in which property?
   a. SelectedText
   b. SelectedValue
   c. Text
   d. TextItem

5. The ________________ event occurs when the user either types a value in the text portion of a combo box or selects a different item in the list portion.
   a. ChangedItem
   b. ChangedValue
   c. SelectedItemChanged
   d. TextChanged

Lesson B Exercises

INTRODUCTORY

1. Use Windows to make a copy of the Gross Pay Solution-Sub folder from Lesson A. Rename the copy Gross Pay Solution-Sub-ComboBox. Open the Gross Pay Solution (Gross Pay Solution.sln) file contained in the Gross Pay Solution-Sub-ComboBox folder. Open the designer window. Replace the Hours list box with a DropDownList combo box. Make the necessary modifications to the code. Save the solution and then start and test the application. Close the Code Editor window and then close the solution.

INTRODUCTORY

2. In this exercise, you create an application that displays the name of the state corresponding to the area code selected in a combo box. Create a Visual Basic Windows application. Use the following names for the solution and project, respectively: Area Code Solution and Area Code Project. Save the application in the VB2012\Chap07 folder. Change the form file's name to Main Form.vb. Change the form's name to frmMain. Add any five area codes to a combo box whose DropDownStyle property is set to DropDownList. When the user clicks an area code, the name of its corresponding state should appear in a label control. Create a suitable interface and then code the application. Save the solution and then start and test the application. Close the Code Editor window and then close the solution.

INTERMEDIATE

3. Create a Visual Basic Windows application. Use the following names for the solution and project, respectively: Planets Solution and Planets Project. Save the application in the VB2012\Chap07 folder. Change the form file's name to Main Form.vb. Change the form's name to frmMain. Create the interface shown in Figure 7-32. The combo box should have the DropDownList style and contain the following planet names: Mercury, Venus, Mars, Jupiter, Saturn, Uranus, Neptune, and Pluto. When the user clicks a planet name, the application should convert the earth weight to the weight on that planet, and then display the converted weight in the label control. Use the Internet to research the formula for making the conversions. Save the solution and then start and test the application. Close the Code Editor window and then close the solution.

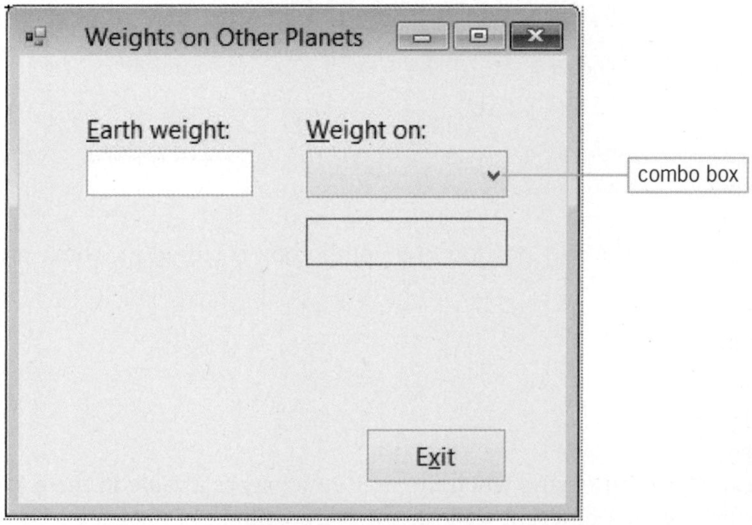

Figure 7-32 Interface for Exercise 3

4. In this exercise, you modify the application from Exercise 3. Use Windows to make a copy of the Planets Solution folder. Rename the copy Planets Solution-Sub. Open the Planets Solution (Planets Solution.sln) file contained in the Planets Solution-Sub folder. Open the designer and Code Editor windows. Modify the code to use an independent Sub procedure to calculate the weight on another planet. Save the solution and then start and test the application. Close the Code Editor window and then close the solution.

INTERMEDIATE

5. In this exercise, you modify the application from Exercise 3. Use Windows to make a copy of the Planets Solution folder. Rename the copy Planets Solution-Function. Open the Planets Solution (Planets Solution.sln) file contained in the Planets Solution-Function folder. Open the designer and Code Editor windows. Modify the code to use a function to calculate and return the weight on another planet. Save the solution and then start and test the application. Close the Code Editor window and then close the solution.

INTERMEDIATE

LESSON C

After studying Lesson C, you should be able to:

- Prevent a form from closing
- Round a number

Creating the Cerruti Company Application

Your task in this chapter is to create an application that calculates an employee's weekly gross pay, federal withholding tax (FWT), Social Security and Medicare (FICA) tax, and net pay. The application's TOE chart is shown in Figure 7-33.

Task	Object	Event
End the application	btnExit	Click
1. Calculate gross pay, FWT, FICA, and net pay 2. Display calculated amounts in appropriate labels	btnCalc	Click
Display calculated amounts (from btnCalc)	lblGross, lblFwt, lblFica, lblNet	None
Clear lblGross, lblFwt, lblFica, and lblNet	txtName, cboAllowances	TextChanged
	lstHours, lstRates	SelectedValueChanged
	radMarried, radSingle	CheckedChanged
Select the existing text	txtName	Enter
Allow only numbers and the Backspace key	cboAllowances	KeyPress
Get and display the name, hours worked, pay rate, marital status, and withholding allowances	txtName, lstHours, lstRates, radMarried, radSingle, cboAllowances	None
Fill lstHours, lstRates, and cboAllowances with values and then select a default item	frmMain	Load
Verify that the user wants to close the application, and then take the appropriate action based on the user's response		FormClosing

Figure 7-33 TOE chart for the Cerruti Company application

START HERE

To open the Cerruti Company application:

1. If necessary, start Visual Studio 2012. Open the Cerruti Solution (Cerruti Solution.sln) file contained in the VB2012\Chap07\Cerruti Solution folder. If necessary, open the designer window. See Figure 7-34.

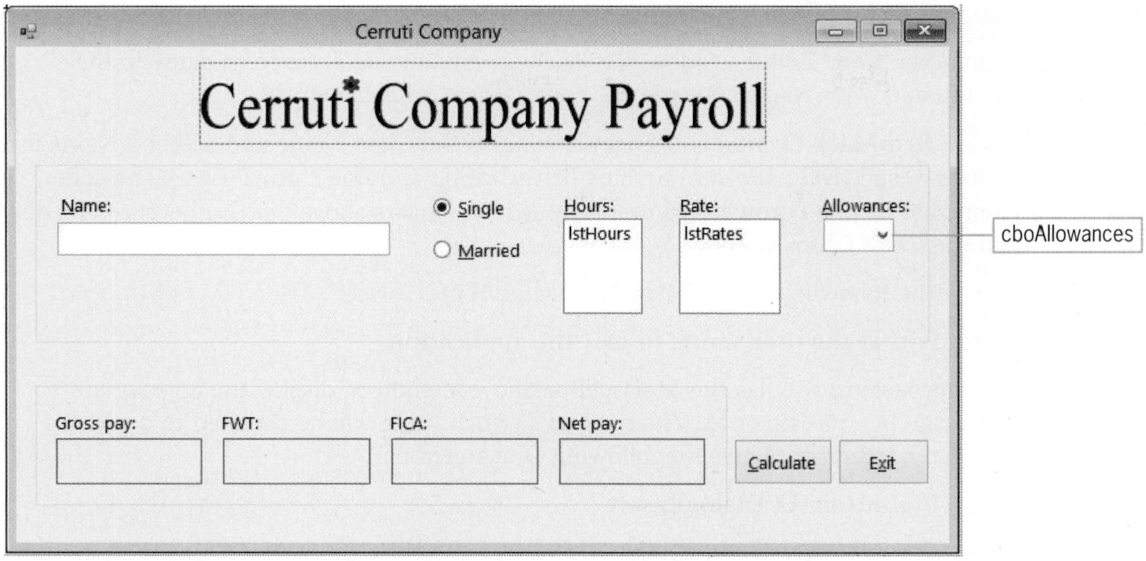

Figure 7-34 User interface for the Cerruti Company application

The interface in Figure 7-34 provides a text box for entering the employee's name, and radio buttons for entering his or her marital status. It also provides list boxes for specifying the hours worked and rate of pay. The combo box in the interface allows the user to either select the number of withholding allowances from the list portion of the control or type a number in the text portion. To complete the Cerruti Company application, you will need to code the btnCalc control's Click event procedure and the form's FormClosing event procedure.

Coding the FormClosing Event Procedure

A form's **FormClosing event** occurs when a form is about to be closed. In most cases, this happens when the computer processes the `Me.Close()` statement in the application's code. However, it also occurs when the user clicks the Close button on the form's title bar. According to the application's TOE chart, the FormClosing event procedure is responsible for verifying that the user wants to close the application, and then taking the appropriate action based on the user's response. Figure 7-35 shows the procedure's pseudocode.

```
frmMain FormClosing event procedure

1. use a message box to ask the user whether he or she wants to exit the application
2. if the user does not want to exit the application
        prevent the form from closing
   end if
```

Figure 7-35 Pseudocode for the FormClosing event procedure

START HERE

To begin coding the FormClosing event procedure:

1. Open the Code Editor window. Replace <your name> and <current date> in the comments with your name and the current date, respectively.
2. Click **(frmMain Events)** and **FormClosing** in the Class Name and Method Name list boxes, respectively. (Be sure to click FormClosing and not FormClosed.) The code template for the FormClosing event procedure appears above the Load event procedure in the Code Editor window.

3. Type the following comment and then press **Enter** twice:

   ' verify that the user wants to exit the application
4. The procedure will use the MessageBox.Show method to display the appropriate message in a message box. The method's return value will be assigned to a variable named `dlgButton`. Enter the following Dim statement:

   Dim dlgButton As DialogResult
5. The message box will contain the "Do you want to exit?" message, Yes and No buttons, and the Exclamation icon. Enter the following statement. Press **Enter** twice after typing the last line in the statement.

```
dlgButton =
    MessageBox.Show("Do you want to exit?",
    "Cerruti Company", MessageBoxButtons.YesNo,
    MessageBoxIcon.Exclamation)
```

If the user selects the No button in the message box, the FormClosing procedure should stop the computer from closing the form. You prevent the computer from closing a form by setting the **Cancel property** of the FormClosing event procedure's `e` parameter to True.

START HERE

To complete the FormClosing event procedure and then test it:

1. Enter the following comment and selection structure:

```
' if the No button was selected, don't close the form
If dlgButton = Windows.Forms.DialogResult.No Then
    e.Cancel = True
End If
```

2. Save the solution and then start the application. Click the **Close** button on the form's title bar. Doing this invokes the FormClosing event procedure, which displays the message box shown in Figure 7-36.

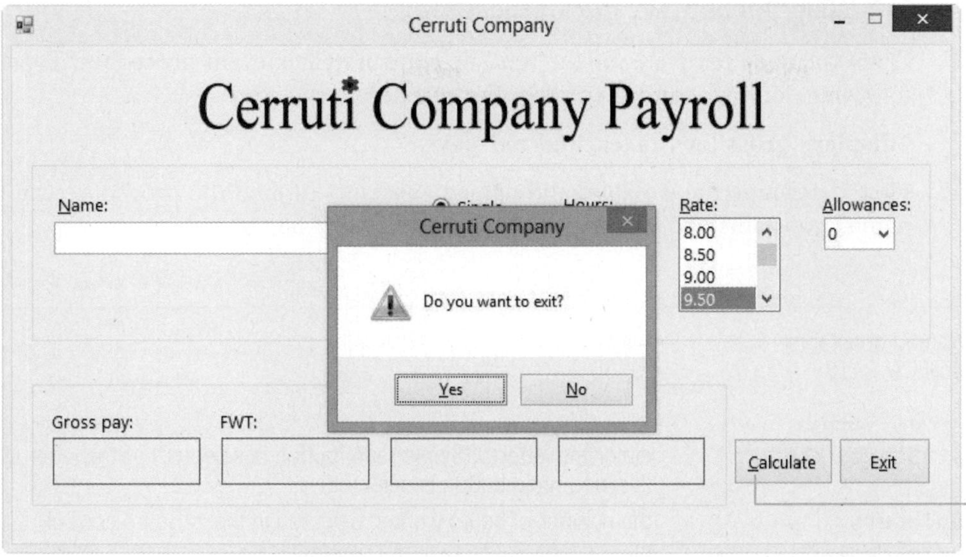

Figure 7-36 Message box displayed by the code in the FormClosing event procedure

3. Click the **No** button in the message box. Notice that the form remains on the screen.
4. Click the **Exit** button. This time, click the **Yes** button in the message box. The application ends.

Coding the btnCalc_Click Procedure

According to the application's TOE chart, the btnCalc control's Click event procedure is responsible for calculating and displaying the gross pay, FWT (federal withholding tax), FICA tax, and net pay. The procedure's pseudocode is shown in Figure 7-37.

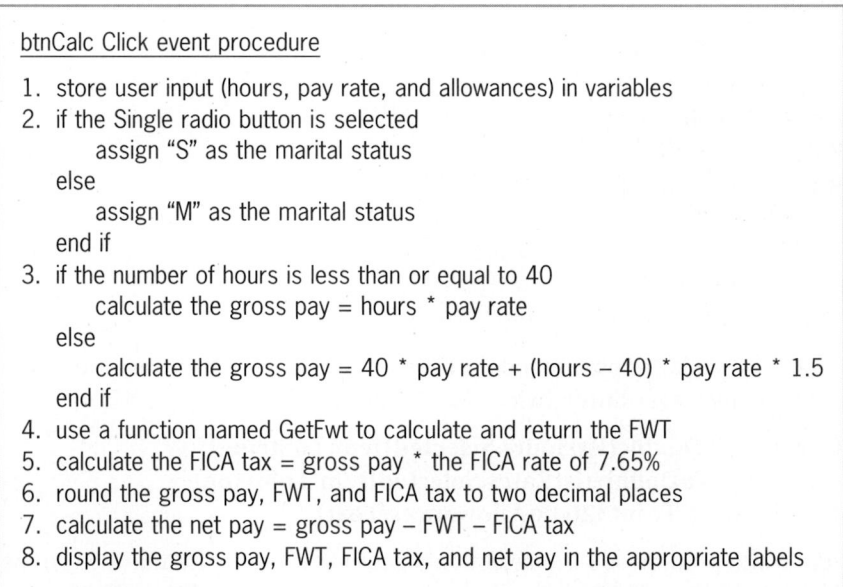

```
btnCalc Click event procedure
1. store user input (hours, pay rate, and allowances) in variables
2. if the Single radio button is selected
        assign "S" as the marital status
   else
        assign "M" as the marital status
   end if
3. if the number of hours is less than or equal to 40
        calculate the gross pay = hours * pay rate
   else
        calculate the gross pay = 40 * pay rate + (hours – 40) * pay rate * 1.5
   end if
4. use a function named GetFwt to calculate and return the FWT
5. calculate the FICA tax = gross pay * the FICA rate of 7.65%
6. round the gross pay, FWT, and FICA tax to two decimal places
7. calculate the net pay = gross pay – FWT – FICA tax
8. display the gross pay, FWT, FICA tax, and net pay in the appropriate labels
```

Figure 7-37 Pseudocode for the btnCalc_Click procedure

START HERE

To begin coding the btnCalc_Click procedure:

1. Open the code template for the btnCalc control's Click event procedure. Type the following comment and then press **Enter** twice:

   ' displays gross pay, taxes, and net pay

2. First, determine the variables and named constants (if any) the procedure will use. The named constants and variables are listed in Figure 7-38.

Named constants	Value
dblFICA_RATE	.0765
Variable names	**Stores**
`strStatus`	either the letter S (Single radio button is selected) or the letter M (Married radio button is selected)
`dblHours`	the number of hours worked selected in the lstHours control
`dblPayRate`	the pay rate selected in the lstRates control
`intAllowances`	the number of withholding allowances either selected or entered in the cboAllowances control
`dblGross`	the gross pay
`dblFwt`	the federal withholding tax calculated and returned by the GetFwt function
`dblFica`	the FICA tax
`dblNet`	the net pay

Figure 7-38 Listing of named constants and variables for the btnCalc_Click procedure

START HERE

To continue coding the btnCalc_Click procedure:

1. Enter the following nine declaration statements. Press **Enter** twice after typing the last declaration statement.

```
Const dblFICA_RATE As Double = .0765
Dim strStatus As String
Dim dblHours As Double
Dim dblPayRate As Double
Dim intAllowances As Integer
Dim dblGross As Double
Dim dblFwt As Double
Dim dblFica As Double
Dim dblNet As Double
```

2. The first step in the procedure's pseudocode is to store the user input in variables. Enter the following statements. Press **Enter** twice after typing the last statement.

```
dblHours = Convert.ToDouble(lstHours.SelectedItem.ToString)
dblPayRate = Convert.ToDouble(lstRates.SelectedItem.ToString)
intAllowances = Convert.ToInt32(cboAllowances.Text)
```

3. The second step in the pseudocode is a selection structure whose condition determines the employee's marital status. Type the selection structure shown in Figure 7-39 and then position the insertion point as indicated in the figure.

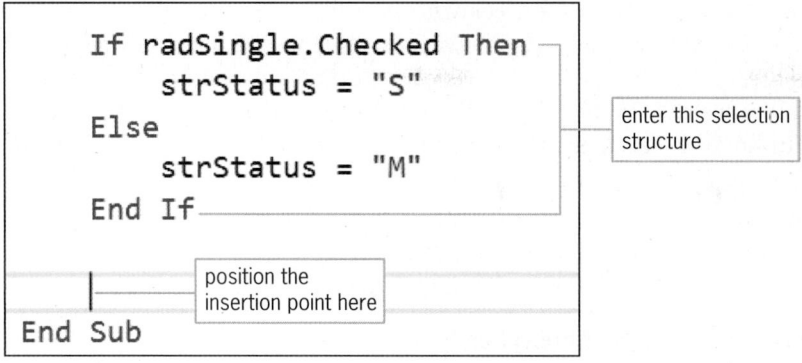

```
    If radSingle.Checked Then
        strStatus = "S"
    Else
        strStatus = "M"
    End If

End Sub
```

enter this selection structure

position the insertion point here

Figure 7-39 Selection structure entered in the procedure

4. The third step in the pseudocode is another selection structure. This selection structure's condition compares the number of hours worked with the number 40. If the number of hours worked is less than or equal to 40, the selection structure's true path should calculate the gross pay by multiplying the number of hours worked by the pay rate. Enter the following comment, If clause, and assignment statement:

   ' calculate gross pay
   If dblHours <= 40 Then
   dblGross = dblHours * dblPayRate

5. If the number of hours worked is greater than 40, the employee is entitled to his or her regular pay rate for the hours worked up to and including 40, and then time and one-half for the hours worked over 40. Enter the Else clause and assignment statement shown in Figure 7-40, and then save the solution.

```
    ' calculate gross pay
    If dblHours <= 40 Then
        dblGross = dblHours * dblPayRate
    Else
        dblGross = 40 * dblPayRate +
            (dblHours - 40) * dblPayRate * 1.5
    End If
End Sub
```

enter the Else clause and the assignment statement

Figure 7-40 Second selection structure entered in the procedure

The fourth step in the procedure's pseudocode uses a function named GetFwt to calculate and return the FWT (federal withholding tax). Before entering the appropriate instruction, you will create the function.

Creating the GetFwt Function

The amount of federal withholding tax (FWT) to deduct from an employee's weekly gross pay is based on his or her weekly taxable wages and filing status, which is either single (including head of household) or married. You calculate the weekly taxable wages by first multiplying the number of withholding allowances by $73.08 (the value of a withholding allowance in 2012), and then subtracting the result from the weekly gross pay. For example, if your weekly gross pay is $400 and you have two withholding allowances, your weekly taxable wages are $253.84. The $253.84 is calculated by multiplying 73.08 by 2 and then subtracting the result (146.16) from 400. You use the weekly taxable wages, along with the filing status and the appropriate weekly Federal Withholding Tax table, to determine the amount of FWT to withhold. The weekly tax tables for the year 2012 are shown in Figure 7-41.

FWT Tables – Weekly Payroll Period

Single person (including head of household)

If the taxable wages are: The amount of income tax to withhold is:

Over	But not over	Base amount	Percentage	Of excess over
	$ 41	0		
$ 41	$ 209	0	10%	$ 41
$ 209	$ 721	$ 16.80 plus	15%	$ 209
$ 721	$1,688	$ 93.60 plus	25%	$ 721
$1,688	$3,477	$ 335.35 plus	28%	$1,688
$3,477	$7,510	$ 836.27 plus	33%	$3,477
$7,510		$2,167.16 plus	35%	$7,510

Married person

If the taxable wages are: The amount of income tax to withhold is

Over	But not over	Base amount	Percentage	Of excess over
	$ 156	0		
$ 156	$ 490	0	10%	$ 156
$ 490	$1,515	$ 33.40 plus	15%	$ 490
$1,515	$2,900	$ 187.15 plus	25%	$1,515
$2,900	$4,338	$ 533.40 plus	28%	$2,900
$4,338	$7,624	$ 936.04 plus	33%	$4,338
$7,624		$2,020.42 plus	35%	$7,624

Figure 7-41 Weekly FWT tables for the year 2012

Each table in Figure 7-41 contains five columns of information. The first two columns list various ranges, also called brackets, of taxable wage amounts. The first column (Over) lists the amount that a taxable wage in that bracket must be over, and the second column (But not over) lists the maximum amount included in the bracket. The remaining three columns (Base amount, Percentage, and Of excess over) tell you how to calculate the tax for each range. For example, assume that you are married and your weekly taxable wages are $388.46. Before you can calculate the amount of your tax, you need to locate your taxable wages in the first two columns of the Married table. Taxable wages of $388.46 fall within the $156 through $490 bracket. After locating the bracket that contains your taxable wages, you then use the remaining three columns in the table to calculate your tax. In this case, you calculate the tax by first subtracting 156 (the amount shown in the Of excess over column) from your taxable wages of 388.46, giving 232.46. You then multiply 232.46 by 10% (the amount shown in the Percentage column), giving 23.25. You then add that amount to the amount shown in the Base amount column (in this case, 0), giving $23.25 as your tax. The calculations are shown in Figure 7-42.

Married with Weekly Taxable Wages of $388.46	
Taxable wages	$ 388.46
Of excess over	– 156.00
	232.46
Percentage	* .10
	23.25
Base amount	+ 0.00
Tax	$ 23.25

Figure 7-42 Example of a FWT calculation

Now calculate the tax for a single taxpayer whose weekly taxable wages are $600. Figure 7-43 shows how the tax amount ($75.45) is calculated.

Single with Weekly Taxable Wages of $600	
Taxable wages	$ 600.00
Of excess over	– 209.00
	391.00
Percentage	* .15
	58.65
Base amount	+ 16.80
Tax	$ 75.45

Figure 7-43 Another example of a FWT calculation

To calculate the federal withholding tax, the GetFwt function needs to know the employee's gross pay amount, number of withholding allowances, and marital status. The gross pay amount and number of withholding allowances are necessary to calculate the taxable wages, and the marital status indicates the appropriate FWT table to use when calculating the tax. The function will receive the necessary information from the btnCalc_Click procedure, which will pass the information when it invokes the function. Recall that the information is stored in the btnCalc_Click procedure's `dblGross`, `intAllowances`, and `strStatus` variables. Figure 7-44 shows the function's pseudocode.

```
GetFwt function
1. calculate the taxable wages = gross pay – number of withholding allowances * 73.08
2. if the marital status is Single
         calculate the FWT using the Single FWT table
   else
         calculate the FWT using the Married FWT table
   end if
3. return the FWT
```

Figure 7-44 Pseudocode for the GetFwt function

START HERE

To create the GetFwt function:

1. Scroll to the top of the Code Editor window. Click the **blank line** below the `' GetFwt function` comment.
2. When it invokes the GetFwt function, the btnCalc_Click procedure will pass the values stored in its `strStatus`, `intAllowances`, and `dblGross` variables. You do not want the GetFwt function to change the contents of the variables, so you will pass a copy of each variable's value (rather than its address). You will store the values passed to the function in three parameters named `strMarital`, `intNumAllow`, and `dblWeekPay`. The GetFwt function will use the information it receives to calculate and return the FWT as a Double number. Type the function header and comment shown in Figure 7-45 and then position the insertion point as indicated in the figure. (Notice that the Code Editor automatically enters the procedure footer for you.)

```
' GetFwt function
Private Function GetFwt(ByVal strMarital As String,
                        ByVal intNumAllow As Integer,
                        ByVal dblWeekPay As Double) As Double
    ' calculates and returns the FWT

    |
End Function
```

enter the function header and the comment

position the insertion point here

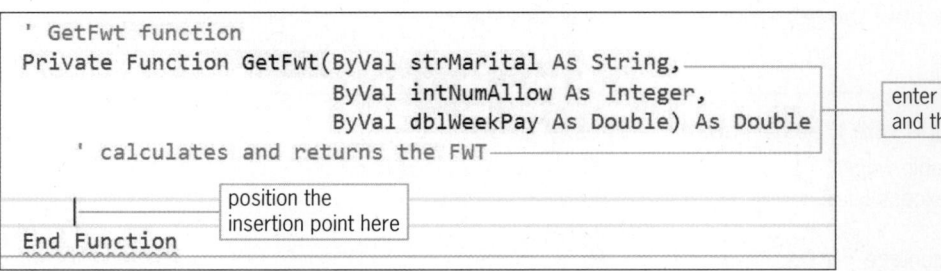

Figure 7-45 GetFwt function header and footer

3. The function will use a named constant for the withholding allowance amount ($73.08). It also will use two additional variables: one to store the taxable wages and the other to store the FWT. Enter the following declaration statements. Press **Enter** twice after typing the last declaration statement.

   Const dblONE_ALLOW As Double = 73.08
   Dim dblTaxWages As Double
   Dim dblTax As Double

4. The first step in the function's pseudocode calculates the taxable wages. Enter the following comment and assignment statement. Press **Enter** twice after typing the assignment statement.

   ' calculate taxable wages
   dblTaxWages =
   dblWeekPay – intNumAllow * dblONE_ALLOW

5. The second step in the pseudocode is a selection structure whose condition determines the marital status. Enter the following comment and If clause:

   ' determine marital status and then calculate FWT
   If strMarital = "S" Then

6. If the `strMarital` variable contains the letter S, the selection structure's true path should calculate the federal withholding tax using the information from the Single tax table. You will find the appropriate code in the Single.txt file. Click **FILE** on the menu bar and then click **Open File**. If necessary, open the Cerruti Company Project folder. Click **Single.txt** in the list of filenames and then click the **Open** button. The Single.txt file appears in a separate window in the IDE. Click **EDIT** on the menu bar and then click

Select All. Press **Ctrl+c** to copy the selected text to the Windows Clipboard, and then close the Single.txt window.

7. The insertion point should be in the blank line below the If clause in the GetFwt function. Press **Ctrl+v** to paste the copied text into the selection structure's true path.
8. Type **Else** and then press **Tab** twice. Type **' strMarital = "M"** and then press **Enter**.
9. If the `strMarital` variable does not contain the letter S, the selection structure's false path should calculate the federal withholding tax using the information from the Married tax table. You will find the appropriate code in the Married.txt file. Click **FILE** and then click **Open File**. Click **Married.txt** in the list of filenames and then click the **Open** button. Click **EDIT** and then click **Select All**. Press **Ctrl+c** to copy the selected text to the Windows Clipboard, and then close the Married.txt window.
10. The insertion point should be in the blank line below the Else clause. Press **Ctrl+v** to paste the copied text into the selection structure's false path.
11. The last step in the function's pseudocode returns the federal withholding tax amount to the statement that invoked the function. The tax amount is stored in the `dblTax` variable. Click **after the letter f** in the End If clause and then press **Enter** twice. Type **Return dblTax** and then click the **blank line** above the Return statement. Save the solution. (You can look ahead to Figure 7-50 to view the function's code.)

Completing the btnCalc_Click Procedure

Now that you have created the GetFwt function, you can invoke the function from the btnCalc_Click procedure. Invoking the GetFwt function is the fourth step listed in the procedure's pseudocode (shown earlier in Figure 7-37).

START HERE

To continue coding the btnCalc_Click event procedure:

1. Locate the btnCalc_Click procedure. Click **after the letter f** in the second End If clause and then press **Enter** twice.
2. Recall that the procedure needs to send the GetFwt function a copy of the values stored in the `strStatus`, `intAllowances`, and `dblGross` variables. The value returned by the function will be assigned to the `dblFwt` variable. Enter the following comment and assignment statement. Press **Enter** twice after typing the assignment statement.

   ' get the FWT
   dblFwt = GetFwt(strStatus, intAllowances, dblGross)
3. The next step in the procedure's pseudocode calculates the FICA tax by multiplying the gross pay amount by the FICA rate. Enter the following comment and assignment statement. Press **Enter** twice after typing the assignment statement.

   ' calculate FICA tax
   dblFica = dblGross * dblFICA_RATE
4. Save the solution.

Rounding Numbers

The sixth step in the procedure's pseudocode rounds the gross pay, FWT, and FICA tax amounts to two decimal places. Rounding these amounts before making the net pay calculation will prevent the "penny off" error from occurring. (You can observe the "penny off" error by completing Exercise 1 at the end of this lesson.) You can use the **Math.Round function** to return a number rounded to a specific number of decimal places. The function's syntax and examples are shown in Figure 7-46. In the syntax, *value* is a numeric expression, and *digits* (which is optional) is an integer indicating how many places to the right of the decimal point are included in the rounding. If the *digits* argument is omitted, the Math.Round function returns an integer.

Math.Round Function

Syntax
Math.Round(*value*[, *digits*]**)**

Examples	Result
`Math.Round(3.235, 2)`	3.24
`Math.Round(6.517, 1)`	6.5
`Math.Round(8.99)`	9

Figure 7-46 Syntax and examples of the Math.Round function

START HERE

To complete the btnCalc_Click procedure:

1. Enter the following comment and assignment statements. Press **Enter** twice after typing the last assignment statement.

```
' round gross pay, FWT, and FICA tax
dblGross = Math.Round(dblGross, 2)
dblFwt = Math.Round(dblFwt, 2)
dblFica = Math.Round(dblFica, 2)
```

2. Next, the procedure should calculate the net pay by subtracting the two tax amounts from the gross pay amount. Enter the following comment and assignment statement. Press **Enter** twice after typing the assignment statement.

```
' calculate net pay
dblNet = dblGross – dblFwt – dblFica
```

3. The last step in the procedure's pseudocode displays the calculated amounts in the appropriate label controls. Enter the following comment and assignment statements:

```
' display calculated amounts
lblGross.Text = dblGross.ToString("N2")
lblFwt.Text = dblFwt.ToString("N2")
lblFica.Text = dblFica.ToString("N2")
lblNet.Text = dblNet.ToString("N2")
```

4. Save the solution.

You will test the application twice, using the data shown in Figure 7-47. The figure also shows the correct amounts for the gross pay, taxes, and net pay.

Test Data

First test

Name:	Sara Huntington
Marital status:	Single
Hours:	40
Pay rate:	$10
Allowances:	1

Gross wages	$ 400.00
Allowance deduction	– 73.08
Taxable wages	326.92
Of excess over	– 209.00
	117.92
Percentage	* .15
	17.688
Base amount	+ 16.80
FWT tax	$ 34.49 (rounded to 2 decimal places)
FICA tax (400 * .0765)	$ 30.60
Net pay (400 – 34.49 – 30.60)	$ 334.91

Second test

Name:	James Perkins
Marital status:	Married
Hours:	42
Pay rate:	$15
Allowances:	2

Gross wages	$ 645.00
Allowance deduction	– 146.16
Taxable wages	498.84
Of excess over	– 490.00
	8.84
Percentage	* .15
	1.326
Base amount	+ 33.40
FWT tax	$ 34.73 (rounded to 2 decimal places)
FICA tax (645 * .0765)	$ 49.34 (rounded to 2 decimal places)
Net pay (645 – 34.73 – 49.34)	$ 560.93

Figure 7-47 Data for testing the Cerruti Company's application

To test the Cerruti Company's application:

START HERE

1. Start the application. Type **Sara Huntington** in the Name box. Click **10.00** in the Rate list box and then click **1** in the Allowances combo box. Click the **Calculate** button. See Figure 7-48. The gross pay, taxes, and net pay agree with the manual calculations from Figure 7-47.

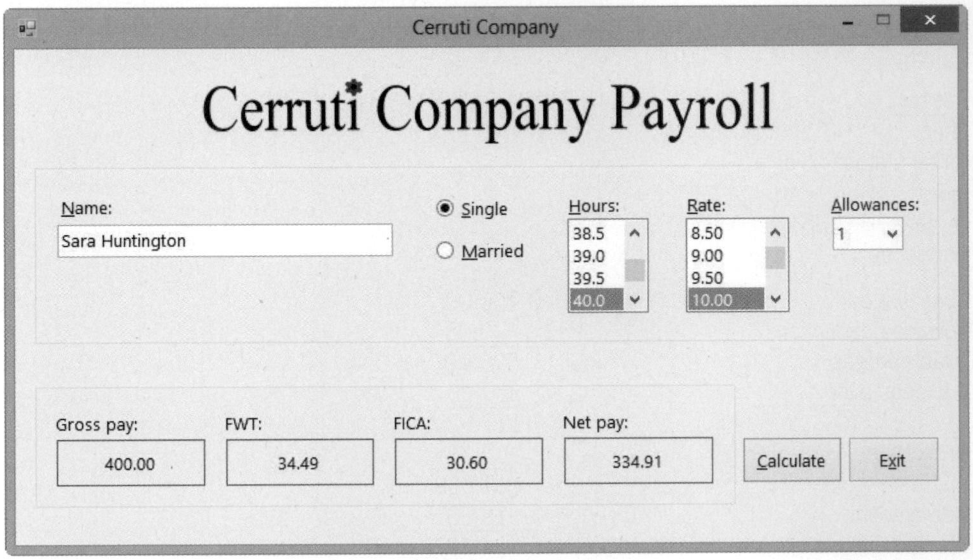

Figure 7-48 Payroll calculations using the first set of test data

2. Change the name entered in the Name box to **James Perkins**. Click the **Married** radio button, click **42** in the Hours list box, and then click **15.00** in the Rate list box. Press **Tab** to move the focus to the Allowances combo box. In addition to selecting the number of allowances in the list portion of the combo box, the user also can type the number in the text portion. Type **2** and then click the **Calculate** button. See Figure 7-49. The gross pay, taxes, and net pay agree with the manual calculations from Figure 7-47.

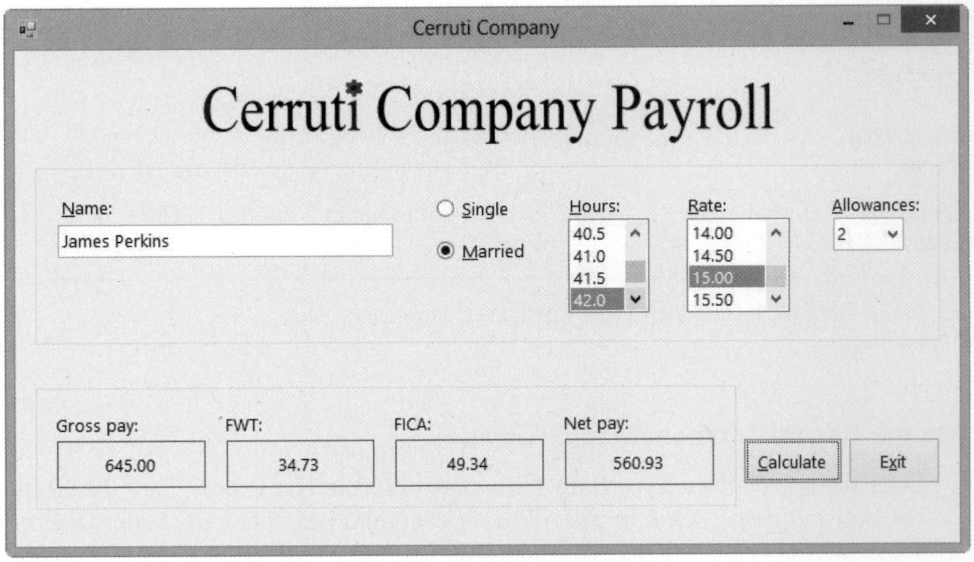

Figure 7-49 Payroll calculations using the second set of test data

3. Click the **Exit** button and then click the **Yes** button. Close the Code Editor window and then close the solution.

Figure 7-50 shows the Cerruti Company application's code.

```
' Name:         Cerruti Project
' Purpose:      Displays gross pay, taxes, and net pay
' Programmer:   <your name> on <current date>

Option Explicit On
Option Strict On
Option Infer Off

Public Class frmMain

    ' GetFwt function
    Private Function GetFwt(ByVal strMarital As String,
                            ByVal intNumAllow As Integer,
                            ByVal dblWeekPay As Double) As Double
        ' calculates and returns the FWT

        Const dblONE_ALLOW As Double = 73.08
        Dim dblTaxWages As Double
        Dim dblTax As Double

        ' calculate taxable wages
        dblTaxWages =
           dblWeekPay - intNumAllow * dblONE_ALLOW

        ' determine marital status and then calculate FWT
        If strMarital = "S" Then
            Select Case dblTaxWages
                Case Is <= 41
                    dblTax = 0
                Case Is <= 209
                    dblTax = 0.1 * (dblTaxWages - 41)
                Case Is <= 721
                    dblTax = 16.8 + 0.15 * (dblTaxWages - 209)
                Case Is <= 1688
                    dblTax = 93.6 + 0.25 * (dblTaxWages - 721)
                Case Is <= 3477
                    dblTax = 335.35 + 0.28 * (dblTaxWages - 1688)
                Case Is <= 7510
                    dblTax = 836.27 + 0.33 * (dblTaxWages - 3477)
                Case Else
                    dblTax = 2167.16 + 0.35 * (dblTaxWages - 7510)
                End Select
        Else    ' strMarital = "M"
            Select Case dblTaxWages
                Case Is <= 156
                    dblTax = 0
                Case Is <= 490
                    dblTax = 0.1 * (dblTaxWages - 156)
                Case Is <= 1515
                    dblTax = 33.4 + 0.15 * (dblTaxWages - 490)
                Case Is <= 2900
                    dblTax = 187.15 + 0.25 * (dblTaxWages - 1515)
```

Figure 7-50 Cerruti Company application's code *(continues)*

(continued)

```
            Case Is <= 4338
                dblTax = 533.4 + 0.28 * (dblTaxWages - 2900)
            Case Is <= 7624
                dblTax = 936.04 + 0.33 * (dblTaxWages - 4338)
            Case Else
                dblTax = 2020.42 + 0.35 * (dblTaxWages - 7624)
        End Select
    End If

    Return dblTax
End Function

Private Sub btnExit_Click(sender As Object,
e As EventArgs) Handles btnExit.Click
    Me.Close()
End Sub

Private Sub txtName_Enter(sender As Object,
e As EventArgs) Handles txtName.Enter
    ' select the existing text

    txtName.SelectAll()
End Sub

Private Sub cboAllowances_KeyPress(sender As Object,
e As Windows.Forms.KeyPressEventArgs)
Handles cboAllowances.KeyPress
    ' allow only numbers and the Backspace key

    If (e.KeyChar < "0" OrElse e.KeyChar > "9")
    AndAlso e.KeyChar <> ControlChars.Back Then
        e.Handled = True
    End If
End Sub

Private Sub ClearLabels(sender As Object,
e As EventArgs) Handles lstHours.SelectedValueChanged,
lstRates.SelectedValueChanged,
radSingle.CheckedChanged, radMarried.CheckedChanged,
txtName.TextChanged, cboAllowances.TextChanged

    lblGross.Text = String.Empty
    lblFwt.Text = String.Empty
    lblFica.Text = String.Empty
    lblNet.Text = String.Empty
End Sub

Private Sub frmMain_FormClosing(sender As Object,
e As FormClosingEventArgs) Handles Me.FormClosing
    ' verify that the user wants to exit the application

    Dim dlgButton As DialogResult
```

Figure 7-50 Cerruti Company application's code *(continues)*

(continued)

```
        dlgButton =
            MessageBox.Show("Do you want to exit?",
            "Cerruti Company", MessageBoxButtons.YesNo,
            MessageBoxIcon.Exclamation)

        ' if the No button was selected, don't close the form
        If dlgButton = Windows.Forms.DialogResult.No Then
            e.Cancel = True
        End If
    End Sub

    Private Sub frmMain_Load(sender As Object,
    e As EventArgs) Handles Me.Load
        ' fill list boxes and combo box with values
        ' then select a default value in each

        For dblHours As Double = 0 To 55 Step 0.5
            lstHours.Items.Add(dblHours.ToString("N1"))
        Next dblHours

        For dblRates As Double = 7.5 To 15.5 Step 0.5
            lstRates.Items.Add(dblRates.ToString("N2"))
        Next dblRates

        For intAllow As Integer = 0 To 10
            cboAllowances.Items.Add(intAllow.ToString)
        Next intAllow

        lstHours.SelectedItem = "40.0"
        lstRates.SelectedItem = "9.50"
        cboAllowances.SelectedIndex = 0
    End Sub

    Private Sub btnCalc_Click(sender As Object,
    e As EventArgs) Handles btnCalc.Click
        ' displays gross pay, taxes, and net pay

        Const dblFICA_RATE As Double = 0.0765
        Dim strStatus As String
        Dim dblHours As Double
        Dim dblPayRate As Double
        Dim intAllowances As Integer
        Dim dblGross As Double
        Dim dblFwt As Double
        Dim dblFica As Double
        Dim dblNet As Double

        dblHours =
             Convert.ToDouble(lstHours.SelectedItem.ToString)
        dblPayRate =
             Convert.ToDouble(lstRates.SelectedItem.ToString)
        intAllowances = Convert.ToInt32(cboAllowances.Text)
```

Figure 7-50 Cerruti Company application's code *(continues)*

(continued)

```

        If radSingle.Checked Then
            strStatus = "S"
        Else
            strStatus = "M"
        End If

        ' calculate gross pay
        If dblHours <= 40 Then
            dblGross = dblHours * dblPayRate
        Else
            dblGross = 40 * dblPayRate +
                (dblHours - 40) * dblPayRate * 1.5
        End If

        ' get the FWT
        dblFwt = GetFwt(strStatus, intAllowances, dblGross)

        ' calculate FICA tax
        dblFica = dblGross * dblFICA_RATE

        ' round gross pay, FWT, and FICA tax
        dblGross = Math.Round(dblGross, 2)
        dblFwt = Math.Round(dblFwt, 2)
        dblFica = Math.Round(dblFica, 2)

        ' calculate net pay
        dblNet = dblGross - dblFwt - dblFica

        ' display calculated amounts
        lblGross.Text = dblGross.ToString("N2")
        lblFwt.Text = dblFwt.ToString("N2")
        lblFica.Text = dblFica.ToString("N2")
        lblNet.Text = dblNet.ToString("N2")

    End Sub
End Class
```

Figure 7-50 Cerruti Company application's code

Lesson C Summary

- To process code when a form is about to be closed:

  Enter the code in the form's FormClosing event procedure. The FormClosing event occurs when the user clicks the Close button on a form's title bar or when the computer processes the `Me.Close()` statement.

- To prevent a form from being closed:

  Set the Cancel property of the FormClosing event procedure's `e` parameter to True, like this: `e.Cancel = True`.

- To round a number to a specific number of decimal places:

  Use the Math.Round function. The function's syntax is **Math.Round(*value*[, *digits*])**, where *value* is a numeric expression, and *digits* (which is optional) is an integer indicating how many places to the right of the decimal point are included in the rounding. If the *digits* argument is omitted, the Math.Round function returns an integer.

Lesson C Key Terms

Cancel property—a property of the `e` parameter in the form's FormClosing event procedure; when set to True, it prevents the form from closing

FormClosing event—occurs when a form is about to be closed, which can happen as a result of the computer processing the `Me.Close()` statement or the user clicking the Close button on the form's title bar

Math.Round function—rounds a number to a specific number of decimal places

Lesson C Review Questions

1. A form's ______________ event is triggered when you click the Close button on its title bar.

   a. Close
   b. CloseForm
   c. FormClose
   d. FormClosing

2. A form's ______________ event is triggered when the computer processes the `Me.Close()` statement.

   a. Close
   b. Closing
   c. FormClose
   d. FormClosing

3. Which of the following statements prevents a form from being closed?

   a. `e.Cancel = False`
   b. `e.Cancel = True`
   c. `e.Close = False`
   d. `sender.Close = False`

4. Which of the following rounds the contents of the `dblNum` variable to three decimal places?

   a. `Math.Round(3, dblNum)`
   b. `Math.Round(dblNum, 3)`
   c. `Round.Math(dblNum, 3)`
   d. `Round.Math(3, dblNum)`

Lesson C Exercises

INTRODUCTORY

1. In this exercise, you will remove the Math.Round function from the payroll application created in the lesson; doing this will allow you to observe the "penny off" error. Use Windows to make a copy of the Cerruti Solution folder. Rename the copy No Rounding Cerruti Solution. Open the Cerruti Solution (Cerruti Solution.sln) file contained in the No Rounding Cerruti Solution folder. Open the designer and Code Editor windows. The Math.Round function appears in three statements in the btnCalc_Click procedure. Type an apostrophe at the beginning of each of the three statements, making them comments. Save the solution and then start the application. Test the application by clicking 38.5 in the Hours list box and 10.50 in the Rate list box. Click the Calculate button. What is wrong with the calculated amounts? Stop the application. Close the Code Editor window and then close the solution.

INTRODUCTORY

2. In this exercise, you modify one of the Gross Pay applications completed in Lesson A. Use Windows to make a copy of the Gross Pay Solution-Sub folder. Rename the copy Gross Pay Solution-Sub-FormClosing. Open the Gross Pay Solution (Gross Pay Solution.sln) file contained in the Gross Pay Solution-Sub- FormClosing folder. Open the designer and Code Editor windows. Code the form's FormClosing event procedure so that it asks the user whether he or she wants to exit the application. Take the appropriate action based on the user's response. Save the solution and then start and test the application. Close the Code Editor window and then close the solution.

INTERMEDIATE

3. In this exercise, you modify the Cerruti Company application from this lesson. Use Windows to make a copy of the Cerruti Solution folder. Rename the copy Cerruti Solution-Sub. Open the Cerruti Solution (Cerruti Solution.sln) file contained in the Cerruti Solution-Sub folder. Open the designer and Code Editor windows. Change the GetFwt function to an independent Sub procedure and then modify the statement that calls the procedure. Save the solution and then start and test the application. Close the Code Editor window and then close the solution.

INTERMEDIATE

4. In this exercise, you modify the Cerruti Company application from this lesson. Use Windows to make a copy of the Cerruti Solution folder from this lesson. Rename the copy Modified Cerruti Solution. Open the Cerruti Solution (Cerruti Solution.sln) file contained in the Modified Cerruti Solution folder. Open the designer and Code Editor windows. Modify the code so that the GetFwt function (rather than btnCalc_Click procedure) determines the selected radio button. Save the solution and then start and test the application. Close the Code Editor window and then close the solution.

INTERMEDIATE

5. The Sweet Life Shoppe sells four varieties of doughnuts: Glazed ($.65), Sugar ($.65), Chocolate ($.85), and Filled ($1.00). It also sells regular coffee ($1.80) and cappuccino ($2.50). The store manager wants an application that she can use to calculate and display a customer's subtotal, 3% sales tax, and total due. Create a Visual Basic Windows application. Use the following names for the solution and project, respectively: Sweet Life Solution and Sweet Life Project. Save the application in the VB2012\Chap07 folder. Change the form file's name to Main Form.vb. Change the form's name to frmMain. Create the interface shown in Figure 7-51. The image for the picture box is stored in the VB2012\Chap07\DonutCoffee.png file. (The image was downloaded from the Open Clip Art Library at *http://openclipart.org*.) Code the application. Use one function to calculate and return the cost of the doughnut. Use another function to calculate and return the cost of the coffee. Use a third function to calculate and return the 3% sales tax. Save the solution and then start and test the application. Close the Code Editor window and then close the solution.

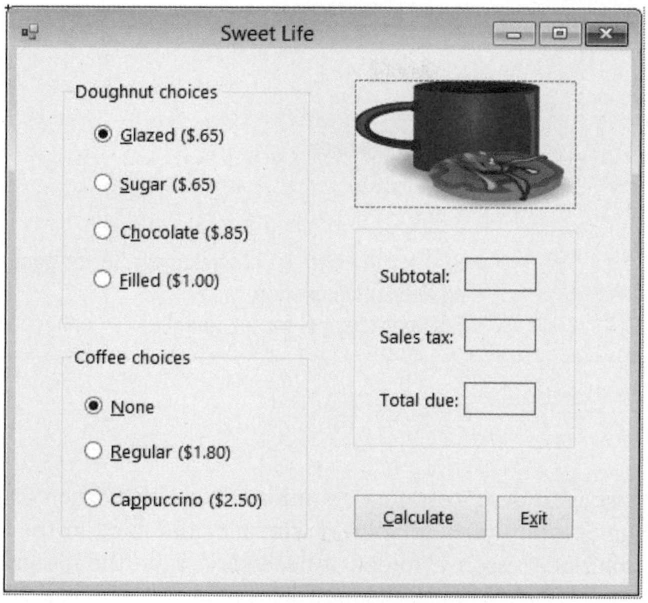

Figure 7-51 User interface for Exercise 5
OpenClipArt.org/gnokii

ADVANCED

6. Create a Visual Basic Windows application. Use the following names for the solution and project, respectively: Cable Direct Solution and Cable Direct Project. Save the application in the VB2012\Chap07 folder. Change the form file's name to Main Form.vb. Change the form's name to frmMain. Create the interface shown in Figure 7-52. The list boxes are named lstPremium and lstConnections. Display numbers from 0 through 20 in the lstPremium control. Display numbers from 0 through 100 in the lstConnections control. The Calculate Total Due button's Click event procedure should calculate and display a customer's cable bill. The cable rates are shown in Figure 7-53. Business customers must have at least one connection. Use two functions: one to calculate and return the total due for business customers, and the other to calculate and return the total due for residential customers. The form's FormClosing event procedure should verify that the user wants to close the application. Code the application. Save the solution and then start and test the application. Close the Code Editor window and then close the solution.

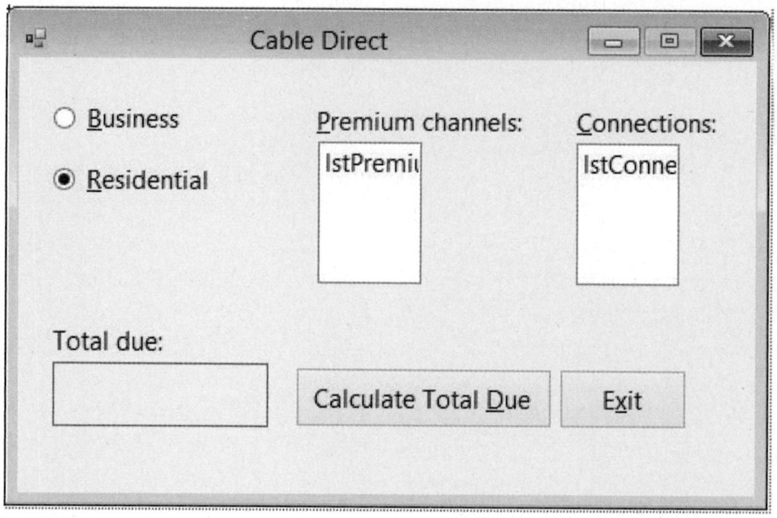

Figure 7-52 User interface for Exercise 6

Residential customers:	
Processing fee:	$4.50
Basic service fee:	$30
Premium channels:	$5 per channel
Business customers:	
Processing fee:	$16.50
Basic service fee:	$80 for the first 10 connections; $4 for each additional connection
Premium channels:	$50 per channel for any number of connections

Figure 7-53 Cable rates for Exercise 6

SWAT THE BUGS

7. The purpose of this exercise is to demonstrate a common error made when using functions. Open the Debug Solution (Debug Solution.sln) file contained in the VB2012\Chap07\Debug Solution-Lesson C folder. If necessary, open the designer window. Start the application. Click 20 in the Length list box and then click 30 in the Width list box. Click the Calculate Area button, which should display the area of a rectangle having a length of 20 feet and a width of 30 feet. Notice that the application is not working properly. Stop the application. Correct the application's code. Save the solution and then start and test the application again. Close the Code Editor window and then close the solution.

CHAPTER 8

String Manipulation

Creating the Frankenstein Game Application

In this chapter, you create the Frankenstein game for Ms. Carlsen, who teaches second grade at Jefferson Elementary School. The game requires two people to play. Currently, Ms. Carlsen thinks of a word that has five letters. She then draws five dashes on the chalkboard—one for each letter in the word. One student is then chosen to guess the word, letter by letter. When the student guesses a correct letter, Ms. Carlsen replaces the appropriate dash or dashes with the letter. For example, if the original word is moose and the student guesses the letter o, Ms. Carlsen changes the five dashes on the chalkboard to -oo--. If the student's letter does not appear in the word, Ms. Carlsen begins drawing a Frankenstein image that contains six parts: a head, a torso, a right arm, a left arm, a right leg, and a left leg. The game is over when the student either guesses all of the letters in the word or makes six incorrect guesses, whichever comes first.

Previewing the Frankenstein Game Application

Before you start the first lesson in this chapter, you will preview the completed application. The application is contained in the VB2012\Chap08 folder.

START HERE

To preview the completed application:

1. Use the Run dialog box to run the Frankenstein (Frankenstein.exe) file contained in the VB2012\Chap08 folder. The application's interface appears on the screen. See Figure 8-1. (The Frankenstein image was downloaded from the Open Clip Art Library at *http://openclipart.org*.) As indicated in the figure, the interface contains a FILE menu. Menus are covered in Lesson B.

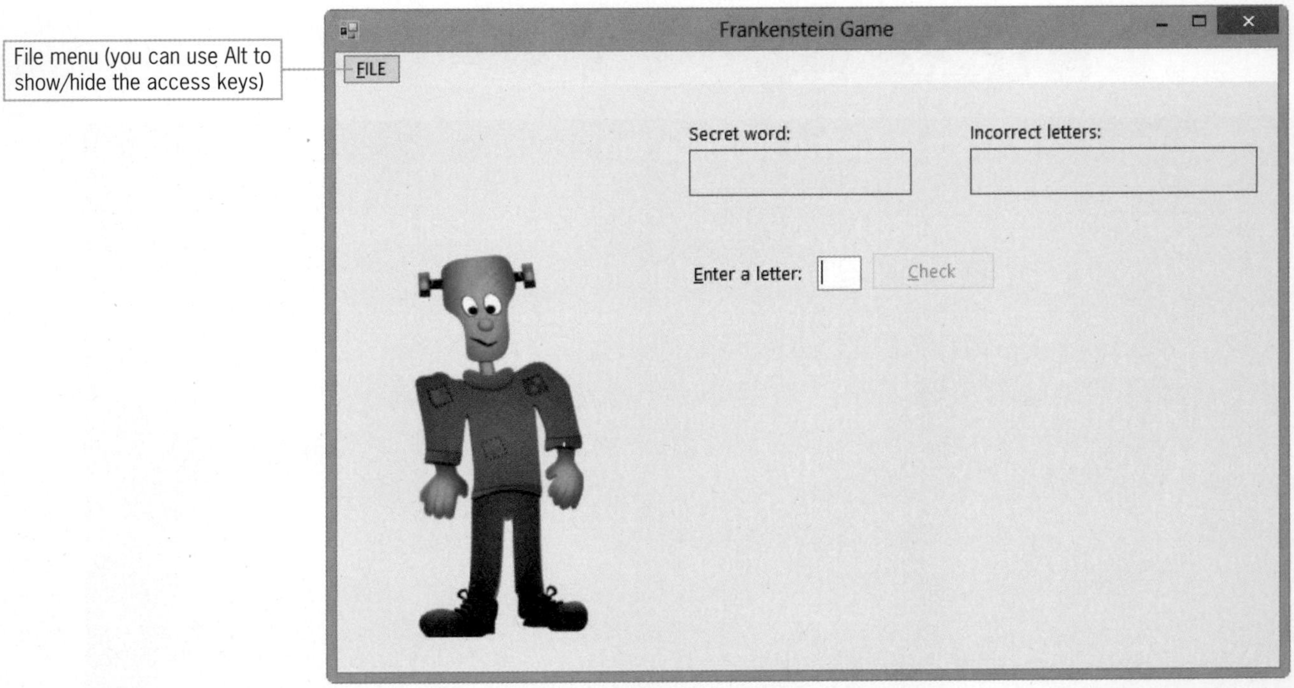

Figure 8-1 Interface for the Frankenstein Game application
OpenClipArt.org/Merlin2525

2. Click **FILE** on the menu bar and then click **New Game**. An input dialog box opens and prompts you to enter a five-letter word.
3. Type **moose** and then press **Enter**. Five dashes (hyphens) appear in the Secret word box. Each dash represents a letter in the word "moose".
4. Type **e** in the Enter a letter text box. The lowercase letter e is changed to its uppercase equivalent because the text box's CharacterCasing property is set to Upper. Press **Enter** to select the Check button, which is the default button on the form. The last dash in the Secret word box is replaced with the uppercase letter E. This indicates that the letter E is the last letter in the secret word.
5. Type **x** in the text box and then press **Enter**. The word "moose" does not contain the letter x, so the application displays X in the Incorrect letters box. It also displays a picture box that contains an image of Frankenstein's head.

6. Type **a** in the text box and then press **Enter**. The application displays A in the Incorrect letters box. It also displays a picture box that contains an image of Frankenstein's head and torso.

7. Type **b** in the text box and then press **Enter**. The application displays B in the Incorrect letters box. It also displays a picture box that contains an image of Frankenstein's head, torso, and right arm.

8. Type **o** in the text box and then press **Enter**. The application replaces the second and third dashes in the Secret word box with the letter O.

9. Now type **m** and **s** in the text box, pressing **Enter** after typing each letter. The application replaces the first and fourth dashes in the Secret word box with the letters M and S, respectively. It also displays the "Great guessing!" message in a message box. See Figure 8-2.

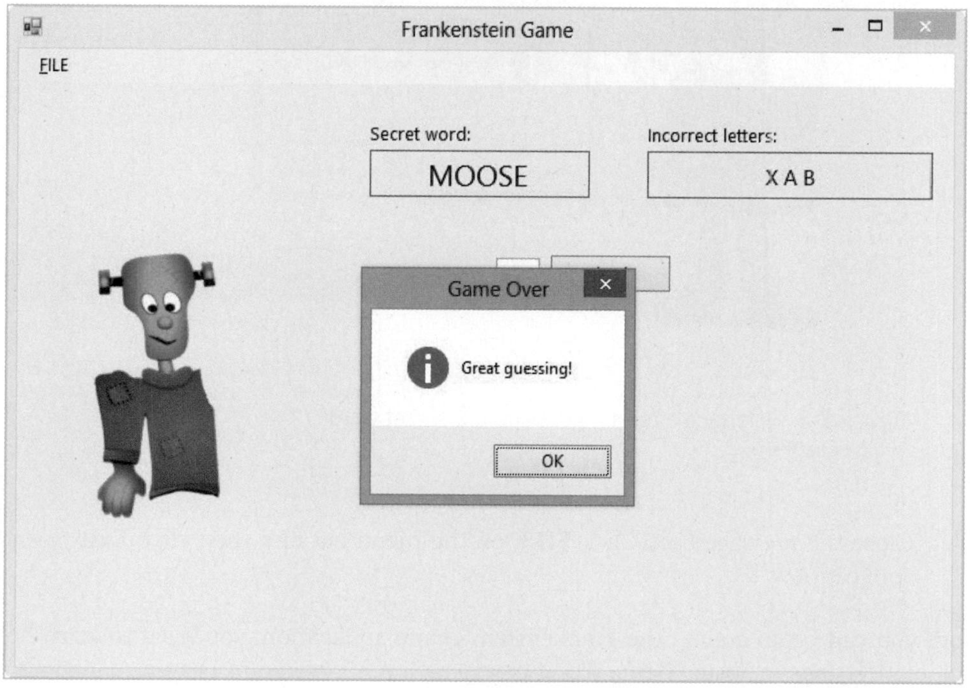

Figure 8-2 Interface after guessing the secret word
OpenClipArt.org/Merlin2525

10. Close the message box. Click **FILE** on the menu bar and then click **New Game**. Type **moo** in the input dialog box and then press **Enter**. The message "5 letters are required" appears in a message box. Close the message box.

11. Press **Ctrl+N** to open the input dialog box. Type **glass** and then press **Enter**. Type **g** in the text box and then press **Enter**. The application replaces the first dash in the Secret word box with the letter G.

12. Now, type the letters **e**, **d**, **p**, **x**, **y**, and **z** in the text box, pressing **Enter** after typing each letter. The letters you entered do not appear in the word "glass", so the application displays the letters in the Incorrect letters box. It also displays Frankenstein's full body and the message "Sorry, the word is GLASS". See Figure 8-3.

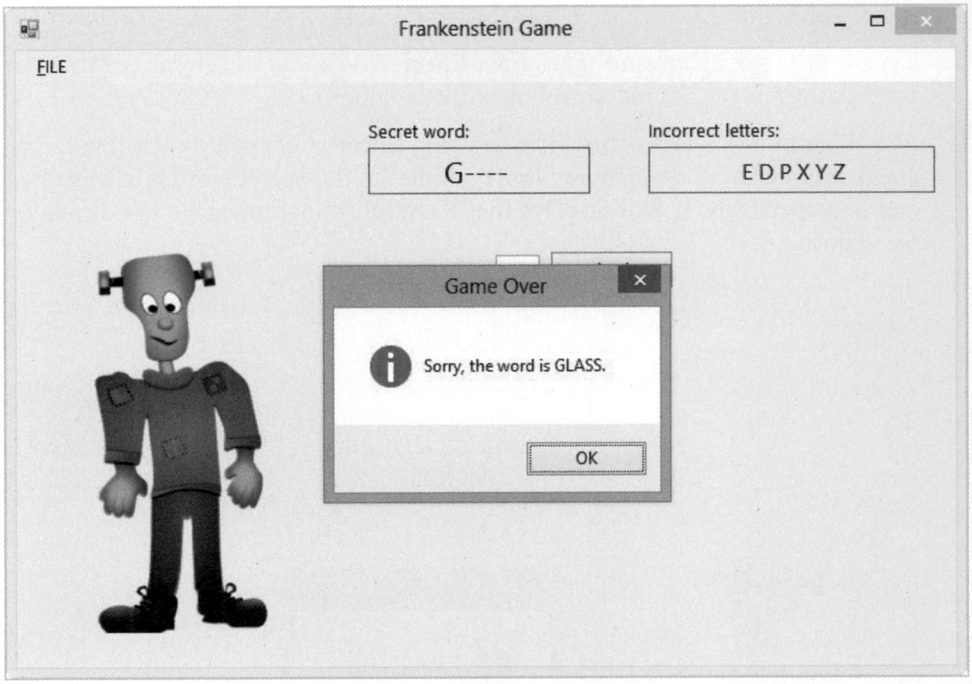

Figure 8-3 Interface after not guessing the secret word
OpenClipArt.org/Merlin2525

13. Close the message box. Click **FILE** on the menu bar and then click **Exit** to end the application.

Before you can begin coding the Frankenstein Game application, you need to learn how to manipulate strings in Visual Basic; string manipulation is covered in Lesson A. You also need to learn how to create a menu. You will learn about the MenuStrip tool in Lesson B, and then use it to add a menu to the Frankenstein Game application's interface. You will code the application in Lessons B and C. Be sure to complete each lesson in full and do all of the end-of-lesson questions and several exercises before continuing to the next lesson.

LESSON A

After studying Lesson A, you should be able to:

- Determine the number of characters in a string
- Remove characters from a string
- Insert characters in a string
- Align the characters in a string
- Search a string
- Access characters in a string
- Compare strings using pattern-matching

Working with Strings

Many times, an application will need to manipulate (process) string data in some way. For example, it may need to look at the first character in an inventory part number to determine the part's location in the warehouse. Or, it may need to search an address to determine the street name. Or, it may need to verify that the input entered by the user is in the expected format. In this lesson, you will learn several ways of manipulating strings in Visual Basic. You will begin by learning how to determine the number of characters in a string.

Determining the Number of Characters in a String

If an application expects the user to enter a seven-digit phone number or a five-digit ZIP code, the application's code should verify that the user's input contains the required number of characters. The number of characters contained in a string is stored as an integer in the string's **Length property**. Figure 8-4 shows the property's syntax and includes examples of using the property. In the syntax, *string* can be a String variable, a String named constant, or the Text property of a control.

Determining the Number of Characters in a String

Syntax
string.**Length**

Example 1
```
strCityState = "Bowling Green, KY"
intNumChars = strCityState.Length
```
assigns the number 17 to the `intNumChars` variable

Example 2
```
intNumChars = txtPhone.Text.Length
```
assigns the number of characters in the txtPhone control's Text property to the `intNumChars` variable

Example 3
```
Do
      strZip = InputBox("5-digit ZIP code", "ZIP")
Loop Until strZip.Length = 5
```
continues prompting the user for a ZIP code until the user enters exactly five characters

Figure 8-4 Syntax and examples of the Length property

Removing Characters from a String

Visual Basic provides the Trim and Remove methods for removing characters from a string. The **Trim method** removes (trims) any space characters from both the beginning and end of a string. The **Remove method**, on the other hand, removes a specified number of characters located anywhere in a string. Figure 8-5 shows the syntax of both methods and includes examples of using the methods. In each syntax, *string* can be a String variable, a String named constant, or the Text property of a control. When processing the Trim and Remove methods, the computer first makes a temporary copy of the *string* in memory. It then performs the specified removal on the copy only. In other words, neither method removes any characters from the original *string*. Both methods return a string with the appropriate characters removed.

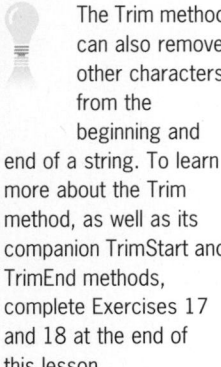

The Trim method can also remove other characters from the beginning and end of a string. To learn more about the Trim method, as well as its companion TrimStart and TrimEnd methods, complete Exercises 17 and 18 at the end of this lesson.

The *startIndex* argument in the Remove method is the index of the first character you want removed from the copy of the *string*. A character's index is an integer that indicates the character's position in the string. The first character in a string has an index of 0; the second character has an index of 1, and so on. The optional *numCharsToRemove* argument is the number of characters you want removed. To remove only the first character from a string, you use 0 as the startIndex and 1 as the numCharsToRemove. To remove the fourth through eighth characters, you use 3 as the startIndex and 5 as the numCharsToRemove. If the numCharsToRemove argument is omitted, the Remove method removes all of the characters from the startIndex position through the end of the string, as shown in Example 3 in Figure 8-5.

Removing Characters from a String

Syntax
string.**Trim**
string.**Remove(***startIndex* [**,** *numCharsToRemove*]**)**

Example 1
```
strName = txtName.Text.Trim
```
assigns the contents of the txtName control's Text property, excluding any leading and trailing spaces, to the `strName` variable

Example 2
```
strCityState = "Dallas, Texas"
txtState.Text = strCityState.Remove(0, 8)
```
assigns the string "Texas" to the txtState control's Text property

Example 3
```
strCityState = "Dallas, Texas"
txtCity.Text = strCityState.Remove(6)
```
assigns the string "Dallas" to the txtCity control's Text property; you can also write the assignment statement as `txtCity.Text = strCityState.Remove(6, 7)`

Example 4
```
strFirst = "John"
strFirst = strFirst.Remove(2, 1)
```
assigns the string "Jon" to the `strFirst` variable

Figure 8-5 Syntax and examples of the Trim and Remove methods

The Product ID Application

You will use the Length property and the Trim method in the Product ID application. The application displays a listing of the product IDs entered by the user. Each product ID must contain exactly five characters.

START HERE

To code and then test the Product ID application:

1. If necessary, start Visual Studio 2012. Open the Product Solution (Product Solution.sln) file contained in the VB2012\Chap08\Product Solution folder. If necessary, open the designer window. The interface provides a text box for entering the product ID.
2. Open the Code Editor window. Replace <your name> and <current date> in the comments with your name and the current date, respectively.
3. Locate the btnAdd_Click procedure. Before verifying the product ID's length, you will remove any leading and trailing spaces from the ID. Click the **blank line** below the `' remove any leading and trailing spaces` comment and then enter the following assignment statement:

   strId = txtId.Text.Trim
4. Now you will determine whether the ID contains exactly five characters. Click the **blank line** below the `' verify length` comment and then enter the following If clause:

   If strId.Length = 5 Then
5. If the ID contains exactly five characters, the selection structure's true path should add the ID to the lstId control; otherwise, its false path should display an appropriate message. Enter the five lines of code indicated in Figure 8-6. (The Trim and Length methods are shaded in the figure.)

```
Private Sub btnAdd_Click(sender As Object,
e As EventArgs) Handles btnAdd.Click
    ' adds a product ID to a list

    Dim strId As String

    ' remove any leading and trailing spaces
    strId = txtId.Text.Trim

    ' verify length
    If strId.Length = 5 Then
        lstId.Items.Add(strId.ToUpper)
    Else
        MessageBox.Show("The ID must contain 5 characters.",
                        "Product ID", MessageBoxButtons.OK,
                        MessageBoxIcon.Information)
    End If

    txtId.Focus()
End Sub
```

enter these five lines of code

Figure 8-6 btnAdd control's Click event procedure

6. Save the solution and then start the application. First, you will enter an ID that contains four characters. Type **bcd2** as the product ID and then click the **Add to List** button. A message box opens and displays the message "The ID must contain 5 characters." Close the message box.

7. Now you will include two leading spaces in the ID. Click **immediately before the letter b** in the text box. Press the **Spacebar** twice and then type the letter **a**. The text box now contains two space characters followed by abcd2. Click the **Add to List** button. ABCD2 appears in the listing of product IDs. See Figure 8-7.

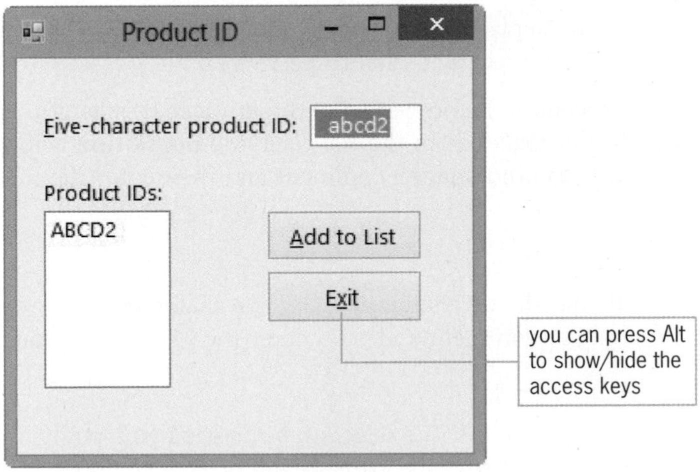

Figure 8-7 Sample run of the Product ID application

8. On your own, test the application using an ID that contains nine characters. Also test it using an ID that contains both leading and trailing spaces. When you are finished testing the application, click the **Exit** button. Close the Code Editor window and then close the solution.

YOU DO IT 1!

Create a Visual Basic Windows application named YouDoIt 1. Save the application in the VB2012\Chap08 folder. Add a text box, a label, and a button to the form. The button's Click event procedure should remove any leading or trailing spaces from the text entered in the text box. If the remaining text contains more than four characters, the button's Click event procedure should display only the first four characters in the label; otherwise, it should display the remaining text in the label. Code the procedure. Save the solution and then start and test the application. Close the solution.

Inserting Characters in a String

Visual Basic's **Insert method** allows you to insert characters anywhere in a string. The method's syntax is shown in Figure 8-8 along with examples of using the method. In the syntax, *string* can be a String variable, a String named constant, or the Text property of a control. When processing the Insert method, the computer first makes a temporary copy of the *string* in memory. It then performs the specified insertion on the copy only. The Insert method does not affect the original *string*. The *startIndex* argument in the Insert method is an integer that specifies where in the string's copy you want the *value* inserted. The integer represents the character's index—in other words, its position in the string. To insert the value at the beginning of a string, you use a startIndex of 0, as shown in Example 1 in Figure 8-8. To insert the value beginning with the eighth character in the string, you use a startIndex of 7, as shown in Example 2. The Insert method returns a string with the appropriate characters inserted.

Inserting Characters in a String

Syntax
string.**Insert(***startIndex*, *value***)**

Example 1
```
strPhone = "111-2222"
txtPhone.Text = strPhone.Insert(0, "(877) ")
```
assigns the string "(877) 111-2222" to the txtPhone control's Text property

Example 2
```
strName = "Joanne Hashem"
strName = strName.Insert(7, "C. ")
```
assigns the string "Joanne C. Hashem" to the `strName` variable

Figure 8-8 Syntax and examples of the Insert method

Aligning the Characters in a String

You can use Visual Basic's PadLeft and PadRight methods to align the characters in a string. The methods do this by inserting (padding) the string with zero or more characters until the string is a specified length; each method then returns the padded string. The **PadLeft method** pads the string on the left, which means it inserts the padded characters at the beginning of the string; doing this right-aligns the characters within the string. The **PadRight method**, on the other hand, pads the string on the right, which means it inserts the padded characters at the end of the string and left-aligns the characters within the string.

Figure 8-9 shows the syntax of both methods and includes examples of using them. In each syntax, *string* can be a String variable, a String named constant, or the Text property of a control. When processing the PadLeft and PadRight methods, the computer first makes a temporary copy of the *string* in memory; it then pads the copy only. The *totalChars* argument in each syntax is an integer that represents the total number of characters you want the string's copy to contain. The optional *padCharacter* argument is the character that each method uses to pad the string until the desired number of characters is reached. If the padCharacter argument is omitted, the default padding character is the space character.

Aligning the Characters in a String

<u>Syntax</u>
string.**PadLeft(***totalChars*[, *padCharacter*]**)**
string.**PadRight(***totalChars*[, *padCharacter*]**)**

<u>Example 1</u>
```
strNumber = "100"
txtNum.Text = strNumber.PadLeft(6)
```
assigns the string "   100" to the txtNum control's Text property

three space characters

<u>Example 2</u>
```
strFirst = "Amy"
strFirst = strFirst.PadRight(10)
```
assigns the string "Amy   " to the `strFirst` variable

seven space characters

<u>Example 3</u>
```
dblNet = 495.84
strFormattedNet =
     dblNet.ToString("C2").PadLeft(10, "*"c)
```
assigns the string "***$495.84" to the `strFormattedNet` variable (Many companies use this type of formatting on their employee paychecks because it makes it more difficult for someone to change the amount.)

Figure 8-9 Syntax and examples of the PadLeft and PadRight methods

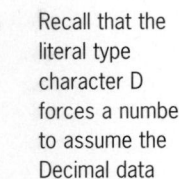

Recall that the literal type character D forces a number to assume the Decimal data type.

Notice that the expression in Example 3 in Figure 8-9 contains the ToString and PadLeft methods. When an expression contains more than one method, the computer processes the methods from left to right. In this case, the computer will process the ToString method before processing the PadLeft method. Also notice the letter c that appears at the end of the *padCharacter* argument in Example 3. The letter c is one of the literal type characters in Visual Basic. As you learned in Chapter 3, a literal type character forces a literal constant to assume a data type other than the one its form indicates. In this case, the letter c forces the `"*"` string in the padCharacter argument to assume the Char (character) data type.

The Net Pay Application

The Net Pay application, which you code in this section, uses the Insert and PadLeft methods. The application allows the user to enter the amount of an employee's net pay. It then displays the net pay with a leading dollar sign, asterisks, and two decimal places. For example, if the net pay is 500, the application will display the net pay as $****500.00.

START HERE

To code and then test the Net Pay application:

1. Open the Net Pay Solution (Net Pay Solution.sln) file contained in the VB2012\Chap08\Net Pay Solution folder. If necessary, open the designer window. The interface provides a text box for entering the net pay.
2. Open the Code Editor window. Replace <your name> and <current date> in the comments with your name and the current date, respectively.
3. Locate the btnFormat_Click procedure. First, you will format the net pay to include two decimal places. Click the **blank line** below the `' format the net pay with two decimal places` comment and then enter the following assignment statement:

   strFormatted = decNet.ToString("N2")

4. Next, you will use the PadLeft method to pad the net pay with asterisks until it contains 10 characters. Click the **blank line** below the `' pad the net pay with asterisks until its length is 10` comment and then enter the following assignment statement:

   strFormatted = strFormatted.PadLeft(10, "*"c)

5. Finally, you will insert a dollar sign at the beginning of the formatted net pay. Click the **blank line** below the `' insert a dollar sign as the first character` comment and then enter the assignment statement indicated in Figure 8-10.

```
Private Sub btnFormat_Click(sender As Object,
e As EventArgs) Handles btnFormat.Click
    ' format the net pay with two decimal places, then
    ' pad with asterisks and insert a dollar sign as the
    ' first character

    Dim decNet As Decimal
    Dim strFormatted As String

    Decimal.TryParse(txtNetPay.Text, decNet)

    ' format the net pay with two decimal places
    strFormatted = decNet.ToString("N2")

    ' pad the net pay with asterisks until its length is 10
    strFormatted = strFormatted.PadLeft(10, "*"c)

    ' insert a dollar sign as the first character
    strFormatted = strFormatted.Insert(0, "$")        enter this assignment statement

    ' display the net pay, then set the focus
    lblFormatted.Text = strFormatted
    txtNetPay.Focus()
End Sub
```

Figure 8-10 btnFormat_Click procedure

6. Save the solution and then start the application. Type **1097** as the net pay and then click the **Format** button. The button's Click event procedure displays $**1,097.00 in the interface, as shown in Figure 8-11. Click the **Exit** button. Close the Code Editor window and then close the solution.

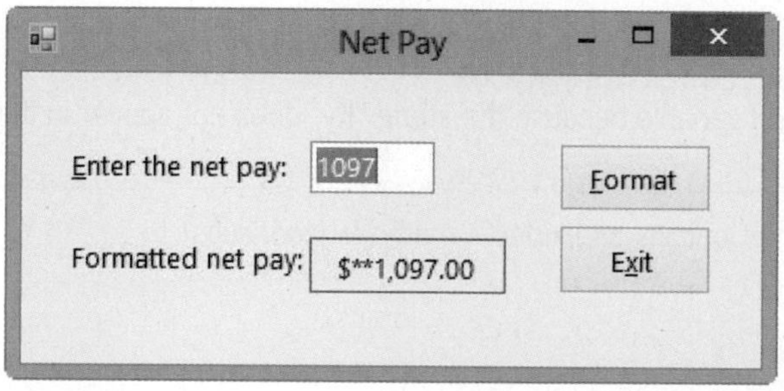

Figure 8-11 Interface showing the formatted net pay

YOU DO IT 2!

Create a Visual Basic Windows application named YouDoIt 2. Save the application in the VB2012\Chap08 folder. Add a text box, a label, and a button to the form. Set the text box's MaxLength property to 5. The button's Click event procedure should assign the contents of the text box to a String variable. It then should remove any leading or trailing spaces from the string stored in the variable. If the variable contains more than three characters, the procedure should insert a number sign (#) as the second character and then pad the variable's value with asterisks until the variable contains 10 characters. Insert the asterisks at the end of the string stored in the variable. Finally, the procedure should display the variable's contents in the label. Code the procedure. Save the solution and then start and test the application. Close the solution.

Searching a String

If you need to determine whether a string contains a specific sequence of characters, you can use either the Contains method or the IndexOf method. Figure 8-12 shows the syntax of both methods. In each syntax, *string* can be a String variable, a String named constant, or the Text property of a control. When processing the methods, the computer first makes a temporary copy of the *string* in memory. It then performs the specified search on the copy only. The *subString* argument in each syntax represents the sequence of characters for which you are searching. Both methods perform a case-sensitive search, which means the case of the subString must match the case of the string in order for both to be considered equal.

Searching a String

Syntax
string.**Contains(***subString***)**
string.**IndexOf(***subString*[, *startIndex*]**)**

Example 1
```
strLocation = "Louisville, KY"
blnIsContained = strLocation.Contains("KY")
```
assigns True to the `blnIsContained` variable because the string "KY" appears in the `strLocation` variable

Example 2
```
strLocation = "Louisville, KY"
blnIsContained = strLocation.Contains("Ky")
```
assigns False to the `blnIsContained` variable because the string "Ky" does not appear in the `strLocation` variable

the Contains method performs a case-sensitive search

Figure 8-12 Syntax and examples of the Contains and IndexOf methods *(continues)*

(continued)

Example 3

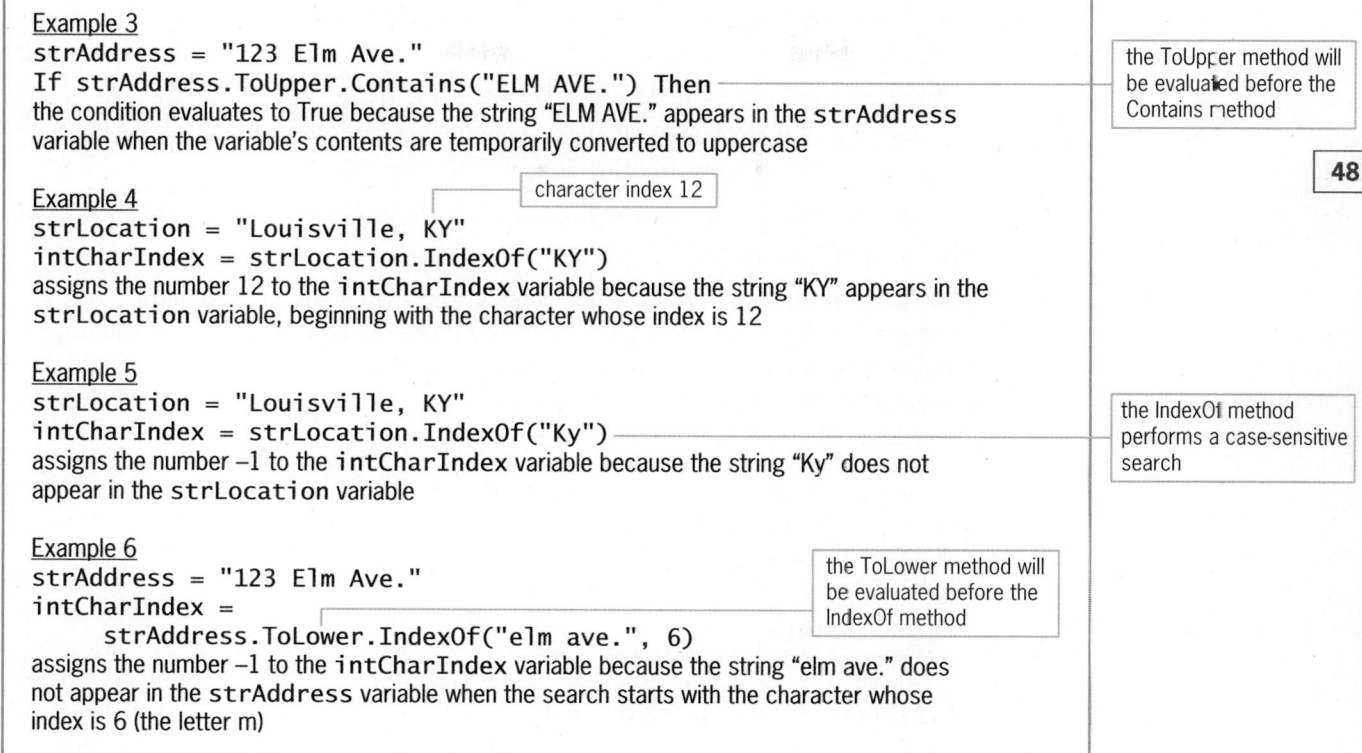

```
strAddress = "123 Elm Ave."
If strAddress.ToUpper.Contains("ELM AVE.") Then
```

the condition evaluates to True because the string "ELM AVE." appears in the `strAddress` variable when the variable's contents are temporarily converted to uppercase

the ToUpper method will be evaluated before the Contains method

Example 4

character index 12

```
strLocation = "Louisville, KY"
intCharIndex = strLocation.IndexOf("KY")
```

assigns the number 12 to the `intCharIndex` variable because the string "KY" appears in the `strLocation` variable, beginning with the character whose index is 12

Example 5

```
strLocation = "Louisville, KY"
intCharIndex = strLocation.IndexOf("Ky")
```

assigns the number −1 to the `intCharIndex` variable because the string "Ky" does not appear in the `strLocation` variable

the IndexOf method performs a case-sensitive search

Example 6

```
strAddress = "123 Elm Ave."
intCharIndex =
     strAddress.ToLower.IndexOf("elm ave.", 6)
```

the ToLower method will be evaluated before the IndexOf method

assigns the number −1 to the `intCharIndex` variable because the string "elm ave." does not appear in the `strAddress` variable when the search starts with the character whose index is 6 (the letter m)

Figure 8-12 Syntax and examples of the Contains and IndexOf methods

The **Contains method**, which appears in Examples 1 through 3 in Figure 8-12, returns the Boolean value True when the subString is contained anywhere in the string; otherwise, it returns the Boolean value False. The Contains method always begins the search with the first character in the string.

The **IndexOf method**, on the other hand, returns an integer: either −1 or a number that is greater than or equal to 0. The −1 indicates that the subString is not contained in the string. A number other than −1 is the character index of the subString's starting position in the string. Unless you specify otherwise, the IndexOf method starts the search with the first character in the string. To specify a different starting location, you use the optional *startIndex* argument. The IndexOf method appears in Examples 4 through 6 in Figure 8-12.

Notice that the expression in Example 3 in Figure 8-12 contains two methods: ToUpper and Contains. Two methods also appear in the expression in Example 6: ToLower and IndexOf. Recall that when an expression contains more than one method, the computer processes the methods from left to right. In this case, the computer will process the ToUpper method before the Contains method in Example 3, and process the ToLower method before the IndexOf method in Example 6.

The City and State Application

The City and State application coded in this section uses the IndexOf method. The application allows the user to enter a string composed of a city name, followed by a comma, a space, and a state name. It then displays the index of the comma contained in the string.

START HERE

To code and then test the City and State application:

1. Open the City State Solution (City State Solution.sln) file contained in the VB2012\Chap08\City State Solution folder. If necessary, open the designer window. The interface provides a text box for entering the string.
2. Open the Code Editor window. Replace <your name> and <current date> in the comments with your name and the current date, respectively.
3. Locate the btnLocate_Click procedure. Click the **blank line** below the `' determine the comma's index` comment.
4. To begin the search with the first character in the string, you can use either `strCityState.IndexOf(",", 0)` or `strCityState.IndexOf(",")`. You will assign the IndexOf method's return value to the `intCommaIndex` variable. Enter the additional assignment statement shown in Figure 8-13.

```
Private Sub btnLocate_Click(sender As Object,
e As EventArgs) Handles btnLocate.Click
    ' locates the comma in a string and then
    ' displays its index

    Dim strCityState As String
    Dim intCommaIndex As Integer

    strCityState = txtCityState.Text

    ' determine the comma's index
    intCommaIndex = strCityState.IndexOf(",")

    lblCommaIndex.Text = intCommaIndex.ToString
    txtCityState.Focus()
End Sub
```

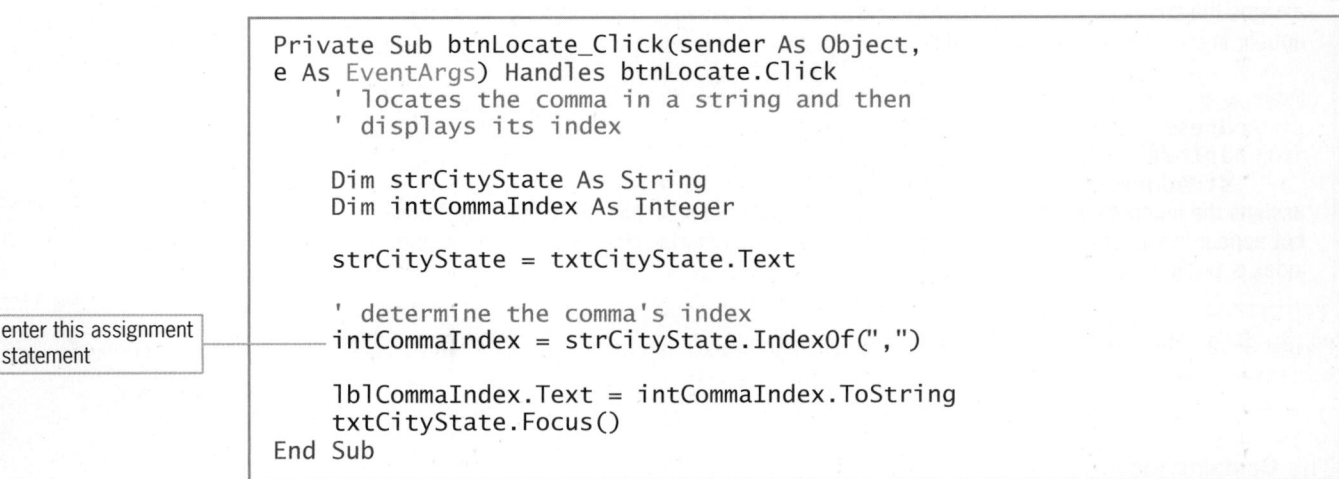

enter this assignment statement

Figure 8-13 btnLocate_Click procedure

5. Save the solution and then start the application. Type **Louisville, KY** in the text box and then click the **Locate the Comma** button. As Figure 8-14 shows, the comma's index is 10. Click the **Exit** button. Close the Code Editor window and then close the solution.

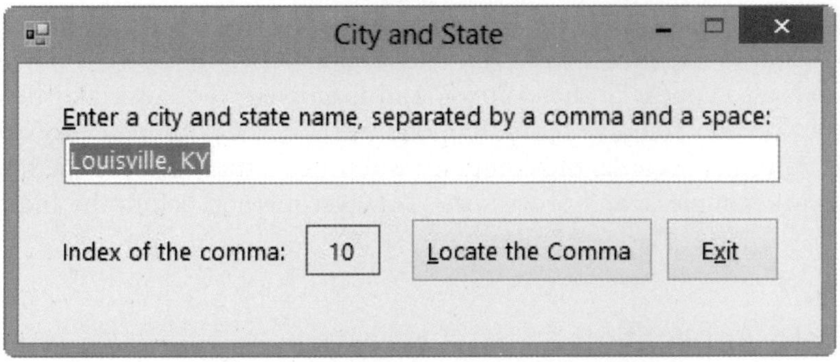

Figure 8-14 Interface showing the comma's index

YOU DO IT 3!

Create a Visual Basic Windows application named YouDoIt 3. Save the application in the VB2012\Chap08 folder. Add a text box, a label, and a button to the form. The button's Click event procedure should determine whether the number 9 appears anywhere in the text box and then display the result (either True or False) in the label. Code the procedure. Save the solution and then start and test the application. Close the solution.

Accessing the Characters in a String

Visual Basic provides the **Substring method** for accessing any number of characters in a string. Figure 8-15 shows the method's syntax and includes examples of using the method. In the syntax, *string* can be a String variable, a String named constant, or the Text property of a control. When processing the Substring method, the computer first makes a temporary copy of the *string* in memory. It then accesses the specified number of characters in the copy only. The *startIndex* argument in the syntax is the index of the first character you want to access in the string's copy. As you already know, the first character in a string has an index of 0. The optional *numCharsToAccess* argument specifies the number of characters you want to access. The Substring method returns a string that contains the number of characters specified in the numCharsToAccess argument, beginning with the character whose index is startIndex. If you omit the numCharsToAccess argument, the Substring method returns all characters from the startIndex position through the end of the string.

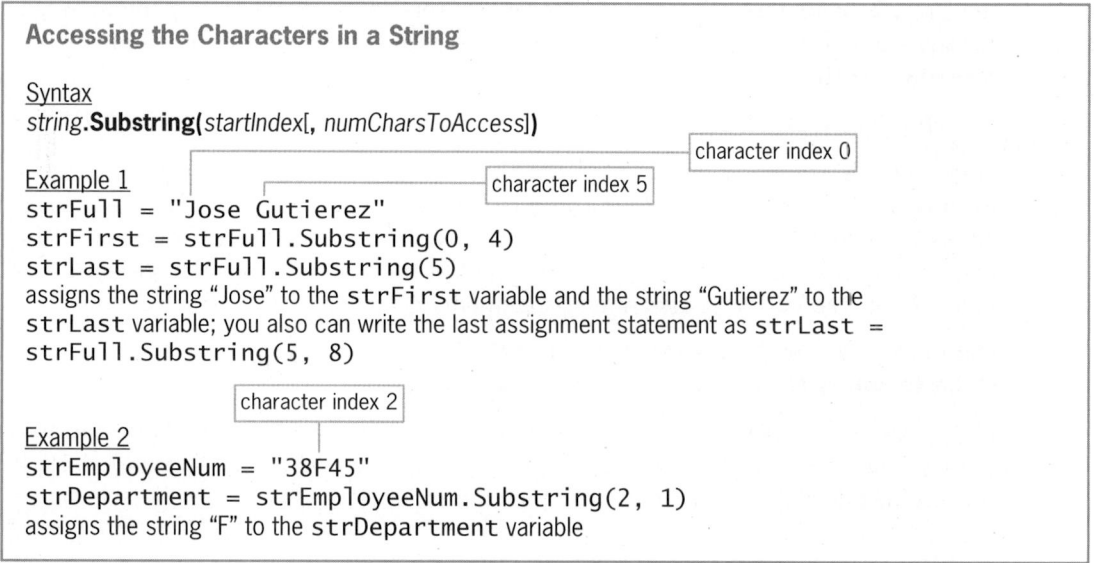

Accessing the Characters in a String

Syntax
string.**Substring(***startIndex*[, *numCharsToAccess*]**)**

Example 1 (callouts: character index 0; character index 5)

```
strFull = "Jose Gutierez"
strFirst = strFull.Substring(0, 4)
strLast = strFull.Substring(5)
```

assigns the string "Jose" to the `strFirst` variable and the string "Gutierez" to the `strLast` variable; you also can write the last assignment statement as `strLast = strFull.Substring(5, 8)`

Example 2 (callout: character index 2)

```
strEmployeeNum = "38F45"
strDepartment = strEmployeeNum.Substring(2, 1)
```

assigns the string "F" to the `strDepartment` variable

Figure 8-15 Syntax and examples of the Substring method

The Rearrange Name Application

You will use the Substring method in the Rearrange Name application. The application's interface provides a text box for entering a person's first name followed by a space and the person's last name. The application rearranges the name so that the last name comes first, followed by a comma, a space, and the first name.

START HERE

To code and then test the Rearrange Name application:

1. Open the Rearrange Name Solution (Rearrange Name Solution.sln) file contained in the VB2012\Chap08\Rearrange Name Solution folder. If necessary, open the designer window.

Ch08A video

2. Open the Code Editor window. Replace <your name> and <current date> in the comments with your name and the current date, respectively.
3. Locate the btnRearrange_Click procedure. The procedure assigns the name entered by the user, excluding any leading or trailing spaces, to the `strName` variable.
4. Before you can rearrange the name stored in the `strName` variable, you need to separate the first name from the last name. To do this, you first search for the space character that appears between the names. Click the **blank line** below the `' search for the space in the name` comment and then enter the following assignment statement, being sure to include a space character between the quotation marks:

   intIndex = strName.IndexOf(" ")

5. If the value in the `intIndex` variable is not –1, it means that the IndexOf method found a space character in the `strName` variable. In that case, the selection structure's true path should continue rearranging the name; otherwise, its false path should display the "Invalid name format" message. Notice that the statement to display the message is already entered in the selection structure's false path. Change the If clause in the procedure to the following:

   If intIndex <> –1 Then

6. Now you will use the value stored in the `intIndex` variable to separate the first name from the last name. Click the **blank line** below the `' separate the first and last names` comment. All of the characters to the left of the space character represent the first name, and all of the characters to the right of the space character represent the last name. Enter the following assignment statements:

   strFirstName = strName.Substring(0, intIndex)
   strLastName = strName.Substring(intIndex + 1)

7. Finally, you will display the rearranged name in the interface. Click the **blank line** above the Else clause. Enter the additional assignment statement indicated in Figure 8-16. Be sure to include a space character after the comma.

```
Private Sub btnRearrange_Click(sender As Object,
e As EventArgs) Handles btnRearrange.Click
    ' rearranges and then displays a name

    Dim strName As String
    Dim strFirstName As String
    Dim strLastName As String
    Dim intIndex As Integer

    ' assign the input to a variable
    strName = txtName.Text.Trim

    ' search for the space in the name
    intIndex = strName.IndexOf(" ")

    ' if the input contains a space
    If intIndex <> -1 Then
        ' separate the first and last names
        strFirstName = strName.Substring(0, intIndex)
        strLastName = strName.Substring(intIndex + 1)

        ' display last name, comma, space, and first name
        lblRearrangedName.Text =
            strLastName & ", " & strFirstName

    Else    ' the name does not contain a space
        MessageBox.Show("Invalid name format",
                        "Rearrange Name",
                        MessageBoxButtons.OK,
                        MessageBoxIcon.Information)
    End If
End Sub
```

enter this assignment statement

Figure 8-16 btnRearrange_Click procedure

8. Save the solution and then start the application. Type **Harold Iberson** as the name and then click the **Rearrange Name** button. The rearranged name appears in the interface, as shown in Figure 8-17. Click the **Exit** button. Close the Code Editor window and then close the solution.

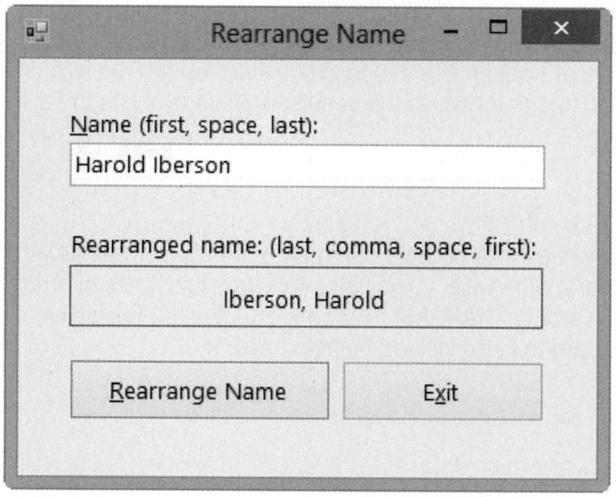

Figure 8-17 Interface showing the rearranged name

YOU DO IT 4!

Create a Visual Basic Windows application named YouDoIt 4. Save the application in the VB2012\Chap08 folder. Add a label and a button to the form. The button's Click event procedure should declare a String variable named `strMessage` and initialize it to the 26 uppercase letters of the alphabet. It then should use the Substring method to display only the letters K, L, M, N, and O in the label. Code the procedure. Save the solution and then start and test the application. Close the solution.

Using Pattern-Matching to Compare Strings

The **Like operator** allows you to use pattern-matching characters to determine whether one string is equal to another string. Figure 8-18 shows the operator's syntax and examples of using the operator. In the syntax, *string* can be a String variable, a String named constant, or the Text property of a control. *Pattern* is a String expression containing one or more of the pattern-matching characters listed in the figure.

Using Pattern-Matching to Compare Strings

<u>Syntax</u>
string **Like** *pattern*

<u>Pattern-matching characters</u>	<u>Matches in *string*</u>
?	any single character
*	zero or more characters
#	any single digit (0 through 9)
[*characterList*]	any single character in the *characterList* (for example, "[A5T]" matches A, 5, or T, whereas "[a–z]" matches any lowercase letter)
[!*characterList*]	any single character *not* in the *characterList* (for example, "[!A5T]" matches any character other than A, 5, or T, whereas "[!a–z]" matches any character that is not a lowercase letter)

<u>Example 1</u>
```
If strFirst.ToUpper Like "B?LL" Then
```
The condition evaluates to True when the string stored in the `strFirst` variable (converted to uppercase) begins with the letter B followed by one character and then the two letters LL; otherwise, it evaluates to False. Examples of strings that would make the condition evaluate to True include "Bill", "Ball", "bell", and "bull". Examples of strings for which the condition would evaluate to False include "BPL", "BLL", and "billy".

<u>Example 2</u>
```
If txtState.Text Like "K*" Then
```
The condition evaluates to True when the value in the txtState control's Text property begins with the letter K followed by zero or more characters; otherwise, it evaluates to False. Examples of strings that would make the condition evaluate to True include "KANSAS", "Ky", and "Kentucky". Examples of strings for which the condition would evaluate to False include "kansas" and "ky".

Figure 8-18 Syntax and examples of the Like operator *(continues)*

(continued)

Example 3

```
Do While strId Like "###*"
```

The condition evaluates to True when the string stored in the `strId` variable begins with three digits followed by zero or more characters; otherwise, it evaluates to False. Examples of strings that would make the condition evaluate to True include "178" and "983Ab". Examples of strings for which the condition would evaluate to False include "X34" and "34Z5".

Example 4

```
If strFirst.ToUpper Like "T[OI]M" Then
```

The condition evaluates to True when the string stored in the `strFirst` variable (converted to uppercase) is either "TOM" or "TIM". When the variable does not contain "TOM" or "TIM"—for example, when it contains "Tam" or "Tommy"—the condition evaluates to False.

Example 5

```
If strLetter Like "[a-z]" Then
```

The condition evaluates to True when the string stored in the `strLetter` variable is one lowercase letter; otherwise, it evaluates to False.

Example 6

```
For intIndex As Integer = 0 To strInput.Length - 1
     strChar = strInput.Substring(intIndex, 1)
     If strChar Like "[!a-zA-Z]" Then
          intNonLetter = intNonLetter + 1
     End If
Next intIndex
```

Compares each character contained in the `strInput` variable with the lowercase and uppercase letters of the alphabet, and counts the number of characters that are not letters.

Example 7

```
If strInput Like "*.*" Then
```

The condition evaluates to True when a period appears anywhere in the `strInput` variable; otherwise, it evaluates to False.

Example 8

```
If strInput.ToUpper Like "[A-Z][A-Z]##" Then
```

The condition evaluates to True when the value in the `strInput` variable (converted to uppercase) is two letters followed by two numbers; otherwise, it evaluates to False.

Figure 8-18 Syntax and examples of the Like operator

As Figure 8-18 indicates, the question mark (?) character in a pattern represents one character only, whereas the asterisk (*) character represents zero or more characters. To represent a single digit in a pattern, you use the number sign (#) character. The last two pattern-matching characters listed in Figure 8-18 contain a *characterList,* which is simply a listing of characters. "[A9M]" is a characterList that contains three characters: A, 9, and M. You also can include a range of values in a characterList. You do this using a hyphen to separate the lowest value in the range from the highest value in the range. For example, to include all lowercase letters in a characterList, you use "[a-z]". To include both lowercase and uppercase letters in the characterList, you use "[a-zA-Z]".

The Like operator compares the string to the pattern; the comparison is case-sensitive. If the string matches the pattern, the Like operator returns the Boolean value True; otherwise, it returns the Boolean value False.

Modifying the Product ID Application

Earlier in this lesson, you coded the Product ID application, which displayed a listing of the product IDs entered by the user. As you may remember, each product ID contained exactly five characters. In the following set of steps, you will modify the application to ensure that the five characters are three letters followed by two numbers.

START HERE

To modify and then test the Product ID application:

1. Use Windows to make a copy of the Product Solution folder. Save the copy in the VB2012\Chap08 folder. Rename the copy Modified Product Solution.
2. Open the Product Solution (Product Solution.sln) file contained in the Modified Product Solution folder. Open the designer window.
3. Open the Code Editor window and locate the btnAdd_Click procedure. Change the `' remove any leading and trailing spaces` comment to the following:

   ' remove any leading and trailing spaces and
   ' then convert to uppercase
4. Change the `strId = txtId.Text.Trim` statement to the following:

   strId = txtId.Text.Trim.ToUpper
5. Replace the `' verify length` comment with the following comments:

   ' verify that the ID contains 3 letters
   ' followed by 2 numbers
6. Change the If clause to the following:

   If strId Like "[A-Z][A-Z][A-Z]##" Then
7. In the statement below the If clause, change `strId.ToUpper` to **strId**. Finally, change the message in the MessageBox.Show method to **"Invalid product ID"**. Figure 8-19 shows the modified procedure. The modified comments and code are shaded in the figure.

```
Private Sub btnAdd_Click(sender As Object,
e As EventArgs) Handles btnAdd.Click
    ' adds a product ID to a list

    Dim strId As String

    ' remove any leading and trailing spaces and
    ' then convert to uppercase
    strId = txtId.Text.Trim.ToUpper

    ' verify that the ID contains 3 letters
    ' followed by 2 numbers
    If strId Like "[A-Z][A-Z][A-Z]##" Then
        lstId.Items.Add(strId)
    Else
        MessageBox.Show("Invalid product ID",
                        "Product ID", MessageBoxButtons.OK,
                        MessageBoxIcon.Information)
    End If

    txtId.Focus()
End Sub
```

Figure 8-19 Modified Click event procedure for the btnAdd control

8. Save the solution and then start the application. First, you will test the application using an invalid ID. Type **abc2f** as the product ID and then click the **Add to List** button. The "Invalid product ID" message appears in a message box. Close the message box.

9. Now you will enter a valid ID. Change the product ID to **abc23** and then click the **Add to List** button. ABC23 appears in the listing of product IDs, as shown in Figure 8-20.

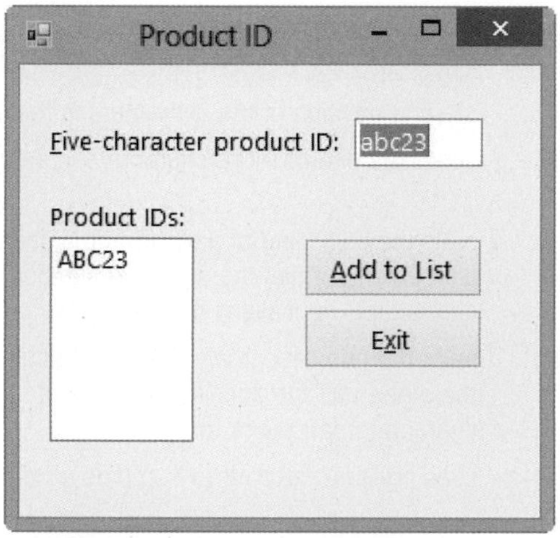

Figure 8-20 Product ID added to the list box

10. On your own, test the application using different valid and invalid IDs. When you are finished testing the application, click the **Exit** button. Close the Code Editor window and then close the solution.

YOU DO IT 5!

Create a Visual Basic Windows application named YouDoIt 5. Save the application in the VB2012\Chap08 folder. Add a text box, a label, and a button to the form. The button's Click event procedure should display the message "OK" when the text box contains two numbers followed by zero or more characters; otherwise, it should display the message "Not OK". Display the message in the label control. Code the procedure. Save the solution and then start and test the application. Close the solution.

Lesson A Summary

- To manipulate strings in Visual Basic:

  Use one of the string manipulation techniques listed in Figure 8-21.

Technique	Syntax	Purpose
Length property	*string*.**Length**	stores an integer that represents the number of characters contained in a string
Trim method	*string*.**Trim**	removes any spaces from both the beginning and end of a string
Remove method	*string*.**Remove(***startIndex*[**,** *numCharsToRemove*]**)**	removes characters from a string
Insert method	*string*.**Insert(***startIndex***,** *value***)**	inserts characters in a string
Contains method	*string*.**Contains(***subString***)**	determines whether a string contains a specific sequence of characters; returns a Boolean value
IndexOf method	*string*.**IndexOf(***subString*[**,** *startIndex*]**)**	determines whether a string contains a specific sequence of characters; returns either –1 or an integer that indicates the starting position of the characters in the string
Substring method	*string*.**Substring(***startIndex*[**,** *numCharsToAccess*]**)**	accesses one or more characters in a string
PadLeft method	*string*.**PadLeft(***totalChars*[**,** *padCharacter*]**)**	pads the beginning of a string with a character until the string has the specified number of characters; right-aligns the string
PadRight method	*string*.**PadRight(***totalChars*[**,** *padCharacter*]**)**	pads the end of a string with a character until the string has the specified number of characters; left-aligns the string
Like operator	*string* **Like** *pattern*	uses pattern-matching to compare strings

Important note: The following additional techniques are covered in the Discovery Exercises at the end of this lesson: the StartsWith and EndsWith methods, the Replace method, the full syntax of the Trim method, the TrimStart and TrimEnd methods, and the Mid statement.

Figure 8-21 String manipulation techniques

Lesson A Key Terms

Contains method—determines whether a string contains a specific sequence of characters; returns a Boolean value

IndexOf method—determines whether a string contains a specific sequence of characters; returns either −1 (if the string does not contain the sequence of characters) or an integer that represents the starting position of the sequence of characters

Insert method—inserts characters anywhere in a string

Length property—stores an integer that represents the number of characters contained in a string

Like operator—uses pattern-matching characters to determine whether one string is equal to another string

PadLeft method—right-aligns a string by inserting characters at the beginning of the string

PadRight method—left-aligns a string by inserting characters at the end of the string

Remove method—removes a specified number of characters located anywhere in a string

Substring method—used to access any number of characters contained in a string

Trim method—removes spaces from both the beginning and end of a string

Lesson A Review Questions

1. The `txtCity` control contains the word "London" followed by two spaces. Which of the following statements removes the two spaces from the control's contents?
   a. `txtCity.Text = txtCity.Trim`
   b. `txtCity.Text = Trim(txtCity.Text)`
   c. `txtCity.Text = txtCity.Text.Trim`
   d. none of the above

2. Which of the following statements assigns the first three characters in the `strPart` variable to the `strCode` variable?
   a. `strCode = strPart.Assign(0, 3)`
   b. `strCode = strPart.Assign(3, 1)`
   c. `strCode = strPart.Sub(0, 3)`
   d. `strCode = strPart.Substring(0, 3)`

3. The `strWord` variable contains the string "Chairs". Which of the following statements changes the contents of the variable to "Chair"?
   a. `strWord = strWord.Remove(5)`
   b. `strWord = strWord.Remove(6, 1)`
   c. `strWord = strWord.Trim(5)`
   d. `strWord = strWord.Trim(6)`

4. Which of the following statements changes the contents of the `strZip` variable from 60521 to 60561?

   a. `strZip = strZip.Insert(3, "6")`
      `strZip = strZip.Remove(4, 1)`

   b. `strZip = strZip.Insert(4, "6")`
      `strZip = strZip.Remove(3, 1)`

   c. `strZip = strZip.Remove(3, 1)`
      `strZip = strZip.Insert(3, "6")`

   d. all of the above

5. Which of the following methods can be used to determine whether the `strAmount` variable contains the dollar sign?

   a. `blnResult = strAmount.Contains("$")`
   b. `intResult = strAmount.IndexOf("$")`
   c. `intResult = strAmount.IndexOf("$", 0)`
   d. all of the above

6. Which of the following statements changes the contents of the `strWord` variable from "sting" to "string"?

   a. `strWord = strWord.AddTo(2, "r")`
   b. `strWord = strWord.Insert(2, "r")`
   c. `strWord = strWord.Insert(3, "r")`
   d. `strWord = strWord.Insert(3, "r"c)`

7. If the `strName` variable contains the string "George Washington", what value will the `strName.IndexOf("Washington")` method return?

   a. –1
   b. 0
   c. 7
   d. 8

8. If the `strWord` variable contains the string "chimes", which of the following statements assigns the fourth character in the variable to the `strLetter` variable?

   a. `strLetter = strWord.Substring(3)`
   b. `strLetter = strWord.Substring(3, 1)`
   c. `strLetter = strWord(4).Substring`
   d. none of the above

9. Which of the following expressions evaluates to True when the `strPart` variable contains the string "123X45"?

   a. `strPart Like "999[A-Z]99"`
   b. `strPart Like "######"`
   c. `strPart Like "###[A-Z]##"`
   d. none of the above

10. Which of the following changes the contents of the `strCityState` variable from Austin Texas to Austin, Texas?

    a. `strCityState = strCityState.Insert(6, ",")`

    b. `strCityState = strCityState.Insert(7, ",")`

    c. `strCityState = strCityState.Insert(8, ",")`

    d. none of the above

11. If the `strMsg` variable contains the string "Today is Monday", which of the following assigns the number 9 to the `intNum` variable?

    a. `intNum = strMsg.Substring(0, "M")`

    b. `intNum = strMsg.Contains("M")`

    c. `intNum = strMsg.IndexOf("M")`

    d. `intNum = strMsg.IndexOf(0, "M")`

12. If the `strName` variable contains the string "Sydney Hart", which of the following changes the contents of the variable to "Sydney D. Hart"?

    a. `strName = strName.Insert(6, "D. ")`

    b. `strName = strName.Insert(7, "D. ")`

    c. `strName = strName.Insert(7, " D.")`

    d. both a and c

13. The `strAmount` variable contains the string "300.89". Which of the following statements changes the contents of the variable to "300.89!!!!"?

    a. `strAmount = strAmount.PadLeft(4, "!"c)`

    b. `strAmount = strAmount.PadRight(4, "!"c)`

    c. `strAmount = strAmount.PadRight(10, "!"c)`

    d. none of the above

14. If the `strAddress` variable contains the string "123 Maple Street", what will the `strAddress.IndexOf("Maple")` method return?

    a. –1

    b. 4

    c. 5

    d. True

15. If the `strAddress` variable contains the string "34 Elm Street", what will the `strAddress.IndexOf("Elm", 4)` method return?

    a. –1

    b. 3

    c. 4

    d. False

Lesson A Exercises

INTRODUCTORY

1. Write a Visual Basic statement that removes the leading and trailing spaces from the txtAddress control.

INTRODUCTORY

2. Write a Visual Basic statement that uses the Insert method to change the contents of the `strWord` variable from "In" to "Indiana".

INTRODUCTORY

3. Using the Insert and Remove methods, write the Visual Basic statements to change the contents of the `strWord` variable from "door" to "floor".

INTRODUCTORY

4. The `strPartNum` variable contains the string "456ANK6". Write a Visual Basic statement that assigns the string "6ANK" from the `strPartNum` variable to the `strCode` variable.

INTRODUCTORY

5. Write the Visual Basic statements to accomplish the following tasks:
   a. Display in the lblSize control the number of characters contained in the `strMsg` variable.
   b. Remove the leading and trailing spaces from the `strCity` variable.
   c. Use the Insert and Remove methods to change the contents of the `strWord` variable from "cater" to "cattle".
   d. Use the Insert method to change the contents of the `strWord` variable from "men" to "women".
   e. Change the contents of the `strPay` variable from "667.99" to "**667.99".

INTRODUCTORY

6. The `strAmount` variable contains the string "3,123,560". Write the Visual Basic statements to change the contents of the variable to "3123560"; use the Remove method.

INTRODUCTORY

7. Write the Visual Basic statement that uses the Contains method to determine whether the `strAddress` variable contains the string "Jefferson Street" (entered in uppercase, lowercase, or a combination of uppercase and lowercase). Assign the method's return value to a Boolean variable named `blnIsContained`.

INTRODUCTORY

8. Open the City Names Solution (City Names Solution.sln) file contained in the VB2012\Chap08\City Names Solution folder. If necessary, open the designer window. The interface allows the user to enter a city name. Code the Add Name button's Click event procedure so that it removes any leading and/or trailing spaces from the city name. If the city name contains at least one character, add the name to the combo box. The procedure should also send the focus to the combo box. Save the solution and then start the application. Test the application by entering spaces before and after the following city names: New York and Miami. Close the Code Editor window and then close the solution.

INTRODUCTORY

9. Open the Item Prices Solution (Item Prices Solution.sln) file contained in the VB2012\Chap08\Item Prices Solution folder. If necessary, open the designer window. Open the Code Editor window. Modify the form's Load event procedure so that it right-aligns the prices listed in the cboRight control and then selects the first price. Save the solution and then start the application. (The prices listed in the cboLeft control should still be left-aligned.) Close the Code Editor window and then close the solution.

INTRODUCTORY

10. Open the Date Solution (Date Solution.sln) file contained in the VB2012\Chap08\Date Solution folder. If necessary, open the designer window. The interface allows the user to enter a date. Code the Change Date button's Click event procedure so that it uses the Insert method to change the year number from *yy* to 20*yy* before displaying the year number in the lblDate control. Save the solution and then start and test the application. Close the Code Editor window and then close the solution.

11. The `strAmount` variable contains the string "3123560". Write the Visual Basic statements to change the variable's contents to "$3,123,560". INTERMEDIATE

12. Open the Sales Tax Solution (Sales Tax Solution.sln) file contained in the VB2012\Chap08\Sales Tax Solution folder. If necessary, open the designer window. The interface allows the user to enter a sales amount and a tax rate. Open the Code Editor window. The btnCalc_Click procedure should determine whether the tax rate ends with a percent sign. If it does, the procedure should remove the percent sign from the rate. Make the appropriate modifications to the code. Save the solution and then start the application. Test the application using the following data: a sales amount of 1000 and a tax rate of 5%, and then a sales amount of 5000 and a tax rate of 7. Close the Code Editor window and then close the solution. INTERMEDIATE

13. Open the Zip Solution (Zip Solution.sln) file contained in the VB2012\Chap08\Zip Solution folder. If necessary, open the designer window. The Display Shipping Charge button's Click event procedure should display the appropriate shipping charge based on the ZIP code entered by the user. To be valid, the ZIP code must contain exactly five digits and the first three digits must be either "605" or "606". The shipping charge for "605" ZIP codes is $25. The shipping charge for "606" ZIP codes is $30. Display an appropriate message if the ZIP code is invalid. Code the procedure. Save the solution and then start the application. Test the application using the following ZIP codes: 60677, 60511, 60344, and 7130. Close the Code Editor window and then close the solution. INTERMEDIATE

14. Open the Social Security Solution (Social Security Solution.sln) file contained in the VB2012\Chap08\Social Security Solution-Remove folder. If necessary, open the designer window. The interface allows the user to enter a Social Security number. Code the Remove Dashes button's Click event procedure so that it first verifies that the Social Security number contains three numbers followed by a hyphen, two numbers, a hyphen, and four numbers. If the Social Security number is in the correct format, the procedure should remove the dashes from the number before displaying the number in the lblNumber control. Save the solution and then start and test the application. Close the Code Editor window and then close the solution. INTERMEDIATE

15. Visual Basic provides the StartsWith and EndsWith methods for determining whether a specific sequence of characters occurs at the beginning or end, respectively, of a string. The StartsWith method's syntax is *string*.**StartsWith(***subString***)**, and the EndsWith method's syntax is *string*.**EndsWith(***subString***)**. Open the City Solution (City Solution.sln) file contained in the VB2012\Chap08\City Solution folder. If necessary, open the designer window. The interface provides a text box for the user to enter the name of a city. The Add to List button's Click event procedure should add the city name to the list box, but only if the city name begins with either the letter L or the letters Ch. The letters can be entered in uppercase, lowercase, or a combination of uppercase and lowercase. Code the procedure. Save the solution and then start and test the application. Close the Code Editor window and then close the solution. DISCOVERY

16. Visual Basic provides the Replace method for replacing a sequence of characters in a string with another sequence of characters. The method's syntax is *string*.**Replace(***oldValue***,** *newValue***)**. When processing the Replace method, the computer makes a temporary copy of the *string* in memory; it then replaces the characters in the copy only. The Replace method returns a string with all occurrences of *oldValue* replaced with *newValue*. Open the Social Security Solution (Social Security Solution.sln) file contained in the VB2012\Chap08\Social Security Solution-Replace folder. If necessary, open the designer window. The interface allows the user to enter a Social Security number. Code the Remove Dashes button's Click event procedure so that it first verifies that the Social Security number is in the correct format. If it is, the procedure should remove the dashes from the number before displaying the number in DISCOVERY

the lblNumber control. Save the solution and then start and test the application. Close the Code Editor window and then close the solution.

DISCOVERY

17. In this lesson, you learned how to use the Trim method to remove space characters from both the beginning and end of a string. You also can use the Trim method to remove other characters. The syntax for doing this is *string*.**Trim**[(*trimChars*)]. The optional *trimChars* argument is a comma-separated list of characters that you want removed (trimmed). For example, if the txtInput control contains the string "#$456#", you can remove the number signs and dollar sign from the control's Text property using the statement `txtInput.Text = txtInput.Text.Trim("#"c, "$"c)`. When processing the Trim method, the computer makes a temporary copy of the *string* in memory; it then removes the characters in the copy only. Open the Trim Method Solution (Trim Method Solution.sln) file contained in the VB2012\Chap08\Trim Method Solution folder. If necessary, open the designer window. Open the Code Editor window and code the btnTrim control's Click event procedure. Save the solution and then start and test the application. Close the Code Editor window and then close the solution.

DISCOVERY

18. Visual Basic provides the TrimStart and TrimEnd methods for removing one or more characters from the beginning or end, respectively, of a string. The TrimStart method's syntax is *string*.**TrimStart**[(*trimChars*)], and the TrimEnd method's syntax is *string*.**TrimEnd**[(*trimChars*)]. The optional *trimChars* argument is a comma-separated list of characters that you want removed (trimmed). For example, if the txtSales control contains the string "$56.80", you can remove the dollar sign from the control's Text property using the statement `txtSales.Text = txtSales.Text.TrimStart("$"c)`. The default value for the *trimChars* argument is the space character (" "c). When processing the TrimStart and TrimEnd methods, the computer makes a temporary copy of the *string* in memory; it then removes the characters from the copy only. Open the Tax Calculator Solution (Tax Calculator Solution.sln) file contained in the VB2012\Chap08\Tax Calculator Solution folder. If necessary, open the designer window. The Calculate button's Click event procedure should calculate and display the sales tax, using the amount entered in the text box and the rate selected in the list box. Code the procedure. Save the solution and then start and test the application. Close the Code Editor window and then close the solution.

DISCOVERY

19. Visual Basic provides the Mid statement for replacing a specified number of characters in a string with another string. The statement's syntax is **Mid(***targetString***,** *start*[**,** *count*]**)** = *replacementString*. In the syntax, the *targetString* argument is the string in which you want characters replaced, and *replacementString* contains the replacement characters. The *start* argument is the position of the first character you want replaced in the targetString. The first character in the targetString is in position 1; the second is in position 2, and so on. The optional *count* argument specifies the number of characters to replace in the targetString. If the count argument is omitted, the Mid statement replaces the lesser of either the number of characters in the replacementString or the number of characters in the targetString from position *start* through the end of the targetString. Open the Area Code Solution (Area Code Solution.sln) file contained in the VB2012\ Chap08\Area Code Solution folder. If necessary, open the designer window. The interface allows the user to enter a phone number, including the area code. Code the Change Area Code button's Click event procedure so that it first verifies that the phone number is in the proper format. If the format is valid, the procedure should use the Mid statement to change the area code to 800 before displaying the phone number in the lblNew control. Save the solution and then start and test the application. Close the Code Editor window and then close the solution.

LESSON B

After studying Lesson B, you should be able to:

- Include a MenuStrip control on a form
- Add elements to a menu
- Assign access keys to menu elements
- Enable and disable a control
- Assign shortcut keys to commonly used menu items
- Code a menu item's Click event procedure
- Include the Like operator in a procedure

Adding a Menu to a Form

The Menus and Toolbars section of the toolbox contains a MenuStrip tool for instantiating a menu strip control. You use a **menu strip control** to include one or more menus on a Windows form. Each menu contains a menu title, which appears on the menu bar at the top of the form. When you click a menu title, its corresponding menu opens and displays a list of options, called menu items. The menu items can be commands (such as Open or Exit), separator bars, or submenu titles. As in all Windows applications, clicking a command on a menu executes the command, and clicking a submenu title opens an additional menu of options. Each of the options on a submenu is referred to as a submenu item. You can use a separator bar to visually group together related items on a menu or submenu. Figure 8-22 identifies the location of these menu elements. Although you can create many levels of submenus, it is best to use only one level in your application because too many layers of submenus can be confusing to the user.

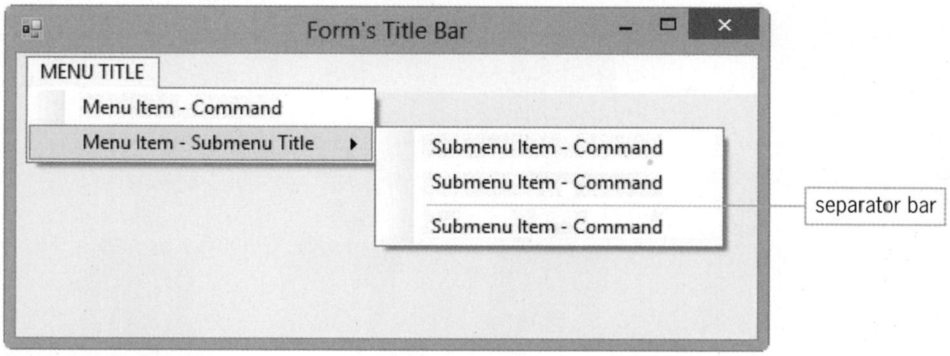

Figure 8-22 Location of menu elements

Each menu element is considered an object; therefore, each has a set of properties associated with it. The most commonly used properties for a menu element are the Name and Text properties. The programmer uses the Name property to refer to the menu element in code. The Text property stores the menu element's caption, which is the text that the user sees when he or she is working with the menu. The caption indicates the purpose of the menu element. Examples of familiar captions for menu elements include Edit, Save As, Copy, and Exit.

Menu title captions should be one word only and entered using uppercase letters. Each menu title should have a unique access key. The access key allows the user to open the menu by pressing the Alt key in combination with the access key. Unlike the captions for menu titles, the captions for menu items typically consist of one to three words. The Windows standard is to use book title capitalization for the menu item captions. Each menu item should have an access key that is unique within its menu. The access key allows the user to select the item by pressing the access key when the menu is open. If a menu item requires additional information from the user, the Windows standard is to place an ellipsis (...) at the end of the caption. The ellipsis alerts the user that the menu item requires more information before it can perform its task.

The menus included in your application should follow the standard Windows conventions. For example, if your application uses a FILE menu, it should be the first menu on the menu bar. FILE menus typically contain commands for opening, saving, and printing files, as well as exiting the application. If your application requires Cut, Copy, and Paste commands, the commands should be placed on an EDIT menu, which is usually the second menu on the menu bar.

Ch08B video

Recall that your task in this chapter is to create the Frankenstein Game application. Most of the application's interface has been created for you. Missing from the interface is a FILE menu that contains three menu items: a New Game command, a separator bar, and an Exit command.

START HERE

To complete the Frankenstein Game application's interface:

1. If necessary, start Visual Studio 2012. Open the Frankenstein Solution (Frankenstein Solution.sln) file contained in the VB2012\Chap08\Frankenstein Solution folder. If necessary, open the designer, Toolbox, and Properties windows. The interface contains five labels, six picture boxes, one text box, and one button.
2. Click the **picHead** control to select it as the reference control. Then Ctrl+Click the other five picture boxes. See Figure 8-23.

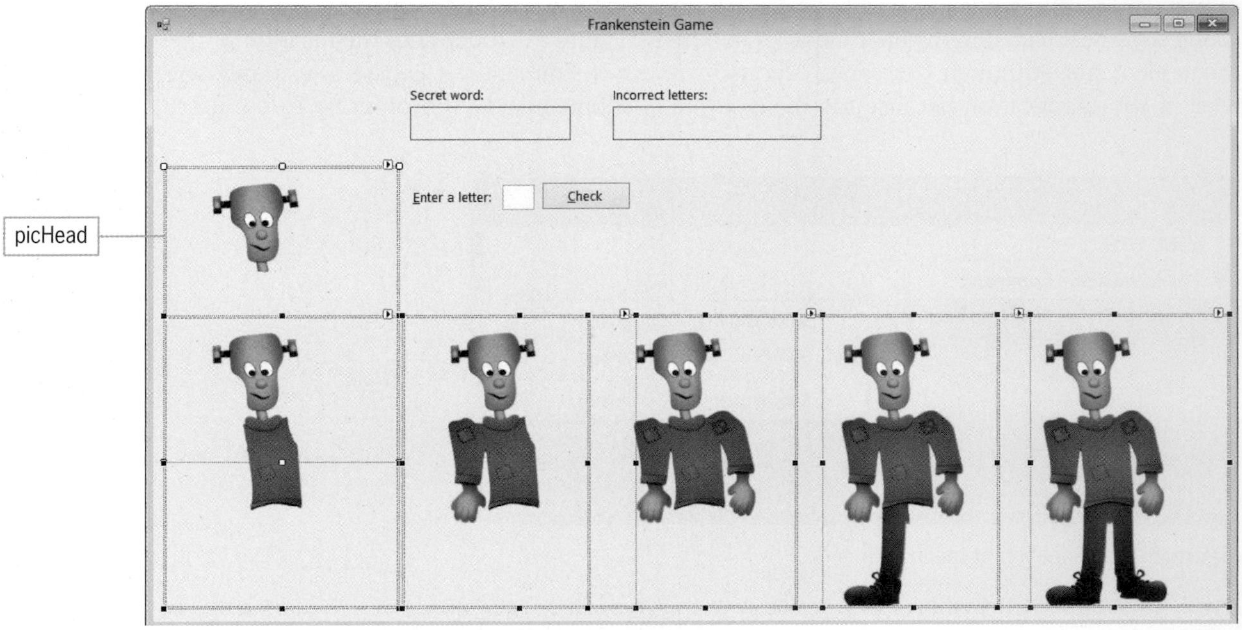

Figure 8-23 Six picture boxes selected in the interface
OpenClipArt.org/Merlin2525

3. Use the Format menu to align the controls by their left and top margins. Click the **form** and change its Size property to **694,486**. Then, lock the controls on the form. See Figure 8-24.

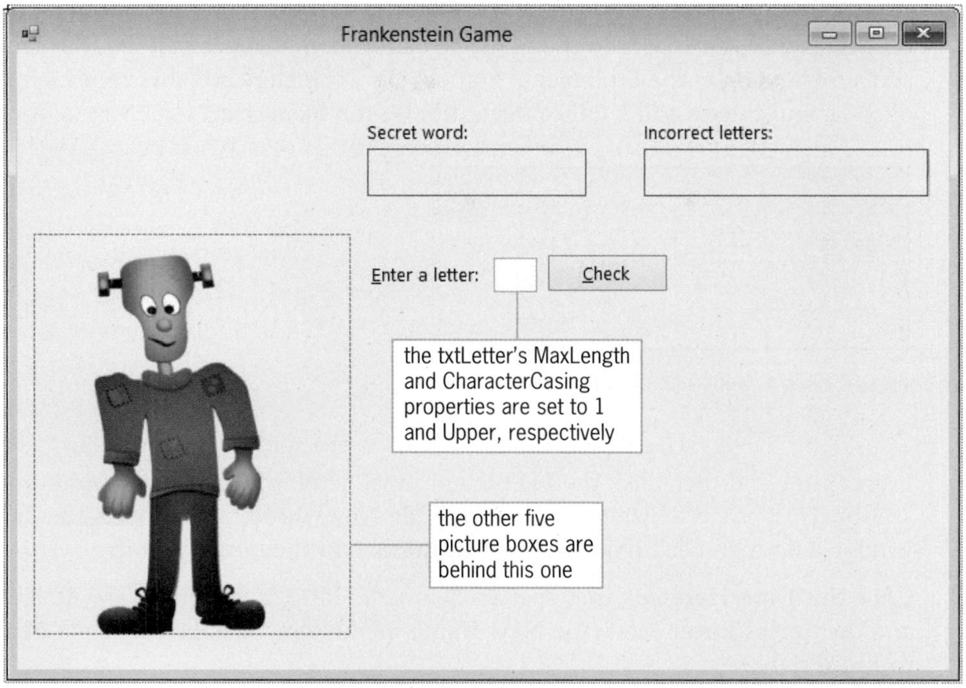

Figure 8-24 Current status of the form
OpenClipArt.org/Merlin2525

4. Click the **MenuStrip** tool, which is located in the Menus & Toolbars section of the toolbox. Drag the mouse pointer to the form and then release the mouse button. A MenuStrip control named MenuStrip1 appears in the component tray, and the words "Type Here" appear in a box below the form's title bar. See Figure 8-25.

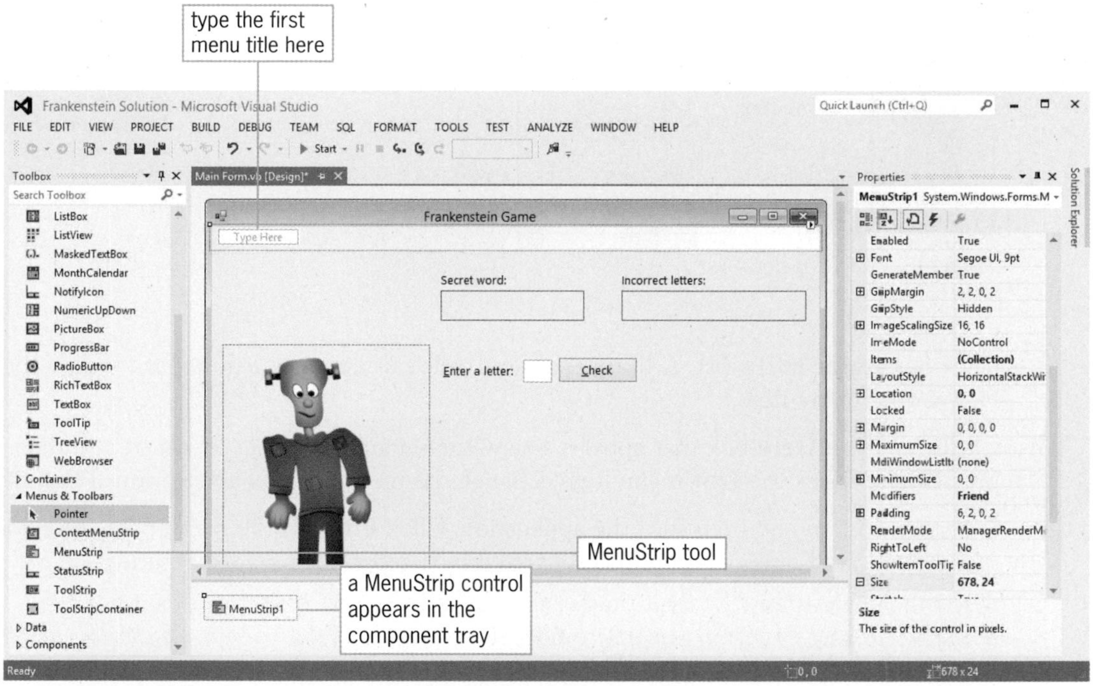

Figure 8-25 MenuStrip control added to the form
OpenClipArt.org/Merlin2525

5. Auto-hide the toolbox. Click the **Type Here** box on the menu bar and then type **&FILE**. See Figure 8-26. You use the Type Here box that appears below the menu title to add a menu item to the FILE menu. You use the Type Here box that appears to the right of the menu title to add another menu title to the menu bar.

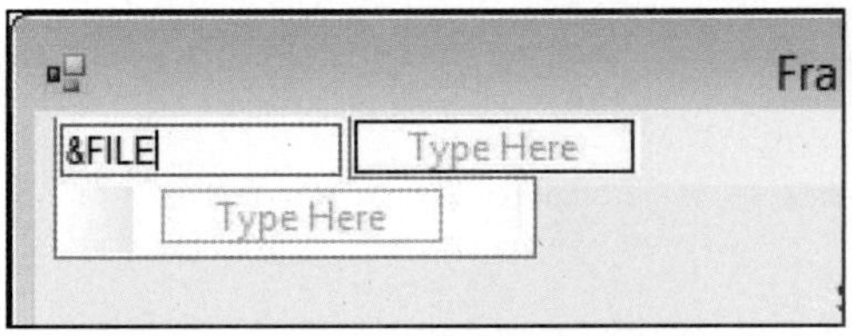

Figure 8-26 Menu title included on the form

6. Press **Enter** and then click the **FILE** menu title. Scroll the Properties window until you see the Text property, which contains &FILE. Now, scroll to the top of the Properties window and then click **(Name)**. Type **mnuFile** and then press **Enter**.
7. Click the **Type Here** box that appears below the FILE menu title. Type **&New Game** and then press **Enter**. Click the **New Game** menu item. Change the menu item's name to **mnuFileNew**.
8. Next, you will add a separator bar to the FILE menu. Place your mouse pointer on the Type Here box that appears below the New Game menu item, but don't click the box. Instead, click the **list arrow** that appears inside the box. See Figure 8-27.

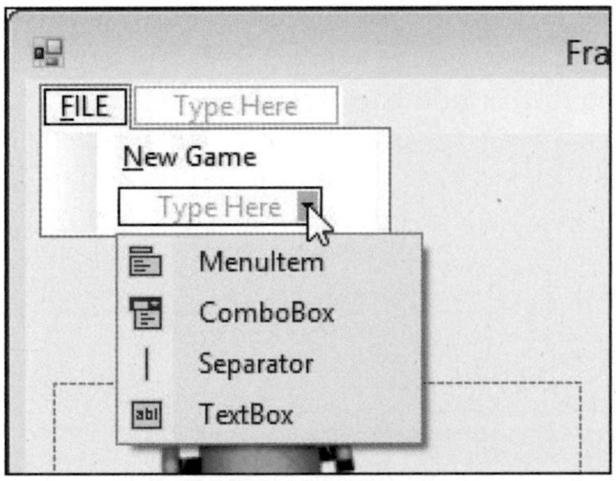

Figure 8-27 Drop-down list

9. Click **Separator** in the list. A horizontal line, called a separator bar, appears below the New Game menu item.
10. Click the **Type Here** box that appears below the separator bar. Type **E&xit** and then press **Enter**. Click the **Exit** menu item. Change the menu item's name to **mnuFileExit**.
11. Save the solution and then start the application. Click **FILE** on the menu bar. The FILE menu opens and offers two options separated by a separator bar. See Figure 8-28.

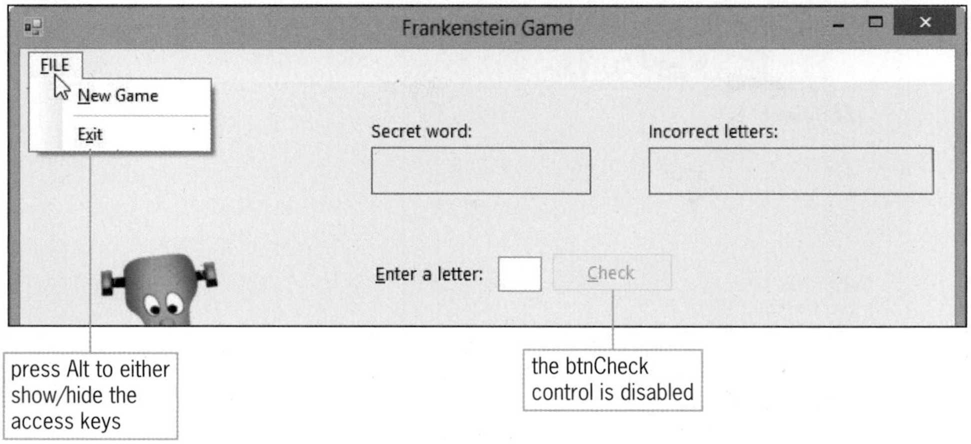

Figure 8-28 File menu opened during run time
OpenClipArt.org/Merlin2525

12. Click the **Close** button on the form's title bar.

As indicated in Figure 8-28, the btnCheck control is disabled, which means it is not currently available to the user. You disable a control by setting its **Enabled property** to False either in the Properties window or in code; you enable it by setting the property to True (the default value). When a control is disabled, it appears dimmed (grayed out) during run time, as shown in the figure. The btnCheck control will remain disabled until the user selects the New Game option on the FILE menu.

Assigning Shortcut Keys to Menu Items

Commonly used menu items should be assigned shortcut keys. The **shortcut keys** appear to the right of a menu item and allow the user to select the item without opening the menu. Examples of familiar shortcut keys include Ctrl+X and Ctrl+V. In Windows applications that have an EDIT menu, Ctrl+X and Ctrl+V are used to select the Cut and Paste commands, respectively, when the EDIT menu is closed. In the Frankenstein Game application, you will assign shortcut keys to the New Game option on the FILE menu.

A menu item's access key can be used only when the menu is open. A menu item's shortcut key can be used only when the menu is closed.

START HERE

To assign shortcut keys to the New Game menu item:

1. Click the **New Game** menu item on the FILE menu. Click **ShortcutKeys** in the Properties window and then click the **list arrow** in the Settings box. A box opens and allows you to specify a modifier and a key. In this case, the modifier and key will be Ctrl and N, respectively. Click the **Ctrl** check box to select it, and then click the **list arrow** that appears in the Key combo box. An alphabetical list of keys appears. Scroll the list until you see the letter N, and then click **N** in the list. See Figure 8-29.

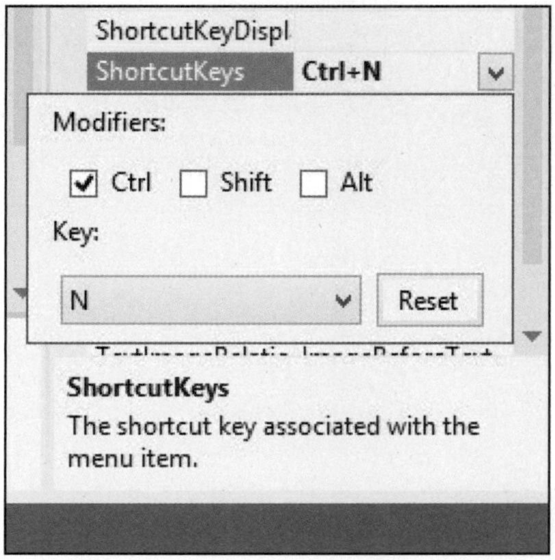

Figure 8-29 Shortcut keys specified in the ShortcutKeys box

2. Press **Enter**. Ctrl+N appears in the ShortcutKeys property in the Properties list. It also appears to the right of the New Game menu item.
3. Auto-hide the Properties window. Save the solution and then start the application. Click **FILE** on the menu bar. See Figure 8-30.

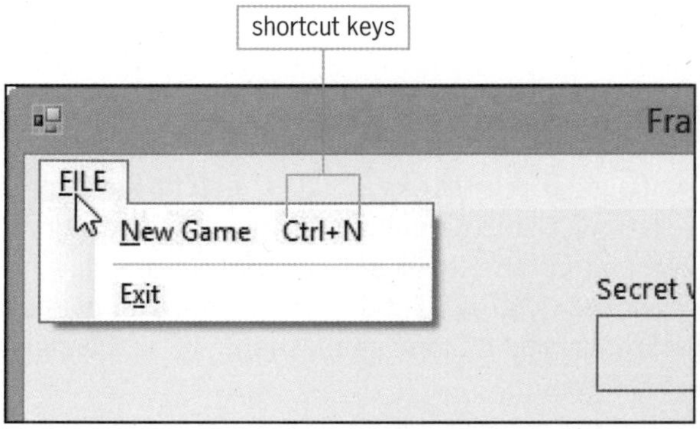

Figure 8-30 Location of the shortcut keys on the menu

4. Click the **Close** button on the form's title bar.

GUI DESIGN TIP Menu Standards

- Menu title captions should be one word and entered using uppercase letters. Each menu title should have a unique access key.
- Menu item captions can be from one to three words. Use book title capitalization and assign a unique access key to each menu item on the same menu.
- Assign unique shortcut keys to commonly used menu items.
- If a menu item requires additional information from the user, place an ellipsis (...) at the end of the item's caption, which is entered in the item's Text property.
- Follow the Windows standards for the placement of menu titles and items.
- Use a separator bar to separate groups of related menu items.

Coding the Exit Menu Item

When the user clicks the Exit option on the FILE menu, the option's Click event procedure should end the application.

To code and then test the Exit menu item:

START HERE

1. Open the Code Editor window, which already contains some code. Replace <your name> and <current date> in the comments with your name and the current date, respectively.
2. Open the code template for the mnuFileExit_Click procedure. Type **Me.Close()** and press **Enter**.
3. Save the solution and then start the application. Click **FILE** on the Frankenstein Game application's menu bar and then click **Exit** to end the application.

Coding the txtLetter Control's KeyPress Event

As indicated earlier in Figure 8-24, the txtLetter's MaxLength and CharacterCasing properties are set to 1 and Upper, respectively. As a result, the text box will accept one character only. If the character is a letter of the alphabet, it will be converted to uppercase. In the next set of steps, you will prevent the text box from accepting a character that is not either a letter of the alphabet or the Backspace key. You can do this using an If...Then...Else statement with the following condition: `e.KeyChar Like "[!A-Za-z]" AndAlso e.KeyChar <> ControlChars.Back`. The sub-condition on the left side of the AndAlso operator will evaluate to True if the user's entry is not one of the uppercase or lowercase letters of the alphabet. The sub-condition on the right side of the AndAlso operator will evaluate to True if the user's entry is not the Backspace key. If both sub-conditions evaluate to True, the compound condition evaluates to True and the text box should not accept the user's entry.

To code and then test the txtLetter control's KeyPress event procedure:

START HERE

1. Open the code template for the txtLetter_KeyPress procedure. Enter the comment and selection structure shown in Figure 8-31.

```
Private Sub txtLetter_KeyPress(sender As Object, e A
    ' allows only letters and the Backspace key

    If e.KeyChar Like "[!A-Za-z]" AndAlso
        e.KeyChar <> ControlChars.Back Then
        e.Handled = True
    End If
End Sub
```

enter this comment and selection structure

Figure 8-31 txtLetter_KeyPress procedure

2. Save the solution and then start the application. Type **a** in the text box. Notice that the letter is changed to its uppercase equivalent, A. Press the **Backspace** key to delete the letter A.
3. Now, try entering a character other than a letter of the alphabet or the Backspace key; you won't be able to do so. Also try entering more than one letter; here, too, you won't be able to do so.
4. Click **FILE** on the Frankenstein Game application's menu bar and then click **Exit** to end the application. Close the Code Editor window and then close the solution.

Lesson B Summary

- To add a MenuStrip control to a form:

  Use the MenuStrip tool, which is located in the Menus & Toolbars section of the toolbox.

- To create a menu:

  Replace the words "Type Here" with the menu element's caption. Assign a meaningful name and a unique access key to each menu element, with the exception of separator bars.

- To include a separator bar on a menu:

  Place your mouse pointer on a Type Here box and then click the list arrow that appears inside the box. Click Separator on the list.

- To enable/disable a control during run time:

  Set its Enabled property to True (enable) or False (disable) either in the Properties window or in code.

- To assign shortcut keys to a menu item:

  Set the menu item's ShortcutKeys property.

Lesson B Key Terms

Enabled property—used to enable (True) or disable (False) a control during run time

Menu strip control—used to include one or more menus on a form

Shortcut keys—appear to the right of a menu item and allow the user to select the item without opening the menu

Lesson B Review Questions

1. The horizontal line in a menu is called ________________.
   a. a menu bar
   b. a separator bar
   c. an item separator
   d. none of the above

2. The underlined letter in a menu element's caption is called ________________.
   a. an access key
   b. a menu key
   c. a shortcut key
   d. none of the above

3. Which of the following allows the user to access a menu item without opening the menu?
   a. an access key
   b. a menu key
   c. shortcut keys
   d. none of the above

4. Which of the following is false?
   a. Menu titles should be one word only.
   b. Each menu title should have a unique access key.
   c. You should assign shortcut keys to commonly used menu titles.
   d. Menu items should be entered using book title capitalization.

5. Which property determines whether a control is available to the user during run time?
   a. Available
   b. Enabled
   c. Unavailable
   d. Disabled

6. Explain the difference between a menu item's access key and its shortcut keys.

Lesson B Exercises

INTRODUCTORY

1. Open the Bonus Solution (Bonus Solution.sln) file contained in the VB2012\Chap08\Bonus Solution folder. If necessary, open the designer window. Add a FILE menu to the form. The FILE menu should contain an Exit menu item that ends the application. Enter the appropriate code in the menu item's Click event procedure. Save the solution and then start the application. Use the Exit option on the FILE menu to end the application. Close the Code Editor window and then close the solution.

INTERMEDIATE

2. Open the Commission Solution (Commission Solution.sln) file contained in the VB2012\Chap08\Commission Solution folder. If necessary, open the designer window. Add a FILE menu and a CALCULATE menu to the form. Include an Exit menu item on the FILE menu. Include two menu items on the CALCULATE menu: 2% Commission and 5% Commission. Assign shortcut keys to the CALCULATE menu's items. When the user clicks the Exit menu item, the application should end. When the user clicks the 2% Commission menu item, the application should calculate and display a 2% commission on the sales entered by the user. When the user clicks the 5% Commission menu item, the application should calculate and display a 5% commission on the sales entered by the user. Enter the appropriate code in each menu item's Click event procedure. Save the solution and then start and test the application. Close the Code Editor window and then close the solution.

LESSON C

After studying Lesson C, you should be able to:

- Include the Length property in a procedure
- Include the Substring method in a procedure
- Include the Remove method in a procedure
- Include the Insert method in a procedure
- Include the Contains method in a procedure

Completing the Frankenstein Game Application

Figure 8-32 shows the Frankenstein Game application's TOE chart. You coded the mnuFileExit_Click and txtLetter_KeyPress procedures in Lesson B. In this lesson, you will complete the application by coding the mnuFileNew_Click and btnCheck_Click procedures.

Task	Object	Event
1. Get a five–letter word from player 1, trim spaces, and convert to uppercase 2. Determine whether the word contains 5 letters 3. If the word contains 5 letters, hide the 6 picture boxes, display 5 dashes in lblWord, clear lblIncorrect, set incorrect guesses counter to 0, clear txtLetter, enable btnCheck, and send focus to txtLetter 4. If the word doesn't contain 5 letters, display "5 letters are required" in a message box	mnuFileNew	Click
1. Search the word for the letter entered by player 2 2. If the letter is contained in the word, replace the appropriate dashes in lblWord; if there aren't any other dashes in the word, the game is over because player 2 guessed the word, so display "Great guessing!" in a message box, disable btnCheck, and set incorrect guesses counter to 0 3. If the letter is not contained in the word, display the letter in lblIncorrect, add 1 to the incorrect guesses counter, and show the appropriate picture box; if player 2 made 6 incorrect guesses, the game is over, so display "Sorry, the word is *word*." in a message box, disable btnCheck, and set incorrect guesses counter to 0 4. Clear txtLetter and send focus to it	btnCheck	Click
End the application	mnuFileExit	Click
Display the Frankenstein images	picHead, picHeadTorso, picHeadTorsoOneArm, picHeadTorsoTwoArms, picHeadTorsoArmsOneLeg, picFullBody	None
Allow only letters and the Backspace key	txtLetter	KeyPress
Display dashes and letters (from mnuFileNew and btnCheck)	lblWord	None
Display the incorrect letters (from mnuFileNew and btnCheck)	lblIncorrect	None

Figure 8-32 TOE chart for the Frankenstein Game application

To open the Frankenstein Game application from Lesson B:

START HERE

1. If necessary, start Visual Studio 2012. Open the Frankenstein Solution (Frankenstein Solution.sln) file contained in the VB2012\Chap08\Frankenstein Solution folder. If necessary, open the designer window. See Figure 8-33.

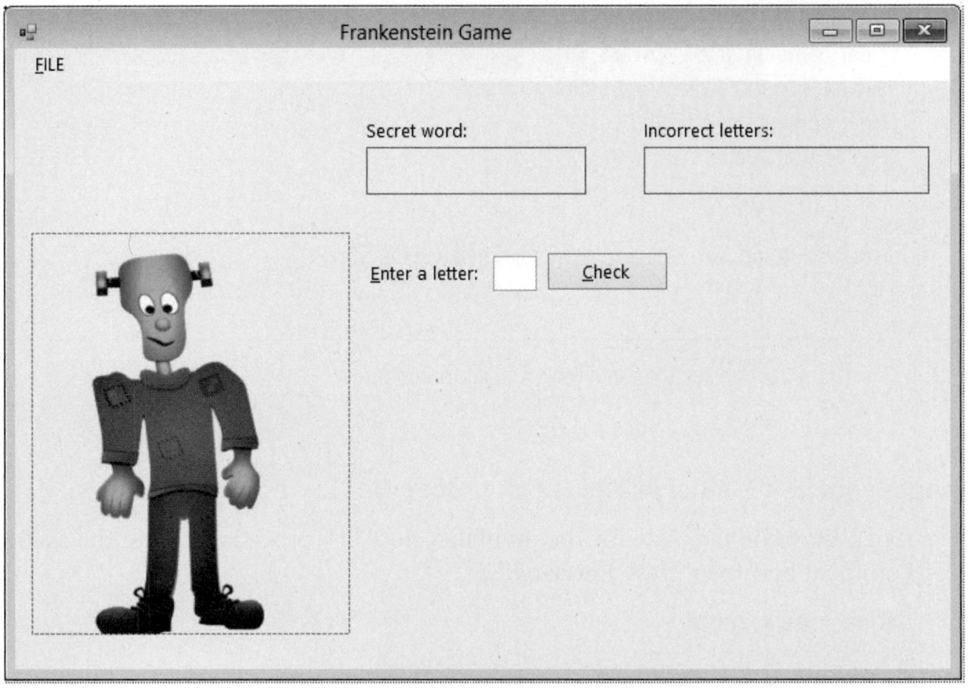

Figure 8-33 Interface for the Frankenstein Game application from Lesson B
OpenClipArt.org/Merlin2525

2. Open the Code Editor window, which already contains some code. The form's Declarations section declares two class-level variables, as shown in Figure 8-34. The `strWord` variable will store the word entered by player 1. The `intIncorrect` variable will keep track of the number of incorrect letters entered by player 2.

```
Public Class frmMain

    Private strWord As String
    Private intIncorrect As Integer
```

class-level variables

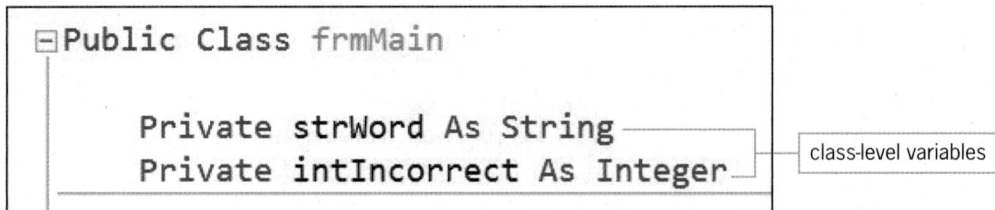

Figure 8-34 Declaration statements for the class-level variables

Coding the FILE Menu's New Game Option

The mnuFileNew_Click procedure is invoked when the user either clicks the New Game option on the FILE menu or presses Ctrl+N (the option's shortcut keys). The procedure should get a five-letter word from player 1 and then verify that the word contains five letters. The procedure's pseudocode is shown in Figure 8-35.

```
mnuFileNew Click event procedure
1. get a 5-letter word from player 1, trim leading and trailing spaces and convert to uppercase
2. if the word contains 5 letters
        hide the 6 picture boxes
        display 5 dashes in lblWord
        clear contents of lblIncorrect
        assign 0 to the intIncorrect counter variable
        clear contents of txtLetter
        enable btnCheck
        send focus to txtLetter
   else
       display "5 letters are required" message in a message box
   end if
```

Figure 8-35 Pseudocode for the mnuFileNew_Click procedure

START HERE

To begin coding the mnuFileNew_Click procedure:

1. Open the code template for the mnuFileNew_Click procedure. Type the following comment and then press **Enter** twice:

   ' start a new game

2. According to its pseudocode, the procedure should begin by getting a five-letter word from player 1. It should trim any leading and trailing spaces from the word and also convert the word to uppercase. Enter the following comment and lines of code. Press **Enter** twice after typing the last line.

```
' get a 5-letter word from player 1
' and then trim and convert to uppercase
strWord = InputBox("Enter a 5-letter word:",
           "Frankenstein Game").Trim.ToUpper
```

Next, the procedure should verify that player 1's word contains exactly five letters. Figure 8-36 shows two ways of accomplishing this task. Example 1 in the figure uses the Length property and the Substring method; both are shaded in the figure. Example 2 uses the Like operator, which also is shaded in the figure. Although the code in both examples produces the same result, Example 2's code is much more concise and easier to understand.

```
Example 1
Dim blnValidWord As Boolean

' determine whether the word contains 5 letters
blnValidWord = True   ' assume word is valid
If strWord.Length <> 5 Then
    blnValidWord = False
Else
    Dim intIndex As Integer
    Do While intIndex < 5 AndAlso blnValidWord = True
        If strWord.Substring(intIndex, 1) Like "[!A-Z]" Then
            blnValidWord = False
        End If
        intIndex = intIndex + 1
    Loop
End If

If blnValidWord = True Then
     instructions to be processed when the word is valid
Else
     instructions to be processed when the word is not valid
End If

Example 2
If strWord Like "[A-Z][A-Z][A-Z][A-Z][A-Z]" Then
     instructions to be processed when the word is valid
Else
     instructions to be processed when the word is not valid
End If
```

Figure 8-36 Two ways of determining whether the word contains five letters

To complete and then test the mnuFileNew_Click procedure:

START HERE

1. Enter the following comment and If clause:

   ' determine whether the word contains 5 letters
   If strWord Like "[A-Z][A-Z][A-Z][A-Z][A-Z]" Then

2. If player 1's word contains five letters, the selection structure's true path should hide the six picture boxes. Enter the following comment and six assignment statements. Press **Enter** twice after typing the last assignment statement.

   ' hide the picture boxes
   picHead.Visible = False
   picHeadTorso.Visible = False
   picHeadTorsoOneArm.Visible = False
   picHeadTorsoTwoArms.Visible = False
   picHeadTorsoArmsOneLeg.Visible = False
   picFullBody.Visible = False

3. Next, the true path should display five dashes (one for each letter in the word) in the lblWord control. It then should clear the contents of the lblIncorrect control, which displays the incorrect letters entered by the user. It also should assign the number 0 to the `intIncorrect` variable, which is a class-level variable that keeps track of the number of incorrect letters entered by the user. Enter the following comments and assignment statements. Press **Enter** twice after typing the last statement.

```
' display 5 dashes in lblWord, clear
' lblIncorrect, and assign 0 to intIncorrect
lblWord.Text = "-----"
lblIncorrect.Text = String.Empty
intIncorrect = 0
```

4. The final three tasks in the selection structure's true path are to clear the contents of the txtLetter control, enable the btnCheck control, and send the focus to the txtLetter control. Enter the following comments and assignment statements:

```
' clear the text box, enable the
' button, set the focus
txtLetter.Text = String.Empty
btnCheck.Enabled = True
txtLetter.Focus()
```

5. Now you need to code the selection structure's false path. According to the pseudocode, the false path should display the "5 letters are required" message when player 1's word does not contain five letters. Enter the following lines of code:

```
Else
    MessageBox.Show("5 letters are required",
                    "Frankenstein Game",
                    MessageBoxButtons.OK,
                    MessageBoxIcon.Information)
```

6. If necessary, delete the blank line above the End If clause.

7. Save the solution and then run the application. Click **FILE** on the menu bar and then click **New Game**. The Frankenstein Game input dialog box opens and prompts you to enter a five-letter word. First, you will enter a valid word. Type **chair** in the dialog box and then press **Enter**. The picture boxes are hidden from view and five dashes appear in the Secret word box. In addition, the Check button is enabled for the user. See Figure 8-37.

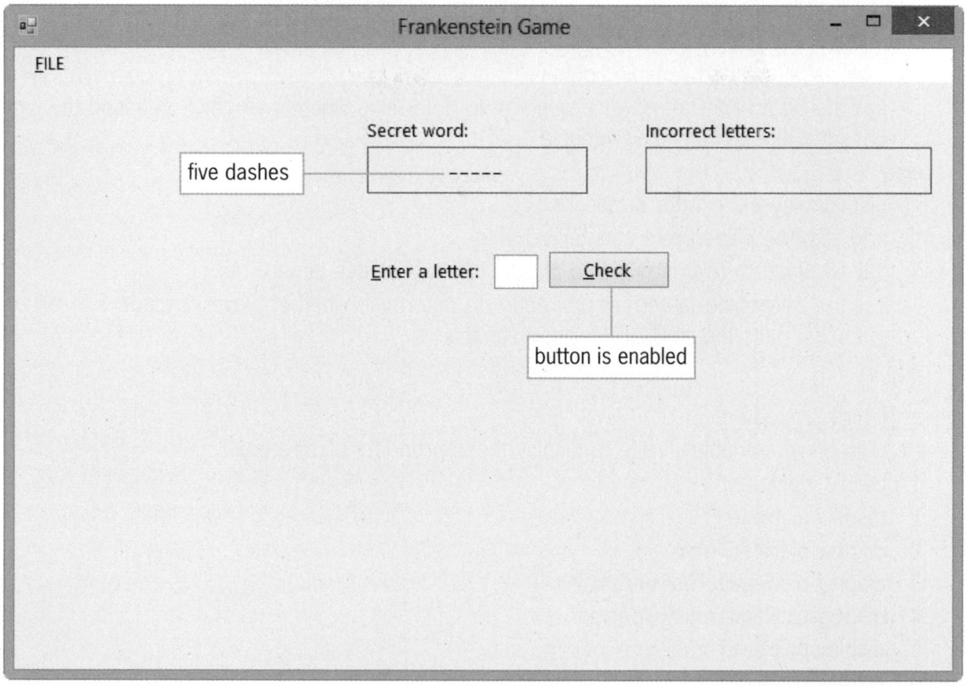

Figure 8-37 Result of entering a valid word

8. Next, you will enter a word that does not contain five letters. Press **Ctrl+n**, which are the shortcut keys for the New Game option. Type **cars3** in the dialog box and then press **Enter**. The message "5 letters are required" appears in a message box. Close the message box.

9. On your own, test the procedure using a word that has less than five letters. Also test it using a word that has more than five letters. In both cases, the message "5 letters are required" should appear in a message box. When you are finished testing the procedure, use the Exit option on the game's FILE menu to end the application.

Completing the Check Button's Click Event Procedure

Figure 8-38 shows the pseudocode for the btnCheck_Click procedure. It also shows the pseudocode for two independent Sub procedures named DisplayPicture and DetermineGameOver. Both independent Sub procedures are used by the btnCheck_Click procedure.

```
btnCheck Click event procedure
1.  repeat for each letter in player 1's word
        if the current letter is the same as the letter entered by player 2
              replace the corresponding dash in lblWord
              assign True to the blnDashReplaced variable
        end if
    end repeat
```

Figure 8-38 Pseudocode for the btnCheck_Click, DisplayPicture, and DetermineGameOver procedures *(continues)*

(continued)

```
2. if the blnDashReplaced variable contains True
       call the DetermineGameOver procedure to determine whether player 2 guessed the word;
       pass the blnDashReplaced variable
   else
       display player 2's letter in lblIncorrect
       add 1 to the intIncorrect counter variable
       call DisplayPicture procedure to display the appropriate picture box
       call the DetermineGameOver procedure to determine whether player 2 made 6 incorrect
       guesses; pass the blnDashReplaced variable
   end if

DisplayPicture procedure
use the intIncorrect variable's value to display the appropriate picture box
   if intNum1 contains:
   1  display picHead
   2  display picHeadTorso
   3  display picHeadTorsoOneArm
   4  display picHeadTorsoTwoArms
   5  display picHeadTorsoArmsOneLeg
   6  display picFullBody

DetermineGameOver procedure
if a dash was replaced in player 1's word
   if there aren't any other dashes in the word
       display "Great guessing!" in a message box
       disable btnCheck
       assign 0 to the intIncorrect counter variable
   end if
else
   if the user entered 6 incorrect letters
       display "Sorry, the word is word." in a message box
       disable btnCheck
       assign 0 to the intIncorrect counter variable
   end if
end if
```

Figure 8-38 Pseudocode for the btnCheck_Click, DisplayPicture, and DetermineGameOver procedures

The DisplayPicture and DetermineGameOver procedures have already been coded for you. The Code Editor window also contains most of the btnCheck_Click procedure's code. You will complete the procedure in the next set of steps.

START HERE

To complete the btnCheck_Click procedure:

1. Locate the btnCheck_Click procedure. The first step in the procedure's pseudocode is a loop that performs its instructions for each letter in player 1's word. The word, which is stored in the `strWord` variable, contains five letters whose indexes are 0, 1, 2, 3, and 4. Click the **blank line** below the `' look at each letter in the word` comment and then enter the following For clause:

   For intIndex As Integer = 0 To 4

2. Change the Next clause to **Next intIndex** and then click the **blank line** below the For clause.

3. According to the pseudocode, the first instruction in the loop is a selection structure that compares the current letter in the `strWord` variable with the letter entered by player 2. Recall from Lesson A that you can use the Substring method to access an individual character in a string. The method's *startIndex* argument is the index of the first character you want to access, and its optional *numCharsToAccess* argument specifies the number of characters you want to access. Enter the following comments and If clause:

   ' if the letter appears in the word,
   ' replace the letter
   If strWord.Substring(intIndex, 1) = strLetter Then

4. If the current letter in the `strWord` variable matches player 2's letter, the selection structure's true path should replace the corresponding dash in the lblWord control with player 2's letter. You can use the Remove and Insert methods to make the replacement. Enter the following assignment statements:

   lblWord.Text =
   lblWord.Text.Remove(intIndex, 1)
   lblWord.Text =
   lblWord.Text.Insert(intIndex, strLetter)

5. Finally, the selection structure's true path should assign the Boolean value True to the `blnDashReplaced` variable to indicate that a replacement was made. Type the additional assignment statement shown in Figure 8-39 and then click the **blank line** below the Next clause.

```
' look at each letter in the word
For intIndex As Integer = 0 To 4
    ' if the letter appears in the word,
    ' replace the letter
    If strWord.Substring(intIndex, 1) = strLetter Then
        lblWord.Text =
            lblWord.Text.Remove(intIndex, 1)
        lblWord.Text =
            lblWord.Text.Insert(intIndex, strLetter)
        blnDashReplaced = True
    End If
Next intIndex
```

enter this assignment statement

Figure 8-39 Additional code entered in the btnCheck_Click procedure

6. Save the solution. Before testing the btnCheck_Click procedure, review the code contained in the DisplayPicture and DetermineGameOver procedures. Notice that the DetermineGameOver procedure uses the Contains method to determine whether there are any dashes in the lblWord control.

START HERE

To test the btnCheck_Click procedure:

1. Start the application. Click **FILE** on the application's menu bar and then click **New Game**. Type **happy** in the input dialog box and then press **Enter**.
2. Type **p** in the Enter a letter text box and then press **Enter**. The letter P replaces two of the dashes in the Secret word box.
3. Type **x** in the text box and then press **Enter**. The letter X appears in the Incorrect letters box. In addition, the picHead control, which shows an image of Frankenstein's head, is now visible.
4. Type the following letters in the text box, pressing **Enter** after typing each one: **a**, **e**, **t**, **y**, and **h**. See Figure 8-40.

Figure 8-40 Result of guessing the secret word
OpenClipArt.org/Merlin2525

5. Close the message box. Now, press **Ctrl+n** and then type **chair** in the input dialog box. Type the following letters in the text box, pressing **Enter** after typing each one: **c**, **e**, **t**, **y**, **a**, **b**, **x**, and **z**. See Figure 8-41.

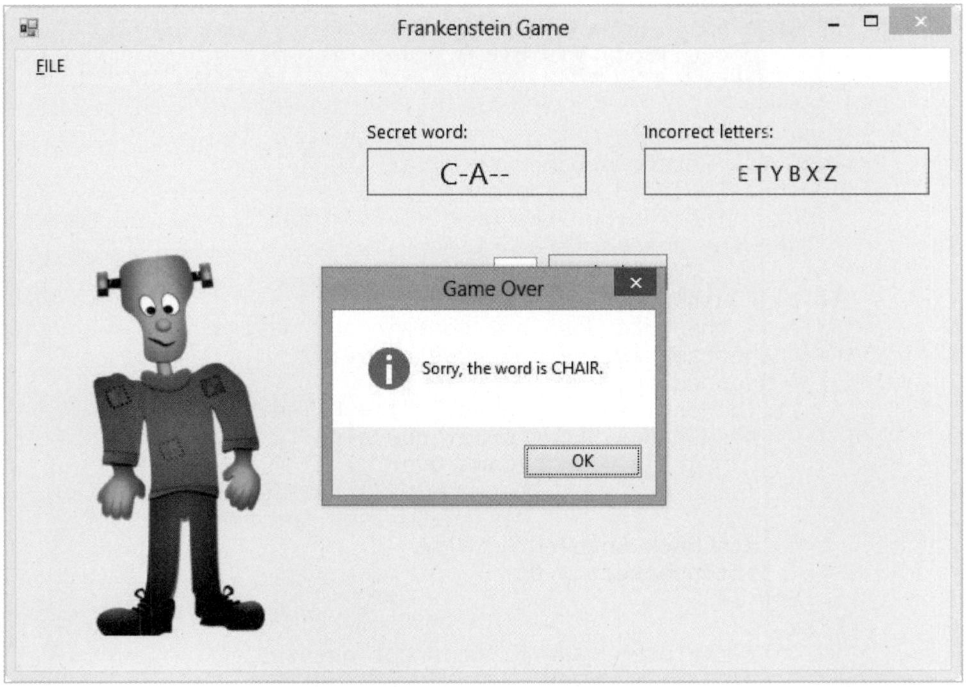

Figure 8-41 Result of not guessing the secret word
OpenClipArt.org/Merlin2525

6. Close the message box. Click **FILE** on the Frankenstein Game application's menu bar and then click **Exit**. Close the Code Editor window and then close the solution. Figure 8-42 shows the application's code.

```
' Name:         Frankenstein Project
' Purpose:      A game that allows the user to guess a
'               word letter-by-letter
' Programmer:   <your name> on <current date>

Public Class frmMain

   Private strWord As String
   Private intIncorrect As Integer

   Private Sub DisplayPicture()
      ' display appropriate picture

      Select Case intIncorrect
         Case 1
            picHead.Visible = True
         Case 2
            picHeadTorso.Visible = True
         Case 3
            picHeadTorsoOneArm.Visible = True
```

Figure 8-42 Frankenstein Game application's code *(continues)*

(continued)

```
            Case 4
                picHeadTorsoTwoArms.Visible = True
            Case 5
                picHeadTorsoArmsOneLeg.Visible = True
            Case 6
                picFullBody.Visible = True
        End Select
    End Sub

    Private Sub DetermineGameOver(ByVal
    blnADashWasReplaced As Boolean)
        ' determine whether the game is over and
        ' take the appropriate action

        If blnADashWasReplaced = True Then
            ' if the word does not contain any dashes,
            ' the game is over because player 2
            ' guessed the word
            If lblWord.Text.Contains("-") = False Then
                MessageBox.Show("Great guessing!",
                                "Game Over",
                                MessageBoxButtons.OK,
                                MessageBoxIcon.Information)
                btnCheck.Enabled = False
                intIncorrect = 0
            End If
        Else
            ' if the user made 6 incorrect guesses,
            ' the game is over
            If intIncorrect = 6 Then
                MessageBox.Show("Sorry, the word is " &
                                strWord & ".",
                               "Game Over",
                                MessageBoxButtons.OK,
                                MessageBoxIcon.Information)
                btnCheck.Enabled = False
                intIncorrect = 0
            End If
        End If
    End Sub

    Private Sub btnCheck_Click(sender As Object,
    e As EventArgs) Handles btnCheck.Click
        ' check if the letter appears in the word

        Dim strLetter As String
        Dim blnDashReplaced As Boolean

        strLetter = txtLetter.Text

        ' look at each letter in the word
        For intIndex As Integer = 0 To 4
            ' if the letter appears in the word,
            ' replace the letter
            If strWord.Substring(intIndex, 1) = strLetter Then
                lblWord.Text =
                    lblWord.Text.Remove(intIndex, 1)
                lblWord.Text =
```

Figure 8-42 Frankenstein Game application's code *(continues)*

(continued)

```
            lblWord.Text.Insert(intIndex, strLetter)
         blnDashReplaced = True
      End If
   Next intIndex

   If blnDashReplaced = True Then
      Call DetermineGameOver(blnDashReplaced)
   Else  ' no dash was replaced
      lblIncorrect.Text =
         lblIncorrect.Text & " " & strLetter
      intIncorrect = intIncorrect + 1
      Call DisplayPicture()
      Call DetermineGameOver(blnDashReplaced)
   End If

   ' clear text box and set focus
   txtLetter.Text = String.Empty
   txtLetter.Focus()
End Sub

Private Sub mnuFileExit_Click(sender As Object,
e As EventArgs) Handles mnuFileExit.Click
   Me.Close()

End Sub

Private Sub txtLetter_KeyPress(sender As Object,
e As KeyPressEventArgs) Handles txtLetter.KeyPress
   ' allows only letters and the Backspace key

   If e.KeyChar Like "[!A-Za-z]" AndAlso
      e.KeyChar <> ControlChars.Back Then
      e.Handled = True
   End If
End Sub

Private Sub mnuFileNew_Click(sender As Object,
e As EventArgs) Handles mnuFileNew.Click
   ' start a new game

   ' get a 5-letter word from player 1
   ' and then trim and convert to uppercase
   strWord = InputBox("Enter a 5-letter word:",
                      "Frankenstein Game").Trim.ToUpper

   ' determine whether the word contains 5 letters
   If strWord Like "[A-Z][A-Z][A-Z][A-Z][A-Z]" Then
      ' hide the picture boxes
      picHead.Visible = False
      picHeadTorso.Visible = False
      picHeadTorsoOneArm.Visible = False
      picHeadTorsoTwoArms.Visible = False
      picHeadTorsoArmsOneLeg.Visible = False
      picFullBody.Visible = False

      ' display 5 dashes in lblWord, clear
      ' lblIncorrect, and assign 0 to intIncorrect
      lblWord.Text = "-----"
```

Figure 8-42 Frankenstein Game application's code *(continues)*

(continued)

```
            lblIncorrect.Text = String.Empty
            intIncorrect = 0

            ' clear the text box, enable the
            ' button, set the focus
            txtLetter.Text = String.Empty
            btnCheck.Enabled = True
            txtLetter.Focus()
        Else
            MessageBox.Show("5 letters are required",
                            "Frankenstein Game",
                            MessageBoxButtons.OK,
                            MessageBoxIcon.Information)
        End If
    End Sub
End Class
```

Figure 8-42 Frankenstein Game application's code

Lesson C Summary

- To determine the length of a string:

  Use the string's Length property.
- To access one or more characters in a string:

  Use the Substring method.
- To use pattern-matching to compare two strings:

  Use the Like operator.
- To remove a specified number of characters located anywhere in a string:

  Use the Remove method.
- To insert characters anywhere in a string:

  Use the Insert method.
- To determine whether a specific character is contained in a string:

  Use the Contains method.

Lesson C Key Terms

There are no key terms in Lesson C.

Lesson C Review Questions

1. The `strName` variable contains 10 characters. Which of the following For clauses will access each character contained in the variable, character by character?

   a. `For intIndex As Integer = 0 To 10`

   b. `For intIndex As Integer = 1 To 10`

   c. `For intIndex As Integer = 0 To strName.Length - 1`

   d. `For intIndex As Integer = 1 To strName.Length - 1`

2. Which of the following changes the contents of the `strName` variable from Tam to Tammy?

   a. `strName = strName.Append(4, "my")`

   b. `strName = strName.Append(3, "my")`

   c. `strName = strName.Insert(4, "my")`

   d. `strName = strName.Insert(3, "my")`

3. If the `strWord` variable contains the string "Irene Turner", what value will the `strWord.Contains("t")` method return?

   a. True

   b. False

   c. 6

   d. 7

4. The `strItem` variable contains uppercase letters only. Which of the following determines whether the variable contains either the word "SHIRT" or the word "SKIRT"?

   a. `If strItem Like "S[HK]IRT" Then`

   b. `If strItem Like "S[H-K]IRT" Then`

   c. `If strItem = "S[HK]IRT" Then`

   d. `If strItem = "SHIRT" AndAlso strItem = "SKIRT" Then`

5. Which of the following returns the Boolean value True when the `strPetName` variable contains the string "Micki"?

   a. `strPetName.Contains("k")`

   b. `strPetName Like "M*"`

   c. `strPetName.Substring(2, 1) = "c"`

   d. all of the above

Lesson C Exercises

INTRODUCTORY

1. Open the Item Number Solution (Item Number Solution.sln) file contained in the VB2012\Chap08\Item Number Solution folder. If necessary, open the designer window. Open the Code Editor window. The btnVerify_Click procedure should determine whether the item number was entered in the required format: three digits, a hyphen, a letter, a hyphen, and two digits. Display an appropriate message indicating whether the format is correct or incorrect. Code the procedure. Save the solution and then start and test the application. Close the Code Editor window and then close the solution.

INTRODUCTORY

2. Open the Color Solution (Color Solution.sln) file contained in the VB2012\Chap08\Color Solution folder. If necessary, open the designer window. The Display Color button's Click event procedure should display the color of the item whose item number is entered by the user. All item numbers contain exactly seven characters. All items are available in four colors: blue, green, red, and white. The fourth character in the item number indicates the item's color, as follows: a B or b indicates Blue, a G or g indicates Green, an R or r indicates Red, and a W or w indicates White. If the item number does not contain exactly seven characters, or if the fourth character is not one of the valid color characters, the procedure should display an appropriate message. Code the procedure. Save the solution and then start and test the application. Close the Code Editor window and then close the solution.

INTERMEDIATE

3. In this exercise, you modify the Frankenstein Game application completed in Lesson C. Use Windows to make a copy of the Frankenstein Solution folder. Rename the copy Modified Frankenstein Solution. Open the Frankenstein Solution (Frankenstein Solution.sln) file contained in the Modified Frankenstein Solution folder. Open the designer and Code Editor windows. Modify the code to allow player 1 to enter a word that contains any number of letters, up to a maximum of 10 letters. Save the solution and then start and test the application. Close the Code Editor window and then close the solution.

INTERMEDIATE

4. Open the Reverse Letters Solution (Reverse Letters Solution.sln) file contained in the VB2012\Chap08\Reverse Letters Solution folder. The interface provides a text box for the user to enter a word. The Reverse Letters button's Click event procedure should display the letters in reverse order. In other words, if the user enters the word "Programming", the procedure should display "gnimmargorP". Code the procedure. Save the solution and then start and test the application. Close the Code Editor window and then close the solution.

INTERMEDIATE

5. Open the Proper Case Solution (Proper Case Solution.sln) file contained in the VB2012\Chap08\Proper Case Solution folder. The interface provides a text box for the user to enter a person's first and last names. The Proper Case button's Click event procedure should display the first and last names in the proper case. In other words, the first and last names should begin with an uppercase letter and the remaining letters should be lowercase. Code the procedure. Save the solution and then start and test the application. Close the Code Editor window and then close the solution.

INTERMEDIATE

6. Open the Part Number Solution (Part Number Solution.sln) file contained in the VB2012\Chap08\Part Number Solution folder. The interface allows the user to enter a part number, which should consist of two numbers followed by either one or two letters. The letter(s) represent the delivery method, as follows: MS represents Mail – Standard, MP represents Mail – Priority, FS represents FedEx – Standard, FO represents FedEx – Overnight, and U represents UPS. Code the Select Delivery button's Click event procedure so that it uses the Like operator to select the appropriate delivery method in the list box. Display an appropriate message when the part number does not contain two numbers followed by one or two letters, or when the letters do not represent a valid delivery method. Save the solution and then start the application. Test the application using the following data: 73mp, 34fs, 12u, 78h, 9FO, 88FO, and 34ms. Close the Code Editor window and then close the solution.

INTERMEDIATE

7. Before completing this exercise, you should complete Lesson A's Discovery Exercise 16. Open the Jacobson Solution (Jacobson Solution.sln) file contained in the VB2012\Chap08\Jacobson Solution folder. The interface provides a text box for entering a password. The password can contain five, six, or seven characters; however, none of the characters can be a space. The Display New Password button should create and display a new password using the following three rules. First, replace all vowels (A, E, I, O, and U) with the letter X. Second, replace all numbers with the letter Z. Third, reverse the

characters in the password. Code the procedure. Save the solution and then start and test the application. Close the Code Editor window and then close the solution.

ADVANCED

8. Each salesperson at Huntington Motors is assigned an ID number that consists of four characters. The first character is either the number 1 or the number 2. A 1 indicates that the salesperson sells new cars, and a 2 indicates that the salesperson sells used cars. The middle two characters are the salesperson's initials, and the last character is either the letter F or the letter P. The letter F indicates that the salesperson is a full-time employee. The letter P indicates that he or she is a part-time employee. Create a Visual Basic Windows application. Use the following names for the solution and project, respectively: Huntington Solution and Huntington Project. Save the application in the VB2012\Chap08 folder. Change the form file's name to Main Form.vb. Change the form's name to frmMain. Create the interface shown in Figure 8-43. The car image in the picture box is contained in the VB2012\Chap08\Car.png file. (The image was downloaded from the Open Clip Art Library at *http://openclipart.org*.) Make the Calculate button the default button. The application should allow the sales manager to enter the ID and number of cars sold for as many salespeople as needed. The application should calculate and display the total number of cars sold by each of the following four categories of employees: full-time employees, part-time employees, employees selling new cars, and employees selling used cars. Code the application. Save the solution and then start and test the application. Close the Code Editor window and then close the solution.

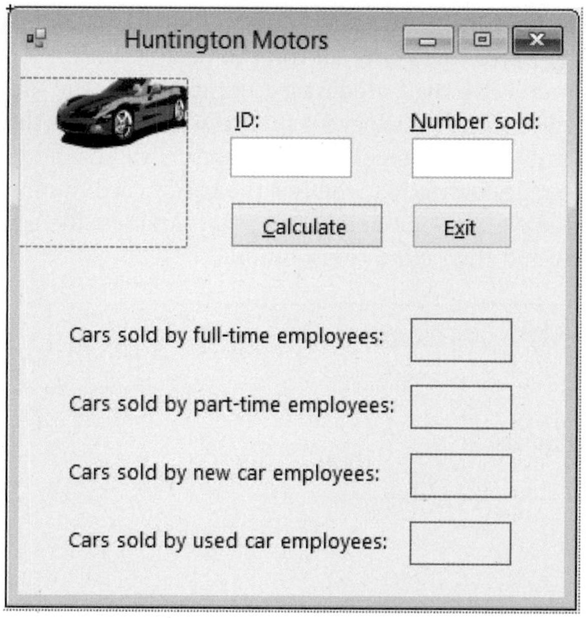

Figure 8-43 Sample interface for Exercise 8

OpenClipArt.org/yves_guillou

ADVANCED

9. Create a Visual Basic Windows application. Use the following names for the solution and project, respectively: Pig Latin Solution and Pig Latin Project. Save the application in the VB2012\Chap08 folder. Change the form file's name to Main Form.vb. Change the form's name to frmMain. Create an interface that allows the user to enter a word. The application should display the word in pig latin form. The rules for converting a word into pig latin form are shown in Figure 8-44. Code the application. Save the solution and then start and test the application. Close the Code Editor window and then close the solution.

1. If the word begins with a vowel (A, E, I, O, or U), then add the string "-way" (a dash followed by the letters w, a, and y) to the end of the word. For example, the pig latin form of the word "ant" is "ant-way".
2. If the word does not begin with a vowel, first add a dash to the end of the word. Then continue moving the first character in the word to the end of the word until the first character is the letter A, E, I, O, U, or Y. Then add the string "ay" to the end of the word. For example, the pig latin form of the word "Chair" is "air-Chay".
3. If the word does not contain the letter A, E, I, O, U, or Y, then add the string "-way" to the end of the word. For example, the pig latin form of "56" is "56-way".

Figure 8-44 Pig latin rules for Exercise 9

ADVANCED

10. Credit card companies typically assign a special digit, called a check digit, to the end of each customer's credit card number. Many methods for creating the check digit have been developed. One simple method is to multiply every other digit in the credit card number by two. You then add the products to the remaining digits to get the total. Finally, you take the last digit in the total and append it to the end of the credit card number, as illustrated in Figure 8-45. Create a Visual Basic Windows application. Use the following names for the solution and project, respectively: Georgetown Solution and Georgetown Project. Save the application in the VB2012\Chap08 folder. Change the form file's name to Main Form.vb. Change the form's name to frmMain. Create the interface shown in Figure 8-46. Make the Verify button the default button. The interface allows the user to enter a five-digit credit card number, with the fifth digit being the check digit. The Verify button's Click event procedure should use the method illustrated in Figure 8-45 to verify that the credit card number is valid. The procedure should display appropriate messages indicating whether the credit card number is valid or invalid. Code the procedure. Save the solution and then start and test the application. Close the Code Editor window and then close the solution.

<u>Check Digit Algorithm</u>

First four digits in credit card number:	1	3	5	7	
Step 1: Multiply the second and fourth digits by 2:		*2		*2	
Result ⟶	1	6	5	14	
Step 2: Add the numbers together:	1 +	6 +	5 +	14	= 26
Step 3: Take the last digit in the sum and append it to the first four digits, resulting in the final credit card number:					13576

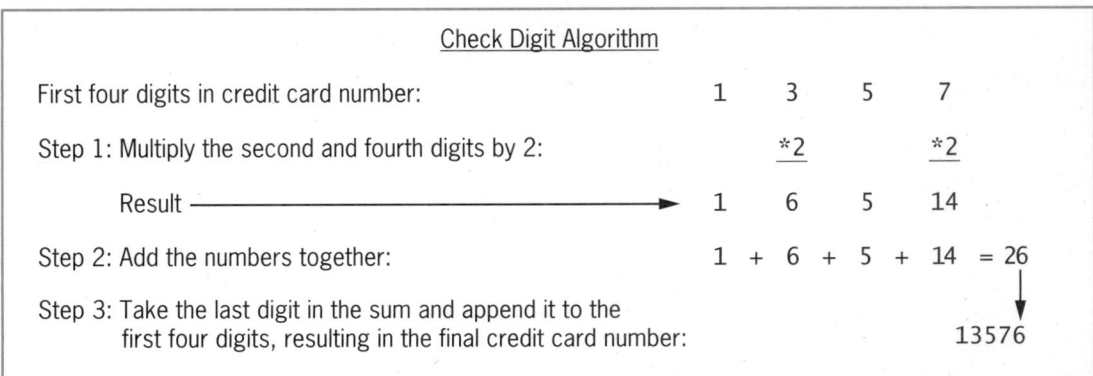

Figure 8-45 Illustration of a check digit algorithm

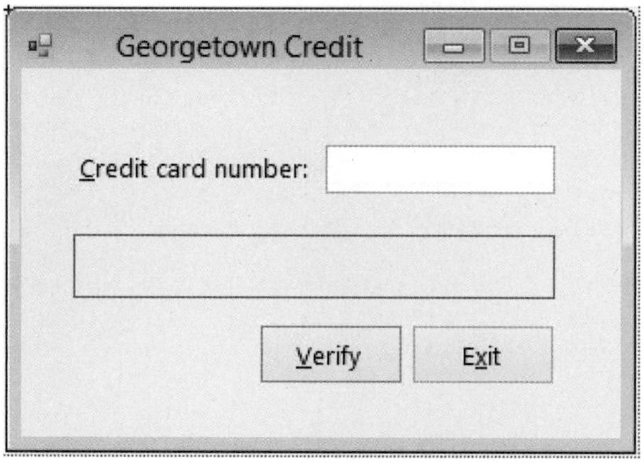

Figure 8-46 Sample interface for Exercise 10

11. Open the Count Solution (Count Solution.sln) file contained in the VB2012\Chap08\ Count Solution folder. If necessary, open the designer window. The interface allows the user to enter a string. Code the Search button's Click event procedure so that it prompts the user to enter the sequence of characters for which he or she wants to search. The procedure should determine the number of times the sequence of characters appears in the string. Use the IndexOf method to search the string for the sequence of characters. Save the solution and then start the application. Enter the string "The weather is beautiful!" (without the quotes) and then click the Search button. Search for the two characters "ea" (without the quotes). The two characters appear twice in the string. On your own, test the application using other data. Close the Code Editor window and then close the solution. ADVANCED

12. Open the Debug Solution (Debug Solution.sln) file contained in the VB2012\Chap08\ Debug Solution 1 folder. If necessary, open the designer window. Open the Code Editor window and review the existing code. Start and then test the application. Notice that the application is not working correctly. Correct the application's code. Save the solution and then start and test the application again. Close the Code Editor window and then close the solution. SWAT THE BUGS

13. Open the Debug Solution (Debug Solution.sln) file contained in the VB2012\Chap08\ Debug Solution 2 folder. If necessary, open the designer window. Open the Code Editor window and review the existing code. Start and then test the application. Notice that the application is not working correctly. Correct the application's code. Save the solution and then start and test the application again. Close the Code Editor window and then close the solution. SWAT THE BUGS

14. Open the Debug Solution (Debug Solution.sln) file contained in the VB2012\Chap08\ Debug Solution 3 folder. If necessary, open the designer window. Open the Code Editor window and review the existing code. Start and then test the application. Notice that the application is not working correctly. Correct the application's code. Save the solution and then start and test the application again. Close the Code Editor window and then close the solution. SWAT THE BUGS

CHAPTER 9

Arrays

Coding the Die Tracker Application

In this chapter, you will code an application that simulates the rolling of a die. The application will display the number of times a die face appears.

Previewing the Die Tracker Application

Before you start the first lesson in this chapter, you will preview the completed application. The application is contained in the VB2012\Chap09 folder.

START HERE

To preview the completed application:

1. Use the Run dialog box to run the Die Tracker (Die Tracker.exe) file contained in the VB2012\Chap09 folder. The application's user interface appears on the screen. (The image in the picture box was downloaded from the Open Clip Art Library at *http://openclipart.org*.)
2. Click the **Roll** button. A die face appears in the picRandDie control and its associated counter label contains the number 1. See Figure 9-1. Because the Roll button's Click event procedure uses random numbers, your die face and counter label may be different from those shown in the figure.

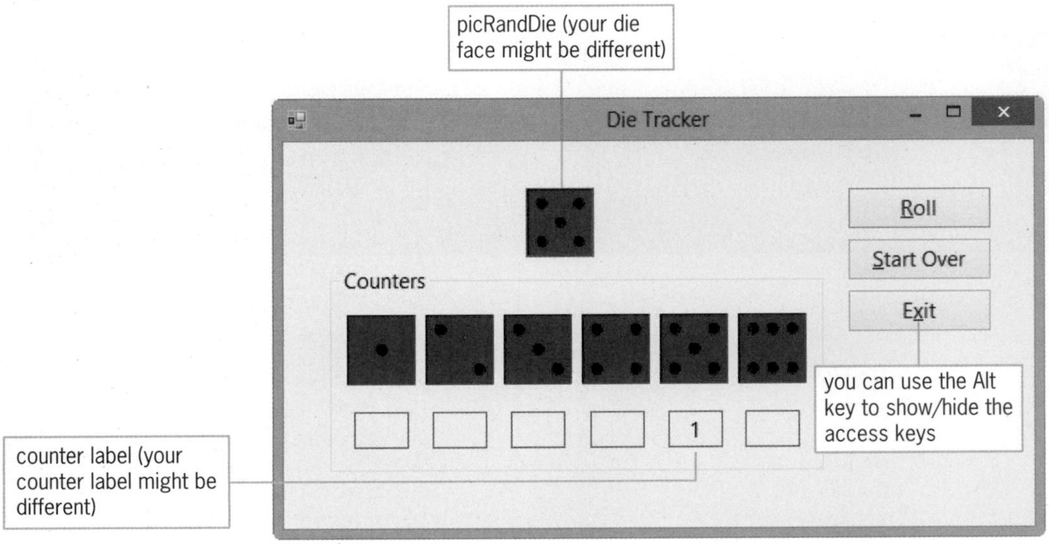

Figure 9-1 Result of clicking the Roll button the first time
OpenClipArt.org/orsonj

3. Click the **Roll** button several more times. Each time you click the Roll button, a die face appears in the picRandDie control and its associated counter label is updated by 1.
4. Now, click the **Start Over** button and then click the **Roll** button. A die face appears in the picRandDie control and its associated counter label contains the number 1.
5. Click the **Exit** button.

Before you can begin coding the Die Tracker application, you need to learn about arrays. One-dimensional arrays are covered in Lessons A and B. Lesson C covers two-dimensional arrays. You will code the Die Tracker application in Lesson B. Be sure to complete each lesson in full and do all of the end-of-lesson questions and several exercises before continuing to the next lesson.

LESSON A

After studying Lesson A, you should be able to:

- Declare and initialize a one-dimensional array
- Store data in a one-dimensional array
- Determine the number of array elements and the highest subscript
- Traverse a one-dimensional array
- Code a loop using the For Each...Next statement
- Compute the total and average of a one-dimensional array's contents
- Find the highest value in a one-dimensional array
- Sort a one-dimensional array

Arrays

All of the variables you have used so far have been simple variables. A **simple variable**, also called a **scalar variable**, is one that is unrelated to any other variable in memory. At times, however, you will encounter situations in which some of the variables *are* related to each other. In those cases, it is easier and more efficient to treat the related variables as a group.

You already are familiar with the concept of grouping. The clothes in your closet are probably separated into groups, such as coats, sweaters, shirts, and so on. Grouping your clothes in this manner allows you to easily locate your favorite sweater because you just need to look through the sweater group rather than through the entire closet. You also probably have your CD (compact disc) collection grouped by either music type or artist. If your collection is grouped by artist, it will take only a few seconds to find all of your Maroon 5 CDs and, depending on the number of Maroon 5 CDs you own, only a short time after that to locate a particular CD.

When you group together related variables, the group is referred to as an array of variables or, more simply, an **array**. You might use an array of 50 variables to store the population of each U.S. state. Or, you might use an array of eight variables to store the sales made in each of your company's eight sales regions. Storing data in an array increases the efficiency of a program because data can be both stored in and retrieved from the computer's internal memory much faster than it can be written to and read from a file on a disk. In addition, after the data is entered into an array, which typically is done at the beginning of a program, the program can use the data as many times as necessary without having to enter the data again. Your company's sales program, for example, can use the sales amounts stored in an array to calculate the total company sales and the percentage that each region contributed to the total sales. It also can use the sales amounts in the array either to calculate the average sales amount or to simply display the sales made in a specific region. As you will learn in this lesson, the variables in an array can be used just like any other variables. You can assign values to them, use them in calculations, display their contents, and so on.

The most commonly used arrays in business applications are one-dimensional and two-dimensional. You will learn about one-dimensional arrays in this lesson and in Lesson B. Two-dimensional arrays are covered in Lesson C. Arrays having more than two dimensions are beyond the scope of this book.

At this point, it is important to point out that arrays are one of the more challenging topics for beginning programmers. Therefore, it is important for you to read and study each section in each lesson thoroughly before moving on to the next section. If you still feel overwhelmed at the end of a lesson, try reading the lesson again, paying particular attention to the examples and procedures shown in the figures.

One-Dimensional Arrays

The variables in an array are stored in consecutive locations in the computer's internal memory. Each variable in an array has the same name and data type. You distinguish one variable in a **one-dimensional array** from another variable in the same array using a unique number. The unique number, which is always an integer, is called a subscript. The **subscript** indicates the variable's position in the array and is assigned by the computer when the array is created in internal memory. The first variable in a one-dimensional array is assigned a subscript of 0, the second a subscript of 1, and so on.

A subscript is also called an index.

You refer to each variable in an array by the array's name and the variable's subscript, which is specified in a set of parentheses immediately following the array name. Figure 9-2 illustrates a one-dimensional array named `strMaroon` that contains three variables. You use `strMaroon(0)`—read "`strMaroon` sub zero"—to refer to the first variable in the array. You use `strMaroon(1)` to refer to the second variable in the array, and use `strMaroon(2)` to refer to the third (and last) variable in the array. The last subscript in an array is always one number less than the total number of variables in the array; this is because array subscripts in Visual Basic (and in many other programming languages) start at 0.

Figure 9-2 Illustration of the one-dimensional `strMaroon` array
Image by Diane Zak; Created with Reallusion CrazyTalk Animator

Declaring a One-Dimensional Array

Before you can use an array in a program, you first must declare (create) it. Figure 9-3 shows two versions of the syntax for declaring a one-dimensional array in Visual Basic. The {Dim | Private | Static} portion in each version indicates that you can select only one of the keywords appearing within the braces. The appropriate keyword depends on whether you are creating a procedure-level array or a class-level array. *ArrayName* is the name of the array, and *dataType* is the type of data the array variables, referred to as **elements**, will store. In syntax Version 1, *highestSubscript* is an integer that specifies the highest subscript in the array. Because the first element in a one-dimensional array has a subscript of 0, the array will contain one element more than the number specified in the highestSubscript argument. In other words, an array whose highest subscript is 2 will contain 3 elements. In syntax Version 2, *initialValues* is a comma-separated list of values you want assigned to the array elements. Also included in Figure 9-3 are examples of using both versions of the syntax.

Declaring a One-Dimensional Array

Syntax – Version 1
{**Dim** | **Private** | **Static**} *arrayName*(*highestSubscript*) **As** *dataType*

Syntax – Version 2
{**Dim** | **Private** | **Static**} *arrayName*() **As** *dataType* = {*initialValues*}

Example 1
```
Dim strMaroon(2) As String
```
declares a three-element procedure-level array named `strMaroon`; each element is automatically initialized using the keyword `Nothing`

Example 2
```
Static intNumbers(4) As Integer
```
declares a static, five-element procedure-level array named `intNumbers`; each element is automatically initialized to 0

Example 3
```
Dim strStates() As String = {"Alaska", "Colorado",
                             "Ohio", "Florida"}
```
declares and initializes a four-element procedure-level array named `strStates`

Example 4
```
Private dblPays() As Double = {13.55, 9.65,
                               8.5, 9.75, 4.5}
```
declares and initializes a five-element class-level array named `dblPays`

Figure 9-3 Syntax versions and examples of declaring a one-dimensional array

Like class-level variables, class-level arrays are declared in the form's Declarations section.

When you use syntax Version 1, the computer automatically initializes each array element when the array is created. If the array's data type is String, each element is initialized using the keyword `Nothing`. As you learned in Chapter 3, variables initialized to `Nothing` do not actually contain the word "Nothing"; rather, they contain no data at all. Elements in a numeric array are initialized to the number 0, and elements in a Boolean array are initialized using the Boolean keyword `False`. Date array elements are initialized to 12:00 AM January 1, 0001.

Rather than having the computer use a default value to initialize each array element, you can use syntax Version 2 to specify each element's initial value when the array is declared. Assigning initial values to an array is often referred to as **populating the array**. You list the initial values in the initialValues section of the syntax, using commas to separate the values, and you enclose the list of values in braces ({}).

Notice that syntax Version 2 does not include the highestSubscript argument; instead, an empty set of parentheses follows the array name. The computer automatically calculates the highest subscript based on the number of values listed in the initialValues section. Because the first subscript in a one-dimensional array is the number 0, the highest subscript is always one number less than the number of values listed in the initialValues section. The Dim statement in Example 3 in Figure 9-3, for instance, creates a four-element array with subscripts of 0, 1, 2, and 3. Similarly, the Private statement in Example 4 creates a five-element array with subscripts of 0, 1, 2, 3, and 4. The arrays are initialized as shown in Figure 9-4.

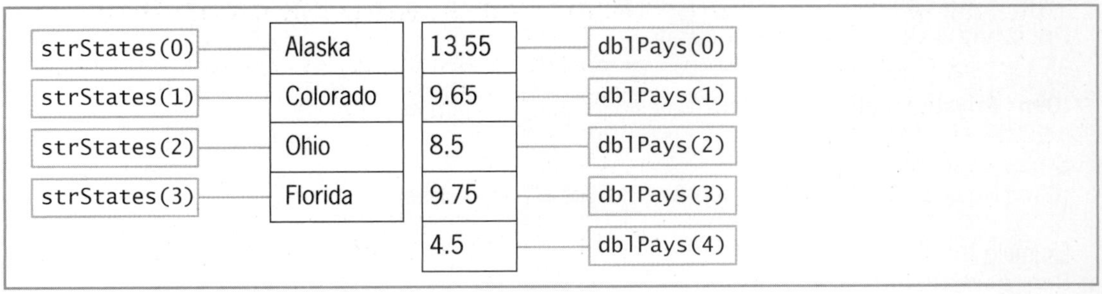

Figure 9-4 Illustration of the `strStates` and `dblPays` arrays

Storing Data in a One-Dimensional Array

After an array is declared, you can use another statement to store a different value in an array element. Examples of such statements include assignment statements and statements that contain the TryParse method. Figure 9-5 shows examples of both types of statements.

Storing Data in a One-Dimensional Array

Example 1

```
strStates(0) = "Kentucky"
```

assigns the string "Kentucky" to the first element in the `strStates` array

Example 2

```
For intX As Integer = 1 To 5
    intNumbers(intX - 1) = intX * intX
Next intX
```

assigns the squares of the numbers from 1 through 5 to the `intNumbers` array

Example 3

```
Dim intSub As Integer
Do While intSub < 5
    intNumbers(intSub) = 100
    intSub += 1
Loop
```

assigns the number 100 to each element in the `intNumbers` array

Example 4

```
dblPays(1) = dblPays(1) * .1
```

multiplies the contents of the second element in the `dblPays` array by .1 and then assigns the result to the element; you also can write this statement as `dblPays(1) *= .1`

Example 5

```
Double.TryParse(txtPay.Text, dblPays(2))
```

assigns either the value entered in the txtPay control (converted to Double) or the number 0 to the third element in the `dblPays` array

Figure 9-5 Examples of statements used to store data in a one-dimensional array

4. Next, you will fill the lstStates control with values. Enter the lines of code shown in either Example 1 or Example 2 in Figure 9-8.

5. Now you will select the first item in the list box. Insert a blank line above the End Sub clause and then enter the following assignment statement:

   lstStates.SelectedIndex = 0

6. Save the solution and then start the application. The form's Load event procedure is processed first. The procedure creates and initializes the `strStates` array. The first time the procedure's loop is processed, the `intSub` variable contains the number 0. Therefore, the Add method in the loop adds the contents of the `strStates(0)` element (Alaska) to the lstStates control. The loop then increases the `intSub` variable's value by 1, giving 1. When the loop is processed the second time, the Add method in the loop adds the contents of the `strStates(1)` element (Colorado) to the lstStates control, and so on. The loop instructions will be repeated for each element in the `strStates` array. The loop stops when the `intSub` variable contains the number 4, which is one number more than the highest subscript in the array. The statement you entered in Step 5 invokes the list box's SelectedValueChanged event procedure. The procedure displays the selected item in the You selected box, as shown in Figure 9-9.

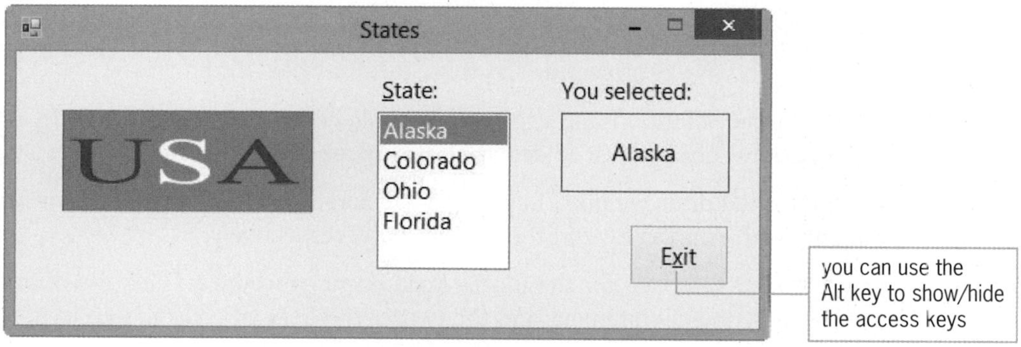

Figure 9-9 Sample run of the States application

7. Click **Ohio** in the list box. Ohio appears in the You selected box.

8. Click the **Exit** button. Close the Code Editor window and then close the solution.

As you learned in Chapter 6, the Visual Basic language provides three statements for coding a loop. You already know how to use the Do...Loop and For...Next statements. You will learn about the For Each...Next statement in the next section.

The For Each...Next Statement

Visual Basic's **For Each...Next statement** provides a convenient way of coding a loop whose instructions you want processed for each element in a group, such as for each variable in an array. An advantage of using the For Each...Next statement to process an array is that your code does not need to keep track of the array subscripts or even know the number of array elements. However, unlike the loop instructions in a Do...Loop or For...Next statement, the instructions in a For Each...Next statement can only read the array values; they cannot permanently modify the values.

Figure 9-10 shows the For Each...Next statement's syntax. The *elementVariableName* that appears in the For Each and Next clauses is the name of a variable that the computer can use to keep track of each element in the *group*. The variable's data type is specified in the `As` *dataType* portion of the For Each clause and must be the same as the group's data type. A variable declared in the For Each clause has block scope and is recognized only by the instructions within the For Each...Next loop. You enter the loop body, which contains the instructions you want the computer to repeat, between the For Each and Next clauses. The example in Figure 9-10 shows how to write the loops from Figure 9-8 using the For Each...Next statement.

Although you do not need to specify the *elementVariableName* in the Next clause, doing so is highly recommended because it makes your code more self-documenting.

You learned about block scope in Chapter 4.

For Each...Next Statement

Syntax
For Each *elementVariableName* **As** *dataType* **In** *group*
    loop body instructions
Next *elementVariableName*

Example
```
For Each strStateElement As String In strStates
     lstStates.Items.Add(strStateElement)
Next strStateElement
```

Figure 9-10 Syntax and an example of the For Each...Next statement

START HERE

To use the For Each...Next statement in the States application:

1. Open the States Solution (States Solution.sln) file contained in the VB2012\Chap09\States Solution-ForEachNext folder. If necessary, open the designer window.
2. Open the Code Editor window. Replace <your name> and <current date> in the comments with your name and the current date, respectively.
3. Locate the code template for the form's Load event procedure. Click the **blank line** above the assignment statement and then enter the lines of code shown in the example in Figure 9-10.
4. Save the solution and then start the application. The four state names appear in the list box, as shown earlier in Figure 9-9. Click **each state name**, one at a time, to verify that the application works correctly.
5. Click the **Exit** button. Close the Code Editor window and then close the solution.

YOU DO IT 2!

Create a Visual Basic Windows application named YouDoIt 2. Save the application in the VB2012\Chap09 folder. Add a button to the form. The button's Click event procedure should declare and initialize a one-dimensional String array. Use any four names to initialize the array. The procedure should display the contents of the array three times: first using the For Each...Next statement, then using the Do...Loop statement, and then using the For...Next statement. Display the array contents in message boxes. (Hint: The procedure will display 12 message boxes.) Code the procedure. Save the solution and then start and test the application. Close the solution.

Calculating the Total and Average Values

Figure 9-11 shows the problem specification for the Brewers Coffee application. The application displays the total number of pounds of coffee sold during a six-month period and the average number of pounds sold each month.

Problem Specification

The store manager at Brewers Coffee wants an application that displays the total number of pounds of coffee sold during a six-month period and the average number of pounds sold each month. Last year, the monthly amounts were as follows: 170.5, 224, 190.5, 193, 250.5, and 236. The application should store the monthly amounts in a six-element one-dimensional array. It then should calculate and display the two output items. The total number of pounds sold is calculated by accumulating the array values. The average number of pounds sold each month is calculated by dividing the total number of pounds sold by the number of array elements.

Figure 9-11 Problem specification for the Brewers Coffee application

To begin coding the Brewers Coffee application:

START HERE

1. Open the Brewers Solution (Brewers Solution.sln) file contained in the VB2012\Chap09\Brewers Solution folder. If necessary, open the designer window. (The image in the picture box was downloaded from the Open Clip Art Library at *http://openclipart.org*.)
2. Open the Code Editor window. Replace <your name> and <current date> in the comments with your name and the current date, respectively.
3. Locate the btnCalc_Click procedure. First, you will declare a one-dimensional array to store the amounts sold during the six-month period. Click the **blank line** above the End Sub clause. Enter the following Dim statement:

   ```
   Dim dblPoundsPerMonth() As Double = {170.5, 224,
                                        190.5, 193,
                                        250.5, 236}
   ```

4. Next, you will declare the variables that will store the total number of pounds sold and the average number of pounds sold. Enter the following Dim statements:

   ```
   Dim dblTotal As Double
   Dim dblAvg As Double
   ```

Figure 9-12 shows three examples of code you could use to accumulate the values stored in the array. In each example, a loop is used to add each array element's value to the `dblTotal` variable. Notice that you need to specify the highest array subscript in the Do...Loop and For...Next statements, but not in the For Each...Next statement. The Do...Loop and For...Next statements must also keep track of the array subscripts; this task is not necessary in the For Each...Next statement. When each loop has finished processing, the `dblTotal` variable contains the total number of pounds sold during the six-month period.

Example 1—Do...Loop statement
```
Dim intHighSub As Integer =
     dblPoundsPerMonth.GetUpperBound(0)
Dim intSub As Integer

' accumulate pounds sold
Do While intSub <= intHighSub
    dblTotal += dblPoundsPerMonth(intSub)
    intSub += 1
Loop
```

Example 2—For...Next statement
```
Dim intHighSub As Integer =
     dblPoundsPerMonth.GetUpperBound(0)

' accumulate pounds sold
For intSub As Integer = 0 To intHighSub
    dblTotal += dblPoundsPerMonth(intSub)
Next intSub
```

Example 3—For Each...Next statement
```
' accumulate pounds sold
For Each dblMonth As Double In dblPoundsPerMonth
    dblTotal += dblMonth
Next dblMonth
```

Figure 9-12 Examples of accumulating the array values

START HERE

To finish coding the Brewers Coffee application:

1. In the btnCalc_Click procedure, enter the comment and code shown in any of the three examples from Figure 9-12.
2. Next, you will calculate the average sold by dividing the value stored in the `dblTotal` variable by the number of array elements. Insert a blank line above the End Sub clause and then enter the following comment and assignment statement:

   ' calculate average
   dblAvg = dblTotal / dblPoundsPerMonth.Length
3. Finally, you can display the total and average numbers of pounds sold. Enter the following comment and assignment statements:

   ' display total and average
   lblTotal.Text = dblTotal.ToString("N2")
   lblAvg.Text = dblAvg.ToString("N2")
4. Save the solution and then start the application. Click the **Calculate** button. See Figure 9-13.

Ch09A video

Figure 9-13 Total and average amounts shown in the interface
OpenClipArt.org/speciwoman

5. Click the **Exit** button. Close the Code Editor window and then close the solution.

YOU DO IT 3!

Create a Visual Basic Windows application named YouDoIt 3. Save the application in the VB2012\Chap09 folder. Add three labels and a button to the form. The button's Click event procedure should declare and initialize a one-dimensional Integer array. Use any five integers to initialize the array. The procedure should total the five integers and then display the result in the labels. Use the Do...Loop statement to calculate the total to display in the first label. Use the For Each...Next statement to calculate the total to display in the second label. Use the For...Next statement to calculate the total to display in the third label. Code the procedure. Save the solution and then start and test the application. Close the solution.

Finding the Highest Value

Figure 9-14 shows the problem specification for the Car Emporium application. The application displays the highest commission amount earned during the month and the number of salespeople who earned that amount.

Problem Specification

The sales manager at Car Emporium wants an application that displays the highest commission earned during the month and the number of salespeople who earned that commission. Last month, the 10 salespeople were paid the following commission amounts: 2500, 3400, 1000, 3400, 2500, 1000, 2850, 3000, 2780, and 1890. The application should store the commission amounts in a 10-element one-dimensional array and then examine each element in the array, looking for the highest amount. The application will need to use a counter variable to keep track of the number of salespeople who were paid the highest commission.

Figure 9-14 Problem specification for the Car Emporium application

START HERE

To open the Car Emporium application:

1. Open the Car Emporium Solution (Car Emporium Solution.sln) file contained in the VB2012\Chap09\Car Emporium Solution folder. If necessary, open the designer window. (The image in the picture box was downloaded from the Open Clip Art Library at *http://openclipart.org.*)
2. Open the Code Editor window. Replace <your name> and <current date> in the comments with your name and the current date, respectively.
3. Locate the btnGet_Click procedure. The procedure already contains the statement to declare and initialize the 10-element array. It also contains the statements to display the two output items.

Figure 9-15 shows the pseudocode and flowchart for the btnGet_Click procedure. The procedure is responsible for determining the highest commission amount stored in the array and the number of salespeople who were paid that amount. You will code the procedure's loop using the For...Next statement; however, you also could use the For Each...Next or Do...Loop statements.

```
btnGet Click event procedure
1. assign the commission stored in the first array element as the highest commission
2. set the number of salespeople counter to 1
3. repeat for each element in the array
       if the commission stored in the current element is equal to the highest commission
              add 1 to the number of salespeople counter
       else
              if the commission stored in the current element is greater than the highest
              commission
                     assign the current element's commission as the highest commission
                     set the number of salespeople counter to 1
              end if
       end if
   end repeat
4. display the highest commission and the number of salespeople who were paid the highest
   commission
```

Figure 9-15 Pseudocode and flowchart for the btnGet_Click procedure *(continues)*

(continued)

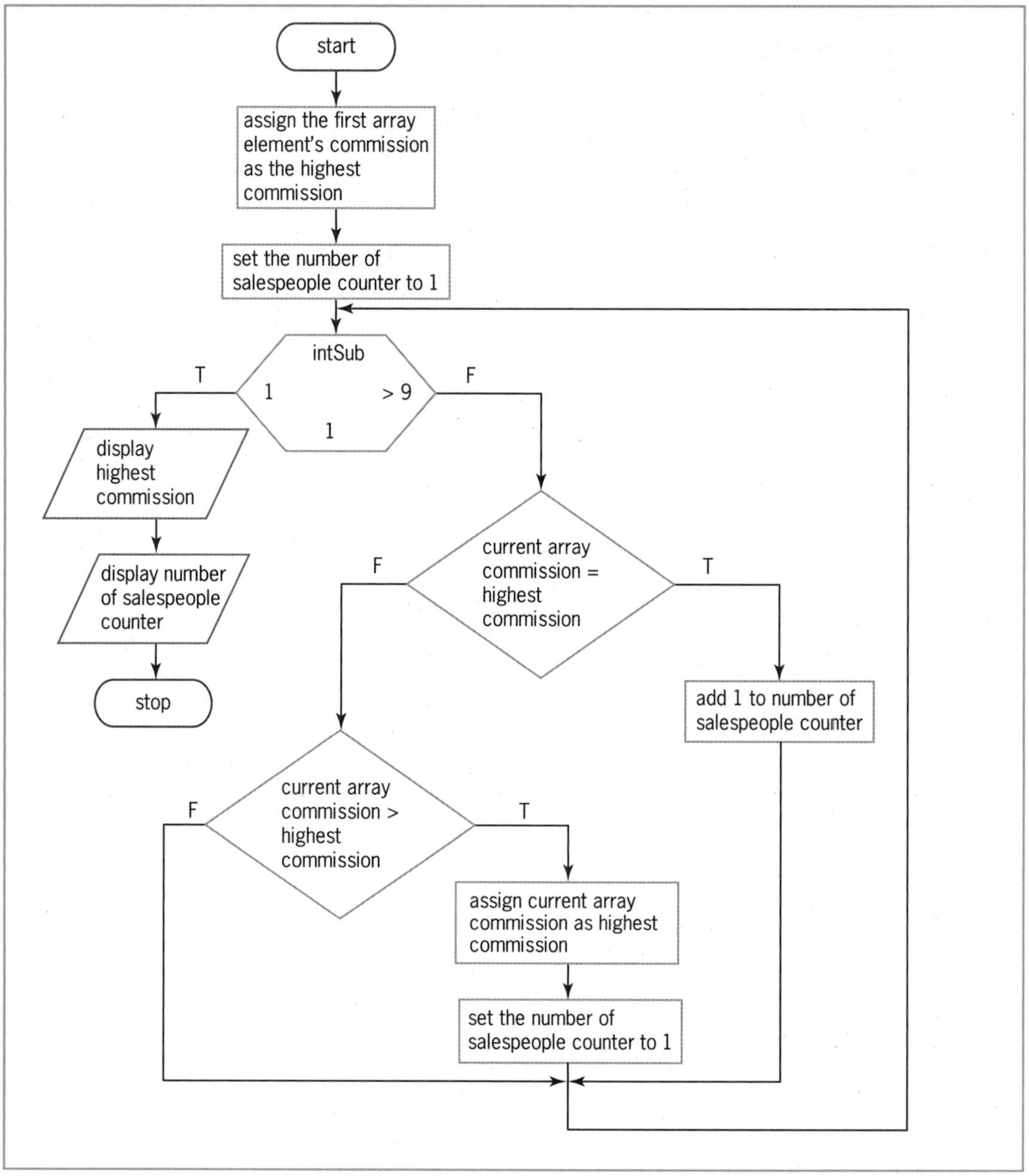

Figure 9-15 Pseudocode and flowchart for the btnGet_Click procedure

To code and then test the btnGet_Click procedure:

START HERE

1. First, you will declare a variable named `intLastSub` and initialize it to the last subscript in the array. The `intLastSub` variable will be used by the For...Next statement to traverse the array. Click the **blank line** below the array declaration statement and then enter the following Dim statement:

   Dim intLastSub As Integer =
   intCommissions.GetUpperBound(0)

2. The procedure will use a variable named `intHighest` to keep track of the highest commission amount in the array. When searching an array for the highest (or lowest) value, it's a common programming practice to initialize the variable to the value stored in the first array element. Enter the following Dim statement:

   Dim intHighest As Integer = intCommissions(0)

3. Next, you will declare and initialize a counter variable to keep track of the number of salespeople whose commission amount matches the value stored in the `intHighest` variable. You will initialize the variable to 1 because, at this point, one salesperson (the first one) was paid the commission amount currently stored in the `intHighest` variable. Type the following Dim statement and then press **Enter** twice:

   Dim intSalespeople As Integer = 1

4. Now you will use the For...Next statement to traverse the second through the last elements in the array. Each element's value will be compared, one at a time, to the value stored in the `intHighest` variable. You don't need to look at the first element because its value is already contained in the `intHighest` variable. Enter the following For clause:

   For intSub As Integer = 1 To intLastSub

5. Change the `Next` clause to **Next intSub**.

6. The first instruction in the loop will determine whether the commission stored in the current array element is equal to the commission stored in the `intHighest` variable. Click the **blank line** below the For clause and then enter the following If clause:

   If intCommissions(intSub) = intHighest Then

7. If both commission amounts are equal, the selection structure's true path will add 1 to the `intSalespeople` counter variable. Enter the following assignment statement:

   intSalespeople += 1

8. If both commission amounts are not equal, the selection structure's false path will determine whether the commission stored in the current array element is greater than the commission stored in the `intHighest` variable. Enter the following Else and If clauses:

   Else
   If intCommissions(intSub) > intHighest Then

9. If the commission in the current array element is greater than the commission in the `intHighest` variable, the nested selection structure's true path should assign the higher value to the `intHighest` variable. It also should reset the number of salespeople counter to 1 because, at this point, only one salesperson was paid that commission amount. Enter the following assignment statements:

   intHighest = intCommissions(intSub)
   intSalespeople = 1

10. If necessary, delete the blank line above the nested End If clause. Save the solution and then start the application. Click the **Get Highest** button. See Figure 9-16.

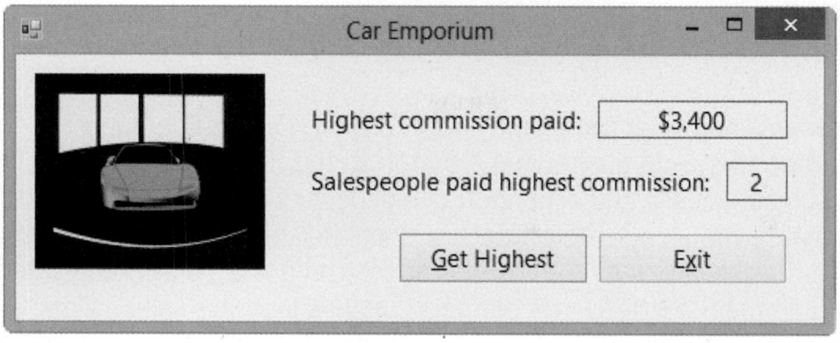

Figure 9-16 Sample run of the Car Emporium application
OpenClipArt.org/majkel

11. Click the **Exit** button. Close the Code Editor window and then close the solution.

Figure 9-17 shows the code entered in the Get Highest button's Click event procedure.

```
Private Sub btnGet_Click(sender As Object,
e As EventArgs) Handles btnGet.Click
    ' displays the highest commission and the
    ' number who were paid that amount

     Dim intCommissions() As Integer = {2500, 3400, 1000,
                                        3400, 2500, 1000,
                                        2850, 3000, 2780, 1890}
     Dim intLastSub As Integer =
         intCommissions.GetUpperBound(0)
     Dim intHighest As Integer = intCommissions(0)
     Dim intSalespeople As Integer = 1

     For intSub As Integer = 1 To intLastSub
         If intCommissions(intSub) = intHighest Then
             intSalespeople += 1
         Else
             If intCommissions(intSub) > intHighest Then
                 intHighest = intCommissions(intSub)
                 intSalespeople = 1
             End If
         End If
     Next intSub
     lblHighest.Text = intHighest.ToString("C0")
     lblSalespeople.Text = intSalespeople.ToString
End Sub
```

assigns the first element's value and the number 1 to the appropriate variables

searches the second through the last array elements

Figure 9-17 Get Highest button's Click event procedure

YOU DO IT 4!

Create a Visual Basic Windows application named YouDoIt 4. Save the application in the VB2012\Chap09 folder. Add a label and a button to the form. The button's Click event procedure should declare and initialize a one-dimensional Double array. Use any six numbers to initialize the array. The procedure should display (in the label) the lowest value stored in the array. Code the procedure using the For...Next statement. Save the solution and then start and test the application. Close the solution.

Sorting a One-Dimensional Array

In some applications, you might need to arrange the contents of an array in either ascending or descending order. Arranging data in a specific order is called **sorting**. When an array is sorted in ascending order, the first element in the array contains the smallest value and the last element contains the largest value. When an array is sorted in descending order, on the other hand, the first element contains the largest value and the last element contains the smallest value.

You can use the **Array.Sort method** to sort the values in a one-dimensional array in ascending order. To sort the values in descending order, you first use the Array.Sort method to sort the values in ascending order, and then use the **Array.Reverse method** to reverse the values. Figure 9-18 shows the syntax of both methods. In each syntax, *arrayName* is the name of a one-dimensional array.

Array.Sort and Array.Reverse Methods

Syntax
Array.Sort(*arrayName***)**
Array.Reverse(*arrayName***)**

Example 1
```
Dim intScores() As Integer = {78, 90, 75, 83}
Array.Sort(intScores)
```
sorts the contents of the array in ascending order, as follows: 75, 78, 83, and 90

Example 2
```
Dim intScores() As Integer = {78, 90, 75, 83}
Array.Reverse(intScores)
```
reverses the contents of the array, placing the values in the following order: 83, 75, 90, and 78

Example 3
```
Dim intScores() As Integer = {78, 90, 75, 83}
Array.Sort(intScores)
Array.Reverse(intScores)
```
sorts the contents of the array in ascending order and then reverses the contents, placing the values in descending order as follows: 90, 83, 78, and 75

Figure 9-18 Syntax and examples of the Array.Sort and Array.Reverse methods

You will use the Array.Sort and Array.Reverse methods in the Continent application, which you finish coding in the next set of steps. The application stores the names of the seven continents in a one-dimensional array named `strContinents`. It then allows the user to display the names in a list box, in either ascending or descending order.

To open the Continent application:

START HERE

1. Open the Continent Solution (Continent Solution.sln) file contained in the VB2012\Chap09\Continent Solution folder. If necessary, open the designer window. (The image in the picture box was downloaded from the Open Clip Art Library at *http://openclipart.org*.)
2. Open the Code Editor window. Replace <your name> and <current date> in the comments with your name and the current date, respectively.

As shown in Figure 9-19, the form's Declarations section contains the statements to declare and initialize the `strContinents` array and the `intLastSub` variable, which stores the highest subscript in the array. The array and variable were declared as class-level memory locations because both need to be accessed by more than one procedure. To complete the application, you need to code the btnAscending_Click and btnDescending_Click procedures.

```
Public Class frmMain

    ' class-level array and variable
    Private strContinents() As String = {"North America", "Africa",
                                         "South America", "Antarctica",
                                         "Australia", "Asia", "Europe"}
    Private intLastSub As Integer = strContinents.GetUpperBound(0)
```

Figure 9-19 Private statements in the form's Declarations section

To code both Click event procedures:

START HERE

1. Locate the btnAscending_Click procedure. The `lstContinents.Items.Clear()` statement in the procedure clears the contents of the list box. Click the **blank line** below the `' sort and display` comment and then enter the following code:

   Array.Sort(strContinents)
   For intSub As Integer = 0 To intLastSub
   lstContinents.Items.Add(strContinents(intSub))
   Next intSub

2. Next, locate the btnDescending_Click procedure. Here, too, the `lstContinents.Items.Clear()` statement clears the contents of the list box. Click the **blank line** below the `' sort and display` comment and then enter the following code:

   Array.Sort(strContinents)
   Array.Reverse(strContinents)
   For intSub As Integer = 0 To intLastSub
   lstContinents.Items.Add(strContinents(intSub))
   Next intSub

Figure 9-20 shows most of the Continent application's code. The Array.Sort and Array.Reverse methods are shaded in the figure.

class-level array and variable declared in the form's Declarations section

```
' class-level array and variable
Private strContinents() As String = {"North America", "Africa",
                                    "South America", "Antarctica",
                                    "Australia", "Asia", "Europe"}
Private intLastSub As Integer = strContinents.GetUpperBound(0)

Private Sub btnAscending_Click(sender As Object,
e As EventArgs) Handles btnAscending.Click
    ' sorts the array values in ascending order

    ' clear the contents of the list box
    lstContinents.Items.Clear()

    ' sort and display
    Array.Sort(strContinents)
    For intSub As Integer = 0 To intLastSub
        lstContinents.Items.Add(strContinents(intSub))
    Next intSub
End Sub

Private Sub btnDescending_Click(sender As Object,
e As EventArgs) Handles btnDescending.Click
    ' sorts the array values in descending order

    ' clear the contents of the list box
    lstContinents.Items.Clear()

    ' sort and display
    Array.Sort(strContinents)
    Array.Reverse(strContinents)
    For intSub As Integer = 0 To intLastSub
        lstContinents.Items.Add(strContinents(intSub))
    Next intSub
End Sub
```

Figure 9-20 Most of the Continent application's code

START HERE

To test the Continent application:

1. Save the solution and then start the application. Click the **Ascending Order** button to display the continent names in ascending order. See Figure 9-21. (The list box's Enabled property is set to False.)

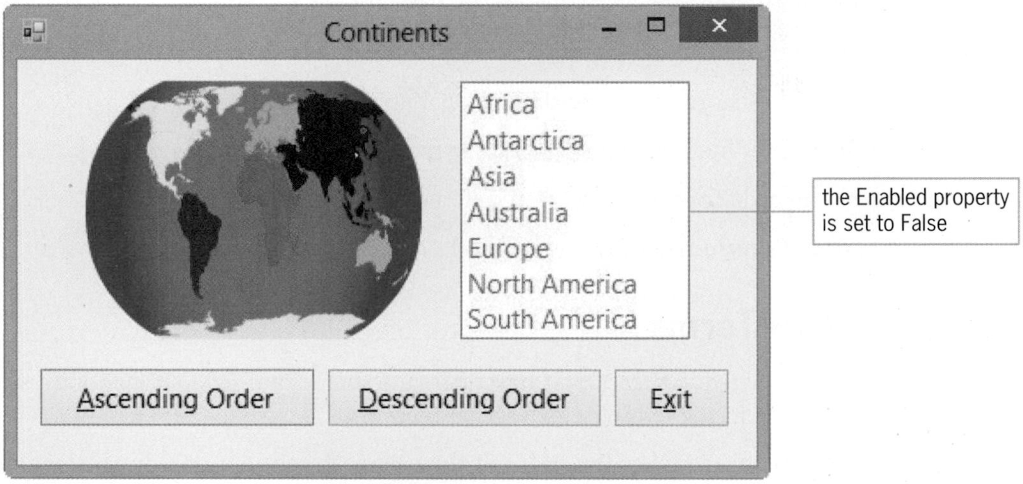

Figure 9-21 Continent names displayed in ascending order
OpenClipArt.org/lyo

2. Click the **Descending Order** button to display the continent names in descending order.
3. Click the **Exit** button. Close the Code Editor window and then close the solution.

Lesson A Summary

- To refer to an element in a one-dimensional array:

  Use the array's name followed by the element's subscript. The subscript is specified in a set of parentheses immediately following the array name.

- To declare a one-dimensional array:

  Use either of the syntax versions shown below. The *highestSubscript* argument in Version 1 is an integer that specifies the highest subscript in the array. Using Version 1's syntax, the computer automatically initializes the array elements. The *initialValues* section in Version 2 is a list of values separated by commas and enclosed in braces. The values are used to initialize each element in the array.

  Version 1: {**Dim** | **Private** | **Static**} *arrayName*(*highestSubscript*) **As** *dataType*

  Version 2: {**Dim** | **Private** | **Static**} *arrayName*() **As** *dataType* = {*initialValues*}

- To determine the number of elements in a one-dimensional array:

  Use the array's Length property as follows: *arrayName*.**Length**. Alternatively, you can add the number 1 to the value returned by the array's GetUpperBound method.

- To determine the highest subscript in a one-dimensional array:

  Use the array's GetUpperBound method as follows: *arrayName*.**GetUpperBound(0)**. Alternatively, you can subtract the number 1 from the value stored in the array's Length property.

- To traverse (or look at) each element in a one-dimensional array:

  Use a loop coded with one of the following statements: Do...Loop, For...Next, or For Each...Next.

- To process instructions for each element in a group:

  Use the For Each...Next statement. The statement's syntax is shown in Figure 9-10.
- To sort the values stored in a one-dimensional array in ascending order:

  Use the Array.Sort method. The method's syntax is **Array.Sort(*arrayName*)**.

- To reverse the order of the values stored in a one-dimensional array:

  Use the Array.Reverse method. The method's syntax is **Array.Reverse(*arrayName*)**.

Lesson A Key Terms

Array—a group of related variables that have the same name and data type and are stored in consecutive locations in the computer's internal memory

Array.Reverse method—reverses the order of the values stored in a one-dimensional array

Array.Sort method—sorts the values stored in a one-dimensional array in ascending order

Elements—the variables in an array

For Each...Next statement—used to code a loop whose instructions you want processed for each element in a group

GetUpperBound method—returns an integer that represents the highest subscript in a specified dimension of an array; when used with a one-dimensional array, the dimension is 0

Length property—one of the properties of an array; stores an integer that represents the number of array elements

One-dimensional array—an array whose elements are identified by a unique subscript

Populating the array—refers to the process of initializing the elements in an array

Scalar variable—another name for a simple variable

Simple variable—a variable that is unrelated to any other variable in the computer's internal memory; also called a scalar variable

Sorting—the process of arranging data in a specific order

Subscript—a unique integer that identifies the position of an element in an array

Lesson A Review Questions

1. Which of the following declares a five-element one-dimensional array?

   a. `Dim dblAmounts(4) As Double`

   b. `Dim dblAmounts(5) As Double`

   c. `Dim dblAmounts(4) As Double =`
      `{3.55, 6.70, 8, 4, 2.34}`

   d. both a and c

2. The `strItems` array is declared as follows: `Dim strItems(20) As String`. The `intSub` variable keeps track of the array subscripts and is initialized to 0. Which of the following Do clauses will process the loop instructions for each element in the array?

   a. `Do While intSub > 20`

   b. `Do While intSub < 20`

   c. `Do While intSub >= 20`

   d. `Do While intSub <= 20`

3. The `intSales` array is declared as follows: `Dim intSales() As Integer = {10000, 12000, 900, 500, 20000}`. The statement `intSales(3) = intSales(3) + 10` will ________________.

   a. replace the 500 amount with 10
   b. replace the 500 amount with 510
   c. replace the 900 amount with 10
   d. replace the 900 amount with 910

4. The `intSales` array is declared as follows: `Dim intSales() As Integer = {10000, 12000, 900, 500, 20000}`. Which of the following loops will correctly add 100 to each array element? The `intSub` variable contains the number 0 before the loop is processed.

   a.
   ```
   Do While intSub <= 4
     intSub = intSub + 100
   Loop
   ```
   b.
   ```
   Do While intSub <= 4
     intSales = intSales + 100
   Loop
   ```
   c.
   ```
   Do While intSub < 5
     intSales(intSub) += 100
   Loop
   ```
   d. none of the above

5. The `intNums` array is declared as follows: `Dim intNums() As Integer = {10, 5, 7, 2}`. Which of the following blocks of code correctly calculates the average value stored in the array? The `intTotal`, `intSub`, and `dblAvg` variables contain the number 0 before the loop is processed.

   a.
   ```
   Do While intSub < 4
     intNums(intSub) = intTotal + intTotal
     intSub += 1
   Loop
   dblAvg = intTotal / intSub
   ```
   b.
   ```
   Do While intSub < 4
     intTotal += intNums(intSub)
     intSub = intSub + 1
   Loop
   dblAvg = intTotal / intSub
   ```
   c.
   ```
   Do While intSub < 4
     intTotal += intNums(intSub)
     intSub += 1
   Loop
   dblAvg = intTotal / intSub - 1
   ```
   d.
   ```
   Do While intSub < 4
     intTotal = intTotal + intNums(intSub)
     intSub = intSub + 1
   Loop
   dblAvg = intTotal / (intSub - 1)
   ```

6. What will the code in Review Question 5's answer a assign to the `dblAvg` variable?
   a. 0
   b. 5
   c. 6
   d. 8

7. What will the code in Review Question 5's answer b assign to the `dblAvg` variable?
   a. 0
   b. 5
   c. 6
   d. 8

8. What will the code in Review Question 5's answer c assign to the `dblAvg` variable?
   a. 0
   b. 5
   c. 6
   d. 8

9. What will the code in Review Question 5's answer d assign to the `dblAvg` variable?
   a. 0
   b. 5
   c. 6
   d. 8

10. Which of the following statements sorts the `intQuantities` array in ascending order?
    a. `Array.Sort(intQuantities)`
    b. `intQuantities.Sort`
    c. `Sort(intQuantities)`
    d. `SortArray(intQuantities)`

11. Which of the following statements assigns (to the `intElements` variable) the number of elements contained in the `intNums` array?
    a. `intElements = Len(intNums)`
    b. `intElements = Length(intNums)`
    c. `intElements = intNums.Len`
    d. `intElements = intNums.Length`

12. Which of the following assigns the string "Rover" to the fifth element in a one-dimensional array named `strPetNames`?
    a. `strPetNames(4) = "Rover"`
    b. `strPetNames[4] = "Rover"`
    c. `strPetNames(5) = "Rover"`
    d. `strPetNames.Items.Add(5) = "Rover"`

13. Which of the following assigns the number 1 to each element in a five-element, one-dimensional Integer array named `intCounters`?

    a.
    ```
    For intSub As Integer = 0 To 4
           intCounters(intSub) = 1
    Next intSub
    ```

    b.
    ```
    Dim intSub As Integer
    Do While intSub < 5
           intCounters(intSub) = 1
           intSub += 1
    Loop
    ```

    c.
    ```
    For intSub As Integer = 1 To 5
           intCounters(intSub - 1) = 1
    Next intSub
    ```

    d. all of the above

14. The `intNums` array is declared as follows: `Dim intNums() As Integer = {10, 5, 7, 2}`. Which of the following blocks of code correctly calculates the average value stored in the array? The `intTotal`, `intSub`, and `dblAvg` variables contain the number 0 before the loop is processed.

    a.
    ```
    For Each intX As Integer In intNums
      intTotal += intX
    Next intX
    dblAvg = intTotal / intNums.Length
    ```

    b.
    ```
    For Each intX As Integer In intNums
      intTotal += intNums(intX)
    Next intX
    dblAvg = intTotal / intX
    ```

    c.
    ```
    For Each intX As Integer In intNums
      intTotal += intNums(intX)
      intX += 1
    Next intX
    dblAvg = intTotal / intX
    ```

    d. none of the above

15. Which of the following statements assigns the `strNames` array's highest subscript to the `intLastSub` variable?

    a. `intLastSub = strNames.Length`

    b. `intLastSub = strNames.GetUpperBound(0) - 1`

    c. `intLastSub = strNames.GetUpperBound(0)`

    d. both a and b

Lesson A Exercises

1. Write the statement to declare a procedure-level one-dimensional array named `intQuantities`. The array should be able to store 15 integers. Then write the statement to store the number 10 in the second element. INTRODUCTORY

2. Write the statement to declare a class-level one-dimensional array named `strFurniture`. The array should be able to store 5 strings. Then write the statement to store the string "Chair" in the third element. INTRODUCTORY

3. Write the statement to declare and initialize a procedure-level one-dimensional array named `dblRates`. Use the following numbers to initialize the array: 5.6, 7.5, and 3.4. INTRODUCTORY

INTRODUCTORY

4. In this exercise, you modify the Car Emporium application coded in the lesson. Use Windows to make a copy of the Car Emporium Solution folder. Rename the copy Modified Car Emporium Solution-DoLoop. Open the Car Emporium Solution (Car Emporium Solution.sln) file contained in the Car Emporium Solution-DoLoop folder. Open the designer window. Modify the btnGet_Click procedure to use the Do...Loop statement rather than the For...Next statement. Save the solution and then start and test the application. Close the Code Editor window and then close the solution.

INTRODUCTORY

5. In this exercise, you modify the Car Emporium application coded in the lesson. Use Windows to make a copy of the Car Emporium Solution folder. Rename the copy Modified Car Emporium Solution-ForEachNext. Open the Car Emporium Solution (Car Emporium Solution.sln) file contained in the Car Emporium Solution-ForEachNext folder. Open the designer window. Modify the btnGet_Click procedure to use the For Each...Next statement rather than the For...Next statement. Save the solution and then start and test the application. Close the Code Editor window and then close the solution.

INTRODUCTORY

6. Open the Chocolate Solution (Chocolate Solution.sln) file contained in the VB2012\Chap09\Chocolate Solution folder. If necessary, open the designer window. Open the Code Editor window.

   a. Enter the statement to declare and initialize a class-level one-dimensional array named `dblPounds`. Use the following numbers to initialize the array: 35.6, 15, 67.9, 78.8, 2.5, and 7.

   b. The btnForNext_Click procedure should display the contents of the `dblPounds` array in the lstPounds control. Use the For...Next statement to code the procedure. Save the solution and then start the application. Test the procedure.

   c. The btnForEachNext_Click procedure should display the contents of the `dblPounds` array in the lstPounds control. Use the For Each...Next statement to code the procedure. Save the solution and then start the application. Test the procedure.

   d. The btnDoLoop_Click procedure should display the contents of the `dblPounds` array in the lstPounds control. Use the Do...Loop statement to code the procedure. Save the solution and then start the application. Test the procedure.

   e. The btnAscend_Click procedure should sort the `dblPounds` array in ascending order. Save the solution and then start the application. Click the Ascending Sort button, and then click the For...Next button.

   f. The btnDescend_Click procedure should sort the `dblPounds` array in descending order. Save the solution and then start the application. Click the Descending Sort button, and then click the Do...Loop button. Close the Code Editor window and then close the solution.

INTRODUCTORY

7. Open the Tips Solution (Tips Solution.sln) file contained in the VB2012\Chap09\Tips Solution folder. If necessary, open the designer window. Open the Code Editor window.

   a. Enter the statement to declare and initialize a class-level one-dimensional array named `intTips`. Use the following numbers to initialize the array: 101, 95, 67, and 83.

   b. The btnForNext_Click procedure should display the average tip. Use the For...Next statement to code the procedure. Save the solution and then start the application. Test the procedure.

c. The btnForEachNext_Click procedure should display the average tip. Use the For Each...Next statement to code the procedure. Save the solution and then start the application. Test the procedure.

d. The btnDoLoop_Click procedure should display the average tip. Use the Do...Loop statement to code the procedure. Save the solution and then start the application. Test the procedure. Close the Code Editor window and then close the solution.

8. In this exercise, you modify the Car Emporium application coded in the lesson. Use Windows to make a copy of the Car Emporium Solution folder. Rename the copy Modified Car Emporium Solution. Open the Car Emporium Solution (Car Emporium Solution.sln) file contained in the Modified Car Emporium Solution folder. Open the designer window. In addition to displaying the highest commission amount and the number of salespeople who were paid the highest amount, the btnGet_Click procedure should display the lowest commission amount and the number of salespeople who were paid the lowest amount. Make the appropriate modifications to the interface and code. Save the solution and then start and test the application. Close the Code Editor window and then close the solution. INTRODUCTORY

9. Open the Sales Solution (Sales Solution.sln) file contained in the VB2012\Chap09\Sales Solution folder. If necessary, open the designer window. The interface allows the user to enter a sales amount. The application should display the number of salespeople selling at least that amount. Open the Code Editor window. The sales amounts are stored in the `intSales` array. Finish coding the application. Save the solution and then start and test the application. Close the Code Editor window and then close the solution. INTERMEDIATE

10. Write the code to multiply by 3 the number stored in the first element in a one-dimensional array named `intNumbers`. Store the result in the `intResult` variable. INTERMEDIATE

11. Write the code to add together the numbers stored in the first and second elements in a one-dimensional array named `intNumbers`. Display the sum in the lblSum control. INTERMEDIATE

12. Open the Quantity Solution (Quantity Solution.sln) file contained in the VB2012\Chap09\Quantity Solution folder. If necessary, open the designer window. Open the Code Editor window. The btnAdd_Click procedure should add the number 1 to each element in the `intQuantities` array and also display the array's contents in the lstQuantities control; use the Do...Loop statement. The btnSubtract_Click procedure should subtract the number 1 from each element in the `intQuantities` array and also display the array's contents in the lstQuantities control; use the For...Next statement. Save the solution and then start and test the application. Close the Code Editor window and then close the solution. INTERMEDIATE

13. Open the Test Scores Solution (Test Scores Solution.sln) file contained in the VB2012\Chap09\Test Scores Solution folder. If necessary, open the designer window. The Average button's Click event procedure should display the number of test scores contained in the one-dimensional array and also the average test score. Code the procedure. Save the solution and then start and test the application. Close the Code Editor window and then close the solution. INTERMEDIATE

14. Open the Update Prices Solution (Update Prices Solution.sln) file contained in the VB2012\Chap09\Update Prices Solution folder. If necessary, open the designer window. The Increase Prices button's Click event procedure should ask the user for a percentage amount by which each price stored in the array should be increased. It then should increase each price by that amount, displaying each increased price (right-aligned with two decimal places) in the list box. (Hint: You can clear the contents of a list box using the Items collection's Clear method.) Save the solution and then start the application. Click the Increase Prices button. Increase each price by 5%. Close the Code Editor window and then close the solution. INTERMEDIATE

ADVANCED

15. In this exercise, you modify the application from Exercise 14. The modified application allows the user to update a specific price. Use Windows to make a copy of the Update Prices Solution folder. Rename the folder Modified Update Prices Solution. Open the Update Prices Solution (Update Prices Solution.sln) file contained in the Modified Update Prices Solution folder. Open the designer window. Modify the Increase Prices button's Click event procedure so it also asks the user to enter a number from 1 through 10. If the user enters the number 1, the procedure should update the first price in the array. If the user enters the number 2, the procedure should update the second price in the array, and so on. Save the solution and then start the application. Click the Increase Prices button. Increase the second price by 10%. Click the Increase Prices button again. This time, increase the tenth price by 5%. (The second price in the list box should still reflect the 10% increase.) Close the Code Editor window and then close the solution.

ADVANCED

16. Open the Scores Solution (Scores Solution.sln) file contained in the VB2012\Chap09\Scores Solution folder. If necessary, open the designer window. Open the Code Editor window and then open the code template for the btnDisplay control's Click event procedure. Declare a 20-element, one-dimensional Integer array named `intScores`. Assign the following 20 numbers to the array: 88, 72, 99, 20, 66, 95, 99, 100, 72, 88, 78, 45, 57, 89, 85, 78, 75, 88, 72, and 88. The procedure should prompt the user to enter a score from 0 through 100. It then should display (in a message box) the number of students who earned that score. Code the procedure. Save the solution and then start the application. Use the application to answer the following questions, and then close the Code Editor window and the solution:

    How many students earned a score of 72?

    How many students earned a score of 88?

    How many students earned a score of 20?

    How many students earned a score of 99?

ADVANCED

17. In this exercise, you modify the application from Exercise 16. The modified application allows the user to display the number of students earning a score within a specific range. Use Windows to make a copy of the Scores Solution folder. Rename the folder Modified Scores Solution. Open the Scores Solution (Scores Solution.sln) file contained in the Modified Scores Solution folder. Open the designer and Code Editor windows. Modify the btnDisplay control's Click event procedure to prompt the user to enter both a minimum score and a maximum score. The procedure then should display (in a message box) the number of students who earned a score within that range. Save the solution and then start the application. Use the application to answer the following questions, and then close the Code Editor window and the solution:

    How many students earned a score from 70 through 79?

    How many students earned a score from 65 through 85?

    How many students earned a score from 0 through 50?

ADVANCED

18. In this exercise, you code an application that generates and displays six unique random numbers for a lottery game. Each lottery number can range from 1 through 54 only. Open the Lottery Game Solution (Lottery Game Solution.sln) file contained in the VB2012\Chap09\Lottery Game Solution folder. If necessary, open the designer window. (The image in the picture box was downloaded from the Open Clip Art Library at *http://openclipart.org*.) Code the Display Lottery Numbers button's Click event procedure so that it displays six unique random numbers in the interface. (Hint: Store the numbers in a one-dimensional array.) Save the solution and then start the

application. Click the Display Lottery Numbers button several times. Each time you click the button, six unique random numbers between 1 and 54 (inclusive) should appear in the interface. Close the Code Editor window and then close the solution.

19. In this exercise, you learn about the ReDim statement.

DISCOVERY

a. Research the Visual Basic ReDim statement. What is the purpose of the statement? What is the purpose of the `Preserve` keyword?

b. Open the ReDim Solution (ReDim Solution.sln) file contained in the VB2012\Chap09\ReDim Solution folder. If necessary, open the designer window. Open the Code Editor window and locate the btnDisplay control's Click event procedure. Study the existing code, and then modify the procedure so that it stores any number of sales amounts in the `intSales` array. (Hint: Declare the array using empty sets of parentheses and braces. Use the ReDim statement to add an element to the array.)

c. Save the solution and then start the application. Click the Display Sales button and then enter the following sales amounts, one at a time: 700, 550, and 800. Click the Cancel button in the input box. The three sales amounts should appear in the list box.

d. Click the Display Sales button again and then enter the following sales amounts, one at a time: 5, 9, 45, 67, 8, and 0. Click the Cancel button in the input box. This time, six sales amounts should appear in the list box. Close the Code Editor window and then close the solution.

LESSON B

After studying Lesson B, you should be able to:

- Associate a list box with a one-dimensional array
- Use a one-dimensional array as an accumulator or a counter
- Explain the relationship between the elements in parallel one-dimensional arrays
- Create parallel one-dimensional arrays
- Locate information in two parallel one-dimensional arrays

Arrays and Collections

Recall that the items in a list box belong to the Items collection.

It's not uncommon for programmers to associate the items in a list box with the values stored in an array. This is because the items in a list box belong to a collection, and collections and arrays have several things in common. First, each is a group of individual objects treated as one unit. Second, each individual object in the group is identified by a unique number. The unique number is called an index when referring to a collection, but a subscript when referring to an array. Third, both the first index in a collection and the first subscript in an array are 0. These commonalities allow you to associate the list box items and array elements by their positions within their respective groups. In other words, you can associate the first item in a list box with the first element in an array, the second item with the second element, and so on.

To associate a list box with an array, you first add the appropriate items to the list box. You then store each item's related value in its corresponding position in the array. You will use a list box and a one-dimensional array in the Rose Performing Arts Center application, which you code next. Figure 9-22 shows the application's problem specification.

Problem Specification

The manager at Rose Performing Arts Center wants an application that displays the price of a ticket. The price is based on the seating section, as shown here. The application's interface should provide a list box from which the user can select the seating section. The application should store the prices in a four-element one-dimensional array, and then use the index of the selected list box item to access the appropriate price from the array.

Section	Price ($)
A	103.00
B	95.00
C	75.50
D	32.50

Figure 9-22 Problem specification for the Rose Performing Arts Center application

START HERE

To begin coding the Rose Performing Arts Center application:

1. If necessary, start Visual Studio 2012. Open the Rose Solution (Rose Solution.sln) file contained in the VB2012\Chap09\Rose Solution folder. If necessary, open the designer window. (The image in the picture box was downloaded from the Open Clip Art Library at *http://openclipart.org*.)
2. Open the Code Editor window. Replace <your name> and <current date> in the comments with your name and the current date, respectively.

3. First, you will fill the list box with values and then select the first item in the list. Open the code template for the form's Load event procedure and then enter the following lines of code:

```
lstSection.Items.Add("A")
lstSection.Items.Add("B")
lstSection.Items.Add("C")
lstSection.Items.Add("D")
lstSection.SelectedIndex = 0
```

4. As the problem specification states, the ticket prices should be stored in a one-dimensional array. You can declare the array in the btnDisplay_Click procedure, making it a procedure-level array. Or, you can declare it in the form's Declarations section, making it a class-level array. In this case, you will use a class-level array so that the array will not need to be created each time the user clicks the Display Price button. Click the **blank line** below the `Public Class frmMain` clause and then press **Enter** to insert another blank line. Enter the following array declaration statement:

```
Private dblPrices() As Double = {103, 95, 75.5, 32.5}
```

The array declaration statement initializes the first array element to 103, which is the price associated with the first item in the list box (A). The remaining array elements are initialized to the prices corresponding to their list box items. The relationship between the list box items and the array elements is illustrated in Figure 9-23.

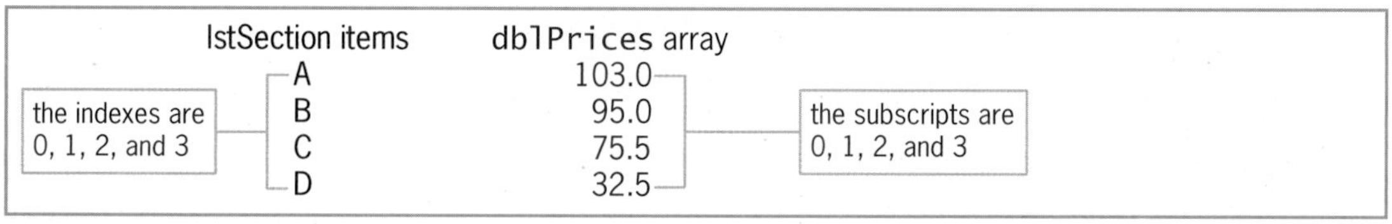

Figure 9-23 Illustration of the relationship between the list box and array

To finish coding the Rose Performing Arts Center application:

START HERE

1. When the user clicks the Display Price button, the button's Click event procedure should display the appropriate price in the Ticket price box. Open the code template for the btnDisplay_Click procedure. Enter the following comments. Press **Enter** twice after typing the second comment.

```
' displays the array price corresponding
' to the selected list box item
```

2. The procedure will use the index of the selected list box item to access the appropriate price from the `dblPrices` array. Enter the following Dim statement:

```
Dim intSub As Integer = lstSection.SelectedIndex
```

3. If the first item is selected in the list box, the Dim statement you entered in Step 2 will initialize the `intSub` variable to 0. If the second item is selected, it will initialize the variable to 1, and so on. As a result, you can use the `intSub` variable to access the appropriate price from the array. Enter the following assignment statement:

```
lblPrice.Text = dblPrices(intSub).ToString("C2")
```

Figure 9-24 shows most of the code for the Rose Performing Arts Center application.

class-level array declared in the form's Declarations section

```
Private dblPrices() As Double = {103, 95, 75.5, 32.5}

PrivateSub frmMain_Load(sender As Object,
e As EventArgs) Handles Me.Load
    lstSection.Items.Add("A")
    lstSection.Items.Add("B")
    lstSection.Items.Add("C")
    lstSection.Items.Add("D")
    lstSection.SelectedIndex = 0

End Sub

Private Sub btnDisplay_Click(sender As Object,
e As EventArgs) Handles btnDisplay.Click
    ' displays the array price corresponding
    ' to the selected list box item

    Dim intSub As Integer = lstSection.SelectedIndex
    lblPrice.Text = dblPrices(intSub).ToString("C2")
End Sub
```

uses the selected item's index as the array subscript

Figure 9-24 Most of the code for the Rose Performing Arts Center application

START HERE

To test the Rose Performing Arts Center application's code:

1. Save the solution and then start the application. Click the **Display Price** button. $103.00 appears in the Ticket price box, as shown in Figure 9-25.

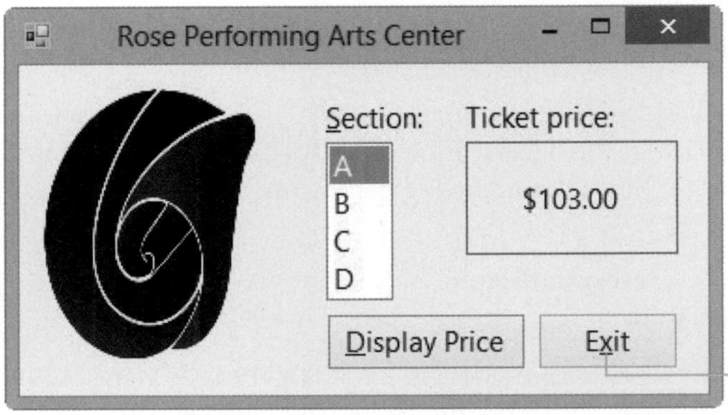

you can use the Alt key to show/hide the access keys

Figure 9-25 Ticket price displayed in the interface

OpenClipArt.org/Merlin2525

2. On your own, verify that the application displays the appropriate ticket price for the remaining list box items.
3. Click the **Exit** button.

If a new item is added to the lstSection control, the programmer will need to enter its corresponding price in the `dblPrices` array. If the programmer neglects to do so, a run time error will occur when the user selects the new item in the list and then clicks the Display Price button. This is because the button's Click event procedure will try to access a memory location that is outside the bounds of the array. Before closing the Rose Performing Arts Center application, you will observe this run time error.

To modify and then test the application's code:

START HERE

1. Click the **blank line** above the End Sub clause in the form's Load event procedure, and then enter the following statement:

   lstSection.Items.Add("E")

2. Save the solution and then start the application. Click **E** in the Section list box and then click the **Display Price** button. A run time error occurs because this seat section does not have a corresponding price in the `dblPrices` array. An arrow points to the statement where the error was encountered, and the statement is highlighted. In addition, the Error Correction window opens and provides information pertaining to the error. In this case, the information indicates that the statement is trying to access an element that is outside the bounds of the array.

3. Place your mouse pointer on `intSub` in the highlighted statement, as shown in Figure 9-26. The `intSub` variable contains the number 4, which is not a valid subscript for the `dblPrices` array. The valid subscripts are 0, 1, 2, and 3.

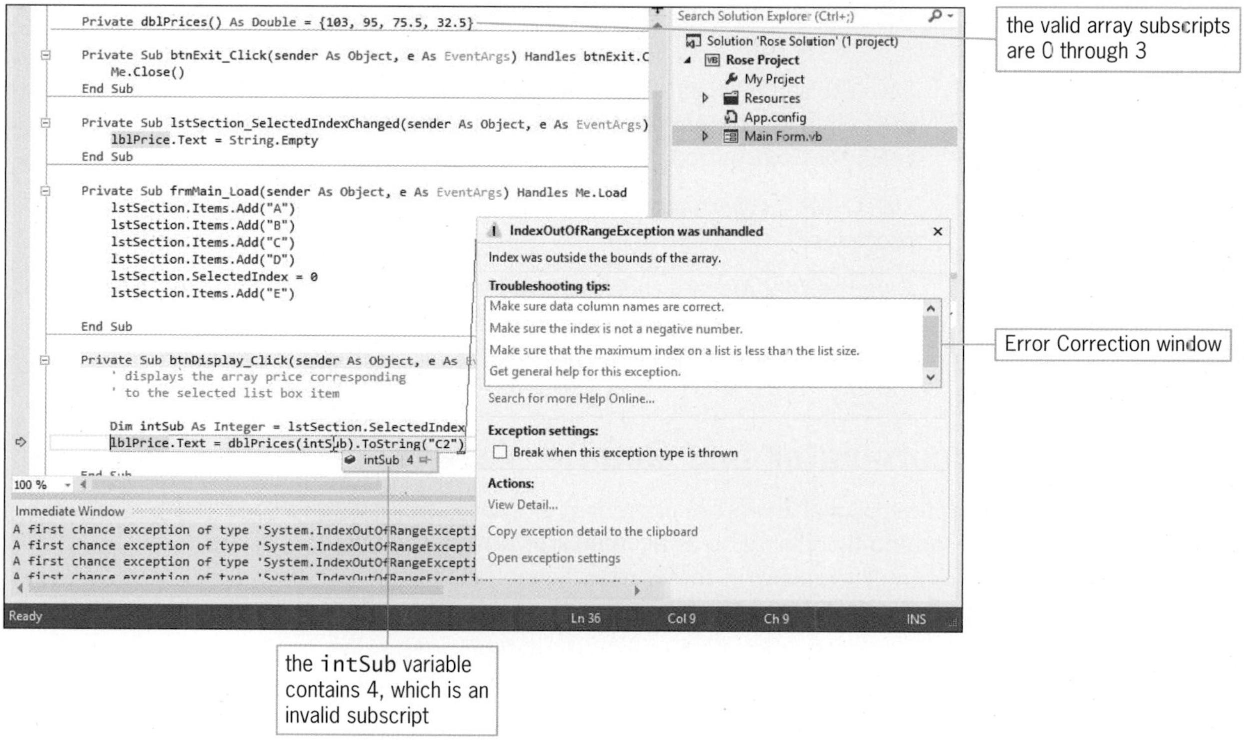

Figure 9-26 Result of the run time error caused by an invalid subscript

4. Click **DEBUG** on the menu bar and then click **Stop Debugging**.

Before accessing an individual array element, you should verify that the subscript you are using is within the acceptable range for the array. The acceptable range would be a number that is greater than or equal to 0 but less than or equal to the highest subscript in the array. In this application, the subscript will always be at least 0 because it is associated with the list box's index. Therefore, in this application, you only need to verify that the subscript is less than or equal to the highest subscript in the array.

START HERE

To continue modifying and testing the application's code:

1. Modify the btnDisplay_Click procedure by adding the selection structure shown in Figure 9-27. Be sure to move the `lblPrice.Text = dblPrices(intSub).ToString("C2")` statement into the selection structure's true path.

```
Private Sub btnDisplay_Click(sender As Object, e As Event
    ' displays the array price corresponding
    ' to the selected list box item

    Dim intSub As Integer = lstSection.SelectedIndex
    If intSub <= dblPrices.GetUpperBound(0) Then
        lblPrice.Text = dblPrices(intSub).ToString("C2")
    Else
        lblPrice.Text = "N/A"
    End If

End Sub
```

add this selection structure

Figure 9-27 Modified btnDisplay_Click procedure

2. Save the solution and then start the application. Click **E** in the Section list box and then click the **Display Price** button. This time, N/A appears in the Ticket price box. Click the **Exit** button.
3. Delete the `lstSection.Items.Add("E")` statement from the form's Load event procedure.
4. Save the solution and then start and test the application to verify that it is still working correctly.
5. Click the **Exit** button. Close the Code Editor window and then close the solution.

Accumulator and Counter Arrays

One-dimensional arrays are often used to either accumulate or count related values; such arrays are commonly referred to as **accumulator arrays** and **counter arrays**, respectively. You will use an accumulator array in the Warren School application, which you finish coding next. The application's problem specification is shown in Figure 9-28.

Problem Specification

Warren School is having its annual Chocolate Fund Raiser event. Students sell the following five types of candy: Choco Bar, Choco Bar-Peanuts, Kit Kat, Peanut Butter Cups, and Take 5 Bar. The school principal wants an application that allows her to enter the amount of each candy type sold by each student. The application's interface will provide a list box for entering the candy type, and a text box for entering the amount sold. The application will use a five-element one-dimensional array to accumulate the amounts sold. It will display the total number sold for each candy type in label controls in the interface.

Figure 9-28 Problem specification for the Warren School application

To open the Warren School application:

START HERE

1. Open the Warren Solution (Warren Solution.sln) file contained in the VB2012\Chap09\Warren Solution folder. If necessary, open the designer window. (The image in the picture box was downloaded from the Open Clip Art Library at *http://openclipart.org.*)

2. Open the Code Editor window. Replace <your name> and <current date> in the comments with your name and the current date, respectively.

The form's Load event procedure fills the list box with the five candy types and then selects the first item in the list. To complete the application, you just need to finish coding the btnAdd_Click procedure, which should accumulate the amounts sold by candy type. The procedure will accomplish its task using a one-dimensional accumulator array named `intCandies`. The array will have five elements, each corresponding to an item listed in the list box. The first array element will correspond to the Choco Bar item, the second array element to the Choco Bar-Peanuts item, and so on. Each array element will be used to accumulate the sales of its corresponding list box item.

To complete the btnAdd_Click procedure:

START HERE

1. Locate the btnAdd_Click procedure. Click the **blank line** below the `' declare array and variables` comment.
2. First, you will declare the `intCandies` array. The array will need to retain its values until the application ends. You can accomplish this by declaring the array in either the form's Declarations section (using the `Private` keyword to make it a class-level array) or in the btnAdd_Click procedure (using the `Static` keyword to make it a static procedure-level array); you will use the latter approach. Like static variables, which you learned about in Chapter 3, static arrays remain in memory and retain their values until the application ends. Enter the following declaration statement:

   Static intCandies(4) As Integer

3. The procedure will also use two Integer variables: one to store the amount sold and one to store the index of the item selected in the list box. Enter the following Dim statements. Press **Enter** twice after typing the last Dim statement.

   Dim intSold As Integer
   Dim intSub As Integer

4. Now you will convert the contents of the txtSold control to Integer and then store the result in the `intSold` variable. Enter the following TryParse method:

   Integer.TryParse(txtSold.Text, intSold)

5. Next, you will assign the index of the selected list box item to the `intSub` variable. Enter the following assignment statement:

   intSub = lstCandy.SelectedIndex

6. You will use the number stored in the `intSub` variable to update the appropriate array element, but only if the number is within the acceptable range for the array. The acceptable range is from 0 through the highest array subscript. As in the previous application, the subscript in this application will always be at least 0 because it is associated with the list box's index. Therefore, you only need to verify that the subscript is less than or equal to the highest subscript in the array. Click the **blank line** below the `' update array value` comment and then enter the following If clause and assignment statement:

If intSub <= intCandies.GetUpperBound(0) Then
intCandies(intSub) += intSold

7. If the `intSub` variable's value is not less than or equal to the highest array subscript, you will display an appropriate message. Enter the following lines of code:

Else
MessageBox.Show("Can't update this candy's sales.",
"Warren School",
MessageBoxButtons.OK,
MessageBoxIcon.Information)

8. If necessary, delete the blank line above the End If clause.
9. Finally, you will enter the code to display the array values in the interface. Click the **blank line** below the `' display array values` comment and then enter the following five assignment statements:

lblChocoBar.Text = intCandies(0).ToString
lblChocoBarPeanuts.Text = intCandies(1).ToString
lblKitKat.Text = intCandies(2).ToString
lblPeanutButCups.Text = intCandies(3).ToString
lblTake5Bar.Text = intCandies(4).ToString

Figure 9-29 shows the code entered in the btnAdd_Click procedure.

static procedure-level array

uses the selected item's index as the array subscript

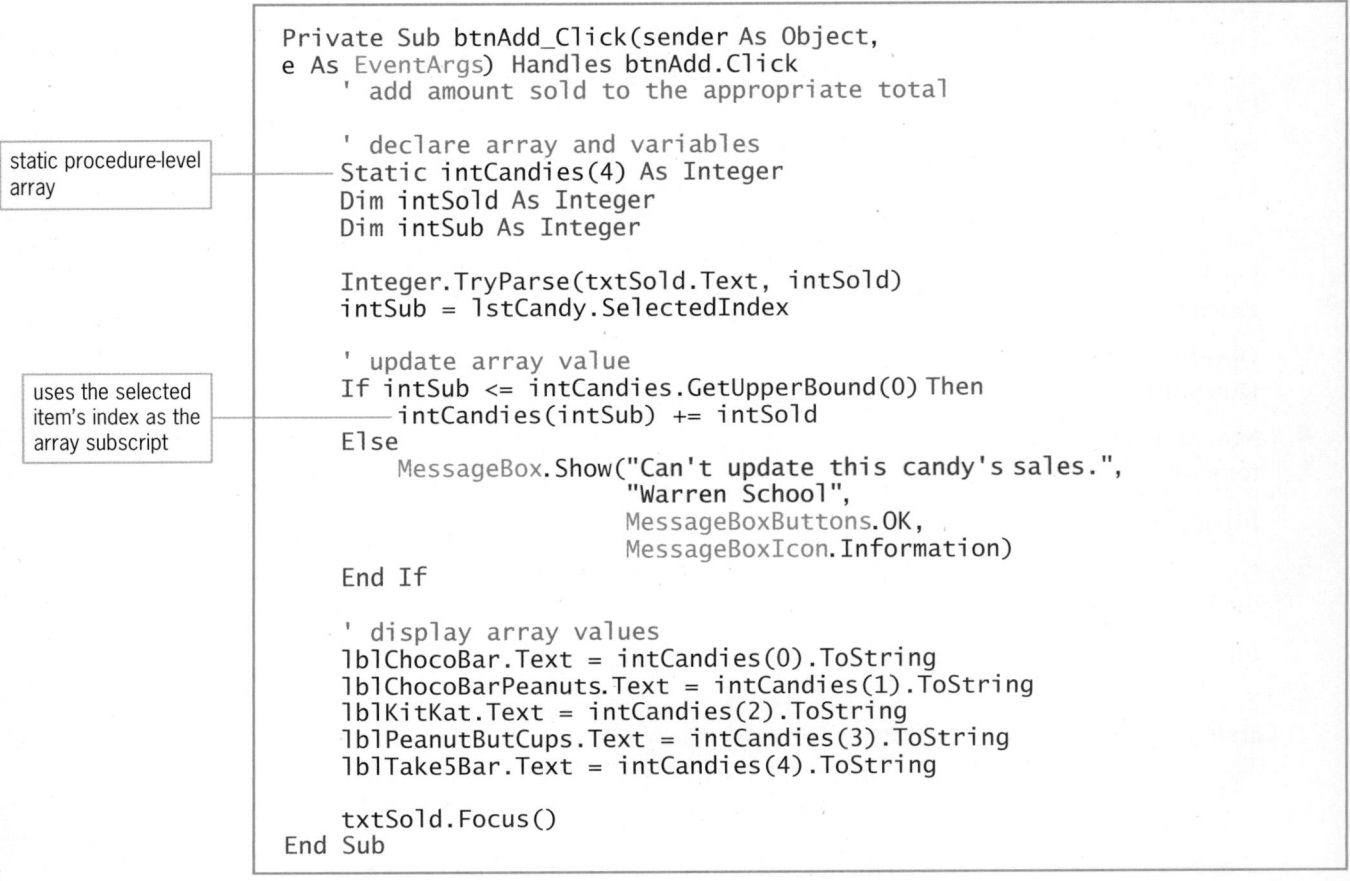

```
Private Sub btnAdd_Click(sender As Object,
e As EventArgs) Handles btnAdd.Click
    ' add amount sold to the appropriate total

    ' declare array and variables
    Static intCandies(4) As Integer
    Dim intSold As Integer
    Dim intSub As Integer

    Integer.TryParse(txtSold.Text, intSold)
    intSub = lstCandy.SelectedIndex

    ' update array value
    If intSub <= intCandies.GetUpperBound(0) Then
        intCandies(intSub) += intSold
    Else
        MessageBox.Show("Can't update this candy's sales.",
                        "Warren School",
                        MessageBoxButtons.OK,
                        MessageBoxIcon.Information)
    End If

    ' display array values
    lblChocoBar.Text = intCandies(0).ToString
    lblChocoBarPeanuts.Text = intCandies(1).ToString
    lblKitKat.Text = intCandies(2).ToString
    lblPeanutButCups.Text = intCandies(3).ToString
    lblTake5Bar.Text = intCandies(4).ToString

    txtSold.Focus()
End Sub
```

Figure 9-29 btnAdd_Click procedure

To test the Warren School application:

START HERE

1. Save the solution and then start the application. Type **100** in the Sold box and then click the **Add to Total** button. The number 100 appears in the Choco Bar label.
2. Click **Kit Kat** in the Candy list box. Change the 100 in the Sold box to **45** and then click the **Add to Total** button. Now change the 45 in the Sold box to **36** and then click the **Add to Total** button. Finally, change the 36 in the Sold box to **–6** (a negative number 6) and then click the **Add to Total** button. See Figure 9-30.

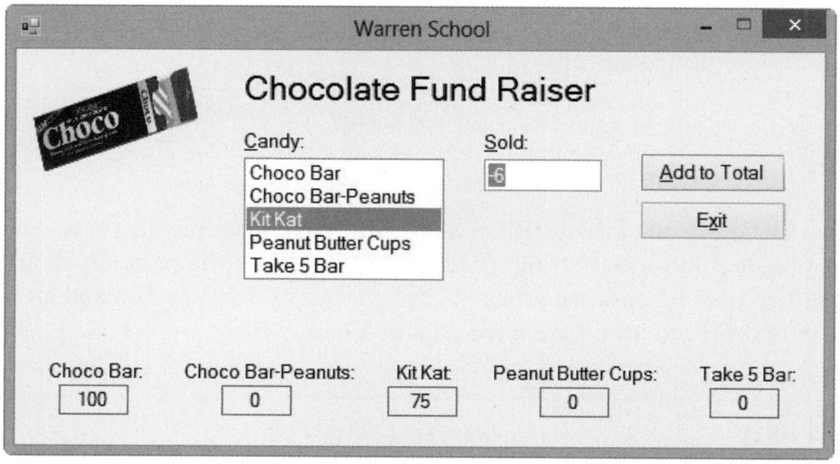

Figure 9-30 Array values displayed in the interface
OpenClipArt.org/kunto

3. On your own, test the application using different candy types and sales amounts.
4. Click the **Exit** button. Close the Code Editor window and then close the solution.

YOU DO IT 5!

Create a Visual Basic Windows application named YouDolt 5. Save the application in the VB2012\Chap09 folder. Add two list boxes and a button to the form. The button's Click event procedure should declare and initialize a one-dimensional Integer array. Use any 10 numbers to initialize the array. The procedure should use the For Each...Next statement to display the contents of the array in the first list box. The procedure should then use the For...Next statement to increase each array element's value by 2. Finally, it should use the Do...Loop statement to display the updated results in the second list box. Code the procedure. Save the solution and then start and test the application. Close the solution.

Parallel One-Dimensional Arrays

Figure 9-31 shows the problem specification for the Treasures Gift Shoppe. The application should display the price of the item corresponding to the ID entered by the gift shop's owner.

Problem Specification

Takoda Tapahe, the owner of a small gift shop named Treasures Gift Shoppe, wants an application that allows her to enter an item's ID. The application should display the item's price. A portion of the gift shop's price list is shown here. The application should store the price list in an array.

Item ID	Price
BX35	13
CR20	10
FE15	12
KW10	24
MM67	4

Figure 9-31 Problem specification for the Treasures Gift Shoppe

As you learned in Lesson A, all of the variables in an array have the same data type. So how can you store a price list that includes a string (the ID) and a number (the price) in an array? One solution is to use two one-dimensional arrays: a String array to store the IDs and an Integer array to store the prices. Both arrays are illustrated in Figure 9-32.

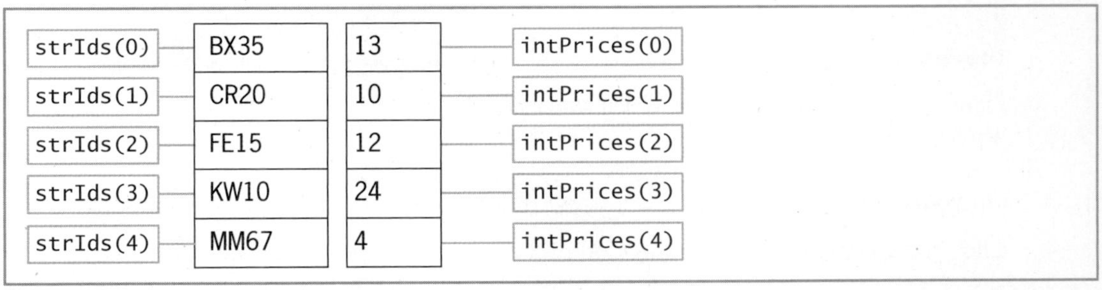

Figure 9-32 Illustration of two parallel one-dimensional arrays

The arrays in Figure 9-32 are referred to as **parallel arrays**, which are two or more arrays whose elements are related by their positions in the arrays; in other words, they are related by their subscripts. The arrays are parallel because each element in the `strIds` array corresponds to the element located in the same position in the `intPrices` array. For example, the item whose product ID is BX35 [`strIds(0)`] has a price of $13 [`intPrices(0)`]. Likewise, the item whose product ID is CR20 [`strIds(1)`] has a price of $10 [`intPrices(1)`]. The same relationship is true for the remaining elements in both arrays. To determine an item's price, you locate the item's ID in the `strIds` array and then view its corresponding element in the `intPrices` array.

START HERE

To begin coding the Treasures Gift Shoppe application:

1. Open the Treasures Solution (Treasures Solution.sln) file contained in the VB2012\Chap09\Treasures Solution-Parallel folder. If necessary, open the designer window. The text box's CharacterCasing and MaxLength properties are set to Upper and 4, respectively. Recall that when a text box's CharacterCasing property is set to Upper, any letters the user types will appear in uppercase. When a text box's MaxLength property is set to 4, the user can enter a maximum of four characters in the text box. See Figure 9-33. (The image in the picture box was downloaded from the Open Clip Art Library at *http://openclipart.org*.)

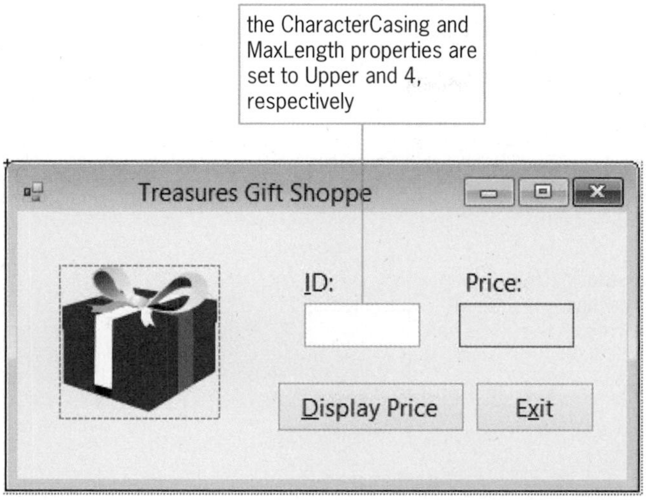

Figure 9-33 User interface for the Treasures Gift Shoppe application
OpenClipArt.org/secretlondon

2. Open the Code Editor window. Replace <your name> and <current date> in the comments with your name and the current date, respectively.

3. First, you will declare and initialize the two parallel one-dimensional arrays. Click the **blank line** below the `' declare parallel arrays` comment in the form's Declarations section, and then enter the following array declaration statements:

```
Private strIds() As String =
    {"BX35", "CR20", "FE15", "KW10", "MM67"}
Private intPrices() As Integer = {13, 10, 12, 24, 4}
```

Figure 9-34 shows the pseudocode and flowchart for the Display Price button's Click event procedure.

```
btnDisplay Click event procedure
1. assign ID to a variable
2. repeat until either the end of the strIds array is reached or the ID is located in the array
       add 1 to the array subscript to search the next element in the array
   end repeat
3. if the ID was located in the strIds array
       display the price contained in the same location in the intPrices array
   else
       display "Invalid ID" message in a message box
   end if
```

Figure 9-34 Pseudocode and flowchart for the btnDisplay_Click procedure *(continues)*

(continued)

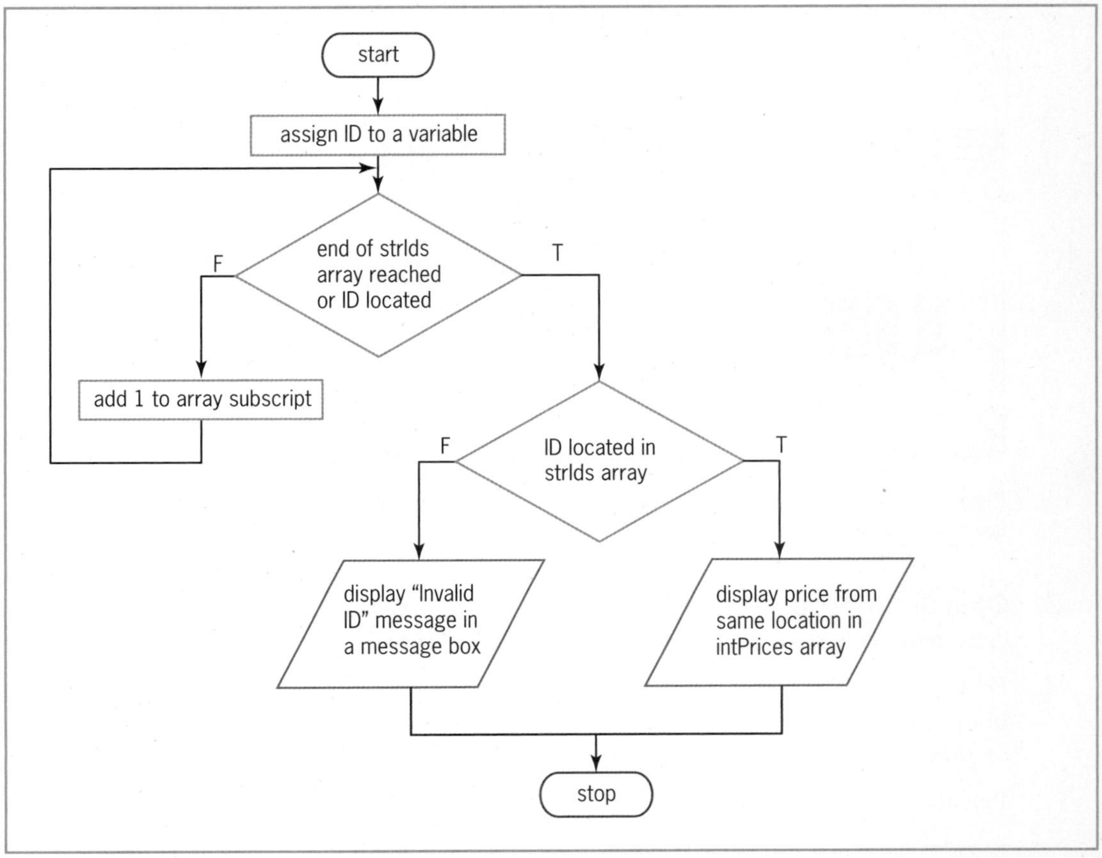

Figure 9-34 Pseudocode and flowchart for the btnDisplay_Click procedure

START HERE

To finish coding the Treasures Gift Shoppe application:

1. Open the btnDisplay_Click procedure. Type the following comment and then press **Enter** twice:

   ' displays the price associated with an ID

2. The procedure will use a String variable to store the ID entered by the user, and use an Integer variable to keep track of the array subscripts while the array is being searched. Enter the following two declaration statements. Press **Enter** twice after typing the second statement.

   Dim strSearchForId As String
   Dim intSub As Integer

3. The first step in the pseudocode and flowchart is to assign the ID to a variable. Type the following assignment statement and then press **Enter** twice:

   strSearchForId = txtId.Text

4. Now you will use a loop to search each element in the `strIds` array, stopping either when the end of the array is reached or when the ID is located in the array. Enter the following comments and code:

```
' search the strIds array for the ID
' continue searching until the end of
' the array or the ID is found
Do Until intSub = strIds.Length OrElse
    strSearchForId = strIds(intSub)
    intSub += 1
Loop
```

5. Finally, you need to use a selection structure to determine why the loop ended. You can make this determination by looking at the value in the `intSub` variable. If the loop ended because it reached the end of the `strIds` array without locating the ID, the `intSub` variable's value will be equal to the array's length. On the other hand, if the loop ended because it located the ID in the `strIds` array, the `intSub` variable's value will be less than the array's length. Insert two blank lines above the End Sub clause. In the blank line immediately above the End Sub clause, enter the following If clause:

```
If intSub < strIds.Length Then
```

6. If the selection structure's condition evaluates to True, it means that the ID was located in the array. In that case, the structure's true path should display the price located in the same position in the `intPrices` array. Otherwise, its false path should display the "Invalid ID" message in a message box. Enter the following lines of code:

```
    lblPrice.Text = intPrices(intSub).ToString("C0")
Else
    MessageBox.Show("Invalid ID", "Treasures",
                    MessageBoxButtons.OK,
                    MessageBoxIcon.Information)
```

7. If necessary, delete the blank line above the End If clause.

Figure 9-35 shows most of the application's code.

parallel one-dimensional arrays declared in the form's Declarations section

searches for the ID in the strIds array

displays the corresponding price from the intPrices array

```
' declare parallel arrays
Private strIds() As String =
    {"BX35", "CR20", "FE15", "KW10", "MM67"}
Private intPrices() As Integer = {13, 10, 12, 24, 4}

Private Sub btnDisplay_Click(sender As Object,
e As EventArgs) Handles btnDisplay.Click
    ' displays the price associated with an ID

    Dim strSearchForId As String
    Dim intSub As Integer

    strSearchForId = txtId.Text

    ' search the strIds array for the ID
    ' continue searching until the end of
    ' the array or the ID is found
    Do Until intSub = strIds.Length OrElse
        strSearchForId = strIds(intSub)
        intSub += 1
    Loop

    If intSub < strIds.Length Then
        lblPrice.Text = intPrices(intSub).ToString("C0")
    Else
        MessageBox.Show("Invalid ID", "Treasures",
                        MessageBoxButtons.OK,
                        MessageBoxIcon.Information)
    End If
End Sub
```

Figure 9-35 Most of the code for the Treasures Gift Shoppe application

START HERE

To test the Treasures Gift Shoppe application:

1. Save the solution and then start the application. Type **cr20** in the ID box and then click the **Display Price** button. $10 appears in the Price box. See Figure 9-36.

Figure 9-36 Sample run of the Treasures Gift Shoppe application

OpenClipArt.org/secretlondon

2. Type **xx44** in the ID box and then click the **Display Price** button. The "Invalid ID" message appears in a message box. Close the message box.
3. On your own, test the application using other valid and invalid IDs. When you are finished testing the application, click the **Exit** button.
4. Close the Code Editor window and then close the solution.

The Die Tracker Application

Recall that your task in this chapter is to create the Die Tracker application. The application simulates the roll of a die and keeps track of the number of times each die face appears.

To open the Die Tracker application:

START HERE

1. Open the Die Solution (Die Solution.sln) file contained in the VB2012\Chap09\ Die Solution folder. If necessary, open the designer window. See Figure 9-37. (The images in the picture boxes were downloaded from the Open Clip Art Library at *http://openclipart.org*.)

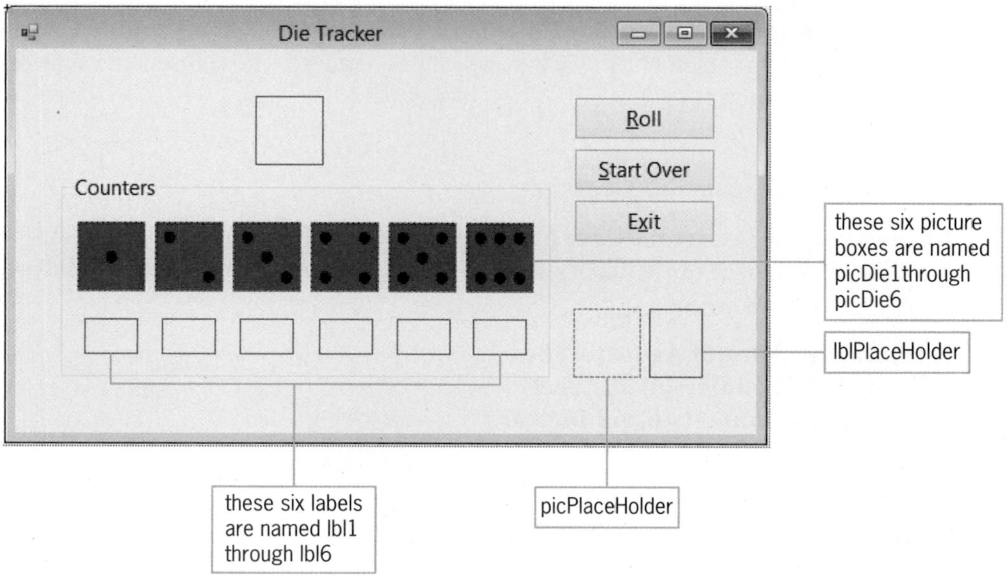

Figure 9-37 User interface for the Die Tracker application
OpenClipArt.org/orsonj

2. Open the Code Editor window. Replace <your name> and <current date> in the comments with your name and the current date, respectively.

The Die Tracker application will use three parallel arrays: a PictureBox array named `picDice`, a Label array named `lblCounters`, and an Integer array named `intCounters`. The arrays are illustrated in Figure 9-38.

Subscripts	picDice array	lblCounters array	intCounters array
0	picPlaceHolder	lblPlaceHolder	0
1	picDie1	lbl1	0
2	picDie2	lbl2	0
3	picDie3	lbl3	0
4	picDie4	lbl4	0
5	picDie5	lbl5	0
6	picDie6	lbl6	0

Figure 9-38 Illustration of the three parallel arrays

You may be wondering why the arrays contain seven elements rather than six elements; after all, there are only six faces on a die. However, the application's code will be much easier to understand if the number of dots on each die corresponds to location of the die's information in the arrays. In other words, the information pertaining to the one-dot die will be contained in the array elements that have a subscript of 1, the two-dot die's information will be contained in the array elements that have a subscript of 2, and so on. When coding the application, the first element in each array will be ignored. (Recall that the first element in an array has a subscript of 0.)

START HERE

To code the Die Tracker application:

1. First, you will declare the three parallel arrays. Click the **blank line** below the `' declare arrays` comment in the form's Declarations section, and then enter the following declaration statements:

   Private picDice(6) As PictureBox
   Private lblCounters(6) as Label
   Private intCounters(6) As Integer

2. Now you will fill the picture box and label arrays with the appropriate controls. You will use the `picPlaceHolder` and `lblPlaceHolder` controls for the first element in their respective arrays. Click the **blank line** above the End Sub clause in the form's Load event procedure and then enter the following assignment statements:

   picDice = {picPlaceHolder, picDie1, picDie2,
   picDie3, picDie4, picDie5, picDie6}
   lblCounters = {lblPlaceHolder, lbl1, lbl2,
   lbl3, lbl4, lbl5, lbl6}

3. Next, you will code the btnRoll_Click procedure. The procedure will use a random number to select one of the six picture boxes from the `picDice` array. Click the **blank line** above the End Sub clause in the btnRoll_Click procedure and then enter the following declaration statements. Press **Enter** twice after typing the second statement.

   Dim randGen As New Random
   Dim intRand As Integer

4. The procedure should generate a random number from 1 through 6. Enter the following comment and assignment statement. Press **Enter** twice after typing the statement.

   ' generate a random number from 1 – 6
   intRand = randGen.Next(1, 7)

5. Now you can use the random number to display the appropriate die face in the `picRandDie` control. Enter the following comment and assignment statement. Press **Enter** twice after typing the statement.

```
' display current roll of the die
picRandDie.Image = picDice(intRand).Image
```


6. You also can use the random number to update the associated counter in the **intCounters** array. Enter the following comment and assignment statement. Press **Enter** twice after typing the statement.

```
' update associated counter
intCounters(intRand) += 1
```

7. Finally, you can use the random number to display the updated counter's value in its associated label control in the `lblCounters` array. Enter the following comment and assignment statement. Press **Enter** twice after typing the statement.

```
' display updated counter
lblCounters(intRand).Text =
    intCounters(intRand).ToString
```

8. The last procedure you need to code is the btnStartOver_Click procedure. The procedure should reset the counters in the `intCounters` array to 0 and also clear the contents of the label controls contained in the `lblCounters` array. Click the **blank line** above the End Sub clause in the btnStartOver_Click procedure and then enter the following loop:

```
For intSub As Integer = 1 To 6
    intCounters(intSub) = 0
    lblCounters(intSub).Text = String.Empty
Next intSub
```

In Step 8, you don't need the loop to access the first element in each array because that element will never change from its initial value.

Figure 9-39 shows most of the application's code.

```
' declare arrays
Private picDice(6) As PictureBox
Private lblCounters(6) As Label
Private intCounters(6) As Integer

Private Sub frmMain_Load(sender As Object,
e As EventArgs) HandlesMe.Load
    ' fill picture box and label arrays

    picDice = {picPlaceHolder, picDie1, picDie2,
               picDie3, picDie4, picDie5, picDie6}
    lblCounters = {lblPlaceHolder, lbl1, lbl2,
                   lbl3, lbl4, lbl5, lbl6}
End Sub

Private Sub btnRoll_Click(sender As Object,
e As EventArgs) Handles btnRoll.Click
    ' calculates and displays the number
    ' of times each die face appears

    Dim randGen As New Random
    Dim intRand As Integer

    ' generate a random number from 1 - 6
    intRand = randGen.Next(1, 7)

    ' display current roll of the die
    picRandDie.Image = picDice(intRand).Image

    ' update associated counter
    intCounters(intRand) += 1

    ' display updated counter
    lblCounters(intRand).Text =
        intCounters(intRand).ToString

End Sub

Private Sub btnStartOver_Click(sender As Object,
e As EventArgs) Handles btnStartOver.Click
    ' reset the counters and clear the
    ' counter labels

    For intSub As Integer = 1 To 6
        intCounters(intSub) = 0
        lblCounters(intSub).Text = String.Empty
    Next intSub
End Sub
```

Figure 9-39 Most of the code for the Die Tracker application

START HERE

To test the Die Tracker application:

1. Save the solution and then start the application. Click the **Roll** button. A die face appears in the picRandDie control and its associated counter label contains the number 1. See Figure 9-40. Because the btnRoll_Click procedure uses random numbers, your die face and counter label might be different from those shown in the figure.

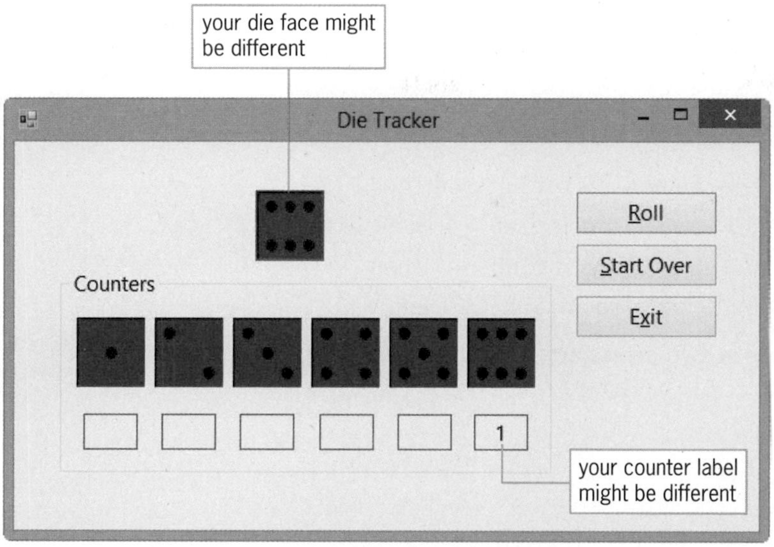

Figure 9-40 Sample run of the Die Tracker application
OpenClipArt.org/orsonj

2. Click the **Roll** button several more times. Each time you click the Roll button, a die face appears in the picRandDie control and its associated counter label is updated by 1.
3. Now, click the **Start Over** button. The button's Click event procedure resets the counters in the `intCounters` array to 0 and also clears the contents of the labels in the `lblCounters` array.
4. Click the **Roll** button. A die face appears in the picRandDie control and its associated counter label contains the number 1.
5. Click the **Exit** button. Close the Code Editor window and then close the solution.

Lesson B Summary

- To associate the items in a list box with the elements in an array:

  Use each list box item's index and each array element's subscript.
- To create parallel one-dimensional arrays:

  Create two or more one-dimensional arrays. When assigning values to the arrays, be sure that the value stored in each element in the first array corresponds to the values stored in the same elements in the other arrays.

Lesson B Key Terms

Accumulator arrays—arrays whose elements are used to accumulate (add together) values

Counter arrays—arrays whose elements are used for counting something

Parallel arrays—two or more arrays whose elements are related by their subscripts (positions) in the arrays

Lesson B Review Questions

1. The `intSales` array is declared as follows: `Dim intSales() As Integer = {10000, 12000, 900, 500, 20000}`. Which of the following If clauses determines whether the `intSub` variable contains a valid subscript for the array?

   a. `If intSub >= 0 AndAlso intSub <= 4 Then`
   b. `If intSub >= 0 AndAlso intSub < 4 Then`
   c. `If intSub >= 0 AndAlso intSub <= 5 Then`
   d. `If intSub > 0 AndAlso intSub < 5 Then`

2. If the elements in two arrays are related by their subscripts, the arrays are called ________________ arrays.

   a. associated
   b. coupled
   c. matching
   d. parallel

3. The `strStates` and `strCapitals` arrays are parallel arrays. If Illinois is stored in the second element in the `strStates` array, where is its capital (Springfield) stored?

   a. `strCapitals(1)`
   b. `strCapitals(2)`

4. The `dblNums` array is a six-element Double array. Which of the following If clauses determines whether the entire array has been searched?

   a. `If intSub = dblNums.Length Then`
   b. `If intSub <= dblNums.Length Then`
   c. `If intSub > dblNums.GetUpperBound(0) Then`
   d. both a and c

Lesson B Exercises

INTRODUCTORY

1. Open the Months Solution (Months Solution.sln) file contained in the VB2012\Chap09\Months Solution-Introductory folder. If necessary, open the designer window. In the form's Load event procedure, declare and initialize a one-dimensional String array. Use the names of the 12 months to initialize the array. Use the For Each...Next statement to display the contents of the array in the list box. The list box's SelectedValueChanged event procedure should display the name of the selected month in the label control. Code the application. Save the solution and then start and test the application. Close the Code Editor window and then close the solution.

INTRODUCTORY

2. Open the Salary Code Solution (Salary Code Solution.sln) file contained in the VB2012\Chap09\Salary Code Solution folder. If necessary, open the designer window. The application should allow the user to select a salary code from the list box. The list box's SelectedIndexChanged event procedure should display the salary associated with the selected code. The salary codes and salaries are listed in Figure 9-41. Code the application, using a class-level array to store the salaries. Save the solution and then start and test the application. Close the Code Editor window and then close the solution.

Salary code	Salary
101	25000
102	35000
103	55000
104	75000
105	80500
106	83000
107	90500

Figure 9-41 Salary codes and salaries for Exercise 2

3. Open the State Capitals Solution (State Capitals Solution.sln) file contained in the VB2012\Chap09\State Capitals Solution folder. If necessary, open the designer window. Open the Code Editor window. The form's Declarations section declares and initializes two parallel one-dimensional arrays named `strStates` and `strCapitals`. Locate the btnDisplay_Click procedure. The procedure should display the contents of the arrays in the list box. Display the information in the following format: the capital name followed by a comma, a space, and the state name. Code the procedure. Save the solution and then start and test the application. Close the Code Editor window and then close the solution. INTRODUCTORY

4. Open the Months Solution (Months Solution.sln) file contained in the VB2012\Chap09\Months Solution-Intermediate folder. Display the names of the 12 months in the list box. Declare and initialize a one-dimensional Integer array named `intDaysInTheMonth`. Use the following 12 integers to initialize the array: 31, 28, 31, 30, 31, 30, 31, 31, 30, 31, 30, and 31. The list box's SelectedIndexChanged event procedure should display (in the Days box) the number of days in the selected month. Code the application. Save the solution and then start and test the application. Close the Code Editor window and then close the solution. INTERMEDIATE

5. In this exercise, you modify the Die Tracker application coded in the lesson. Use Windows to make a copy of the Die Solution folder. Rename the copy Modified Die Solution. Open the Die Solution (Die Solution.sln) file contained in the Modified Die Solution folder. Code the application without using the picPlaceHolder and lblPlaceHolder controls. Remove both controls from the interface. Be sure to change the *highestSubscript* argument in the three array declaration statements to 5. Save the solution and then start and test the application. Close the Code Editor window and then close the solution. INTERMEDIATE

6. Open the Car Sales Solution (Car Sales Solution.sln) file contained in the VB2012\Chap09\Car Sales Solution folder. The interface allows the user to enter the number of each car type sold by each salesperson. The Add to Total button should use an array to accumulate the numbers sold by car type. It also should display (in the labels) the total number sold for each car type. Code the application. Save the solution and then start and test the application. Close the Code Editor window and then close the solution. INTERMEDIATE

7. In this exercise, you code an application that allows Professor Jacoby to display a grade based on the number of points he enters. The grading scale is shown in Figure 9-42. Open the Jacoby Solution (Jacoby Solution.sln) file contained in the VB2012\Chap09\Jacoby Solution folder. Store the minimum points in a one-dimensional Integer array named `intPoints`. Store the grades in a one-dimensional String array named `strGrades`. The arrays should be parallel arrays. The Display button's Click event procedure should search the `intPoints` array for the number of points entered by the INTERMEDIATE

user. It then should display the corresponding grade from the `strGrades` array. Save the solution and then start and test the application. Close the Code Editor window and then close the solution.

Minimum points	Maximum points	Grade
0	299	F
300	349	D
350	399	C
400	449	B
450	500	A

Figure 9-42 Grading scale for Exercise 7

INTERMEDIATE

8. In this exercise, you code an application that allows Professor Kensington to display a grade based on the number of points she enters. The grading scale is shown in Figure 9-43. Open the Kensington Solution (Kensington Solution.sln) file contained in the VB2012\Chap09\Kensington Solution folder. Professor Kensington will enter the total possible points in the Possible points box. The Create Grading Scale button's Click event procedure should store the minimum number of points and the grades in two parallel one-dimensional arrays. The Display Grade button's Click event procedure should display the grade corresponding to the number of points entered in the Earned points box. Save the solution and then start the application. Enter 300 in the Possible points box and then click the Create Grading Scale button. Enter 185 in the Earned points box and then click the Display Grade button. The letter D should appear in the Grade box. Now, enter 290 in the Earned points box and then click the Display Grade button. The letter A should appear in the Grade box. Next, enter 500 in the Possible points box and then click the Create Grading Scale button. Enter 363 in the Earned points box and then click the Display Grade button. The letter C should appear in the Grade box. Test the application using different values for the possible and earned points. Close the Code Editor window and then close the solution.

Minimum points	Grade
90% of the total possible points	A
80% of the total possible points	B
70% of the total possible points	C
60% of the total possible points	D
0	F

Figure 9-43 Grading scale for Exercise 8

INTERMEDIATE

9. Open the Laury Solution (Laury Solution.sln) file contained in the VB2012\Chap09\Laury Solution folder. The Display Shipping button's Click event procedure should display a shipping charge that is based on the number of items a customer orders. The order amounts and shipping charges are listed in Figure 9-44. Store the minimum order amounts and shipping charges in parallel arrays. Display the appropriate shipping charge with a dollar sign and two decimal places. Code the application. Save the solution and then start and test the application. Close the Code Editor window and then close the solution.

Minimum order	Maximum order	Shipping charge
1	10	15
11	50	10
51	100	5
101	No maximum	0

Figure 9-44 Order amounts and shipping charges for Exercise 9

10. In this exercise, you code a modified version of the Die Tracker application coded in the lesson. Open the Dice Solution (Dice Solution.sln) file contained in the VB2012\Chap09\Dice Solution-Advanced folder. The application should simulate the roll of two dice (rather than one die). It also should display the total amount rolled. In other words, if one die shows two dots and the other shows four dots, the number 6 should appear in the Total box. The application should keep track of the number of times each total (from 2 through 12) is rolled. Code the application. Save the solution and then start and test the application. Close the Code Editor window and then close the solution. ADVANCED

11. Create a Visual Basic Windows application. Use the following names for the solution and project, respectively: Stock Market Solution and Stock Market Project. Save the application in the VB2012\Chap09 folder. Change the form file's name to Main Form.vb. Change the form's name to frmMain. The application should declare a Double array that contains 30 elements. Each element will store the price of a stock. Initialize the first 10 elements using the following values: 2.25, 2.4, 1.97, 1.97, 1.99, 1.97, 2.25, 2.87, 2.5, and 2.4. Use your own values to initialize the remaining 20 elements. The application should display the following items: the average price of the stock, the number of days the stock price increased from the previous day, the number of days the stock price decreased from the previous day, and the number of days the stock price stayed the same as the previous day. Create a suitable interface and then code the application. Display the average price with a dollar sign and two decimal places. Save the solution and then start and test the application. Close the Code Editor window and then close the solution. ADVANCED

LESSON C

After studying Lesson C, you should be able to:

- Declare and initialize a two-dimensional array
- Store data in a two-dimensional array
- Sum the values in a two-dimensional array
- Search a two-dimensional array

Two-Dimensional Arrays

As you learned in Lesson A, the most commonly used arrays in business applications are one-dimensional and two-dimensional. You can visualize a one-dimensional array as a column of variables in memory. A **two-dimensional array**, on the other hand, resembles a table in that the variables (elements) are in rows and columns. You can determine the number of elements in a two-dimensional array by multiplying the number of its rows by the number of its columns. An array that has four rows and three columns, for example, contains 12 elements.

Each element in a two-dimensional array is identified by a unique combination of two subscripts that the computer assigns to the element when the array is created. The subscripts specify the element's row and column positions in the array. Elements located in the first row in a two-dimensional array are assigned a row subscript of 0, elements in the second row are assigned a row subscript of 1, and so on. Similarly, elements located in the first column in a two-dimensional array are assigned a column subscript of 0, elements in the second column are assigned a column subscript of 1, and so on.

You refer to each element in a two-dimensional array by the array's name and the element's row and column subscripts, with the row subscript listed first and the column subscript listed second. The subscripts are separated by a comma and specified in a set of parentheses immediately following the array name. For example, to refer to the element located in the first row, first column in a two-dimensional array named `strCds`, you use `strCds(0, 0)`—read "`strCds` sub zero comma zero." Similarly, to refer to the element located in the second row, third column, you use `strCds(1, 2)`. Notice that the subscripts are one number less than the row and column in which the element is located. This is because the row and column subscripts start at 0 rather than at 1. You will find that the last row subscript in a two-dimensional array is always one number less than the number of rows in the array. Likewise, the last column subscript is always one number less than the number of columns in the array. Figure 9-45 illustrates the elements contained in the two-dimensional `strCds` array.

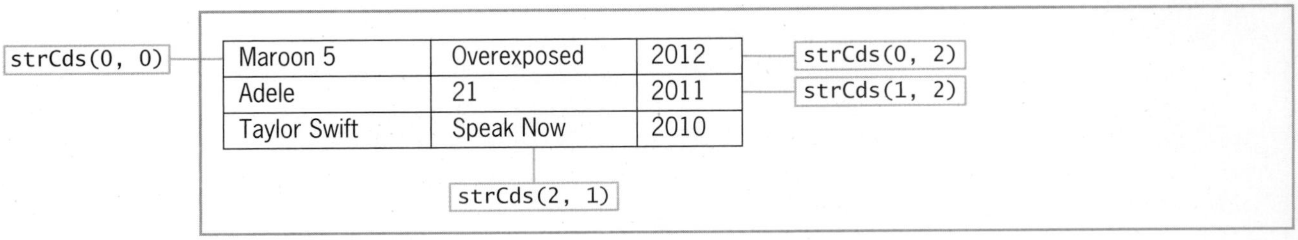

Figure 9-45 Names of some of the elements in the `strCds` array

Figure 9-46 shows two versions of the syntax for declaring a two-dimensional array in Visual Basic. The figure also includes examples of using both syntax versions. In each version, *arrayName* is the name of the array and *dataType* is the type of data the array variables will store.

Declaring a Two-Dimensional Array

Syntax – Version 1

{**Dim** | **Private** | **Static**} *arrayName*(*highestRowSubscript*, *highestColumnSubscript*) **As** *dataType*

Syntax – Version 2

{**Dim** | **Private** | **Static**} *arrayName*(,) **As** *dataType* = {{*initialValues*},...{*initialValues*}}

Example 1

```
Dim strNames(5, 2) As String
```

declares a six-row, three-column procedure-level array named `strNames`; each element is automatically initialized using the keyword `Nothing`

Example 2

```
Static intNumbers(4, 3) As Integer
```

declares a static, five-row, four-column procedure-level array named `intNumbers`; each element is automatically initialized to 0

Example 3

```
Private strCds(,) As String =
        {{"Maroon 5", "Overexposed", "2012"},
         {"Adele", "21", "2011"},
         {"Taylor Swift", "Speak Now", "2010"}}
```

declares and initializes a three-row, three-column class-level array named `strCds` (the array is illustrated in Figure 9-45)

Example 4

```
Private dblSales(,) As Double = {{75.33, 9.65},
                                 {23.55, 6.89},
                                 {4.5, 89.3}}
```

declares and initializes a three-row, two-column class-level array named `dblPrices`

Figure 9-46 Syntax versions and examples of declaring a two-dimensional array

In Version 1's syntax, *highestRowSubscript* and *highestColumnSubscript* are integers that specify the highest row and column subscripts, respectively, in the array. When the array is created, it will contain one row more than the number specified in the highestRowSubscript argument and one column more than the number specified in the highestColumnSubscript argument. This is because the first row and column subscripts in a two-dimensional array are 0. When you declare a two-dimensional array using Version 1's syntax, the computer automatically initializes each element in the array when the array is created.

You would use Version 2's syntax when you want to specify each variable's initial value. You do this by including a separate *initialValues* section, enclosed in braces, for each row in the array. If the array has two rows, then the statement that declares and initializes the array should have two initialValues sections. If the array has five rows, then the declaration statement should have five initialValues sections. Within the individual initialValues sections, you enter one or more values separated by commas. The number of values to enter corresponds to the number of columns in the array. If the array contains 10 columns, then each individual initialValues section should contain 10 values. In addition to the set of braces enclosing each individual initialValues section, Version 2's syntax also requires all of the initialValues sections to be enclosed in a set of braces. When using Version 2's syntax, be sure to include a comma within the parentheses that follow the array's name. The comma indicates that the array is a two-dimensional array. (Recall that a comma is used to separate the row subscript from the column subscript in a two-dimensional array.)

After an array is declared, you can use another statement to store a different value in an array element. Examples of such statements include assignment statements and statements that contain the TryParse method. Figure 9-47 shows examples of both types of statements, using three of the arrays declared in Figure 9-46.

Storing Data in a Two-Dimensional Array

Example 1
```
strNames(0, 1) = "Sarah"
```
assigns the string "Sarah" to the element located in the first row, second column in the `strNames` array

Example 2
```
For intRow As Integer = 0 To 4
    For intColumn As Integer = 0 To 3
        intNumbers(intRow, intColumn) += 1
    Next intColumn
Next intRow
```
adds the number 1 to the contents of each element in the `intNumbers` array

Example 3
```
Dim intRow As Integer
Dim intCol As Integer
Do While intRow <= 2
    intCol = 0
    Do While intCol <= 1
        dblSales(intRow, intCol) = 100
        intCol = intCol + 1
    Loop
    intRow = intRow + 1
Loop
```
assigns the number 100 to each element in the `dblSales` array

Example 4
```
dblSales(2, 1) = dblSales(2, 1) * .1
```
multiplies the value contained in the third row, second column in the `dblSales` array by .1 and then assigns the result to the element; you can also write this statement as `dblSales(2, 1) *= .1`

Example 5
```
Double.TryParse(txtSales.Text, dblSales(0, 0))
```
assigns either the value entered in the txtSales control (converted to Double) or the number 0 to the element located in the first row, first column in the `dblSales` array

Figure 9-47 Examples of statements used to store data in a two-dimensional array

In Lesson A, you learned how to use the GetUpperBound method to determine the highest subscript in a one-dimensional array. You can also use the GetUpperBound method to determine the highest row and column subscripts in a two-dimensional array, as shown in Figure 9-48.

Using a Two-Dimensional Array's GetUpperBound Method

Syntax to determine the highest row subscript
arrayName.**GetUpperBound(0)** — the row dimension is always 0

Syntax to determine the highest column subscript
arrayName.**GetUpperBound(1)** — the column dimension is always 1

Example
```
Dim strOrders(10, 3) As String
Dim intHighestRowSub As Integer
Dim intHighestColumnSub As Integer
intHighestRowSub = strOrders.GetUpperBound(0)
intHighestColumnSub = strOrders.GetUpperBound(1)
```
assigns the numbers 10 and 3 to the `intHighestRowSub` and `intHighestColumnSub` variables, respectively

Figure 9-48 Syntax and an example of a two-dimensional array's GetUpperBound method

Traversing a Two-Dimensional Array

Recall that you use a loop to traverse a one-dimensional array. To traverse a two-dimensional array, you typically use two loops: an outer loop and a nested loop. One of the loops keeps track of the row subscript and the other keeps track of the column subscript. You can code the loops using either the For...Next statement or the Do...Loop statement. Rather than using two loops to traverse a two-dimensional array, you can also use one For Each...Next loop. However, recall that the instructions in a For Each...Next loop can only read the array values; they cannot permanently modify the values.

Figure 9-49 shows examples of loops that traverse the `strMonths` array, displaying each element's value in the lstMonths control. Both loops in Example 1 are coded using the For...Next statement. However, either one of the loops could be coded using the Do...Loop statement instead. Or, both loops could be coded using the Do...Loop statement, as shown in Example 2. The loop in Example 3 is coded using the For Each...Next statement.

Traversing a Two-Dimensional Array

```
Private strMonths(,) As String = {{"Jan", "31"},
                                   {"Feb", "28"},
                                   {"Mar", "31"},
                                   {"Apr", "30"}}
```

Example 1

```
Dim intHighRow As Integer = strMonths.GetUpperBound(0)
Dim intHighCol As Integer = strMonths.GetUpperBound(1)
For intR As Integer = 0 To intHighRow
    For intC As Integer = 0 To intHighCol
        lstMonths.Items.Add(strMonths(intR, intC))
    Next intC
Next intR
```

displays the contents of the `strMonths` array in the lstMonths control; the array values are displayed row by row, as follows: Jan, 31, Feb, 28, Mar, 31, Apr, and 30

Example 2

```
Dim intHighRow As Integer = strMonths.GetUpperBound(0)
Dim intHighCol As Integer = strMonths.GetUpperBound(1)
Dim intR As Integer
Dim intC As Integer
Do While intC <= intHighCol
    intR = 0
    Do While intR <= intHighRow
        lstMonths.Items.Add(strMonths(intR, intC))
        intR += 1
    Loop
    intC += 1
Loop
```

displays the contents of the `strMonths` array in the lstMonths control; the array values are displayed column by column, as follows: Jan, Feb, Mar, Apr, 31, 28, 31, and 30

Example 3

```
For Each strElement As String In strMonths
    lstMonths.Items.Add(strElement)
Next strElement
```

displays the contents of the `strMonths` array in the lstMonths control; the array values are displayed as follows: Jan, 31, Feb, 28, Mar, 31, Apr, and 30

Figure 9-49 Examples of loops used to traverse a two-dimensional array

Totaling the Values Stored in a Two-Dimensional Array

Figure 9-50 shows the problem specification for the Jenko Booksellers application. The application displays the total of the sales stored in a two-dimensional array.

Problem Specification

Jenko Booksellers sells paperback and hardcover books in each of its three stores. The sales manager wants an application that displays the total sales made in the previous month. The sales amounts for the previous month are shown here. The application will store the sales amounts in a two-dimensional array that has three rows and two columns. Each row will contain the data pertaining to one of the three stores. The sales amounts for paperback books will be stored in the first column. The second column will contain the sales amounts for hardcover books. The application will need to total the values stored in the array.

	Paperback sales ($)	Hardcover sales ($)
Store 1	1200.33	2350.75
Store 2	3677.80	2456.05
Store 3	750.67	1345.99

Figure 9-50 Problem specification for the Jenko Booksellers application

START HERE

To code and then test the Jenko Booksellers application:

1. If necessary, start Visual Studio 2012. Open the Jenko Solution (Jenko Solution.sln) file contained in the VB2012\Chap09\Jenko Solution folder. If necessary, open the designer window. (The image in the picture box was downloaded from the Open Clip Art Library at *http://openclipart.org*.)
2. Open the Code Editor window. Replace <your name> and <current date> in the comments with your name and the current date, respectively.
3. Locate the btnCalc_Click procedure. First, you will declare and initialize a two-dimensional array to store the sales amounts. The array will contain three rows (one for each store) and two columns. The first column will contain the paperback book sales, and the second column will contain the hardcover book sales. Click the **blank line** immediately above the `' total the sales amounts stored in the array` comment and then enter the following array declaration statement:

```
Dim dblSales(,) As Double = {{1200.33, 2350.75},
                             {3677.8, 2456.05},
                             {750.67, 1345.99}}
```

4. Now you will declare a variable that the procedure can use to accumulate the sales amounts stored in the array. Enter the following declaration statement:

```
Dim dblTotal As Double
```

5. Next, you will enter a loop that totals the values stored in the array. Click the **blank line** below the `' total the sales amounts stored in the array` comment and then enter the following lines of code:

```
For Each dblElement As Double in dblSales
    dblTotal = dblTotal + dblElement
Next dblElement
```

6. Finally, you will display the total sales. Insert a blank line below the `Next dblElement` clause and then enter the additional assignment statement indicated in Figure 9-51.

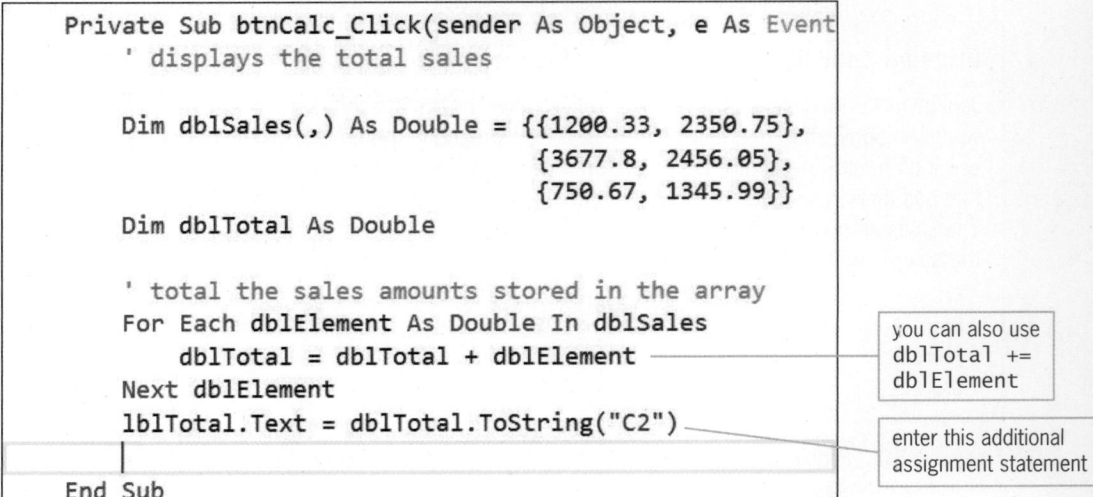

```
Private Sub btnCalc_Click(sender As Object, e As Event
    ' displays the total sales

    Dim dblSales(,) As Double = {{1200.33, 2350.75},
                                  {3677.8, 2456.05},
                                  {750.67, 1345.99}}
    Dim dblTotal As Double

    ' total the sales amounts stored in the array
    For Each dblElement As Double In dblSales
        dblTotal = dblTotal + dblElement
    Next dblElement
    lblTotal.Text = dblTotal.ToString("C2")

End Sub
```

you can also use dblTotal += dblElement

enter this additional assignment statement

Figure 9-51 btnCalc_Click procedure

7. Save the solution and then start the application. Click the **Calculate** button. $11,781.59 appears in the Total sales box, as shown in Figure 9-52.

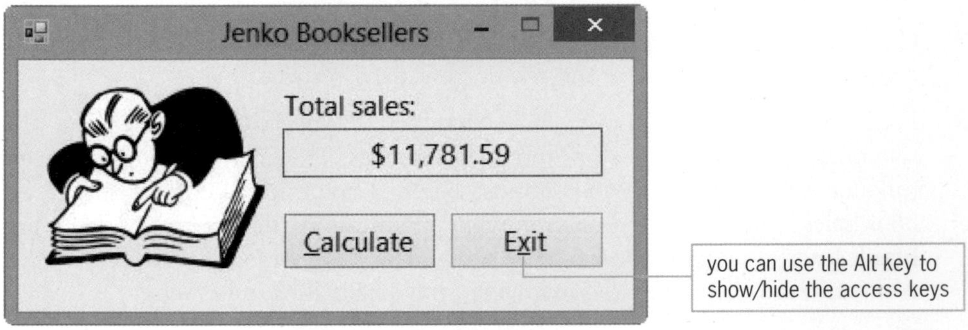

Figure 9-52 Total sales displayed in the interface
OpenClipArt.org/johnny_automatic

8. Click the **Exit** button. Close the Code Editor window and then close the solution.

Searching a Two-Dimensional Array

In Lesson B, you coded the Treasures Gift Shoppe application. As you may remember, the application stores the gift shop's price list in two parallel one-dimensional arrays: a String array for the item IDs and an Integer array for the corresponding prices. It then searches the String array for the ID entered by the user. If the ID is in the array, the application displays its corresponding price from the Integer array; otherwise, it displays an appropriate message in a message box. Instead of using two parallel one-dimensional arrays for the price list, you can use a two-dimensional array. To do this, you store the IDs in the first column of the array, and store the corresponding prices in the second column. However, you will need to treat the prices as strings because all of the data in a two-dimensional array must have the same data type.

To use a two-dimensional array to code the Treasures Gift Shoppe application:

START HERE

1. Open the Treasures Solution (Treasures Solution.sln) file contained in the VB2012\Chap09\Treasures Solution-Two-Dimensional folder. If necessary, open the designer window. The text box's CharacterCasing and MaxLength properties are set to Upper and 4, respectively.
2. Open the Code Editor window. Replace <your name> and <current date> in the comments with your name and the current date, respectively.
3. First, you will declare and initialize the two-dimensional array. Click the **blank line** below the `' declare two-dimensional array` comment in the form's Declarations section, and then enter the following array declaration statement:

```
Private strItems(,) As String = {{"BX35", "13"},
                                  {"CR20", "10"},
                                  {"FE15", "12"},
                                  {"KW10", "24"},
                                  {"MM67", "4"}}
```

4. Open the btnDisplay_Click procedure. Type the following comment and then press **Enter** twice:

```
' displays the price associated with an ID
```

5. The procedure will use a String variable to store the ID entered by the user, and use an Integer variable to keep track of the row subscripts while the array is being searched. Enter the following two declaration statements. Press **Enter** twice after typing the second statement.

```
Dim strSearchForId As String
Dim intRow As Integer
```

6. Now you will assign the ID to the `strSearchForId` variable. Type the following assignment statement and then press **Enter** twice:

```
strSearchForId = txtId.Text
```

7. Next, you will use a loop to search each element in the first column in the `strItems` array, stopping either when the end of the first column is reached or when the ID is located in the first column. Enter the following comments and code:

```
' search the first column for the ID
' continue searching until the end of
' the first column or the ID is found
Do Until intRow > strItems.GetUpperBound(0) OrElse
    strSearchForId = strItems(intRow, 0)
    intRow += 1
Loop
```

8. Finally, you need to use a selection structure to determine why the loop ended. You can make this determination by looking at the value in the `intRow` variable. If the loop ended because it reached the end of the array's first column without locating the ID, the `intRow` variable's value will be greater than the highest row subscript. On the other hand, if the loop ended because it located the ID in the first column, the `intRow` variable's value will be less than or equal to the highest row subscript. Insert two blank lines above the End Sub clause. In the blank line immediately above the End Sub clause, enter the following If clause:

```
If intRow <= strItems.GetUpperBound(0) Then
```

9. If the selection structure's condition evaluates to True, it means that the ID was located in the first column of the array. In that case, the structure's true path should display the price contained in the same row as the ID, but in the second column in the array. For example, if the ID is contained in the `strItems(3, 0)` element, then its associated price is contained in the `strItems(3, 1)` element. However, recall that the price is stored as a string in the `strItems` array. In order to use the ToString method to format the price with a dollar sign and zero decimal places, you first need to convert the price to a numeric data type. (Recall that the ToString method is used with numeric variables.) Enter the following lines of code:

```
Dim intPrice As Integer
Integer.TryParse(strItems(intRow, 1), intPrice)
lblPrice.Text = intPrice.ToString("C0")
```

10. On the other hand, if the selection structure's condition evaluates to False, the structure's false path should display the "Invalid ID" message in a message box. Enter the following lines of code:

```
Else
    MessageBox.Show("Invalid ID", "Treasures",
                    MessageBoxButtons.OK,
                    MessageBoxIcon.Information)
```

11. If necessary, delete the blank line above the End If clause.

Figure 9-53 shows most of the application's code.

```
' declare two-dimensional array
Private strItems(,) As String = {{"BX35", "13"},
                                 {"CR20", "10"},
                                 {"FE15", "12"},
                                 {"KW10", "24"},
                                 {"MM67", "4"}}

Private Sub btnDisplay_Click(sender As Object,
e As EventArgs) Handles btnDisplay.Click
    ' displays the price associated with an ID

    Dim strSearchForId As String
    Dim intRow As Integer

    strSearchForId = txtId.Text

    ' search the first column for the ID
    ' continue searching until the end of
    ' the first column or the ID is found
    Do Until intRow > strItems.GetUpperBound(0) OrElse
        strSearchForId = strItems(intRow, 0)
        intRow += 1
    Loop

    If intRow <= strItems.GetUpperBound(0) Then
        Dim intPrice As Integer
        Integer.TryParse(strItems(intRow, 1), intPrice)
        lblPrice.Text = intPrice.ToString("C0")
    Else
        MessageBox.Show("Invalid ID", "Treasures",
                        MessageBoxButtons.OK,
                        MessageBoxIcon.Information)
    End If
End Sub
```

two-dimensional array declaration

searches for the ID in the array's first column

assigns the corresponding price from the array's second column

Figure 9-53 Most of the code for the Treasures Gift Shoppe application

To test the Treasures Gift Shop application:

START HERE

1. Save the solution and then start the application. Type **kw10** in the ID box and then click the **Display Price** button. $24 appears in the Price box. See Figure 9-54.

Figure 9-54 Interface showing the price for item ID KW10

2. Type **xx44** in the ID box and then click the **Display Price** button. The "Invalid ID" message appears in a message box. Close the message box.

3. On your own, test the application using other valid and invalid IDs. When you are finished testing the application, click the **Exit** button.

4. Close the Code Editor window and then close the solution.

Lesson C Summary

- To declare a two-dimensional array:

  Use either of the syntax versions shown below. In Version 1, the *highestRowSubscript* and *highestColumnSubscript* arguments are integers that specify the highest row and column subscripts, respectively, in the array. Using Version 1's syntax, the computer automatically initializes the array elements. In Version 2, the *initialValues* section is a list of values separated by commas and enclosed in braces. You include a separate initialValues section for each row in the array. Each initialValues section should contain the same number of values as there are columns in the array.

  Version 1: {**Dim** | **Private** | **Static**} *arrayName*(*highestRowSubscript*, *highestColumnSubscript*) **As** *dataType*

  Version 2: {**Dim** | **Private** | **Static**} *arrayName*(,) **As** *dataType* = {{*initialValues*},...{*initialValues*}}

- To refer to an element in a two-dimensional array:

  Use the syntax *arrayName*(*rowSubscript*, *columnSubscript*).

- To determine the highest row subscript in a two-dimensional array:

  Use the GetUpperBound method as follows: *arrayName*.**GetUpperBound(0)**.

- To determine the highest column subscript in a two-dimensional array:

  Use the GetUpperBound method as follows: *arrayName*.**GetUpperBound(1)**.

Lesson C Key Term

Two-dimensional array—an array made up of rows and columns; each element has the same name and data type and is identified by a unique combination of two subscripts: a row subscript and a column subscript

Lesson C Review Questions

1. Which of the following declares a two-dimensional array that has three rows and four columns?

   a. `Dim decNums(2, 3) As Decimal`

   b. `Dim decNums(3, 4) As Decimal`

   c. `Dim decNums(3, 2) As Decimal`

   d. `Dim decNums(4, 3) As Decimal`

2. The `intSales` array is declared as follows: `Dim intSales(,) As Integer = {{1000, 1200, 900, 500, 2000}, {350, 600, 700, 800, 100}}`. The `intSales(1, 3) = intSales(1, 3) + 10` statement will ______________.

   a. replace the 900 amount with 910
   b. replace the 500 amount with 510
   c. replace the 700 amount with 710
   d. replace the 800 amount with 810

3. The `intSales` array is declared as follows: `Dim intSales(,) As Integer = {{1000, 1200, 900, 500, 2000}, {350, 600, 700, 800, 100}}`. The `intSales(0, 4) = intSales(0, 4 - 2)` statement will ______________.

   a. replace the 500 amount with 1200
   b. replace the 2000 amount with 900
   c. replace the 2000 amount with 1998
   d. result in an error

4. The `intSales` array is declared as follows: `Dim intSales(,) As Integer = {{1000, 1200, 900, 500, 2000}, {350, 600, 700, 800, 100}}`. Which of the following If clauses determines whether the `intRow` and `intCol` variables contain valid row and column subscripts, respectively, for the array?

   a.
```
If intSales(intRow, intCol) >= 0 AndAlso
      intSales(intRow, intCol) < 5 Then
```
   b.
```
If intSales(intRow, intCol) >= 0 AndAlso
      intSales(intRow, intCol) <= 5 Then
```
   c.
```
If intRow >= 0 AndAlso intRow < 3 AndAlso
      intCol >= 0 AndAlso intCol < 6 Then
```
   d.
```
If intRow >= 0 AndAlso intRow < 2 AndAlso
      intCol >= 0 AndAlso intCol < 5 Then
```

5. Which of the following statements assigns the string "California" to the element located in the third column, fifth row in the two-dimensional `strStates` array?

   a. `strStates(3, 5) = "California"`
   b. `strStates(5, 3) = "California"`
   c. `strStates(4, 2) = "California"`
   d. `strStates(2, 4) = "California"`

6. Which of the following assigns the number 0 to each element in a two-row, four-column Integer array named `intSums`?

   a.
```
For intRow As Integer = 0 To 1
    For intCol As Integer = 0 To 3
        intSums(intRow, intCol) = 0
    Next intCol
Next intRow
```

b.
```
Dim intRow As Integer
Dim intCol As Integer
Do While intRow < 2
      intCol = 0
      Do While intCol < 4
            intSums(intRow, intCol) = 0
            intCol += 1
      Loop
      intRow += 1
Loop
```

c.
```
For intX As Integer = 1 To 2
      For intY As Integer = 1 To 4
            intSums(intX - 1, intY - 1) = 0
      Next intY
Next intX
```

d. all of the above

7. Which of the following returns the highest column subscript in a two-dimensional array named `decPays`?

   a. `decPays.GetUpperBound(1)`
   b. `decPays.GetUpperBound(0)`
   c. `decPays.GetUpperSubscript(0)`
   d. `decPays.GetHighestColumn(0)`

Lesson C Exercises

INTRODUCTORY

1. Write the statement to declare a procedure-level two-dimensional array named `intBalances`. The array should have four rows and six columns. Then write the statement to store the number 100 in the element located in the second row, fourth column.

INTRODUCTORY

2. Write a loop to store the number 10 in each element in the `intBalances` array from Exercise 1. Use the For...Next statement.

INTRODUCTORY

3. Rewrite the code from Exercise 2 using a Do...Loop statement.

INTRODUCTORY

4. Write the statement to assign the Boolean value True to the variable located in the third row, first column of a two-dimensional Boolean array named `blnAnswers`.

INTRODUCTORY

5. Write the Private statement to declare a two-dimensional Integer array named `intOrders` that has three rows and two columns. Use the following values to initialize the array: 1, 2, 10, 20, 100, 200.

INTRODUCTORY

6. Write the statements that determine the highest row and highest column subscripts in a two-dimensional array named `strTypes`. The statements should assign the subscripts to the `intHighRow` and `intHighCol` variables, respectively.

INTRODUCTORY

7. Write the statement that determines the number of elements in a two-dimensional array named `strTypes`. The statement should assign the number to the `intNumTypes` variable.

INTERMEDIATE

8. Open the Westin Solution (Westin Solution.sln) file contained in the VB2012\Chap09\Westin Solution folder. Open the Code Editor window. The btnForEach_Click procedure should use the For Each...Next statement to display the contents of the `strParts` array in the lstForEachParts control. The btnFor_Click procedure should display the contents of the `strParts` array in the lstForParts control, column by column. Save the solution and then start and test the application. Close the Code Editor window and then close the solution.

9. Open the Bonus Solution (Bonus Solution.sln) file contained in the VB2012\Chap09\Bonus Solution folder. Open the Code Editor window. The btnCalc_Click procedure should total the numbers stored in the following three array elements: the first row, first column; the second row, third column; and the third row, fourth column. Display the sum in the lblSum control. Save the solution and then start and test the application. Close the Code Editor window and then close the solution. INTERMEDIATE

10. Open the Inventory Solution (Inventory Solution.sln) file contained in the VB2012\Chap09\Inventory Solution folder. Open the Code Editor window. The btnCalc_Click procedure should multiply the value stored in each array element by 2 and then display the result in the list box. Use two For...Next statements. Save the solution and then start and test the application. Close the Code Editor window and then close the solution. INTERMEDIATE

11. Open the Laury Solution (Laury Solution.sln) file contained in the VB2012\Chap09\Laury Solution-TwoDimensional folder. The application should display a shipping charge that is based on the number of items a customer orders. The order amounts and shipping charges are listed in Figure 9-55. Code the application. Store the minimum order amounts and shipping charges in a two-dimensional array. Display the appropriate shipping charge with a dollar sign and two decimal places. Save the solution and then start and test the application. Close the Code Editor window and then close the solution. INTERMEDIATE

Minimum order	Maximum order	Shipping charge
1	10	15
11	50	10
51	100	5
101	No maximum	0

Figure 9-55 Order amounts and shipping charges for Exercise 11

12. In this exercise, you code an application that allows Professor Carver to display a grade based on the number of points he enters. The grading scale is shown in Figure 9-56. Open the Carver Solution (Carver Solution.sln) file contained in the VB2012\Chap09\Carver Solution-TwoDimensional folder. Code the application. Store the minimum points and grades in a two-dimensional array. Save the solution and then start and test the application. Close the Code Editor window and then close the solution. ADVANCED

Minimum points	Maximum points	Grade
0	299	F
300	349	D
350	399	C
400	449	B
450	500	A

Figure 9-56 Grading scale for Exercise 12

ADVANCED

13. The sales manager at Conway Enterprises wants an application that she can use to display the total domestic, total international, and total company sales made during a six-month period. The sales amounts are shown in Figure 9-57. Create a Visual Basic Windows application. Use the following names for the solution and project, respectively: Conway Solution and Conway Project. Save the application in the VB2012\Chap09 folder. Change the form file's name to Main Form.vb. Change the form's name to frmMain. Create a suitable interface and then code the application. Store the sales amounts in a two-dimensional array. Save the solution and then start and test the application. Close the Code Editor window and then close the solution.

Month	Domestic sales ($)	International sales ($)
1	100,000	150,000
2	90,000	120,000
3	75,000	210,000
4	88,000	50,000
5	125,000	220,000
6	63,000	80,000

Figure 9-57 Sales amounts for Exercise 13

ADVANCED

14. Open the Harrison Solution (Harrison Solution.sln) file contained in the VB2012\Chap09\Harrison Solution folder. The btnDisplay_Click procedure should display the largest number stored in the first column of the array. Code the procedure using the For...Next statement. Save the solution and then start and test the application. Close the Code Editor window and then close the solution.

ADVANCED

15. Open the Count Solution (Count Solution.sln) file contained in the VB2012\Chap09\Count Solution folder. Code the Display button's Click event procedure so that it displays the number of times each of the numbers from 1 through 9 appears in the `intNumbers` array. (Hint: Store the counts in a one-dimensional array.) Save the solution and then start the application. Click the Display button to display the nine counts. Close the Code Editor window and then close the solution.

SWAT THE BUGS

16. Open the Debug Solution (Debug Solution.sln) file contained in the VB2012\Chap09\Debug Solution folder. Open the Code Editor window and review the existing code. The first column in the `strNames` array contains first names, and the second column contains last names. The btnDisplay_Click procedure should display the first and last names in the lstFirst and lstLast controls, respectively. Correct the code to remove the jagged lines. Save the solution and then start the application. Click the Display button. Notice that the application is not working correctly. Correct the errors in the application's code. Save the solution and then start and test the application. Close the Code Editor window and then close the solution.

CHAPTER 10

Structures and Sequential Access Files

Creating the CD Collection Application

In this chapter, you will create an application that keeps track of a person's CD collection. The application will save each CD's name, the artist's name, and the CD price in a sequential access file named CDs.txt. When the application is started, it will display the contents of the file in a list box. The application will allow the user to add information to the file and also remove information from the file.

Previewing the CD Collection Application

Before you start the first lesson in this chapter, you will preview the completed application. The application is contained in the VB2012\Chap10 folder.

START HERE

To preview the completed application:

1. Use the Run dialog box to run the CD (CD.exe) file contained in the VB2012\Chap10 folder. The application's user interface appears on the screen, with the contents of the CDs.txt file displayed in the list box. Notice that the list box contains three columns. You will learn how to align columns of information in Lesson C.
2. First, you will add a new CD to the list box. Click the **Add** button. Type **Uncovered** as the CD name and then press **Enter**. Type **Elvis Presley** as the artist name and then press **Enter**. Type **6.99** as the price and then press **Enter**. The information you entered appears in the list box. See Figure 10-1.

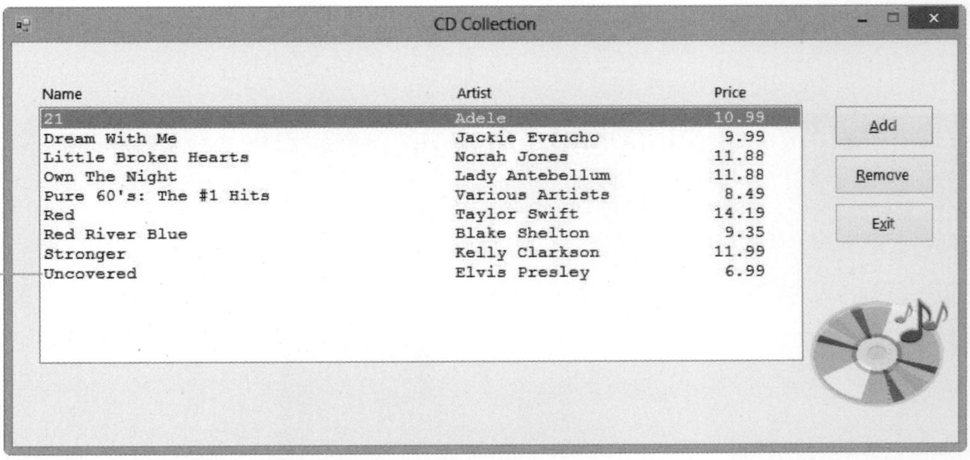

Figure 10-1 CD information added to the list box
OpenClipArt.org/ilnanny/Cristian Pozzessere

3. Now you will remove the Own The Night CD from the list box. Click **Own The Night** in the list box and then click the **Remove** button. The information pertaining to the CD is removed from the list box.
4. Click the **Exit** button to end the application. The application saves the contents of the list box in the CDs.txt sequential access file. You will learn about sequential access files in Lesson B.
5. Use Windows to open the VB2012\Chap10 folder. Right-click **CDs.txt** in the list of filenames. Point to **Open with** and then click **Notepad**. See Figure 10-2.

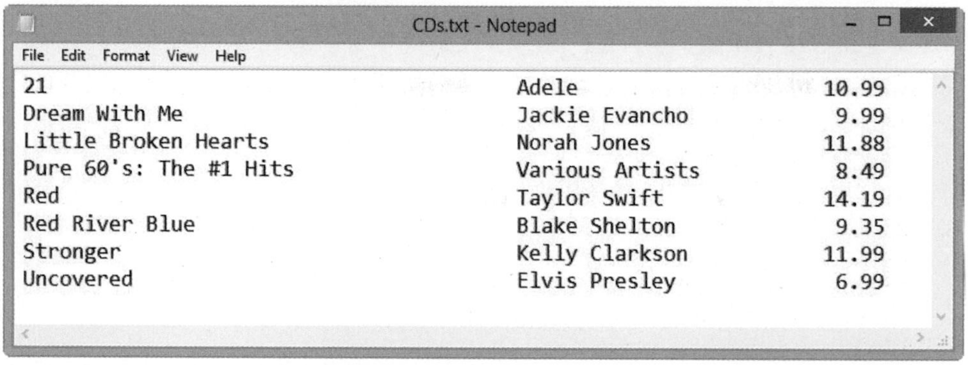

21	Adele	10.99
Dream With Me	Jackie Evancho	9.99
Little Broken Hearts	Norah Jones	11.88
Pure 60's: The #1 Hits	Various Artists	8.49
Red	Taylor Swift	14.19
Red River Blue	Blake Shelton	9.35
Stronger	Kelly Clarkson	11.99
Uncovered	Elvis Presley	6.99

Figure 10-2 Contents of the CDs.txt file

6. Close Notepad. Start the application again. The list box displays the current contents of the CDs.txt file, which includes the CD information added in Step 2 but does not include the CD information removed in Step 3.
7. Click the **Exit** button to end the application.

In Lesson A, you will learn how to create a structure in Visual Basic. Lesson B covers sequential access files. You will code the CD Collection application in Lesson C. Be sure to complete each lesson in full and do all of the end-of-lesson questions and several exercises before continuing to the next lesson.

LESSON A

After studying Lesson A, you should be able to:

- Create a structure
- Declare and use a structure variable
- Pass a structure variable to a procedure
- Create an array of structure variables

Structures

Most programmers use the Class statement (rather than the Structure statement) to create data types that contain procedures. You will learn about the Class statement in Chapter 11.

You also can include an array in a structure. This topic is explored in Exercises 9 and 10 at the end of this lesson.

The data types used in previous chapters, such as the Integer and Double data types, are built into the Visual Basic language. You also can create your own data types in Visual Basic using the **Structure statement**. Data types created by the Structure statement are referred to as **user-defined data types** or **structures**. Figure 10-3 shows the statement's syntax. The structure's name is typically entered using Pascal case. Between the Structure and End Structure clauses, you define the members included in the structure. The members can be variables, constants, or procedures. However, in most cases, the members will be variables; such variables are referred to as **member variables**.

Each member variable's definition contains the keyword `Public` followed by the variable's name, which is typically entered using camel case. Following the variable's name is the keyword `As` and the variable's *dataType*. The dataType identifies the type of data the member variable will store and can be any of the standard data types available in Visual Basic; it also can be another structure (user-defined data type). The Employee structure shown in the example in Figure 10-3 contains four member variables: three String variables and one Double variable. In most applications, you enter the Structure statement in the form's Declarations section, which begins with the Public Class clause and ends with the End Class clause.

Structure Statement

Syntax

Structure *structureName*
    Public *memberVariableName1* **As** *dataType*
    [**Public** *memberVariableNameN* **As** *dataType*]
End Structure

Example

```
Structure Employee
    Public strId As String
    Public strFirst As String
    Public strLast As String
    Public dblPay As Double
End Structure
```

Figure 10-3 Syntax and an example of the Structure statement

The Structure statement allows the programmer to group related items into one unit: a structure. However, keep in mind that the Structure statement merely defines the structure members; it does not reserve any memory locations inside the computer. You reserve memory locations by declaring a structure variable.

Declaring and Using a Structure Variable

After entering the Structure statement in the Code Editor window, you then can use the structure to declare a variable. Variables declared using a structure are often referred to as **structure variables**. The syntax for creating a structure variable is shown in Figure 10-4. The figure also includes examples of declaring structure variables using the Employee structure from Figure 10-3.

Declaring a Structure Variable

Syntax
{**Dim** | **Private**} *structureVariableName* **As** *structureName*

Example 1
```
Dim hourly As Employee
```
declares a procedure-level Employee structure variable named `hourly`

Example 2
```
Private salaried As Employee
```
declares a class-level Employee structure variable named `salaried`

Figure 10-4 Syntax and examples of declaring a structure variable

Similar to the way the `Dim intAge As Integer` instruction declares an Integer variable named `intAge`, the `Dim hourly As Employee` instruction in Example 1 declares an Employee variable named `hourly`. However, unlike the `intAge` variable, the `hourly` variable contains four member variables. In code, you refer to the entire structure variable by its name—in this case, `hourly`. You refer to a member variable by preceding its name with the name of the structure variable in which it is defined. You use the dot member access operator (a period) to separate the structure variable's name from the member variable's name. For instance, to refer to the member variables within the `hourly` structure variable, you use `hourly.strId`, `hourly.strFirst`, `hourly.strLast`, and `hourly.dblPay`. The `Private salaried As Employee` instruction in Example 2 in Figure 10-4 declares a class-level Employee variable named `salaried`. The names of the member variables within the `salaried` variable are `salaried.strId`, `salaried.strFirst`, `salaried.strLast`, and `salaried.dblPay`.

The dot member access operator indicates that `strId`, `strFirst`, `strLast`, and `dblPay` are members of the `hourly` and `salaried` variables.

The member variables in a structure variable can be used just like any other variables. You can assign values to them, use them in calculations, display their contents, and so on. Figure 10-5 shows various ways of using the member variables created by the statements shown in Figure 10-4.

Using a Member Variable

Example 1
```
hourly.strLast = "Hamilton"
```
assigns the string "Hamilton" to the `hourly.strLast` member variable

Example 2
```
hourly.dblPay = hourly.dblPay * 1.02
```
multiplies the contents of the `hourly.dblPay` member variable by 1.02 and then assigns the result to the member variable; you also can write the statement as `hourly.dblPay *= 1.02`

Example 3
```
lblSalary.Text = salaried.dblPay.ToString("C2")
```
formats the value contained in the `salaried.dblPay` member variable and then displays the result in the lblSalary control

Figure 10-5 Examples of using a member variable

Programmers use structure variables when they need to pass a group of related items to a procedure for further processing. This is because it's easier to pass one structure variable rather than many individual variables. Programmers also use structure variables to store related items in an array, even when the members have different data types. In the next two sections, you will learn how to pass a structure variable to a procedure and also store a structure variable in an array.

Passing a Structure Variable to a Procedure

The sales manager at Norbert Pool & Spa Depot wants an application that determines the amount of water required to fill a rectangular pool. To perform this task, the application will need to calculate the volume of the pool. You calculate the volume by first multiplying the pool's length by its width and then multiplying the result by the pool's depth. Assuming the length, width, and depth are measured in feet, this gives you the volume in cubic feet. To determine the number of gallons of water, you multiply the number of cubic feet by 7.48 because there are 7.48 gallons in one cubic foot.

START HERE

To open and then test the Norbert application:

1. If necessary, start Visual Studio 2012. Open the Norbert Solution (Norbert Solution.sln) file contained in the VB2012\Chap10\Norbert Solution folder. If necessary, open the designer window. (The image in the picture box was downloaded from the Open Clip Art Library at *http://openclipart.org.*)

2. Start the application. Type **100** in the Length box, **30** in the Width box, and **4** in the Depth box. Click the **Calculate** button. The required number of gallons appears in the interface. See Figure 10-6.

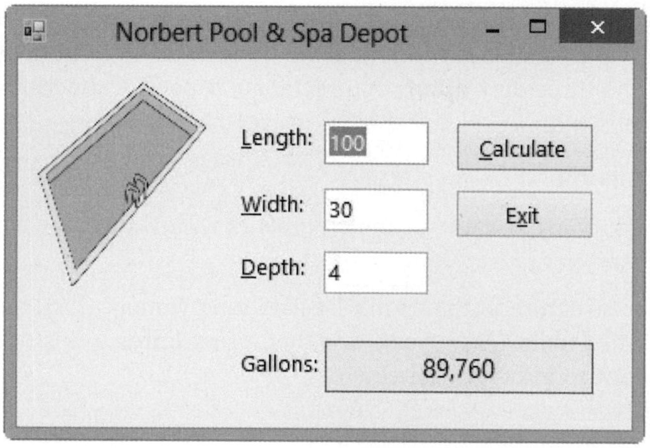

Figure 10-6 Interface showing the required number of gallons
OpenClipArt.org/laobc

3. Click the **Exit** button to end the application, and then open the Code Editor window.

Figure 10-7 shows the GetGallons function and the btnCalc_Click procedure. The procedure calls the GetGallons function, passing it three variables *by value*. The GetGallons function uses the values to calculate the number of gallons required to fill the pool. The function returns the number of gallons as a Double number to the procedure, which assigns the value to the `dblGallons` variable.

```
Public Function GetGallons(ByVal dblLen As Double,
                           ByVal dblWid As Double,
                           ByVal dblDep As Double) As Double
    ' calculates and returns the number of gallons

    Const dblGAL_PER_CUBIC_FOOT As Double = 7.48

    Return dblLen * dblWid * dblDep * dblGAL_PER_CUBIC_FOOT
End Function

Private Sub btnCalc_Click(sender As Object,
e As EventArgs) Handles btnCalc.Click
    ' displays the number of gallons

    Dim dblPoolLength As Double
    Dim dblPoolWidth As Double
    Dim dblPoolDepth As Double
    Dim dblGallons As Double

    Double.TryParse(txtLength.Text, dblPoolLength)
    Double.TryParse(txtWidth.Text, dblPoolWidth)
    Double.TryParse(txtDepth.Text, dblPoolDepth)

    dblGallons =
        GetGallons(dblPoolLength, dblPoolWidth, dblPoolDepth)
    lblGallons.Text = dblGallons.ToString("N0")

    txtLength.Focus()
End Sub
```

receives three variables *by value*

returns the number of gallons

declares three variables to store the input data

passes three variables to the GetGallons function

Figure 10-7 Code for the Norbert Pool & Spa Depot application (without a structure)

A more convenient way of coding the application is to use a structure to group together the input items: length, width, and depth. It's logical to group the three items because they are related; each represents one of the three dimensions of a rectangular pool. A descriptive name for the structure would be Dimensions.

START HERE

To use a structure in the application:

1. Replace <your name> and <current date> in the comments with your name and the current date, respectively.
2. First, you will declare the structure in the form's Declarations section. Click the **blank line** immediately below the Public Class clause and then press **Enter** to insert another blank line. Enter the following Structure statement:

```
Structure Dimensions
    Public dblLength As Double
    Public dblWidth As Double
    Public dblDepth As Double
End Structure
```

3. Locate the btnCalc_Click procedure. The procedure will use a structure variable (rather than three separate variables) to store the input items. Replace the first three Dim statements with the following Dim statement:

```
Dim poolSize As Dimensions
```

4. Now you will store each input item in its corresponding member in the structure variable. In the three TryParse methods, change `dblPoolLength`, `dblPoolWidth`, and `dblPoolDepth` to **poolSize.dblLength**, **poolSize.dblWidth**, and **poolSize.dblDepth**, respectively.
5. Next, consider the changes you will need to make to the statement that invokes the GetGallons function. Instead of sending three separate variables to the function, you now need to send only one variable: the structure variable. When you pass a structure variable to a procedure, all of its members are passed automatically. Although passing one structure variable rather than three separate variables may not seem like a huge advantage, consider the convenience of passing one structure variable rather than 10 separate variables! Change the statement that invokes the GetGallons function to **dblGallons = GetGallons(poolSize)**. Don't be concerned about the jagged line that appears below `GetGallons(poolSize)` in the statement. It will disappear when you modify the GetGallons function in the next step.
6. Locate the GetGallons function. The function will now receive a Dimensions structure variable rather than three Double variables. Like the Double variables, the structure variable will be passed *by value* because the function does not need to change any member's value. Change the function's header to the following:

```
Public Function GetGallons(ByVal pool As Dimensions) As Double
```

7. Now you will use the members of the structure variable to calculate the number of gallons. Change the Return statement as follows:

```
Return pool.dblLength * pool.dblWidth *
    pool.dblDepth * dblGAL_PER_CUBIC_FOOT
```

Figure 10-8 shows the Structure statement, the GetGallons function, and the btnCalc_Click procedure. The procedure calls the GetGallons function, passing it a structure variable *by value*. The GetGallons function uses the values contained in the structure variable to calculate the number of gallons required to fill the pool. The function returns the number of gallons as a Double number to the procedure, which assigns the value to the `dblGallons` variable.

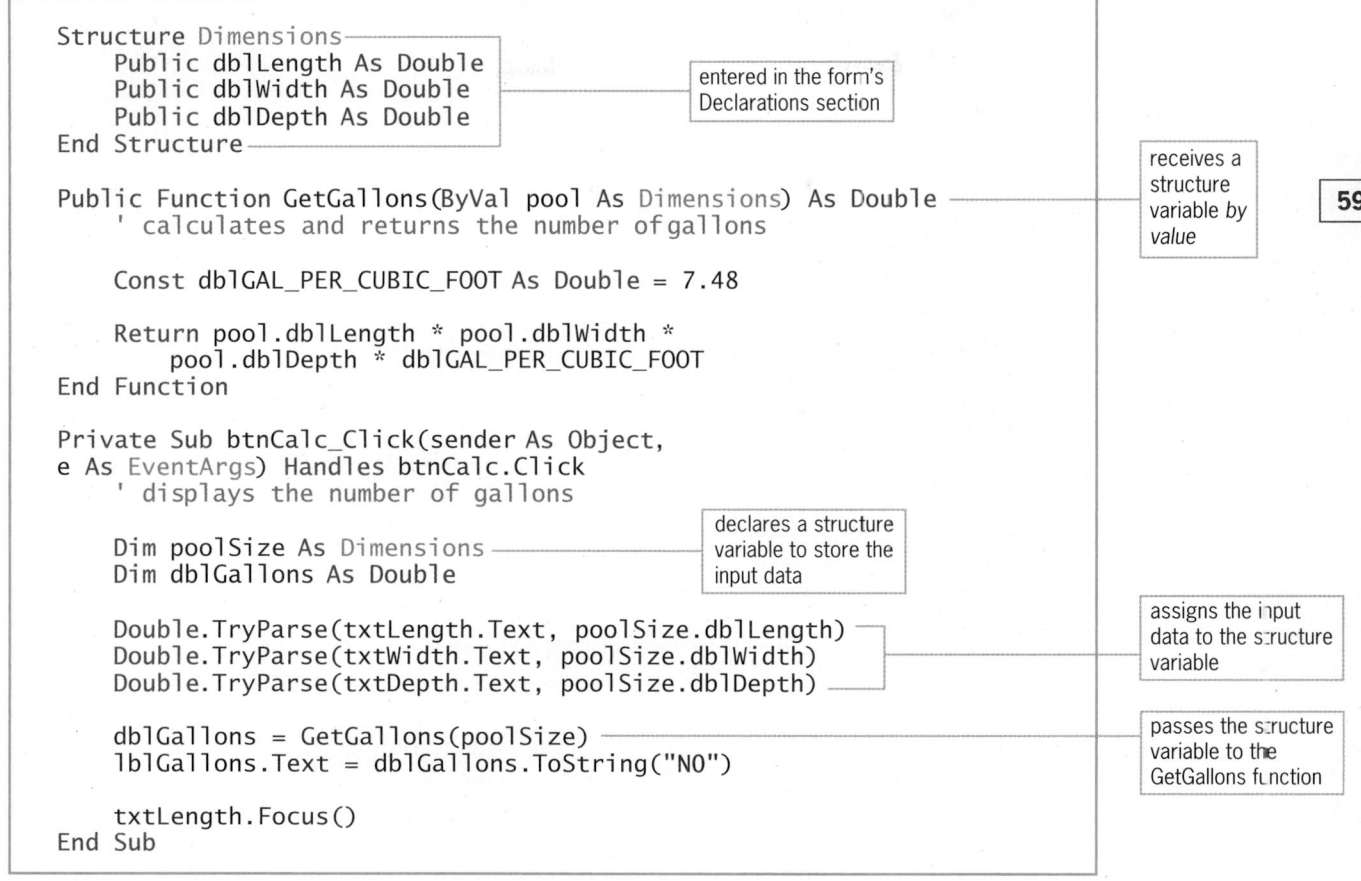

```
Structure Dimensions
    Public dblLength As Double
    Public dblWidth As Double
    Public dblDepth As Double
End Structure

Public Function GetGallons(ByVal pool As Dimensions) As Double
    ' calculates and returns the number of gallons

    Const dblGAL_PER_CUBIC_FOOT As Double = 7.48

    Return pool.dblLength * pool.dblWidth *
        pool.dblDepth * dblGAL_PER_CUBIC_FOOT
End Function

Private Sub btnCalc_Click(sender As Object,
e As EventArgs) Handles btnCalc.Click
    ' displays the number of gallons

    Dim poolSize As Dimensions
    Dim dblGallons As Double

    Double.TryParse(txtLength.Text, poolSize.dblLength)
    Double.TryParse(txtWidth.Text, poolSize.dblWidth)
    Double.TryParse(txtDepth.Text, poolSize.dblDepth)

    dblGallons = GetGallons(poolSize)
    lblGallons.Text = dblGallons.ToString("N0")

    txtLength.Focus()
End Sub
```

entered in the form's Declarations section

receives a structure variable *by value*

declares a structure variable to store the input data

assigns the input data to the structure variable

passes the structure variable to the GetGallons function

Figure 10-8 Code for the Norbert Pool & Spa Depot application (with a structure)

To test the modified code:

START HERE

1. Save the solution and then start the application. Type **100**, **30**, and **4** in the Length, Width, and Depth boxes, respectively. Press **Enter** to select the Calculate button. The required number of gallons (89,760) appears in the interface, as shown earlier in Figure 10-6.
2. Click the **Exit** button. Close the Code Editor window and then close the solution.

YOU DO IT 1!

Create a Visual Basic Windows application named YouDoIt 1. Save the application in the VB2012\Chap10 folder. Add two text boxes, a label, and a button to the form. Open the Code Editor window. Create a structure named Rectangle. The structure should have two members: one for the rectangle's length and the other for its width. The button's Click event procedure should declare a Rectangle variable named `myRectangle`. It then should assign the text box values to the variable's members. Next, the procedure should pass the `myRectangle` variable to a function that calculates and returns the area of the rectangle. Finally, the procedure should display the function's return value in the label. Code the procedure. Save the solution and then start and test the application. Close the solution.

Creating an Array of Structure Variables

As mentioned earlier, another advantage of using a structure is that a structure variable can be stored in an array, even when its members have different data types. The Treasures Gift Shoppe application from Chapter 9 can be used to illustrate this concept. The problem specification is shown in Figure 10-9.

Problem Specification

Takoda Tapahe, the owner of a small gift shop named Treasures Gift Shoppe, wants an application that allows her to enter an item's ID. The application should display the item's price. A portion of the gift shop's price list is shown here. The application should store the price list in an array.

Item ID	Price
BX35	13
CR20	10
FE15	12
KW10	24
MM67	4

Figure 10-9 Problem specification for the Treasures Gift Shoppe

In Chapter 9, you coded the Treasures Gift Shoppe application in two different ways. In Lesson B, you coded it using two parallel one-dimensional arrays: one having the String data type and the other having the Integer data type. In Lesson C, you coded it using a two-dimensional String array. In this lesson, you will code the application using a one-dimensional array of structure variables. (Notice that there are many different ways of solving the same problem.) Each structure variable will contain two member variables: a String variable for the ID and an Integer variable for the price.

START HERE

To open the Treasures Gift Shoppe application:

1. Open the Treasures Solution (Treasures Solution.sln) file contained in the VB2012\Chap10\Treasures Solution-Structure folder. If necessary, open the designer window. See Figure 10-10. (The image in the picture box was downloaded from the Open Clip Art Library at *http://openclipart.org*.)

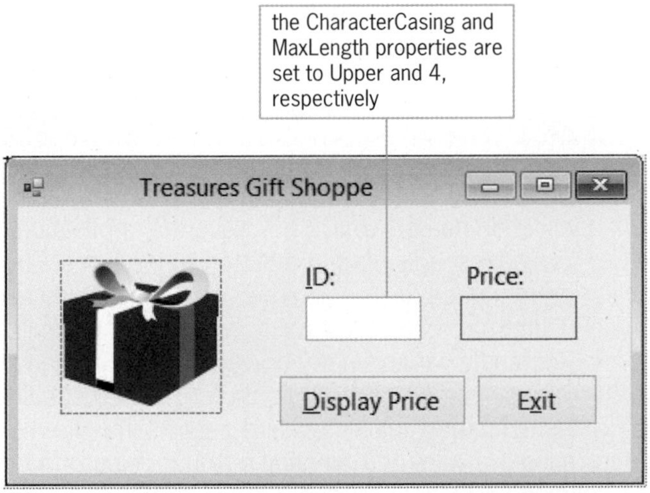

Figure 10-10 Interface for the Treasures Gift Shoppe application

2. Open the Code Editor window. Replace <your name> and <current date> in the comments with your name and the current date, respectively.

Figure 10-11 shows the code entered in both the form's Declarations section and the btnDisplay_Click procedure. The code, which comes from Chapter 9's Lesson B, uses two parallel one-dimensional arrays. In the remainder of this lesson, you will modify the code to use a structure.

```
' declare parallel arrays
Private strIds() As String =
    {"BX35", "CR20", "FE15", "KW10", "MM67"}
Private intPrices() As Integer = {13, 10, 12, 24, 4}


Private Sub btnDisplay_Click(sender As Object,
e As EventArgs) Handles btnDisplay.Click
    ' displays the price associated with an ID

    Dim strSearchForId As String
    Dim intSub As Integer

    strSearchForId = txtId.Text

    ' search the strIds array for the ID
    ' continue searching until the end of
    ' the array or the ID is found
    Do Until intSub = strIds.Length OrElse
        strSearchForId = strIds(intSub)
        intSub += 1
    Loop

    If intSub < strIds.Length Then
        lblPrice.Text = intPrices(intSub).ToString("C0")
    Else
        MessageBox.Show("Invalid ID", "Treasures",
                        MessageBoxButtons.OK,
                            MessageBoxIcon.Information)
    End If
End Sub
```

form's Declarations section

btnDisplay_Click

Figure 10-11 Code for the Treasures Gift Shoppe application (without a structure)

START HERE

To begin modifying the code to use a structure:

1. First, you will declare a structure named ProductInfo. The structure will contain two members: one for the item ID and one for the price. Click the **blank line** immediately below the Public Class clause and then press **Enter** to insert another blank line. Enter the following Structure statement:

   Structure ProductInfo
   Public strId As String
   Public intPrice As Integer
   End Structure

2. If necessary, insert a blank line below the End Structure clause.

3. Rather than using two parallel one-dimensional arrays to store the price list, the procedure will use a one-dimensional array of ProductInfo structure variables. Change the `' declare parallel arrays` comment to **' declare array of structure variables**.

4. Now, replace the two array declaration statements with the following statement:

   Private priceList(4) As ProductInfo

Next, you need to store the five IDs and prices in the `priceList` array. You will have the form's Load event procedure perform that task. Keep in mind that each element in the array is a structure variable, and each structure variable contains two member variables: `strId` and `intPrice`. You refer to a member variable in an array element using the syntax shown in Figure 10-12. The figure also indicates how you would refer to some of the member variables contained in the `priceList` array. For example, to refer to the `strId` member contained in the first array element, you use `priceList(0).strId`. Similarly, you use `priceList(4).intPrice` to refer to the `intPrice` member contained in the last array element.

Referring to a Member Variable in an Array Element

Syntax
arrayName(*subscript*).*memberVariableName*

Examples using the `priceList` array

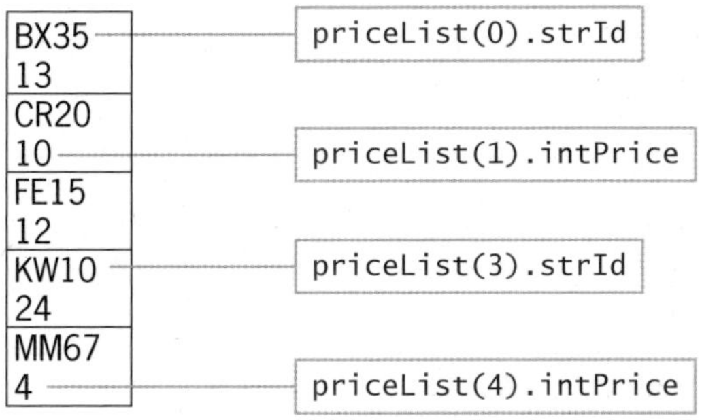

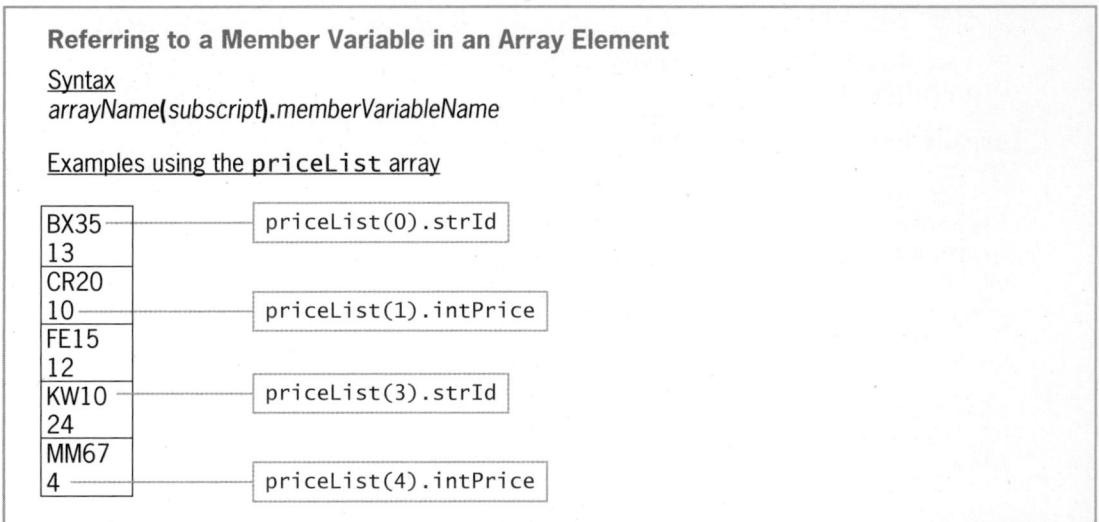

Figure 10-12 Syntax and examples of referring to member variables in an array

START HERE

To continue modifying the code:

1. Open the form's Load event procedure. Type the following comment and then press **Enter** twice:

   ' fill array with IDs and prices

2. Enter the following comment and assignment statements:

```
priceList(0).strId = "BX35"
priceList(0).intPrice = 13
priceList(1).strId = "CR20"
priceList(1).intPrice = 10
priceList(2).strId = "FE15"
priceList(2).intPrice = 12
priceList(3).strId = "KW10"
priceList(3).intPrice = 24
priceList(4).strId = "MM67"
priceList(4).intPrice = 4
```

3. Locate the btnDisplay_Click procedure. The loop now needs to search the `priceList` array (rather than the `strIds` array). Change `strIds` in the `' search the strIds array for the ID` comment to **priceList**.

4. The loop should search each element in the `priceList` array, comparing the value contained in the current element's `strId` member with the value stored in the `strSearchForId` variable. The loop should stop searching either when the end of the array is reached or when the ID is found. Change the Do clause to the following:

   Do Until intSub = priceList.Length OrElse
   strSearchForId = priceList(intSub).strId

You can also write the first expression in the Do loop's condition as `intSub > priceList.GetUpperBound(0)`.

5. The selection structure in the procedure determines why the loop ended and then takes the appropriate action. Currently, the statement's condition compares the value contained in the `intSub` variable with the value stored in the `strIds` array's Length property. Recall that a one-dimensional array's Length property stores an integer that represents the number of elements in the array. You will need to modify the condition so that it compares the `intSub` variable's value with the value stored in the `priceList` array's Length property. Change `strIds.Length` in the If clause to **priceList.Length**.

6. If the value contained in the `intSub` variable is less than the number of array elements, the loop ended because the ID was located in the array. In that case, the selection structure's true path should display the corresponding price. Change the assignment statement below the If clause as follows:

   lblPrice.Text =
   priceList(intSub).intPrice.ToString("C0")

7. On the other hand, if the value in the `intSub` variable is not less than the number of array elements, the loop ended because it reached the end of the array without finding the ID. In that case, the selection structure's false path should display the "Invalid ID" message in a message box. The appropriate code is already entered in the selection structure's false path.

Figure 10-13 shows the Structure statement, the btnDisplay_Click procedure, and the frmMain_Load procedure. The code pertaining to the structure is shaded in the figure.

form's Declarations section

btnDisplay_Click

frmMain_Load

```
Structure ProductInfo
    Public strId As String
    Public intPrice As Integer
End Structure

' declare array of structure variables
Private priceList(4) As ProductInfo

Private Sub btnDisplay_Click(sender As Object,
e As EventArgs) Handles btnDisplay.Click
    ' displays the price associated with an ID

    Dim strSearchForId As String
    Dim intSub As Integer

    strSearchForId = txtId.Text

    ' search the priceList array for the ID
    ' continue searching until the end of
    ' the array or the ID is found
    Do Until intSub = priceList.Length OrElse
        strSearchForId = priceList(intSub).strId
        intSub += 1
    Loop

    If intSub < priceList.Length Then
        lblPrice.Text =
            priceList(intSub).intPrice.ToString("C0")
    Else
        MessageBox.Show("Invalid ID", "Treasures",
                        MessageBoxButtons.OK,
                        MessageBoxIcon.Information)
    End If
End Sub

Private Sub frmMain_Load(sender As Object,
e As EventArgs) Handles Me.Load
    ' fill array with IDs and prices

    pricelist(0).strId = "BX35"
    pricelist(0).intPrice = 13
    pricelist(1).strId = "CR20"
    pricelist(1).intPrice = 10
    pricelist(2).strId = "FE15"
    pricelist(2).intPrice = 12
    pricelist(3).strId = "KW10"
    pricelist(3).intPrice = 24
    pricelist(4).strId = "MM67"
    pricelist(4).intPrice = 4

End Sub
```

Figure 10-13 Code for the Treasures Gift Shoppe application (with a structure)

START HERE

To test the application's code:

1. Save the solution and then start the application. Type **fe15** in the ID box and then click the **Display Price** button. $12 appears in the Price box, as shown in Figure 10-14.

Figure 10-14 Interface showing the price for product ID FE15
OpenClipArt.org/secretlondon

2. Click the **Exit** button. Close the Code Editor window and then close the solution.

Lesson A Summary

- To create a structure (user-defined data type):

  Use the Structure statement. The statement's syntax is shown in Figure 10-3. In most applications, you enter the Structure statement in the form's Declarations section.

- To declare a structure variable:

  Use the following syntax: {**Dim** | **Private**} *structureVariableName* **As** *structureName*.

- To refer to a member within a structure variable:

  Use the syntax *structureVariableName***.***memberVariableName*.

- To create an array of structure variables:

  Declare the array using the structure as the data type.

- To refer to a member within a structure variable stored in an array:

  Use the syntax *arrayName*(*subscript*)**.***memberVariableName*.

Lesson A Key Terms

Member variables—the variables contained in a structure

Structure statement—used to create user-defined data types, called structures

Structure variables—variables declared using a structure as the data type

Structures—data types created by the Structure statement; allow the programmer to group related items into one unit; also called user-defined data types

User-defined data types—data types created by the Structure statement; also called structures

Lesson A Review Questions

1. Which statement is used to create a user-defined data type?
   a. Declare
   b. Define
   c. Structure
   d. UserType

2. A structure variable named `course` contains a member variable named `strNum`. Which of the following statements assigns the string "CIS250" to the member variable?
   a. `course.strNum = "CIS250"`
   b. `course&strNum = "CIS250"`
   c. `strNum.course = "CIS250"`
   d. none of the above

3. An array is declared using the statement `Dim onOrder(10) As Items`. Which of the following statements assigns the number 50 to the `intQuantity` member variable contained in the last array element?
   a. `onOrder.intQuantity(10) = 50`
   b. `Items.onOrder.intQuantity = 50`
   c. `onOrder(9).intQuantity = 50`
   d. `onOrder(10).intQuantity = 50`

4. An application uses a structure named Employee. Which of the following statements declares a five-element array of Employee structure variables?
   a. `Dim workers(4) As Employee`
   b. `Dim workers(5) As Employee`
   c. `Dim workers As Employee(4)`
   d. `Dim workers As Employee(5)`

5. In most applications, the Structure statement is entered in the form's ______________.
   a. Declarations section
   b. Definition section
   c. Load event procedure
   d. User-defined section

Lesson A Exercises

INTRODUCTORY

1. Write a Structure statement that defines a structure named Book. The structure contains three member variables named `strTitle`, `strAuthor`, and `decPrice`. Then write a Dim statement that declares a Book variable named `fiction`.

INTRODUCTORY

2. Write a Structure statement that defines a structure named Tape. The structure contains four member variables named `strName`, `strArtist`, `strSongLength`, and `intSongNum`. Then write a Private statement that declares a Tape variable named `blues`.

INTRODUCTORY

3. An application contains the Structure statement shown here. Write a Dim statement that declares a Computer variable named `homeUse`. Then, write an assignment statement that assigns the string "IB-50" to the `strModel` member. Finally, write an assignment statement that assigns the number 2400 to the `dblCost` member.

```
Structure Computer
    Public strModel As String
    Public dblCost As Double
End Structure
```

4. An application contains the Structure statement shown here. Write a Dim statement that declares a MyFriend variable named `school`. Then, write assignment statements that assign the value in the txtFirst control to the `strFirst` member and assign the value in the txtLast control to the `strLast` member. Finally, write assignment statements that assign the value in the `strLast` member to the lblLast control and assign the value in the `strFirst` member to the lblFirst control. INTRODUCTORY

```
Structure MyFriend
    Public strLast As String
    Public strFirst As String
End Structure
```

5. An application contains the Structure statement shown here. Write a Private statement that declares a 10-element one-dimensional array of Computer variables. Name the array `business`. Then, write an assignment statement that assigns the string "HPP405" to the `strModel` member contained in the first array element. Finally, write an assignment statement that assigns the number 3600 to the `decCost` member contained in the first array element. INTERMEDIATE

```
Structure Computer
    Public strModel As String
    Public decCost As Decimal
End Structure
```

6. An application contains the Structure statement shown here. Write a Dim statement that declares a five-element one-dimensional array of MyFriend variables. Name the array `home`. Then, write an assignment statement that assigns the value in the txtName control to the `strName` member contained in the last array element. Finally, write an assignment statement that assigns the value in the txtBirthday control to the `strBirthday` member contained in the last array element. INTERMEDIATE

```
Structure MyFriend
    Public strName As String
    Public strBirthday As String
End Structure
```

7. In this exercise, you modify the Treasures Gift Shoppe application completed in the lesson. Use Windows to make a copy of the Treasures Solution-Structure folder. Rename the folder Modified Treasures Solution-Structure. Open the Treasures Solution (Treasures Solution.sln) file contained in the Modified Treasures Solution-Structure folder. Open the designer window. The modified application should display both the name and price corresponding to the ID entered by the user. Make the appropriate modifications to the interface and the code (including the Structure statement). The names of the products are shown in Figure 10-15. Save the solution and then start and test the application. Close the Code Editor window and then close the solution. INTERMEDIATE

Product ID	Name
BX35	Necklace
CR20	Bracelet
FE15	Jewelry box
KW10	Doll
MM67	Ring

Figure 10-15 Product information for Exercise 7

INTERMEDIATE

8. Open the Middleton Solution (Middleton Solution.sln) file contained in the VB2012\Chap10\Middleton Solution folder. If necessary, open the designer window. The application should display a grade based on the number of points entered by the user. The grading scale is shown in Figure 10-16. Open the Code Editor window. Create a structure that contains two members: an Integer variable for the minimum points and a String variable for the grades. Use the structure to declare a class-level one-dimensional array that has five elements. In the form's Load event procedure, store the minimum points and grades in the array. The application should search the array for the number of points earned and then display the appropriate grade from the array. Code the application. Save the solution and then start and test the application. Close the Code Editor window and then close the solution.

Minimum Points	Maximum Points	Grade
0	299	F
300	349	D
350	419	C
420	469	B
470	500	A

Figure 10-16 Grade information for Exercise 8

DISCOVERY

9. Open the Average Solution (Average Solution.sln) file contained in the VB2012\Chap10\Average Solution folder. If necessary, open the designer window. The application should display a student's name and the average of five test scores entered by the user.

   a. Open the Code Editor window. Create a structure named StudentInfo. The structure should contain two members: a String variable for the student's name and a Double array for the test scores. An array contained in a structure cannot be assigned an initial size, so you will need to include an empty set of parentheses after the array name, like this: `Public dblScores() As Double`.

   b. Open the code template for the btnCalc control's Click event procedure. First, use the StudentInfo structure to declare a structure variable. Next, research the Visual Basic ReDim statement. Use the ReDim statement to declare the array's size. The array should have five elements.

   c. The btnCalc_Click procedure should use the InputBox function to get the student's name. It should also use a repetition structure and the InputBox function to get the five test scores from the user, storing each in the array. The procedure should display the student's name and average test score in the lblAverage control.

   d. Save the solution and then start and test the application. Close the Code Editor window and then close the solution.

DISCOVERY

10. In this exercise, you modify the application from Exercise 9. Use Windows to make a copy of the Average Solution folder. Rename the folder Modified Average Solution. Open the Average Solution (Average Solution.sln) file contained in the Modified Average Solution folder. Open the designer window. Change the font used in the lblAverage control to Courier New. Change the control's TextAlign property to TopLeft and then resize the control to display four lines of text. Open the Code Editor window. Modify the application to calculate the average of five test scores for each of four students. (Hint: Use an array of structure variables.) Display each student's name and average test score in the lblAverage control. Save the solution and then start and test the application. Close the Code Editor window and then close the solution.

LESSON B

After studying Lesson B, you should be able to:

- Open and close a sequential access file
- Write data to a sequential access file
- Read data from a sequential access file
- Determine whether a sequential access file exists
- Test for the end of a sequential access file

Sequential Access Files

In addition to getting data from the keyboard and sending data to the computer screen, an application can also get data from and send data to a file on a disk. Getting data from a file is referred to as "reading the file," and sending data to a file is referred to as "writing to the file." Files to which data is written are called **output files** because the files store the output produced by an application. Files that are read by the computer are called **input files** because an application uses the data in these files as input.

Ch10B video

Most input and output files are composed of lines of text that are both read and written sequentially. In other words, they are read and written in consecutive order, one line at a time, beginning with the first line in the file and ending with the last line in the file. Such files are referred to as **sequential access files** because of the manner in which the lines of text are accessed. They are also called **text files** because they are composed of lines of text. Examples of text stored in sequential access files include an employee list, a memo, or a sales report.

Writing Data to a Sequential Access File

An item of data—such as the string "Robert"—is viewed differently by a human being and a computer. To a human being, the string represents a person's name; to a computer, it is merely a sequence of characters. Programmers refer to a sequence of characters as a **stream of characters**.

In Visual Basic, you use a **StreamWriter object** to write a stream of characters to a sequential access file. Before you create the StreamWriter object, you first declare a variable to store the object in the computer's internal memory. Figure 10-17 shows the syntax and an example of declaring a StreamWriter variable. The IO in the syntax stands for Input/Output.

Declaring a StreamWriter Variable

Syntax

{**Dim** | **Private**} *streamWriterVariableName* **As IO.StreamWriter**

Example

```
Dim outFile As IO.StreamWriter
```

declares a StreamWriter variable named `outFile`

Figure 10-17 Syntax and an example of declaring a StreamWriter variable

You will use a StreamWriter variable in the Game Show Contestants application, which you code in this lesson. The application will write the names of contestants to a sequential access file. It also will subsequently read the names and display them in a list box.

To begin coding the Game Show Contestants application:

START HERE

1. If necessary, start Visual Studio 2012. Open the Game Show Solution (Game Show Solution.sln) file contained in the VB2012\Chap10\Game Show Solution folder. If necessary, open the designer window. See Figure 10-18.

Figure 10-18 Interface for the Game Show Contestants application

2. Open the Code Editor window. Replace <your name> and <current date> in the comments with your name and the current date, respectively.
3. Locate the btnWrite_Click procedure. Click the **blank line** below the `' declare a StreamWriter variable` comment and then enter the following declaration statement:

   Dim outFile As IO.StreamWriter

After declaring a StreamWriter variable, you can use the syntax shown in Figure 10-19 to create a StreamWriter object. As the figure indicates, creating a StreamWriter object involves opening a sequential access file using either the CreateText method or the AppendText method. You use the **CreateText method** to open a sequential access file for output. When you open a file for output, the computer creates a new, empty file to which data can be written. If the file already exists, the computer erases the contents of the file before writing any data to it. You use the **AppendText method** to open a sequential access file for append. When a file is opened for append, new data is written after any existing data in the file. If the file does not exist, the computer creates the file for you. In addition to opening the file, both methods automatically create a StreamWriter object to represent the file in the application. You assign the StreamWriter object to a StreamWriter variable, which you use to refer to the file in code. Figure 10-19 also includes examples of using both methods.

CreateText and AppendText Methods

Syntax
IO.File.*method***(***fileName***)**

method	Description
CreateText	opens a sequential access file for output
AppendText	opens a sequential access file for append

Example 1
```
outFile = IO.File.CreateText("employee.txt")
```
opens the employee.txt file for output; creates a StreamWriter object and assigns it to the `outFile` variable

Example 2
```
outFile = IO.File.AppendText("F:\Chap10\report.txt")
```
opens the report.txt file for append; creates a StreamWriter object and assigns it to the `outFile` variable

Figure 10-19 Syntax and examples of the CreateText and AppendText methods

When processing the statement in Example 1, the computer searches for the employee.txt file in the default folder, which is the current project's bin\Debug folder. If the file exists, its contents are erased and the file is opened for output; otherwise, a new, empty file is created and opened for output. The statement then creates a StreamWriter object and assigns it to the `outFile` variable.

Unlike the *fileName* argument in Example 1, the *fileName* argument in Example 2 contains a folder path. When processing the statement in Example 2, the computer searches for the report.txt file in the Chap10 folder on the F drive. If the computer locates the file, it opens the file for append. If it does not find the file, it creates a new, empty file and then opens the file for append. Like the statement in Example 1, the statement in Example 2 creates a StreamWriter object and assigns it to the `outFile` variable. When deciding whether to include the folder path in the fileName argument, keep in mind that a USB drive may have a different letter designation on another computer. Therefore, you should specify the folder path only when you are sure that it will not change.

When the user clicks the Write to File button in the Game Show Contestants interface, the name entered in the Name box should be added to the end of the existing names in the file. Therefore, you will need to open the sequential access file for append. A descriptive name for a file that stores the names of contestants is contestants.txt. Although it is not a requirement, the "txt" (short for "text") filename extension is commonly used when naming sequential access files; this is because the files contain text.

START HERE

To continue coding the btnWrite_Click procedure:

1. Click the **blank line** below the `' open the file for append` comment and then enter the following statement:

   outFile = IO.File.AppendText("contestants.txt")

After opening a file for either output or append, you can begin writing data to it using either the **Write method** or the **WriteLine method**. The difference between both methods is that the WriteLine method writes a newline character after the data. Figure 10-20 shows the syntax and an example of both methods. As the figure indicates, when using the Write method, the next character written to the file will appear immediately after the letter o in the string "Hello". When using the WriteLine method, however, the next character written to the file will appear on the line immediately below the string. You do not need to include the file's name in either method's syntax because the data will be written to the file associated with the StreamWriter variable.

Write and WriteLine Methods

Syntax
streamWriterVariableName.**Write(***data***)**
streamWriterVariableName.**WriteLine(***data***)**

Example	Result	
Example 1 `outFile.Write("Hello")`	Hello|	the next character will appear immediately after the o
Example 2 `outFile.WriteLine("Hello")`	Hello |	the next character will appear on the next line

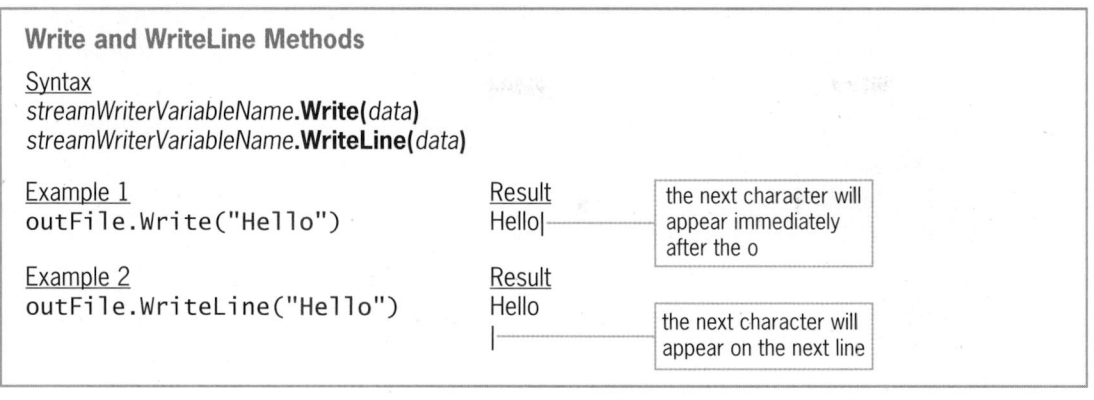

Figure 10-20 Syntax and examples of the Write and WriteLine methods

Each contestant's name should appear on a separate line in the file, so you will use the WriteLine method to write each name to the file.

START HERE

To continue coding the btnWrite_Click procedure:

1. Click the **blank line** below the `' write the name on a separate line in the file` comment and then enter the following statement:

   outFile.WriteLine(txtName.Text)

Closing an Output Sequential Access File

You should use the **Close method** to close an output sequential access file as soon as you are finished using it. This ensures that the data is saved and it makes the file available for use elsewhere in the application. The syntax to close an output sequential access file is shown in Figure 10-21 along with an example of using the method. Here again, notice that you use the StreamWriter variable to refer to the file you want to close.

Close Method (Output Sequential Access File)

Syntax
streamWriterVariableName.**Close()**

Example
`outFile.Close()`
closes the file associated with the `outFile` variable

Figure 10-21 Syntax and an example of closing an output sequential access file

START HERE

To finish coding and then test the btnWrite_Click procedure:

1. Click the **blank line** below the `' close the file` comment and then enter the following statement:

   outFile.Close()

2. Save the solution and then start the application. Type **Sophie Jacoby** in the Name box and then click the **Write to File** button. Use the application to write the following four names to the file:

   Christopher Mills
   Khalid Patel
   Marsha Coffee
   Sara Chen

3. Click the **Exit** button. Now you will open the contestants.txt file to verify its contents. Click **FILE** on the menu bar and then click **Open File**. Open the project's bin\Debug folder. Click **contestants.txt** in the list of filenames and then click the **Open** button. The contestants.txt window opens and shows the five names contained in the file. See Figure 10-22.

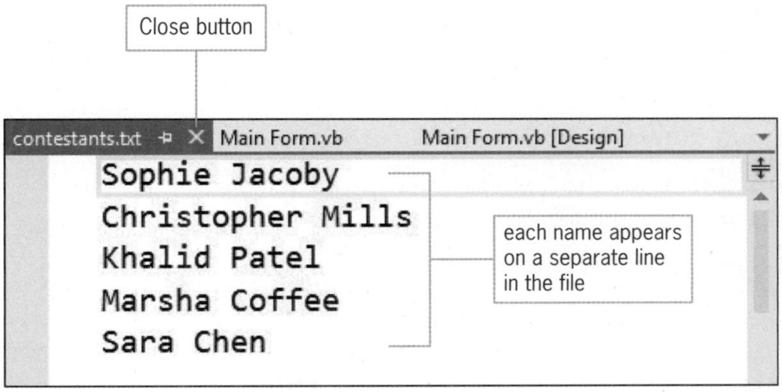

Figure 10-22 Names contained in the contestants.txt file

4. Close the contestants.txt window by clicking its **Close** button.

Reading Data from a Sequential Access File

In Visual Basic, you use a **StreamReader object** to read data from a sequential access file. Before creating the StreamReader object, you first declare a variable to store the object in the computer's internal memory. Figure 10-23 shows the syntax and an example of declaring a StreamReader variable. As mentioned earlier, the IO in the syntax stands for Input/Output.

Declaring a StreamReader Variable

Syntax
{**Dim** | **Private**} *streamReaderVariableName* **As IO.StreamReader**

Example
```
Dim inFile As IO.StreamReader
```
declares a StreamReader variable named `inFile`

Figure 10-23 Syntax and an example of declaring a StreamReader variable

To begin coding the Read from File button's Click event procedure:

START HERE

1. Locate the btnRead_Click procedure. Click the **blank line** below the `' declare variables` comment and then enter the following declaration statement:

   Dim inFile As IO.StreamReader

After declaring a StreamReader variable, you can use the **OpenText method** to open a sequential access file for input, which will automatically create a StreamReader object. When a file is opened for input, the computer can read the lines of text stored in the file. Figure 10-24 shows the OpenText method's syntax along with an example of using the method. The *fileName* argument in the example does not include a folder path, so the computer will search for the employee.txt file in the default folder, which is the current project's bin\Debug folder. If the computer finds the file, it opens the file for input. If the computer does not find the file, a run time error occurs. You assign the StreamReader object created by the OpenText method to a StreamReader variable, which you use to refer to the file in code.

OpenText Method

Syntax
IO.File.OpenText(*fileName***)**

Example
```
inFile = IO.File.OpenText("employee.txt")
```
opens the employee.txt file for input; creates a StreamReader object and assigns it to the `inFile` variable

Figure 10-24 Syntax and an example of the OpenText method

The run time error that occurs when the computer cannot locate the file you want opened for input will cause the application to end abruptly. You can use the Exists method to avoid this run time error. Figure 10-25 shows the method's syntax and includes an example of using the method. If the *fileName* argument does not include a folder path, the computer searches for the file in the current project's bin\Debug folder. The **Exists method** returns the Boolean value True if the file exists; otherwise, it returns the Boolean value False.

Exists Method

Syntax
IO.File.Exists(*fileName***)**

Example
```
If IO.File.Exists("employee.txt") Then
```
determines whether the employee.txt file exists in the current project's bin\Debug folder; you also can write the If clause as `If IO.File.Exists("employee.txt") = True Then`

Figure 10-25 Syntax and an example of the Exists method

To continue coding the btnRead_Click procedure:

START HERE

1. Click the **blank line** below the `' determine whether the file exists` comment and then enter the following If clause:

   If IO.File.Exists("contestants.txt") Then

2. If the file exists, you will use the OpenText method to open the file. Enter the following comment and assignment statement. Press **Enter** twice after typing the assignment statement.

   ' open the file for input
   inFile = IO.File.OpenText("contestants.txt")

3. If the file does not exist, you will display an appropriate message. Enter the additional lines of code shown in Figure 10-26.

```
' determine whether the file exists
If IO.File.Exists("contestants.txt") Then
    ' open the file for input
    inFile = IO.File.OpenText("contestants.txt")

Else
    MessageBox.Show("Can't find the file",
                    "Game Show Contestants",
                    MessageBoxButtons.OK,
                    MessageBoxIcon.Information)
End If
```

enter these five lines of code

Figure 10-26 Additional code entered in the procedure

After opening a file for input, you can use the **ReadLine method** to read the file's contents, one line at a time. A **line** is defined as a sequence (stream) of characters followed by the newline character. The ReadLine method returns a string that contains only the sequence of characters in the current line. The returned string does not include the newline character at the end of the line. In most cases, you assign the string returned by the ReadLine method to a String variable. Figure 10-27 shows the ReadLine method's syntax and includes an example of using the method. The ReadLine method does not require you to provide the file's name because it uses the file associated with the StreamReader variable.

ReadLine Method

Syntax
streamReaderVariableName.**ReadLine**

Example
```
Dim strMessage As String
strMessage = inFile.ReadLine
```
reads a line of text from the sequential access file associated with the `inFile` variable and assigns the line, excluding the newline character, to the `strMessage` variable

Figure 10-27 Syntax and an example of the ReadLine method

In most cases, an application will need to read each line of text contained in a sequential access file, one line at a time. You can do this using a loop along with the Peek method. The **Peek method** "peeks" into the file to determine whether the file contains another character to read. If the file contains another character, the Peek method returns the character; otherwise, it returns the number –1 (a negative 1). The Peek method's syntax is shown in Figure 10-28 along with an example of using the method. The Do clause in the example tells the computer to process the loop instructions until the Peek method returns the number –1, which indicates that there are no more characters to read. In other words, the Do clause tells the computer to process the loop instructions until the end of the file is reached.

Peek Method

Syntax
streamReaderVariableName.**Peek**

Example
```
Dim strLineOfText As String
Do Until inFile.Peek = -1
    strLineOfText = inFile.ReadLine
    MessageBox.Show(strLineOfText)
Loop
```
reads each line of text from the sequential access file associated with the `inFile` variable, line by line; each line (excluding the newline character) is assigned to the `strLineOfText` variable and is then displayed in a message box

Figure 10-28 Syntax and an example of the Peek method

START HERE

To continue coding the btnRead_Click procedure:

1. First, you will declare a variable to store the string returned by the ReadLine method. Each line in the contestants.txt file represents a name, so you will call the variable `strName`. Click the **blank line** below the Dim statement and then enter the following declaration statement:

   Dim strName As String

2. The Do clause is next. Click the **blank line** below the statement that opens the contestants.txt file. Enter the following comment and Do clause, being sure to type the minus sign before the number 1:

   ' process loop instructions until end of file
   Do Until inFile.Peek = –1

3. The first instruction in the loop should read a line of text and assign it (excluding the newline character) to the `strName` variable. Enter the following comment and assignment statement:

   ' read a name
   strName = inFile.ReadLine

4. Now, you will add the name to the Contestants list box. Enter the following comment and statement:

   ' add name to list box
   lstContestants.Items.Add(strName)

5. If necessary, delete the blank line above the Loop clause.

Closing an Input Sequential Access File

Just as you do with an output sequential access file, you should use the Close method to close an input sequential access file as soon as you are finished using it. Doing this makes the file available for use elsewhere in the application. The syntax to close an input sequential access file is shown in Figure 10-29 along with an example of using the method. Notice that you use the StreamReader variable to refer to the file you want to close.

Close Method (Input Sequential Access File)

Syntax
streamReaderVariableName.**Close()**

Example
`inFile.Close()`
closes the file associated with the `inFile` variable

Figure 10-29 Syntax and an example of closing an input sequential access file

START HERE

To finish coding the btnRead_Click procedure:

1. Click **after the letter p** in the Loop clause and then press **Enter** to insert a blank line. Enter the following comment and statement:

   ' close the file
   inFile.Close()

Figure 10-30 shows the code entered in the btnWrite_Click and btnRead_Click procedures.

```
Private Sub btnWrite_Click(sender As Object,
e As EventArgs) Handles btnWrite.Click
    ' writes a name to a sequential access file

    ' declare a StreamWriter variable
    Dim outFile As IO.StreamWriter

    ' open the file for append
    outFile = IO.File.AppendText("contestants.txt")

    ' write the name on a separate line in the file
    outFile.WriteLine(txtName.Text)

    ' close the file
    outFile.Close()

    ' clear the list box and then set the focus
    lstContestants.Items.Clear()
    txtName.Focus()
End Sub

Private Sub btnRead_Click(sender As Object,
e As EventArgs) Handles btnRead.Click
    ' reads names from a sequential access file
    ' and displays them in the interface

    ' declare variables
    Dim inFile As IO.StreamReader
    Dim strName As String

    ' clear previous names from the list box
    lstContestants.Items.Clear()
```

Figure 10-30 Click event procedures for the btnWrite and btnRead controls *(continues)*

(continued)

```
        ' determine whether the file exists
        If IO.File.Exists("contestants.txt") Then
            ' open the file for input
            inFile = IO.File.OpenText("contestants.txt")
            ' process loop instructions until end of file
            Do Until inFile.Peek = -1
                ' read a name
                strName = inFile.ReadLine
                ' add name to list box
                lstContestants.Items.Add(strName)
            Loop
            ' close the file
            inFile.Close()

        Else
            MessageBox.Show("Can't find the file",
                            "Game Show Contestants",
                            MessageBoxButtons.OK,
                            MessageBoxIcon.Information)
        End If
    End Sub
```

Figure 10-30 Click event procedures for the btnWrite and btnRead controls

To test the application's code:

START HERE

1. Save the solution and then start the application. Click the **Read from File** button. The five names contained in the contestants.txt file appear in the Contestants box, as shown in Figure 10-31.

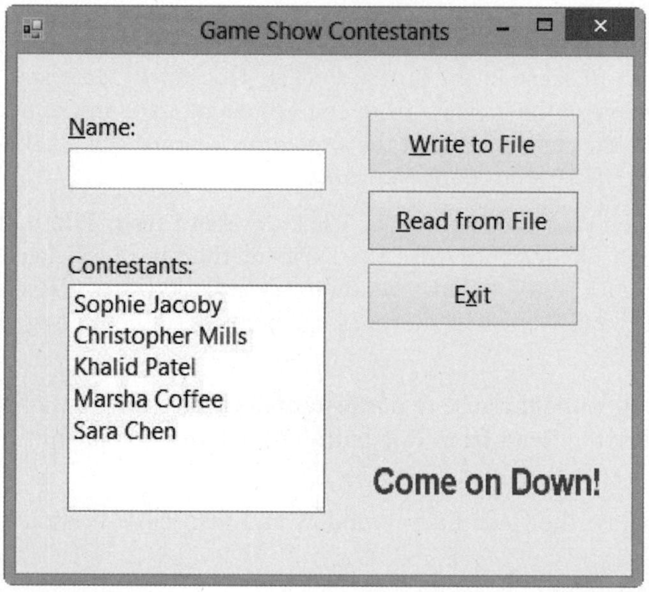

Figure 10-31 Five contestant names listed in the Contestants box

2. Type **James Miller** in the Name box and then click the **Write to File** button.
3. On your own, add the following three names to the file:

   Cheryl Smith
   Serena Kaplan
   Matthew Howenwald

4. Click the **Read from File** button to display the nine names in the list box. See Figure 10-32.

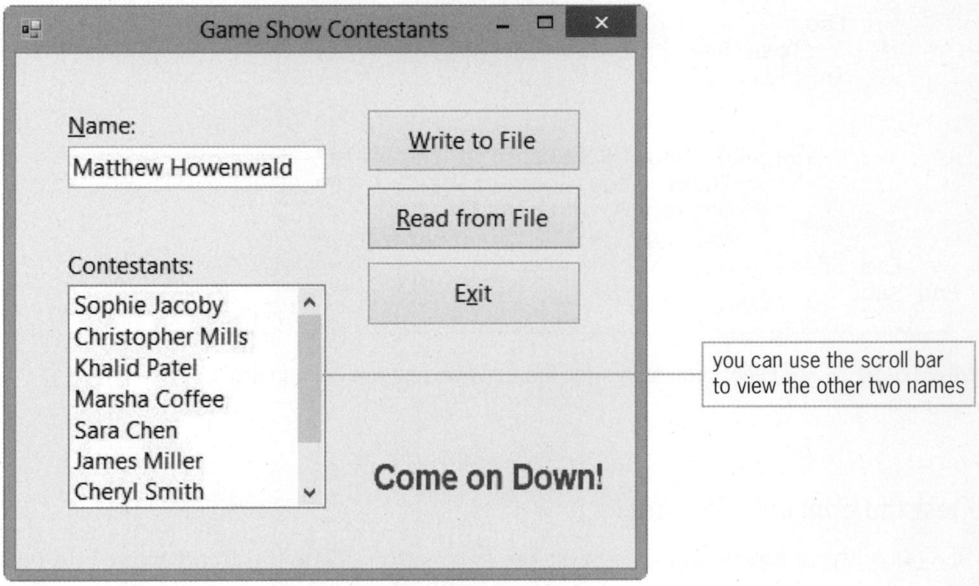

Figure 10-32 Nine contestant names listed in the list box

5. Click the **Exit** button.
6. Next, you will modify the If clause in the btnRead_Click procedure. More specifically, you will change the filename in the If clause from contestants.txt to contestant.txt. Doing this will allow you to test the code entered in the selection structure's false path. Change `contestants.txt` in the If clause to **contestant.txt**.
7. Save the solution and then start the application. Click the **Read from File** button. Because the contestant.txt file does not exist, the Exists method in the If clause returns the Boolean value False. As a result, the instruction in the selection structure's false path displays the "Can't find the file" message in a message box. Close the message box and then click the **Exit** button.
8. Change `contestant.txt` in the If clause to **contestants.txt**. Save the solution and then start the application. Click the **Read from File** button, which displays the nine names in the list box.
9. Click the **Exit** button. Close the Code Editor window and then close the solution.

YOU DO IT 2!

Create a Visual Basic Windows application named YouDoIt 2. Save the application in the VB2012\Chap10 folder. Add a label and two buttons to the form. The first button's Click event procedure should use the InputBox function to get one or more numbers from the user. Each number should be saved on a separate line in a sequential access file. The second button's Click event procedure should total the numbers contained in the sequential access file and then display the total in the label control. Code the procedures. Save the solution and then start and test the application. Close the solution.

Lesson B Summary

- To write data to a sequential access file:

  Declare a StreamWriter variable and then use either the CreateText method or the AppendText method to open a sequential access file. Assign the method's return value to the StreamWriter variable. Use either the Write method or the WriteLine method to write the data to the file. Close the file using the Close method.

- To read data from a sequential access file:

  Declare a StreamReader variable. Use the Exists method to determine whether the sequential access file exists. If the file exists, use the OpenText method to open the file. Assign the method's return value to the StreamReader variable. Use the ReadLine and Peek methods to read the data from the file. Close the file using the Close method.

- To determine whether a sequential access file exists:

  Use the Exists method. The method's syntax is **IO.File.Exists(***fileName***)**. The method returns the Boolean value True if the file exists; otherwise, it returns the Boolean value False.

- To determine whether the end of a sequential access file has been reached:

  Use the Peek method. The method's syntax is *streamReaderVariableName***.Peek**. The method returns the number –1 when the end of the file has been reached; otherwise, it returns the next character in the file.

Lesson B Key Terms

AppendText method—used with a StreamWriter variable to open a sequential access file for append

Close method—used with either a StreamWriter variable or a StreamReader variable to close a sequential access file

CreateText method—used with a StreamWriter variable to open a sequential access file for output

Exists method—used to determine whether a file exists

Input files—files from which an application reads data

Line—a sequence (stream) of characters followed by the newline character

OpenText method—used with a StreamReader variable to open a sequential access file for input

Output files—files to which an application writes data

Peek method—used with a StreamReader variable to determine whether a file contains another character to read

ReadLine method—used with a StreamReader variable to read a line of text from a sequential access file

Sequential access files—files composed of lines of text that are both read and written sequentially; also called text files

Stream of characters—a sequence of characters

StreamReader object—used to read a sequence (stream) of characters from a sequential access file

StreamWriter object—used to write a sequence (stream) of characters to a sequential access file

Text files—another name for sequential access files

Write method—used with a StreamWriter variable to write data to a sequential access file; differs from the WriteLine method in that it does not write a newline character after the data

WriteLine method—used with a StreamWriter variable to write data to a sequential access file; differs from the Write method in that it writes a newline character after the data

Lesson B Review Questions

1. Which of the following opens the employ.txt file and allows the computer to write new data to the end of the file's existing data?

   a. `outFile = IO.File.AddText("employ.txt")`

   b. `outFile = IO.File.AppendText("employ.txt")`

   c. `outFile = IO.File.InsertText("employ.txt")`

   d. `outFile = IO.File.WriteText("employ.txt")`

2. If the file to be opened exists, the ________ method erases the file's contents.

   a. AppendText

   b. CreateText

   c. InsertText

   d. OpenText

3. Which of the following reads a line of text from a sequential access file and assigns the line (excluding the newline character) to the `strText` variable?

   a. `inFile.Read(strText)`

   b. `inFile.ReadLine(strText)`

   c. `strText = inFile.ReadLine`

   d. `strText = inFile.Read(line)`

4. The Peek method returns ________ when the end of the file is reached.

   a. −1

   b. 0

   c. the last character in the file

   d. the newline character

5. Which of the following can be used to determine whether the employ.txt file exists?
   a. `If IO.File.Exists("employ.txt") Then`
   b. `If IO.File("employ.txt").Exists Then`
   c. `If IO.Exists("employ.txt") = True Then`
   d. `If IO.Exists.File("employ.txt") = True Then`

6. The OpenText method creates a ______________ object.
   a. File
   b. SequenceReader
   c. StreamWriter
   d. none of the above

7. The AppendText method creates a ______________ object.
   a. File
   b. SequenceReader
   c. StreamWriter
   d. none of the above

Lesson B Exercises

1. Write the code to declare a variable named `outFile` that can be used to write data to a sequential access file. Then write the statement to open a sequential access file named sales.txt for output. INTRODUCTORY

2. Write the code to declare a variable named `inFile` that can be used to read data from a sequential access file. Then write the statement to open a sequential access file named sales.txt for input. INTRODUCTORY

3. Write the code to close the sequential access file associated with a StreamWriter variable named `outFile`. INTRODUCTORY

4. Write an If clause that determines whether a sequential access file exists. The file's name is sales.txt. INTRODUCTORY

5. Write a Do clause that determines whether the end of a sequential access file has been reached. The file is associated with a StreamReader variable named `inFile`. INTRODUCTORY

6. Open the Gross Pay Solution (Gross Pay Solution.sln) file contained in the VB2012\Chap10\Gross Pay Solution folder. If necessary, open the designer window. The interface provides a text box for entering a gross pay amount. The Save button should write the gross pay amount to a sequential access file named gross.txt. Save the file in the project's bin\Debug folder. The Display button should read the gross pay amounts from the gross.txt file and display each (formatted with a dollar sign and two decimal places) in the list box. Right-align the numbers in the list box. Open the Code Editor window. Code the Click event procedures for the btnSave and btnDisplay controls. Save the solution and then start the application. Write the following 10 gross pay amounts to the file: 600, 1250, 750.67, 350.75, 2000, 450, 125.89, 560, 1400, and 555.78. Click the Display button to display the gross pay amounts in the interface. Close the Code Editor window and then close the solution. INTRODUCTORY

7. Open the Name Solution (Name Solution.sln) file contained in the VB2012\Chap10\Name Solution folder. If necessary, open the designer window. Open the Code Editor window. Open the names.txt file contained in the project's bin\Debug folder. The sequential access file contains five names. Close the names.txt window. The btnDisplay INTERMEDIATE

control's Click event procedure should read the five names contained in the names.txt file, storing each in a five-element one-dimensional array. The procedure should sort the array in descending order and then display the contents of the array in the list box. Code the procedure. Save the solution and then start and test the application. Close the Code Editor window and then close the solution. (If you need to recreate the names.txt file, open the file in a window in the IDE. Delete the contents of the file and then type the following five names, pressing Enter after typing each name: Joanne, Zelda, Abby, Ben, and Linda.)

INTERMEDIATE

8. Open the Salary Solution (Salary Solution.sln) file contained in the VB2012\Chap10\Salary Solution folder. If necessary, open the designer window. Open the Code Editor window and study the existing code. The code stores six salary amounts in a one-dimensional array named `intSalaries`. Each salary amount corresponds to a salary code from 1 through 6. Code 1's salary is stored in the `intSalaries(0)` element in the array, code 2's salary is stored in the `intSalaries(1)` element, and so on. The btnDisplay_Click procedure prompts the user to enter a salary code. It then displays the amount associated with the code. Currently, the Private statement assigns the six salary amounts to the array. Modify the code so that the form's Load event procedure reads the salary amounts from the salary.txt file and stores each in the array. The salary.txt file is contained in the project's bin\Debug folder. Save the solution and then start and test the application. Close the Code Editor window and then close the solution.

INTERMEDIATE

9. Open the Test Scores Solution (Test Scores Solution.sln) file contained in the VB2012\Chap10\Test Scores Solution folder. If necessary, open the designer window. Open the Code Editor window. The btnSave control's Click event procedure should allow the user to enter an unknown number of test scores, saving each score in a sequential access file. The btnCount control's Click event procedure should display (in a message box) the number of scores stored in the file. Code both procedures. Save the solution and then start and test the application. Close the Code Editor window and then close the solution.

INTERMEDIATE

10. In this exercise, you code an application that reads five numbers from a sequential access file and stores the numbers in a one-dimensional array. The application then increases each number by 1 and writes the numbers to the file. The application also displays the current contents of the sequential access file. Open the Numbers Solution (Numbers Solution.sln) file contained in the VB2012\Chap10\Numbers Solution folder. If necessary, open the designer window. Open the Code Editor window. Code the btnDisplay_Click procedure so it reads the five numbers stored in the numbers.txt file and displays the numbers in the list box. The numbers.txt file is contained in the project's bin\Debug folder. Currently, the file contains the numbers 1 through 5. Code the btnUpdate_Click procedure so it reads the five numbers from the numbers.txt file and stores the numbers in an array. It then should increase each number in the array by 1 and write the array contents to an empty numbers.txt file. Save the solution and then start the application. Click the Display button. The numbers 1 through 5 appear in the interface. Click the Update button and then click the Display button. The numbers 2 through 6 appear in the interface. Close the Code Editor window and then close the solution. (If you need to recreate the numbers.txt file, open the file in a window in the IDE. Delete the contents of the file and then type the numbers 1 through 5, pressing Enter after typing each number.)

ADVANCED

11. During July and August of each year, the Political Awareness Organization (PAO) sends a questionnaire to the voters in its district. The questionnaire asks the voter for his or her political party (Democratic, Republican, or Independent) and age. From the returned questionnaires, the organization's secretary tabulates the number of Democrats, Republicans, and Independents in the district. The secretary wants an

application that she can use to save each respondent's information (political party and age) to a sequential access file. The application should also calculate and display the number of voters in each political party. Create a Visual Basic Windows application. Use the following names for the solution and project, respectively: PAO Solution and PAO Project. Save the application in the VB2012\Chap10 folder. Change the form file's name to Main Form.vb. Change the form's name to frmMain. Create the interface shown in Figure 10-33. The Party list box should contain three items: Democratic, Republican, and Independent. The Age text box should accept only numbers and the Backspace key. Code the Click event procedures for the Write to File and Display Totals buttons. Save the solution and then start and test the application. Close the Code Editor window and then close the solution.

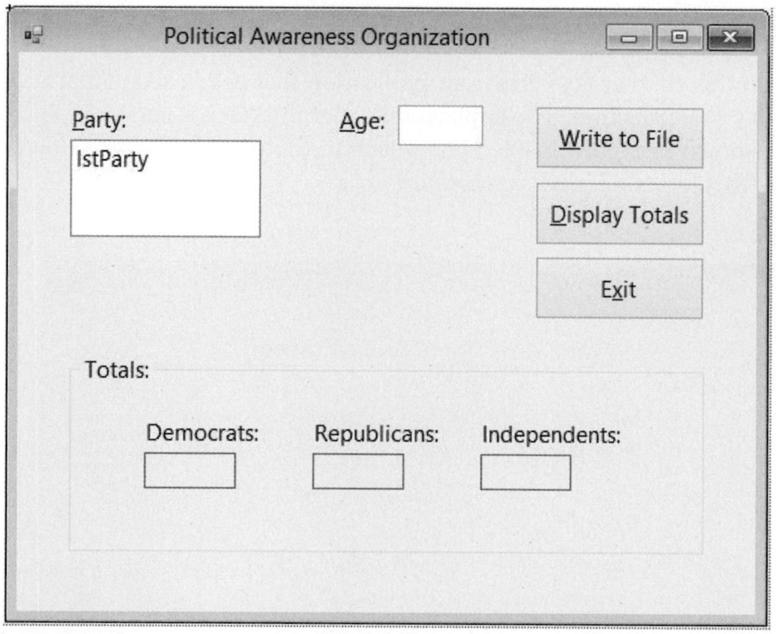

Figure 10-33 Interface for Exercise 11

12. In this exercise, you modify the application from Exercise 11. Use Windows to make a copy of the PAO Solution folder. Rename the folder Modified PAO Solution. Open the PAO Solution (PAO Solution.sln) file contained in the Modified PAO Solution folder. Open the designer window and then open the Code Editor window. Modify the code to use a structure in the btnDisplay_Click procedure. Save the solution and then start and test the application. Close the Code Editor window and then close the solution. ADVANCED

13. Open the Debug Solution (Debug Solution.sln) file contained in the VB2012\Chap10\Debug Solution folder. Open the Code Editor window and study the existing code. Start the application. Test the application using Sue and 1000, and then using Pete and 5000. A run time error occurs. Read the error message. Click DEBUG on the menu bar and then click Stop Debugging. Open the bonus.txt file contained in the project's bin\Debug folder. Notice that the file is empty. Close the bonus.txt window. Locate and correct the error in the code. Save the solution and then start and test the application again. Verify that the bonus.txt file contains the two names and bonus amounts. Close the Code Editor window and then close the solution. SWAT THE BUGS

LESSON C

After studying Lesson C, you should be able to:

- Add an item to a list box while an application is running
- Align columns of information
- Remove an item from a list box while an application is running
- Save list box items in a sequential access file
- Write records to a sequential access file

Coding the CD Collection Application

Recall that your task in this chapter is to create an application that uses a sequential access file to keep track of a person's CD collection. The application's user interface is shown in Figure 10-34, and its TOE chart is shown in Figure 10-35. (The image in the picture box was downloaded from the Open Clip Art Library at *http://openclipart.org.*)

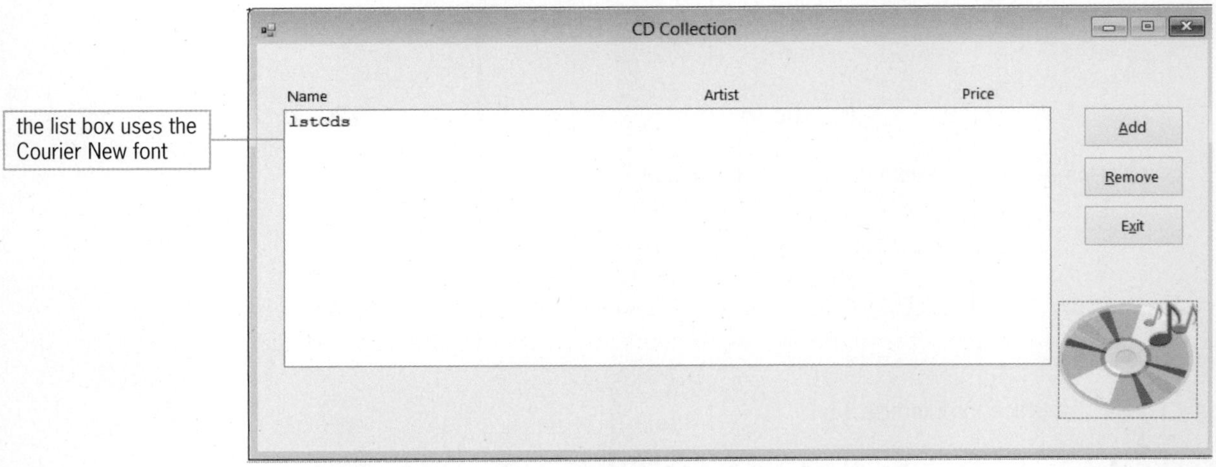

Figure 10-34 Interface for the CD Collection application
OpenClipArt.org/ilnanny/Cristian Pozzessere

Task	Object	Event
Read the CDs.txt file and assign its contents to lstCds Save the contents of lstCds in the CDs.txt file	frmMain	Load FormClosing
End the application	btnExit	Click
1. Get CD name, artist name, and price 2. Add CD name, artist name, and price to lstCds	btnAdd	Click
Remove the selected line from lstCds	btnRemove	Click
Display the CD name, artist name, and price	lstCds	None

Figure 10-35 TOE chart for the CD Collection application

START HERE

To open the CD Collection application and then view the CDs.txt file:

1. If necessary, start Visual Studio 2012. Open the CD Solution (CD Solution.sln) file contained in the VB2012\Chap10\CD Solution folder. If necessary, open the designer window.
2. Open the Code Editor window. Replace <your name> and <current date> in the comments with your name and the current date, respectively.
3. Click **FILE** on the menu bar and then click **Open File**. Open the project's bin\Debug folder. Click **CDs.txt** in the list of filenames and then click the **Open** button. The CDs.txt window shows the information contained in the file. The CD names are listed in the first column, the artist names in the second column, and the CD prices in the third column. See Figure 10-36.

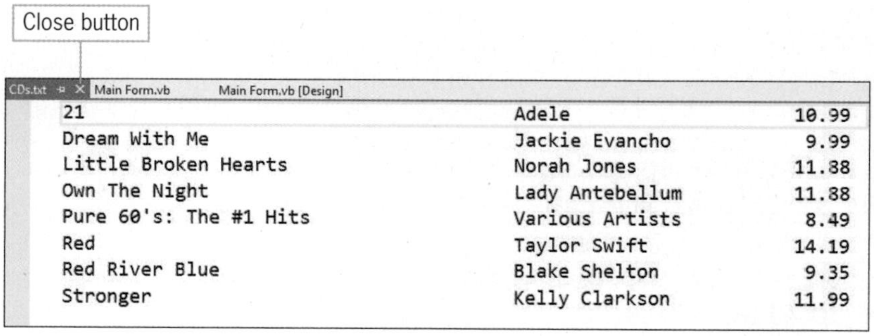

21	Adele	10.99
Dream With Me	Jackie Evancho	9.99
Little Broken Hearts	Norah Jones	11.88
Own The Night	Lady Antebellum	11.88
Pure 60's: The #1 Hits	Various Artists	8.49
Red	Taylor Swift	14.19
Red River Blue	Blake Shelton	9.35
Stronger	Kelly Clarkson	11.99

Figure 10-36 CDs.txt window

4. Close the CDs.txt window by clicking its **Close** button.

The TOE chart indicates that five procedures need to be coded. The Code Editor window already contains the code for the btnExit_Click procedure. You will need to code only the form's Load and FormClosing event procedures and the Click event procedures for the btnAdd and btnRemove controls. You will code the form's Load event procedure first.

Coding the Form's Load Event Procedure

The form's Load event procedure is responsible for displaying the contents of the CDs.txt file in the list box. The procedure's pseudocode is shown in Figure 10-37.

```
frmMain Load event procedure

if the CDs.txt sequential access file exists
    open the file for input
    repeat until the end of the file
        read a line from the file
        add the line to the lstCds control
    end repeat
    close the file
    select the first line in the lstCds control
else
    display the "Can't find the CDs.txt file" message
end if
```

Figure 10-37 Pseudocode for the form's Load event procedure

START HERE

To code and then test the form's Load event procedure:

1. As you learned in Lesson B, you use a StreamReader object to read data from a sequential access file. Before creating the StreamReader object, you first declare a variable to store the object in the computer's internal memory. Locate the frmMain_Load procedure. Click the **blank line** below the `' declare variables` comment and then enter the following declaration statement:

   Dim inFile As IO.StreamReader

2. The procedure will also need a variable to store the string returned by the ReadLine method when reading the file. Type the following declaration statement and then press **Enter** twice:

   Dim strInfo As String

3. According to its pseudocode, the procedure should display an appropriate message if the CDs.txt file does not exist. Enter the comment and selection structure shown in Figure 10-38, and then position the insertion point as shown in the figure.

```
    Dim inFile As IO.StreamReader
    Dim strInfo As String

    ' verify that the file exists
    If IO.File.Exists("CDs.txt") Then
        |
    Else
        MessageBox.Show("Can't find the CDs.txt file",
                        "CD Collection",
                        MessageBoxButtons.OK,
                        MessageBoxIcon.Information)
    End If
End Sub
```

enter this comment and selection structure

position the insertion point here

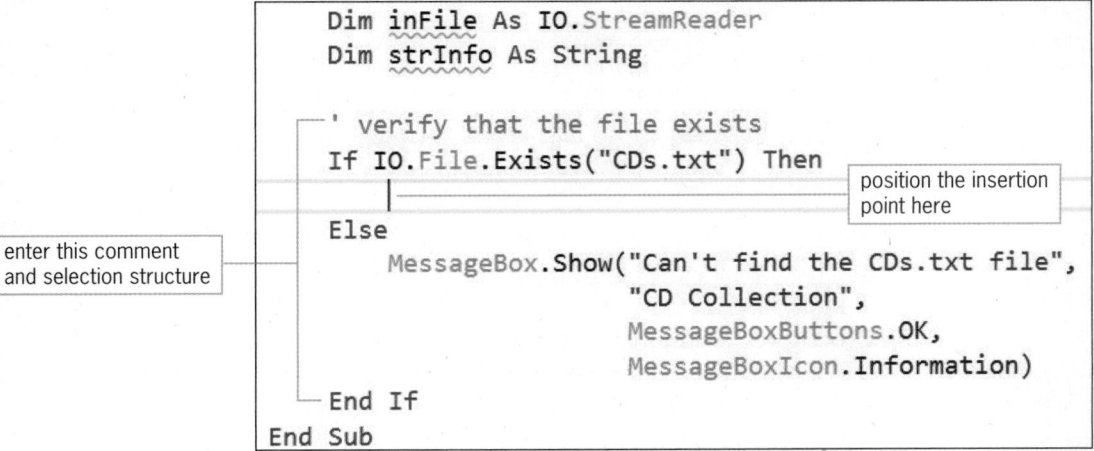

Figure 10-38 Additional comment and code entered in the Load event procedure

4. If the file exists, the procedure should open the file for input. Enter the following comment and assignment statement:

   ' open the file for input
   inFile = IO.File.OpenText("CDs.txt")

5. Next, the procedure should use a loop to read each line from the file, adding each to the list box. Enter the following comment and lines of code:

   ' process loop instructions until end of file
   Do Until inFile.Peek = –1
   strInfo = inFile.ReadLine
   lstCds.Items.Add(strInfo)
   Loop

6. After the loop ends, the procedure should close the file. Click **after the letter p** in the Loop clause and then press **Enter**. Type **inFile.Close()** and then press **Enter**.

7. The last task in the selection structure's true path is to select the first line in the list box. Enter the following comment and line of code:

   ' select the first line in the list box
   lstCds.SelectedIndex = 0

8. Save the solution and then start the application. The information contained in the CDs.txt file appears in the list box, as shown in Figure 10-39. (Recall that you can use the Alt key to show/hide the access keys.)

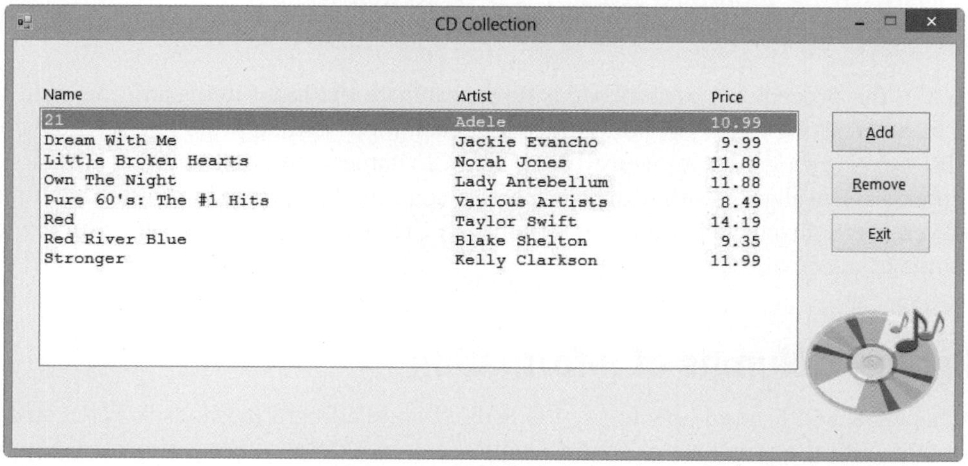

Figure 10-39 Contents of the CDs.txt file shown in the list box
OpenClipArt.org/ilnanny/Cristian Pozzessere

9. Click the **Exit** button.

Coding the btnAdd_Click Procedure

According to the application's TOE chart, the btnAdd control's Click event procedure should get a CD name, an artist name, and a price from the user, and then display that information in the list box. Figure 10-40 shows the procedure's pseudocode.

btnAdd Click event procedure

1. use the InputBox function to get the CD name, artist name, and price
2. concatenate the CD name, artist name, and price, and then add the concatenated string to the lstCds control

Figure 10-40 Pseudocode for the btnAdd_Click procedure

To begin coding the btnAdd_Click procedure:

START HERE

1. Locate the btnAdd_Click procedure and then click the **blank line** below the `' declare variables` comment. The procedure will use four String variables: three to store the input items and one to store the concatenated string. It also will use a Double variable to store the numeric equivalent of the CD price. Enter the following five declaration statements:

   Dim strName As String
   Dim strArtist As String

Dim strPrice As String
Dim strConcatenatedInfo As String
Dim dblPrice As Double

2. Now you will use the InputBox function to get the CD information from the user. Click the **blank line** below the `' get the CD information` comment and then enter the following assignment statements:

strName = InputBox("CD name:", "CD Collection")
strArtist = InputBox("Artist:", "CD Collection")
strPrice = InputBox("Price:", "CD Collection")

Step 2 in the procedure's pseudocode is to concatenate the input items and then add the concatenated string to the list box. Notice that each input item appears in a separate column in the list box shown earlier in Figure 10-39. The CD names and artist names in the first two columns are left-aligned within their respective column. The prices in the third column, however, are right-aligned within the column. In the next section, you will learn how to align columns of information.

Aligning Columns of Information

In Chapter 8, you learned how to use the PadLeft and PadRight methods to pad a string with a character until the string is a specified length. Each method's syntax is shown in Figure 10-41. Recall that when processing the methods, the computer first makes a temporary copy of the *string* in memory; it then pads the copy only. The *totalChars* argument in each syntax is an integer that represents the total number of characters you want the string's copy to contain. The optional *padCharacter* argument is the character that each method uses to pad the string until it reaches the desired number of characters. If the padCharacter argument is omitted, the default padding character is the space character. You can use the PadLeft and PadRight methods to align columns of information, as shown in the examples in Figure 10-41.

In Example 1, you also need to set the lstPrices control's Font property to a fixed-spaced font, such as Courier New. A fixed-spaced font uses the same amount of space to display each character.

Aligning Columns of Information

Syntax
string.**PadLeft(***totalChars*[, *padCharacter*]**)**
string.**PadRight(***totalChars*[, *padCharacter*]**)**

Example 1
```
Dim strPrice As String
For dblPrice As Double = 9 To 11 Step 0.5
    strPrice = dblPrice.ToString("N2").PadLeft(5)
    lstPrices.Items.Add(strPrice)
Next dblPrice
```

Result
```
 9.00
 9.50
10.00
10.50
11.00
```

Figure 10-41 Examples of aligning columns of information *(continues)*

(continued)

Example 2

```
Dim outFile As IO.StreamWriter
Dim strHeading As String =
    "Name" & Strings.Space(11) & "City"
Dim strName As String
Dim strCity As String

outFile = IO.File.CreateText("Example2.txt")
outFile.WriteLine(strHeading)

strName = InputBox("Enter name:", "Name")
Do While strName <> String.Empty
    strCity = InputBox("Enter city:", "City")
    outFile.WriteLine(strName.PadRight(15) & strCity)
    strName = InputBox("Enter name:", "Name")
Loop
outFile.Close()
```

contains the Strings.Space method

Result (when the user enters the following: Janice, Paris, Sue, Rome)

```
Name           City
Janice         Paris
Sue            Rome
```

Figure 10-41 Examples of aligning columns of information

Example 1's code aligns a column of numbers by the decimal point. Notice that you first format each number in the column to ensure that each has the same number of digits to the right of the decimal point. You then use the PadLeft method to insert spaces at the beginning of the number (if necessary); this right-aligns the number within the column. Because each number has the same number of digits to the right of the decimal point, aligning each number on the right will align each by its decimal point.

Example 2's code shows how you can align the second column of information when the first column contains strings with varying lengths. First, you use either the PadRight or PadLeft method to ensure that each string in the first column contains the same number of characters. You then concatenate the padded string to the information in the second column. Example 2's code, for instance, uses the PadRight method to ensure that each name in the first column contains exactly 15 characters. It then concatenates the 15 characters with the string stored in the `strCity` variable before writing the concatenated string to a sequential access file. Because each name has 15 characters, each city entry will automatically appear beginning in character position 16 in the file. Example 2 also shows how you can use the **Strings.Space method** to include a specific number of space characters in a string. The method's syntax is `Strings.Space(`*number*`)`, in which *number* is an integer representing the number of spaces to include.

START HERE

To complete and then test the btnAdd_Click procedure:

1. Click the **blank line** below the `' and 5 spaces for the price` comment. First, you will format the price to ensure that it contains two decimal places. Enter the following lines of code:

```
Double.TryParse(strPrice, dblPrice)
strPrice = dblPrice.ToString("N2")
```

2. Now you will concatenate the three input items, reserving 40 characters for the CD name, 25 characters for the artist name, and 5 characters for the price. You will left-align the first two columns but right-align the last column. Enter the following assignment statement:

```
strConcatenatedInfo = strName.PadRight(40) &
    strArtist.PadRight(25) & strPrice.PadLeft(5)
```

3. Now you will add the concatenated string to the list box. Click the **blank line** below the `' add the information to the list box` comment and then enter the following line of code:

```
lstCds.Items.Add(strConcatenatedInfo)
```

4. Save the solution and then start the application. Click the **Add** button. Type **Lotus** as the CD name and then press **Enter**. Type **Christina Aguilera** as the artist name and then press **Enter**. Type **11.99** as the price and then press **Enter**. The Add button's Click event procedure adds the CD information to the list box. The list box's Sorted property is set to True, so the information you entered appears in the fourth line of the list box. See Figure 10-42.

the CD information you entered appears in alphabetical order by the CD name

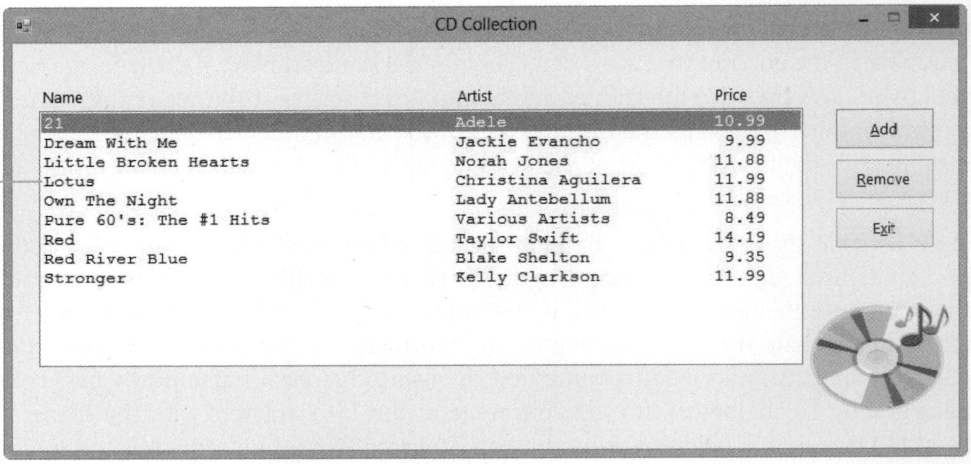

Figure 10-42 CD information added to the list box
OpenClipArt.org/ilnanny/Cristian Pozzessere

5. Click the **Exit** button.

Coding the btnRemove_Click Procedure

According to the application's TOE chart, the btnRemove control's Click event procedure should remove the selected line from the lstCds control. The procedure's pseudocode is shown in Figure 10-43.

```
btnRemove Click event procedure
if a line is selected in the lstCds control
    remove the line from the control
end if
```

Figure 10-43 Pseudocode for the btnRemove_Click procedure

You remove an item from a list box using either the Items collection's Remove method or its RemoveAt method. Figure 10-44 shows each method's syntax and includes an example of using each method. In each syntax, *object* is the name of the list box control. The **Remove method** removes the item whose value is specified in its *item* argument. The **RemoveAt method** removes the item whose index is specified in its *index* argument.

Remove and RemoveAt Methods (Items Collection)

Syntax
object.**Items.Remove(***item***)**
object.**Items.RemoveAt(***index***)**

Example 1 – Remove
`lstAnimal.Items.Remove("Cat")`
removes the Cat item from the lstAnimal control

Example 2 – RemoveAt
`lstAnimal.Items.RemoveAt(0)`
removes the first item from the lstAnimal control

Figure 10-44 Syntax and examples of the Items collection's Remove and RemoveAt methods

To code and then test the btnRemove_Click procedure:

START HERE

1. Locate the btnRemove_Click procedure. If a line is selected in the list box, the list box's SelectedIndex property will contain the line's index; otherwise, it will contain –1. Therefore, if the SelectedIndex property does not contain the number –1, the procedure should remove the selected line from the list box. Click the **blank line** below the second comment and then enter the following selection structure:

   ```
   If lstCds.SelectedIndex <> -1 Then
       lstCds.Items.RemoveAt(lstCds.SelectedIndex)
   End If
   ```

2. Save the solution and then start the application. Click **Red** in the list box and then click the **Remove** button. The button's Click event procedure removes the Red CD from the list box.
3. Click the **Exit** button.

Coding the Form's FormClosing Event Procedure

The last procedure you need to code is the form's FormClosing event procedure. According to the application's TOE chart, the procedure is responsible for saving the contents of the lstCds control in the CDs.txt file. Figure 10-45 shows the procedure's pseudocode.


```
frmMain FormClosing event procedure
1.  open the CDs.txt file for output
2.  repeat for each line in the list box
        write the line to the file
    end repeat
3.  close the file
```

Figure 10-45 Pseudocode for the form's FormClosing event procedure

START HERE

To code and then test the form's FormClosing event procedure:

1. Locate the frmMain_FormClosing procedure. As you learned in Lesson B, you use a StreamWriter object to write data to a sequential access file. Before creating the StreamWriter object, you first declare a variable to store the object in the computer's internal memory. Click the **blank line** below the `' declare a StreamWriter variable` comment and then enter the following declaration statement:

   Dim outFile As IO.StreamWriter

2. Step 1 in the pseudocode is to open the CDs.txt file for output. Click the **blank line** below the `' open the file for output` comment and then enter the following line of code:

   outFile = IO.File.CreateText("CDs.txt")

3. The next step in the pseudocode is a loop that will write each line from the list box to the file. Click the **blank line** below the `' write each line in the list box` comment and then enter the following loop:

   ```
   For intIndex As Integer = 0 To lstCds.Items.Count – 1
       outFile.WriteLine(lstCds.Items(intIndex))
   Next intIndex
   ```

4. The last step in the pseudocode is to close the file. Click the **blank line** below the `' close the file` comment and then enter the following line of code:

   outFile.Close()

5. Save the solution and then start the application. Click the **Add** button. Use the input boxes to enter the following CD name, artist, and price: **Lotus**, **Christina Aguilera**, and **11.99**. The Add button's Click event procedure adds the CD information to the list box.

6. Click the **Exit** button. The computer processes the `Me.Close()` statement in the Exit button's Click event procedure; doing this invokes the form's FormClosing event. The FormClosing event procedure saves the contents of the list box to the CDs.txt file.

7. Now you will verify that the CD information you entered was saved to the CDs.txt file. Click **FILE** on the menu bar and then click **Open File**. Open the project's bin\Debug folder. Click **CDs.txt** in the list of filenames and then click the **Open** button. The CD information you entered appears in the fourth line in the file, as shown in Figure 10-46.

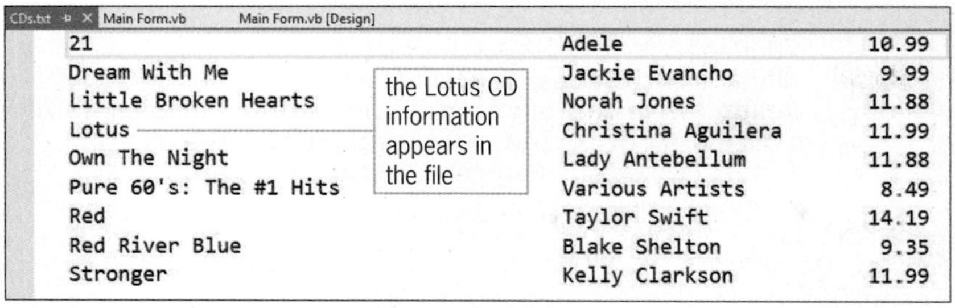

21	Adele	10.99
Dream With Me	Jackie Evancho	9.99
Little Broken Hearts	Norah Jones	11.88
Lotus	Christina Aguilera	11.99
Own The Night	Lady Antebellum	11.88
Pure 60's: The #1 Hits	Various Artists	8.49
Red	Taylor Swift	14.19
Red River Blue	Blake Shelton	9.35
Stronger	Kelly Clarkson	11.99

Figure 10-46 CD information saved in the CDs.txt file

8. Close the CDs.txt window by clicking its **Close** button. Start the application again. Click **Lotus** in the list box and then click the **Remove** button. The button's Click event procedure removes the CD information from the list box.
9. Click the **Exit** button. Now you will verify that the CDs.txt file does not contain the CD information you removed from the list box. Open the CDs.txt file. See Figure 10-47. Notice that the Lotus CD's information does not appear in the file. Close the CDs.txt window.

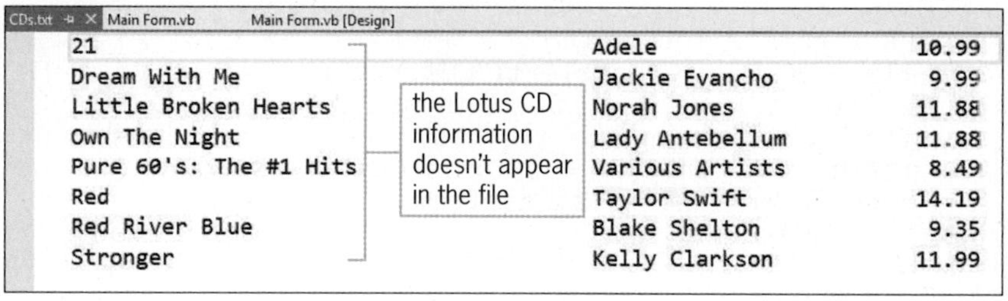

21	Adele	10.99
Dream With Me	Jackie Evancho	9.99
Little Broken Hearts	Norah Jones	11.88
Own The Night	Lady Antebellum	11.88
Pure 60's: The #1 Hits	Various Artists	8.49
Red	Taylor Swift	14.19
Red River Blue	Blake Shelton	9.35
Stronger	Kelly Clarkson	11.99

Figure 10-47 Current contents of the CDs.txt file

10. Close the Code Editor window and then close the solution.

Figure 10-48 shows the code for the CD Collection application.

```
' Name:         CD Project
' Purpose:      Adds and deletes list box entries
'               Reads information from a sequential access file
'               Writes information to a sequential access file
' Programmer:   <your name> on <current date>

Option Explicit On
Option Strict On
Option Infer Off

Public Class frmMain

    Private Sub btnExit_Click(sender As Object,
    e As EventArgs) Handles btnExit.Click
        Me.Close()
    End Sub

    Private Sub frmMain_FormClosing(sender As Object,
    e As Windows.Forms.FormClosingEventArgs
    ) Handles Me.FormClosing
        ' save the list box information

        ' declare a StreamWriter variable
        Dim outFile As IO.StreamWriter

        ' open the file for output
        outFile = IO.File.CreateText("CDs.txt")

        ' write each line in the list box
        For intIndex As Integer = 0 To lstCds.Items.Count - 1
            outFile.WriteLine(lstCds.Items(intIndex))
        Next intIndex

        ' close the file
        outFile.Close()

    End Sub

    Private Sub frmMain_Load(sender As Object,
    e As EventArgs) Handles Me.Load
        ' fills the list box with data
        ' stored in a sequential access file

        ' declare variables
        Dim inFile As IO.StreamReader
        Dim strInfo As String

        ' verify that the file exists
        If IO.File.Exists("CDs.txt") Then
            ' open the file for input
            inFile = IO.File.OpenText("CDs.txt")
            ' process loop instructions until end of file
```

Figure 10-48 Code for the CD Collection application *(continues)*

(continued)

```
            Do Until inFile.Peek = -1
               strInfo = inFile.ReadLine
               lstCds.Items.Add(strInfo)
            Loop
            inFile.Close()
            ' select the first line in the list box
            lstCds.SelectedIndex = 0

        Else
            MessageBox.Show("Can't find the CDs.txt file",
                            "CD Collection",
                            MessageBoxButtons.OK,
                            MessageBoxIcon.Information)
        End If
    End Sub

    Private Sub btnAdd_Click(sender As Object,
    e As EventArgs) Handles btnAdd.Click
        ' adds CD information to the list box

        ' declare variables
        Dim strName As String
        Dim strArtist As String
        Dim strPrice As String
        Dim strConcatenatedInfo As String
        Dim dblPrice As Double

        ' get the CD information
        strName = InputBox("CD name:", "CD Collection")
        strArtist = InputBox("Artist:", "CD Collection")
        strPrice = InputBox("Price:", "CD Collection")

        ' format the price, then concatenate the
        ' input items, using 40 spaces for the
        ' CD name, 25 spaces for the artist name,
        ' and 5 spaces for the price
        Double.TryParse(strPrice, dblPrice)
        strPrice = dblPrice.ToString("N2")
        strConcatenatedInfo = strName.PadRight(40) &
           strArtist.PadRight(25) & strPrice.PadLeft(5)

        ' add the information to the list box
        lstCds.Items.Add(strConcatenatedInfo)

    End Sub

    Private Sub btnRemove_Click(sender As Object,
    e As EventArgs) Handles btnRemove.Click
        ' removes the selected line from the list box

        ' if a line is selected, remove the line
        If lstCds.SelectedIndex <> -1 Then
           lstCds.Items.RemoveAt(lstCds.SelectedIndex)
        End If
    End Sub
End Class
```

Figure 10-48 Code for the CD Collection application

Lesson C Summary

- To align columns of information:

  Use the PadLeft and PadRight methods.

- To align a column of numbers by the decimal point:

  Format each number in the column to ensure that each has the same number of digits to the right of the decimal point, and then use the PadLeft method to right-align the numbers.

- To include a specific number of spaces in a string:

  Use the Strings.Space method. The method's syntax is **Strings.Space(***number***)**, in which *number* is an integer that represents the number of spaces to include.

- To remove an item from a list box:

  Use either the Items collection's Remove method or its RemoveAt method. The Remove method's syntax is *object***.Items.Remove(***item***)**, where *item* is the value of the item you want to remove. The RemoveAt method's syntax is *object***.Items.RemoveAt(***index***)**, where *index* is the index of the item you want removed.

Lesson C Key Terms

Remove method—used to specify the value of the item to remove from a list box

RemoveAt method—used to specify the index of the item to remove from a list box

Strings.Space method—used to include a specific number of spaces in a string

Lesson C Review Questions

1. Which of the following opens a sequential access file named "MyFriends.txt" for input?

   a. `inFile = IO.File.Input("MyFriends.txt")`

   b. `inFile = IO.InputFile("MyFriends.txt")`

   c. `inFile = IO.File.InputText("MyFriends.txt")`

   d. `inFile = IO.File.OpenText("MyFriends.txt")`

2. Which of the following right-aligns the contents of the `strNumbers` variable?

   a. `strNumbers = strNumbers.PadLeft(10)`

   b. `strNumbers = strNumbers.PadRight(10)`

   c. `strNumbers = strNumbers.AlignLeft(10)`

   d. `strNumbers = strNumbers.RightAlign(10)`

3. Which of the following removes the fourth item from the lstFriends control?

   a. `lstFriends.Items.Remove(4)`

   b. `lstFriends.Items.RemoveAt(4)`

   c. `lstFriends.Items.RemoveIndex(3)`

   d. none of the above

4. Which of the following determines whether an item is selected in the lstFriends control?

   a. `If lstFriends.SelectedIndex >= 0 Then`

   b. `If lstFriends.SelectedItem <> -1 Then`

   c. `If lstFriends.IndexSelected = -1 Then`

   d. none of the above

5. The lstFriends control contains five items. Which of the following writes the last item to the file associated with the `outFile` variable?

   a. `outFile.WriteLine(lstFriends.Items(5))`

   b. `outFile.WriteLine(lstFriends.Items(4))`

   c. `outFile.WriteLine(lstFriends.Index(4))`

   d. none of the above

Lesson C Exercises

1. In this exercise, you modify the CD Collection application coded in the lesson. Use Windows to make a copy of the CD Solution folder. Rename the copy CD Solution-Verify Save. Open the CD Solution (CD Solution.sln) file contained in the CD Solution-Verify Save folder. Open the designer and Code Editor windows. The FormClosing event procedure should verify that the user wants to save the changes made to the list box. It then should take the appropriate action based on the user's response. Modify the code accordingly. Save the solution and then start and test the application. Close the Code Editor window and then close the solution. INTRODUCTORY

2. In this exercise, you modify the CD Collection application coded in the lesson. Use Windows to make a copy of the CD Solution folder. Rename the copy CD Solution-Verify Remove. Open the CD Solution (CD Solution.sln) file contained in the CD Solution-Verify Remove folder. Open the designer and Code Editor windows. The btnRemove_Click procedure should verify that the user wants to remove the selected CD information from the list box. Use the message "Do you want to remove the *x* CD?", where *x* is the name of the CD. The procedure should take the appropriate action based on the user's response. Modify the code accordingly. Save the solution and then start and test the application. Close the Code Editor window and then close the solution. INTERMEDIATE

3. Open the Friends Solution (Friends Solution.sln) file contained in the VB2012\Chap10\Friends Solution folder. If necessary, open the designer window. The Add button should add the name entered in the text portion of the combo box to the list portion, but only if the name is not already in the list. The Remove button should remove (from the list portion of the combo box) the name either entered in the text portion or selected in the list portion. The form's FormClosing event procedure should save the combo box items in a sequential access file named MyFriends.txt. The form's Load event procedure should read the names from the MyFriends.txt file and add each to the combo box. Code the application. Save the solution and then start and test the application. Close the Code Editor window and then close the solution. INTERMEDIATE

4. In this exercise, you modify the CD Collection application coded in the lesson. Use Windows to make a copy of the CD Solution folder. Rename the copy CD Solution-No Duplicate. Open the CD Solution (CD Solution.sln) file contained in the CD Solution-No Duplicate folder. Open the designer and Code Editor windows. Before getting the artist name and price, the btnAdd_Click procedure should determine whether the CD name is already included in the list box. If the list box contains the CD name, the procedure should display an appropriate message and then not add the CD to the list. Save the solution and then start and test the application. Close the Code Editor window and then close the solution. INTERMEDIATE

5. In this exercise, you modify the CD Collection application coded in the lesson. Use Windows to make a copy of the CD Solution folder. Rename the copy CD Solution-Undo. Open the CD Solution (CD Solution.sln) file contained in the CD Solution-Undo folder. Open the designer window. Add an Undo Remove button to the form. The Undo Remove button's Click event procedure should restore the last line removed by the INTERMEDIATE

Remove button. Open the Code Editor window and make the necessary modifications to the code. Save the solution and then start and test the application. Close the Code Editor window and then close the solution.

INTERMEDIATE

6. In this exercise, you modify the CD Collection application coded in the lesson. Use Windows to make a copy of the CD Solution folder. Rename the copy CD Solution-Structure. Open the CD Solution (CD Solution.sln) file contained in the CD Solution-Structure folder. Open the designer and Code Editor windows. Create a structure for the input information and then use the structure in the btnAdd_Click procedure. Save the solution and then start and test the application. Close the Code Editor window and then close the solution.

INTERMEDIATE

7. Glovers Industries stores the item numbers and prices of its products in a sequential access file named ItemInfo.txt. The company's sales manager wants an application that displays the price corresponding to the item selected in a list box.
   a. Open the Glovers Solution (Glovers Solution.sln) file contained in the VB2012\Chap10\Glovers Solution folder. If necessary, open the designer window.
   b. Open the Code Editor window. Open the ItemInfo.txt file, which is contained in the project's bin\Debug folder. Notice that the item number and price appear on separate lines in the file. Close the ItemInfo.txt window.
   c. Define a structure named Product. The structure should contain two member variables: a String variable to store the item number and a Double variable to store the price.
   d. Declare a class-level array that contains five Product structure variables.
   e. The form's Load event procedure should read the item numbers and prices from the ItemInfo.txt file and store them in the class-level array. It also should add the item numbers to the list box. Code the procedure.
   f. When the user selects an item in the list box, the item's price should appear in the lblPrice control. Code the appropriate procedure.
   g. Save the solution and then start and test the application. Close the Code Editor window and then close the solution.

ADVANCED

8. Each year, WKRK-Radio polls its audience to determine the best Super Bowl commercial. The choices are as follows: Budweiser, FedEx, E*TRADE, and Pepsi. The station manager wants an application that allows him to enter a caller's choice. The choice should be saved in a sequential access file. The application also should display the number of votes for each commercial. Create a Visual Basic Windows application. Use the following names for the solution and project, respectively: WKRK Solution and WKRK Project. Save the application in the VB2012\Chap10 folder. Change the form file's name to Main Form.vb. Change the form's name to frmMain. Create the interface shown in Figure 10-49, and then code the application. Save the solution and then start and test the application. Close the Code Editor window and then close the solution.

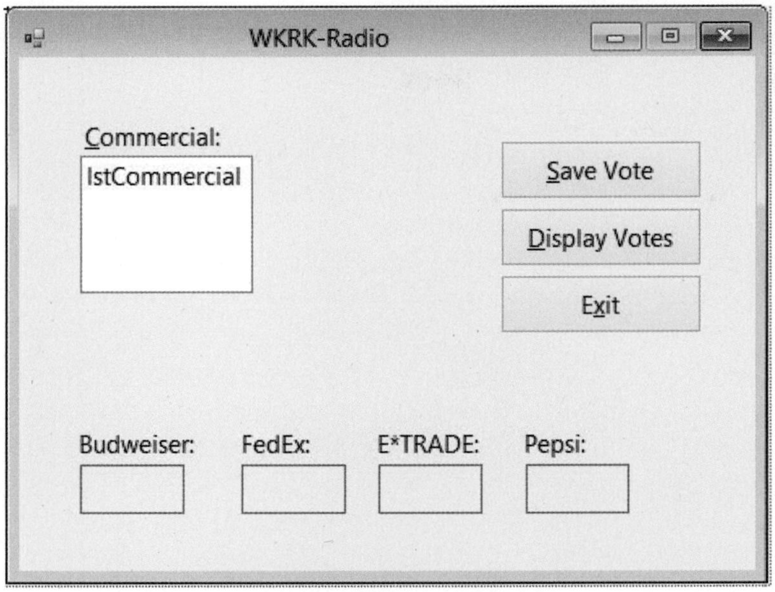

Figure 10-49 Interface for Exercise 8

ADVANCED

9. Kensington Industries stores the item numbers and prices of the items it sells in a sequential access file named ItemInfo.txt. The company's sales manager wants an application that displays the price corresponding to the item selected in a list box.

   a. Open the Kensington Solution (Kensington Solution.sln) file contained in the VB2012\Chap10\Kensington Solution folder. Open the Code Editor window and then open the ItemInfo.txt file contained in the project's bin\Debug folder. Each line contains an item's number followed by a comma and the price. Close the ItemInfo.txt window.

   b. Define a structure named Item. The structure should contain two member variables: a String variable to store the item number and a Decimal variable to store the price.

   c. Declare a class-level array that contains five Item structure variables.

   d. Code the form's Load event procedure so that it reads the item numbers and prices from the ItemInfo.txt file. The procedure should store the item numbers and prices in the class-level array. It also should add the item numbers to the list box.

   e. When the user selects an item in the list box, the item's price should appear in the lblPrice control. Code the appropriate procedure.

   f. Save the solution and then start and test the application. Close the Code Editor window and then close the solution.

CHAPTER 11

Classes and Objects

Creating the Woods Manufacturing Application

In this chapter, you will create an application that calculates and displays the gross pay for salaried and hourly employees. Salaried employees are paid twice per month. Therefore, each salaried employee's gross pay is calculated by dividing his or her annual salary by 24. Hourly employees are paid weekly. The gross pay for an hourly employee is calculated by multiplying the number of hours the employee worked during the week by his or her hourly pay rate. The application will also display a report showing each employee's number, name, and gross pay.

Previewing the Woods Manufacturing Application

Before you start the first lesson in this chapter, you will preview the completed application. The application is contained in the VB2012\Chap11 folder.

START HERE

To preview the completed application:

1. Use the Run dialog box to run the Woods (Woods.exe) file contained in the VB2012\Chap11 folder. The application's user interface appears on the screen.
2. First, you will calculate the gross pay for Charika Jones. Charika worked 30 hours and earns $10.50 per hour. Her employee number is 5618. Type **5618** and **Charika Jones** in the Number and Name boxes, respectively. Scroll the Hours list box and then click **30.0** in the list. Click **10.50** in the Rate list box. Click the **Calculate** button. $315.00 appears in the Gross pay box, and Charika's information appears in the Report box. See Figure 11-1. (Recall that you can use the Alt key to show/hide the access keys.)

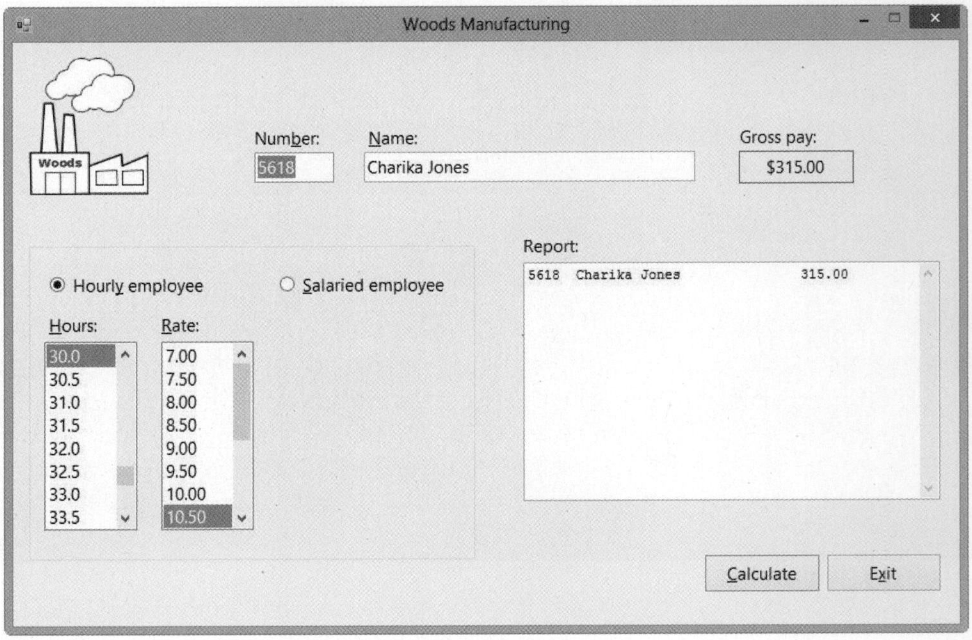

Figure 11-1 Interface showing Charika's gross pay and information
OpenClipArt.org/Improulx

3. Now you will calculate the gross pay for a salaried employee earning $24,000 per year. Type **9999** and **Chris Beshier** in the Number and Name boxes, respectively. Click the **Salaried employee** radio button. Scroll the Annual salary list box and then click **24000** in the list. Click the **Calculate** button. $1,000.00 appears in the Gross pay box, and Chris's information appears below Charika's information in the Report box. See Figure 11-2.

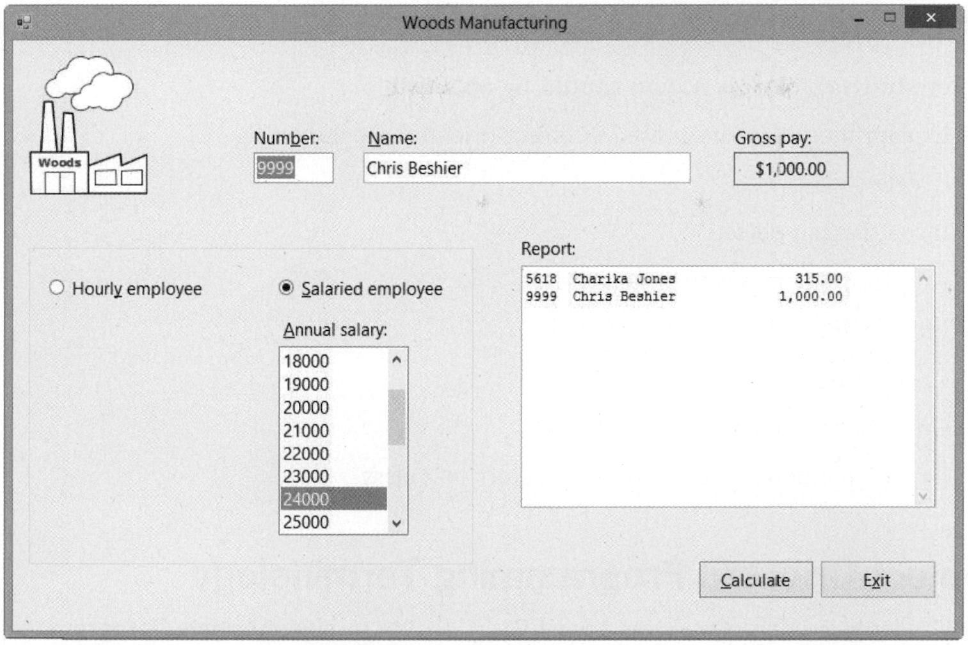

Figure 11-2 Interface showing Chris's gross pay and information
OpenClipArt.org/Improulx

4. Click the **Exit** button to end the application.

In Lesson A, you will learn about object-oriented programming (OOP). More specifically, you will learn how to define a class and how to use the class to instantiate an object. You will also learn how to utilize the instantiated object in an application. Lesson B will teach you how to include ReadOnly and auto-implemented properties in a class. You will also learn how to overload a class method. You will code the Woods Manufacturing application in Lesson B. Lesson C covers an advanced OOP topic: inheritance. Be sure to complete each lesson in full and do all of the end-of-lesson questions and several exercises before continuing to the next lesson.

LESSON A

After studying Lesson A, you should be able to:

- Explain the terminology used in object-oriented programming
- Create a class
- Instantiate an object
- Add Property procedures to a class
- Include data validation in a class
- Create a default constructor
- Create a parameterized constructor
- Include methods other than constructors in a class

Object-Oriented Programming Terminology

As you learned in the Overview, Visual Basic 2012 is an **object-oriented programming language**, which is a language that allows the programmer to use objects to accomplish a program's goal. An object is anything that can be seen, touched, or used. In other words, an object is nearly any *thing*. The objects used in an object-oriented program can take on many different forms. The text boxes, list boxes, and buttons included in most Windows applications are objects, and so are the application's named constants and variables. An object also can represent something found in real life, such as a wristwatch or a car.

Every object in an object-oriented program is created from a **class**, which is a pattern that the computer uses to create the object. Using object-oriented programming (**OOP**) terminology, objects are **instantiated** (created) from a class, and each object is referred to as an **instance** of the class. A button control, for example, is an instance of the Button class. The button is instantiated when you drag the Button tool from the toolbox to the form. A String variable, on the other hand, is an instance of the String class and is instantiated the first time you refer to the variable in code. Keep in mind that the class itself is not an object. Only an instance of a class is an object.

Every object has **attributes**, which are the characteristics that describe the object. Attributes are also called properties. Included in the attributes of buttons and text boxes are the Name and Text properties. List boxes have a Name property as well as a Sorted property.

In addition to attributes, every object also has behaviors. An object's **behaviors** include methods and events. **Methods** are the operations (actions) that the object is capable of performing. For example, a button can use its Focus method to send the focus to itself. Similarly, a String variable can use its ToUpper method to temporarily convert its contents to uppercase. **Events**, on the other hand, are the actions to which an object can respond. A button's Click event, for instance, allows the button to respond to a mouse click.

A class contains—or, in OOP terms, it **encapsulates**—all of the attributes and behaviors of the object it instantiates. The term "encapsulate" means "to enclose in a capsule." In the context of OOP, the "capsule" is a class.

Creating a Class

In previous chapters, you instantiated objects using classes that are built into Visual Basic, such as the TextBox and Label classes. You used the instantiated objects in a variety of ways in many different applications. In some applications, you used a text box to enter a name, while in other applications you used it to enter a sales tax rate. Similarly, you used label controls to identify text boxes and also to display the result of calculations. The ability to use an object for more than one purpose saves programming time and money—an advantage that contributes to the popularity of object-oriented programming.

You also can define your own classes in Visual Basic and then create instances (objects) from those classes. You define a class using the **Class statement**, which you enter in a class file. Figure 11-3 shows the statement's syntax and lists the steps for adding a class file to an open project. Although it is not a requirement, the convention is to use Pascal case for the class name. The names of Visual Basic classes (for example, Integer and TextBox) also follow this naming convention. Within the Class statement, you define the attributes and behaviors of the objects the class will create. In most cases, the attributes are represented by Private variables and Public properties. The behaviors are represented by methods, which are usually Sub or Function procedures. (You also can include Event procedures in a Class statement. However, that topic is beyond the scope of this book.)

Class Statement

Syntax

Public Class *className*
    attributes section
    behaviors section
End Class

Adding a class file to an open project

1. Click PROJECT on the menu bar and then click Add Class. The Add New Item dialog box opens with Class selected in the middle column of the dialog box.
2. Type the name of the class followed by a period and the letters vb in the Name box, and then click the Add button.

Figure 11-3 Syntax of the Class statement

The creation of a good class, which is one whose objects can be used in a variety of ways by many different applications, requires a lot of planning.

Figure 11-4 shows an example of the Class statement entered in a class file. The three Option statements included in the figure have the same meaning in a class file as they have in a form file.

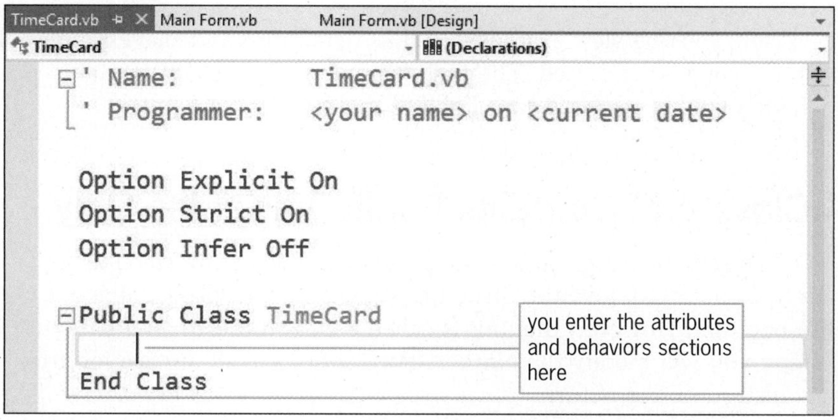

Figure 11-4 Class statement entered in the TimeCard.vb class file

After you define a class, you can use either of the syntax versions in Figure 11-5 to instantiate one or more objects. In both versions, *className* is the name of the class, and *variableName* is the name of a variable that will represent the object. The difference between both versions relates to when the object is actually created. The computer creates the object only when it processes the statement containing the `New` keyword. (You will learn more about the `New` keyword later in this lesson.) Also included in Figure 11-5 is an example of using each version of the syntax.

Instantiating an Object from a Class

Syntax – Version 1
{**Dim** | **Private**} *variableName* **As** *className*
variableName = **New** *className*

Syntax – Version 2
{**Dim** | **Private**} *variableName* **As New** *className*

Example 1 (using syntax version 1)

```
Private hoursInfo As TimeCard
hoursInfo = New TimeCard
```

the Private instruction creates a TimeCard variable named `hoursInfo`; the assignment statement instantiates a TimeCard object and assigns it to the `hoursInfo` variable

Example 2 (using syntax version 2)

```
Dim hoursInfo As New TimeCard
```

the Dim instruction creates a TimeCard variable named `hoursInfo` and also instantiates a TimeCard object, which it assigns to the `hoursInfo` variable

Figure 11-5 Syntax and examples of instantiating an object

In Example 1, the `Private hoursInfo As TimeCard` instruction creates a class-level variable that can represent a TimeCard object; however, it does not create the object. The object isn't created until the computer processes the `hoursInfo = New TimeCard` statement, which uses the TimeCard class to instantiate a TimeCard object. The statement assigns the object to the `hoursInfo` variable. In Example 2, the `Dim hoursInfo As New TimeCard` instruction creates a procedure-level variable named `hoursInfo`. It also instantiates a TimeCard object and assigns it to the variable.

In the remainder of this lesson, you will view examples of class definitions and also examples of code in which objects are instantiated and used. The first example is a class that contains attributes only, with each attribute represented by a Public variable.

Example 1—A Class that Contains Public Variables Only

In its simplest form, the Class statement can be used in place of the Structure statement, which you learned about in Chapter 10. Like the Structure statement, the Class statement groups related items into one unit. However, the unit is called a class rather than a structure. In the following set of steps, you will modify the Norbert Pool & Spa Depot application from Chapter 10 to use a class instead of a structure.

START HERE

To begin modifying the Norbert Pool & Spa Depot application:

1. If necessary, start Visual Studio 2012. Open the Norbert Solution (Norbert Solution.sln) file contained in the VB2012\Chap11\Norbert Solution folder. If necessary, open the

designer window. (The image in the picture box was downloaded from the Open Clip Art Library at *http://openclipart.org.*)

2. Open the Code Editor window. Figure 11-6 shows the Structure statement, the GetGallons function, and the btnCalc_Click procedure. The Structure statement groups together the three dimensions of a rectangular pool: length, width, and depth. The event procedure declares a structure variable and then fills the variable's members with values. It then passes the structure variable to the GetGallons function, which calculates and returns the number of gallons required to fill the pool. The event procedure displays the returned value in the lblGallons control.

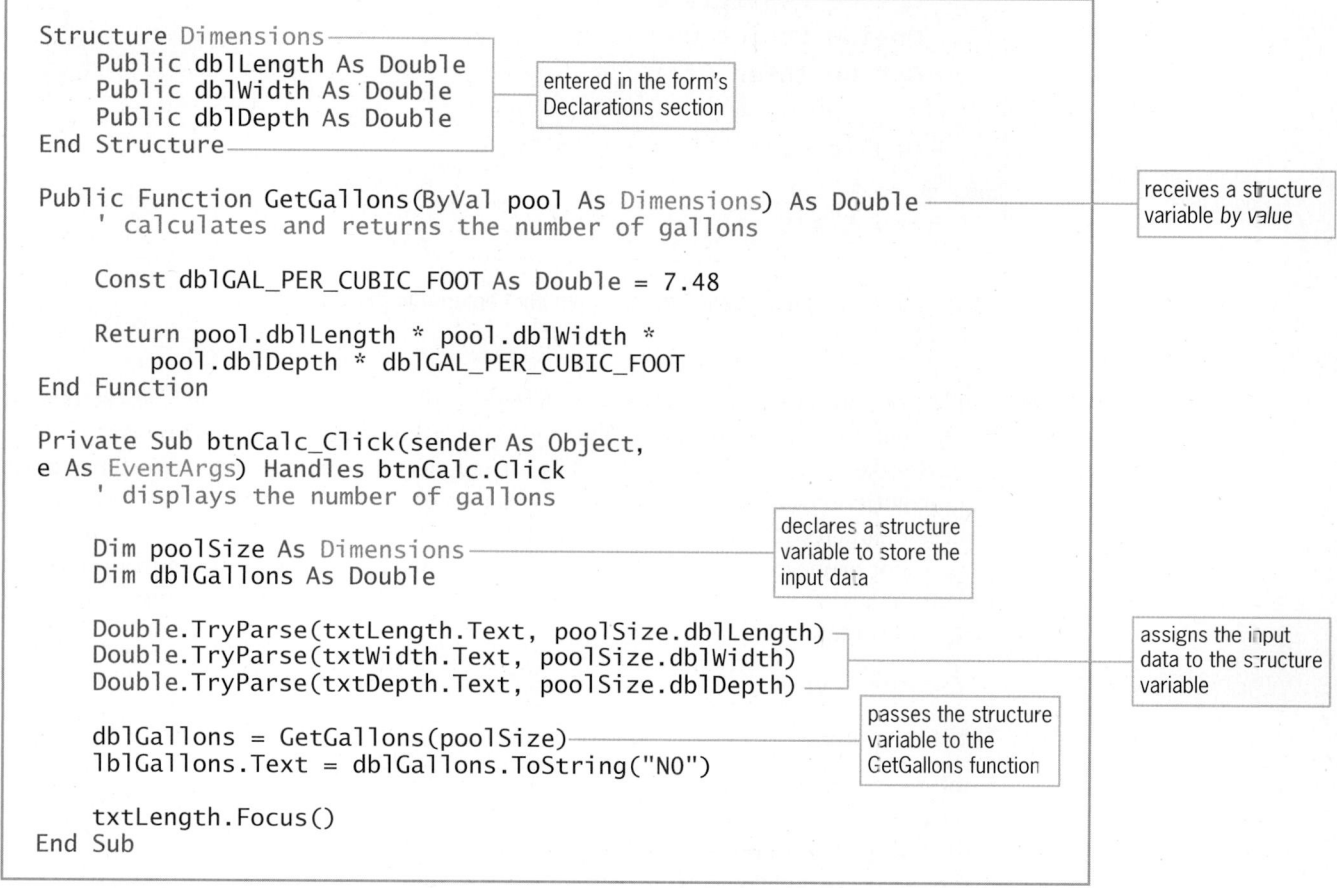

```
Structure Dimensions
    Public dblLength As Double
    Public dblWidth As Double
    Public dblDepth As Double
End Structure

Public Function GetGallons(ByVal pool As Dimensions) As Double
    ' calculates and returns the number of gallons

    Const dblGAL_PER_CUBIC_FOOT As Double = 7.48

    Return pool.dblLength * pool.dblWidth *
        pool.dblDepth * dblGAL_PER_CUBIC_FOOT
End Function

Private Sub btnCalc_Click(sender As Object,
e As EventArgs) Handles btnCalc.Click
    ' displays the number of gallons

    Dim poolSize As Dimensions
    Dim dblGallons As Double

    Double.TryParse(txtLength.Text, poolSize.dblLength)
    Double.TryParse(txtWidth.Text, poolSize.dblWidth)
    Double.TryParse(txtDepth.Text, poolSize.dblDepth)

    dblGallons = GetGallons(poolSize)
    lblGallons.Text = dblGallons.ToString("N0")

    txtLength.Focus()
End Sub
```

entered in the form's Declarations section

receives a structure variable *by value*

declares a structure variable to store the input data

assigns the input data to the structure variable

passes the structure variable to the GetGallons function

Figure 11-6 Code for the Norbert Pool & Spa Depot application (with a structure)

3. First, you will add a class file to the project. Click **PROJECT** on the menu bar and then click **Add Class**. The Add New Item dialog box opens with Class selected in the middle column of the dialog box. Type **RectangularPool.vb** in the Name box. As you learned in Chapter 1, the .vb in a filename indicates that the file contains Visual Basic code.

4. Click the **Add** button. The computer adds the RectangularPool.vb file to the project. It also opens the file, which contains the Class statement, in a separate window. Temporarily display the Solution Explorer window, if necessary, to verify that the class file's name appears in the window.

5. Insert a blank line above the Class statement and then enter the comments and Option statements shown in Figure 11-7. (Replace <your name> and <current date> in the comments with your name and the current date, respectively.) Also, position the insertion point as shown in the figure.

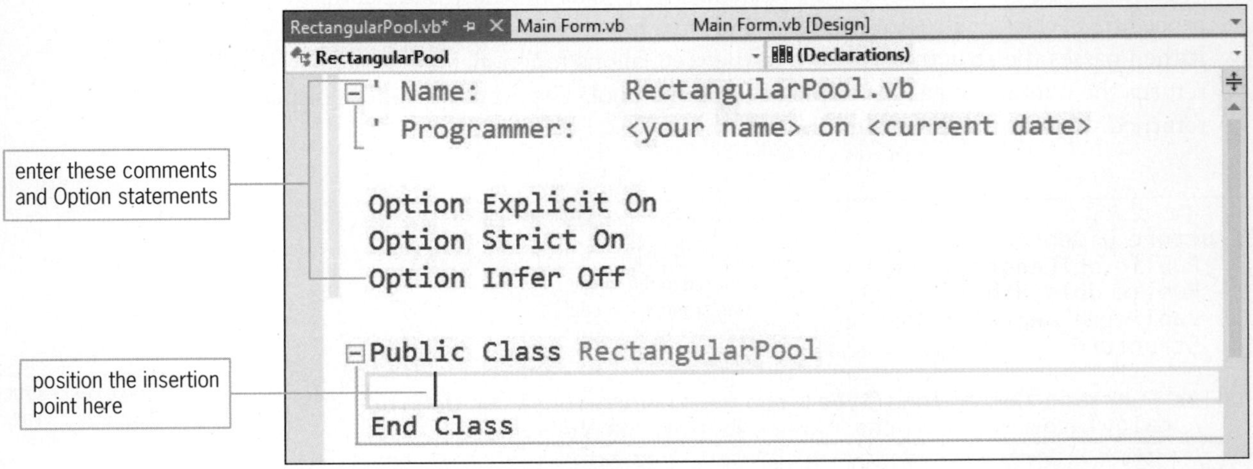

Figure 11-7 Comments and Option statements entered in the class file

A RectangularPool object has three attributes: length, width, and depth. In the Class statement, each attribute will be represented by a Public variable. When a variable in a class is declared using the `Public` keyword, it can be accessed by any application that contains an instance of the class. The convention is to use Pascal case for the names of the Public variables in a class, and to omit the three-character ID that indicates the variable's data type. This is because Public variables represent properties that will be seen by anyone using an object created from the class. The properties of Visual Basic objects, such as the Text and StartPosition properties, also follow this naming convention.

START HERE

To enter the Public variables in the class definition:

1. Enter the following three Public statements:

   Public Length As Double
   Public Width As Double
   Public Depth As Double

2. Delete the blank line above the End Class clause, if necessary, and then save the solution.

Now you will modify the application's code to use the RectangularPool class rather than the Dimensions structure.

START HERE

To modify the code to use the RectangularPool class:

1. Click the **Main Form.vb** tab to return to the form's Code Editor window. Replace <your name> and <current date> in the comments with your name and the current date, respectively.
2. First, delete the Structure statement from the form's Declarations section.
3. Next, locate the btnCalc_Click procedure. The procedure will instantiate a RectangularPool object. Replace the `Dim poolSize As Dimensions` instruction with the following instruction:

   Dim customerPool As New RectangularPool

4. Now you will modify the three TryParse methods to use the object's Public variables. Highlight (select) `poolSize.dblLength` in the first TryParse method. Type **customerPool.** and then click the **Common** tab (if necessary). The Public variables appear in the IntelliSense list, as shown in Figure 11-8.

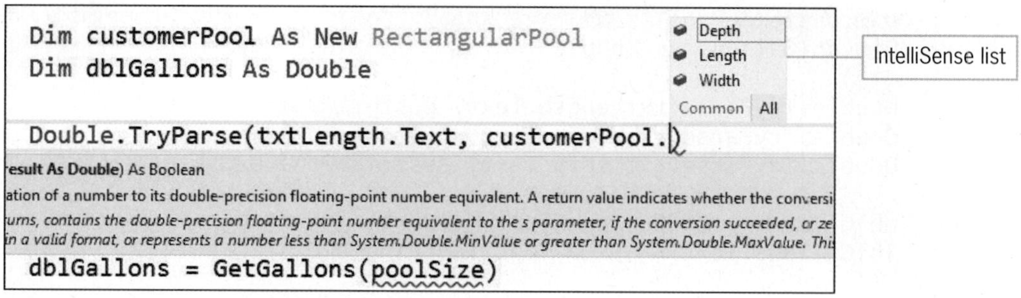

Dim customerPool As New RectangularPool
Dim dblGallons As Double
Depth
Length
Width
Common
All
IntelliSense list
Double.TryParse(txtLength.Text, customerPool.
esult As Double) As Boolean
ation of a number to its double-precision floating-point number equivalent. A return value indicates whether the conversi
urns, contains the double-precision floating-point number equivalent to the s parameter, if the conversion succeeded, or ze
in a valid format, or represents a number less than System.Double.MinValue or greater than System.Double.MaxValue. Thi
dblGallons = GetGallons(poolSize)

Figure 11-8 Public variables included in the IntelliSense list

5. Click **Length** and then press **Tab**. Now change `poolSize.dblWidth` and `poolSize.dblDepth` in the remaining TryParse methods to **customerPool.Width** and **customerPool.Depth**, respectively.
6. The procedure needs to pass the customerPool object (rather than the poolSize structure) to the GetGallons function. Change `poolSize` in the `dblGallons = GetGallons(poolSize)` statement to **customerPool**.
7. Locate the GetGallons function. The function will need to receive a RectangularPool object rather than a Dimensions structure. Change `Dimensions` in the function header to **RectangularPool**.
8. Finally, change `dblLength`, `dblWidth`, and `dblDepth` in the Return statement to **Length**, **Width**, and **Depth**, respectively. Recall that Length, Width, and Depth are the names of the RectangularPool object's properties.

Figure 11-9 shows the Class statement, the GetGallons function, and the btnCalc_Click procedure. The changes made to the original function and procedure (both of which are shown earlier in Figure 11-6) are shaded in the figure.

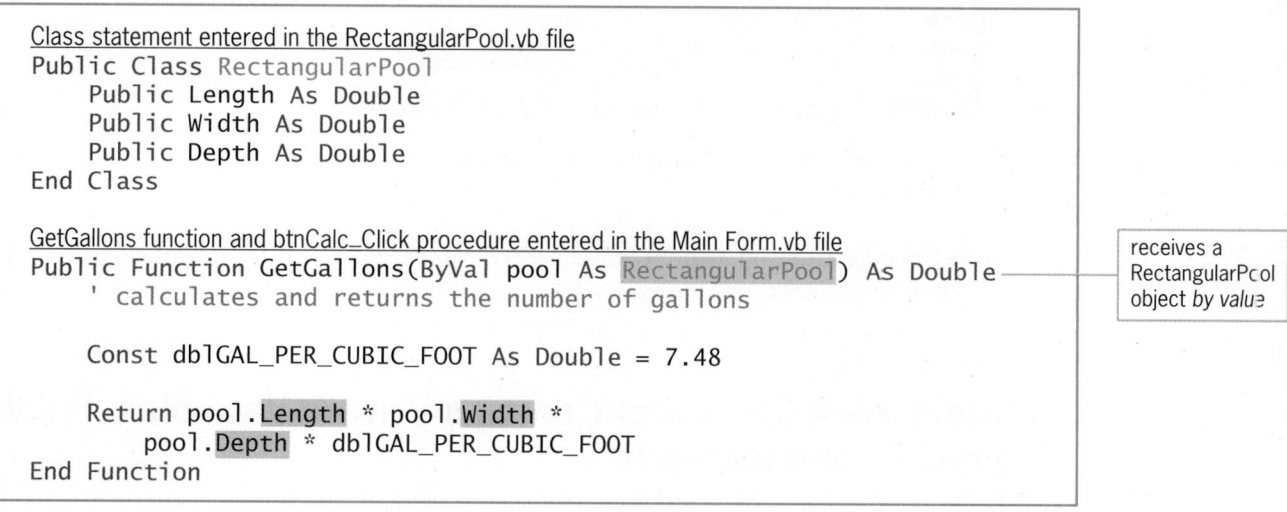

Class statement entered in the RectangularPool.vb file

```
Public Class RectangularPool
    Public Length As Double
    Public Width As Double
    Public Depth As Double
End Class
```

GetGallons function and btnCalc_Click procedure entered in the Main Form.vb file

```
Public Function GetGallons(ByVal pool As RectangularPool) As Double
    ' calculates and returns the number of gallons

    Const dblGAL_PER_CUBIC_FOOT As Double = 7.48

    Return pool.Length * pool.Width *
        pool.Depth * dblGAL_PER_CUBIC_FOOT
End Function
```

receives a RectangularPool object *by value*

Figure 11-9 Class statement, GetGallons function, and btnCalc_Click procedure *(continues)*

(continued)

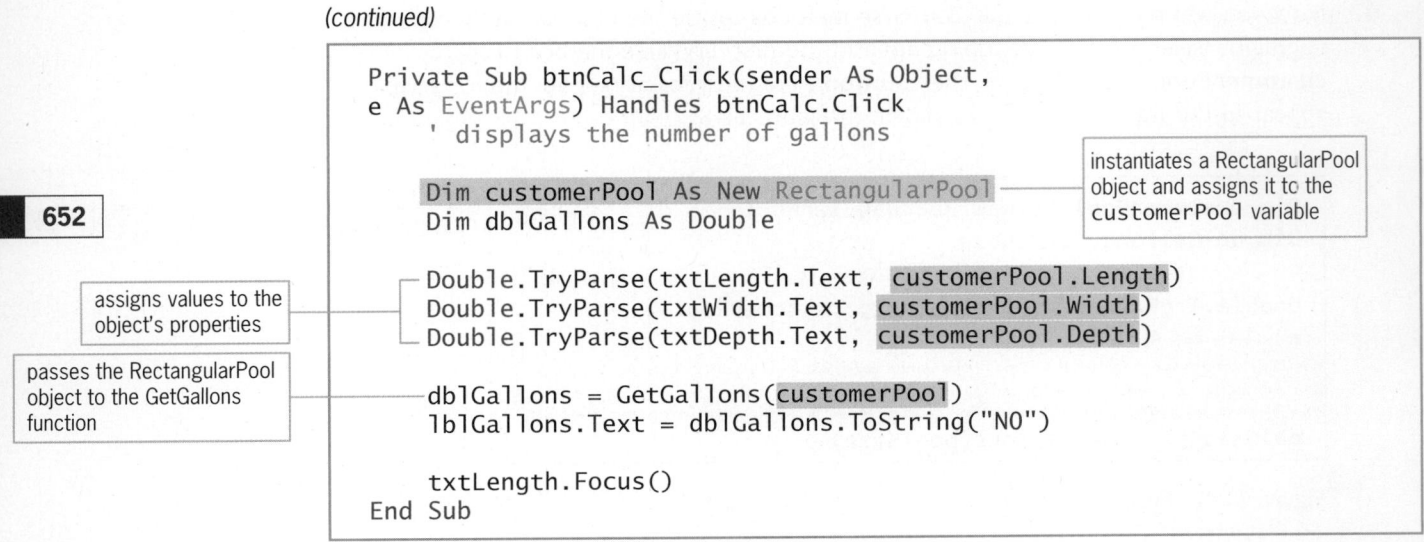

```
Private Sub btnCalc_Click(sender As Object,
e As EventArgs) Handles btnCalc.Click
    ' displays the number of gallons

    Dim customerPool As New RectangularPool
    Dim dblGallons As Double

    Double.TryParse(txtLength.Text, customerPool.Length)
    Double.TryParse(txtWidth.Text, customerPool.Width)
    Double.TryParse(txtDepth.Text, customerPool.Depth)

    dblGallons = GetGallons(customerPool)
    lblGallons.Text = dblGallons.ToString("N0")

    txtLength.Focus()
End Sub
```

instantiates a RectangularPool object and assigns it to the `customerPool` variable

assigns values to the object's properties

passes the RectangularPool object to the GetGallons function

Figure 11-9 Class statement, GetGallons function, and btnCalc_Click procedure

START HERE

To test the modified code:

1. Save the solution and then start the application. Type **60** in the Length box, **30** in the Width box, and **5** in the Depth box. Click the **Calculate** button to display the required number of gallons of water. See Figure 11-10.

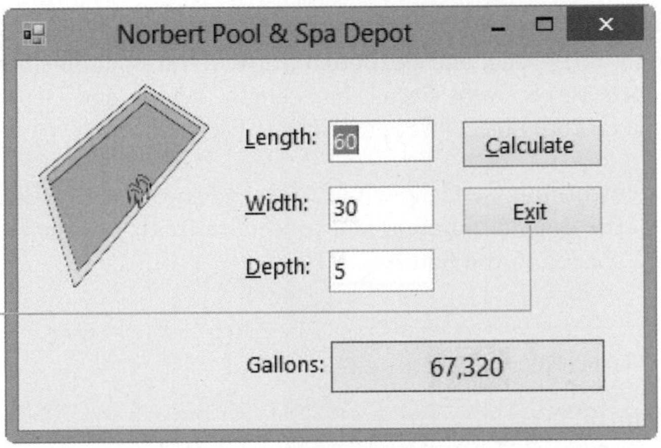

you can use the Alt key to show/hide the access keys

Figure 11-10 Interface showing the number of gallons

OpenClipArt.org/laobc

2. Click the **Exit** button. Close the Main Form.vb and RectangularPool.vb windows and then close the solution.

Example 2—A Class that Contains Private Variables, Public Properties, and Methods

Although you can define a class that contains only attributes represented by Public variables—like the RectangularPool class shown in Figure 11-9—that is rarely done. The disadvantage of using Public variables in a class is that a class cannot control the values assigned to its Public variables. As a result, the class cannot validate the values to ensure they are appropriate for the variables. Furthermore, most classes contain not only attributes, but behaviors as well. This is because the purpose of a class in OOP is to encapsulate the properties that describe an object, the methods that allow the object to perform tasks, and the events that allow the object to respond to actions. In this section, you will create a class that contains data validation code and methods. (Including events in a class is beyond the scope of this book.) The class will be used in the Carpets Galore application, which calculates and displays the number of square yards of carpeting required to carpet a rectangular floor. It also calculates and displays the cost of the carpet.

START HERE

To add a class file to the Carpets Galore application:

1. Open the Carpets Galore Solution (Carpets Galore Solution.sln) file contained in the VB2012\Chap11\Carpets Galore Solution folder. If necessary, open the designer window. The interface provides list boxes for the user to enter the length and width of a room's floor and the price of a square yard of carpet. See Figure 11-11. (The image in the picture box was downloaded from the Open Clip Art Library at *http://openclipart.org*.)

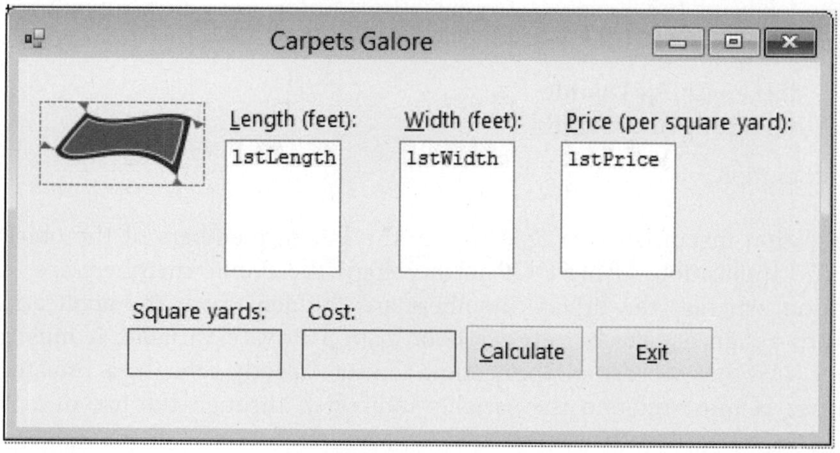

Figure 11-11 Interface for the Carpets Galore application
OpenClipArt.org/Artmaker

2. Use the PROJECT menu to add a new class file to the project. Name the class file **Rectangle.vb**. Insert a blank line above the Class statement and then enter the comments and Option statements shown in Figure 11-12. (Replace <your name> and <current date> in the comments with your name and the current date, respectively.) Also, position the insertion point as shown in the figure.

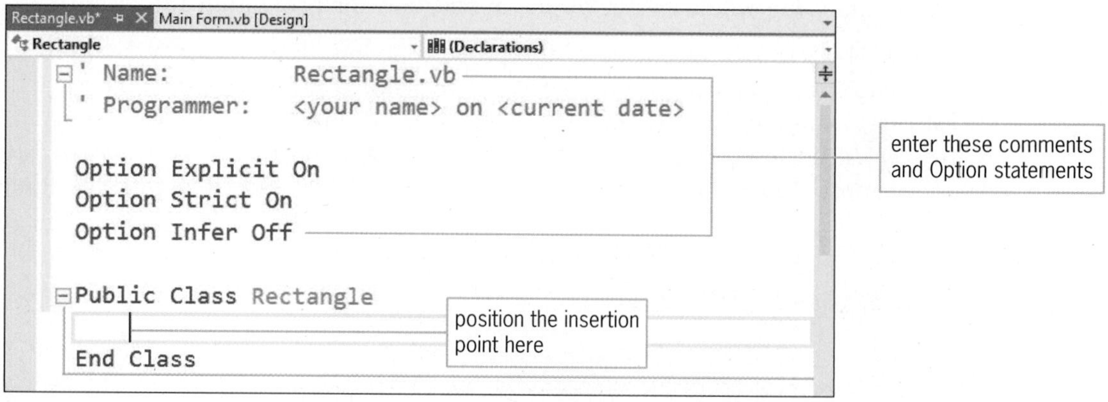

Figure 11-12 Comments and Option statements entered in the class file

A room's floor is a rectangular object that has two attributes: length and width. Rather than using Public variables to represent both attributes, the Rectangle class will use Private variables and Property procedures.

Private Variables and Property Procedures

Unlike a class's Public variables, its Private variables are not visible to applications that contain an instance of the class. Because of this, the names of the Private variables will not appear in the IntelliSense list as you are coding, nor will they be recognized within the application's code. A class's Private variables can be used only by instructions within the class itself. The naming convention for a class's Private variables is to use the underscore as the first character in the name and then camel case for the remainder of the name. Following this naming convention, you will use the names `_dblLength` and `_dblWidth` for the Private variables in the Rectangle class.

START HERE

To include Private variables in the Rectangle class:

1. Enter the following two Private statements. Press **Enter** twice after typing the last statement.

   Private _dblLength As Double
   Private _dblWidth As Double

2. Save the solution.

When an application instantiates an object, only the Public members of the object's class are visible to the application. Using OOP terminology, the Public members are "exposed" to the application, whereas the Private members are "hidden" from the application. For an application to assign data to or retrieve data from a Private variable, it must use a Public property. In other words, an application cannot directly refer to a Private variable in a class. Rather, it must refer to the variable indirectly, through the use of a Public property.

You create a Public property using a **Property procedure**, whose syntax is shown in Figure 11-13. A Public Property procedure creates a property that is visible to any application that contains an instance of the class. In most cases, a Property procedure header begins with the keywords `Public Property`. However, as the syntax indicates, the header can also include one of the following keywords: `ReadOnly` or `WriteOnly`. The **ReadOnly keyword** indicates that the property's value can be retrieved (read) by an application, but the application cannot set (write to) the property. The property would get its value from the class itself rather than from the application. The **WriteOnly keyword** indicates that an application can set the property's value, but it cannot retrieve the value. In this case, the value would be set by the application for use within the class.

The Length property of a one-dimensional array is an example of a ReadOnly property.

As Figure 11-13 shows, the name of the property follows the `Property` keyword in the header. You should use nouns and adjectives to name a property and enter the name using Pascal case, as in Side, Bonus, and AnnualSales. Following the property name is an optional *parameterList* enclosed in parentheses, the keyword `As`, and the property's *dataType*. The dataType must match the data type of the Private variable associated with the Property procedure.

Property Procedure

Syntax

Public [**ReadOnly** | **WriteOnly**] **Property** *propertyName*[**(***parameterList***)**] **As** *dataType*
  Get
    [*instructions*]
    Return *privateVariable*
  End Get
  Set(value As *dataType***)**
    [*instructions*]
    privateVariable = {**value** | *defaultValue*}
  End Set
End Property

Example 1 – an application can both retrieve and set the Side property's value

```
Private _intSide As Integer

Public Property Side As Integer
      Get
            Return _intSide
      End Get
      Set(value As Integer)
            If value > 0 Then
                  _intSide = value
            Else
                  _intSide = 0
            End If
      End Set
End Property
```

Example 2 – an application can retrieve, but not set, the Bonus property's value

```
Private _dblBonus As Double

Public ReadOnly Property Bonus As Double
      Get
            Return _dblBonus
      End Get
End Property
```

Example 3 – an application can set, but not retrieve, the AnnualSales property's value

```
Private _decAnnualSales As Decimal

Public WriteOnly Property AnnualSales As Decimal
      Set(value As Decimal)
            _decAnnualSales = value
      End Set
End Property
```

Figure 11-13 Syntax and examples of a Property procedure

Between a Property procedure's header and footer, you include a Get block of code, a Set block of code, or both Get and Set blocks of code. The appropriate block or blocks of code to include depends on the keywords contained in the procedure header. If the header contains the `ReadOnly` keyword, you include only a Get block of code in the Property procedure. The code contained in the **Get block** allows an application to retrieve the contents of the Private variable associated with the property. In the Property procedure shown in Example 2 in Figure 11-13, the `ReadOnly` keyword indicates that an application can retrieve the contents of the Bonus property, but it cannot set the property's value.

If the header contains the `WriteOnly` keyword, on the other hand, you include only a Set block of code in the procedure. The code in the **Set block** allows an application to assign a value to the Private variable associated with the property. In the Property procedure shown in Example 3 in Figure 11-13, the `WriteOnly` keyword indicates that an application can assign a value to the AnnualSales property, but it cannot retrieve the property's contents.

If the Property procedure header does not contain the `ReadOnly` or `WriteOnly` keywords, you include both a Get block of code and a Set block of code in the procedure, as shown in Example 1 in Figure 11-13. In this case, an application can both retrieve and set the Side property's value.

The Get block in a Property procedure contains the **Get statement**, which begins with the Get clause and ends with the End Get clause. Most times, you will enter only the `Return` *privateVariable* instruction within the Get statement. The instruction returns the contents of the Private variable associated with the property. In Example 1 in Figure 11-13, the `Return _intSide` statement returns the contents of the `_intSide` variable, which is the Private variable associated with the Side property. Similarly, the `Return _dblBonus` statement in Example 2 returns the contents of the `_dblBonus` variable, which is the Private variable associated with the Bonus property. Example 3 does not contain a Get statement because the AnnualSales property is designated as a `WriteOnly` property.

The Set block contains the **Set statement**, which begins with the Set clause and ends with the End Set clause. The Set clause's `value` parameter temporarily stores the value that is passed to the property by the application. The `value` parameter's *dataType* must match the data type of the Private variable associated with the Property procedure. You can enter one or more instructions between the Set and End Set clauses. One of the instructions should assign the contents of the `value` parameter to the Private variable associated with the property. In Example 3 in Figure 11-13, the `_decAnnualSales = value` statement assigns the contents of the property's `value` parameter to the Private `_decAnnualSales` variable.

In the Set statement, you often will include instructions to validate the value received from the application before assigning it to the Private variable. The Set statement in Example 1 in Figure 11-13 includes a selection structure that determines whether the side measurement received from the application is greater than 0. If it is, the `_intSide = value` instruction assigns the integer stored in the `value` parameter to the Private `_intSide` variable. Otherwise, the `_intSide = 0` instruction assigns a default value (in this case, 0) to the variable. The Property procedure in Example 2 in Figure 11-13 does not contain a Set statement because the Bonus property is designated as a `ReadOnly` property.

START HERE

To enter a Property procedure for each Private variable in the Rectangle class:

1. The insertion point should be positioned in the blank line above the End Class clause. Enter the following Property procedure header and Get clause. When you press Enter after typing the Get clause, the Code Editor automatically enters the End Get clause, the Set statement, and the End Property clause.

   Public Property Length As Double
   Get

2. Recall that in most cases, the Get statement simply returns the contents of the Private variable associated with the Property procedure. Type the following statement, but don't press Enter:

   Return _dblLength

3. The Set statement should assign either the contents of its `value` parameter or a default value to the Private variable associated with the Property procedure. In this case, you will assign the integer stored in the `value` parameter only when the integer is greater than 0;

otherwise, you will assign the number 0. Click the **blank line** above the End Set clause and then enter the following selection structure:

If value > 0 Then
_dblLength = value
Else
_dblLength = 0
End If

4. Save the solution. Figure 11-14 shows the Length Property procedure associated with the `_dblLength` variable.

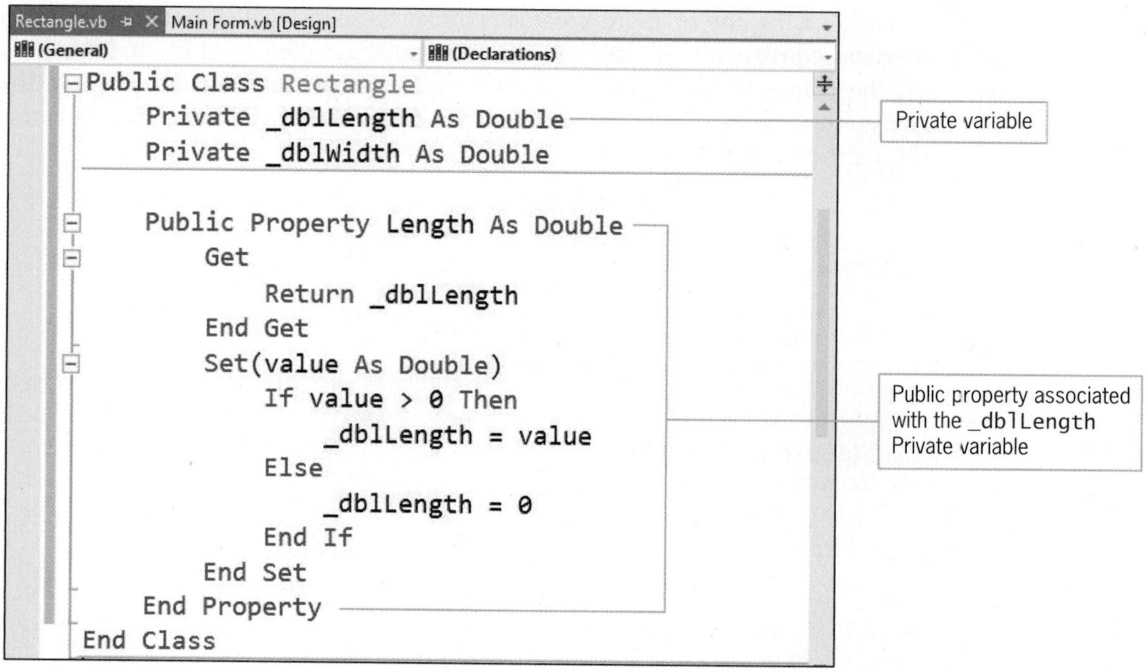

Figure 11-14 Length Property procedure entered in the class

5. Now you will enter a Property procedure for the `_dblWidth` variable. Insert two blank lines below the End Property clause, and then enter the following Property procedure header and Get clause:

Public Property Width As Double
Get

6. Type the following Return statement, but don't press Enter:

Return _dblWidth

7. Click the **blank line** above the End Set clause and then enter the following selection structure:

If value > 0 Then
_dblWidth = value
Else
_dblWidth = 0
End If

8. Save the solution.

You have finished entering the class's Private variables and Property procedures. The class's methods are next. The first method you will learn about is a constructor.

Constructors

Most classes contain at least one constructor. A **constructor** is a class method, always named New, whose sole purpose is to initialize the class's Private variables. Constructors never return a value, so they are always Sub procedures rather than Function procedures. The syntax for creating a constructor is shown in Figure 11-15. Notice that a constructor's *parameterList* is optional. A constructor that has no parameters, like the constructor in Example 1, is called the **default constructor**. A class can have only one default constructor. A class that contains one or more parameters, like the constructor in Example 2, is called a **parameterized constructor**. A class can have as many parameterized constructors as needed. However, the parameterList in each parameterized constructor must be unique within the class. The method name (in this case, New) combined with its optional parameterList is called the method's **signature**.

Constructor

Syntax
Public Sub New([*parameterList*]**)**
instructions to initialize the class's Private variables
End Sub

Example 1 (default constructor)
```
Public Sub New()
    _dblLength = 0
    _dblWidth = 0
End Sub
```
initializes the Private variables directly

Example 2 (parameterized constructor)
```
Public Sub New (ByVal dblL As Double,
                ByVal dblW As Double)
    Length = dblL
    Width = dblW
End Sub
```
uses the Public properties to initialize the Private variables indirectly

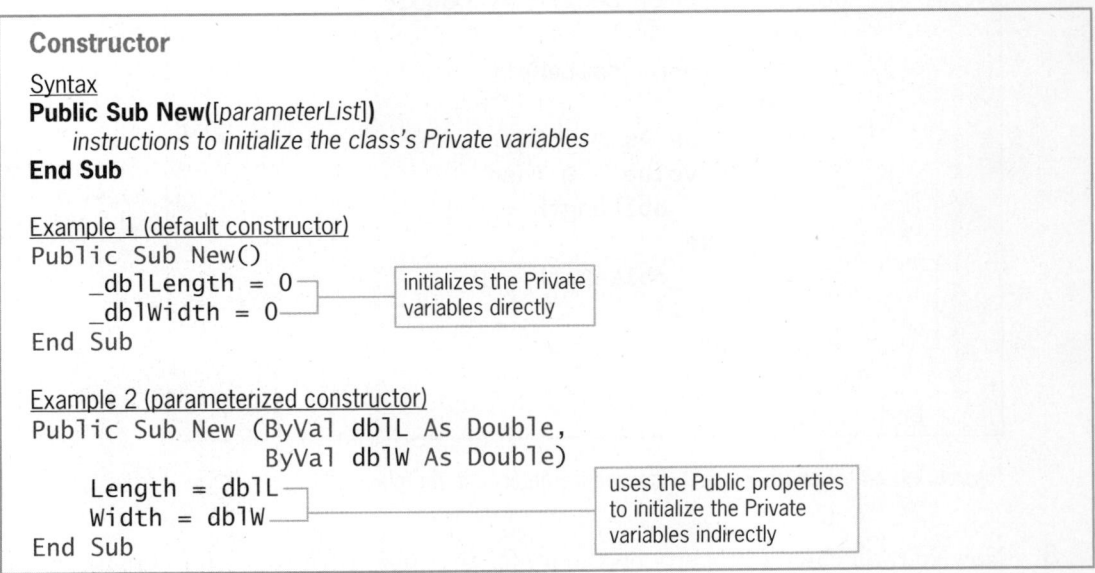

Figure 11-15 Syntax and examples of a constructor

When an object is instantiated, the computer uses one of the class's constructors to initialize the class's Private variables. If a class contains more than one constructor, the computer determines the appropriate constructor by matching the number, data type, and position of the arguments in the statement that instantiates the object with the number, data type, and position of the parameters listed in each constructor's parameterList. The statements in Examples 1 and 2 in Figure 11-16 will invoke the default constructor because neither statement contains any arguments. The statements in Examples 3 and 4 will invoke the parameterized constructor because both statements contain two arguments whose data type is Double.

```
Example 1 – invokes the default constructor
Dim floor As New Rectangle

Example 2 – invokes the default constructor
floor = New Rectangle

Example 3 – invokes the parameterized constructor
Dim floor As New Rectangle(10.5, 12.5)

Example 4 – invokes the parameterized constructor
floor = New Rectangle(dblRoomLen, dblRoomWid)
```

Figure 11-16 Statements that invoke the constructors shown in Figure 11-15

The `Dim randGen As New Random` statement from Chapter 5 instantiates a Random object and invokes the class's default constructor.

A default constructor is allowed to initialize the class's Private variables directly. The default constructor shown earlier in Example 1 in Figure 11-15, for instance, assigns the number 0 to the class's Private `_dblLength` and `_dblWidth` variables. Parameterized constructors, on the other hand, should use the class's Public properties to access the Private variables indirectly. This is because the values passed to a parameterized constructor come from the application rather than from the class itself. Values that originate outside of the class should always be assigned to the Private variables indirectly, through the Public properties. Doing this ensures that the Property procedure's Set block, which typically contains validation code, is processed. The parameterized constructor shown earlier in Example 2 in Figure 11-15, for instance, uses the Public Length property to initialize the Private `_dblLength` variable, thereby invoking the validation code in the Length property. It also uses the Public Width property to initialize the Private `_dblWidth` variable; doing this invokes the Width property's validation code.

START HERE

To include a default constructor in the Rectangle class:

1. Insert two blank lines below the Width property's End Property clause, and then enter the following default constructor:

```
Public Sub New()
    _dblLength = 0
    _dblWidth = 0
End Sub
```

Methods Other than Constructors

Except for constructors, which must be Sub procedures, the other methods in a class can be either Sub procedures or Function procedures. Recall from Chapter 7 that the difference between these two types of procedures is that a Function procedure returns a value after performing its assigned task, whereas a Sub procedure does not return a value. Figure 11-17 shows the syntax for a method that is not a constructor. Like property names, method names should be entered using Pascal case. However, unlike property names, the first word in a method name should be a verb, and any subsequent words should be nouns and adjectives. Figure 11-17 also includes two examples of a method that allows a Rectangle object to calculate its area. Notice that you can write the method as either a Function procedure or a Sub procedure.

Method That Is Not a Constructor

Syntax

Public {**Sub** | **Function**} *methodName*(*[parameterList]*) [**As** *dataType*]
    instructions
End {**Sub** | **Function**}

Example 1 – Function procedure

```
Public Function GetArea() As Double
     Return _dblLength * _dblWidth
End Function
```

Example 2 – Sub procedure

```
Public Sub GetArea(ByRef dblA As Double)
     dblA = _dblLength * _dblWidth
End Sub
```

Figure 11-17 Syntax and examples of a method that is not a constructor

START HERE

To enter the GetArea method from Example 1:

1. Insert two blank lines below the default constructor's End Sub clause, and then enter the following GetArea method:

   ```
   Public Function GetArea() As Double
       Return _dblLength * _dblWidth
   End Function
   ```

2. The Rectangle class definition is now complete. Save the solution.

Coding the Carpets Galore Application

The Calculate button's Click event procedure is the only procedure you need to code in the Carpets Galore application. Figure 11-18 shows the procedure's pseudocode.

btnCalc Click event procedure

1. instantiate a Rectangle object to represent the floor
2. declare variables to store the price per square yard, required number of square yards, and carpet cost
3. assign the input data to the appropriate properties and variable
4. calculate the required number of square yards by dividing the floor's area by 9
5. calculate the carpet cost by multiplying the price per square yard by the required number of square yards
6. display the required number of square yards and the carpet cost

Figure 11-18 Pseudocode for the Calculate button's Click event procedure

START HERE

To code the Calculate button's Click event procedure:

1. Click the **designer window's tab** and then open the Code Editor window. Replace <your name> and <current date> in the comments with your name and the current date, respectively.

2. Locate the btnCalc_Click procedure. The first step in the pseudocode is to instantiate a Rectangle object to represent the room's floor. Enter the following Dim statement in the blank line below the `' instantiate a Rectangle object` comment:

   Dim floor As New Rectangle

3. Now you will declare variables to store the price of a square yard of carpet, the number of square yards needed, and the cost of the carpet. You won't need variables to store the floor's length and width measurements because the procedure will assign those values to the Rectangle object's Length and Width properties. Click the **blank line** below the `' declare variables` comment, and then enter the following three Dim statements:

   Dim dblPriceSqYd As Double
   Dim dblSqYards As Double
   Dim dblCost As Double

4. Next, you will assign the length and width entries to the Rectangle object's Length and Width properties, respectively. You also will assign the price entry to the `dblPriceSqYd` variable. Click the **blank line** below the `' assign values to the object's Public properties` comment, and then enter the three TryParse methods shown in Figure 11-19. Notice that when you press the period after typing `floor` in the first two TryParse methods, the `floor` object's Length and Width properties appear in the IntelliSense list.

```
' assign values to the object's Public properties
Double.TryParse(lstLength.SelectedItem.ToString, floor.Length)
Double.TryParse(lstWidth.SelectedItem.ToString, floor.Width)
Double.TryParse(lstPrice.SelectedItem.ToString, dblPriceSqYd)
```

Figure 11-19 TryParse methods entered in the procedure

5. The fourth step in the pseudocode calculates the required number of square yards by dividing the floor's area (which is in square feet) by the number 9. You need to divide by 9 because there are 9 square feet in a square yard. You can use the Rectangle object's GetArea method to calculate and return the area of the floor. Click the **blank line** below the `' calculate the square yards` comment, and then enter the following assignment statement. Here again, notice that when you press the period after typing `floor`, the `floor` object's GetArea method appears in the IntelliSense list.

   dblSqYards = floor.GetArea / 9

6. The next step in the pseudocode calculates the cost of the carpet by multiplying the price per square yard by the required number of square yards. Enter the following assignment statement in the blank line below the `' calculate the carpet cost` comment:

   dblCost = dblPriceSqYd * dblSqYards

7. The last step in the pseudocode displays the required number of square yards and the carpet cost. Click the **blank line** below the `' display output` comment, and then enter the following assignment statements:

   lblSquareYards.Text = dblSqYards.ToString("N1")
   lblCost.Text = dblCost.ToString("C2")

8. Delete the blank line above the btnCalc_Click procedure's End Sub clause, if necessary.

Figure 11-20 shows the Rectangle class definition contained in the Rectangle.vb file. It also shows the btnCalc_Click procedure contained in the Main Form.vb file.

Class statement entered in the Rectangle.vb file

```
Public Class Rectangle
    Private _dblLength As Double
    Private _dblWidth As Double

    Public Property Length As Double
        Get
            Return _dblLength
        End Get
        Set(value As Double)
            If value > 0 Then
                _dblLength = value
            Else
                _dblLength = 0
            End If
        End Set
    End Property

    Public Property Width As Double
        Get
            Return _dblWidth
        End Get
        Set(value As Double)
            If value > 0 Then
                _dblWidth = value
            Else
                _dblWidth = 0
            End If
        End Set
    End Property

    Public Sub New()
        _dblLength = 0
        _dblWidth = 0
    End Sub

    Public Function GetArea() As Double
        Return _dblLength * _dblWidth
    End Function
End Class
```

Figure 11-20 Rectangle class definition and btnCalc_Click procedure *(continues)*

(continued)

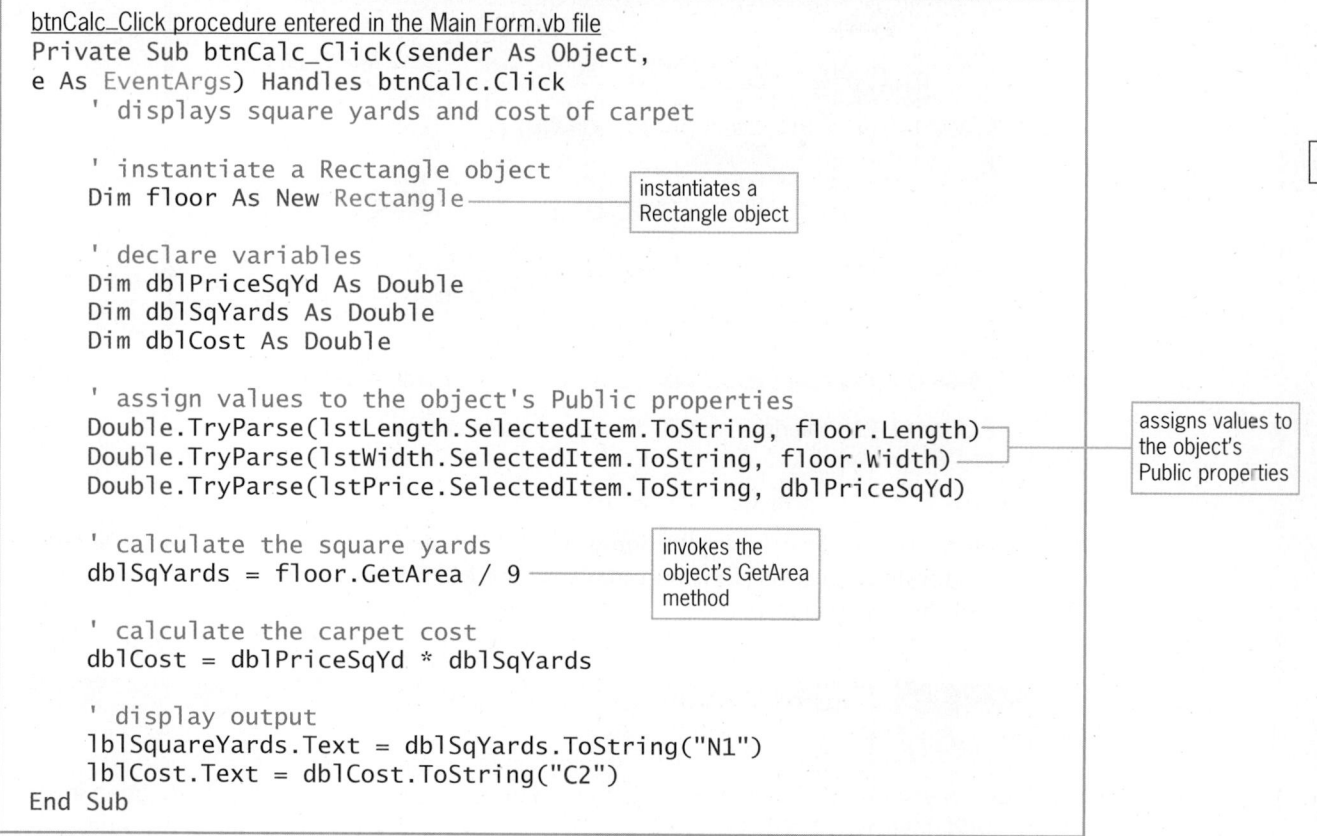

btnCalc_Click procedure entered in the Main Form.vb file

```
Private Sub btnCalc_Click(sender As Object,
e As EventArgs) Handles btnCalc.Click
    ' displays square yards and cost of carpet

    ' instantiate a Rectangle object
    Dim floor As New Rectangle

    ' declare variables
    Dim dblPriceSqYd As Double
    Dim dblSqYards As Double
    Dim dblCost As Double

    ' assign values to the object's Public properties
    Double.TryParse(lstLength.SelectedItem.ToString, floor.Length)
    Double.TryParse(lstWidth.SelectedItem.ToString, floor.Width)
    Double.TryParse(lstPrice.SelectedItem.ToString, dblPriceSqYd)

    ' calculate the square yards
    dblSqYards = floor.GetArea / 9

    ' calculate the carpet cost
    dblCost = dblPriceSqYd * dblSqYards

    ' display output
    lblSquareYards.Text = dblSqYards.ToString("N1")
    lblCost.Text = dblCost.ToString("C2")
End Sub
```

instantiates a Rectangle object

assigns values to the object's Public properties

invokes the object's GetArea method

Figure 11-20 Rectangle class definition and btnCalc_Click procedure

To test the Carpets Galore application:

START HERE

1. Save the solution and then start the application. Click **9.0** and **8.5** in the Length and Width list boxes, respectively. Click **9.50** in the Price list box and then click the **Calculate** button. The `Dim floor As New Rectangle` instruction in the button's Click event procedure instantiates a Rectangle object. At this point, the computer processes the class's default constructor, which initializes the object's Private variables to the number 0. The next three Dim statements in the procedure create and initialize three Double variables. Next, the TryParse methods assign the appropriate values to the Rectangle object's Public properties and to the `dblPriceSqYd` variable. The procedure then calculates the required number of square yards of carpet, using the Rectangle object's GetArea method to calculate and return the area of the floor. Finally, the procedure calculates the cost of the carpet and then displays both the required number of square yards and the cost. See Figure 11-21.

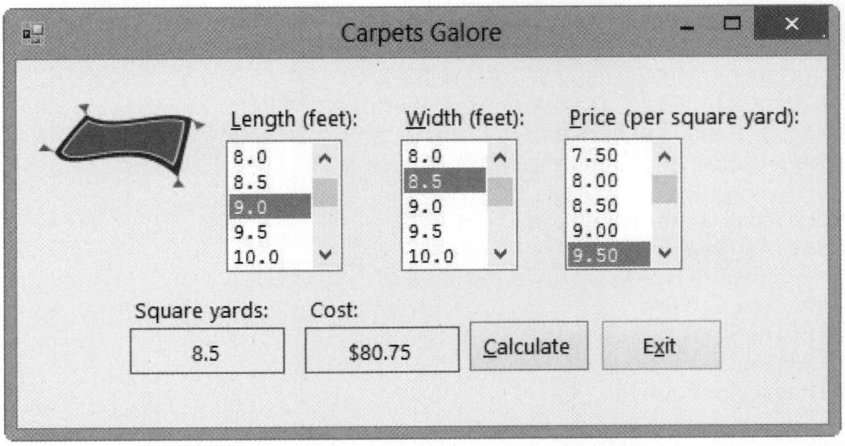

Figure 11-21 Interface showing the square yards and cost
OpenClipArt.org/Artmaker

2. On your own, test the application using different lengths, widths, and prices. When you are finished, click the **Exit** button. Close the Main Form.vb and Rectangle.vb windows and then close the solution.

YOU DO IT 1!

Create a Visual Basic Windows application named YouDoIt 1. Save the application in the VB2012\Chap11 folder. Add a text box, a label, and a button to the form. Add a class file named Circle.vb to the project. Define a class named Circle. The class should contain one attribute: the circle's radius. It also should contain a default constructor and a method that calculates and returns the circle's area. Use the following formula to calculate the area: 3.141592 * $radius^2$. Open the form's Code Editor window. The button's Click event procedure should display the circle's area, using the radius entered by the user. Code the procedure. Save the solution and then start and test the application. Close the solution.

Example 3—A Class that Contains a Parameterized Constructor

In this example, you will add a parameterized constructor to the Rectangle class created in Example 2. Recall that a parameterized constructor is simply a constructor that has parameters. You then will modify the Carpets Galore application to use the parameterized constructor.

START HERE

To add a parameterized constructor to the Rectangle.vb file:

1. Use Windows to make a copy of the Carpets Galore Solution folder from Example 2. Rename the copy Modified Carpets Galore Solution. Open the Carpets Galore Solution (Carpets Galore Solution.sln) file contained in the Modified Carpets Galore Solution folder. Open the designer window.
2. Right-click **Rectangle.vb** in the Solution Explorer window and then click **View Code**.

3. Locate the default constructor. Click the **blank line** below the default constructor's End Sub clause and then press **Enter** twice to insert two blank lines. Press the **up arrow** key on your keyboard and then enter the following parameterized constructor:

Public Sub New(ByVal dblL As Double, ByVal dblW As Double)
Length = dblL
Width = dblW
End Sub

4. Save the solution and then close the Rectangle.vb window.

Figure 11-22 shows the Rectangle class's default and parameterized constructors. Unlike the default constructor, which automatically initializes the Private variables to 0 when a Rectangle object is created, a parameterized constructor allows an application to specify the object's initial values. In this case, the initial values must have the Double data type because the constructor's parameterList contains two Double variables. You include the initial values, enclosed in a set of parentheses, in the statement that instantiates the object. In other words, you include them in the statement that contains the `New` keyword, such as the `Dim floor As New Rectangle(10.5, 12.5)` statement or the `floor = New Rectangle(dblRoomLen, dblRoomWid)` statement.

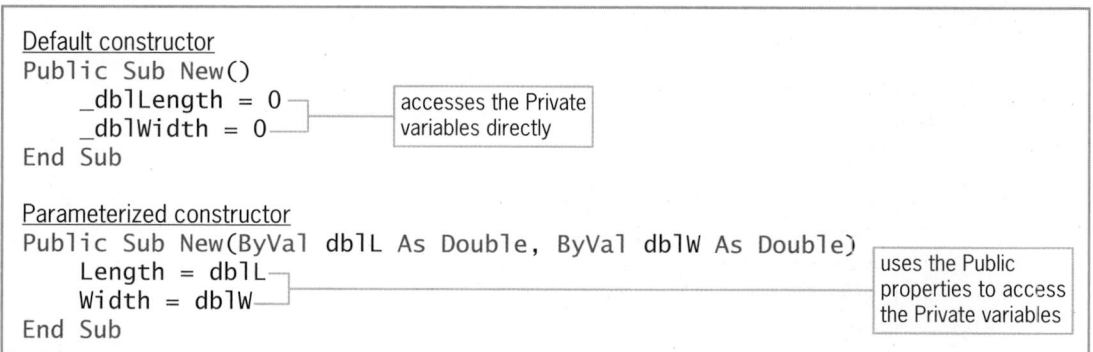

Default constructor
```
Public Sub New()
    _dblLength = 0
    _dblWidth = 0
End Sub
```
accesses the Private variables directly

Parameterized constructor
```
Public Sub New(ByVal dblL As Double, ByVal dblW As Double)
    Length = dblL
    Width = dblW
End Sub
```
uses the Public properties to access the Private variables

Figure 11-22 Default and parameterized constructors

START HERE

To use the parameterized constructor in the modified application:

1. Open the form's Code Editor window. Locate the btnCalc_Click procedure. Change the first comment in the procedure to **' declare a variable for a Rectangle object**.
2. Delete the `New` keyword from the first Dim statement. The statement should now say `Dim floor As Rectangle`.
3. Click the **blank line** below the last Dim statement, and then enter the following two declaration statements:

Dim dblRoomLen As Double
Dim dblRoomWid As Double

4. In the first TryParse method, replace `floor.Length` with **dblRoomLen**. Then, in the second TryParse method, replace `floor.Width` with **dblRoomWid**.
5. Click the **blank line** below the last TryParse method and then press **Enter**. Enter the following comment and assignment statement:

' instantiate and initialize a Rectangle object
floor = New Rectangle(dblRoomLen, dblRoomWid)

The modifications made to the original code, shown earlier in Figure 11-20, are shaded in Figure 11-23.

Modified Class statement entered in the Rectangle.vb file

```
Public Class Rectangle
    Private _dblLength As Double
    Private _dblWidth As Double

    Public Property Length As Double
        Get
            Return _dblLength
        End Get
        Set(value As Double)
            If value > 0 Then
                _dblLength = value
            Else
                _dblLength = 0
            End If
        End Set
    End Property

    Public Property Width As Double
        Get
            Return _dblWidth
        End Get
        Set(value As Double)
            If value > 0 Then
                _dblWidth = value
            Else
                _dblWidth = 0
            End If
        End Set
    End Property

    Public Sub New()
        _dblLength = 0
        _dblWidth = 0
    End Sub

    Public Sub New(ByVal dblL As Double, ByVal dblW As Double)
        Length = dblL
        Width = dblW
    End Sub

    Public Function GetArea() As Double
        Return _dblLength * _dblWidth
    End Function
End Class
```

parameterized constructor

Figure 11-23 Modified Rectangle class definition and btnCalc_Click procedure *(continues)*

(continued)

<u>Modified btnCalc_Click procedure entered in the Main Form.vb file</u>

```
Private Sub btnCalc_Click(sender As Object,
e As EventArgs) Handles btnCalc.Click
    ' displays square yards and cost of carpet

    ' declare a variable for a Rectangle object
    Dim floor As Rectangle

    ' declare variables
    Dim dblPriceSqYd As Double
    Dim dblSqYards As Double
    Dim dblCost As Double
    Dim dblRoomLen As Double
    Dim dblRoomWid As Double

    ' assign values to the object's Public properties
    Double.TryParse(lstLength.SelectedItem.ToString, dblRoomLen)
    Double.TryParse(lstWidth.SelectedItem.ToString, dblRoomWid)
    Double.TryParse(lstPrice.SelectedItem.ToString, dblPriceSqYd)

    ' instantiate and initialize a Rectangle object
    floor = New Rectangle(dblRoomLen, dblRoomWid)

    ' calculate the square yards
    dblSqYards = floor.GetArea / 9

    ' calculate the carpet cost
    dblCost = dblPriceSqYd * dblSqYards

    ' display output
    lblSquareYards.Text = dblSqYards.ToString("N1")
    lblCost.Text = dblCost.ToString("C2")
End Sub
```

declares a variable that can store a Rectangle object

uses the parameterized constructor to instantiate and initialize a Rectangle object

Figure 11-23 Modified Rectangle class definition and btnCalc_Click procedure

When the user clicks the Calculate button, the `Dim floor As Rectangle` instruction in the btnCalc_Click procedure creates a variable that can store a Rectangle object; but it does not create the object. The remaining Dim statements create and initialize five Double variables. Next, the TryParse methods assign the input values to the `dblRoomLen`, `dblRoomWid`, and `dblPriceSqYd` variables.

The next statement in the procedure, `floor = New Rectangle(dblRoomLen, dblRoomWid)`, instantiates a Rectangle object. The two Double arguments in the statement tell the computer to use the parameterized constructor to initialize the Rectangle object's Private variables. In this case, the computer passes the two Double arguments (*by value*) to the parameterized constructor, which stores them in its `dblL` and `dblW` parameters. The assignment statements in the constructor then assign the parameter values to the Rectangle object's Public Length and Width properties.

When you assign a value to a property, the computer passes the value to the property's Set statement, where it is stored in the Set statement's `value` parameter. In this case, the selection structure in the Length property's Set statement compares the value stored in the `value` parameter with the number 0. If the value is greater than 0, the selection structure's true path assigns the value to the Private `_dblLength` variable; otherwise, its false path assigns the number 0 to the variable. Similarly, the selection structure in the Width property's Set statement compares the value stored in the `value` parameter with the number 0. If the value is greater than 0, the selection structure's true path assigns the value to the Private `_dblWidth` variable; otherwise, its false path assigns the number 0 to the variable. Notice that a parameterized constructor uses the class's Public properties to access the Private variables indirectly. This is because the values passed to a parameterized constructor come from the application rather than from the class itself. As mentioned earlier, values that originate outside of the class should always be assigned to the Private variables indirectly, through the Public properties. Doing this ensures that the Property procedure's Set block, which typically contains validation code, is processed.

After the Rectangle object is instantiated and its Private variables are initialized, the btnCalc_Click procedure uses the object's GetArea method to calculate and return the area of the floor. The procedure uses the area to calculate the required number of square yards of carpet. Finally, the procedure calculates the cost of the carpet and then displays both the required number of square yards and the cost.

START HERE

To test the modified Carpets Galore application:

1. Save the solution and then start the application. Click **12.0** and **13.0** in the Length and Width list boxes, respectively. Click **14.50** in the Price list box and then click the **Calculate** button. See Figure 11-24.

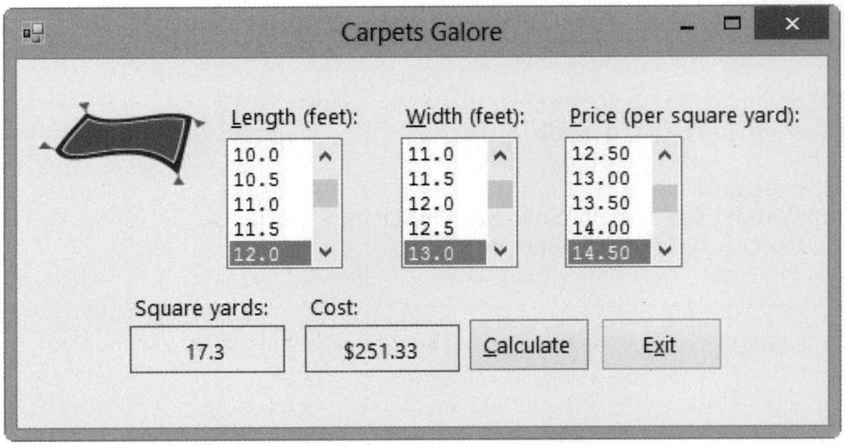

Figure 11-24 Square yards and cost shown in the interface
OpenClipArt.org/Artmaker

2. On your own, test the application using different lengths, widths, and prices. When you are finished, click the **Exit** button. Close the Main Form.vb window and then close the solution.

Example 4—Reusing a Class

In Examples 2 and 3, you used the Rectangle class to create an object that represented the floor in a room. In this example, you will use the Rectangle class to create an object that represents a square pizza. A square is simply a rectangle that has four equal sides. As mentioned earlier, the ability to use an object—in this case, a Rectangle object—for more than one purpose saves programming time and money, which contributes to the popularity of object-oriented programming.

To add the Rectangle.vb file to the Pete's Pizzeria application:

START HERE

1. Open the Pizzeria Solution (Pizzeria Solution.sln) file contained in the VB2012\Chap11\Pizzeria Solution folder. If necessary, open the designer window. The interface provides text boxes for entering the side measurements of both the entire pizza and a pizza slice. The application will use both measurements to calculate the number of pizza slices that can be cut from the entire pizza. See Figure 11-25.

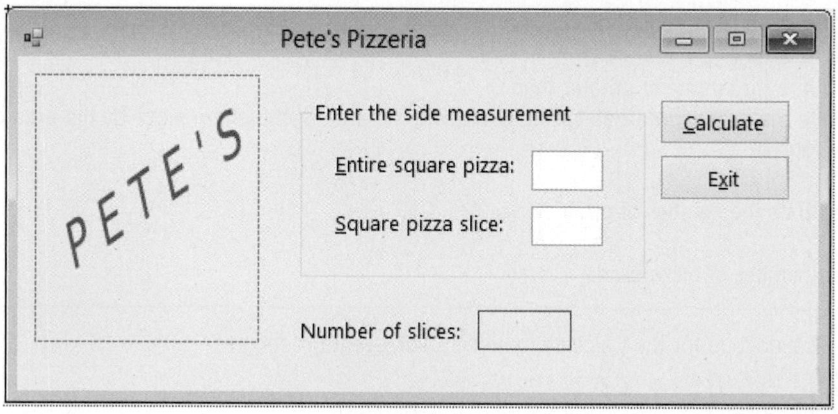

Figure 11-25 Interface for the Pete's Pizzeria application

2. First, you will copy the Rectangle.vb class file from the modified Carpets Galore application to the Pete's Pizzeria application. Use Windows to copy the Rectangle.vb file from the VB2012\Chap11\Modified Carpets Galore Solution\Carpets Galore Project folder to the Pizzeria Solution\Pizzeria Project folder. (If you did not complete the modified Carpets Galore application, you can copy the Rectangle.vb file contained in the VB2012\Chap11 folder.)
3. Next, you will add the Rectangle.vb file to the Pete's Pizzeria project. Click **PROJECT** on the menu bar and then click **Add Existing Item**. Open the Pizzeria Project folder (if necessary) and then click **Rectangle.vb** in the list of filenames. Click the **Add** button. Temporarily display the Solution Explorer window (if necessary) to verify that the Rectangle.vb file was added to the project.

Figure 11-26 shows the pseudocode for the Calculate button's Click event procedure.

```
btnCalc Click event procedure
1. instantiate a Rectangle object to represent the entire square pizza
2. instantiate a Rectangle object to represent a square pizza slice
3. declare variables to store the area of the entire pizza, the area of a pizza slice, and the number of
   slices
4. assign the input data to the properties of the appropriate Rectangle object
5. calculate the area of the entire pizza
6. calculate the area of a pizza slice
7. if the area of a pizza slice is greater than 0
      calculate the number of pizza slices by dividing the area of the entire pizza by the area of a
      pizza slice
   else
      assign 0 as the number of pizza slices
   end if
8. display the number of pizza slices
```

Figure 11-26 Pseudocode for the Calculate button's Click event procedure

START HERE

To code the Calculate button's Click event procedure:

1. Open the Code Editor window. Replace <your name> and <current date> in the comments with your name and the current date, respectively.

2. Locate the btnCalc_Click procedure. The first two steps in the pseudocode are to instantiate two Rectangle objects to represent the entire pizza and a pizza slice. Click the **blank line** above the End Sub clause, and then enter the following Dim statements:

   Dim entirePizza As New Rectangle
   Dim pizzaSlice As New Rectangle

3. The third step in the pseudocode is to declare variables to store the area of the entire pizza, the area of a pizza slice, and the number of slices. You won't need variables to store the side measurements entered by the user because the procedure will assign those values to each Rectangle object's Length and Width properties. Enter the following three Dim statements. Press **Enter** twice after typing the last Dim statement.

   Dim dblEntireArea As Double
   Dim dblSliceArea As Double
   Dim dblSlices As Double

4. The fourth step in the pseudocode assigns the side measurements to the properties of the appropriate Rectangle object. Enter the following four lines of code. Notice that when you press the period after typing either `entirePizza` or `pizzaSlice`, the object's Length and Width properties appear in the IntelliSense list. Press **Enter** twice after typing the last line.

   Double.TryParse(txtEntirePizza.Text, entirePizza.Length)
   Double.TryParse(txtEntirePizza.Text, entirePizza.Width)
   Double.TryParse(txtPizzaSlice.Text, pizzaSlice.Length)
   Double.TryParse(txtPizzaSlice.Text, pizzaSlice.Width)

5. The fifth and sixth steps in the pseudocode calculate the areas of both the entire pizza and a pizza slice, respectively. You can accomplish both tasks using the Rectangle object's GetArea method. Because the method already contains the code needed to calculate the area of a rectangle, you do not need to waste time planning and then reentering the code. Enter the following comment and assignment statements:

' calculate areas
dblEntireArea = entirePizza.GetArea
dblSliceArea = pizzaSlice.GetArea

6. The seventh step in the pseudocode is a selection structure that determines whether the pizza slice area is greater than 0. You need to make this determination because the area is used as the divisor when calculating the number of pizza slices. If the area is greater than 0, the selection structure's true path should calculate the number of pizza slices; otherwise, its false path should assign 0 as the number of pizza slices. Enter the following comment and selection structure:

' calculate number of slices
If dblSliceArea > 0 Then
    dblSlices = dblEntireArea / dblSliceArea
Else
    dblSlices = 0
End If

7. The last step in the pseudocode displays the number of pizza slices. Insert a blank line below the End If clause and then enter the following comment and assignment statement:

' display number of slices
lblSlices.Text = dblSlices.ToString("N1")

8. Delete the blank line above the End Sub clause, if necessary.

The btnCalc_Click procedure is shown in Figure 11-27.

```
Private Sub btnCalc_Click(sender As Object,
e As EventArgs) Handles btnCalc.Click
    ' displays the number of square pizza slices
    ' that can be cut from a square pizza

    Dim entirePizza As New Rectangle
    Dim pizzaSlice As New Rectangle
    Dim dblEntireArea As Double
    Dim dblSliceArea As Double
    Dim dblSlices As Double

    Double.TryParse(txtEntirePizza.Text, entirePizza.Length)
    Double.TryParse(txtEntirePizza.Text, entirePizza.Width)
    Double.TryParse(txtPizzaSlice.Text, pizzaSlice.Length)
    Double.TryParse(txtPizzaSlice.Text, pizzaSlice.Width)

    ' calculate areas
    dblEntireArea = entirePizza.GetArea
    dblSliceArea = pizzaSlice.GetArea
    ' calculate number of slices
    If dblSliceArea > 0 Then
        dblSlices = dblEntireArea / dblSliceArea
    Else
        dblSlices = 0
    End If
    ' display number of slices
    lblSlices.Text = dblSlices.ToString("N1")
End Sub
```

instantiates two Rectangle objects

assigns values to each object's Public properties

invokes each object's GetArea method

Figure 11-27 btnCalc_Click procedure

START HERE

To test the application's code:

1. Save the solution and then start the application. First, you will determine the number of 4-inch slices that can be cut from a 12-inch pizza. Type **12** in the Entire square pizza box and then type **4** in the Square pizza slice box. Click the **Calculate** button. As Figure 11-28 indicates, nine 4-inch square pizza slices can be cut from a 12-inch square pizza.

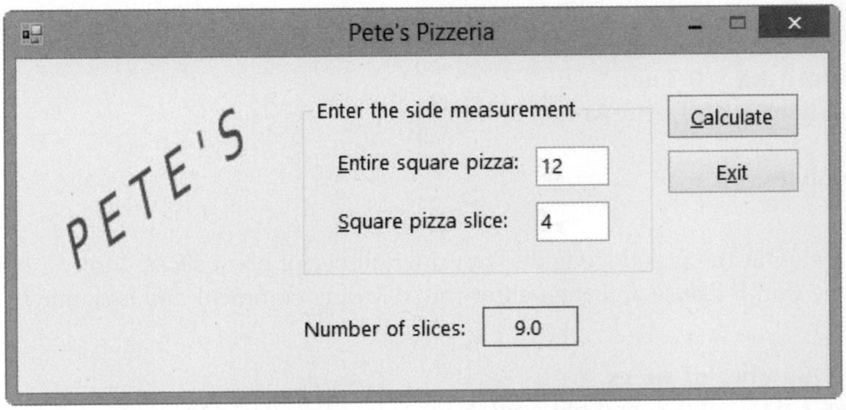

Figure 11-28 Number of pizza slices shown in the interface

2. On your own, test the application using different side measurements. When you are finished, click the **Exit** button. Close the Code Editor window and then close the solution.

Lesson A Summary

- To define a class:

  Use the Class statement. The statement's syntax is shown in Figure 11-3.

- To add a class file to a project:

  Click PROJECT on the menu bar and then click Add Class. In the Name box, type the name of the class followed by a period and the letters vb, and then click the Add button.

- To instantiate (create) an object from a class:

  Use either of the syntax versions shown in Figure 11-5.

- To create a Property procedure:

  Use the syntax shown in Figure 11-13. The Get block allows an application to retrieve the contents of the Private variable associated with the Property procedure. The Set block allows an application to assign a value to the Private variable associated with the Property procedure.

- To create a constructor:

  Use the syntax shown in Figure 11-15. A constructor that has no parameters is called the default constructor. A class can have only one default constructor. A constructor that has one or more parameters is called a parameterized constructor. A class can have as many parameterized constructors as needed. All constructors are Sub procedures that are named New. Each constructor must have a unique parameterList (if any) within the class.

- To create a method other than a constructor:

  Use the syntax shown in Figure 11-17.

Lesson A Key Terms

Attributes—the characteristics that describe an object

Behaviors—an object's methods and events

Class—a pattern that the computer follows when instantiating (creating) an object

Class statement—the statement used to define a class in Visual Basic

Constructor—a method whose instructions are automatically processed each time the class is used to instantiate an object; used to initialize the class's Private variables; always a Sub procedure named New

Default constructor—a constructor that has no parameters; a class can have only one default constructor

Encapsulates—an OOP term that means "contains"

Events—the actions to which an object can respond

Get block—the section of a Property procedure that contains the Get statement

Get statement—appears in a Get block in a Property procedure; contains the code that allows an application to retrieve the contents of the Private variable associated with the property

Instance—an object created from a class

Instantiated—the process of creating an object from a class

Methods—the actions that an object is capable of performing

Object-oriented programming language—a programming language that allows the use of objects to accomplish a program's goal

OOP—an acronym for object-oriented programming

Parameterized constructor—a constructor that contains one or more parameters

Property procedure—creates a Public property that an application can use to access a Private variable in a class

ReadOnly keyword—used when defining a Property procedure; indicates that the property's value can only be retrieved (read) by an application

Set block—the section of a Property procedure that contains the Set statement

Set statement—appears in a Set block in a Property procedure; contains the code that allows an application to assign a value to the Private variable associated with the property; may also contain validation code

Signature—a method's name combined with its optional parameterList

WriteOnly keyword—used when defining a Property procedure; indicates that an application can only set the property's value

Lesson A Review Questions

1. The name of a class file ends with ______________.
   a. .cla
   b. .cls
   c. .vb
   d. none of the above

2. A constructor is ______________.
   a. a Function procedure
   b. a Property procedure
   c. a Sub procedure
   d. either a Function procedure or a Sub procedure

3. The Item class contains a Private variable named `_dblCost`. The variable is associated with the Public Cost property. An application instantiates an Item object and assigns it to a variable named `phone`. Which of the following can be used by the application to assign the number 150.65 to the `_dblCost` variable?
   a. `phone.Cost = 150.65`
   b. `item.Cost = 150.65`
   c. `phone._dblCost = 150.65`
   d. `item._dblCost = 150.65`

4. The Item class in Review Question 3 also contains a Public method named GetTax. The method is a Function procedure. Which of the following can be used by the application from Review Question 3 to invoke the GetTax method?
   a. `dblNewCost = Call GetTax`
   b. `dblNewCost = phone.GetTax`
   c. `dblNewCost = item.GetTax`
   d. `dblNewCost = phone.GetTax(_dblCost)`

5. Which of the following statements is false?
   a. A class can contain only one constructor.
   b. An example of a behavior is the `SetTime` method in a Time class.
   c. An object created from a class is referred to as an instance of the class.
   d. An instance of a class is considered an object.

6. A Private variable in a class can be accessed directly by a Public method in the same class.
   a. True
   b. False

7. An application can access the Private variables in a class ______________.
   a. directly
   b. using properties created by Public Property procedures
   c. through Private procedures contained in the class
   d. none of the above

8. To hide a variable or method contained in a class, you declare the variable or method using the keyword ________.
   a. `Hide`
   b. `Invisible`
   c. `Private`
   d. `ReadOnly`

9. Which of the following is the name of the Item class's default constructor?
   a. Item
   b. ItemConstructor
   c. Default
   d. New

10. Which of the following instantiates an Item object and assigns it to the `phone` variable?
    a. `Dim phone As Item`
    b. `Dim phone As New Item`
    c. `Dim phone As Item`
       `phone = New Item`
    d. both b and c

11. If you need to validate a value before assigning it to a Private variable, you enter the validation code in the ________ block in a Property procedure.
    a. Assign
    b. Get
    c. Set
    d. Validate

12. The Return statement is entered in the ________ statement in a Property procedure.
    a. Get
    b. Set

13. A class contains a Private variable named `_strState`. The variable is associated with a Public property named State. Which of the following is the best way for a parameterized constructor to assign the value stored in its `strName` parameter to the variable?
    a. `_strState = strName`
    b. `State = strName`
    c. `_strState = State.strName`
    d. `State = _strName`

Lesson A Exercises

1. A class contains more than one constructor. Explain how the computer determines the appropriate constructor to use when instantiating an object. INTRODUCTORY
2. Write a Class statement that defines a class named Book. The class contains three Public variables named `Title`, `Author`, and `Cost`. The `Title` and `Author` variables are String variables. The `Cost` variable is a Decimal variable. Then use the syntax shown in INTRODUCTORY

Version 1 in Figure 11-5 to declare a variable that can store a Book object; name the variable `fiction`. Also write a statement that instantiates the Book object and assigns it to the `fiction` variable.

INTRODUCTORY

3. Rewrite the Class statement from Exercise 2 so that it uses Private variables rather than Public variables. Be sure to include the Property procedures and default constructor.

INTRODUCTORY

4. Write a Class statement that defines a class named Tape. The class contains four Private String variables named `_strName`, `_strArtist`, `_strSongNumber`, and `_strLength`. Name the corresponding properties TapeName, Artist, SongNumber, and Length. Then, use the syntax shown in Version 2 in Figure 11-5 to create a Tape object, assigning it to a variable named `blues`.

INTRODUCTORY

5. The Television class definition is shown in Figure 11-29. Write a Dim statement that uses the default constructor to instantiate a Television object in an application. The Dim statement should assign the object to a variable named `flatScreen`. Next, write assignment statements that the application can use to assign the string "78XR5" and the number 567.99 to the Model and Price properties, respectively. Finally, write an assignment statement that the application can use to invoke the GetNewPrice function. Assign the function's return value to a variable named `dblNewPrice`.

```
Public Class Television
    Private _strModel As String
    Private _dblPrice As Double

    Public Property Model As String
        Get
            Return _strModel
        End Get
        Set(value As String)
            _strModel = value
        End Set
    End Property

    Public Property Price As Double
        Get
            Return _dblPrice
        End Get
        Set(value As Double)
            _dblPrice = value
        End Set
    End Property

    Public Sub New()
        _strModel = String.Empty
        _dblPrice = 0
    End Sub

    Public Sub New(ByVal strM As String, ByVal dblP As Double)
        Model = strM
        Price = dblP
    End Sub

    Public Function GetNewPrice() As Double
        Return _dblPrice * 1.08
    End Function
End Class
```

Figure 11-29 Television class definition

6. Using the Television class shown in Figure 11-29, write a Dim statement that uses the parameterized constructor to instantiate a Television object. Pass the parameterized constructor the string "89MM5" and the number 699.99. The Dim statement should assign the object to a variable named `myTv`. INTRODUCTORY

7. An application contains the statement `Dim myNewTv As Television`. Using the Television class shown in Figure 11-29, write an assignment statement that instantiates a Television object and initializes it using the `strName` and `dblPrice` variables. The statement should assign the object to the `myNewTv` variable. INTRODUCTORY

8. In this exercise, you modify the Pete's Pizzeria application completed in the lesson. Use Windows to make a copy of the Pizzeria Solution folder. Rename the copy Pizzeria Solution–Parameterized. Open the Pizzeria Solution (Pizzeria Solution.sln) file contained in the Pizzeria Solution–Parameterized folder. Open the designer and Code Editor windows. Modify the btnCalc_Click procedure to use the Rectangle class's parameterized constructor. Save the solution and then start and test the application. Close the Code Editor window and then close the solution. INTRODUCTORY

9. In this exercise, you modify the Norbert Pool & Spa Depot application completed in the lesson. Use Windows to make a copy of the Norbert Solution folder. Rename the copy Norbert Solution–Introductory. Open the Norbert Solution (Norbert Solution.sln) file contained in the Norbert Solution–Introductory folder. Open the designer window and then open the RectangularPool.vb file. Modify the RectangularPool class so that it uses Private variables and Public Property procedures rather than Public variables. Include both a default constructor and a parameterized constructor in the class. Save the solution and then start and test the application. Close the Code Editor window and then close the solution. INTRODUCTORY

10. In this exercise, you modify the Norbert Pool & Spa Depot application from Exercise 9. Use Windows to make a copy of the Norbert Solution–Introductory folder. Rename the copy Norbert Solution–Intermediate. Open the Norbert Solution (Norbert Solution.sln) file contained in the Norbert Solution–Intermediate folder. INTERMEDIATE

    a. Open the designer window. Add two labels to the form. Position one of the labels below the Gallons: label, and then change its Text property to Cost:. Position the other label below the lblGallons control and then change its Name, TextAlign, AutoSize, and BorderStyle properties to lblCost, MiddleCenter, False, and FixedSingle, respectively. Remove the contents of its Text property and then size the control appropriately. Also change the control's Font and BackColor properties to match the lblGallons control.

    b. Open the RectangularPool.vb file. Add a method named GetVolume to the RectangularPool class. The method should calculate and return the volume of a RectangularPool object. The formula for calculating the volume is *length * width * depth*. Save the solution and then close the RectangularPool.vb window.

    c. Open the form's Code Editor window. The btnCalc_Click procedure should use the RectangularPool object's GetVolume method to determine the pool's volume. It then should pass only the pool's volume to the GetGallons function. The procedure should also calculate and display the cost of filling the pool with water. The charge for water is $1.75 per 1000 gallons (or .00175 per gallon). Make the necessary modifications to the code.

    d. Save the solution and then start and test the application. Close the Code Editor window and then close the solution.

11. In this exercise, you create an application that can be used to estimate the cost of laying sod on a rectangular piece of property. INTERMEDIATE

    a. Create a Visual Basic Windows application. Use the following names for the solution and project, respectively: Harston Solution and Harston Project. Save the application in the VB2012\Chap11 folder. Change the form file's name to Main Form.vb. Change the form's name to frmMain.

b. Use Windows to copy the Rectangle.vb file from the VB2012\Chap11 folder to the VB2012\Chap11\Harston Solution\Harston Project folder. Use the PROJECT menu to add the Rectangle.vb class file to the project.

c. Create the interface shown in Figure 11-30. The image for the picture box is stored in the VB2012\Chap11\Landscape.png file. (The image was downloaded from the Open Clip Art Library at *http://openclipart.org*.)

d. Open the form's Code Editor window and then code the application. Save the solution and then start and test the application. Close the Code Editor window and then close the solution.

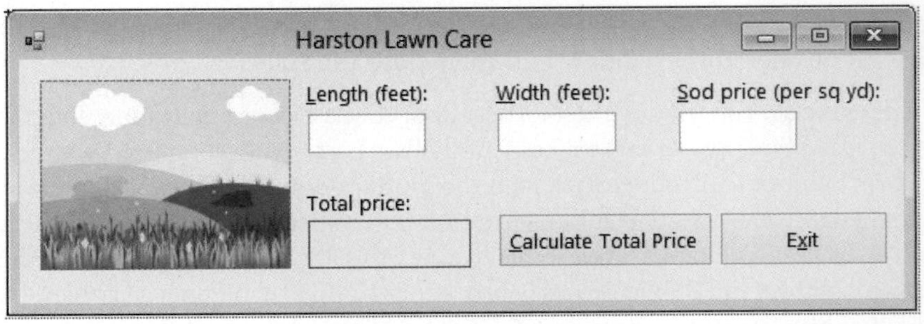

Figure 11-30 Interface for Exercise 11
OpenClipArt.org/rg1024

INTERMEDIATE

12. In this exercise, you create an application that can be used to calculate the cost of installing a fence around a rectangular area.

a. Create a Visual Basic Windows application. Use the following names for the solution and project, respectively: Fence Solution and Fence Project. Save the application in the VB2012\Chap11 folder. Change the form file's name to Main Form.vb. Change the form's name to frmMain.

b. Use Windows to copy the Rectangle.vb file from the VB2012\Chap11 folder to the Fence Solution\Fence Project folder. Use the PROJECT menu to add the Rectangle.vb class file to the project. Add a method named GetPerimeter to the Rectangle class. The GetPerimeter method should calculate and return the perimeter of a rectangle. To calculate the perimeter, the method will need to add together the length and width measurements and then multiply the sum by 2.

c. Create the interface shown in Figure 11-31. The image for the picture box is stored in the VB2012\Chap11\Fence.png file. (The image was downloaded from the Open Clip Art Library at *http://openclipart.org*.)

d. Open the form's Code Editor window and then code the application, which should calculate and display the cost of installing the fence.

e. Save the solution and then start the application. Test the application using 120 feet as the length, 75 feet as the width, and 10 as the cost per linear foot of fencing. The installation cost should be $3,900.00. Close the Main Form.vb and Rectangle.vb windows and then close the solution.

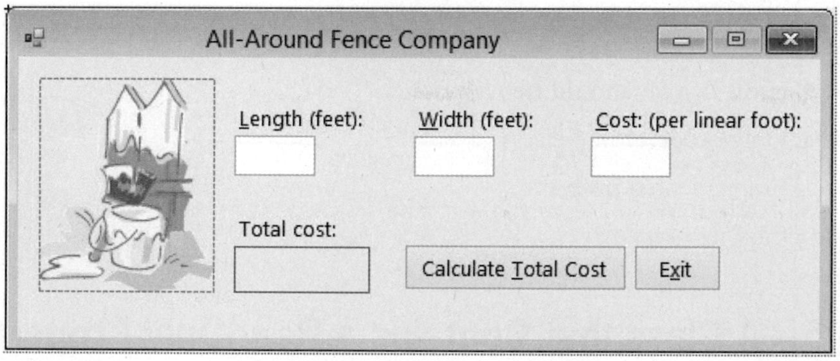

Figure 11-31 Interface for Exercise 12
OpenClipArt.org/liftarn

ADVANCED

13. In this exercise, you define a Triangle class. You also create an application that allows the user to display either a Triangle object's area or its perimeter. The formula for calculating the area of a triangle is 1/2 * *base* * *height*. The formula for calculating the perimeter of a triangle is $a + b + c$, where a, b, and c are the lengths of the sides.

    a. Create a Visual Basic Windows application. Use the following names for the solution and project, respectively: Math Triangle Solution and Math Triangle Project. Save the application in the VB2012\Chap11 folder. Change the form file's name to Main Form.vb. Change the form's name to frmMain.

    b. Create the interface shown in Figure 11-32. The image for the picture box is stored in the VB2012\Chap11\Triangle.png file. (The image was downloaded from the Open Clip Art Library at *http://openclipart.org.*)

    c. Add a class file to the project. Name the class file Triangle.vb. The Triangle class should verify that the dimensions are greater than zero before assigning the values to the Private variables. The class should also include a method to calculate the area of a triangle and a method to calculate the perimeter of a triangle. Save the solution and then close the Triangle.vb window.

    d. Open the form's Code Editor window. Use the InputBox function to get the appropriate data from the user. Save the solution and then start and test the application. Close the Code Editor window and then close the solution.

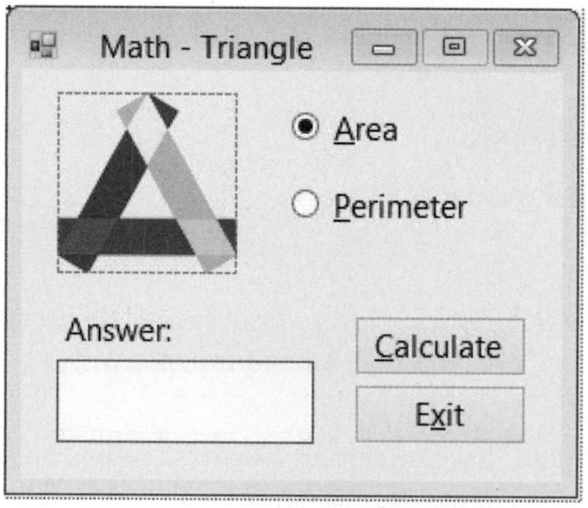

Figure 11-32 Interface for Exercise 13
OpenClipArt.org/10binary

LESSON B

After studying Lesson B, you should be able to:

- Include a ReadOnly property in a class
- Create an auto-implemented property
- Overload a method in a class

Example 5—A Class that Contains a ReadOnly Property

In Lesson A, you learned that a Property procedure's header can include the `ReadOnly` keyword. Recall that the `ReadOnly` keyword indicates that the property's value can be retrieved (read) by an application, but the application cannot set (write to) the property. A ReadOnly property gets its value from the class itself rather than from the application. In the next set of steps, you will add a ReadOnly property to a class named CourseGrade. You will also add the default constructor and a method that will assign the appropriate grade to the Private variable associated with the ReadOnly property. You will use the ReadOnly property and the method in the Grade Calculator application, which you will finish coding in the second set of steps. The application displays a grade based on two test scores entered by the user.

START HERE

To modify the CourseGrade class:

1. If necessary, start Visual Studio 2012. Open the Grade Solution (Grade Solution.sln) file contained in the VB2012\Chap11\Grade Solution folder. If necessary, open the designer window. The interface provides list boxes for entering two test scores that can range from 0 to 100 points each. See Figure 11-33. (The image in the picture box was downloaded from the Open Clip Art Library at *http://openclipart.org.*)

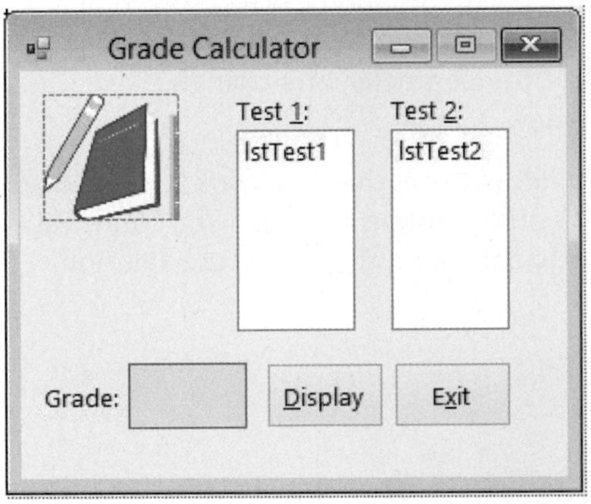

Figure 11-33 Interface for the Grade Calculator application
OpenClipArt.org/Minduka

2. Right-click **CourseGrade.vb** in the Solution Explorer window and then click **View Code**. Replace <your name> and <current date> in the comments with your name and the current date, respectively.

3. The CourseGrade class should contain three attributes: two test scores and a letter grade. The Private variable for the letter grade is missing from the code. Click the **blank line** below the `Private _intScore2 As Integer` statement and then enter the following Private statement:

   Private _strGrade As String

4. Now you will create a Public property for the Private `_strGrade` variable. You will make the property ReadOnly so that the class (rather than the Grade Calculator application) determines the appropriate grade. By making the property ReadOnly, the application will only be able to retrieve the grade; it will not be able to change the grade. Click the **blank line** immediately above the End Class clause and then enter the following Property procedure header. Notice that when you press Enter after typing the header, the Code Editor automatically includes the Get block of code and the End Property clause in the procedure. It does not enter the Set block of code because the header contains the `ReadOnly` keyword.

   Public ReadOnly Property Grade As String

5. Type the following Return statement in the blank line below the Get clause, but don't press Enter:

   Return _strGrade

6. Next, you will enter the default constructor in the class. The default constructor will initialize the Private variables when a CourseGrade object is instantiated. Insert two blank lines above the End Class clause. Click the **blank line** immediately above the clause (if necessary) and then enter the following default constructor:

```
Public Sub New()
    _intScore1 = 0
    _intScore2 = 0
    _strGrade = String.Empty
End Sub
```

7. Finally, you will enter the DetermineGrade method, which will assign the appropriate letter grade to the `_strGrade` variable. The method will be a Sub procedure because it will not need to return a value to the application that calls it. Insert two blank lines above the End Class clause, and then enter the following procedure header in the blank line immediately above the clause:

   Public Sub DetermineGrade()

8. Now enter the following Select Case statement:

```
Select Case _intScore1 + _intScore2
   Case Is >= 180
         _strGrade = "A"
   Case Is >= 160
         _strGrade = "B"
   Case Is >= 140
         _strGrade = "C"
   Case Is >= 120
         _strGrade = "D"
   Case Else
         _strGrade = "F"
End Select
```

9. Save the solution.

Now that you have finished defining the class, you can use the class to instantiate a CourseGrade object in the Grade Calculator application.

START HERE

To complete the Grade Calculator application:

1. Click the **designer window's tab** and then open the form's Code Editor window. Replace <your name> and <current date> in the comments with your name and the current date, respectively.

2. Locate the btnDisplay_Click procedure. First, you will instantiate a CourseGrade object. Click the **blank line** above the second comment in the procedure and then enter the following Dim statement:

   Dim studentGrade As New CourseGrade

3. Now you will assign the test scores, which are selected in the list boxes, to the object's properties. Click the **blank line** below the second comment in the procedure and then enter the following TryParse methods:

   Integer.TryParse(lstTest1.SelectedItem.ToString,
   studentGrade.Score1)
   Integer.TryParse(lstTest2.SelectedItem.ToString,
   studentGrade.Score2)

4. Next, you will use the object's DetermineGrade method to determine the appropriate grade. Click the **blank line** below the `' object's DetermineGrade method` comment and then enter the following Call statement:

   Call studentGrade.DetermineGrade()

5. Finally, you will display the grade, which is stored in the object's ReadOnly Grade property. Click the **blank line** below the `' object's ReadOnly property` comment. Type the following code, but don't press Enter:

   lblGrade.Text = studentGrade.

6. Click **Grade** in the IntelliSense list. If necessary, click the **Common** tab. See Figure 11-34. The message that appears next to the IntelliSense list indicates that the Grade property is ReadOnly.

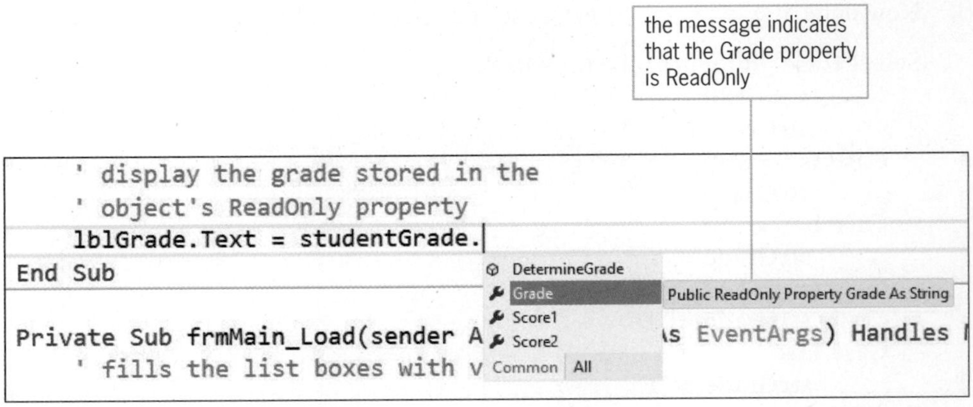

Figure 11-34 ReadOnly property message

7. Press **Tab** to include the Grade property in the assignment statement.

Figure 11-35 shows the CourseGrade class definition and the btnDisplay_Click procedure.

Class statement entered in the CourseGrade.vb file

```
Public Class CourseGrade
    Private _intScore1 As Integer
    Private _intScore2 As Integer
    Private _strGrade As String

    Public Property Score1 As Integer
        Get
            Return _intScore1
        End Get
        Set(value As Integer)
            _intScore1 = value
        End Set
    End Property

    Public Property Score2 As Integer
        Get
            Return _intScore2
        End Get
        Set(value As Integer)
            _intScore2 = value
        End Set
    End Property

    Public ReadOnly Property Grade As String
        Get
            Return _strGrade
        End Get
    End Property

    Public Sub New()
        _intScore1 = 0
        _intScore2 = 0
        _strGrade = String.Empty
    End Sub

    Public Sub DetermineGrade()
        Select Case _intScore1 + _intScore2
            Case Is >= 180
                _strGrade = "A"
            Case Is >= 160
                _strGrade = "B"
            Case Is >= 140
                _strGrade = "C"
            Case Is >= 120
                _strGrade = "D"
            Case Else
                _strGrade = "F"
        End Select
    End Sub
End Class
```

Figure 11-35 CourseGrade class definition and btnDisplay_Click procedure *(continues)*

(continued)

btnDisplay_Click procedure entered in the Main Form.vb file

```
Private Sub btnDisplay_Click(sender As Object,
e As EventArgs) Handles btnDisplay.Click
    ' calculates and displays a letter grade

    Dim studentGrade As New CourseGrade

    ' assign test scores to object's properties
    Integer.TryParse(lstTest1.SelectedItem.ToString,
                     studentGrade.Score1)
    Integer.TryParse(lstTest2.SelectedItem.ToString,
                     studentGrade.Score2)

    ' calculate the grade using the
    ' object's DetermineGrade method
    Call studentGrade.DetermineGrade()

    ' display the grade stored in the
    ' object's ReadOnly property
    lblGrade.Text = studentGrade.Grade
End Sub
```

calls the object's DetermineGrade method

refers to the object's ReadOnly Grade property

Figure 11-35 CourseGrade class definition and btnDisplay_Click procedure

START HERE

To test the Grade Calculator application:

1. Save the solution and then start the application. Click **74** and **89** in the Test 1 and Test 2 list boxes, respectively, and then click the **Display** button. The letter B appears in the Grade box, as shown in Figure 11-36. (Recall that you can use the Alt key to show/hide the access keys.)

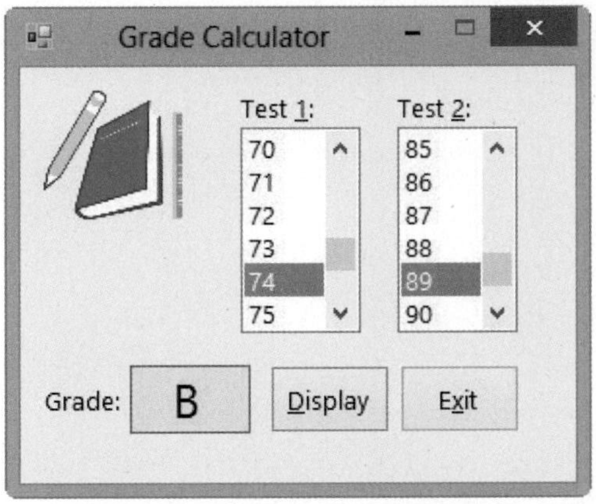

Figure 11-36 Grade shown in the interface

OpenClipArt.org/Minduka

2. On your own, test the application using different test scores. When you are finished, click the **Exit** button. Close the Main Form.vb and CourseGrade.vb windows and then close the solution.

Example 6—A Class that Contains Auto-Implemented Properties

The **auto-implemented properties** feature in Visual Basic enables you to specify the property of a class in one line of code, as shown in Figure 11-37. When you enter the line of code in the Code Editor window, Visual Basic automatically creates a hidden Private variable that it associates with the property. It also automatically creates hidden Get and Set blocks. The Private variable's name will be the same as the property's name, but it will be preceded by an underscore. For example, if you create an auto-implemented property named City, Visual Basic will create a hidden Private variable named `_City`. The auto-implemented properties feature provides a shorter syntax for you to use when creating a class: You don't need to create the Private variable associated with a property, nor do you need to enter the property's Get and Set blocks of code. However, keep in mind that you will need to use the standard syntax if you want to add validation code to the Set block, or if you want the property to be either ReadOnly or WriteOnly.

Auto-Implemented Property

Syntax
Public Property *propertyName* **As** *dataType*

Example 1
```
Public Property City As Integer
```
creates a Public property named City, a hidden Private variable named `_City`, and hidden Get and Set blocks

Example 2
```
Public Property Sales As Integer
```
creates a Public property named Sales, a hidden Private variable named `_Sales`, and hidden Get and Set blocks

Figure 11-37 Syntax and examples of creating an auto-implemented property

In the next set of steps, you will modify the CourseGrade class from Example 5 to use two auto-implemented properties.

To modify the CourseGrade class:

START HERE

1. Use Windows to make a copy of the Grade Solution folder from Example 5. Rename the copy Modified Grade Solution. Open the Grade Solution (Grade Solution.sln) file contained in the Modified Grade Solution folder. Open the designer window.
2. Open the **CourseGrade.vb** file's Code Editor window. First, replace the `Private _intScore1 As Integer` and `Private _intScore2 As Integer` statements with the following statements:

   Public Property Score1 As Integer
   Public Property Score2 As Integer
3. Next, delete the Score1 and Score2 Property procedures. (Don't delete the Grade property procedure.)

4. Now change `_intScore1` and `_intScore2` in the default constructor to **_Score1** and **_Score2**, respectively. (Recall that the name of the Private variable associated with an auto-implemented property is the property's name preceded by an underscore.)

5. Finally, change `_intScore1` and `_intScore2` in the DetermineGrade method to **_Score1** and **_Score2**, respectively.

Figure 11-38 shows the modified class definition. The code pertaining to the two auto-implemented properties (Score1 and Score2) is shaded in the figure. You cannot use the auto-implemented properties feature for the Grade property because that property is ReadOnly.

auto-implemented properties

a ReadOnly property cannot be an auto-implemented property

```
Public Class CourseGrade
    Public Property Score1 As Integer
    Public Property Score2 As Integer
    Private _strGrade As String

    Public ReadOnly Property Grade As String
        Get
            Return _strGrade
        End Get
    End Property

    Public Sub New()
        _Score1 = 0
        _Score2 = 0
        _strGrade = String.Empty
    End Sub

    Public Sub DetermineGrade()
        Select Case _Score1 + _Score2
            Case Is >= 180
                _strGrade = "A"
            Case Is >= 160
                _strGrade = "B"
            Case Is >= 140
                _strGrade = "C"
            Case Is >= 120
                _strGrade = "D"
            Case Else
                _strGrade = "F"
        End Select
    End Sub
End Class
```

Figure 11-38 Modified CourseGrade class definition

START HERE

To test the modified Grade Calculator application:

1. Save the solution and then start the application. Click **86** and **95** in the Test 1 and Test 2 list boxes, respectively, and then click the **Display** button. The letter A appears in the Grade box.

2. On your own, test the application using different test scores. When you are finished, click the **Exit** button. Close the CourseGrade.vb window and then close the solution.

YOU DO IT 2!

Create a Visual Basic Windows application named YouDoIt 2. Save the application in the VB2012\Chap11 folder. Add a text box, a label, and a button to the form. Add a class file named Square.vb to the project. Define a class named Square. The class should contain an auto-implemented property that will store the side measurement of a square. It also should contain a default constructor and a method that calculates and returns the square's perimeter. Use the following formula to calculate the perimeter: 4 * *side*. Open the form's Code Editor window. The button's Click event procedure should display the square's perimeter, using the side measurement entered by the user. Code the procedure. Save the solution and then start and test the application. Close the solution.

Example 7—A Class that Contains Overloaded Methods

In this example, you will use a class named Employee to instantiate an object. Employee objects have the attributes and behaviors listed in Figure 11-39.

Attributes of an Employee object
employee number
employee name

Behaviors of an Employee object
1. An employee object can initialize its attributes using values provided by the class.
2. An employee object can initialize its attributes using values provided by the application in which it is instantiated.
3. An employee object can calculate and return the gross pay for salaried employees. The gross pay is calculated by dividing the salaried employee's annual salary by 24, because the salaried employees are paid twice per month.
4. An employee object can calculate and return the gross pay for hourly employees. The gross pay is calculated by multiplying the number of hours the employee worked during the week by his or her pay rate.

Figure 11-39 Attributes and behaviors of an Employee object

Figure 11-40 shows the Employee class defined in the Employee.vb file. The class contains two auto-implemented properties and four methods. The two New methods are the class's default and parameterized constructors. Notice that the default constructor initializes the class's Private variables directly, while the parameterized constructor uses the class's Public properties to initialize the Private variables indirectly. As you learned in Lesson A, using a Public property in this manner ensures that the computer processes any validation code associated with the property. Even though the Number and EmpName properties in Figure 11-40 do not have any validation code, you should use the properties in the parameterized constructor in case validation code is added to the class in the future.

```
Public Class Employee
    Public Property Number As String
    Public Property EmpName As String

    Public Sub New()
        _Number = String.Empty
        _EmpName = String.Empty
    End Sub

    Public Sub New(ByVal strNum As String,
                   ByVal strName As String)
        Number = strNum
        EmpName = strName
    End Sub

    Public Function GetGross(ByVal dblSalary As Double) As Double
        ' calculates the gross pay for salaried
        ' employees, who are paid twice per month

        Return dblSalary / 24
    End Function

    Public Function GetGross(ByVal dblHours As Double,
                             ByVal dblRate As Double) As Double
        ' calculates the weekly gross pay for hourly employees

        Return dblHours * dblRate
    End Function
End Class
```

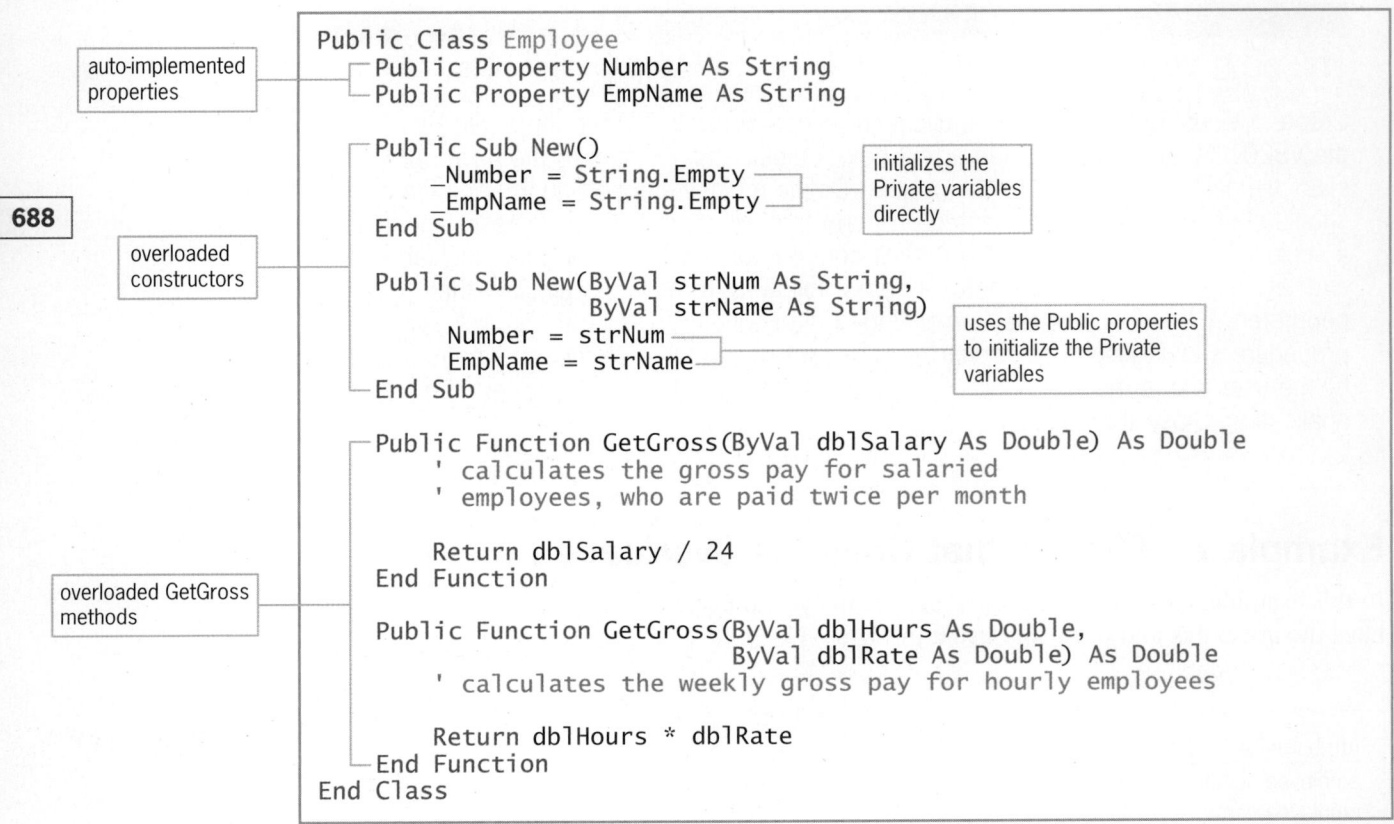

auto-implemented properties

initializes the Private variables directly

overloaded constructors

uses the Public properties to initialize the Private variables

overloaded GetGross methods

Figure 11-40 Employee class definition

When two or more methods have the same name but different parameters, the methods are referred to as **overloaded methods**. The two constructors in Figure 11-40 are considered overloaded methods because each is named New and each has a different parameterList. You can overload any of the methods contained in a class, not just constructors. The two GetGross methods in the figure are also overloaded methods because they have the same name but a different parameterList.

You already are familiar with overloaded methods because you have used several of the ones built into Visual Basic. Examples of such methods include ToString, TryParse, Convert.ToDecimal, and MessageBox.Show. The Code Editor's IntelliSense feature displays a box that allows you to view a method's signatures, one signature at a time. Recall that a method's signature includes its name and optional parameterList. The box shown in Figure 11-41 displays the first of the ToString method's four signatures. You use the up and down arrows in the box to display the other signatures. If a class you create contains overloaded methods, the signatures of those methods will also be displayed in the IntelliSense box.

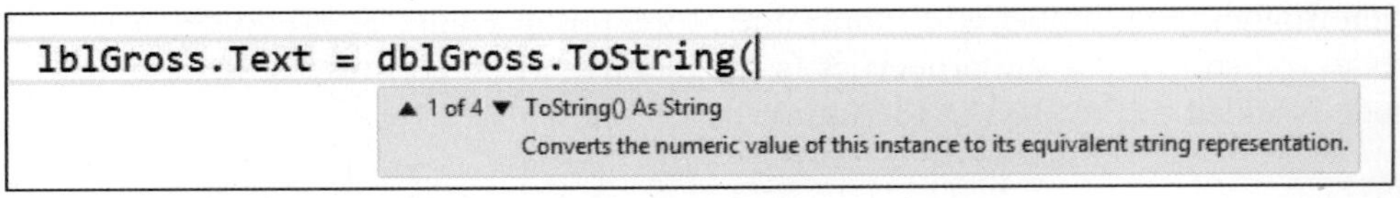
lblGross.Text = dblGross.ToString(
▲ 1 of 4 ▼ ToString() As String
Converts the numeric value of this instance to its equivalent string representation.

Figure 11-41 First of the ToString method's signatures

Overloading is useful when two or more methods require different parameters to perform essentially the same task. Both overloaded constructors in the Employee class, for example, initialize the class's Private variables. However, the default constructor does not need to be passed any information to perform the task, whereas the parameterized constructor requires two items of information (the employee number and name). Similarly, both GetGross methods in the Employee class calculate and return a gross pay amount. However, the first GetGross method performs its task for salaried employees and requires an application to pass it one item of information: the employee's annual salary. The second GetGross method performs its task for hourly employees and requires two items of information: the number of hours the employee worked and his or her rate of pay. Rather than using two overloaded GetGross methods, you could have used two methods having different names, such as GetSalariedGross and GetHourlyGross. The advantage of overloading the GetGross method is that you need to remember the name of only one method.

You will use the Employee class when coding the Woods Manufacturing application, which displays the gross pay for salaried and hourly employees. Salaried employees are paid twice per month. Therefore, each salaried employee's gross pay is calculated by dividing his or her annual salary by 24. Hourly employees are paid weekly. The gross pay for an hourly employee is calculated by multiplying the number of hours the employee worked during the week by his or her hourly pay rate. The application also displays a report showing each employee's number, name, and gross pay.

To view the class file contained in the Woods Manufacturing application:

START HERE

1. Open the Woods Solution (Woods Solution.sln) file contained in the VB2012\Chap11\ Woods Solution folder. If necessary, open the designer window. See Figure 11-42. (The image in the picture box was downloaded from the Open Clip Art Library at *http://openclipart.org.*)

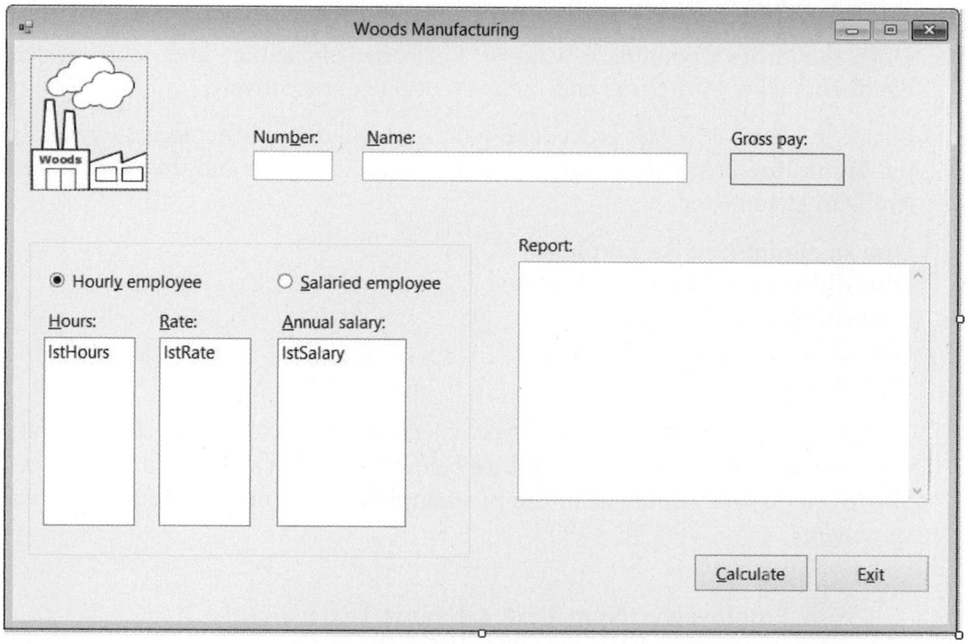

Figure 11-42 Interface for the Woods Manufacturing application
OpenClipArt.org/lmproulx

2. Open the Employee.vb file in the Code Editor window. The class definition from Figure 11-40 appears in the window.

3. Replace <your name> and <current date> in the comments with your name and the current date, respectively. Save the solution and then close the Employee.vb window.

You will need to code only the Calculate button's Click event procedure. The procedure's pseudocode is shown in Figure 11-43.

```
btnCalc Click event procedure
1. declare variables to store an Employee object, the annual salary, hours worked, hourly pay rate, and
   gross pay
2. instantiate an Employee object to represent an employee; initialize the object's variables using the
   number and name entered in the text boxes
3. if the Hourly employee radio button is selected
      assign the hours worked and hourly pay rate to the appropriate variables
      use the Employee object's GetGross method to calculate the gross pay for an hourly employee
   else
      assign the annual salary to the appropriate variable
      use the Employee object's GetGross method to calculate the gross pay for a salaried employee
   end if
4. display the gross pay and the report
5. send the focus to the txtNum control
```

Figure 11-43 Pseudocode for the Calculate button's Click event procedure

START HERE

To code the Calculate button's Click event procedure:

1. Open the form's Code Editor window. Replace <your name> and <current date> in the comments with your name and the current date, respectively.

2. Locate the btnCalc_Click procedure. First, you will declare the necessary variables. Click the **blank line** below the `' declare variables` comment and then enter the following five Dim statements:

   Dim ourEmployee As Employee
   Dim dblAnnualSalary As Double
   Dim dblHours As Double
   Dim dblHourRate As Double
   Dim dblGross As Double

3. Now you will instantiate an Employee object, using the text box values to initialize the object's variables. Click the **blank line** below the `' instantiate and initialize an Employee object` comment in the procedure and then enter the following assignment statement:

   ourEmployee =
   New Employee(txtNum.Text, txtName.Text)

4. The third step in the pseudocode determines the selected radio button and then takes the appropriate action. Click the **blank line** below the `' determine the selected radio button` comment and then enter the following If clause:

   If radHourly.Checked Then

5. If the Hourly employee radio button is selected, the selection structure's true path should use the Employee object's GetGross method to calculate the gross pay for an hourly employee. Enter the following comment and lines of code:

   ' calculate the gross pay for an hourly employee
   Double.TryParse(lstHours.SelectedItem.ToString, dblHours)
   Double.TryParse(lstRate.SelectedItem.ToString, dblHourRate)
   dblGross = ourEmployee.GetGross(dblHours, dblHourRate)

6. If the Salaried employee radio button is selected, the selection structure's false path should use the Employee object's GetGross method to calculate the gross pay for a salaried employee. Enter the additional comment and lines of code indicated in Figure 11-44.

```
    dblGross = ourEmployee.GetGross(dblHours, dblHourRate)
Else
    ' calculate the gross pay for a salaried employee
    Double.TryParse(lstSalary.SelectedItem.ToString,
                    dblAnnualSalary)
    dblGross = ourEmployee.GetGross(dblAnnualSalary)
End If
```

enter this comment and these lines of code

Figure 11-44 Additional comment and code entered in the false path

7. Next, you need to display the gross pay and the report. Click the **blank line** below the `' display the gross pay and report` comment and then enter the following lines of code:

   lblGross.Text = dblGross.ToString("C2")
   txtReport.Text = txtReport.Text &
   ourEmployee.Number.PadRight(6) &
   ourEmployee.EmpName.PadRight(25) &
   dblGross.ToString("N2").PadLeft(9) & ControlChars.NewLine

8. The last step in the pseudocode is to set the focus. The code for this step has already been entered in the Code Editor window.

Figure 11-45 shows the btnCalc_Click procedure.

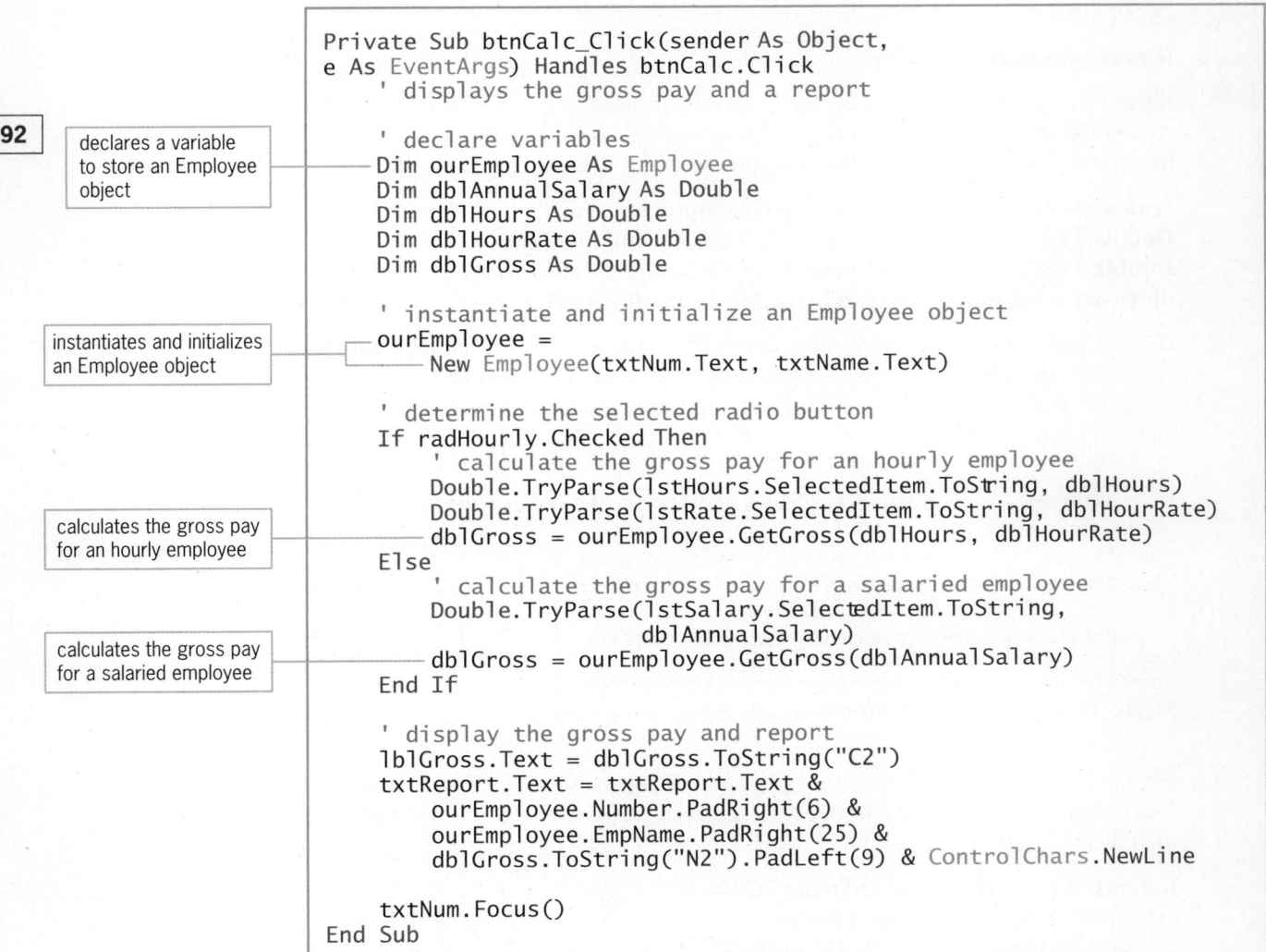

declares a variable to store an Employee object

instantiates and initializes an Employee object

calculates the gross pay for an hourly employee

calculates the gross pay for a salaried employee

```
Private Sub btnCalc_Click(sender As Object,
e As EventArgs) Handles btnCalc.Click
    ' displays the gross pay and a report

    ' declare variables
    Dim ourEmployee As Employee
    Dim dblAnnualSalary As Double
    Dim dblHours As Double
    Dim dblHourRate As Double
    Dim dblGross As Double

    ' instantiate and initialize an Employee object
    ourEmployee =
        New Employee(txtNum.Text, txtName.Text)

    ' determine the selected radio button
    If radHourly.Checked Then
        ' calculate the gross pay for an hourly employee
        Double.TryParse(lstHours.SelectedItem.ToString, dblHours)
        Double.TryParse(lstRate.SelectedItem.ToString, dblHourRate)
        dblGross = ourEmployee.GetGross(dblHours, dblHourRate)
    Else
        ' calculate the gross pay for a salaried employee
        Double.TryParse(lstSalary.SelectedItem.ToString,
                        dblAnnualSalary)
        dblGross = ourEmployee.GetGross(dblAnnualSalary)
    End If

    ' display the gross pay and report
    lblGross.Text = dblGross.ToString("C2")
    txtReport.Text = txtReport.Text &
        ourEmployee.Number.PadRight(6) &
        ourEmployee.EmpName.PadRight(25) &
        dblGross.ToString("N2").PadLeft(9) & ControlChars.NewLine

    txtNum.Focus()
End Sub
```

Figure 11-45 btnCalc_Click procedure

START HERE

To test the Woods Manufacturing application:

1. Save the solution and then start the application. Type **1004** and **Jake Johnson** in the Number and Name boxes, respectively. Click **9.00** in the Rate list box and then click the **Calculate** button. $360.00 appears in the Gross pay box, and Jake's information appears in the Report box. See Figure 11-46.

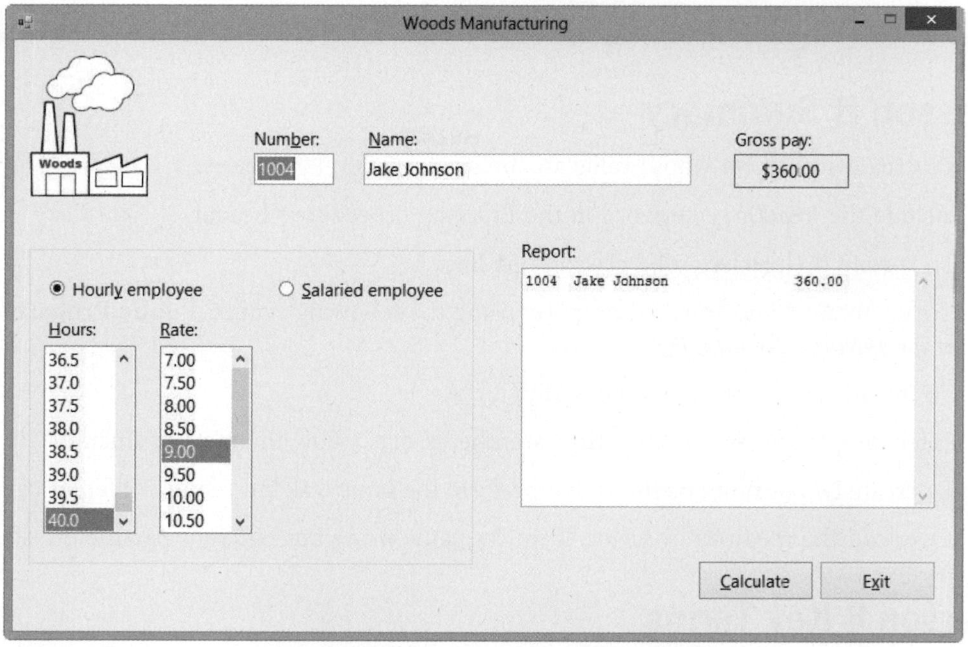

Figure 11-46 Jake's gross pay and information shown in the interface
OpenClipArt.org/Improulx

2. Type **1009** and **Sherri Hammel** in the Number and Name boxes, respectively. Click the **Salaried employee** radio button. Scroll the Annual salary list box and then click **32000** in the list. Click the **Calculate** button. The button's Click event procedure displays the gross pay amount ($1,333.33) in the Gross pay box. It also adds Sherri's information to the Report box. See Figure 11-47.

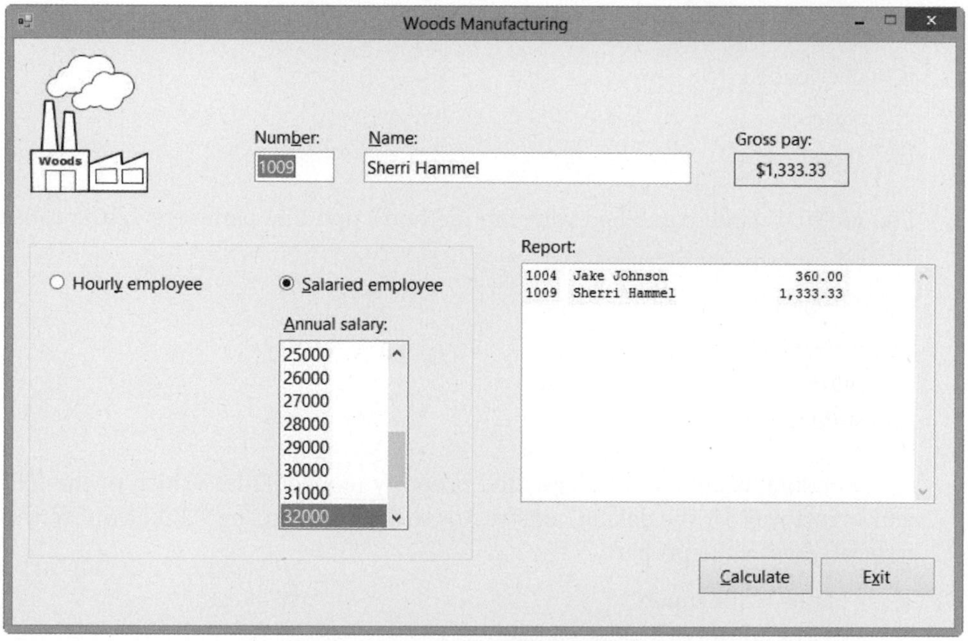

Figure 11-47 Sherri's gross pay and information shown in the interface
OpenClipArt.org/Improulx

3. Click the **Exit** button. Close the Code Editor window and then close the solution.

Lesson B Summary

- To create a property whose value an application can only retrieve:

  Include the `ReadOnly` keyword in the Property procedure's header.

- To specify the property of a class in one line:

  Create an auto-implemented property using the following syntax: **Public Property** *propertyName* **As** *dataType.*

- To include a parameterized method in a class:

  Enter the parameters between the parentheses that follow the method's name.

- To create two or more methods that perform the same task but require different parameters:

  Overload the methods by giving them the same name but different parameterLists.

Lesson B Key Terms

Auto-implemented properties—the feature that enables you to specify the property of a class in one line

Overloaded methods—two or more class methods that have the same name but different parameterLists

Lesson B Review Questions

1. Two or more methods that have the same name but different parameterLists are referred to as ______________ methods.

   a. loaded
   b. overloaded
   c. parallel
   d. signature

2. The method name combined with the method's optional parameterList is called the method's ______________.

   a. autograph
   b. inscription
   c. signature
   d. statement

3. A class contains an auto-implemented property named Title. Which of the following is the correct way for the default constructor to assign the string "Unknown" to the variable associated with the property?

   a. `_Title = "Unknown"`
   b. `_Title.strTitle = "Unknown"`
   c. `Title = "Unknown"`
   d. none of the above

4. A ReadOnly property can be an auto-implemented property.

   a. True

   b. False

5. The Purchase class contains a ReadOnly property named Tax. The property is associated with the Private `_dblTax` variable. A button's Click event procedure instantiates a Purchase object and assigns it to the `currentSale` variable. Which of the following is valid in the Click event procedure?

   a. `lblTax.Text = currentSale.Tax.ToString("C2")`

   b. `currentSale.Tax = 15`

   c. `currentSale.Tax = dblPrice * .05`

   d. all of the above

Lesson B Exercises

1. What are overloaded methods and why are they used? INTRODUCTORY

2. Write the Property procedure for a ReadOnly property named TaxRate. The property is associated with the `_decTaxRate` variable. INTRODUCTORY

3. Write the code for an auto-implemented property named Bonus. The property's data type is Decimal. INTRODUCTORY

4. Write the class definition for a class named Worker. The class should include Private variables and Property procedures for a Worker object's name and salary. The salary may contain a decimal place. The class also should contain two constructors: the default constructor and a parameterized constructor. INTRODUCTORY

5. Rewrite the code from Exercise 4 using auto-implemented properties. INTRODUCTORY

6. Add a method named GetNewSalary to the Worker class from Exercise 5. The method should calculate a Worker object's new salary, which is based on a raise percentage provided by the application using the object. Before calculating the new salary, the method should verify that the raise percentage is greater than or equal to 0. If the raise percentage is less than 0, the method should assign 0 as the new salary. INTRODUCTORY

7. In this exercise, you modify the Norbert Pool & Spa Depot application completed in Lesson A. Use Windows to make a copy of the Norbert Solution folder. Rename the copy Norbert Solution–Auto–Implemented. Open the Norbert Solution (Norbert Solution.sln) file contained in the Norbert Solution–Auto–Implemented folder. Open the designer window. Modify the RectangularPool class so that it uses Public auto-implemented properties rather than Public variables. Include a default constructor in the class. Save the solution and then start and test the application. Close the Code Editor window and then close the solution. INTRODUCTORY

8. Open the Hire Date Solution (Hire Date Solution.sln) file contained in the VB2012\Chap11\Hire Date Solution folder. Open the designer window. INTRODUCTORY

   a. Open the FormattedDate.vb file. Add a default constructor and a parameterized constructor to the class. Also add a method that returns the month and day numbers, separated by a slash (/).

   b. Open the form's Code Editor window. The btnDefault_Click and btnParameterized_Click procedures should display the hire date in the following format: *month/day*. For example, if the numbers 3 and 2 are selected in the Month and Day list boxes, respectively, the Click event procedures should display 3/2 in the Hire date box. Code the btnDefault_Click procedure using the FormattedDate class's default constructor. Code the btnParameterized_Click procedure using the class's parameterized constructor.

c. Save the solution and then start and test the application. Close the Main Form.vb and FormattedDate.vb windows and then close the solution.

INTERMEDIATE

9. Open the Salary Solution (Salary Solution.sln) file contained in the VB2012\Chap11\Salary Solution folder. Open the Worker.vb class file and then enter the Worker class definition from Exercises 5 and 6. Save the solution and then close the Worker.vb window. Open the form's Code Editor window. Use the comments in the btnCalc_Click procedure to enter the missing instructions. Save the solution and then start the application. Test the application by entering your name, a current salary amount of 54000, and a raise percentage of 10 (for 10%). The new salary should be $59,400.00. Close the Code Editor window and then close the solution.

INTERMEDIATE

10. In this exercise, you modify the Grade Calculator application coded in the lesson. Use Windows to make a copy of the Grade Solution folder. Rename the copy Grade Solution–Intermediate. Open the Grade Solution (Grade Solution.sln) file contained in the Grade Solution–Intermediate folder. Open the designer window.

a. Open the CourseGrade.vb file. Modify the DetermineGrade method so that it accepts the maximum number of points that can be earned on both tests. (Currently, the maximum number of points is 200: 100 points per test.) For an A grade, the student must earn at least 90% of the total number of points. For a B, C, and D grade, the student must earn at least 80%, 70%, and 60%, respectively. If the student earns less than 60% of the total points, the grade is F. Make the appropriate modifications to the class and then save the solution.

b. Add a label control and a text box to the form. Change the label control's Text property to "&Maximum points" (without the quotation marks). Change the text box's name to txtMax.

c. Open the form's Code Editor window. The text box should accept only numbers and the Backspace key. The maximum number allowed in the text box should be 400. Each list box should display numbers from 0 through 200. Make the necessary modifications to the code.

d. Save the solution and then start and test the application. Close the CourseGrade.vb and Main Form.vb windows and then close the solution.

ADVANCED

11. Each member of Glasgow Health Club must pay monthly dues that consist of a basic fee and one or more optional charges. The basic monthly fee for a single membership is $50; for a family membership, it is $90. If the member has a single membership, the additional monthly charges are $30 for tennis, $25 for golf, and $20 for racquetball. If the member has a family membership, the additional monthly charges are $50 for tennis, $35 for golf, and $30 for racquetball. The application should display the member's basic fee, additional charges, and monthly dues. Create a Visual Basic Windows application. Use the following names for the solution and project, respectively: Glasgow Solution and Glasgow Project. Save the application in the VB2012\Chap11 folder. Change the form file's name to Main Form.vb. Change the form's name to frmMain. Create the interface shown in Figure 11-48 and then code the application. Be sure to use a class in your code. Save the solution and then start and test the application. Close the Code Editor windows and then close the solution.

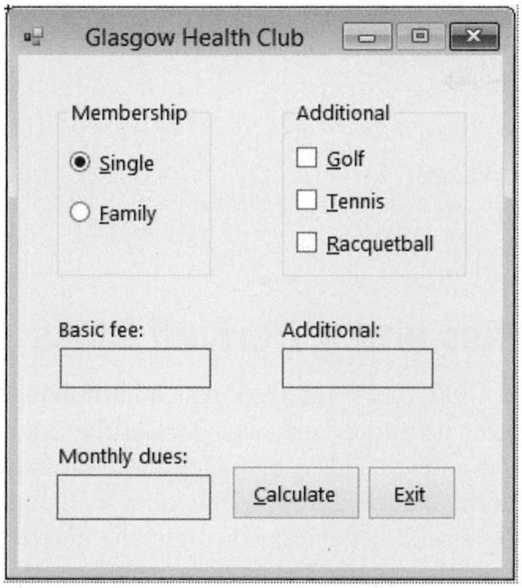

Figure 11-48 Interface for Exercise 11

12. Karen Miller, the manager of the Accounts Payable department at Serenity Photos, wants an application that keeps track of the checks written by her department. More specifically, she wants to record (in a sequential access file) the check number, date, payee, and amount of each check. Create a Visual Basic Windows application. Use the following names for the solution and project, respectively: Serenity Solution and Serenity Project. Save the application in the VB2012\Chap11 folder. Change the form file's name to Main Form.vb. Change the form's name to frmMain. Create the interface shown in Figure 11-49. The image for the picture box is stored in the VB2012\Chap11\Flower.png file. (The image was downloaded from the Open Clip Art Library at *http://openclipart.org*.) Code the application. Be sure to use a class in your code. Save the solution and then start and test the application. Close the Code Editor windows and then close the solution.

ADVANCED

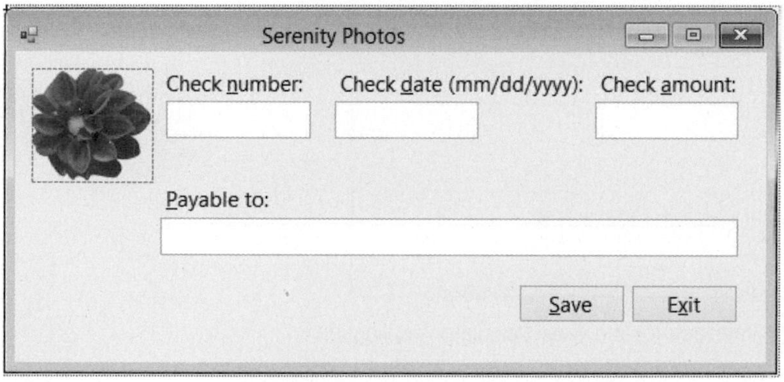

Figure 11-49 Interface for Exercise 12
OpenClipArt.org/yves_guillou

LESSON C

After studying Lesson C, you should be able to:

- Create a derived class
- Refer to the base class using the `MyBase` keyword
- Override a method in the base class

Example 8—Using a Base Class and a Derived Class

You can create one class from another class; in OOP, this is referred to as **inheritance**. The new class is called the **derived class** and it inherits the attributes and behaviors of the original class, called the **base class**. You indicate that a class is a derived class by including the Inherits clause in the derived class's Class statement. The **Inherits clause** is simply the keyword `Inherits` followed by the name of the class whose attributes and behaviors you want the derived class to inherit. You enter the Inherits clause immediately below the Public Class clause in the derived class.

You will use a base class named Square and a derived class named Cube to code the Area Calculator application. The application calculates and displays either the area of a square or the surface area of a cube.

START HERE

To open the Area Calculator application and then view the class file:

1. If necessary, start Visual Studio 2012. Open the Area Solution (Area Solution.sln) file contained in the VB2012\Chap11\Area Solution folder. If necessary, open the designer window. The interface provides a text box for entering the side measurement. See Figure 11-50.

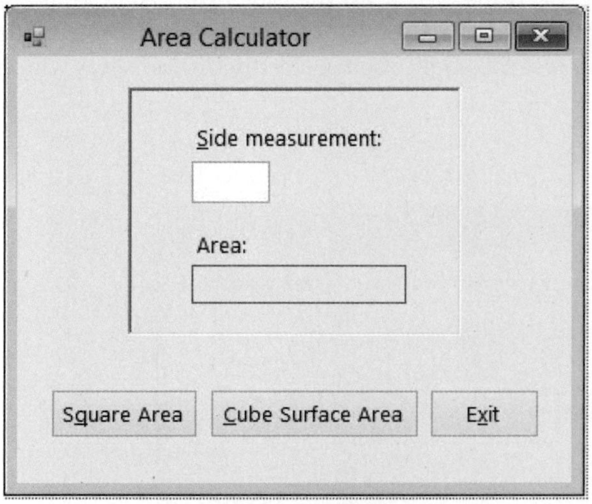

Figure 11-50 Interface for the Area Calculator application

2. Right-click **Shapes.vb** in the Solution Explorer window and then click **View Code**. Replace <your name> and <current date> in the comments with your name and the current date, respectively. The Shapes.vb file contains the Square class definition. See Figure 11-51.

```
' Name:          Shapes.vb
' Programmer:    <your name> on <current date>

Option Explicit On
Option Strict On
Option Infer Off

' base class
Public Class Square
    Public Property Side As Double

    Public Sub New()
        _Side = 0
    End Sub

    Public Sub New(ByVal dblS As Double)
        Side = dblS
    End Sub

    Public Function GetArea() As Double
        ' returns the area of a square
        Return _Side ^ 2
    End Function
End Class

' derived class
```

Square class definition

Figure 11-51 Contents of the Shapes.vb file

The Square class contains a Public property named Side, two constructors, and a method named GetArea. The Side property represents an attribute of a Square object: its side measurement. Each time a Square object is instantiated, the computer will use one of the two constructors to initialize the object. An application can use the class's GetArea method to calculate the area of a Square object. Notice that you calculate the area by raising the Square object's side measurement to the second power. The GetArea method will return the area to the statement that invoked the method.

In this section, you will create a derived class from the Square class. The derived class will inherit only the base class's Side attribute and GetArea method. It will not inherit the two constructors because constructors are never inherited. You will name the derived class Cube.

To create a derived class named Cube:

START HERE

1. Click the **blank line** below the `' derived class` comment and then enter the following two lines of code. Press **Enter** twice after typing the Inherits clause.

   Public Class Cube
   Inherits Square

2. As already mentioned, the Cube class will not inherit the Square class's constructors. Therefore, it will need its own constructors. Enter the following procedure header for the default constructor:

   Public Sub New()

3. Insert two blank lines above the Cube class's End Class clause. In the blank line immediately above the End Class clause, enter the following procedure header for the parameterized constructor:

   Public Sub New(ByVal dblS As Double)

Recall that when a Square object is instantiated, the computer uses one of the Square class's constructors to initialize the object. When a Cube object is instantiated, its constructors will call upon the base class's constructors to initialize the object. You refer to the base class using the **MyBase** keyword. For example, the `MyBase.New()` statement tells the computer to process the code contained in the base class's default constructor. Similarly, the `MyBase.New(dblS)` statement tells the computer to process the code contained in the base class's parameterized constructor.

START HERE

To finish coding the Cube class's constructors:

1. Click the **blank line** below the default constructor's procedure header and then type the following statement, but don't press Enter:

   MyBase.New()

2. Click the **blank line** below the parameterized constructor's procedure header and then type the following statement, but don't press Enter:

   MyBase.New(dblS)

Recall that the Square (base) class contains a method that calculates and returns the area of a Square object; the method's name is GetArea. You will also include a GetArea method in the Cube (derived) class. However, the Cube class's GetArea method will calculate and return the surface area of a Cube object. The formula for calculating the surface area is $sideMeasurement^2 * 6$. The GetArea method in the Cube class will use the Square class's GetArea method to calculate and return the first part of the formula: $sideMeasurement^2$. It then will simply multiply the return value by 6 to get the surface area of a Cube object.

In order to use the same method name—in this case, GetArea—in both a base class and a derived class, the method's procedure header in the base class will need to contain the Overridable keyword, and the method's procedure header in the derived class will need to contain the Overrides keyword. The **Overridable** keyword in the base class indicates that the method can be overridden by any class that is derived from the base class. In other words, classes derived from the Square (base) class will provide their own GetArea method. The **Overrides** keyword in the derived class indicates that the method overrides (replaces) the same method contained in the base class. In this case, for example, the GetArea method in the Cube class replaces the GetArea method in the Square class.

START HERE

To finish coding the Cube class:

1. Locate the GetArea function in the Square class. Change the procedure header to the following:

   Public Overridable Function GetArea() As Double

2. Now, insert two blank lines above the Cube class's End Class clause. (Be sure to insert the lines in the Cube class.) Beginning in the blank line above the End Class clause, enter the following GetArea method:

```
Public Overrides Function GetArea() As Double
    Return MyBase.GetArea * 6
End Function
```

3. Save the solution.

Figure 11-52 shows the Square and Cube class definitions contained in the Shapes.vb file.

```
' base class
Public Class Square
    Public Property Side As Double

    Public Sub New()
        _Side = 0
    End Sub

    Public Sub New(ByVal dblS As Double)
        Side = dblS
    End Sub

    Public Overridable Function GetArea() As Double
        ' returns the area of a square
        Return _Side ^ 2
    End Function
End Class

' derived class
Public Class Cube
    Inherits Square

    Public Sub New()
        MyBase.New()
    End Sub

    Public Sub New(ByVal dblS As Double)
        MyBase.New(dblS)
    End Sub

    Public Overrides Function GetArea() As Double
        Return MyBase.GetArea * 6
    End Function
End Class
```

indicates that the method can be overridden in the derived class
the derived class inherits from the base class
invokes the base class's default constructor
invokes the base class's parameterized constructor
indicates that the method overrides the one in the base class

Figure 11-52 Modified Square and Cube class definitions

To complete the Area Calculator application, you still need to code the Click event procedures for the Square Area and Cube Surface Area buttons in the interface. The Square Area button's Click event procedure will calculate and display the area of a square. Similarly, the Cube Surface Area button's Click event procedure will calculate and display the surface area of a cube. You will code the Square Area button's Click event procedure first.

To code and then test the Square Area button's Click event procedure:

START HERE

1. Click the **designer window's tab** and then open the form's Code Editor window.
2. Locate the btnSquare_Click procedure. First, you will instantiate a Square object. Click the **blank line** immediately above the End Sub clause and then enter the following Dim statement:

   Dim mySquare As New Square

3. Next, you will declare a variable to store the mySquare object's area. Type the following Dim statement and then press **Enter** twice:

   Dim dblArea As Double

4. Now you will assign the side measurement, which is entered by the user, to the mySquare object's Side property. Type the following TryParse method and then press **Enter** twice:

   Double.TryParse(txtSide.Text, mySquare.Side)

5. Next, you will use the mySquare object's GetArea method to calculate the area. You will assign the method's return value to the `dblArea` variable. Enter the following comment and assignment statement:

   ' calculate the area
   dblArea = mySquare.GetArea

6. Finally, you will display the area in the lblArea control. Enter the following comment and assignment statement:

   ' display the area
   lblArea.Text = "Square: " & dblArea.ToString("N1")

7. If necessary, delete the blank line above the End Sub clause.

8. Save the solution and then start the application. Type **12** in the Side measurement box and then click the **Square Area** button. The message "Square: 144.0" appears in the Area box. See Figure 11-53. (Recall that you can use the Alt key to show/hide the access keys.)

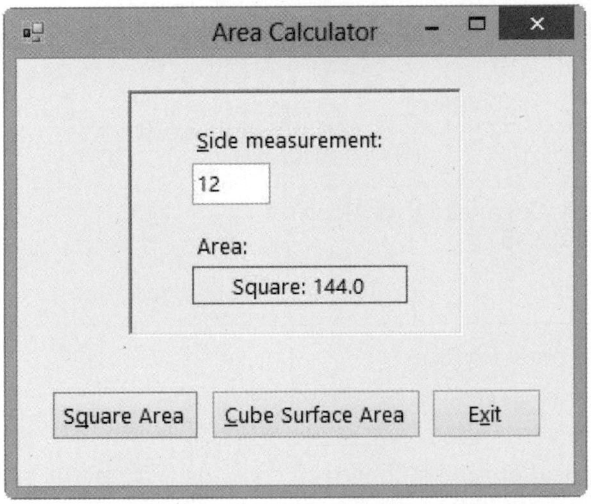

Figure 11-53 Interface showing the square's area

9. Click the **Exit** button.

Finally, you will code the Cube Surface Area button's Click event procedure.

START HERE

To code and then test the Cube Surface Area button's Click event procedure:

1. Locate the btnCube_Click procedure. First, you will instantiate a Cube object. Click the **blank line** immediately above the End Sub clause and then enter the following Dim statement:

   Dim myCube As New Cube

2. Next, you will declare a variable to store the myCube object's area. Type the following Dim statement and then press **Enter** twice:

   Dim dblArea As Double

3. Now you will assign the side measurement to the myCube object's Side property. Type the following TryParse method and then press **Enter** twice:

   Double.TryParse(txtSide.Text, myCube.Side)

4. Next, you will use the myCube object's GetArea method to calculate the area. You will assign the method's return value to the `dblArea` variable. Enter the following comment and assignment statement:

   ' calculate the area
   dblArea = myCube.GetArea

5. Finally, you will display the area in the lblArea control. Enter the following comment and assignment statement:

   ' display the area
   lblArea.Text = "Cube: " & dblArea.ToString("N1")

6. If necessary, delete the blank line above the End Sub clause.

7. Save the solution and then start the application. Type **12** in the Side measurement box and then click the **Cube Surface Area** button. The message "Cube: 864.0" appears in the Area box.

8. Click the **Exit** button. Close the form's Code Editor window and the Shapes.vb window, and then close the solution.

Figure 11-54 shows the btnSquare_Click and btnCube_Click procedures.

```
Private Sub btnSquare_Click(sender As Object,
e As EventArgs) Handles btnSquare.Click
    ' displays the area of a square

    Dim mySquare As New Square
    Dim dblArea As Double

    Double.TryParse(txtSide.Text, mySquare.Side)

    ' calculate the area
    dblArea = mySquare.GetArea
    ' display the area
    lblArea.Text = "Square: " & dblArea.ToString("N1")
End Sub

Private Sub btnCube_Click(sender As Object,
e As EventArgs) Handles btnCube.Click
    ' displays the surface area of a cube

    Dim myCube As New Cube
    Dim dblArea As Double

    Double.TryParse(txtSide.Text, myCube.Side)

    ' calculate the area
    dblArea = myCube.GetArea
    ' display the area
    lblArea.Text = "Cube: " & dblArea.ToString("N1")
End Sub
```

Figure 11-54 btnSquare_Click and btnCube_Click procedures

Lesson C Summary

- To allow a derived class to inherit the attributes and behaviors of a base class:

  Enter the Inherits clause immediately below the Public Class clause in the derived class. The Inherits clause is the keyword `Inherits` followed by the name of the base class.

- To refer to the base class:

  Use the `MyBase` keyword.

- To indicate that a method in the base class can be overridden (replaced) in the derived class:

  Use the `Overridable` keyword in the method's header in the base class.

- To indicate that a method in the derived class overrides (replaces) a method in the base class:

  Use the `Overrides` keyword in the method's header in the derived class.

Lesson C Key Terms

Base class—the original class from which another class is derived

Derived class—a class that inherits the attributes and behaviors of a base class

Inheritance—the ability to create one class from another class

Inherits clause—entered immediately below the Public Class clause in a derived class; specifies the name of the base class associated with the derived class

MyBase—a keyword used in a derived class to refer to the base class

Overridable—a keyword that can appear in a method's header in a base class; indicates that the method can be overridden by any class that is derived from the base class

Overrides—a keyword that can appear in a method's header in a derived class; indicates that the method overrides the method with the same name in the base class

Lesson C Review Questions

1. Which of the following clauses allows a derived class named Cat to have the same attributes and behaviors as its base class, which is named Animal?

   a. `Inherited Animal`

   b. `Inherits Animal`

   c. `Inherited Cat`

   d. `Inherits Cat`

2. A base class contains a method named GetTax. Which of the following procedure headers can be used in the base class to indicate that a derived class can provide its own code for the method?

   a. `Public Inherits Sub GetTax()`

   b. `Public Overridable Sub GetTax()`

   c. `Public Overrides Sub GetTax()`

   d. `Public Overriding Sub GetTax()`

3. A base class contains a method named GetTax. Which of the following procedure headers can be used in the derived class to indicate that it is providing its own code for the method?

   a. `Public Inherits Sub GetTax()`

   b. `Public Overridable Sub GetTax()`

   c. `Public Overrides Sub GetTax()`

   d. `Public Overriding Sub GetTax()`

4. The Salaried class is derived from a base class named Employee. Which of the following statements can be used by the Salaried class to invoke the Employee class's default constructor?

   a. `MyBase.New()`

   b. `MyEmployee.New()`

   c. `Call Employee.New`

   d. none of the above

Lesson C Exercises

INTRODUCTORY

1. Open the Formula Solution (Formula Solution.sln) file contained in the VB2012\Chap11\Formula Solution folder. If necessary, open the designer window. Open the Areas.vb file, which contains the Parallelogram class definition. The class contains two Public properties and two constructors. It also contains a GetArea method that calculates the area of a parallelogram.

   a. Create a derived class named Triangle. The derived class should inherit the properties and GetArea method from the Parallelogram class. However, the Triangle class's GetArea method should calculate the area of a triangle. The formula for calculating the area of a triangle is *base* * *height* / 2. Be sure to include a default constructor and a parameterized constructor in the derived class.

   b. The Calculate button's Click event procedure should display either the area of a parallelogram or the area of a triangle. The appropriate area to display depends on the radio button selected in the interface. Code the button's Click event procedure.

   c. Save the solution and then start and test the application. Close the form's Code Editor window and the Areas.vb window, and then close the solution.

INTERMEDIATE

2. Open the Kerry Sales Solution (Kerry Sales Solution.sln) file contained in the VB2012\Chap11\Kerry Sales Solution folder. If necessary, open the designer window.

   a. Open the Payroll.vb file. Create a base class named Bonus. The class should contain two Public properties: a String property named SalesId and a Double property named Sales. Include a default constructor and a parameterized constructor in the class. Also include a GetBonus method (function) that calculates a salesperson's bonus using the following formula: *sales* * .05.

   b. Create a derived class named PremiumBonus. The derived class's GetBonus method should calculate the bonus as follows: *sales* * .05 + (*sales* – 2500) * .01. Be sure to include a default constructor and a parameterized constructor in the derived class.

   c. Open the form's Code Editor window and locate the btnCalc_Click procedure. Finish coding the procedure, using the comments as a guide.

   d. Save the solution and then start and test the application. Close the form's Code Editor window and the Payroll.vb window, and then close the solution.

SWAT THE BUGS

3. Open the Debug Solution (Debug Solution.sln) file contained in the VB2012\Chap11\Debug Solution folder. If necessary, open the designer window. Open the Code Editor windows for the form and class file. Review the existing code. Correct the code to remove the jagged lines in the Shape and Circle class definitions. Save the solution and then start and test the application. Notice that the application is not working correctly. Locate and correct the errors in the code. Save the solution and then start and test the application again. Close the Code Editor windows and then close the solution.

CHAPTER 12

Web Applications

Creating the DJ Tom Application

In this chapter, you will create a Web application for DJ (disc jockey) Tom. Although DJ Tom can be hired for any event, his specialty is weddings. Therefore, he has requested a Web page that allows the user to enter the names of the bride and groom, the wedding date, an e-mail address, and the name of the first song to be danced by the newly married couple. The Web page will provide a Submit button that displays a message on the page. The message will contain the information entered by the user.

Previewing the DJ Tom Application

Before you start the first lesson in this chapter, you will preview the completed application. The application is contained in the VB2012\Chap12 folder.

START HERE

To preview the completed application:

1. If necessary, start Visual Studio 2012 or Visual Studio Express 2012 for Web.
2. Click **FILE** on the menu bar and then click **Open Web Site**. The Open Web Site dialog box appears. If necessary, click the **File System** button. Click the **DJTom-Preview** folder contained in the VB2012\Chap12 folder and then click the **Open** button. If a message box appears and asks whether you want to use IIS Express or the Visual Studio Development Server, click the **Yes** button to use IIS Express.
3. If the Default.aspx Web page does not appear in the Document window, right-click **Default.aspx** in the Solution Explorer window and then click **View Designer**.
4. Press **Ctrl+F5** to start the application. The Web page appears in a browser window. (If the message "Intranet settings are turned off by default" appears, click the Don't show this message again button.)
5. Click the **Bride** box and then type **Carlita**. Press **Tab** and then type **John** as the groom's name.
6. Click **any date** in the calendar.
7. Click the **E-mail box** and then type **anyEmail@domain.com**.
8. Click the **down arrow** in the First song box and then click **The Way You Look Tonight**.
9. Click the **Submit** button. A message appears in a purple box on the Web page. See Figure 12-1. (The top of your browser window may look slightly different from the one shown in Figure 12-1.)

your message may show a different date

Figure 12-1 Result of clicking the Submit button

10. Close the browser window. Click **FILE** on the Visual Studio 2012 (or Visual Studio Express 2012 for Web) menu bar and then click **Close Solution**. If you are asked whether you want to save the changes to the DJTom-Preview.sln file, click the **No** button. Click **FILE** and then click **Exit**.

In Lesson A, you will learn how to create static Web pages. Dynamic Web pages are covered in Lessons B and C. You will code the DJ Tom application in Lesson C. Be sure to complete each lesson in full and do all of the end-of-lesson questions and several exercises before continuing to the next lesson.

LESSON A

After studying Lesson A, you should be able to:

- Define basic Web terminology
- Create a Web application
- Add Web pages to an application
- Customize a Web page
- Add static text to a Web page
- Format a Web page's static text
- View a Web page in full screen view
- Add a link button and an image to a Web page
- Start a Web application
- Close and open a Web application
- Reposition a control on a Web page

Web Applications

The Internet is the world's largest computer network, connecting millions of computers located all around the world. One of the most popular features of the Internet is the World Wide Web, often referred to simply as the Web. The Web consists of documents called **Web pages** that are stored on Web servers. A **Web server** is a computer that contains special software that "serves up" Web pages in response to requests from client computers. A **client computer** is a computer that requests information from a Web server. The information is requested and subsequently viewed through the use of a program called a Web browser or, more simply, a **browser**. Currently, the two most popular browsers are Microsoft Internet Explorer and Mozilla Firefox.

Many Web pages are static. A **static Web page** is a document whose purpose is merely to display information to the viewer. Static Web pages are not interactive. The only interaction that can occur between static Web pages and the user is through links that allow the user to "jump" from one Web page to another. Figures 12-2 and 12-3 show examples of static Web pages created for Jumping Jack Toy Store. The Web page in Figure 12-2 shows the store's name, address, and telephone number. The page also provides a link to the Web page shown in Figure 12-3. That page shows the store's business hours and provides a link for returning to the first Web page. You will create both Web pages in this lesson.

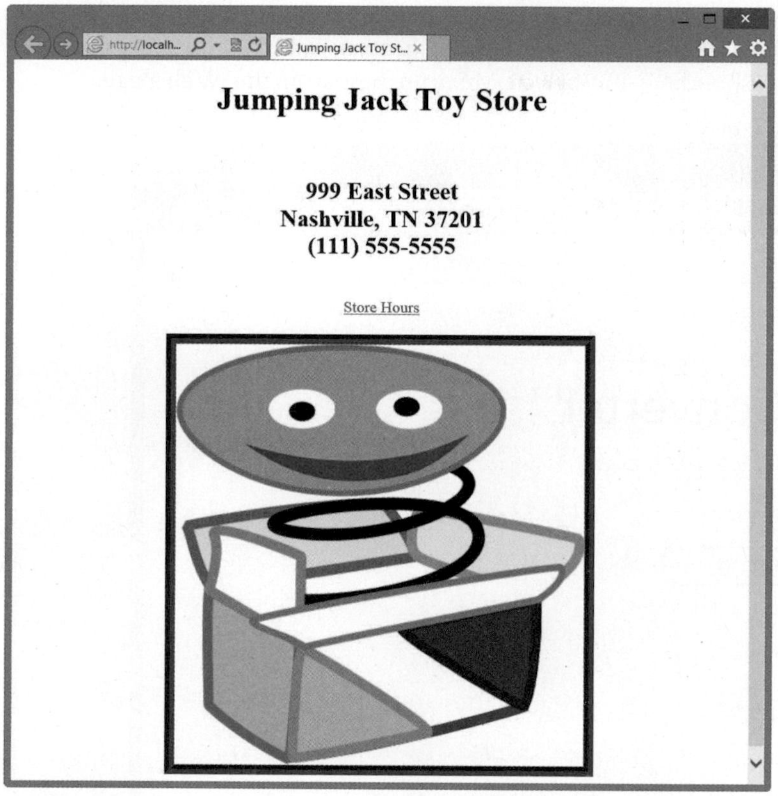

Figure 12-2 Example of a static Web page
OpenClipArt.org/Anonymous

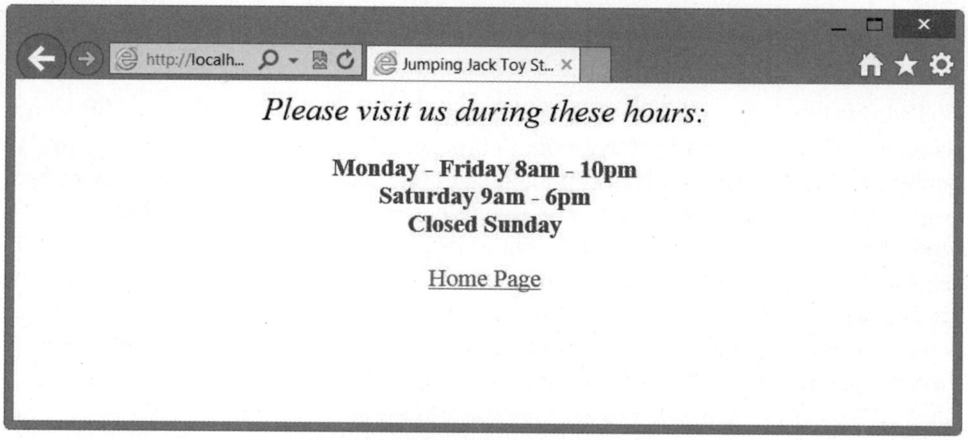

Figure 12-3 Another example of a static Web page

Although static Web pages provide a means for a store to list its location and hours, a company wanting to do business on the Web must be able to do more than just list information: It must be able to interact with customers through its Web site. The Web site should allow customers to submit inquiries, select items for purchase, and submit payment information. It also should allow the company to track customer inquiries and process customer orders. Tasks such as these can be accomplished using dynamic Web pages.

Unlike a static Web page, a **dynamic Web page** is interactive in that it can accept information from the user and also retrieve information for the user. Examples of dynamic Web pages include forms for purchasing merchandise online and for submitting online resumes. Figure 12-4 shows an example of a dynamic Web page that converts American dollars to Mexican pesos. To use the Web page, you enter the number of American dollars in the American dollars box and then click the Submit button. The button's Click event procedure displays the corresponding number of Mexican pesos on the Web page.

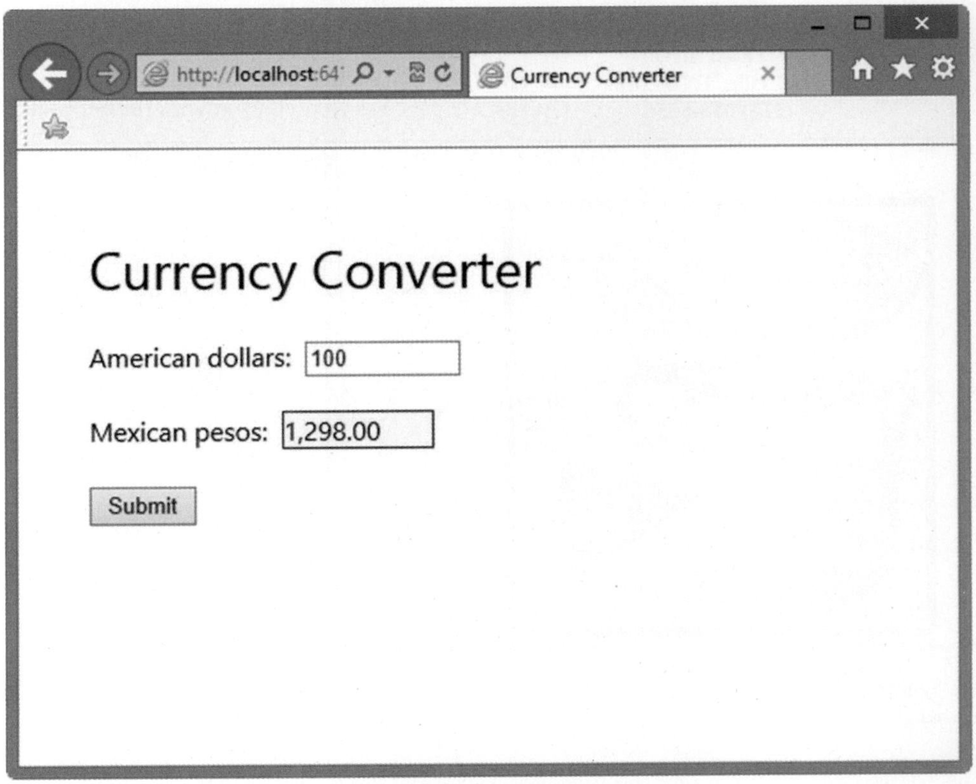

Figure 12-4 Example of a dynamic Web page

The Web applications created in this chapter use a technology called ASP.NET 4.5. **ASP** stands for "active server page" and refers to the type of Web page created by the ASP technology. All ASP pages contain HTML (Hypertext Markup Language) tags that tell the client's browser how to render the page on the computer screen. For example, the instruction <h1>Hello</h1> uses the opening <h1> tag and its closing </h1> tag to display the word "Hello" as a heading on the Web page. Many ASP pages also contain ASP tags that specify the controls to include on the Web page. In addition to the HTML and ASP tags, dynamic ASP pages contain code that tells the objects on the Web page how to respond to the user's actions. In this chapter, you will write the appropriate code using the Visual Basic programming language.

When a client computer's browser sends a request for an ASP page, the Web server locates the page and then sends the appropriate HTML instructions to the client. The client's browser uses the instructions to render the Web page on the computer screen. If the Web page is a dynamic one, like the Currency Converter page shown in Figure 12-4, the user can interact with the page by entering data. In most cases, the user then clicks a button on the Web page to submit the data to the server for processing. When the server receives the data, it executes the Visual Basic code associated with the Web page. It then sends back the appropriate HTML, which now includes the result of processing the code and data, to the client for rendering in the browser window. Using the Currency Converter Web page as an example, the user first enters the number of American dollars and then clicks the Submit button, which submits the user's entry to the Web server. The server executes the Visual Basic code to convert the American dollars to Mexican pesos and then sends back the HTML, which now includes the number of Mexican pesos. Notice that the Web page's HTML is interpreted and executed by the client computer, whereas the program code is executed by the Web server. Figure 12-5 illustrates the relationship between the client computer and the Web server.

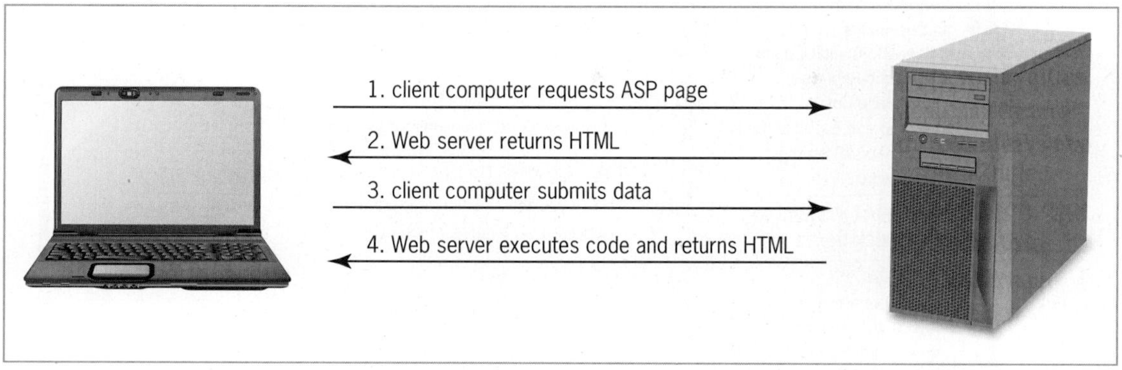
1. client computer requests ASP page
2. Web server returns HTML
3. client computer submits data
4. Web server executes code and returns HTML

Figure 12-5 Illustration of the relationship between a client computer and a Web server

This lesson covers static Web pages. Dynamic Web pages are covered in Lessons B and C.

Creating a Web Application

You create a Web application in Visual Basic using Visual Studio 2012 for Web, which is available either as a stand-alone product (called Visual Studio Express 2012 for Web) or as part of Visual Studio 2012. You can download a free copy of Visual Studio Express 2012 for Web from Microsoft's Web site. At the time of this writing, the address is *http://www.microsoft.com/visualstudio/eng/products/visual-studio-express-for-web*. The following steps show you how to configure the Express edition. You should perform these steps only if you are using Visual Studio Express 2012 for Web.

To configure Visual Studio Express 2012 for Web:

START HERE

1. *Windows 8*: If necessary, tap the **Windows logo** key to switch to the Windows 8 tile-based mode and then click the **VS Express for Web** tile.

   Windows 7: Click the **Start** button on the Windows 7 taskbar and then point to **All Programs**. Click **Microsoft Visual Studio Express 2012** on the All Programs menu and then click **Visual Studio Express 2012 for Web**.

2. Click **TOOLS** on the menu bar, and then click **Options** to open the Options dialog box. Click the **Projects and Solutions** node. Use the information shown in Figure 12-6 to select and deselect the appropriate check boxes.

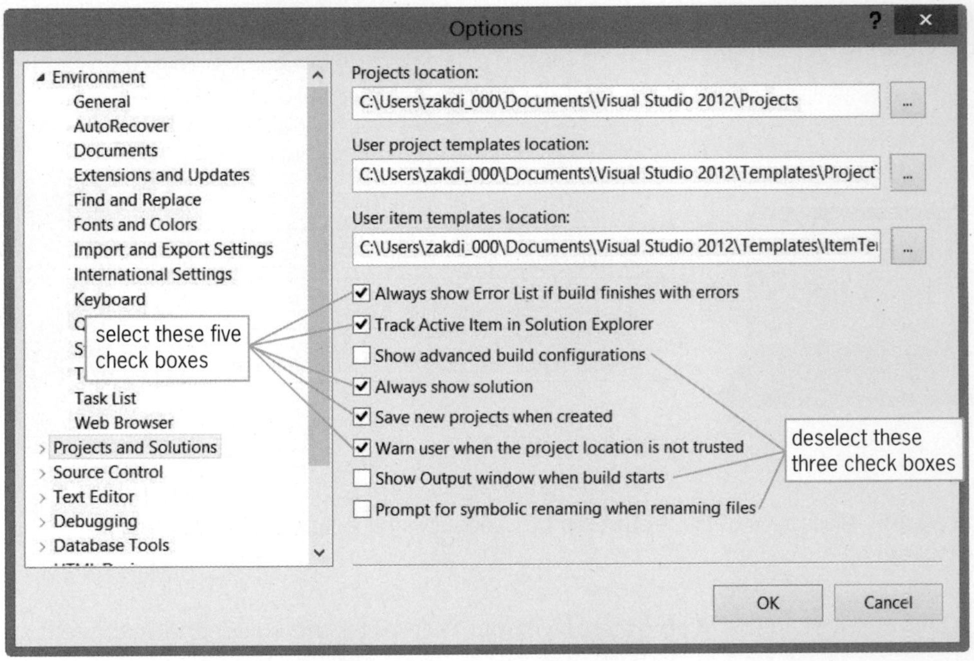

Figure 12-6 Options dialog box

3. Click the **OK** button to close the Options dialog box.
4. Click **TOOLS** on the menu bar and then point to **Settings**. If necessary, click **Expert Settings** to select it.

In the next set of steps, you begin creating the Jumping Jack Toy Store Web application.

START HERE

To begin creating the Web application:

1. If necessary, start Visual Studio 2012 or Visual Studio Express 2012 for Web.
2. If necessary, open the Solution Explorer and Properties windows and auto-hide the Toolbox window.
3. Click **FILE** on the menu bar and then click **New Web Site** to open the New Web Site dialog box. If necessary, click **Visual Basic** in the Installed Templates list. Click **ASP.NET Empty Web Site** in the middle column of the dialog box.
4. If necessary, change the entry in the Web location box to **File System**. The File System selection allows you to store your Web application in any folder on either your computer or a network drive.
5. In this chapter, you will be instructed to store your Web applications in the VB2012\Chap12 folder on the E drive; however, you should use the drive letter that contains your data disk. In the box that appears next to the Web location box, replace the existing text with **E:\VB2012\Chap12\JumpingJack**. Figure 12-7 shows the completed New Web Site dialog box. Your dialog box will look slightly different if you are using Visual Studio Express 2012 for Web.

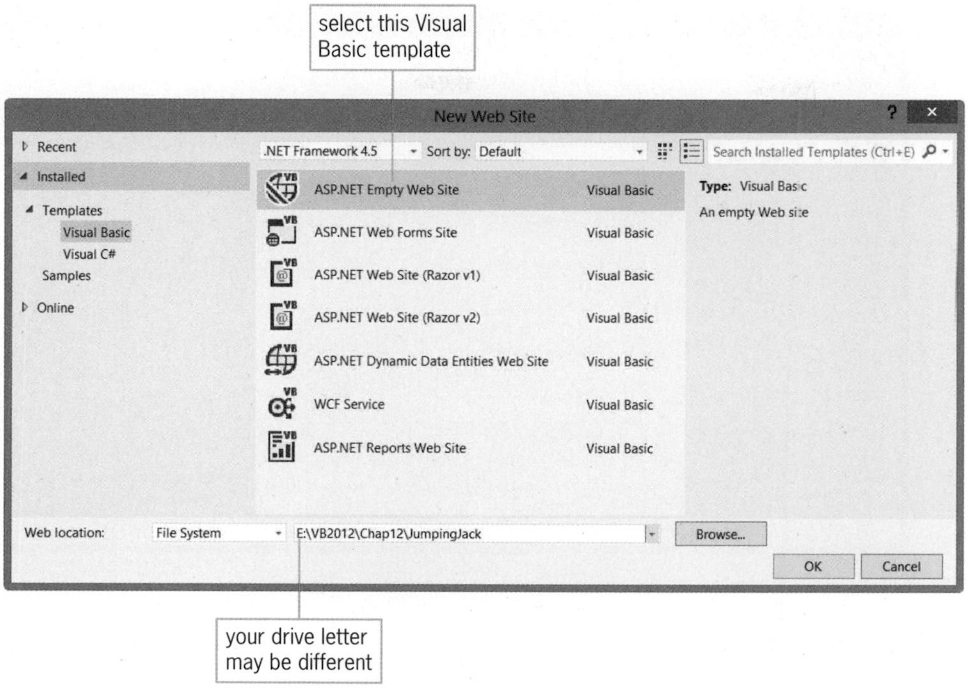

Figure 12-7 New Web Site dialog box

6. Click the **OK** button to close the dialog box. The computer creates an empty Web application named JumpingJack.

Adding the Default.aspx Web Page to the Application

After creating an empty Web application, you need to add a Web page to it. The first Web page added to an application is usually named Default.aspx.

To add the Default.aspx Web page to the application:

START HERE

1. Click **WEBSITE** on the menu bar and then click **Add New Item** to open the Add New Item dialog box. (If WEBSITE does not appear on the menu bar, click the Web application's name in the Solution Explorer window.)
2. If necessary, click **Visual Basic** in the Installed list and then (if necessary) click **Web Form** in the middle column of the dialog box. Verify that the Place code in separate file check box is selected, and that the Select master page check box is not selected. As indicated in Figure 12-8, the Web page will be named Default.aspx.

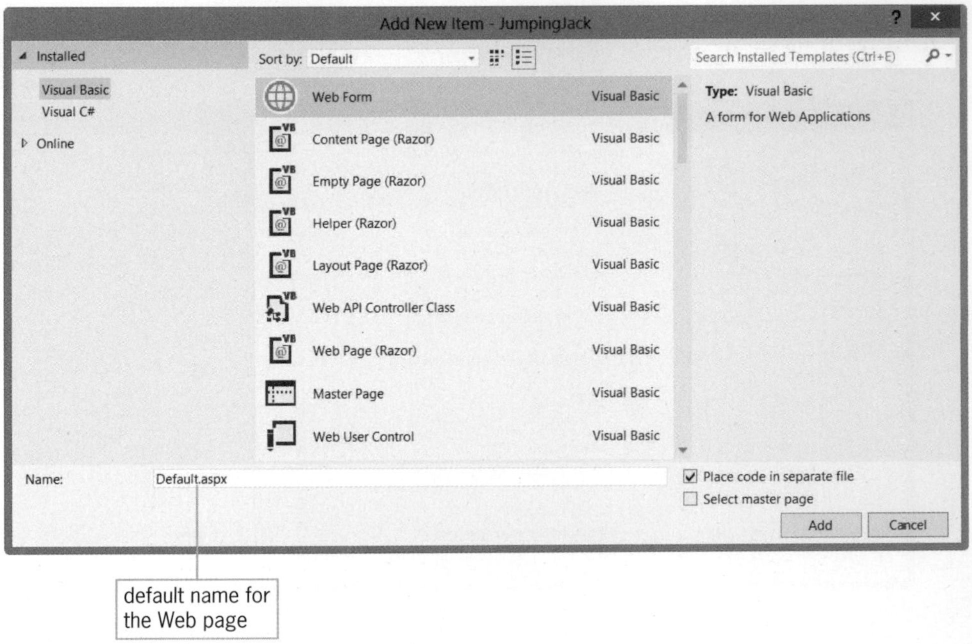

Figure 12-8 Add New Item dialog box

3. Click the **Add** button to display the Default.aspx page in the Document window. If necessary, click the **Design** tab that appears at the bottom of the IDE. When the Design tab is selected, the Web page appears in Design view in the Document window, as shown in Figure 12-9. You can use Design view to add text and controls to the Web page. If the Formatting toolbar does not appear on your screen, click **VIEW** on the menu bar, point to **Toolbars**, and then click **Formatting**. If the div tag does not appear in the Document window, click either the <**div**> button at the bottom of the IDE or the **rectangle** below the body tag.

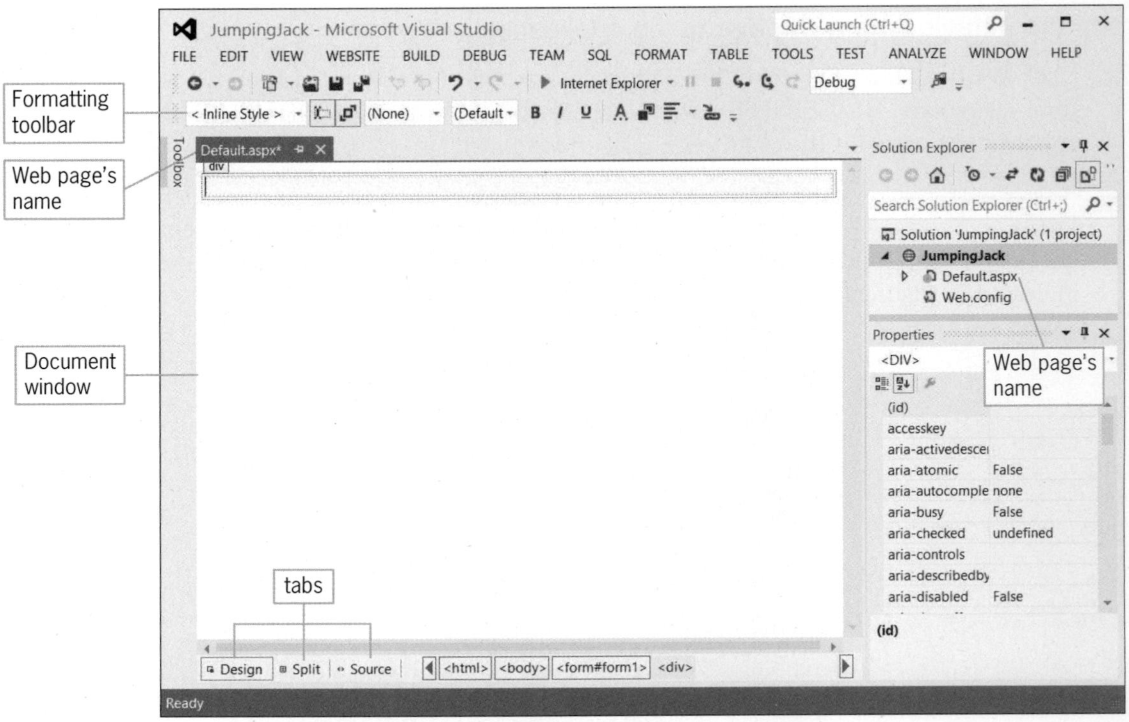

Figure 12-9 Default.aspx Web page shown in Design view

4. Click the **Source** tab to display the Web page in Source view. This view shows the HTML and ASP tags that tell a browser how to render the Web page. The tags are automatically generated for you as you are creating the Web page in Design view. Currently, the Web page contains only HTML tags.
5. Click the **Split** tab to split the Document window into two parts. The upper half displays the Web page in Source view, and the lower half displays it in Design view.
6. Click the **Design** tab to return to Design view, and then auto-hide the Solution Explorer window.

Including a Title on a Web Page

You can use the Properties window to include a title on a Web page. The properties appear in the Properties window when you select DOCUMENT in the window's Object box.

START HERE

To include a title on the Web page:

1. Click the **down arrow** button in the Properties window's Object box and then click **DOCUMENT** in the list. (If DOCUMENT does not appear in the Object box, click the Design tab.) The DOCUMENT object represents the Web page.
2. If necessary, click the **Alphabetical** button in the Properties window to display the properties in alphabetical order. Click **Title** in the Properties list. Type **Jumping Jack Toy Store** in the Settings box and then press **Enter**.
3. Auto-hide the Properties window. Save the application either by clicking the **Save All** button on the Standard toolbar or by clicking the **Save All** option on the FILE menu.

Adding Static Text to a Web Page

All Web pages contain some text that the user is not allowed to edit, such as a company name or the caption that identifies a text box. Text that cannot be changed by the user is referred to as **static text**. You can add static text to a Web page by simply typing the text on the page itself; or, you can use a label control that you dragged to the Web page from the Toolbox window. In this lesson, you will type the static text on the Web page.

START HERE

To add static text to the Web page:

1. If necessary, click **inside the rectangle** that appears below the div tag at the top of the Document window. The div tag defines a division in a Web page. (If the div tag does not appear in the Document window, click the <div> button at the bottom of the IDE.)
2. Enter the following four lines of text. Press **Enter** twice after typing the last line.

   Jumping Jack Toy Store
   999 East Street
   Nashville, TN 37201
   (111) 555-5555

3. Save the application.

You can use either the FORMAT menu or the Formatting toolbar to format the static text on a Web page. Figure 12-10 indicates some of the tools available on the Formatting toolbar.

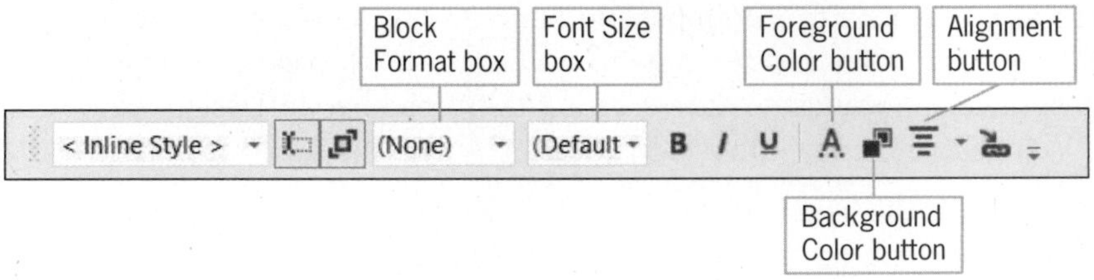

Figure 12-10 Formatting toolbar

START HERE

To use the Formatting toolbar to format the static text:

1. Select (highlight) the Jumping Jack Toy Store text on the Web page. Click the **down arrow** in the Block Format box on the Formatting toolbar. (If the Formatting toolbar does not appear on your screen, click VIEW on the menu bar, point to Toolbars, and then click Formatting.) See Figure 12-11.

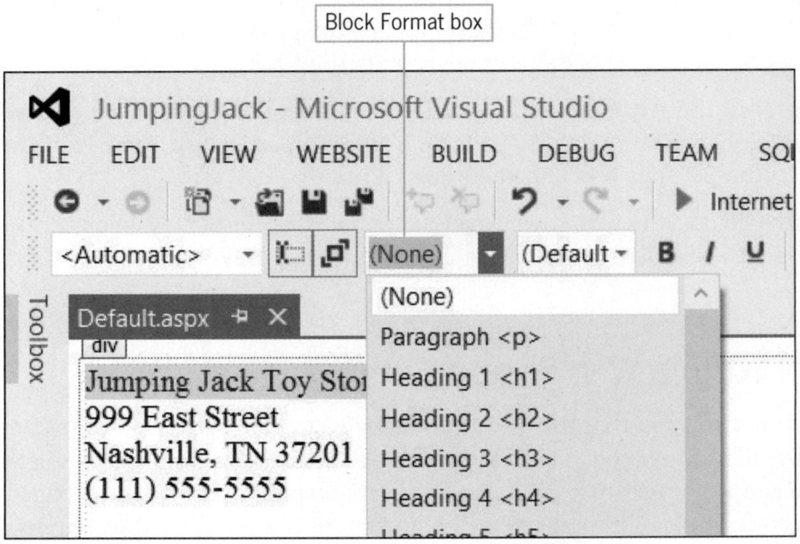

Figure 12-11 Result of clicking the arrow in the Block Format box

2. Click **Heading 1 <h1>**.
3. Select the address and phone number text on the Web page. Click the **down arrow** in the Block Format box and then click **Heading 2 <h2>**.
4. Now, you will use the Formatting toolbar's Alignment button to center all of the static text. Select all of the static text on the Web page and then click the **down arrow** on the Alignment button. See Figure 12-12.

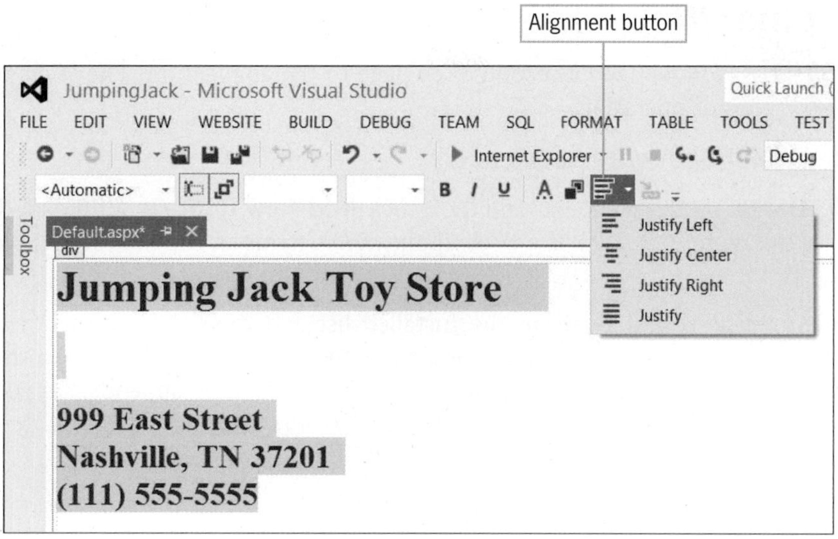

Figure 12-12 Result of clicking the Alignment button

5. Click **Justify Center**. The selected text appears centered, horizontally, on the Web page. Click **anywhere below the phone number** to deselect the text, and then save the application.

Viewing a Web Page in Full Screen View

While you are designing a Web page, you can use the Full Screen option on the VIEW menu to determine how the Web page will appear to the user.

START HERE

To view the Web page using the Full Screen option:

1. Click **VIEW** on the menu bar and then click **Full Screen**. See Figure 12-13. Although not identical to viewing in a browser window, full screen view provides a quick and easy way to verify the placement of controls and text on the Web page.

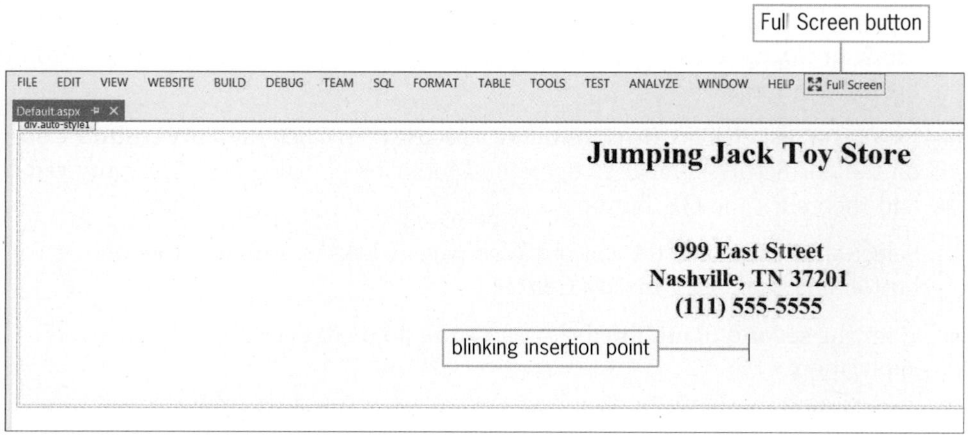

Figure 12-13 Default.aspx Web page displayed in full screen view

2. Click the **Full Screen** button to return to the standard view. (If you mistakenly clicked the window's Close button, click the Full Screen button, right-click Default.aspx in the Solution Explorer window, and then click View Designer.)

Adding Another Web Page to the Application

In the next set of steps, you will add a second Web page to the application. The Web page will display the store's hours of operation.

START HERE

To add another Web page to the application:

1. Click **WEBSITE** on the menu bar and then click **Add New Item**. (If WEBSITE does not appear on the menu bar, click the Web application's name in the Solution Explorer window.)
2. If necessary, click **Visual Basic** in the Installed list and then (if necessary) click **Web Form** in the middle column of the dialog box. Change the filename in the Name box to **Hours** and then click the **Add** button. The computer appends the .aspx extension on the filename and then displays the Hours.aspx Web page in the Document window.
3. Temporarily display the Solution Explorer window. Notice that the window now contains the Hours.aspx filename.
4. Click the **Hours.aspx** tab and then temporarily display the Properties window. Click the **down arrow** button in the Properties window's Object box and then click **DOCUMENT** in the list. Change the Web page's Title property to **Jumping Jack Toy Store**.
5. Click the **Hours.aspx** tab. The blinking insertion point should be inside the rectangle that appears below the div tag. (If the div tag does not appear in the Document window, click the <div button> at the bottom of the IDE.) Type **Please visit us during these hours:** and press **Enter** twice.
6. Now, enter the following three lines of text. Press **Enter** twice after typing the last line.

   Monday – Friday 8am – 10pm
   Saturday 9am – 6pm
   Closed Sunday

7. Select the **Please visit us during these hours:** text. Click the **down arrow** in the Font Size box and then click **x-large (24 pt)**. Also click the ***I*** (Italic) button on the Formatting toolbar.
8. Select the three lines of text that contain the store hours. Click the **down arrow** in the Font Size box and then click **large (18 pt)**. Also click the **B** (Bold) button on the Formatting toolbar.
9. Now, you will change the color of the selected text. Click the **Foreground Color** button on the Formatting toolbar to open the More Colors dialog box. Click **any red hexagon** and then click the **OK** button.
10. Select all of the static text on the Web page. Click the **down arrow** on the Alignment button and then click **Justify Center**.
11. Click the **second blank line** below the store hours to deselect the text, and then save the application.

Adding a Link Button Control to a Web Page

The Toolbox window provides tools for adding controls to a Web page. In the next set of steps, you will add a **link button control** to both Web pages. The link button control on the Default.aspx page will display the Hours.aspx page. The link button control on the Hours.aspx page will return the user to the Default.aspx Web page.

START HERE

To add a link button control to both Web pages:

1. First, you will add a link button control to the Hours.aspx page. Permanently display the Toolbox window. Expand the Standard node, if necessary, and then click the **LinkButton** tool. Drag your mouse pointer to the location shown in Figure 12-14 and then release the mouse button.

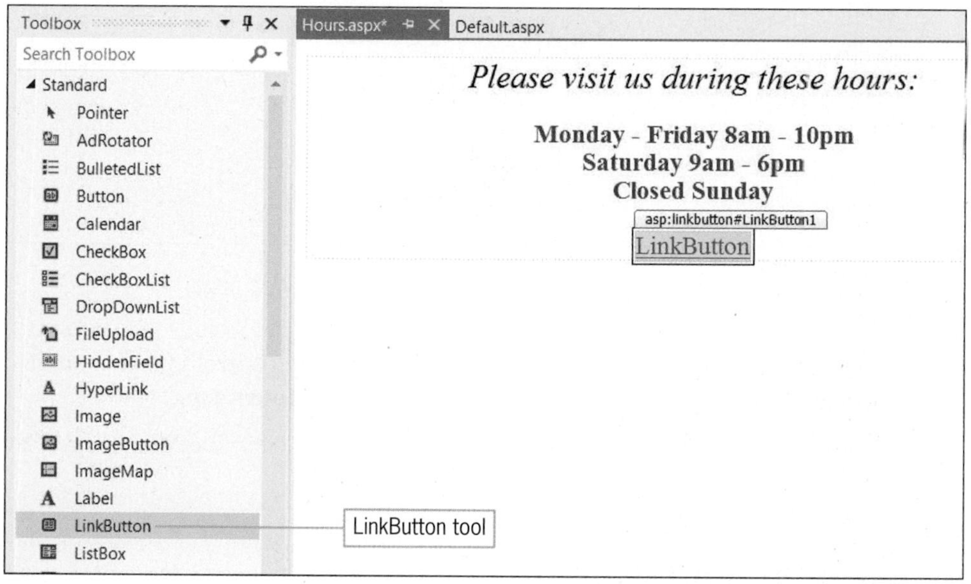

Figure 12-14 Link button control added to the Hours.aspx Web page

2. Temporarily display the Properties window. Change the control's Text property to **Home Page**. Click **PostBackUrl** in the Properties list and then click the **...** (ellipsis) button to open the Select URL dialog box. Click **Default.aspx** in the Contents of folder list. See Figure 12-15.

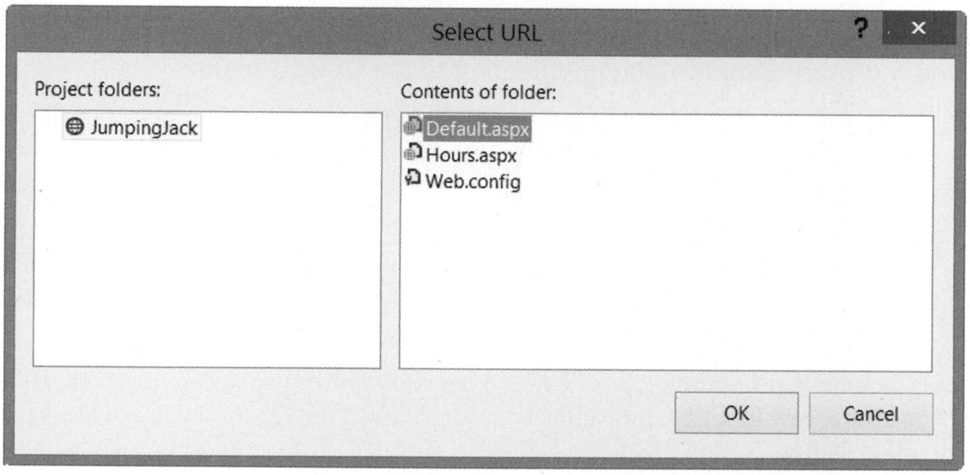

Figure 12-15 Select URL dialog box

3. Click the **OK** button to close the dialog box and then click the **Web page**.
4. Now, you will add a link button control to the Default.aspx page. Click the **Default.aspx** tab. Click the **LinkButton** tool. Drag your mouse pointer to the location shown in Figure 12-16 and then release the mouse button.

Figure 12-16 Link button control added to the Default.aspx Web page

5. Temporarily display the Properties window. Change the control's Text property to **Store Hours** and then change its PostBackUrl property to **Hours.aspx**.
6. Click the **OK** button to close the dialog box and then click the **Web page**. Save the application.

Starting a Web Application

Typically, you start a Web application either by pressing Ctrl+F5 or by clicking the Start Without Debugging option on the DEBUG menu. The method you use—the shortcut keys or the menu option—is a matter of personal preference. If you prefer to use a menu option, you might need to add the Start Without Debugging option to the DEBUG menu because the option is not automatically included on the menu in either Visual Studio 2012 or Visual Studio Express 2012 for Web. You can add the option to the menu by performing the next set of steps. If you prefer to use the Ctrl+F5 shortcut keys, you can skip the next set of steps.

START HERE

To add the Start Without Debugging option to the DEBUG menu:

1. First, you will determine whether your DEBUG menu already contains the Start Without Debugging option. Click **DEBUG** on the menu bar. If the DEBUG menu contains the Start Without Debugging option, close the menu by clicking **DEBUG** again, and then skip the remaining steps in this set of steps.
2. If the DEBUG menu does *not* contain the Start Without Debugging option, close the menu by clicking **DEBUG** again. Click **TOOLS** on the menu bar and then click **Customize** to open the Customize dialog box.
3. Click the **Commands** tab. The Menu bar radio button should be selected. Click the **down arrow** in the Menu bar list box. Scroll down the list until you see Debug, and then click **Debug**.
4. Click the **Add Command** button to open the Add Command dialog box, and then click **Debug** in the Categories list. Scroll down the Commands list until you see Start Without Debugging, and then click **Start Without Debugging**. Click the **OK** button to close the Add Command dialog box.
5. Click the **Move Down** button until the Start Without Debugging option appears below the Start/Continue option, as shown in Figure 12-17.

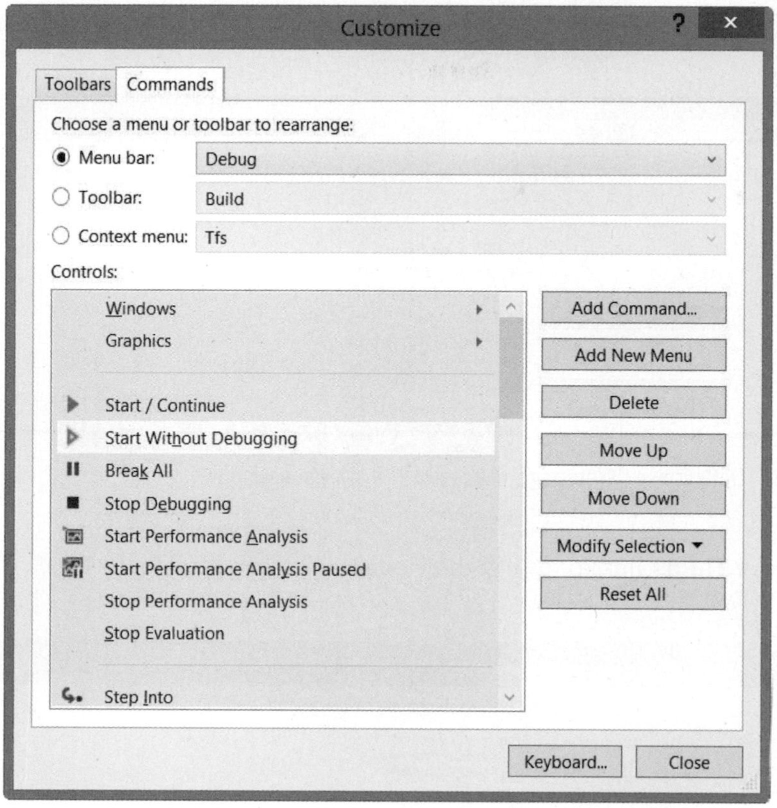

Figure 12-17 Customize dialog box

6. Click the **Close** button to close the dialog box.

When you start a Web application in either Visual Studio 2012 or Visual Studio Express 2012 for Web, the computer creates a temporary Web server that allows you to view your Web page in a browser. Keep in mind, however, that your Web page will need to be placed on an actual Web server for others to view it.

START HERE

To start the Jumping Jack Toy Store Web application:

1. Start the Web application either by pressing **Ctrl+F5** or by clicking the **Start Without Debugging** option on the DEBUG menu. (If the message "Intranet settings are turned off by default." appears, click the Don't show this message again button.) Your browser requests the Default.aspx page from the Web server. The server locates the page and then sends the appropriate HTML instructions to your browser for rendering on the screen. Notice that the value in the page's Title property appears on the page's tab in the browser window. See Figure 12-18.

Figure 12-18 Default.aspx Web page displayed in a browser window

2. Click the **Store Hours** link to display the Hours.aspx page. See Figure 12-19.

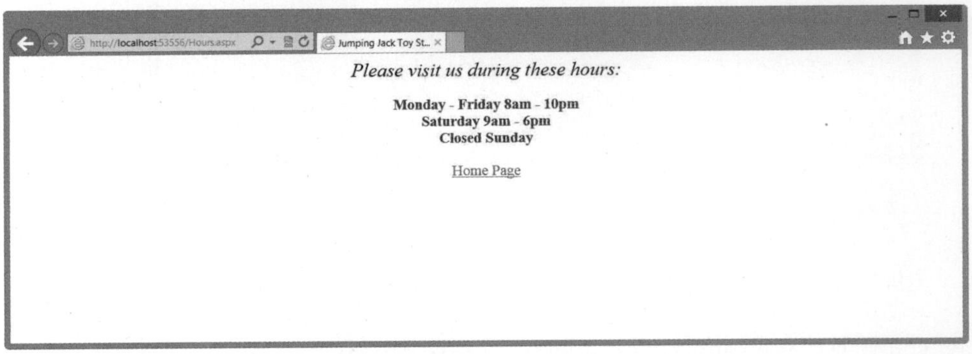

Figure 12-19 Hours.aspx Web page displayed in a browser window

3. Click the **Home Page** link to display the Default.aspx page, and then close the browser window. If necessary, close the Performance Explorer window.

Adding an Image to a Web Page

In the next set of steps, you will add an image to the Default.aspx page. The image is stored in the VB2012\Chap12\ToyStore.png file. The image was downloaded from the Open Clip Art Library at *http://openclipart.org*.

START HERE

To add an image to the Web page:

1. First, you will need to add the image file to the application. Click **WEBSITE** on the menu bar and then click **Add Existing Item**. Open the VB2012\Chap12 folder. Click the **down arrow** in the box that controls the file types and then click **All Files (*.*)** in the list. Click **ToyStore.png** in the list of filenames and then click the **Add** button.
2. Insert a blank line below the Store Hours link button control. Click the **blank line** below the control and then press **Enter** to insert another blank line. Click the **Image** tool in the toolbox. Drag your mouse pointer to the location shown in Figure 12-20 and then release the mouse button.

Figure 12-20 Image control added to the Default.aspx Web page

3. Temporarily display the Properties window. Click **ImageUrl** in the Properties list, if necessary, and then click the **...** (ellipsis) button to open the Select Image dialog box. Click **ToyStore.png** in the Contents of folder section and then click the **OK** button.
4. Next, you will put a border around the image control and also change the border's width to 10 pixels. Change the image control's BorderStyle property to **Groove**, and then change its BorderWidth property to **10**. Press **Enter** after typing the number 10.
5. Now, you will change the color of the image's border to red. Click **BorderColor** in the Properties list and then click the **...** (ellipsis) button. When the More Colors dialog box opens, click **any red hexagon**. Click the **OK** button to close the dialog box and then click the **Web page**.
6. Auto-hide the toolbox. Save and then start the application. See Figure 12-21.

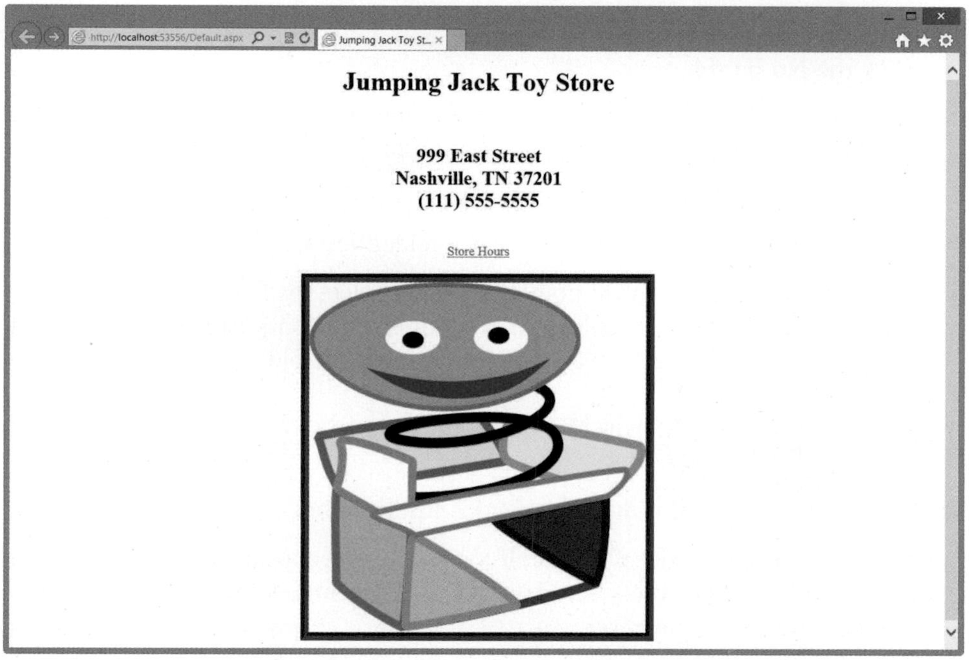

Figure 12-21 Default.aspx Web page
OpenClipArt.org/Anonymous

7. Verify that the browser window is not maximized. Place your mouse pointer on the window's right border and then drag the border to the left to make the window narrower. Notice that the text and image remain centered in the visible portion of the window. Now, drag the right border to the right to make the window wider. Here again, the text and image remain centered in the visible portion of the window.
8. Close the browser window.

Closing and Opening an Existing Web Application

You can use the FILE menu to close and also open an existing Web application.

START HERE

To close and then open the Jumping Jack Toy Store application:

1. Click **FILE** on the menu bar and then click **Close Solution** to close the application.
2. Now, you will open the application. Click **FILE** on the menu bar, and then click **Open Web Site** to open the Open Web Site dialog box. If necessary, click the **File System** button. If necessary, click the **JumpingJack** folder, which is contained in the VB2012\Chap12 folder. Click the **Open** button. If a message box appears and asks whether you want to use IIS Express or the Visual Studio Development Server, click the **Yes** button to use IIS Express.
3. If the Default.aspx Web page is not open in the Document window, right-click **Default.aspx** in the Solution Explorer window and then click **View Designer**.

Repositioning a Control on a Web Page

At times, you may want to reposition a control on a Web page. In this section, you will move the image and link button controls to different locations on the Default.aspx Web page. First, however, you will create a new Web application and then copy the Jumping Jack Toy Store files to the application.

START HERE

To create a new Web application and then copy files to the application:

1. Close the Jumping Jack Toy Store application. If you are prompted to save the solution, click the **No** button.
2. Use the New Web Site option on the FILE menu to create an empty Web application named **JumpingJack2**. Save the application in the VB2012\Chap12 folder.
3. Close the JumpingJack2 application.
4. Use Windows to open the JumpingJack2 folder. Delete the Web.config file.
5. Use Windows to open the JumpingJack folder. Select the folder's contents, which include six files (Default.aspx, Default.aspx.vb, Hours.aspx, Hours.aspx.vb, ToyStore.png, and Web.config). Copy the six files to the JumpingJack2 folder.

Now, you will open the JumpingJack2 application and move the two controls to different locations on the Default.aspx Web page.

START HERE

To move the controls in the JumpingJack2 application:

1. Open the JumpingJack2 Web site. If a message box appears and asks whether you want to use IIS Express or the Visual Studio Development Server, click the **Yes** button to use IIS Express.
2. Right-click **Default.aspx** in the Solution Explorer window and then click **View Designer**.

3. First, you will move the image control from the bottom of the Web page to the top of the Web page. If necessary, click **immediately before the first letter J** in the Jumping Jack Toy Store heading. Press **Enter** to insert a blank line above the heading.
4. Click the **image control** on the Web page. Drag the image control to the blank line immediately above the heading, and then release the mouse button.
5. Next, you will move the link button control to the empty area below the store's name. Click the **link button control**. Drag the control to the empty area below the store's name, and then release the mouse button.
6. Click **FILE** on the menu bar and then click **Save Default.aspx**.
7. Start the application. See Figure 12-22.

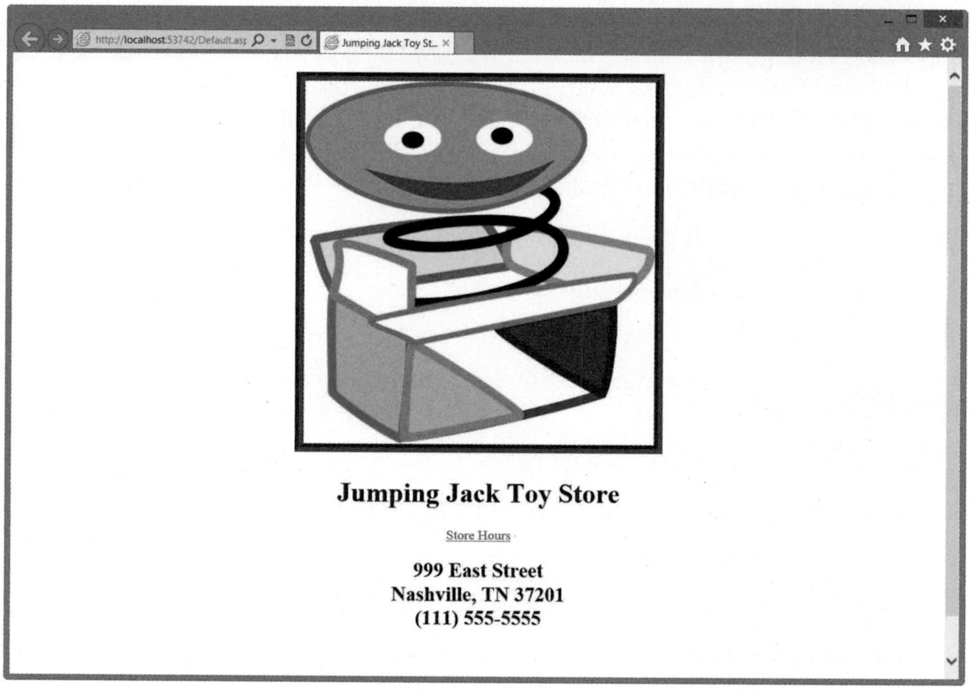

Figure 12-22 Modified Default.aspx Web page
OpenClipArt.org/Anonymous

8. Close the browser window and then close the application.

YOU DO IT 1!

Create an empty Web application named YouDoIt 1. Save the application in the VB2012\Chap12 folder. Add two Web pages to the application: one named Default.aspx and one named Address.aspx. The Default.aspx page should contain your name and a link button control. Change the link button control's Text property to Address. The control should display the Address.aspx page. The Address.aspx page should contain your address and a link button control. Change this link button control's Text property to Name. The control should display the Default.aspx page. Save the application and then start and test it. Close the browser window and then close the application.

Lesson A Summary

- To create an empty Web application:

  Start Visual Studio 2012 or Visual Studio Express 2012 for Web. Click FILE on the menu bar and then click New Web Site to open the New Web Site dialog box. If necessary, click Visual Basic in the Installed Templates list. Click ASP.NET Empty Web Site in the middle column of the dialog box. If necessary, change the entry in the Web location box to File System. In the box that appears next to the Web location box, enter the location where you want the Web application saved. Also enter the application's name. Click the OK button to close the New Web Site dialog box.

- To add a Web page to a Web application:

  Open the Web application. Click WEBSITE on the menu bar and then click Add New Item to open the Add New Item dialog box. (If WEBSITE does not appear on the menu bar, click the Web application's name in the Solution Explorer window.) If necessary, click Visual Basic in the Installed list and then (if necessary) click Web Form in the middle column of the dialog box. Verify that the Place code in separate file check box is selected, and that the Select master page check box is not selected. Enter an appropriate name in the Name box. Click the Add button to display the Web page in the Document window. If necessary, click the Design tab that appears at the bottom of the IDE.

- To add a title to a Web page:

  Set the DOCUMENT's Title property.

- To add static text to a Web page:

  Either type the text on the Web page or use a label control that you dragged to the Web page from the Toolbox window.

- To format the static text on a Web page:

  Use either the FORMAT menu or the Formatting toolbar.

- To display a Web page in full screen view:

  Click VIEW on the menu bar and then click Full Screen.

- To add a link button control to a Web page:

  Use the LinkButton tool in the toolbox to drag a link button control to the Web page, and then set the control's Text and PostBackUrl properties.

- To display a Web page in a browser window:

  Start the Web application either by pressing Ctrl+F5 or by clicking the Start Without Debugging option on the DEBUG menu.

- To add an image file to an application:

  Click WEBSITE on the menu bar and then click Add Existing Item. Open the appropriate folder and then click the image filename. Click the Add button.

- To add an image control to a Web page:

  Use the Image tool in the toolbox to drag an image control to the Web page, and then set the image control's ImageUrl property.

- To close a Web application:

  Click FILE on the menu bar and then click Close Solution.

- To open an existing Web application:

  Click FILE on the menu bar and then click Open Web Site. If necessary, click the File System button in the Open Web Site dialog box. Click the name of the Web site and then click the Open button. If necessary, right-click the Web page's name in the Solution Explorer window and then click View Designer.

- To reposition a control on a Web page:

  Drag the control to the new location.

Lesson A Key Terms

ASP—stands for "active server page"

Browser—a program that allows a client computer to request and view Web pages

Client computer—a computer that requests information from a Web server

Dynamic Web page—an interactive document that can accept information from the user and also retrieve information for the user

Link button control—allows the user to "jump" from one Web page to another

Static text—text that the user is not allowed to edit

Static Web page—a non-interactive document whose purpose is merely to display information to the viewer

Web pages—the documents stored on Web servers

Web server—a computer that contains special software that "serves up" Web pages in response to requests from client computers

Lesson A Review Questions

1. A computer that requests an ASP page from a Web server is called a ______________ computer.
   a. browser
   b. client
   c. requesting
   d. none of the above

2. A ______________ is a program that uses HTML to render a Web page on the computer screen.
   a. browser
   b. client
   c. server
   d. none of the above

3. An online form used to purchase a product is an example of a ______________ Web page.
   a. dynamic
   b. static

4. The first Web page in an empty Web application is automatically assigned the name ______________.
   a. Default.aps
   b. Default1.vb
   c. Default.aspx
   d. WebFormDefault.aspx

5. The HTML instructions in a Web page are processed by the ________.
   a. client computer
   b. Web server

6. The text that appears on the application's tab in the browser window is determined by the ________ property.
   a. Application object's Name
   b. Application object's Title
   c. Document object's Tab Name
   d. Document object's Title

Lesson A Exercises

INTRODUCTORY

1. Create an empty Web application named Caroline. Save the application in the VB2012\Chap12 folder. Add a new Web page named Default.aspx to the application. Change the DOCUMENT object's Title property to Caroline's Pet Shoppe. Create a Web page similar to the one shown in Figure 12-23. The static text should be centered, horizontally, on the page. Save and then start the application. Close the browser window and then close the application.

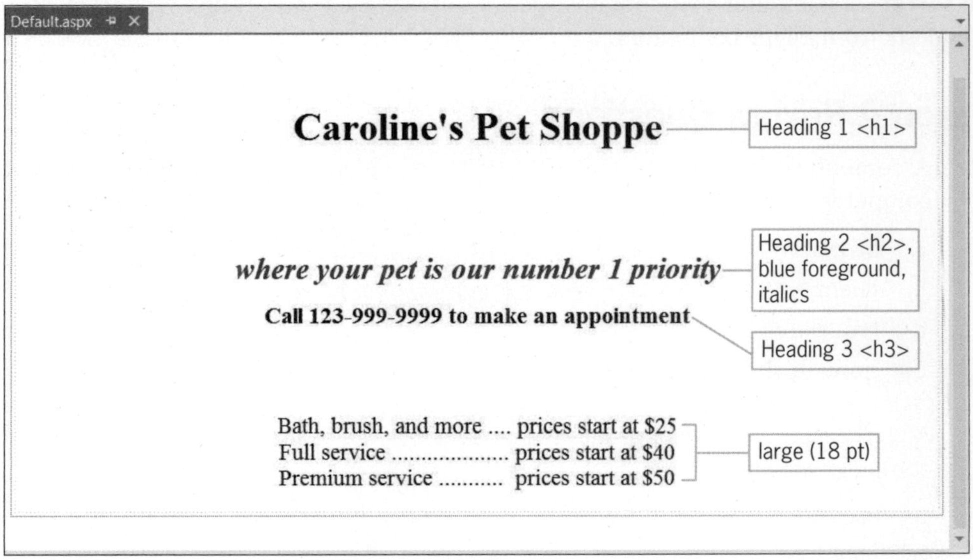

Figure 12-23 Web page for Caroline's Pet Shoppe

INTRODUCTORY

2. Create an empty Web application named AppleOrchard. Save the application in the VB2012\Chap12 folder. Add a new Web page named Default.aspx to the application. Change the DOCUMENT object's Title property to Apple Orchard Farm. Create a Web page similar to the one shown in Figure 12-24. The image on the Web page is stored in the VB2012\Chap12\Apple.png file. (The image was downloaded from the Open Clip Art Library at *http://openclipart.org*. Hint: To position the image as shown in the figure, click the image and then use the Position option on the FORMAT menu. Click the Left button in the Wrapping style section.) Save and then start the application. Close the browser window and then close the application.

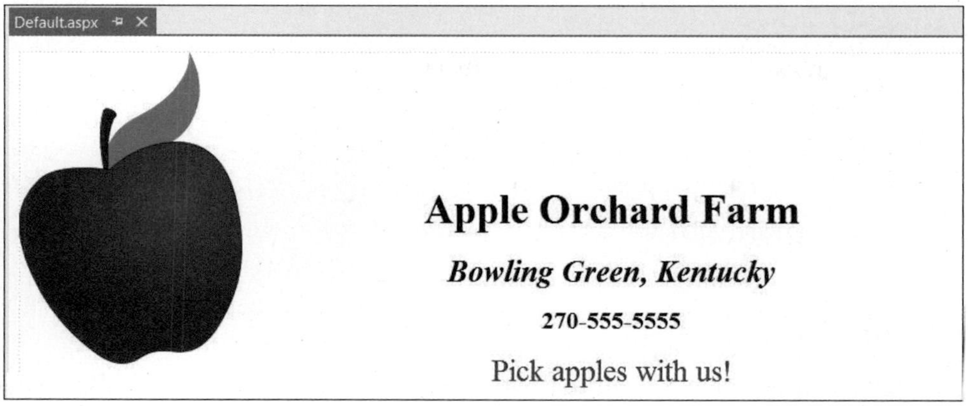

Figure 12-24 Web page for Apple Orchard Farm
OpenClipArt.org/Ana Paula

INTERMEDIATE

3. Create an empty Web application named Hearthstone. Save the application in the VB2012\Chap12 folder. Add two new Web pages named Default.aspx and Message.aspx to the application. Change each DOCUMENT object's Title property to Hearthstone Heating and Cooling. Create Web pages similar to the ones shown in Figures 12-25 and 12-26. The image on the Web page is stored in the VB2012\Chap12\Thermostat.png file. (The image was downloaded from the Open Clip Art Library at *http://openclipart.org*. Hint: To position the image as shown in the figure, click the image and then use the Position option on the FORMAT menu. Click the Left button in the Wrapping style section.) The static text and link button control on the Default.aspx page should be centered, horizontally, on the page. Save and then start the application. Close the browser window and then close the application.

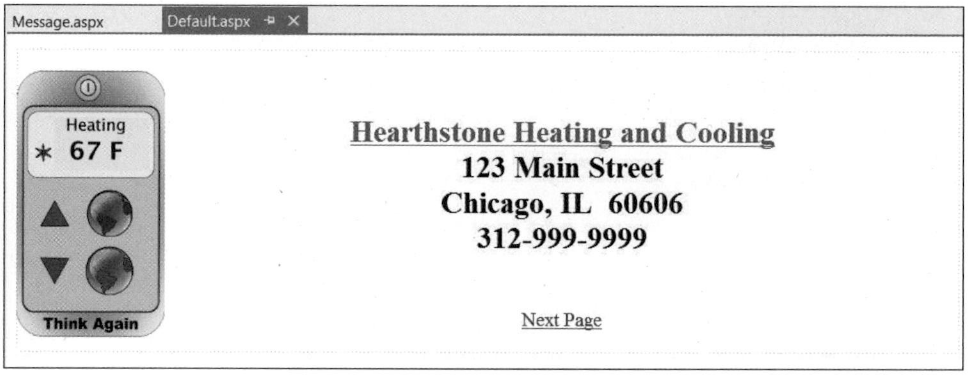

Figure 12-25 Default.aspx Web page for Hearthstone Heating and Cooling
OpenClipArt.org/motudo

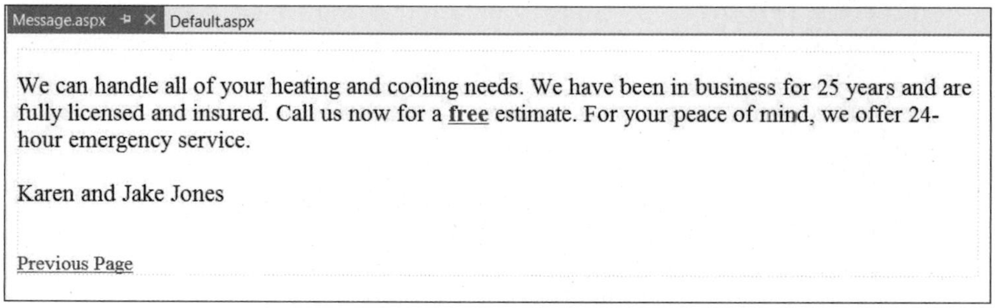

Figure 12-26 Message.aspx Web page for Hearthstone Heating and Cooling

LESSON B

After studying Lesson B, you should be able to:

- Add a text box, a label, and a button to a Web page
- Code a control on a Web page
- Use a RequiredFieldValidator control

Dynamic Web Pages

A dynamic Web page contains controls with which the user can interact. It also contains code that tells the controls how to respond to the user's actions. In this lesson, you will create a dynamic Web page that displays the number of tablespoons and teaspoons required when the user wants to either increase a recipe or decrease it. The user will need to enter the number of teaspoons required in the original recipe and whether he or she wants to double the recipe, triple it, halve it, and so on.

Before you add any text or controls to a Web page, you should plan the page's layout. Figure 12-27 shows a sketch of the Web page for the Recipe application. The Web page will contain static text and the following controls: an image, two text boxes, two labels, and a button. You will add the static text in the next set of steps.

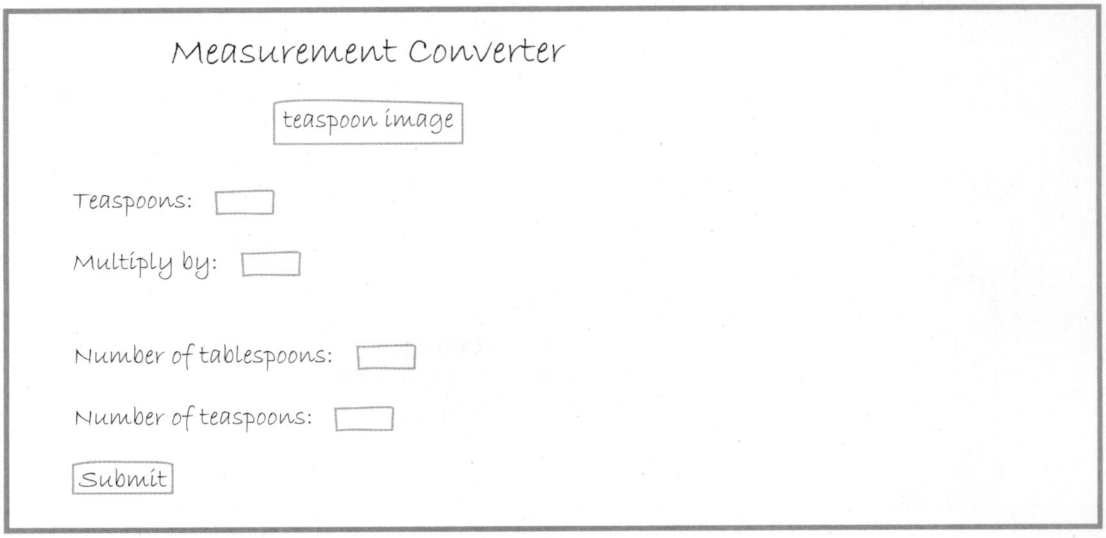

Figure 12-27 Sketch of the Recipe application's Web page

START HERE

To add the static text to the partially-completed Recipe Web application:

1. If necessary, start Visual Studio 2012 or Visual Studio Express 2012 for Web.
2. If necessary, open the Solution Explorer, Properties, and Toolbox windows.
3. Click **FILE** on the menu bar, and then click **Open Web Site**. If necessary, click the **File System** button in the Open Web Site dialog box. Click the **Recipe** folder, which is contained in the VB2012\Chap12 folder, and then click the **Open** button. If a message box appears and asks whether you want to use IIS Express or the Visual Studio Development Server, click the **Yes** button to use IIS Express.

4. If the Default.aspx Web page is not open in the Document window, right-click **Default.aspx** in the Solution Explorer window and then click **View Designer**. Position the blinking insertion point as shown in Figure 12-28. (The teaspoon image was downloaded from the Open Clip Art Library at *http://openclipart.org*.)

Figure 12-28 Partially-completed interface for the Recipe Web application
OpenClipArt.org/mazeo

5. With the insertion point positioned as shown in Figure 12-28, press **Tab** twice. Type **Teaspoons:**, press the **Spacebar** three times, and then press **Enter** twice.
6. Press **Tab** twice. Type **Multiply by:**, press the **Spacebar** twice, and then press **Enter** twice.
7. Press **Tab** twice. Type **Number of tablespoons:**, press the **Spacebar** twice, and then press **Enter** twice.
8. Press **Tab** twice. Type **Number of teaspoons:**, press the **Spacebar** four times, and then press **Enter** twice. See Figure 12-29.

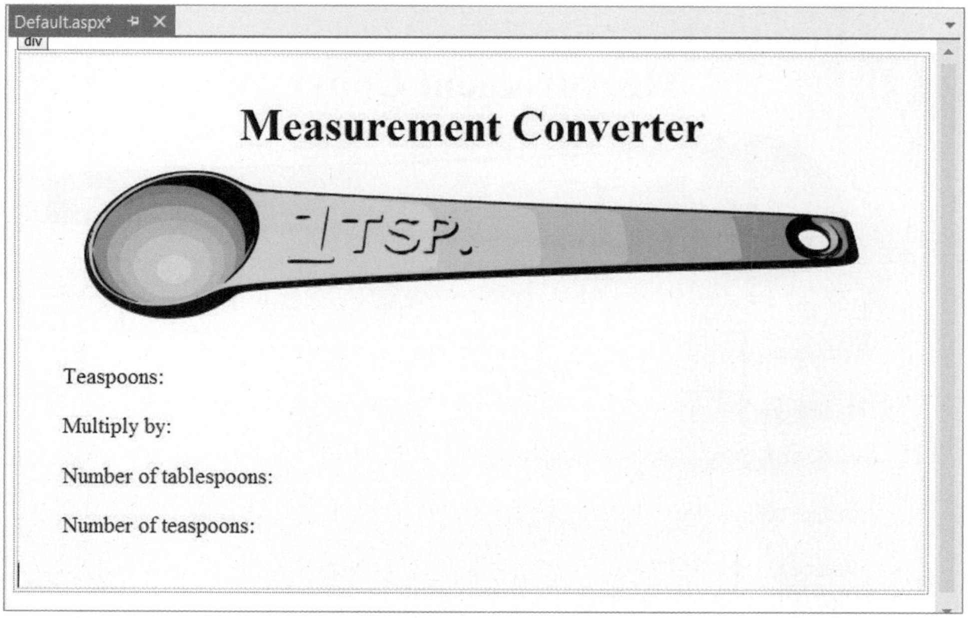

Figure 12-29 Static text added to the Web page
OpenClipArt.org/mazeo

In addition to the image control and static text, the Web page will contain two text boxes, two labels, and a button. You will add those controls next.

START HERE

To add controls to the page:

1. Drag a text box control from the toolbox to the Web page. Position the control immediately after the three spaces that follow the "Teaspoons:" text, and then release the mouse button.
2. Unlike Windows controls, Web controls have an ID property rather than a Name property. Use the Properties window to set the TextBox1 control's ID property (which appears at the top of the Properties list) to **txtOriginalTeaspoons**. Also set its Width property to **45px**. (The px stands for pixels.)
3. Drag another text box control to the Web page. Position the control immediately after the two spaces that follow the "Multiply by:" text, and then release the mouse button. Set the text box's ID and Width properties to **txtMultiplyBy** and **45px**, respectively.
4. Drag a label control to the Web page. Position the control immediately after the two spaces that follow the "Number of tablespoons:" text, and then release the mouse button. Set the control's ID property to **lblTablespoons**, and then delete the contents of its Text property. (The control's name appears in the label during design time, but it won't when the application is started.)
5. Drag another label control to the Web page. Position the control immediately after the four spaces that follow the "Number of teaspoons:" text, and then release the mouse button. Set the control's ID property to **lblTeaspoons**, and then delete the contents of its Text property.
6. Click the **blank line** that is two lines below the "Number of teaspoons:" text, and then press **Tab** twice. Drag a button control to the Web page. Position the control immediately after the insertion point in the blank line, and then release the mouse button. Set the Button1 control's ID and Text properties to **btnSubmit** and **Submit**, respectively.
7. Select the static text and all of the controls that appear below the teaspoon image, except the Submit button. See Figure 12-30.

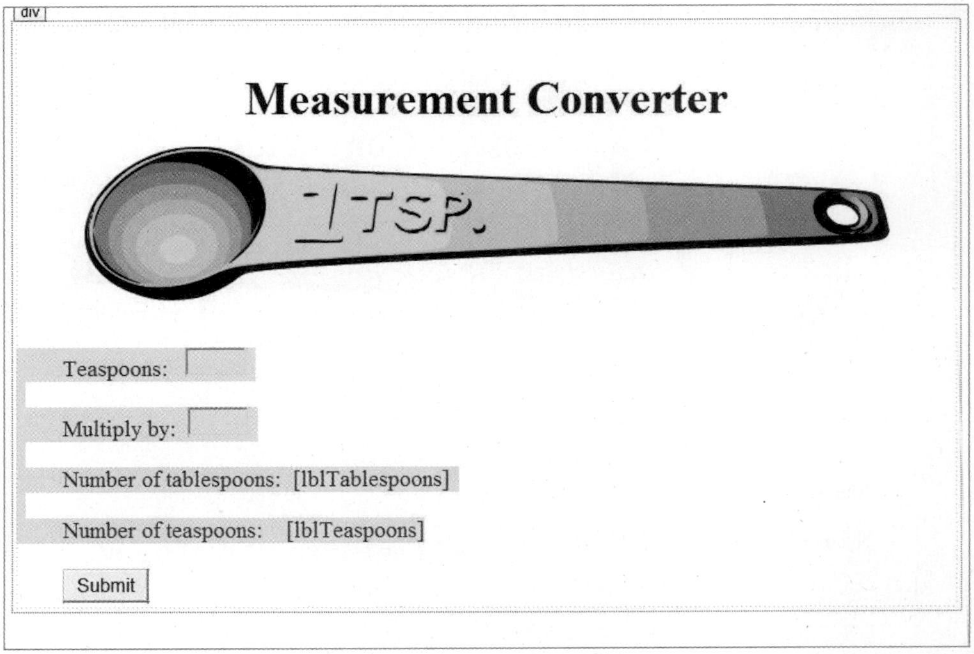

Figure 12-30 Selected text and controls
OpenClipArt.org/mazeo

8. Click the **down arrow** in the Font Size box and then click **large (18 pt)**.
9. Click the **Submit** button, and then use the Font Size box to change the button's font to **medium (14 pt)**.
10. Save the application. (If necessary, click the Save button in the dialog box.) Start the application by pressing **Ctrl+F5**. The Web page appears in a browser window. See Figure 12-31.

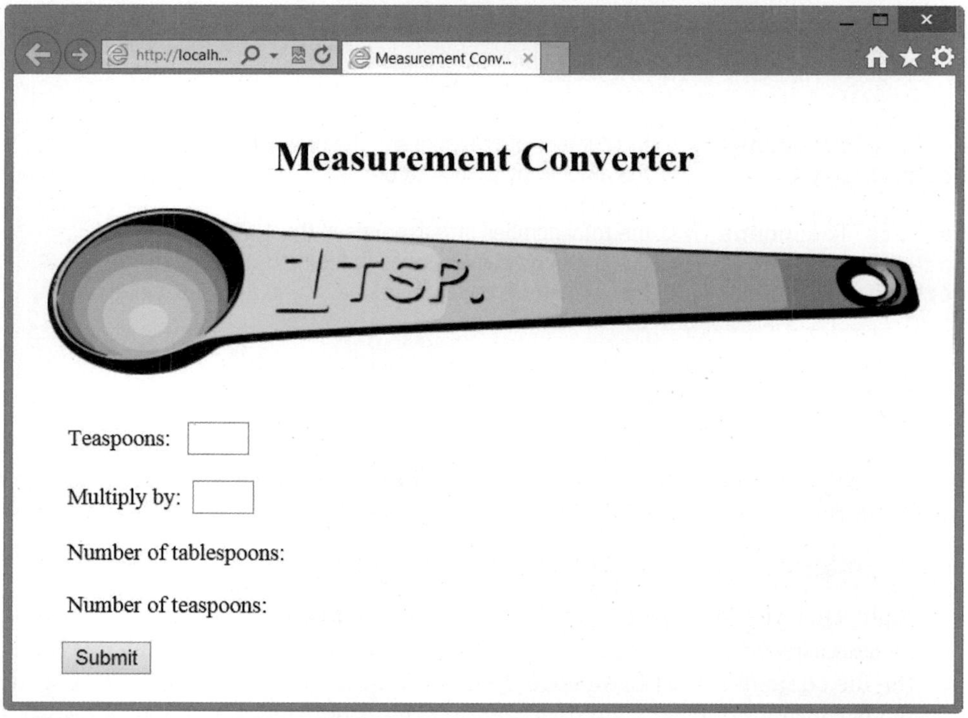

Figure 12-31 Web page displayed in a browser window
OpenClipArt.org/mazeo

11. Close the browser window. Auto-hide the Solution Explorer, Properties, and Toolbox windows.

Coding the Submit Button's Click Event Procedure

In the following set of steps, you will code the Submit button's Click event procedure so that it displays both the number of tablespoons and the number of teaspoons required when either increasing or decreasing a recipe. The procedure's pseudocode is shown in Figure 12-32 along with a list of the variables the procedure will use.

btnSubmit Click event procedure
1. store user input (the number of teaspoons in the original recipe and the amount by which the recipe should be increased or decreased) in variables
2. calculate the total number of teaspoons required in the new recipe by multiplying the number of teaspoons in the original recipe by the amount by which the original recipe should be increased or decreased
3. calculate the number of tablespoons in the new recipe by using integer division to divide the total number of teaspoons in the new recipe by 3
4. calculate the number of teaspoons remaining in the new recipe by using the Mod operator to divide the total number of teaspoons in the new recipe by 3
5. display, in label controls, the number of tablespoons in the new recipe and the number of teaspoons remaining in the new recipe

Variable names	Stores
`decOrigTeaspoons`	the number of teaspoons in the original recipe
`decMultiplyBy`	the amount by which the original recipe should be increased or decreased
`decTotalTeaspoons`	the total number of teaspoons in the new recipe
`intNewTablespoons`	the number of tablespoons in the new recipe
`decNewTeaspoons`	the number of teaspoons remaining in the new recipe

Figure 12-32 Pseudocode and variables for the btnSubmit_Click procedure

As you do when coding a control on a Windows form, you enter the code for a control on a Web page in the Code Editor window.

START HERE

To code the Submit button's Click event procedure:

1. Right-click the **Web page** and then click **View Code** on the context menu. The Default.aspx.vb window opens. Recall that the .vb extension on a filename indicates that the file contains Visual Basic code. In this case, the file is referred to as the code-behind file because it contains code that supports the Web page. Temporarily display the Solution Explorer window. If necessary, click the **Default.aspx** node. See Figure 12-33.

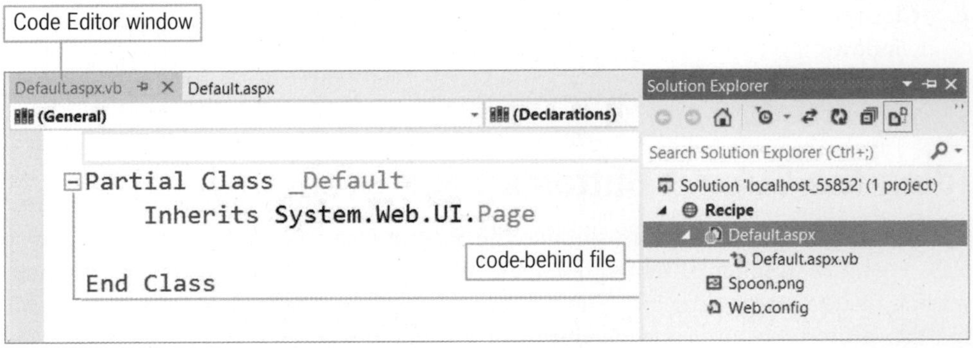

Figure 12-33 Code Editor and Solution Explorer windows

2. Enter the following comments above the Partial Class clause. Replace <your name> and <current date> with your name and the current date, respectively. Press **Enter** twice after typing the last comment.

```
' Name:           Recipe
' Purpose:        Display number of tablespoons
'                 and teaspoons
' Programmer:     <your name> on <current date>
```

3. Now, enter the following Option statements:

```
Option Explicit On
Option Strict On
Option Infer Off
```

4. Open the btnSubmit control's Click event procedure. Enter the following comments. Press **Enter** twice after typing the second comment.

```
' calculates number of tablespoons
' and teaspoons
```

5. Next, you will declare the procedure's variables. Enter the following Dim statements. Press **Enter** twice after typing the last Dim statement.

```
Dim decOrigTeaspoons As Decimal
Dim decMultiplyBy As Decimal
Dim decTotalTeaspoons As Decimal
Dim intNewTablespoons As Integer
Dim decNewTeaspoons As Decimal
```

6. The first step in the procedure's pseudocode is to store the input items in variables. Enter the following two TryParse methods. Press **Enter** twice after typing the second TryParse method.

```
Decimal.TryParse(txtOriginalTeaspoons.Text, decOrigTeaspoons)
Decimal.TryParse(txtMultiplyBy.Text, decMultiplyBy)
```

7. The second step in the pseudocode calculates the total number of teaspoons required for the new recipe. Enter the following assignment statement:

```
decTotalTeaspoons = decOrigTeaspoons * decMultiplyBy
```

8. The third step in the pseudocode calculates the number of tablespoons in the new recipe. Enter the following assignment statement. (Recall that the integer division operator requires its operands to be integers, and it returns the quotient as an integer.)

```
intNewTablespoons = Convert.ToInt32(decTotalTeaspoons) \ 3
```

9. The fourth step in the pseudocode calculates the number of teaspoons remaining in the new recipe. Type the following assignment statement and then press **Enter** twice. (Recall that the Mod operator divides its operands and then returns the remainder.)

```
decNewTeaspoons = decTotalTeaspoons Mod 3
```

10. The last step in the pseudocode displays the output in label controls. Enter the following two assignment statements:

```
lblTablespoons.Text = intNewTablespoons.ToString("N0")
lblTeaspoons.Text = decNewTeaspoons.ToString("N2")
```

Figure 12-34 shows the code entered in the btnSubmit control's Click event procedure.

```
Protected Sub btnSubmit_Click(sender As Object, e As EventArgs) Han
    ' calculates number of tablespoons
    ' and teaspoons

    Dim decOrigTeaspoons As Decimal
    Dim decMultiplyBy As Decimal
    Dim decTotalTeaspoons As Decimal
    Dim intNewTablespoons As Integer
    Dim decNewTeaspoons As Decimal

    Decimal.TryParse(txtOriginalTeaspoons.Text, decOrigTeaspoons)
    Decimal.TryParse(txtMultiplyBy.Text, decMultiplyBy)

    decTotalTeaspoons = decOrigTeaspoons * decMultiplyBy
    intNewTablespoons = Convert.ToInt32(decTotalTeaspoons) \ 3
    decNewTeaspoons = decTotalTeaspoons Mod 3

    lblTablespoons.Text = intNewTablespoons.ToString("N0")
    lblTeaspoons.Text = decNewTeaspoons.ToString("N2")

End Sub
```

Figure 12-34 btnSubmit_Click procedure

In the next set of steps, you will test the application to verify that it is working correctly.

START HERE

To test the Recipe application:

1. Save the application, and then start it by pressing **Ctrl+F5**. Your browser requests the Default.aspx page from the server. The server locates the page and then sends the appropriate HTML instructions to your browser for rendering on the screen.
2. First, we'll triple a recipe that requires 1 and 1/4 (or .25) teaspoons of some ingredient. Type **1.25** and **3** in the Teaspoons and Multiply by boxes, respectively. Click the **Submit** button; doing this submits your entry to the server, along with a request for additional services. (If the message "Do you want AutoComplete to remember web form entries?" appears, click the No button.) The server processes the code contained in the button's Click event procedure and then sends the appropriate HTML to the browser for rendering on the screen. As Figure 12-35 indicates, the new recipe requires 1 tablespoon and 3/4 (0.75) teaspoon of the ingredient.

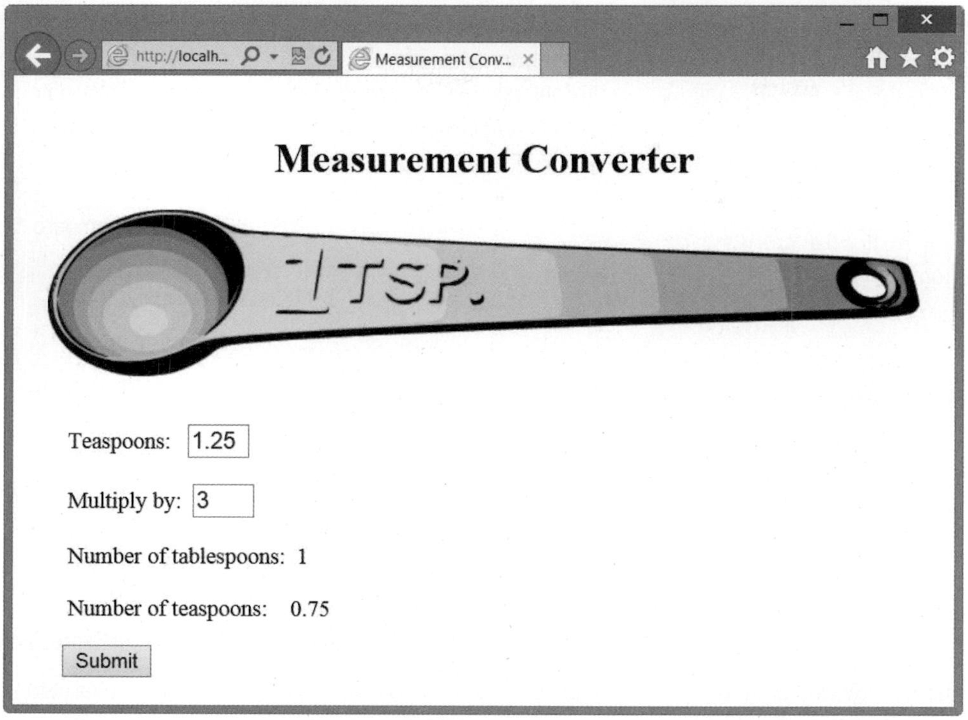

Figure 12-35 Result of clicking the Submit button
OpenClipArt.org/mazeo

3. Now we'll halve a recipe that requires 1 teaspoon of some ingredient. Change the entries in the Teaspoons and Multiply by boxes to **1** and **.5**, respectively. Click the **Submit** button. The Web page indicates that the new recipe requires 1/2 (0.50) teaspoon of the ingredient.
4. Close the browser window and then close the Code Editor window.

Validating User Input

The Validation section of the toolbox provides several tools for validating user input. The tools are referred to as **validator tools**. The name, purpose, and important properties of each validator tool are listed in Figure 12-36. In the Recipe application, you will use a RequiredFieldValidator control to verify that the user entered the two input items.

Name	Purpose	Properties
CompareValidator	compare an entry with a constant value or the property stored in a control	ControlToCompare ControlToValidate ErrorMessage Operator Type ValueToCompare
CustomValidator	verify that an entry passes the specified validation logic	ClientValidationFunction ControlToValidate ErrorMessage
RangeValidator	verify that an entry is within the specified minimum and maximum values	ControlToValidate ErrorMessage MaximumValue MinimumValue Type
RegularExpressionValidator	verify that an entry matches a specific pattern	ControlToValidate ErrorMessage ValidationExpression
RequiredFieldValidator	verify that a control contains data	ControlToValidate ErrorMessage
ValidationSummary	display all of the validation error messages in a single location on a Web page	DisplayMode HeaderText

Figure 12-36 Validator tools

START HERE

To verify that the user entered the two input items:

1. Click **to the immediate right of the txtOriginalTeaspoons control** and then press the **Spacebar** three times.
2. Permanently display the Toolbox window. If necessary, expand the Validation section. Click the **RequiredFieldValidator** tool and then drag your mouse pointer to the Web page. Position your mouse pointer to the right of the txtOriginalTeaspoons control and then release the mouse button. The RequiredFieldValidator1 control appears on the Web page.
3. Temporarily display the Properties window. Set the following properties for the RequiredFieldValidator1 control:

   ControlToValidate: **txtOriginalTeaspoons**
   ErrorMessage: **Required entry**
   ForeColor: choose a red hexagon

4. Click **to the immediate right of the txtMultiplyBy control** and then press the **Spacebar** three times. Click the **RequiredFieldValidator** tool and then drag your mouse pointer to the Web page, positioning it to the right of the txtMultiplyBy control. Release the mouse button. Set the following properties for the RequiredFieldValidator2 control:

   ControlToValidate: **txtMultiplyBy**
   ErrorMessage: **Required entry**
   ForeColor: choose a red hexagon

5. Click an **empty area** of the Web page, and then auto-hide the Toolbox window. Save the application.
6. Start the application by pressing **Ctrl+F5**. Click the **Submit** button without entering any values. (If a Web page opens and displays the "Server Error in '/' Application." message, refer to the Important note that follows Figure 12-37.) Each RequiredFieldValidator control displays the "Required entry" message, as shown in Figure 12-37.

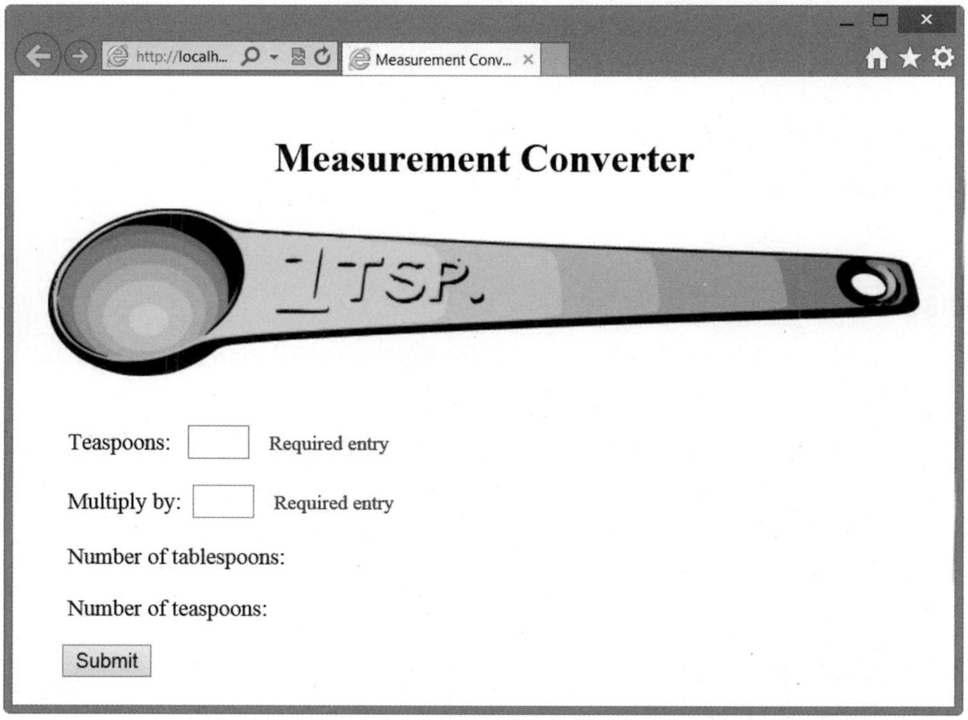

Figure 12-37 Result of clicking the Submit button when both text boxes are empty
OpenClipArt.org/mazeo

Important note: At the time of this writing, there was an unresolved issue with some of the validator controls. Until this problem is fixed, you can use the following workaround: First, close the browser window. Next, right-click Web.config in the Solution Explorer window and then click Open. Change both occurrences of "4.5" to "4.0", and then save the application. Close the Web.config window and then repeat Step 6.

7. Type **3** in the Teaspoons box and then click the **Submit** button. This time, the "Required entry" message appears only next to the Multiply by text box.
8. Type **2** in the Multiply by box and then click the **Submit** button. The Web page indicates that the new recipe requires 2 tablespoons of the ingredient.
9. Close the browser window and then close the application.

YOU DO IT 2!

Create an empty Web application named YouDoIt 2. Save the application in the VB2012\Chap12 folder. Add a Web page named Default.aspx to the application. The Web page should contain a text box, a label, and a button. When the user clicks the button, the application should multiply the number entered in the text box by 2 and then display the result in the label. Include a RequiredFieldValidator control on the Web page. Save the application and then start and test it. Close the application.

Lesson B Summary

- To code a control on a Web page:

  Enter the code in the Code Editor window.

- To validate user input on a Web page:

  Use one or more of the validator tools contained in the Validation section of the toolbox. The controls are summarized in Figure 12-36.

Lesson B Key Term

Validator tools—the tools contained in the Validation section of the toolbox; used to validate user input on a Web page

Lesson B Review Questions

1. In code, you refer to a control on a Web page using the control's ________________ property.
   a. Caption
   b. ID
   c. Name
   d. Text

2. The Visual Basic code in a Web page is processed by the ________________.
   a. client computer
   b. Web server

3. You can use a ________________ control to verify that a control on a Web page contains data.
   a. RequiredFieldValidator
   b. RequiredField
   c. RequiredValidator
   d. none of the above

4. You can use a ________________ control to verify that an entry on a Web page is within a minimum and maximum value.
   a. MinMaxValidation
   b. MaxMinValidation
   c. EntryValidator
   d. RangeValidator

Lesson B Exercises

INTRODUCTORY

1. Create an empty Web application named SquareArea. Save the application in the VB2012\Chap12 folder.
   a. Add a new Web page named Default.aspx to the application. Change the DOCUMENT object's Title property to Square Area.

b. Use Figure 12-38 as a guide when designing the Web page. The square image is contained in the VB2012\Chap12\Square.png file. (The image was downloaded from the Open Clip Art Library at *http://openclipart.org*. Hint: To position the image as shown in the figure, click the image and then use the Position option on the FORMAT menu. Click the Left button in the Wrapping style section.) Set the CompareValidator control's ControlToValidate, Operator, Type, and ValueToCompare properties to txtSide, Greater Than, Double, and 0, respectively. Also set the control's ErrorMessage and ForeColor properties appropriately.

c. Open the Code Editor window. Use comments to document the application's name and purpose, as well as your name and the current date. Also enter the appropriate Option statements. Code the Calculate Area button's Click event procedure. Display the area with two decimal places.

d. Save and then start the application. (If necessary, refer to the Important note that appears after Figure 12-37 in the lesson.) Test the application using positive and negative numbers, as well as the number 0. Close the browser window. Close the Code Editor window and then close the application.

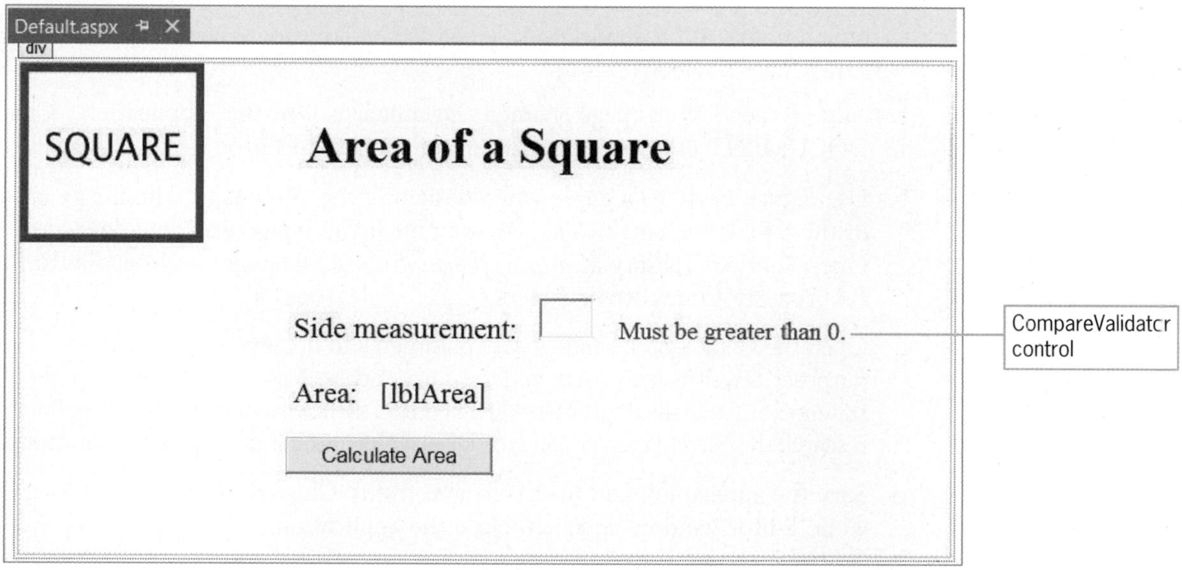

Figure 12-38 Web page for Exercise 1

INTRODUCTORY

2. Create an empty Web application named Multiplication. Save the application in the VB2012\Chap12 folder.

   a. Add a new Web page named Default.aspx to the application. Change the DOCUMENT object's Title property to Multiplication Calculator.

   b. Use Figure 12-39 as a guide when designing the Web page. The calculator image is contained in the VB2012\Chap12\Calculator.png file. (The image was downloaded from the Open Clip Art Library at *http://openclipart.org*.)

   c. Add two RequiredFieldValidator controls to the Web page. The controls should verify that both text boxes contain data. Display appropriate messages.

   d. Open the Code Editor window. Use comments to document the application's name and purpose, as well as your name and the current date. Also enter the appropriate Option statements. Code the Calculate button's Click event procedure. Display the product with two decimal places.

   e. Save the application and then start it. (If necessary, refer to the Important note that appears after Figure 12-37 in the lesson.) Test the application. Close the browser window. Close the Code Editor window and then close the application.

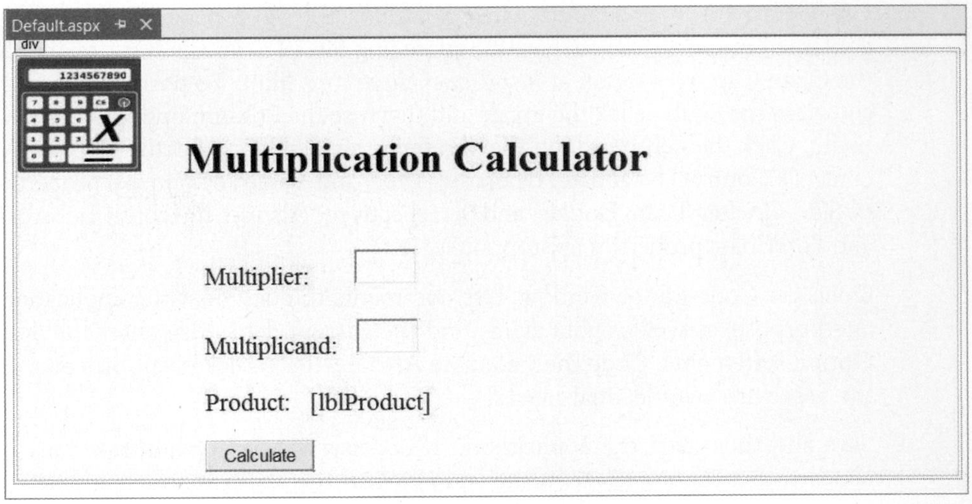

Figure 12-39 Web page for Exercise 2
OpenClipArt.org/gsagri04

INTRODUCTORY

3. Create an empty Web application named DollarToEuro. Save the application in the VB2012\Chap12 folder.

   a. Add a new Web page named Default.aspx to the application. Change the DOCUMENT object's Title property to Dollars to Euros.

   b. Use Figure 12-40 as a guide when designing the Web page. The image is contained in the VB2012\Chap12\ClickHere.png file. (The image was downloaded from the Open Clip Art Library at *http://openclipart.org*.) Change the ImageButton control's ID property to imgBtnClickHere.

   c. Open the Code Editor window. Use comments to document the application's name and purpose, as well as your name and the current date. Also enter the appropriate Option statements. Code the imgBtnClickHere control's Click event procedure. Use the Internet to research the current conversion rate. Display the number of euros with four decimal places.

   d. Save the application and then start and test it. Close the browser window. Close the Code Editor window and then close the application.

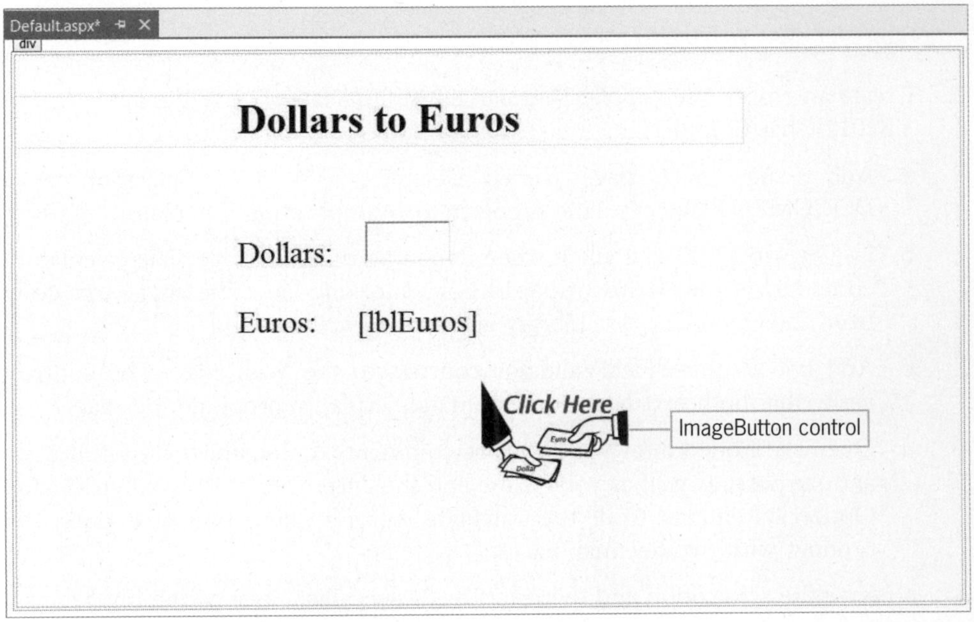

Figure 12-40 Web page for Exercise 3
OpenClipArt.org/Onsemeliot

4. Create an empty Web application named ZipCode. Save the application in the VB2012\Chap12 folder. INTERMEDIATE

   a. Add a new Web page named Default.aspx to the application. Change the DOCUMENT object's Title property to ZIP Code Verifier.

   b. Use Figure 12-41 as a guide when designing the Web page. Use labels for the static text. Also, use the Segoe UI font for the static text and controls. Use a RequiredFieldValidator control to verify that the text box is not empty. Use a RegularExpressionValidator control to verify that the ZIP code is in the appropriate format.

   c. Save and then start the application. (If necessary, refer to the Important note that appears after Figure 12-37 in the lesson.) Test the application by clicking the text box and then pressing Enter. The RequiredFieldValidator control should display the "Please enter a ZIP code." message. Now, test it using the following ZIP codes: 606123, 60612, 60611-3, and 60611-3456. The RegularExpressionValidator control should display the "Incorrect format" message for the first and third ZIP codes. Close the browser window. Close the Code Editor window and then close the application.

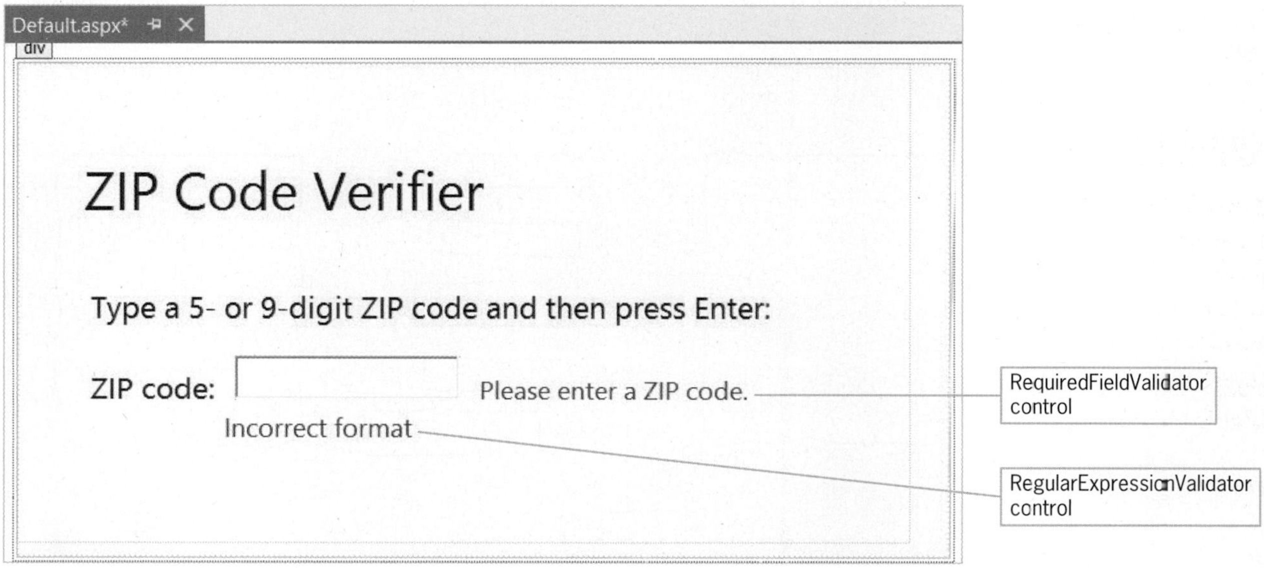

Figure 12-41 Web page for Exercise 4

5. Create an empty Web application named Temperature. Save the application in the VB2012\Chap12 folder. Add a new Web page named Default.aspx to the application. Change the DOCUMENT object's Title property to Temperature Converter. The Web page should allow the user to enter a temperature in degrees Fahrenheit. When the user clicks a button on the Web page, the button's Click event procedure should display the temperature converted to Celsius. Save and then start and test the application. Close the browser window. Close the Code Editor window and then close the application. INTERMEDIATE

6. Create an empty Web application named Measurement. Save the application in the VB2012\Chap12 folder. Add a new Web page named Default.aspx to the application. Change the DOCUMENT object's Title property to Inches to Centimeters. The Web page should allow the user to enter the number of inches. When the user clicks a button on the Web page, the button's Click event procedure should display the number of inches converted to centimeters. Save and then start and test the application. Close the browser window. Close the Code Editor window and then close the application. INTERMEDIATE

LESSON C

After studying Lesson C, you should be able to:

- Make changes to the Web page in Source view
- Create columns using the <div> tag
- Utilize an ASP table in a Web page
- Add a calendar to a Web page
- Add a drop-down list box to a Web page
- Create a new line using the <br /> tag

Creating the DJ Tom Application

Recall that your task is to create a Web application for DJ (disc jockey) Tom. The application's Web page should allow the user to enter the names of the bride and groom, the wedding date, an e-mail address, and the name of the first song to be danced by the newly married couple. The Web page should provide a Submit button that displays a message on the page. The message should contain the input items. A sketch of the Web page is shown in Figure 12-42.

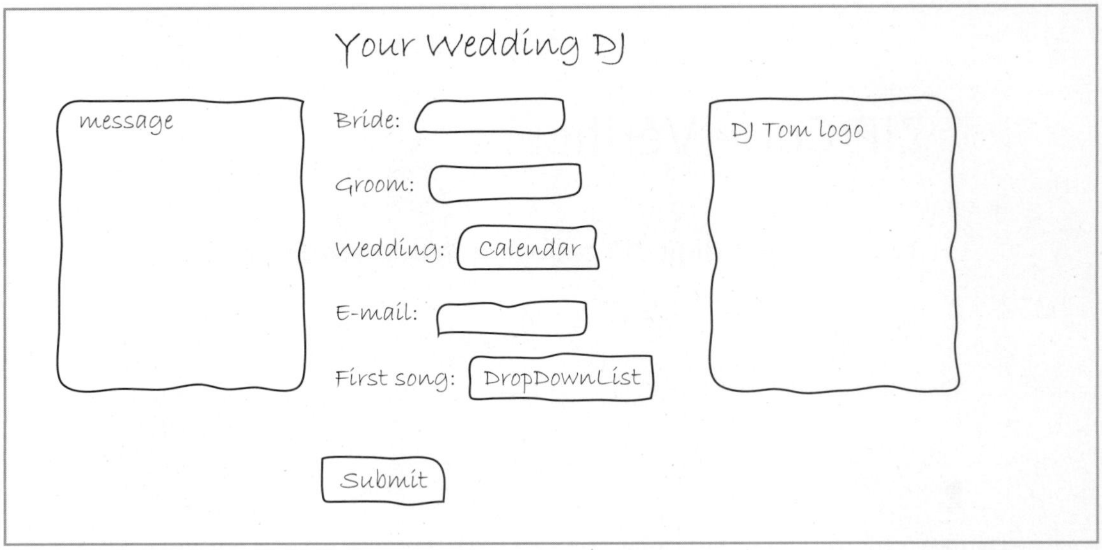

Figure 12-42 Sketch of the DJ Tom application's Web page

START HERE

To create the DJ Tom Web application:

1. If necessary, start Visual Studio 2012 or Visual Studio Express 2012 for Web.
2. If necessary, auto-hide the Solution Explorer, Properties, and Toolbox windows.
3. Create an empty Web application named **DJTom**. Save the application in the VB2012\Chap12 folder.
4. Use the Add New Item option on the WEBSITE menu to add a Web page named Default.aspx to the application. Change the DOCUMENT object's Title property to **DJ Tom**.

First, you will set the font for the text in the Web page. You can do this by switching to Source view and then setting one of the style attribute's properties in the <body> tag. More specifically, you set the style attribute's **font-family property**.

START HERE

To set the font for the text, and then continue creating the Web page:

1. Click the **Source** button at the bottom of the IDE and then locate the <body> tag.
2. You can use the style attribute's font-family property to specify one or more fonts to use for the Web page's text. For example, the `style="font-family:Segoe UI, Arial, Sans-Serif"` attribute tells the browser to use the Segoe UI font when displaying text. However, if the Segoe UI font is not available, the browser should use the Arial font. If neither of those two fonts is available, the browser should use an available sans serif font. Modify the <body> tag as shown in Figure 12-43. The modifications are shaded in the figure.

```
</head>
<body style="font-family:'Segoe UI', Arial, sans-serif">
    <form id="form1" runat="server">
```

Figure 12-43 Modified <body> tag

3. Click the **Design** tab at the bottom of the IDE. If necessary, click **inside the rectangle** that appears below the div tag at the top of the Document window. (If the div tag does not appear on the Web page, click the <div> button at the bottom of the IDE.) Type **Your Wedding DJ** and press **Enter**.
4. If necessary, use the VIEW menu to display the Formatting toolbar. Select (highlight) the **Your Wedding DJ** text.
5. Click the **down arrow** in the Block Format box and then click **Heading 1 <h1>** in the list. Click the **down arrow** on the Alignment button and then click **Justify Center**. Click **an empty area** of the Web page to deselect the text.

Creating a Columnar Layout

The content in many Web pages is laid out in a columnar format, similar to a newspaper. The sketch of DJ Tom's Web page (shown earlier in Figure 12-42) indicates that the page contains three columns. The first column displays a message, the second column displays the data entry controls, and the third column displays DJ Tom's logo. You can divide a Web page into columns using the **<div> tag**.

START HERE

To divide DJ Tom's Web page into three columns:

1. Click the **Source** tab and then click the **blank line** below the `<br />` tag. (You will learn about the `<br />` tag later in this lesson.) If necessary, press **Tab** to align the insertion point with the tag.
2. The first column, which you will name "MessageColumn", will occupy 30% of the page. You will change the column's background color to purple and then specify that the column should appear on the left side of the page. Type **<div>**. The Source view editor automatically enters the closing </div> tag for you. Click **immediately after the letter v** in the <div> tag and then press the **Spacebar**. Complete the tag by entering the text shaded in Figure 12-44, and then position the insertion point as shown in the figure.

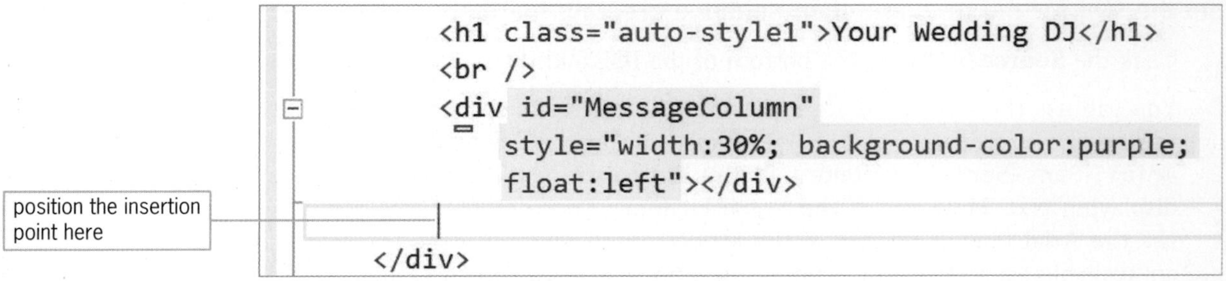
<h1 class="auto-style1">Your Wedding DJ</h1>

<div id="MessageColumn"
style="width:30%; background-color:purple;
float:left"></div>
</div>
position the insertion point here

Figure 12-44 Completed <div> tag for the first column

3. Now you will use another <div> tag to create the second column. This column will occupy 39% of the Web page and appear next to the first column. Type the following <div> tag:

   <div id="ContentColumn" style="width:39%; float:left"></div>

4. Click **immediately after the </div> tag** from Step 3 and then press **Enter**. The third column will occupy 30% of the Web page and appear on the right side of the page. Type the following <div> tag:

   <div id="LogoColumn" style="width:30%; float:right"></div>

5. Click the **Design** tab. Three columns appear in the Web page. See Figure 12-45.

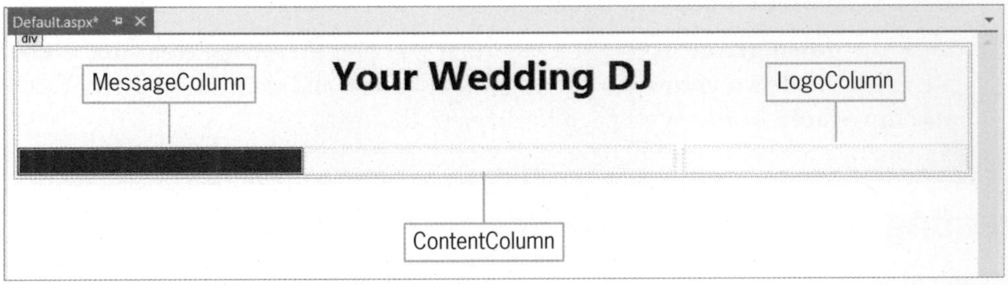
Default.aspx*
div
MessageColumn
Your Wedding DJ
LogoColumn
ContentColumn

Figure 12-45 Web page showing the three columns

6. Permanently display the Toolbox and Properties windows. Drag a label control into the MessageColumn. Set the control's ID and ForeColor properties to **lblMsg** and **White**, respectively. Also remove the contents of its Text property.

7. Before dragging an image control to the Web page, you will add the DJ Tom image file to the application. Click **WEBSITE** on the menu bar and then click **Add Existing Item**. Open the VB2012\Chap12 folder. Click the **down arrow** in the box that controls the file types and then click **All Files (*.*)** in the list. Click **DJ.png** in the list of filenames and then click the **Add** button.

8. Now drag an image control into the LogoColumn. Set the control's ImageUrl property to **DJ.png** and then click an **empty area** on the Web page to deselect the control.

Using an ASP Table

The Table tool in the Standard section of the toolbox creates an **ASP table control**. The control displays information in a row and column format, similar to a spreadsheet, and is often used to align the information on a Web page. The ASP table control you will use in DJ Tom's Web page will have six rows and two columns. The intersection of a row and a column in a table is called a **cell**.

START HERE

To add an ASP table to the Web page:

1. Click the **Table** tool located in the Standard section of the toolbox. Drag a table control into the ContentColumn and then release the mouse button. (The HTML section of the toolbox also has a Table tool. Be sure to use the Table tool listed in the Standard section.) See Figure 12-46.

Figure 12-46 ASP table control added to the ContentColumn

2. Set the table control's CellSpacing property, which controls the spacing between the table cells, to **40**. Set the control's HorizontalAlign property to **Center**.
3. Now you will begin defining the table rows. Click **Rows** in the Properties window and then click the **...** (ellipsis) button in the Settings box. The TableRow Collection Editor dialog box opens. Click the **Add** button and then click **(ID)** in the list of TableRow properties. Type **tblRow1** and press **Enter**. See Figure 12-47.

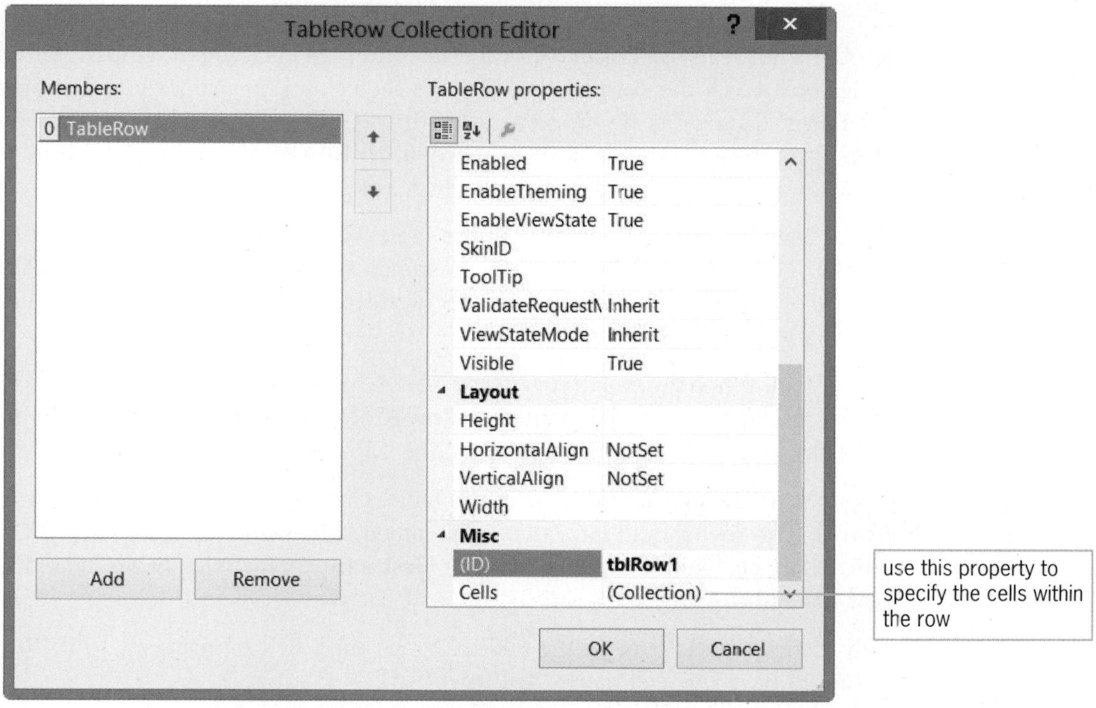

Figure 12-47 TableRow Collection Editor dialog box

4. The row will have two cells: one will contain the text "Bride:" and the other will contain a text box for entering the bride's name. Click **Cells** in the list of TableRow properties and then click the **...** (ellipsis) button in the Settings box. The TableCell Collection Editor dialog box opens.

5. Click the **Add** button. Change the cell's Text property to **Bride:** and press **Enter**. Change its ID property to **tblRow1Col1** and press **Enter**. See Figure 12-48.

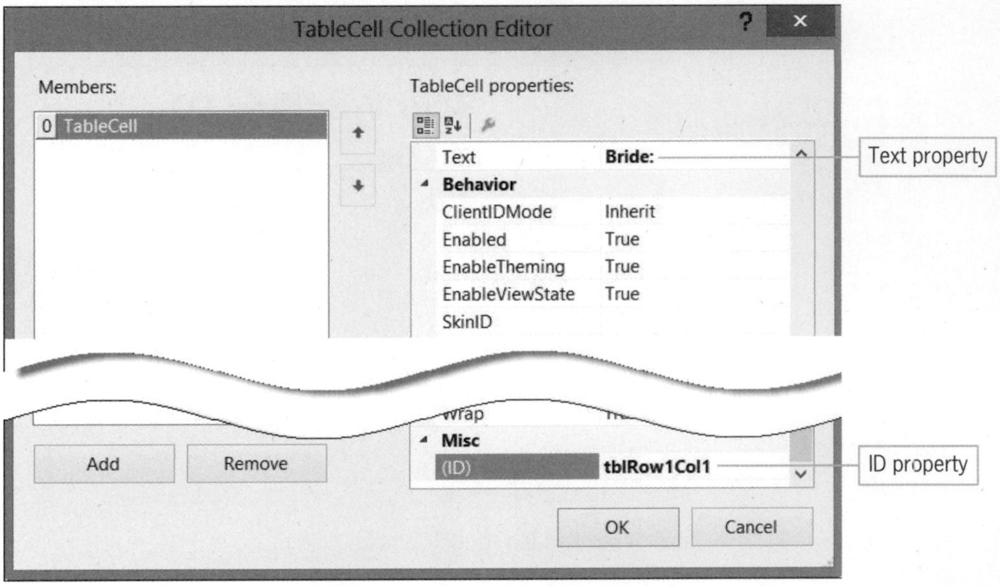

Figure 12-48 TableCell Collection Editor dialog box

6. Click the **Add** button again. Change the cell's ID property to **tblRow1Col2** and press **Enter**. Click the **OK** button. The TableCell Collection Editor dialog box closes and you are returned to the TableRow Collection Editor dialog box.

7. Now you will define the second row in the table. Click the **Add** button in the TableRow Collection Editor dialog box. Set the row's ID property to **tblRow2** and press **Enter**.

8. Click **Cells** in the list of TableRow properties and then click the **...** (ellipsis) button in the Settings box. Click the **Add** button. Change the cell's Text property to **Groom:** and press **Enter**. Change its ID property to **tblRow2Col1** and press **Enter**. Click the **Add** button again. Change the cell's ID property to **tblRow2Col2** and press **Enter**. Click the **OK** button to close the TableCell Collection Editor dialog box.

9. On your own, define the third row in the table. Change the row's ID property to **tblRow3**. The row should have two cells named **tblRow3Col1** and **tblRow3Col2**. The tblRow3Col1 cell should contain the text **Wedding:**. Close the TableCell Collection Editor dialog box.

10. On your own, define the fourth row in the table. Change the row's ID property to **tblRow4**. The row should have two cells named **tblRow4Col1** and **tblRow4Col2**. The tblRow4Col1 cell should contain the text **E-mail:**. Close the TableCell Collection Editor dialog box.

11. On your own, define the fifth row in the table. Change the row's ID property to **tblRow5**. The row should have two cells named **tblRow5Col1** and **tblRow5Col2**. The tblRow5Col1 cell should contain the text **First song:**. Close the TableCell Collection Editor dialog box.

12. Finally, define the last row in the table. Change the row's ID property to **tblRow6**. The row should have one cell named **tblRow6Col1**.

13. Click the **OK** button to close the TableCell Collection Editor dialog box, and then click the **OK** button to close the TableRow Collection Editor dialog box.

14. Auto-hide the Toolbox and Properties windows and then save the application.

Figure 12-49 shows the table on the Web page.

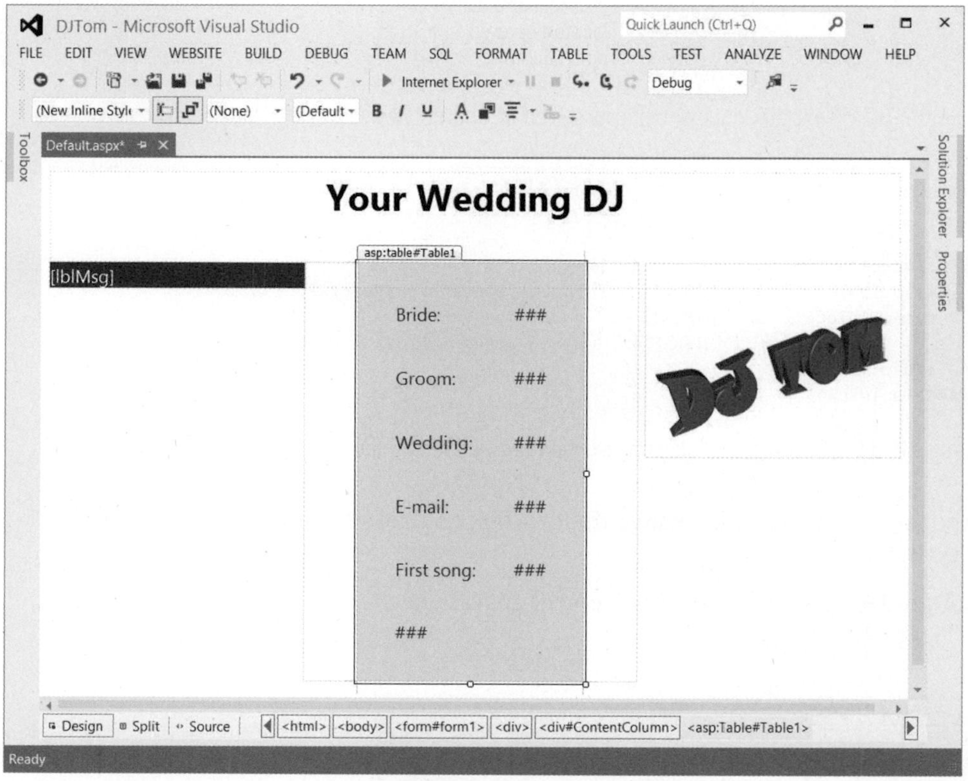

Figure 12-49 Table containing six rows and two columns

Dragging Controls in Source View

In the next set of steps, you will open the Web page in Source view and then drag the controls to the appropriate cells in the table.

To drag controls to the table in Source view:

START HERE

1. Click the **Your Wedding DJ** text to deselect the table control and then click the **Source** tab at the bottom of the IDE.

2. Permanently display the Toolbox window. First, you will drag a text box into the cell located next to the Bride: text. That cell is located in the second column of the first row in the table. Locate the line that contains the opening and closing tags for the tblRow1Col2 cell. The line says `<asp:TableCell ID="tblRow1Col2" runat="server"></asp:TableCell>`. Click **immediately before the cell's closing tag** (which says `</asp:TableCell>`) and then press **Enter**. Click the **TextBox** tool in the toolbox. Press and hold down the left mouse button as you drag your mouse pointer to the location shown in Figure 12-50.

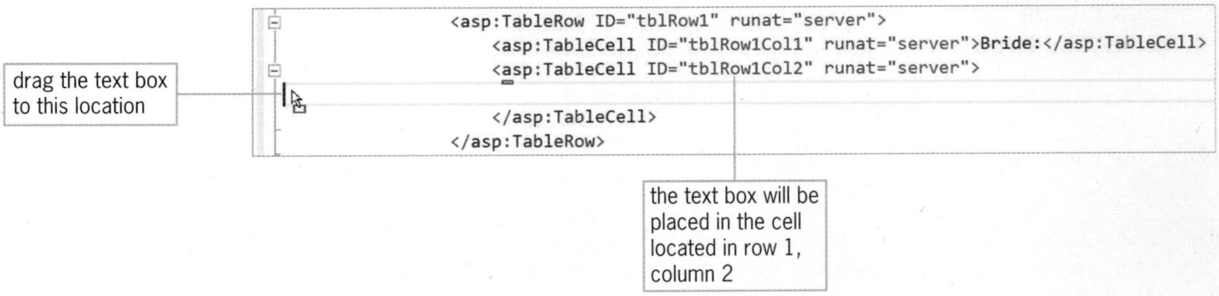
<asp:TableRow ID="tblRow1" runat="server">
<asp:TableCell ID="tblRow1Col1" runat="server">Bride:</asp:TableCell>
<asp:TableCell ID="tblRow1Col2" runat="server">
</asp:TableCell>
</asp:TableRow>
drag the text box to this location
the text box will be placed in the cell located in row 1, column 2

Figure 12-50 Text box control being dragged in Source view

3. Release the mouse button. See Figure 12-51.

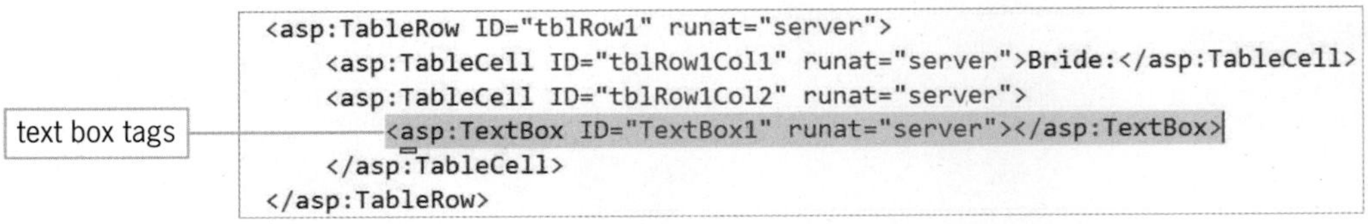
<asp:TableRow ID="tblRow1" runat="server">
<asp:TableCell ID="tblRow1Col1" runat="server">Bride:</asp:TableCell>
<asp:TableCell ID="tblRow1Col2" runat="server">
<asp:TextBox ID="TextBox1" runat="server"></asp:TextBox>
</asp:TableCell>
</asp:TableRow>
text box tags

Figure 12-51 Opening and closing text box tags added to the table instructions

4. In the <asp:TextBox> tag, change the text box control's ID property from "TextBox1" to **"txtBride"**.

5. Click the **Design** tab. A text box control appears in the second cell in row 1. See Figure 12-52.

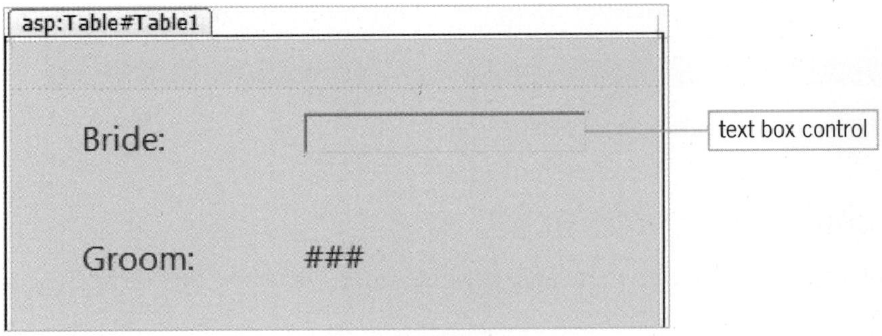
asp:Table#Table1
Bride:
Groom:
###
text box control

Figure 12-52 Text box control shown in the table

6. Click the **Your Wedding DJ** text to deselect the table control and then click the **Source** tab.

7. Now you will place a text box in the cell located in the second row, second column in the table. Locate the line that contains the opening and closing tags for the tblRow2Col2 cell. The line says `<asp:TableCell ID="tblRow2Col2" runat="server"></asp:TableCell>`. Click **immediately before the cell's closing tag** and then press **Enter**. Drag a text box control to the blank line above the closing tag and then release the mouse button. Change the text box's ID property to **"txtGroom"**.

8. Next, you will add a calendar control to the cell located in the second column of the table's third row. Locate the line that contains the opening and closing tags for the tblRow3Col2 cell. Click **immediately before the cell's closing tag** and then press **Enter**. Click the **Calendar** tool in the toolbox. Drag a calendar control to the blank line above the closing tag and then release the mouse button. Change the calendar's ID property to **"calWedding"**.

9. Now you will add a text box to the cell located in the second column of the fourth row. Locate the line that contains the opening and closing tags for the tblRow4Col2 cell. Click **immediately before the cell's closing tag** and then press **Enter**. Drag a text box control to the blank line above the closing tag and then release the mouse button. Change the text box's ID property to **"txtEmail"**.

10. Next, you will place a drop-down list control in the cell located in the second column of the fifth row. Locate the line that contains the opening and closing tags for the tblRow5Col2 cell. Click **immediately before the cell's closing tag** and then press **Enter**. Click the **DropDownList** tool in the toolbox. Drag a drop-down list control to the blank line above the closing tag and then release the mouse button. Change the drop-down list's ID property to **"ddlSongs"**.

11. Finally, you will add a button to the last row in the table. Locate the line that contains the opening and closing tags for the tblRow6Col1 cell. Click **immediately before the cell's closing tag** and then press **Enter**. Drag a button control to the blank line above the closing tag and then release the mouse button. Change the button's ID property to **"btnSubmit"** and change its Text property to **"Submit"**.

12. Save the application. Auto-hide the toolbox and then click the **Design** tab. Click the **Your Wedding DJ** text to deselect the table control.

Figure 12-53 shows the controls added to the table. (Your calendar may show a different month and year.)

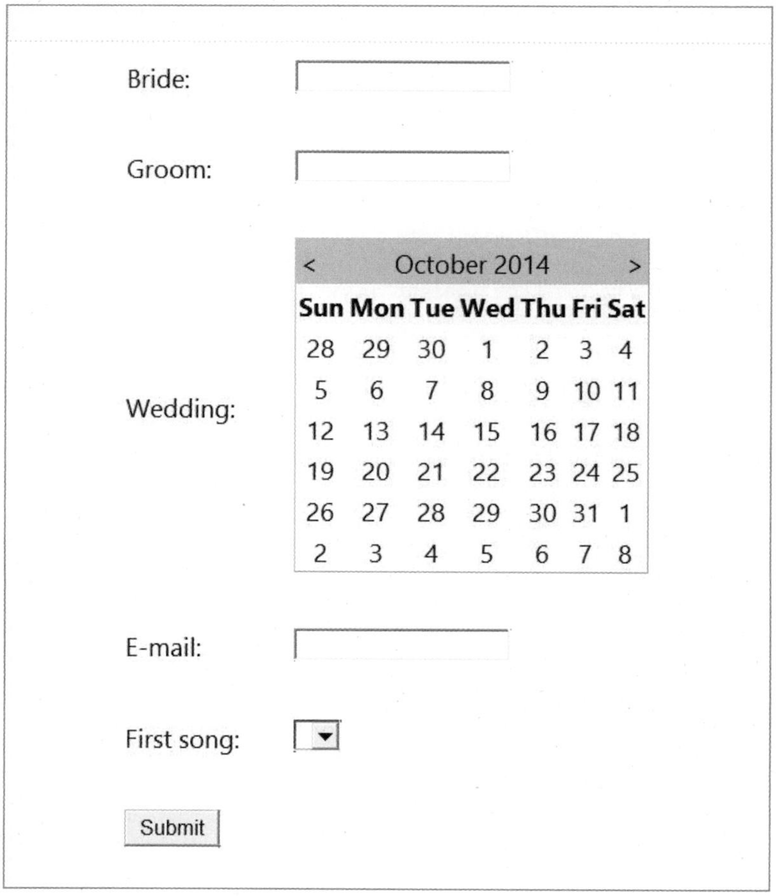

Figure 12-53 Controls added to the table

Adding Items to a DropDownList Control

Currently, the drop-down list control on DJ Tom's Web page does not contain any items. You add items to a drop-down list control using the **<asp:ListItem> tag**. In the next set of steps, you will add the following four song titles to the control: From This Moment On, At Last, Because You Loved Me, and The Way You Look Tonight.

To add items to the drop-down list control:

START HERE

1. Click the **Source tab**. Locate the line that contains the opening and closing tags for the ddlSongs control. The line says `<asp:DropDownList ID="ddlSongs" runat="server">`. Click **immediately before the control's closing tab** and then press **Enter**.
2. Type **<asp:ListItem Text="From This Moment On">**. When you type the > symbol, the Source view editor automatically enters the closing </asp:ListItem> tag for you. See Figure 12-54.

```
<asp:DropDownList ID="ddlSongs" runat="server">
    <asp:ListItem Text="From This Moment On"></asp:ListItem>
</asp:DropDownList>
```

the closing tag is automatically entered for you

Figure 12-54 First song title added to the drop-down list control

3. Click **after the** > in the list item's closing tag and then press **Enter**. Enter the three additional <asp:ListItem> tags indicated in Figure 12-55.

enter these three <asp:ListItem> tags

```
<asp:DropDownList ID="ddlSongs" runat="server">
    <asp:ListItem Text="From This Moment On"></asp:ListItem>
    <asp:ListItem Text="At Last"></asp:ListItem>
    <asp:ListItem Text="Because You Loved Me"></asp:ListItem>
    <asp:ListItem Text="The Way You Look Tonight"></asp:ListItem>
</asp:DropDownList>
```

Figure 12-55 Additional song titles added to the drop-down list control

4. Save the application and then click the **Design** tab. Click the **Your Wedding DJ** text to deselect the table control.
5. Start the application and then click the **down arrow** in the drop-down list control. The song titles appear as shown in Figure 12-56.

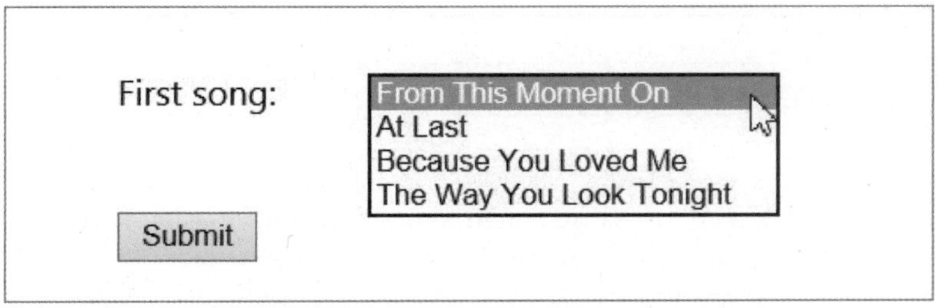

Figure 12-56 Song titles displayed in the drop-down list control

6. Close the browser window.

Coding DJ Tom's Web Page

Now that the interface is complete, you can code the Web page's Submit button. The button's Click event procedure will display a message in the lblMsg control, which is contained in the MessageColumn on the Web page.

START HERE

To code the Submit button's Click event procedure:

1. Right-click the **Web page** and then click **View Code** to open the Code Editor window. Enter the following comments. Replace <your name> and <current date> with your name and the current date, respectively. Press **Enter** twice after typing the last comment.

```
' Name:         DJTom
' Purpose:      Display a message
' Programmer:   <your name> on <current date>
```

2. Now enter the following Option statements:

```
Option Explicit On
Option Strict On
Option Infer Off
```

3. Open the code template for the btnSubmit_Click procedure. Type the following comment and then press **Enter** twice:

```
' displays the user's input in a message
```

4. First, you will declare variables to store the five input items. Enter the following Dim statements. Press **Enter** twice after typing the last Dim statement.

```
Dim strBride As String
Dim strGroom As String
Dim strWedDate As String
Dim strEmail As String
Dim strSong As String
```

5. Now you will assign the names of the bride and groom to the appropriate variables. Enter the following assignment statements:

```
strBride = txtBride.Text.Trim
strGroom = txtGroom.Text.Trim
```

6. Next, you will assign the date selected in the Calendar control to the `strWedDate` variable. The selected date is stored in the control's SelectedDate property. You can use the ToShortDateString method to convert the date to the String data type, formatting it as follows: mm/dd/yyyy. Enter the following assignment statement:

```
strWedDate = calWedding.SelectedDate.ToShortDateString
```

The Calendar control also has a ToLongDateString method that formats the date as follows: day of the week, month name, day number, year number.

7. Now you will assign the e-mail address to the `strEmail` variable. Enter the following assignment statement:

```
strEmail = txtEmail.Text.Trim
```

8. Next, you will assign the item selected in the drop-down list control to the `strSong` variable. The selected item is stored in the control's SelectedItem property. Type the following assignment statement and then press **Enter** twice:

```
strSong = ddlSongs.SelectedItem.ToString
```

9. Finally, you will display the user's input in the lblMsg control. Enter the following lines of code:

```
lblMsg.Text = "Thank you "& strBride & " and " &
    strGroom & " for visiting my Web site. " &
    "Wedding date: " & strWedDate &
    "E-mail address: " & strEmail &
    "Song: " & strSong
```

Next, you will test the Submit button's Click event procedure to verify that its code is working correctly.

START HERE

To test the Submit button's Click event procedure:

1. Save and then start the application. Click the **Bride** box and then type **Pam**. Press **Tab** and then type **Nathan** in the Groom box.
2. Click **any date** in the Calendar control. Click the **E-mail** box and then type **anyEmail@domain.com**. Click the **down arrow** in the drop-down list control and then click **Because You Loved Me** in the list.
3. Click the **Submit** button. The button's Click event procedure displays the message shown in Figure 12-57 in the lblMsg control. (Your message may contain a different date.) Notice that the message is difficult to read. It would be better if the "Thank you" message, the wedding date, the e-mail address, and the song title appeared on separate lines in the control. You will learn how to accomplish this in the next section.

lblMsg control
Thank you Pam and Nathan for visiting my Web site. Wedding date: 10/25/2014E-mail address: anyEmail@domain.comSong: Because You Loved Me

Figure 12-57 Message displayed in the lblMsg control

4. Close the browser window.

Using the
 Tag

At times, you may need to break the text on a Web page in a specific location. You can do this using the <br /> tag. The "br" in the tag stands for "break." The **
 tag** in a Web page is similar to the ControlChars.NewLine constant in a Windows form; both are used to create a new line. In DJ Tom's Web page, you will use the <br /> tag to separate the wedding date information from the "Thank you" message. You also will use it to display the e-mail information and song information on separate lines in the lblMsg control.

START HERE

To use the <br /> tag in the lblMsg control:

1. Modify the assignment statement that displays the message in the lblMsg control. The modifications are shaded in Figure 12-58. (Although the <br /> tags appear at the beginning of the lines in Figure 12-58, the tags can appear anywhere within a line.)

```
Protected Sub btnSubmit_Click(sender As Object,
e As EventArgs) Handles btnSubmit.Click
    ' displays the user's input in a message

    Dim strBride As String
    Dim strGroom As String
    Dim strWedDate As String
    Dim strEmail As String
    Dim strSong As String

    strBride = txtBride.Text.Trim
    strGroom = txtGroom.Text.Trim
    strWedDate = calWedding.SelectedDate.ToShortDateString
    strEmail = txtEmail.Text.Trim
    strSong = ddlSongs.SelectedItem.ToString

    lblMsg.Text = "Thank you " & strBride & " and " &
        strGroom & " for visiting my Web site. " &
        "<br /><br />Wedding date: " & strWedDate &
        "<br />E-mail address: " & strEmail &
        "<br />Song: " & strSong

End Sub
```

Figure 12-58 Modified btnSubmit_Click procedure

2. Save and then start the application. Click the **Bride** box and then type **Tammy**. Press **Tab** and then type **Christopher** in the Groom box.
3. Click **any date** in the Calendar control. Click the **E-mail** box and then type **anyEmail@domain.com**. Click the **down arrow** in the drop-down list control and then click **At Last** in the list.
4. Click the **Submit** button. The button's Click event procedure displays the message shown in Figure 12-59 in the lblMsg control. (Your message may contain a different date.)

Figure 12-59 Message displayed on separate lines in the lblMsg control

5. Close the browser window. Close the Code Editor window and then close the application.

Lesson C Summary

- To set the font for the text on a Web page:

  Assign one or more fonts to the style attribute's font-family property in the <body> tag.

- To divide a Web page into columns:

  Use the <div> tag. Use the id attribute to assign a name to the column. Assign a percentage to the style attribute's width property. Assign either left or right to the style attribute's float property.

- To use an ASP table:

  Use the Table tool located in the Standard section of the toolbox to add a table control to the Web page. The table's CellSpacing property specifies the spacing between the table cells. Its HorizontalAlign property determines its alignment on the Web page. Use the Rows property to add rows and columns (cells) to the table. It's helpful to set the ID property for each row and each cell.

- To place a control in an ASP table:

  Open the Web page in Source view. Drag the control to a location immediately before the desired cell's closing tag.

- To add items to a drop-down list control:

  Use a separate <asp:ListItem> tag for each item. In each tag, set the item's Text property. Place the tags between the drop-down list control's opening and closing tags.

- To determine the date selected in a Calendar control:

  Use the control's SelectedDate property.

- To format the date selected in a Calendar control:

  Use the control's ToShortDateString method to format the date as follows: mm/dd/yyyy. Use the control's ToLongDateString method to format the date as follows: day of the week, month name, day number, year number.

- To determine the item selected in a drop-down list control:

  Use the control's SelectedItem property.

- To create a new line on a Web page from code:

  Use the <br /> tag.

Lesson C Key Terms

<asp:ListItem> tag—used to add items to a drop-down list control

**
 tag**—used to create a new line on a Web page or in a control

<div> tag—creates a division on a Web page; can be used to divide a Web page into columns

ASP table control—displays information in a row and column format; can be used to align information on a Web page

Cell—the intersection of a row and a column in a table

font-family property—a property of the style attribute in the <body> tag; assigns one or more fonts to be used for text

Lesson C Review Questions

1. Which of the following specifies the fonts to use for the text on a Web page?
   a. `style="font-family:Segoe UI, Arial, Sans-Serif"`
   b. `style="fonts:Segoe UI, Arial, Sans-Serif"`
   c. `style:"font-family=Segoe UI, Arial, Sans-Serif"`
   d. `style:"fonts=Segoe UI, Arial, Sans-Serif"`

2. Which of the following specifies that Col3 should occupy 15% of the Web page and be positioned on the right?
   a. `<div id="Col3" "width:15%; position:right">`
   b. `<div id="Col3" style="width:15%; float:right">`
   c. `<div id="Col3" "position:right; column:15%">`
   d. `<div id="Col3" style="width:15%; position:right">`

3. Which of the following adds the word "Alaska" to a drop-down list control?
   a. `<asp:ListItem Caption="Alaska">`
   b. `<asp:ListItem Item="Alaska">`
   c. `<asp:Item Text="Alaska">`
   d. none of the above

4. The item selected in a drop-down list control is stored in the control's ________________ property.
   a. Item
   b. Selected
   c. SelectedItem
   d. none of the above

5. The date selected in a Calendar control is stored in the control's ________________ property.
   a. Date
   b. SelectedDate
   c. DateSelection
   d. none of the above

6. You can use the ________________ tag to display text on the next line in a control.
   a.
   b. <break>
   c. <newline>
   d. none of the above

Lesson C Exercises

INTRODUCTORY

1. In this exercise, you modify the DJ Tom application from this lesson.

   a. Create an empty Web application named DJTomIntro1. Save the application in the VB2012\Chap12 folder. Close the DJTomIntro1 application.

   b. Use Windows to open the DJTomIntro1 folder. Delete the Web.config file.

   c. Use Windows to open the DJTom folder. Select the folder's contents. Copy the selected contents to the DJTomIntro1 folder.

   d. Open the DJTomIntro1 Web site. Right-click Default.aspx in the Solution Explorer window and then click View Designer.

   e. Drag a RegularExpressionValidator control to the Web page. Don't be concerned about the control's location. The control will verify the format of the e-mail address entered by the user. Click ErrorMessage in the Properties window, press the Spacebar twice and then type Invalid. Now, change the ValidationExpression and ControlToValidate properties to Internet e-mail address and "txtEmail", respectively. Click the Source tab. Cut the control's entire asp tag and then paste the tag before the txtEmail control's </asp:TableCell> closing tag. Click the Design tab.

   f. Save and then start and test the application. (If necessary, refer to the Important note that appears after Figure 12-37 in Lesson B.) Close the browser window and then close the application.

INTRODUCTORY

2. In this exercise, you modify the DJ Tom application from this lesson.

   a. Create an empty Web application named DJTomIntro2. Save the application in the VB2012\Chap12 folder. Close the DJTomIntro2 application.

   b. Use Windows to open the DJTomIntro2 folder. Delete the Web.config file.

   c. Use Windows to open the DJTom folder. Select the folder's contents. Copy the selected contents to the DJTomIntro2 folder.

   d. Open the DJTomIntro2 Web site. Right-click Default.aspx in the Solution Explorer window and then click View Designer.

   e. Open the Web page in Source view. Add four song titles to the drop-down list control.

   f. Save and then start and test the application. Close the browser window and then close the application.

INTERMEDIATE

3. In this exercise, you modify the DJ Tom application from this lesson.

   a. Create an empty Web application named DJTomIntermediate. Save the application in the VB2012\Chap12 folder. Close the DJTomIntermediate application.

   b. Use Windows to open the DJTomIntermediate folder. Delete the Web.config file.

   c. Use Windows to open the DJTom folder. Select the folder's contents. Copy the selected contents to the DJTomIntermediate folder.

   d. Open the DJTomIntermediate Web site. Right-click Default.aspx in the Solution Explorer window and then click View Designer.

   e. Open the Web page in Source view. Locate the asp tag for the last table row. Change tblRow6 and tblRow6Col1 to tblRow8 and tblRow8Col1, respectively. Add two rows to the table. The rows should be added above the last row and each should contain two cells. In the first new row, enter the text "Father/Daughter:" (without the quotes) in the first column and then place a drop-down list control in the second column.

In the second new row, enter the text "Mother/Son:" (without the quotes) in the first column and then place a drop-down list control in the second column. Add the titles of any four songs to the drop-down list control in the first new row. Add the titles of any three songs to the drop-down list control in the second new row.

f. Save the application and then switch to Design view. Open the Code Editor window and modify the code to display the additional user input in the lblMsg control.

g. Save and then start and test the application. Close the browser window. Close the Code Editor window and then close the application.

4. Create an empty Web application named MarketFoods. Save the application in the VB2012\Chap12 folder. Add a new Web page named Default.aspx to the application. Change the DOCUMENT object's Title property to Market Foods. Create a Web page similar to the sketch shown in Figure 12-60. The DropDownList control should contain the store numbers listed in Figure 12-61. When the user clicks the Submit button, the button's Click event procedure should display the names of the manager and assistant manager on the Web page. Open the Code Editor window. Enter the appropriate comments and Option statements. Code the Submit button's Click event procedure. Save and then start and test the application. Close the browser window. Close the Code Editor window and then close the application. INTERMEDIATE

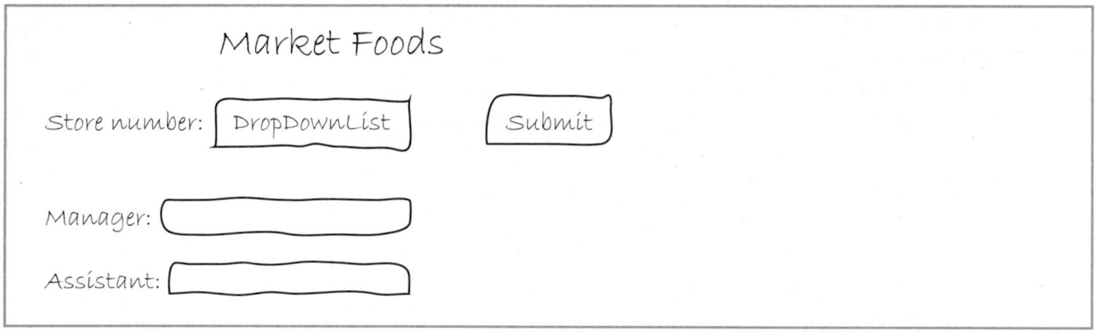

Figure 12-60 Sketch for Exercise 4

Store number	Manager	Assistant manager
1001	Jeffrey Jefferson	Paula Hendricks
1002	Barbara Millerton	Sung Lee
1003	Inez Baily	Homer Gomez
1004	Lou Chan	Jake Johansen
1005	Henry Abernathy	Ingrid Nadkarni

Figure 12-61 Store information for Exercise 4

5. Create an empty Web application named SalesTax. Save the application in the VB2012\Chap12 folder. Add a new Web page named Default.aspx to the application. Change the DOCUMENT object's Title property to Sales Tax Calculator. Create a Web page similar to the sketch shown in Figure 12-62. When the user enters the sales amount and then clicks the Calculate button, the button's Click event procedure should calculate and display a 5% sales tax and a 6% sales tax. Code the procedure. Save and then start and test the application. Close the browser window. Close the Code Editor window and then close the application. INTERMEDIATE

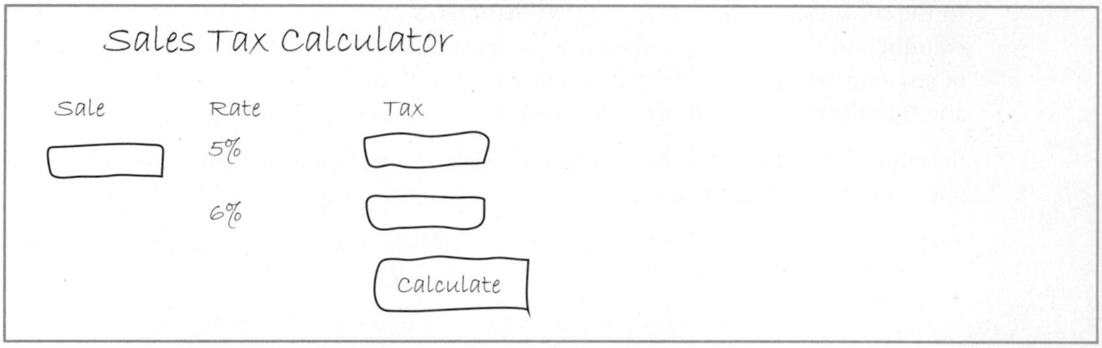

Figure 12-62 Sketch for Exercise 5

ADVANCED

6. Create an empty Web application named SkateAway. Save the application in the VB2012\ Chap12 folder. Add a new Web page named Default.aspx to the application. Change the DOCUMENT object's Title property to Skate-Away Sales. The Skate-Away Sales company sells skateboards by phone. The skateboards are priced at $100 each and are available in two colors: yellow and blue. The application should allow the salesperson to enter the customer's name and the numbers of blue and yellow skateboards ordered. It should calculate the total number of skateboards ordered and the total price of the order, including a 5% sales tax. Create a suitable Web page and then code the application. Save and then start and test the application. Close the browser window. Close the Code Editor window and then close the application.

CHAPTER 13

Working with Access Databases and LINQ

Creating the Paradise Bookstore Application

In this chapter, you will create an application for the manager of the Paradise Bookstore, Louise Pantello. Each book in the bookstore is associated with a number that uniquely identifies it. The number is stored in a Microsoft Access database named Books, along with the book's title, author, price, and quantity in stock. The application will allow Ms. Pantello to view either all of the information stored in the database or only the information for the books written by the author whose name (or partial name) she enters. She can also use it to display the total value of the books in the store.

Previewing the Paradise Bookstore Application

Before you start the first lesson in this chapter, you will preview the completed application. The application is contained in the VB2012\Chap13 folder.

START HERE

To preview the completed application:

1. Use the Run dialog box to run the Paradise (Paradise.exe) file contained in the VB2012\Chap13 folder. The 11 records stored in the Books database appear in a DataGridView control, which you will learn about in Lesson A.
2. First, you will display only the books written by Carol Smith. Click the **Author** text box and then type **Smith, C** (be sure to include a space after the comma). Click the **Go** button. Three records appear in the DataGridView control, as shown in Figure 13-1. (Recall that you can use the Alt key to show/hide the access keys.)

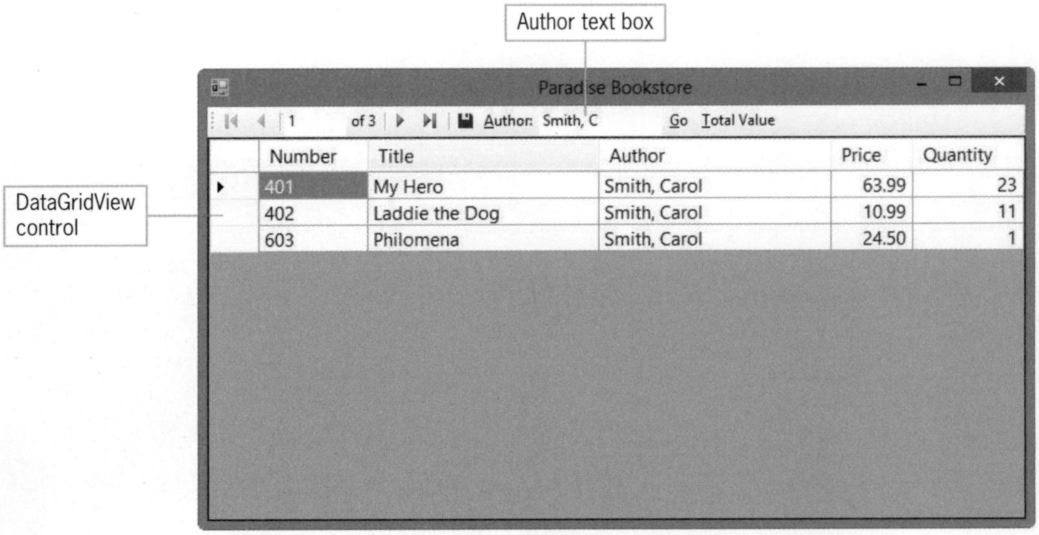

Figure 13-1 Books written by Carol Smith

3. Now you will display all of the records again. Delete the contents of the Author text box and then click the **Go** button. The 11 records appear in the DataGridView control.
4. Finally, click the **Total Value** button to display the total value of the books in the store. See Figure 13-2.

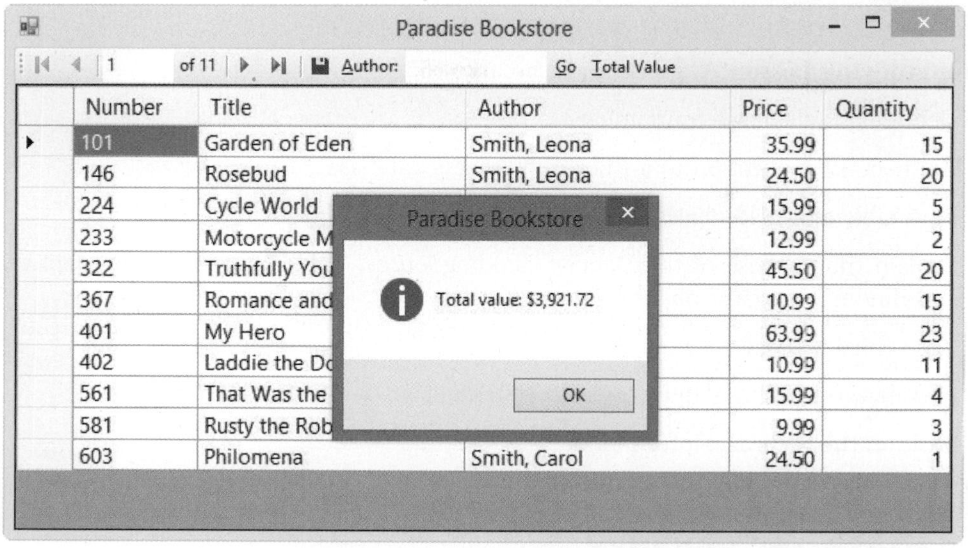

Figure 13-2 Total value of the inventory

5. Click the **OK** button to close the message box. Click the **Close** button on the form's title bar to stop the application.

In Lesson A, you will learn how to connect an application to a Microsoft Access database, and then display the information in one or more controls in the interface. Lesson B will show you how to query a database using LINQ, which stands for Language Integrated Query. You will complete the Paradise Bookstore application in Lesson C. Be sure to complete each lesson in full and do all of the end-of-lesson questions and several exercises before continuing to the next lesson.

LESSON A

After studying Lesson A, you should be able to:

- Define basic database terminology
- Connect an application to a Microsoft Access database
- Bind table and field objects to controls
- Explain the purpose of the DataSet, BindingSource, TableAdapter, TableAdapterManager, and BindingNavigator objects
- Customize a DataGridView control
- Handle errors using the Try...Catch statement
- Position the record pointer in a dataset

Database Terminology

In order to maintain accurate records, most businesses store information about their employees, customers, and inventory in computer databases. A **computer database** is an electronic file that contains an organized collection of related information. Many products exist for creating computer databases; such products are called database management systems (or DBMS). Some of the most popular database management systems are Microsoft Access, Microsoft SQL Server, and Oracle. You can use Visual Basic to access the data stored in databases created by these database management systems. As a result, companies can use Visual Basic to create a standard interface that allows employees to access information stored in a variety of database formats. Instead of learning each DBMS's user interface, the employee needs to know only one interface. The actual format of the database is unimportant and will be transparent to the user.

Many people use databases to keep track of their medical records, compact disc collections, and even golf scores.

In this chapter, you will learn how to access the data stored in Microsoft Access databases. Databases created using Microsoft Access are relational databases. A **relational database** stores information in tables composed of columns and rows, similar to the format used in a spreadsheet. The databases are called relational because the information in the tables can be related in different ways.

Each column in a relational database's table represents a field and each row represents a record. A **field** is a single item of information about a person, place, or thing—such as a name, a salary amount, a Social Security number, or a price. A **record** is a group of related fields that contain all of the necessary data about a specific person, place, or thing. The college you are attending keeps a student record on you. Examples of fields contained in your student record include your Social Security number, name, address, phone number, credits earned, and grades earned. A group of related records is called a **table**. Each record in a table pertains to the same topic and contains the same type of information. In other words, each record in a table contains the same fields.

A relational database can contain one or more tables. A one-table database would be a good choice for storing information about the college courses you have taken. An example of such a table is shown in Figure 13-3. Each record in the table contains four fields: an ID field that indicates the department name and course number, a course title field, a field listing the number of credit hours, and a grade field.

ID	Title	Hours	Grade
ACC110	Accounting Procedures	3	A
ENG101	English Composition I	3	B
CIS156	Visual Basic 2012	3	A
BIO111	Environmental Biology	3	C

Figure 13-3 Example of a one-table relational database

Most tables have a **primary key**, which is a field that uniquely identifies each record. In the table shown in Figure 13-3, you could use either the ID field or the Title field as the primary key because the data in those fields will be unique for each record.

You might use a two-table database to store information about a CD (compact disc) collection. You would store the general information about each CD, such as the CD's name and the artist's name, in the first table. The information about the songs on each CD, such as their title and track number, would be stored in the second table. You would need to use a common field—for example, a CD number—to relate the records contained in both tables.

Figure 13-4 shows an example of a two-table database that stores CD information. The first table is referred to as the **parent table**, and the second table is referred to as the **child table**. The CdNum field is the primary key in the parent table because it uniquely identifies each record in the table. The CdNum field in the child table is used solely to link the song title and track information to the appropriate CD in the parent table. In the child table, the CdNum field is called the **foreign key**.

Parent and child tables are also referred to as master and detail tables, respectively

CdNum	Name	Artist
01	Greatest Hits	Shania Twain
02	Music From Another Dimension	Aerosmith

the two tables are related by the CdNum field

CdNum	SongTitle	Track
01	That Don't Impress Me Much	1
01	From This Moment On	2
01	You're Still The One	3
02	Beautiful	1
02	Tell Me	2
02	Another Last Goodbye	3

Figure 13-4 Example of a two-table relational database

Storing data in a relational database offers many advantages. The computer can retrieve data stored in a relational format both quickly and easily, and the data can be displayed in any order. The information in the CD database, for example, can be arranged by artist name, song title, and so on. You also can control the amount of information you want to view from a relational database. You can view all of the information in the CD database, only the information pertaining to a certain artist, or only the names of the songs contained on a specific CD.

Connecting an Application to a Microsoft Access Database

In this lesson, you will use a Microsoft Access database named Employees. The database contains one table, which is named tblEmploy. The table data is shown in Figure 13-5. The table contains seven fields and 17 records. The Emp_Number field is the primary key because it uniquely identifies each record in the table. The Status field contains the employment status, which is either the letter F (for full-time) or the letter P (for part-time). The Code field identifies the employee's department: 1 for Accounting, 2 for Advertising, 3 for Personnel, and 4 for Inventory.

field names

records

Emp_Number	Last_Name	First_Name	Hired	Rate	Status	Code
100	Benton	Jack	3/5/2001	$15.00	F	2
101	Jones	Carol	4/2/2001	$15.60	F	2
102	Ismal	Asaad	1/15/2002	$10.00	P	1
103	Rodriguez	Carl	5/6/2002	$12.00	P	3
104	Iovanelli	Rebecca	8/15/2002	$20.00	F	1
105	Nyugen	Thomas	10/20/2002	$11.00	P	3
106	Vine	Martha	2/5/2003	$9.50	P	2
107	Smith	Jefferson	5/14/2003	$17.50	F	2
108	Gerber	Sarah	9/24/2004	$21.00	F	3
109	Jones	Samuel	1/10/2005	$13.50	F	4
110	Smith	John	5/6/2005	$9.00	P	4
111	Krutchen	Jerry	5/7/2006	$9.00	P	4
112	Smithson	Jose	6/27/2009	$14.50	F	1
113	Johnson	Leshawn	7/20/2009	$10.00	P	4
114	Jerod	James	4/9/2010	$10.00	P	4
115	Simons	Pam	6/8/2011	$9.00	P	2
116	Sorenson	Harry	3/4/2012	$15.00	F	3

Figure 13-5 Data contained in the tblEmploy table

Before an application can access the data stored in a database, it needs to be connected to the database. You can make the connection using the Data Source Configuration Wizard. The wizard allows you to specify the data you want to access. The computer makes a copy of the specified data and stores the copy in its internal memory. The copy of the data you want to access is called a **dataset**. In the following set of steps, you will connect the Morgan Industries application to the Employees database.

START HERE

To connect the Morgan Industries application to the Employees database:

1. If necessary, start Visual Studio 2012. Open the Morgan Industries Solution (Morgan Industries Solution.sln) file contained in the VB2012\Chap13\Morgan Industries Solution–DataGridView folder. If necessary, open the designer window.
2. Auto-hide the Properties and Toolbox windows, and permanently display the Solution Explorer window.
3. If necessary, click **VIEW** on the menu bar, point to **Other Windows**, and then click **Data Sources** to open the Data Sources window. If necessary, click the **Auto Hide** button to permanently display the Data Sources window.
4. Click **Add New Data Source** in the Data Sources window to start the Data Source Configuration Wizard. If necessary, click **Database** on the Choose a Data Source Type screen. See Figure 13-6. (If you want to display the Wizard's access keys, press the Alt key.)

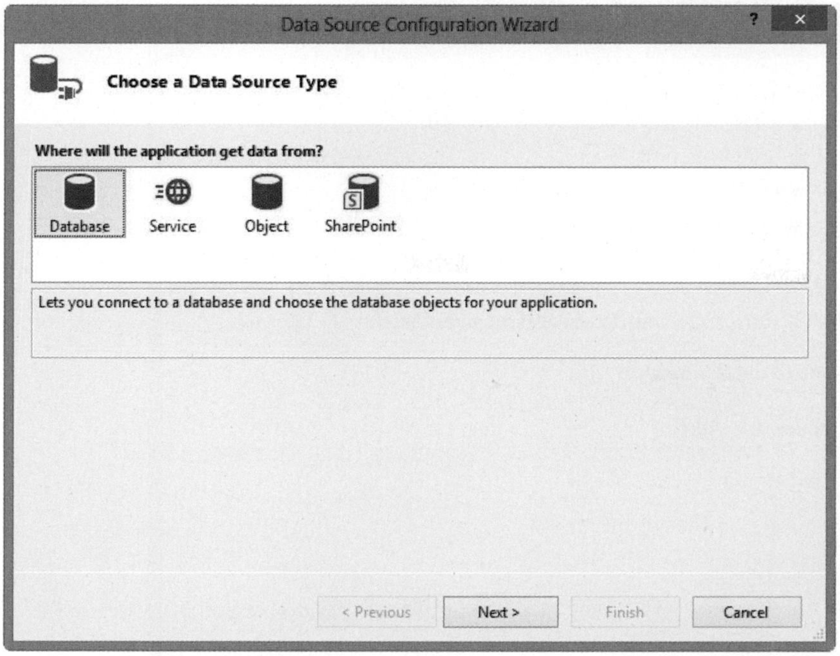

Figure 13-6 Choose a Data Source Type screen

5. Click the **Next** button to display the Choose a Database Model screen. If necessary, click **Dataset**.
6. Click the **Next** button to display the Choose Your Data Connection screen. Click the **New Connection** button to open the Add Connection dialog box. If Microsoft Access Database File (OLE DB) does not appear in the Data source box, click the **Change** button to open the Change Data Source dialog box, click **Microsoft Access Database File**, and then click the **OK** button.
7. Click the **Browse** button in the Add Connection dialog box to open the Select Microsoft Access Database File dialog box. Open the VB2012\Chap13\Access Databases folder and then click **Employees.accdb** in the list of filenames. Click the **Open** button. Figure 13-7 shows the completed Add Connection dialog box.

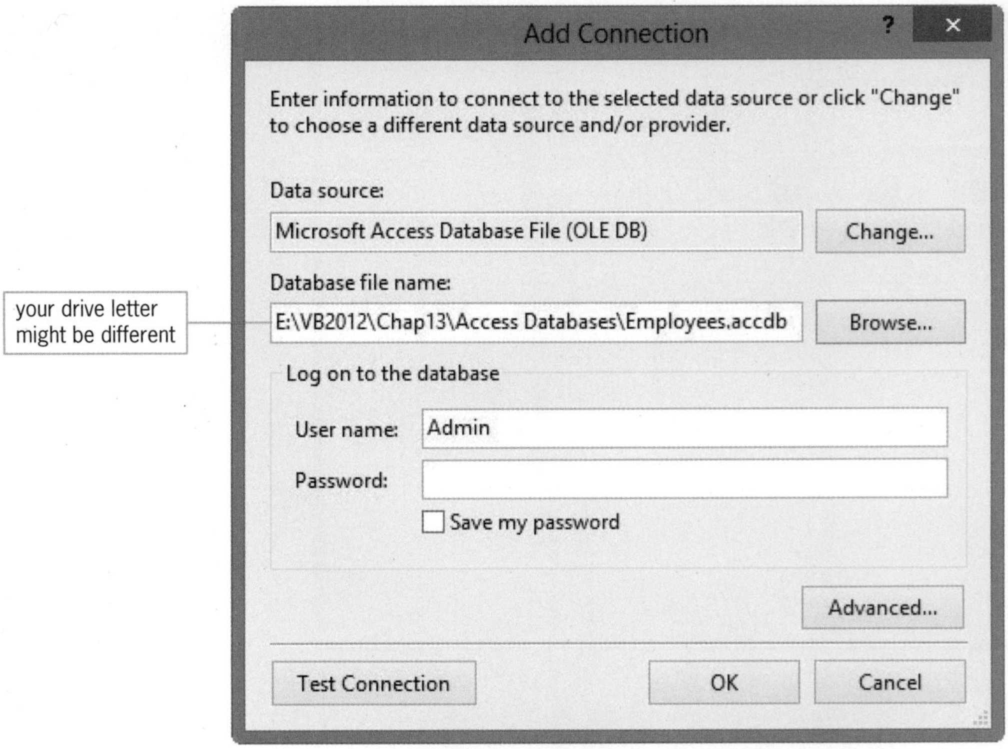

Figure 13-7 Completed Add Connection dialog box

8. Click the **Test Connection** button. The "Test connection succeeded." message appears in a message box. Close the message box.
9. Click the **OK** button to close the Add Connection dialog box. Employees.accdb appears in the Choose Your Data Connection screen. Click the **Next** button. The message box shown in Figure 13-8 opens. The message asks whether you want to include the database file in the current project. By including the file in the current project, you can more easily copy the application and its database to another computer.

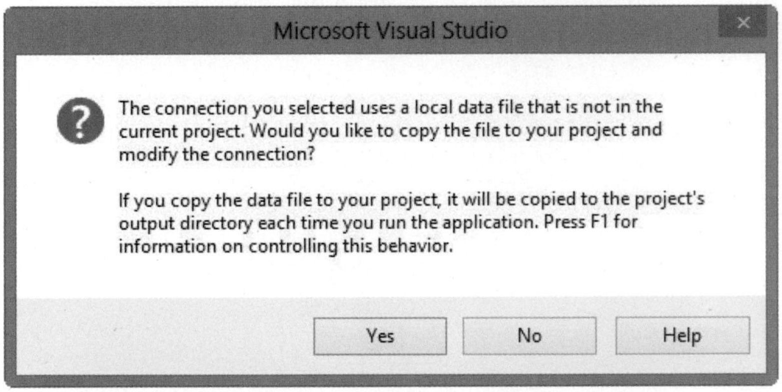

Figure 13-8 Message regarding copying the database file

10. Click the **Yes** button to add the Employees.accdb file to the application's project folder in the Solution Explorer window. The Save the Connection String to the Application Configuration File screen appears next. The name of the connection string, EmployeesConnectionString, appears on the screen. If necessary, select the **Yes, save the connection as** check box.

11. Click the **Next** button to display the Choose Your Database Objects screen. You use this screen to select the table and/or field objects to include in the dataset, which is automatically named EmployeesDataSet.

12. Expand the Tables node and then expand the tblEmploy node. In this application, you need the dataset to include all of the fields in the table. Click the **empty box** next to tblEmploy. Doing this selects the table and field check boxes, as shown in Figure 13-9.

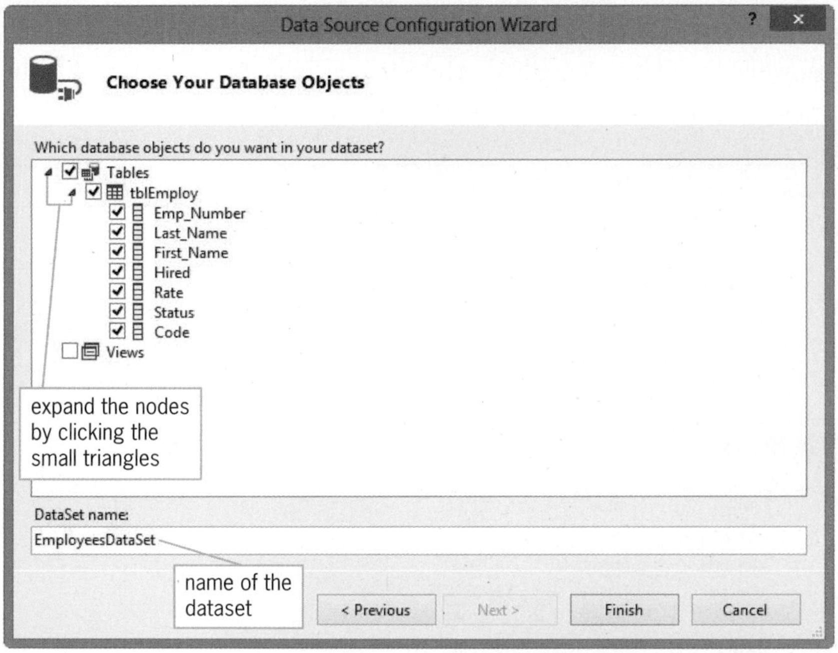

Figure 13-9 Objects selected in the Choose Your Database Objects screen

13. Click the **Finish** button. The computer adds the EmployeesDataSet to the Data Sources and Solution Explorer windows. Expand the tblEmploy node in the Data Sources window. As shown in Figure 13-10, the dataset contains one table object and seven field objects.

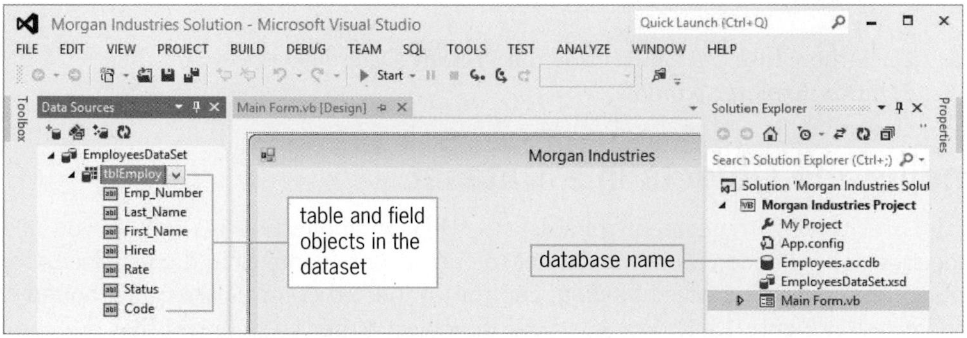

Figure 13-10 Result of running the Data Source Configuration Wizard

Previewing the Contents of a Dataset

You can view the fields and records contained in a dataset by right-clicking the dataset's name in the Data Sources window and then clicking Preview Data.

START HERE

To view the contents of the EmployeesDataSet:

1. Right-click **EmployeesDataSet** in the Data Sources window, and then click **Preview Data** to open the Preview Data dialog box.
2. Click the **Preview** button. As Figure 13-11 shows, the EmployeesDataSet contains 17 records (rows), each having seven fields (columns). Notice the information that appears in the Select an object to preview box in the figure. EmployeesDataSet is the name of the dataset in the application, and tblEmploy is the name of the table included in the dataset. Fill and GetData are methods. The Fill method populates an existing table with data, while the GetData method creates a new table and populates it with data.

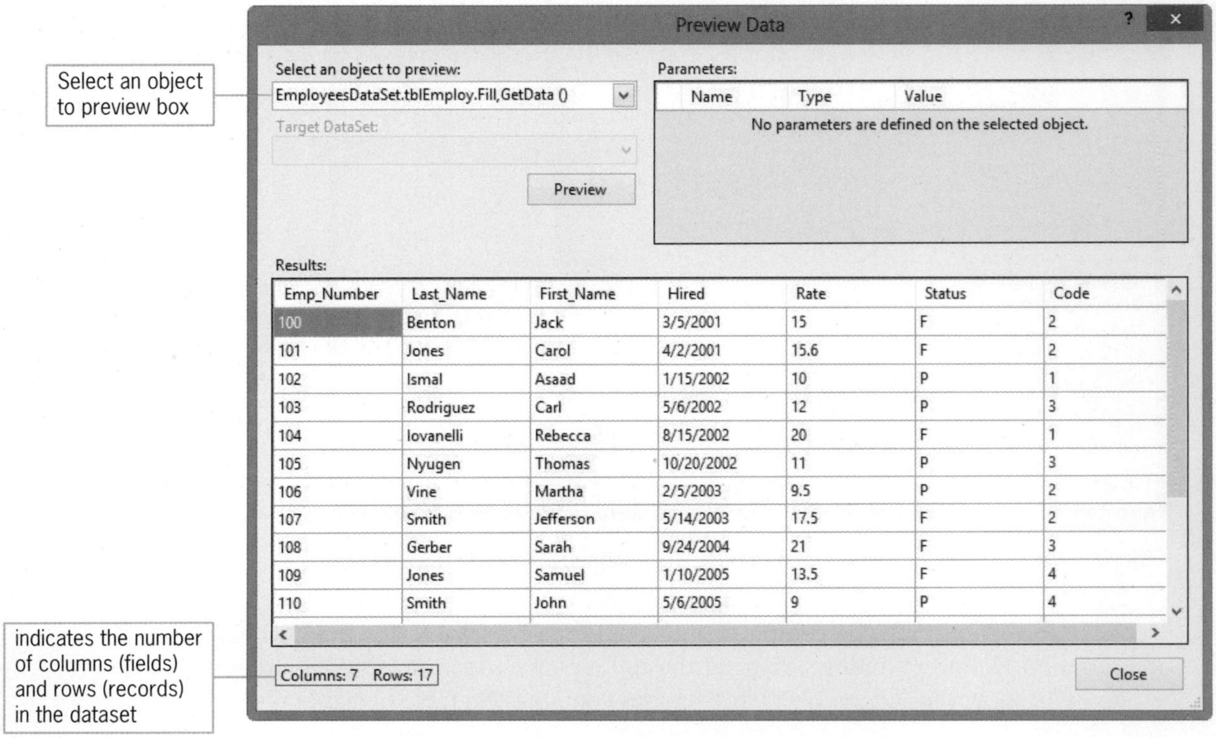

Figure 13-11 Data displayed in the Preview Data dialog box

3. Click the **Close** button to close the Preview Data dialog box, and then auto-hide the Solution Explorer window.

Binding the Objects in a Dataset

Bound controls are also referred to as data-aware controls.

For the user to view the contents of a dataset while an application is running, you need to connect one or more objects in the dataset to one or more controls in the interface. Connecting an object to a control is called **binding**, and the connected controls are called **bound controls**. As indicated in Figure 13-12, you can bind the object either to a control that the computer creates for you or to an existing control in the interface. First, you will learn how to have the computer create a bound control.

Binding an Object in a Dataset

To have the computer create a control and then bind an object to it:
In the Data Sources window, click the object you want to bind. If necessary, use the object's list arrow to change the control type. Drag the object to an empty area on the form and then release the mouse button.

To bind an object to an existing control:
In the Data Sources window, click the object you want to bind. Drag the object to the control on the form and then release the mouse button. Alternatively, you can click the control on the form and then use the Properties window to set the appropriate property or properties. (Refer to the *Binding to an Existing Control* section later in this lesson.)

Figure 13-12 Ways to bind an object in a dataset

Having the Computer Create a Bound Control

When you drag an object from a dataset to an empty area on the form, the computer creates a control and automatically binds the object to it. The icon that appears before the object's name in the Data Sources window indicates the type of control the computer will create. For example, the icon next to tblEmploy in Figure 13-13 indicates that a DataGridView control will be created when you drag the tblEmploy table object to the form. A DataGridView control displays the table data in a row and column format, similar to a spreadsheet. You will learn more about the DataGridView control in the next section. The icon next to each of the seven field objects, on the other hand, indicates that the computer creates a text box when a field object is dragged to the form.

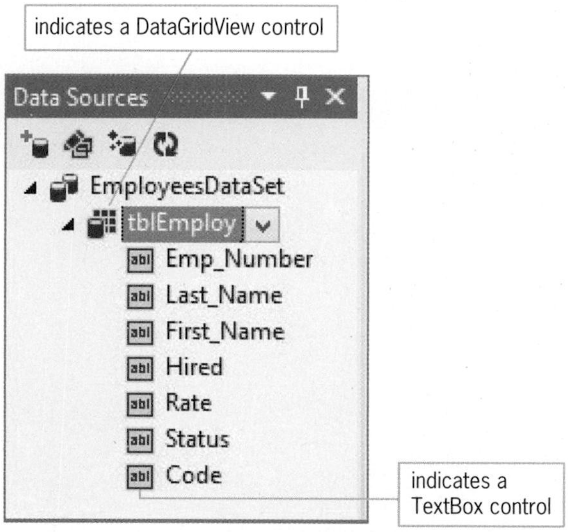

Figure 13-13 Icons in the Data Sources window

When an object is selected in the Data Sources window, you can use the list arrow that appears next to the object's name to change the type of control the computer creates. For example, to display the table data in separate text boxes rather than in a DataGridView control, you click tblEmploy in the Data Sources window and then click the tblEmploy list arrow, as shown in Figure 13-14. Clicking Details in the list tells the computer to create a separate control for each field in the table.

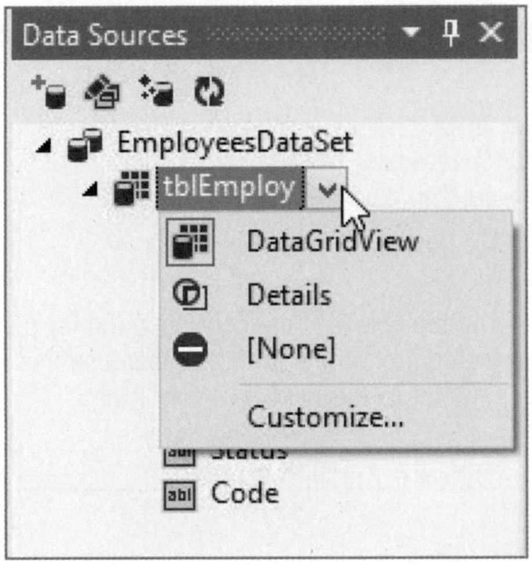

Figure 13-14 Result of clicking the tblEmploy object's list arrow

Similarly, to display the Last_Name field's data in a label control rather than in a text box, you first click Last_Name in the Data Sources window. You then click the field's list arrow, as shown in Figure 13-15, and then click Label in the list.

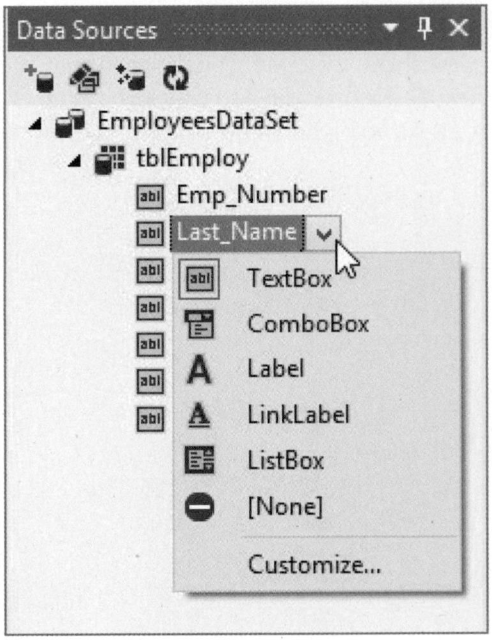

Figure 13-15 Result of clicking the Last_Name object's list arrow

In the following set of steps, you will drag the tblEmploy object from the Data Sources window to the form, using the default control type for a table.

START HERE

To bind the tblEmploy object to a DataGridView control:

1. If necessary, click **tblEmploy** in the Data Sources window to select the tblEmploy object. Drag the tblEmploy object from the Data Sources window to the form and then release the mouse button. The computer adds a DataGridView control to the form, and it binds the tblEmploy object to the control. See Figure 13-16.

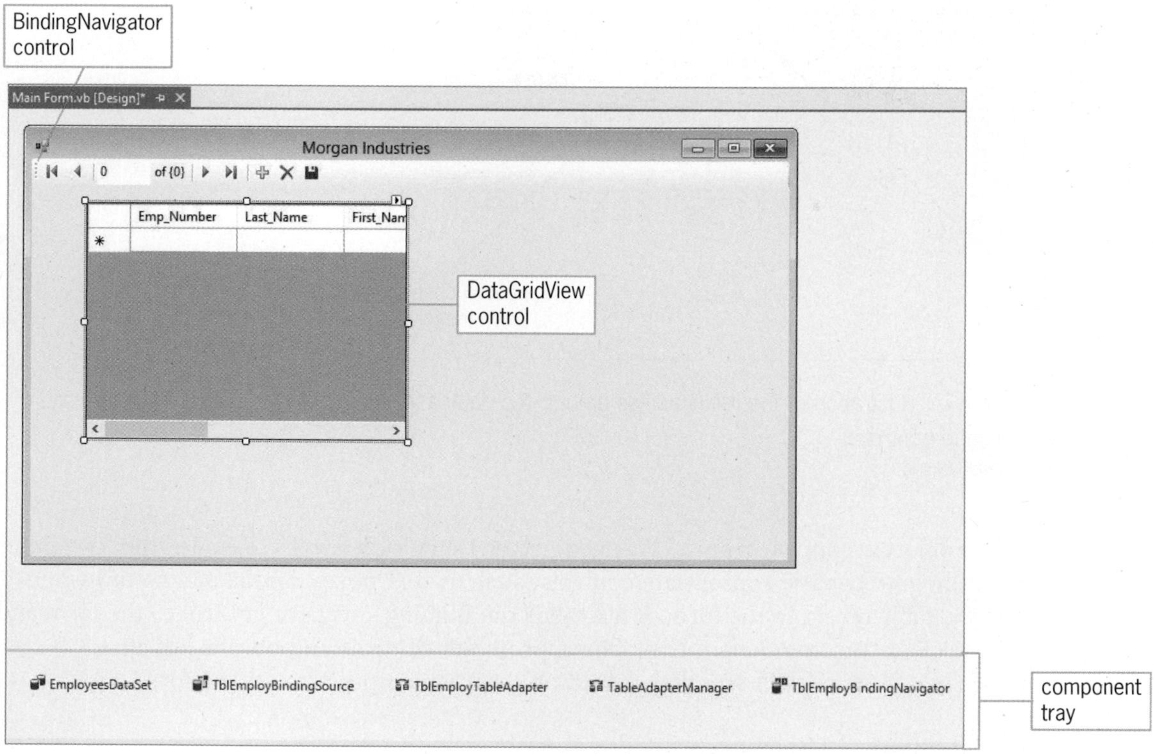

Figure 13-16 Result of dragging the table object to the form

As Figure 13-16 shows, besides adding a DataGridView control to the form, the computer also adds a BindingNavigator control. When an application is running, you can use the **BindingNavigator control** to move from one record to the next in the dataset, as well as to add or delete a record and save any changes made to the dataset. The computer also places five objects in the component tray: a DataSet, BindingSource, TableAdapter, TableAdapterManager, and BindingNavigator. As you learned in Chapter 1, the component tray stores objects that do not appear in the user interface while an application is running. An exception to this is the BindingNavigator object, which appears as the BindingNavigator control during both design time and run time.

The **TableAdapter object** connects the database to the **DataSet object**, which stores the information you want to access from the database. The TableAdapter is responsible for retrieving the appropriate information from the database and storing it in the DataSet. It also can be used to save to the database any changes made to the data contained in the DataSet. However, in most cases, you will use the **TableAdapterManager object** to save the changes because it can handle saving data to multiple tables in the DataSet.

The **BindingSource object** provides the connection between the DataSet and the bound controls on the form. The TblEmployBindingSource in Figure 13-16, for example, connects the EmployeesDataSet to two bound controls: a DataGridView control and a BindingNavigator control. The TblEmployBindingSource allows the DataGridView control to display the data contained in the EmployeesDataSet. It also allows the BindingNavigator control to access the records stored in the EmployeesDataSet. Figure 13-17 illustrates the relationships among the database, the objects in the component tray, and the bound controls on the form.

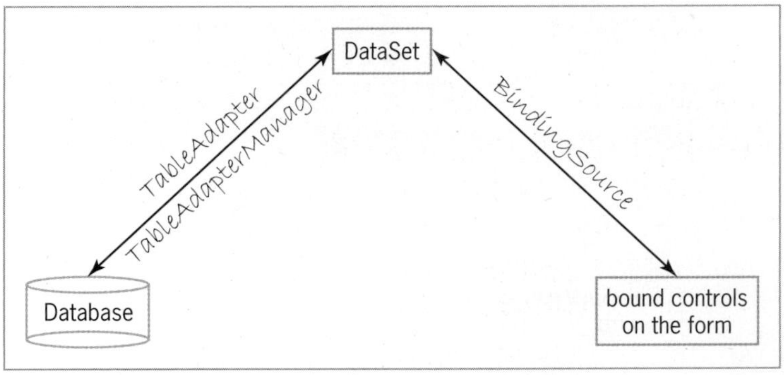

Figure 13-17 Illustration of the relationships among the database, the objects in the component tray, and the bound controls

If a table object's control type is changed from DataGridView to Details, the computer automatically provides the appropriate controls (such as text boxes, labels, and so on) when you drag the table object to the form. It also adds the BindingNavigator control to the form and the five objects to the component tray. The appropriate controls and objects are also automatically included when you drag a field object to an empty area on the form.

The DataGridView Control

The **DataGridView control** is one of the most popular controls for displaying table data because it allows you to view a great deal of information at the same time. The control displays the data in a row and column format, similar to a spreadsheet. Each row represents a record, and each column represents a field. The intersection of a row and column in a DataGridView control is called a **cell**.

Like the PictureBox control, the DataGridView control has a task list. The task list is shown in Figure 13-18 along with a description of each task.

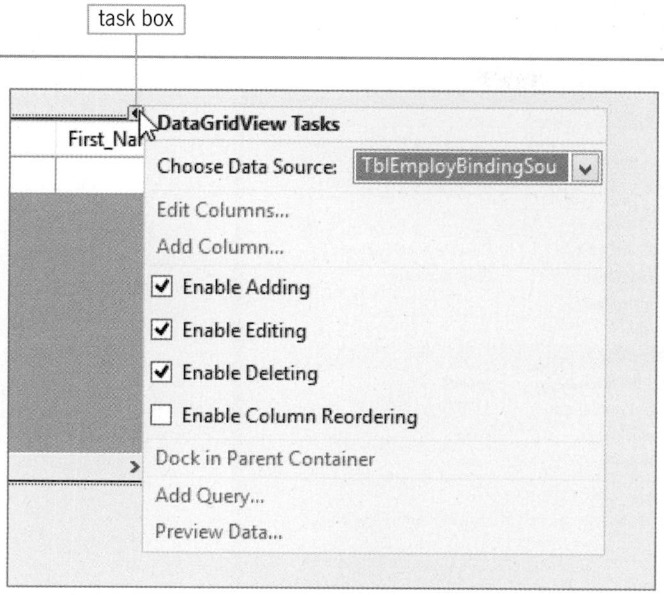

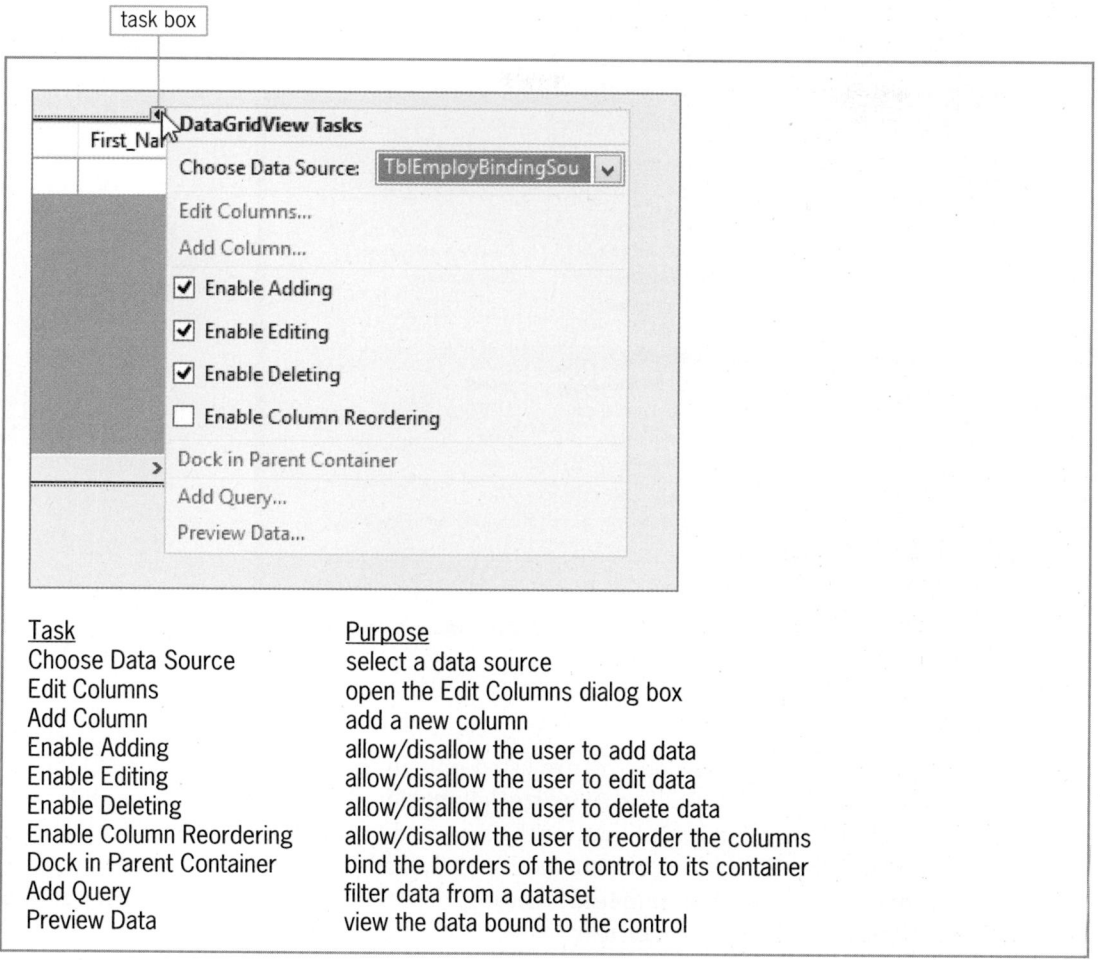

Task	Purpose
Choose Data Source	select a data source
Edit Columns	open the Edit Columns dialog box
Add Column	add a new column
Enable Adding	allow/disallow the user to add data
Enable Editing	allow/disallow the user to edit data
Enable Deleting	allow/disallow the user to delete data
Enable Column Reordering	allow/disallow the user to reorder the columns
Dock in Parent Container	bind the borders of the control to its container
Add Query	filter data from a dataset
Preview Data	view the data bound to the control

Figure 13-18 DataGridView control's task list

Figure 13-19 shows the Edit Columns dialog box, which opens when you click Edit Columns on the DataGridView control's task list. You can use the Edit Columns dialog box during design time to add columns to the control, remove columns from the control, and reorder the columns. You also can use it to set the properties of the bound columns. For example, you can use a column's DefaultCellStyle property to format the column's data, and also to change the column's width and alignment. You can use a column's HeaderText property, on the other hand, to change a column's heading.

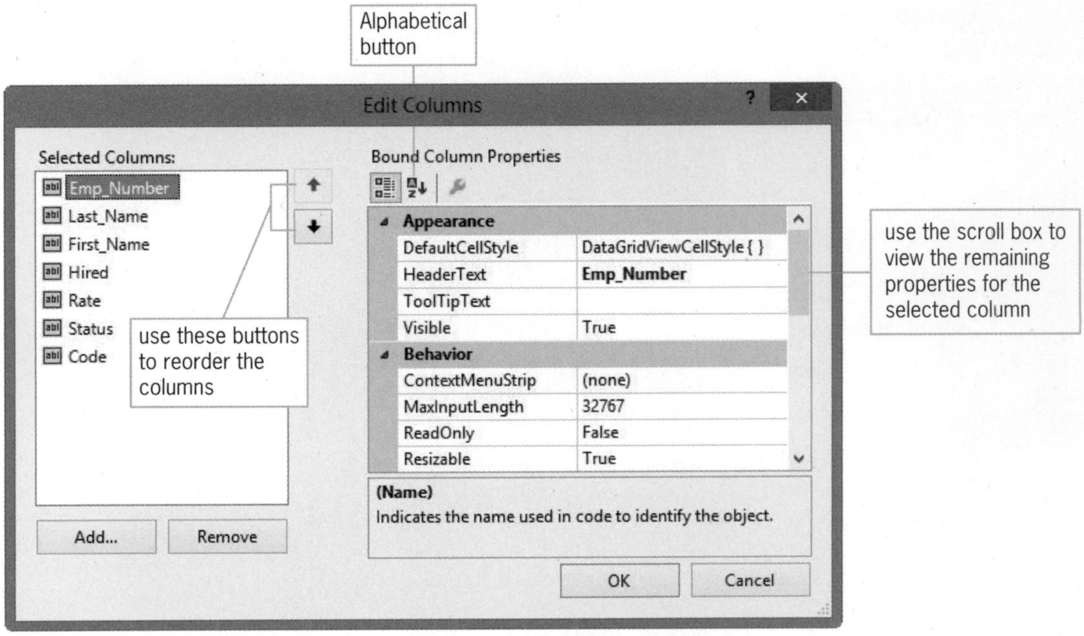

Figure 13-19 Edit Columns dialog box

Some properties of a DataGridView control are listed only in the Properties window. One such property is AutoSizeColumnsMode. The **AutoSizeColumnsMode property** has seven different settings that determine the way the column widths are sized in the DataGridView control. The Fill setting automatically adjusts the column widths so that all of the columns exactly fill the display area of the control. The ColumnHeader setting, on the other hand, automatically adjusts the column widths based on the header text.

START HERE

To improve the appearance of the DataGridView control:

1. Temporarily display the Properties window. Click **AutoSizeColumnsMode** in the Properties list and then set the property to **Fill**.
2. Click the **TblEmployDataGridView control** to close the Properties window. Now, click the control's **task box** and then click **Dock in Parent Container**. The DataGridView control expands to the size of the form. This is because the Dock in Parent Container option anchors the control's borders to the borders of its container, which (in this case) is the form.
3. Next, you will change the header text on several of the columns. Click **Edit Columns** in the task list. Click the **Alphabetical** button (shown earlier in Figure 13-19) to display the property names in alphabetical order. Emp_Number is currently selected in the Selected Columns list. Click **HeaderText** in the Bound Column Properties list and then type **Employee Number** and press **Enter**.
4. Click **Last_Name** in the Selected Columns list and then change the HeaderText property to **Last Name**. On your own, change the First_Name column's HeaderText property to **First Name**. Also change the Rate column's HeaderText property to **Pay Rate**.
5. Now you will have the DataGridView control format the pay rates to show two decimal places. With Pay Rate selected in the Selected Columns list, click **DefaultCellStyle** and then click the **...** (ellipsis) button to open the CellStyle Builder dialog box. Click **Format** and then click the **...** (ellipsis) button to open the Format String Dialog box. Click **Numeric** in the Format type list and then verify that the number 2 appears in the Decimal places box. See Figure 13-20.

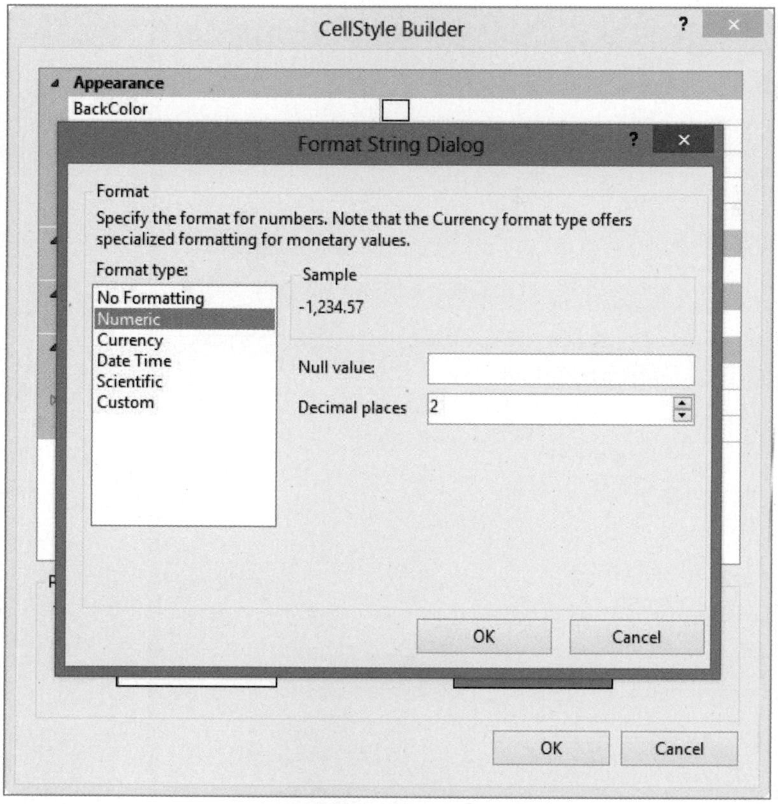

Figure 13-20 Completed Format String Dialog box

6. Click the **OK** button to close the Format String Dialog box. You are returned to the CellStyle Builder dialog box.
7. Next, you will have the DataGridView control align the pay rates in the Pay Rate column. Click **Alignment** and then set the property to **MiddleRight**. See Figure 13-21.

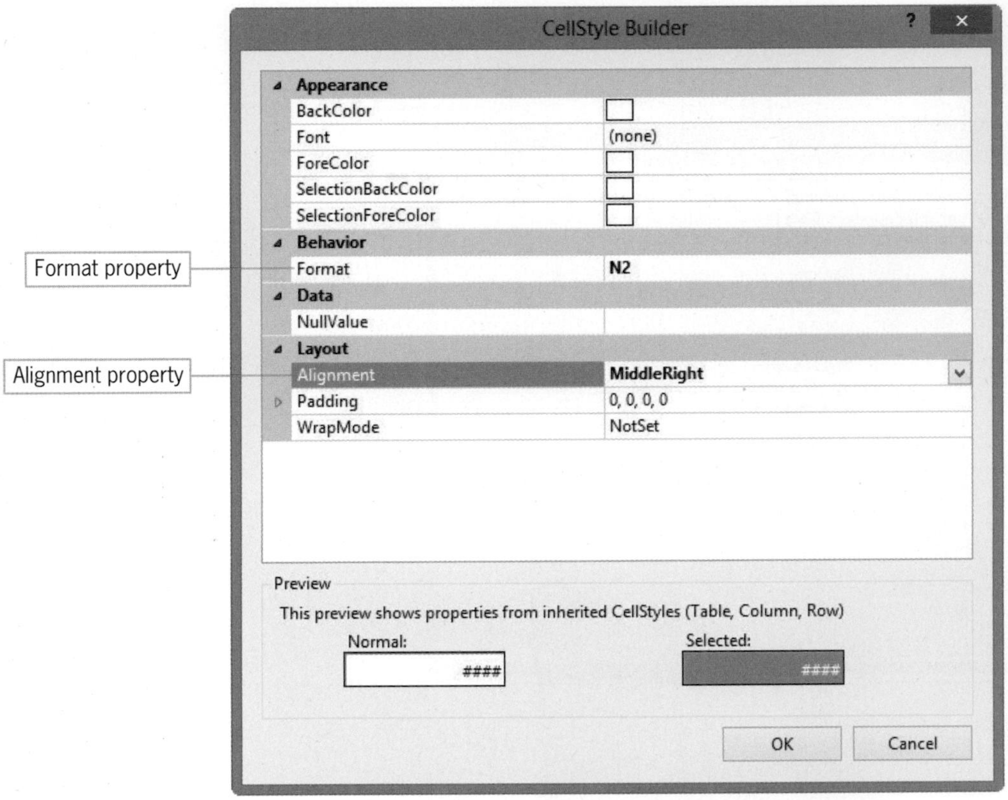

Figure 13-21 Completed CellStyle Builder dialog box

8. Click the **OK** button to close the CellStyle Builder dialog box and then click the **OK** button to close the Edit Columns dialog box.
9. Click the **DataGridView** control to close its task list. Auto-hide the Data Sources window, and then save the solution.

Figure 13-22 shows the DataGridView control after completing the previous set of steps. You won't see the effect of the formatting and aligning the pay rates until the application is started.

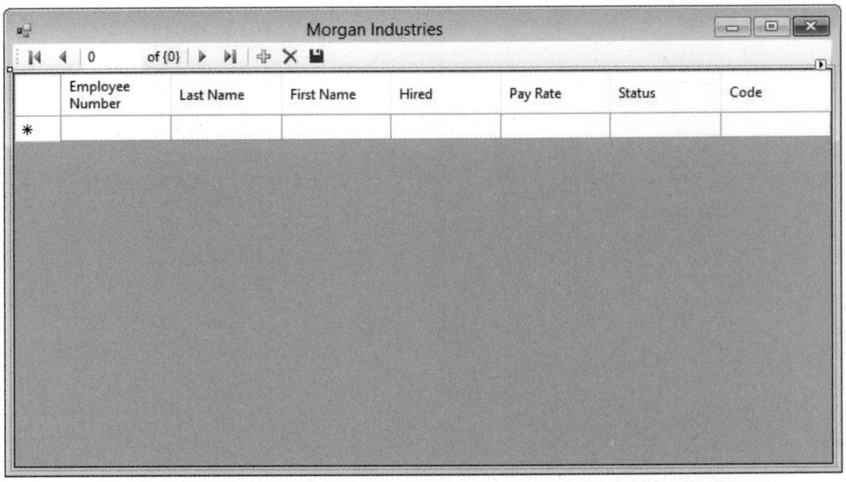

Figure 13-22 DataGridView control after setting some of its properties

Visual Basic Code

In addition to adding the appropriate controls and objects to the application when a table or field object is dragged to the form, the computer also enters some code in the Code Editor window.

START HERE

To view the code automatically entered in the Code Editor window:

1. Open the Code Editor window. Replace <your name> and <current date> in the comments with your name and the current date, respectively.

2. The two procedures shown in Figure 13-23 were automatically entered when the tblEmploy object was dragged to the form. (In your Code Editor window, the first procedure header and also the comments in the second procedure will appear on one line.)

```
Private Sub TblEmployBindingNavigatorSaveItem_Click(sender As Object,
        e As EventArgs) Handles TblEmployBindingNavigatorSaveItem.Click
    Me.Validate()
    Me.TblEmployBindingSource.EndEdit()
    Me.TableAdapterManager.UpdateAll(Me.EmployeesDataSet)

End Sub

Private Sub frmMain_Load(sender As Object, e As EventArgs) Handles MyBase.Load
    'TODO: This line of code loads data into the
    'EmployeesDataSet.tblEmploy' table. You can move, or remove it, as needed.
    Me.TblEmployTableAdapter.Fill(Me.EmployeesDataSet.tblEmploy)

End Sub
```

Figure 13-23 Code automatically entered in the Code Editor window

As you learned in Chapter 1, the keyword Me refers to the current form.

The form's Load event procedure uses the TableAdapter object's Fill method to retrieve the data from the database and store it in the DataSet object. In most applications, the code to fill a dataset belongs in the form's Load event procedure. However, as the comments in the procedure indicate, you can either move or delete the code.

The TblEmployBindingNavigatorSaveItem_Click procedure is processed when you click the Save Data button (the disk) on the BindingNavigator control. The procedure's code validates the changes made to the data before saving the data to the database. Two methods are involved in the save operation: the BindingSource object's EndEdit method and the TableAdapterManager's UpdateAll method. The EndEdit method applies any pending changes (such as new records, deleted records, or changed records) to the dataset. The UpdateAll method commits the dataset changes to the database. Because it is possible for an error to occur when saving data to a database, you should add error handling code to the Save Data button's Click event procedure.

Handling Errors in the Code

An error that occurs while an application is running is called an **exception**. If your code does not contain specific instructions for handling the exceptions that may occur, Visual Basic handles them for you. Typically, it does this by displaying an error message and then abruptly terminating the application. You can prevent your application from behaving in such an unfriendly manner by taking control of the exception handling in your code; you can do this using the **Try...Catch statement**.

When an error occurs in a procedure's code during run time, programmers say that the procedure "threw an exception."

Figure 13-24 shows the basic syntax of the Try...Catch statement and includes examples of using the syntax. The basic syntax contains a Try block and a Catch block. Within the Try block you place the code that could possibly generate an exception. When an exception occurs in the Try block's code, the computer processes the code contained in the Catch block; it then skips to the code following the End Try clause. A description of the exception that occurred is stored in the Message property of the Catch block's `ex` parameter. You can access the description using the code `ex.Message`, as shown in Example 2 in the figure.

Try...Catch Statement

Basic syntax
Try
one or more statements that might generate an exception
Catch ex As Exception
one or more statements to execute when an exception occurs
End Try

Example 1
```
Private Sub btnDisplay_Click(sender As Object,
e As EventArgs) Handles btnDisplay.Click
    Dim inFile As IO.StreamReader
    Dim strLine As String

    Try
        inFile = IO.File.OpenText("names.txt")
        Do Until inFile.Peek = -1
            strLine = inFile.ReadLine
            lstNames.Items.Add(strLine)
        Loop
        inFile.Close()
    Catch ex As Exception
        MessageBox.Show("File error", "JK's",
                        MessageBoxButtons.OK,
                        MessageBoxIcon.Information)
    End Try
End Sub
```

Example 2
```
Private Sub TblSalesBindingNavigatorSaveItem_Click(
sender As Object, e As EventArgs
) Handles TblSalesBindingNavigatorSaveItem.Click
    Try
        Me.Validate()
        Me.TblSalesBindingSource.EndEdit()
        Me.TableAdapterManager.UpdateAll(Me.SalesDataSet)
    Catch ex As Exception
        MessageBox.Show(ex.Message, "Sales Data",
                        MessageBoxButtons.OK,
                        MessageBoxIcon.Information)
    End Try
End Sub
```

Figure 13-24 Basic syntax and examples of the Try...Catch statement

The Try...Catch statement also has a Finally block. The code in the Finally block is processed whether or not an exception is thrown within the Try block.

START HERE

To include a Try...Catch statement in the Save Data button's Click event procedure:

1. Insert two blank lines above the `Me.Validate()` statement in the TblEmployBindingNavigatorSaveItem_Click procedure.
2. In the blank line above the `Me.Validate()` statement, type **Try** and press **Enter**. The Code Editor automatically enters the `Catch ex As Exception` and `End Try` clauses for you.
3. Select (highlight) the three statements that appear below the `End Try` clause, and also the blank line below the statements. Press **Ctrl+x** to place the selected lines on the Clipboard. Click the **blank line** below the `Try` clause and then press **Ctrl+v**.

4. If the three statements in the Try block do not produce (throw) an exception, the Try block should display the "Changes saved" message; otherwise, the Catch block should display a description of the exception. Enter the two MessageBox.Show methods indicated in Figure 13-25.

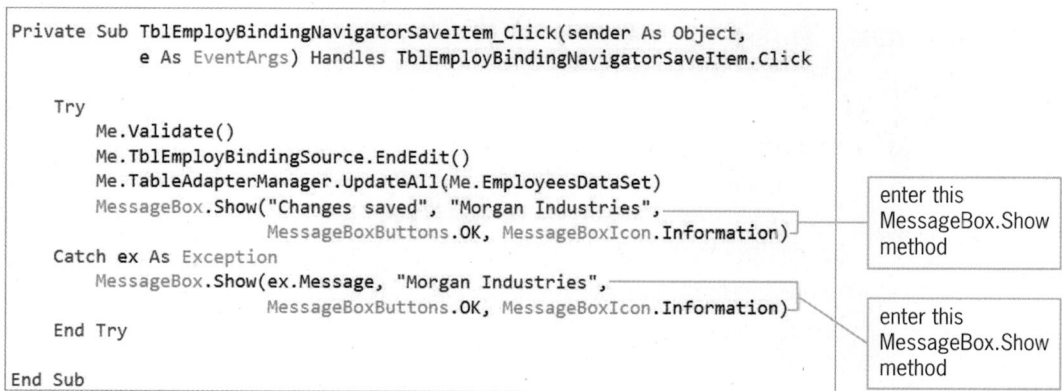

```
Private Sub TblEmployBindingNavigatorSaveItem_Click(sender As Object,
          e As EventArgs) Handles TblEmployBindingNavigatorSaveItem.Click

    Try
        Me.Validate()
        Me.TblEmployBindingSource.EndEdit()
        Me.TableAdapterManager.UpdateAll(Me.EmployeesDataSet)
        MessageBox.Show("Changes saved", "Morgan Industries",
                        MessageBoxButtons.OK, MessageBoxIcon.Information)
    Catch ex As Exception
        MessageBox.Show(ex.Message, "Morgan Industries",
                        MessageBoxButtons.OK, MessageBoxIcon.Information)
    End Try

End Sub
```

enter this MessageBox.Show method

enter this MessageBox.Show method

Figure 13-25 Completed Click event procedure for the Save Data button

5. Save the solution and then start the application. The statement in the form's Load event procedure (shown earlier in Figure 13-23) retrieves the appropriate data from the Employees database and loads the data into the EmployeesDataSet. The data is displayed in the DataGridView control, which is bound to the tblEmploy table contained in the dataset. See Figure 13-26.

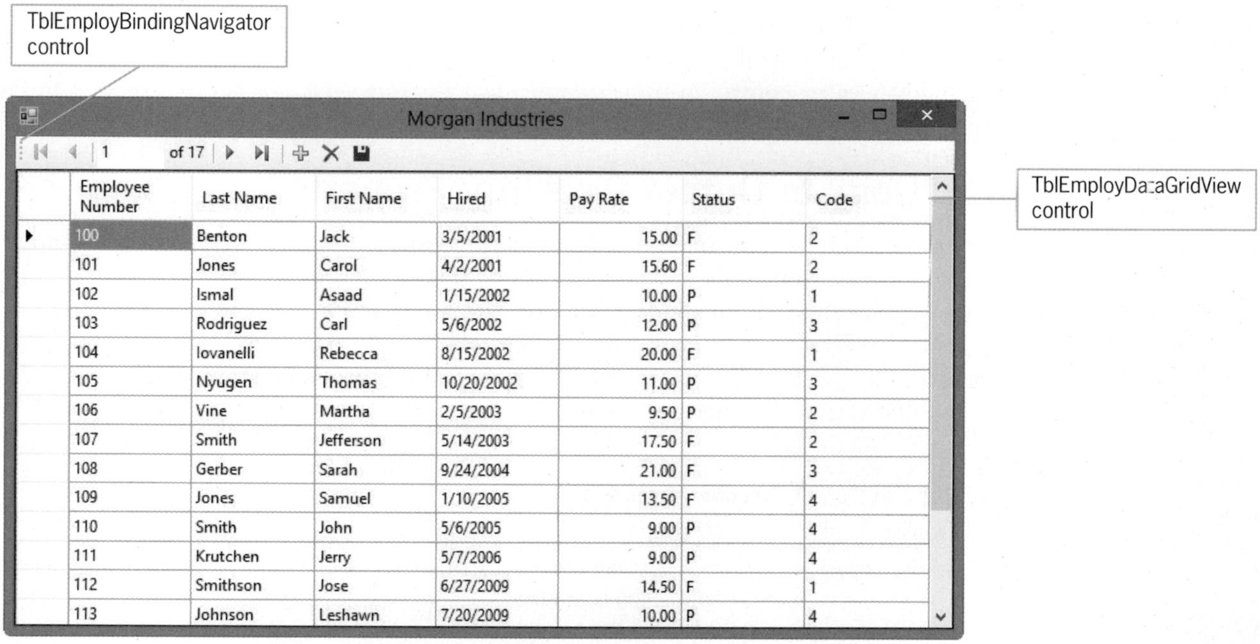

Employee Number	Last Name	First Name	Hired	Pay Rate	Status	Code
100	Benton	Jack	3/5/2001	15.00	F	2
101	Jones	Carol	4/2/2001	15.60	F	2
102	Ismal	Asaad	1/15/2002	10.00	P	1
103	Rodriguez	Carl	5/6/2002	12.00	P	3
104	Iovanelli	Rebecca	8/15/2002	20.00	F	1
105	Nyugen	Thomas	10/20/2002	11.00	P	3
106	Vine	Martha	2/5/2003	9.50	P	2
107	Smith	Jefferson	5/14/2003	17.50	F	2
108	Gerber	Sarah	9/24/2004	21.00	F	3
109	Jones	Samuel	1/10/2005	13.50	F	4
110	Smith	John	5/6/2005	9.00	P	4
111	Krutchen	Jerry	5/7/2006	9.00	P	4
112	Smithson	Jose	6/27/2009	14.50	F	1
113	Johnson	Leshawn	7/20/2009	10.00	P	4

Figure 13-26 Dataset displayed in the DataGridView control

6. You can use the arrow keys on your keyboard to move the highlight to a different cell in the DataGridView control. When a cell is highlighted, you can modify its contents by simply typing the new data. Press the ↓ key to move the highlight to the next record, and then press the → key to move it to the next field.

7. The BindingNavigator control provides buttons for accessing the first, last, previous, and next records in the dataset. When you rest your mouse pointer on one of these buttons,

a tooltip appears and indicates the button's purpose. Rest your mouse pointer on the Move last button, as shown in Figure 13-27.

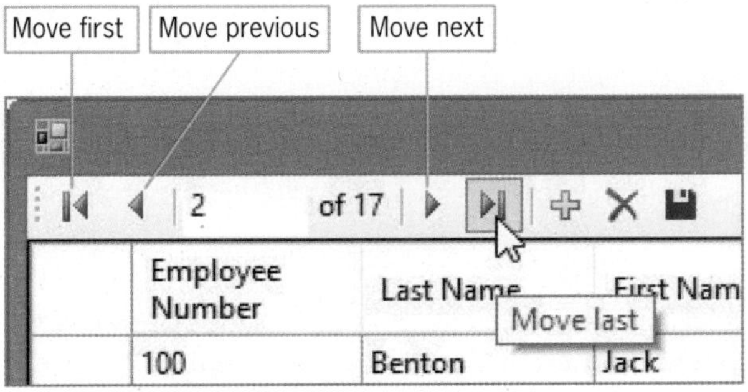

Figure 13-27 Tooltip for the Move last button

8. Click the **Move last** button to move the highlight to the last record, and then click the **Move first** button to move the highlight to the first record.
9. You can also use the BindingNavigator control to access a record by its record number. The records are numbered 1, 2, 3, and so on. Click the **Current position** box, which contains the number 1. Replace the 1 with a **6** and then press **Enter**. The highlight moves to the record for employee number 105, which is the sixth record.
10. Click the **Close** button on the form's title bar to stop the application.

The BindingNavigator control also provides buttons for adding a new record to the dataset, deleting a record from the dataset, and saving the changes made to the dataset. You can add additional items (such as buttons and text boxes) to a BindingNavigator control and also delete items from the control. You will learn how to add items to and delete items from a BindingNavigator control in the *Customizing a BindingNavigator Control* section in Lesson B.

The Copy to Output Directory Property

When the Data Source Configuration Wizard connected the Morgan Industries application to the Employees database, it added the database file (Employees.accdb) to the application's project folder. (You can verify this in the Solution Explorer window.) A database file contained in a project is referred to as a local database file. The way Visual Basic saves changes to a local database file is determined by the file's **Copy to Output Directory property**. Figure 13-28 lists the values that can be assigned to the property.

Copy to Output Directory Property

Property setting	Meaning
Do not copy	the file in the project folder is not copied to the bin\Debug folder when the application is started
Copy always	the file in the project folder is copied to the bin\Debug folder each time the application is started
Copy if newer	when an application is started, the computer compares the date on the file in the project folder with the date on the file in the bin\Debug folder; the file from the project folder is copied to the bin\Debug folder only when its date is newer

Figure 13-28 Settings for the Copy to Output Directory property

When a file's Copy to Output Directory property is set to its default setting, Copy always, the file is copied from the project folder to the project folder's bin\Debug folder each time you start the application. In this case, the Employees.accdb file is copied from the Morgan Industries Project folder to the Morgan Industries Project\bin\Debug folder. As a result, the file will appear in two different folders in the solution. When you click the Save Data button on the BindingNavigator control, any changes made in the DataGridView control are recorded only in the file stored in the bin\Debug folder; the file stored in the project folder is not changed. The next time you start the application, the file in the project folder is copied to the bin\Debug folder, overwriting the file that contains the changes. You can change this behavior by setting the database file's Copy to Output Directory property to Copy if newer. The Copy if newer setting tells the computer to compare the dates on both files to determine which file has the newer (more current) date. If the database file in the project folder has the newer date, the computer should copy it to the bin\Debug folder; otherwise, it shouldn't copy it.

To change the Employees.accdb file's Copy to Output Directory property:

START HERE

1. Temporarily display the Solution Explorer window. Right-click **Employees.accdb** and then click **Properties**. Change the Employees.accdb file's Copy to Output Directory property to **Copy if newer**.
2. Save the solution and then start the application.
3. Click the **Add new** button (the plus sign) to add a new record to the end of the DataGridView control. Type **117** as the employee number, press **Tab**, and then type **Horowitz** as the last name. Press **Tab** and then type **Penny** as the first name. Now, enter **8/9/2012**, **10**, **P**, and **3** in the Hired, Pay Rate, Status, and Code fields, respectively. Press **Enter** after typing the number 3.
4. Click the **Move first** button to move the highlight to the Code field in the first record. When a cell is highlighted, you can modify its existing data by simply typing the new data. Type **3** and press **Enter** to change the entry in Jack Benton's Code field.
5. Click the **Save Data** button (the disk). The "Changes saved" message appears in a message box. Close the message box, and then click the **Close** button on the form's title bar to stop the application.
6. Start the application again. The DataGridView control contains the change you made to Jack Benton's Code field. Scroll down the control to verify that it contains the record you added.
7. Click **117** in the Employee Number field and then click the **Delete** button (the X) to delete the record. Now, click the **Move first** button to move the highlight to the first record, and then change Jack Benton's Code field from 3 to **2**.
8. Click the **Save Data** button. The "Changes saved" message appears in a message box. Close the message box, and then click the **Close** button on the form's title bar to stop the application.
9. Start the application again to verify that your changes were saved, and then stop the application. Close the Code Editor window and then close the solution.

YOU DO IT 1!

Create a Visual Basic Windows application named YouDoIt 1. Save the application in the VB2012\Chap13 folder. Connect the application to the CD database. The database is stored in the CD.accdb file, which is contained in the VB2012\Chap13\Access Databases folder. The database contains one table named tblCds. The table contains 13 records. Each record contains three fields: CdName, Artist, and Price. Display the records in a DataGridView control. Include the Try...Catch statement in the Save Data button's Click event procedure. Also, change the database file's Copy to Output Directory property appropriately. Save the solution and then start and test the application. Close the Code Editor window and then close the solution.

Binding to an Existing Control

As indicated earlier in Figure 13-12, you can bind an object in a dataset to an existing control on a form. The easiest way to do this is by dragging the object from the Data Sources window to the control. However, you also can click the control and then set one or more properties in the Properties window. The appropriate property (or properties) to set depends on the control you are binding. For example, you use the DataSource property to bind a DataGridView control. However, you use the DataSource and DisplayMember properties to bind a ListBox control. To bind label and text box controls, you use the DataBindings/Text property.

When you drag an object from the Data Sources window to an existing control, the computer does not create a new control; instead, it binds the object to the existing control. Because a new control does not need to be created, the computer ignores the control type specified for the object in the Data Sources window. Therefore, it is not necessary to change the control type in the Data Sources window to match the existing control's type. In other words, you can drag an object that is associated with a text box in the Data Sources window to a label control on the form. The computer will bind the object to the label, but it will not change the label to a text box.

In the next set of steps, you will open a different version of the Morgan Industries application. You will connect the application to the Employees database and then begin binding objects from the dataset to existing label controls in the interface. In this version of the application, you will not need to change the database file's Copy to Output Directory property to Copy if newer because the user will not be adding, deleting, or editing the records in the dataset.

START HERE

To connect an application to a database and then bind an object to an existing control:

1. Open the Morgan Industries Solution (Morgan Industries Solution.sln) file contained in the VB2012\Chap13\Morgan Industries Solution–Labels folder. If necessary, open the designer window. See Figure 13-29.

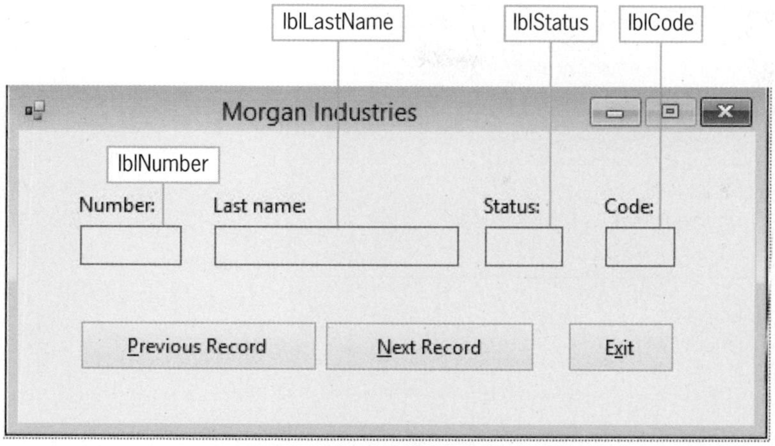

Figure 13-29 A different version of the Morgan Industries application

2. Permanently display the Data Sources window and then click **Add New Data Source** to start the Data Source Configuration Wizard. If necessary, click **Database** on the Choose a Data Source Type screen.

3. Click the **Next** button to display the Choose a Database Model screen. If necessary, click **Dataset**.

4. Click the **Next** button to display the Choose Your Data Connection screen. Click the **New Connection** button to open the Add Connection dialog box. If Microsoft Access Database File (OLE DB) does not appear in the Data source box, click the **Change** button to open the Change Data Source dialog box, click **Microsoft Access Database File**, and then click the **OK** button.

5. Click the **Browse** button in the Add Connection dialog box. Open the VB2012\Chap13\Access Databases folder and then click **Employees.accdb** in the list of filenames. Click the **Open** button. Click the **Test Connection** button in the Add Connection dialog box. The "Test connection succeeded." message appears in a message box. Close the message box.

6. Click the **OK** button to close the Add Connection dialog box. Click the **Next** button on the Choose Your Data Connection screen and then click the **Yes** button to add the Employees.accdb file to the application's project folder.

7. If necessary, select the **Yes, save the connection as** check box on the Save the Connection String to the Application Configuration File screen. Click the **Next** button to display the Choose Your Database Objects screen.

8. Expand the Tables node and then expand the tblEmploy node. In this application, you will include only four fields in the dataset. Click the **empty box** that appears next to each of the following four field names: Emp_Number, Last_Name, Status, and Code. Click the **Finish** button. The computer adds the EmployeesDataSet to the Data Sources window. Expand the tblEmploy node in the Data Sources window. The dataset contains one table object and four field objects.

9. Click **Emp_Number** in the Data Sources window and then drag the field object to the lblNumber control. Release the mouse button. The computer binds the control and adds the DataSet, BindingSource, TableAdapter, and TableAdapterManager objects to the component tray. See Figure 13-30.

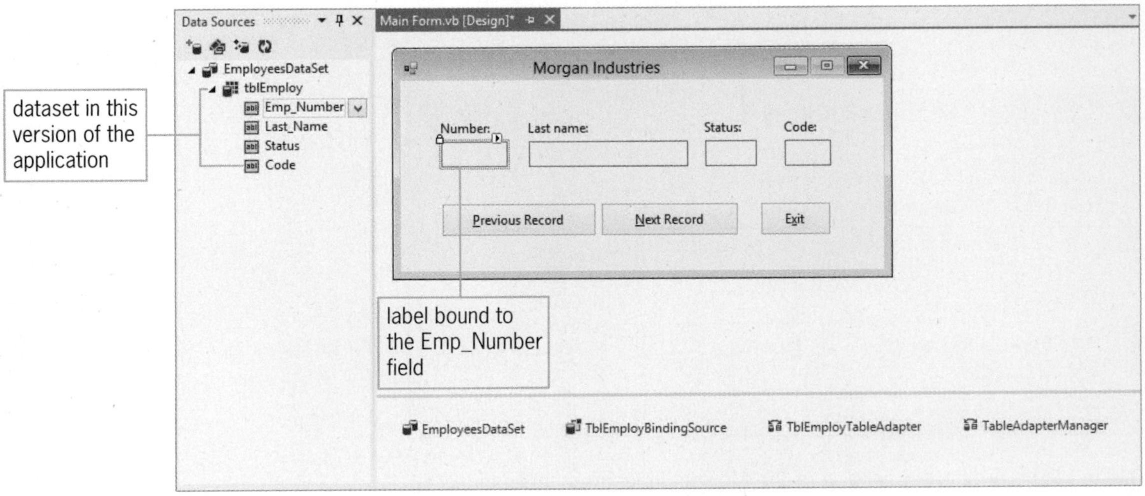

Figure 13-30 Result of binding a field to an existing control

Notice that when you drag an object from the Data Sources window to an existing control, the computer does not add a BindingNavigator object to the component tray, nor does it add a BindingNavigator control to the form. You can use the BindingNavigator tool, which is located in the Data section of the toolbox, to add a BindingNavigator control and object to the application. You then would set the control's DataSource property to the name of the BindingSource object (in this case, TblEmployBindingSource).

Besides adding the objects shown in Figure 13-30 to the component tray, the computer also enters (in the Code Editor window) the Load event procedure shown earlier in Figure 13-23. Recall that the procedure uses the TableAdapter object's Fill method to retrieve the data from the database and store it in the DataSet object.

START HERE

To bind the remaining objects in the dataset to existing controls:

1. On your own, drag the Last_Name, Status, and Code field objects to the lblLastName, lblStatus, and lblCode controls, respectively.
2. Auto-hide the Data Sources window and then save the solution. Start the application. Only the first record in the dataset appears in the interface. See Figure 13-31.

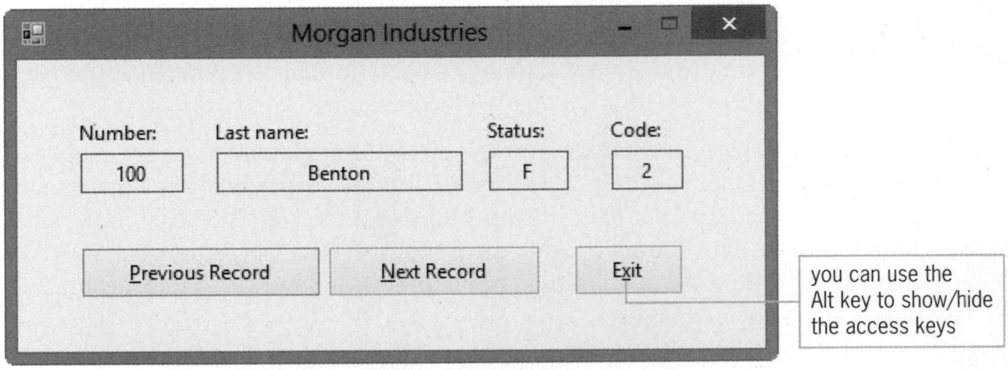

Figure 13-31 First record displayed in the interface

3. Because the interface does not contain a BindingNavigator control, which would allow you to move from one record to the next, you will need to code the Next Record and Previous Record buttons to view the remaining records. Click the **Exit** button to stop the application.

Coding the Next Record and Previous Record Buttons

The BindingSource object uses an invisible record pointer to keep track of the current record in the dataset. It stores the position of the record pointer in its **Position property**. The first record is in position 0, the second is in position 1, and so on. Figure 13-32 shows the Position property's syntax and includes examples of using the property.

BindingSource Object's Position Property

Syntax
bindingSourceName.**Position**

Example 1
```
intRecordNum = TblEmployBindingSource.Position
```
assigns the current record's position to the `intRecordNum` variable

Example 2
```
TblEmployBindingSource.Position = 4
```
moves the record pointer to the fifth record in the dataset

Example 3
```
TblEmployBindingSource.Position += 1
```
moves the record pointer to the next record in the dataset

Figure 13-32 Syntax and examples of the BindingSource object's Position property

Rather than using the Position property to position the record pointer in a dataset, you can use the BindingSource object's Move methods. The **Move methods** move the record pointer to the first, last, next, or previous record in the dataset. Figure 13-33 shows each Move method's syntax and includes examples of using two of the methods.

BindingSource Object's Move Methods

Syntax
bindingSourceName.**MoveFirst()**
bindingSourceName.**MoveLast()**
bindingSourceName.**MoveNext()**
bindingSourceName.**MovePrevious()**

Example 1
```
TblEmployBindingSource.MoveFirst()
```
moves the record pointer to the first record in the dataset

Example 2
```
TblEmployBindingSource.MoveNext()
```
moves the record pointer to the next record in the dataset

Figure 13-33 Syntax and examples of the BindingSource object's Move methods

START HERE

To code the Next Record and Previous Record buttons, and then test the code:

1. Open the Code Editor window. Replace <your name> and <current date> in the comments with your name and the current date, respectively.
2. When the user clicks the Next Record button, the button's Click event procedure should move the record pointer to the next record in the dataset. Similarly, when the user clicks the Previous Record button, the button's Click event procedure should move the record pointer to the previous record in the dataset. Open the code templates for the btnNext_Click and btnPrevious_Click procedures. Enter the comments and Move methods shown in Figure 13-34.

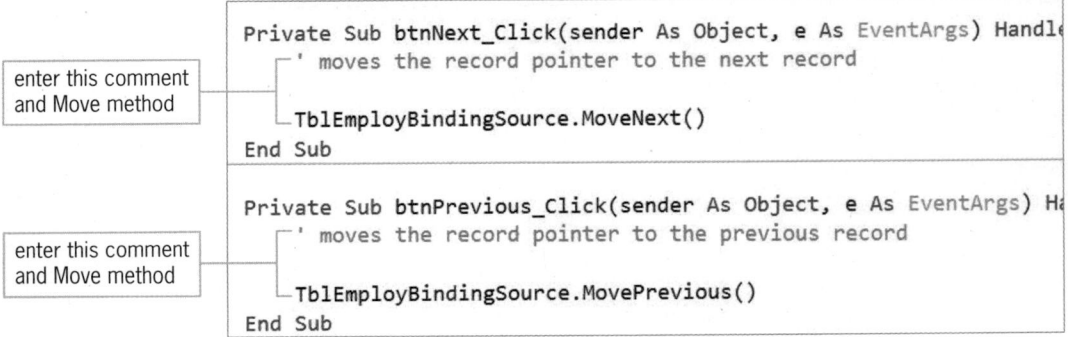

enter this comment and Move method

```
Private Sub btnNext_Click(sender As Object, e As EventArgs) Handl
    ' moves the record pointer to the next record

    TblEmployBindingSource.MoveNext()
End Sub
```

enter this comment and Move method

```
Private Sub btnPrevious_Click(sender As Object, e As EventArgs) Ha
    ' moves the record pointer to the previous record

    TblEmployBindingSource.MovePrevious()
End Sub
```

Figure 13-34 btnNext_Click and btnPrevious_Click procedures

3. Save the solution and then start the application. Click the **Next Record** button to display the second record. Continue clicking the **Next Record** button until the last record appears in the interface.
4. Click the **Previous Record** button until the first record appears in the interface, and then click the **Exit** button. Close the Code Editor window and then close the solution.

YOU DO IT 2!

Create a Visual Basic Windows application named YouDoIt 2. Save the application in the VB2012\Chap13 folder. Add three labels and two buttons to the form. Connect the application to the CD database. The database is stored in the CD.accdb file, which is contained in the VB2012\Chap13\Access Databases folder. The database contains one table named tblCds. The table contains 13 records. Each record contains three fields: CdName, Artist, and Price. Display the records, one at a time, in the labels. Use the buttons to display the next and previous records. Save the solution and then start and test the application. Close the Code Editor window and then close the solution.

Lesson A Summary

- To connect an application to a database:

  Use the Data Source Configuration Wizard. To start the wizard, open the Data Sources window by clicking VIEW on the menu bar, pointing to Other Windows, and then clicking Data Sources. Then, click Add New Data Source in the Data Sources window.

- To preview the data contained in a dataset:

  Right-click the dataset's name in the Data Sources window, click Preview Data, and then click the Preview button in the Preview Data dialog box.

- To have the computer create a control and then bind an object to it:

  In the Data Sources window, click the object you want to bind. If necessary, use the object's list arrow to change the control type. Drag the object to an empty area on the form and then release the mouse button.

- To bind an object to an existing control:

  In the Data Sources window, click the object you want to bind. Drag the object to the control on the form and then release the mouse button. Alternatively, you can click the control on the form and then use the Properties window to set the appropriate property or properties. (Refer to the *Binding to an Existing Control* section in this lesson.)

- To have the columns exactly fill the display area in a DataGridView control:

  Set the DataGridView control's AutoSizeColumnsMode property to Fill.

- To anchor the DataGridView control to the borders of its container:

  Click the Dock in Parent Container option in the DataGridView control's task list. You can also set the DataGridView control's Dock property in the Properties window.

- To handle exceptions (errors) that occur during run time:

  Use the Try...Catch statement.

- To move the record pointer in a dataset during run time:

  You can use a BindingNavigator control. You also can use either the BindingSource object's Position property or one of its Move methods.

Lesson A Key Terms

AutoSizeColumnsMode property—determines the way the column widths are sized in a DataGridView control

Binding—the process of connecting an object in a dataset to a control on a form

BindingNavigator control—can be used to add, delete, and save records and also to move the record pointer from one record to another in a dataset

BindingSource object—connects a DataSet object to the bound controls on a form

Bound controls—the controls connected to an object in a dataset

Cell—the intersection of a row and column in a DataGridView control

Child table—a table linked to a parent table

Computer database—an electronic file that contains an organized collection of related information

Copy to Output Directory property—a property of a database file; determines when and if the file is copied from the project folder to the project folder's bin\Debug folder

DataGridView control—displays data in a row and column format

Dataset—a copy of the data (database fields and records) that can be accessed by an application

DataSet object—stores the information you want to access from a database

Exception—an error that occurs while an application is running

Field—a single item of information about a person, place, or thing

Foreign key—the field used to link a child table to a parent table

Move methods—methods of a BindingSource object; used to move the record pointer to the first, last, next, or previous record in a dataset

Parent table—a table linked to a child table

Position property—a property of a BindingSource object; stores the position of the record pointer

Primary key—a field that uniquely identifies each record in a table

Record—a group of related fields that contain all of the necessary data about a specific person, place, or thing

Relational database—a database that stores information in tables composed of columns (fields) and rows (records)

Table—a group of related records

TableAdapter object—connects a database to a DataSet object

TableAdapterManager object—handles saving data to multiple tables in a dataset

Try...Catch statement—used for exception handling in a procedure

Lesson A Review Questions

1. Which of the following objects connects a database to a DataSet object?
   a. BindingSource
   b. DataBase
   c. DataGridView
   d. TableAdapter
2. The ______________ property stores an integer that represents the location of the record pointer in a dataset.
   a. BindingNavigator object's Position
   b. BindingSource object's Position
   c. TableAdapter object's Position
   d. none of the above
3. If the record pointer is positioned on record number 7 in a dataset, which of the following will move the record pointer to record number 8?
   a. `TblBooksBindingSource.GoNext()`
   b. `TblBooksBindingSource.Move(8)`
   c. `TblBooksBindingSource.MoveNext()`
   d. `TblBooksBindingSource.PositionNext`
4. A ______________ is an organized collection of related information stored in a computer file.
   a. database
   b. dataset
   c. field
   d. record

5. The information in a ______________ database is stored in tables.

   a. columnar
   b. relational
   c. sorted
   d. tabular

6. Which of the following objects provides the connection between a DataSet object and a control on a form?

   a. Bound
   b. Binding
   c. BindingSource
   d. Connecting

7. Which of the following statements retrieves data from the Friends database and stores it in the FriendsDataSet?

   a. `Me.FriendsDataSet.Fill(Friends.accdb)`
   b. `Me.TblNamesBindingSource.Fill(Me.FriendsDataSet)`
   c. `Me.TblNamesBindingNavigator.Fill(Me.FriendsDataSet.tblNames)`
   d. `Me.TblNamesTableAdapter.Fill(Me.FriendsDataSet.tblNames)`

8. If an application contains the `Catch ex As Exception` clause, which of the following can be used to access the exception's description?

   a. `ex.Description`
   b. `ex.Exception`
   c. `ex.Message`
   d. `Exception.Description`

9. If the current record is the ninth record in a dataset that contains 10 records, which of the following statements will position the record pointer on the tenth record?

   a. `TblEmployBindingSource.Position = 9`
   b. `TblEmployBindingSource.Position =`
      `TblEmployBindingSource.Position + 1`
   c. `TblEmployBindingSource.MoveLast()`
   d. all of the above

10. The field that links a child table to a parent table is called the ______________.

    a. foreign key in the child table
    b. foreign key in the parent table
    c. link key in the parent table
    d. primary key in the child table

11. The process of connecting a control to an object in a dataset is called ______________.

    a. assigning
    b. binding
    c. joining
    d. none of the above

12. Which of the following is true?
    a. Data stored in a relational database can be retrieved both quickly and easily by the computer.
    b. Data stored in a relational database can be displayed in any order.
    c. A relational database stores data in a column and row format.
    d. all of the above

Lesson A Exercises

INTRODUCTORY

1. In this exercise, you modify one of the Morgan Industries applications from the lesson. Use Windows to make a copy of the Morgan Industries Solution–Labels folder. Rename the copy Modified Morgan Industries Solution–Labels. Open the Morgan Industries Solution (Morgan Industries Solution.sln) file contained in the Modified Morgan Industries Solution–Labels folder. Open the designer window. Modify the Next Record and Previous Record buttons' Click event procedures to use the Position property rather than the MoveNext and MovePrevious methods. Save the solution and then start and test the application. Close the Code Editor window and then close the solution.

INTRODUCTORY

2. Sydney Industries records the item number, name, and price of each of its products in a database named Products. The Products database is stored in the VB2012\Chap13\Access Databases\Products.accdb file. The database contains a table named tblProducts. The table contains 10 records, each composed of three fields. The ItemNum and ItemName fields contain text; the Price field contains numbers. Open the Sydney Solution (Sydney Solution.sln) file contained in the VB2012\Chap13\Sydney Solution–DataGridView folder. If necessary, open the designer window. Connect the application to the Products database. Change the database file's Copy to Output Directory property to Copy if newer. Bind the table to a DataGridView control and then make the necessary modifications to the control. Open the Code Editor window and enter the Try...Catch statement in the Save Data button's Click event procedure. Include appropriate messages. Save the solution and then start and test the application. Close the Code Editor window and then close the solution.

INTRODUCTORY

3. Sydney Industries records the item number, name, and price of each of its products in a database named Products. The Products database is stored in the VB2012\Chap13\Access Databases\Products.accdb file. The database contains a table named tblProducts. The table contains 10 records, each composed of three fields. The ItemNum and ItemName fields contain text; the Price field contains numbers. Open the Sydney Solution (Sydney Solution.sln) file contained in the VB2012\Chap13\Sydney Solution–Labels folder. If necessary, open the designer window. Connect the application to the Products database. Bind the appropriate objects to the existing label controls. Open the Code Editor window. Code the Click event procedures for the Next Record and Previous Record buttons. Save the solution and then start and test the application. Close the Code Editor window and then close the solution.

INTRODUCTORY

4. The MusicBox database is stored in the VB2012\Chap13\Access Databases\MusicBox.accdb file. The database contains a table named tblBox. The table contains 10 records, each composed of four text fields. Open the MusicBox Solution (MusicBox Solution.sln) file contained in the VB2012\Chap13\MusicBox Solution–DataGridView folder. If necessary, open the designer window. Connect the application to the MusicBox database. Change the database file's Copy to Output Directory property to Copy if newer. Bind the table to a DataGridView control and then make the necessary modifications to the control. Open the Code Editor window and enter the Try...Catch statement in the Save Data button's Click event procedure. Include appropriate messages. Save the solution and then start and test the application. Close the Code Editor window and then close the solution.

5. The MusicBox database is stored in the VB2012\Chap13\Access Databases\MusicBox.accdb file. The database contains a table named tblBox. The table contains 10 records, each composed of four text fields. Open the MusicBox Solution (MusicBox Solution.sln) file contained in the VB2012\Chap13\MusicBox Solution–Labels folder. If necessary, open the designer window. Connect the application to the MusicBox database. Bind the appropriate objects to the existing label controls. Open the Code Editor window. Code the Click event procedures for the Next Record and Previous Record buttons. Save the solution and then start and test the application. Close the Code Editor window and then close the solution. INTRODUCTORY

6. The MusicBox database is stored in the VB2012\Chap13\Access Databases\MusicBox.accdb file. The database contains a table named tblBox. The table contains 10 records, each composed of four text fields. Open the MusicBox Solution (MusicBox Solution.sln) file contained in the VB2012\Chap13\MusicBox Solution–ListBox folder. If necessary, open the designer window. Connect the application to the MusicBox database. Bind the Shape, Source, and Song field objects to the existing label controls. Then, set the lstId control's DataSource and DisplayMember properties to TblMusicBoxBindingSource and ID, respectively. Save the solution and then start the application. Test the application by clicking each entry in the list box. Close the solution. INTERMEDIATE

7. In this exercise, you modify one of the Morgan Industries applications from the lesson. INTERMEDIATE

    a. Use Windows to make a copy of the Morgan Industries Solution–Labels folder. Rename the copy Morgan Industries Solution–ListBox. Open the Morgan Industries Solution (Morgan Industries Solution.sln) file contained in the Morgan Industries Solution–ListBox folder. Open the designer window.

    b. Unlock the controls and then delete the lblNumber control from the form. Also delete the Previous Record and Next Record buttons and their Click event procedures. Add a list box to the form. Change the list box's name to lstNumber. Assign an access key to the list box. Make any needed modifications to the interface. Lock the controls and then set the tab order appropriately.

    c. Set the lstNumber control's DataSource and DisplayMember properties appropriately. Save the solution and then start the application. Test the application by clicking each entry in the list box. Close the solution.

LESSON B

After studying Lesson B, you should be able to:

- Query a dataset using LINQ
- Customize a BindingNavigator control
- Use the LINQ aggregate operators

Creating a Query

You can arrange the records stored in a dataset in any order. For example, the records in the EmployeesDataSet from Lesson A can be arranged by employee number, pay rate, status, and so on. You can also control the number of records you want to view at any one time. You can view all of the records in the EmployeesDataSet; or, you can choose to view only the records for the part-time employees. You use a **query** to specify both the records to select in a dataset and the order in which to arrange the records. You can create a query in Visual Basic 2012 using a language feature called **Language Integrated Query** or, more simply, **LINQ**.

Figure 13-35 shows the basic syntax of LINQ when used to select and arrange records in a dataset. In the syntax, *variableName* and *elementName* can be any names you choose, as long as the name follows the naming rules for variables. In other words, there is nothing special about the `records` and `employee` names used in the examples. The Where and Order By clauses are optional parts of the syntax. You use the **Where clause**, which contains a *condition*, to limit the records you want to view. Similar to the condition in the If...Then...Else and Do...Loop statements, the condition in a Where clause specifies a requirement that must be met for a record to be selected. The **Order By clause** is used to arrange (sort) the records in either ascending (the default) or descending order by one or more fields.

Using LINQ to Select and Arrange Records in a Dataset

Basic syntax

Dim *variableName* **= From** *elementName* **In** *dataset.table*
    [**Where** *condition*]
    [**Order By** *elementName.fieldName1* [**Ascending** | **Descending**]
        [, *elementName.fieldNameN* [**Ascending** | **Descending**]]]
    Select *elementName*

Example 1

```
Dim records = From employee In EmployeesDataSet.tblEmploy
              Select employee
```

selects all of the records in the dataset

Figure 13-35 Basic LINQ syntax and examples for selecting and arranging records in a dataset *(continues)*

(continued)

Example 2
```
Dim records = From employee In EmployeesDataSet.tblEmploy
              OrderBy employee.Code
              Select employee
```
selects all of the records in the dataset and arranges them in ascending order by the Code field

Example 3
```
Dim records = From employee In EmployeesDataSet.tblEmploy
              Where employee.Status.ToUpper = "P"
              Select employee
```
selects only the part-time employee records in the dataset

Example 4
```
Dim records = From employee In EmployeesDataSet.tblEmploy
              Where employee.Last_Name.ToUpper Like"J*"
              OrderBy employee.Code Descending
              Select employee
```
selects from the dataset only the employee records whose last name begins with the letter J, and arranges them in descending order by the Code field

Figure 13-35 Basic LINQ syntax and examples for selecting and arranging records in a dataset

Notice that the syntax shown in Figure 13-35 does not require you to specify the data type of the variable in the Dim statement. Instead, the syntax allows the computer to infer the data type from the value being assigned to the variable. However, for this inference to take place, you must set Option Infer to On (rather than to Off, as you have been doing). You can do this by entering the `Option Infer On` statement in the General Declarations section of the Code Editor window.

Figure 13-35 also includes examples of using the LINQ syntax. The statement in Example 1 selects all of the records in the dataset and assigns the records to the `records` variable. The statement in Example 2 performs the same task; however, the records are assigned in ascending order by the Code field. If you are sorting records in ascending order, you do not need to include the keyword `Ascending` in the Order By clause because `Ascending` is the default sort order. The statement in Example 3 assigns only the records for part-time employees to the `records` variable. The statement in Example 4 uses the Like operator and the asterisk pattern-matching character to select only records whose Last_Name field begins with the letter J. (You learned about the Like operator and pattern-matching characters in Chapter 8.)

The syntax and examples in Figure 13-35 merely assign the selected and/or arranged records to a variable. To actually view the records, you need to assign the variable's contents to the DataSource property of a BindingSource object. The syntax for doing this is shown in Figure 13-36 along with an example of using the syntax. Any control that is bound to the BindingSource object will display the appropriate field(s) when the application is started.

Assigning a LINQ Variable's Contents to a BindingSource Object

Basic syntax
bindingSource.**DataSource** = *variableName*.**AsDataView**

Example
`TblEmployBindingSource.DataSource = records.AsDataView`
assigns the contents of the `records` variable (from Figure 13-35) to the TblEmployBindingSource object

Figure 13-36 Syntax and an example of assigning a LINQ variable's contents to a BindingSource object

START HERE

To use LINQ to select specific records in the Morgan Industries application:

1. If necessary, start Visual Studio 2012. Open the Morgan Industries Solution (Morgan Industries Solution.sln) file contained in the VB2012\Chap13\Morgan Industries Solution-LINQ folder. If necessary, open the designer window. The Find Last Name button in the interface will display records whose Last_Name field begins with one or more characters entered by the user.
2. Open the Code Editor window. Replace <your name> and <current date> in the comments with your name and the current date, respectively.
3. The btnFind_Click procedure will use LINQ to select the appropriate records. Therefore, you will change the Option Infer setting from Off to On. Locate the `Option Infer Off` statement and then change `Off` to **On**. Press the **Tab** key and then type **' using LINQ**.
4. Locate the btnFind_Click procedure. The procedure uses the InputBox function to prompt the user either to enter one or more characters or to leave the input area empty. The user's response is converted to uppercase and assigned to the `strFindName` variable. Click the **blank line** above the procedure's End Sub clause.
5. First, you will enter the LINQ statement to select the appropriate records. The condition in the statement's Where clause will use the Like operator and the asterisk pattern-matching character to compare the contents of each record's Last_Name field with the user's entry followed by zero or more characters. Enter the following lines of code:

```
Dim records = From employee In EmployeesDataSet.tblEmploy
              Where employee.Last_Name.ToUpper Like
              strFindName & "*"
              Select employee
```

6. Now you will display the contents of the `records` variable in the DataGridView control. You do this by assigning the variable to the TblEmployBindingSource object's DataSource property. Press **Enter** to insert another blank line and then enter the following assignment statement:

```
TblEmployBindingSource.DataSource = records.AsDataView
```

Figure 13-37 shows the code entered in the General Declarations section and the btnFind_Click procedure.

General Declarations section

```
Option Explicit On
Option Strict On
Option Infer On ' using LINQ
```

set Option Infer to On in the General Declarations section

btnFind_Click procedure

```
Private Sub btnFind_Click(sender As Object,
e As EventArgs) Handles btnFind.Click
    ' selects records whose last name
    ' begins with the user's entry

    Const strPROMPT As String = "One or more letters " &
            "(leave empty to retrieve all records):"

    ' get the last name
    Dim strFindName As String =
    InputBox(strPROMPT, "Find Last Name").ToUpper

    ' select records matching the last name
    Dim records = From employee In EmployeesDataSet.tblEmploy
                  Where employee.Last_Name.ToUpper Like
                  strFindName & "*"
                  Select employee

    TblEmployBindingSource.DataSource = records.AsDataView

End Sub
```

LINQ code to select the records

assigns the LINQ variable to the BindingSource object

Figure 13-37 Code entered in the General Declarations section and btnFind Click event procedure

To test the btnFind_Click procedure:

START HERE

1. Save the solution and then start the application. The 17 records in the dataset appear in the DataGridView control.
2. Click the **Find Last Name** button. First, you will find all of the records whose Last_Name field begins with the letter S. Type **s** and press **Enter**. Five records appear in the DataGridView control. See Figure 13-38. (Recall that you can use the Alt key to show/hide the access keys.)

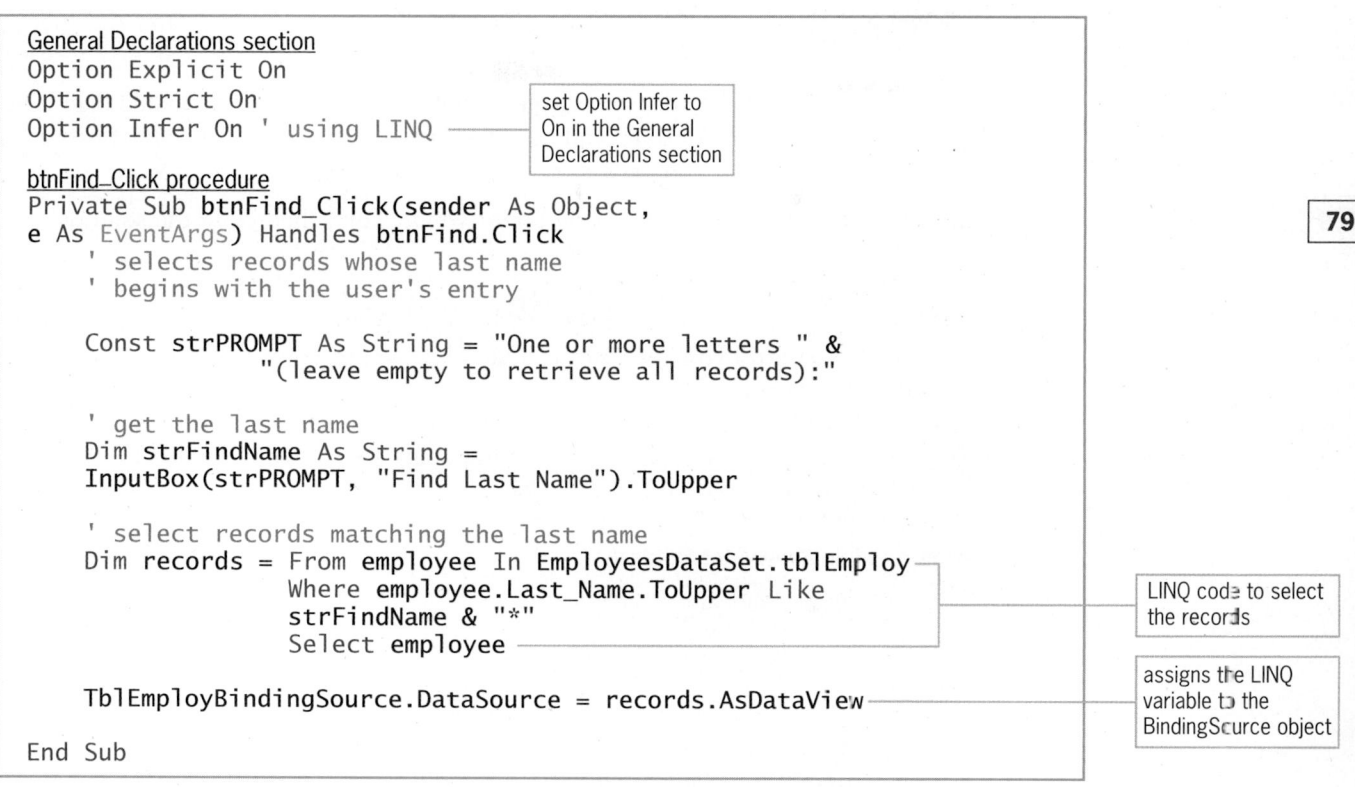

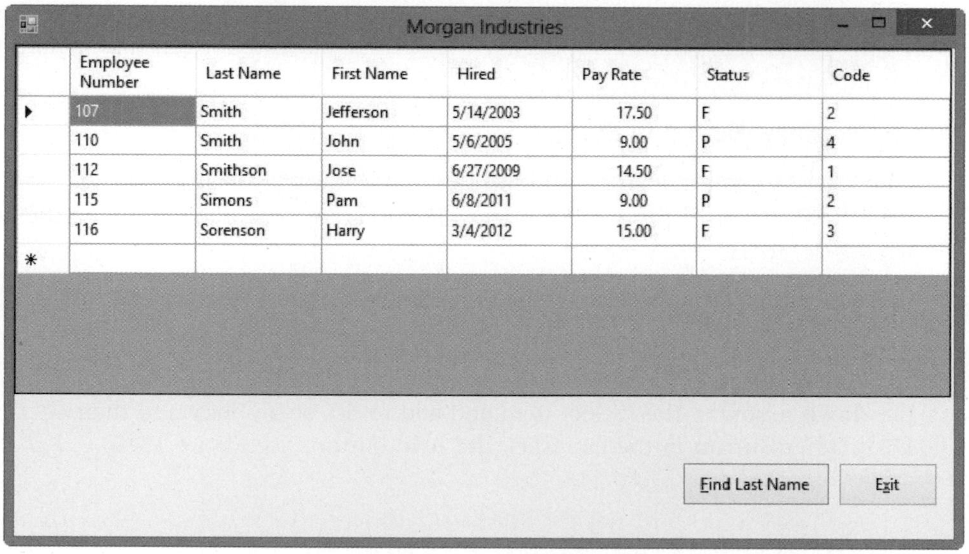

Morgan Industries
Employee Number | Last Name | First Name | Hired | Pay Rate | Status | Code
107 | Smith | Jefferson | 5/14/2003 | 17.50 | F | 2
110 | Smith | John | 5/6/2005 | 9.00 | P | 4
112 | Smithson | Jose | 6/27/2009 | 14.50 | F | 1
115 | Simons | Pam | 6/8/2011 | 9.00 | P | 2
116 | Sorenson | Harry | 3/4/2012 | 15.00 | F | 3
Find Last Name
Exit

Figure 13-38 Employees whose last name begins with the letter S

3. Now you will display all of the records. Click the **Find Last Name** button and then press **Enter**.

4. You can click a column header to sort the records in order by the associated field. Click **Code** to display the records in ascending order by the Code field. Now click **Code** again to display the records in descending order by the Code field.

5. Click the **Exit** button. Close the Code Editor window and then close the solution.

Customizing a BindingNavigator Control

The BindingNavigator control contains buttons that allow you to move to a different record in the dataset, add or delete a record, and save any changes made to the dataset. At times, you may want to include additional items on the control, such as another button, a text box, or a drop-down button. The steps for adding and deleting items are shown in Figure 13-39.

Customizing a BindingNavigator Control

To add an item to a BindingNavigator control:

1. Click the BindingNavigator control's task box and then click Edit Items to open the Items Collection Editor window.
2. If necessary, click the "Select item and add to list below" arrow.
3. Click the item you want to add to the BindingNavigator control and then click the Add button.
4. If necessary, you can use the up and down arrows to reposition the item.

To delete an item from a BindingNavigator control:

1. Click the BindingNavigator control's task box and then click Edit Items to open the Items Collection Editor window.
2. In the Members list, click the item you want to remove and then click the *X* button.

Figure 13-39 Instructions for customizing a BindingNavigator control

In the following set of steps, you will add a DropDownButton to the BindingNavigator control in the Morgan Industries application. The DropDownButton will display a menu that contains three options: All Employees, Full-time Employees, and Part-time Employees. The All Employees option will display the average pay rate for all employees. The Full-time Employees and Part-time Employees options will display the average pay rate for full-time employees and part-time employees, respectively.

START HERE

To add a DropDownButton to the BindingNavigator control:

1. Open the Morgan Industries Solution (Morgan Industries Solution.sln) file contained in the VB2012\Chap13\Morgan Industries Solution–Aggregate folder. Open the designer window.

2. Click an **empty area** on the TblEmployBindingNavigator control and then click the control's **task box**.

3. Click **Edit Items** in the task list to open the Items Collection Editor dialog box. Click the **down arrow** in the "Select item and add to list below" box and then click **DropDownButton** in the list. Click the **Add** button. See Figure 13-40.

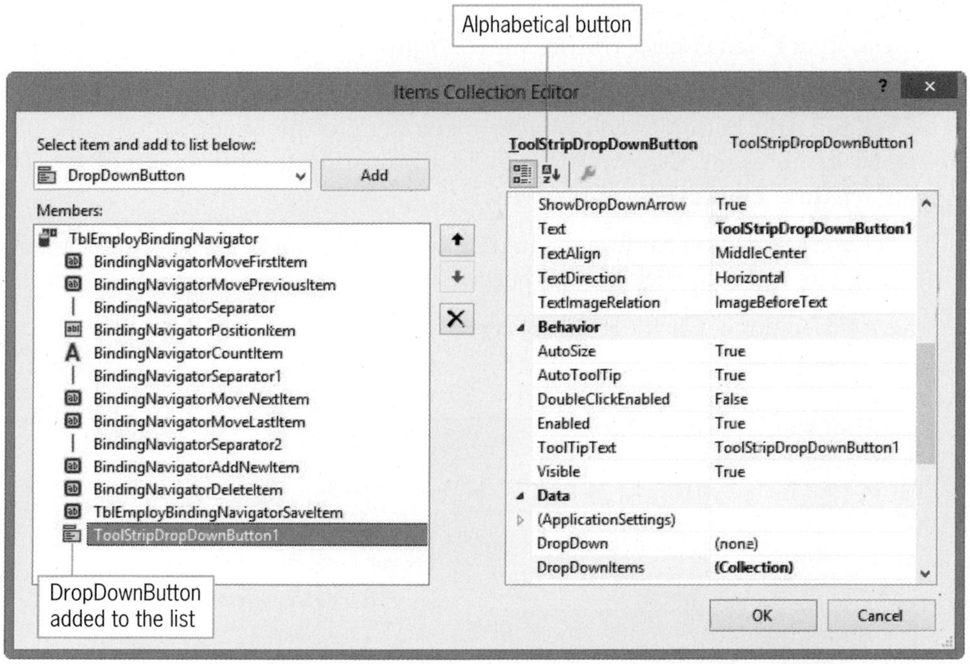

Figure 13-40 Items Collection Editor dialog box

4. Click the **Alphabetical** button to display the property names in alphabetical order. Click **(Name)** in the properties list and then type **ddbAverage** and press **Enter**. Change the DisplayStyle and Text properties to **Text** and **A&verage Pay Rate**, respectively.

5. Click **DropDownItems** in the Properties list and then click the **...** (ellipsis) button. Click the **Add** button to add a menu item to the DropDownButton. Click the **Alphabetical** button to display the property names in alphabetical order. Change the menu item's Name, DisplayStyle, and Text properties to **mnuAverageAll**, **Text**, and **&All Employees**, respectively. See Figure 13-41.

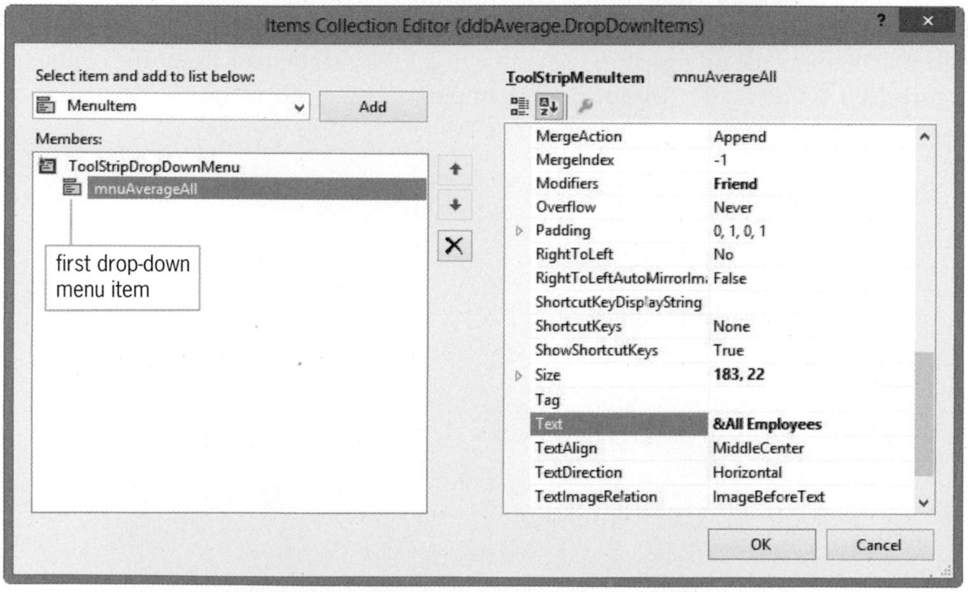

Figure 13-41 DropDownItems property in the Items Collection Editor dialog box

6. Click the **Add** button to add another menu item to the DropDownButton. Change the menu item's Name, DisplayStyle, and Text properties to **mnuAverageFull**, **Text**, and **&Full-time Employees**, respectively.
7. Click the **Add** button to add another menu item to the DropDownButton. Change the menu item's Name, DisplayStyle, and Text properties to **mnuAveragePart**, **Text**, and **&Part-time Employees**, respectively.
8. Click the **OK** button to close the Items Collection Editor (ddbAverage.DropDownItems) dialog box and then click the **OK** button to close the Items Collection Editor dialog box.
9. Save the solution. Click the **down arrow** on the Average Pay Rate button. See Figure 13-42.

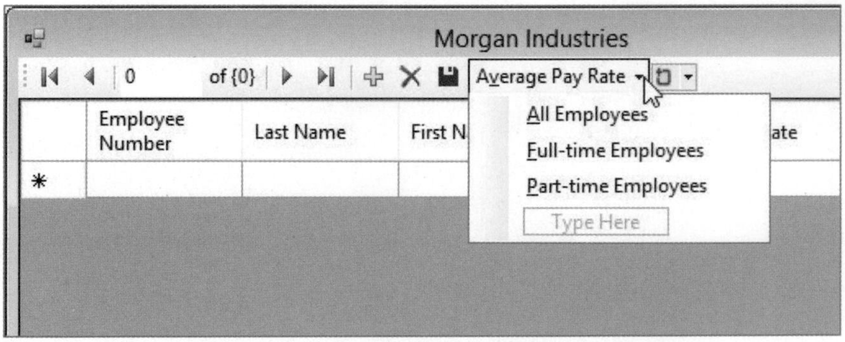

Figure 13-42 DropDownButton added to the TblEmployBindingNavigator control

10. Click the form's **title bar** to close the Average Pay Rate menu.

Using the LINQ Aggregate Operators

LINQ provides several aggregate operators that you can use when querying a dataset. The most commonly used aggregate operators are Average, Count, Max, Min, and Sum. An **aggregate operator** returns a single value from a group of values. The Sum operator, for example, returns the sum of the values in the group, whereas the Min operator returns the smallest value in the group. You include an aggregate operator in a LINQ statement using the syntax shown in Figure 13-43. The figure also includes examples of using the syntax.

LINQ Aggregate Operators

Syntax

Dim *variableName* [**As** *dataType*] =
    Aggregate *elementName* **In** *dataset.table*
    [**Where** *condition*]
    Select *elementName.fieldName*
    Into *aggregateOperator*()

Example 1

```
Dim dblAvgRate As Double =
      Aggregate employee In EmployeesDataSet.tblEmploy
      Select employee.Rate Into Average()
```

calculates the average of the pay rates in the dataset and assigns the result to the `dblAvgRate` variable

Example 2

```
Dim dblMaxRate As Double =
      Aggregate employee In EmployeesDataSet.tblEmploy
      Where employee.Status.ToUpper = "P"
      Select employee.Rate Into Max()
```

finds the highest pay rate for a part-time employee and assigns the result to the `dblMaxRate` variable

Example 3

```
Dim intCounter As Integer =
      Aggregate employee In EmployeesDataSet.tblEmploy
      Where employee.Code = 2
      Into Count()
```

counts the number of employees whose department code is 2 and assigns the result to the `intCounter` variable (The Count operator doesn't need the Select clause.)

Figure 13-43 Syntax and examples of the LINQ aggregate operators

In the following set of steps, you will use the Average aggregate operator to calculate the average pay rate for all employees, part-time employees, and full-time employees.

To code the menu items on the DropDownButton control:

START HERE

1. Open the Code Editor window. Replace <your name> and <current date> in the comments with your name and the current date, respectively.
2. Open the code template for the mnuAverageAll item's Click event procedure. Type the following comment and then press **Enter** twice:

   ' displays the average pay rate for all employees

3. Enter the following three lines of code. Press **Enter** twice after typing the last line.

```
Dim dblAverage As Double =
    Aggregate employee In EmployeesDataSet.tblEmploy
    Select employee.Rate Into Average()
```

4. Next, enter the following five lines of code:

```
MessageBox.Show("Average pay rate for all employees: " &
                dblAverage.ToString("C2"),
                "Morgan Industries",
                MessageBoxButtons.OK,
                MessageBoxIcon.Information)
```

5. Open the code template for the mnuAverageFull item's Click event procedure. Type the following comment and then press **Enter** twice:

   ' displays the average pay rate for full-time employees

6. Enter the following four lines of code. Press **Enter** twice after typing the last line.

```
Dim dblAverage As Double =
    Aggregate employee In EmployeesDataSet.tblEmploy
    Where employee.Status.ToUpper = "F"
    Select employee.Rate Into Average()
```

7. Next, enter the following five lines of code:

```
MessageBox.Show("Average pay rate for full-time employees: " &
                dblAverage.ToString("C2"),
                "Morgan Industries",
                MessageBoxButtons.OK,
                MessageBoxIcon.Information)
```

8. Open the code template for the mnuAveragePart item's Click event procedure. Type the following comment and then press **Enter** twice:

   ' displays the average pay rate for part-time employees

9. On your own, enter the appropriate LINQ statement and MessageBox.Show method.

Figure 13-44 shows the code entered in each menu item's Click event procedure.

Important note: Instead of using the Dim statement to both declare and assign a LINQ value to a variable, you can declare the variable in the Dim statement and then use an assignment statement to assign the LINQ value to it. For example, you can replace the Dim statement in the mnuAverageAll_Click procedure in Figure 13-44 with the following two statements:

```
Dim dblAverage As Double
dblAverage = Aggregate employee In EmployeesDataSet.tblEmploy
             Select employee.Rate Into Average()
```

```
Private Sub mnuAverageAll_Click(sender As Object,
e As EventArgs) Handles mnuAverageAll.Click
    ' displays the average pay rate for all employees

    Dim dblAverage As Double =
        Aggregate employee In EmployeesDataSet.tblEmploy
        Select employee.Rate Into Average()

    MessageBox.Show("Average pay rate for all employees: " &
                    dblAverage.ToString("C2"),
                    "Morgan Industries",
                    MessageBoxButtons.OK,
                    MessageBoxIcon.Information)

End Sub

Private Sub mnuAverageFull_Click(sender As Object,
e As EventArgs) Handles mnuAverageFull.Click
    ' displays the average pay rate for full-time employees

    Dim dblAverage As Double =
        Aggregate employee In EmployeesDataSet.tblEmploy
        Where employee.Status.ToUpper = "F"
        Select employee.Rate Into Average()

    MessageBox.Show("Average pay rate for full-time employees: " &
                    dblAverage.ToString("C2"),
                    "Morgan Industries",
                    MessageBoxButtons.OK,
                    MessageBoxIcon.Information)

End Sub

Private Sub mnuAveragePart_Click(sender As Object,
e As EventArgs) Handles mnuAveragePart.Click
    ' displays the average pay rate for part-time employees

    Dim dblAverage As Double =
        Aggregate employee In EmployeesDataSet.tblEmploy
        Where employee.Status.ToUpper = "P"
        Select employee.Rate Into Average()

    MessageBox.Show("Average pay rate for part-time employees: " &
                    dblAverage.ToString("C2"),
                    "Morgan Industries",
                    MessageBoxButtons.OK,
                    MessageBoxIcon.Information)

End Sub
```

calculates the average pay rate for all employees

calculates the average pay rate for full-time employees

calculates the average pay rate for part-time employees

Figure 13-44 Code entered in each menu item's Click event procedure

To test the code in each menu item's Click event procedure:

START HERE

1. Save the solution and then start the application. Click the **down arrow** on the Average Pay Rate button and then click **All Employees**. (Or, you can press **Alt+v** and then type the letter **a**.) The average pay rate for all employees appears in a message box, as shown in Figure 13-45.

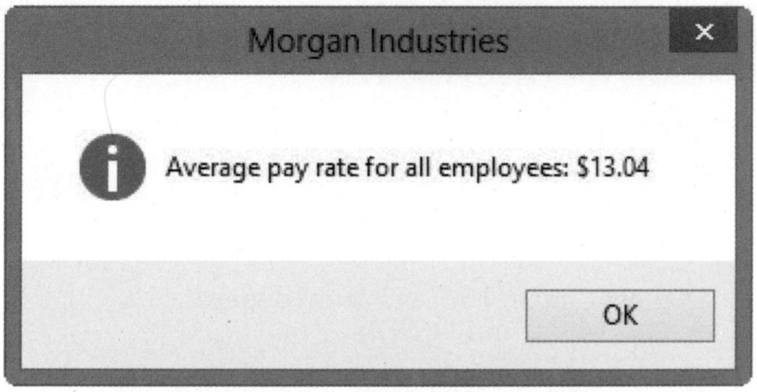

Figure 13-45 Message box showing the average pay rate for all employees

2. Close the message box. Click the **down arrow** on the Average Pay Rate button and then click **Full-time Employees**. The message indicates that the average pay rate for full-time employees is $16.51.
3. Close the message box. Click the **down arrow** on the Average Pay Rate button and then click **Part-time Employees**. The message indicates that the average pay rate for part-time employees is $9.94.
4. Close the message box and then click the **Close** button on the form's title bar. Close the Code Editor window and then close the solution.

Lesson B Summary

- To use LINQ to select and arrange records in a dataset:

  Use the following syntax:

  Dim *variableName* = **From** *elementName* **In** *dataset.table*
  [**Where** *condition*]
  [**Order By** *elementName.fieldName1* [**Ascending** | **Descending**]
  [, *elementName.fieldNameN* [**Ascending** | **Descending**]]]
  Select *elementName*

- To assign a LINQ variable's contents to a BindingSource object:

  Use the following syntax: *bindingSource*.**DataSource** = *variableName*.**AsDataView**

- To add items to a BindingNavigator control:

  Click the BindingNavigator control's task box and then click Edit Items to open the Items Collection Editor window. If necessary, click the "Select item and add to list below" arrow. Click the item you want to add to the BindingNavigator control and then click the Add button. If necessary, you can use the up and down arrows to reposition the item.

- To delete items from a BindingNavigator control:

  Click the BindingNavigator control's task box and then click Edit Items to open the Items Collection Editor window. In the Members list, click the item you want to remove and then click the *X* button.

- To use the LINQ aggregate operators:

  Use the following syntax:

  > **Dim** *variableName* [**As** *dataType*] =
  > **Aggregate** *elementName* **In** *dataset.table*
  > [**Where** *condition*]
  > **Select** *elementName.fieldName*
  > **Into** *aggregateOperator*()

Lesson B Key Terms

Aggregate operator—an operator that returns a single value from a group of values; LINQ provides the Average, Count, Max, Min, and Sum aggregate operators

Language Integrated Query—LINQ; the query language built into Visual Basic 2012

LINQ—an acronym for Language Integrated Query

Order By clause—used in LINQ to arrange the records in a dataset

Query—specifies the records to select in a dataset and the order in which to arrange the records

Where clause—used in LINQ to limit the records you want to view in a dataset

Lesson B Review Questions

1. Which of the following will select only records whose City field begins with an uppercase letter T?

   a.
   ```
   Dim records = From StoresDataSet.tblStores
       Select City Like "T*"
   ```
   b.
   ```
   Dim records = From tblStores
       Where tblStores.City Like "T*"
       Select city
   ```
   c.
   ```
   Dim records =
       From store In StoresDataSet.tblStores
       Where store.City Like "T*"
       Select store
   ```
   d.
   ```
   Dim records =
       From store In StoresDataSet.tblStores
       Where tblStores.City Like "T*"
       Select store
   ```

2. Which of the following calculates the sum of the values stored in a numeric field named Quantity?

   a.
   ```
   Dim dblTotal As Double =
       Aggregate item In ItemsDataSet.tblItems
       Select item.Quantity
       Into Sum()
   ```
   b.
   ```
   Dim dblTotal As Double =
       From item In ItemsDataSet.tblItems
       Select item.Quantity
       Into Sum()
   ```

c.
```
Dim dblTotal As Double =
    From item In ItemsDataSet.tblItems
    Aggregate item.Quantity
    Into Sum()
```

d.
```
Dim dblTotal As Double =
    From item In ItemsDataSet.tblItems
    Sum item.Quantity
```


3. Which of the following statements selects all of the records in the tblItems table?

a.
```
Dim records =
    From item In ItemsDataSet.tblItems
    Select All item
```

b.
```
Dim records =
    From item In ItemsDataSet.tblItems
    Select item
```

c.
```
Dim records =
    Select item From ItemsDataSet.tblItems
```

d.
```
Dim records = From ItemsDataSet.tblItems
    Select tblItems.item
```

4. The tblCities table contains a numeric field named Population. Which of the following statements selects all cities having a population that exceeds 15000?

a.
```
Dim records =
    From city In CitiesDataSet.tblCities
    Where Population > 15000
    Select city
```

b.
```
Dim records =
    From city In CitiesDataSet.tblCities
    Select city.Population > 15000
```

c.
```
Dim records =
    From city In CitiesDataSet.tblCities
    Where city.Population > 15000
    Select city
```

d.
```
Dim records =
    Select city.Population > 15000
    From tblCities
```

5. The tblCities table contains a numeric field named Population. Which of the following statements calculates the total population of all of the cities in the table?

a.
```
Dim intTotal As Integer =
    Aggregate city In CitiesDataSet.tblCities
    Select city.Population
    Into Sum()
```

b.
```
Dim intTotal As Integer =
    Sum city In CitiesDataSet.tblCities
    Select city.Population
    Into Total()
```

c.
```
Dim intTotal As Integer =
    Aggregate CitiesDataSet.tblCities.city
    Select city.Population
    Into Sum()
```

d.
```
Dim intTotal As Integer =
    Sum city In CitiesDataSet.tblCities.Population
```

6. In a LINQ statement, the ______________ clause limits the records that will be selected.

   a. Limit
   b. Order By
   c. Select
   d. Where

Lesson B Exercises

INTRODUCTORY

1. The tblMagInfo table contains three fields. The Code and Cost fields are numeric. The Magazine field contains text. The dataset's name is MagsDataSet.

   a. Write a LINQ statement that arranges the records in ascending order by the Magazine field.
   b. Write a LINQ statement that selects records having a code of 3.
   c. Write a LINQ statement that selects records having a cost of at least $2.
   d. Write a LINQ statement that selects the Funtime magazine.

INTRODUCTORY

2. In this exercise, you modify one of the Morgan Industries applications from the lesson. Use Windows to make a copy of the Morgan Industries Solution–Aggregate folder. Rename the copy Modified Morgan Industries Solution–Aggregate. Open the Morgan Industries Solution (Morgan Industries Solution.sln) file contained in the Modified Morgan Industries Solution–Aggregate folder. Open the designer window.

   a. Click an empty area on the TblEmployBindingNavigator control and then click the control's task box. Click Edit Items in the task list to open the Items Collection Editor dialog box. Add a DropDownButton to the control. Change the DropDownButton's name to ddbDepartment. Change its DisplayStyle and Text properties to Text and &Department, respectively.
   b. Use the DropDownItems property to add four menu items to the DropDownButton: Accounting, Advertising, Personnel, and Inventory. Be sure to change each menu item's name, as well as its DisplayStyle and Text properties.
   c. Each menu item should display (in a message box) the number of employees in the department. Code 1 is Accounting, Code 2 is Advertising, Code 3 is Personnel, and Code 4 is Inventory. Open the Code Editor window and code each menu item's Click event procedure.
   d. Save the solution and then start and test the application. Close the Code Editor window and then close the solution.

INTRODUCTORY

3. Open the Magazine Solution (Magazine Solution.sln) file contained in the VB2012\Chap13\Magazine Solution–Introductory folder. If necessary, open the designer window. The application is connected to the Magazines database, which is stored in the Magazines.accdb file. The database contains a table named tblMagazine; the table has three fields. The Cost field is numeric. The Code and MagName fields contain text. Start the application to view the records contained in the dataset, and then stop the application. Open the Code Editor window. The btnCode_Click procedure should display the record whose Code field contains EX33. The btnName_Click procedure should display only the Visual Basic record. The btnAll_Click procedure should display all of the records. Code the procedures. Save the solution and then start and test the application. Close the Code Editor window and then close the solution.

INTERMEDIATE

4. Using the information from Exercise 1, write a LINQ statement that selects magazines whose names begin with the letter G (in either uppercase or lowercase). Then write a LINQ statement that calculates the average cost of a magazine.

INTERMEDIATE

5. Open the Magazine Solution (Magazine Solution.sln) file contained in the VB2012\Chap13\Magazine Solution–Intermediate folder. If necessary, open the designer window. The application is connected to the Magazines database stored in the Magazines.accdb file. The database contains a table named tblMagazine; the table has three fields. The Cost field is numeric. The Code and MagName fields contain text.

   a. Start the application to view the records contained in the dataset, and then stop the application.
   b. Open the Code Editor window. Code the btnAll_Click procedure so that it displays all of the records.
   c. Code the btnCost_Click procedure so that it displays records having a cost of $4 or more.
   d. Code the btnName_Click procedure so that it displays only magazines whose names begin with the letter C (in either uppercase or lowercase).
   e. Code the btnAverage_Click procedure so that it displays the average cost of a magazine. Display the average in a message box.
   f. Save the solution and then start and test the application. Close the Code Editor window and then close the solution.

INTERMEDIATE

6. Open the MusicBox Solution (MusicBox Solution.sln) file contained in the VB2012\Chap13\MusicBox Solution–LINQ folder. If necessary, open the designer window. The application is connected to the MusicBox database stored in the MusicBox.accdb file. The database contains a table named tblBox. The table contains 10 records, each composed of four text fields.
   a. Start the application to view the records contained in the dataset, and then stop the application.
   b. Open the Code Editor window. Code the btnAll_Click procedure so that it displays all of the records.
   c. Code the btnShape_Click procedure so that it displays the records for music boxes having the shape selected by the user.
   d. Code the btnSource_Click procedure so that it displays either the records for music boxes received as gifts or the records for music boxes that were purchased by the user.
   e. Code the btnCount_Click procedure to display the number of music boxes in the dataset.
   f. Save the solution and then start and test the application. Close the Code Editor window and then close the solution.

LESSON C

After studying Lesson C, you should be able to:

- Prevent the user from adding and deleting records
- Remove buttons from a BindingNavigator control
- Add a label, a text box, and a button to a BindingNavigator control

Completing the Paradise Bookstore Application

Your task in this chapter is to create an application for the Paradise Bookstore. The application will use a DataGridView control to display the records contained in a Microsoft Access database named Books. It will also allow the store manager to enter an author's name (or part of a name) and then display only the books written by that author. In addition, it will allow the store manager to display the total value of the books in the store.

The Books database is stored in the Books.accdb file, which is contained in the VB2012\Chap13\Access Databases folder. The database contains one table named tblBooks. The table has five fields and 11 records. The BookNumber, Price, and QuantityInStock fields are numeric. The Title and Author fields contain text. The fields and records contained in the tblBooks table are shown in Figure 13-46.

BookNumber	Title	Author	Price	QuantityInStock
101	Garden of Eden	Smith, Leona	$35.99	15
146	Rosebud	Smith, Leona	$24.50	20
224	Cycle World	Russel, John	$15.99	5
233	Motorcycle Mania	Russel, John	$12.99	2
322	Truthfully Yours	Staven, Harriet	$45.50	20
367	Romance and You	Staven, Harriet	$10.99	15
401	My Hero	Smith, Carol	$63.99	23
402	Laddie the Dog	Smith, Carol	$10.99	11
561	That Was the Day	Handel, Pat	$15.99	4
581	Rusty the Robot	Handel, Pat	$9.99	3
603	Philomena	Smith, Carol	$24.50	1

Figure 13-46 tblBooks table in the Books database

To modify the DataGridView and BindingNavigator controls in the Paradise Bookstore application:

START HERE

1. If necessary, start Visual Studio 2012. Open the Paradise Bookstore Solution (Paradise Bookstore Solution.sln) file contained in the VB2012\Chap13\Paradise Bookstore Solution folder. If necessary, open the designer window.
2. In this application, the user will not be allowed to add or delete records. Click the **TblBooksDataGridView** control. Click the control's **task box** to open its task list. Click the **Enable Adding** and **Enable Deleting** check boxes to deselect both check boxes. Click the form's **title bar** to close the task list.
3. Click the **TblBooksBindingNavigator** control and then click its **task box**. Click **Edit Items** on the task list. Click **BindingNavigatorAddNewItem** in the Members list and then click the **X** button to remove the item from the list. This also removes the Add new button (the plus sign) from the TblBooksBindingNavigator control.

4. The BindingNavigatorDeleteItem should be selected in the Members list. Click the **X** button to remove the item from the list. This also removes the Delete button (the letter *X*) from the TblBooksBindingNavigator control.
5. Now you will add a label and a text box for entering the author's name. Click the **down arrow** in the "Select item and add to list below" box and then click **Label** in the list. Click the **Add** button. Click the **Alphabetical** button to display the property names in alphabetical order. Click **Text** in the properties list (if necessary) and then type **&Author:** and press **Enter**.
6. Click the **down arrow** in the "Select item and add to list below" box and then click **TextBox** in the list. Click the **Add** button. Change the text box's name to **txtAuthor**.
7. Next, you will add a button that, when clicked, will display the books written by the author whose name (or part of the name) is entered in the text box. Click the **down arrow** in the "Select item and add to list below" box and then click **Button** in the list. Click the **Add** button. Change the button's name to **btnGo**. Also change its DisplayStyle and Text properties to **Text** and **&Go**, respectively.
8. Finally, you will add a button for displaying the total value of the books. Click the **Add** button again to add another button to the BindingNavigator control. Change the button's name to **btnTotal**. Also change its DisplayStyle and Text properties to **Text** and **&Total Value**, respectively. See Figure 13-47.

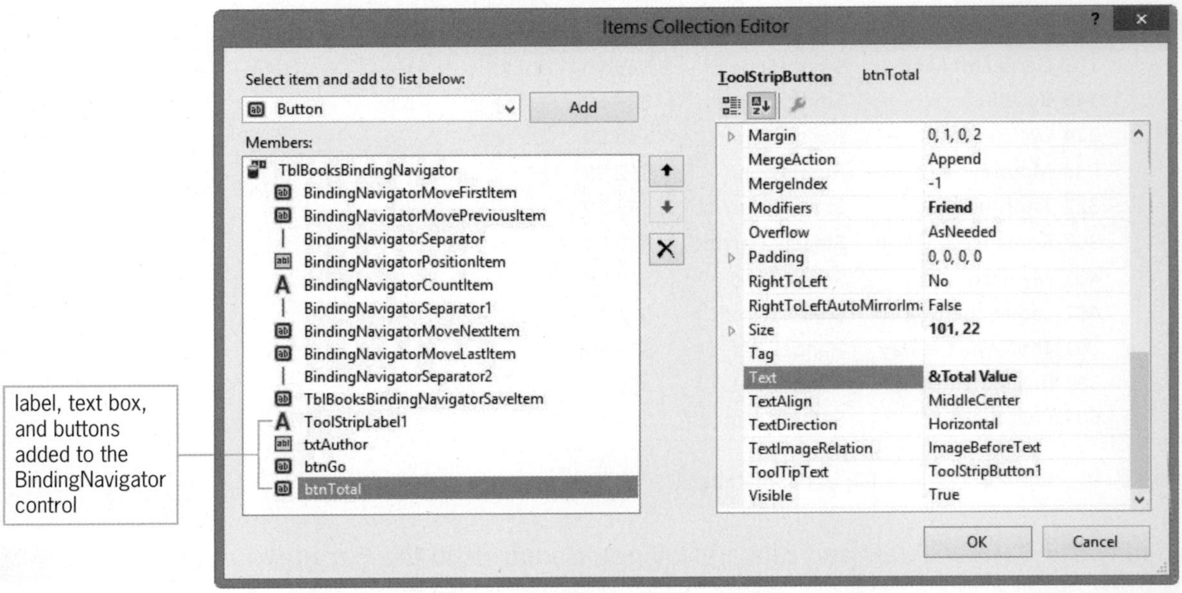

Figure 13-47 Completed Items Collection Editor dialog box

9. Click the **OK** button to close the dialog box, and then click the form's **title bar**. See Figure 13-48.

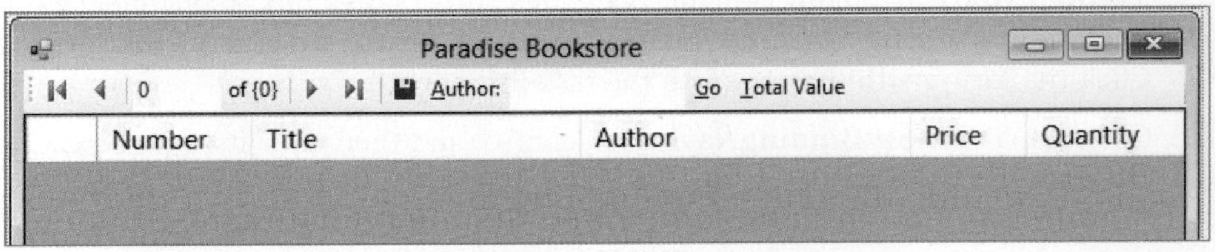

Figure 13-48 Completed TblBooksBindingNavigator control

Coding the Paradise Bookstore Application

The Go button's Click event procedure should display only records whose Author field begins with the one or more characters entered in the txtAuthor control. If the text box is empty, the Go button should display all of the records.

START HERE

To code and then test the Go button's Click event procedure:

1. Open the Code Editor window. Replace <your name> and <current date> in the comments with your name and the current date, respectively.

2. Open the code template for the btnGo control's Click event procedure. Type the following comment and then press **Enter** twice:

   ' display records for a specific author

3. You can use LINQ to select the appropriate records. Enter the following lines of code. Press **Enter** twice after typing the last line.

```
Dim records = From book In BooksDataSet.tblBooks
              Where book.Author.ToUpper Like
              txtAuthor.Text.ToUpper & "*"
              Select book
```

4. Now you will display the records in the DataGridView control. As you learned in Lesson B, you do this by assigning the `records` variable to the BindingSource object's DataSource property. Enter the following line of code:

   TblBooksBindingSource.DataSource = records.AsDataView

5. Save the solution and then start the application. Click the **Author** text box (or press **Alt+a**) and then type the letter **s**. Click the **Go** button (or press **Alt+g**). The DataGridView control shows only the seven books written by authors whose names begin with the letter s. See Figure 13-49.

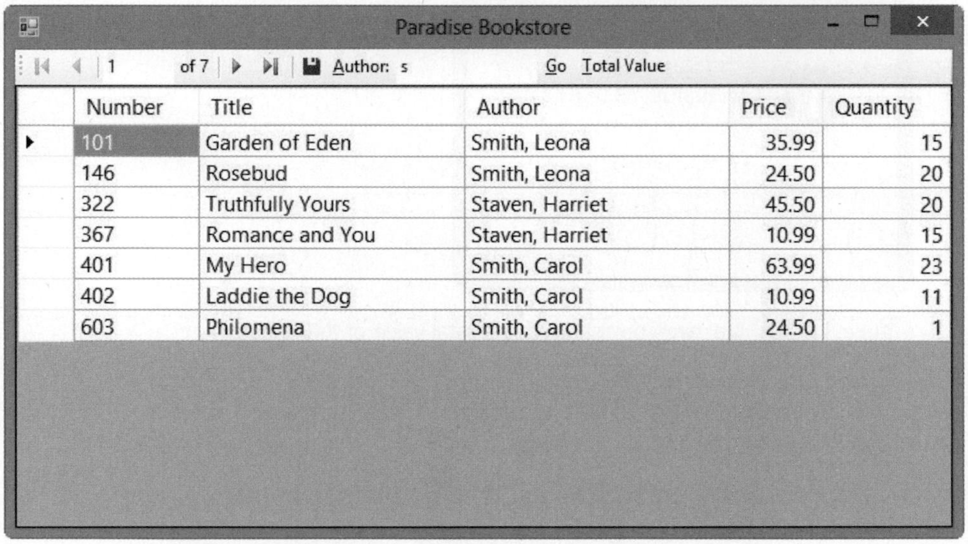
Paradise Bookstore
1 of 7
Author: s
Go Total Value
Number Title Author Price Quantity
101 Garden of Eden Smith, Leona 35.99 15
146 Rosebud Smith, Leona 24.50 20
322 Truthfully Yours Staven, Harriet 45.50 20
367 Romance and You Staven, Harriet 10.99 15
401 My Hero Smith, Carol 63.99 23
402 Laddie the Dog Smith, Carol 10.99 11
603 Philomena Smith, Carol 24.50 1

Figure 13-49 Books written by authors whose names begin with s

6. Remove the letter s from the Author text box and then click the **Go** button. All of the records appear in the DataGridView control.

7. Click the **Close** button on the form's title bar to stop the application.

The Total Value button's Click event procedure should display the total value of the books in the store. The total value is calculated by multiplying the quantity of each book by its price and then adding together the results.

START HERE

To code and then test the Total Value button's Click event procedure:

1. Open the code template for the btnTotal control's Click event procedure. Type the following comment and then press **Enter** twice:

   ' display the total value of the inventory

2. You can use the Sum aggregate operator to accumulate the results of multiplying each book's quantity by its price. The quantity and price are stored in the QuantityInStock and Price fields, respectively. Enter the following lines of code. Press **Enter** twice after typing the last line.

```
Dim dblTotal As Double =
    Aggregate book In BooksDataSet.tblBooks
    Select book.QuantityInStock * book.Price
    Into Sum()
```

3. Now display the total value in a message box. Enter the following lines of code:

```
MessageBox.Show("Total value: " &
                dblTotal.ToString("C2"),
                "Paradise Bookstore",
                MessageBoxButtons.OK,
                MessageBoxIcon.Information)
```

4. Save the solution and then start the application. Click the **Total Value** button (or press **Alt+t**). The total value of the inventory appears in a message box. See Figure 13-50.

Figure 13-50 Message box showing the total value of the inventory

5. Close the message box, and then click the **Close** button on the form's title bar to stop the application.
6. Close the Code Editor window and then close the solution.

Figure 13-51 shows the code entered in the btnGo and btnTotal Click event procedures.

```
Private Sub btnGo_Click(sender As Object,
e As EventArgs) Handles btnGo.Click
    ' display records for a specific author

    Dim records = From book In BooksDataSet.tblBooks
                  Where book.Author.ToUpper Like
                  txtAuthor.Text.ToUpper & "*"
                  Select book

    TblBooksBindingSource.DataSource = records.AsDataView

End Sub

Private Sub btnTotal_Click(sender As Object,
e As EventArgs) Handles btnTotal.Click
    ' display the total value of the inventory

    Dim dblTotal As Double =
        Aggregate book In BooksDataSet.tblBooks
        Select book.QuantityInStock * book.Price
        Into Sum()

        MessageBox.Show("Total value: " &
                        dblTotal.ToString("C2"),
                        "Paradise Bookstore",
                        MessageBoxButtons.OK,
                        MessageBoxIcon.Information)

End Sub
```

Figure 13-51 btnGo_Click and btnTotal_Click procedures

Lesson C Summary

- To prevent the user from adding or deleting records in a DataGridView control:

  Click the DataGridView control's task box and then deselect the Enable Adding and Enable Deleting check boxes.

- To delete items from a BindingNavigator control:

  Click the BindingNavigator control's task box and then click Edit Items. In the Members list, click the item you want to remove. Click the *X* button.

- To add controls to a BindingNavigator control:

  Click the BindingNavigator control's task box and then click Edit Items. Use the "Select item and add to list below" box and Add button to add the appropriate control.

Lesson C Key Terms

There are no key terms in Lesson C.

Lesson C Review Questions

1. The Enable Deleting check box in a ________ control's task list determines whether a record can be deleted from the control.

   a. BindingNavigator
   b. BindingSource
   c. DataBindingNavigator
   d. DataGridView

2. Using the Books database from the lesson, which of the following will select book number 401? The BookNumber field is numeric.

   a.
   ```
   Dim records = From book In BooksDataSet.tblBooks
         Where book.BookNumber = "401"
         Select book
   ```
   b.
   ```
   Dim records = From book In BooksDataSet.tblBooks
         Select book.BookNumber = 401
   ```
   c.
   ```
   Dim records = From book In BooksDataSet.tblBooks
         Where book.BookNumber = 401
         Select book
   ```
   d.
   ```
   Dim records = From book In BooksDataSet.tblBooks
         Select BookNumber = 401
   ```

3. Using the Books database from the lesson, which of the following determines the number of records in the dataset?

   a.
   ```
   Dim intNumRecords As Integer =
         Aggregate book In BooksDataSet.tblBooks
         In Counter()
   ```
   b.
   ```
   Dim intNumRecords As Integer =
         Aggregate book In BooksDataSet.tblBooks
         Into Count()
   ```
   c.
   ```
   Dim intNumRecords As Integer =
         Aggregate book In BooksDataSet.tblBooks
         Into Sum()
   ```
   d.
   ```
   Dim intNumRecords As Integer =
         Aggregate book In BooksDataSet.tblBooks
         Into Total()
   ```

4. Using the Books database from the lesson, which of the following determines the total number of books in the bookstore?

   a.
   ```
   Dim intNumBooks As Integer =
         Aggregate book In BooksDataSet.tblBooks
         Select book.QuantityInStock
         Into Count()
   ```
   b.
   ```
   Dim intNumBooks As Integer =
         Aggregate book In BooksDataSet.tblBooks
         Select book.QuantityInStock
         Into Sum()
   ```
   c.
   ```
   Dim intNumBooks As Integer =
         Aggregate book In BooksDataSet.tblBooks
         Into Sum()
   ```
   d.
   ```
   Dim intNumBooks As Integer =
         Aggregate book In BooksDataSet.tblBooks
         Into Total()
   ```

5. Using the Books database from the lesson, which of the following determines the number of books whose price is at least $20?

   a.
```
Dim intNum As Integer =
    Aggregate book In BooksDataSet.tblBooks
    Where book.Price > 20
    Into Count()
```

   b.
```
Dim intNum As Integer =
    Aggregate book In BooksDataSet.tblBooks
    Where book.Price >= 20
    Into Sum()
```

   c.
```
Dim intNum As Integer =
    Aggregate book In BooksDataSet.tblBooks
    Where book.Price >= 20
    Select book
```

   d.
```
Dim intNum As Integer =
    Aggregate book In BooksDataSet.tblBooks
    Where book.Price >= 20
    Into Count()
```

Lesson C Exercises

1. Open the Addison Playhouse Solution (Addison Playhouse Solution.sln) file contained in the VB2012\Chap13\Addison Playhouse Solution folder. If necessary, open the designer window. Connect the application to a Microsoft Access database named Play. The database is stored in the VB2012\Chap13\Access Databases\Play.accdb file. The Play database contains one table named tblReservations. The table has 20 records. Each record has three fields: a numeric field named Seat and two text fields named Patron and Phone. The application should display the contents of the Play database in a DataGridView control. It should also allow the user to add, delete, modify, and save records. Enter the Try...Catch statement in the Save Data button's Click event procedure. Save the solution and then start and test the application. Close the Code Editor window and then close the solution. INTRODUCTORY

2. Open the Sports Action Solution (Sports Action Solution.sln) file contained in the VB2012\Chap13\Sports Action Solution folder. If necessary, open the designer window. Connect the application to a Microsoft Access database named Sports. The database is stored in the VB2012\Chap13\Access Databases\Sports.accdb file. The database contains one table named tblScores. The table contains 10 records. Each record has five fields that store the following information: a unique number that identifies the game, the date the game was played, the name of the opposing team, the home team's score, and the opposing team's score. The application should display each record contained in the Sports database, one at a time, in label controls. (Hint: First, change each field object's control type to Label in the Data Sources window. Then, change the table object's control type to Details before dragging it to the form.) The user should not be allowed to add, delete, edit, or save records. Include a button on a BindingNavigator control to allow the user to display the average of the home team's scores. Open the Code Editor window and code the application. Save the solution and then start and test the application. Close the Code Editor window and then close the solution. INTRODUCTORY

3. The sales manager at JW Industries records the item number, name, and price of the company's products in a database named Items. The Items database is stored in the VB2012\Chap13\Access Databases\Items.accdb file. The database contains one table named tblItems. The table contains 10 records, each composed of three fields. The ItemNum and ItemName fields contain text, and the Price field contains numbers. The sales manager wants an application that displays the records in a DataGridView control. INTERMEDIATE

The application should not allow records to be added or deleted. The application should allow the sales manager to display records whose item number matches one or more characters he enters. In addition, it should allow him to display the average price.

a. Create a Visual Basic Windows application. Use the following names for the solution and project, respectively: JW Solution, JW Project. Save the application in the VB2012\Chap13 folder. Change the form file's name to Main Form.vb. Change the form's name to frmMain.

b. Connect the application to the Items database and then drag the tblItems object to the form. Make the appropriate modifications to the DataGridView and BindingNavigator controls.

c. Open the Code Editor window and code the application. Save the solution and then start and test the application. Close the Code Editor window and then close the solution.

INTERMEDIATE

4. In this exercise, you use a Microsoft Access database named Courses. The database is stored in the VB2012\Chap13\Access Databases\Courses.accdb file. The database contains one table named tblCourses. The table has 10 records. Each record has the following four fields: ID, Title, CreditHours, and Grade. The CreditHours field is numeric; the other fields contain text.

   a. Open the College Courses Solution (College Courses Solution.sln) file contained in the VB2012\Chap13\College Courses Solution folder. If necessary, open the designer window. Connect the application to the Courses database. Drag the table into the group box control and then dock the DataGridView control in its parent container. (In this case, the parent container is the group box control.) Use the task list to disable Adding, Editing, and Deleting. Change the DataGridView control's AutoSizeColumnsMode property to Fill. Change its RowHeadersVisible and Enabled properties to False. Also change its SelectionMode property to FullRowSelect.

   b. Remove the BindingNavigator control from the form by deleting the BindingNavigator object from the component tray.

   c. Open the Code Editor window. Delete the Save Data button's Click event procedure. Code the Next Record and Previous Record buttons. Code the Grade Display button so it allows the user to display either all the records or only the records matching a specific grade.

   d. Save the solution and then start and test the application. Close the Code Editor window and then close the solution.

INTERMEDIATE

5. In this exercise, you use a Microsoft Access database named Trips. The database keeps track of a person's business and pleasure trips. The database is stored in the VB2012\Chap13\Access Databases\Trips.accdb file. The database contains one table named tblTrips. The table has 10 records. Each record has the following four text fields: TripDate, Origin, Destination, BusinessPleasure. The user should be able to display the number of trips from a specific origin to a specific destination, such as from Chicago to Atlanta. He or she should also be able to display the total number of business trips and the total number of pleasure trips.

   a. Create a Visual Basic Windows application. Use the following names for the solution and project, respectively: Trips Solution and Trips Project. Save the application in the VB2012\Chap13 folder. Change the form file's name to Main Form.vb. Change the form's name to frmMain.

b. Connect the application to the Trips database and then drag the tblTrips object to the form. Make the appropriate modifications to the DataGridView control.

c. Open the Code Editor window and code the application. Be sure to enter the Try... Catch statement in the Save Data button's Click event procedure. (Hint: You can use a logical operator in the Where clause.) Save the solution and then start the application. Use the application to answer the following questions:

How many trips were made from Chicago to Nashville?

How many trips were made from Atlanta to Los Angeles?

How many business trips were taken?

How many pleasure trips were taken?

d. Close the Code Editor window and then close the solution.

ADVANCED

6. In this exercise, you use a Microsoft Access database named Calories. The database keeps track of the calories consumed during the day. The database is stored in the VB2012\Chap13\Access Databases\Calories.accdb file. The database contains one table named tblCalories. The table has 10 records. Each record has the following six fields: Day, Breakfast, Lunch, Dinner, Dessert, and Snack. The Day field is a text field; the other fields are numeric. The user should be able to display the total number of calories consumed in the entire dataset. He or she should also be able to display the total calories consumed for a specific meal, such as the total calories consumed for breakfasts, lunches, dinners, desserts, or snacks. In addition, the user should be able to display the total calories consumed on a specific day, the number of days in which more than 1200 calories were consumed, and the average number of calories consumed per day.

a. Create a Visual Basic Windows application. Use the following names for the solution and project, respectively: Calorie Counter Solution and Calorie Counter Project. Save the application in the VB2012\Chap13 folder. Change the form file's name to Main Form.vb. Change the form's name to frmMain.

b. Connect the application to the Calories database and then drag the tblCalories object to the form. Make the appropriate modifications to the DataGridView control.

c. Open the Code Editor window and code the application. Save the solution and then start the application. Use the application to answer the following questions:

How many calories were consumed in the entire dataset?

How many calories were consumed for desserts?

How many calories were consumed on 12/21/2013?

How many days were more than 1200 calories consumed?

What is the average number of calories consumed per day?

d. Close the Code Editor window and then close the solution.

ADVANCED

7. In this exercise, you modify the College Courses application from Exercise 4. Use Windows to make a copy of the College Courses Solution folder. Rename the copy Modified College Courses Solution. Open the College Courses Solution (College Courses Solution.sln) file contained in the Modified College Courses Solution folder. Open the designer window. Add a Calculate GPA button to the form. Open the Code Editor window. Code the Calculate GPA button's Click event procedure so that it displays the student's GPA. (An A grade is worth 4 points, a B is worth 3 points, and so on.) Display the GPA in a message box. Save the solution and then start and test the application. Close the Code Editor window and then close the solution.

SWAT THE BUGS

8. Open the Debug Solution (Debug Solution.sln) file contained in the VB2012\Chap13\Debug Solution folder. The application is connected to the Friends database stored in the Friends.accdb file. The database contains one table named tblFriends. The table contains nine records. Open the Code Editor window and review the existing code. Correct the code to remove the jagged line that appears below one of the lines of code. Save the solution and then start the application. Click the Fill button, then click the Next and Previous buttons. Notice that the application is not working correctly. Correct the application's code. Save the solution and then start and test the application again. Close the Code Editor window and then close the solution.

CHAPTER 14

Access Databases and SQL

Creating the Academy Award Winners Application

In this chapter, you will create an application that uses a Microsoft Access database named Movies to keep track of the Academy Award winners for Best Picture. The Movies database will store the title of each movie, the year the movie won the award, the name of the director, and the movie's running time. The application will allow the user to add records to the database and also delete records from the database.

Previewing the Academy Award Winners Application

Before you start the first lesson in this chapter, you will preview the completed application. The application is contained in the VB2012\Chap14 folder.

START HERE

To preview the completed application:

1. Use the Run dialog box to run the Academy (Academy.exe) file contained in the VB2012\Chap14 folder. The interface displays the records in a DataGridView control. As Figure 14-1 indicates, the record for the year 2002 is missing. (Recall that you can use the Alt key to show/hide the access keys.)

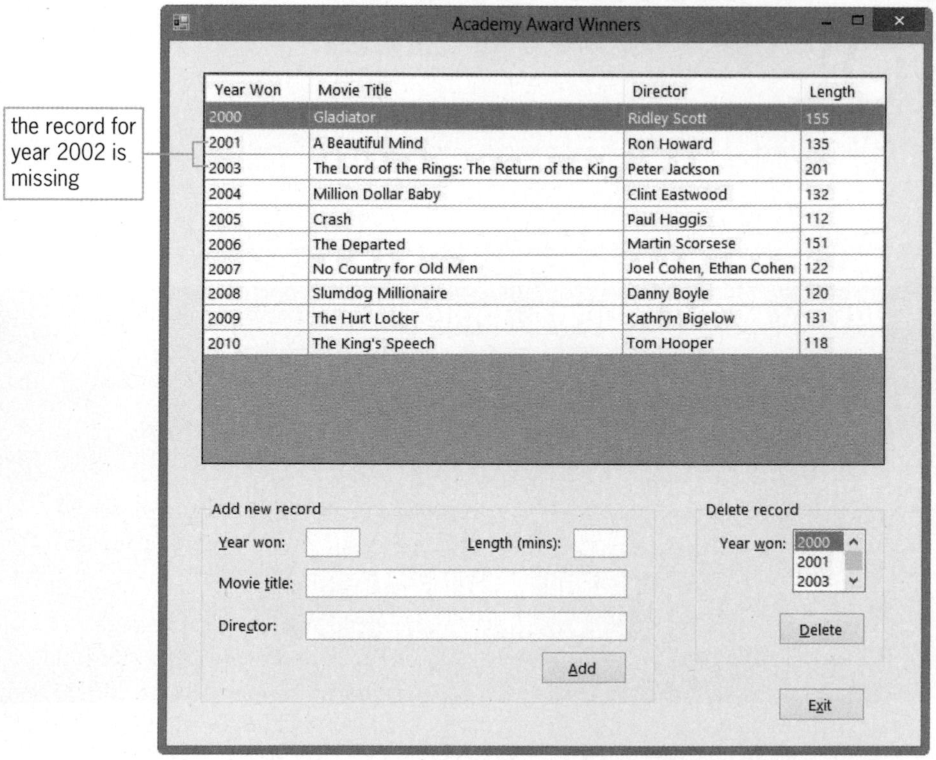

Figure 14-1 Academy Award Winners application

2. First, you will add the missing record to the database. Click the **Year won** text box in the Add new record section of the interface. Type **2002** and then press **Tab**. Type **113**, **Chicago**, and **Rob Marshall** in the Length, Movie title, and Director boxes, respectively. Click the **Add** button. The record you added appears in numerical order by the year number. See Figure 14-2.

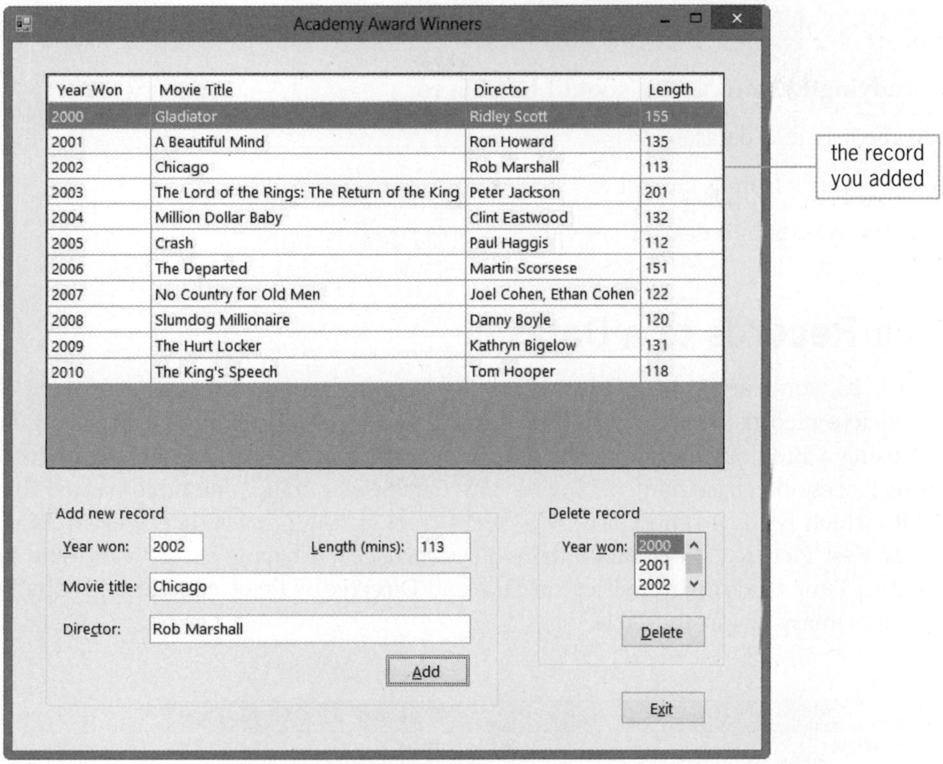

Figure 14-2 Result of adding the missing record

3. Next, you'll verify that the record was saved to the database. Click the **Exit** button to end the application, and then run the Academy (Academy.exe) file again. The record for the year 2002 appears in the DataGridView control.
4. Now, you'll delete the record. Click **2002** in the first column of the DataGridView control; doing this highlights (selects) the entire record. It also selects the 2002 value in the Delete record section. Click the **Delete** button. The "Delete winner from year 2002?" message appears in a message box. Click the **Yes** button to delete the record. The computer removes the record from the DataGridView control, the dataset, and the database.
5. Click **2009** in the first column of the DataGridView control, and then click the **Delete** button. This time, click the **No** button in the Confirm Delete message box. The record remains in the DataGridView control, the dataset, and the database.
6. Click the **Exit** button to end the application, and then run the Academy (Academy.exe) file again. Notice that the 2002 record, which you deleted in Step 4, does not appear in the DataGridView control.
7. Click the **Exit** button.

In Lesson A, you will learn how to add records to a dataset, delete records from a dataset, and sort the records in a dataset. You will also learn how to save (to a database) the changes made to a dataset. Lessons B and C cover SQL, which stands for Structured Query Language. You will create the Academy Award Winners application in Lesson C. Be sure to complete each lesson in full and do all of the end-of-lesson questions and several exercises before continuing to the next lesson.

LESSON A

After studying Lesson A, you should be able to:

- Add records to a dataset
- Delete records from a dataset
- Sort the records in a dataset

Adding Records to a Dataset

In Chapter 13, you learned how to use a BindingNavigator control to add records to a dataset and also delete records from a dataset. In this lesson, you will learn how to perform both tasks without using a BindingNavigator control. The records will be added to and deleted from a Microsoft Access database named Movies. The database contains one table named tblMovies. The table, which is shown in Figure 14-3, keeps track of the movies that won an Academy Award for Best Picture. The table contains 11 records, each having three fields. The YearWon and RunningTime fields are numeric; the Title and DirectedBy fields contain text. The YearWon field is the primary key in the table.

YearWon	Title	DirectedBy	RunningTime
2000	Gladiator	Ridley Scott	155
2001	A Beautiful Mind	Ron Howard	135
2002	Chicago	Rob Marshall	113
2003	The Lord of the Rings: The Return of the King	Peter Jackson	201
2004	Million Dollar Baby	Clint Eastwood	132
2005	Crash	Paul Haggis	112
2006	The Departed	Martin Scorsese	151
2007	No Country for Old Men	Joel Cohen, Ethan Cohen	122
2008	Slumdog Millionaire	Danny Boyle	120
2009	The Hurt Locker	Kathryn Bigelow	131
2010	The King's Speech	Tom Hooper	118

Figure 14-3 Data contained in the tblMovies table

START HERE

To open the Academy Award Winners application:

1. If necessary, start Visual Studio 2012. Open the Academy Award Solution (Academy Award Solution.sln) file contained in the VB2012\Chap14\Academy Award Solution folder. If necessary, open the designer window. The Academy Award Winners application is already connected to the Movies database, and the Movies.accdb file's Copy to Output Directory property is set to Copy if newer. The application's interface contains a DataGridView control named TblMoviesDataGridView. The control is bound to the tblMovies table in the dataset. The application also contains four objects in its component tray. See Figure 14-4.

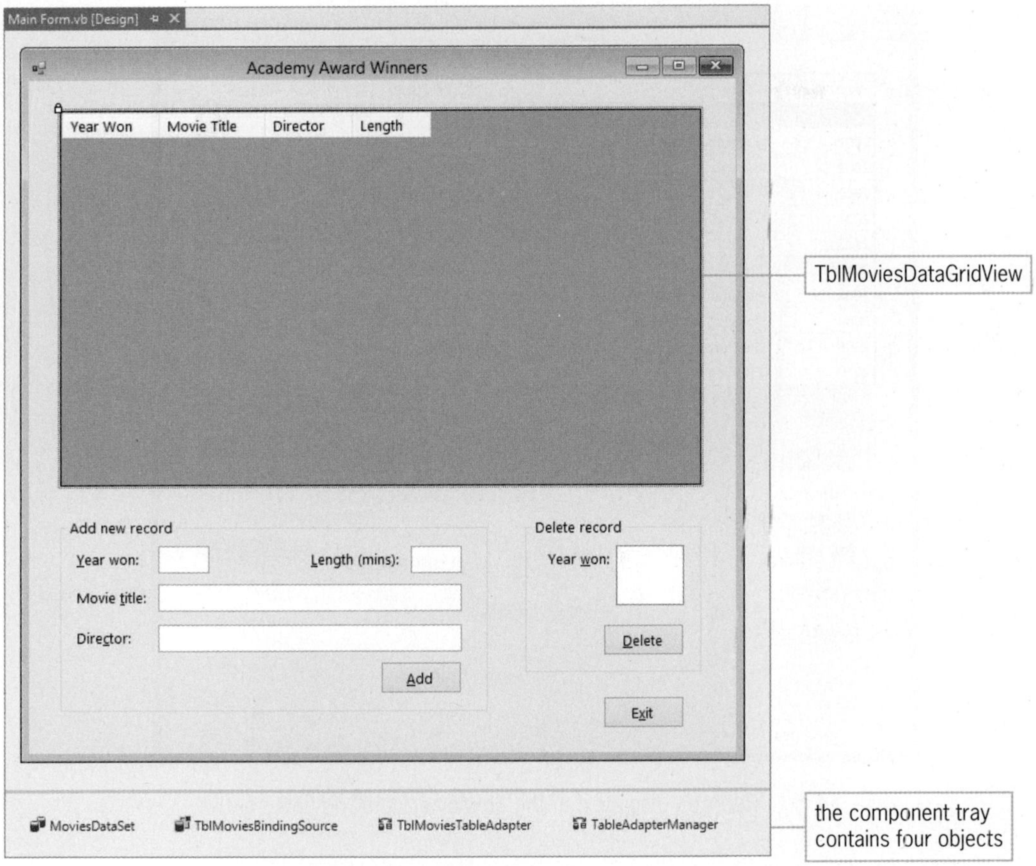

Figure 14-4 Interface for the Academy Award Winners application

2. Start the application. The records in the dataset appear in the TblMoviesDataGridView control. The control's AutoSizeColumnsMode, ReadOnly, SelectionMode, and StandardTab properties are set to DisplayedCells, True, FullRowSelect, and True, respectively. Its AllowUserToAddRows, AllowUserToDeleteRows, and RowHeadersVisible properties are set to False. The lstDeleteYear control is bound to the YearWon field in the dataset; this is accomplished by setting the control's DataSource and DataMember properties to TblMoviesBindingSource and YearWon, respectively. See Figure 14-5. (Recall that you can use the Alt key to show/hide the access keys.)

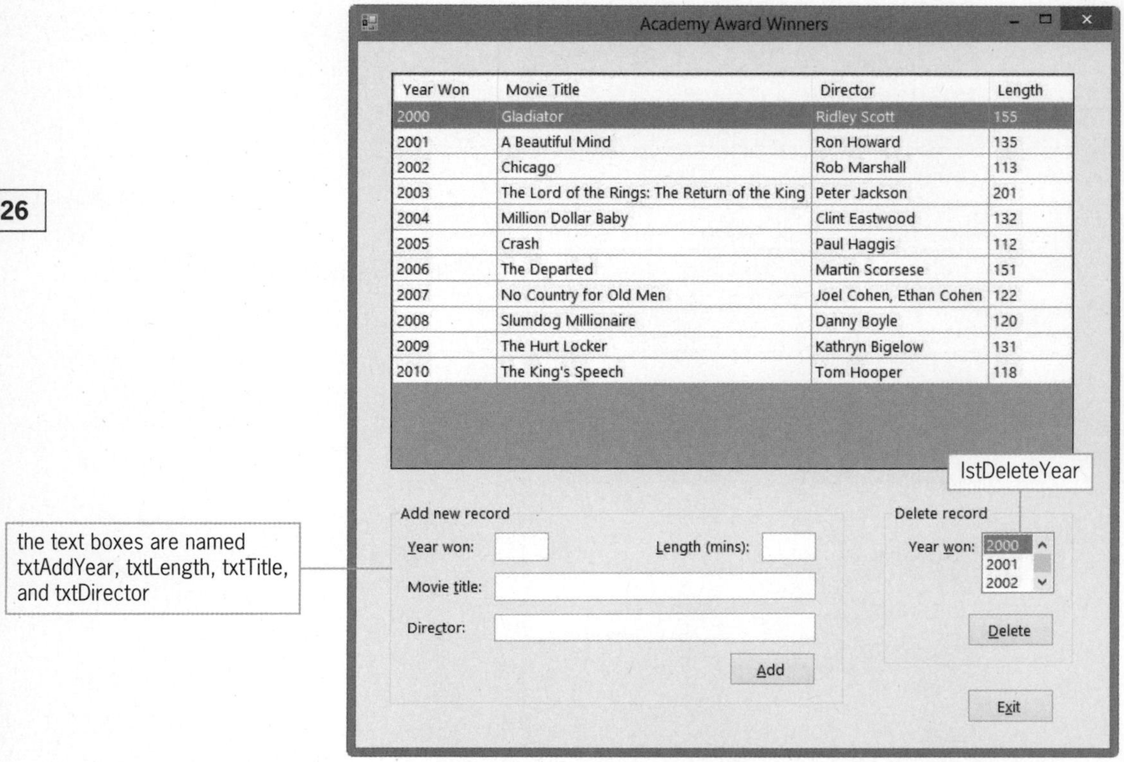

Figure 14-5 Records displayed in the TblMoviesDataGridView control

3. Press the **down arrow** key on your keyboard, slowly, several times. Each time the highlight moves to a different row in the DataGridView control, the value in the current row's YearWon field is highlighted in the lstDeleteYear control.
4. Click the **Exit** button to end the application.

The Add button's Click event procedure should add the record entered in the four text boxes to the MoviesDataSet. Visual Basic provides several ways of adding records to a dataset. In this lesson, you will use the syntax shown in Figure 14-6. The figure also includes examples of using the syntax.

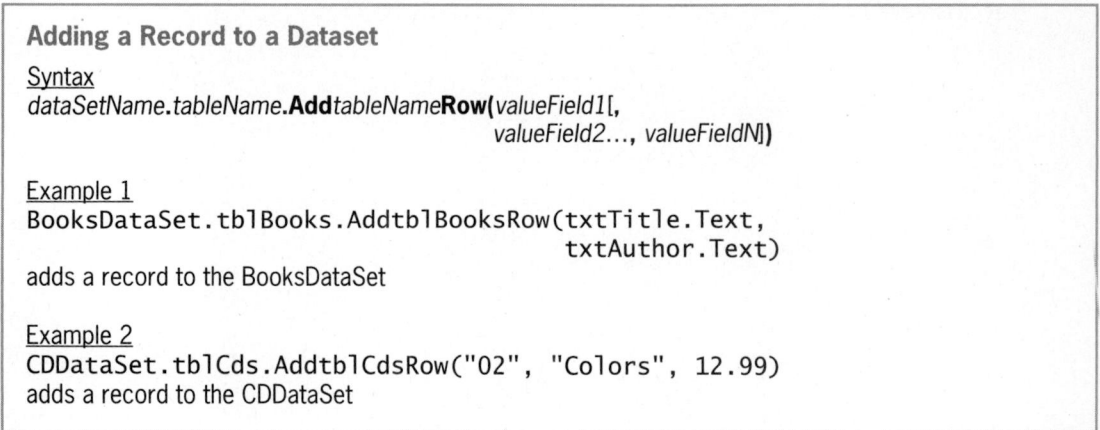

Adding a Record to a Dataset

Syntax

dataSetName.*tableName*.**Add***tableName***Row(***valueField1*[, *valueField2*..., *valueFieldN*]**)**

Example 1

```
BooksDataSet.tblBooks.AddtblBooksRow(txtTitle.Text,
                                     txtAuthor.Text)
```

adds a record to the BooksDataSet

Example 2

```
CDDataSet.tblCds.AddtblCdsRow("02", "Colors", 12.99)
```

adds a record to the CDDataSet

Figure 14-6 Syntax and examples of adding a record to a dataset

START HERE

To begin coding the Add button's Click event procedure:

1. Open the Code Editor window. Replace <your name> and <current date> in the comments with your name and the current date, respectively.
2. Locate the btnAdd_Click procedure and then click the **blank line** above the End Sub clause.
3. Recall that the YearWon and RunningTime fields in the dataset are numeric. Therefore, you will need to convert the values entered in the txtAddYear and txtLength controls to numbers before storing each in its associated field. Enter the following four statements. Press **Enter** twice after typing the last statement.

```
Dim intYear As Integer
Dim intLength As Integer
Integer.TryParse(txtAddYear.Text, intYear)
Integer.TryParse(txtLength.Text, intLength)
```

4. Now, you will use the syntax from Figure 14-6 to add the record to the MoviesDataSet. Enter the following statement:

```
MoviesDataSet.tblMovies.AddtblMoviesRow(intYear,
                                        txtTitle.Text,
                                        txtDirector.Text,
                                        intLength)
```

5. Save the solution and then start the application. In the Add new record section of the interface, type **2011** in the Year won box, **100** in the Length box, **The Artist** in the Movie title box, and **Michael Hazanavicius** in the Director box. Click the **Add** button. The new record appears as the last record in the DataGridView control, as shown in Figure 14-7.

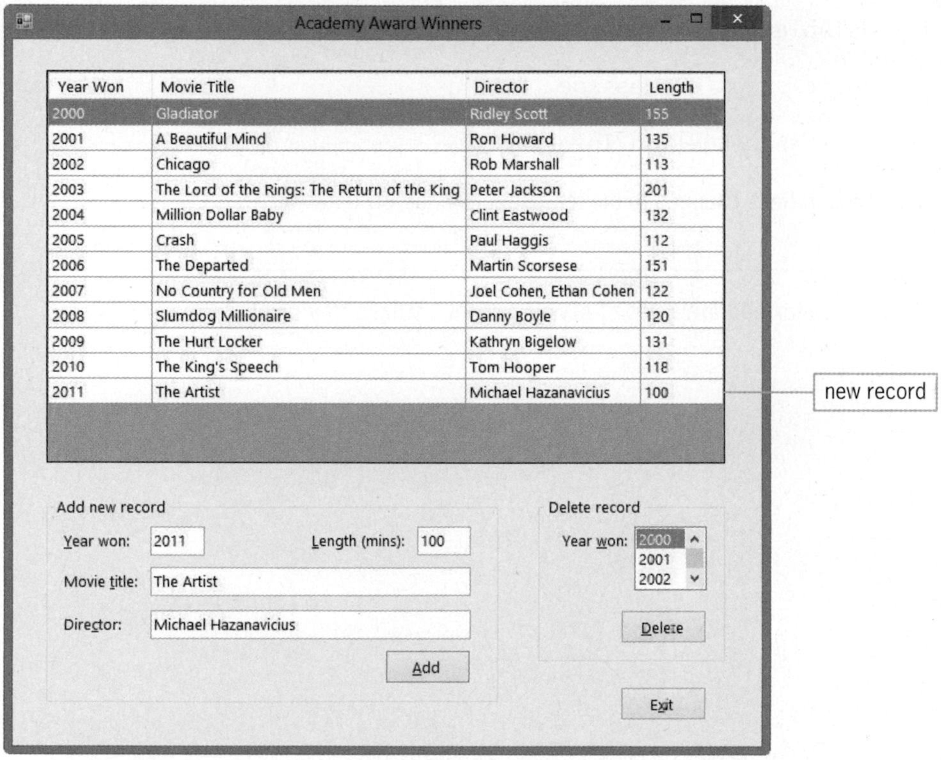

Figure 14-7 New record added to the DataGridView control

6. Click the **Exit** button and then start the application again. Notice that the new record is missing from the DataGridView control. This is because the Add button's Click event procedure contains only the code for adding a record to a dataset. It does not yet contain the code for actually saving the record to the Movies database. You will add that code in the next set of steps. Click the **Exit** button.

Figure 13-17 in Chapter 13 illustrates the relationships among the database, the objects in the component tray, and the bound controls.

For the changes made to a dataset to be permanent, you need to save the changes to the database associated with the dataset. Here too, Visual Basic provides several ways of performing this task. In this lesson, you will use the TableAdapter object's **Update method**. As you learned in Chapter 13, the TableAdapter object connects the database to the DataSet object.

The Update method's syntax is shown in Figure 14-8 along with examples of using the syntax. Because it is possible for an error to occur when saving data to a database, you should place the Update method within the Try block of a Try...Catch statement, as shown in the examples.

Saving Dataset Changes to a Database

Syntax

tableAdapterName.**Update(***dataSetName.tableName***)**

Example 1

```
Try
   TblBooksTableAdapter.Update(BooksDataSet.tblBooks)
Catch ex As Exception
   MessageBox.Show(ex.Message, "Books",
          MessageBoxButtons.OK,
          MessageBoxIcon.Information)
End Try
```

saves the BooksDataSet's changes to the tblBooks table in the Books database

Example 2

```
Try
   TblCdsTableAdapter.Update(CDDataSet.tblCds)
Catch ex As Exception
   MessageBox.Show(ex.Message, "CDs",
          MessageBoxButtons.OK,
          MessageBoxIcon.Information)
End Try
```

saves the CDDataSet's changes to the tblCds table in the CD database

Figure 14-8 Syntax and examples of saving dataset changes to a database

START HERE

To finish coding the btnAdd_Click procedure, and then test it:

1. Enter the additional lines of code indicated in Figure 14-9.

```
                                        intLength)
    Try
        TblMoviesTableAdapter.Update(MoviesDataSet.tblMovies)
    Catch ex As Exception
        MessageBox.Show(ex.Message, "Add Record",
                        MessageBoxButtons.OK,
                        MessageBoxIcon.Information)
    End Try
End Sub
```

enter these seven lines of code

Figure 14-9 Additional code entered in the btnAdd_Click procedure

2. Save the solution and then start the application. In the Add new record section of the interface, type **2011**, **100**, **The Artist**, and **Michael Hazanavicius** in the appropriate boxes. Click the **Add** button. The new record is added to the end of the records in the DataGridView control, as shown earlier in Figure 14-7.
3. Now observe what happens when you try to add a duplicate record to the dataset. In this case, a duplicate record is a record whose YearWon field value is already in the dataset. (Recall that the YearWon field is the primary key in the tblMovies table.) Click the **Add** button again. A run time error occurs when the computer attempts to process the AddtblMoviesRow function. The run time error occurs because the 2011 value is already present in the dataset. See Figure 14-10.

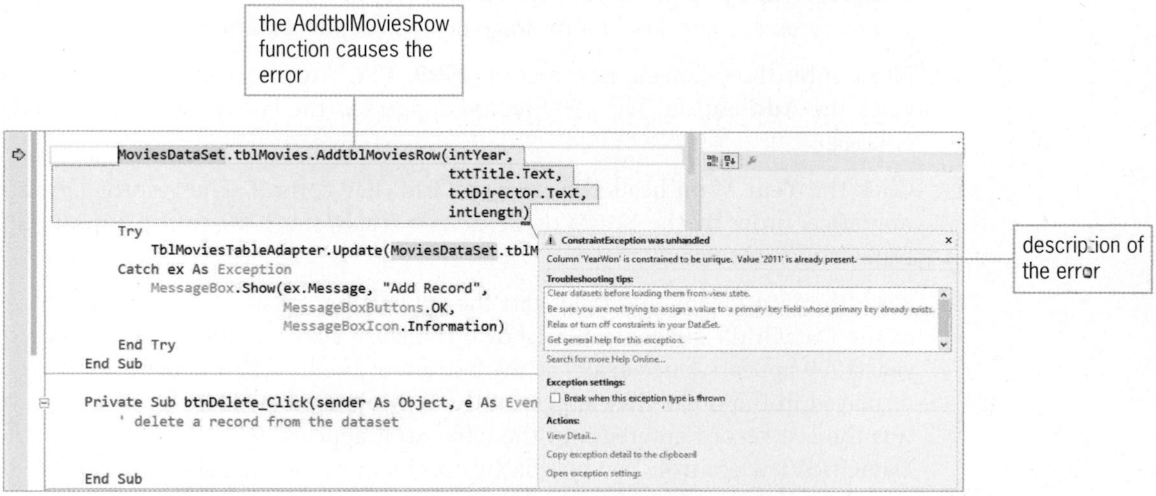

Figure 14-10 Result of trying to add a duplicate record

4. Click **DEBUG** on the menu bar and then click **Stop Debugging**. You can fix this problem by placing the AddtblMoviesRow function in a Try...Catch statement. Enter the outer Try...Catch statement shown in Figure 14-11. Be sure to move the AddtblMoviesRow function and the existing Try...Catch statement into the Try section of the outer Try...Catch statement.

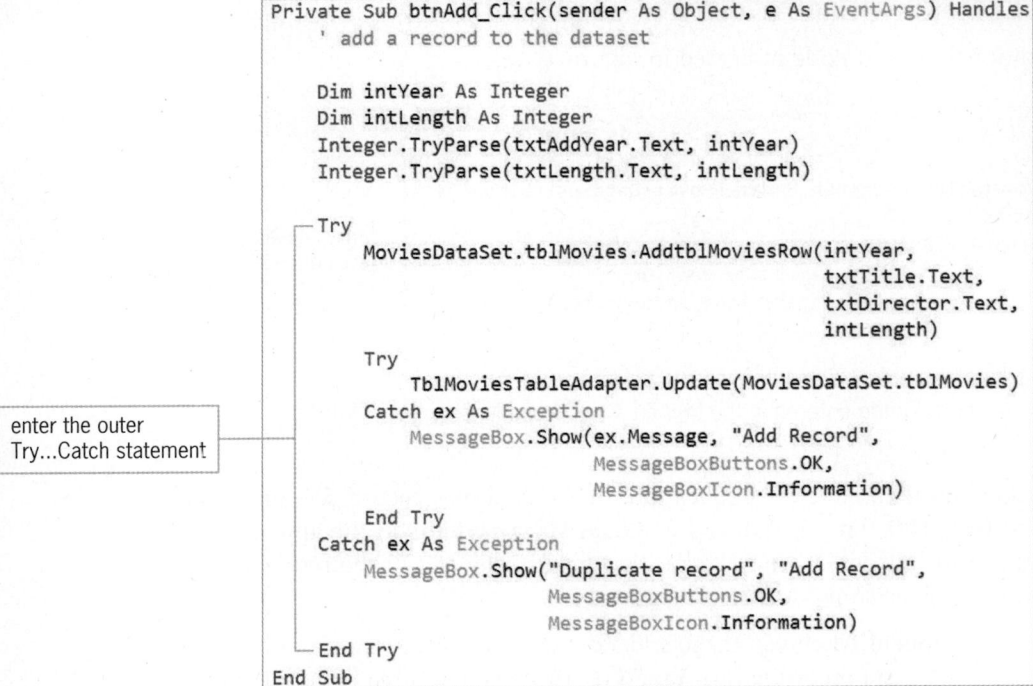

```
Private Sub btnAdd_Click(sender As Object, e As EventArgs) Handles
    ' add a record to the dataset

    Dim intYear As Integer
    Dim intLength As Integer
    Integer.TryParse(txtAddYear.Text, intYear)
    Integer.TryParse(txtLength.Text, intLength)

    Try
        MoviesDataSet.tblMovies.AddtblMoviesRow(intYear,
                                                txtTitle.Text,
                                                txtDirector.Text,
                                                intLength)
        Try
            TblMoviesTableAdapter.Update(MoviesDataSet.tblMovies)
        Catch ex As Exception
            MessageBox.Show(ex.Message, "Add Record",
                            MessageBoxButtons.OK,
                            MessageBoxIcon.Information)
        End Try
    Catch ex As Exception
        MessageBox.Show("Duplicate record", "Add Record",
                        MessageBoxButtons.OK,
                        MessageBoxIcon.Information)
    End Try
End Sub
```

enter the outer Try...Catch statement

Figure 14-11 Completed btnAdd_Click procedure

5. Save the solution and then start the application. In the Add new record section of the interface, type **2011** in the Year won box and then click the **Add** button. The "Duplicate record" message appears in a message box. Close the message box.
6. Next, enter the following new record: **1999**, **122**, **American Beauty**, **Sam Mendes**. Click the **Add** button. The 1999 record appears as the last record in the DataGridView control.
7. Click the **Year Won** header in the DataGridView control. The records now appear in numerical order by the YearWon field. As a result, the 1999 record appears first in the DataGridView control.
8. Click the **Exit** button and then start the application again. The two new records appear in the DataGridView control, as shown in Figure 14-12. Notice that the record for the year 1999 appears, once again, at the bottom of the list. This is because the records are displayed in the order they appear in the tblMovies table. The record for the year 1999 was the last record entered into the table, so it appears as the last record in the DataGridView control. You will fix this problem in the next section.

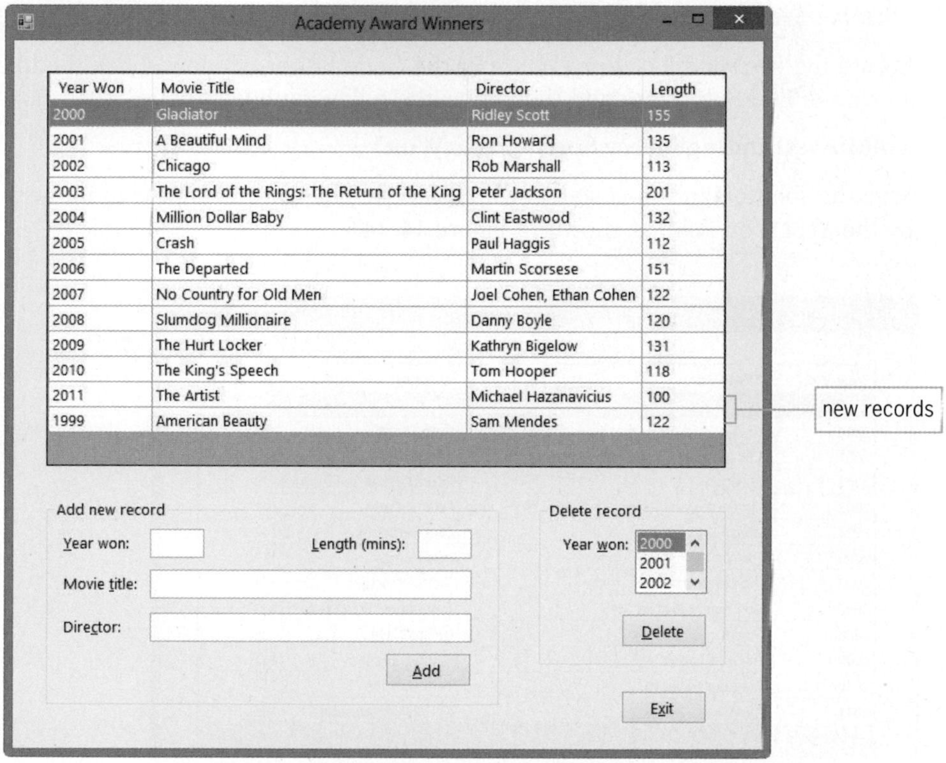

Figure 14-12 New records displayed in the DataGridView control

9. Click the **Exit** button.

Sorting the Records in a Dataset

As you observed in the previous set of steps, you can sort the records in a DataGridView control by clicking the appropriate header while the application is running. You also can use the BindingSource object's **Sort method** in code. The method's syntax is shown in Figure 14-13 along with examples of using the syntax. If you want the records in a dataset to appear in a particular order when the application is started, you enter the Sort method in the form's Load event procedure.

Sorting the Records in a Dataset

Syntax
bindingSourceName.**Sort** = *fieldName*

Example 1
```
TblBooksBindingSource.Sort = "Author"
```
sorts the records by the Author field

Example 2
```
TblCdsBindingSource.Sort = "Cost"
```
sorts the records by the Cost field

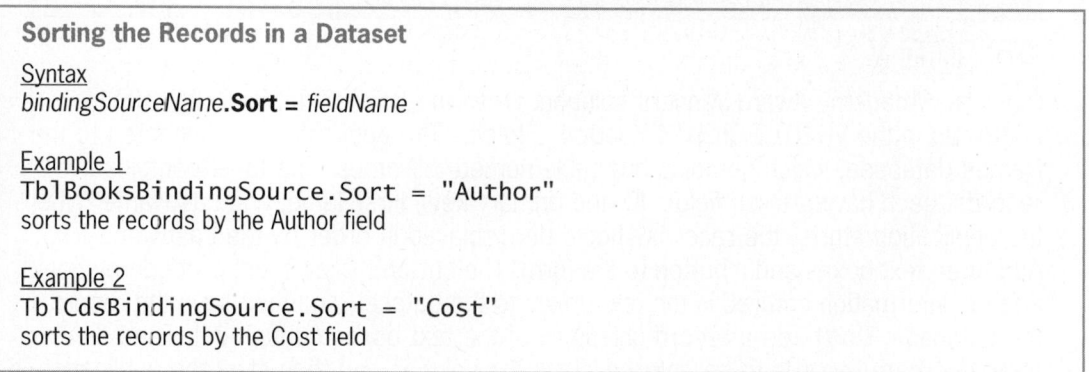

Figure 14-13 Syntax and examples of sorting the records in a dataset

START HERE

To sort the records by the YearWon field:

1. Locate the frmMain_Load procedure in the Code Editor window. Click the **blank line** above the End Sub clause and then enter the following line of code:

   TblMoviesBindingSource.Sort = "YearWon"

2. Save the solution and then start the application. The records appear in numerical order by the YearWon field, as shown in Figure 14-14.

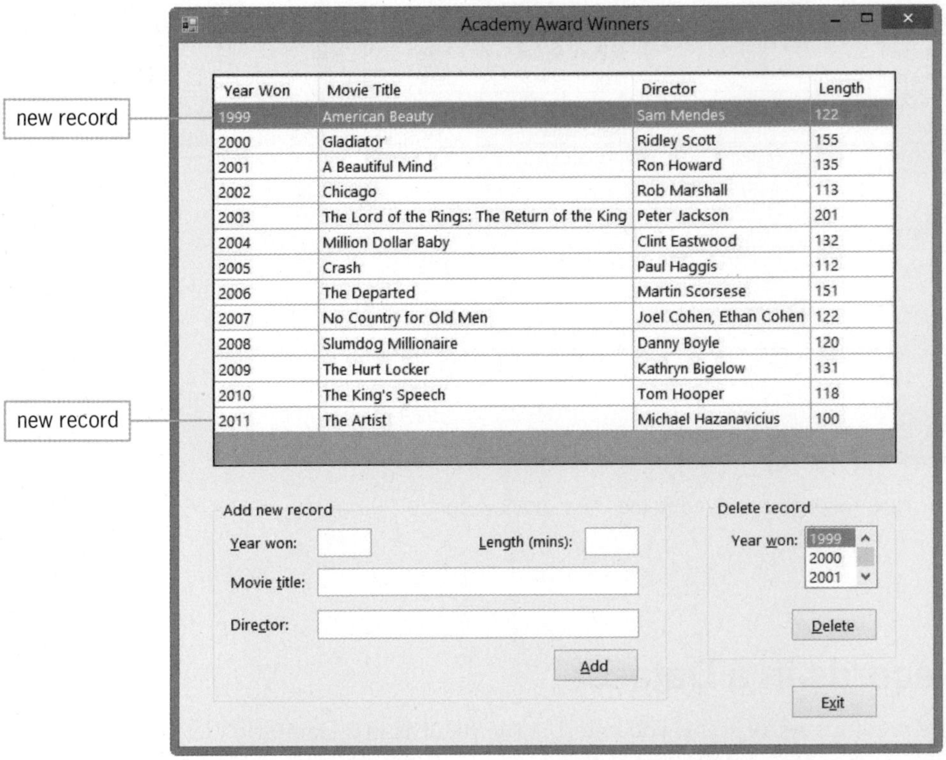

Figure 14-14 Records sorted by the YearWon field

3. Click the **Exit** button.

YOU DO IT 1!

Close the Academy Award Winners solution. Open the YouDoIt 1 (YouDoIt 1.sln) file contained in the VB2012\Chap14\YouDoIt 1 folder. The application is connected to the Names database, which contains one table named tblNames. The table contains five records, each having three fields: ID (the primary key), FirstName, and LastName. When the application starts, the records should be displayed in order by the LastName field. Add three text boxes and a button to the form. The button's Click event procedure should add the information entered in the text boxes to the dataset, and then save the record in the database. Don't add a record unless all of the text boxes contain data, and don't allow duplicate records to be entered. Save the solution and then start the application. Add your name to the database. Then, try adding a duplicate record. Close the Code Editor window and then close the solution.

Deleting Records from a Dataset

The Delete button's Click event procedure should search the dataset for the record whose YearWon field contains the value selected in the lstDeleteYear control. Before deleting the record, the procedure should display a message that asks the user to confirm the deletion. You will use the MessageBox.Show method to both display the message and get the user's response.

START HERE

To begin coding the Delete button's Click event procedure:

1. If necessary, open the Academy Award Winners solution. Locate the btnDelete_Click procedure and then click the **blank line** above the End Sub clause. The procedure will use a DialogResult variable to store the value returned by the MessageBox.Show method. Enter the following statement:

   Dim dlgButton As DialogResult

2. Now, enter the MessageBox.Show method shown in Figure 14-15, and then position the insertion point as indicated in the figure. Notice that the message box will have Yes and No buttons.

```
Private Sub btnDelete_Click(sender As Object, e As EventArgs) Handles btn
    ' delete a record from the dataset

    Dim dlgButton As DialogResult
    dlgButton =
        MessageBox.Show("Delete winner from year " &
                        lstDeleteYear.Text & "?", "Confirm Delete",
                        MessageBoxButtons.YesNo,
                        MessageBoxIcon.Exclamation)

    |
End Sub
```

enter these five lines of code

position the insertion point here

Figure 14-15 MessageBox.Show method entered in the btnDelete_Click procedure

3. The procedure will delete the record only when the user selects the Yes button in the message box. Enter the following If clause:

   If dlgButton = Windows.Forms.DialogResult.Yes Then

4. Save the solution.

Before the btnDelete_Click procedure can delete the record from the dataset, it first must locate the record. Visual Basic provides several ways of locating records in a dataset. In this lesson, you will use the syntax shown in Figure 14-16. The figure also includes examples of using the syntax.

Locating a Record in a Dataset

Syntax
dataRowVariable =
    dataSetName.tableName.**FindBy***fieldName*(*value*)

Example 1
```
Dim row As DataRow
row = BooksDataSet.tblBooks.FindById(123)
```
The assignment statement searches the dataset for the record whose Id field contains 123, and then assigns the record to the `row` variable.

Example 2
```
Dim findRow As DataRow
findRow = CDDataSet.tblCds.FindByArtist("Cher")
```
The assignment statement searches the dataset for the record whose Artist field contains "Cher", and then assigns the record to the `findRow` variable.

Figure 14-16 Syntax and examples of locating a record in a dataset

START HERE

To continue coding the btnDelete_Click procedure:

1. First, enter the following declaration statement below the If clause:

   Dim row As DataRow

2. As mentioned earlier, the YearWon field in the dataset is numeric. Therefore, you will need to convert the year contained in the lstDeleteYear control to a number before searching for the record in the dataset. Enter the following statements:

   Dim intYear As Integer
   Integer.TryParse(lstDeleteYear.Text, intYear)

3. Now, you will use the syntax from Figure 14-16 to locate the appropriate record. Enter the following statement:

   row =
   MoviesDataSet.tblMovies.FindByYearWon(intYear)

4. Save the solution.

After locating the appropriate record and assigning it to a DataRow variable, you can use the variable's **Delete method** to delete the record. Figure 14-17 shows the method's syntax and includes an example of using the method.

Deleting a Record from a Dataset

Syntax
dataRowVariable.**Delete()**

Example
```
Dim row As DataRow
row = BooksDataSet.tblBooks.FindByTitle("Money")
row.Delete()
```
The Delete method deletes the record associated with the `row` variable.

Figure 14-17 Syntax and an example of deleting a record from a dataset

To finish coding the btnDelete_Click procedure:

START HERE

1. Enter the following statement:

   row.Delete()

2. As you learned earlier, the changes made to a dataset are not permanent until they are saved to the database associated with the dataset. Recall that you can save the changes using the TableAdapter object's Update method. Also recall that you should enter the Update method within the Try block of a Try...Catch statement. Enter the additional code shown in Figure 14-18.

```
                         MessageBoxIcon.Exclamation)

If dlgButton = Windows.Forms.DialogResult.Yes Then
    Dim row As DataRow
    Dim intYear As Integer
    Integer.TryParse(lstDeleteYear.Text, intYear)
    row =
        MoviesDataSet.tblMovies.FindByYearWon(intYear)
    row.Delete()
    Try
        TblMoviesTableAdapter.Update(MoviesDataSet.tblMovies)
    Catch ex As Exception
        MessageBox.Show(ex.Message, "Delete Record",
                        MessageBoxButtons.OK,
                        MessageBoxIcon.Information)
    End Try
End If
```

enter these seven lines of code

Figure 14-18 Additional code entered in the btnDelete_Click procedure

3. Save the solution and then start the application. The first record is highlighted in the DataGridView control, and the value of the record's YearWon field (1999) is highlighted in the list box.

4. Click the **Delete** button. The message box shown in Figure 14-19 appears on the screen. (Recall that you can use the Alt key to show/hide the access keys.)

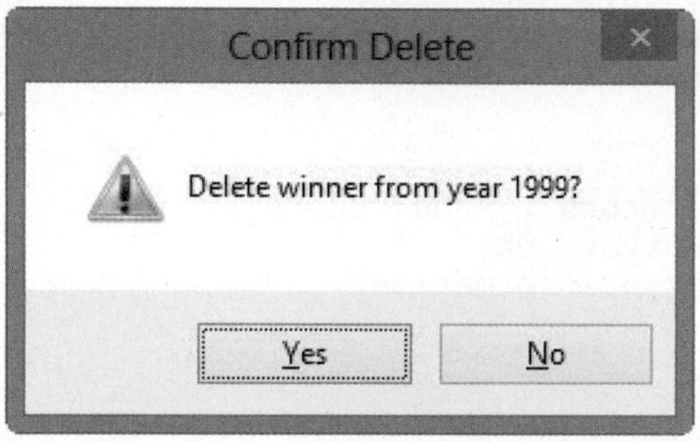

Figure 14-19 Message box displayed by the btnDelete_Click procedure

5. Click the **Yes** button in the message box. The computer deletes the record from the dataset, the DataGridView control, and the database. It also deletes the 1999 entry from the list box.

6. Next, click **2005** in the Year Won column. The record for the year 2005 is highlighted in the DataGridView control, and the value of the record's YearWon field (2005) is highlighted in the list box. Click the **Delete** button, and then click the **No** button in the message box. The record remains in the dataset, the DataGridView control, and the database. The 2005 entry also remains in the list box.

7. Finally, scroll down the list box until you see 2011, and then click **2011** in the list. Click the **Delete** button and then click the **Yes** button. The computer deletes the record from the dataset, the DataGridView control, and the database. It also deletes the 2011 entry from the list box.
8. Click the **Exit** button and then start the application again. Notice that the 2005 record remains in the dataset, but the 1999 and 2011 records were deleted.
9. Click the **Exit** button to end the application. Close the Code Editor window and then close the solution.

Figure 14-20 shows the frmMain_Load, btnAdd_Click, and btnDelete_Click procedures.

```
Private Sub frmMain_Load(sender As Object,
e As EventArgs) Handles MyBase.Load
    'TODO: This line of code loads data into the
    'MoviesDataSet.tblMovies' table. You can move, or
    remove it, as needed.
    Me.TblMoviesTableAdapter.Fill(Me.MoviesDataSet.tblMovies)
    TblMoviesBindingSource.Sort = "YearWon"

End Sub

Private Sub btnAdd_Click(sender As Object,
e As EventArgs) Handles btnAdd.Click
    ' add a record to the dataset

    Dim intYear As Integer
    Dim intLength As Integer
    Integer.TryParse(txtAddYear.Text, intYear)
    Integer.TryParse(txtLength.Text, intLength)

    Try
        MoviesDataSet.tblMovies.AddtblMoviesRow(intYear,
                                        txtTitle.Text,
                                        txtDirector.Text,
                                        intLength)
        Try
            TblMoviesTableAdapter.Update(MoviesDataSet.tblMovies)
        Catch ex As Exception
            MessageBox.Show(ex.Message, "Add Record",
                            MessageBoxButtons.OK,
                            MessageBoxIcon.Information)
        End Try

    Catch ex As Exception
        MessageBox.Show("Duplicate record", "Add Record",
                        MessageBoxButtons.OK,
                        MessageBoxIcon.Information)
    End Try
End Sub

Private Sub btnDelete_Click(sender As Object,
e As EventArgs) Handles btnDelete.Click
    ' delete a record from the dataset

    Dim dlgButton As DialogResult
    dlgButton =
        MessageBox.Show("Delete winner from year " &
                        lstDeleteYear.Text & "?", "Confirm Delete",
                        MessageBoxButtons.YesNo,
                        MessageBoxIcon.Exclamation)
```

Notice that you can nest the Try...Catch statement.

Figure 14-20 frmMain_Load, btnAdd_Click, and btnDelete_Click procedures *(continues)*

(continued)

```
If dlgButton = Windows.Forms.DialogResult.Yes Then
        Dim row As DataRow
        Dim intYear As Integer
        Integer.TryParse(lstDeleteYear.Text, intYear)
        row =
            MoviesDataSet.tblMovies.FindByYearWon(intYear)
        row.Delete()
        Try
            TblMoviesTableAdapter.Update(MoviesDataSet.tblMovies)
        Catch ex As Exception
            MessageBox.Show(ex.Message, "Delete Record",
                            MessageBoxButtons.OK,
                            MessageBoxIcon.Information)
        End Try
    End If
End Sub
```

Figure 14-20 frmMain_Load, btnAdd_Click, and btnDelete_Click procedures

Lesson A Summary

- To add a record to a dataset:

  Use the following syntax:

  dataSetName.tableName.**Add***tableName***Row(***valueField1*[, *valueField2…*, *valueFieldN*])

- To save dataset changes to a database:

  Use the TableAdapter object's Update method. The method's syntax is:

  tableAdapterName.**Update(***dataSetName.tableName***)**

- To sort the records in a dataset:

  Use the BindingSource object's Sort method. The method's syntax is:

  bindingSourceName.**Sort** = *fieldName*

- To locate a record in a dataset:

  Use the following syntax:

  dataRowVariable = *dataSetName.tableName*.**FindBy***fieldName*(*value*)

- To delete a record from a dataset:

  Use a DataRow variable's Delete method. The syntax is:

  dataRowVariable.**Delete()**

Lesson A Key Terms

Delete method—a method of a DataRow variable; used to delete a record from a dataset

Sort method—a method of the BindingSource object; used to sort a dataset in order by a specific field

Update method—a method of the TableAdapter object; used to save a dataset's changes to its associated database

Lesson A Review Questions

1. The FriendsDataSet contains a table named tblFriends. The table contains two text fields named FName and LName. Which of the following will add a new record to the dataset?
   a. `FriendsDataSet.tblFriends.AddFriendsRow(strF, strL)`
   b. `FriendsDataSet.tblFriends.AddRowToFriends(strF, strL)`
   c. `FriendsDataSet.tblFriends.AddtblFriendsRow(strF, strL)`
   d. `FriendsDataSet.AddtblFriendsRow(strF, strL)`

2. Two records were added to the FriendsDataSet from Review Question 1. Which of the following will save the records in the Friends database?
   a. `TblFriendsBindingSource.Save(FriendsDataSet.tblFriends)`
   b. `TblFriendsBindingSource.Update(FriendsDataSet.tblFriends)`
   c. `TblFriendsTableAdapter.Save(FriendsDataSet.tblFriends)`
   d. `TblFriendsTableAdapter.Update(FriendsDataSet.tblFriends)`

3. The FriendsDataSet from Review Question 1 is associated with the TblFriendsBindingSource and TblFriendsTableAdapter objects. Which of the following will sort the records by the LName field?
   a. `TblFriendsBindingSource.Sort = "LName"`
   b. `TblFriendsBindingSource.Sort("LName")`
   c. `TblFriendsTableAdapter.Sort = "LName"`
   d. none of the above

4. Using the FriendsDataSet from Review Question 1, which of the following will locate the record whose last name is Winkler, and then assign the record to the `row` variable?
   a. `row =`
      `FriendsDataSet.tblFriends.FindLName("Winkler")`
   b. `row =`
      `FriendsDataSet.tblFriends.FindByLName("Winkler")`
   c. `row =`
      `FriendsDataSet.tblFriends.Find("Winkler")`
   d. `row =`
      `FriendsDataSet.FindByLName("Winkler")`

5. Which of the following will delete the record associated with a DataRow variable named `findRow`?
   a. `findRow.Delete()`
   b. `findRow.Remove()`
   c. `delete(findRow)`
   d. none of the above

Lesson A Exercises

INTRODUCTORY

1. In this exercise, you modify the Academy Award Winners application from the lesson. Use Windows to make a copy of the Academy Award Solution folder. Rename the copy Modified Academy Award Solution. Open the Academy Award Solution (Academy Award Solution.sln) file contained in the VB2012\Chap14\Modified Academy Award Solution folder. Open the designer and Code Editor windows. Modify the btnAdd_Click procedure so that it adds a

record only when the four text boxes contain data. In addition, save the movie title and director name without any leading or trailing spaces. Save the solution and then start and test the application. Close the Code Editor window and then close the solution.

2. Open the HR Sales Solution (HR Sales Solution.sln) file contained in the VB2012\Chap14\HR Sales Solution folder. If necessary, open the designer window. The application is connected to the Sales database. The database contains a table named tblSales. The table contains five records, each having four numeric fields named RecordNum (the primary key), YearNum, MonthNum, and Sales. The Add button's Click event procedure should allow the user to add records to the database, but only when the four text boxes contain data. All of the records in the database must be unique. The records should appear in numerical order by the record number. Code the application. Save the solution and then start and test the application. Close the Code Editor window and then close the solution. INTRODUCTORY

3. Open the Sydney Solution (Sydney Solution.sln) file contained in the VB2012\Chap14\Sydney Solution folder. If necessary, open the designer window. The application is connected to the Products database. The database contains a table named tblProducts. The table contains 10 records, each composed of three fields. The ItemNum (primary key) and ItemName fields contain text; the Price field contains numbers. The Add button's Click event procedure should allow the user to add records to the database, but only when the three text boxes contain data. All of the records in the database must be unique. The Delete button's Click event procedure should allow the user to delete records from the database. The records should appear in order by the item number when the application is started. Code the application. Save the solution and then start and test the application. Close the Code Editor window and then close the solution. INTRODUCTORY

4. Open the Morgan Industries Solution (Morgan Industries Solution.sln) file contained in the VB2012\Chap14\Morgan Industries Solution folder. If necessary, open the designer window. The application is connected to the Employees database. The database contains one table, which is named tblEmploy. The table contains seven fields and 17 records. The Emp_Number field is the primary key. The Status field contains the employment status, which is either the letter F (for full-time) or the letter P (for part-time). The Code field identifies the employee's department: 1 for Accounting, 2 for Advertising, 3 for Personnel, and 4 for Inventory. The Add button's Click event procedure should allow the user to add records to the database, but only when the user provides all of the employee information. All of the records in the database must be unique. The Delete button's Click event procedure should allow the user to delete records from the database. The records should appear in order by the employee number when the application is started. Code the application. Be sure to code each text box's Enter event procedure. Also code the KeyPress event procedures for the Number, Rate, Status, and Code text boxes. Save the solution and then start and test the application. Close the Code Editor window and then close the solution. INTERMEDIATE

5. In this exercise, you modify the HR Sales application from Exercise 2. Use Windows to make a copy of the HR Sales Solution folder. Rename the copy HR Sales Solution-LINQ. Open the HR Sales Solution (HR Sales Solution.sln) file contained in the HR Sales Solution-LINQ folder. Open the designer window. Add a button to the form. Change the button's name to btnTotal. Change its Text property to &Total Sales. The button's Click event procedure should display the total sales amount in a message box. (Hint: Use one of the LINQ aggregate operators, which you learned about in Chapter 13.) Save the solution and then start and test the application. Close the Code Editor window and then close the solution. INTERMEDIATE

ADVANCED

6. In this exercise, you modify the Academy Award Winners application from this lesson. Use Windows to make a copy of the Academy Award Solution folder. Rename the copy Academy Award Solution-Advanced. Open the Academy Award Solution (Academy Award Solution.sln) file contained in the Academy Award Solution-Advanced folder. Open the designer and Code Editor windows.

   a. Use the Delete button, followed by the Yes button, to delete the 11 records from the dataset. Then, click the Delete button again, followed by the Yes button. A run time error occurs because the `row.Delete()` statement is attempting to delete a record that does not exist. See Figure 14-21.

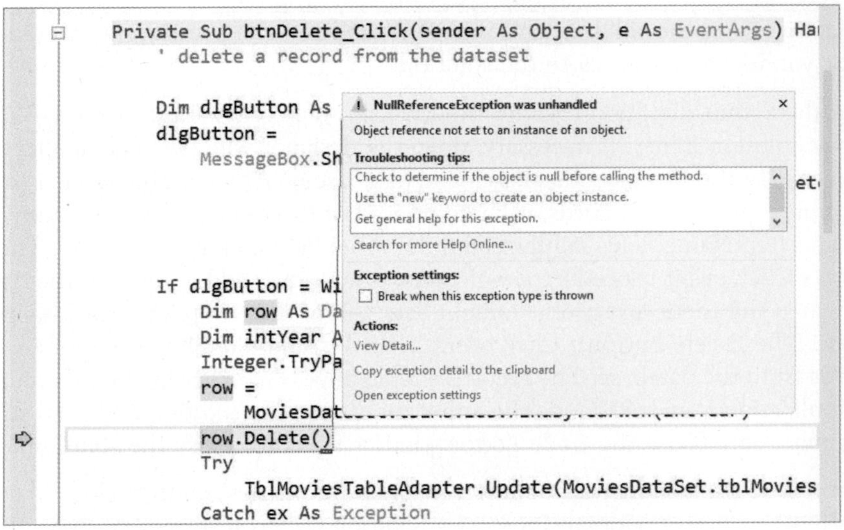

Figure 14-21 Result of trying to delete a non-existent record

   b. Click DEBUG on the menu bar and then click Stop Debugging. To fix the problem, you will have the computer determine whether the `row` variable contains a data row. Insert a blank line above the `row.Delete()` statement. Type `If row Is Nothing Then`, press Enter twice, type `Else`, and then press Enter. In the selection structure's true path, enter a MessageBox.Show method that displays the "No record found" message. Move the `row.Delete()` and Try...Catch statements into the selection structure's false path.

   c. Save the solution and then start the application. Click the Delete button, followed by the Yes button. The "No record found" message appears in a message box. Close the message box. Click the Exit button. Close the Code Editor window and then close the solution.

DISCOVERY

7. Open the Friends Solution (Friends Solution.sln) file contained in the VB2012\Chap14\Friends Solution folder. Open the designer and Code Editor windows. Currently, the form's Load event procedure sorts the records in alphabetical order by the last name. Modify the procedure so that it sorts the records in alphabetical order by first name within last name. Save the solution and then start and test the application. Close the Code Editor window and then close the solution.

LESSON B

After studying Lesson B, you should be able to:

- Query a database using the SQL SELECT statement
- Create queries using the Query Builder dialog box

Structured Query Language

As you learned in Chapter 13, you use a query to specify both the records to select from a database and the order in which to arrange the records. In Chapter 13, you created the queries using LINQ (Language Integrated Query). In this chapter, you will use a different query language, called SQL. You can pronounce SQL either as *ess-cue-el* or as *sequel.*

SQL, which stands for **Structured Query Language**, is a set of statements that allows you to access and manipulate the data stored in many database management systems on computers of all sizes, from large mainframes to small microcomputers. You can use SQL statements—such as SELECT, INSERT, and DELETE—to perform common database tasks. Examples of these tasks include storing, retrieving, updating, deleting, and sorting data.

In this lesson, you will use the SQL SELECT statement to query the Movies database from Lesson A. The tblMovies table in the database contains the 11 records shown in Figure 14-22. Each record has four fields. The YearWon and RunningTime fields are numeric; the Title and DirectedBy fields contain text.

YearWon	Title	DirectedBy	RunningTime
2000	Gladiator	Ridley Scott	155
2001	A Beautiful Mind	Ron Howard	135
2002	Chicago	Rob Marshall	113
2003	The Lord of the Rings: The Return of the King	Peter Jackson	201
2004	Million Dollar Baby	Clint Eastwood	132
2005	Crash	Paul Haggis	112
2006	The Departed	Martin Scorsese	151
2007	No Country for Old Men	Joel Cohen, Ethan Cohen	122
2008	Slumdog Millionaire	Danny Boyle	120
2009	The Hurt Locker	Kathryn Bigelow	131
2010	The King's Speech	Tom Hooper	118

Figure 14-22 Contents of the tblMovies table

The SELECT Statement

The **SELECT statement** is the most commonly used statement in SQL. You can use it to specify the fields and records you want to view, and also to control the order in which the fields and records appear when they are displayed. The statement's basic syntax is shown in Figure 14-23. In the syntax, *fieldList* is one or more field names separated by commas, and *tableName* is the name of the table containing the fields. The WHERE and ORDER BY clauses are optional parts of the syntax. You use the **WHERE clause**, which contains a *condition*, to limit the records you want to view. Similar to the condition in the If...Then...Else and Do...Loop statements, the condition in a WHERE clause specifies a requirement that must be met for a record to be selected. The **ORDER BY clause** is used to arrange the records in either ascending (the default) or descending order by one or more fields. Although you do not have to capitalize the keywords `SELECT`, `FROM`, `WHERE`, `ORDER BY`, and `DESC` in a SELECT statement, many programmers do so for clarity.

SELECT Statement

Basic syntax
SELECT *fieldList* **FROM** *tableName*
    [**WHERE** *condition*]
    [**ORDER BY** *fieldName* [**DESC**]]

Example 1
```
SELECT YearWon, Title, DirectedBy, RunningTime FROM tblMovies
```
selects all of the fields and records in the tblMovies table

Example 2
```
SELECT YearWon, Title, DirectedBy, RunningTime FROM tblMovies
      WHERE YearWon >= 2006
```
selects all of the fields from records for the year 2006 and later

Example 3
```
SELECT YearWon FROM tblMovies WHERE Title = 'Chicago'
```
selects the YearWon field from the Chicago record

Example 4
```
SELECT YearWon, Title, DirectedBy, RunningTime FROM tblMovies
      ORDER BY Title
```
selects all of the fields and records in the tblMovies table and then sorts the records in ascending order by the Title field

Example 5
```
SELECT Title, RunningTime FROM tblMovies
      WHERE Title LIKE 'The %'
      ORDER BY RunningTime DESC
```
selects the Title and RunningTime fields from records whose title begins with the word "The" followed by a space and zero or more characters, and then sorts the records in descending order by the RunningTime field

Figure 14-23 Syntax and examples of the SELECT statement

The SELECT statement in Example 1 in Figure 14-23 tells the computer to select all of the fields and records from the tblMovies table. The SELECT statement in Example 2 uses the WHERE clause to limit the records that will be selected. In this case, the statement tells the computer to select all of the fields, but only from records for the year 2006 and later. The SELECT statement in Example 3 tells the computer to select the YearWon field, but only from the Chicago record. At this point, you may be wondering why the word "Chicago" in Example 3 appears in single quotes, but the number 2006 in Example 2 does not. The single quotes around the value in the WHERE clause's condition are necessary only when you are comparing a text field with a literal constant. Recall that the Title field contains text, whereas the YearWon field contains numbers. Text comparisons in SQL are not case-sensitive. Therefore, you can also write the WHERE clause in Example 3 as `WHERE Title = 'chicago'`.

The SELECT statement in Example 4 in Figure 14-23 selects all of the fields and records from the tblMovies table and then sorts the records in ascending order by the Title field. The SELECT statement in Example 5 shows how you can use the **LIKE operator** along with the **%** (percent sign) wildcard character in the WHERE clause. The statement tells the computer to select the Title and RunningTime fields from records whose title begins with the word "The" followed by a space and zero or more characters. The statement then sorts the records in descending order by the RunningTime field.

Creating a Query

In this section, you will use the Academy Award Winners application to test the SELECT statements from Figure 14-23.

START HERE

To use the Academy Award Winners application to test the SELECT statements:

1. If necessary, start Visual Studio 2012. Open the Academy Award Solution (Academy Award Solution.sln) file contained in the VB2012\Chap14\Academy Award Solution-SQL folder. If necessary, open the designer window. The application is already connected to the Movies database.
2. Start the application. The dataset appears in the DataGridView control. See Figure 14-24. (Recall that you can use the Alt key to show/hide the access keys.)

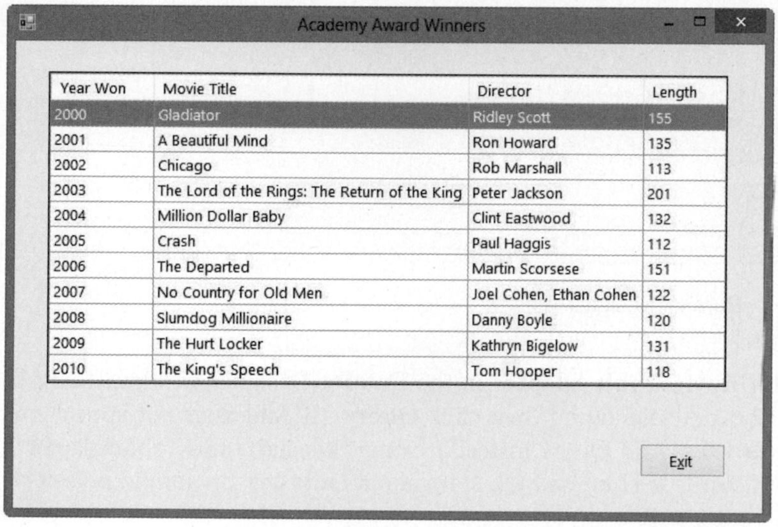

Year Won	Movie Title	Director	Length
2000	Gladiator	Ridley Scott	155
2001	A Beautiful Mind	Ron Howard	135
2002	Chicago	Rob Marshall	113
2003	The Lord of the Rings: The Return of the King	Peter Jackson	201
2004	Million Dollar Baby	Clint Eastwood	132
2005	Crash	Paul Haggis	112
2006	The Departed	Martin Scorsese	151
2007	No Country for Old Men	Joel Cohen, Ethan Cohen	122
2008	Slumdog Millionaire	Danny Boyle	120
2009	The Hurt Locker	Kathryn Bigelow	131
2010	The King's Speech	Tom Hooper	118

Figure 14-24 Contents of the dataset displayed in the DataGridView control

3. Click the **Exit** button to end the application. Right-click **MoviesDataSet.xsd** in the Solution Explorer window. The .xsd file, called the dataset's schema file, contains information about the tables, fields, records, and properties included in the MoviesDataSet. Click **Open** to open the DataSet Designer window. See Figure 14-25.

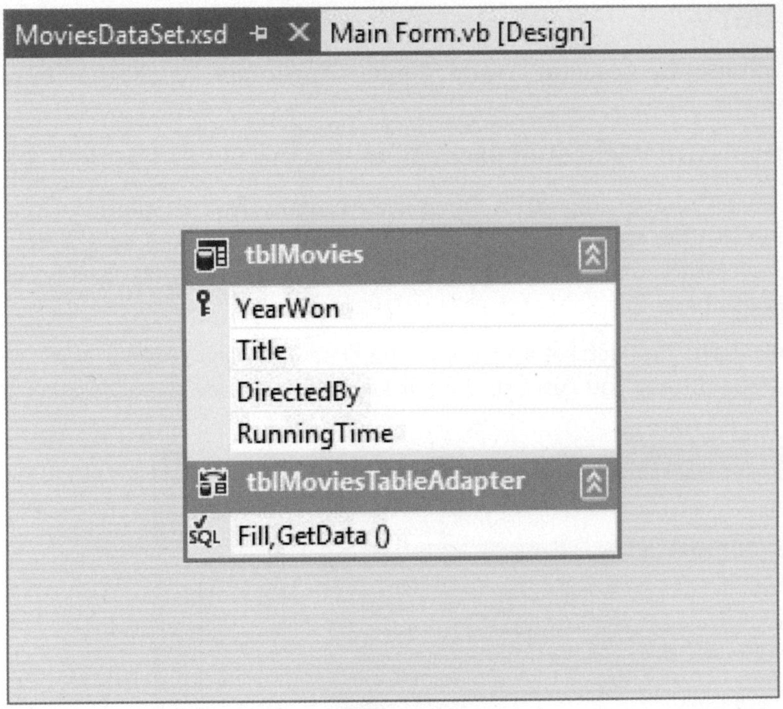

Figure 14-25 DataSet Designer window

4. Right-click **tblMoviesTableAdapter** in the DataSet Designer window. Point to **Add** on the shortcut menu and then click **Query**. (If Add does not appear on the shortcut menu, click Add Query instead.) Doing this starts the TableAdapter Query Configuration Wizard. The Use SQL statements radio button should be selected, as shown in Figure 14-26.

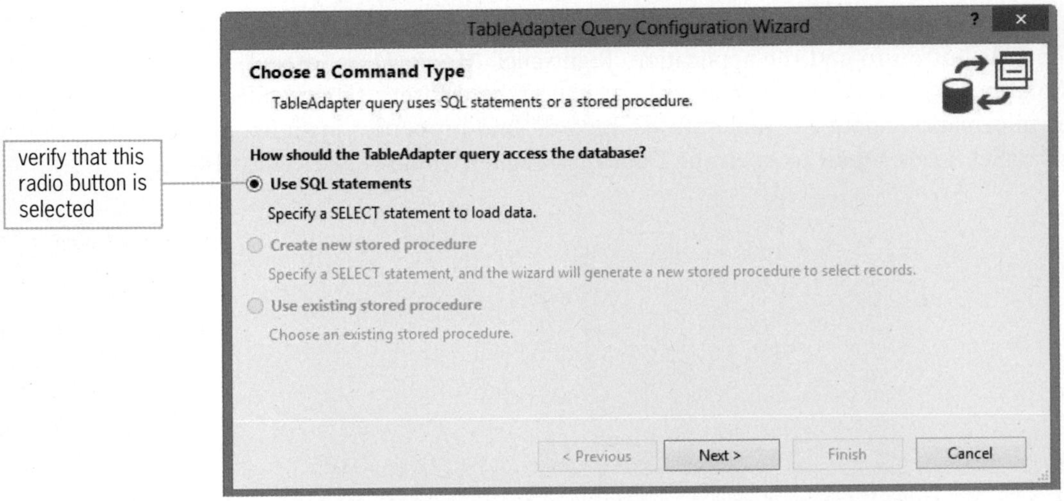

Figure 14-26 Choose a Command Type screen

5. Click the **Next** button to display the Choose a Query Type screen. The "SELECT which returns rows" radio button should be selected, as shown in Figure 14-27.

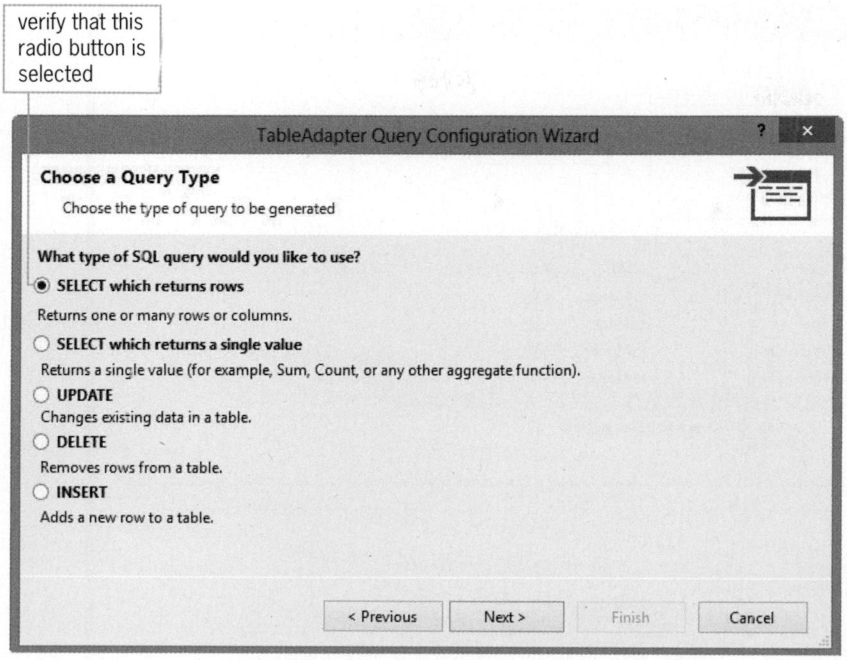

Figure 14-27 Choose a Query Type screen

6. Click the **Next** button to display the Specify a SQL SELECT statement screen. The SELECT statement in the "What data should the table load?" box tells the computer to select all of the fields and records from the tblMovies table. See Figure 14-28.

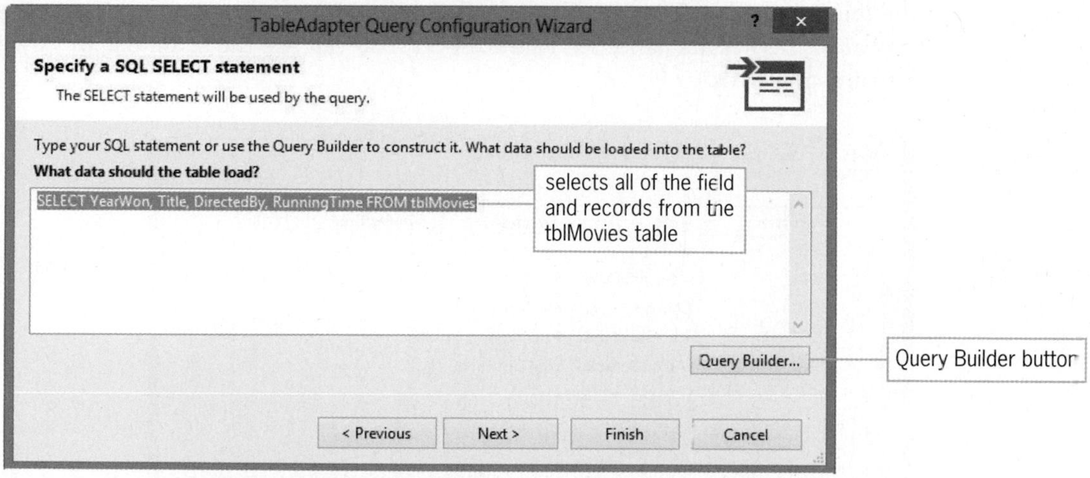

Figure 14-28 Specify a SQL SELECT statement screen

You can type a different SELECT statement in the "What data should the table load?" box shown in Figure 14-28. Or, you can use the Query Builder dialog box to construct the statement for you. In the next set of steps, you will use the Query Builder dialog box.

To test the SELECT statements from Figure 14-23:

START HERE

1. Click the **Query Builder** button to open the Query Builder dialog box. See Figure 14-29. The table's primary key appears boldfaced in the Diagram pane.

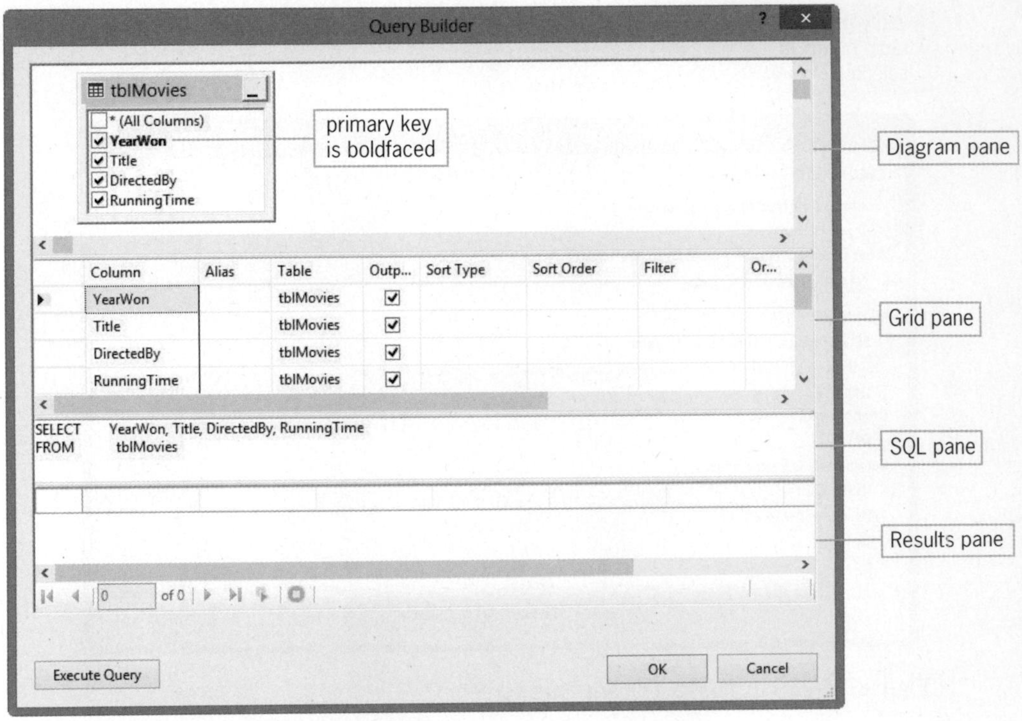

Figure 14-29 Query Builder dialog box

2. The SQL pane contains the same SELECT statement shown in Example 1 in Figure 14-23. The statement tells the computer to select all of the fields and records contained in the tblMovies table. Click the **Execute Query** button to run the query. The query results appear in the Results pane. See Figure 14-30. You can use the scroll bar to view the remaining records.

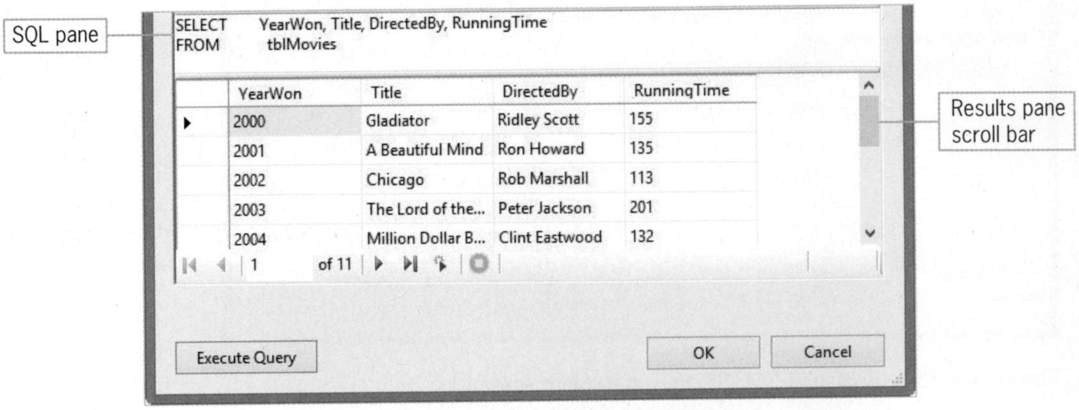

YearWon	Title	DirectedBy	RunningTime
2000	Gladiator	Ridley Scott	155
2001	A Beautiful Mind	Ron Howard	135
2002	Chicago	Rob Marshall	113
2003	The Lord of the...	Peter Jackson	201
2004	Million Dollar B...	Clint Eastwood	132

Figure 14-30 Records listed in the Results pane

3. Next, you will create a query that selects all of the fields, but only from records for the year 2006 and later. In the Grid pane, click the **blank cell** in the YearWon field's Filter column. Type **>= 2006** and press **Enter**. The Filter column entry tells the Query Builder to include the `WHERE (YearWon >= 2006)` clause in the SELECT statement. The funnel symbol that appears in the Diagram pane indicates that the YearWon field is used to filter the records. Notice the Query Changed message and icon that appear in the Results pane. The message and icon alert you that the information displayed in the Results pane

is not from the current query. See Figure 14-28. (For clarity, the Query Builder places the WHERE clause's condition in parentheses; however, the parentheses are not a requirement of the SELECT statement.)

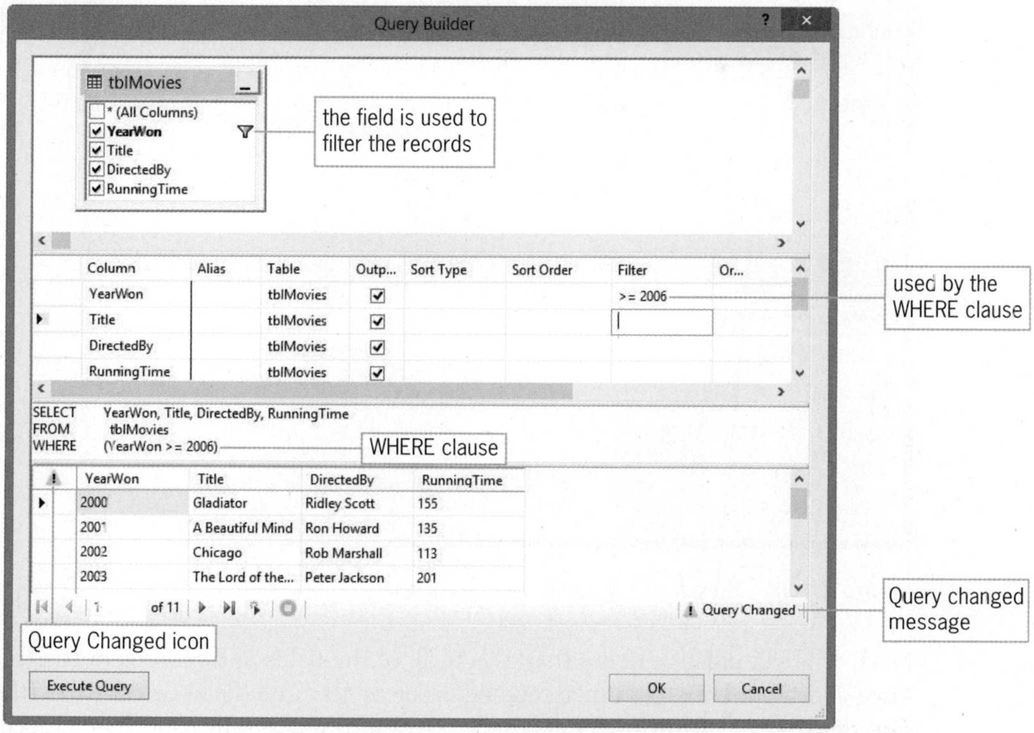

Figure 14-31 SELECT statement containing a WHERE clause

4. Click the **Execute Query** button to run the current query. If necessary, scroll the Results pane to verify that it contains only the records for the years 2006 through 2010.

5. Next, you will create a query that selects only the YearWon field for the Chicago record. Select (highlight) the **>= 2006** entry in the YearWon field's Filter column and then press **Delete**. Click the **blank cell** in the Title field's Filter column. Type **Chicago** and press **Enter**. The Query Builder changes the entry in the Filter column to `= 'Chicago'`. It also enters the `WHERE (Title = 'Chicago')` clause in the SELECT statement.

6. Now, click the **Title**, **DirectedBy**, and **RunningTime** check boxes in the Diagram pane to remove the check marks. The Query Builder changes the first line in the SELECT statement to `SELECT YearWon`. Click the **Execute Query** button. See Figure 14-32.

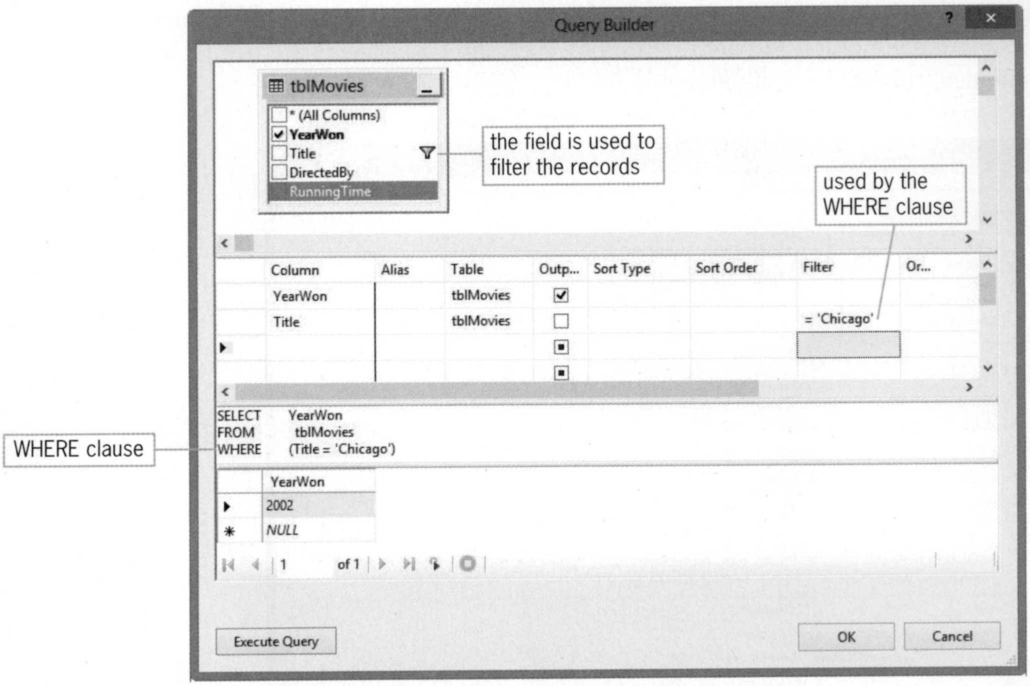

Figure 14-32 Result of executing the current query

7. Next, you will create a query that selects all of the fields and records in the tblMovies table and then sorts them in ascending order by the Title field. Select the **Title**, **DirectedBy**, and **RunningTime** check boxes in the Diagram pane. The Query Builder changes the first line in the SELECT statement to `SELECT YearWon, Title, DirectedBy, RunningTime`. Delete the `= 'Chicago'` entry from the Filter column in the Grid pane, and then press **Enter**. The Query Builder removes the WHERE clause from the SELECT statement.

8. Now, click the **blank cell** in the Title field's Sort Type column and then click the **list arrow** in the cell. Click **Ascending** and then press **Enter**. The word "Ascending" appears as the Title field's Sort Type, and the number 1 appears as its Sort Order. The number 1 indicates that the Title field is the primary field in the sort. As a result, the Query Builder adds the `ORDER BY Title` clause to the SELECT statement. Click the **Execute Query** button. See Figure 14-33.

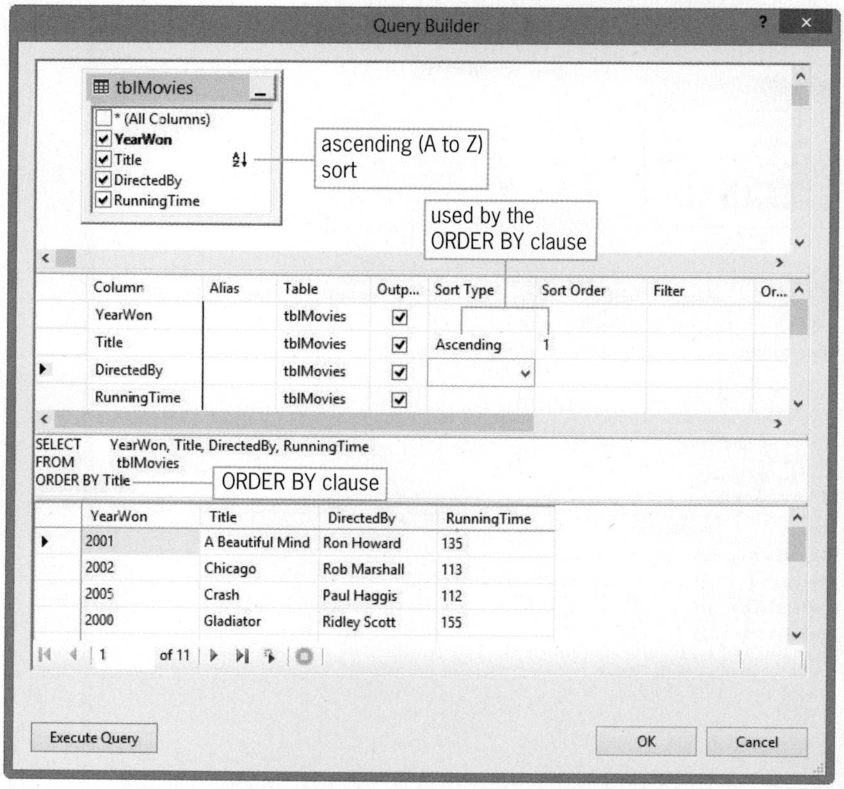

Figure 14-33 Records displayed in ascending order by the Title field

9. On your own, create the query for Figure 14-23's Example 5. The query should select the Title and RunningTime fields from records whose title begins with the word "The" followed by a space and zero or more characters. The query should sort the records in descending order by the RunningTime field. Figure 14-34 shows the query along with the result of executing it.

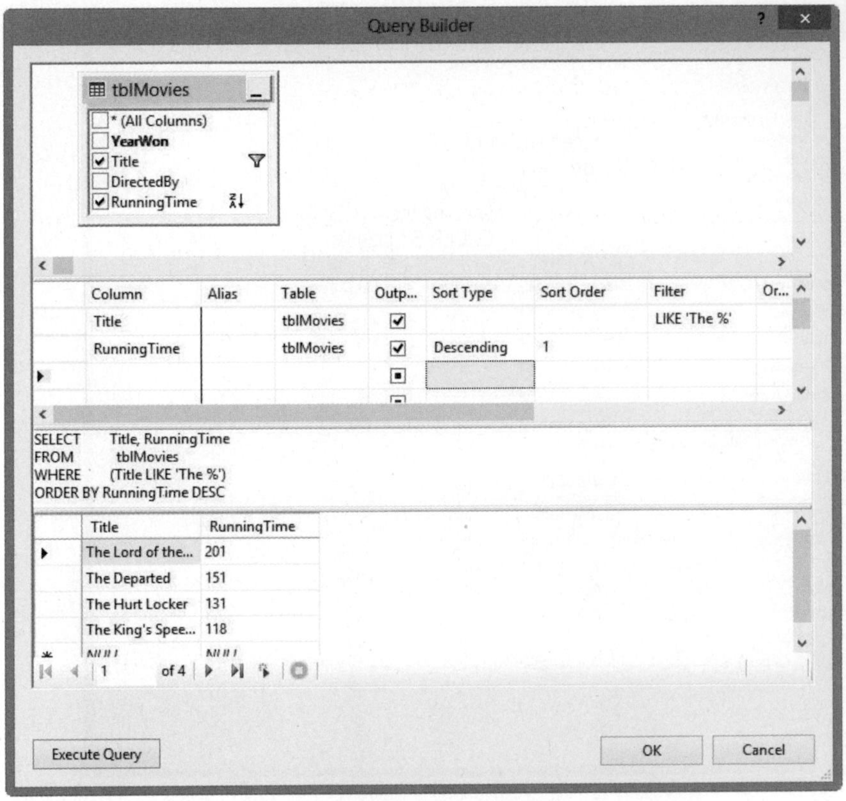

Figure 14-34 Records displayed by the current query

10. Click the **Cancel** button in the Query Builder dialog box and then click the **Cancel** button in the TableAdapter Query Configuration Wizard dialog box.

11. Save the solution. Close the MoviesDataSet.xsd window and then close the solution.

Lesson B Summary

- To query a database using SQL:

  Use the SELECT statement. The statement's basic syntax is:

  SELECT *fieldList* **FROM** *tableName*
  [**WHERE** *condition*]
  [**ORDER BY** *fieldName* [**DESC**]]

- To limit the records you want to view:

  Use the SELECT statement's WHERE clause.

- To sort the selected records:

  Use the SELECT statement's ORDER BY clause.

- To open the DataSet Designer window:

  Right-click the name of the dataset's schema file in the Solution Explorer window and then click Open. The schema filename ends with .xsd.

- To start the TableAdapter Query Configuration Wizard:

  Open the DataSet Designer window and then right-click the table adapter's name. Point to Add on the shortcut menu and then click Query. (If Add does not appear on the shortcut menu, click Add Query instead.)

- To open the Query Builder dialog box:

  Start the TableAdapter Query Configuration Wizard. Click the Next button and then click the Next button again to display the Specify a SQL SELECT statement screen. Click the Query Builder button.

- To represent zero or more characters in the WHERE clause's condition:

  Use the % wildcard.

Lesson B Key Terms

%—a wildcard character used in the condition in a SELECT statement's WHERE clause; represents zero or more characters

LIKE operator—used with a wildcard character in the condition in a SELECT statement's WHERE clause

ORDER BY clause—used in a SELECT statement to sort the selected records

SELECT statement—the SQL statement that allows you to specify the fields and records to select, and also the order in which the fields and records appear when displayed

SQL—an acronym for Structured Query Language

Structured Query Language—SQL; a set of statements that allows you to access and manipulate the data stored in a database

WHERE clause—used in a SELECT statement to limit the records to be selected

Lesson B Review Questions

1. SQL stands for ________________.
   a. Select Query Language
   b. Semi-Quick Language
   c. Structured Quick Language
   d. Structured Query Language

2. Which of the following SELECT statements will select the First and Last fields from the tblNames table?
   a. `SELECT First AND Last FROM tblNames`
   b. `SELECT First OR Last FROM tblNames`
   c. `SELECT First, Last FROM tblNames`
   d. `SELECT ONLY First, Last FROM tblNames`

3. Which of the following SELECT statements will select the SSN field from the tblPayInfo table, and then sort the records in descending order by the SSN field?
   a. `SELECT SSN FROM tblPayInfo DESC`
   b.
   ```
   SELECT SSN FROM tblPayInfo
       ORDER BY SSN DESC
   ```
   c.
   ```
   SELECT SSN FROM tblPayInfo
       WHERE SSN DESC
   ```
   d.
   ```
   SELECT SSN FROM tblPayInfo
       SORT SSN DESC
   ```

4. Which of the following SELECT statements will select only records whose Status field contains the letter A? The Status field is contained in the tblWorker table.

   a. `SELECT Id, Name, Status FROM tblWorker`
      `WHERE Status = 'A'`

   b. `SELECT Id, Name, Status FROM tblWorker`
      `ORDER BY Status = 'A'`

   c. `SELECT Id, Name, Status FROM tblWorker`
      `FOR Status = 'A'`

   d. `SELECT Id, Name, Status FROM tblWorker`
      `SELECT Status = 'A'`

5. The tblState table contains a text field named State. Which of the following SELECT statements will select the State and Capital fields from only the Kansas and Kentucky records?

   a. `SELECT State, Capital FROM tblState`
      `WHERE State LIKE 'K'`

   b. `SELECT State, Capital FROM tblState`
      `WHERE State LIKE 'K*'`

   c. `SELECT State, Capital FROM tblState`
      `WHERE State LIKE 'K%'`

   d. `SELECT State, Capital FROM tblState`
      `WHERE State LIKE 'K#'`

6. The tblState table contains a numeric field named Population. Which of the following SELECT statements will select the State and Capital fields from only states with populations that exceed 5,000,000?

   a. `SELECT State, Capital FROM tblState`
      `WHERE Population > 5000000`

   b. `SELECT State, Capital FROM tblState`
      `WHERE Population > '5000000'`

   c. `SELECT State, Capital FROM tblState`
      `WHERE Population > "5000000"`

   d. `SELECT State, Capital FROM tblState`
      `SELECT Population > 5000000`

7. In a SELECT statement, which clause is used to limit the records that will be selected?

   a. LIMIT

   b. ORDER BY

   c. ONLY

   d. WHERE

8. If a funnel symbol appears next to a field's name in the Query Builder dialog box, it indicates that the field is ______________.

   a. used in an ORDER BY clause in a SELECT statement

   b. used in a WHERE clause in a SELECT statement

   c. the primary key

   d. the foreign key

9. The SQL SELECT statement performs case sensitive comparisons.
   a. True
   b. False

Lesson B Exercises

INTRODUCTORY

1. The tblMagazine table contains three fields. The Cost field is numeric. The Code and MagName fields contain text.
   a. Write a SQL SELECT statement that arranges the records in descending order by the Cost field.
   b. Write a SQL SELECT statement that selects only the MagName and Cost fields from records having a code of PG10.
   c. Write a SQL SELECT statement that selects only the MagName and Cost fields from records having a cost of $3 or more.
   d. Write a SQL SELECT statement that selects the Visual Basic record.
   e. Write a SQL SELECT statement that selects only the MagName field from records whose magazine names begin with the letter C.
   f. Open the Magazine Solution (Magazine Solution.sln) file contained in the VB2012\Chap14\Magazine Solution-SQL folder. If necessary, open the designer window. The application is connected to the Magazines database. Start the application to view the records contained in the dataset, and then stop the application. Open the DataSet Designer window and then start the TableAdapter Query Configuration Wizard. Open the Query Builder dialog box. Use the dialog box to test your SELECT statements from Steps a through e.
   g. Close the Query Builder dialog box and the TableAdapter Query Configuration Wizard dialog box. Save the solution. Close the MagazinesDataSet.xsd window and then close the solution.

INTRODUCTORY

2. The tblEmploy table contains seven fields. The Emp_Number, Rate, and Code fields are numeric. The Last_Name, First_Name, Hired, and Status fields contain text. The Status field contains either the letter F (for full-time) or the letter P (for part-time). The Code field identifies the employee's department: 1 for Accounting, 2 for Advertising, 3 for Personnel, and 4 for Inventory.
   a. Write a SQL SELECT statement that selects all of the fields and records in the table, and then sorts the records in ascending order by the Code field.
   b. Write a SQL SELECT statement that selects only the Emp_Number, Last_Name, and First_Name fields from all of the records.
   c. Write a SQL SELECT statement that selects only the records for full-time employees.
   d. Write a SQL SELECT statement that selects the Emp_Number and Rate fields for employees in the Personnel department.
   e. Write a SQL SELECT statement that selects the Emp_Number and Last_Name fields for employees having a last name of Smith.
   f. Write a SQL SELECT statement that selects the Emp_Number and Last_Name fields for employees having a last name that begins with the letter S.

g. Write a SQL SELECT statement that selects only the first and last names for part-time employees, and then sorts the records in descending order by the Last_Name field.

h. Open the Morgan Industries Solution (Morgan Industries Solution.sln) file contained in the VB2012\Chap14\Morgan Industries Solution-SQL folder. If necessary, open the designer window. The application is connected to the Employees database from Chapter 13. Start the application to view the records contained in the dataset, and then stop the application. Open the DataSet Designer window and then start the TableAdapter Query Configuration Wizard. Open the Query Builder dialog box. Which field in the table is the primary key? How can you tell that it is the primary key?

i. Use the Query Builder dialog box to test your SELECT statements from Steps a through g.

j. Close the Query Builder dialog box and the TableAdapter Query Configuration Wizard dialog box. Save the solution. Close the EmployeesDataSet.xsd window and then close the solution.

LESSON C

After studying Lesson C, you should be able to:

- Create a parameter query
- Save a query
- Invoke a query from code
- Add records to a dataset using the SQL INSERT statement
- Delete records from a dataset using the SQL DELETE statement

Parameter Queries

In Lesson B, you learned how to create queries that search for records meeting a specific criteria, such as `Title = 'Chicago'` and `YearWon >= 2006`. Most times, however, you will not know ahead of time the values to include in the criteria. For example, the next time the user runs the query, he or she may want to view the Gladiator record (`Title = 'Gladiator'`) rather than the Chicago record. Or, the user may want to view the movies that won the Academy Award in the year 2007 and later (`YearWon >= 2007`). When you don't know the specific value to include in the criteria, you use a parameter query.

A **parameter query** is a query that uses the parameter marker in place of the criteria's value. The **parameter marker** is a question mark (**?**). Figure 14-35 shows examples of parameter queries using the tblMovies table from Lessons A and B.

Parameter Queries

Example 1

```
SELECT YearWon, Title, DirectedBy, RunningTime FROM tblMovies
      WHERE Title = ?
```

selects all of the fields from the record whose title is represented by the parameter marker

Example 2

```
SELECT YearWon, Title, DirectedBy, RunningTime FROM tblMovies
      WHERE YearWon >= ?
```

selects all of the fields from records whose YearWon field contains a value that is greater than or equal to the value represented by the parameter marker

Figure 14-35 Examples of parameter queries

In this section, you will open the Academy Award Winners application and then use it to test the SELECT statements from Figure 14-35.

To test the first SELECT statement from Figure 14-35:

START HERE

1. If necessary, start Visual Studio 2012. Open the Academy Award Solution (Academy Award Solution.sln) file contained in the VB2012\Chap14\Academy Award Solution-Parameter Queries folder. If necessary, open the designer window. The application is already connected to the Movies database.
2. Start the application. The dataset shown in Figure 14-36 appears in the DataGridView control.

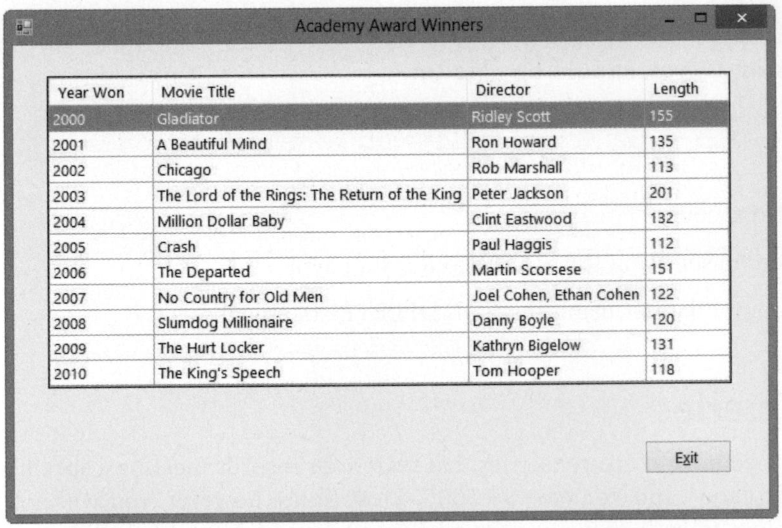

Figure 14-36 Records displayed in the DataGridView control

3. Click the **Exit** button to end the application. Right-click **MoviesDataSet.xsd** in the Solution Explorer window, and then click **Open** to open the DataSet Designer window.
4. Right-click **tblMoviesTableAdapter** in the DataSet Designer window. Point to **Add** on the shortcut menu and then click **Query** to start the TableAdapter Query Configuration Wizard. (If Add does not appear on the shortcut menu, click Add Query instead.)
5. Verify that the Use SQL statements radio button is selected. Click the **Next** button to display the Choose a Query Type screen. Verify that the "SELECT which returns rows" radio button is selected. Click the **Next** button to display the Specify a SQL SELECT statement screen. Click the **Query Builder** button to open the Query Builder dialog box.
6. First, you will create a query that selects the Chicago record. In the Grid pane, click the **blank cell** in the Title field's Filter column. Type **?** and press **Enter**. The Filter column entry tells the Query Builder to include the `WHERE (Title = ?)` clause in the SELECT statement.
7. Click the **Execute Query** button to run the query. The Query Parameters dialog box opens. Type **Chicago** in the Value column. See Figure 14-37.

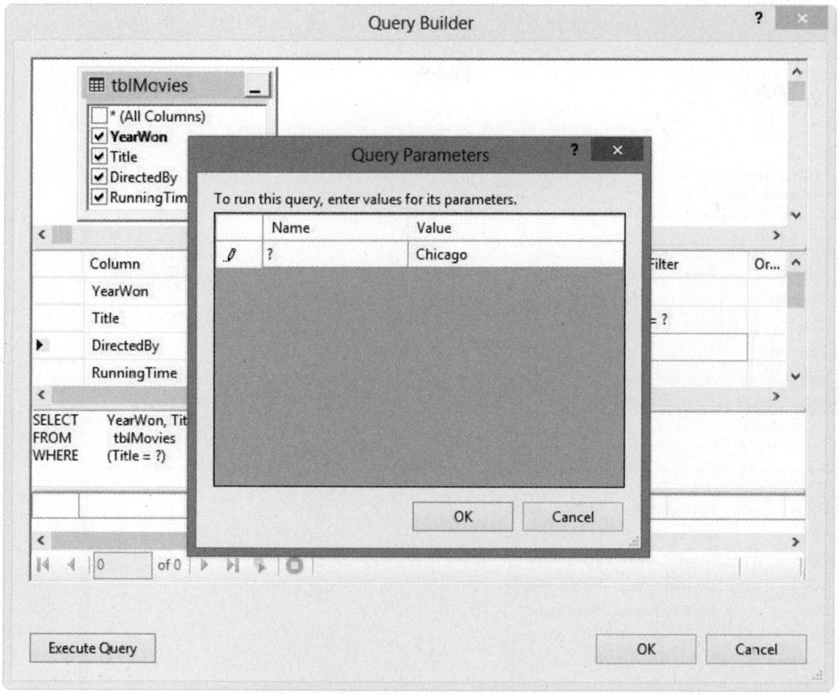

Figure 14-37 Query Parameters dialog box

8. Click the **OK** button to close the Query Parameters dialog box. The Chicago record appears in the Results pane.

9. Now, you will run the query again. This time, however, you will select the Gladiator record. Click the **Execute Query** button to run the query. Type **Gladiator** in the Value column of the Query Parameters dialog box and then click the **OK** button. The Gladiator record appears in the Results pane.

Next, you will create a query for Example 2 from Figure 14-35.

To test the second SELECT statement from Figure 14-35:

START HERE

1. Delete the = ? from the Title field's Filter column. Now, type **>= ?** in the YearWon field's Filter column and then press **Enter**. Click the **Execute Query** button to run the query. Type **2006** in the Value column of the Query Parameters dialog box and then click the **OK** button. Five records appear in the Results pane. See Figure 14-38.

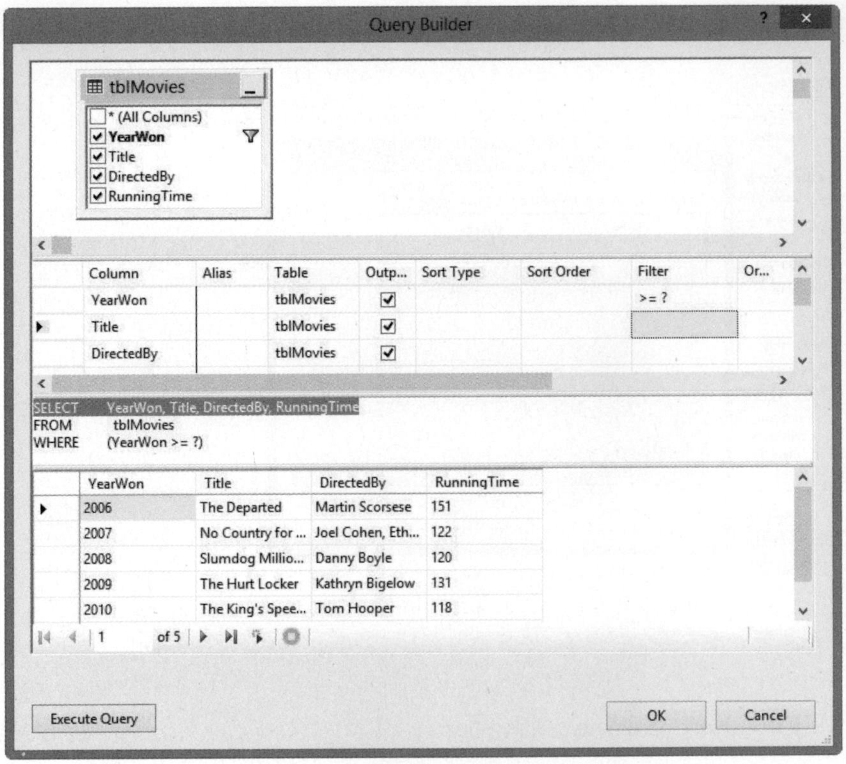

Figure 14-38 Records with a YearWon field value of at least 2006

2. Now, you will run the query again. This time, however, you will select records for the year 2009 and later. Click the **Execute Query** button to run the query. Type **2009** in the Value column of the Query Parameters dialog box and then click the **OK** button. This time, only two records appear in the Results pane.
3. Click the **Cancel** button in the Query Builder dialog box and then click the **Cancel** button in the TableAdapter Query Configuration Wizard dialog box.
4. Save the solution. Close the MoviesDataSet.xsd window and then close the solution.

Saving a Query

In order for an application to use a query during run time, you will need to save the query and then invoke it from code. You save a query that contains the SELECT statement by associating the query with one or more methods. The TableAdapter Query Configuration Wizard provides an easy way of performing this task.

START HERE

To use the TableAdapter Query Configuration Wizard to save a query:

1. Open the Academy Award Solution (Academy Award Solution.sln) file contained in the VB2012\Chap14\Academy Award Solution-Save Query folder. If necessary, open the designer window. The application is connected to the Movies database. The application allows the user to display either all of the records or only the record for the year entered in the txtYear control.
2. Start the application. The dataset shown in Figure 14-39 appears in the DataGridView control. The user can choose to display either all of the records or only the record whose YearWon field matches the value entered in the txtYear control.

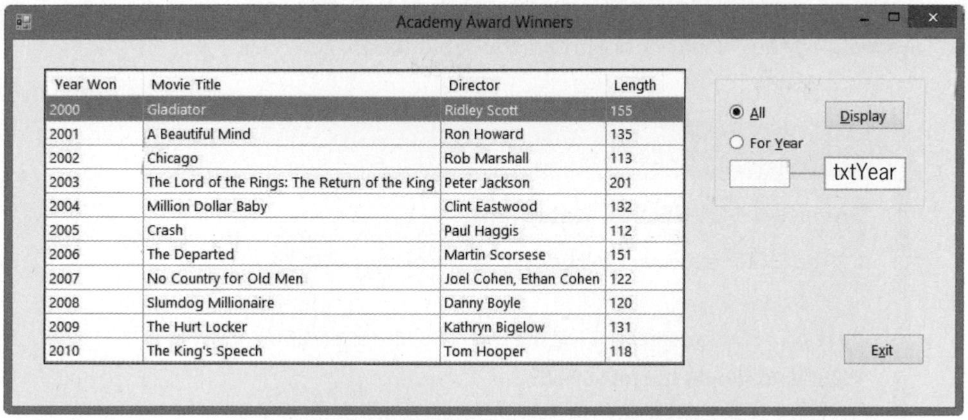

Figure 14-39 Interface for the Academy Award Winners application in Lesson C

3. Click the **Exit** button to end the application. Right-click **MoviesDataSet.xsd** in the Solution Explorer window and then click **Open** to open the DataSet Designer window.
4. Right-click **tblMoviesTableAdapter** in the DataSet Designer window. Point to **Add** on the shortcut menu and then click **Query** to start the TableAdapter Query Configuration Wizard. (If Add does not appear on the shortcut menu, click Add Query instead.)
5. Verify that the Use SQL statements radio button is selected. Click the **Next** button to display the Choose a Query Type screen. Verify that the "SELECT which returns rows" radio button is selected. Click the **Next** button to display the Specify a SQL SELECT statement screen. As shown in Figure 14-40, the "What data should the table load?" box contains the default query, which selects all of the fields and records in the table.

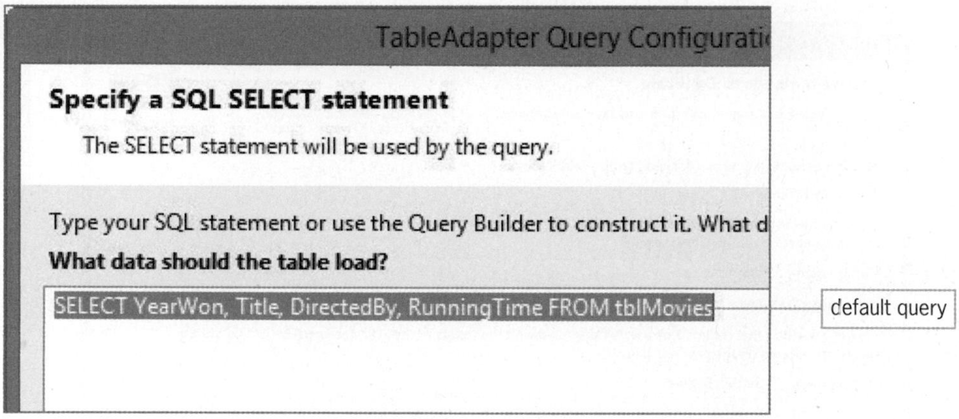

Figure 14-40 Default query in the Specify a SQL SELECT statement screen

6. You can invoke the default query using the TableAdapter object's Fill method. Click the **Query Builder** button to open the Query Builder dialog box.
7. Recall that the interface provides the txtYear control for the user to enter a year number. You will create a parameter query that allows the user to display the Academy Award winner for that year. In the Grid pane, click the **blank cell** in the YearWon field's Filter column. Type **?** and press **Enter**. The Query Builder adds the `WHERE (YearWon = ?)` clause to the SELECT statement.
8. Click the **Execute Query** button to run the query. The Query Parameters dialog box opens. Type **2004** in the Value column and then click the **OK** button to close the dialog box. The 2004 record appears in the Results pane.

9. Click the **OK** button to close the Query Builder dialog box. The parameter query appears in the "What data should the table load?" box. See Figure 14-41.

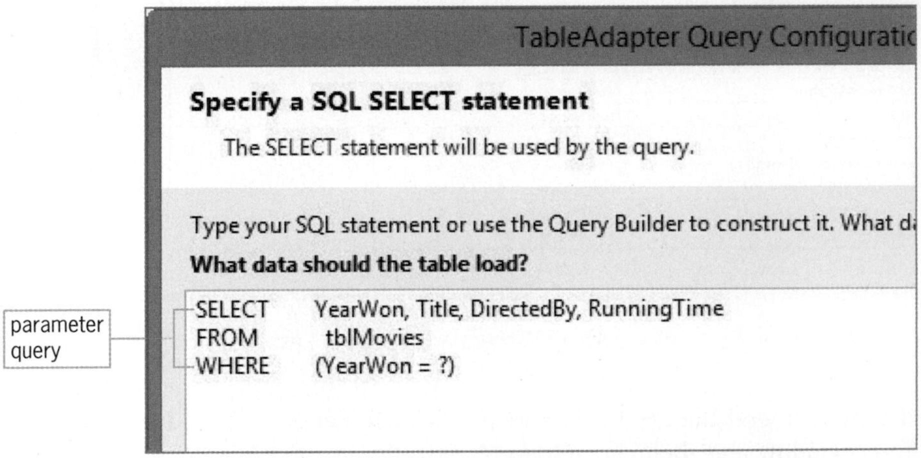

Figure 14-41 Parameter query in the Specify a SQL SELECT statement screen

10. Click the **Next** button to display the Choose Methods to Generate screen. If necessary, select the **Fill a DataTable** and **Return a DataTable** check boxes. Change the Fill a DataTable method's name from FillBy to **FillByYear**. Change the Return a DataTable method's name from GetDataBy to **GetDataByYear**. See Figure 14-42. As the figure indicates, the FillByYear and GetDataByYear methods are associated with the parameter query you created. Therefore, you can use the methods to invoke the query during run time.

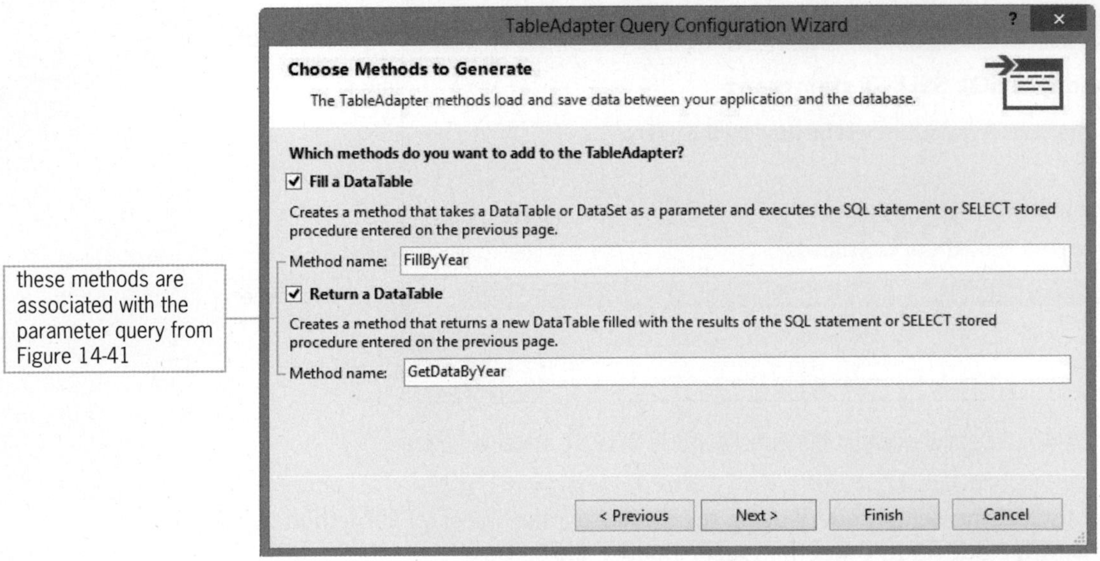

Figure 14-42 Completed Choose Methods to Generate screen

11. Click the **Next** button to display the Wizard Results screen. See Figure 14-43.

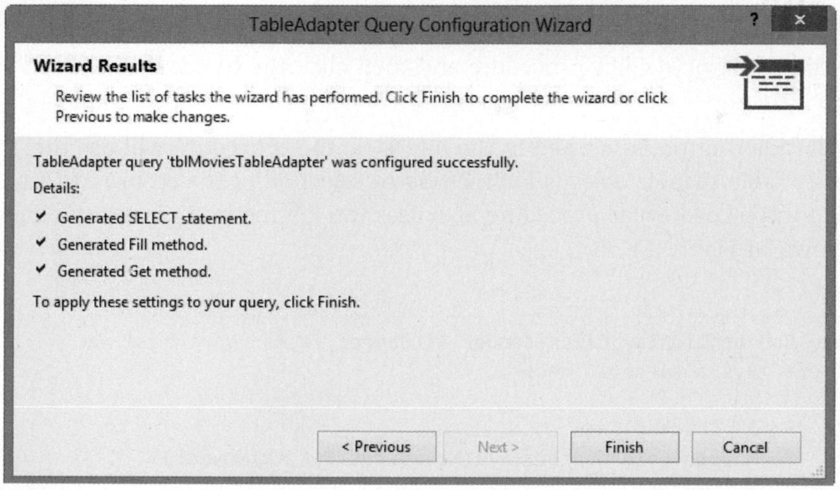

Figure 14-43 Wizard Results screen

12. Click the **Finish** button. The FillByYear and GetDataByYear methods are added to the DataSet Designer window, as shown in Figure 14-44.

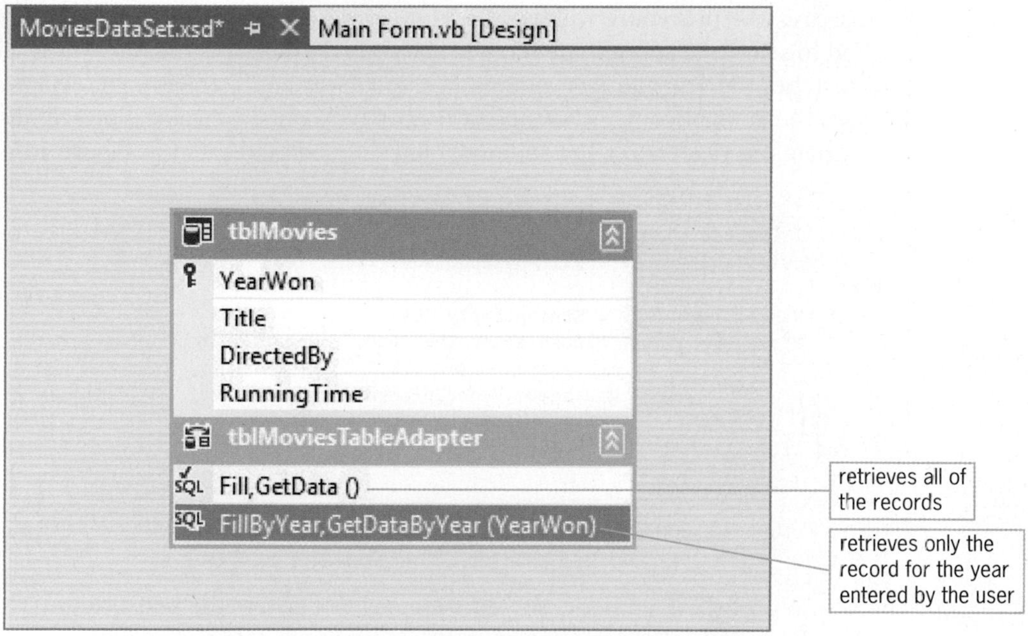

Figure 14-44 Method names included in the DataSet Designer window

13. Save the solution and then close the MoviesDataSet.xsd window.

Invoking a Query from Code

You can invoke a query during run time by entering its associated methods in a procedure. In the next set of steps, you will enter the appropriate methods in the Display button's Click event procedure.

START HERE

To code the Display button's Click event procedure:

1. Open the Code Editor window. Replace <your name> and <current date> in the comments with your name and the current date, respectively.
2. Locate the btnDisplay_Click procedure and then click the **blank line** above the End Sub clause.

3. If the All radio button is selected in the interface, the procedure will use the TblMoviesTableAdapter object's Fill method to select all of the records. (Recall that the form's Load event procedure also uses the Fill method.) Enter the lines of code shown in Figure 14-45.

enter these lines of code

```
Private Sub btnDisplay_Click(sender As Object, e As EventArgs) Ha
    ' displays a specific record

    If radAll.Checked Then
        TblMoviesTableAdapter.Fill(MoviesDataSet.tblMovies)

    End If
End Sub
```

Figure 14-45 If clause and Fill method entered in the procedure

4. If the All radio button is not selected, it means that the For Year radio button is selected. In that case, the procedure will use the TblMoviesTableAdapter object's FillByYear method to select the appropriate record. The record to select is the one whose YearWon field matches the year number entered in the txtYear control. First, you will determine whether the control contains a value. If it does not contain a value, you will display an appropriate message. Enter the additional lines of code indicated in Figure 14-46.

enter these lines of code

```
If radAll.Checked Then
    TblMoviesTableAdapter.Fill(MoviesDataSet.tblMovies)
Else
    If txtYear.Text.Trim = String.Empty Then
        MessageBox.Show("Please enter the year.", "Year Entry",
                        MessageBoxButtons.OK,
                        MessageBoxIcon.Information)

    End If
End If
```

Figure 14-46 Additional code entered in the procedure

5. The YearWon field is numeric, so you will need to convert the text box entry to a number. Enter the following lines of code:

   Else
   Dim intYear As Integer
   Integer.TryParse(txtYear.Text, intYear)

6. Next, you will invoke the TblMoviesTableAdapter object's FillByYear method. Because the method is associated with a parameter query, you will need to include the parameter information in the method. Enter the additional lines of code indicated in Figure 14-47.

```
Private Sub btnDisplay_Click(sender As Object, e As EventArgs) Handles
    ' displays a specific record

    If radAll.Checked Then
        TblMoviesTableAdapter.Fill(MoviesDataSet.tblMovies)
    Else
        If txtYear.Text.Trim = String.Empty Then
            MessageBox.Show("Please enter the year.", "Year Entry",
                            MessageBoxButtons.OK,
                            MessageBoxIcon.Information)
        Else
            Dim intYear As Integer
            Integer.TryParse(txtYear.Text, intYear)
            TblMoviesTableAdapter.FillByYear(MoviesDataSet.tblMovies,
                                             intYear)
        End If
    End If
End Sub
```

enter these lines of code

year number for the parameter query

Figure 14-47 btnDisplay_Click procedure

7. Save the solution and then start the application. Click the **For Year** radio button and then click the **Display** button. The "Please enter the year." message appears in a message box. Close the message box.
8. Click the **text box** located below the For Year radio button. Type **2008** and then click the **Display** button. Only the 2008 record appears in the DataGridView control. See Figure 14-48.

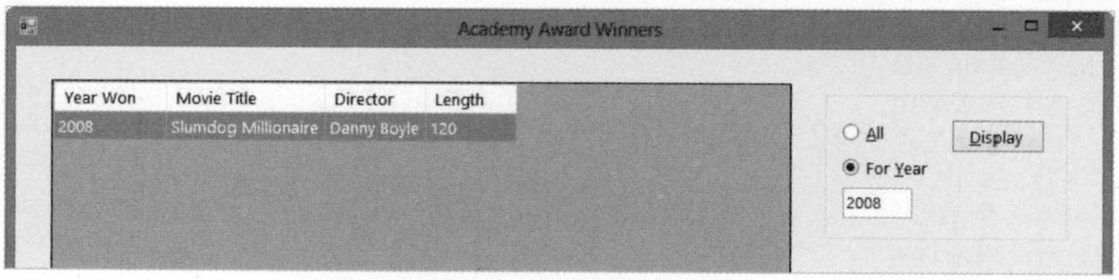

Figure 14-48 2008 record shown in the interface

9. Click the **All** radio button, and then click the **Display** button to display all of the records in the DataGridView control.
10. Click the **Exit** button. Close the Code Editor window and then close the solution.

The INSERT and DELETE Statements

SQL provides the **INSERT statement** for inserting records into a database, and the **DELETE statement** for deleting records from a database. Figures 14-49 and 14-50 show the syntax and examples of the INSERT and DELETE statements, respectively.

INSERT Statement

Syntax
INSERT INTO *tableName*(*fieldName1*, *fieldName2*,...*fieldNameN*)
    VALUES (*field1Value*, *field2Value*,...*fieldNValue*)

Example 1
```
INSERT INTO 'tblMovies' ('YearWon', 'Title',
                         'DirectedBy', 'RunningTime')
     VALUES (1997, 'Titanic', 'James Cameron', 194)
```

Example 2
```
INSERT INTO 'tblMovies' ('YearWon', 'Title',
                         'DirectedBy', 'RunningTime')
     VALUES (1994, 'Forrest Gump', 'Robert Zemeckis', 141)
```

Example 3—parameter query
```
INSERT INTO 'tblMovies' ('YearWon', 'Title',
                         'DirectedBy', 'RunningTime')
     VALUES (?, ?, ?, ?)
```

Figure 14-49 Syntax and examples of the SQL INSERT statement

DELETE Statement

Syntax
DELETE FROM *tableName* **WHERE** *condition*

Example 1
```
DELETE FROM tblMovies
     WHERE YearWon = 1997
```

Example 2
```
DELETE FROM tblMovies
     WHERE Title = 'Forrest Gump'
```

Example 3—parameter query
```
DELETE FROM tblMovies
     WHERE YearWon = ?
```

Figure 14-50 Syntax and examples of the SQL DELETE statement

In the next two sets of steps, you will use the TableAdapter Query Configuration Wizard to create Insert and Delete queries for the Movies database in the Academy Award Winners application. An **Insert query** uses the INSERT statement to add a record to a database. A **Delete query** uses the DELETE statement to delete a record from a database.

START HERE

To create an Insert query in the Academy Award Winners application:

1. Open the Academy Award Solution (Academy Award Solution.sln) file contained in the VB2012\Chap14\Academy Award Solution-InsertDelete folder. If necessary, open the designer window. The application is already connected to the Movies database. Start the application to view the records contained in the dataset. See Figure 14-51.

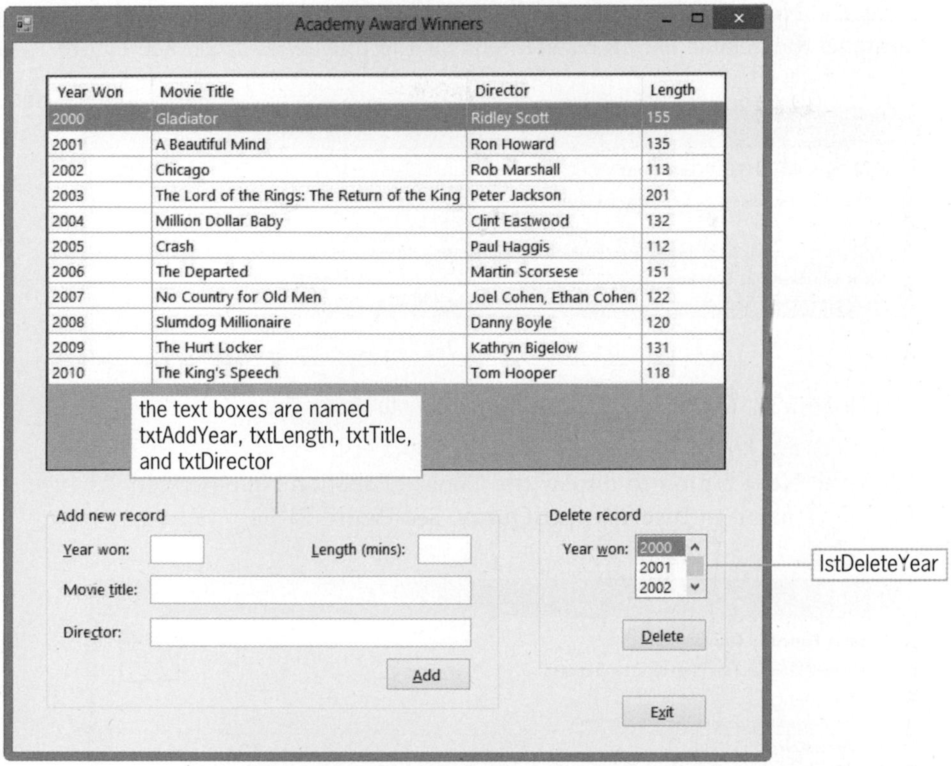

Figure 14-51 Records displayed in the TblMoviesDataGridView control

2. Click the **Exit** button to end the application. First, you will create the Insert query. Right-click **MoviesDataSet.xsd** in the Solution Explorer window and then click **Open** to open the DataSet Designer window.
3. Right-click **tblMoviesTableAdapter** in the DataSet Designer window. Point to **Add** on the shortcut menu and then click **Query** to start the TableAdapter Query Configuration Wizard. (If Add does not appear on the shortcut menu, click Add Query instead.)
4. Verify that the Use SQL statements radio button is selected, and then click the **Next** button to display the Choose a Query Type screen. Click the **INSERT** radio button. See Figure 14-52.

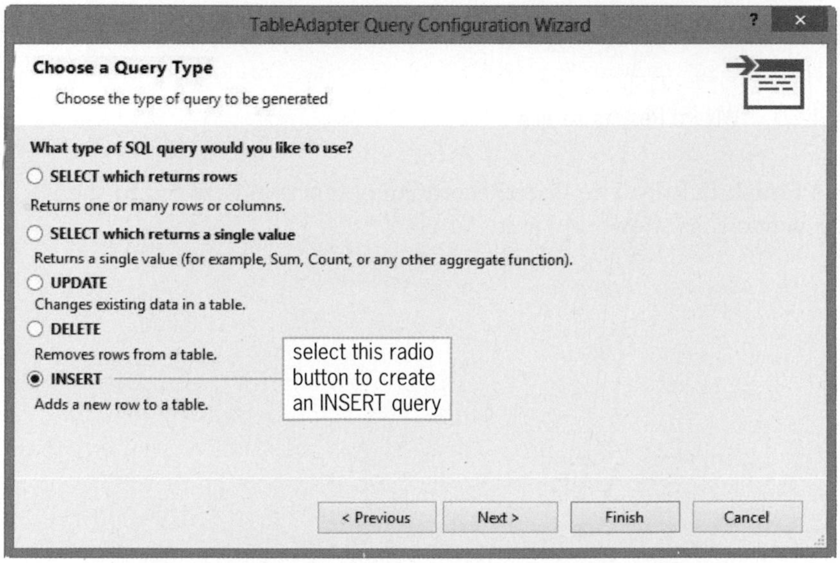

Figure 14-52 Choose a Query Type screen

5. Click the **Next** button to display the Specify a SQL INSERT statement screen, which contains the default INSERT statement for the tblMovies table. See Figure 14-53.

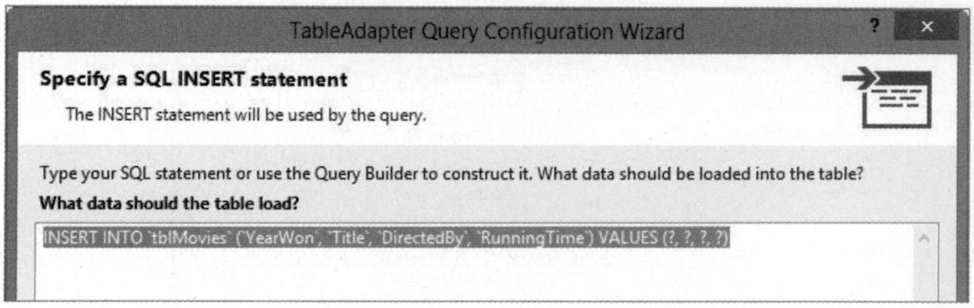

Figure 14-53 Default INSERT statement for the tblMovies table

6. Click the **Next** button to display the Choose Function Name screen. Change the function's name to **InsertRecordQuery**. See Figure 14-54.

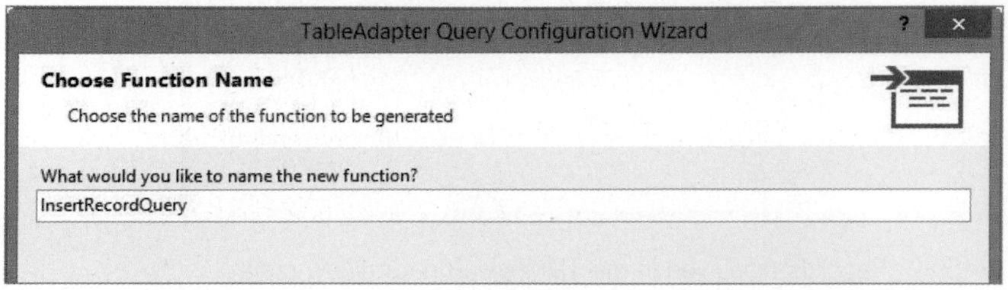

Figure 14-54 Choose Function Name screen

7. Click the **Next** button to display the Wizard Results screen. See Figure 14-55.

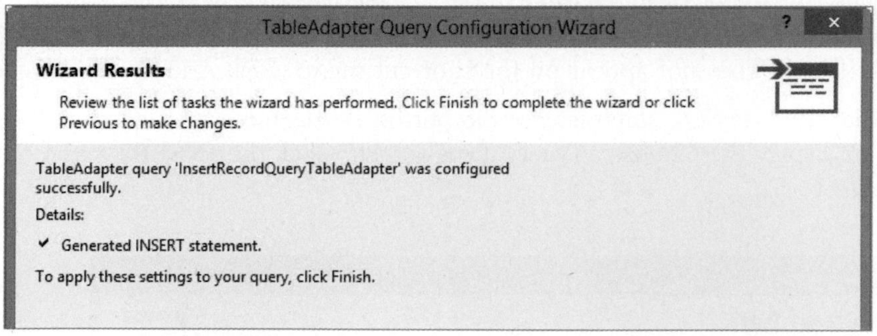

Figure 14-55 Wizard Results screen

8. Click the **Finish** button. The InsertRecordQuery function is added to the DataSet Designer window, as shown in Figure 14-56.

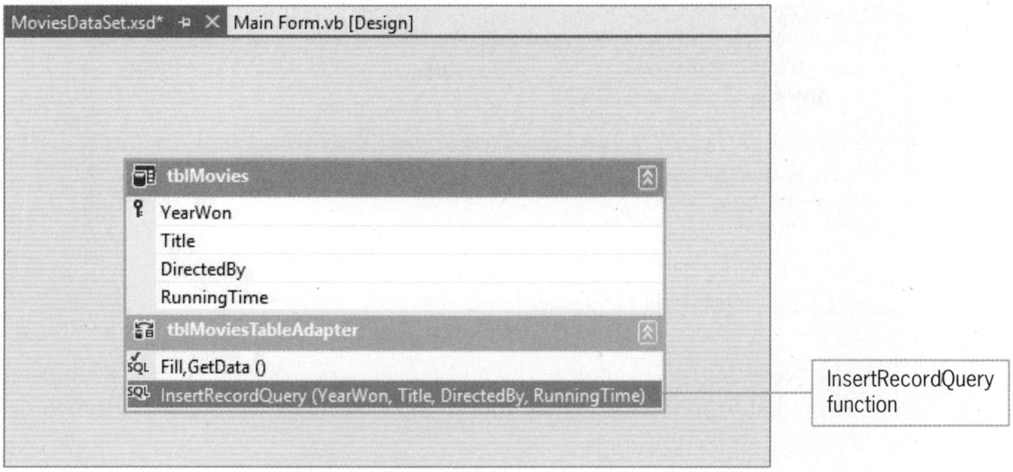

Figure 14-56 InsertRecordQuery function

Now, you will create a Delete query.

START HERE

To create a Delete query:

1. Right-click **tblMoviesTableAdapter** in the DataSet Designer window. Click **Add Query** on the shortcut menu to start the TableAdapter Query Configuration Wizard. (If Add Query does not appear on the shortcut menu, point to Add and then click Query.)
2. Verify that the Use SQL statements radio button is selected. Click the **Next** button to display the Choose a Query Type screen.
3. Click the **DELETE** radio button and then click the **Next** button to display the Specify a SQL DELETE statement screen, which contains the default DELETE statement for the tblMovies table.
4. Click the **Query Builder** button. Change the statement in the SQL pane of the Query Builder dialog box as shown in Figure 14-57. (Don't be concerned about the values in the Grid pane.)

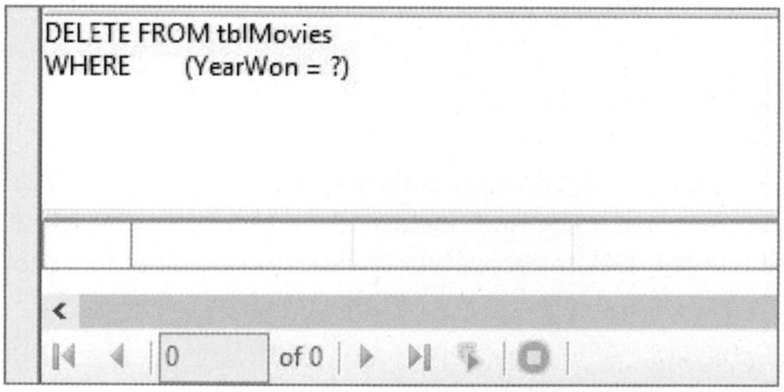

Figure 14-57 SQL pane in the Query Builder dialog box

5. Click the **OK** button. The DELETE statement shown in Figure 14-58 appears in the Specify a SQL DELETE statement screen.

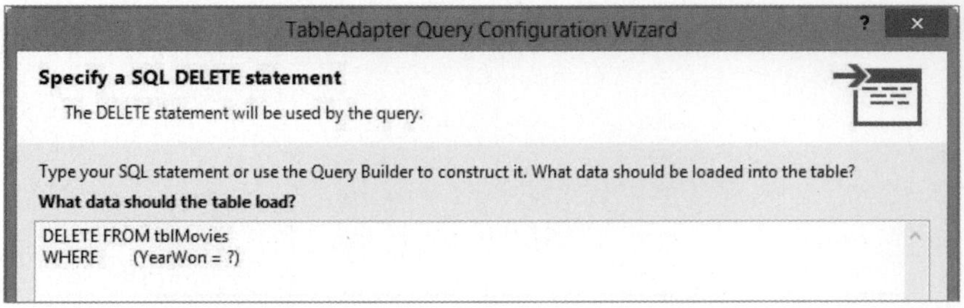

Figure 14-58 SQL DELETE statement

6. Click the **Next** button to display the Choose Function Name screen. Change the function's name to **DeleteRecordQuery**, and then click the **Next** button to display the Wizard Results screen.
7. Click the **Finish** button to add the DeleteRecordQuery function to the DataSet Designer window. See Figure 14-59.

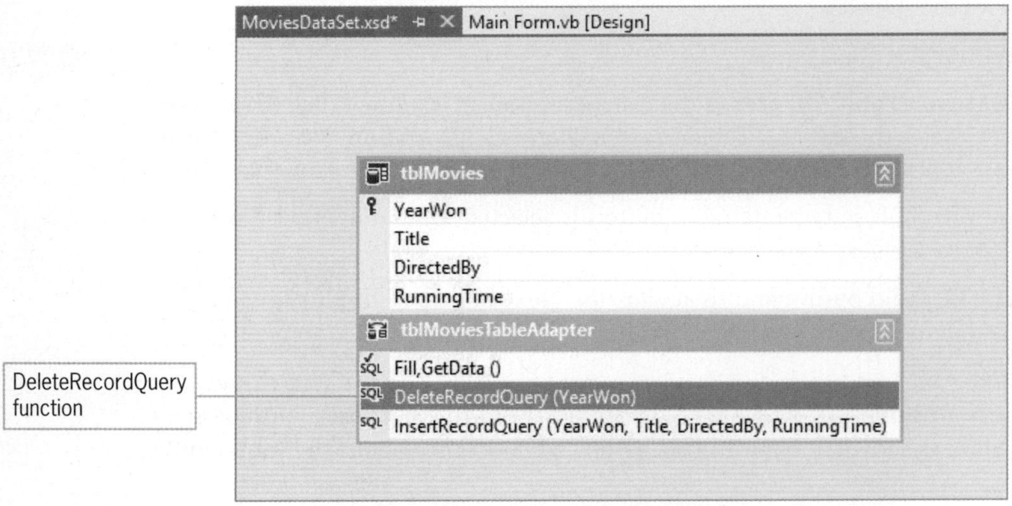

Figure 14-59 DeleteRecordQuery function

8. Save the solution and then close the MoviesDataSet.xsd window.

In the next set of steps, you will code the Click event procedures for the Add and Delete buttons. The Add button will use the InsertRecordQuery function to add a record to the Movies database. The Delete button will use the DeleteRecordQuery function to delete a record from the Movies database.

START HERE

To code the Add and Delete buttons:

1. Open the Code Editor window. Locate the btnAdd_Click procedure and then click the **blank line** above the End Sub clause. First, you will determine whether the four text boxes contain data. If at least one of the text boxes is empty, the procedure will display an appropriate message. Enter the selection structure shown in Figure 14-60.

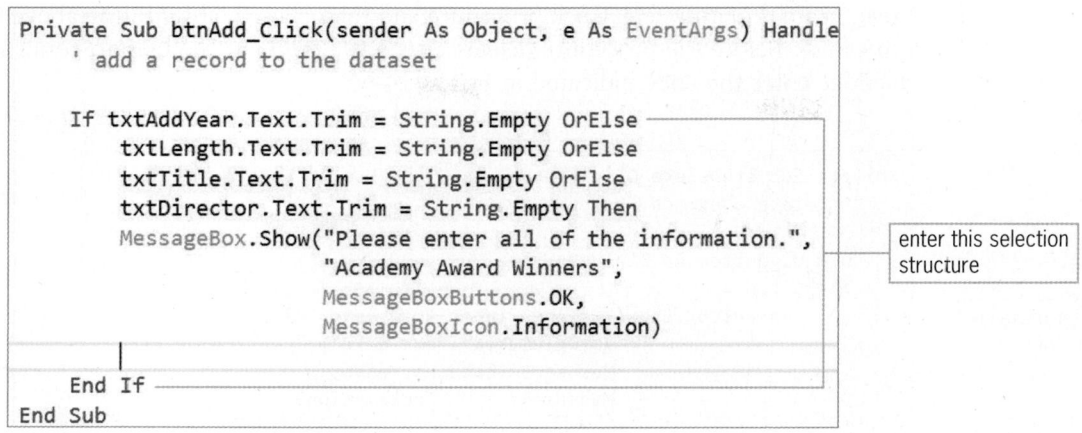

```
Private Sub btnAdd_Click(sender As Object, e As EventArgs) Handle
    ' add a record to the dataset

    If txtAddYear.Text.Trim = String.Empty OrElse
        txtLength.Text.Trim = String.Empty OrElse
        txtTitle.Text.Trim = String.Empty OrElse
        txtDirector.Text.Trim = String.Empty Then
        MessageBox.Show("Please enter all of the information.",
                        "Academy Award Winners",
                        MessageBoxButtons.OK,
                        MessageBoxIcon.Information)

    End If
End Sub
```

enter this selection structure

Figure 14-60 Selection structure entered in the btnAdd_Click procedure

2. If all of the text boxes contain data, you will need to convert the values in the txtAddYear and txtLength controls to numbers before you can add them to the database; this is because the YearWon and RunningTime fields in the table are numeric. Enter the following lines of code:

Else
Dim intYear As Integer
Dim intLength As Integer
Integer.TryParse(txtAddYear.Text, intYear)
Integer.TryParse(txtLength.Text, intLength)

3. Now, you will use the TblMoviesTableAdapter object's InsertRecordQuery function to add the record to the database. You then will use the object's Fill method to retrieve the appropriate data from the database. However, as you learned in Lesson A, a run time error will occur if you try to add a duplicate record to a dataset. Recall that in this case, a duplicate record is a record whose YearWon field value is already in the dataset. Therefore, you will enter the InsertRecordQuery function and Fill method in a Try...Catch statement. Enter the additional lines of code shown in Figure 14-61.

```
Else
    Dim intYear As Integer
    Dim intLength As Integer
    Integer.TryParse(txtAddYear.Text, intYear)
    Integer.TryParse(txtLength.Text, intLength)
    Try
        TblMoviesTableAdapter.InsertRecordQuery(intYear,
                                txtTitle.Text.Trim,
                                txtDirector.Text.Trim,
                                intLength)
        TblMoviesTableAdapter.Fill(MoviesDataSet.tblMovies)
    Catch ex As Exception
        MessageBox.Show("Duplicate record", "Add Record",
                MessageBoxButtons.OK,
                MessageBoxIcon.Information)
    End Try
End If
```

enter these lines of code

Figure 14-61 Additional lines of code entered in the btnAdd_Click procedure

4. Next, locate the btnDelete_Click procedure and then click the **blank line** above the End Sub clause. Before the procedure deletes a record, it will ask the user to confirm the deletion. Enter the code indicated in Figure 14-62.

enter these six lines of code

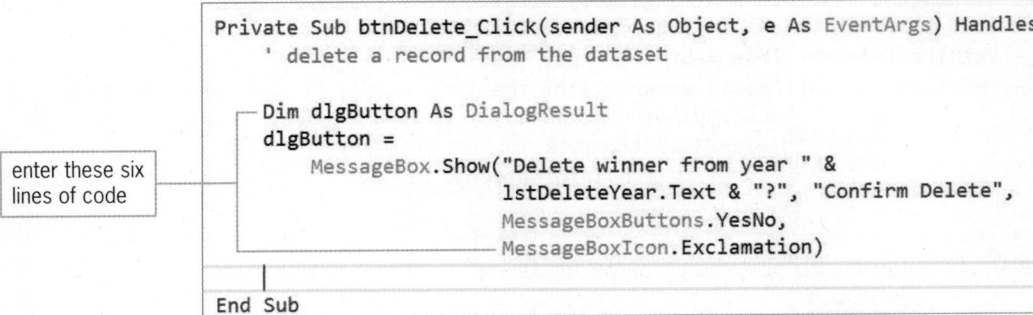

```
Private Sub btnDelete_Click(sender As Object, e As EventArgs) Handles
    ' delete a record from the dataset

    Dim dlgButton As DialogResult
    dlgButton =
        MessageBox.Show("Delete winner from year " &
                        lstDeleteYear.Text & "?", "Confirm Delete",
                        MessageBoxButtons.YesNo,
                        MessageBoxIcon.Exclamation)

End Sub
```

Figure 14-62 Additional code entered in the btnDelete_Click procedure

5. If the user confirms the deletion, you will need to convert the value in the lstDeleteYear control to a number because the YearWon field in the table is numeric. Enter the following lines of code:

   If dlgButton = Windows.Forms.DialogResult.Yes Then
   Dim intYear As Integer
   Integer.TryParse(lstDeleteYear.Text, intYear)

6. Now you will use the TblMoviesTableAdapter object's DeleteRecordQuery function to delete the record from the database. You then will use the object's Fill method to retrieve the appropriate data from the database. Enter the additional lines of code shown in Figure 14-63.

enter these two lines of code

```
                        MessageBoxIcon.Exclamation)
If dlgButton = Windows.Forms.DialogResult.Yes Then
    Dim intYear As Integer
    Integer.TryParse(lstDeleteYear.Text, intYear)
    TblMoviesTableAdapter.DeleteRecordQuery(intYear)
    TblMoviesTableAdapter.Fill(MoviesDataSet.tblMovies)
End If
```

Figure 14-63 Additional code entered in the selection structure

Figure 14-64 shows the code entered in the frmMain_Load, btnAdd_Click, and btnDelete_Click procedures.

```
Private Sub frmMain_Load(sender As Object,
e As EventArgs) Handles MyBase.Load
    'TODO: This line of code loads data into the
    'MoviesDataSet.tblMovies' table. You can move, or
     remove it, as needed.
    Me.TblMoviesTableAdapter.Fill(Me.MoviesDataSet.tblMovies)
    TblMoviesBindingSource.Sort = "YearWon"
End Sub

Private Sub btnAdd_Click(sender As Object,
e As EventArgs) Handles btnAdd.Click
    ' add a record to the dataset

    If txtAddYear.Text.Trim = String.Empty OrElse
        txtLength.Text.Trim = String.Empty OrElse
        txtTitle.Text.Trim = String.Empty OrElse
        txtDirector.Text.Trim = String.Empty Then
        MessageBox.Show("Please enter all of the information.",
                        "Academy Award Winners",
                        MessageBoxButtons.OK,
                        MessageBoxIcon.Information)
    Else
        Dim intYear As Integer
        Dim intLength As Integer
        Integer.TryParse(txtAddYear.Text, intYear)
        Integer.TryParse(txtLength.Text, intLength)
        Try
            TblMoviesTableAdapter.InsertRecordQuery(intYear,
                                        txtTitle.Text.Trim,
                                        txtDirector.Text.Trim,
                                        intLength)
            TblMoviesTableAdapter.Fill(MoviesDataSet.tblMovies)
        Catch ex As Exception
            MessageBox.Show("Duplicate record", "Add Record",
                            MessageBoxButtons.OK,
                            MessageBoxIcon.Information)

        End Try
    End If
End Sub

Private Sub btnDelete_Click(sender As Object,
e As EventArgs) Handles btnDelete.Click
    ' delete a record from the dataset

    Dim dlgButton As DialogResult
    dlgButton =
    MessageBox.Show("Delete winner from year " &
                    lstDeleteYear.Text & "?", "Confirm Delete",
                    MessageBoxButtons.YesNo,
                    MessageBoxIcon.Exclamation)
    If dlgButton = Windows.Forms.DialogResult.Yes Then
        Dim intYear As Integer
        Integer.TryParse(lstDeleteYear.Text, intYear)
        TblMoviesTableAdapter.DeleteRecordQuery(intYear)
        TblMoviesTableAdapter.Fill(MoviesDataSet.tblMovies)
    End If
End Sub
```

Figure 14-64 Most of the application's code

START HERE

To test the Add and Delete buttons:

1. Save the solution and then start the application. Click the **Add** button. The "Please enter all of the information." message appears in a message box. Close the message box.
2. Next, try to add a duplicate record. In the Add new record section, type **2010** in the Year won box, **181** in the Length box, **Dances with Wolves** in the Movie title box, and **Kevin Costner** in the Director box. Click the **Add** button. The "Duplicate record" message appears in a message box. Close the message box.
3. Change the 2010 in the Year won box to **1990**, and then click the **Add** button. The new record appears at the top of the list in the DataGridView control. This is because the frmMain_Load procedure contains the `TblMoviesBindingSource.Sort = "YearWon"` statement, which sorts the records in numerical order by the YearWon field. You learned about the BindingSource object's Sort method in Lesson A.
4. Now, add the following record to the database: **2011**, **100**, **The Artist**, **Michael Hazanavicius**. When you click the Add button, the record appears at the end of the list in the DataGridView control. See Figure 14-65.

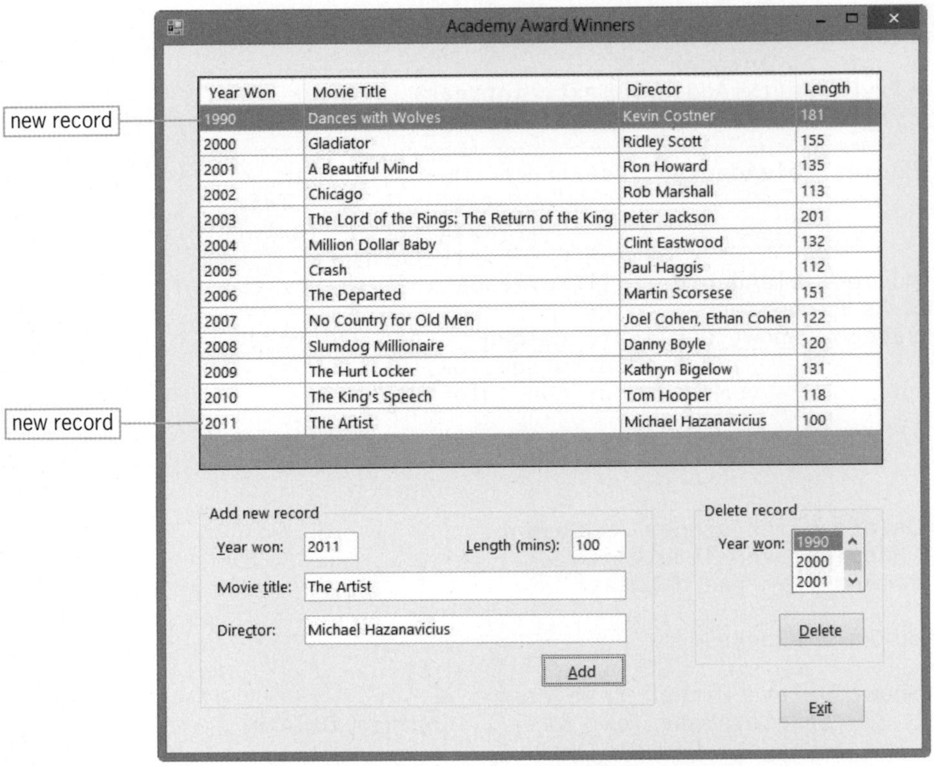

Figure 14-65 Two records added to the database

5. Click the **Exit** button to end the application, and then start the application again to verify that both new records appear in the DataGridView control.
6. Next, you will delete the record for the year 2011. Click **2011** in the DataGridView control. Notice that 2011 now appears in the lstDeleteYear control. This is because the list box is bound to the YearWon field in the dataset. Click the **Delete** button. The "Delete winner from year 2011?" message appears in the Confirm Delete message box. Click the **Yes** button to delete the record.
7. On your own, delete the record for the year 1990.

8. Click **2005** in the DataGridView control and then click the **Delete** button. When the Confirm Delete message box appears, click the **No** button. The record remains in the DataGridView control.
9. Click the **Exit** button to end the application, and then start the application again to verify that only the records for the years 1990 and 2011 were deleted.
10. Click the **Exit** button to end the application. Close the Code Editor window and then close the solution.

Lesson C Summary

- To create a parameter query:

  Use a question mark in place of the criteria's value in the WHERE clause.
- To save a query that contains the SELECT statement:

  Use the TableAdapter Query Configuration Wizard to associate the query with one or more methods.
- To save a query that contains either the INSERT statement or the DELETE statement:

  Use the TableAdapter Query Configuration Wizard to associate the query with a function.
- To invoke a query from code:

  Enter the query's method or function in a procedure.
- To use SQL to insert records into a database:

  Use the INSERT statement.
- To use SQL to delete records from a database:

  Use the DELETE statement.

Lesson C Key Terms

?—the parameter marker in a parameter query

Delete query—a query that uses the DELETE statement to delete a record from a database

DELETE statement— the SQL statement used to delete a record from a database

Insert query—a query that uses the INSERT statement to add a record to a database

INSERT statement—the SQL statement used to insert a record into a database

Parameter marker—a question mark (?)

Parameter query—a query that uses the parameter marker (?) in place of the criteria's value

Lesson C Review Questions

1. When used in a parameter query, which of the following WHERE clauses will allow you to select the records for employees working more than 40 hours?

   a. `WHERE Hours >= 40`

   b. `WHERE Hours > ?`

   c. `WHERE Hours > #`

   d. `WHERE Hours < ?`

2. The FillByCity method is associated with a parameter query. Which of the following invokes the method, passing it the contents of the txtCity control's Text property?

   a. `TblCityTableAdapter.FillByCity(CityDataSet.tblCity, txtCity.Text)`

   b. `TblCityTableAdapter.FillByCity(txtCity.Text)`

   c. `TblCityBindingSource.FillByCity(CityDataSet.tblCity, txtCity.Text)`

   d. `CityDataSet.FillByCity(txtCity.Text)`

3. You can use the SQL ______________ statement to add a record to a database.

   a. ADD
   b. ADD INTO
   c. APPEND
   d. INSERT

4. You can use the SQL ______________ statement to remove a record from a database.

   a. DELETE
   b. DETACH
   c. ERASE
   d. REMOVE

Lesson C Exercises

INTRODUCTORY

1. Open the JM Sales Solution (JM Sales Solution.sln) file contained in the VB2012\Chap14\JM Sales Solution folder. If necessary, open the designer window. The application is connected to the AnnualSales database. The tblSales table in the database contains five records. Each record has two numeric fields: YearNum (the primary key) and Sales. The Add button's Click event procedure should allow the user to add records to the database. The Delete button's Click event procedure should allow the user to delete records (by year number) from the database. Use SQL to code the procedures. Save the solution and then start and test the application. Be sure to try adding a record whose year number matches an existing year number. Stop the application. Close the Code Editor window and then close the solution.

INTERMEDIATE

2. Open the Addison Playhouse Solution (Addison Playhouse Solution.sln) file contained in the VB2012\Chap14\Addison Playhouse Solution folder. If necessary, open the designer window. The application is connected to the Play database. The tblReservations table in the database contains 20 records. Each record has three fields: a numeric field named Seat (the primary key) and two text fields named Patron and Phone. The application should allow the user to add records to the database and also delete records (by seat number) from the database. It should also allow the user to enter a seat number and then view the associated record. In addition, it should allow the user to view the records whose Patron field begins with the one or more characters the user enters. (Hint: Use `LIKE ? & '%'` as the filter.) The records should always appear in order by the seat number. Code the application. Save the solution and then start and test the application. Close the Code Editor window and then close the solution.

INTERMEDIATE

3. Open the Polter Solution (Polter Solution.sln) file contained in the VB2012\Chap14\Polter Solution folder. If necessary, open the designer window. The application is connected to the Products database. The tblProducts table in the database contains 10 records. Each record has three fields. The ItemNum (primary key) and ItemName fields contain text; the Price field contains numbers. The application should allow the user to view the record associated with a specific item number. It should also allow the user to enter a price and then view the records whose prices are at least that amount. The records should appear in order by the item number when the application is started. Code the application. Save the solution and then start and test the application. Close the Code Editor window and then close the solution.

ADVANCED

4. Open the Morgan Industries Solution (Morgan Industries Solution.sln) file contained in the VB2012\Chap14\Morgan Industries Solution-Advanced folder. If necessary, open the designer window. The application is connected to the Employees database. The tblEmploy table in the database contains seven fields and 17 records. The Emp_Number field is the primary key. The Status field contains the employment status, which is either the letter F (for full-time) or the letter P (for part-time). The Code field identifies the employee's department: 1 for Accounting, 2 for Advertising, 3 for Personnel, and 4 for Inventory. The records should appear in order by the employee number when the application is started. The application should allow the user to display all of the records, only the part-time records, only the full-time records, and only the records for a specific department. Use the InputBox function to get the department code. Code the application. Save the solution and then start and test the application. Close the Code Editor window and then close the solution.

APPENDIX A

Finding and Fixing Program Errors

After studying Appendix A, you should be able to:

- Locate syntax errors using the Error List window
- Locate a logic error by stepping through the code
- Locate logic errors using breakpoints
- Fix syntax and logic errors
- Identify a run time error

Finding and Fixing Syntax Errors

As you learned in Chapter 2, a syntax error occurs when you break one of a programming language's rules. Most syntax errors are a result of typing errors that occur when entering instructions, such as typing `Me.Clse()` instead of `Me.Close()`. The Code Editor detects most syntax errors as you enter the instructions. However, if you are not paying close attention to your computer screen, you may not notice the errors. In the next set of steps, you will observe what happens when you start an application that contains a syntax error.

START HERE

To start debugging the Total Sales Calculator application:

1. Start Visual Studio 2012. Open the Total Sales Solution (Total Sales Solution.sln) file contained in the VB2012\AppA\Total Sales Solution folder. If necessary, open the designer window. The application calculates and displays the total of the sales amounts entered by the user. See Figure A-1. (The image in the picture box was downloaded from the Open Clip Art Library at *http://openclipart.org*.)

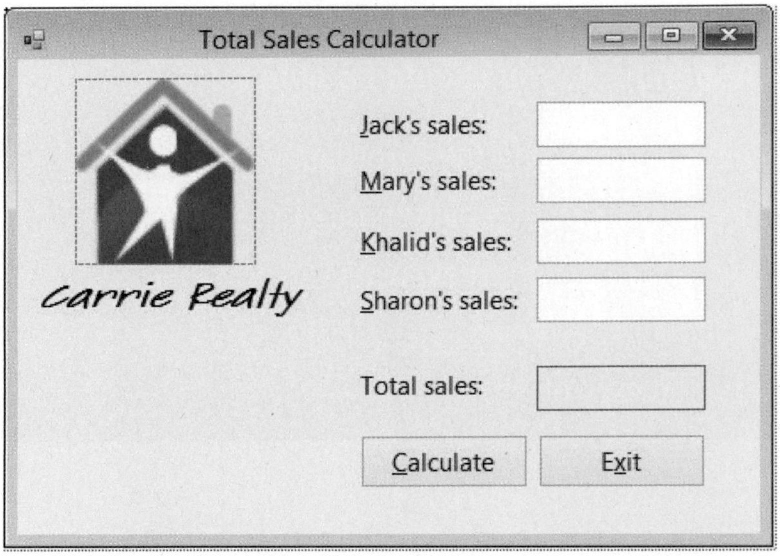

Figure A-1 Total Sales Calculator application
OpenClipArt.org/luc

2. Open the Code Editor window. Figure A-2 shows the code entered in the btnCalc_Click procedure. The jagged blue lines alert you that three lines of code contain a syntax error.

```
Private Sub btnCalc_Click(sender As Object, e As EventArg
    ' calculates and displays the total sales

    ' declare variables
    Dim intJack As Integer
    Dim intMary As Integer
    Dim intKhalid As Integer
    Dim intSharon As Integer
    Dim intTotal As Intger

    ' assign input to variables
    Integer.TryParse(txtJack.Text, intJack
    Integer.TryParse(txtMary.Text, intMary)
    Integer.TryParse(txtKhalid.Text, intKhalid)
    Integer.TryParse(txtSharon.Text, intSharon)

    ' calculate total sales
    inTotal = intJack + intMary + intKhalid + intSharon

    ' display total sales
    lblTotal.Text = intTotal.ToString("C0")
End Sub
```

syntax error

syntax error

syntax error

Figure A-2 btnCalc_Click procedure

3. Start the application. If the dialog box shown in Figure A-3 appears, click the **No** button.

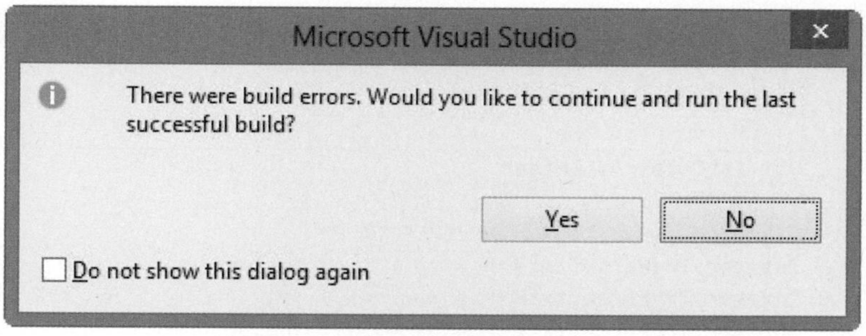

Figure A-3 Dialog box

4. The Error List window opens at the bottom of the IDE, and the Code Editor displays a red rectangle next to each error in the code. If necessary, click the **first error message** in the Error List window. See Figure A-4. The Error List window indicates that the code contains three errors, and it provides a description of each error and the location of each error in the code. The red rectangles indicate that the Code Editor has some suggestions for fixing the errors.

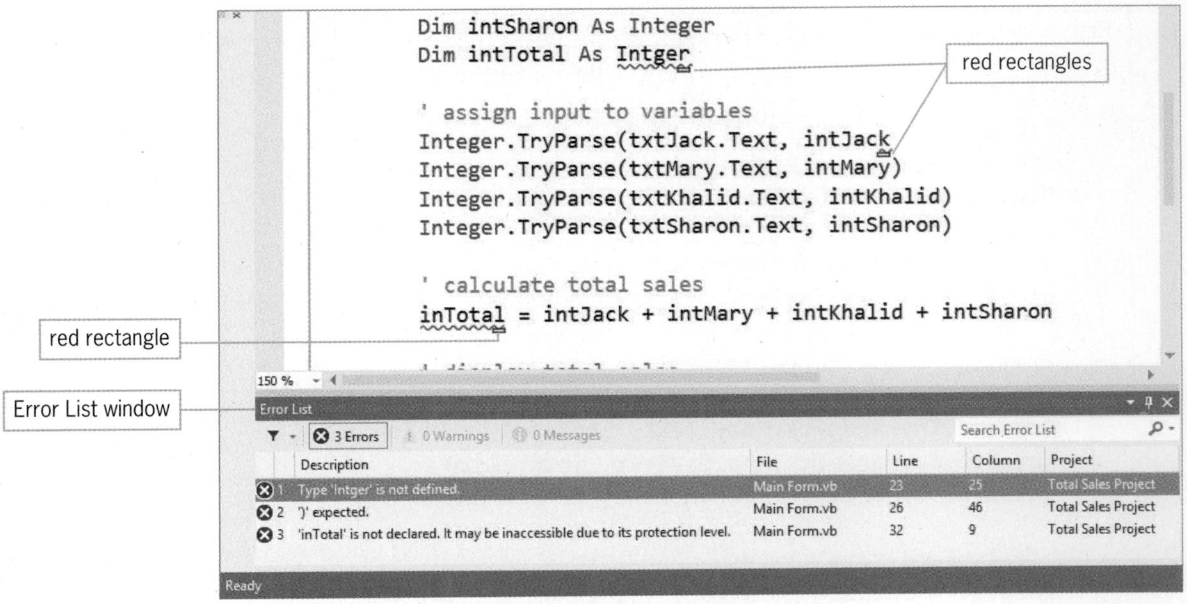

Figure A-4 Error List window

Important note: You can change the size of the Error List window by positioning your mouse pointer on the window's top border until the mouse pointer becomes a vertical line with an arrow at the top and bottom. Then press and hold down the left mouse button while you drag the border either up or down.

5. Double-click the **first error message** in the Error List window. The Code Editor opens the Error Correction window shown in Figure A-5.

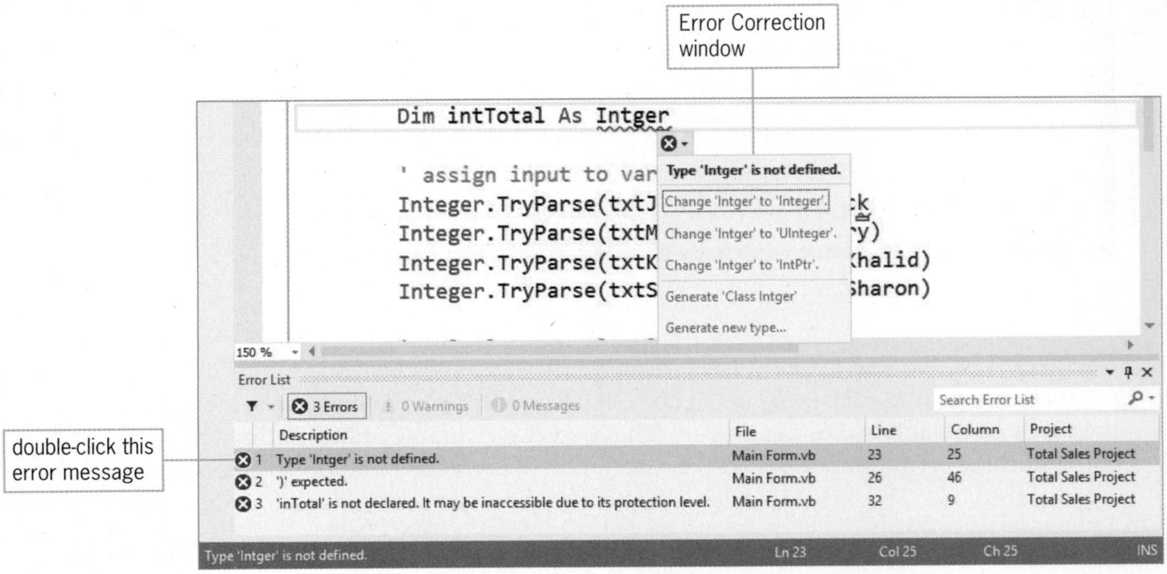

Figure A-5 List of suggestions for fixing the typing error

6. The first error is simply a typing error: The programmer meant to type `Integer`. You can either type the missing `e` yourself or click the appropriate suggestion in the Error Correction window. Click **Change 'Intger' to 'Integer'.** in the list. The Code Editor makes the change in the Dim statement and also removes the error from the Error List window.

7. Double-click the **first error message** in the Error List window. Move the scroll bar in the Error Correction window all the way to the right. The window indicates that the missing parenthesis will be inserted at the end of the assignment statement that contains the syntax error. See Figure A-6.

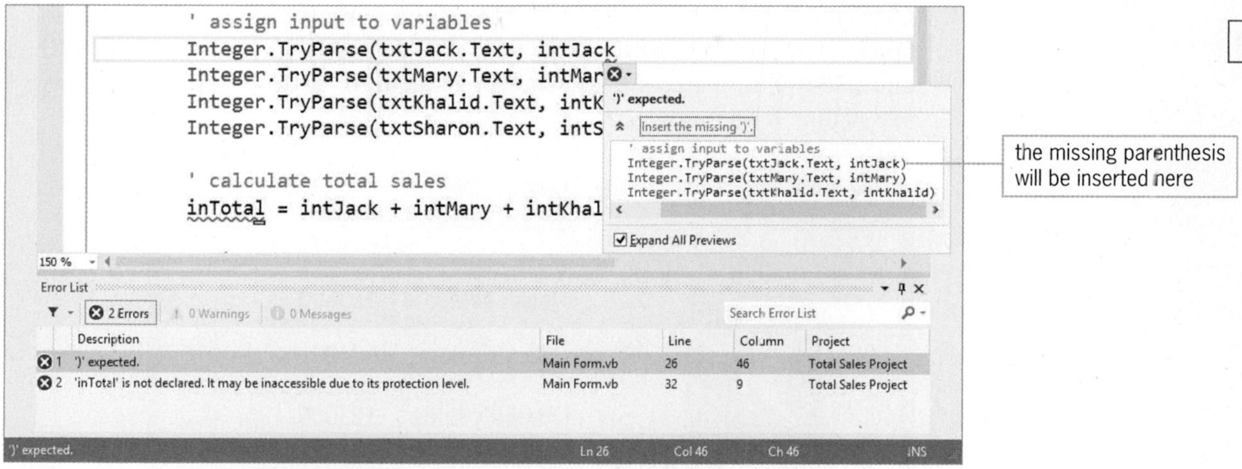

Figure A-6 List of suggestions for fixing the missing parenthesis error

8. Click the **Insert the missing ')'.** suggestion to insert the missing parenthesis. The Code Editor removes the error from the Error List window.

9. Only one error message remains in the Error List window. The error's description indicates that the Code Editor does not recognize the name `inTotal`. Double-click the **remaining error message** in the Error List window. See Figure A-7.

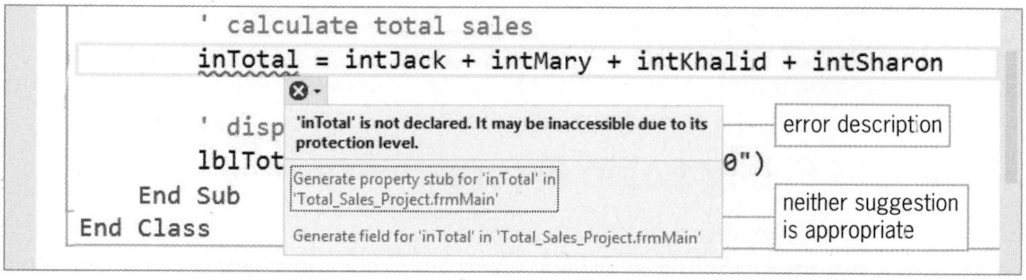

Figure A-7 Error Correction window for the last error message

Neither of the suggestions listed in the Error Correction window in Figure A-7 is appropriate for fixing the error. Therefore, you will need to come up with your own solution to the problem. You do this by studying the line of code that contains the error. First, notice that the unrecognized name (`inTotal`) appears on the left side of an assignment statement. This tells you that the name belongs to something that can store information—either a control or a variable. It doesn't refer to the Text property, so it's most likely the name of a variable. Looking at the beginning of the procedure, where the variables are declared, you will notice that the procedure declares a variable named `intTotal`. Obviously, the programmer mistyped the variable's name.

START HERE

To finish debugging the Total Sales Calculator application:

1. Change `inTotal` to **intTotal** in the assignment statement and then move the insertion point to another line in the Code Editor window. When you move the insertion point, the Code Editor removes the error message from the Error List window.
2. Close the Error List window. Save the solution and then start the application. Test the application using **125600** as Jack's sales, **98700** as Mary's sales, **165000** as Khalid's sales, and **250400** as Sharon's sales. Click the **Calculate** button. The total sales are $639,700. See Figure A-8.

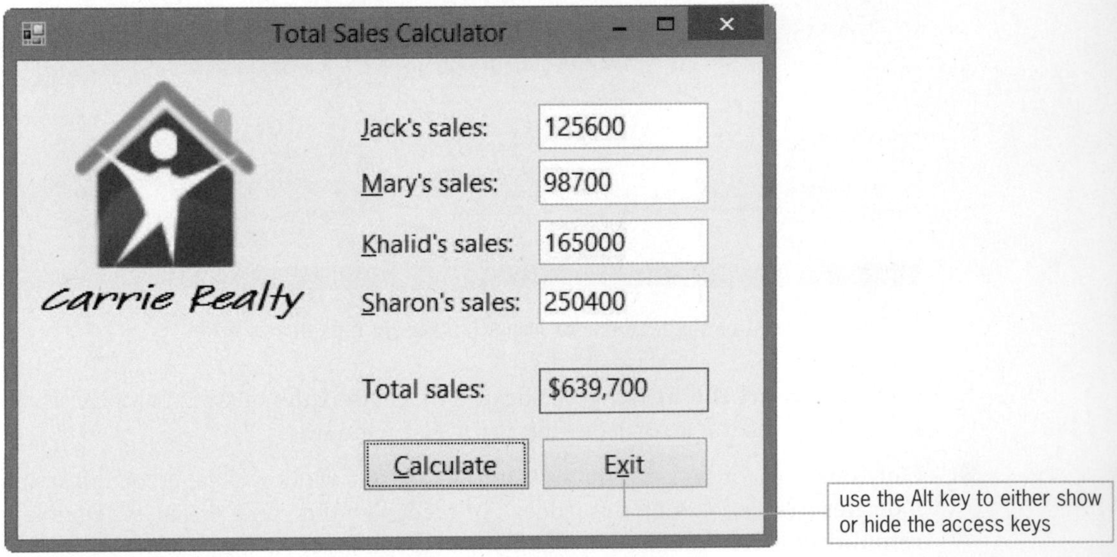

Figure A-8 Sample run of the Total Sales Calculator application
OpenClipArt.org/luc

3. Click the **Exit** button. Close the Code Editor window and then close the solution.

Finding and Fixing Logic Errors

Unlike syntax errors, logic errors are much more difficult to find because they do not trigger an error message from the Code Editor. A logic error can occur for a variety of reasons, such as forgetting to enter an instruction or entering the instructions in the wrong order. Some logic errors occur as a result of calculation statements that are correct syntactically but incorrect mathematically. For example, consider the statement `dblRadiusSquared = dblRadius + dblRadius`, which is supposed to calculate the square of the number stored in the `dblRadius` variable. The statement's syntax is correct, but it is incorrect mathematically because you square a number by multiplying it by itself, not by adding it to itself. In the next two sections, you will debug two applications that contain logic errors.

START HERE

To debug the Discount Calculator application:

1. Open the Discount Solution (Discount Solution.sln) file contained in the VB2012\AppA\Discount Solution folder. If necessary, open the designer window. See Figure A-9. The application calculates and displays three discount amounts, which are based on the price entered by the user.

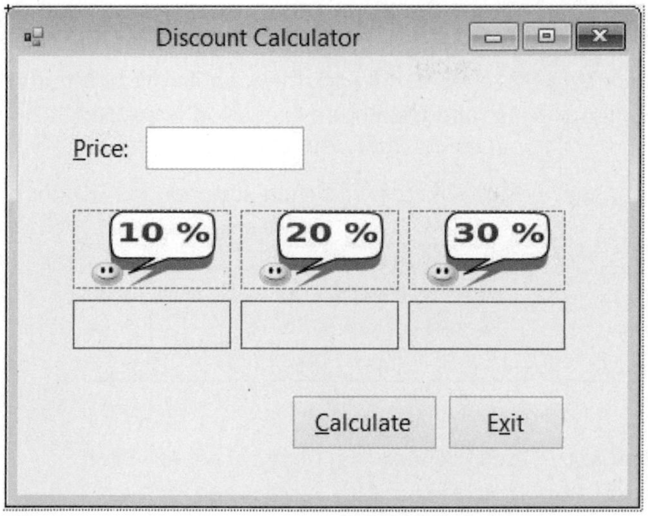

Figure A-9 Discount Calculator application

2. Open the Code Editor window. Figure A-10 shows the code entered in the btnCalc_Click procedure.

```
Private Sub btnCalc_Click(sender As Object, e As E
    ' calculates and displays a 10%, 20%, and
    ' 30% discount on an item's price

    ' declare variables
    Dim decPrice As Decimal
    Dim decDiscount10 As Decimal
    Dim decDiscount20 As Decimal
    Dim decDiscount30 As Decimal

    ' calculate discounts
    decDiscount10 = decPrice * 0.1D
    decDiscount20 = decPrice * 0.2D
    decDiscount30 = decPrice * 0.3D

    ' display discounts
    lbl10.Text = decDiscount10.ToString("N2")
    lbl20.Text = decDiscount20.ToString("N2")
    lbl30.Text = decDiscount30.ToString("N2")
End Sub
```

Figure A-10 btnCalc_Click procedure

3. Start the application. Type **100** in the Price box and then click the **Calculate** button. The interface shows that each discount is 0.00, which is incorrect. Click the **Exit** button.

4. You'll use the DEBUG menu to run the Visual Basic debugger, which is a tool that helps you locate the logic errors in your code. Click **DEBUG** on the menu bar. The menu's Step Into option will start your application and allow you to step through your code. It does this by executing the code one statement at a time, pausing immediately before

each statement is executed. Click **Step Into**. Type **100** in the Price box and then click the **Calculate** button. The debugger highlights the first instruction to be executed, which is the btnCalc_Click procedure header. In addition, an arrow points to the instruction, as shown in Figure A-11, and the code's execution is paused.

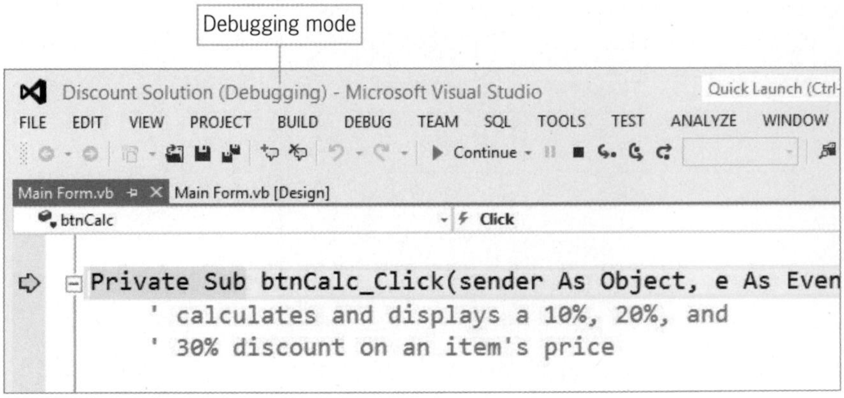

Figure A-11 Result of using the DEBUG menu's Step Into option

5. You can use either the DEBUG menu's Step Into option or the F8 key on your keyboard to tell the computer to execute the highlighted instruction. Press the **F8** key. After the computer processes the procedure header, the debugger highlights the next statement to be processed, which is the `decDiscount10 = decPrice * 0.1D` statement. It then pauses execution of the code. (The Dim statements are skipped over because they are not considered executable by the debugger.)

6. While the execution of a procedure's code is paused, you can view the contents of controls and variables that appear in the highlighted statement and also in the statements above it in the procedure. Before you view the contents of a control or variable, however, you should consider the value you expect to find. Before the `decDiscount10 = decPrice * 0.1D` statement is processed, the `decDiscount10` variable should contain its initial value, 0. (Recall that the Dim statement initializes numeric variables to 0.) Place your mouse pointer on `decDiscount10` in the highlighted statement. The variable's name (`decDiscount10`) and current value (0D) appear in a small box, as shown in Figure A-12. The letter D indicates that the data type of the value—in this case, 0—is Decimal. At this point, the `decDiscount10` variable's value is correct.

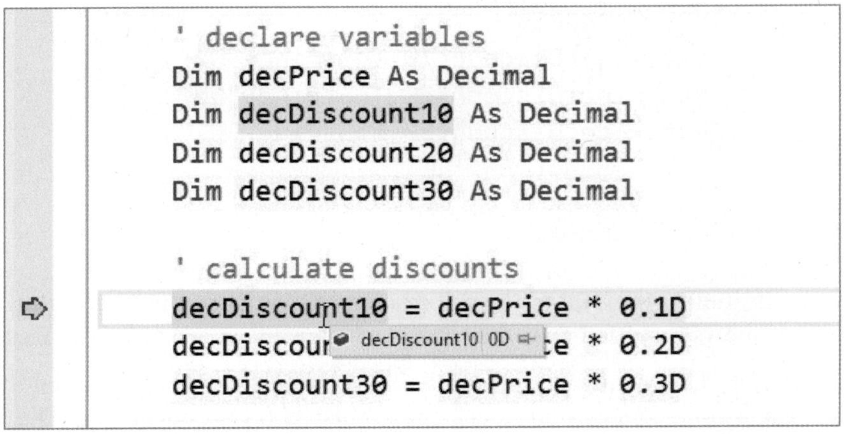

Figure A-12 Value stored in `decDiscount10` before the highlighted statement is executed

7. Now consider the value you expect the `decPrice` variable to contain. Before the highlighted statement is processed, the `decPrice` variable should contain the number 100, which is the value you entered in the Price box. Place your mouse pointer on `decPrice` in the highlighted statement. As Figure A-13 shows, the `decPrice` variable contains 0D, which is its initial value. Consider why the variable's value is incorrect. In this case, the value is incorrect because no statement above the highlighted statement assigns the Price box's value to the `decPrice` variable. In other words, a statement is missing from the procedure.

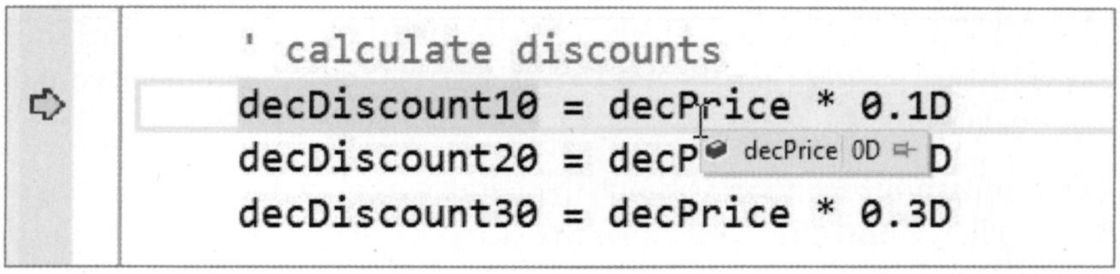
' calculate discounts
decDiscount10 = decPrice * 0.1D
decDiscount20 = decP
decPrice 0D
D
decDiscount30 = decPrice * 0.3D

Figure A-13 Value stored in `decPrice` before the highlighted statement is executed

8. Click **DEBUG** on the menu bar and then click **Stop Debugging** to stop the debugger. Click the **blank line** below the last Dim statement and then press **Enter** to insert another blank line. Now, enter the following comment and TryParse method:

   ' assign price to a variable
   Decimal.TryParse(txtPrice.Text, decPrice)

9. Save the solution. Click **DEBUG** on the menu bar and then click **Step Into**. Type **100** in the Price box and then click the **Calculate** button. Press **F8** to process the procedure header. The debugger highlights the TryParse method and then pauses execution of the code.

10. Before the TryParse method is processed, the txtPrice control's Text property should contain 100, which is the value you entered in the Price box. Place your mouse pointer on `txtPrice.Text` in the TryParse method. The box shows that the Text property contains the expected value. The 100 is enclosed in quotation marks because it is considered a string.

11. The `decPrice` variable should contain its initial value, 0D. Place your mouse pointer on `decPrice` in the TryParse method. The box shows that the variable contains the expected value.

12. Press **F8** to process the TryParse method. The debugger highlights the `decDiscount10 = decPrice * 0.1D` statement before pausing execution of the code. Place your mouse pointer on `decPrice` in the TryParse method, as shown in Figure A-14. Notice that after the method is processed by the computer, the `decPrice` variable contains the number 100D, which is correct.

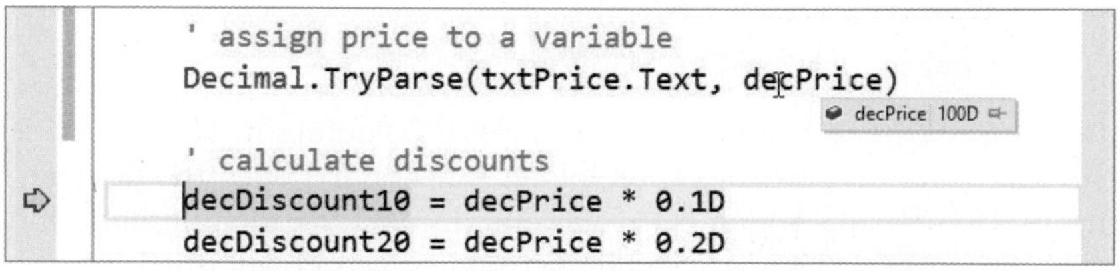
' assign price to a variable
Decimal.TryParse(txtPrice.Text, decPrice)
decPrice 100D
' calculate discounts
decDiscount10 = decPrice * 0.1D
decDiscount20 = decPrice * 0.2D

Figure A-14 Value stored in `decPrice` after the TryParse method is executed

13. Before the highlighted statement is processed, the `decDiscount10` variable should contain its initial value, and the `decPrice` variable should contain the value assigned to it by the TryParse method. Place your mouse pointer on `decDiscount10` in the highlighted statement. The box shows that the variable contains 0D, which is correct. Place your mouse pointer on `decPrice` in the highlighted statement. The box shows that the variable contains 100D, which also is correct.

14. After the highlighted statement is processed, the `decPrice` variable should still contain 100D. However, the `decDiscount10` variable should contain 10D, which is 10% of 100. Press **F8** to execute the highlighted statement, and then place your mouse pointer on `decDiscount10` in the statement. The box shows that the variable contains the expected value. On your own, verify that the `decPrice` variable in the statement contains the appropriate value.

15. To continue program execution without the debugger, click **DEBUG** on the menu bar and then click **Continue**. This time, the correct discount amounts appear in the interface. See Figure A-15.

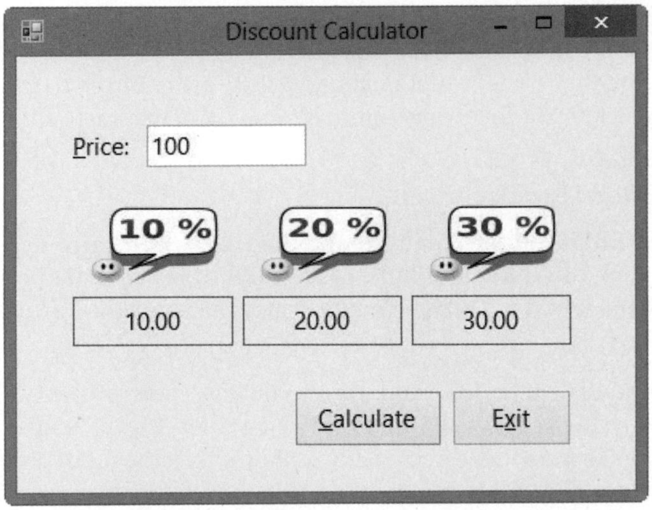

Figure A-15 Sample run of the Discount Calculator application

16. Click the **Exit** button. Close the Code Editor window and then close the solution.

Setting Breakpoints

Stepping through code one line at a time is not the only way to search for logic errors. You also can use a breakpoint to pause execution at a specific line in the code. You will learn how to set a breakpoint in the next set of steps.

START HERE

To begin debugging the Hours Worked application:

1. Open the Hours Worked Solution (Hours Worked Solution.sln) file contained in the VB2012\AppA\Hours Worked Solution folder. If necessary, open the designer window. See Figure A-16. The application calculates and displays the total number of hours worked in four weeks. (The image in the picture box was downloaded from the Open Clip Art Library at *http://openclipart.org*.)

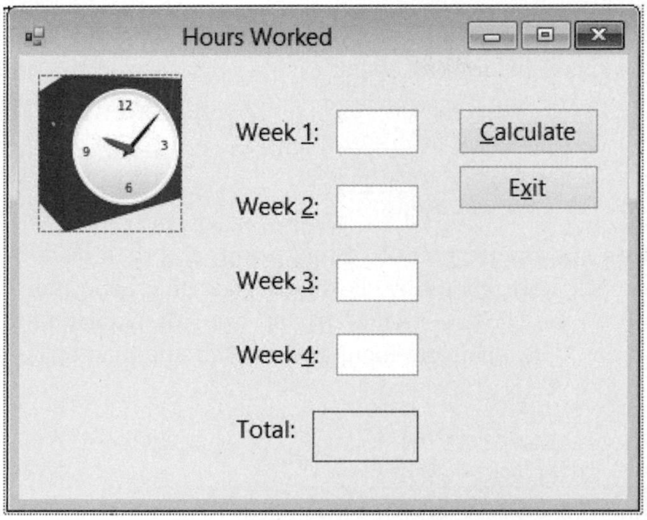

Figure A-16 Hours Worked application

OpenClipArt.org/AirW

2. Open the Code Editor window. Figure A-17 shows the code entered in the btnCalc_Click procedure.

```
Private Sub btnCalc_Click(sender As Object, e As EventArgs)
    ' calculates and displays the total number
    ' of hours worked during 4 weeks

    ' declare variables
    Dim dblWeek1 As Double
    Dim dblWeek2 As Double
    Dim dblWeek3 As Double
    Dim dblWeek4 As Double
    Dim dblTotal As Double

    ' assign input to variables
    Double.TryParse(txtWeek1.Text, dblWeek1)
    Double.TryParse(txtWeek2.Text, dblWeek2)
    Double.TryParse(txtWeek3.Text, dblWeek2)
    Double.TryParse(txtWeek4.Text, dblWeek4)

    ' calculate total hours worked
    dblTotal = dblWeek1 + dblWeek2 + dblWeek3 + dblWeek4

    ' display total hours worked
    lblTotal.Text = dblTotal.ToString("N1")
End Sub
```

Figure A-17 btnCalc_Click procedure

3. Start the application. Type **10.5**, **25**, **33**, and **40** in the Week 1, Week 2, Week 3, and Week 4 boxes, respectively, and then click the **Calculate** button. The interface shows that the total number of hours is 83.5, which is incorrect; it should be 108.5. Click the **Exit** button.

The statement that calculates the total number of hours worked is not giving the correct result. Rather than having the computer pause before processing each line of code in the procedure, you will have it pause only before processing the calculation statement. You do this by setting a breakpoint on the statement.

To finish debugging the Hours Worked application:

START HERE

1. Right-click the **calculation statement**, point to **Breakpoint**, and then click **Insert Breakpoint**. (You also can set a breakpoint by clicking the statement and then using the Toggle Breakpoint option on the DEBUG menu. Or, you can simply click in the gray margin next to the statement.) The debugger highlights the statement and places a circle next to it, as shown in Figure A-18.

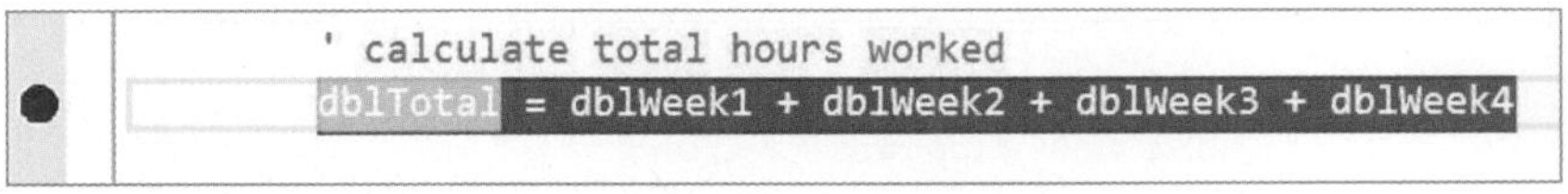
' calculate total hours worked
dblTotal = dblWeek1 + dblWeek2 + dblWeek3 + dblWeek4

Figure A-18 Breakpoint set in the procedure

2. Start the application. Type **10.5**, **25**, **33**, and **40** in the Week 1, Week 2, Week 3, and Week 4 boxes, respectively, and then click the **Calculate** button. The computer begins processing the code contained in the button's Click event procedure. It stops processing when it reaches the breakpoint statement, which it highlights. The highlighting indicates that the statement is the next one to be processed. Notice that a yellow arrow now appears in the red dot next to the breakpoint. See Figure A-19.

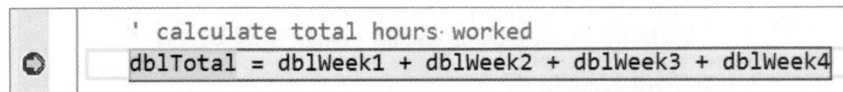

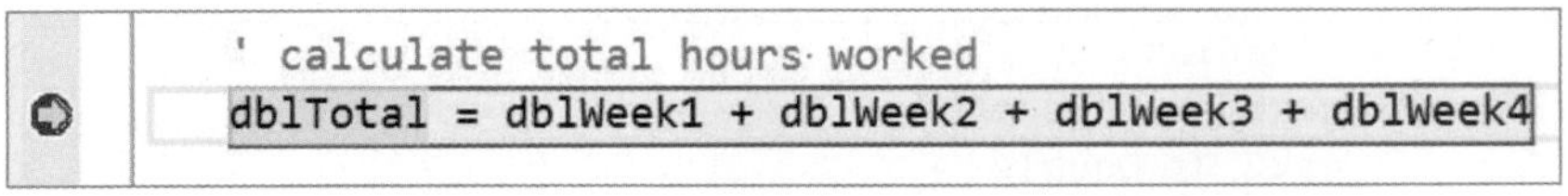
' calculate total hours worked
dblTotal = dblWeek1 + dblWeek2 + dblWeek3 + dblWeek4

Figure A-19 Result of the computer reaching the breakpoint

3. Before viewing the values contained in each variable in the highlighted statement, consider the values you expect to find. Before the calculation statement is processed, the `dblTotal` variable should contain its initial value (0). Place your mouse pointer on `dblTotal` in the highlighted statement. The box shows that the variable's value is 0.0, which is correct. (You can verify the variable's initial value by placing your mouse pointer on `dblTotal` in its declaration statement.) Don't be concerned that 0.0 appears rather than 0. The .0 indicates that the value's data type is Double.

4. The other four variables should contain the numbers 10.5, 25, 33, and 40, which are the values you entered in the text boxes. On your own, view the values contained in the `dblWeek1`, `dblWeek2`, `dblWeek3`, and `dblWeek4` variables. Notice that two of the variables (`dblWeek1` and `dblWeek4`) contain the correct values (10.5 and 40.0). The `dblWeek2` variable, however, contains 33.0 rather than 25.0, and the `dblWeek3` variable contains its initial value (0.0) rather than the number 33.0.

5. Two of the TryParse methods are responsible for assigning the text box values to the `dblWeek2` and `dblWeek3` variables. Looking closely at the four TryParse methods in the procedure, you will notice that the third one is incorrect. After converting the contents of the txtWeek3 control to a number, the method should assign the number to the `dblWeek3` variable rather than to the `dblWeek2` variable. Click **DEBUG** on the menu bar and then click **Stop Debugging**.

6. Change `dblWeek2` in the third TryParse method to **dblWeek3**.
7. Now you can remove the breakpoint. Right-click the **statement containing the breakpoint**, point to **Breakpoint**, and then click **Delete Breakpoint**. (Or, you can simply click the breakpoint circle.)
8. Save the solution and then start the application. Type **10.5**, **25**, **33**, and **40** in the Week 1, Week 2, Week 3, and Week 4 boxes, respectively, and then click the **Calculate** button. The interface shows that the total number of hours is 108.5, which is correct. See Figure A-20.

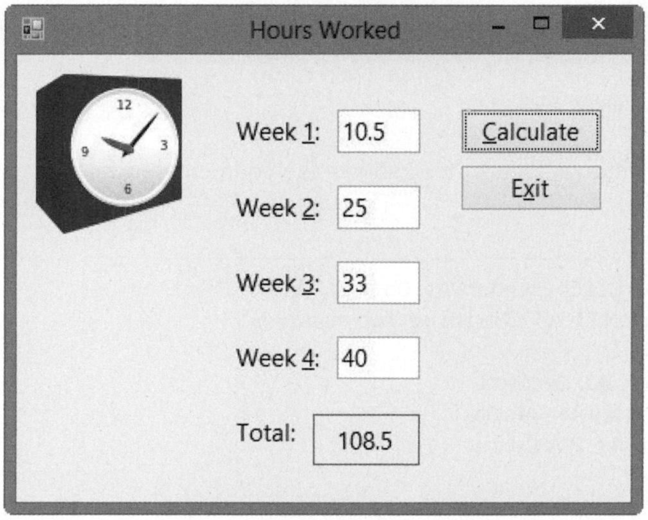

Figure A-20 Sample run of the Hours Worked application
OpenClipArt.org/AirW

9. On your own, test the application using other values for the hours worked in each week. When you are finished testing, click the **Exit** button. Close the Code Editor window and then close the solution.

Run Time Errors

In addition to syntax and logic errors, programs can also have run time errors. A run time error is an error that occurs while an application is running. As you will observe in the following set of steps, an expression that attempts to divide a value by the number 0 will result in a run time error. This is because, as in math, division by zero is not allowed.

To use the Quotient Calculator application to observe a run time error:

START HERE

1. Open the Quotient Solution (Quotient Solution.sln) file contained in the VB2012\AppA\Quotient Solution folder. If necessary, open the designer window. See Figure A-21. The interface provides two text boxes for the user to enter two numbers. The Calculate button's Click event procedure divides the number in the txtNumerator control by the number in the txtDenominator control and then displays the result, called the quotient, in the lblQuotient control.

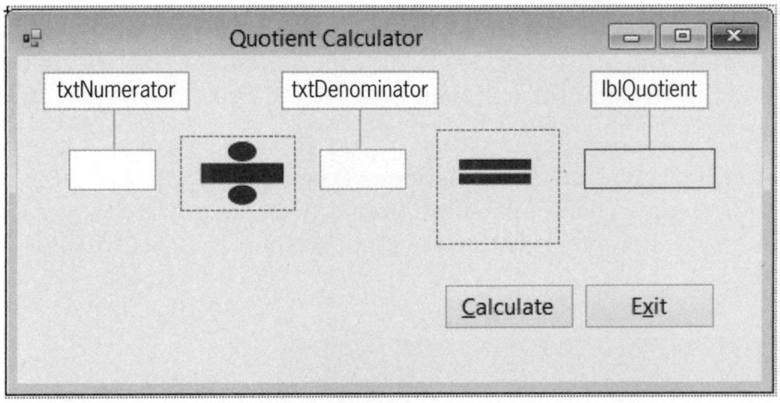

Figure A-21 Quotient Calculator application

2. Open the Code Editor window. Figure A-22 shows the code entered in the btnCalc_Click procedure.

```
Private Sub btnCalc_Click(sender As Object, e As EventArgs) I
    ' display the result of dividing two numbers

    Dim decNumerator As Decimal
    Dim decDenominator As Decimal
    Dim decQuotient As Decimal

    Decimal.TryParse(txtNumerator.Text, decNumerator)
    Decimal.TryParse(txtDenominator.Text, decDenominator)

    decQuotient = decNumerator / decDenominator

    lblQuotient.Text = decQuotient.ToString("N2")
End Sub
```

Figure A-22 Code entered in the btnCalc_Click procedure

3. Start the application. Type **100** and **5** in the txtNumerator and txtDenominator controls, respectively, and then click the **Calculate** button. The interface shows that the quotient is 20.00, which is correct.

4. Now, delete the 5 from the txtDenominator control and then click the **Calculate** button. A run time error occurs. The Error Correction window indicates that the highlighted statement, which also has an arrow pointing to it, is attempting to divide by zero. The troubleshooting tips section of the window advises you to "Make sure the value of the denominator is not zero before performing a division operation." See Figure A-23.

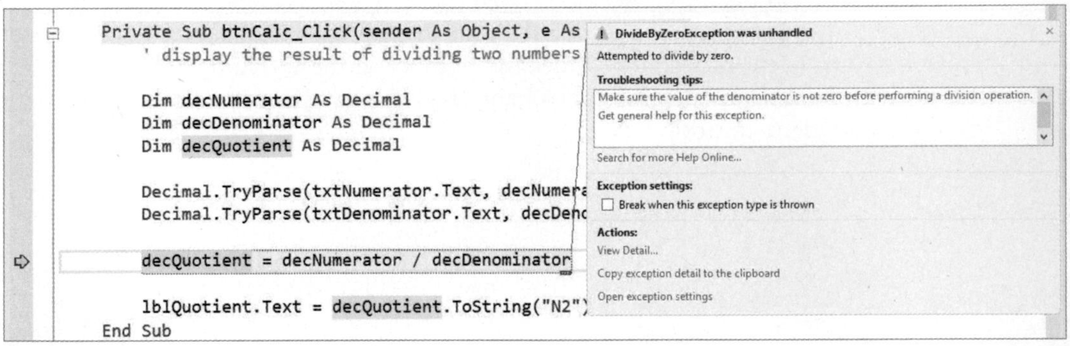

Figure A-23 Run time error caused by attempting to divide by zero

When the txtDenominator control is empty, or when it contains a character that cannot be converted to a number, the second TryParse method in the procedure stores the number 0 in the `decDenominator` variable. If the `decDenominator` variable contains 0, the statement that calculates the quotient will produce a run time error because the variable is used as the denominator in the calculation. To prevent this error from occurring, you will need to tell the computer to calculate the quotient only when the `decDenominator` variable contains a value other than 0. You do this using a selection structure, which is covered in Chapter 4 in this book.

START HERE

To add a selection structure to the Quotient Calculator application:

1. Click **DEBUG** on the menu bar and then click **Stop Debugging**.
2. Enter the selection structure shown in Figure A-24. Be sure to move the calculation statement into the selection structure's true path, as shown.

```
Private Sub btnCalc_Click(sender As Object, e As EventArgs)
    ' display the result of dividing two numbers

    Dim decNumerator As Decimal
    Dim decDenominator As Decimal
    Dim decQuotient As Decimal

    Decimal.TryParse(txtNumerator.Text, decNumerator)
    Decimal.TryParse(txtDenominator.Text, decDenominator)

    If decDenominator <> 0 Then
        decQuotient = decNumerator / decDenominator
    End If

    lblQuotient.Text = decQuotient.ToString("N2")
End Sub
```

enter this selection structure

Figure A-24 Selection structure entered in the procedure

3. Start the application. Type **100** and **5** in the txtNumerator and txtDenominator controls, respectively, and then click the **Calculate** button. The interface shows that the quotient is 20.00, which is correct.
4. Now, delete the 5 from the txtDenominator control and then click the **Calculate** button. Instead of a run time error, the number 0.00 appears in the interface. See Figure A-25.

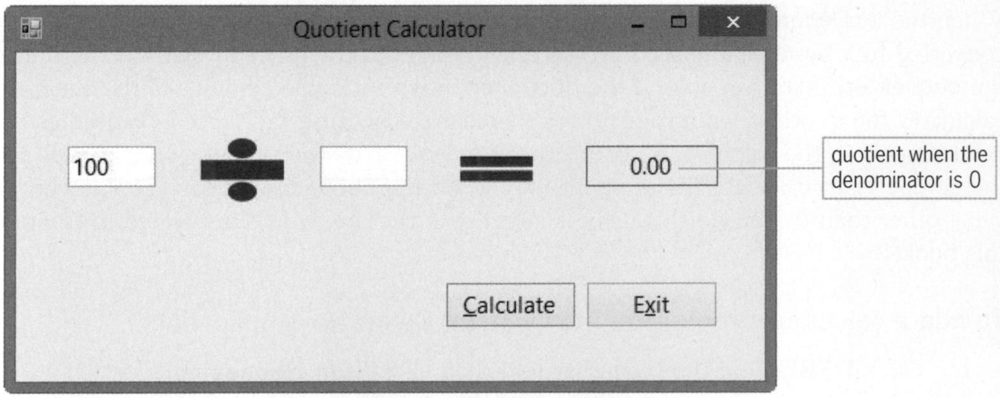

Figure A-25 Result of including the selection structure in the btnCalc_Click procedure

5. Click the **Exit** button. Close the Code Editor window and then close the solution.

Appendix A Summary

- To find the syntax errors in a program:

  Look for jagged lines in the Code Editor window. Or, start the application and then look in the Error List window.

- To find the logic errors in a program:

  Either step through the code in the Code Editor window or set a breakpoint.

- To step through your code:

  Use either the Step Into option on the DEBUG menu or the F8 key on your keyboard.

- To set a breakpoint:

  Right-click the line of code on which you want to set the breakpoint. Point to Breakpoint and then click Insert Breakpoint. You also can click the line of code and then use the Toggle Breakpoint option on the DEBUG menu. In addition, you can click in the gray margin next to the line of code.

- To remove a breakpoint:

  Right-click the line of code containing the breakpoint, point to Breakpoint, and then click Delete Breakpoint. You also can simply click the breakpoint circle in the margin.

- To determine whether a variable contains the number 0:

  Use a selection structure.

Review Questions

1. The process of locating and fixing any errors in a program is called ________.
   a. bug-proofing
   b. bug-eliminating
   c. debugging
   d. error removal

2. While stepping through code, the debugger highlights the statement that ________.
   a. was just executed
   b. will be executed next
   c. contains the error
   d. none of the above

3. Logic errors are listed in the Error List window.
   a. True
   b. False

4. Which key is used to step through code?
   a. F5
   b. F6
   c. F7
   d. F8

5. While stepping through the code in the Code Editor window, you can view the contents of controls and variables that appear in the highlighted statement only.
   a. True
   b. False

6. You use ________ to pause program execution at a specific line in the code.
   a. a breakpoint
   b. the Error List window
   c. the Step Into option on the DEBUG menu
   d. the Stop Debugging option on the DEBUG menu

7. If the `intTotalScore` and `intTests` variables contain the numbers 200 and 0, respectively, the statement `dblAvg = intTotalScore / intTests` will ________.
   a. assign 0 to the `dblAvg` variable
   b. result in a syntax error
   c. result in a logic error
   d. result in a run time error

8. If the `intTotalScore` and `intTests` variables contain the numbers 0 and 10, respectively, the statement `dblAvg = intTotalScore / intTests` will ________.
   a. assign 0 to the `dblAvg` variable
   b. result in a syntax error
   c. result in a logic error
   d. result in a run time error

9. The statement `Constant dblRATE As Double` is an example of a ________.
   a. correct statement
   b. logic error
   c. syntax error
   d. run time error

10. When entered in a procedure, which of the following statements will result in a syntax error?
    a. `Me.Clse()`
    b. `Integer.TryPars(txtHours.Text, intHours)`
    c. `Dim decRate as Decimel`
    d. all of the above

Exercises

INTRODUCTORY

1. Open the Commission Calculator Solution (Commission Calculator Solution.sln) file contained in the VB2012\AppA\Commission Calculator Solution folder. Use what you learned in the chapter to debug the application. When you are finished debugging the application, close the Code Editor window and then close the solution.

INTRODUCTORY

2. Open the New Pay Solution (New Pay Solution.sln) file contained in the VB2012\AppA\New Pay Solution folder. Use what you learned in the chapter to debug the application. When you are finished debugging the application, close the Code Editor window and then close the solution.

INTRODUCTORY

3. Open the Hawkins Solution (Hawkins Solution.sln) file contained in the VB2012\AppA\Hawkins Solution folder. Use what you learned in the chapter to debug the application. When you are finished debugging the application, close the Code Editor window and then close the solution.

INTRODUCTORY

4. Open the Allenton Solution (Allenton Solution.sln) file contained in the VB2012\AppA\Allenton Solution folder. Use what you learned in the chapter to debug the application. When you are finished debugging the application, close the Code Editor window and then close the solution.

INTERMEDIATE

5. Open the Martins Solution (Martins Solution.sln) file contained in the VB2012\AppA\Martins Solution folder. Use what you learned in the chapter to debug the application. When you are finished debugging the application, close the Code Editor window and then close the solution.

INTERMEDIATE

6. Open the Average Score Solution (Average Score Solution.sln) file contained in the VB2012\AppA\Average Score Solution folder. Use what you learned in the chapter to debug the application. When you are finished debugging the application, close the Code Editor window and then close the solution.

ADVANCED

7. Open the Beachwood Solution (Beachwood Solution.sln) file contained in the VB2012\AppA\Beachwood Solution folder. Use what you learned in the chapter to debug the application. When you are finished debugging the application, close the Code Editor window and then close the solution.

ADVANCED

8. Open the Framington Solution (Framington Solution.sln) file contained in the VB2012\AppA\Framington Solution folder. Use what you learned in the chapter to debug the application. When you are finished debugging the application, close the Code Editor window and then close the solution.

APPENDIX B

GUI Design Guidelines

Chapter 1—Lesson C

FormBorderStyle, ControlBox, MaximizeBox, MinimizeBox, and StartPosition Properties

- A splash screen should not have Minimize, Maximize, or Close buttons, and its borders should not be sizable. In most cases, a splash screen's FormBorderStyle property is set to either None or FixedSingle. Its StartPosition property is set to CenterScreen.
- A form that is not a splash screen should always have a Minimize button and a Close button, but you can choose to disable the Maximize button. Typically, the FormBorderStyle property is set to Sizable; however, it also can be set to FixedSingle. Most times, the form's StartPosition property is set to CenterScreen.

Chapter 2—Lesson A

Layout and Organization of the User Interface

- Organize the user interface so that the information flows either vertically or horizontally, with the most important information always located in the upper-left corner of the interface.
- Group related controls together using either white (empty) space or one of the tools from the Containers section of the toolbox.
- Use a label to identify each text box in the user interface. Also use a label to identify other label controls that display program output. The label text should be meaningful, be from one to three words only, and appear on one line. Left-align the text within the label, and position the label either above or to the left of the control it identifies. Enter the label text using sentence capitalization, and follow the label text with a colon (:).
- Display a meaningful caption on the face of each button. The caption should indicate the action the button will perform when clicked. Enter the caption using book title capitalization. Place the caption on one line and use from one to three words only.
- When a group of buttons are stacked vertically, each button in the group should be the same height and width. When a group of buttons are positioned horizontally, each button in the

group should be the same height. In a group of buttons, the most commonly used button is typically placed first in the group.

- Align the borders of the controls wherever possible to minimize the number of different margins appearing in the interface.

Chapter 2—Lesson B

Adding Graphics

- Use graphics sparingly. If the graphic is used solely for aesthetics, use a small graphic and place it in a location that will not distract the user.

Selecting Font Types, Styles, and Sizes

- Use only one font type (typically Segoe UI) for all of the text in the interface.
- Use no more than two different font sizes in the interface.
- Avoid using italics and underlining because both font styles make text difficult to read.
- Limit the use of bold text to titles, headings, and key items that you want to emphasize.

Selecting Colors

- Build the interface using black, white, and gray. Only add color if you have a good reason to do so.
- Use white, off-white, or light gray for the background. Use black for the text.
- Never use a dark color for the background or a light color for the text. A dark background is hard on the eyes, and light-colored text can appear blurry.
- Limit the number of colors in an interface to three, not including white, black, and gray. The colors you choose should complement each other.
- Never use color as the only means of identification for an element in the interface.

Setting the BorderStyle Property of a Text Box or Label

- Keep the BorderStyle property of text boxes at the default setting: Fixed3D.
- Keep the BorderStyle property of identifying labels at the default setting: None.
- Set to FixedSingle the BorderStyle property of labels that display program output, such as those that display the result of a calculation.
- In Windows applications, a control that contains data that the user is not allowed to edit does not usually appear three-dimensional. Therefore, avoid setting a label control's BorderStyle property to Fixed3D.

Setting the AutoSize Property of a Label

- Keep the AutoSize property of identifying labels at the default setting: True.
- In most cases, change to False the AutoSize property of label controls that display program output.

Assigning Access Keys

- Assign a unique access key to each control that can accept user input.
- When assigning an access key to a control, use the first letter of the control's caption or identifying label, unless another letter provides a more meaningful association. If you can't use the first letter and no other letter provides a more meaningful association, then use a distinctive consonant. Lastly, use a vowel or a number.

Using the TabIndex Property to Control the Focus

- Assign a TabIndex value (starting with 0) to each control in the interface, except for controls that do not have a TabIndex property. The TabIndex values should reflect the order in which the user will want to access the controls.
- To allow users to access a text box using the keyboard, assign an access key to the text box's identifying label. Set the identifying label's TabIndex property to a value that is one number less than the value stored in the text box's TabIndex property.

Chapter 3—Lesson B

InputBox Function's Prompt and Title Capitalization

- Use sentence capitalization for the prompt, but book title capitalization for the title.

Assigning a Default Button

- The default button should be the button that is most often selected by the user, except in cases where the tasks performed by the button are both destructive and irreversible. If a form contains a default button, it typically is the first button.

Chapter 4—Lesson B

Labeling a Group Box

- Use sentence capitalization for the optional identifying label, which is entered in the group box's Text property.

MessageBox.Show Method

- Use sentence capitalization for the *text* argument, but book title capitalization for the *caption* argument.
- Display the Exclamation icon to alert the user that he or she must make a decision before the application can continue. You can phrase the message as a question. These message boxes typically contain more than one button.
- Display the Information icon along with an OK button in a message box that displays an informational message.
- Display the Stop icon to alert the user of a serious problem that must be corrected before the application can continue.
- The default button in the message box should be the one that represents the user's most likely action, as long as that action is not destructive.

Chapter 5—Lesson B

Radio Button Standards

- Use radio buttons to limit the user to one choice in a group of related but mutually exclusive choices.
- The minimum number of radio buttons in a group is two and the recommended maximum number is seven.
- The label in the radio button's Text property should be entered using sentence capitalization.
- Assign a unique access key to each radio button in an interface.

- Use a container (such as a group box) to create separate groups of radio buttons. Only one button in each group can be selected at any one time.
- Designate a default radio button in each group of radio buttons.

Check Box Standards

- Use check boxes to allow the user to select any number of choices from a group of one or more independent and nonexclusive choices.
- The label in the check box's Text property should be entered using sentence capitalization.
- Assign a unique access key to each check box in an interface.

Chapter 6—Lesson C

List Box Standards

- A list box should contain a minimum of three items.
- A list box should display a minimum of three items and a maximum of eight items at a time.
- Use a label control to provide keyboard access to the list box. Set the label's TabIndex property to a value that is one number less than the list box's TabIndex value.
- List box items are either arranged by use, with the most used entries appearing first in the list, or sorted in ascending order.

Default List Box Item

- If a list box allows the user to make only one selection, a default item should be selected when the interface first appears. The default item should be either the item selected most frequently or the first item in the list. However, if a list box allows more than one selection at a time, you do not select a default item.

Chapter 7—Lesson B

Combo Box Standards

- Use a label control to provide keyboard access to a combo box. Set the label's TabIndex property to a value that is one number less than the combo box's TabIndex value.
- Combo box items are either arranged by use, with the most used entries appearing first in the list, or sorted in ascending order.

Chapter 8—Lesson B

Menu Standards

- Menu title captions should be one word and entered using uppercase letters. Each menu title should have a unique access key.
- Menu item captions can be from one to three words. Use book title capitalization and assign a unique access key to each menu item on the same menu.
- Assign unique shortcut keys to commonly used menu items.
- If a menu item requires additional information from the user, place an ellipsis (...) at the end of the item's caption, which is entered in the item's Text property.
- Follow the Windows standards for the placement of menu titles and items.
- Use a separator bar to separate groups of related menu items.

APPENDIX C

Visual Basic Conversion Functions

Syntax	Return data type	Range for *expression*
CBool(*expression*)	Boolean	Any valid String or numeric expression
CByte(*expression*)	Byte	0 through 255 (unsigned)
CChar(*expression*)	Char	Any valid String expression; value can be 0 through 65535 (unsigned); only the first character is converted
CDate(*expression*)	Date	Any valid representation of a date and time
CDbl(*expression*)	Double	–1.79769313486231570E+308 through –4.94065645841246544E-324 for negative values; 4.94065645841246544E-324 through 1.79769313486231570E +308 for positive values
CDec(*expression*)	Decimal	+/–79,228,162,514,264,337,593,543,950,335 for zero-scaled numbers, that is, numbers with no decimal places; for numbers with 28 decimal places, the range is +/– 7.9228162514264337593543950335; the smallest possible non-zero number is .0000000000000000000000000001 (+/–1E-28)
CInt(*expression*)	Integer	–2,147,483,648 through 2,147,483,647; fractional parts are rounded
CLng(*expression*)	Long	–9,223,372,036,854,775,808 through 9,223,372,036,854,775,807; fractional parts are rounded
CObj(*expression*)	Object	Any valid expression
CSByte(*expression*)	SByte (signed Byte)	–128 through 127; fractional parts are rounded
CShort(*expression*)	Short	–32,768 through 32,767; fractional parts are rounded
CSng(*expression*)	Single	–3.402823E+38 through –1.401298E-45 for negative values; 1.401298E-45 through 3.402823E+38 for positive values
CStr(*expression*)	String	Depends on the expression
CUInt(*expression*)	UInt	0 through 4,294,967,295 (unsigned)
CULng(*expression*)	ULng	0 through 18,446,744,073,709,551,615 (unsigned)
CUShort(*expression*)	UShort	0 through 65,535 (unsigned)

APPENDIX D

Visual Basic 2012 Cheat Sheet

Statements

Assignment

object.property = *expression*
variableName = *expression*

Updating a counter

counterVariable = *counterVariable* {+ | –} *constantValue*
counterVariable {+= | –=} *constantValue*

Updating an accumulator

accumulatorVariable = *accumulatorVariable* {+ | –} *value*
accumulatorVariable {+= | –=} *value*

Option Explicit

when set to On, prevents the computer from creating an undeclared variable
Option Explicit [**On** | **Off**]

Option Strict

when set to On, prevents the computer from making implicit type conversions that may result in a loss of data
Option Strict [**On** | **Off**]

Option Infer

when set to Off, prevents the computer from inferring a variable's data type
Option Infer [**On** | **Off**]

Do...Loop

Pretest loop

Do {**While** | **Until**} *condition*
    loop body instructions to be processed either while the condition is true or until the condition becomes true
Loop

Posttest loop

Do
    loop body instructions to be processed either while the condition is true or until the condition becomes true
Loop {**While** | **Until**} *condition*

For Each...Next

For Each *elementVariableName* **As** *dataType* **In** *group*
    loop body instructions
Next *elementVariableName*

For...Next

For *counterVariableName* [**As** *dataType*] = *startValue* **To** *endValue* [**Step** *stepValue*]
    loop body instructions
Next *counterVariableName*

stepValue	Loop body processed when	Loop ends when
positive number	counter's value <= *endValue*	counter's value > *endValue*
negative number	counter's value >= *endValue*	counter's value < *endValue*

If...Then...Else

If *condition* **Then**
    statement block to be processed when the condition is true
[**ElseIf** *condition2*
    statement block to be processed when the first condition is false and condition2 is true]
[**Else**
    statement block to be processed when all previous conditions are false]
End If

Logic errors in selection structures

1. Using a compound condition rather than a nested selection structure
2. Reversing the decisions in the outer and nested selection structures
3. Using an unnecessary nested selection structure
4. Including an unnecessary comparison in a condition

Select Case

Select Case *selectorExpression*
    Case *expressionList1*
        instructions for the first Case
    [**Case** *expressionList2*
        instructions for the second Case]
    [**Case** *expressionListN*
        instructions for the Nth Case]
    [**Case Else**
        instructions for when the selectorExpression does not match any of the expressionLists]
End Select

Case *smallest value in the range* **To** *largest value in the range*
Case Is *comparisonOperator value*

Try...Catch
Try
one or more statements that might generate an exception
Catch ex As Exception
one or more statements to execute when an exception occurs
End Try

Variable and Named Constant Declaration

{**Dim** | **Private** | **Static**} *variableName* **As** *dataType* [= *initialValue*]
[**Private**] **Const** *constantName* **As** *dataType* = *expression*

Data Types

Boolean	a logical value (True, False)
Char	one Unicode character
Date	date and time information
Decimal	a number with a decimal place
Double	a number with a decimal place
Integer	integer
Long	integer
Object	data of any type
Short	integer
Single	a number with a decimal place
String	text

Rules for Naming Variables

1. The name must begin with a letter or an underscore.
2. The name can contain only letters, numbers, and the underscore character. No punctuation characters, special characters, or spaces are allowed in the name.
3. Although the name can contain thousands of characters, 32 characters is the recommended maximum number of characters to use.
4. The name cannot be a reserved word, such as `Sub` or `Double`.

Type Conversion Rules

1. Strings will not be implicitly converted to numbers.
2. Numbers will not be implicitly converted to strings.
3. Wider data types will not be implicitly demoted to narrower data types.
4. Narrower data types will be implicitly promoted to wider data types.

Operators and Precedence

^	exponentiation	1
–	negation	2
*, /	multiplication and division	3
\	integer division	4
Mod	modulus (remainder) arithmetic	5
+, –	addition and subtraction	6
&	concatenation	7
=, <>, >, >=, <, <=	equal to, not equal to, greater than, greater than or equal to, less than, less than or equal to	8
Not	reverses the truth-value of the condition; True becomes False, and False becomes True	9
And	all sub-conditions must be true for the compound condition to evaluate to True	10
AndAlso	same as the And operator, except performs short-circuit evaluation	10
Or	only one of the sub-conditions needs to be true for the compound condition to evaluate to True	11
OrElse	same as the Or operator, except performs short-circuit evaluation	11
Xor	one and only one of the sub-conditions can be true for the compound condition to evaluate to True	12

Arithmetic Assignment

variableName arithmeticAssignmentOperator value

Operator	Purpose
+=	addition assignment
–=	subtraction assignment
*=	multiplication assignment
/=	division assignment

Printing

Print the interface during design time

Make the designer window the active window. Use the Windows Snipping tool to take a picture of the interface, save the picture, and then print it. Or, tap the Print Screen key, start an application that can display a picture, open a new document (if necessary), and then press Ctrl+v.

Print the interface during run time

Add a PrintForm control (object) to the component tray.
object.**PrintAction = Printing.PrintAction.***destination*
object.**Print()**

destination	Purpose
`PrintToPreview`	sends the printout to the Print Preview window
`PrintToPrinter`	sends the printout to the printer

Print the code during design time

Make the Code Editor window the active window. Collapse any code you do not want to print. Click the Print option on the FILE menu. Select/deselect the Hide collapsed regions and/or Include line numbers check boxes. Click the OK button.

Generate Random Numbers

Integers
Dim *randomObjectName* **As New Random**
randomObjectName.**Next(***minValue*, *maxValue*)

Double numbers
Dim *randomObjectName* **As New Random**
(*maxValue* – *minValue* + **1**) * *randomObjectName*.**NextDouble** + *minValue*

Methods

Convert
converts a number from one data type to another
Convert.*method*(*value*)

Focus
sends the focus to an object
object.**Focus()**

MessageBox.Show
displays a message box
MessageBox.Show(*text*, *caption*, *buttons*, *icon*[, *defaultButton*])
dialogResultVariable = **MessageBox.Show(**text, *caption*, *buttons*, *icon*[, *defaultButton*])

SelectAll
selects the contents of a text box
textbox.**SelectAll()**

Strings.Space
includes a specific number of spaces in a string
Strings.Space(*number*)

ToString
formats a number
numericVariableName.**ToString(***formatString*)

TryParse
converts a string to a number
dataType.**TryParse(***string*, *numericVariableName*)
booleanVariable = *dataType*.**TryParse(***string*, *numericVariableName*)

Functions

Format
formats a number
Format(*expression*, *style*)

InputBox
InputBox(*prompt*[, *title*][, *defaultResponse*])

Val
converts a string to a Double number
Val(*string***)**

Independent Sub Procedure

Private Sub *procedureName*([*parameterList*])
    statements
End Sub
Call *procedureName*([*argumentList*])

Function Procedure

Private Function *procedureName*([*parameterList*]) **As** *dataType*
    statements
    Return *expression*
End Function

Internally Document the Code

Start the comment with an apostrophe followed by an optional space.

Control the Characters Accepted by a Text Box

Example

```
Private Sub txtAge_KeyPress(sender As Object,
e As KeyPressEventArgs) Handles txtAge.KeyPress
    ' allows the text box to accept only numbers
    ' and the Backspace key

    If (e.KeyChar < "0" OrElse e.KeyChar > "9") AndAlso
      e.KeyChar <> ControlChars.Back Then
      e.Handled = True
    End If
End Sub
```

Prevent a Form from Closing (FormClosing Event Procedure)

```
e.Cancel = True
```

Working with Strings

Accessing characters
string.**Substring(***startIndex*[, *numCharsToAccess*])

Aligning the characters
string.**PadLeft(***totalChars*[, *padCharacter*])
string.**PadRight(***totalChars*[, *padCharacter*])

Comparing using pattern-matching
string **Like** *pattern*

Pattern-matching characters	Matches in *string*
?	any single character
*	zero or more characters
#	any single digit (0 through 9)
[*characterList*]	any single character in the *characterList* (for example, "[A5T]" matches A, 5, or T, whereas "[a–z]" matches any lowercase letter)
[!*characterList*]	any single character *not* in the *characterList* (for example, "[!A5T]" matches any character other than A, 5, or T, whereas "[!a–z]" matches any character that is not a lowercase letter)

Concatenation
string **&** *string* [...**&** *string*]

Converting to uppercase or lowercase
string.**ToUpper**
string.**ToLower**

Determining the number of characters
string.**Length**

Inserting characters
string.**Insert(***startIndex*, *value***)**

Removing characters
string.**Trim**
string.**Remove(***startIndex*[, *numCharsToRemove*]**)**

Searching
string.**Contains(***subString***)**
string.**IndexOf(***subString*[, *startIndex*]**)**

List/Combo Boxes

Add items
object.**Items.Add(***item***)**

Clear items
object.**Items.Clear()**

Determine the selected item
object.**SelectedItem**
object.**SelectedIndex**

Perform a task when the selected item changes
Code the SelectedValueChanged or SelectedIndexChanged events.

Remove items
object.**Items.Remove(***item***)**
object.**Items.RemoveAt(***index***)**

Select an item
object.**SelectedItem** = *item*
object.**SelectedIndex** = *itemIndex*

One-Dimensional Arrays

Array declaration

{**Dim** | **Private** | **Static**} *arrayName*(*highestSubscript*) **As** *dataType*
{**Dim** | **Private** | **Static**} *arrayName*() **As** *dataType* = {*initialValues*}

Highest subscript

arrayName.**GetUpperBound(0)**
arrayName.**Length – 1**

Number of elements

arrayName.**Length**
arrayName.**GetUpperBound(0) + 1**

Reversing

Array.Reverse(*arrayName***)**

Sorting (ascending order)

Array.Sort(*arrayName***)**

Traversing

```
Dim strCities() As String = {"Boston", "Chicago",
                             "Louisville", "Tampa"}
```

Example 1—For...Next

```
Dim intHigh As Integer = strCities.GetUpperBound(0)
For intSub As Integer = 0 To intHigh
     MessageBox.Show(strCities(intSub))
Next intSub
```

Example 2—Do...Loop

```
Dim intHigh As Integer = strCities.Length - 1
Dim intSub As Integer
Do While intSub <= intHigh
     lstCities.Items.Add(strCities(intSub))
     intSub += 1
Loop
```

Example 3—For Each...Next

```
For Each strCity As String In strCities
      MessageBox.Show(strCity)
Next strCity
```

Two-dimensional Arrays

Array declaration

{**Dim** | **Private** | **Static**} *arrayName*(*highestRowSubscript*, *highestColumnSubscript*) **As** *dataType*
{**Dim** | **Private** | **Static**} *arrayName*(,) **As** *dataType* = {{*initialValues*}, ...{*initialValues*}}

Highest column subscript

arrayName.**GetUpperBound(1)**

Highest row subscript

arrayName.**GetUpperBound(0)**

Traversing

```
Dim strMonths(,) As String = {{"Jan", "31"},
                              {"Feb", "28"},
                              {"Mar", "31"},
                              {"Apr", "30"}}
```

Example 1 – For...Next (displays contents row by row)

```
Dim intHighRow As Integer = strMonths.GetUpperBound(0)
Dim intHighCol As Integer = strMonths.GetUpperBound(1)
For intR As Integer = 0 To intHighRow
    For intC As Integer = 0 To intHighCol
        lstMonths.Items.Add(strMonths(intR, intC))
    Next intC
Next intR
```

Example 2 – Do...Loop (displays contents column by column)

```
Dim intHighRow As Integer = strMonths.GetUpperBound(0)
Dim intHighCol As Integer = strMonths.GetUpperBound(1)
Dim intR As Integer
Dim intC As Integer
Do While intC <= intHighCol
    intR = 0
    Do While intR <= intHighRow
        lstMonths.Items.Add(strMonths(intR, intC))
        intR += 1
    Loop
    intC += 1
Loop
```

Example 3 – For Each...Next (displays contents row by row)

```
For Each strElement As String In strMonths
     lstMonths.Items.Add(strElement)
Next strElement
```

Sequential Access Files

Close a file
streamWriterVariableName.**Close()**
streamReaderVariableName.**Close()**

Create a StreamReader object
IO.File.OpenText(*fileName***)**

Create a StreamWriter object
IO.File.*method***(***fileName***)**

method	Description
CreateText	opens a sequential access file for output
AppendText	opens a sequential access file for append

Declare StreamWriter and StreamReader variables
{**Dim** | **Private**} *streamWriterVariableName* **As IO.StreamWriter**
{**Dim** | **Private**} *streamReaderVariableName* **As IO.StreamReader**

Determine whether a file exists
IO.File.Exists(*fileName***)**

Read data from a file
streamReaderVariableName.**ReadLine**

Determine whether a file contains another character to read
streamReaderVariableName.**Peek**

Write data to a file
streamWriterVariableName.**Write(***data***)**
streamWriterVariableName.**WriteLine(***data***)**

Structures

Declare a structure variable
{**Dim** | **Private**} *structureVariableName* **As** *structureName*

Declare an array of structure variables
Use the structureName as the array's dataType.

Definition
Structure *structureName*
    Public *memberVariableName1* **As** *dataType*
    [**Public** *memberVariableNameN* **As** *dataType*]
End Structure

Member variable within a structure variable
structureVariableName.*memberVariableName*

Member variable within an array of structure variables
arrayName(*subscript*).*memberVariableName*

Databases

Connect an application to an Access database

1. Open the application's solution file.
2. If necessary, open the Data Sources window by clicking VIEW on the menu bar, pointing to Other Windows, and then clicking Data Sources.
3. Click Add New Data Source in the Data Sources window to start the Data Source Configuration Wizard, which displays the Choose a Data Source Type screen. If necessary, click Database.
4. Click the Next button and then continue using the wizard to specify the data source and the name of the database file. The data source for an Access database is Microsoft Access Database File (OLE DB).

Preview the contents of a dataset

1. Right-click the dataset's name in the Data Sources window and then click Preview Data.
2. Click the Preview button.
3. When you are finished previewing the data, close the dialog box.

Bind an object in a dataset

<u>To have the computer create a control and then bind an object to it:</u>

In the Data Sources window, click the object you want to bind. If necessary, use the object's list arrow to change the control type. Drag the object to an empty area on the form and then release the mouse button.

<u>To bind an object to an existing control:</u>

In the Data Sources window, click the object you want to bind. Drag the object to the control on the form and then release the mouse button. Alternatively, you can click the control on the form and then use the Properties window to set the appropriate property or properties.

Customizing a BindingNavigator control

To add an item to a BindingNavigator control:

1. Click the BindingNavigator control's task box and then click Edit Items to open the Items Collection Editor window.
2. If necessary, click the "Select item and add to list below" arrow.
3. Click the item you want to add to the BindingNavigator control and then click the Add button.
4. If necessary, you can use the up and down arrows to reposition the item.

To delete an item from a BindingNavigator control:

1. Click the BindingNavigator control's task box and then click Edit Items to open the Items Collection Editor window.
2. In the Members list, click the item you want to remove and then click the *X* button.

Determine the location of the record pointer
bindingSourceName.**Position**

Move the record pointer
bindingSourceName.**MoveFirst()**
bindingSourceName.**MoveLast()**
bindingSourceName.**MoveNext()**
bindingSourceName.**MovePrevious()**

Add a record to a dataset
dataSetName.tableName.**Add***tableName***Row(***valueField1*[,
valueField2..., *valueFieldN*])

Save dataset changes to a database
tableAdapterName.**Update(***dataSetName.tableName*)

Sort the records in a dataset
bindingSourceName.**Sort** = *fieldName*

Locate a record in a dataset
dataRowVariable =
dataSetName.tableName.**FindBy***fieldName*(*value*)

Delete a record from a dataset
dataRowVariable.**Delete()**

LINQ

Select and arrange records
Dim *variableName* = **From** *elementName* **In** *dataset.table*
[**Where** *condition*]
[**Order By** *elementName.fieldName1* [**Ascending** | **Descending**]
[, *elementName.fieldName*N [**Ascending** | **Descending**]]]
Select *elementName*

Assign a LINQ variable's contents to a BindingSource control
bindingSource.**DataSource** = *variableName*.**AsDataView**

LINQ aggregate operators

The aggregate operators are Average, Count, Max, Min, and Sum. The Count operator does not need the Select clause.

Dim *variableName* [**As** *dataType*] =
Aggregate *elementName* **In** *dataset.table*
[**Where** *condition*]
Select *elementName.fieldName*
Into *aggregateOperator*()

SQL

Selecting fields and records

SELECT *fieldList* **FROM** *tableName*
[**WHERE** *condition*]
[**ORDER BY** *fieldName* [**DESC**]]

Add a record to a dataset

INSERT INTO *tableName*(*fieldName1*, *fieldName2*,...*fieldNameN*)
VALUES (*field1Value*, *field2Value*,...*fieldNValue*)

Delete a record from a dataset

DELETE FROM *tableName* **WHERE** *condition*

Classes

Define a class

Public Class *className*
attributes section
behaviors section
End Class

Instantiate an object

Syntax – Version 1

{**Dim** | **Private**} *variableName* **As** *className*
variableName = **New** *className*

Syntax – Version 2

{**Dim** | **Private**} *variableName* **As New** *className*

Create a Property procedure

Public [**ReadOnly** | **WriteOnly**] **Property** *propertyName*[(*parameterList*)] **As** *dataType*
Get
[*instructions*]
Return *privateVariable*
End Get
Set(value As *dataType*)
[*instructions*]
privateVariable = {**value** | *defaultValue*}
End Set
End Property

Create a constructor

Public Sub New([*parameterList*])
instructions to initialize the class's Private variables
End Sub

Create a method that is not a constructor
Public {**Sub** | **Function**} *methodName*([*parameterList*]) [**As** *dataType*]
    instructions
End {**Sub** | **Function**}

Create an auto-implemented property
Public Property *propertyName* **As** *dataType*

Most Commonly Used Properties

Windows Form

AcceptButton	specify a default button that will be selected when the user presses the Enter key
CancelButton	specify a cancel button that will be selected when the user presses the Esc key
ControlBox	indicate whether the form contains the Control box and Minimize, Maximize, and Close buttons
Font	specify the font to use for text
FormBorderStyle	specify the appearance and behavior of the form's border
MaximizeBox	specify the state of the Maximize button
MinimizeBox	specify the state of the Minimize button
Name	give the form a meaningful name (use frm as the ID)
StartPosition	indicate the starting position of the form
Text	specify the text that appears in the form's title bar and on the taskbar

Button

Enabled	indicate whether the button can respond to the user's actions
Font	specify the font to use for text
Image	specify the image to display on the button's face
ImageAlign	indicate the alignment of the image on the button's face
Name	give the button a meaningful name (use btn as the ID)
TabIndex	indicate the position of the button in the Tab order
Text	specify the text that appears on the button

CheckBox

Checked	indicate whether the check box is selected or unselected
Font	specify the font to use for text
Name	give the check box a meaningful name (use chk as the ID)
TabIndex	indicate the position of the check box in the Tab order
Text	specify the text that appears inside the check box

ComboBox

DropDownStyle	indicate the style of the combo box
Font	specify the font to use for text
Name	give the combo box a meaningful name (use cbo as the ID)
SelectedIndex	get or set the index of the selected item
SelectedItem	get or set the value of the selected item
Sorted	specify whether the items in the list portion are sorted
TabIndex	indicate the position of the combo box in the Tab order
Text	get or set the value that appears in the text portion

DataGridView

AutoSizeColumnsMode	control the way the column widths are sized
DataSource	indicate the source of the data to display in the control
Dock	define which borders of the control are bound to its container
Name	give the data grid view control a meaningful name (use dgv as the ID)

GroupBox

Name	give the group box a meaningful name (use grp as the ID)
Padding	specify the internal space between the edges of the group box and the edges of the controls contained within the group box
Text	specify the text that appears in the upper-left corner of the group box

Label

AutoSize	enable/disable automatic sizing
BorderStyle	specify the appearance of the label's border
Font	specify the font to use for text
Name	give the label a meaningful name (use lbl as the ID)
TabIndex	specify the position of the label in the Tab order
Text	specify the text that appears inside the label
TextAlign	specify the position of the text inside the label

ListBox

Font	specify the font to use for text
Name	give the list box a meaningful name (use lst as the ID)
SelectedIndex	get or set the index of the selected item
SelectedItem	get or set the value of the selected item
SelectionMode	indicate whether the user can select zero choices, one choice, or more than one choice
Sorted	specify whether the items in the list are sorted

PictureBox

Image	specify the image to display
Name	give the picture box a meaningful name (use pic as the ID)
SizeMode	specify how the image should be displayed
Visible	hide/display the picture box

RadioButton

Checked	indicate whether the radio button is selected or unselected
Font	specify the font to use for text
Name	give the radio button a meaningful name (use rad as the ID)
Text	specify the text that appears inside the radio button

TextBox

BackColor	indicate the background color of the text box
CharacterCasing	specify whether the text should remain as is or be converted to either uppercase or lowercase
Font	specify the font to use for text
ForeColor	indicate the color of the text inside the text box
Name	give the text box a meaningful name (use txt as the ID)
MaxLength	specify the maximum number of characters the text box will accept
Multiline	control whether the text can span more than one line
PasswordChar	specify the character to display when entering a password
ReadOnly	specify whether the text can be edited
ScrollBars	indicate whether scroll bars appear on a text box (used with a multiline text box)
TabIndex	specify the position of the text box in the Tab order
TabStop	indicate whether the user can use the Tab key to give focus to the text box
Text	get or set the text that appears inside the text box

Timer

Name	give the timer a meaningful name (use tmr as the ID)
Enabled	stop/start the timer
Interval	indicate the number of milliseconds between each Tick event

APPENDIX E

Case Projects

Your Special Day Catering (Chapters 1 – 3)

Create an application for Your Special Day Catering. The interface should allow the user to enter the customer ID, the bride's name, the groom's name, and the date of the wedding reception. It also should allow the user to enter the number of beef dinners, the number of chicken dinners, and the number of vegetarian dinners ordered for the reception. The interface should display the total number of dinners ordered, the total price of the order without sales tax, the sales tax, and the total price of the order with sales tax. Each dinner costs $26.75, and the sales tax rate is 5%. Include an appropriate image in the interface. (You can find many different images on the Open Clip Art Library Web site at *http://openclipart.org.*)

Crispies Bagels and Bites (Chapters 1 – 3)

Create an application for Crispies Bagels and Bites. The interface should allow the salesclerk to enter the number of bagels, donuts, and cups of coffee a customer orders. Bagels are 99¢, donuts are 75¢, and coffee is $1.20 per cup. The application should calculate and display the total price of the order without sales tax, the sales tax, and the total price of the order with sales tax. The sales tax rate is 6%. Include an appropriate image in the interface. (You can find many different images on the Open Clip Art Library Web site at *http://openclipart.org.*)

High Roll Game (Chapters 1 – 5)

The High Roll game requires two players. When the application is started, it should get each player's name and then display the names in the interface. Each player will roll two dice. The application should calculate the total roll for each player and then compare both totals. The application should display one of the following messages: "Tie", "*player 1's name* wins", or "*player 2's name* wins". The application should keep track of the number of times player 1 wins, the number of times player 2 wins, and the number of ties. You can use either your own die images or the ones contained in the VB2012\AppE folder. (The die images were downloaded from the Open Clip Art Library at *http://openclipart.org.*)

Mortgage Calculator (Chapters 1 – 5)

Research Visual Basic's Financial.Pmt method. Create an application that calculates and displays three monthly mortgage payments. The application should use the loan amount and annual interest rate provided by the user, and terms of 15 years, 25 years, and 30 years. The application should also display the total amount paid at the end of 15 years, 25 years, and 30 years.

Math Practice (Chapters 1 – 5)

Create an application that can be used to practice adding , subtracting, multiplying, and dividing numbers. The application should display a math problem on the screen, and then allow the student to enter the answer and also verify that the answer is correct. The application should give the student as many chances as necessary to answer the problem correctly. The math problems should use random integers from 1 through 20 only. The subtraction problems should never ask the student to subtract a larger number from a smaller one. The division problems should never ask the student to divide a smaller number by a larger number. Also, the division problems should always result in a whole number. The application should keep track of the number of correct and incorrect responses made by the student.

Loan Payment Calculator (Chapters 1 – 7)

Research Visual Basic's Financial.Pmt method. Create an application that calculates and displays the monthly payments on a loan. The application should use the loan amount provided by the user, rates of 3% to 7%, and terms of 3, 4, and 5 years.

Savings Calculator (Chapters 1 – 7)

Research Visual Basic's Financial.FV (Future Value) method. Create an application that allows the user to enter the amount a customer plans to deposit in a savings account each month, and whether the money will be deposited at either the beginning or the end of the month. The application should calculate and display the value of the account at the end of 5 years, 10 years, 15 years, 20 years, and 25 years. The interest rate is 3% and is compounded monthly.

Tax Deductible Calculator (Chapters 1 – 8)

Create an interface that provides text boxes for entering the following business expenses: lodging, travel, meals, and entertainment. Lodging and travel are 100% tax deductible; meals and entertainment are only 50% tax deductible. The application should calculate and display the total expenses, the amount that is tax deductible, and the percentage that is tax deductible. The text boxes should accept only numbers, the period, and the Backspace key. The application should display an error message if a text box contains more than one period.

State Finder (Chapters 1 – 8)

Create an interface that provides a text box for the user to enter one or more characters. The interface should also include a list box containing the names of the 50 states. When the user clicks a button in the interface, the button's Click event procedure should select the first list box item that begins with the character(s) entered by the user. For example, if the user enters the letter K, the procedure should select Kansas in the list box. However, if the user enters the letters Ke, the procedure should select Kentucky.

Shopping Cart (Chapters 1 – 10)

The shopping cart application should list the names of 10 different DVDs in a list box, and also store the associated prices in a one-dimensional array. To purchase a DVD, the user needs to click its name in the list box and then click an Add to Cart button. The button's Click event procedure should display the DVD's name and price in another list box, which will represent the shopping cart. The interface should also provide a Remove from Cart button. The application should display the cost of the items in the shopping cart, the sales tax, the shipping charge, and the total cost. The sales tax rate is 4%. The shipping charge is $1 per DVD, up to a maximum shipping charge of $5.

Airplane Seats (Chapters 1 – 10)

Create an interface that contains 18 controls arranged in six rows and three columns. You can use label controls, picture boxes, or buttons. The seats in the first row are designated 1A, 1B, and 1C. The seats in the second row are designated 2A, 2B, and 2C, and so on. When the user clicks one of the 18 controls, the application should display the passenger's name, seat designation, and ticket price. The application should use a sequential access file for the passenger information, a structure, and an array.

Theater Seats (Chapters 1 – 11)

Create an interface that contains 10 controls arranged in five rows and two columns. You can use label controls, picture boxes, or buttons. The seats in the first row are designated A1 and B1. The seats in the second row are designated A2 and B2, and so on. When the user clicks one of the 10 controls, the application should display the patron's name, seat designation, and ticket price. The application should use a sequential access file for the patron information, a class, and an array.

Roll Em Again (Chapters 1 – 11)

Code the Roll Em Game from Chapter 5's Lesson C using a class for the pair of dice.

Rosette Catering (Chapters 1 – 12)

Create a Web application for Rosette Catering. The interface should allow the user to enter the customer ID, the bride's name, the groom's name, and the date of the wedding reception. It should also allow the user to enter the number of chicken dinners, the number of pasta dinners, and the number of vegetarian dinners ordered for the reception. The interface should display the total number of dinners ordered, the total price of the order without sales tax, the sales tax, and the total price of the order with sales tax. Each dinner costs $21, and the sales tax rate is 3%. Include an appropriate image in the interface. (You can find many different images on the Open Clip Art Library Web site at *http://openclipart.org*.)

Jefferson Realty (Chapters 1 – 13)

Create a Microsoft Access database that contains one table named tblHomes. The table should contain 10 records, each having five fields. The ID and ZIP code fields should contain text. (Be sure to use several different ZIP codes.) The number of bedrooms, number of bathrooms, and price fields should be numeric. Create an application that displays the contents of the database in a DataGridView control. The user should not be allowed to add or delete records. The application should allow the user to display the records for a specific number of bedrooms, a specific number of bathrooms, or a specific ZIP code. It also should allow the user to display the average home price for the entire database and also for a specific ZIP code.

Foxmore Realty (Chapters 1 – 14)

Create a Microsoft Access database that contains one table named tblHomes. The table should contain 10 records, each having six fields. The ID, city, and state fields should contain text. The number of bedrooms, number of bathrooms, and price fields should be numeric. Create an application that displays the contents of the database in a DataGridView control. If necessary, remove the BindingNavigator control from the application. The application should allow the user to insert and delete records. It also should allow the user to display the records for a specific number of bedrooms, a specific number of bathrooms, a specific ZIP code, or a specific combination of bedrooms and bathrooms.

Index

Note: Page numbers in **boldface** type indicate where key terms are defined; page numbers followed by an asterisk (*) refer to Appendix F, available online at www.cengagebrain.com.

C

D

E

G

H

I

O

P

Q

R

S

WORKING PAPERS

TO ACCOMPANY

FINANCIAL ACCOUNTING

SECOND EDITION

▶ JERRY J. WEYGANDT *Ph.D., C.P.A.*
Arthur Andersen Alumni Professor of Accounting
University of Wisconsin
Madison, Wisconsin

▶ DONALD E. KIESO *Ph.D., C.P.A.*
KPMG Peat Marwick Emeritus Professor of Accountancy
Northern Illinois University
DeKalb, Illinois

▶ PAUL D. KIMMEL *Ph.D., C.P.A.*
Associate Professor of Accounting
University of Wisconsin
Milwaukee, Wisconsin

PREPARED BY

▶ ANNE LEE BAIN, *M.A., C.P.A.*
Assistant Professor of Accounting
St. Cloud State University
St. Cloud, Minnesota

JOHN WILEY & SONS, INC.
New York • Chichester • Weinheim • Brisbane • Singapore • Toronto

ISBN 0-471-18268-0

Printed in the United States of America

10 9 8 7 6 5 4 3 2 1

Printed and bound by Courier Kendallville, Inc.

Note To The Student

These **Working Papers** contain solution forms for all Brief Exercises, Exercises, Problems, Alternate Problems, and Comprehensive Problems in **Financial Accounting, Second Edition** by Weygandt, Kieso, and Kimmel. From the *Broadening Your Perspective* section at the end of each chapter, the **Working Papers** also contain solution forms for each Financial Reporting Problem, Decision Case, Comparative Analysis Case, Group Activity, Ethics Case and Critical Thinking Case. There are, however, no **Working Paper** solution forms for any of the Questions that begin the end-of-chapter materials or for any of the Communication Activities that appear in the *Broadening Your Perspective* section.

In general, the **Working Papers** follow the organization of the textbook. To maximize the use of space, however, forms for the Exercises occasionally appear out of order, and exercises or problems that require 11" x 17" sheets are separately bound in the back of this volume. In addition, the **Working Papers** for all Group Activities appear at the end of each chapter's set of solution forms, for ease in locating them.

Name

Section

Date

Exercise 1-5

Roberta Mendez & Co.

Name

Section

Date

Exercise 1-6

Debra Company

(a)

(b)

(c)

Name

Section

Date

Exercise 1-7

Kate Cordova, Inc., & Maxim Enterprises

(a)

(b)

(c)

(d)

Name **Exercise 1-8**

Section

Date **Tone Kon Co.**

Name

Section

Date

#9

#10

Name

Section

Date

Exercises 1-11 to 1-12

#11

#12

Name **Problem 1-1**

Section

Date **Alschuler Travel Agency, Inc.**

(a)

ALSCHULER TRAVEL AGENCY

	Assets							=	Liabilities	+	Stockholders' Equity		
Trans-action	Cash	+	Accounts Receivable	+	Supplies	+	Office Equip-ment	=	Accounts Payable	+	Common Stock	+	Retained Earnings
1.													
2.													
3.													
4.													
5.													
6.													
7.													
8.													
9.													
10.													

Name

Section

Date

Problem 1-1 Concluded

Alschuler Travel Agency, Inc.

(b)

Name

Section

Date

Problem 1-2

Hillary Brennan Corporation

(a)

HILLARY BRENNAN CORPORATION

	Assets							=	Liabilities			+	Stockholder's Equity		
Trans-action	Cash	+	Accounts Receivable	+	Supplies	+	Office Equipment	=	Notes Payable	+	Accounts Payable	+	Common Stock	+	Retained Earnings
Bal.	$4,000	+	$1,500	+	$500	+	$5,000	=		+	$4,200	+	$6,500	+	$300
1.															
2.															
3.															
4.															
5.															
6.															
7.															
8.															

Name

Section

Date

Problem 1-2 Continued

Hillary Brennan Corporation

(b)

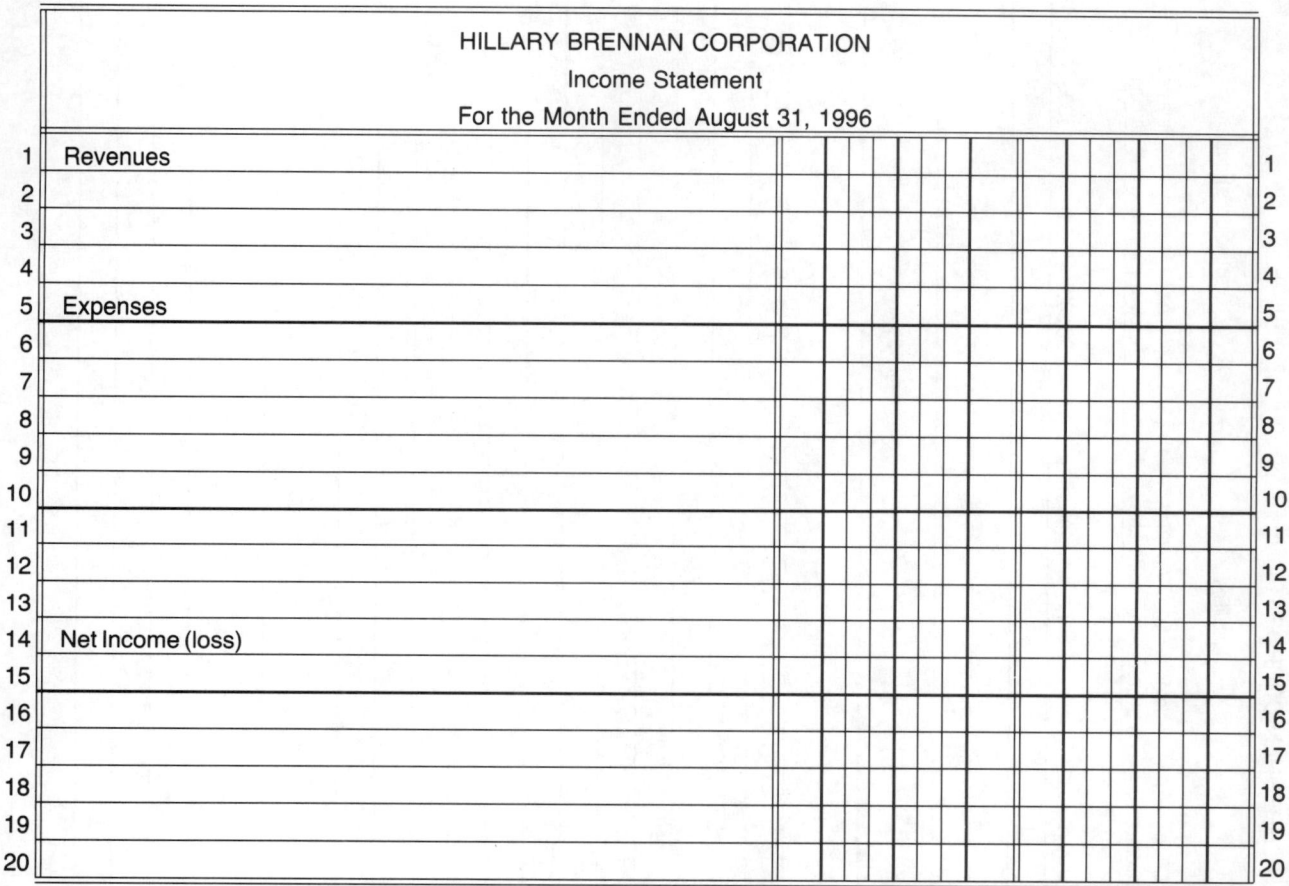

HILLARY BRENNAN CORPORATION
Income Statement
For the Month Ended August 31, 1996

Revenues		
Expenses		
Net Income (loss)		

HILLARY BRENNAN CORPORATION
Retained Earnings Statement
For the Month Ended August 31, 1996

Name
Section
Date

Problem 1-2 Concluded

Hillary Brennan Corporation

(b) (Continued)

HILLARY BRENNAN CORPORATION
Balance Sheet
August 31, 1996

Assets

Liabilities and Stockholders' Equity

Name | **Problem 1-3**

Section

Date | **Cindy Crawford Cosmetics**

CINDY CRAWFORD COSMETICS
Income Statement
For the Month Ended June 30, 1996

Revenues

Expenses

Net Income (loss)

CINDY CRAWFORD COSMETICS
Retained Earnings Statement
For the Month Ended June 30, 1996

CINDY CRAWFORD COSMETICS

Balance Sheet

June 30, 1996

Assets

Liabilities and Stockholders' Equity

Name Section Date

Problem 1-4

Charlie Doss Consulting Co.

(a)

CHARLIE DOSS CONSULTING CO.
Income Statement
For the Month Ended March 31, 1996

1	Revenues		1
2			2
3			3
4			4
5	Expenses		5
6			6
7			7
8			8
9			9
10			10
11			11
12			12
13			13
14	Net Income (loss)		14
15			15
16			16
17			17
18			18
19			19
20			20

(b)

CHARLIE DOSS CONSULTING CO.
Retained Earnings Statement
For the Month Ended March 31, 1996

1			1
2			2
3			3
4			4
5			5
6			6
7			7
8			8
9			9
10			10
11			11
12			12
13			13
14			14
15			15

Name | | Problem 1-5
Section
Date | | Zarle Company

(a)	Zarle Company	Wasicsko Company	McKane Company	Russe Company

(b)

ZARLE COMPANY
Retained Earnings Statement
For the Year Ended December 31, 1996

(c)

Name **Problem 1-1A**

Section

Date **Better Bob, Inc.**

(a)

BETTER BOB, INC.

	Assets							=	Liabilities	+	Stockholders' Equity		
Trans-action	Cash	+	Accounts Receivable	+	Supplies	+	Equip-ment	=	Accounts Payable	+	Common Stock	+	Retained Earnings
1.													
2.													
3.													
4.													
5.													
6.													
7.													
8.													
9.													
10.													
11.													

Name

Section

Date

Problem 1-1A Concluded

Better Bob, Inc.

(b)

Name | **Problem 1-2A**

Section

Date | **Cook Corporation**

(a)

COOK CORPORATION

	Assets							=	Liabilities			+	Stockholders' Equity		
Trans-actions	Cash	+	Accounts Receivable	+	Supplies	+	Office Equipment	=	Notes Payable	+	Accounts Payable	+	Common Stock	+	Retained Earnings
Bal.	$9,000	+	$1,700	+	$600	+	$6,000	=		+	$3,600	+	$13,000	+	$700
1.															
2.															
3.															
4.															
5.															
6.															
7.															
8.															

Name **Problem 1-2A Continued**

Section

Date **Cook Corporation**

(b)

COOK CORPORATION

Income Statement

For the Month Ended September 30, 1996

Revenues		
Expenses		
Net Income (loss)		

COOK CORPORATION

Retained Earnings Statement

For the Month Ended September 30, 1996

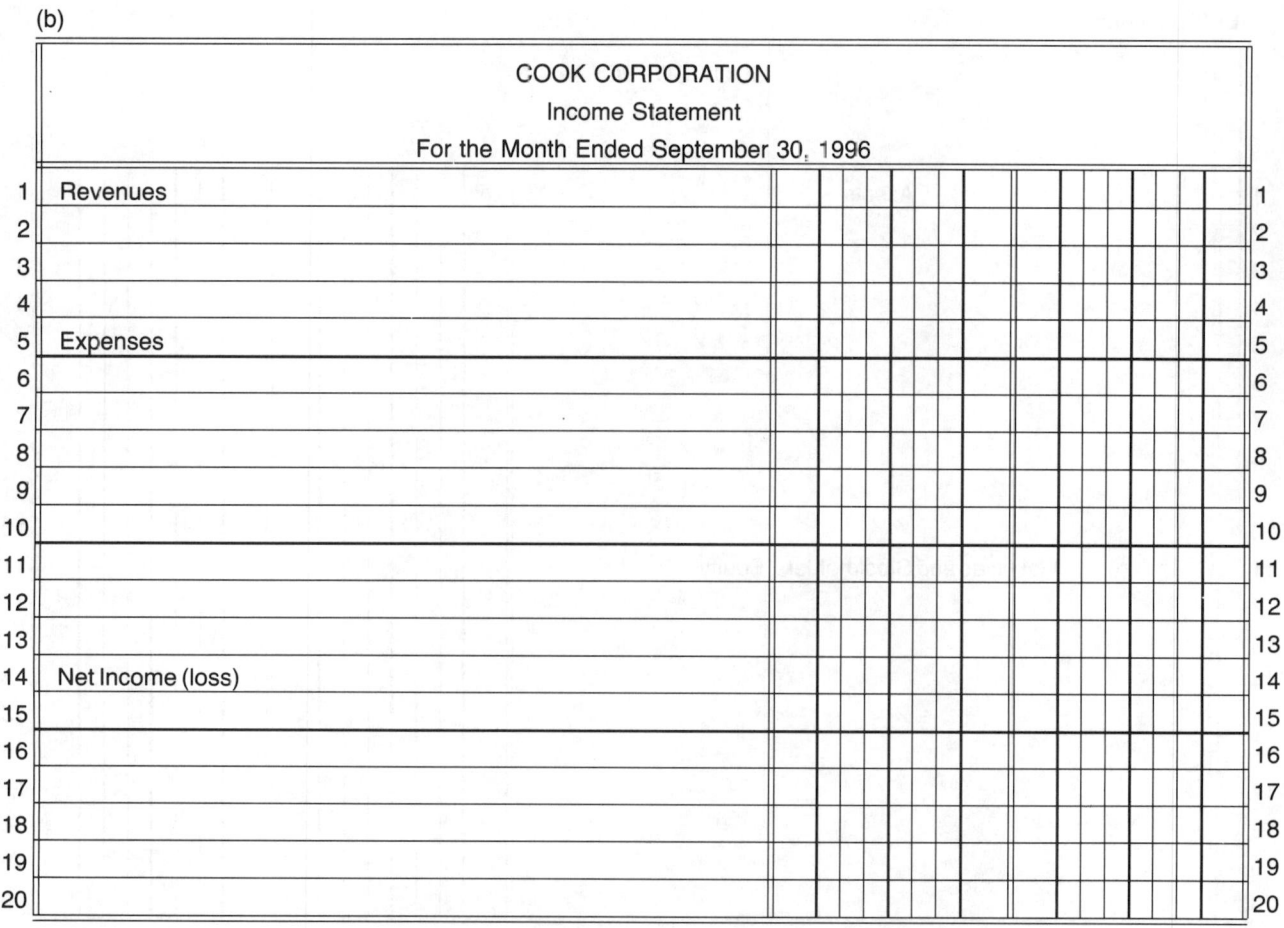

Name **Problem 1-2A Concluded**

Section

Date **Cook Corporation**

(b) (Continued)

COOK CORPORATION

Balance Sheet

September 30, 1996

Assets

Liabilities and Stockholders' Equity

Name | **Problem 1-3A**

Section

Date | **Skyline Flying School, Inc.**

(a)

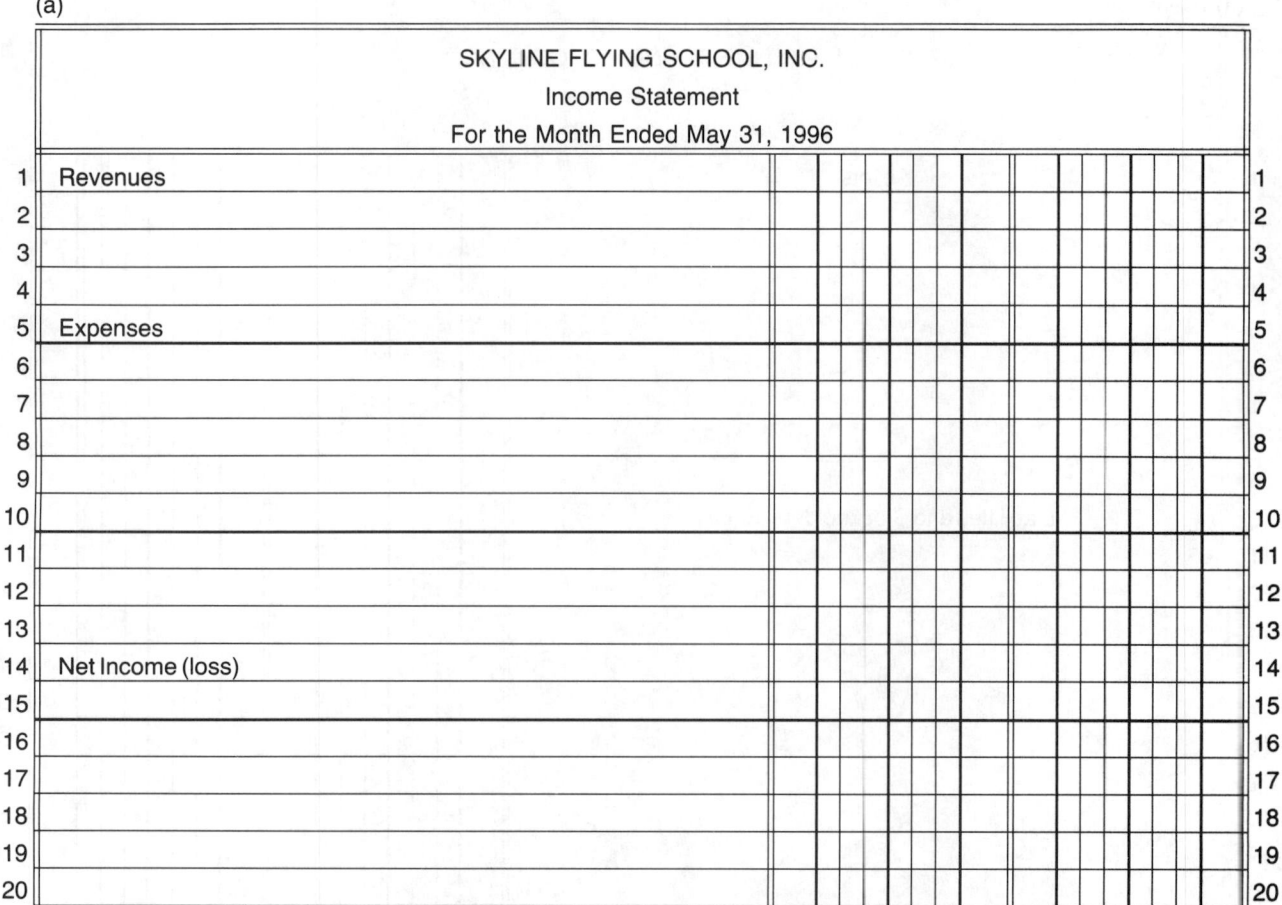

SKYLINE FLYING SCHOOL, INC.
Income Statement
For the Month Ended May 31, 1996

Revenues		
Expenses		
Net Income (loss)		

SKYLINE FLYING SCHOOL, INC.
Retained Earnings Statement
For the Month Ended May 31, 1996

Name

Section

Date

Problem 1-3A Continued

Skyline Flying School, Inc.

(a) (Continued)

SKYLINE FLYING SCHOOL, INC.
Balance Sheet
May 31, 1996

Assets

Liabilities and Stockholders' Equity

(b)

SKYLINE FLYING SCHOOL, INC.
Income Statement
For the Month Ended May 31, 1996

Revenues

Expenses

Net Income (loss)

Name
Section
Date

Problem 1-3A Concluded

Skyline Flying School, Inc.

(b) (Continued)

SKYLINE FLYING SCHOOL, INC.
Retained Earnings Statement
For the Month Ended May 31, 1996

Name Problem 1-4A

Section

Date Michael Bolton Corp.

(a)

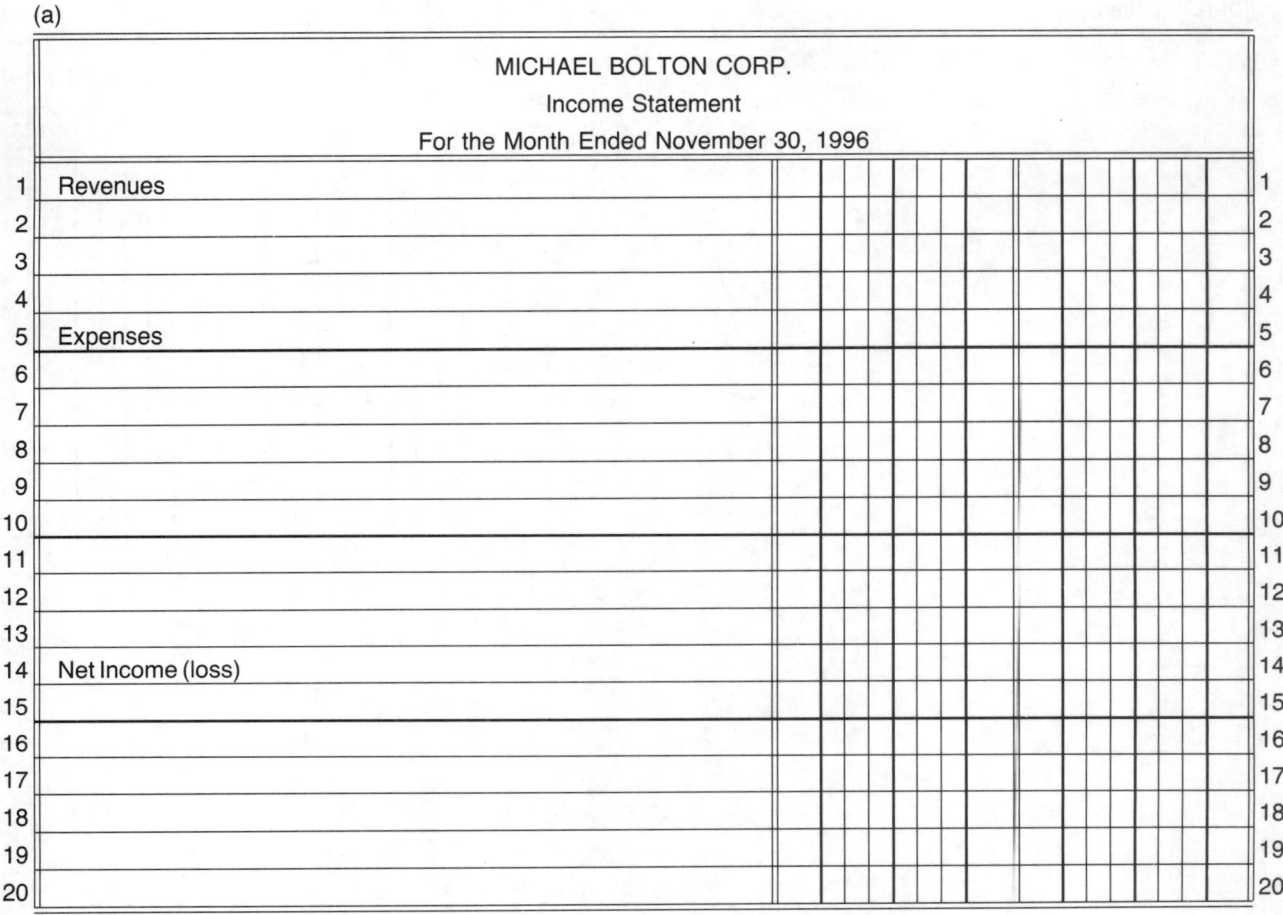

MICHAEL BOLTON CORP.
Income Statement
For the Month Ended November 30, 1996

Revenues

Expenses

Net Income (loss)

(b)

MICHAEL BOLTON CORP.
Retained Earnings Statement
For the Month Ended November 30, 1996

Name

Section

Date

Problem 1-5A

Selena Company

(a)	Yanni Company	Selena Company	Candlebox Company	Winans Company

(b)

SELENA COMPANY

Retained Earnings Statement

For the Year Ended December 31, 1996

(c)

Name

Section

Date

PepsiCo, Inc.

(1)

(2)

(3)

(4)

(5)

(6)

Name | **Chapter 1 Comparative Analysis Problem**

Section

Date | **The Coca-Cola Company vs. PepsiCo, Inc.**

	Coca-Cola	PepsiCo.
(a)		

(b)

Name

Section

Date

MINI-CASE ONE Med/Waste, Inc.

(a)

(b)

(c)

MINI-CASE TWO Lincoln Village Properties, Inc.

Name

Section

Date

(a)

(b)

PARBUSTER CORPORATION

Balance Sheet

March 31,1996

Assets

Liabilities and Stockholders' Equity

Name

Section

Date

Parbuster Corporation

(c)

(d)

Name | Chapter 1 Ethics Case

Section

Date | Chapter 1 Critical Thinking Case

ETHICS CASE | Joe Catmus, job candidate

(a)

(b)

(c)

CRITICAL THINKING CASE | Air Transportation Holding Company, Inc.

(a)

(b)

(c)

Name | **Chapter 1 Group Activity**

Section

Date | **Hattie Company**

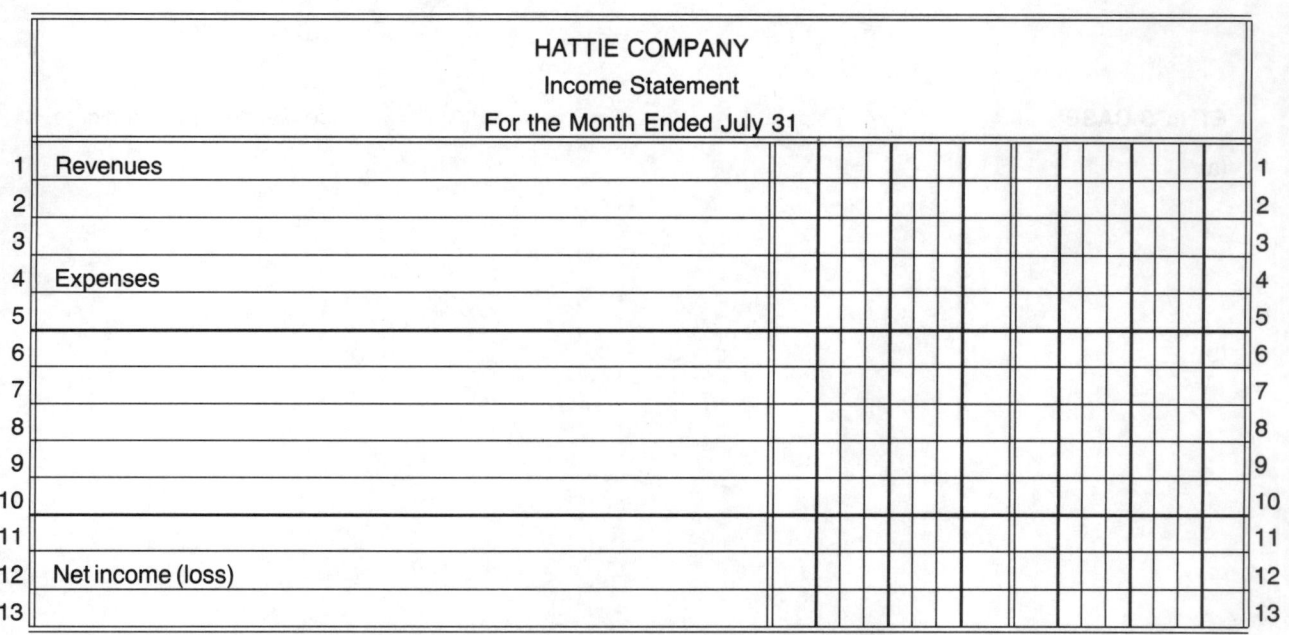

HATTIE COMPANY
Income Statement
For the Month Ended July 31

Revenues		
Expenses		
Net income (loss)		

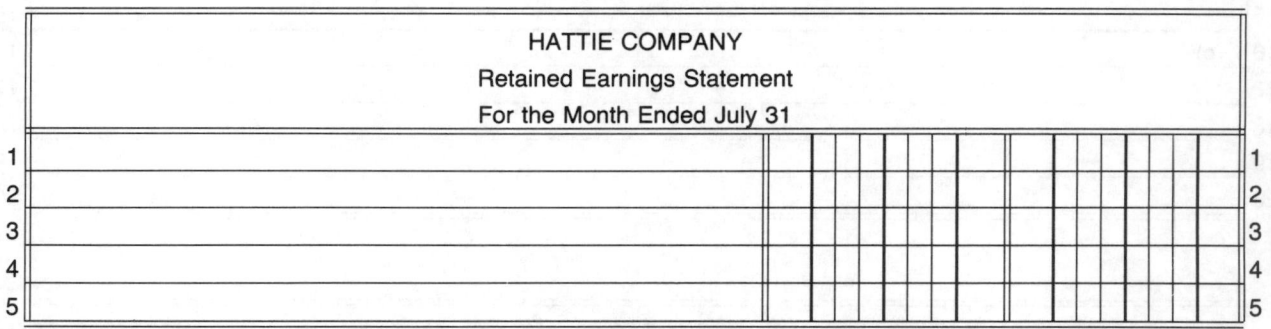

HATTIE COMPANY
Retained Earnings Statement
For the Month Ended July 31

HATTIE COMPANY
Balance Sheet
July 31

Assets		
Liabilities and Stockholders' Equity		

Name

Section

Date

Name

Section

Date

Name

Section

Date

Exercise 2-6

Lush Landscaping Corporation

(a)

General Journal

Date	Account Titles and Explanation	Ref.	Debit	Credit

Name

Section

Date

Exercise 2-6 Concluded

Lush Landscaping Corporation

(b)

	Debit	Credit

Name **Exercise 2-7**

Section

Date **Holly Corp.**

(a) General Journal

Trans-action	Account Titles and Explanation	Ref.	Debit	Credit

Name

Section

Date

Exercise 2-7 Concluded

Holly Corp.

(b)

	Debit	Credit

Name

Section

Date

Exercise 2-8

Craig Stevenson Corporation

(a)

General Journal J1

Date	Account Titles and Explanation	Ref.	Debit	Credit

(b)

Cash No. 101

Date	Explanation	Ref.	Debit	Credit	Balance

Equipment No. 157

Date	Explanation	Ref.	Debit	Credit	Balance

Accounts Payable No. 201

Date	Explanation	Ref.	Debit	Credit	Balance

Common Stock No. 311

Date	Explanation	Ref.	Debit	Credit	Balance

Dividends No. 332

Date	Explanation	Ref.	Debit	Credit	Balance

Name

Section

Date

Exercises 2-9 to 2-10

#9	(a)	(b)	(c)
Error	In Balance?	Difference	Larger Column
1. Credit posting of $400 to Accounts Receivable was omitted	No	$400	Debit
2.			
3.			
4.			
5.			
6.			

#10

	Debit	Credit

Name **Problem 2-3 Continued**

Section

Date **Jane's Laundry Corp.**

(a) and (c) (Continued)

Common Stock No. 311

Date	Explanation	Ref.	Debit	Credit	Balance

Dividends No. 332

Date	Explanation	Ref.	Debit	Credit	Balance

Laundry Revenue No. 426

Date	Explanation	Ref.	Debit	Credit	Balance

Salaries Expense No. 726

Date	Explanation	Ref.	Debit	Credit	Balance

Utilities Expense No. 732

Date	Explanation	Ref.	Debit	Credit	Balance

(d)

JANE'S LAUNDRY CORP.
Trial Balance
October 31, 1996

		Debit	Credit	
1	Cash			1
2	Accounts Receivable			2
3	Supplies			3
4	Equipment			4
5	Accounts Payable			5
6	Unearned Revenue			6
7	Common Stock			7
8	Dividends			8
9	Laundry Revenue			9
10	Salaries Expense			10
11	Utilities Expense			11
12				12
13				13

Name　　　　　　　　　　　　　　　　　　　　　　　　　　　　　**Problem 2-3 Concluded**

Section

Date　　　　　　　　　　　　　　　　　　　　　　　　　　　　　**Jane's Laundry Corp.**

(b)　　　　　　　　General Journal　　　　　　　　J1

	Date	Account Titles and Explanation	Ref.	Debit	Credit	
1						1
2						2
3						3
4						4
5						5
6						6
7						7
8						8
9						9
10						10
11						11
12						12
13						13
14						14
15						15
16						16
17						17
18						18
19						19
20						20
21						21
22						22
23						23
24						24
25						25
26						26
27						27
28						28
29						29
30						30
31						31
32						32
33						33
34						34
35						35
36						36
37						37
38						38
39						39
40						40

Name **Problem 2-4**

Section

Date **Thom Wargo Corp.**

THOM WARGO CORP.
Trial Balance
June 30, 1996

	Debit	Credit

Name **Problem 2-5**

Section

Date **Star Theater Corp.**

(a) and (c)

Cash No. 101

Date	Explanation	Ref.	Debit	Credit	Balance

Accounts Receivable No. 112

Date	Explanation	Ref.	Debit	Credit	Balance

Land No. 140

Date	Explanation	Ref.	Debit	Credit	Balance

Buildings No. 145

Date	Explanation	Ref.	Debit	Credit	Balance

Equipment No. 157

Date	Explanation	Ref.	Debit	Credit	Balance

Accounts Payable No. 201

Date	Explanation	Ref.	Debit	Credit	Balance

Name | Problem 2-5 Continued

Section

Date | Star Theater Corp.

(a) and (c) (Continued)

Common Stock — No. 311

Date	Explanation	Ref.	Debit	Credit	Balance

Admission Revenue — No. 405

Date	Explanation	Ref.	Debit	Credit	Balance

Concession Revenue — No. 406

Date	Explanation	Ref.	Debit	Credit	Balance

Advertising Expense — No. 610

Date	Explanation	Ref.	Debit	Credit	Balance

Film Rental Expense — No. 632

Date	Explanation	Ref.	Debit	Credit	Balance

Salaries Expense — No. 726

Date	Explanation	Ref.	Debit	Credit	Balance

Name
Section
Date

Problem 2-5 Continued

Star Theater Corp.

(b) General Journal J1

	Date	Account Titles and Explanation	Ref.	Debit	Credit	
1						1
2						2
3						3
4						4
5						5
6						6
7						7
8						8
9						9
10						10
11						11
12						12
13						13
14						14
15						15
16						16
17						17
18						18
19						19
20						20
21						21
22						22
23						23
24						24
25						25
26						26
27						27
28						28
29						29
30						30
31						31
32						32
33						33
34						34
35						35
36						36
37						37
38						38
39						39
40						40

Name | **Problem 2-5 Concluded**

Section

Date | **Star Theater Corp.**

(d)

STAR THEATER CORP.
Trial Balance
March 31, 1996

	Debit	Credit
Cash		
Accounts Receivable		
Land		
Buildings		
Equipment		
Accounts Payable		
Common Stock		
Admission Revenue		
Concession Revenue		
Advertising Expense		
Film Rental Expense		
Salaries Expense		

Name **Problem 2-1A**

Section

Date **Frontier Park Corp.**

General Journal J1

Date	Account Titles and Explanation	Ref.	Debit	Credit

Name

Section

Date

Problem 2-2A

Iva Holz Inc., CPA

(a) General Journal J1

Date	Account Titles and Explanation	Ref.	Debit	Credit

Name

Section

Date

Problem 2-2A Continued

Iva Holz Inc., CPA

(b)

Cash — No. 101

Date	Explanation	Ref.	Debit	Credit	Balance

Accounts Receivable — No. 112

Date	Explanation	Ref.	Debit	Credit	Balance

Supplies — No. 126

Date	Explanation	Ref.	Debit	Credit	Balance

Accounts Payable — No. 201

Date	Explanation	Ref.	Debit	Credit	Balance

Unearned Fees — No. 205

Date	Explanation	Ref.	Debit	Credit	Balance

Common Stock — No. 311

Date	Explanation	Ref.	Debit	Credit	Balance

Name Problem 2-2A Concluded

Section

Date Iva Holz Inc., CPA

(b) (Continued)

Fees Earned No. 400

Date	Explanation	Ref.	Debit	Credit	Balance

Salaries Expense No. 726

Date	Explanation	Ref.	Debit	Credit	Balance

Rent Expense No. 729

Date	Explanation	Ref.	Debit	Credit	Balance

(c)

IVA HOLZ INC., CPA
Trial Balance
April 30, 1996

		Debit	Credit	
1	Cash			1
2	Accounts Receivable			2
3	Supplies			3
4	Accounts Payable			4
5	Unearned Fees			5
6	Common Stock			6
7	Fees Earned			7
8	Salaries Expense			8
9	Rent Expense			9
10				10
11				11

Name **Problem 2-3A**

Section

Date **Sterling Dry Cleaners Inc.**

(a) and (c)

Cash No. 101

Date	Explanation	Ref.	Debit	Credit	Balance

Accounts Receivable No. 112

Date	Explanation	Ref.	Debit	Credit	Balance

Supplies No. 126

Date	Explanation	Ref.	Debit	Credit	Balance

Equipment No. 157

Date	Explanation	Ref.	Debit	Credit	Balance

Accounts Payable No. 201

Date	Explanation	Ref.	Debit	Credit	Balance

Unearned Revenue No. 206

Date	Explanation	Ref.	Debit	Credit	Balance

Name Problem 2-3A Continued

Section

Date Sterling Dry Cleaners Inc.

(a) and (c) (Continued)

Common Stock No. 311

Date	Explanation	Ref.	Debit	Credit	Balance

Retained Earnings No. 320

Date	Explanation	Ref.	Debit	Credit	Balance

Dividends No. 332

Date	Explanation	Ref.	Debit	Credit	Balance

Dry Cleaning Revenue No. 428

Date	Explanation	Ref.	Debit	Credit	Balance

Repair Expense No. 622

Date	Explanation	Ref.	Debit	Credit	Balance

Salaries Expense No. 726

Date	Explanation	Ref.	Debit	Credit	Balance

Utilities Expense No. 732

Date	Explanation	Ref.	Debit	Credit	Balance

Name
Section
Date

Sterling Dry Cleaners Inc.

(b) General Journal J1

Date	Account Titles and Explanation	Ref.	Debit	Credit

(d)

STERLING DRY CLEANERS INC.
Trial Balance
July 31, 1996

	Debit	Credit
Cash		
Accounts Receivable		
Supplies		
Equipment		
Accounts Payable		
Unearned Revenue		
Common Stock		
Retained Earnings		
Dividends		
Dry Cleaning Revenue		
Salaries Expense		
Utilities Expense		
Repair Expense		

Name | **Problem 2-4A**
Section
Date | **Saginaw Corporation**

SAGINAW CORPORATION
Trial Balance
May 31, 1996

	Debit	Credit

Name **Problem 2-5A**

Section

Date **Lake Theater Inc.**

(a) and (c)

Cash — No. 101

Date	Explanation	Ref.	Debit	Credit	Balance

Accounts Receivable — No. 112

Date	Explanation	Ref.	Debit	Credit	Balance

Prepaid Rentals — No. 136

Date	Explanation	Ref.	Debit	Credit	Balance

Land — No. 140

Date	Explanation	Ref.	Debit	Credit	Balance

Buildings — No. 145

Date	Explanation	Ref.	Debit	Credit	Balance

Equipment — No. 157

Date	Explanation	Ref.	Debit	Credit	Balance

Accounts Payable — No. 201

Date	Explanation	Ref.	Debit	Credit	Balance

Name | **Problem 2-5A Continued**

Section

Date | **Lake Theater**

(a) and (c) (Continued)

Mortgage Payable — No. 275

Date	Explanation	Ref.	Debit	Credit	Balance

Common Stock — No. 311

Date	Explanation	Ref.	Debit	Credit	Balance

Admission Revenue — No. 405

Date	Explanation	Ref.	Debit	Credit	Balance

Concession Revenue — No. 406

Date	Explanation	Ref.	Debit	Credit	Balance

Advertising Expense — No. 610

Date	Explanation	Ref.	Debit	Credit	Balance

Film Rental Expense — No. 632

Date	Explanation	Ref.	Debit	Credit	Balance

Salaries Expense — No. 726

Date	Explanation	Ref.	Debit	Credit	Balance

Name

Section

Date

Problem 2-5A Continued

Lake Theater Inc.

(b) General Journal J1

Date	Account Titles and Explanation	Ref.	Debit	Credit

Name

Section

Date

Problem 2-5A Concluded

Lake Theater Inc.

(d)

LAKE THEATER INC.
Trial Balance
April 30, 1996

	Debit	Credit
Cash		
Accounts Receivable		
Prepaid Rentals		
Land		
Buildings		
Equipment		
Accounts Payable		
Mortgage Payable		
Common Stock		
Admission Revenue		
Concession Revenue		
Advertising Expense		
Film Rental Expense		
Salaries Expense		

Name

Section

Date

(a) Account	(1) Side of Account for: Increase	(1) Side of Account for: Decrease	(2) Normal Balance
Accounts payable			
Accounts receivable			
Interest expense			
Land			
Income taxes payable			
Interest Income			
Advertising expense			
Prepaid expenses			

(b) 1.

2.

3.

(c) 1.

2.

Name

Section

Date

The Coca-Cola Company vs. PepsiCo, Inc.

(a)

	Normal balance
Coca-Cola Company-	
Account receivable	
Land	
Loans and notes payable	
Common stock	
Interest expense	
PepsiCo, Inc.-	
Inventories	
Machinery and Equipment	
Short-Term borrowing	
Retained earnings	
Interest income	

(a) 1.

2.

3.

4.

Name

Section

Date

MINI-CASE ONE Bob Evans Farms, Inc.

(a)

(b)

(c)

MINI-CASE TWO Chieftain International, Inc.

(a)

(b)

(c)

Name Chapter 2 Decision Case

Section

Date Lucy Riding Academy Inc.

General Journal

Date	Account Titles and Explanation	Ref.	Debit	Credit
(a)				
(b)				
(c)				
(d)				

Name

Section

Date

ETHICS CASE

Zarle Company

(a)

(b)

(c)

CRITICAL THINKING CASE

Automated Security Holdings

(a)

(b)

(c)

Name

Section

Date

Category	(a) (1) Increase/Decrease	(a) (2) Normal balance	(b) Example of an Increase transaction
Assets			
Liabilities			
Common stock			
Dividends			
Revenues			
Expenses			

Name

Section

Date

Name

Section

Date

Name | Exercise 3-9

Section

Date | Apachi Company

APACHI COMPANY
Income Statement
For the Year Ended August 31, 1996

APACHI COMPANY
Retained Earnings Statement
For the Year Ended August 31, 1996

APACHI COMPANY
Balance Sheet
August 31, 1996

Name

Section

Date

Exercise 3-10

Cash vs. Accrual

(a)

(b)

(c)

Name
Section
Date

***Exercise 3-11**

Devereaux Company

(a)

CASH

FEES EARNED

INSURANCE EXPENSE

SUPPLIES EXPENSE

(b)

PREPAID INSURANCE

INSURANCE EXPENSE

SUPPLIES

SUPPLIES EXPENSE

UNEARNED FEES

FEES EARNED

(c)

Name

Section

Date

Problem 3-1

Scenic Tours Inc.

(a)

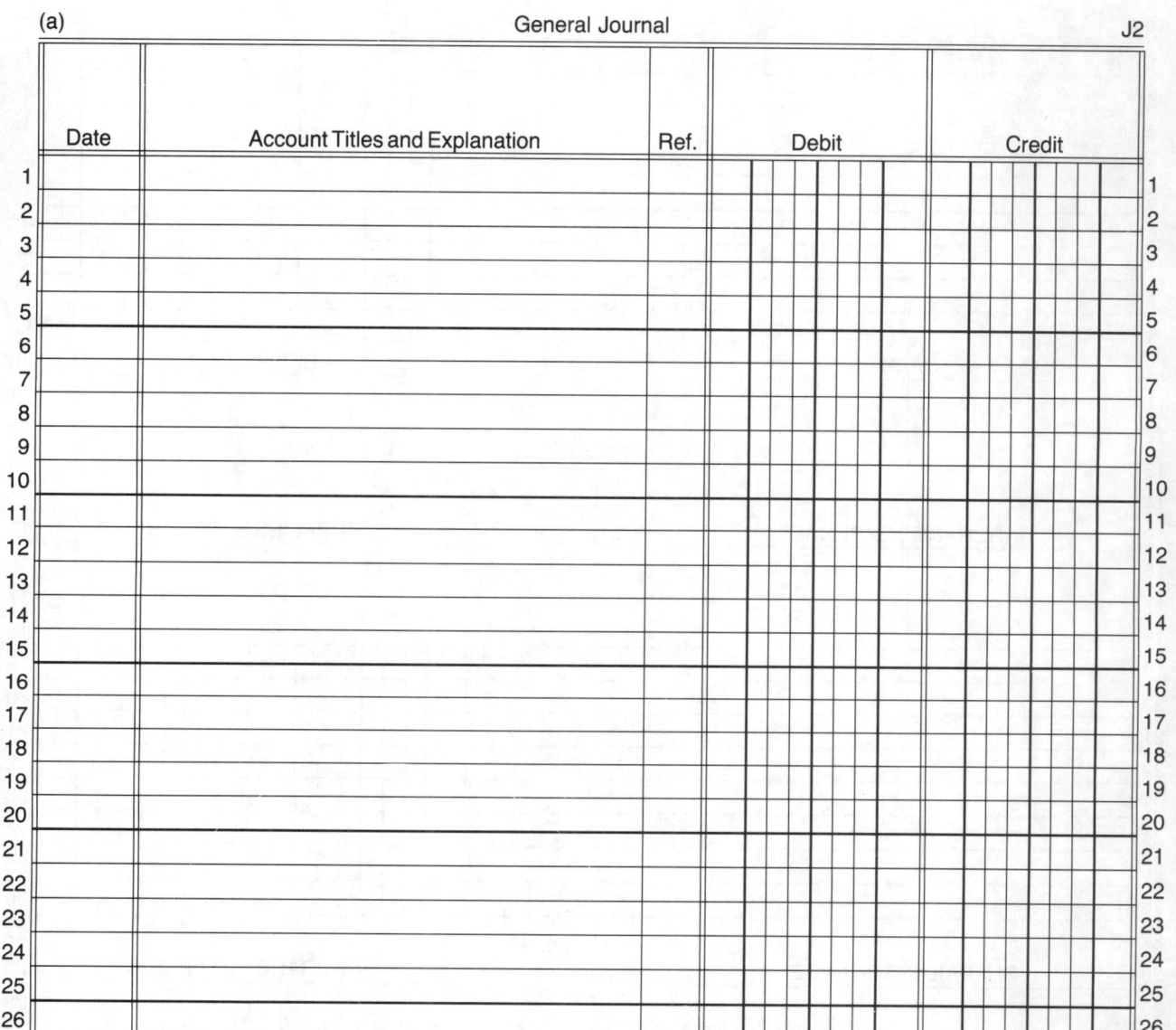

General Journal

J2

Date	Account Titles and Explanation	Ref.	Debit	Credit

Cash

Date	Explanation	Ref.	Debit	Credit	Balance

Accounts Receivable

Date	Explanation	Ref.	Debit	Credit	Balance

Name

Section

Date

Problem 3-1 Continued

Scenic Tours Inc.

(b) (Continued)

Prepaid Insurance

Date	Explanation	Ref.	Debit	Credit	Balance

Office Equipment

Date	Explanation	Ref.	Debit	Credit	Balance

Accumulated Depreciation — Office Equipment

Date	Explanation	Ref.	Debit	Credit	Balance

Buses

Date	Explanation	Ref.	Debit	Credit	Balance

Accumulated Depreciation — Buses

Date	Explanation	Ref.	Debit	Credit	Balance

Salaries Payable

Date	Explanation	Ref.	Debit	Credit	Balance

Interest Payable

Date	Explanation	Ref.	Debit	Credit	Balance

Notes Payable

Date	Explanation	Ref.	Debit	Credit	Balance

Name

Section

Date

Problem 3-1 Continued

Scenic Tours Inc.

(b) (Continued)

Unearned Fees

Date	Explanation	Ref.	Debit	Credit	Balance

Common Stock

Date	Explanation	Ref.	Debit	Credit	Balance

Fees Earned

Date	Explanation	Ref.	Debit	Credit	Balance

Salaries Expense

Date	Explanation	Ref.	Debit	Credit	Balance

Advertising Expense

Date	Explanation	Ref.	Debit	Credit	Balance

Gas and Oil Expense

Date	Explanation	Ref.	Debit	Credit	Balance

Insurance Expense

Date	Explanation	Ref.	Debit	Credit	Balance

Name

Section

Date

***Problem 3-6 Continued**

Global Graphics Company

(b)

GLOBAL GRAPHICS COMPANY

Adjusted Trial Balance

June 30, 1996

	Debit	Credit

(c)

GLOBAL GRAPHICS COMPANY

Income Statement

For the Six Months Ended June 30, 1996

Name | *Problem 3-6 Concluded

Section

Date | Global Graphics Company

(c) (Continued)

GLOBAL GRAPHICS COMPANY
Retained Earnings Statement
For the Six Months Ended June 30, 1996

GLOBAL GRAPHICS COMPANY
Balance Sheet
June 30, 1996

Assets

Liabilities and Stockholders' Equity

Name

Section

Date

Problem 3-1A

Ortega Security Service Inc.

(a)

General Journal

J15

Date	Account Titles and Explanation	Ref.	Debit	Credit

(b)

Cash

Date	Explanation	Ref.	Debit	Credit	Balance

Accounts Receivable

Date	Explanation	Ref.	Debit	Credit	Balance

(b) (Continued)

Prepaid Insurance

Date	Explanation	Ref.	Debit	Credit	Balance

Automobiles

Date	Explanation	Ref.	Debit	Credit	Balance

Accumulated Depreciation — Automobiles

Date	Explanation	Ref.	Debit	Credit	Balance

Notes Payable

Date	Explanation	Ref.	Debit	Credit	Balance

Accounts Payable

Date	Explanation	Ref.	Debit	Credit	Balance

Interest Payable

Date	Explanation	Ref.	Debit	Credit	Balance

Salaries Payable

Date	Explanation	Ref.	Debit	Credit	Balance

Name **Problem 3-1A Continued**

Section

Date **Ortega Security Service Inc.**

(b) (Continued)

Unearned Fees

Date	Explanation	Ref.	Debit	Credit	Balance

Common Stock

Date	Explanation	Ref.	Debit	Credit	Balance

Fees Earned

Date	Explanation	Ref.	Debit	Credit	Balance

Salaries Expense

Date	Explanation	Ref.	Debit	Credit	Balance

Repairs Expense

Date	Explanation	Ref.	Debit	Credit	Balance

Gas and Oil Expense

Date	Explanation	Ref.	Debit	Credit	Balance

Insurance Expense

Date	Explanation	Ref.	Debit	Credit	Balance

Name | Problem 3-1A Continued
Section
Date | Ortega Security Service Inc.

(b) (Continued)

Depreciation Expense — Automobiles

Date	Explanation	Ref.	Debit	Credit	Balance

Interest Expense

Date	Explanation	Ref.	Debit	Credit	Balance

(c)

ORTEGA SECURITY SERVICE INC.
Adjusted Trial Balance
December 31, 1996

		Debit	Credit	
1				1
2				2
3				3
4				4
5				5
6				6
7				7
8				8
9				9
10				10
11				11
12				12
13				13
14				14
15				15
16				16
17				17
18				18
19				19
20				20
21				21
22				22
23				23
24				24
25				25

Name

Section

Date

Problem 3-2A

Highland Cove Resort Inc.

(a)

General Journal

J1

Date	Account Titles and Explanation	Ref.	Debit	Credit

(b)

Cash

Date	Explanation	Ref.	Debit	Credit	Balance

Accounts Receivable

Date	Explanation	Ref.	Debit	Credit	Balance

Name | **Problem 3-2A Continued**
Section
Date | **Highland Cove Resort Inc.**

(b) (Continued)

Prepaid Insurance

Date	Explanation	Ref.	Debit	Credit	Balance

Supplies

Date	Explanation	Ref.	Debit	Credit	Balance

Land

Date	Explanation	Ref.	Debit	Credit	Balance

Cottages

Date	Explanation	Ref.	Debit	Credit	Balance

Accumulated Depreciation — Cottages

Date	Explanation	Ref.	Debit	Credit	Balance

Furniture

Date	Explanation	Ref.	Debit	Credit	Balance

Accumulated Depreciation — Furniture

Date	Explanation	Ref.	Debit	Credit	Balance

(b) (Continued)

Accounts Payable

Date	Explanation	Ref.	Debit	Credit	Balance

Unearned Rent Revenue

Date	Explanation	Ref.	Debit	Credit	Balance

Salaries Payable

Date	Explanation	Ref.	Debit	Credit	Balance

Interest Payable

Date	Explanation	Ref.	Debit	Credit	Balance

Mortgage Payable

Date	Explanation	Ref.	Debit	Credit	Balance

Common Stock

Date	Explanation	Ref.	Debit	Credit	Balance

Dividends

Date	Explanation	Ref.	Debit	Credit	Balance

Name

Section

Date

Problem 3-2A Continued

Highland Cove Resort Inc.

(b) (Continued)

Rent Revenue

Date	Explanation	Ref.	Debit	Credit	Balance

Salaries Expense

Date	Explanation	Ref.	Debit	Credit	Balance

Utilities Expense

Date	Explanation	Ref.	Debit	Credit	Balance

Repair Expense

Date	Explanation	Ref.	Debit	Credit	Balance

Insurance Expense

Date	Explanation	Ref.	Debit	Credit	Balance

Supplies Expense

Date	Explanation	Ref.	Debit	Credit	Balance

Depreciation Expense — Cottages

Date	Explanation	Ref.	Debit	Credit	Balance

(b) (Continued)

Depreciation Expense — Furniture

Date	Explanation	Ref.	Debit	Credit	Balance

Interest Expense

Date	Explanation	Ref.	Debit	Credit	Balance

(c)

HIGHLAND COVE RESORT INC.
Adjusted Trial Balance
August 31, 1996

		Debit	Credit	
1				1
2				2
3				3
4				4
5				5
6				6
7				7
8				8
9				9
10				10
11				11
12				12
13				13
14				14
15				15
16				16
17				17
18				18
19				19
20				20
21				21
22				22
23				23
24				24
25				25
26				26
27				27

(d)

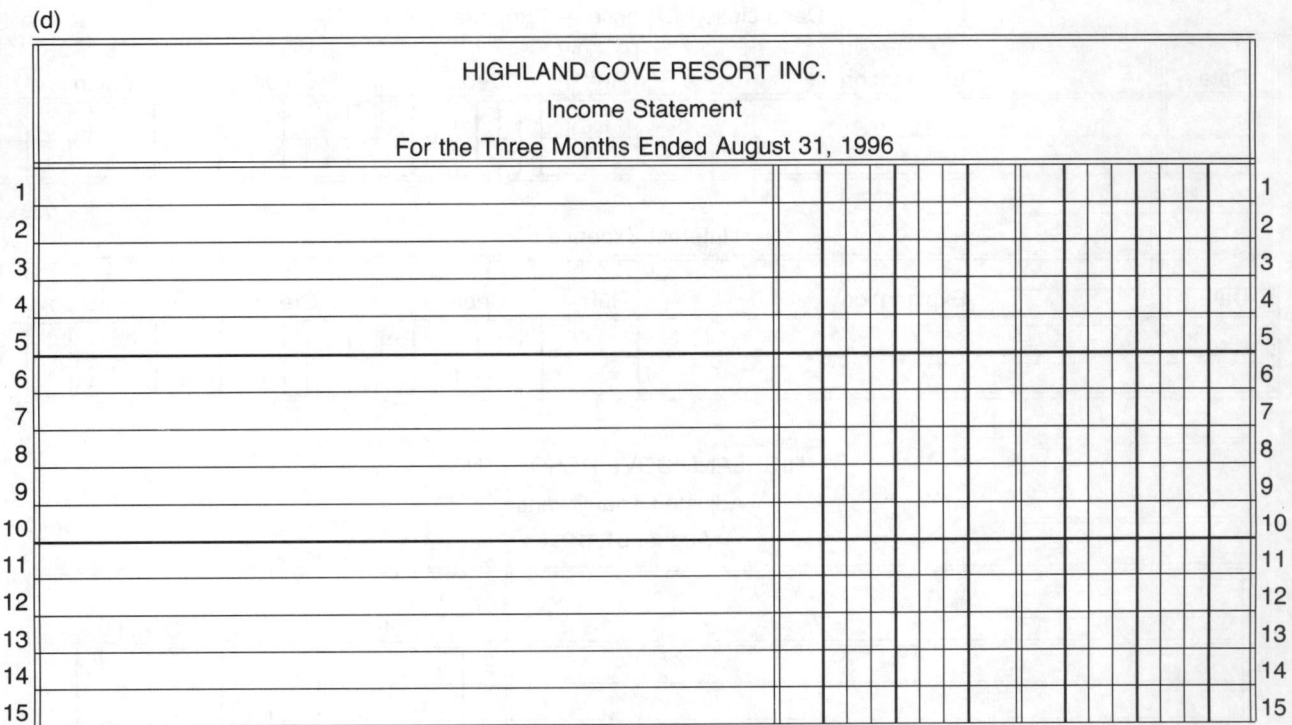

HIGHLAND COVE RESORT INC.
Income Statement
For the Three Months Ended August 31, 1996

HIGHLAND COVE RESORT INC.
Retained Earnings Statement
For the Three Months Ended August 31, 1996

Name **Problem 3-5A**

Section

Date **Rijo Equipment Repair Corp.**

(a), (c) and (e)

Cash — No. 101

Date	Explanation	Ref.	Debit	Credit	Balance

Accounts Receivable — No. 112

Date	Explanation	Ref.	Debit	Credit	Balance

Supplies — No. 126

Date	Explanation	Ref.	Debit	Credit	Balance

Store Equipment — No. 153

Date	Explanation	Ref.	Debit	Credit	Balance

Accumulated Depreciation – Store Equipment — No. 154

Date	Explanation	Ref.	Debit	Credit	Balance

Problem 3-5A Continued

Rijo Equipment Repair Corp.

(a), (c) and (e) (Continued)

Accounts Payable — No. 201

Date	Explanation	Ref.	Debit	Credit	Balance

Unearned Service Revenue — No. 209

Date	Explanation	Ref.	Debit	Credit	Balance

Salaries Payable — No. 212

Date	Explanation	Ref.	Debit	Credit	Balance

Common Stock — No. 311

Date	Explanation	Ref.	Debit	Credit	Balance

Retained Earnings — No. 320

Date	Explanation	Ref.	Debit	Credit	Balance

Service Revenue — No. 407

Date	Explanation	Ref.	Debit	Credit	Balance

Name Problem 3-5A Continued

Section

Date Rijo Equipment Repair Corp.

(a), (c) and (e) (Continued)

Depreciation Expense No. 615

Date	Explanation	Ref.	Debit	Credit	Balance

Supplies Expense No. 631

Date	Explanation	Ref.	Debit	Credit	Balance

Salaries Expense No. 726

Date	Explanation	Ref.	Debit	Credit	Balance

Rent Expense No. 729

Date	Explanation	Ref.	Debit	Credit	Balance

(b) General Journal J1

Date	Account Titles and Explanation	Ref.	Debit	Credit

(b)(Continued)

General Journal J1

Date	Account Titles and Explanation	Ref.	Debit	Credit

(e)

General Journal J2

Date	Account Titles and Explanation	Ref.	Debit	Credit
	Adjusting Entries			

Name | **Problem 3-5A Continued**

Section

Date | **Rijo Equipment Repair Corp.**

(d) and (f)

RIJO EQUIPMENT REPAIR CORP.

Trial Balances

September 30, 1996

	Before Adjustment		After Adjustment	
	Dr.	Cr.	Dr.	Cr.

(g)

RIJO EQUIPMENT REPAIR CORP.

Income Statement

For the Month Ended September 30, 1996

Name
Section
Date

Problem 3-5A Continued

Rijo Equipment Repair Corp.

(g) (Continued)

RIJO EQUIPMENT REPAIR CORP.
Retained Earnings Statement
For the Month Ended September 30, 1996

RIJO EQUIPMENT REPAIR CORP.
Balance Sheet
September 30, 1996

Assets	
Liabilities and Stockholders' Equity	

Name

Section

Date

PepsiCo, Inc.

(a)

(b)

(c)

(d)

(e)

Name

Section

Date

Chapter 3 Comparative Analysis Problem

The Coca-Cola Company vs. PepsiCo, Inc.

(a)	Coca-Cola	PepsiCo
1. Prepaid expenses		
2. Total accrued expenses		
3. Depreciation expense		
4. Interest expense		

(b)	Coca-Cola		PepsiCo	
	Dr.	Cr.	Dr.	Cr.

Name

Section

Date

Chapter 3 Ethics Case

Chapter 3 Critical Thinking Case

ETHICS CASE Diamond Company

(a)

(b)

(c)

CRITICAL THINKING CASE Laser Recording Systems Incorporated

(a)

(b)

(c)

Name

Section

Date

Chapter 3 Group Activity

Type of Adjustment	Account Relationship	Accounts Before Adjustment	Adjusting Entry	Balance Sheet Effects of No Adjusting Entry	Income Statement Effects of No Adjusting Entry

Presentation Notes:

Name

Section

Date

Name

Section

Date

	Account Titles	Trial Balance		Adjusting Entries		Adjusted Trial Balance		Income Statement		Balance Sheet	
		Debit	Credit	Debit	Credit	Debit	Credit	Debit	Credit	Debit	Credit
1											
2											
3											
4											
5											
6											
7											
8											
9											
10											
11											
12											
13											
14											
15											
16											
17											
18											
19											
20											
21											
22											
23											
24											
25											
26											
27											
28											

Name
Section
Date

Exercise 4-2

Rey Sanchez Company

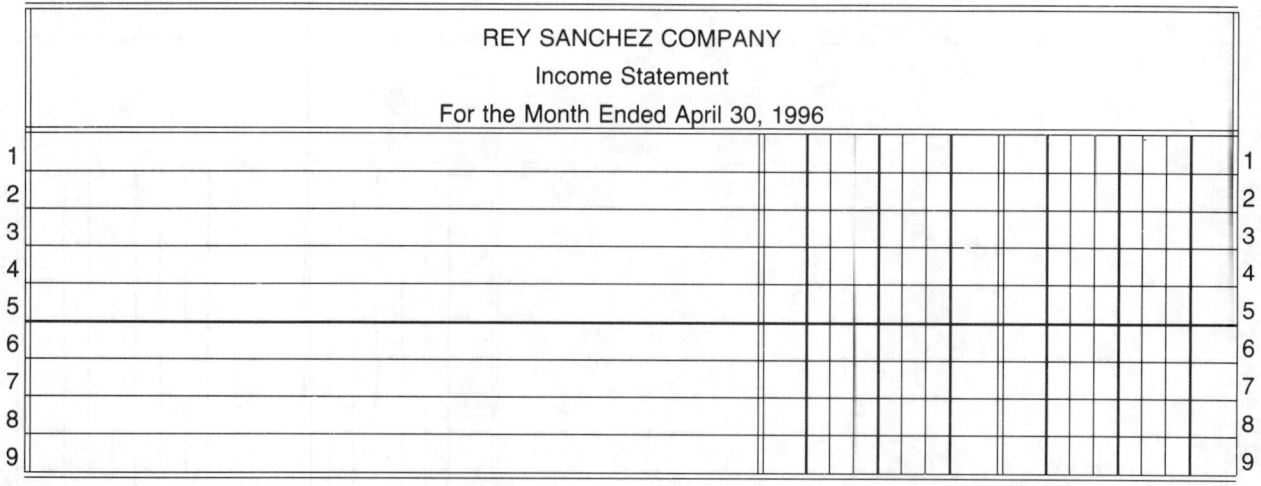

REY SANCHEZ COMPANY
Income Statement
For the Month Ended April 30, 1996

REY SANCHEZ COMPANY
Retained Earnings Statement
For the Month Ended April 30, 1996

REY SANCHEZ COMPANY
Balance Sheet
April 30, 1996

Assets

Liabilities and Stockholders' Equity

Name

Section

Date

Exercise 4-3

Rey Sanchez Company

(a)

(b)

INCOME SUMMARY

RETAINTED EARNINGS

(c)

REY SANCHEZ COMPANY

Post-Closing Trial Balance

April 30, 1996

Additional working papers for this problem are at the back of this book.

(b)

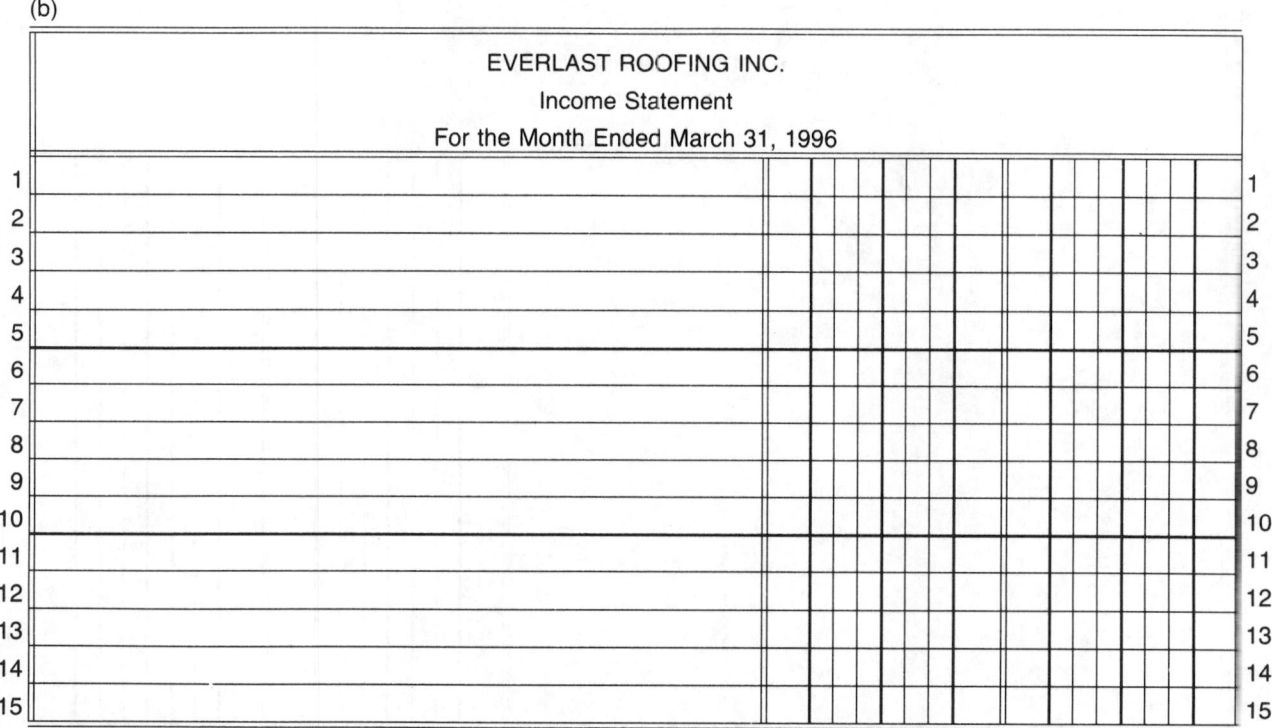

EVERLAST ROOFING INC.
Income Statement
For the Month Ended March 31, 1996

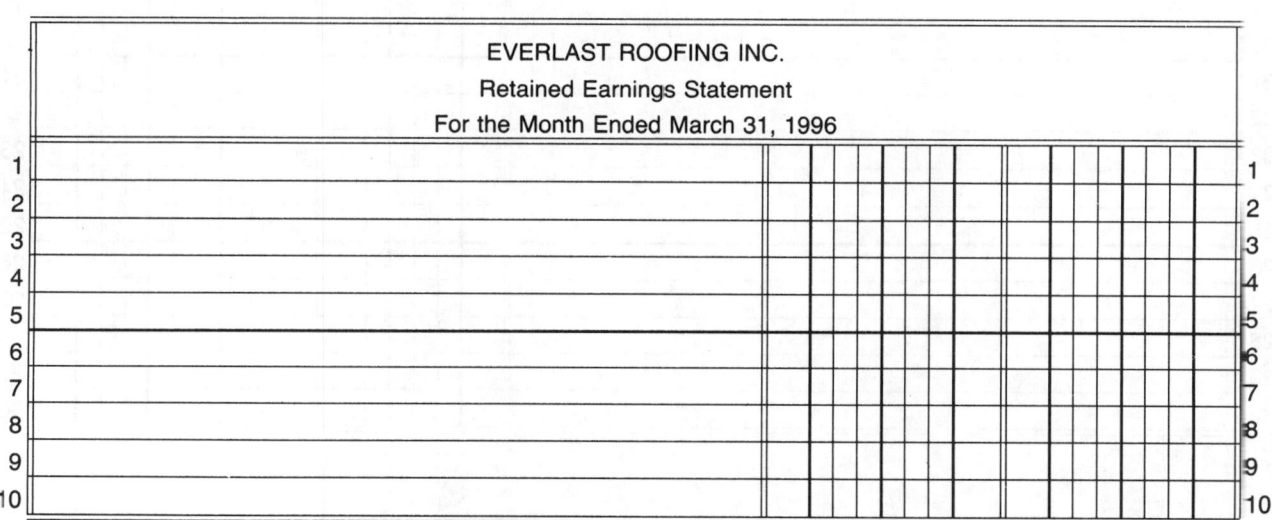

EVERLAST ROOFING INC.
Retained Earnings Statement
For the Month Ended March 31, 1996

Name | **Problem 4-1 Continued**

Section

Date | **Everlast Roofing Inc.**

(b) (Continued)

EVERLAST ROOFING INC.

Balance Sheet

March 31, 1996

Assets

Liabilities and Stockholders' Equity

Name | Problem 4-1 Concluded
Section
Date | **Everlast Roofing Inc.**

(c) General Journal

	Date	Account Titles and Explanation	Ref.	Debit	Credit	
1		Adjusting Entries				1
2						2
3						3
4						4
5						5
6						6
7						7
8						8
9						9
10						10
11						11
12						12
13						13
14						14
15						15
16						16

(d) General Journal

	Date	Account Titles and Explanation	Ref.	Debit	Credit	
1		Closing Entries				1
2						2
3						3
4						4
5						5
6						6
7						7
8						8
9						9
10						10
11						11
12						12
13						13
14						14
15						15
16						16

Name

Section

Date

Problem 4-2

Diaz Company

(a)

DIAZ COMPANY
Partial Work Sheet
For the Year Ended December 31, 1996

No.	Account Titles	Adjusted Trial Balance		Income Statement		Balance Sheet	
		Dr.	Cr.	Dr.	Cr.	Dr.	Cr.

Name Problem 4-2 Continued

Section

Date Diaz Company

(b)

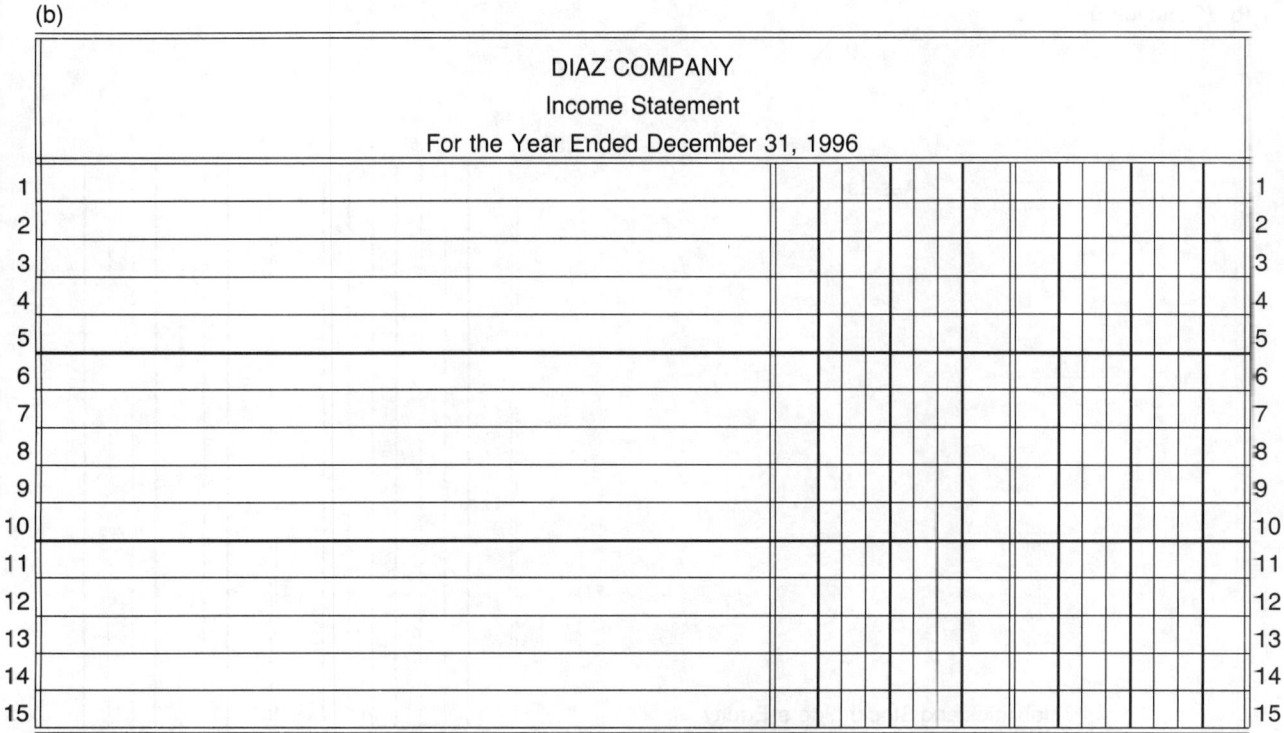

DIAZ COMPANY
Income Statement
For the Year Ended December 31, 1996

1			1
2			2
3			3
4			4
5			5
6			6
7			7
8			8
9			9
10			10
11			11
12			12
13			13
14			14
15			15

DIAZ COMPANY
Retained Earnings Statement
For the Year Ended December 31, 1996

1			1
2			2
3			3
4			4
5			5
6			6

(b) (Continued)

DIAZ COMPANY
Balance Sheet
December 31, 1996

Assets

Liabilities and Stockholders' Equity

Name | | Problem 4-2 Continued
Section
Date | | Diaz Company

(c) General Journal J14

Date	Account Titles and Explanation	Ref.	Debit	Credit

(d) Common Stock No. 311

Date	Explanation	Ref.	Debit	Credit	Balance

Retained Earnings No. 320

Date	Explanation	Ref.	Debit	Credit	Balance

Dividends No. 332

Date	Explanation	Ref.	Debit	Credit	Balance

Name | Problem 4-2 Continued

Section

Date | Diaz Company

(d) (Continued)

Income Summary | No. 350

Date	Explanation	Ref.	Debit	Credit	Balance

Fees Earned | No. 400

Date	Explanation	Ref.	Debit	Credit	Balance

Advertising Expense | No. 610

Date	Explanation	Ref.	Debit	Credit	Balance

Supplies Expense | No. 631

Date	Explanation	Ref.	Debit	Credit	Balance

Depreciation Expense | No. 711

Date	Explanation	Ref.	Debit	Credit	Balance

Insurance Expense | No. 722

Date	Explanation	Ref.	Debit	Credit	Balance

Name

Section

Date

Additional working papers for this problem are at the back of this book.

(b)

PORTER MANAGEMENT SERVICES INC.
Balance Sheet
December 31, 1996

Assets		
Liabilities and Stockholders' Equity		

Name | **Problem 4-4 Continued**

Section

Date | **Porter Management Services Inc.**

(c) and (d) General Journal

Date	Account Titles and Explanation	Ref.	Debit	Credit
	Adjusting Entries			
	Closing Entries			

Name | Problem 4-6 Concluded

Section

Date | Campus TV Repair Corp.

Additional working papers for this problem are at the back of this book.

(b)

CAMPUS TV REPAIR CORP.
Trial Balance
April 30, 1996

		Debit	Credit	
1				1
2				2
3				3
4				4
5				5
6				6
7				7
8				8
9				9
10				10
11				11
12				12
13				13
14				14
15				15
16				16
17				17
18				18
19				19
20				20
21				21
22				22
23				23
24				24
25				25
26				26
27				27
28				28
29				29
30				30
31				31
32				32
33				33
34				34
35				35

Name **Problem 4-1A Continued**

Section

Date **Nancy Zarl Corp.**

Additional working papers for this problem are at the back of this book.

(b)

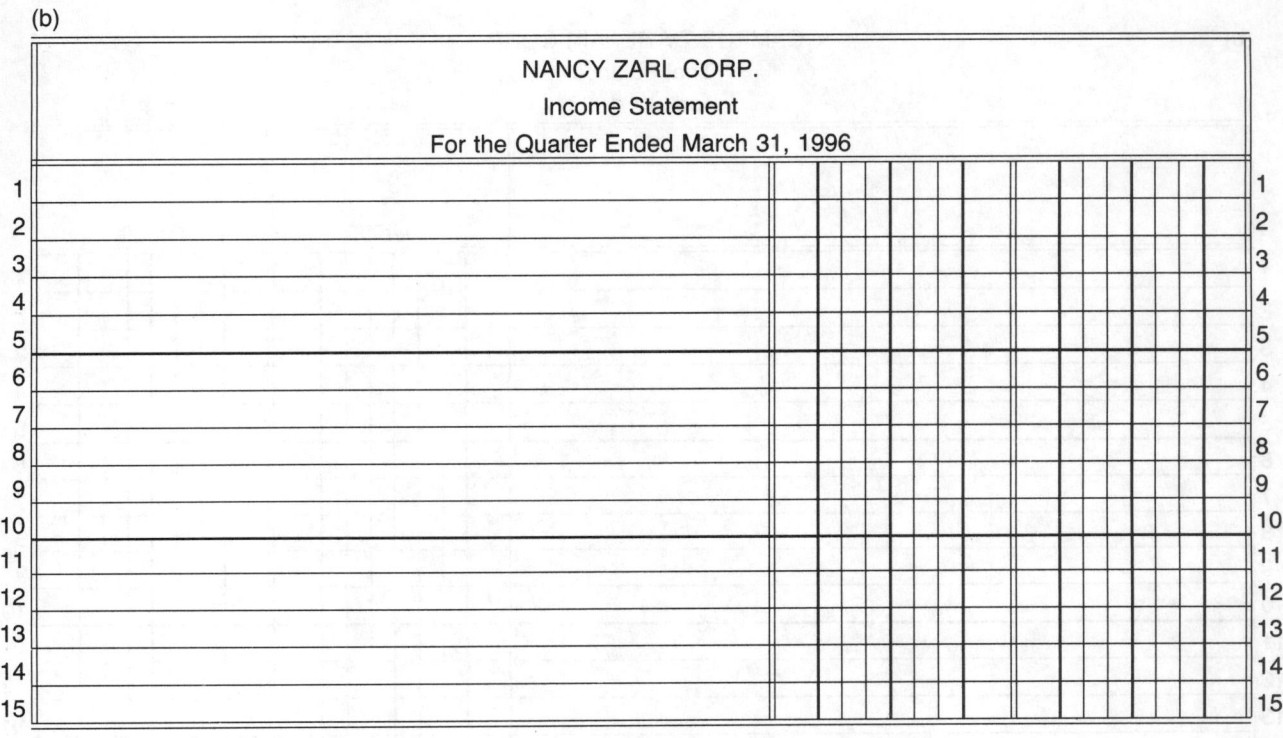

NANCY ZARL CORP.
Income Statement
For the Quarter Ended March 31, 1996

NANCY ZARL CORP.
Retained Earnings Statement
For the Quarter Ended March 31, 1996

Name

Section

Date

Problem 4-1A Continued

Nancy Zarl Corp.

(b) (Continued)

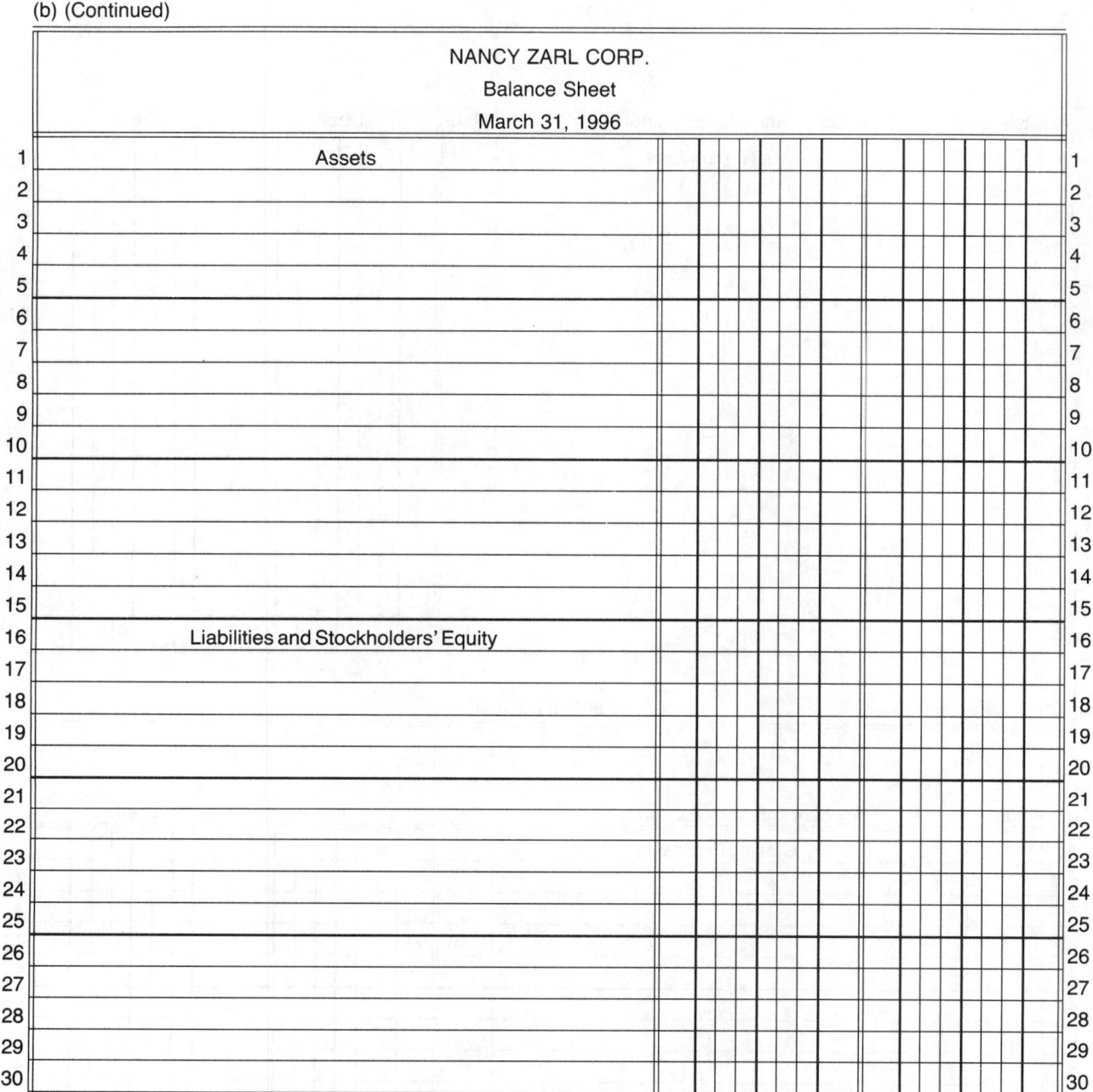

NANCY ZARL CORP.

Balance Sheet

March 31, 1996

Assets

Liabilities and Stockholders' Equity

Name

Section

Date

Problem 4-1A Concluded

Nancy Zarl Corp.

(c)

General Journal

	Date	Account Titles and Explanation	Ref.	Debit	Credit	
1		Adjusting Entries				1
2						2
3						3
4						4
5						5
6						6
7						7
8						8
9						9
10						10
11						11
12						12
13						13
14						14
15						15
16						16

(d)

General Journal

	Date	Account Titles and Explanation	Ref.	Debit	Credit	
1		Closing Entries				1
2						2
3						3
4						4
5						5
6						6
7						7
8						8
9						9
10						10
11						11
12						12
13						13
14						14
15						15
16						16
17						17
18						18
19						19

Name

Section

Date

Problem 4-2A

Ohno Company

(a)

OHNO COMPANY

Partial Work Sheet

For the Year Ended December 31, 1996

No.	Account Titles	Adjusted Trial Balance Dr.	Adjusted Trial Balance Cr.	Income Statement Dr.	Income Statement Cr.	Balance Sheet Dr.	Balance Sheet Cr.	
1								1
2								2
3								3
4								4
5								5
6								6
7								7
8								8
9								9
10								10
11								11
12								12
13								13
14								14
15								15
16								16
17								17
18								18
19								19
20								20
21								21
22								22
23								23
24								24
25								25
26								26
27								27
28								28
29								29
30								30

Name

Section

Date

Problem 4-2A Continued

Ohno Company

(b)

OHNO COMPANY

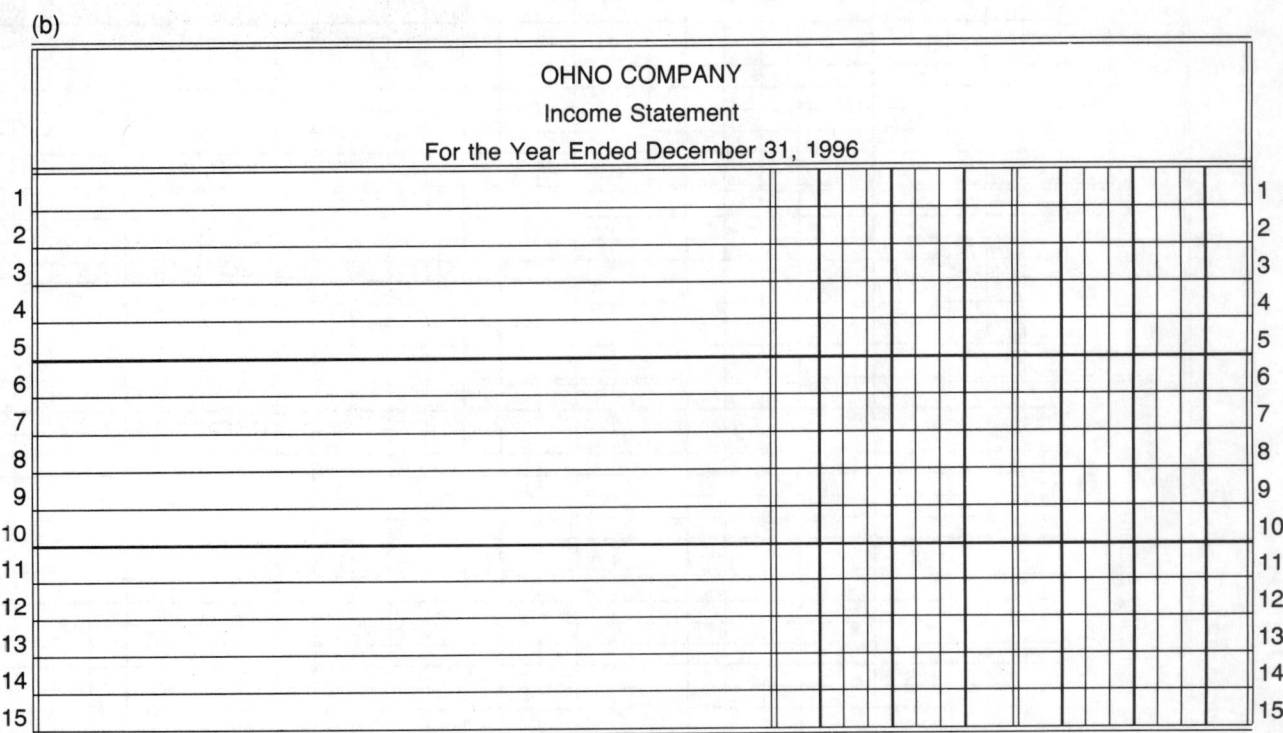

Income Statement

For the Year Ended December 31, 1996

OHNO COMPANY

Retained Earnings Statement

For the Year Ended December 31, 1996

Name

Section

Date

Problem 4-2A Continued

Ohno Company

(b) (Continued)

OHNO COMPANY

Balance Sheet

December 31, 1996

Assets

Liabilities and Stockholders' Equity

Name | **Problem 4-2A Continued**

Section

Date | **Ohno Company**

(c) General Journal J14

Date	Account Titles and Explanation	Ref.	Debit	Credit

(d) Common Stock No. 311

Date	Explanation	Ref.	Debit	Credit	Balance

Name

Section

Date

Problem 4-2A Continued

Ohno Company

(d) (Continued)

Retained Earnings — No. 320

Date	Explanation	Ref.	Debit	Credit	Balance

Dividends — No. 332

Date	Explanation	Ref.	Debit	Credit	Balance

Income Summary — No. 350

Date	Explanation	Ref.	Debit	Credit	Balance

Fees Earned — No. 400

Date	Explanation	Ref.	Debit	Credit	Balance

Advertising Expense — No. 610

Date	Explanation	Ref.	Debit	Credit	Balance

Supplies Expense — No. 631

Date	Explanation	Ref.	Debit	Credit	Balance

Name

Section

Date

Problem 4-2A Concluded

Ohno Company

(d) (Continued)

Depreciation Expense — No. 711

Date	Explanation	Ref.	Debit	Credit	Balance

Insurance Expense — No. 722

Date	Explanation	Ref.	Debit	Credit	Balance

Salaries Expense — No. 726

Date	Explanation	Ref.	Debit	Credit	Balance

Interest Expense — No. 905

Date	Explanation	Ref.	Debit	Credit	Balance

(e)

OHNO COMPANY
Post-Closing Trial Balance
December 31, 1996

		Debit	Credit	
1				1
2				2
3				3
4				4
5				5
6				6
7				7
8				8
9				9
10				10
11				11
12				12
13				13
14				14

Name

Section

Date

Problem 4-3A

Batavia Company

(a)

BATAVIA COMPANY

Income Statement

For the Year Ended December 31, 1996

BATAVIA COMPANY

Retained Earnings Statement

For the Year Ended December 31, 1996

Name

Section

Date

(a) (Continued)

BATAVIA COMPANY

Balance Sheet

December 31, 1996

Assets

Liabilities and Stockholders' Equity

(b)

General Journal

J14

Date	Account Titles and Explanation	Ref.	Debit	Credit

Name | Problem 4-3A Concluded

Section

Date | Batavia Company

(c)

General Ledger Accounts

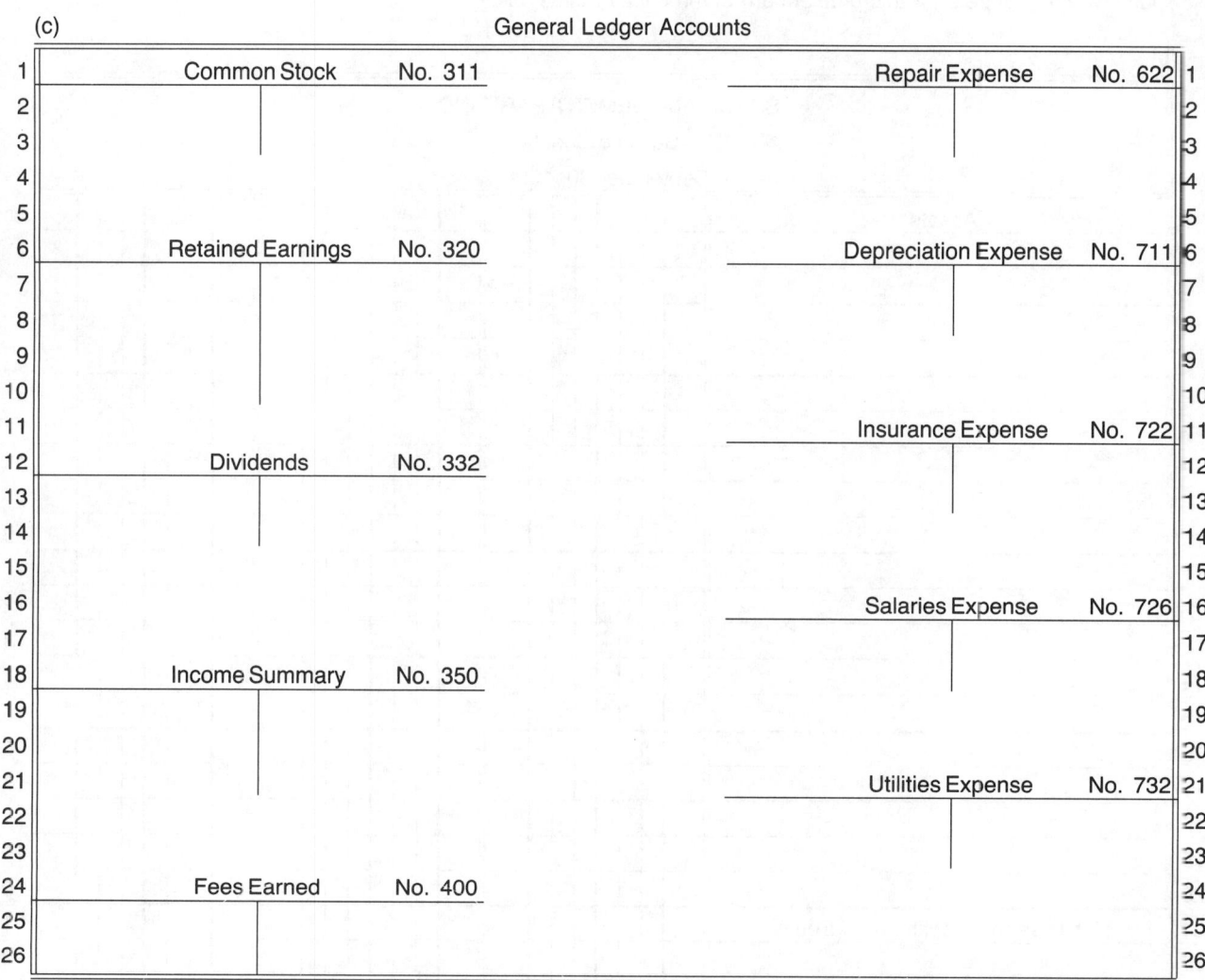

Account	No.
Common Stock	No. 311
Retained Earnings	No. 320
Dividends	No. 332
Income Summary	No. 350
Fees Earned	No. 400
Repair Expense	No. 622
Depreciation Expense	No. 711
Insurance Expense	No. 722
Salaries Expense	No. 726
Utilities Expense	No. 732

(d)

BATAVIA COMPANY
Post-Closing Trial Balance
December 31, 1996

	Debit	Credit

Name
Section
Date

Additional working papers for this problem are at the back of this book.

(b)

SPACE AMUSEMENT PARK INC.
Balance Sheet
September 30, 1996

Assets

Liabilities and Stockholders' Equity

Name | Problem 4-4A Continued

Section

Date | Space Amusement Park Inc.

(c) and (d) General Journal

Date	Account Titles and Explanation	Ref.	Debit	Credit
	Adjusting Entries			
	Closing Entries			

Name

Section

Date

Problem 4-4A Concluded

Space Amusement Park Inc.

(e)

SPACE AMUSEMENT PARK INC.
Post-Closing Trial Balance
September 30, 1996

	Debit	Credit

Name **Problem 4-5A**

Section

Date **Helga's Carpet Cleaners Inc.**

Additional working papers for this problem are at the back of this book.

(a) General Journal J1

Date	Account Titles and Explanation	Ref.	Debit	Credit

(a), (d) and (f)

Cash — No. 101

Date	Explanation	Ref.	Debit	Credit	Balance

Accounts Receivable — No. 112

Date	Explanation	Ref.	Debit	Credit	Balance

Cleaning Supplies — No. 128

Date	Explanation	Ref.	Debit	Credit	Balance

Prepaid Insurance — No. 130

Date	Explanation	Ref.	Debit	Credit	Balance

Equipment — No. 157

Date	Explanation	Ref.	Debit	Credit	Balance

Accumulated Depreciation - Equipment — No. 158

Date	Explanation	Ref.	Debit	Credit	Balance

Name | **Problem 4-5A Continued**

Section

Date | **Helga's Carpet Cleaners Inc.**

(a), (d) and (f) (Continued)

Accounts Payable — No. 201

Date	Explanation	Ref.	Debit	Credit	Balance

Salaries Payable — No. 212

Date	Explanation	Ref.	Debit	Credit	Balance

Common Stock — No. 311

Date	Explanation	Ref.	Debit	Credit	Balance

Retained Earnings — No. 320

Date	Explanation	Ref.	Debit	Credit	Balance

Dividends — No. 332

Date	Explanation	Ref.	Debit	Credit	Balance

Income Summary — No. 350

Date	Explanation	Ref.	Debit	Credit	Balance

Name | Problem 4-5A Continued

Section

Date | Helga's Carpet Cleaners Inc.

(a), (d) and (f) (Continued)

Fees Earned — No. 400

Date	Explanation	Ref.	Debit	Credit	Balance

Gas & Oil Expense — No. 633

Date	Explanation	Ref.	Debit	Credit	Balance

Cleaning Supplies Expense — No. 634

Date	Explanation	Ref.	Debit	Credit	Balance

Depreciation Expense — No. 711

Date	Explanation	Ref.	Debit	Credit	Balance

Insurance Expense — No. 722

Date	Explanation	Ref.	Debit	Credit	Balance

Salaries Expense — No. 726

Date	Explanation	Ref.	Debit	Credit	Balance

(e)

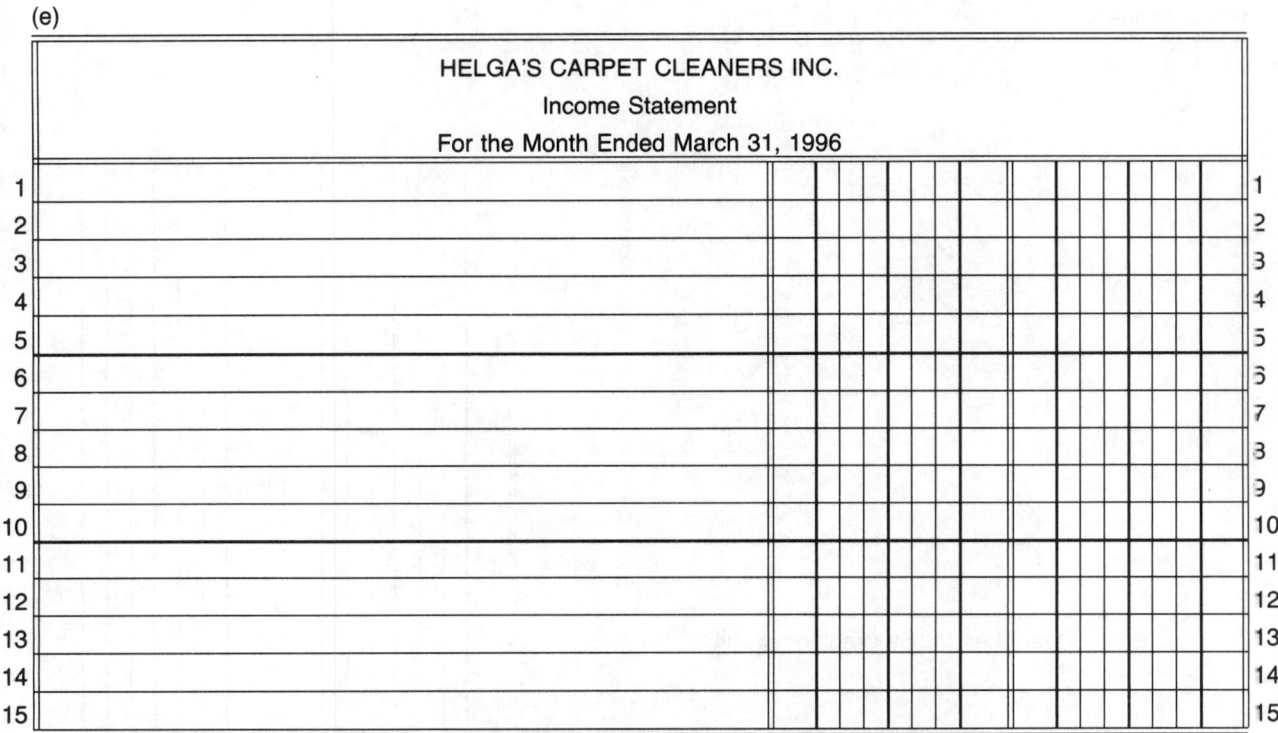

HELGA'S CARPET CLEANERS INC.
Income Statement
For the Month Ended March 31, 1996

HELGA'S CARPET CLEANERS INC.
Retained Earnings Statement
For the Month Ended March 31, 1996

(e) (Continued)

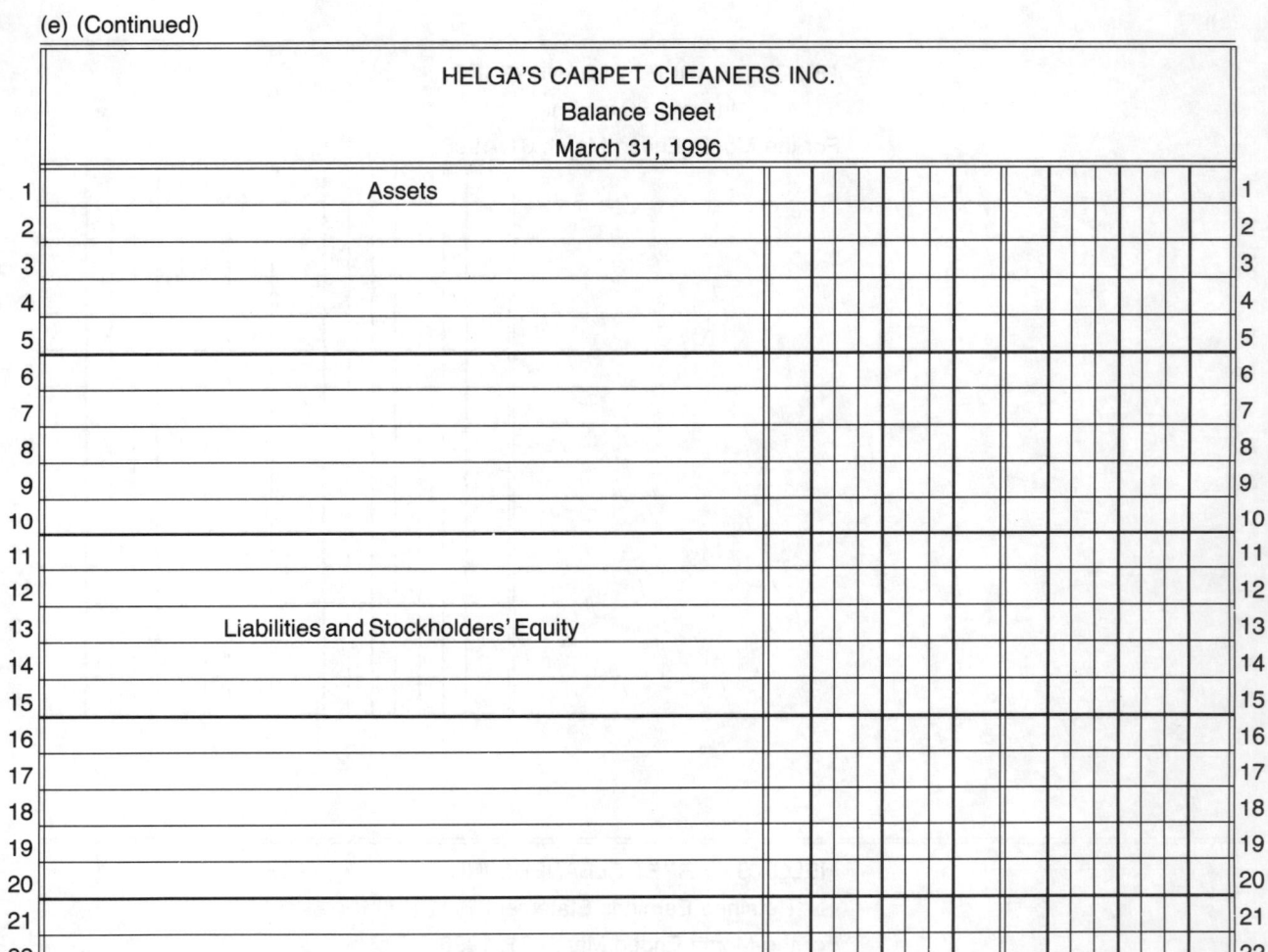

HELGA'S CARPET CLEANERS INC.
Balance Sheet
March 31, 1996

Assets		
Liabilities and Stockholders' Equity		

(g)

HELGA'S CARPET CLEANERS INC.
Post-Closing Trial Balance
March 31, 1996

	Debit	Credit

Name　　　　　　　　　　　　　　　　　　　　　　　　　　　　**Problem 4-5A Continued**

Section

Date　　　　　　　　　　　　　　　　　　　　　　　　　　　　**Helga's Carpet Cleaners Inc.**

(d) General Journal J2

	Date	Account Titles and Explanation	Ref.	Debit	Credit	
1		Adjusting Entries				1
2						2
3						3
4						4
5						5
6						6
7						7
8						8
9						9
10						10
11						11
12						12
13						13
14						14
15						15
16						16

(f) General Journal J3

	Date	Account Titles and Explanation	Ref.	Debit	Credit	
1		Closing Entries				1
2						2
3						3
4						4
5						5
6						6
7						7
8						8
9						9
10						10
11						11
12						12
13						13
14						14
15						15
16						16
17						17

Name
Section
Date

PepsiCo, Inc.

1.

2.

3.

4.

5.

6.

Name

Section

Date

Chapter 4 Comparative Analysis Problem

The Coca-Cola Company vs. PepsiCo, Inc.

	Coca-Cola	PepsiCo.
(a)		
1. Total current assets		
2. Net property, plant, and equipment		
3. Total current liabilities		
4. Total stockholders' (shareholders') equity		

(b)

Name

Section

Date

MINI-CASE Case Corporation

(a)

(b)

(c)

General Ledger Account	Income Statement Item

Name

Section

Date

(d)

Revenues

Net sales

Interest income and other income

Expenses

Cost of goods sold

Selling, general and administrative

Research, development and engineering

Interest expense

Other, net

Income from operations before taxes

Name

Section

Date

(a)

MOODY JANITORIAL SERVICE INC.
Balance Sheet
December 31, 1996

Assets

Liabilities and Stockholders' Equity

Retained earnings calculation:

(b)

Name
Section
Date

Chapter 4 Ethics Case

Chapter 4 Critical Thinking Case

ETHICS CASE Breathless Perfume Company

(a)

(b)

(c)

CRITICAL THINKING CASE Bethlehem Corporation

(a)

(b)

(c)

Name

Section

Date

Current assets

Property, plant, and equipment

Long-term investments

Intangible assets

Current liabilities

Long-term liabilities

Stockholders' equity

Name

Section

Date

Name

Section

Date

Name
Section
Date

Problem 5-3 Continued

Mesa Wholesale Company

(b) (Continued)

MESA WHOLESALE COMPANY
Retained Earnings Statement
For the Year Ended December 31, 1998

MESA WHOLESALE COMPANY
Balance Sheet
December 31, 1998

Assets

Liabilities and Stockholders' Equity

Name

Section

Date

Problem 5-3 Continued

Mesa Wholesale Company

(c)

General Journal

Date	Account Titles and Explanation	Ref.	Debit	Credit
	Adjusting Entries			

(d)

General Journal

Date	Account Titles and Explanation	Ref.	Debit	Credit
	Closing Entries			

Name **Problem 5-3 Concluded**

Section

Date **Mesa Wholesale Company**

(e)

MESA WHOLESALE COMPANY

Post-Closing Trial Balance

December 31, 1998

	Debit	Credit

Name

Section

Date

Problem 5-4

Metro Department Store

(a)

METRO DEPARTMENT STORE

Income Statement

For the Year Ended November 30, 1998

Name | **Problem 5-4 Continued**

Section

Date | **Metro Department Store**

(a) (Continued)

METRO DEPARTMENT STORE

Retained Earnings Statement

For the Year Ended November 30, 1998

(b) General Journal

Date	Account Titles and Explanation	Ref.	Debit	Credit
	Adjusting Entries			

Name

Section

Date

Problem 5-4 Continued

Metro Department Store

(a) (Continued)

METRO DEPARTMENT STORE

Balance Sheet

December 31, 1998

Assets

Liabilities and Stockholders' Equity

Name | **Problem 5-4 Concluded**

Section

Date | **Metro Department Store**

(c) General Journal

Date	Account Titles and Explanation	Ref.	Debit	Credit
	Closing Entries			

Name Problem 5-5

Section

Date Chi Chi's Pro Shop

(a) General Journal J1

Date	Account Titles and Explanation	Ref.	Debit	Credit

Name

Section

Date

Problem 5-5 Continued

Chi Chi's Pro Shop

(b)

Cash — No. 101

Date	Explanation	Ref.	Debit	Credit	Balance

Accounts Receivable — No. 112

Date	Explanation	Ref.	Debit	Credit	Balance

Merchandise Inventory — No. 120

Date	Explanation	Ref.	Debit	Credit	Balance

Accounts Payable — No. 201

Date	Explanation	Ref.	Debit	Credit	Balance

Name

Section

Date

Problem 5-5 Concluded

Chi Chi's Pro Shop

(b) (Continued)

Common Stock No. 311

Date	Explanation	Ref.	Debit	Credit	Balance

Sales No. 401

Date	Explanation	Ref.	Debit	Credit	Balance

Sales Returns and Allowances No. 412

Date	Explanation	Ref.	Debit	Credit	Balance

Cost of Goods Sold No. 501

Date	Explanation	Ref.	Debit	Credit	Balance

(c)

CHI CHI'S PRO SHOP
Trial Balance
April 30, 1998

		Debit	Credit	
1				1
2				2
3				3
4				4
5				5
6				6
7				7
8				8
9				9
10				10

Name **Problem 5-1A**

Section

Date **Nisson Distributing Company**

(a) General Journal J1

	Date	Account Titles and Explanation	Ref.	Debit	Credit	
1						1
2						2
3						3
4						4
5						5
6						6
7						7
8						8
9						9
10						10
11						11
12						12
13						13
14						14
15						15
16						16
17						17
18						18
19						19
20						20
21						21
22						22
23						23
24						24
25						25
26						26
27						27
28						28
29						29
30						30
31						31
32						32
33						33
34						34
35						35
36						36
37						37
38						38
39						39
40						40

Name

Section

Date

Problem 5-1A Continued

Nisson Distributing Company

(a) (Continued) General Journal J1

	Date	Account Titles and Explanation	Ref.	Debit	Credit	
1						1
2						2
3						3
4						4
5						5
6						6
7						7
8						8
9						9
10						10
11						11
12						12
13						13
14						14
15						15
16						16
17						17
18						18
19						19
20						20

(b)

Cash No. 101

Date	Explanation	Ref.	Debit	Credit	Balance

Name | **Problem 5-1A Continued**

Section

Date | **Nisson Distributing Company**

(b) (Continued)

Accounts Receivable — No. 112

Date	Explanation	Ref.	Debit	Credit	Balance

Merchandise Inventory — No. 120

Date	Explanation	Ref.	Debit	Credit	Balance

Accounts Payable — No. 201

Date	Explanation	Ref.	Debit	Credit	Balance

Common Stock — No. 311

Date	Explanation	Ref.	Debit	Credit	Balance

Name
Section
Date

Problem 5-1A Continued

Nisson Distributing Company

(b) (Continued)

Sales — No. 401

Date	Explanation	Ref.	Debit	Credit	Balance

Sales Returns and Allowances — No. 412

Date	Explanation	Ref.	Debit	Credit	Balance

Sales Discounts — No. 414

Date	Explanation	Ref.	Debit	Credit	Balance

Cost of Goods Sold — No. 501

Date	Explanation	Ref.	Debit	Credit	Balance

Freight-out — No. 644

Date	Explanation	Ref.	Debit	Credit	Balance

Name

Section

Date

Problem 5-1A Concluded

Nisson Distributing Company

(c)

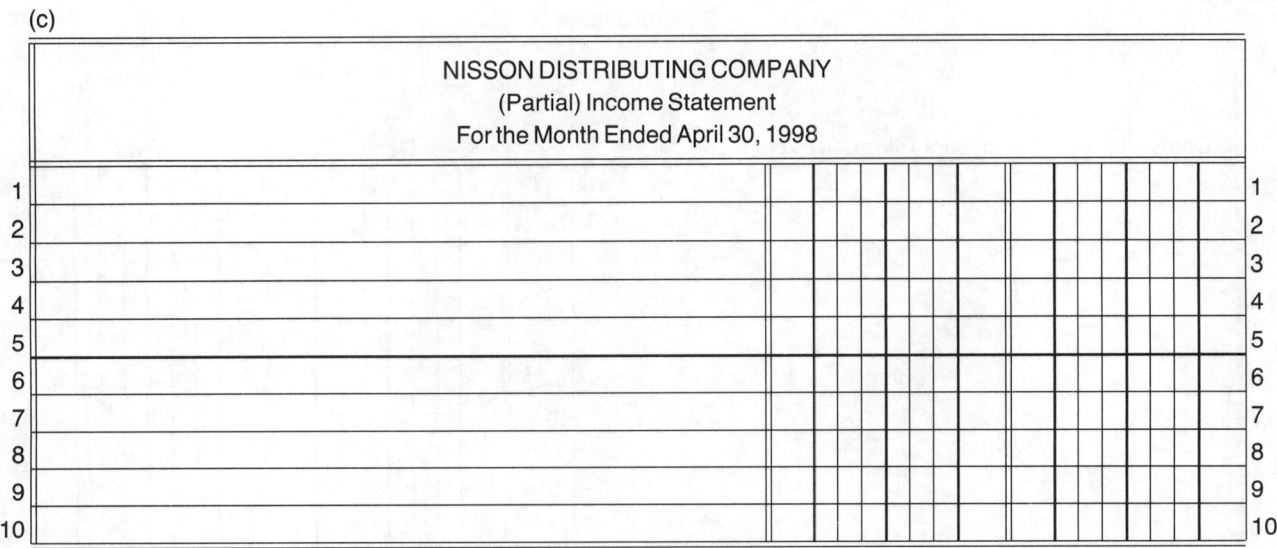

NISSON DISTRIBUTING COMPANY
(Partial) Income Statement
For the Month Ended April 30, 1998

Name

Section

Date

Problem 5-2A

Varsity Auto Sales

General Journal

Date	Account Titles and Explanation	Ref.	Debit	Credit

Name

Section

Date

Problem 5-3A Continued

Ivanna Fashion Center

Additional working papers for this problem are at the back of this book.

(b)

IVANNA FASHION CENTER

Income Statement

For the Year Ended November 30, 1998

Name

Section

Date

Problem 5-3A Continued

Ivanna Fashion Center

(b) (Continued)

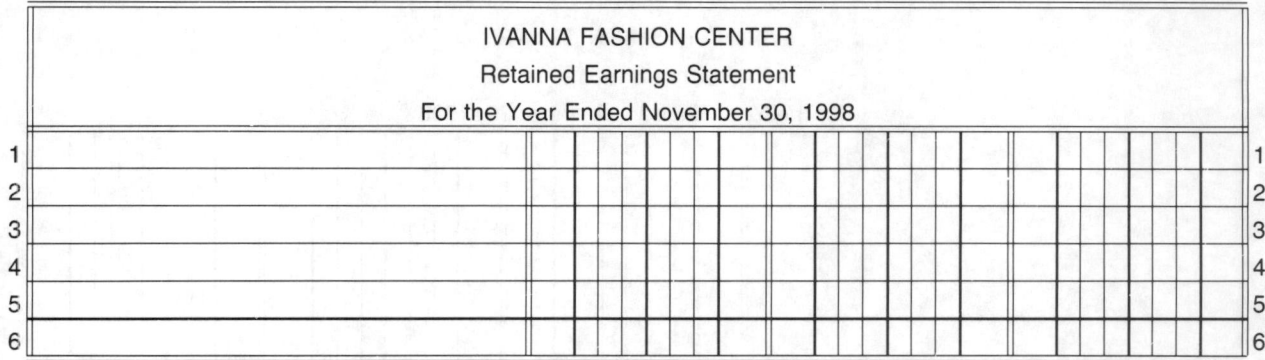

IVANNA FASHION CENTER

Retained Earnings Statement

For the Year Ended November 30, 1998

IVANNA FASHION CENTER

Balance Sheet

November 30, 1998

Assets

Liabilities and Stockholders' Equity

Name

Section

Date

Problem 5-3A Continued

Ivanna Fashion Center

(c) General Journal

Date	Account Titles and Explanation	Ref.	Debit	Credit
	Adjusting Entries			

(d) General Journal

Date	Account Titles and Explanation	Ref.	Debit	Credit
	Closing Entries			

(d) (Continued) General Journal

Date	Account Titles and Explanation	Ref.	Debit	Credit

(e)

IVANNA FASHION CENTER
Post-Closing Trial Balance
November 30, 1998

	Debit	Credit

Name **Problem 5-4A**

Section

Date **N-Mart Department Store**

(a)

N-MART DEPARTMENT STORE

Income Statement

For the Year Ended December 31, 1998

Name

Section

Date

Problem 5-4A Continued

N-Mart Department Store

(a) (Continued)

N-MART DEPARTMENT STORE

Retained Earnings Statement

For the Year Ended December 31, 1998

(b) General Journal

Date	Account Titles and Explanation	Ref.	Debit	Credit
	Adjusting Entries			

(a) (Continued)

N-MART DEPARTMENT STORE
Balance Sheet
December 31, 1998

Assets

Liabilities and Stockholders' Equity

Name | Problem 5-5A

Section

Date | B. J.'s Tennis Shop

(a) General Journal J1

Date	Account Titles and Explanation	Ref.	Debit	Credit

Name

Section

Date

Problem 5-5 Continued

B. J.'s Tennis Shop

(a) (Continued) General Journal J1

Date	Account Titles and Explanation	Ref.	Debit	Credit

(b)

Cash No. 101

Date	Explanation	Ref.	Debit	Credit	Balance

Accounts Receivable No. 112

Date	Explanation	Ref.	Debit	Credit	Balance

Name

Section

Date

Problem 5-5A Continued

B. J.'s Tennis Shop

(b) (Continued)

Merchandise Inventory — No. 120

Date	Explanation	Ref.	Debit	Credit	Balance

Accounts Payable — No. 201

Date	Explanation	Ref.	Debit	Credit	Balance

Common Stock — No. 311

Date	Explanation	Ref.	Debit	Credit	Balance

Sales — No. 401

Date	Explanation	Ref.	Debit	Credit	Balance

Name | Problem 5-5A Concluded
Section
Date | B. J.'s Tennis Shop

(b) (Continued)

Sales Returns and Allowances — No. 412

Date	Explanation	Ref.	Debit	Credit	Balance

Cost of Goods Sold — No. 501

Date	Explanation	Ref.	Debit	Credit	Balance

(c)

B. J.'S TENNIS SHOP
Trial Balance
April 30, 1998

		Debit	Credit	
1				1
2				2
3				3
4				4
5				5
6				6
7				7
8				8
9				9
10				10

Name

Section

Date

Chapter 5 Financial Reporting Problem

PepsiCo, Inc.

(a)

(b)

(c)

MINI-CASE ONE (Continued) Kellogg Company

Percentage change in	1993 to 1994	1992 to 1993
Net income		

MINI-CASE TWO McDonnell Douglas

(a)

(b)

(c)

(a)

(1)

FEDCO DEPARTMENT STORE

Income Statement

For the Year Ended December 31, 1999

(2)

FEDCO DEPARTMENT STORE

Income Statement

For the Year Ended December 31, 1999

(b)

(c)

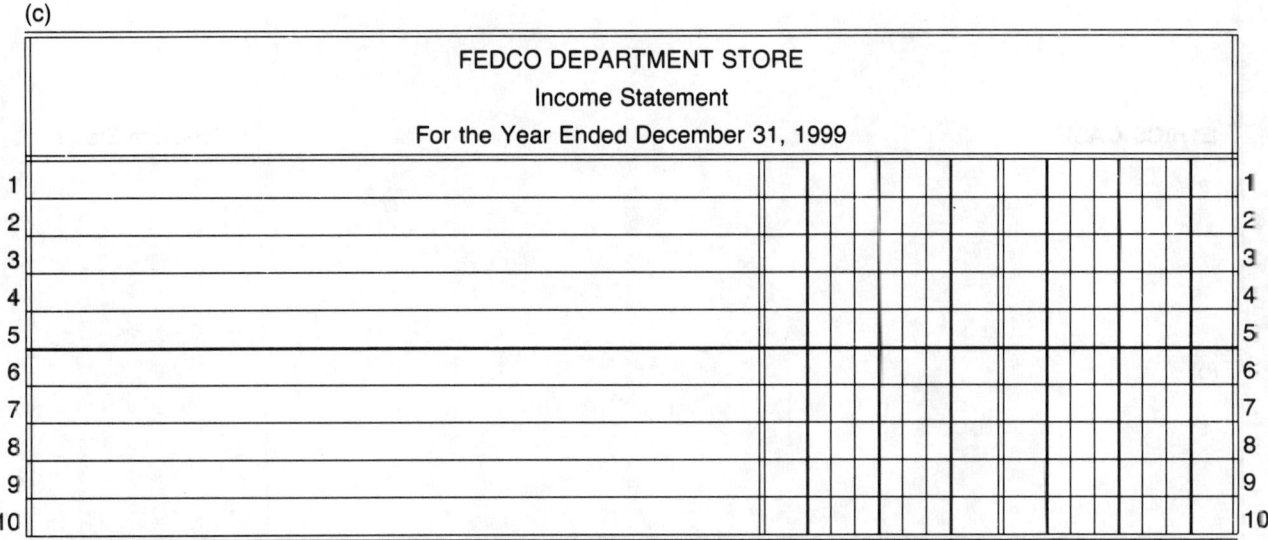

FEDCO DEPARTMENT STORE
Income Statement
For the Year Ended December 31, 1999

Name | Chapter 5 Ethics Case

Section

Date | Chapter 5 Critical Thinking Case

ETHICS CASE Yorkshire Stores

(a)

(b)

(c)

CRITICAL THINKING CASE A.L. Laboratories

(a)

(b)

(c)

Name

Section

Date

Chapter 5 Group Activity

Grant Company

(a) Net sales

(b) Gross profit

(c) Income from operations

(d) Net income

Name

Section

Date

Name

Section

Date

Name | Problem 6-5

Section

Date | Lee's Leathers Inc.

(a)

LEE'S LEATHERS INC.

Income Statement

For the Year Ended January 31, 1997

Name

Section

Date

Problem 6-5 Concluded

Lee's Leathers Inc.

(b) and (c)

(b)

(c)

Name
Section
Date

Problem 6-1A

Qwik Printers

(1)

(2)

(3)

Name

Section

Date

Problem 6-1A Concluded

Qwik Printers

(4)

(5)

(6)

Name **Problem 6-2A**

Section

Date **Chita, Inc.**

(1)

(2)

(3)

Name

Section

Date

Problem 6-2A Concluded

Chita, Inc.

(4)

(5)

Name

Section

Date

Problem 6-3A

1.

2.

3.

4.

5.

6.

7.

8.

Name | **Problem 6-4A**

Section

Date | **North Shore Outfitters, Inc.**

(a)

NORTH SHORE OUTFITTERS, INC.
Balance Sheet
October 31, 1997

Assets

Liabilities and Stockholders' Equity

(b) and (c)

(b)

(c)

Name

Section

Date

Problem 6-5A

Inigo Jones Galleries, Inc.

(a)

INIGO JONES GALLERIES, INC.

Income Statement

For the Year Ended December 31, 1997

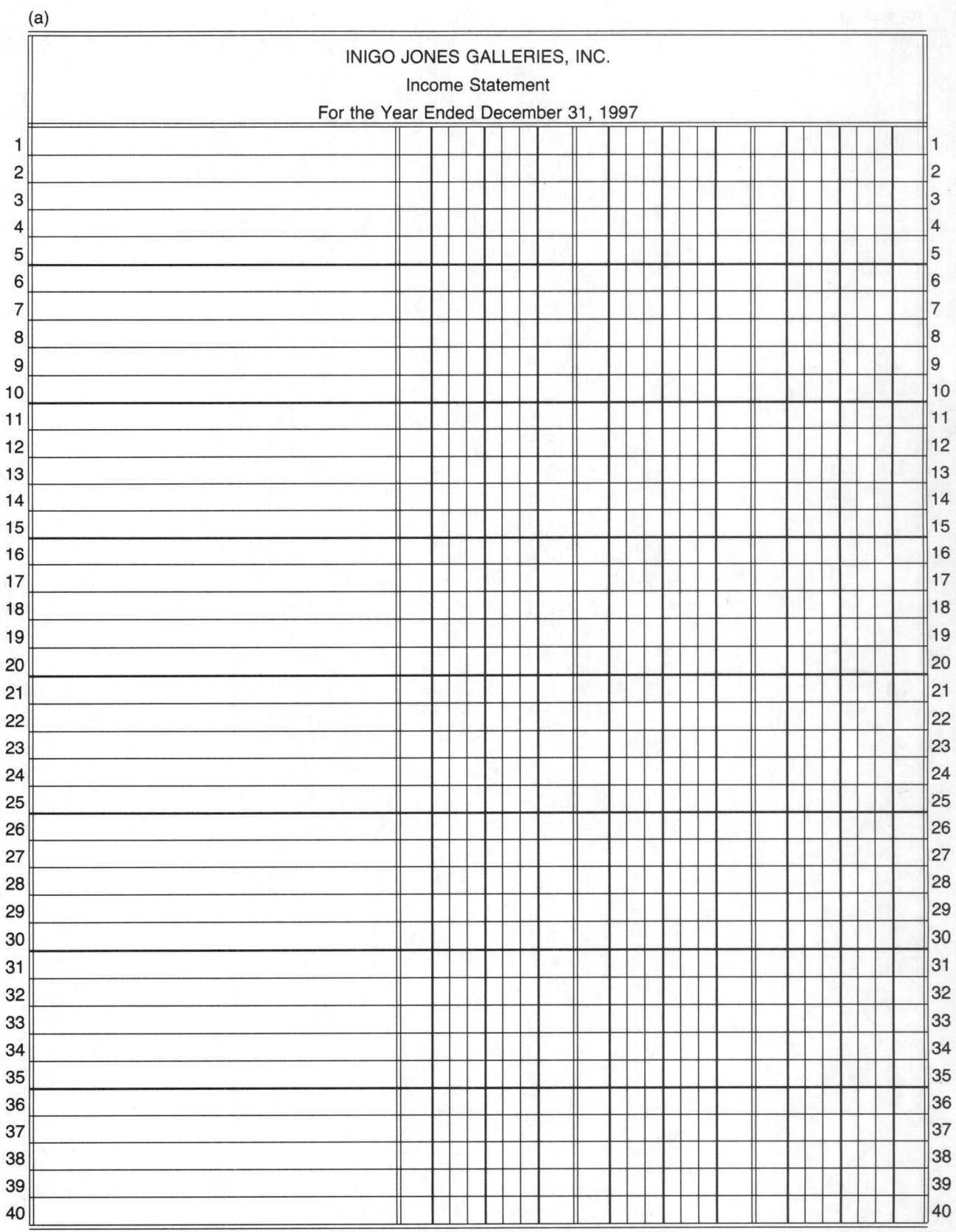

Name

Section

Date

Problem 6-5A Concluded

Inigo Jones Galleries, Inc.

(b) and (c)

(b)

(c)

Name

Section

Date

Chapter 6 Comprehensive Problem

Do-Re-Mi Corporation

(a) Multiple-step format

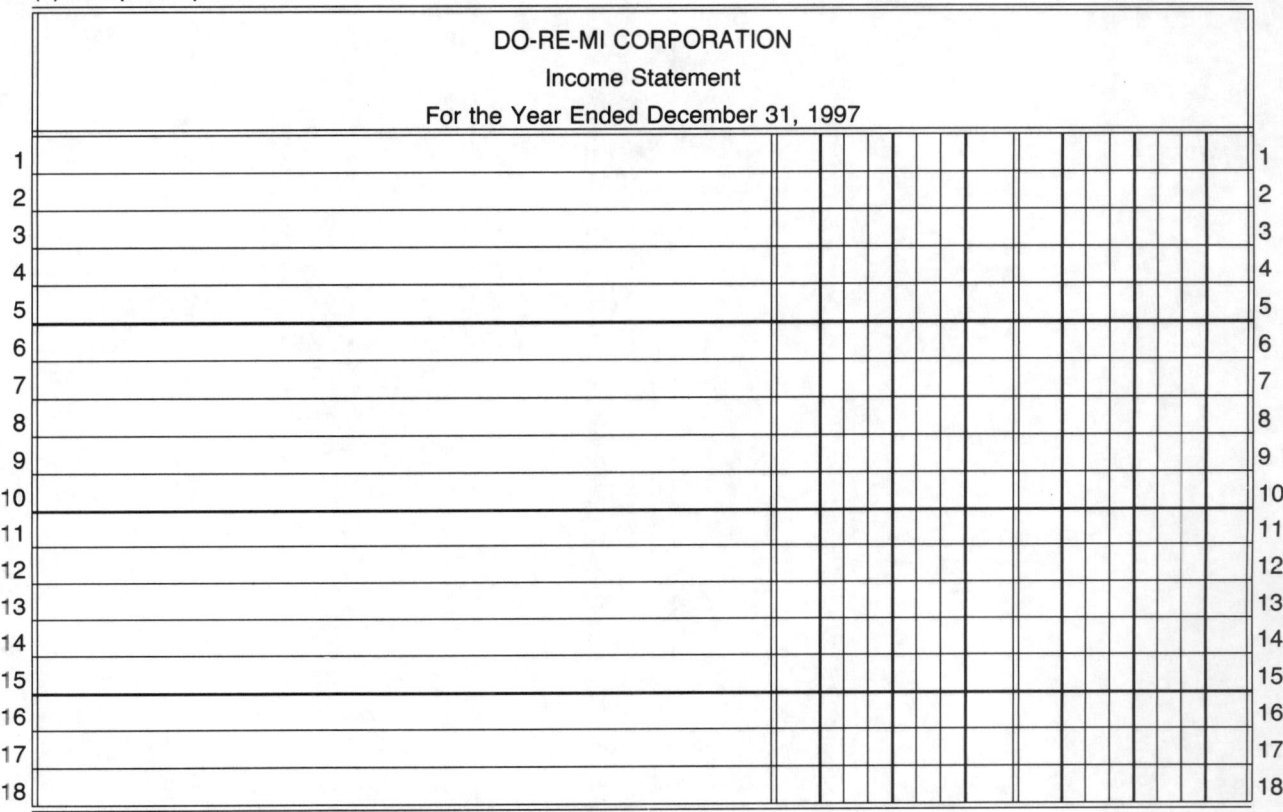

DO-RE-MI CORPORATION
Income Statement
For the Year Ended December 31, 1997

(b) Single-step format

DO-RE-MI CORPORATION
Income Statement
For the Year Ended December 31, 1997

Name

Section

Date

(c)

DO-RE-MI CORPORATION

Retained Earnings Statement

For the Year Ended December 31, 1997

(d)

DO-RE-MI CORPORATION

Balance Sheet

December 31, 1997

Assets

Liabilities and Stockholders' Equity

(e) and (f)

(e)

(f)

Name

Section

Date

(g)

Name

Section

Date

(a)

(b)

(c)

(d)

Name

Section

Date

(e)

(f)

(g)

Name **Chapter 6 Comparative Analysis Problem**

Section

Date **The Coca-Cola Company vs. PepsiCo, Inc.**

(a)	Coca-Cola	PepsiCo.
1. Current ratio		
2. Working capital		
3. Profit margin percentage		
4. Return on assets		
5. Return on common stockholders' equity		
6. Debt to total assets		

(b) Liquidity:

(b) (Continued)

Profitability:

Solvency:

MINI-CASE ONE The North Face, Inc.

(a) Liquidity:

(b) Solvency:

Name
Section
Date

MINI-CASE TWO RJR Nabisco and Phillip Morris

(a) Profit margin percentage:

Return on assets:

Return on common stockholders' equity:

(b)

Name

Section

Date

Exemplar Manufacturing, Merchandising, and Mining Companies

(a)

(b)

Name

Section

Date

(c)

(d)

Name

Section

Date

ETHICS CASE Redondo Corporation

(a)

(b)

(c)

CRITICAL THINKING CASE Weyerhaeuser Company

(a)

(b)

xxx

Name

Section

Date

Concept:

Rationale for NOT eliminating it:

Concept:

Rationale for NOT eliminating it:

Concept:

Rationale for NOT eliminating it:

Concept:

Rationale for NOT eliminating it:

Name

Section

Date

Concept:

Rationale for NOT eliminating it:

Concept:

Rationale for NOT eliminating it:

Concept:

Rationale for NOT eliminating it:

Concept:

Rationale for NOT eliminating it:

Name

Section

Date

Concept:

Rationale for NOT eliminating it:

Concept:

Rationale for NOT eliminating it:

Concept:

Rationale for NOT eliminating it:

Concept:

Rationale for NOT eliminating it:

Name

Section

Date

Name

Section

Date

Name

Section

Date

Name **Exercise 7-1**

Section

Date **Marino's Pizza**

1.

2.

3.

4.

5.

6.

Name

Section

Date

Exercise 7-2

Tolan Company

(a) Weakness	Principle Violated	(b) Recommended Change
1.		
2.		
3.		
4.		
5.		

Name

Section

Date

Exercise 7-3

Ann's Boutique Shoppe

(a)		(b)
Weakness	Principle Violated	Suggested Improvement
1.		
2.		
3.		
4.		
5.		

Name

Section

Date

Exercise 7-4

O'Malley Company

(a) Weaknesses	(b) Suggested Improvement
1.	
2.	
3.	
4.	
5.	
6.	
7.	
8.	

Name

Section

Date

#5

#6

(a)

ONO LOKO COMPANY

Bank Reconciliation

January 31

(b)

Name

Section

Date

Exercise 7-10

Kuwait Company

(a)

(b)

(c)

(d)

Name

Section

Date

Problem 7-1

Red River Theater

(a)

Principles	Application to Red River Theater

(b)

Name **Problem 7-2**

Section

Date **MTR Company**

General Journal

Date	Account Titles and Explanation	Ref.	Debit	Credit

Name | **Problem 7-2 Concluded**

Section

Date | **MTR Company**

(b)

Petty Cash

Date	Explanation	Ref.	Debit	Credit	Balance

(c)

Name

Section

Date

Problem 7-5

Mayo Company

(a)

MAYO COMPANY

Bank Reconciliation

August 31, 1996

Computations

Name | **Problem 7-5 Concluded**

Section

Date | **Mayo Company**

(b) General Journal

	Date	Account Titles and Explanation	Ref.	Debit	Credit	
1						1
2						2
3						3
4						4
5						5
6						6
7						7
8						8
9						9
10						10
11						11
12						12
13						13
14						14
15						15

Name

Section

Date

Problem 7-1A

Segal Office Supply Company

	Principles	Application to Cash Disbursements
1		
2		
3		
4		
5		
6		
7		
8		
9		
10		
11		
12		
13		
14		
15		
16		
17		
18		
19		
20		
21		
22		
23		
24		
25		
26		
27		
28		
29		
30		
31		
32		
33		
34		
35		
36		
37		
38		
39		
40		

Name

Section

Date

Problem 7-2A

Dockers Company

(a) General Journal J1

Date	Account Titles and Explanation	Ref.	Debit	Credit

Name **Problem 7-2A Concluded**

Section

Date **Dockers Company**

(b)

Petty Cash

Date	Explanation	Ref.	Debit	Credit	Balance

(c)

Name **Problem 7-3A**

Section

Date **Maloney Company**

(a)

MALONEY COMPANY

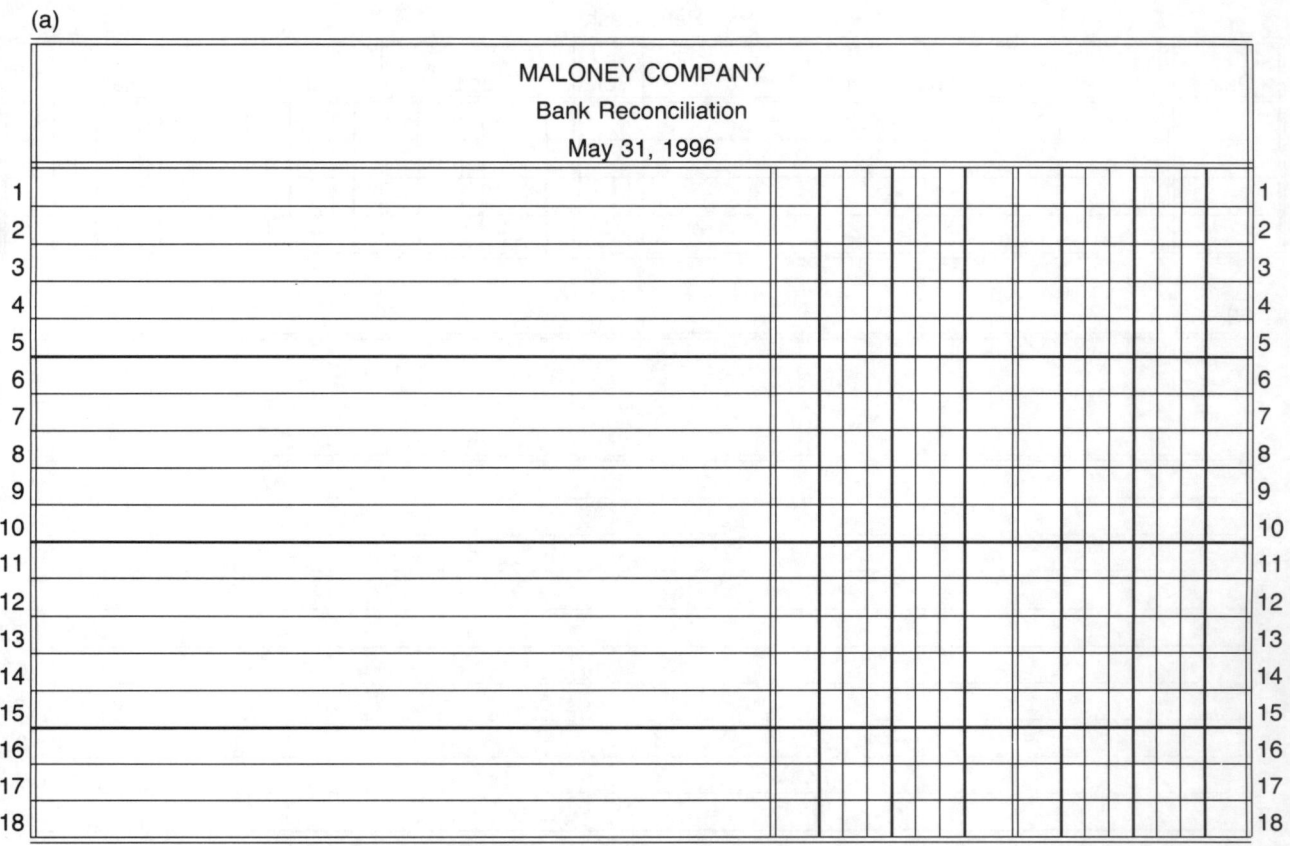

Bank Reconciliation

May 31, 1996

(b) General Journal

Date	Account Titles and Explanation	Ref.	Debit	Credit

Name

Section

Date

Problem 7-4A

Sandra Company

(a)

SANDRA COMPANY

Bank Reconciliation

December 31, 1996

(b) General Journal

Date	Account Titles and Explanation	Ref.	Debit	Credit

Name

Section

Date

Problem 7-5A

Palmeiro Company

(a)

PALMEIRO COMPANY

Bank Reconciliation

July 31, 1996

Computations

(b) General Journal

	Date	Account Titles and Explanation	Ref.	Debit	Credit	
1						1
2						2
3						3
4						4
5						5
6						6
7						7
8						8
9						9
10						10
11						11
12						12
13						13
14						14
15						15

Name

Section

Date

Problem 7-6A

Acura Company

(a)

ACURA COMPANY

Bank Reconciliation

October 31, 1996

(b) and (c)

Name
Section
Date

MINI-CASE Microsoft, Inc.

(a)

(b)

(c)

(d)

(e)

Name

Section

Date

Chapter 7 Decision Case

Local Church

(a)

(b)

(c)

Name

Section

Date

Name

Section

Date

Name **Exercises 8-7 to 8-8**

Section

Date

#7

#8

Name

Section

Date

Exercises 8-9 to 8-10

#9

#10

Name | **Problem 8-5**

Section

Date | **Bon Ton Company**

(a) General Journal

Date	Account Titles and Explanation	Ref.	Debit	Credit

(b)

Notes Receivable

Date	Explanation	Ref.	Debit	Credit	Balance

Accounts Receivable

Date	Explanation	Ref.	Debit	Credit	Balance

Interest Receivable

Date	Explanation	Ref.	Debit	Credit	Balance

(c)

BON TON COMPANY
(Partial) Balance Sheet
December 31, 1996

Assets		
Current Assets		

Name **Problem 8-6**

Section

Date **Comaneci Company**

General Journal

Date	Account Titles and Explanation	Ref.	Debit	Credit

Name **Problem 8-1A**

Section

Date **Bordeaux Inc.**

(a)

General Journal

Date	Account Titles and Explanation	Ref.	Debit	Credit

(b)

ACCOUNTS RECEIVABLE

ALLOWANCE FOR DOUBTFUL ACCOUNTS

(c) and (d)

Name

Section

Date

Problem 8-2A

Volkov Company

(a)

(b)

(c)

(d)

(e)

Name | Problem 8-3A

Section

Date | Deep Canyon Company

(a), (b), and (c)

General Journal

	Date	Account Titles and Explanation	Ref.	Debit	Credit	
1	(a)					1
2						2
3						3
4						4
5						5
6	(b)					6
7						7
8						8
9						9
10						10
11						11
12						12
13						13
14						14
15						15
16						16
17						17
18						18
19	(c)					19
20						20
21						21
22						22

(a) and (b)

Bad Debts Expense

	Date	Explanation	Ref.	Debit	Credit	Balance	
1							1
2							2
3							3

Allowance for Doubtful Accounts

	Date	Explanation	Ref.	Debit	Credit	Balance	
1							1
2							2
3							3
4							4
5							5
6							6
7							7

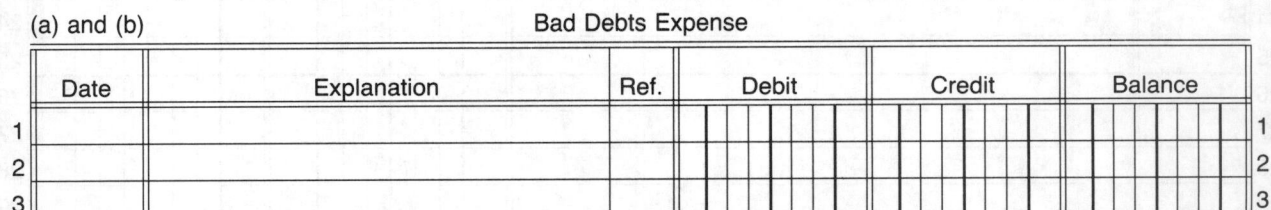

Name **Problem 8-4A**

Section

Date **Huang Co.**

General Journal

Date	Account Titles and Explanation	Ref.	Debit	Credit
(a)				
(b)				
(c)				
(d)				

Name Problem 8-5A

Section

Date Selica Company

(a) General Journal

Date	Account Titles and Explanation	Ref.	Debit	Credit

Name _______________ **Problem 8-5A Concluded**

Section _______________

Date _______________ **Selica Company**

(b)

Notes Receivable

Date	Explanation	Ref.	Debit	Credit	Balance

Accounts Receivable

Date	Explanation	Ref.	Debit	Credit	Balance

Interest Receivable

Date	Explanation	Ref.	Debit	Credit	Balance

(c)

SELICA COMPANY
(Partial) Balance Sheet
October 31, 1996

Assets			
Current Assets			

Name | **Problem 8-6A**

Section

Date | **Ricardo Company**

General Journal

	Date	Account Titles and Explanation	Ref.	Debit	Credit	
1						1
2						2
3						3
4						4
5						5
6						6
7						7
8						8
9						9
10						10
11						11
12						12
13						13
14						14
15						15
16						16
17						17
18						18
19						19
20						20
21						21
22						22
23						23
24						24
25						25
26						26
27						27
28						28
29						29
30						30
31						31
32						32
33						33
34						34
35						35
36						36
37						37
38						38
39						39
40						40

(a)

ARVADA COMPANY
Accounts Receivable Aging Schedule
May 31, 1997

	Proportion of Total %	Amount in Category	Probability of Non-Collection %	Estimated Uncollectible Amount

(b)

ARVADA COMPANY
Analysis of Allowance for Doubtful Accounts
May 31, 1997

Adjusting entry:		

1. Steps to Improve	2. Risks and Costs Involved

Name

Section

Date

Chapter 8 Group Activity

(a)

(b)

Name

Section

Date

Name

Section

Date

Name
Section
Date

Name

Section

Date

Name

Section

Date

Exercises 9-*10 to 9-11

#10	Women's Department		Men's Department	
	Cost	Retail	Cost	Retail

#11	1998	1999

Name

Section

Date

Exercise 9-12

Aruba Company

	1998	1999

(b)

(c)

Name ***Problem 9-6**

Section

Date **Barker's Book Store**

(a)

	Hardcovers		Paperbacks	
	Cost	Retail	Cost	Retail

(b)

Hardcovers:

Paperbacks:

Name ***Problem 9-7**

Section

Date **Save-Mart Center**

Date		Purchases	Sales	Balance
(a) (1)	FIFO			
(2)	Average Cost			
(3)	LIFO			

(b)

Name

Section

Date

Problem 9-1A

B.J.'s Tennis Shop

(a) General Journal J1

Date	Account Titles and Explanation	Ref.	Debit	Credit

Name Problem 9-1A Continued
Section
Date B.J.'s Tennis Shop

(a) (Continued) General Journal

	Date	Account Titles and Explanation	Ref.	Debit	Credit	
1						1
2						2
3						3
4						4
5						5
6						6
7						7
8						8
9						9
10						10

(b)

Cash No. 101

Date	Explanation	Ref.	Debit	Credit	Balance

Accounts Receivable No. 112

Date	Explanation	Ref.	Debit	Credit	Balance

Merchandise Inventory No. 120

Date	Explanation	Ref.	Debit	Credit	Balance

Name **Problem 9-1A Continued**

Section

Date **B.J.'s Tennis Shop**

(b) (Continued)

Accounts Payable No. 201

Date	Explanation	Ref.	Debit	Credit	Balance

Common Stock No. 311

Date	Explanation	Ref.	Debit	Credit	Balance

Sales No. 401

Date	Explanation	Ref.	Debit	Credit	Balance

Sales Returns and Allowances No. 412

Date	Explanation	Ref.	Debit	Credit	Balance

Purchases No. 510

Date	Explanation	Ref.	Debit	Credit	Balance

Purchase Returns and Allowances No. 512

Date	Explanation	Ref.	Debit	Credit	Balance

(b) (Continued) Purchase Discounts

Date	Explanation	Ref.	Debit	Credit	Balance

Freight-in

Date	Explanation	Ref.	Debit	Credit	Balance

(c)

B.J.'S TENNIS SHOP
Trial Balance
April 30, 1998

		Debit	Credit	
1				1
2				2
3				3
4				4
5				5
6				6
7				7
8				8
9				9
10				10
11				11
12				12

(d)

B.J.'S TENNIS SHOP
(Partial) Income Statement
For the Month Ended April 30, 1998

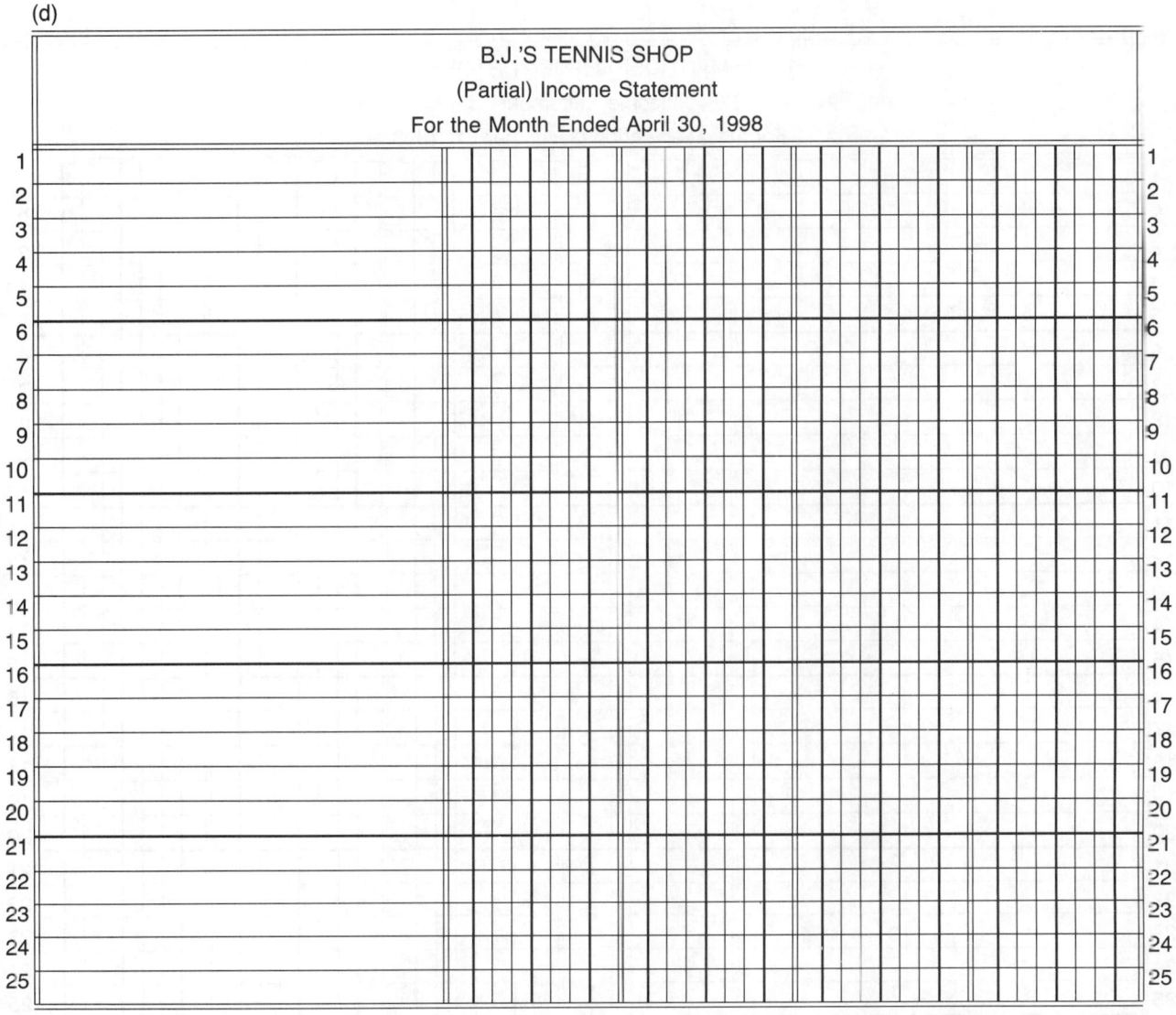

Name

Section

Date

Problem 9-2A

N-Mart Department Store

N-MART DEPARTMENT STORE

Income Statement

For the Year Ended December 31, 1998

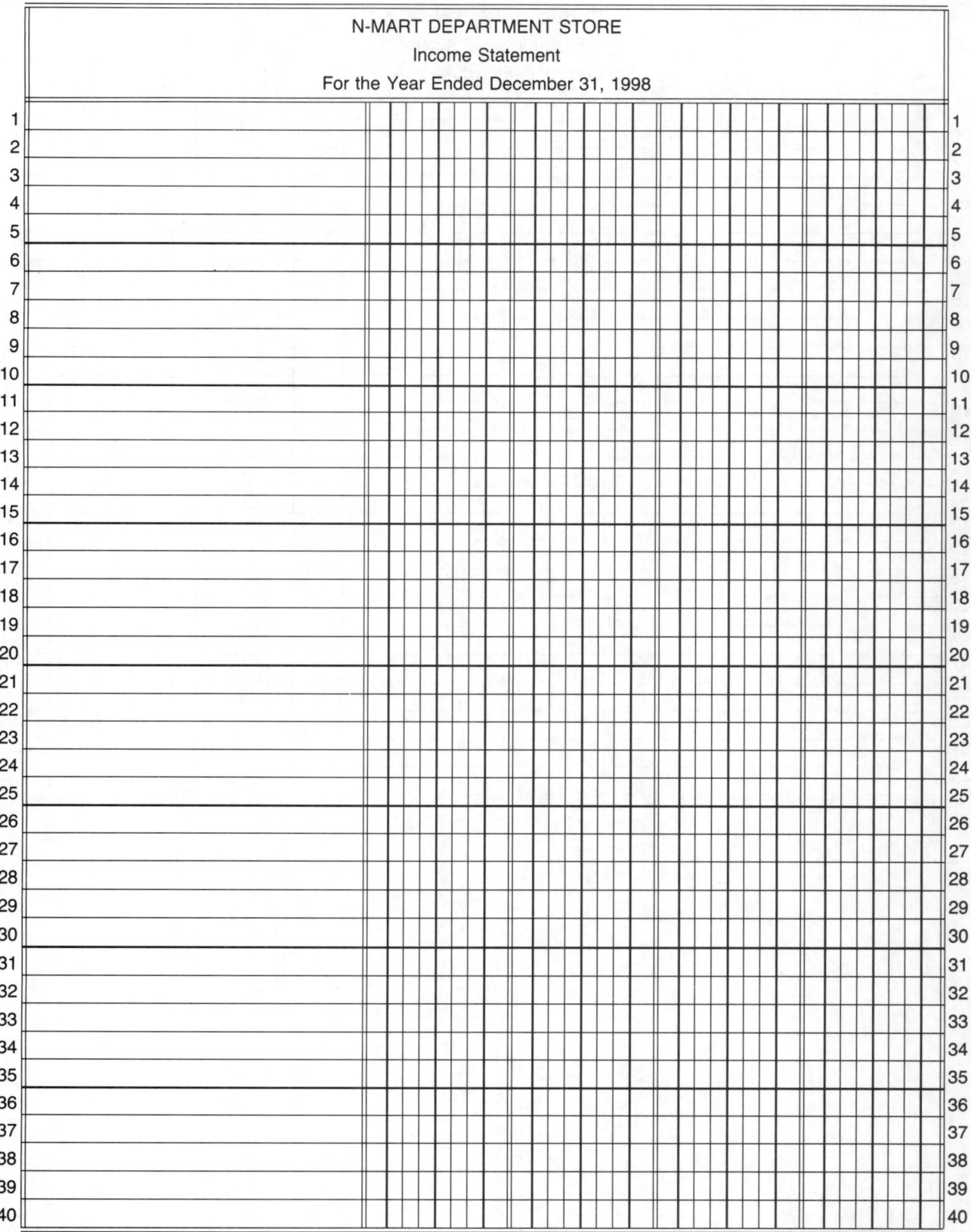

Name ____________________ **Problem 9-2A Continued**

Section ____________________

Date ____________________ **N-Mart Department Store**

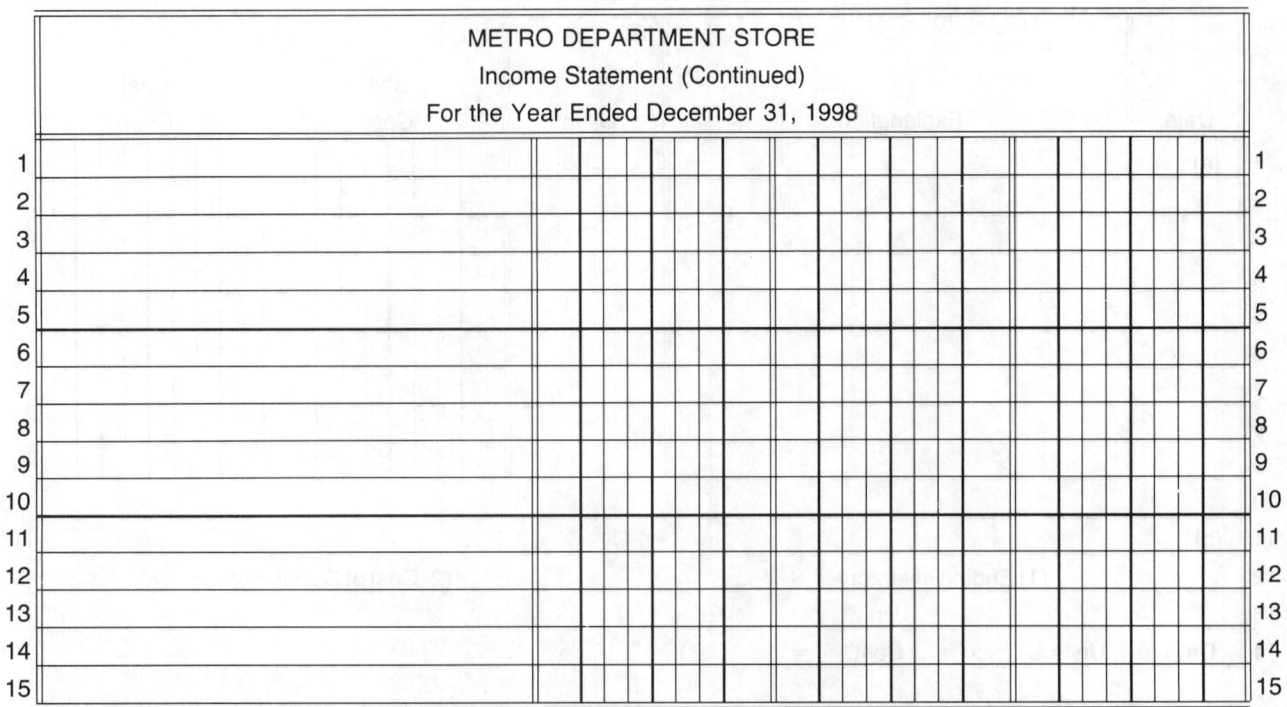

METRO DEPARTMENT STORE
Income Statement (Continued)
For the Year Ended December 31, 1998

Name Problem 9-3A

Section

Date Steward Company

(a) and (b)

Cost of Goods Available for Sale

Date	Explanation	Units	Unit Cost	Total Cost
(a)				

(b) FIFO

(1) Ending Inventory (2) Cost of Goods Sold

Date	Units	×	Unit Cost	=	Total Cost

Proof of Cost of Goods Sold

Date	Units	×	Unit Cost	=	Total Cost

LIFO

(1) Ending Inventory (2) Cost of Goods Sold

Date	Units	×	Unit Cost	=	Total Cost

(b) (Continued) and (c)

(b) (Continued) Proof of Cost of Goods Sold

Date	Units	×	Unit Cost	=	Total Cost

AVERAGE COST

(1) Ending Inventory

(2) Cost of Goods Sold

Units	×	Unit Cost	=	Total Cost

(c)

	FIFO	LIFO	Average Cost
Summary —			
Inventory value:			
Cost of goods sold:			

Name

Section

Date

Problem 9-4A

Real Novelty Inc.

(a)

REAL NOVELTY INC.
Condensed Income Statements
For the Year Ended December 31, 1998

	FIFO	LIFO

(b) (1)

(2)

(3)

(4)

(5)

Name *Problem 9-5A

Section

Date Vanessa Company

(a) February

(b) Estimated Inventory Loss

Name

Section

Date

Problem 9-6A

Martinez Department Store

(a)

	Sporting Goods		Jewelry and Cosmetics	
	Cost	Retail	Cost	Retail

(b)

Sporting Goods:

Jewelry and Cosmetics:

Name ***Problem 9-7A**

Section

Date **Family Home Appliance Mart**

Date		Purchases	Sales	Balance
(a) (1)	FIFO			
(2)	Average Cost			
(3)	LIFO			

(b)

Name

Section

Date

PepsiCo, Inc.

(a)

(b)

(c)

(d)

(e)

Name

Section

Date

MINI-CASE TWO Nike/Reebok

(a)

(b)

(c)

(d)

Name

Section

Date

Chapter 9 Decision Case

Gibson Company

(a) (1) Sales

(2) Purchases

*(b)

	1997	1996

*(c)

Name **Chapter 9 Ethics Case**

Section

Date **Chapter 9 Critical Thinking Case**

ETHICS CASE Lonergan Wholesale Company

(a)

(b)

(c)

CRITICAL THINKING CASE General Motors Corporation

(a)

(b)

(c)

Name

Section

Date

Name

Section

Date

Name

Section

Date

Name

Section

Date

Name

Section

Date

Name

Section

Date

Exercise 10-8

Mueller Company and Evert Company

Mueller Company:

Evert Company:

Name

Section

Date

Exercise 10-9

Abner's Delivery Company and Wainwright's Express Delivery

(a) Abner's Delivery Company:

(b) Wainwright's Express Delivery:

Name

Section

Date

Exercises 10-10 to 10-11

#10

(a)

(b)

#11

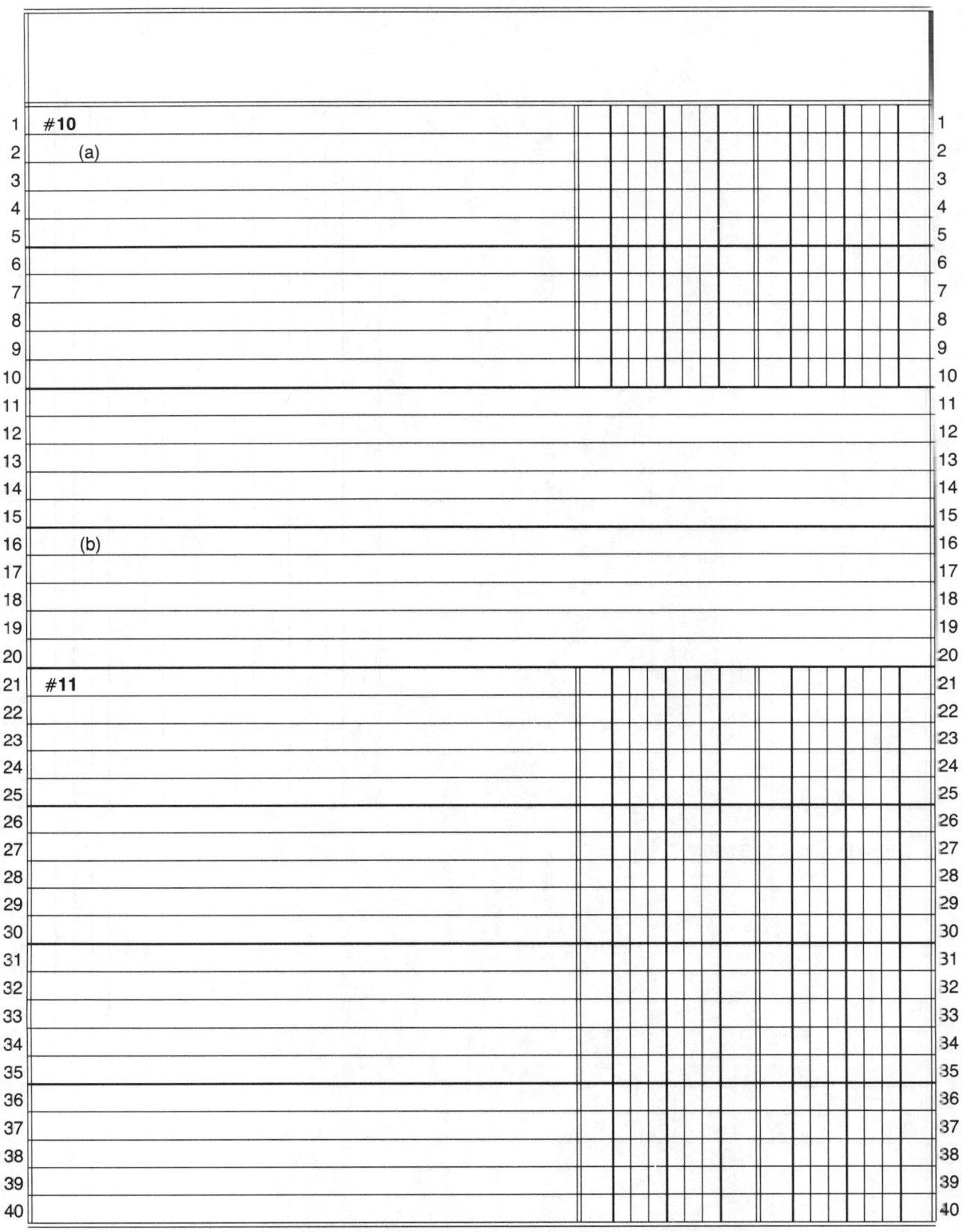

Name

Section

Date

Exercise 10-12

Collins Company

Ending balances, 12/31/96:

Name **Problem 10-1**

Section

Date **Jay Weiseman Company**

Item	Land	Building	Other Accounts	
			Amount	Title
1.				
2.				
3.				
4.				
5.				
6.				
7.				
8.				
9.				
10.				

Name
Section
Date

Problem 10-2
Wind Company

	Year	Computation	Cumulative, 12/31
(a)		MACHINE 1	
	1993		
	1994		
	1995		
	1996		
		MACHINE 2	
	1994		
	1995		
	1996		
		MACHINE 3	
	1996		
(b)		MACHINE 2	Expense
	(1) 1994		
	(2) 1995		

Name

Section

Date

Problem 10-4 Continued

Jerry Hamsmith Corporation

(a) (Continued) and (b)

General Journal

Date	Account Titles and Explanation	Ref.	Debit	Credit
(b)				

Name

Section

Date

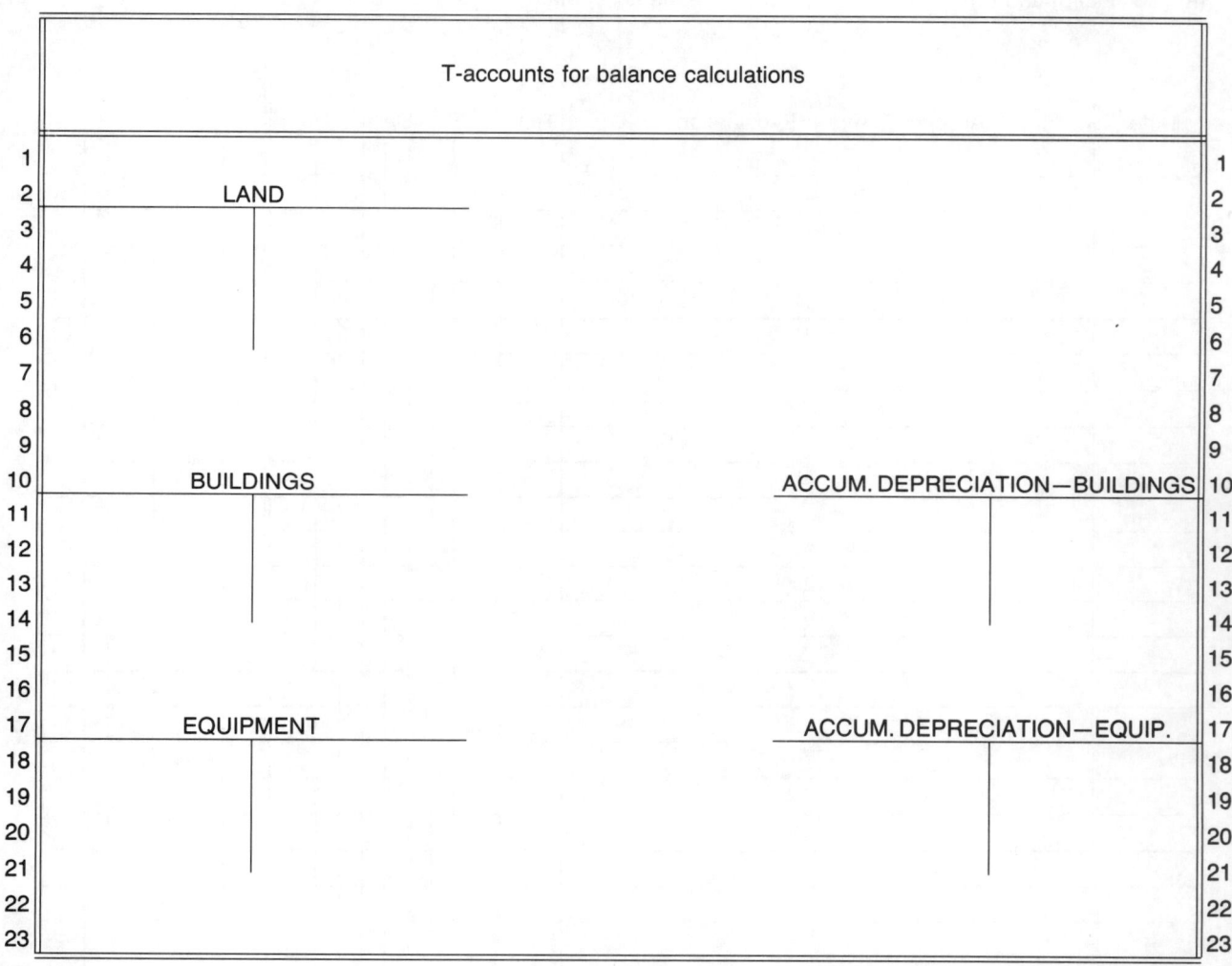

T-accounts for balance calculations

LAND

BUILDINGS

ACCUM. DEPRECIATION—BUILDINGS

EQUIPMENT

ACCUM. DEPRECIATION—EQUIP.

(c)

JERRY HAMSMITH CORPORATION

Partial Balance Sheet

December 31, 1997

Name **Problem 10-5**

Section

Date **Express Co.**

General Journal

Date	Account Titles and Explanation	Ref.	Debit	Credit
(a)				
(b)				
(c)				
(d)				

Name — Problem 10-5 Concluded

Section

Date — Express Co.

General Journal

Date	Account Titles and Explanation	Ref.	Debit	Credit
(d)	(Continued)			
(e)				

Name

Section

Date

Problem 10-6

Roberts Corporation

General Journal

Date	Account Titles and Explanation	Debit	Credit
(a)			
(b)			

(c)

(d)

Name | **Problem 10-7**

Section

Date | **Riley Corporation**

General Journal

	Account Titles and Explanation	Debit	Credit
1.			
2.			

Name

Section

Date

Problem 10-1A

Julie Kadlec Company

Item	Land	Building	Other Accounts Amount	Other Accounts Title
1.				
2.				
3.				
4.				
5.				
6.				
7.				
8.				
9.				
10.				

Name | **Problem 10-2A**

Section

Date | **Rapid Transportation**

Year	Computation	Cumulative, 12/31
(a)	BUS 1	
1994		
1995		
1996		
	BUS 2	
1994		
1995		
1996		
	BUS 3	
1995		
1996		
(b)	BUS 2	Expense
(1) 1994		
(2) 1995		

Name **Problem 10-3A**

Section

Date **Scott Piper Corporation**

(a)

STRAIGHT-LINE DEPRECIATION

	Computation				Annual	End of Year	
Year	Depreciable Cost	×	Depreciation Rate	=	Depreciation Expense	Accum. Depreciation	Book Value
1996							
1997							
1998							
1999							
2000							

DOUBLE DECLINING-BALANCE DEPRECIATION

	Computation				Annual	End of Year	
Year	Book Value Beginning of Year	×	Depreciation Rate	=	Depreciation Expense	Accum. Depreciation	Book Value
1996							
1997							
1998							
1999							
2000							

(b) and (c)

(b)

(c)

Name — Problem 10-4A

Section

Date — Yount Corporation

(a) General Journal

Date	Account Titles and Explanation		Debit	Credit

(a) (Continued) and (b) General Journal

Date	Account Titles and Explanation		Debit	Credit
(b)				

T-accounts for balance calculations

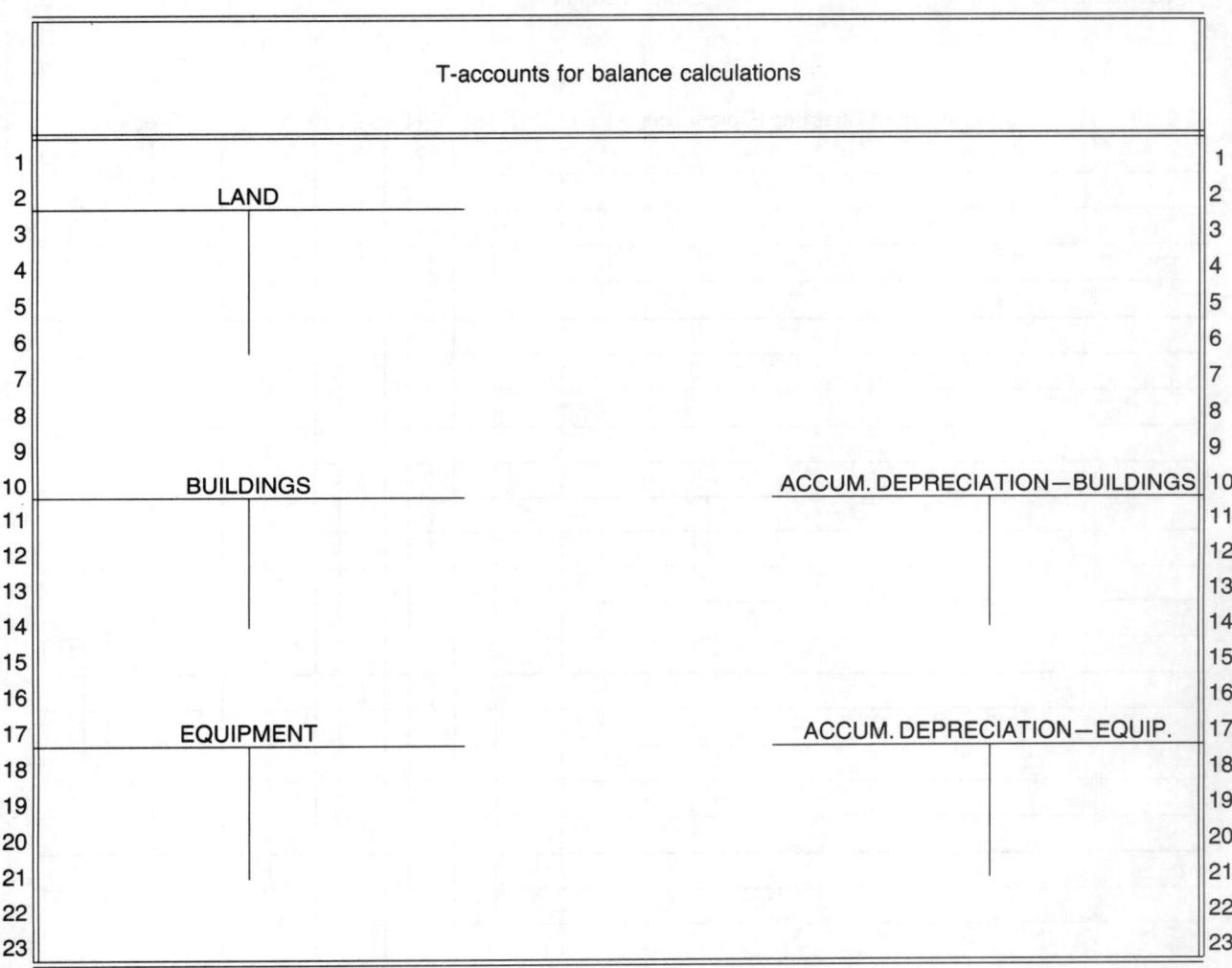

LAND

BUILDINGS

ACCUM. DEPRECIATION—BUILDINGS

EQUIPMENT

ACCUM. DEPRECIATION—EQUIP.

(c)

YOUNT CORPORATION
Partial Balance Sheet
December 31, 1997

Name | **Problem 10-5A**

Section

Date | **Walker Co.**

General Journal

Date	Account Titles and Explanation	Ref.	Debit	Credit
(a)				
(b)				
(c)				
(d)				

Name

Section

Date

Walker Co.

General Journal

Date	Account Titles and Explanation	Ref.	Debit	Credit
(d)	(Continued)			
(e)				

Name

Section

Date

Problem 10-6A

Eikel Company

General Journal

Date	Account Titles and Explanation	Debit	Credit
(a)			
(b)			
(c)			

Name
Section
Date

Problem 10-7A

Glover Company

General Journal

	Account Titles and Explanation	Debit	Credit
1.			
2.			

MINI-CASE ONE Microsoft vs Oracle

(a)

(b)

(c)

Name
Section
Date

MINI-CASE TWO Merck vs. Johnson & Johnson

(a)

(b)

(c)

(d)

MINI-CASE THREE Boeing vs. McDonnell Douglas

(a)

(b)

(c)

(d)

(a) Tammy Company — Straight-line method

Hamline Company — Double-declining-balance method

Year	Asset	Computation	Annual Depreciation	Accumulated Depreciation
1994				
1995				
1996				

(b)

Year	Tammy Co. Net Income	Hamline Co. Net Income as Adjusted	Computations for Hamline Company
1994			
1995			
1996			

(c)

Name

Section

Date

ETHICS CASE Imporia Container Company

(a)

(b)

(c)

Name

Section

Date

CRITICAL THINKING CASE Clark Equipment Company

(a)

(b)

(c)

Name

Section

Date

(a)

(b)

Name

Section

Date

Name
Section
Date

Name

Section

Date

Name

Section

Date

Name

Section

Date

***Exercise 11-13**

Cleveland Company

Period	(A) Interest to Be Paid (in Cash)	(B) Interest Expense to Be Recorded	(C) Premium Amortization	(D) Unamortized Premium	(E) Carrying Value of the Bonds

(a) Jan. 1

(b) July 1

(c) Dec. 31

Name **Problem 11-1**

Section

Date **Calcutta Company**

(a) and (b) General Journal

Date	Account Titles and Explanation	Ref.	Debit	Credit
(a)				
(b)				

(c)

CALCUTTA COMPANY

Partial Balance Sheet

January 31, 1996

Current liabilities	

Name **Problem 11-2**

Section

Date **Eldorado Company**

(a) General Journal

	Date	Account Titles and Explanation	Ref.	Debit	Credit	
1						1
2						2
3						3
4						4
5						5
6						6
7						7
8						8
9						9
10						10
11						11
12						12
13						13
14						14
15						15
16						16
17						17
18						18
19						19
20						20
21						21
22						22
23						23
24						24
25						25
26						26
27						27
28						28
29						29
30						30
31						31
32						32
33						33
34						34
35						35
36						36
37						37
38						38
39						39
40						40

(b)

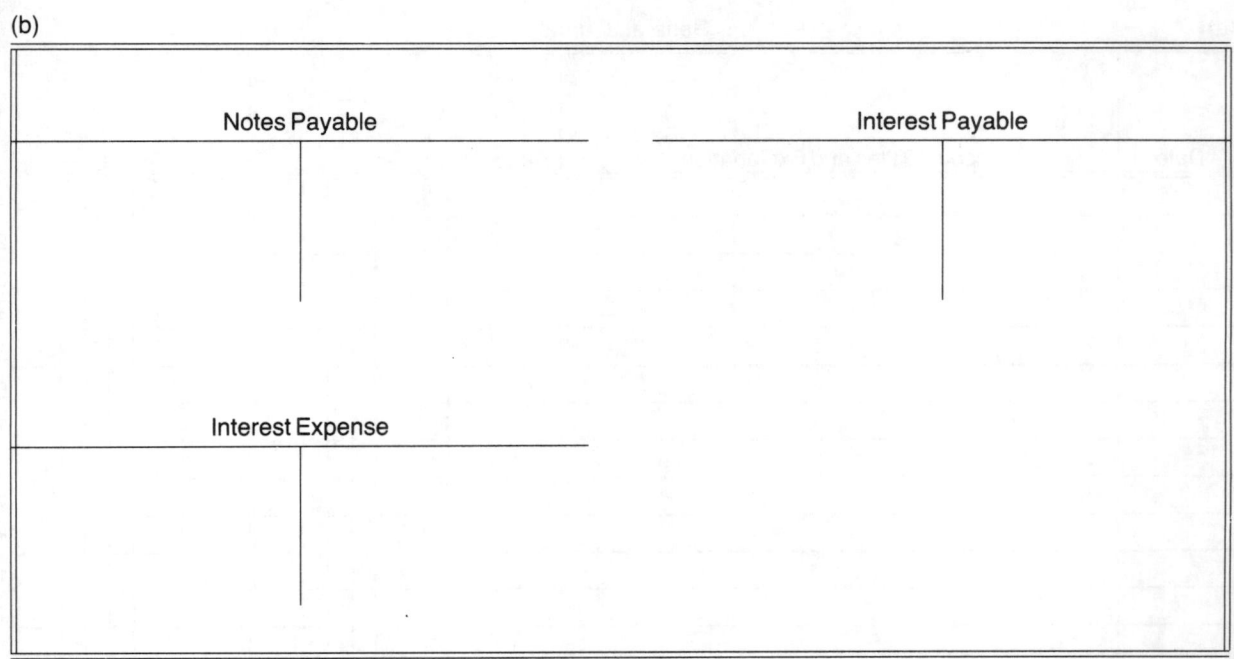

Notes Payable	

Interest Payable	

Interest Expense	

(c)

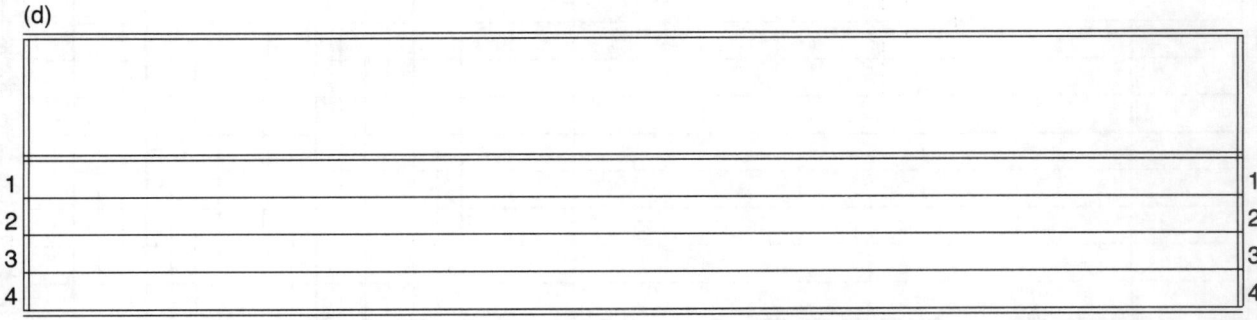

ELDORADO COMPANY
Partial Balance Sheet
December 31

1	Current liabilities			1
2				2
3				3
4				4
5				5
6				6

(d)

1		1
2		2
3		3
4		4

Name **Problem 11-6**

Section

Date **Nankin Electronics**

(a)

Semiannual Interest Period	Cash Payment	Interest Expense	Reduction of Principal	Principal Balance

(b) and (c) General Journal

Date	Account Titles and Explanation	Debit	Credit
(b)	1995		
	1996		
(c)	Current liabilities:		
	Long-term liabilities:		

Name | *Problem 11-7

Section

Date | Global Satellites

(a), (c), (d), and (e)

General Journal

	Date	Account Titles and Explanation	Debit	Credit	
1	(a)	1996			1
2					2
3					3
4					4
5					5
6					6
7	(c)				7
8					8
9					9
10					10
11					11
12					12
13					13
14	(d)	1997			14
15					15
16					16
17					17
18					18
19					19
20					20
21	(e)				21
22					22
23					23
24					24
25					25
26					26
27					27

(b)

GLOBAL SATELLITES
Bond Discount Amortization
Effective Interest Method — Semiannual Interest Payments
9% Bonds Issued at 10%

	Semiannual Interest Periods	(A) Interest to be Paid	(B) Interest Expense to be Recorded	(C) Discount Amortization	(D) Unamortized Discount	(E) Carrying Value of Bonds	
1							1
2							2
3							3
4							4
5							5
6							6

Name

Section

Date

***Problem 11-8**

Saudi Chemical Company

General Journal

Date	Account Titles and Explanation	Debit	Credit
(a) (1)	1996		
(2)			
(3)	1997		
(4)			
(b)			
(c) (1)			
(2)			
(3)			
(4)			

Name | Problem 11-1A

Section

Date | El Paso Company

(a) and (b)

General Journal

Date	Account Titles and Explanation	Ref.	Debit	Credit
(a)				
(b)				

(c)

EL PASO COMPANY
Partial Balance Sheet
January 31, 1996

Current liabilities	

Name
Section
Date

Problem 11-2A

Montego Electric

(a) and (c)

General Journal

Date	Account Titles and Explanation	Debit	Credit
(a)			
(c)	1996		
	1997		

Name

Section

Date

Problem 11-2A Concluded

Montego Electric

(b)

	Period	(A) Interest to Be Paid (in Cash)	(B) Interest Expense to Be Recorded	(C) Discount Amortization	(D) Unamortized Discount	(E) Carrying Value of the Bonds	
1							1
2							2
3							3
4							4
5							5
6							6
7							7
8							8
9							9

(d)

	MONTEGO ELECTRIC (Partial) Balance Sheet December 31, 1997			
1				1
2				2
3				3
4				4
5				5
6				6
7				7
8				8

Name **Problem 11-3A**

Section

Date **San Diego Company**

General Journal

Date	Account Titles and Explanation	Debit	Credit
(a)			
(b)			
(c)	Premium:		
	Discount:		

Name
Section
Date

Problem 11-4A

Walenda Oil Company

General Journal

Date	Account Titles and Explanation	Debit	Credit
(a)			
(b)			
(c)			
(d)			

Name | **Problem 11-5A**

Section

Date | **Elite Electronics**

(a)

Semiannual Interest	Cash Payment	Interest Expense	Reduction of Principal	Principal Balance

(b) and (c) General Journal

Date	Account Titles and Explanation	Debit	Credit
(b)	1995		
	1996		
(c)	Current liabilities:		
	Long-term liabilities:		

Name ***Problem 11-6A**

Section

Date **Mt. Vernon Corporation**

(a), (c), (d), and (e) General Journal

Date	Account Titles and Explanation	Debit	Credit
(a)	1996		
(c)			
(d)	1997		
(e)			

(b)

MT. VERNON CORPORATION
Bond Premium Amortization
Effective Interest Method — Semiannual Interest Payments
12% Bonds Issued at 10%

Semiannual Interest Periods	(A) Interest to be Paid	(B) Interest Expense	(C) Premium Amortization	(D) Unamortized Premium	(E) Carrying Value Bonds

Name | *Problem 11-7A

Section

Date | Cherokee Company

General Journal

Date	Account Titles and Explanation	Debit	Credit
(a) (1)	1996		
(2)			
(3)	1997		
(4)			
(b)			
(c) (1)			
(2)			
(3)			
(4)			

Name

Section

Date

PepsiCo, Inc., and Didde Industries, Inc.

A. PepsiCo, Inc.

(a)

(b)

(c)

Type of current liability	Amount (in 000's)

B. Didde Industries, Inc.

(a)

(b)

MINI-CASE TWO Northland Cranberries

(a)

(b)

(c)

Name

Section

Date

Jerry Mall Corporation

(a)

(b)

Name

Section

Date

Jerry Mall Corporation

(c)

Name

Section

Date

Chapter 11 Ethics Case

Chapter 11 Critical Thinking Case

ETHICS CASE Custom Medical Corporation

(a)

(b)

(c)

CRITICAL THINKING CASE Apache Corporation

(a)

(b)

Name

Section

Date

Chapter 11 Group Activity 1

Notes Payable

Sales Taxes Payable

Payroll and payroll taxes payable

Name

Section

Date

Unearned Revenues

Current Maturities of Long-Term Debt

Financial Statement Presentation

Name
Section
Date

(1) (a)

(b)

(c) Balance sheet

Income statement

(2) (a)

(b)

(c) Balance sheet

Income statement

Name

Section

Date

(3) (a)

(b)

(c) Balance sheet

Income statement

(4) (a)

(b)

(c) Balance sheet

Income statement

Name

Section

Date

Name

Section

Date

Name

Section

Date

Name

Section

Date

Name **Exercises 12-7 to 12-8**

Section

Date

Date	Account Titles and Explanation	Debit	Credit
#7			
#8			

Name

Section

Date

Exercises 12-9 to 12-10

#9 (1)

(2)

#10

	Before Action	After Stock Dividend	After Stock Split
Stockholders' equity			

Name **Exercises 12-11 to 12-12**

Section

Date

#11

#12

Name

Section

Date

#13

Account	Paid-in Capital		Retained Earnings	Other
	Capital Stock	Additional Paid-in Capital		

(a) **#15***

ALUMINIUM COMPANY OF AMERICA
(Partial) Balance Sheet
December 31, 19xx
(dollar amounts in millions)

Stockholders' equity

(b)

Name | **Exercise 12-14**
Section
Date | **Ozabal Inc.**

OZABAL INC.
(Partial) Balance Sheet
December 31

Stockholders' equity	

Name

Section

Date

#16*

(a) (b)

#17*

(a)

(b)

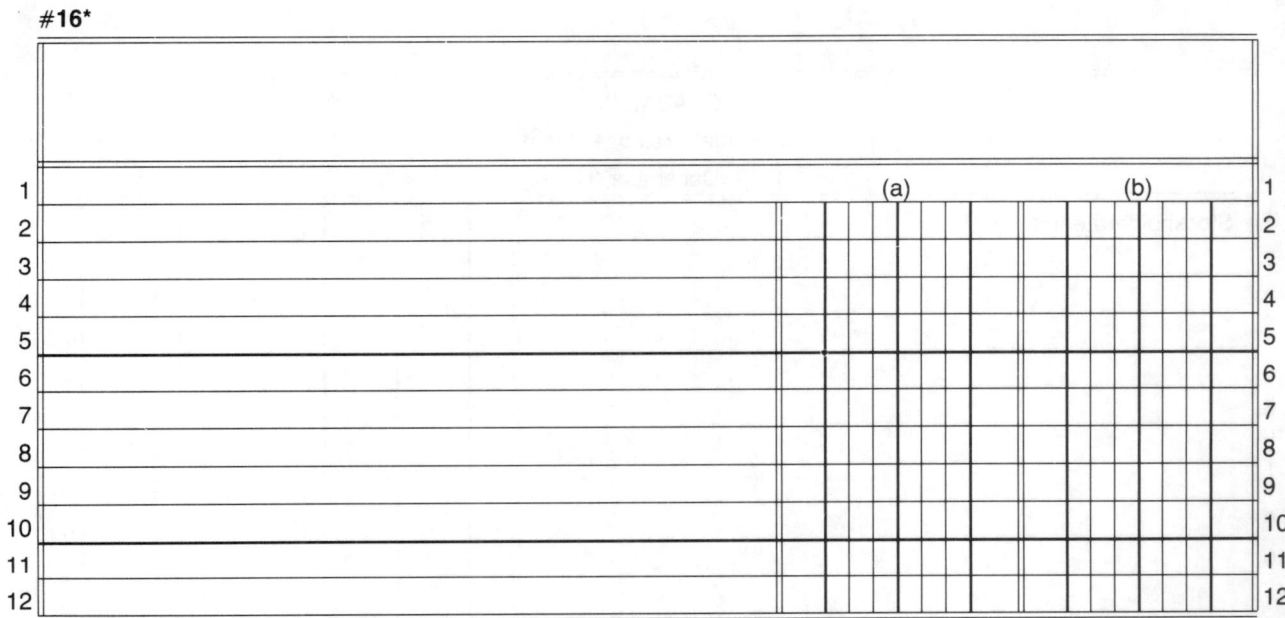

Name **Problem 12-1**

Section

Date **Jackie Remmers Corporation**

(a) General Journal J1

Date	Account Titles and Explanation	Ref.	Debit	Credit

?

Name **Problem 12-1 Continued**

Section

Date **Jackie Remmers Corporation**

(b)

Preferred Stock

	Date	Explanation	Ref.	Debit	Credit	Balance	
1							1
2							2
3							3
4							4
5							5

Paid-in Capital in Excess of Par Value — Preferred Stock

	Date	Explanation	Ref.	Debit	Credit	Balance	
1							1
2							2
3							3
4							4
5							5

Common Stock

	Date	Explanation	Ref.	Debit	Credit	Balance	
1							1
2							2
3							3
4							4
5							5
6							6
7							7
8							8

Paid-in Capital in Excess of Stated Value — Common Stock

	Date	Explanation	Ref.	Debit	Credit	Balance	
1							1
2							2
3							3
4							4
5							5
6							6
7							7
8							8

(b)

Preferred Stock

	Date	Explanation	Ref.	Debit	Credit	Balance	
1							1
2							2

Common Stock

	Date	Explanation	Ref.	Debit	Credit	Balance	
1							1
2							2
3							3
4							4

Paid-in Capital in Excess of Par Value — Preferred Stock

	Date	Explanation	Ref.	Debit	Credit	Balance	
1							1
2							2

Paid-in Capital in Excess of Stated Value — Common Stock

	Date	Explanation	Ref.	Debit	Credit	Balance	
1							1
2							2
3							3
4							4

Retained Earnings

	Date	Explanation	Ref.	Debit	Credit	Balance	
1							1
2							2
3							3

Treasury Stock — Common

	Date	Explanation	Ref.	Debit	Credit	Balance	
1							1
2							2
3							3
4							4

Paid-in Capital from Treasury Stock — Common

	Date	Explanation	Ref.	Debit	Credit	Balance	
1							1
2							2

Name

Section

Date

Problem 12-3 Concluded

Chung Corporation

(c)

CHUNG CORPORATION

(Partial) Balance Sheet

December 31, 1996

Stockholders' equity

(d)

Name **Problem 12-4**

Section

Date **V. Conway Company**

(a)

V. CONWAY COMPANY
Retained Earnings Statement
For the Year Ended December 31, 1996

(b)

V. CONWAY COMPANY
(Partial) Balance Sheet
December 31, 1996

Stockholder's equity

Name | Problem 12-5
Section
Date | Reno Corporation

(a)

RETAINED EARNINGS

(b)

RENO CORPORATION
Retained Earnings Statement
For the Year Ended December 31, 1996

(c)

RENO CORPORATION
(Partial) Balance Sheet
December 31, 1996

Stockholders' equity

Name

Section

Date

Problem 12-6

Largent Corporation

(a)

General Journal

Account Titles and Explanation	Debit	Credit
(1)		
(2)		
(3)		
(4)		

Name **Problem 12-6 Concluded**

Section

Date **Largent Corporation**

(b)

LARGENT CORPORATION

(Partial) Balance Sheet

December 31, 1996

Stockholders' equity

Name | **Problem 12-7**

Section

Date | **Wirth Corporation**

(a) General Journal

Date	Account Titles and Explanation	Debit	Credit

(b) Common Stock

Date	Explanation	Ref.	Debit	Credit	Balance

Name

Section

Date

Problem 12-7 Concluded

Wirth Corporation

(b) Continued

Paid-in Capital in Excess of Par Value

	Date	Explanation	Ref.	Debit	Credit	Balance	
1							1
2							2
3							3

Retained Earnings

	Date	Explanation	Ref.	Debit	Credit	Balance	
1							1
2							2
3							3
4							4
5							5
6							6

Common Stock Dividends Distributable

	Date	Explanation	Ref.	Debit	Credit	Balance	
1							1
2							2
3							3

(c)

WIRTH CORPORATION
(Partial) Balance Sheet
December 31, 1997

1	Stockholders' equity			1
2				2
3				3
4				4
5				5
6				6
7				7
8				8
9				9
10				10
11				11
12				12
13				13
14				14
15				15

Name *Problem 12-8

Section

Date Dublin Corporation

(a)

DUBLIN CORPORATION
(Partial) Balance Sheet
December 31, 1996

Stockholders' equity

(b)

Name *Problem 12-9

Section

Date **Cedeno Inc.**

CEDENO INC.
Stockholders' Equity Statement
For the Year Ending December 31, 1996
(in thousands)

	Common Stock	Paid-in Capital in Excess of Par Value	Stock Dividends Distrib-utable	Treasury Stock	Retained Earnings	Total

Name

Section

Date

Problem 12-1A

Wetland Corporation

(a) General Journal J5

Date	Account Titles and Explanation	Ref.	Debit	Credit

Name

Section

Date

Problem 12-1A Continued

Wetland Corporation

(b)

Preferred Stock

	Date	Explanation	Ref.	Debit	Credit	Balance	
1							1
2							2
3							3

Paid-in Capital in Excess of Par Value — Preferred Stock

	Date	Explanation	Ref.	Debit	Credit	Balance	
1							1
2							2
3							3

Common Stock

	Date	Explanation	Ref.	Debit	Credit	Balance	
1							1
2							2
3							3
4							4
5							5
6							6
7							7

Paid-in Capital in Excess of Stated Value — Common Stock

	Date	Explanation	Ref.	Debit	Credit	Balance	
1							1
2							2
3							3
4							4
5							5
6							6
7							7

Name | **Problem 12-1A Concluded**

Section

Date | **Wetland Corporation**

(c)

WETLAND CORPORATION
(Partial) Balance Sheet
December 31, 1996

Stockholders' equity		

Name | **Problem 12-2A**

Section

Date | **Rena Rhoda Corporation**

(a) General Journal J10

Date	Account Titles and Explanation	Ref.	Debit	Credit

(b) Paid-in Capital from Treasury Stock

Date	Explanation	Ref.	Debit	Credit	Balance

(b) (Continued)

Treasury Stock

Date	Explanation	Ref.	Debit	Credit	Balance

Retained Earnings

Date	Explanation	Ref.	Debit	Credit	Balance

(c)

RENA RHODA CORPORATION
(Partial) Balance Sheet
December 31, 1996

Stockholders' equity		

Name **Problem 12-3A**

Section

Date **Capozza Corporation**

(a) General Journal J5

Date	Account Titles and Explanation	Ref.	Debit	Credit

(b)

Preferred Stock

	Date	Explanation	Ref.	Debit	Credit	Balance	
1							1
2							2

Common Stock

	Date	Explanation	Ref.	Debit	Credit	Balance	
1							1
2							2
3							3
4							4

Paid-in Capital in Excess of Par Value — Preferred Stock

	Date	Explanation	Ref.	Debit	Credit	Balance	
1							1
2							2

Paid-in Capital in Excess of Stated Value — Common Stock

	Date	Explanation	Ref.	Debit	Credit	Balance	
1							1
2							2
3							3
4							4

Retained Earnings

	Date	Explanation	Ref.	Debit	Credit	Balance	
1							1
2							2
3							3

Treasury Stock — Common

	Date	Explanation	Ref.	Debit	Credit	Balance	
1							1
2							2
3							3
4							4

Paid-in Capital from Treasury Stock — Common

	Date	Explanation	Ref.	Debit	Credit	Balance	
1							1
2							2

(c)

CAPOZZA CORPORATION
(Partial) Balance Sheet
December 31, 1996

Stockholders' equity

(d)

Name

Section

Date

Problem 12-4A

Casey Stengel Corporation

(a) General Journal

Date	Account Titles and Explanation	Debit	Credit

(b) Common Stock

Date	Explanation	Ref.	Debit	Credit	Balance

Name

Section

Date

Problem 12-4A Concluded

Casey Stengel Corporation

(b) (Continued)

Paid-in Capital in Excess of Par Value

	Date	Explanation	Ref.	Debit	Credit	Balance	
1							1
2							2
3							3

Retained Earnings

	Date	Explanation	Ref.	Debit	Credit	Balance	
1							1
2							2
3							3
4							4
5							5
6							6

Common Stock Dividends Distributable

	Date	Explanation	Ref.	Debit	Credit	Balance	
1							1
2							2
3							3

(c)

CASEY STENGEL CORPORATION

(Partial) Balance Sheet

December 31, 1996

1	Stockholders' equity			1
2				2
3				3
4				4
5				5
6				6
7				7
8				8
9				9
10				10
11				11
12				12
13				13
14				14
15				15

Name

Section

Date

Problem 12-5A

K. Schipper Company

(c)

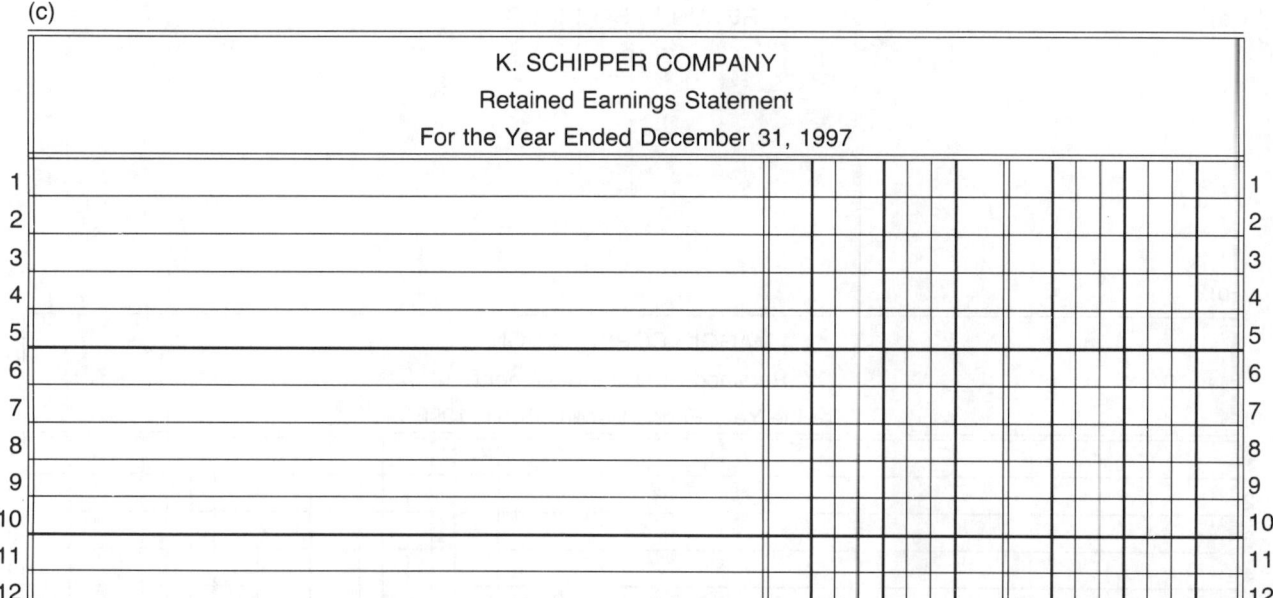

K. SCHIPPER COMPANY
Retained Earnings Statement
For the Year Ended December 31, 1997

(d)

K. SCHIPPER COMPANY
(Partial) Balance Sheet
December 31, 1997

Stockholder's equity

Name | Problem 12-6A

Section

Date | Maggio Corporation

(a)

RETAINED EARNINGS

(b)

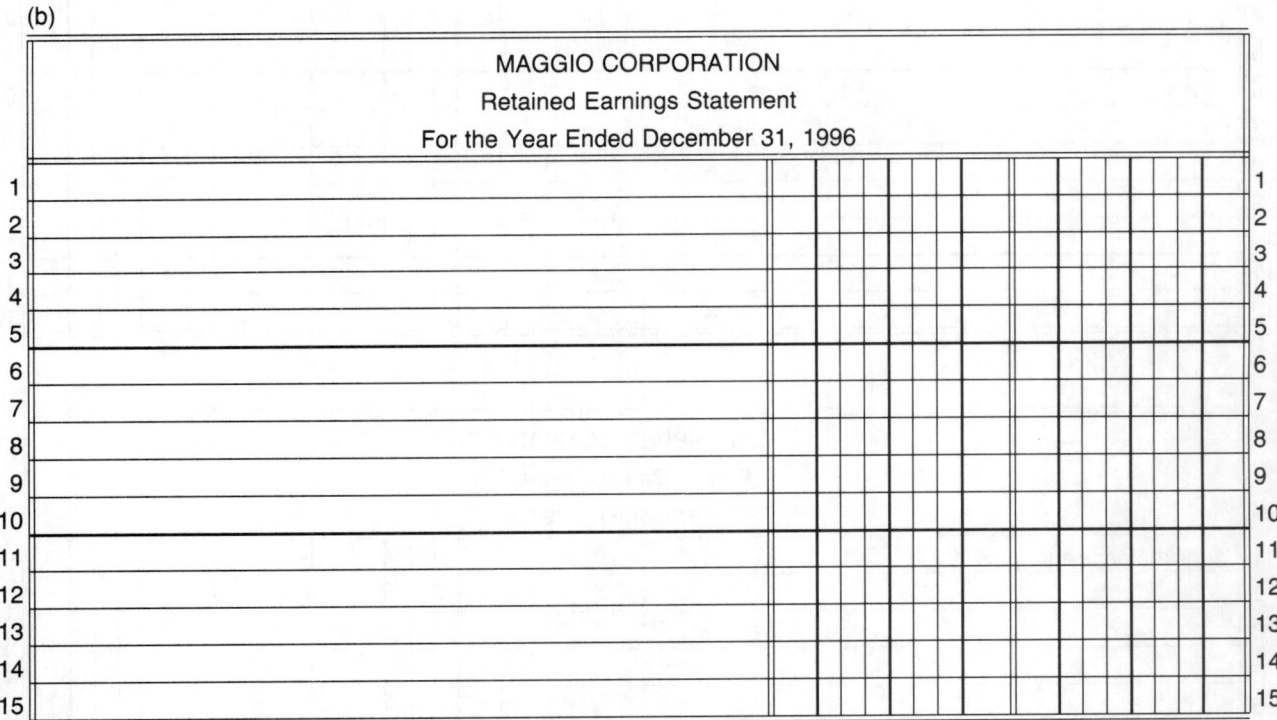

MAGGIO CORPORATION
Retained Earnings Statement
For the Year Ended December 31, 1996

1			1
2			2
3			3
4			4
5			5
6			6
7			7
8			8
9			9
10			10
11			11
12			12
13			13
14			14
15			15

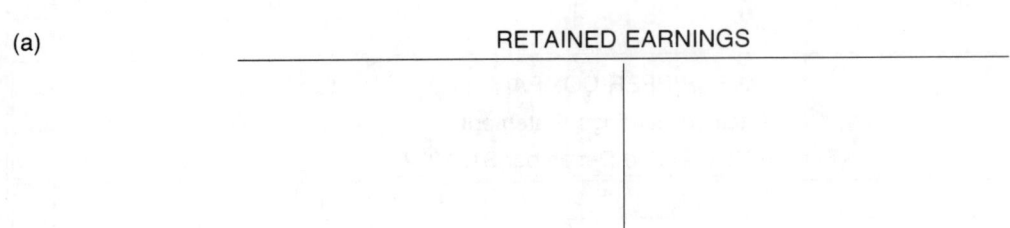

Name

Section

Date

Problem 12-6A Concluded

Maggio Corporation

(c)

MAGGIO CORPORATION

(Partial) Balance Sheet

December 31, 1996

1	Stockholders' equity			1
2				2
3				3
4				4
5				5
6				6
7				7
8				8
9				9
10				10
11				11
12				12
13				13
14				14
15				15
16				16
17				17
18				18
19				19
20				20
21				21
22				22
23				23
24				24
25				25
26				26
27				27
28				28
29				29
30				30
31				31
32				32
33				33
34				34
35				35

Name *Problem 12-7A

Section

Date Shirley Denson Corporation

(a)

SHIRLEY DENSON CORPORATION

(Partial) Balance Sheet

December 31, 1996

Stockholders' equity

(b)

Name

Section

Date

ETHICS CASE A Simplex Chemical Corporation

(a)

(b)

(c)

CRITICAL THINKING CASE A Diebold, Incorporated

(a)

(b)

(c)

ETHICS CASE B Flambeau Corporation

(a)

(b)

(c)

CRITICAL THINKING CASE B Barrister Information Systems Corp.

(a)

(b)

Name

Section

Date

Honest and Accurate CPAs

(a) 1.

2.

(b) 1.

2.

Name

Section

Date

Name

Section

Date

Name

Section

Date

Name

Section

Date

Exercises 13-1 to 13-2

Date	Account Titles and Explanation	Debit	Credit
#1			
#2			

Name **Exercises 13-3 to 13-4**

Section

Date

Date	Account Titles and Explanation	Debit	Credit
#3			
#4			

Name

Section

Date

Exercises 13-5 to 13-6

Date	Account Titles and Explanation	Debit	Credit
#5			
#6			

Name

Section

Date

Exercise 13-7

Nielson, Inc.

(a) and (b)

(a)

(b)

(c)

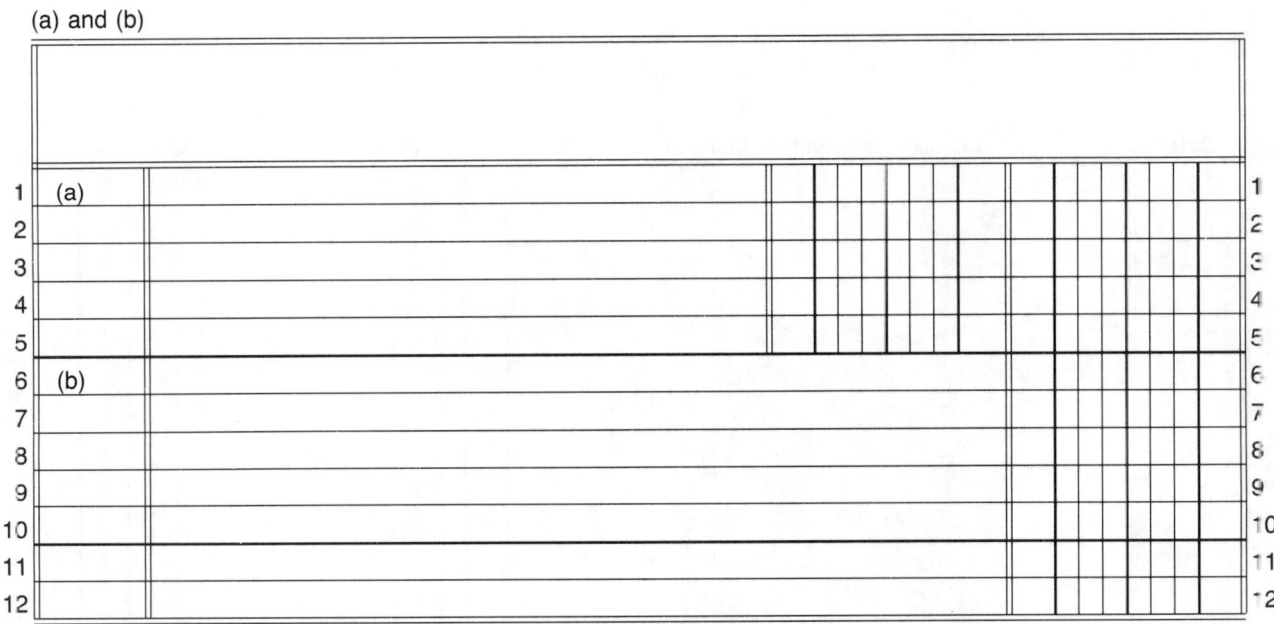

Name

Section

Date

Exercise 13-8

Felipe Company

Date	Account Titles and Explanation	Debit	Credit

Name

Section

Date

***Exercises 13-9 to 13-10**

SWISS CORPORATION AND SUBSIDIARY
Worksheet — Consolidated Balance Sheet
January 1, 1996

	Swiss Corporation	Arco, Inc.	Eliminations		Consolidated Data
			Debit	Credit	
#9					
#10					

Name

Section

Date

Problem 13-1

Lund Corporation

(a) and (b)

General Journal

Date	Account Titles and Explanation	Debit	Credit
(a)	1996		
	1997		
(b)	1996		

(c)

Name

Section

Date

Problem 13-2

Reed Company

(a)

General Journal

Date	Account Titles and Explanation	Debit	Credit

STOCK INVESTMENTS

DEBT INVESTMENTS

Name
Section
Date

(b)

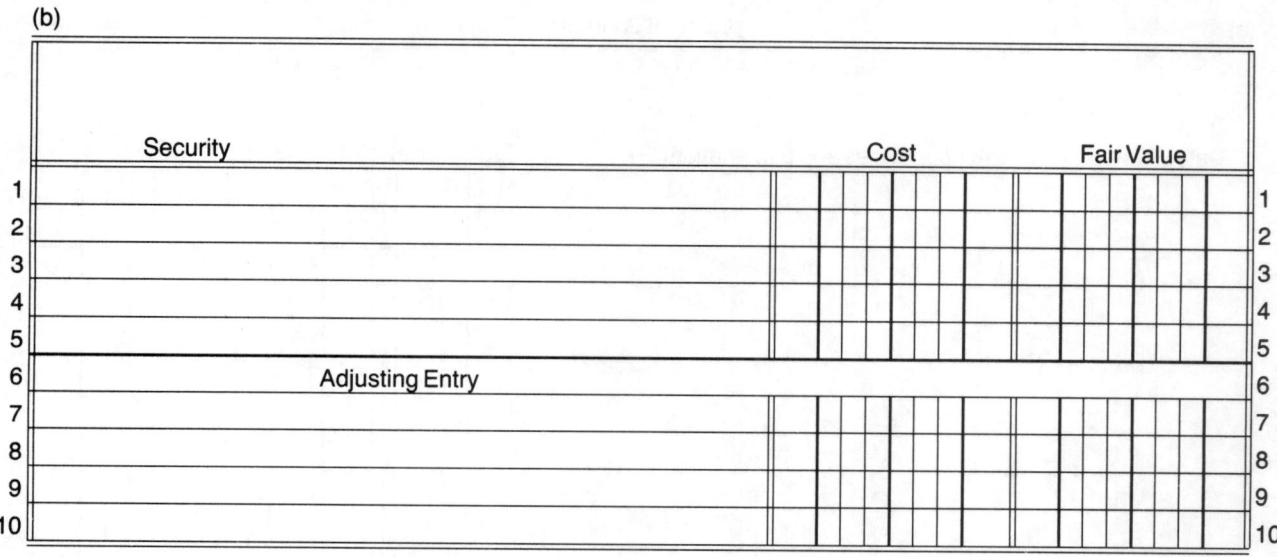

Security	Cost	Fair Value
Adjusting Entry		

(c) and (d)

(c)

(d)

Name **Problem 13-3**

Section

Date **Harmon Associates**

(a) General Journal

Date	Account Titles and Explanation	Debit	Credit

STOCK INVESTMENTS

Name

Section

Date

Problem 13-3 Concluded

Harmon Associates

(b)

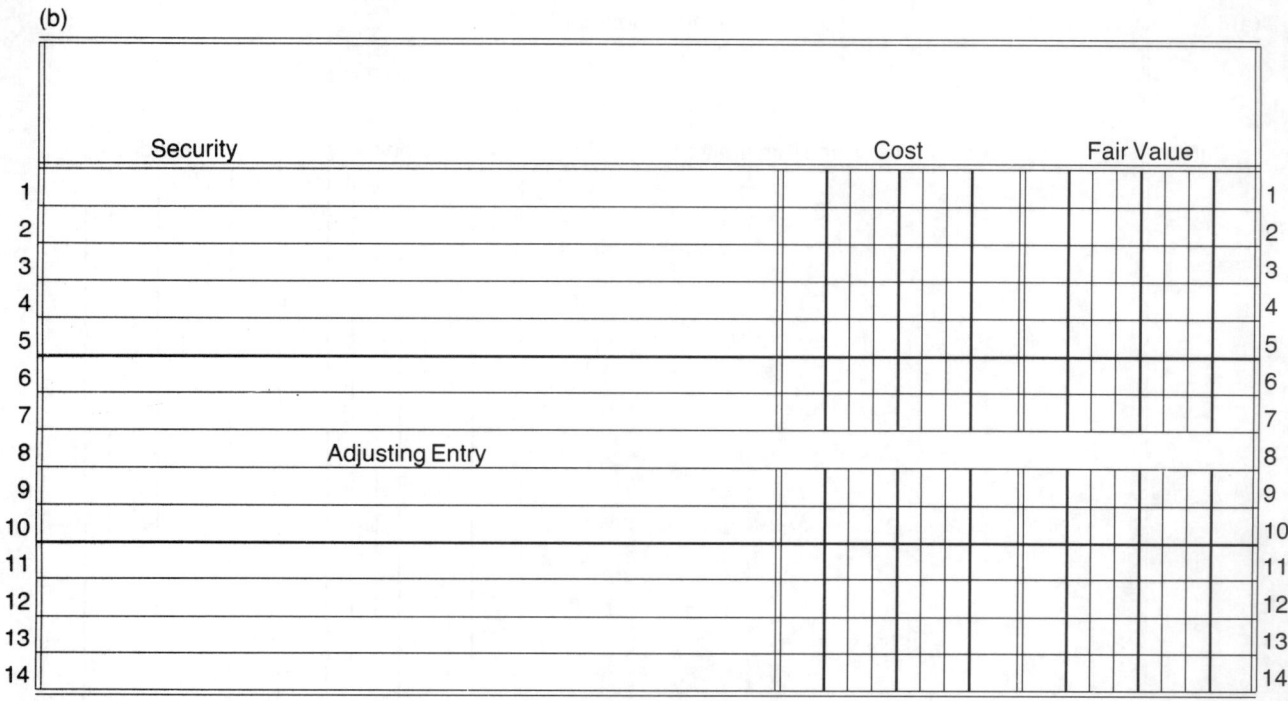

Security	Cost	Fair Value

Adjusting Entry

(c)

Balance Sheet Presentation at December 31, 1996

Investments

Stockholders' Equity

Name

Section

Date

Problem 13-4

Cardinal Concrete

(a) and (b)

General Journal

Date	Account Titles and Explanation	Debit	Credit
(a)	1996		
(b)	1996		

Name

Section

Date

Problem 13-4 Concluded

Cardinal Concrete

(c)

	Cost Method	Equity Method

Name **Problem 13-5**

Section

Date **Hi-Tech Company**

(a) General Journal

Date	Account Titles and Explanation	Debit	Credit

(b)

Investment in Awixa Corporation Common Stock		Investment in HAL Corporation Common Stock	

(b) (Continued)

Investment in Renda Corporation Preferred Stock	

Investment in Mintor Corporation Common Stock	

(c)

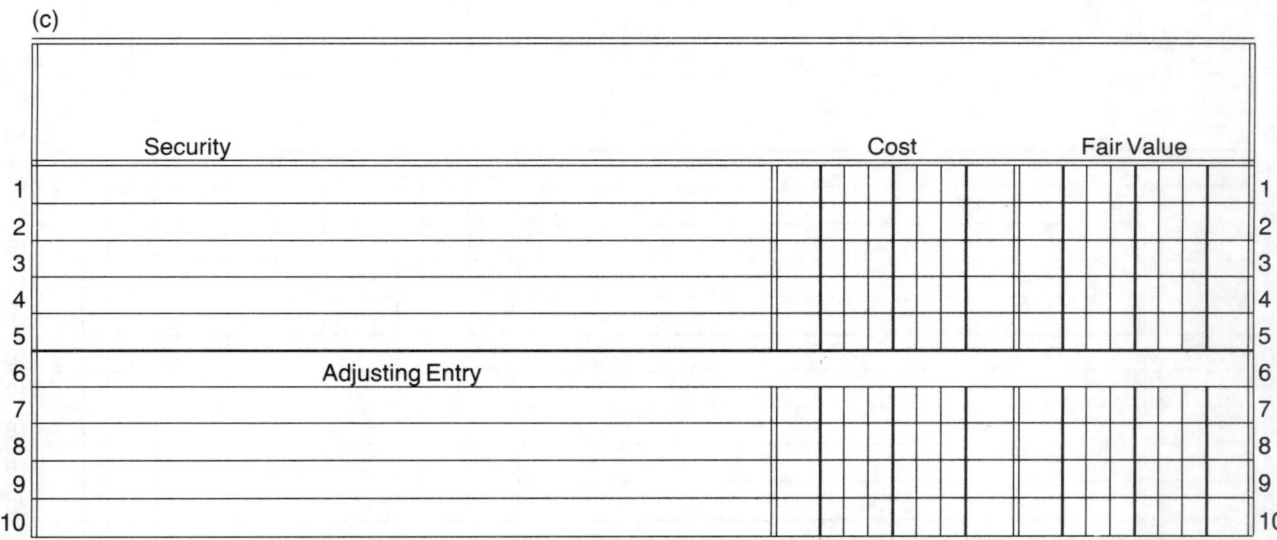

	Security	Cost	Fair Value	
1				1
2				2
3				3
4				4
5				5
6	Adjusting Entry			6
7				7
8				8
9				9
10				10

(d)

	Balance Sheet Presentation at December 31, 1996			
1	Investments			1
2				2
3				3
4				4
5				5
6	Stockholders' Equity			6
7				7
8				8
9				9
10				10
11				11
12				12

Name

Section

Date

Problem 13-6

Oklahoma Corporation

OKLAHOMA CORPORATION

Consolidated Balance Sheet

December 31, 1996

Assets				

Name **Problem 13-6 Concluded**

Section

Date **Oklahoma Corporation**

OKLAHOMA CORPORATION

Consolidated Balance Sheet (continued)

December 31, 1996

Liabilities and Stockholders' Equity		

Name ***Problem 13-7**

Section

Date **Neal Company**

(a) General Journal

Date	Account Titles and Explanation	Debit	Credit

(c)

NEAL COMPANY AND SUBSIDIARY
Consolidated Balance Sheet
December 31, 1996

Assets

Liabilities and Stockholders' Equity

Name

Section

Date

***Problem 13-7 Concluded**

Neal Company

(b)

NEAL COMPANY AND SUBSIDIARY
Work Sheet — Consolidated Balance Sheet
December 31, 1996

	Neal Company	Wheaton Company	Eliminations Dr.	Eliminations Cr.	Consolidated Data
Assets					
Liabilities and Stock-holders' Equity					

Name **Problem 13-1A**

Section

Date **Givarz Corporation**

(a) and (b) General Journal

Date	Account Titles and Explanation	Debit	Credit
(a)	1996		
	1997		
(b)	1996		

(c)

Name

Section

Date

Problem 13-2A

Mead Company

(a) General Journal

Date	Account Titles and Explanation	Debit	Credit

STOCK INVESTMENTS

DEBT INVESTMENTS

Name

Section

Date

Problem 13-2A Concluded

Mead Company

(b)

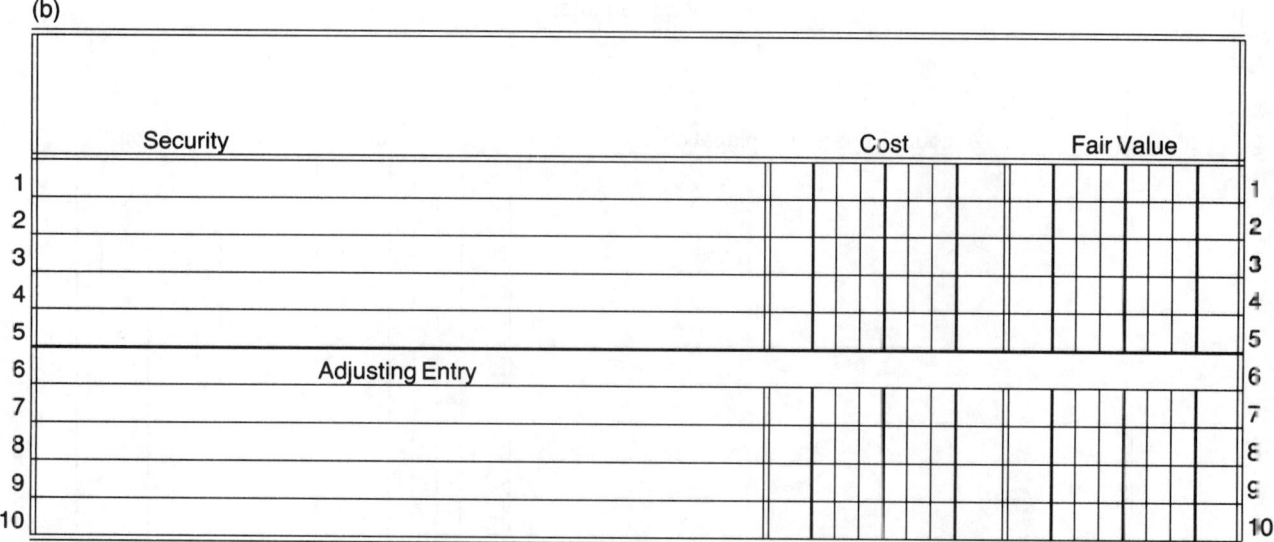

Security	Cost	Fair Value
Adjusting Entry		

(c) and (d)

(c)	
(d)	

Name **Problem 13-3A**

Section

Date **Karen Associates**

(a) General Journal

Date	Account Titles and Explanation	Debit	Credit

STOCK INVESTMENTS

Name **Problem 13-3A Concluded**

Section

Date **Karen Associates**

(b)

Security	Cost	Fair Value
Adjusting Entry		

(c)

Balance Sheet Presentation at December 31, 1997

Investments		
Stockholders' Equity		

Name **Problem 13-4A**

Section

Date **DFM Services**

(a) and (b) General Journal

Date	Account Titles and Explanation	Debit	Credit
(a)			
(b)			

Name

Section

Date

Problem 13-4A Concluded

DFM Services

(c)

			Cost Method	Equity Method	
1					1
2					2
3					3
4					4
5					5
6					6
7					7
8					8
9					9
10					10

Name

Section

Date

Problem 13-5A

Alameda Corporation

ALAMEDA CORPORATION
Consolidated Balance Sheet
December 31, 1996

Assets

ALAMEDA CORPORATION
Consolidated Balance Sheet (continued)
December 31, 1996

Liabilities and Stockholders' Equity

Name

Section

Date

***Problem 13-6A**

Linger Corporation

(a)

General Journal

Date	Account Titles and Explanation	Debit	Credit

(c)

LINGER CORPORATION AND SUBSIDIARY

Consolidated Balance Sheet

December 31, 1996

Assets		
Liabilities and Stockholders' Equity		

Name *Problem 13-6A Concluded

Section

Date **Linger Corporation**

(b)

LINGER CORPORATION AND SUBSIDIARY
Work Sheet — Consolidated Balance Sheet
December 31, 1996

	Linger Corporation	Chrissy Foods	Eliminations Dr.	Eliminations Cr.	Consolidated Data
Assets					
Liabilities and Stock-					
holders' Equity					

Name

Section

Date

PepsiCo, Inc.

(a)

	1995	1994

(b)

(c)

(d)

(e)

Name

Section

Date

The Coca-Cola Company vs. PepsiCo, Inc.

(a)	Coca-Cola	PepsiCo.
1. Cash used in investing activities		
2. Cash used for acquisitions and investments		
3. Total investments in unconsolidated affiliates at December 31, 1995		

(b)

Name
Section
Date

MINI-CASE ONE Key Corp.

(a)

(b)

(c)

(d)

Name

Section

Date

Chapter 13 Decision Case

Revell Corporation

Name
Section
Date

Name

Section

Date

ETHICS CASE Scott Krieter Financial Services Company

CRITICAL THINKING CASE SPS Technologies, Inc.

Name

Section

Date

(a)

(b)

(c)

Name

Section

Date

Name

Section

Date

Name

Section

Date

Balance Sheet Accounts	Balance 1/1/96	Reconciling Items Debit	Reconciling Items Credit	Balance 12/31/96
Statement of Cash Flows Effects				

Name

Section

Date

Exercises 14-1 to 14-2

#1

#2

Name **Problem 14-3**

Section

Date **Vail Company**

(Direct)

VAIL COMPANY

(Partial) Statement of Cash Flows

For the Year Ended December 31, 1996

Cash flows from operating activities

Computations—

(1) Cash receipts from customers:

(2) Cash payments for operating expesnes:

(3) Cash payments for income taxes:

Name Problem 14-4

Section

Date Vail Company

(Indirect)

VAIL COMPANY

(Partial) Statement of Cash Flows

For the Year Ended December 31, 1996

Cash flows from operating activities

Name

Section

Date

Problem 14-8

Fern Galenti, Inc.

(Direct)

FERN GALENTI, INC.

Statement of Cash Flows

For the Year Ended December 31, 1996

Name

Section

Date

Problem 14-8 Concluded

Fern Galenti, Inc.

Computations—

(1) Cash receipts from customers:

(2) Cash payments to suppliers:

(3) Cash payments for operating expenses:

Computation of loss on sale of plant assets—

Name **Problem 14-1A**

Section

Date **Tina Maria Company**

(Indirect)

TINA MARIA COMPANY
(Partial) Statement of Cash Flows
For the Year Ended December 31, 1996

Cash flows from operating activities

Name | Problem 14-2A
Section
Date | Tina Maria Company

(Direct)

TINA MARIA COMPANY
(Partial) Statement of Cash Flows
For the Year Ended December 31, 1996

Computations—

(1) Cash receipts from customers:

(2) Cash payments to suppliers:

(3) Cash payments for operating expenses:

Name

Section

Date

Problem 14-3A

Hanalei International Inc.

(Direct)

HANALEI INTERNATIONAL INC.

(Partial) Statement of Cash Flows

For the Year Ended December 31, 1996

Computations—

(1) Cash receipts from customers:

(2) Cash payments for operating expenses:

(3) Cash payments for income taxes:

Name **Problem 14-4A**

Section

Date **Hanalei International Inc.**

(Indirect)

HANALEI INTERNATIONAL INC.
(Partial) Statement of Cash Flows
For the Year Ended December 31, 1996

Cash flows from operating activities

Name | Problem 14-5A
Section
Date | Sean Seymor Company

(a) | (Indirect)

SEAN SEYMOR COMPANY
Statement of Cash Flows
For the Year Ended December 31, 1996

(b)

1.

2.

3.

Name

Section

Date

Problem 14-6A

Sean Seymor Company

(Direct)

SEAN SEYMOR COMPANY

Statement of Cash Flows

For the Year Ended December 31, 1996

Computations —

(1) Cash receipts from customers:

Name

Section

Date

Problem 14-6A Concluded

Sean Seymor Company

(a) (Continued)

Computations (continued)

(2) Cash payments to suppliers:

(3) Cash payments for income taxes:

(b)

1.

2.

3.

Name

Section

Date

Problem 14-7A

Norway Company

NORWAY COMPANY

Statement of Cash Flows

For the Year Ended December 31, 1996

Cash proceeds from sale of plant assets—

Name

Section

Date

Problem 14-8A

Norway Company

(Direct)

NORWAY COMPANY

Statement of Cash Flows

For the Year Ended December 31, 1996

Name
Section
Date

Norway Company

Computations—

(1) Cash receipts from customers:

(2) Cash payments to suppliers:

(3) Cash payments for operating expenses:

Cash proceeds from sale of plant assets—

Name

Section

Date

Problem 14-9A

Cortina Company

(Indirect)

CORTINA COMPANY

Statement of Cash Flows

For the Year Ended December 31, 1996

Name *Problem 14-10A

Section

Date **Norway Company**

NORWAY COMPANY
Work Sheet — Statement of Cash Flows
For the Year Ended December 31, 1996

Balance Sheet Accounts	Balance 12/31/95	Reconciling Items Debit	Reconciling Items Credit	Balance 12/31/96
Debits				
Credits				
Statement of Cash Flows Effects				

Name

Section

Date

Chapter 14 Financial Reporting Problem

PepsiCo, Inc.

(a)

(b)

(c)

(d)

(e)

(f)

(g)

Name

Section

Date

Chapter 14 Comparative Analysis Problem

The Coca-Cola Company vs. PepsiCo, Inc.

(a)	Coca-Cola	PepsiCo.
1. Current cash debt coverage		
2. Cash return on sales		
3. Cash debt coverage		

(b)

Name

Section

Date

MINI-CASE ONE Mattel Corporation

(a)

(b)

MINI-CASE TWO Vermont Teddy Bear Co.

(a)

(b)

(a)

(b)

L. L. BEAN TRADING COMPANY
Statement of Cash Flows
For the Year Ended January 31, 1997

(b) (Continued)

L. L. BEAN TRADING COMPANY
Statement of Cash Flows
For the Year Ended January 31, 1997

Computation of net income (loss)—

Name | **Chapter 14 Ethics Case**

Section

Date | **Chapter 14 Critical Thinking Case**

ETHICS CASE Puebla Corporation

(a)

(b)

(c)

CRITICAL THINKING CASE Praxair Incorporated

(a)

(b)

(c)

Name

Section

Date

(a) For a severely financially troubled firm:

Operating—

Investing—

Financing—

(b) For a recently formed firm that is experiencing rapid growth:

Operating—

Investing—

Financing—

Name

Section

Date

Name

Section

Date

Name

Section

Date

Name

Section

Date

Name

Section

Date

Name

Section

Date

Name

Section

Date

Exercises 15-1 to 15-2

#1

Horizontal Analysis

MERCHANDISE INC.
Condensed Balance Sheet
December 31,

	1996	1995	Increase (Decrease)	
			Amount	Percent

#2

Vertical Analysis

FLEETWOOD CORPORATION
Condensed Income Statements
For the Years Ended December 31,

	1997		1996	
	Amount	Percent	Amount	Percent

Name   **Exercise 15-3**

Section

Date   **Oklahoma Corporation**

(a) Horizontal Analysis

OKLAHOMA CORPORATION
Comparative Balance Sheet
December 31,

	1996	1995	Increase (Decrease)	
			Amount	Percent

(b) Vertical Analysis

OKLAHOMA CORPORATION
Comparative Balance Sheets
December 31,

	1997		1996	
	Amount	Percent	Amount	Percent

Name

Section

Date

#4

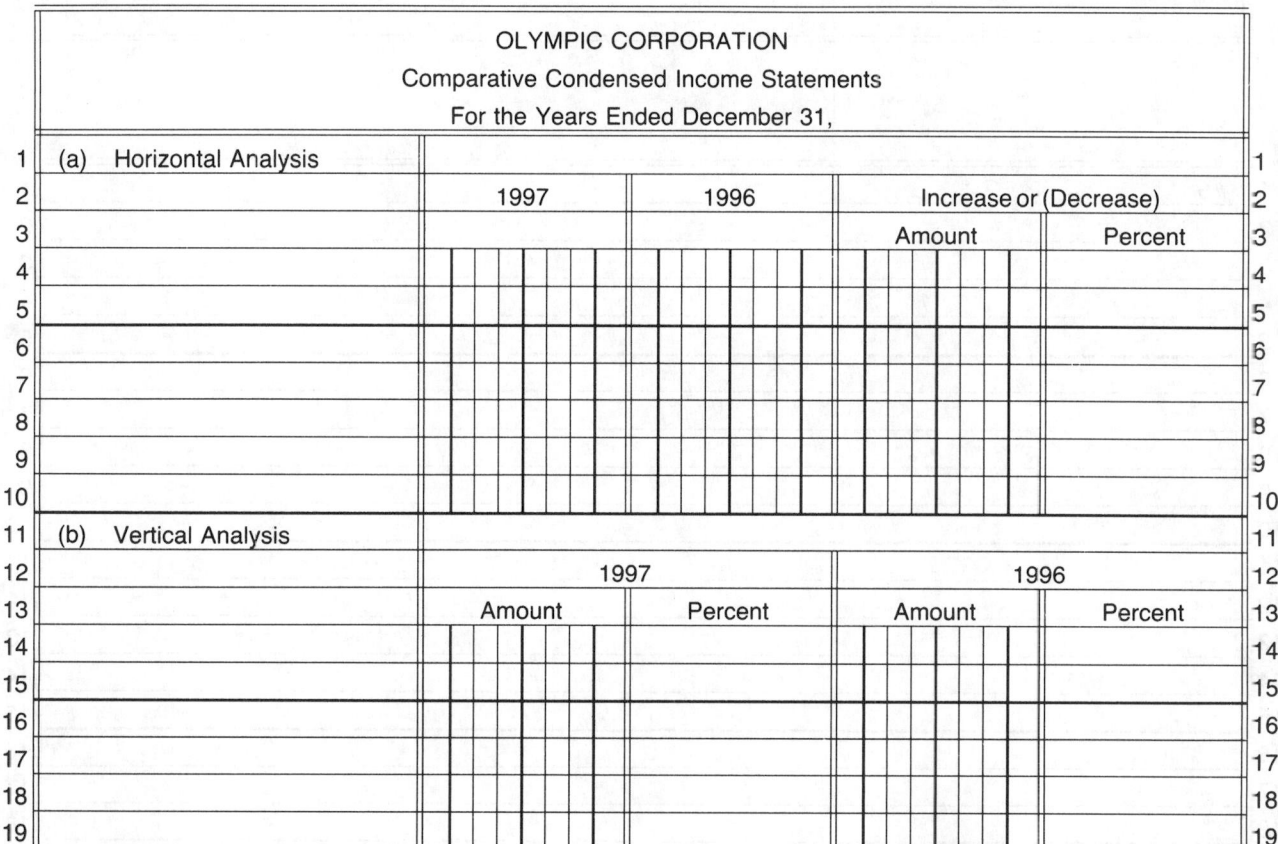

OLYMPIC CORPORATION

Comparative Condensed Income Statements

For the Years Ended December 31,

(a) Horizontal Analysis

	1997	1996	Increase or (Decrease)	
			Amount	Percent

(b) Vertical Analysis

	1997		1996	
	Amount	Percent	Amount	Percent

#5

(a)

(b)

	Nordstrom	J C Penney	Industry

Name

Section

Date

#6

#7

Name

Exercises 15-8 to 15-9

Section

Date

#8

#9

Name

Section

Date

Exercise 15-10

Shaker Corporation

(a)

(b)

(c)

(d)

Name Exercise 15-11

Section

Date Davis Company

DAVIS COMPANY

(Partial) Income Statement

For the Year Ended December 31, 1995

Name **Exercise 15-12**

Section

Date **Energy Enterprises**

(a)

(b)

(c)

(d)

(e)

(f)

Name | **Problem 15-1**

Section

Date | **Chen Company and Couric Company**

(a)

VERTICAL ANALYSIS
Condensed Income Statements
For the Year Ended December 31, 1996

	CHEN COMPANY		COURIC COMPANY	
	Dollars	Percent	Dollars	Percent

(b)

Name

Section

Date

Problem 15-2

Magic Johnson Company

(a) Earnings per share

(b) Return on common stockholders' equity

(c) Return on assets

(d) Current ratio

(e) Acid-test ratio

(f) Receivables turnover

(g) Inventory turnover

Name

Section

Date

Problem 15-2 Concluded

Magic Johnson Company

(h) Times interest earned

(i) Asset turnover

(j) Debt to total assets

(k) Current cash debt coverage

(l) Cash return on sales

(m) Cash debt coverage

Name | | Problem 15-3
Section
Date | | Pitka Corporation

(a)

	1995	1996
(1) Profit margin on sales		
(2) Asset turnover		
(3) Earnings per share		
(4) Price-earnings ratio		
(5) Payout ratio		
(6) Debt to total assets		

(b)

Name | **Problem 15-4**

Section

Date | **Caroline Company**

(a)

1995	1996	Change
LIQUIDITY		
Current ratio		
Acid-test ratio		
Receivables turnover		
Inventory turnover		
Liquidity analysis:		
PROFITABILITY		
Profit margin		
Asset turnover		
Return on assets		
Earnings per share		
Profitability analysis:		

(b)

1996	1997	Change
(1) Return on common stockholders' equity		
(2) Debt to total assets		
(3) Price-earnings ratio		

Name

Section

Date

Problem 15-5

Kmart Corporation and Wal-Mart Stores, Inc.

(a)

Ratio	Kmart	Wal-Mart
(1) Current Ratio		
(2) Receivables turnover		
(3) Inventory turnover		
(4) Profit margin		
(5) Asset turnover		
(6) Return on assets		
(7) Return on common stockholders' equity		
(8) Debt to total assets		

(a) (Continued)

Ratio	Kmart	Wal-Mart
(9) Times interest earned		
(10) Current cash debt coverage		
(11) Cash return on sales		
(12) Cash debt coverage		

(b)

Name

Section

Date

Problem 15-6

Ultra Vision Company

(a) Current ratio

(b) Acid-test ratio

(c) Receivables turnover

(d) Inventory turnover

(e) Profit margin

(f) Asset turnover

(g) Return on assets

(h) Return on common stockholders' equity

Name

Section

Date

Problem 15-6 Concluded

Ultra Vision Company

(i) Earnings per share

(j) Price-earnings

(k) Payout

(l) Debt to total assets

(m) Times interest earned

Name
Section
Date

Problem 15-7

Vienna Corporation

Name

Section

Date

Problem 15-7 Concluded

Vienna Corporation

VIENNA CORPORATION Income Statement For the Year Ended December 31, 1996	
Sales	$11000000
Cost of goods sold	
Gross profit	
Operating expenses	1665000
Income from operations	
Other expenses and losses	
Interest expense	
Income before taxes	
Income tax expense	560000
Net income	

VIENNA CORPORATION Balance Sheet December 31, 1996	
ASSETS	
Current Assets	
Cash	$450000
Accounts receivable (net)	
Inventory	
Total current assets	
Plant assets (net)	4620000
Total assets	
LIABILITIES AND STOCKHOLDERS' EQUITY	
Current liabilities	
Long-term notes payable	
Total liabilities	
Common stock, $1 par	3000000
Retained earnings	400000
Total stockholders' equity	3400000
Total liabilities and stockholders' equity	

Name **Problem 15-1A**

Section

Date **Brooks Company and Shields Company**

(a)

VERTICAL ANALYSIS

Condensed Income Statements

For the Year Ended December 31, 1996

	BROOKS COMPANY		SHIELDS COMPANY	
	Dollars	Percent	Dollars	Percent

(b)

Name
Section
Date

Problem 15-2A

Marti Rosen Company

(a) Earnings per share

(b) Return on common stockholders' equity

(c) Return on assets

(d) Current ratio

(e) Acid-test ratio

(f) Receivables turnover

(g) Inventory turnover

Name

Section

Date

Problem 15-2A Concluded

Marti Rosen Company

(h) Times interest earned

(i) Asset turnover

(j) Debt to total assets

(k) Current cash debt coverage

(l) Cash return on sales

(m) Cash debt coverage

Name

Section

Date

Problem 15-3A

Los Colinas Corporation

(a)

1995	1996
(1) Profit margin on sales	
(2) Asset turnover	
(3) Earnings per share	
(4) Price-earnings ratio	
(5) Payout ratio	
(6) Debt to total assets	

(b)

Name
Section
Date

Problem 15-4A

Star Track Company

(a)

1995	1996	Change
LIQUIDITY		
Current ratio		
Acid-test ratio		
Receivables turnover		
Inventory turnover		
Liquidity analysis:		
PROFITABILITY		
Profit margin		
Asset turnover		
Return on assets		
Earnings per share		
Profitability analysis:		

Name　　　　　　　　　　　　　　　　　　　　　**Problem 15-4A Concluded**

Section

Date　　　　　　　　　　　　　　　　　　　　　**Star Track Company**

(b)

1996	1997	Change
(1) Return on common stockholders' equity		
(2) Debt to total assets		
(3) Price-earnings ratio		

Name

Section

Date

Problem 15-5A

Bethlehem Steel Corporation and Inland Steel Company

(a)

Ratio	Bethlehem Steel	Inland Steel
(1) Current Ratio		
(2) Receivables turnover		
(3) Inventory turnover		
(4) Profit margin		
(5) Asset turnover		
(6) Return on assets		
(7) Return on common stockholders' equity		
(8) Debt to total assets		

Name

Section

Date

Problem 15-5A Concluded

Bethlehem Steel Corporation and Inland Steel Company

(a) (Continued)

Ratio	Bethlehem Steel	Inland Steel
(9) Times interest earned		
(10) Current cash debt coverage		
(11) Cash return on sales		
(12) Cash debt coverage		

(b)

Name

Section

Date

Chapter 15 Financial Reporting Problem

PepsiCo, Inc.

(a)

PEPSICO, INC.
Trend Analysis of Net Sales and Income from Continuing Operations
For the Five Years Ended December 30, 1995

	1995	1994	1993	1992	1991
(1) Net sales					
					100%
(2) Income from continuing operations					
					100%

Analysis:

(b)

	1995	1994
(1) Profit margin		
(2) Asset turnover		
(3) Return on assets		
(4) Return on common equity		

(b) (Continued)

Analysis:

(c)

1995	1994
(1) Debt to total assets	
(2) Times interest earned	

Analysis:

(d)

Name

Section

Date

Chapter 15 Comparative Analysis Problem

The Coca-Cola Company vs. PepsiCo, Inc.

(a)	Coca-Cola	PepsiCo.
1. (1) Percentage increase in net sales		
(2) Percentage increase in net income		
2. (1) Percentage Increase in total assets		
(2) Percentage increase in total stockholders' equity		
3. (1) Earnings per share		
(2) Price-earnings ratio		

(b)

Name

Section

Date

Manitowoc Company and Caterpiller Corporation

(a)

Section

(b) and (c)

(b)

(c)

(a)

(b)

Name

Section

Date

ETHICS CASE Fairly Industries

(a)

(b)

(c)

Name

Section

Date

CRITICAL THINKING CASE The Coca-Cola Company

(a)	Cola-Cola	PepsiCo.
Current ratio		
Acid-test ratio		
Current cash debt coverage		
Receivables turnover		
Inventory turnover		

(c)

(d) Profitability ratio	Cola-Cola	PepsiCo.
Profit margin		
Asset turnover		
Return on assets		
Return on common stockholders' equity		

(e)

Name

Section

Date

Sears, Roebuck and Co.

(a) and (b)

(a) (1) Profit margin percentage on income from continuing operations

Profit margin percentage on net income

(2) Return on common stockholders' equity

(3) Return on assets

(4) Times interest earned

(b)

Name

Section

Date

Sears, Roebuck and Co.

(c) and (d)

(c)

(d)

Name

Section

Date

Horizontal analysis—

Vertical analysis—

Ratio analysis—liquidity—

Ratio analysis—profitability—

Ratio analysis—solvency—

Name

Section

Date

Name

Section

Date

Name

Section

Date

Name

Section

Date

Name

Section

Date

Name

Section

Date

Name
Section
Date

Name

Section

Date

Name

Section

Date

Name

Section

Date

#1

#2

Name | **Exercise C-3**

Section

Date | **Ahmad Company**

(a)

AHMAD COMPANY
Payroll Register
For the Week Ending January 31

Employee	Total Hours	Earnings		
		Regular	Overtime	Gross Pay
A. Hope				
B. Innes				
C. Stone				

(a) (Continued)

AHMAD COMPANY
Payroll Register (continued)
For the Week Ending January 31

	Deductions				Net Pay
	FICA Taxes	Federal Income Taxes	Health Insurance	Total	
A.					
B.					
C.					

(b)

General Journal

Date		Debit	Credit

Name

Section

Date

Exercises C-4 to C-5

#4

#5

Name

Section

Date

Problem C-1

Lindy, Selina, and Winker Companies

(a) Weaknesses	(b) Recommended Procedures
1.	
2.	
3.	

Name
Section
Date

Problem C-2

Banner Drug Store

(a)

BANNER DRUG STORE

Payroll Register

For the Week Ended February 15, 1996

Employee	Hours	Earnings			Deductions					Net Pay	Store Wages Exp.	Office Wages Exp.
		Regular	Over-time	Gross Pay	FICA Taxes	Fed. Inc. Tax	State Inc. Tax	United Fund	Total			
B. Creek												
C. Crowley												
E. Irvine												
G. Klamath												
Totals												

Name **Problem C-2 Concluded**

Section

Date **Banner Drug Store**

(b), (c), and (d) General Journal

Date	Account Titles and Explanation	Debit	Credit
(b)			
(c)			
(d)			

Name

Section

Date

Problem C-3

Carlos Costa Company

General Journal

Date	Account Titles and Explanation	Debit	Credit
(a)			
(b)			

Name Problem C-4

Section

Date Valley Electric Company

(a) and (b) General Journal

Date	Account Titles and Explanation	Debit	Credit
(a)			
(b)			

(c)

Employee	Wages, Tips, Other Comp.	Fed. Inc. Tax Withheld	State Inc. Tax Withheld	FICA Wages	FICA Tax Withheld
A. Osa					
B. Bama					

Name

Section

Date

Problem C-1A

Chen Wee Company

(a) Weaknesses	(b) Recommended Procedures
1.	
2.	
3.	

Name

Section

Date

Problem C-2A

Sure-Value Hardware

(a)

SURE-VALUE HARDWARE

Payroll Register

For the Week Ended March 15, 1996

Employee	Hours	Earnings			Deductions					Net Pay	Store Wages Exp.	Office Wages Exp.
		Regular	Over-time	Gross Pay	FICA Taxes	Fed. Inc. Tax	State Inc. Tax	United Fund	Total			
A. Pima												
C. Zuni												
E. Hopi												
G. Mohav												
Totals												

Name

Section

Date

Problem C-2A Concluded

Sure-Value Hardware

(b), (c), and (d)

General Journal

Date	Account Titles and Explanation	Debit	Credit
(b)			
(c)			
(d)			

Name **Problem C-3A**

Section

Date **Amora Company**

General Journal

Date	Account Titles and Explanation	Ref.	Debit	Credit
(a)				
(b)				

Name | **Problem C-4A**

Section

Date | **Wynn Electrical Repair Company**

(a) and (b) General Journal

	Date	Account Titles and Explanation	Debit	Credit	
1	(a)				1
2					2
3					3
4					4
5					5
6					6
7					7
8					8
9					9
10					10
11					11
12	(b)				12
13					13
14					14
15					15
16					16
17					17
18					18
19					19
20					20

(c)

	Employee	Wages, Tips, Other Comp.	Fed. Inc. Tax Withheld	State Inc. Tax Withheld	FICA Wages	FICA Tax Withheld	
1							1
2	A. Ute						2
3							3
4	B. Yuma						4
5							5
6							6
7							7
8							8
9							9
10							10

Name | **Appendix C Decision Case**

Section

Date | **Quicko Processing Company**

(a)

QUICKO PROCESSING COMPANY
Comparative Employee Costs
Annual Estimates

HIAWATHA SERVICES, INC.

	Number of Employees	Days Worked	Daily Rate	Cost

PERMANENT EMPLOYEES

Salaries		
Additional payroll costs		

(b)

Name
Section
Date

ETHICS CASE **Spicy-Saucey Restaurant**

(a)

(b)

(c)

(d)

Name

Section

Date

Date	Explanation	Ref.	Debit	Credit	Balance

Date	Explanation	Ref.	Debit	Credit	Balance

Date	Explanation	Ref.	Debit	Credit	Balance

Date	Explanation	Ref.	Debit	Credit	Balance

Name

Section

Date

Name **Exercises D-1 to D-2**

Section

Date

#1

#2

Name | Exercise D-3

Section

Date | Crampton Company

General Ledger

Accounts Receivable

Date	Explanation	Ref.	Debit	Credit	Balance

Accounts Receivable Subsidiary Ledger

Date	Explanation	Ref.	Debit	Credit	Balance

Date	Explanation	Ref.	Debit	Credit	Balance

Date	Explanation	Ref.	Debit	Credit	Balance

Date	Explanation	Ref.	Debit	Credit	Balance

Date	Explanation	Ref.	Debit	Credit	Balance

Name

Section

Date

Exercises D-3 (continued) to D-4

#3 (Continued)

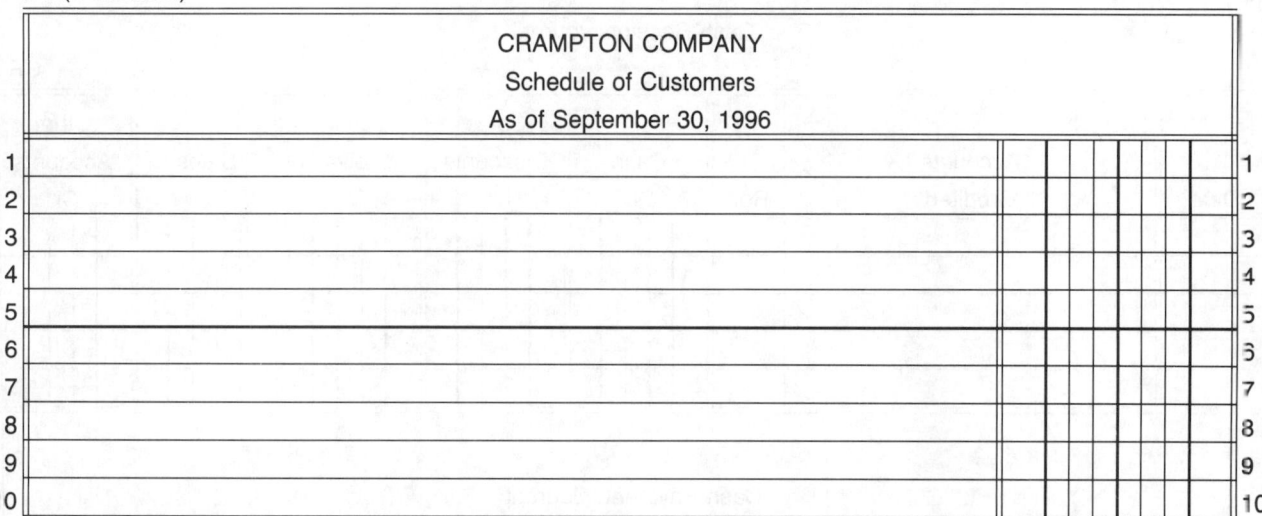

CRAMPTON COMPANY Schedule of Customers As of September 30, 1996	

#4

Sales Journal S1

Date	Account Debited	Ref.	Accounts Rec. (Dr.) Sales (Cr.)

Purchases Journal P1

Date	Account Credited (Debited)	Ref.	Other Accounts Dr.	Purchases Dr.	Freight-in Dr.	Accounts Payable Cr.

Name

Section

Date

Exercises D-5 to D-6

#5

Cash Receipts Journal

CR1

Date	Accounts Credited	Ref.	Cash Dr.	Sales Discounts Dr.	Accounts Receivable Cr.	Sales Cr.	Other Accounts Cr.

Cash Payments Journal

CP1

Date	Ck. No.	Accounts Debited	Ref.	Other Accounts Dr.	Accounts Payable Dr.	Purchase Discounts Cr.	Cash Cr.

#6

Name

Section

Date

Exercise D-7

Vernor Company

(a)

(b)

Name

Section

Date

Exercises D-8, D-9, and D-11

#8

#9

#11

Name | **Exercise D-10**

Section

Date | **Alps Company**

(a) Purchases Journal P1

Date	Account Credited	Ref.	Purchases (Dr.) Accounts Pay. Cr

(b) General Journal

Date	Account Titles and Explanation	Debit	Credit

Name | **Problem D-1**
Section
Date | **Kimbell Company**

(a) Cash Receipts Journal CR1

Date	Accounts Credited	Ref.	Cash Dr.	Sales Discounts Dr.	Accounts Receivable Cr.	Sales Cr.	Other Accounts Cr.

(b) *General Ledger*

Accounts Receivable No. 112

Date	Explanation	Ref.	Debit	Credit	Balance

Name

Section

Date

Problem D-1 Concluded

Kimbell Company

(b) (Continued)

Accounts Receivable Subsidiary Ledger

Block & Son

Date	Explanation	Ref.	Debit	Credit	Balance

Field Co.

Date	Explanation	Ref.	Debit	Credit	Balance

Green Bros.

Date	Explanation	Ref.	Debit	Credit	Balance

Mastin Co.

Date	Explanation	Ref.	Debit	Credit	Balance

(c)

1		1
2		2
3		3
4		4
5		5
6		6

Name **Problem D-2**

Section

Date **Creek Company**

(a) Cash Payments Journal CP1

Date	Ck. No.	Accounts Debited	Ref.	Other Accounts Dr.	Accounts Payable Dr.	Purchases Dr.	Purchase Discounts Cr.	Cash Cr.

(b) *General Ledger*

Accounts Payable

Date	Explanation	Ref.	Debit	Credit	Balance

Name
Section
Date

Problem D-2 Concluded

Creek Company

(b) (Continued)

Accounts Payable Subsidiary Ledger

R. Huff & Co.

Date	Explanation	Ref.	Debit	Credit	Balance

G. Paul

Date	Explanation	Ref.	Debit	Credit	Balance

R. Snyder

Date	Explanation	Ref.	Debit	Credit	Balance

Wicks Bros.

Date	Explanation	Ref.	Debit	Credit	Balance

(c)

1			1
2			2
3			3
4			4
5			5
6			6

Name

Section

Date

Problem D-3

Ventura Company

(a)

Purchases Journal P1

Date	Accounts Credited (Debited)	Ref.	Other Accounts Dr.	Purchases Dr.	Freight-in Dr.	Accounts Payable Cr.

Sales Journal S1

Date	Account Debited	Ref.	Accounts Rec. (Dr.) Sales (Cr.)

Name

Section

Date

Problem D-3 Continued

Ventrua Company

(a) (Continued)

General Journal

Date	Account Titles and Explanation	Ref.	Debit	Credit

(b)

General Ledger

Accounts Receivable

No. 112

Date	Explanation	Ref.	Debit	Credit	Balance

Supplies

No. 126

Date	Explanation	Ref.	Debit	Credit	Balance

Name

Section

Date

Problem D-3 Continued

Ventura Company

(b) (Continued)

Equipment — No. 157

Date	Explanation	Ref.	Debit	Credit	Balance

Accounts Payable — No. 201

Date	Explanation	Ref.	Debit	Credit	Balance

Sales — No. 401

Date	Explanation	Ref.	Debit	Credit	Balance

Sales Returns and Allowances — No. 412

Date	Explanation	Ref.	Debit	Credit	Balance

Purchases — No. 510

Date	Explanation	Ref.	Debit	Credit	Balance

Purchase Returns and Allowances — No. 512

Date	Explanation	Ref.	Debit	Credit	Balance

Name

Section

Date

Problem D-3 Continued

Ventura Company

(b) (Continued)

Freight-in — No. 516

Date	Explanation	Ref.	Debit	Credit	Balance

Advertising Expense — No. 610

Date	Explanation	Ref.	Debit	Credit	Balance

Accounts Receivable Subsidiary Ledger

Penner Company

Date	Explanation	Ref.	Debit	Credit	Balance

Hendrix Bros.

Date	Explanation	Ref.	Debit	Credit	Balance

Nelles Company

Date	Explanation	Ref.	Debit	Credit	Balance

Name

Section

Date

Problem D-3 Continued

Ventura Company

(b) (Continued)

Accounts Payable Subsidiary Ledger

Acme Freight

Date	Explanation	Ref.	Debit	Credit	Balance

Vons Company

Date	Explanation	Ref.	Debit	Credit	Balance

Engle Supply

Date	Explanation	Ref.	Debit	Credit	Balance

Golden Company

Date	Explanation	Ref.	Debit	Credit	Balance

Dorn Company

Date	Explanation	Ref.	Debit	Credit	Balance

Name

Section

Date

Problem D-3 Concluded

Ventura Company

(b) (Continued)

Ball Advertising

Date	Explanation	Ref.	Debit	Credit	Balance

(c)

Accounts receivable balance:

Subsidiary account balances:

Accounts payable balance:

Subsidiary account balances:

Name

Section

Date

Problem D-4

Susan Company

(a), (b), and (c)

Sales Journal S1

Date	Account Debited	Invoice Number	Ref.	Accounts Rec. (Dr.) Sales (Cr.)

Purchases Journal P1

Date	Account Credited	Ref.	Purchases (Dr.) Accounts Pay. (Cr.)

General Journal G1

	Date	Account Titles and Explanation	Ref.	Debit	Credit	
1						1
2						2
3						3
4						4
5						5
6						6
7						7
8						8
9						9
10						10

Name | **Problem D-4 Concluded**

Section

Date | **Susan Company**

(a), (b), and (c) (Continued) Cash Receipts Journal CR1

Date	Accounts Credited	Ref.	Cash Dr.	Sales Discounts Dr.	Accounts Receivable Cr.	Sales Cr.	Other Accounts Cr.

Cash Payments Journal CP1

Date	Accounts Debited	Ref.	Other Accounts Dr.	Accounts Payable Dr.	Purchase Discounts Cr.	Cash Cr.

Name **Problem D-5**

Section

Date **Taco Co.**

(a), (d) and (g)

General Ledger

Cash No. 101

Date	Explanation	Ref.	Debit	Credit	Balance

Accounts Receivable No. 112

Date	Explanation	Ref.	Debit	Credit	Balance

Supplies No. 126

Date	Explanation	Ref.	Debit	Credit	Balance

Equipment No. 157

Date	Explanation	Ref.	Debit	Credit	Balance

Accumulated Depreciation — Equipment No. 158

Date	Explanation	Ref.	Debit	Credit	Balance

Accounts Payable No. 201

Date	Explanation	Ref.	Debit	Credit	Balance

Common Stock No. 301

Date	Explanation	Ref.	Debit	Credit	Balance

(a), (d) and (g) (Continued)

Dividends No. 306

Date	Explanation	Ref.	Debit	Credit	Balance

Sales No. 401

Date	Explanation	Ref.	Debit	Credit	Balance

Sales Discounts No. 414

Date	Explanation	Ref.	Debit	Credit	Balance

Purchases No. 510

Date	Explanation	Ref.	Debit	Credit	Balance

Purchase Returns and Allowances No. 512

Date	Explanation	Ref.	Debit	Credit	Balance

Purchase Discounts No. 514

Date	Explanation	Ref.	Debit	Credit	Balance

Name

Section

Date

Problem D-5 Continued

Taco Co.

(a), (d) and (g) (Continued)

Supplies Expense

No. 631

Date	Explanation	Ref.	Debit	Credit	Balance

Depreciation Expense

No. 711

Date	Explanation	Ref.	Debit	Credit	Balance

(b)

Purchases Journal

P1

Date	Account Credited	Ref.	Purchases (Dr.) Acc. Pay. (Cr.)

Cash Payments Journal

CP1

Date	Accounts Debited	Ref.	Other Accounts Dr.	Accounts Payable Dr.	Purchase Discounts Cr.	Cash Cr.

Name **Problem D-5 Continued**

Section

Date **Taco Co.**

(c) *Accounts Receivable Subsidiary Ledger*

H. Adams

Date	Explanation	Ref.	Debit	Credit	Balance

B. Chambers

Date	Explanation	Ref.	Debit	Credit	Balance

R. Babcock

Date	Explanation	Ref.	Debit	Credit	Balance

L. Dawson

Date	Explanation	Ref.	Debit	Credit	Balance

Accounts Payable Subsidiary Ledger

J. Able

Date	Explanation	Ref.	Debit	Credit	Balance

S. Healy

Date	Explanation	Ref.	Debit	Credit	Balance

L. Held

Date	Explanation	Ref.	Debit	Credit	Balance

Name	Problem D-5 Continued
Section	
Date	Taco Co.

(c) (Continued)

R. Landly

Date	Explanation	Ref.	Debit	Credit	Balance

(e)

TACO CO.
Trial Balance
February 28, 1996

		Debit	Credit	
1	Cash			1
2	Accounts Receivable			2
3	Supplies			3
4	Equipment			4
5	Accumulated Depreciation—Equipment			5
6	Accounts Payable			6
7	Common Stock			7
8	Dividends			8
9	Sales			9
10	Sales Discounts			10
11	Purchases			11
12	Purchase Returns and Allowances			12
13	Purchase Discounts			13
14				14
15				15

(f)

1	Accounts receivable control account:			1
2				2
3	Accounts receivable subsidiary accounts:			3
4				4
5				5
6				6
7				7
8	Accounts payable control account:			8
9				9
10	Accounts payable subsidiary accounts:			10
11				11
12				12

Name

Section

Date

(g) General Journal G1

Date	Account Titles and Explanation	Ref.	Debit	Credit
	Adjusting Entries			

(h)

TACO CO.
Adjusted Trial Balance
February 28, 1996

	Debit	Credit
Cash		
Accounts Receivable		
Supplies		
Equipment		
Accumulated Depreciation—Equipment		
Accounts Payable		
Common Stock		
Dividends		
Sales		
Sales Discounts		
Purchases		
Purchase Returns and Allowances		
Purchase Discounts		
Supplies Expense		
Depreciation Expense		

Name **Problem D-6**

Section

Date **Garcia Co.**

(b) Sales Journal S1

Date	Account Debited	Ref.	Accounts Rec. (Dr.) Sales Cr.

Purchases Journal P1

Date	Account Credited	Ref.	Purchases (Dr.) Accounts Pay. Cr.

General Journal G1

	Date	Account Titles and Explanation	Ref.	Debit	Credit	
1						1
2						2
3						3
4						4
5						5
6						6
7						7
8						8
9						9
10						10
11						11
12						12
13						13
14						14
15						15

(b) (Continued)

Cash Receipts Journal CR1

Date	Accounts Credited	Ref.	Cash Dr.	Sales Discounts Dr.	Accounts Receivable Cr.	Sales Cr.	Other Accounts Cr.

Cash Payments Journal CP1

Date	Accounts Debited	Ref.	Other Accounts Dr.	Accounts Payable Dr.	Purchase Discounts Cr.	Cash Cr.

(a) and (c)

General Ledger

Cash No. 101

Date	Explanation	Ref.	Debit	Credit	Balance

Name **Problem D-6 Continued**

Section

Date **Garcia Company**

(a) and (c)

Accounts Receivable No. 112

Date	Explanation	Ref.	Debit	Credit	Balance

Notes Receivable No. 115

Date	Explanation	Ref.	Debit	Credit	Balance

Merchandise Inventory No. 120

Date	Explanation	Ref.	Debit	Credit	Balance

Equipment No. 157

Date	Explanation	Ref.	Debit	Credit	Balance

Accumulated Depreciation — Equipment No. 158

Date	Explanation	Ref.	Debit	Credit	Balance

Notes Payable No. 200

Date	Explanation	Ref.	Debit	Credit	Balance

Name

Section

Date

Problem D-6 Continued

Garcia Company

(a) and (c) (Continued)

Accounts Payable No. 201

Date	Explanation	Ref.	Debit	Credit	Balance

Common Stock No. 301

Date	Explanation	Ref.	Debit	Credit	Balance

Sales No. 401

Date	Explanation	Ref.	Debit	Credit	Balance

Sales Returns and Allowances No. 412

Date	Explanation	Ref.	Debit	Credit	Balance

Sales Discounts No. 414

Date	Explanation	Ref.	Debit	Credit	Balance

Purchases No. 510

Date	Explanation	Ref.	Debit	Credit	Balance

Purchase Returns and Allowances No. 512

Date	Explanation	Ref.	Debit	Credit	Balance

Name

Section

Date

Problem D-6 Continued

Garcia Co.

(a) and (c) (Continued)

Purchase Discounts — No. 514

Date	Explanation	Ref.	Debit	Credit	Balance

Freight-in — No. 516

Date	Explanation	Ref.	Debit	Credit	Balance

Sales Salaries Expense — No. 627

Date	Explanation	Ref.	Debit	Credit	Balance

Office Salaries Expense — No. 727

Date	Explanation	Ref.	Debit	Credit	Balance

Rent Expense — No. 729

Date	Explanation	Ref.	Debit	Credit	Balance

Accounts Receivable Subsidiary Ledger

R. Barton

Date	Explanation	Ref.	Debit	Credit	Balance

B. Cole

Date	Explanation	Ref.	Debit	Credit	Balance

Name

Section

Date

Problem D-6 Continued

Garcia Co.

(a) and (c) (Continued)

S. Devine

Date	Explanation	Ref.	Debit	Credit	Balance

B. Senton

Date	Explanation	Ref.	Debit	Credit	Balance

Accounts Payable Subsidiary Ledger

D. Lapeska

Date	Explanation	Ref.	Debit	Credit	Balance

S. Field

Date	Explanation	Ref.	Debit	Credit	Balance

R. Gilson

Date	Explanation	Ref.	Debit	Credit	Balance

D. Harms

Date	Explanation	Ref.	Debit	Credit	Balance

S. Warren

Date	Explanation	Ref.	Debit	Credit	Balance

(d)

GARCIA CO.
Trial Balance
January 31, 1997

	Debit	Credit
Cash		
Accounts Receivable		
Notes Receivable		
Merchandise Inventory		
Equipment		
Accumulated Depreciation—Equipment		
Notes Payable		
Accounts Payable		
Common Stock		
Sales		
Sales Returns and Allowances		
Sales Discounts		
Purchases		
Purchase Returns and Allowances		
Purchase Discounts		
Freight-in		
Sales Salaries Expense		
Office Salaries Expense		
Rent Expense		

(e)

Accounts receivable subsidiary ledger:		
Accounts receivable control:		
Accounts payable subsidiary ledger:		
Accounts payable control:		

Name **Appendix D Financial Reporting Problem**

Section

Date **Hunt Co. Mini Practice Set**

(a) Sales Journal S1

Date	Account Debited	Invoice No.	Ref.	Accounts Rec. Dr. Sales Cr.

Purchases Journal P1

Date	Account Credited	Terms	Ref.	Purchases Dr. Accounts Pay. Cr.

(a) (Continued) Cash Receipts Journal CR1

Date	Accounts Credited	Ref.	Cash Dr.	Sales Discounts Dr.	Accounts Receivable Cr.	Sales Cr.	Other Accounts Cr.

Cash Payments Journal CP1

Date	Accounts Debited	Ref.	Other Accounts Dr.	Accounts Payable Dr.	Office Supplies Dr.	Purchase Discounts Cr.	Cash Cr.

Name | **Appendix D Financial Reporting Problem Continued**

Section

Date | **Hunt Co. Mini Practice Set**

(a) General Journal G1

Date	Account Titles and Explanation	Ref.	Debit	Credit

Name
Section
Date

(e) General Journal G2

Date	Account Titles and Explanation	Ref.	Debit	Credit
	Adjusting Entries			
	Closing Entries			

(b) and (e)

General Ledger

Cash No. 101

Date	Explanation	Ref.	Debit	Credit	Balance

Accounts Receivable No. 112

Date	Explanation	Ref.	Debit	Credit	Balance

Notes Receivable No. 115

Date	Explanation	Ref.	Debit	Credit	Balance

Merchandise Inventory No. 120

Date	Explanation	Ref.	Debit	Credit	Balance

Office Supplies No. 125

Date	Explanation	Ref.	Debit	Credit	Balance

Prepaid Insurance No. 130

Date	Explanation	Ref.	Debit	Credit	Balance

Section

Date

(b) and (e) (Continued)

Equipment No. 157

Date	Explanation	Ref.	Debit	Credit	Balance

Accumulated Depreciation - Equipment No. 158

Date	Explanation	Ref.	Debit	Credit	Balance

Notes Payable No. 200

Date	Explanation	Ref.	Debit	Credit	Balance

Accounts Payable No. 201

Date	Explanation	Ref.	Debit	Credit	Balance

Interest Payable No. 230

Date	Explanation	Ref.	Debit	Credit	Balance

Common Stock No. 311

Date	Explanation	Ref.	Debit	Credit	Balance

(b) and (e) (Continued)

Retained Earnings No. 320

Date	Explanation	Ref.	Debit	Credit	Balance

Dividends No. 332

Date	Explanation	Ref.	Debit	Credit	Balance

Income Summary No. 350

Date	Explanation	Ref.	Debit	Credit	Balance

Sales No. 401

Date	Explanation	Ref.	Debit	Credit	Balance

Sales Returns and Allowances No. 412

Date	Explanation	Ref.	Debit	Credit	Balance

Sales Discounts No. 414

Date	Explanation	Ref.	Debit	Credit	Balance

(b) and (e) (Continued)

Interest Revenue No. 430

Date	Explanation	Ref.	Debit	Credit	Balance

Purchases No. 510

Date	Explanation	Ref.	Debit	Credit	Balance

Purchase Returns and Allowances No. 512

Date	Explanation	Ref.	Debit	Credit	Balance

Purchase Discounts No. 514

Date	Explanation	Ref.	Debit	Credit	Balance

Freight-in No. 516

Date	Explanation	Ref.	Debit	Credit	Balance

Sales Salaries Expense No. 627

Date	Explanation	Ref.	Debit	Credit	Balance

(b) and (e) (Continued)

Depreciation Expense — No. 711

Date	Explanation	Ref.	Debit	Credit	Balance

Interest Expense — No. 718

Date	Explanation	Ref.	Debit	Credit	Balance

Insurance Expense — No. 722

Date	Explanation	Ref.	Debit	Credit	Balance

Office Salaries Expense — No. 727

Date	Explanation	Ref.	Debit	Credit	Balance

Office Supplies Expense — No. 728

Date	Explanation	Ref.	Debit	Credit	Balance

Rent Expense — No. 729

Date	Explanation	Ref.	Debit	Credit	Balance

(b) and (e) (Continued)

Accounts Receivable Subsidiary Ledger

R. Dansig

Date	Explanation	Ref.	Debit	Credit	Balance

J. Eaton

Date	Explanation	Ref.	Debit	Credit	Balance

B. Jaggar

Date	Explanation	Ref.	Debit	Credit	Balance

S. Lowell

Date	Explanation	Ref.	Debit	Credit	Balance

B. Sargent

Date	Explanation	Ref.	Debit	Credit	Balance

(b) and (e) (Continued) *Accounts Receivable Subsidiary Ledger*

D. Landell

Date	Explanation	Ref.	Debit	Credit	Balance

S. Lee

Date	Explanation	Ref.	Debit	Credit	Balance

R. Mannon

Date	Explanation	Ref.	Debit	Credit	Balance

D. Nordin

Date	Explanation	Ref.	Debit	Credit	Balance

S. Walden

Date	Explanation	Ref.	Debit	Credit	Balance

(d)

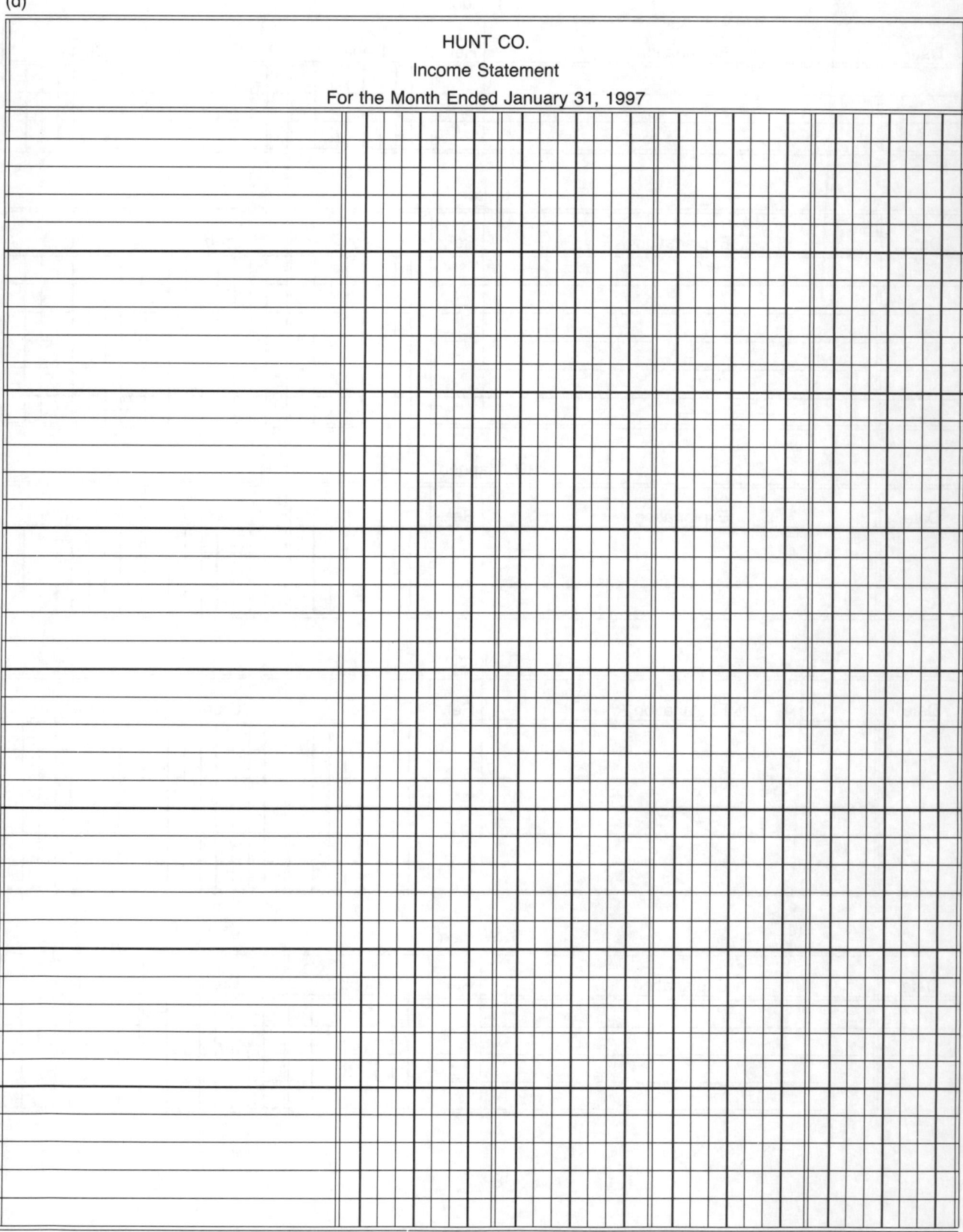

HUNT CO.
Income Statement
For the Month Ended January 31, 1997

Name

Section

Date

(d) (Continued)

HUNT CO.
Retained Earnings Statement
For the Month Ended January 31, 1997

HUNT CO.
Balance Sheet
January 31, 1997

Assets

Liabilities and Stockholders' Equity

(f)

HUNT CO.
Post-Closing Trial Balance
January 31, 1997

	Account Titles and Explanation	Debit	Credit	
1				1
2				2
3				3
4				4
5				5
6				6
7				7
8				8
9				9
10				10
11				11
12				12
13				13
14				14
15				15
16				16
17				17
18				18
19				19
20				20
21	Accoounts receivable balance:			21
22				22
23	Subsidiary account balances:			23
24				24
25				25
26				26
27				27
28				28
29				29
30	Accounts payable balance:			30
31				31
32	Subsidiary account balances:			32
33				33
34				34
35				35
36				36
37				37
38				38
39				39
40				40

Name
Section
Date

(a)

Name

Section

Date

Appendix D Decision Case Concluded

Smith & Young

(a) (Continued), (b), and (c)

(a) (Continued)

(b)

(c)

Name

Section

Date

Appendix D Ethics Case

Apprendix D Critical Thinking Case

ETHICS CASE Triport Products Company

(a)

(b)

(c)

CRITICAL THINKING CASE Alco Standard Corporation

(a)

(b)

Name

Section

Date

Appendix D Group Activity

Hard Hat Construction

Sales journal—

Purchases journal—

Cash receipts journal—

Cash payments journal—

General journal—

Control and subsidiary accounts—

Name

Section

Date

Name | Exercise E-1
Section
Date | Red Cliff Company

(a)

	Estimate	Units Defective	Units Outstanding

(b)

(c)

Name

Section

Date

Exercise E-2

Murphy Company

(a)

MURPHY COMPANY

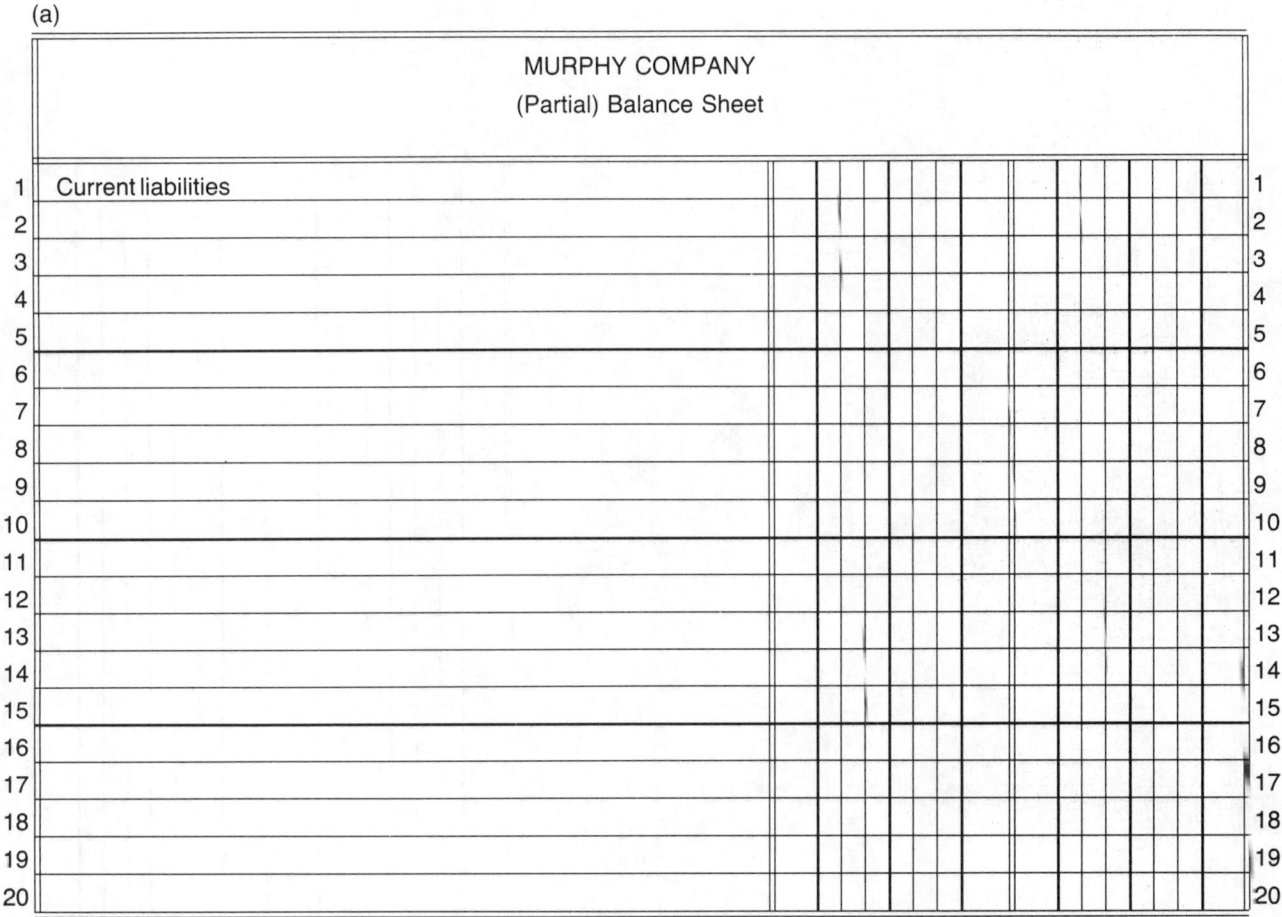

(Partial) Balance Sheet

Current liabilities		

(b)

Name

Section

Date

Exercises E-3 to E-4

#3

#4

Name **Problem E-1**

Section

Date **Carroll Company**

(a) General Journal

Date	Account Titles and Explanation	Debit	Credit

Name

Section

Date

Problem E-1 Concluded

Carroll Company

(b)

General Journal

Date	Account Titles and Explanation	Debit	Credit

(c)

CARROLL COMPANY
Partial Balance Sheet
January 31, 1996

Current liabilities		

Name **Problem E-2**

Section

Date **Casper Enterprises**

(a)

(b)

(c)

Name

Section

Date

Problem E-1A

Midler Company

(a) General Journal

Date	Account Titles and Explanation	Debit	Credit

Name | **Problem E-1A Concluded**

Section

Date | **Midler Company**

(b)

General Journal

Date	Account Titles and Explanation	Debit	Credit

(c)

MIDLER COMPANY

Partial Balance Sheet

January 31, 1996

Current liabilities		

Name Problem E-2A

Section

Date Brett Inc.

(a)

(b)

(c)

Name

Section

Date

PepsiCo, Inc., and CF Industries, Inc.

A. PepsiCo

1.

2.

3.

4.

5.

B. CF Industries

Name
Section
Date

Appendix E Decision Case

Express, Inc.

(a)

(b)

(c)

WORK SHEETS FOLLOW